MW00807631

The Complete
BIBLICAL LIBRARY

THE OLD TESTAMENT STUDY BIBLE

GENESIS

The Complete
BIBLICAL LIBRARY

The Complete Biblical Library: The Old Testament. Volume 1: STUDY BIBLE, GENESIS World
Copyright © 1994 Dagengruppen AB, Stockholm, Sweden.
© Published 1994 by World Library Press, Inc., Springfield, Missouri, 65804, U.S.A.
All rights reserved.
No part of this publication may be reproduced or transmitted in any form or by any means, electronic or mechanical, including photocopy, recording, or any information storage and retrieval system, without permission in writing from the publisher.
Printed in the United States of America 1994 by R.R. Donnelley and Sons Company, Chicago, Illinois 60606. International Standard Book Number 1-884642-25-X.

THE NEW TESTAMENT
Study Bible, Greek-English Dictionary,
Harmony of the Gospels

THE OLD TESTAMENT
Study Bible, Hebrew-English Dictionary
Harmony of the Historical Accounts

THE BIBLE ENCYCLOPEDIA

INTERNATIONAL EDITOR
THORALF GILBRANT

EXECUTIVE EDITOR
Gregory A. Lint, M.Div.

NATIONAL EDITORS

U.S.A.
Stanley M. Horton, Th.D.

NORWAY
Erling Utnem, Bishop
Arthur Berg, B.D.

DENMARK
Jorgen Glenthoj, Th.M.

SWEDEN
Hugo Odeberg, Ph.D., D.D.
Bertil E. Gartner, D.D.
Thorsten Kjall, M.A.
Stig Wikstrom, D.Th.M.

FINLAND
Aapelii Saarisal, Ph.D.
Valter Luoto, Pastor
Matti Liljequist, B.D.

HOLLAND
Herman ter Welle, Pastor
Hank Courtz, Drs.

INTERNATIONAL AND
INTERDENOMINATIONAL
BIBLE STUDY SYSTEM

THE OLD TESTAMENT STUDY BIBLE

GENESIS

WORLD LIBRARY PRESS INC.
Springfield, Missouri, U.S.A.

Contributors

VERSE-BY-VERSE COMMENTARY

Stanley M. Horton, Th.D.

VARIOUS VERSIONS

John E. Veazey, B.A.
Rev. Gary L. Sherman
Rev. Paul D. Sherman
Rev. Robert D. Gay
Joel E. Labertew, B.A.

REVIEW BOARD

Gleason L. Archer, Jr., Ph.D.
Roger D. Cotton, Th.D.
Stanley M. Horton, Th.D.

TECHNICAL ASSISTANCE

Editorial Team: Melissa L. Gunckel, B.A. (editorial assistant); Jess L. Leeper, B.A. (Hebrew assistance); Pamela S. Behling, B.S. (proofreader).

Computer Consultant: Martin D. Crossland, Ph.D.

Art Director: Terry Van Someren, B.F.A.

Table of Contents

PREFACE

A word of introduction is in order for this first Old Testament volume of many volumes to come. With the completion of the New Testament portion of *The Complete Biblical Library* there was much acclaim, then the long task of planning and setting into motion the Old Testament project.

During the formative years, the final planning stages and the production, the editors have sought to infuse the Old Testament project with the basic focuses of: usability to all; compatibility with the New Testament series; adherence to the fundamental doctrine of the inspiration of the Scriptures and, of course, accuracy to whatever point is humanly and reasonably possible.

Differences from the New Testament series are barely noticeable in the dictionary volumes. In the Study Bibles, however, we have sought certain improvements. The interlinear proceeds from left to right from one word to the next, although Hebrew normally reads right to left. This will be more usable to the non-Hebrew reader and of little consequence to those familiar with Hebrew. Moreover, there is precedent for this within the discipline of Israeli music. The most obvious benefit is that the translation line has been afforded a much greater degree of readability. Other changes include the textual apparatus being discussed within the commentary wherever significant, since we have only the Masoretic texts today; and the various versions section being placed in a horizontal band between the original language and the commentary, so as to be more accessible from both.

It is, then, our privilege and with great pleasure that we present to you, Genesis, the first volume of *The Complete Biblical Library--Old Testament Series.*

Thoralf Gilbrant, International Editor

Gregory A. Lint, Executive Editor

Introduction

This volume of the *Old Testament Study Bible* is part of a 20-volume set entitled *The Complete Biblical Library: Old Testament* series. It is designed to provide the information needed for a basic understanding of the Old Testament--useful for scholars but also for students and laypeople.

The Complete Biblical Library: Old Testament series consists of a 16-volume *Study Bible* and a 4-volume *Hebrew-English Dictionary.* They are closely linked. You will find information about the *Study Bible's* features later in the Introduction. The *Hebrew-English Dictionary* (HED) lists all the Hebrew words of the Old Testament in their alphabetic order with an article explaining the background, significance, and meaning of the words. The HED also provides a concordance showing each place the words appear in the Old Testament, a list of synonyms and related words, and many other features for a full understanding of each word.

FEATURES OF THE STUDY BIBLE

The *Study Bible* is a combination of study materials which will help scholar and layperson achieve a better understanding of the Old Testament and its language. All of these helps are available in various forms, but bringing them together in combination will save many hours of research. Many scholars do not have in their personal libraries all the volumes necessary to provide the information so readily available here.

The Complete Biblical Library accomplishes an unusual task: to help scholars in their research and to make available to laypersons the tools by which to acquire knowledge which up to this time has been available only to scholars. Following are the major divisions of the *Study Bible:*

Overview

Each volume contains an encyclopedic survey of the Old Testament book. It provides a general outline, discusses matters about which there may be a difference of opinion, and provides background information regarding the history, cultures, literature, and philosophy of the era covered by the book.

Interlinear

Following the principle of providing help for both the scholar and the layperson, a unique interlinear has been supplied. Most interlinears, if not all, give the Hebrew text and the meanings of the words. This interlinear contains five parts:

1. *Hebrew Text.* This is the original language of the Old Testament as we have it today.

2. *Grammatical Forms.* These are shown above each Hebrew word, beneath its assigned number. Each word's part of speech is identified (construct's being italicized). This information is repeated, along with the Hebrew word, in the *Hebrew-English Dictionary* where more details may be found.

3. *Transliteration.* No other interlinears provide this. Its purpose is to familiarize laypersons with the proper pronunciation of Hebrew words so they will feel comfortable when using them in teaching situations. Information on pronunciation is found on page 10 which shows the Hebrew alphabet.

4. *Translation.* The basic meaning of each Hebrew word is found beneath it. Rather then merely compiling past interlinears, a fresh translation was made.

5. *Assigned Numbers.* The unique numbering system of *The Complete Biblical Library* makes cross-reference study between the *Study Bible* and the *Hebrew-English Dictionary* the ultimate in simplicity. Each Hebrew word has been assigned a number.

The *Hebrew-English Dictionary* then follows with the same cross-referencing plan with each word listed in alphabetical sequence and labeled with the proper number. If further study on a certain word is desired, information can be found by locatings its number in the dictionary.

Various Versions

The various versions section contains a vast comparison of the Old Testament versions. The King James Version is shown in boldface type; then from more than 20 other versions, various ways the Hebrew phrase may be translated can be found. The Hebrew language of ancient times was such a rich language that to obtain the full meaning of words, several synonyms may be needed.

Verse-by-Verse Commentary

Many scholars have combined their knowledge and skills to provide a reliable commentary. Providing a basic understanding of every verse in the Old Testament, the commentary opens up the nuances of the Hebrew Old Testament.

HEBREW TRANSLATION

No word-for-word translation can be fully "literal" and still express all the nuances of the original language. Rather the purpose is to help the reader find the English word which most correctly expresses the original Hebrew word in that particular context. The Hebrew language is so rich in meaning that the same word may have a slightly different meaning in another context.

Language idioms offer a special translation problem. Idioms are expressions that have a meaning which cannot be derived from the conjoined meanings of its elements. The Hebrew language abounds in such phrases which cannot be translated literally if they are to make any sense to the English reader.

LITERARY AND BIBLICAL STANDARDS

Hundreds of qualified scholars and specialists in particular fields have participated in producing *The Complete Biblical Library.* Great care has been taken to maintain high standards of scholarship and ethics, involving scholars in Review Boards for the *Study Bible* and the *Hebrew-English Dictionary.* There has been particular concern about giving proper credit for citations from other works and writers have been instructed to show care in this regard. Any deviation from this principle has been inadvertent and unintentional.

Obviously, with writers coming from widely differing backgrounds, there are differences of opinion as to how to interpret certain passages. But, the focus of The Complete Bibilical Library is always from a conservative and evangelical standpoint upholding Scripture as the inspired word of God. When there are strong differences on the meaning of a particular passage, we have felt it best to present the contrasting viewpoints.

STUDY HELPS

As you come to the Scripture section of this volume, you will find correlated pages for your study. The facing pages are designed to complement each other, so you will have a better understanding of the Word of God. Each two-page spread will deal with a group of verses.

First is the interlinear with its fivefold helps: (1) the Hebrew text in which the Old Testament was written; (2) the transliteration, showing how to pronounce each word; (3) the translation of each word; (4) an assigned number (you will need this number to learn more about the word in the *Hebrew-English Dictionary*, companion to the *Study Bible*); and (5) the grammatical forms of each Hebrew word.

The second part of each two-page spread contains two features. The *Various Versions* section provides an expanded understanding of the various ways Hebrew words or phrases can be translated. The phrase from the King James Version appears in boldface print, then other meaningful ways the Hebrew language has been translated follow. This feature will bring you the riches of the language of the Old Testament. The Verse-by-Verse Commentary refers to each verse giving a sufficient basic explanation. Significant viewpoints are discussed in addition to the author's.

THE HEBREW ALPHABET

א	aleph	’ (glottal stop)
ב	beth	b, v
ג	gimel	g, gh
ד	daleth	d, dh
ה	he	h
ו	waw	w, v
ז	zayin	z
ח	heth	ch
ט	teth	t̲ (hardened)
י	yodh	y
כ, ךְ, ך	kaph	k, kh
ל	lamedh	l
מ, ם	mem	m
נ	nun	n
ס	samekh	s̲ (hardened)
ע	ayin	‘ (aspiration)
פ, ף	pe	p, ph
צ, ץ	tsadhe	ts
ק	qoph	q
ר	resh	r
שׂ	sin	s
שׁ	shin	sh
ת	taw	t, th

INTERLINEAR COMPONENTS

A & B: Number

The first line of each record of the interlinear is a numeral which refers to the *Hebrew-English Dictionary*. The numbers should be referenced *only* by the digits before the decimal. Most words have an ordinary numeral. Only the verbs have the extended system.

The digits after the decimal refer to the standard verb chart found in Hebrew Grammars. The first digit after the decimal refers to the "mood" of the verb (simple, passive, causative, intensive, reflexive); the second refers to the "tense" (perfect, imperfect, jussive, imperative, infinitive, or participle); the third refers to the person, gender and number (such as 3rd masculine singular).

C: Location or Grammar

The second line of the interlinear is the description of the grammatical construction of the Hebrew word. Describing a Hebrew word in this manner is called locating the word. You will notice there is often more than one word written as a single Hebrew word. This is because related words are often joined. A full listing of abbreviations and brief explanation may be found at the end of the book.

D: Hebrew

This is the original language of the Old Testament as we have it today. The Hebrew text of the interlinear is a comparative text, provided by The Original Word Publishers of Roswell, Georgia.

E: Transliteration

This is the key to pronouncing the word. The transliteration matches that found in the Septuagint research of the *New Testament Greek-English Dictionary* of *The Complete Biblical Library.*

F: Translation

This is a fresh translation prepared by the executive editor and the commentary writer.

Genesis 1:1-6

THE FIRST BOOK OF MOSES CALLED

GENESIS בְּרֵאשִׁית

A

1:1	904, 7519	1282.111	435	881	8452	881	800
	prep, art, n fs	v Qal pf 3ms	n mp	do	art, n md	cj, do	art, n fs
	בְּרֵאשִׁית	בָּרָא	אֱלֹהִים	אֵת	הַשָּׁמַיִם	וְאֵת	הָאָרֶץ
	b^{e}rē'shîth	bārā'	'ĕlōhîm	'ēth	hashshāmayim	w^{e}'ēth	hā'ārets
	in the beginning	created	God		the heavens	and	the earth

B

2.	800	2030.112	8744	958	2932	6142, 6686
	cj, art, n fs	v Qal pf 3fs	n ms	cj, n ms	cj, n ms	prep, *n mp*
	וְהָאָרֶץ	הָיְתָה	תֹהוּ	וָבֹהוּ	וְחֹשֶׁךְ	עַל־פְּנֵי
	w^{e}hā'ārets	hāy^{e}thāh	thōhû	wāvōhû	w^{e}chōshekh	'al-p^{e}nê
	and the earth	it was	formless	and empty	and darkness	over the surface of

8745	7593	435	7646.353	6142, 6686	4448
n fs	cj, *n fs*	n mp	v Piel ptc fs	prep, *n mp*	art, n md
תְהוֹם	וְרוּחַ	אֱלֹהִים	מְרַחֶפֶת	עַל־פְּנֵי	הַמָּיִם
th^{e}hôm	w^{e}rûach	'ĕlōhîm	m^{e}rachepheth	'al-p^{e}nê	hammāyim
the deep	and the Spirit of	God	hovering	over the surface of	the waters

C

3.	569.121	435	2030.121	214	2030.121, 214	4.	7495.121
	cj, v Qal impf 3ms	n mp	v Qal juss 3ms	n ms	cj, v Qal impf 3ms, n ms		cj, v Qal impf 3ms
	וַיֹּאמֶר	אֱלֹהִים	יְהִי	אוֹר	וַיְהִי־אוֹר		וַיַּרְא
	wayyō'mer	'ĕlōhîm	y^{e}hî	'ôr	wayhî-'ôr		wayyar'
	and He said	God	let there be	light	and there was light		and He saw

435	881, 214	3706, 3005	950.521	435	1033	214
n mp	do, art, n ms	prep, adj	cj, v Hiphil impf 3ms	n mp	prep	art, n ms
אֱלֹהִים	אֶת־הָאוֹר	כִּי־טוֹב	וַיַּבְדֵּל	אֱלֹהִים	בֵּין	הָאוֹר
'ĕlōhîm	'eth-hā'ôr	kî-ṭôv	wayyavdēl	'ĕlōhîm	bên	hā'ôr
God	the light	that good	and He separated	God	between	the light

D

1033	2932	5.	7410.121	435	3937, 214	3219	3937, 2932
cj, prep	art, n ms		cj, v Qal impf 3ms	n mp	prep, art, n ms	n ms	cj, prep, art, n ms
וּבֵין	הַחֹשֶׁךְ		וַיִּקְרָא	אֱלֹהִים	לָאוֹר	יוֹם	וְלַחֹשֶׁךְ
ûvên	hachōshekh		wayyiqrā'	'ĕlōhîm	lā'ôr	yôm	w^{e}lachōshekh
and between	the darkness		and He named	God	the light	day	and the darkness

7410.111	4050	2030.121, 6394	2030.121, 1269	3219	259
v Qal pf 3ms	n ms	cj, v Qal impf 3ms, n ms	cj, v Qal impf 3ms, n ms	n ms	num
קָרָא	לָיְלָה	וַיְהִי־עֶרֶב	וַיְהִי־בֹקֶר	יוֹם	אֶחָד
qārā'	lāy^{e}lāh	wayhî-'erev	wayhî-vōqer	yôm	'echādh
He named	night	and it was evening	and it was morning	day	one

E

6.	569.121	435	2030.121	7842	904, 8761	4448
	cj, v Qal impf 3ms	n mp	v Qal juss 3ms	n ms	prep, *n ms*	art, n md
	וַיֹּאמֶר	אֱלֹהִים	יְהִי	רָקִיעַ	בְּתוֹךְ	הַמָּיִם
	wayyō'mer	'ĕlōhîm	y^{e}hî	rāqîa'	b^{e}thôkh	hammāyim
	and He said	God	let there be	expanse	in the middle of	the waters

F

2030.121	950.551	1033	4448	3937, 4448	7.	6449.121
cj, v Qal juss 3ms	v Hiphil ptc ms	prep	n md	prep, n md		cj, v Qal impf 3ms
וִיהִי	מַבְדִּיל	בֵּין	מַיִם	לָמָיִם		וַיַּעַשׂ
wîhî	mavdîl	bên	mayim	lāmāyim		wayya'as
and let it be	what separates	between	waters	from the waters		and He made

THE FIRST BOOK OF MOSES CALLED

GENESIS

Expanded Interlinear
Various Versions
Verse-by-Verse Commentary

THE FIRST BOOK OF MOSES CALLED

GENESIS בְּרֵאשִׁית

1:1	**904, 7519**	**1282.111**	**435**	**881**	**8452**	**881**	**800**
	prep, art, n fs	v Qal pf 3ms	n mp	do	art, n md	cj, do	art, n fs
	בְּרֵאשִׁית	בָּרָא	אֱלֹהִים	אֵת	הַשָּׁמַיִם	וְאֵת	הָאָרֶץ
	bere'shîth	bārā'	'ĕlōhîm	'ēth	hashshāmayim	we'ēth	hā'ārets
	in the beginning	created	God		the heavens	and	the earth

2.	**800**	**2030.112**	**8744**	**958**	**2932**	**6142, 6686**
	cj, art, n fs	v Qal pf 3fs	n ms	cj, n ms	cj, n ms	prep, *n mp*
	וְהָאָרֶץ	הָיְתָה	תֹהוּ	וָבֹהוּ	וְחֹשֶׁךְ	עַל־פְּנֵי
	wehā'ārets	hāyethāh	thōhû	wāvōhû	wechōshekh	'al-penê
	and the earth	it was	formless	and empty	and darkness	over the surface of

8745	**7593**	**435**	**7646.353**	**6142, 6686**	**4448**
n fs	cj, *n fs*	n mp	v Piel ptc fs	prep, *n mp*	art, n md
תְהוֹם	וְרוּחַ	אֱלֹהִים	מְרַחֶפֶת	עַל־פְּנֵי	הַמָּיִם
thehôm	werûach	'ĕlōhîm	merachepheth	'al-penê	hammāyim
the deep	and the Spirit of	God	hovering	over the surface of	the waters

3.	**569.121**	**435**	**2030.121**	**214**	**2030.121, 214**	**4.**	**7495.121**
	cj, v Qal impf 3ms	n mp	v Qal juss 3ms	n ms	cj, v Qal impf 3ms, n ms		cj, v Qal impf 3ms
	וַיֹּאמֶר	אֱלֹהִים	יְהִי	אוֹר	וַיְהִי־אוֹר		וַיַּרְא
	wayyō'mer	'ĕlōhîm	yehî	'ôr	wayhî-'ôr		wayyar'
	and He said	God	let there be	light	and there was light		and He saw

435	**881, 214**	**3706, 3005**	**950.521**	**435**	**1033**	**214**
n mp	do, art, n ms	prep, adj	cj, v Hiphil impf 3ms	n mp	prep	art, n ms
אֱלֹהִים	אֶת־הָאוֹר	כִּי־טוֹב	וַיַּבְדֵּל	אֱלֹהִים	בֵּין	הָאוֹר
'ĕlōhîm	'eth-hā'ôr	kî-ṭôv	wayyavdēl	'ĕlōhîm	bên	hā'ôr
God	the light	that good	and He separated	God	between	the light

1. In the beginning God created the heaven and the earth: ... When God set about to create, *Anchor* ... By periods God created, *Fenton* ... At the first, *BB*.

2. And the earth was without form, and void: ... unorganized and empty, *Fenton* ... a shapeless, chaotic mass, *LIVB* ... a formless waste, *Anchor*.

and darkness was upon the face of the deep: ... raging ocean that covered everything was engulfed, *NAB* ... covered its convulsed surface, *Berkeley* ... the abyss, *AMT*.

And the spirit of God moved upon the face of the waters: ... a tempestous wind raging over the surface, *AMT* ... an awesome wind, *Anchor* ... the power of God, *Good News*.

3. And God said, Let there be light: and there was light: ... Let light be; and light is, *Young* ... and light appeared, *LIVB*.

4. And God saw the light, that it was good: and God divided the light from the darkness: ... God gazed upon that beautiful light, *Berkeley*.

Genesis, the book of beginnings, might be called the "seed plot" of all the great teachings of the Bible, for they are all found in it, at least in initial form. In the first 11 chapters, God's dealings with humankind as a whole are covered at lightning speed. With chapter 12, Genesis slows down to a walking pace, however, and deals with the beginnings of God's plan of redemption through Abraham and his immediate decendants.

The book also shows a blood line, a line of descent that is related to God's promise given to Abraham. This line of descent ultimately leads to the one who will bring final fulfillment of that promise, our Lord Jesus Christ. In that line we find Abraham chosen to fulfill God's promise and Lot dropped, Isaac chosen and Ishmael dropped, Jacob chosen and Esau dropped. Those chosen were all younger sons, showing mere human inheritance was not enough. Each one was brought to the place where they expressed faith, thus, all were chosen by grace through faith. Nor were they chosen simply to receive blessing for themselves, but they were chosen as servants to bring blessing to others. The key people in this line of descent in Genesis give us a person pattern as a simple outline of the book: Adam (ch. 1-4), Noah (ch. 5-11), Abraham (ch. 12-25), Jacob (ch. 26-36), Joseph (ch. 37-50).

Genesis chapters 1-2:4 gives us an overview of creation emphasizing God's actions. Notice that in every sentence God is explicitly creating, speaking, observing, or doing something.

1:1. Genesis, however, in the Hebrew puts the emphasis on the word "beginning." Other ancient religions did not see a real beginning or a God great enough to create the entire universe out of nothing. If they discussed creation, it was always creation out of something else, such as earth, air, fire, and water, slime, or a giant's body. Ancient people's view of history was cyclical, with everything repeating itself forever, without any ultimate goal or eternal hope.

But the Bible shows a linear view of history, with a real beginning and a future consummation and an end to the history of this world that will bring glory to God and blessing to all believers as well as judgment to those who reject God's grace.

"Created" (Heb., *bara'*) is always used of God's divine creative activity, never of human activity. The word is also u sed of what He creates to bring judgment. (See Num. 16:30, where "if the Lord make a new thing" is literally, "if the LORD [Yahweh] creates a creation.") Thus the use of bara' draws attention to the fact that the creation in the beginning was totally new. There never had been a creation or a created universe before.

From verse 2 on, the attention is given to God's activity in relation to the earth rather than to the heavens. God does not discuss what exists in the rest of the universe. In fact. the Bible as a whole focuses on life on earth.

1:2. God did not create the earth with people already living on it. In the beginning it did not have the form needed for human habitation. Darkness covered the surface of the primeval ocean, and the earth "was" empty of inhabitants. Some wish to interpret the word "was" to mean "became," as if verse 1 represented a prior creation. However, a different Hebrew construction would be needed if "became" were the true meaning. Rather than referring to a ruin, the words "without form and void," that is, "formless and empty" refer to a bud stage. In this stage of preparation with the Holy Spirit hovering over the primeval ocean, God was preparing for the fruition of creation which would take place during the following 6 days of creation.

The 6 creation days involve eight distinct creative acts, each beginning with "And God said." The days show sequence and climax leading up to the creation of the man and the woman in the image of God. The days also show correspondence, in that light on the first day corresponds to lights on the fourth day ("lightbearers," including the sun and stars giving off light, and the moon reflecting light). The firmament (that is, the expanse of the atmospheric heaven) on the second day parallels the fifth day where the birds fly across the expanse of the sky and the fish that fill the expanse of the seas. The dry land and vegetation on the third day corresponds to the animals and humankind on the sixth day that live on the land and eat the vegetation. The days also show balance, for one distinct creative act occurs on the first day (introduced by "And God said"), one on the second day, and two on the third day. There is one "And God said" on the fourth day, one on the fifth day, and two on the sixth day. This is significant because it draws attention to the creation of humankind as separate and distinct from the creation of animals.

1:3. On the first day, "and there was light" could be translated, "and light proceeded to come into being." That is, this chapter is giving a summary of God's creative acts. In chapter two God used several steps in the creation of man and woman. Possibly, several steps were taken by God in His divine creative acts on the other days, but we are not told about them. Instead, the focus is on the creation of humankind and God's purpose for us.

1:4. God, being the personal God He is, made a judgment and saw the light was "good." By "good," He meant it was perfectly suited for His purposes and would benefit and bless the creation of the earth that He had made. The separation of light from darkness was good for humankind, giving opportunity for rest.

1:5. God named the light "day" and the darkness, "night," no such a distinction had been made before. Here day is used of the light portion of the 24 hours (the earth was probably rotating on its axis from the beginning, thus giving 24 hour days). The reference to the evening and morning shows the

1033	2932		7410.121	435	3937, 214	3219	3937, 2932
cj, prep	art, n ms	**5.**	cj, v Qal impf 3ms	n mp	prep, art, n ms	n ms	cj, prep, art, n ms
וּבֵין	הַחֹשֶׁךְ		וַיִּקְרָא	אֱלֹהִים	לָאוֹר	יוֹם	וְלַחֹשֶׁךְ
ûvên	hachōshekh		wayyiqŏrā'	'ĕlōhîm	lā'ôr	yôm	w^{e}lachōshekh
and between	the darkness		and He named	God	the light	day	and the darkness

7410.111	4050	2030.121, 6394	2030.121, 1269	3219	259
v Qal pf 3ms	n ms	cj, v Qal impf 3ms, n ms	cj, v Qal impf 3ms, n ms	n ms	num
קָרָא	לָיְלָה	וַיְהִי־עֶרֶב	וַיְהִי־בֹקֶר	יוֹם	אֶחָד
qārā'	lāy^{e}lāh	wayhî-'erev	wayhî-vōqer	yôm	'echādh
He named	night	and it was evening	and it was morning	day	one

	569.121	435	2030.121	7842	904, 8761	4448
6.	cj, v Qal impf 3ms	n mp	v Qal juss 3ms	n ms	prep, *n ms*	art, n md
	וַיֹּאמֶר	אֱלֹהִים	יְהִי	רָקִיעַ	בְּתוֹךְ	הַמָּיִם
	wayyō'mer	'ĕlōhîm	y^{e}hî	rāqîa'	b^{e}thôkh	hammāyim
	and He said	God	let there be	expanse	in the middle of	the waters

2030.121	950.551	1033	4448	3937, 4448		6449.121
cj, v Qal juss 3ms	v Hiphil ptc ms	prep	n md	prep, art, n md	**7.**	cj, v Qal impf 3ms
וִיהִי	מַבְדִּיל	בֵּין	מַיִם	לָמָּיִם		וַיַּעַשׂ
wîhî	mavdîl	bên	mayim	lāmāyim		wayya'as
and let it be	what separates	between	waters	from the waters		and He made

435	881, 7842	950.521	1033	4448	866	4623, 8809
n mp	do, art, n ms	v Hiphil impf 3ms	prep	art, n md	rel part	prep, prep
אֱלֹהִים	אֶת־הָרָקִיעַ	וַיַּבְדֵּל	בֵּין	הַמַּיִם	אֲשֶׁר	מִתַּחַת
'ĕlōhîm	'eth-hārāqîa'	wayyavdēl	bên	hammayim	'ăsher	mittachath
God	the expanse	and He separated	between	the waters	which	under

3937, 7842	1033	4448	866	4623, 6142	3937, 7842
prep, art, n ms	cj, prep	art, n md	rel part	prep, prep	prep, art, n ms
לָרָקִיעַ	וּבֵין	הַמַּיִם	אֲשֶׁר	מֵעַל	לָרָקִיעַ
lārāqîa'	ûvên	hammayim	'ăsher	mē'al	lārāqîa'
the expanse	and between	the waters	which	above	the expanse

2030.121, 3772		7410.121	435	3937, 7842	8452	2030.121, 6394
cj, v Qal impf 3ms, adv	**8.**	cj, v Qal impf 3ms	n mp	prep, art, n ms	n md	cj, v Qal impf 3ms, n ms
וַיְהִי־כֵן		וַיִּקְרָא	אֱלֹהִים	לָרָקִיעַ	שָׁמָיִם	וַיְהִי־עֶרֶב
wayhî-khēn		wayyiqŏrā'	'ĕlōhîm	lārāqîa'	shāmāyim	wayhî-'erev
and it was so		and He named	God	the expanse	heavens	and it was evening

2030.121, 1269	3219	8529		569.121	435	7245.226
cj, v Qal impf 3ms, n ms	n ms	num	**9.**	cj, v Qal impf 3ms	n mp	v Niphal juss 3mp
וַיְהִי־בֹקֶר	יוֹם	שֵׁנִי		וַיֹּאמֶר	אֱלֹהִים	יִקָּווּ
wayhî-vōqer	yôm	shēnî		wayyō'mer	'ĕlōhîm	yiqqāwû
and it was morning	day	second		and He said	God	let them gather

4448	4263, 8809	8452	420, 4887	259	7495.222	3114
art, n md	prep, prep	art, n md	prep, n ms	num	cj, v Niphal juss 3fs	art, n fs
הַמַּיִם	מִתַּחַת	הַשָּׁמַיִם	אֶל־מָקוֹם	אֶחָד	וְתֵרָאֶה	הַיַּבָּשָׁה
hammayim	mittachath	hashshāmayim	'el-māqôm	'echādh	w^{e}thērā'eh	hayyabbāshāh
the waters	under	the heavens	to place	one	and let it appear	the dry land

2030.121, 3772		7410.121	435	3937, 3114	800	3937, 4885
cj, v Qal impf 3ms, adv	**10.**	cj, v Qal impf 3ms	n mp	prep, art, n fs	n fs	cj, art, prep, *n ms*
וַיְהִי־כֵן		וַיִּקְרָא	אֱלֹהִים	לַיַּבָּשָׁה	אֶרֶץ	וּלְמִקְוֵה
wayhî-khēn		wayyiqŏrā'	'ĕlōhîm	layyabbāshāh	'erets	ûlămiqŏwēh
and it was so		and He named	God	the dry land	earth	and the gathering of

4448	7410.111	3328	7495.121	435	3706, 3005	11. 569.121
art, n md	v Qal pf 3ms	n mp	cj, v Qal impf 3ms	n mp	prep, adj	cj, v Qal impf 3ms
הַמָּיִם	קָרָא	יַמִּים	וַיַּרְא	אֱלֹהִים	כִּי־טוֹב	וַיֹּאמֶר
hammayim	qārā'	yammîm	wayyar'	'ĕlōhîm	kî-ṭôv	wayyō'mer
the waters	He named	seas	and He saw	God	that good	and He said

435	1939.522	800	1940	6448	2319.551	2320
n mp	v Hiphil juss 3fs	art, n fs	*n ms*	n ms	v Hiphil ptc ms	n ms
אֱלֹהִים	תַּדְשֵׁא	הָאָרֶץ	דֶּשֶׁא	עֵשֶׂב	מַזְרִיעַ	זֶרַע
'ĕlōhîm	tadhshē'	hā'ārets	deshe'	'ēsev	mazrîa'	zera'
God	let it sprout	the earth	vegetation of	plants	yielding	seed

5. And God called the light Day, and the darkness he called Night. And the evening and the morning were the first day: ... it was the first day, *REB* ... the close and the dawn of the first age, *Berkeley*.

6. And God said, Let there be a firmament in the midst of the waters, and let it divide the waters from the waters: ... Let the vapors separate to form the sky above and the oceans below, *LIVB* ... a vault between, *REB* ... a dome in the middle of, *NAB* ... a solid arch stretching over ... , parting, *BB*.

7. And God made the firmament, and divided the waters which were under the firmament from the waters which were above the firmament: and it was so: ... made a dome, and it separated, *Good News* ... the arch for a division, *BB*.

8. And God called the firmament Heaven. And the evening and the morning were the second day: ... named the expanse the Heavens. The close and the dawn of the second age, *Berkeley* ... named the dome Sky, *Good News*.

9. And God said, Let the waters under the heaven be gathered together unto one place, and let the dry land appear: and it was so: ... collected in one place, *Berkeley* ... a single area, that the dry land may be visible, *Anchor* ... will emerge, *LIVB* ... a single basin, *NAB*.

10. And God called the dry land Earth; and the gathering together of the waters called he Seas: and God saw that it was good: ... God was pleased with what he saw, *Anchor* ... and God admired their beauty, *Berkeley*.

creative acts were distinct and separate from each other and were not part of a gradual evolutionary process. "Evening" indicated God was through with that creative act. "Morning" indicated God was ready to begin the next one.

Bible believers give several interpretations to the word "day" in this chapter. The twenty-four hour day theory takes them be ordinary days and nothing else. The interval and restitution theory (also called the "gap" theory) interprets verse 2 to represent an interval after the original creation and shows them to be days of re-creation. The day-age theory takes them to represent ages of various length, perhaps overlapping, with distinct creative acts followed by periods of development. All these theories reject the theory of atheistic evolution by purely natural means.

1:6-8. The creation of the firmament (literally, the expanse) seems to be the creation of an atmospheric blanket around the earth with the seas. It seems that ancient people understood that the primeval ocean was the bottom face of the expanse and the skies the top face. One theory is that in doing this, God lifted what was probably a cloud blanket over the surface of the primeval ocean, and thus it floated in the upper face of the expanse as a cloud blanket in the sky, giving waters above and below. Thus, "heaven" refers to the atmospheric heaven including the sky (as the Hebrew word often means).

1:9-10. Causing dry land to appear must have made tremendous geological changes in the surface of the earth. Surveys of the ocean floor and the mid-Atlantic rift indicate that all the continents were once joined together in a supercontinent, which fits verse 9. Some believe the changes that came at the time of Noah's flood may have broken the single land mass apart.

1:11-13. On the third day also God commanded the land to produce grass (including cereal grains), the herb (seed-bearing plants including vegetables), and fruit trees bearing fruit. Nothing is said here about many other forms of plant life such as algae on the one hand or coniferous trees on the other. We can be sure that God created them along with all other plant life, but the account in this chap-

6320	6780	6449.151	6780	3937, 4464	866	2320, 904
n ms	n ms	v Qal act ptc ms	n ms	prep, n ms	rel part	n ms, ps 3ms, prep, ps 3ms
עֵץ	פְּרִי	עֹשֶׂה	פְּרִי	לְמִינוֹ	אֲשֶׁר	זַרְעוֹ־בוֹ
ʽēts	perî	ʽōseh	perî	leminô	ʼăsher	zarʽô-vô
trees	fruit	producing	fruit	according to its kind	which	its seed in it

6142, 800	2030.121, 3772	12.	3428.522	800	1940	6448
prep, art, n fs	cj, v Qal impf 3ms, adv		cj, v Hiphil impf 3fs	art, n fs	*n ms*	n ms
עַל־הָאָרֶץ	וַיְהִי־כֵן		וַתּוֹצֵא	הָאָרֶץ	דֶּשֶׁא	עֵשֶׂב
ʽal-hāʼārets	wayhî-khēn		wattôtsēʼ	hāʼārets	desheʼ	ʽēsev
on the earth	and it was so		and it produced	the earth	vegetation of	plants

2319.551	2320	3937, 4464	6320	6449.151, 6780	6780	866
v Hiphil ptc ms	n ms	prep, n ms, ps 3ms	cj, n ms	v Qal act ptc ms, n ms	n ms	rel part
מַזְרִיעַ	זֶרַע	לְמִינֵהוּ	וְעֵץ	עֹשֶׂה־פְּרִי	פְּרִי	אֲשֶׁר
mazrîaʽ	zeraʽ	leminēhû	weʼēts	ʽōseh-perî	perî	ʼăsher
yielding	seed	according to its kind	and trees	producing fruit	fruit	which

2320, 904	3937, 4464	7495.121	435	3706, 3005
n ms, ps 3ms, prep, ps 3ms	prep, n ms, ps 3ms	cj, v Qal impf 3ms	n mp	prep, adj
זַרְעוֹ־בוֹ	לְמִינֵהוּ	וַיַּרְא	אֱלֹהִים	כִּי־טוֹב
zarʽô-vô	leminēhû	wayyarʼ	ʼĕlōhîm	kî-ṭôv
its seed in it	according to its kind	and He saw	God	that good

13.	2030.121, 6394	2030.121, 1269	3219	8389	14.	569.121
	cj, v Qal impf 3ms, n ms	cj, v Qal impf 3ms, n ms	n ms	num		cj, v Qal impf 3ms
	וַיְהִי־עֶרֶב	וַיְהִי־בֹקֶר	יוֹם	שְׁלִישִׁי		וַיֹּאמֶר
	wayhî-ʽerev	wayhî-vōqer	yôm	shelîshî		wayyōʼmer
	and it was evening	and it was morning	day	third		and He said

435	2030.121	4115	904, 7842	8452	3937, 950.541	1033
n mp	v Qal juss 3ms	n mp	prep, *n ms*	art, n md	prep, v Hiphil inf con	prep
אֱלֹהִים	יְהִי	מְאֹרֹת	בִּרְקִיעַ	הַשָּׁמַיִם	לְהַבְדִּיל	בֵּין
ʼĕlōhîm	yehî	meʼōrōth	birqîaʽ	hashshāmayim	lehavdîl	bên
God	let them be	lights	in the expanse of	the heavens	to separate	between

3219	1033	4050	2030.116	3937, 225	3937, 4287	3937, 3219
art, n ms	cj, prep	art, n ms	cj, v Qal pf 3cp	prep, n mp	cj, prep, n mp	cj, prep, n mp
הַיּוֹם	וּבֵין	הַלָּיְלָה	וְהָיוּ	לְאֹתֹת	וּלְמוֹעֲדִים	וּלְיָמִים
hayyôm	ûvên	hallāyelāh	wehāyû	leʼōthōth	ûlămôʽădhîm	ûlăyāmîm
the day	and between	the night	and they will be	for signs	and for seasons	and for days

8523	15.	2030.116	4115	904, 7842	8452	3937, 213.541
cj, n fp		cj, Qal pf 3cp	cj, n mp	prep, *n ms*	art, n md	prep, v Hiphil inf con
וְשָׁנִים		וְהָיוּ	לִמְאוֹרֹת	בִּרְקִיעַ	הַשָּׁמַיִם	לְהָאִיר
weshānîm		wehāyû	limʼôrōth	birqîaʽ	hashshāmayim	lehāʼîr
and years		and they will be	for lights	in the expanse of	the heavens	to give light

6142, 800	2030.121, 3772	16.	6449.121	435	881, 8529	4115
prep, art, n fs	cj, v Qal impf 3ms, adv		cj, v Qal impf 3ms	n mp	do, num	art, n mp
עַל־הָאָרֶץ	וַיְהִי־כֵן		וַיַּעַשׂ	אֱלֹהִים	אֶת־שְׁנֵי	הַמְּאֹרֹת
ʽal-hāʼārets	wayhî-khēn		wayyaʽas	ʼĕlōhîm	ʼeth-shenê	hammeʼōrōth
on the earth	and it was so		and He made	God	two	the lights

1448	881, 4115	1448	3937, 4617	3219	881, 4115	7277
art, adj	do, art, n ms	art, adj	prep, *n fs*	art, n ms	cj, do, art, n ms	art, adj
הַגְּדֹלִים	אֶת־הַמָּאוֹר	הַגָּדֹל	לְמֶמְשֶׁלֶת	הַיּוֹם	וְאֶת־הַמָּאוֹר	הַקָּטֹן
haggedhōlîm	ʼeth-hammāʼôr	haggādhōl	lememsheleth	hayyôm	weʼeth-hammāʼôr	haqqāṭōn
the great	the light	the greater	for ruling of	the day	and the light	the lesser

3937, 4617 prep, *n fs* לְמֶמְשֶׁלֶת l^{e}memsheleth for ruling of	4050 art, n ms הַלַּיְלָה hallaylāh the night	881 cj, do וְאֵת w^{e}'ēth and	3676 art, n mp הַכּוֹכָבִים hakkôkhāvîm the stars	**17.**	5598.121 cj, v Qal pf 3ms וַיִּתֵּן wayyittēn and He placed	881 do, ps 3mp אֹתָם 'ōthām them	435 n mp אֱלֹהִים 'ĕlōhîm God

904, 7842 prep, *n ms* בִּרְקִיעַ birqîa' in the expanse of	8452 art, n md הַשָּׁמָיִם hashshāmāyim the heavens	3937, 213.541 prep, v Hiphil inf con לְהָאִיר l^{e}hā'îr to give light	6142, 800 prep, art, n fs עַל־הָאָרֶץ 'al-hā'ārets on the earth	**18.**	3937, 5090.141 cj, prep, v Qal inf con וְלִמְשֹׁל w^{e}limshōl and to rule

904, 3219 prep, art, n ms בַּיּוֹם bayyôm over the day	904, 4050I cj, prep, art, n ms וּבַלַּיְלָה ûvallaylāh and over the night	3937, 950.541 cj, prep, v Hiphil inf con וּלֲהַבְדִּיל ûlăhavdîl and to separate	1033 prep בֵּין bên between	214 art, n ms הָאוֹר hā'ôr the light	1033 cj, prep וּבֵין ûvên and between	2932 art, n ms הַחֹשֶׁךְ hachōshekh the darkness

11. And God said, Let the earth bring forth grass, the herb yielding seed, and the fruit tree yielding fruit after his kind, whose seed is in itself, upon the earth: and it was so: ... seed-bearing vegetation, *Berkeley* ... burst forth with growth, *Anchor* ... bud forth, *Geneva* ... cause grass to spring up, *Darby.*

12. And the earth brought forth grass, and herb yielding seed after his kind, and the tree yielding fruit, whose seed was in itself, after his kind: and God saw that it was good: ... produced growth, *Anchor* ... the seed-bearing herbage according to every species, as well as reproductive fruit trees, *Berkeley* ... the bud of the herb, *Geneva.*

13. And the evening and the morning were the third day: ... the third age, *Fenton.*

14. And God said, Let there be lights in the firmament of the heaven to divide the day from the night; and let them be for signs, and for seasons, and for days, and years: ... Let reflectors appear, *Fenton* ... lights in the dome of the sky, *NAB* ... lights in the arch of heaven, *BB.*

15. And let them be for lights in the firmament of the heaven to give light upon the earth: and it was so: ... and serve as luminaries, *NAB* ... shine in the sky to give light to the earth, *Good News.*

16. And God made two great lights; the greater light to rule the day, and the lesser light to rule the night: he made the stars also: ... two larger lights, *Good News* ... two large luminaries, ... accompanied by the stars, *Berkeley.*

17. And God set them in the firmament of the heaven to give light upon the earth: ... fixed them in the heavenly expanse, *Fenton* ... in the vault of the heavens, *REB* ... He placed lights in the sky to shine on the earth, *Good News.*

18. And to rule over the day and over the night, and to divide the light from the darkness: and God saw that it was good: ... to dominate the day and the night, *Anchor* ... to govern the day and the night, *NAB* ... God saw they were beautiful, *Fenton.*

19. And the evening and the morning were the fourth day: ... the fourth age, *Fenton* ... This all happened on the fourth day, *LIVB.*

20. And God said, Let the waters bring forth abundantly the moving creature that hath life, and fowl that may fly above the earth in the

---

ter is focusing on God's preparation of food for humankind. We are not told everything we would like to know. It is enough to see the land proceeding to produce what God commanded.

1:14-19. The fourth day tells of the sun, moon and stars. They would serve as signs to mark seasons, days and years. The calendar sequence of time is important. Some wonder how there could be evening and morning on the first three days if the sun had not yet been created. There may have been a cosmic source of light at first. But the first verse indicates God created the whole heaven and earth. Furthermore, because the Hebrew of verses 16-17 uses verb forms indicating a completed action, the verse could well be translated "God had made two great lights" and "God had set them in the expanse of the sky."

Thus, on the fourth day some believe God caused at least a partial breakup of the cloud blanket so that now the sun and moon could be seen from the surface of the earth and could "govern" the day and the night.

7495.121	435	3706, 3005	19.	2030.121, 6394	2030.121, 1269	3219
cj, v Qal impf 3ms	n mp	prep, adj		cj, v Qal impf 3ms, n ms	cj, v Qal impf 3ms, n ms	n ms
וַיַּרְא	אֱלֹהִים	כִּי־טוֹב		וַיְהִי־עֶרֶב	וַיְהִי־בֹקֶר	יוֹם
wayyar'	'ĕlōhîm	kî-ṯôv		wayhî-‘erev	wayhî-vōqer	yôm
and He saw	God	that good		and it was evening	and it was morning	day

7536	20.	569.121	435	8650.126	4448	8651	5497
num		cj, v Qal impf 3ms	n mp	v Qal juss 3mp	art, n md	*n ms*	*n fs*
רְבִיעִי		וַיֹּאמֶר	אֱלֹהִים	יִשְׁרְצוּ	הַמַּיִם	שֶׁרֶץ	נֶפֶשׁ
r^{e}vî‘î		wayyō'mer	'ĕlōhîm	yishr^{e}tsû	hammayim	sherets	nephesh
fourth		and He said	God	let them teem	the waters	swarms of	creatures of

2516	5991	5990.321	6142, 800	6142, 6686	7842
n fs	cj, n ms	v Polel juss 3ms	prep, art, n fs	prep, *n mp*	*n ms*
חַיָּה	וְעוֹף	יְעוֹפֵף	עַל־הָאָרֶץ	עַל־פְּנֵי	רְקִיעַ
chayyāh	w^{e}‘ôph	y^{e}‘ôphēph	‘al-hā'ārets	‘al-p^{e}nê	r^{e}qîa‘
living things	and birds	let them fly	above the earth	over the surface of	the expanse of

8452	21.	1282.121	435	881, 8906	1448	881
art, n md		cj, v Qal impf 3ms	n mp	do, art, n mp	art, adj mp	cj, do
הַשָּׁמָיִם		וַיִּבְרָא	אֱלֹהִים	אֶת־הַתַּנִּינִם	הַגְּדֹלִים	וְאֵת
hashshāmāyim		wayyivrā'	'ĕlōhîm	'eth-hattannînim	hagg^{e}dhōlîm	w^{e}'ēth
the heavens		and He created	God	the sea creatures	the great	and

3725, 5497	2516	7718.153	866	8650.116	4448
adj, n fs	art, n fs	art, v Qal act ptc fs	rel part	v Qal pf 3cp	art, n md
כָּל־נֶפֶשׁ	הַחַיָּה	הָרֹמֶשֶׂת	אֲשֶׁר	שָׁרְצוּ	הַמַּיִם
kol-nephesh	hachayyāh	hārōmesheth	'āsher	shārtsû	hammayim
every creature of	the living things	that which teems	which	they teemed	the waters

3937, 4464	881	3725, 5991	3796	3937, 4464	7495.121
prep, n ms, ps 3mp	cj, do	adj, *n ms*	n fs	prep, n ms, ps 3ms	cj, v Qal impf 3ms
לְמִינֵהֶם	וְאֵת	כָּל־עוֹף	כָּנָף	לְמִינֵהוּ	וַיַּרְא
l^{e}mînēhem	w^{e}'ēth	kol-‘ôph	kānāph	l^{e}mînēhû	wayyar'
according to their kind	and	every bird of	wings	according to its kind	and He saw

435	3706, 3005	22.	1313.321	881	435	3937, 569.141
n mp	prep, adj		cj, v Piel impf 3ms	do, ps 3mp	n mp	prep, v Qal inf con
אֱלֹהִים	כִּי־טוֹב		וַיְבָרֶךְ	אֹתָם	אֱלֹהִים	לֵאמֹר
'ĕlōhîm	kî-ṯôv		way^{e}vārekh	'ōthām	'ĕlōhîm	lē'mōr
God	that good		and He blessed	them	God	saying

6759.133	7528.133	4527.133	881, 4448	904, 3328	5991
v Qal impv 2mp	cj, v Qal impv 2mp	cj, v Qal impv 2mp	do, art, n md	prep, art, n mp	cj, art, n ms
פְּרוּ	וּרְבוּ	וּמִלְאוּ	אֶת־הַמַּיִם	בַּיַּמִּים	וְהָעוֹף
p^{e}rû	ûr^{e}vû	ûmil'û	'eth-hammayim	bayyammîm	w^{e}hā‘ôph
be fruitful	and multiply	and fill	the waters	in the seas	and the birds

7528.121	904, 800	23.	2030.121, 6394	2030.121, 1269	3219	2653
v Qal juss 3ms	prep, art, n fs		cj, v Qal impf 3ms, n ms	cj, v Qal impf 3ms, n ms	n ms	num
יִרֶב	בָּאָרֶץ		וַיְהִי־עֶרֶב	וַיְהִי־בֹקֶר	יוֹם	חֲמִישִׁי
yirev	bā'ārets		wayhî-‘erev	wayhî-vōqer	yôm	chămîshî
let them multiply	on the earth		and it was evening	and it was morning	day	fifth

24.	569.121	435	3428.522	800	5497	2516
	cj, v Qal impf 3ms	n mp	v Hiphil juss 3fs	art, n fs	*n fs*	n fs
	וַיֹּאמֶר	אֱלֹהִים	תּוֹצֵא	הָאָרֶץ	נֶפֶשׁ	חַיָּה
	wayyō'mer	'ĕlōhîm	tôtsē'	hā'ārets	nephesh	chayyāh
	and He said	God	let it bring forth	the earth	creatures of	living things

3937, 4464 prep, n ms, ps 3fs לְמִינָהּ lᵉmînāhh according to its kind	966 n fs בְּהֵמָה bᵉhēmāh animals	7719 cj, n ms וָרֶמֶשׂ wāremes and creeping things	2516, 800 cj, *n fs*, n fs וְחַיְתוֹ־אֶרֶץ wᵉchayᵉthô-'erets and living things of the earth

3937, 4464 prep, n ms, ps 3fs לְמִינָהּ lᵉmînāhh according to its kind	2030.121, 3772 cj, v Qal impf 3ms, adv וַיְהִי־כֵן wayhî-khēn and it was so	**25.**	6449.121 cj, v Qal impf 3ms וַיַּעַשׂ wayya'as and He made	435 n mp אֱלֹהִים 'ĕlōhîm God	881, 2516 do, *n fs* אֶת־חַיַּת 'eth-chayyath the living things of

open firmament of heaven: ... swarm with swarms of living souls, *Darby* ... Let the water be filled with many kinds of living beings, *Good News* ... Let the waters teem with shoals of living creatures, *MLB.*

21. And God created great whales: ... great sea-beasts, *BB* . . the monsters of the deep, *Fenton* ... And God prepareth the great monsters, *Young.*

and every living creature that moveth, which the waters brought forth abundantly, after their kind, and every winged fowl after his kind: and God saw that it was good: ... and all kinds of swimming creatures with which the water teems, *NAB* ... gliding creatures, *Goodspeed.*

22. And God blessed them, saying, Be fruitful, and multiply, and fill the waters in the seas, and let fowl multiply in the earth: ... Be fertile and increase, *Anchor* ... told the creatures...to reproduce, *Good News* ... Multiply and stock the oceans, he told them, and to the birds he said, Let your numbers increase. Fill the earth, *LIVB.*

23. And the evening and the morning were the fifth day: ... That ended the fifth day, *LIVB* ... the fifth age, *Fenton.*

24. And God said, Let the earth bring forth the living creature after his kind, cattle, and creeping thing, and beast of the earth after his kind: and it was so: ... give birth to all sorts of living things, *BB* ... all kinds of animal life: domestic and wild, large and small, *Good News* ... animal life according to its species, in quadrupeds, reptiles and all wild animals, answering to their species, *Fenton.*

25. And God made the beast of the earth after his kind, and cattle after their kind, and every thing that creepeth upon the earth after his kind: and God saw that it was good: ... and he was pleased with what he saw, *Good News* ... all sorts of wild animals and cattle and reptiles, *LIVB* ... various species of the animals of the Earth, ...the several species of quadrupeds, ...the different species of reptiles; and God admired their beauty, *Fenton.*

1:20-23. On the fifth day, God said "Let the waters bring forth abundantly the moving creature that hath life, and fowl that may fly above the earth in the open firmament of heaven." But He did not say, "And the waters produced the moving creatures" nor did He say, "And the sky produced the birds." (Compare verse 12.) Instead, the word *bara'* is used, indicating a unique step in God's creative activity. Special attention is given also to God blessing them (that is enabling them to move on in His plan) and commanding them to be fruitful and multiply.

1:24-25. On the sixth day, God commanded the land to produce all varieties of land animals. God again took an active part and made all the animals. "Made" (Heb. *'asah*) is a more general word than *bara'* but the parallel with verse 21 indicates here it too is emphasizing divine creative activity. All were made to reproduce "after their kind." "Kind" is a broad term in the Hebrew. In Leviticus 11, where specific kinds are named, the word can be seen to correspond to what scientists might call superfamilies. That is God did not have to create every sort of dog from the St. Bernard to the Pekinese. He probably created a dog with a good supply of inheritance factors that could separate out into the various species of the dog family. Similarly, He probably created cattle that could differentiate out into the various kinds we have today.

1:26-28. Finally, in the climactic act of creation, God created humankind. He did not say "Let the land produce humankind." He gave special attention to the creation of the human race. The command was given to Himself, when He said, "Let us make man in our image (or pattern), after our likeness (with similarity and potential).

Some scholars believe that "Let us" was simply a plural of majesty. More likely, it is the earliest

800	**3937, 4464**	**881, 966**	**3937, 4464**	**881**
art, n fs	prep, n ms, ps 3fs	cj, do, art, n fs	prep, n ms, ps 3fs	cj, do
הָאָרֶץ	לְמִינָהּ	וְאֶת־הַבְּהֵמָה	לְמִינָהּ	וְאֵת
hā'ārets	lemînāhh	we'eth-habbehēmāh	lemînāhh	we'ēth
the earth	according to its kind	and the animals	according to their kind	and

3725, 7719	**124**	**3937, 4464**	**7495.121**	**435**
adj, *n ms*	art, n fs	prep, n ms, ps 3ms	cj, v Qal impf 3ms	n mp
כָּל־רֶמֶשׂ	הָאֲדָמָה	לְמִינֵהוּ	וַיַּרְא	אֱלֹהִים
kol-remes	hā'ădhāmāh	lemînēhû	wayyar'	'ĕlōhîm
every creeping thing of	the ground	according to its kind	and He saw	God

3706, 3005		**569.121**	**435**	**6449.120**	**119**	**904, 7021**
prep, adj	**26.**	cj, v Qal impf 3ms	n mp	v Qal juss 1cp	n ms	prep, n ms, ps 1cp
כִּי־טוֹב		וַיֹּאמֶר	אֱלֹהִים	נַעֲשֶׂה	אָדָם	בְּצַלְמֵנוּ
kî-ṯôv		wayyō'mer	'ĕlōhîm	na'ăseh	'ādhām	betsalmēnû
that good		and He said	God	let us make	humankind	in our image

3626, 1883	**7575.126**	**904, 1761**	**3328**	**904, 5591**
prep, n fs, ps 1cp	cj, v Qal impf 3mp	prep, *n fs*	art, n ms	cj, prep, *n ms*
כִּדְמוּתֵנוּ	וְיִרְדּוּ	בִדְגַת	הַיָּם	וּבְעוֹף
kidhmûthēnû	weyirdû	vidhghath	hayyām	ûv'ôph
according to our likeness	and they will rule	over the fish of	the sea	and over the birds of

8452	**904, 966**	**904, 3725, 800**	**904, 3725, 7719**
art, n md	cj, prep, art, n fs	cj, prep, *adj*, art n fs	cj, prep, *adj*, art, *n ms*
הַשָּׁמַיִם	וּבַבְּהֵמָה	וּבְכָל־הָאָרֶץ	וּבְכָל־הָרֶמֶשׂ
hashshāmayim	ûvabbehēmāh	ûvekhāl-hā'ārets	ûvekhāl-hāremes
the air	and over the animals	and over all the earth	and over every creeping thing

7718.151	**6142, 800**		**1282.121**	**435**	**881, 119**
art, v Qal act ptc ms	prep, art, n fs	**27.**	cj, v Qal impf 3ms	n mp	do, art, n ms
הָרֹמֵשׂ	עַל־הָאָרֶץ		וַיִּבְרָא	אֱלֹהִים	אֶת־הָאָדָם
hārōmēs	'al-hā'ārets		wayyivrā'	'ĕlōhîm	'eth-hā'ādhām
the creepers	on the earth		and He created	God	the humankind

904, 7021	**904, 7021**	**435**	**1282.111**	**881**	**2227**	**5531**
prep, *n ms*, ps 3ms	prep, *n ms*	n mp	v Qal pf 3ms	do, ps 3ms	n ms	cj, n fs
בְּצַלְמוֹ	בְּצֶלֶם	אֱלֹהִים	בָּרָא	אֹתוֹ	זָכָר	וּנְקֵבָה
betsalmô	betselem	'ĕlōhîm	bārā'	'ōthô	zākhār	ûnqēvāh
in His image	in the image of	God	He created	him	male	and female

1282.111	**881**		**1313.321**	**881**	**435**	**569.121**
v Qal pf 3ms	do, ps 3mp	**28.**	cj, v Piel impf 3ms	do, ps 3mp	n mp	cj, v Qal impf 3ms
בָּרָא	אֹתָם		וַיְבָרֶךְ	אֹתָם	אֱלֹהִים	וַיֹּאמֶר
bārā'	'ōthām		wayevārekh	'ōthām	'ĕlōhîm	wayyō'mer
He created	them		and He blessed	them	God	and He said

3937	**435**	**6759.133**	**7528.133**	**4527.133**	**881, 800**
prep, ps 3mp	n mp	v Qal impv 2mp	cj, v Qal impv 2mp	cj, v Qal impv 2mp	do, art, n fs
לָהֶם	אֱלֹהִים	פְּרוּ	וּרְבוּ	וּמִלְאוּ	אֶת־הָאָרֶץ
lāhem	'ĕlōhîm	perû	ûrevû	ûmil'û	'eth-hā'ārets
to them	God	be fruitful	and multiply	and fill	the earth

3653.133	**7575.133**	**904, 1761**	**3328**	**904, 5991**	**8452**
cj, v Qal impv 2mp, ps 3fs	cj, v Qal impv 2mp	prep, *n fs*	art, n ms	cj, prep, *n ms*	art, n md
וְכִבְשֻׁהָ	וּרְדוּ	בִּדְגַת	הַיָּם	וּבְעוֹף	הַשָּׁמַיִם
wekhivshuāh	ûredhû	bidhghath	hayyām	ûve'ôph	hashshāmayim
and subdue it	and rule	over the fish of	the sea	and over the birds of	the sky

904, 3725, 2516	7718.153	6142, 800		569.121	435
cj, prep, *adj*, n fs	art, v Qal act ptc fs	prep, art, n fs		cj, v Qal impf 3ms	n mp
וּבְכָל־חַיָּה	הָרֹמֶשֶׂת	עַל־הָאָרֶץ	**29.**	וַיֹּאמֶר	אֱלֹהִים
ûvekhol-chayyāh	hārōmeseth	'al-hā'ārets		wayyō'mer	'ĕlōhîm
and over every living thing of	the creeping things	on the earth		and He said	God

2079	5595.115	3937	881, 3725, 6448	2319.151	2320	866
intrj	v Qal pf 1cs	prep, ps 2mp	do, *adj*, n ms	v Qal act ptc ms	n ms	rel part
הִנֵּה	נָתַתִּי	לָכֶם	אֶת־כָּל־עֵשֶׂב	זֹרֵעַ	זֶרַע	אֲשֶׁר
hinnēh	nāthattî	lākhem	'eth-kāl-'ēsev	zōrēa'	zera'	'ăsher
behold	I have given	to you	every plant	producing seed	seed	which

26. And God said, Let us make man in our image, after our likeness: ... I will make man in my image, after my likeness, *Anchor* ... someone like ourselves, *LIVB* ... Let Us make men under Our Shadow, as Our Representatives, *Fenton* ... they will be like us and resemble us, *Good News*.

and let them have dominion over the fish of the sea, and over the fowl of the air, and over the cattle, and over all the earth, and over every creeping thing that creepeth upon the earth: ... They will have power over the fish, the birds, and all animals, domestic and wild, large and small, *Good News* ... to be the master of all life upon the earth and in the skies and in the seas, *MLB*.

27. So God created man in his own image, in the image of God created he him; male and female created he them: ... In the divine image created he him, *Anchor* ... making them to be like himself, *Good News* ... under His own Shadow, ...and constituting them male and female, *Fenton* ... in the image of God He prepared him, a male and a female, *Young* ... So God made man like his Maker...Man and maid, *LIVB*.

28. And God blessed them, and God said unto them, Be fruitful, and multiply, and replenish the earth, and subdue it: and have dominion over the fish of the sea, and over the fowl of the air, and over every living thing that moveth upon the earth: ... Have many children, so that your descendants will live all over the earth and bring it under their control. I am putting you in charge of the fish, the birds, and all the wild animals, *Good News*.

29. And God said, Behold, I have given you every herb bearing seed, which is upon the face of all the earth, and every tree, in the which is the fruit of a tree yielding seed; to you it shall be for meat: ... I have provided all kinds of grain and all kinds of fruit for you to eat, *Good News* ... for food every fruit and grain-bearing plant as well as fruit and seed-bearing trees and all vegetation, *Fenton* ... it shall be food for you, *NASB*.

30. And to every beast of the earth,

reflection of the Trinity. Because the world in Moses' day was not ready to understand the Trinity, and because the unity of God needed to be emphasized in contrast to the many gods of the pagans, verse 27 immediately says, "So God created man in his own image." Verse 27 draws attention to male and female who were God's special creation and who bore the image of God. Though standing upright seems to be important to indicate the authority they had over the other created beings, the image and likeness was not primarily physical, for God is Spirit (John 4:24; 1 Tim. 1:17; 6:16, cf. 1 Ki. 8:27). When Jesus was incarnated He had to be made "in human likeness"--He did not have that likeness as part of His nature before (Phil. 2:7-8). Ephesians 4:24 indicates that the likeness to God is a matter of "true righteousness and holiness." That is, it refers to the inner nature, not the physical body. The image and likeness also enables us to have fellowship with God. But it does not mean we are gods or can become gods. We were created dependent beings (Ps. 8:5), and even in the new heavens and the new earth we shall continue to be dependent on the light and energy that God provides through Christ as we both serve God and reign with Christ (Rev. 21:23; 22:3-5).

God blessed both male and female and commanded them to be fruitful and increase in number. Thus, children and a godly family were a priority in God's purpose for humankind. Ultimately this would mean the bringing of many into His Kingdom and glory (1 Thess. 2:12; Heb. 2:10).

1:29-31. The image of God also made it possible for humankind to be given the authority to rule over the rest of God's creation on the earth. This is a delegated responsibility, however, and human

6142, 6686	3725, 800	881, 3725, 6320	866, 904	6780, 6320
prep, *n mp*	*adj*, art, n fs	cj, do, *adj*, art, n ms	rel part, prep, ps 3ms	*n ms*, n ms
עַל־פְּנֵי	כָל־הָאָרֶץ	וְאֶת־כָּל־הָעֵץ	אֲשֶׁר־בּוֹ	פְּרִי־עֵץ
'al-p^{e}nê	khol-hā'ārets	w^{e}'eth-kol-hā'ēts	'ăsher-bô	ph^{e}rî-'ēts
on the surface of	all the earth	and all the trees	which on it	fruit of a tree

2319.151	2320	3937	2030.121	3937, 403		3937, 3725, 2516
v Qal act ptc ms	n ms	prep, ps 2mp	v Qal impf 3ms	prep, n fs	**30.**	cj, prep, *adj*, *n fs*
זֹרֵעַ	זָרַע	לָכֶם	יִהְיֶה	לְאָכְלָה		וּלְכָל־חַיַּת
zōrē'a	zāra'	lākhem	yihyeh	l^{e}'ākh^{e}lāh		ûlăkhol-chayyath
producing seed	seed	to you	it will be	for food		and to every living thing of

800	3937, 3725, 5991	8452	3937, 3725	7718.151	6142, 800
art, n fs	cj, prep, *adj*, *n ms*	art, n md	cj, prep, *adj*	v Qal act ptc ms	prep, art, n fs
הָאָרֶץ	וּלְכָל־עוֹף	הַשָּׁמַיִם	וּלְכֹל	רוֹמֵשׂ	עַל־הָאָרֶץ
hā'ārets	ûlăkhol-'ôph	hashshāmayim	ûlăkhōl	rômēs	'al-hā'ārets
the earth	and to every bird of	the air	and to every	creeping thing	on the earth

866, 904	5497	2516	881, 3725, 3537	6448	3937, 403
rel part, prep, ps 3ms	*n fs*	n fs	do, *adj*, *n ms*	n ms	prep, n fs
אֲשֶׁר־בּוֹ	נֶפֶשׁ	חַיָּה	אֶת־כָּל־יֶרֶק	עֵשֶׂב	לְאָכְלָה
'ăsher-bô	nephesh	chayyāh	'eth-kol-yereq	'ēsev	l^{e}'ākh^{e}lāh
which in it	the breath of	life	every green plant of	plants	for food

2030.121, 3772		7495.121	435	881, 3725, 866	6449.111	2079, 3005
cj, v Qal impf 3ms, adv	**31.**	cj, v Qal impf 3ms	n mp	do, *adj*, rel part	v Qal pf 3ms	cj, intrj, adj
וַיְהִי־כֵן		וַיַּרְא	אֱלֹהִים	אֶת־כָּל־אֲשֶׁר	עָשָׂה	וְהִנֵּה־טוֹב
wayhî-khēn		wayyar'	'ĕlōhîm	'eth-kol-'ăsher	'āsāh	w^{e}hinnēh-ṭôv
and it was so		and He saw	God	everything that	He made	and behold good

4108	2030.121, 6394	2030.121, 1269	3219	8676		3735.426
adv	cj, v Qal impf 3ms, n ms	cj, v Qal impf 3ms, n ms	n ms	art, num	**2:1**	cj, v Pual impf 3mp
מְאֹד	וַיְהִי־עֶרֶב	וַיְהִי־בֹקֶר	יוֹם	הַשִּׁשִּׁי		וַיְכֻלּוּ
m^{e}'ōdh	wayhî-'erev	wayhî-vōqer	yôm	hashshishshî		way^{e}khullû
very	and it was evening	and it was morning	day	the sixth		and they were finished

8452	800	3725, 6893		3735.321	435	904, 3219
art, n md	cj, art, n fs	cj, *adj*, n ms, ps 3mp	**2.**	cj, v Piel impf 3ms	n mp	prep, art, n ms
הַשָּׁמַיִם	וְהָאָרֶץ	וְכָל־צְבָאָם		וַיְכַל	אֱלֹהִים	בַּיּוֹם
hashshāmayim	w^{e}hā'ārets	w^{e}khol-ts^{e}vā'ām		waykhal	'ĕlōhîm	bayyôm
the heavens	and the earth	and all their hosts		and He finished	God	on the day

8113	4536	866	6449.111	8139.121	904, 3219	8113
art, num	n fs, ps 3fs	rel part	v Qal pf 3ms	cj, v Qal impf 3ms	prep, art, n ms	art, num
הַשְּׁבִיעִי	מְלַאכְתּוֹ	אֲשֶׁר	עָשָׂה	וַיִּשְׁבֹּת	בַּיּוֹם	הַשְּׁבִיעִי
hashsh^{e}vî'î	m^{e}la'khtô	'ăsher	'āsāh	wayyishbōth	bayyôm	hashsh^{e}vî'î
the seventh	His work	which	He did	and He ceased	on the day	the seventh

4623, 3725, 4536	866	6449.111		1313.321	435	881, 3219
prep, *adj*, n fs, ps 3ms	rel part	v Qal pf 3ms	**3.**	cj, v Piel impf 3ms	n mp	do, *n ms*
מִכָּל־מְלַאכְתּוֹ	אֲשֶׁר	עָשָׂה		וַיְבָרֶךְ	אֱלֹהִים	אֶת־יוֹם
mikkol-m^{e}la'khtô	'ăsher	'āsāh		way^{e}vārekh	'ĕlōhîm	'eth-yôm
from all His work	which	He did		and He blessed	God	the day of

8113	7227.321	881	3706	904	8139.111	4623, 3725, 4536
art, num	cj, v Piel impf 3ms	do, ps 3ms	cj	prep, ps 3ms	v Qal pf 3ms	prep, *adj*, n fs, ps 3ms
הַשְּׁבִיעִי	וַיְקַדֵּשׁ	אֹתוֹ	כִּי	בוֹ	שָׁבַת	מִכָּל־מְלַאכְתּוֹ
hashsh^{e}vî'î	way^{e}qaddēsh	'ōthô	kî	vô	shāvath	mikkol-m^{e}la'khtô
the seventh	and He made holy	it	because	on it	He ceased	from all His work

and to every fowl of the air, and to every thing that creepeth upon the earth, wherein there is life, I have given every green herb for meat: and it was so: ... To all...in which there is a living spirit, I give all the green plants for food, *Goodspeed* ... I have provided grass and leafy plants for food, *Good News*.

31. And God saw every thing that he had made, and, behold, it was very good: ... it was very beautiful, *Fenton* ... He was very pleased, *Good News* ... everything He had made was excellent, indeed, *MLB*.

And the evening and the morning were the sixth day: ... This ended the sixth day, *LIVB* ... Thus the close came, and the dawn came of the sixth age, *Fenton*.

2:1. Thus the heavens and the earth were finished, and all the host of them: ... with all their mighty throng, *NEB* ... were successfully completed, with all that they contained, *LIVB* ... in all their vast array, *NIV*.

2. And on the seventh day God ended his work which he had made; and he rested on the seventh day from all his work which he had made: ... God completed all the work he had been doing, *NEB* ... finished what he had been doing and stopped working, *Good News* ... desisting on the seventh day from all his work, *Goodspeed* ... God rested at the seventh age, *Fenton*.

3. And God blessed the seventh day, and sanctified it: because that in it he had rested from all his work which God created and made: ... he had desisted from all his work, *Goodspeed* ... made it holy, *BB, NCB, NEB, REB,* ... hallowed it, *RSV, Fenton*.

---

beings are held accountable for how they treat the plant and animal world. God told them to subdue the earth, that is bring it under control. God had placed many wonderful elements in the earth. This, then, was a command to learn about the earth and its riches, not through exploiting it, but by exploring it and using it in a way that would glorify God, the earth's Maker. If sin had not entered into the earth, physical science would surely have made much more progress in ancient times.

Humans were also to rule over the fish, birds and land creatures. This was an approval from God for biological science. It meant learning about the fish, animals and birds, giving some government in their use that would give glory to God.

Initially, humankind as well as animals and birds were given green plants for food. Adam and Eve were initially vegetarians. (This was changed after the flood. See Gen. 9:3.) After the final act of creation, God viewed His work and pronounced it very good (exceedingly good). He had now completed His plan of creation, and everything was in balance, perfectly suited to His divine purpose. Thus, we cannot blame God for the world's present condition (as chapter 3 will explain).

2:1. Verses 1-4 actually conclude the subject of chapter 1. The Bible had no chapter divisions until the 13th century A.D. when a preacher added them while riding horseback from one preaching place to another. He did well on the whole, but sometimes he made the division in the wrong place.

The sixth day finished the work of creation. "All the host of them" indicates the earth was no longer formless or empty, as it was in 1:2.

2:2. The first word of this verse uses the Hebrew verb form which indicates completed action. God had finished all His created work and on the seventh day He ceased from His work of creation. The word "rested" basically means "ceased" (e.g. when a lawyer "rests" his case, he means he has ceased his arguments). Thus, God is not presently creating new universes. This does not mean God was tired, however, or ceased working. Rather, He gave Himself to a new work of upholding His creation (cf. Col. 1:17, "by him [Christ] all things consist [hold together]," that is, the universe would fall apart if it were not for our Lord). Since the fall of humankind, He has given Himself to carry out His great plan of redemption. As Jesus said, "My Father worketh hitherto, and I work" (John 5:17).

2:3. God blessed the seventh day and sanctified it, that is, set it apart because His work of creation was complete. No mention is made of an evening and a morning for the seventh day. Some take this to mean that the seventh day has not ended and we are still in it--and will be in it until God creates the new heavens and the new earth. This gave a precedent for Israel to set apart and dedicate the seventh day to worship of the LORD (Exo. 20:11). We are not under law, and the New Testament calls for us to seek a "sabbath rest" where we cease from our own (selfish) works and enter a rest in which we remain every day (Heb. 4:9-11). God also intended that people should have a cycle of rest for their good and for a time of worship.

866, 1282.111	435	3937, 6449.141		431	8765	8452
rel part, v Qal pf 3ms	n mp	prep, v Qal inf con	**4.**	dem pron	*n fp*	art, n md
אֲשֶׁר־בָּרָא	אֱלֹהִים	לַעֲשׂוֹת		אֵלֶּה	תוֹלְדוֹת	הַשָּׁמַיִם
'ăsher-bārā'	'ĕlōhîm	la'ăsôth		'ēlleh	thôl^{e}dhôth	hashshāmayim
which He created	God	to make		these	the accounts of	the heavens

800	904, 1282.241	904, 3219	6449.141	3176	435	800
cj, art, n fs	cj, v Niphal inf con, ps 3mp	prep, *n ms*	v Qal inf con	pn	n mp	n fs
וְהָאָרֶץ	בְּהִבָּרְאָם	בְּיוֹם	עֲשׂוֹת	יְהוָה	אֱלֹהִים	אֶרֶץ
w^{e}hā'ārets	b^{e}hibbār'ām	b^{e}yôm	'ăsôth	y^{e}hwāh	'ĕlōhîm	'erets
and the earth	in their creating	on day of	making	Yahweh	God	earth

8452		3725	7944	7898	3071	2030.121	904, 800
cj, n md	**5.**	cj, *adj*	*n ms*	art, n ms	adv	v Qal impf 3ms	prep, n fs
וְשָׁמָיִם		וְכֹל	שִׂיחַ	הַשָּׂדֶה	טֶרֶם	יִהְיֶה	בָּאָרֶץ
w^{e}shāmāyim		w^{e}khōl	sîach	hassādheh	ṯerem	yihyeh	vā'ārets
and heavens		and all	the shrubs of	the field	not yet	they were	on the earth

3725, 6448	7898	3071	7048.121	3706	3940	4442.511
cj, *adj, n ms*	art, n ms	adv	v Qal impf 3ms	cj	neg part	v Hiphil pf 3ms
וְכָל־עֵשֶׂב	הַשָּׂדֶה	טֶרֶם	יִצְמָח	כִּי	לֹא	הִמְטִיר
w^{e}khol-'ēsev	hassādheh	ṯerem	yitsmāch	kî	lō'	himṯîr
and all the plants of	the field	not yet	they sprouted	because	not	He caused it to rain

3176	435	6142, 800	119	375	3937, 5856.141	881, 124
pn	n mp	prep, art, n fs	cj, n ms	sub	prep, v Qal inf con	do, art, n fs
יְהוָה	אֱלֹהִים	עַל־הָאָרֶץ	וְאָדָם	אַיִן	לַעֲבֹד	אֶת־הָאֲדָמָה
y^{e}hwāh	'ĕlōhîm	'al-hā'ārets	w^{e}'ādhām	'ayin	la'ăvōdh	'eth-hā'ădhāmāh
Yahweh	God	on the earth	and man	there was not	to cultivate	the ground

	105	6148.121	4623, 800	8615.511	881, 3725, 6686	124
6.	cj, n ms	v Qal impf 3ms	prep, art, n fs	v Hiphil pf 3ms	do, *adj, n ms*	art, n fs
	וְאֵד	יַעֲלֶה	מִן־הָאָרֶץ	וְהִשְׁקָה	אֶת־כָּל־פְּנֵי	הָאֲדָמָה
	w^{e}'ēdh	ya'ăleh	min-hā'ārets	w^{e}hishqāh	'eth-kol-p^{e}nê	hā'ădhāmāh
	but a mist	it went up	from the earth	and it watered	all the surface of	the ground

	3443.121	3176	435	881, 119	6312	4623, 124
7.	v Qal impf 3ms	pn	n mp	do, art, n ms	n ms	prep, art, n fs
	וַיִּיצֶר	יְהוָה	אֱלֹהִים	אֶת־הָאָדָם	עָפָר	מִן־הָאֲדָמָה
	wayyîtser	y^{e}hwāh	'ĕlōhîm	'eth-hā'ādhām	'āphār	min-hā'ădhāmāh
	and He formed	Yahweh	God	the man	dust	from the ground

5483.121	904, 653	5580	2508	2030.121	119	3937, 5497
cj, v Qal impf 3ms	prep, n mp, ps 3ms	*n fs*	n mp	cj, v Qal impf 3ms	art, n ms	prep, n fs
וַיִּפַּח	בְּאַפָּיו	נִשְׁמַת	חַיִּים	וַיְהִי	הָאָדָם	לְנֶפֶשׁ
wayyippach	b^{e}'appāv	nishmath	chayyîm	wayhî	hā'ādhām	l^{e}nephesh
and He breathed	into his nostrils	the breath of	life	and he became	the man	being

4. These are the generations of the heavens and of the earth when they were created, in the day that the LORD God made the earth and the heavens: ... This is the account, *NASB, NIV* ... These were the productions, *Fenton* ... This is the story, *NEB, NCB*.

5. And every plant of the field before it was in the earth, and every herb of the field before it grew: ... there was not yet any field shrub, *NCB* ... before the Ever-Living God had scattered them, *Fenton*.

for the LORD God had not caused it to rain upon the earth: ... Jehovah Elohim had not caused it to rain, *Darby* ... for God Yahweh had not sent rain, *Anchor*.

and there was not a man to till the ground: ... no man to do work on the land, *BB* ... no man to cultivate, *Berkeley, MLB* ... nor was there anyone to farm the soil, *LIVB*.

6. But there went up a mist from

the earth, and watered the whole face of the ground: ... A flood used to rise out of the earth, *NEB* ... streams came up, *NIV* ... Moisture used to well up out of the earth, *REB* ... a vapor used to rise, *Berkeley, MLB.*

7. And the LORD God formed man of the dust of the ground: ... Lord God formed a human being, *REB* ... God Yahweh formed man from clods in the soil, *Anchor* ... And Jehovah Elohim formed Man, *Darby.*

and breathed into his nostrils the breath of life; and man became a living soul: ... breathed into his nostrils the life of animals; but man became a life-containing soul, *Fenton* ... became a living person, *LIVB.*

2:4. The Hebrew uses the phrase *'elleh tholedoth,* "these are the generations [progeny] of..." This phrase is used ten times in Genesis and provides the framework of the book. It is the key to Moses' own outline of its contents. In the latter part of the Book it is used in two ways. In 25:12, "the generations of Ishmael" is followed by a list of names only, for Ishmael's descendants do not carry on the chosen line. In 25:19, "the generations of Isaac" is followed, not by a list of names, but by the events in the life of Jacob, who was the next one to carry on the chosen line. In 36:1, "the generations of Esau" is followed by a list of names, for Esau did not carry on the chosen line either. But 37:2, "the generations of Jacob" is followed by the events in the life of Joseph and his brothers who would carry on the chosen line and become the chosen nation.

From these examples we see that the phrase "these are the generations of ..." is transitional. Thus, in 2:4, it means the book is through dealing with the heavens and earth in general and will now focus on the details of the creation of humankind. Note that "the day" here includes all six of the creation days of chapter one.

The first chapter was chronological and emphasized a doctrine of a sovereign, transcendent, yet personal God in relation to humankind. The second chapter is topical and gives us a doctrine of humanity in relation to God. The center of attention is the step-by-step creation of the first man and the first woman. Thus, other things are mentioned when they are brought into relation with Adam.

Notice God is now referred to as LORD God (Hebrew, *Yahweh Elohim*). Elohim is from a root word that speaks of power. Yahweh is God's personal name that speaks of His entire being in action, especially in his relationships where He is with people. It is also his covenant-keeping name and means "He will [actively] continue to be." The consonants of Yahweh were written in the New Latin as JHVH. Shortly before New Testament times, Jews began to substitute the word Adonai, "Lord," for this personal name. In modern times people combined the consonants of the personal name JHVH with the vowels of the Hebrew word for Lord to give the nonbiblical form "Jehovah."

Beginning in the 18th century unbelieving scholars began to theorize that the Pentateuch was composed of separate documents which they eventually said were not written by Moses but by later writers or groups of writers and editors: a "J" document using the name Yahweh for God, an "E" document using the term Elohim for God, a "D" document consisting of Deuteronomy, and a "P" document written by priestly writers who included editorial notes throughout. These JEDP documents, they claimed, were not patched together in the present form of the Pentateuch until near the time of Ezra. However, the usage of the names fits the context, Elohim emphasizing God's power and Yahweh emphasizing His personal relationships with His people. Archaeological discoveries provide much evidence that the entire Pentateuch fits the time of Moses and not the later time. As Bible-believing scholars we accept the Bible's own claim that Moses wrote the Pentateuch, the first five books of the Bible. To doubt that Moses is the author contradicts Jesus himself (e.g. Matt. 19:7,8; John 7:19).

In Genesis 1, the emphasis is on God's power shown in creation. Chapter 2 is also dealing with creation, but it shows God's personal attention to the creation of man and woman, which could explain the use of LORD God, the compound name.

2:5-6. This goes back to the third creation day and draw attention to God's purpose to create plants for the benefit of human beings. If the theory of the cloud blanket is correct, it would have kept an even temperature over the whole earth. This would mean no warm fronts, cold fronts, and thus, no rain. Gentle on-shore breezes during the day and off-shore breezes at night, with the high humidity would bring in a heavy mist that watered the land as verse 6 suggests. Finally, beginning with the fourth creation day there were seasons and rain.

2:7. Verse 7 points to the sixth creation day and gives details of the latter part of it. It lets us

2516		5378.121	3176	435	1629	904, 5942	4623, 7208
n fs	**8.**	cj, v Qal impf 3ms	pn	n mp	n ms	prep, pn	prep, n ms
חַיָּה		וַיִּטַּע	יְהוָה	אֱלֹהִים	גַּן	בְּעֵדֶן	מִקֶּדֶם
chayyāh		wayyitta‘	y^{e}hwāh	'ĕlōhîm	gan	b^{e}‘ēdhen	miqqedhem
living being		and He planted	Yahweh	God	garden	in Eden	of the east

7947.121	8427	881, 119	866	3443.111		7048.521
cj, v Qal impf 3ms	adv	do, art, n ms	rel part	v Qal pf 3ms	**9.**	cj, v Hiphil impf 3ms
וַיָּשֶׂם	שָׁם	אֶת־הָאָדָם	אֲשֶׁר	יָצָר		וַיַּצְמַח
wayyāsem	shām	'eth-hā'ādhām	'ăsher	yātsār		wayyatsmach
and He put	there	the humankind	which	He formed		and He caused to grow

3176	435	4623, 124	3725, 6320	2629.255	3937, 4920	3005
pn	n mp	prep, art, n fs	adj, n ms	v Niphal ptc ms	prep, n ms	cj, adj
יְהוָה	אֱלֹהִים	מִן־הָאֲדָמָה	כָּל־עֵץ	נֶחְמָד	לְמַרְאֶה	וְטוֹב
y^{e}hwāh	'ĕlōhîm	min-hā'ădhāmāh	kol-‘ēts	nechmādh	l^{e}mar'eh	w^{e}ṭôv
Yahweh	God	from the ground	every tree	pleasing	for sight	and good

3937, 4120	6320	2522	904, 8761	1629	6320	1907
prep, n ms	cj, *n ms*	art, n mp	prep, sub	art, n ms	cj, *n ms*	art, *n fs*
לְמַאֲכָל	וְעֵץ	הַחַיִּים	בְּתוֹךְ	הַגָּן	וְעֵץ	הַדַּעַת
l^{e}ma'ăkhol	w^{e}‘ēts	hachayyîm	b^{e}thôkh	haggān	w^{e}‘ēts	hadda‘ath
for food	and the tree of	the life	in the middle of	the garden	and the tree of	the knowledge of

3005	7737II		5282	3428.151	4623, 5942	8615.541
adj	cj, adj	**10.**	cj, n ms	v Qal act ptc ms	prep, pn	prep, v Hiphil inf con
טוֹב	וָרָע		וְנָהָר	יֹצֵא	מֵעֵדֶן	לְהַשְׁקוֹת
ṭôv	wārā‘		w^{e}nāhār	yōtsē'	mē‘ēdhen	l^{e}hashqôth
good	and evil		and a river	going out	from Eden	to water

881, 1629	4623, 8427	6754.221	2030.111	3937, 727	7513		8428
do, art, n ms	cj, prep, adv	v Niphal impf 3ms	cj, Qal pf 3ms	prep, num	n mp	**11.**	*n ms*
אֶת־הַגָּן	וּמִשָּׁם	יִפָּרֵד	וְהָיָה	לְאַרְבָּעָה	רָאשִׁים		שֵׁם
'eth-haggān	ûmishshām	yippārēdh	w^{e}hāyāh	l^{e}'arbā‘āh	rā'shîm		shēm
the garden	and from there	it divided	and it became	four	heads		the name of

259	6618	2000	5621.151	881	3725, 800	2434
art, num	pn	pers pron	art, v Qal act ptc ms	do	*adj, n fs*	art, pn
הָאֶחָד	פִּישׁוֹן	הוּא	הַסֹּבֵב	אֵת	כָּל־אֶרֶץ	הַחֲוִילָה
hā'echādh	pîshôn	hû'	hassōvēv	'ēth	kol-'erets	hachwîlāh
the first	Pishon	it	the one that flows around		all the land of	the Havilah

866, 8427	2174		2174	800	2000	3005	8427
rel part, adv	art, n ms	**12.**	cj, *n ms*	art, n fs	art, dem pron	adj	adv
אֲשֶׁר־שָׁם	הַזָּהָב		וּזֲהַב	הָאָרֶץ	הַהִוא	טוֹב	שָׁם
'ăsher-shom	hazzāhāv		ûzăhav	hā'ārets	hahiw'	ṭôv	shām
where there	the gold		and the gold of	the land	the that	good	there

952	63	8172		8428, 5282	8529	1556
art, n ms	cj, *n fs*	art, n ms	**13.**	cj, *n ms*, art, n ms	art, num	pn
הַבְּדֹלַח	וְאֶבֶן	הַשֹּׁהַם		וְשֵׁם־הַנָּהָר	הַשֵּׁנִי	גִּיחוֹן
habb^{e}dhōlach	w^{e}'even	hashshōham		w^{e}shēm-hannāhār	hashshēnî	gîchôn
the bdellium	and the stone of	the onyx		and the name of the river	the second	Gihon

2000	5621.151	881	3725, 800	3688		8428, 5282
pers pron	art, v Qal act ptc ms	do	*adj, n fs*	pn	**14.**	cj, *n ms*, art, n ms
הוּא	הַסּוֹבֵב	אֵת	כָּל־אֶרֶץ	כּוּשׁ		וְשֵׁם־הַנָּהָר
hû'	hassōvēv	'ēth	kol-'erets	kûsh		w^{e}shēm-hannāhār
it	the one that flows around		all the land of	Cush		and the name of the river

8. And the LORD God planted a garden eastward in Eden; and there he put the man whom he had formed.

9. And out of the ground made the LORD God to grow every tree that is pleasant to the sight, and good for food; the tree of life also in the midst of the garden, and the tree of knowledge of good and evil: ... the tree of knowing good and evil, *Berkeley* ... Tree of Conscience, *LIVB.*

10. And a river went out of Eden to water the garden; and from thence it was parted, and became into four heads: ... hath become four chief rivers, *Young* ... becomes four branches, *NAB* ... became four main streams, *Darby*, ... river watering the garden flowed from there it divided; it had four headstreams, *NIV.*

11. The name of the first is Pison: ... Pishon, *Anchor, NKJV, NRSV, KJVII.*

that is it which compasseth the whole land of Havilah, where there is gold: ... flows around all the land, *MLB* ... skirts the whole land, *REB* ... encircles all the land of Heliva, *NCB.*

12. And the gold of that land is good: ... high quality gold, *Berkeley* ... excellent, *NAB* ... gold is choice, *Anchor.*

there is bdellium and the onyx stone: ... aromatic resin and onyx, *NIV* ... gum resin and cornelians, *REB* ... bdolach and the shoham stone, *Young* ... lapis lazuli are also there, *NAB, Anchor.*

13. And the name of the second river is Gihon: ... is Jihon, *Fenton.*

the same is it that compasseth the whole land of Ethiopia: ... Chus, *NCB* ... Kush, *Fenton* ... Cush, *NIV, NASB, KJVII.*

14. And the name of the third river is Hiddekel: ... Tigris, *NEB, BB, RSV.*

that is it which goeth toward the east of Assyria: ... Asshur, *NIV, REB* ... Asher, *LIVB.*

And the fourth river is Euphrates: ... Phrat, *Young* ... Frath, *Fenton.*

15. And the LORD God took the man, and put him into the garden

---

know that the man (Heb. *hā'ădām*) was created first. Adam is used later in Hebrew for humankind in general, but was initially the name of the first man. Adam comes from a root word which means to be red or red-brown like tropical soil. So God carefully molded the body of the man (*hā'ădām*) out of the dark red dust of the ground (Heb., *hā'ădām āh*). Then God breathed into man's nostrils and he became a living soul (literally, "soul of life"), that is a living person, or a physical being with individuality. "Soul of life" does not refer to a theological soul. The same phrase is used in 1:20-21, 24 of fish and animals and simply means they were living individuals. So Adam became a living individual. But he was more than the animals, for God breathed into him the breath of life. This suggests human beings have a unique relationship to God because we are made in the image and likeness of God and are intended to have fellowship with God. Nothing else in God's creation received the breath of God.

2:8. In addition to the general creation of plant life on the third creation day, God by the sixth day had planted a beautiful garden, specially prepared for Adam. It was eastward in Eden ("land of delight"), possibly near what is now the Persian Gulf.

2:9-14. These verses are possibly a parenthesis giving more information about the garden. It was full of trees bearing delicious fruit, but in the middle of the garden were both the tree of life and the tree of the knowledge of good and evil. A river flowed out of Eden through the garden and divided into four heads. The first two, the Pishon and the Gihon are not easy to identify today. The Pishon and the land of Havilah, however, must have been known in Moses' day, for he knew of the gold and jewels that came from there. The Gihon went around the land of Cush. In most of the Old Testament, Cush means Ethiopia. But there is another Cush in the east which is more likely the meaning here. The other two rivers are well known. The Hiddekel is the Tigris and the Euphrates remains the great river of the Middle East. The relationships of the rivers, however, must have been changed, probably due to great changes in the earth's geography during Noah's flood.

2:15-19. Here a continuation is found from verse 9 by adding that Adam was given work to do, such as cultivating, trimming and caring for the garden (otherwise the garden could have become a jungle). This work would be healthy and also a joy, thus, God made him a responsible being sharing in part of the work of taking care of God's creation. God never intended for His gifts to be neglected, misused, or wasted. He is active. People should be active, serving God where He has put them.

Adam was created a moral being with the power of free choice. God placed the tree of the

8389	2408	2000	2050.151	7209	831	5282
art, num	pn	pers pron	art, v Qal act ptc ms	*n fs*	pn	cj, art, n ms
הַשְּׁלִישִׁי	חִדֶּקֶל	הוּא	הַהֹלֵךְ	קִדְמַת	אַשּׁוּר	וְהַנָּהָר
hashsh^{e}lîshî	chiddeqel	hû'	hahōlēkh	qidhmath	'ashshûr	w^{e}hannāhār
the third	Hiddekel	it	the one that flows	east of	Assyria	and the river

7536	2000	6828		4089.121	3176	435	881, 119
art, num	pers pron	pn	**15.**	cj, v Qal impf 3ms	pn	n mp	do, art, n ms
הָרְבִיעִי	הוּא	פְרָת		וַיִּקַּח	יְהוָה	אֱלֹהִים	אֶת־הָאָדָם
hār^{e}vî'î	hû'	ph^{e}rāth		wayyiqqach	y^{e}hwāh	'ĕlōhîm	'eth-hā'ādhām
the fourth	it	Euphrates		and He took	Yahweh	God	the man

5299.521	904, 1629, 5942	3937, 5856.141	3937, 8490
cj, v Hiphil impf 3ms, ps 3ms	prep, *n ms*, pn	prep, v Qal inf con, ps 3fs	cj, prep, v Qal inf con, ps 3fs
וַיַּנִּחֵהוּ	בְגַן־עֵדֶן	לְעָבְדָהּ	וּלְשָׁמְרָהּ
wayyannichēhû	v^{e}ghan-'ēdhen	l^{e}'āv^{e}dhāhh	ûlăshāmrāhh
and He put him	in the garden of Eden	to till it	and to care for it

	6943	3176	435	6142, 119	3937, 569.141	4623, 3725
16.	cj, v Piel impf 3ms	pn	n mp	prep, art, n ms	prep, v Qal inf con	prep, adj
	וַיְצַו	יְהוָה	אֱלֹהִים	עַל־הָאָדָם	לֵאמֹר	מִכֹּל
	waytsaw	y^{e}hwāh	'ĕlōhîm	'al-hā'ādhām	lē'mōr	mikkōl
	and He commanded	Yahweh	God	to the man	saying	from every

6320, 1629	404.142	404.123		4623, 6320	1907	3005
n ms, art, n ms	v Qal inf abs	v Qal impf 2ms	**17.**	cj, prep, *n ms*	art, *n fs*	adj
עֵץ־הַגָּן	אָכֹל	תֹּאכֵל		וּמֵעֵץ	הַדַּעַת	טוֹב
'ēts-haggān	'ākhōl	tō'khēl		ûmē'ēts	hadda'ath	ṯôv
tree of the garden	eating	you may eat		but from the tree of	the knowledge of	good

7737II	3940	404.123	4623	3706	904, 3219	404.141
cj, adj	neg part	v Qal impf 2ms	prep, ps 3ms	cj	prep, *n ms*	v Qal inf con, ps 2ms
וָרָע	לֹא	תֹאכַל	מִמֶּנּוּ	כִּי	בְּיוֹם	אֲכָלְךָ
wārā'	lō'	thō'khal	mimmennû	kî	b^{e}yôm	'ăkhāl^{e}khā
and evil	not	you will eat	from it	because	on the day of	your eating

4623	4322.142	4322.123		569.121	3176	435	3940, 3005
prep, ps 3ms	v Qal inf abs	v Qal impf 2ms	**18.**	cj, v Qal impf 3ms	pn	n mp	neg part, adj
מִמֶּנּוּ	מוֹת	תָּמוּת		וַיֹּאמֶר	יְהוָה	אֱלֹהִים	לֹא־טוֹב
mimmennû	môth	tāmûth		wayyō'mer	y^{e}hwāh	'ĕlōhîm	lō'-ṯôv
from it	dying	you will die		and He said	Yahweh	God	not good

2030.141	119	3937, 940	6449.125, 3937	6039	3626, 5224
v Qal inf con	art, n ms	prep, n ms, ps 3ms	v Qal impf 1cs, prep, ps 3ms	n ms	prep, prep, ps 3ms
הֱיוֹת	הָאָדָם	לְבַדּוֹ	אֶעֱשֶׂה־לּוֹ	עֵזֶר	כְּנֶגְדּוֹ
hĕyôth	hā'ādhām	l^{e}vaddô	'e'ĕsehh-lô	'ēzer	k^{e}neghdô
to be	the man	by himself	I will make for him	help	like his counterpart

	3443.121	3176	435	4623, 124	3725, 2516	7898
19.	cj, v Qal impf 3ms	pn	n mp	prep, art, n fs	*adj, n fs*	art, n ms
	וַיִּצֶר	יְהוָה	אֱלֹהִים	מִן־הָאֲדָמָה	כָּל־חַיַּת	הַשָּׂדֶה
	wayyitser	y^{e}hwāh	'ĕlōhîm	min-hā'ădhāmāh	kol-chayyath	hassādheh
	so He formed	Yahweh	God	from the ground	every animal of	the field

881	3725, 5991	8452	971.521	420, 119	3937, 7495.141
cj, do	*adj, n ms*	art, n md	cj, v Hiphil impf 3ms	prep, art, n ms	prep, v Qal inf con
וְאֵת	כָּל־עוֹף	הַשָּׁמַיִם	וַיָּבֵא	אֶל־הָאָדָם	לִרְאוֹת
w^{e}'ēth	kol-'ôph	hashshāmayim	wayyāvē'	'el-hā'ādhām	lir'ôth
and	every bird of	the air	and He brought	to the man	to see

4242, 7410.121, 3937	3725	866	7410.121, 3937	119	5497
intrg, v Qal impf 3ms, prep, ps 3ms	cj, adj	rel part	v Qal impf 3ms, prep, ps 3ms	art, n ms	*n fs*
מַה־יִּקְרָא־לוֹ	וְכֹל	אֲשֶׁר	יִקְרָא־לוֹ	הָאָדָם	נֶפֶשׁ
mah-yiqŏrā'-lô	w^{e}khōl	'ăsher	yiqŏrā'-lô	hā'ādhām	nephesh
what he would name it	and all	that	he named them	the man	creatures of

2516	2000	8428		7410.121	119	8428
n fs	pers pron	n ms, ps 3ms		cj, v Qal impf 3ms	art, n ms	n mp
חַיָּה	הוּא	שְׁמוֹ	**20.**	וַיִּקְרָא	הָאָדָם	שֵׁמוֹת
chayyāh	hû'	sh^{e}mô		wayyiqŏrā'	hā'ādhām	shēmôth
living things	that	its name		and he named	the man	names

3937, 3725, 966	3937, 5991	8452	3937, 3725	2516	7898	3937, 119
prep, *adj*, art, n ms	cj, prep, *n ms*	art, n md	cj, prep, adj	*n fs*	art, n ms	cj, prep, n ms
לְכָל־הַבְּהֵמָה	וּלְעוֹף	הַשָּׁמַיִם	וּלְכֹל	חַיַּת	הַשָּׂדֶה	וּלְאָדָם
l^{e}khāl-habb^{e}hēmāh	ûl'ôph	hashshāmayim	ûlăkhōl	chayyath	hassādheh	ûlă'ādhām
to every animal	and to the birds of	the sky	and to every	living thing of	the field	but for man

of Eden to dress it and to keep it: ... cultivate, *NASB* ... work and take care of, *NIV* ... settled him in to care for it, *NAB.*

16. And the LORD God commanded the man, saying, Of every tree of the garden thou mayest freely eat: ... gave the man this warning, *LIVB* ... gave the man orders, *BB* ... Jehovah Elohim commanded, *Darby.*

17. But of the tree of the knowledge of good and evil, thou shalt not eat of it: for in the day that thou eatest thereof thou shalt surely die: ... Tree of Conscience - for its fruit will open your eyes to make you aware of right and wrong, *LIVB* ... you must die, *NCB* ... doomed to die, *NAB.*

18. And the LORD God said, It is not good that the man should be alone: ... to be in solitude, *Fenton.*

I will make him an help meet for him: ... helper as his counterpart, *Young* ... who is like him, *Goodspeed* ... helper suited to his needs, *LIVB* ... completing him, *MLB* ... an aid fit for him, *Anchor.*

19. And out of the ground the LORD God formed every beast of the field, and every fowl of the air; and brought them unto Adam to see what he would call them: ... took some soil from the ground, *Good News* ... molded out of the ground, *Goodspeed.*

and whatsoever Adam called every living creature, that was the name thereof: ... whatever the man with the Living Soul, *Fenton.*

knowledge of good and evil in the Garden giving an opportunity to choose to obey Him instead of pleasing the self. Because God is a just God and cannot look on sin with indifference, a penalty was provided for disobedience. As a moral being Adam was accountable for his actions, and eating from that tree would bring death (which in the Bible has the primary meaning of separation). The Hebrew uses an infinite absolute here to emphasize the certainty of death, literally, "dying you shall die," means "you shall surely die." In other parts of the Old Testament the same phrase is used of sudden death (see 1 Sam. 14:44; 22:16; 1 Ki. 2:37;), but since Adam was both a spiritual and physical being, spiritual death (separation from God) would be immediate and physical death would come later.

God also created Adam to be a social being. Verse 8 says it was not good for him to be alone. Therefore God determined to make a help "meet" for him, that is, corresponding to him or as his counterpart--like him mentally, physically, and spiritually. The word "help" is most often used of God being a help to His people and does not indicate any inferiority or subordination. The man and the woman were meant to be partners, each contributing their full abilities to the well being of each other and the family, as well as to the glory of God.

Before God created the woman He prepared Adam by bringing to him all kinds of animals and birds which He had already formed out of the ground. Now God gave Adam the opportunity of naming them all. "Name" in the Hebrew indicates the nature and character.

Verse 19 says whatever Adam called every living creature ("living soul"), that was its name. Adam was created as an intelligent being, who took time to observe the habits of each kind of bird and animal, and give it a name befitting its nature.

3940, 4834.111	6039	3626, 5224	21.	5489.521	3176	435
neg part, v Qal pf 3ms	n ms	prep, prep, ps 3ms		cj, v Hiphil impf 3ms	pn	n mp
לֹא־מָצָא	עֵזֶר	כְּנֶגְדּוֹ		וַיַּפֵּל	יְהוָה	אֱלֹהִים
lō'-mātsā'	‘ēzer	k^{e}neghdô		wayyappēl	y^{e}hwāh	'ĕlōhîm
he did not find	help	like his counterpart		and He caused to fall	Yahweh	God

8976	6142, 119	3583.121	4089.121	259	4623, 7029
n fs	prep, art, n ms	cj, v Qal impf 3ms	cj, v Qal impf 3ms	num	prep, n fp, ps 3ms
תַּרְדֵּמָה	עַל־הָאָדָם	וַיִּישָׁן	וַיִּקַּח	אַחַת	מִצַּלְעֹתָיו
tardēmāh	‘al-hā’ādhām	wayyîshān	wayyiqqach	'achath	mitstsal‘ōthâv
deep sleep	on the man	and he was sleeping	and He took	one	from his ribs

5646	1340	8809	22.	1161.121	3176	435	881, 7029
cj, v Qal impf 3ms	n ms	n fs, ps 3fs		cj, v Qal impf 3ms	pn	n mp	do, art, n fs
וַיִּסְגֹּר	בָּשָׂר	תַּחְתֶּנָּה		וַיִּבֶן	יְהוָה	אֱלֹהִים	אֶת־הַצֵּלָע
wayyisgōr	bāsār	tachtennāh		wayyiven	y^{e}hwāh	'ĕlōhîm	'eth-hatstsēlā‘
and He closed	flesh	its underside		and He built	Yahweh	God	the rib

866, 4089.111	4623, 119	3937, 828	971.521	420, 119
rel part, v Qal pf 3ms	prep, art, n ms	prep, n fs	cj, v Hiphil impf 3ms, ps 3fs	prep, art, n ms
אֲשֶׁר־לָקַח	מִן־הָאָדָם	לְאִשָּׁה	וַיְבִאֶהָ	אֶל־הָאָדָם
'ăsher-lāqach	min-hā’ādhām	l^{e}'ishshāh	way^{e}vi'ehā	'el-hā’ādhām
which He had taken	from the man	into a woman	and He brought her	to the man

23.	569.121	119	2148	6718	6344	4623, 6344	1340
	cj, v Qal impf 3ms	art, n ms	dem pron	art, n fs	n fs	prep, n fp, ps 1cs	cj, n ms
	וַיֹּאמֶר	הָאָדָם	זֹאת	הַפַּעַם	עֶצֶם	מֵעֲצָמַי	וּבָשָׂר
	wayyō'mer	hā’ādhām	zō'th	happa‘am	‘etsem	mē‘ătsāmay	ûvāsār
	and he said	the man	this	this time	bone	from my bones	and flesh

4623, 1340	3937, 2148	7410.221	828	3706	4623, 382	4089.412, 2148
prep, n ms, ps 1cs	prep, dem pron	v Niphal impf 3ms	n fs	cj	prep, n ms	v Pual pf 3fs, dem pron
מִבְּשָׂרִי	לְזֹאת	יִקָּרֵא	אִשָּׁה	כִּי	מֵאִישׁ	לֻקֳחָה־זֹּאת
mibb^{e}sārî	l^{e}zō'th	yiqqārē'	'ishshāh	kî	mē'îsh	luqŏchāh-zō'th
from my flesh	this	it will be named	woman	because	from man	she was taken this

24.	6142, 3772	6013.121, 382	881, 1	881, 524	1740.111	904, 828
	prep, adv	v Qal impf 3ms, n ms	do, n ms, ps 3ms	cj, do, n fs, ps 3ms	cj, v Qal pf 3ms	prep, n fs, ps 3ms
	עַל־כֵּן	יַעֲזָב־אִישׁ	אֶת־אָבִיו	וְאֶת־אִמּוֹ	וְדָבַק	בְּאִשְׁתּוֹ
	‘al-kēn	ya‘ăzāv-'îsh	'eth-'āvîw	w^{e}'eth-'immô	w^{e}dhāvaq	b^{e}'ishtô
	therefore	man leaves	his father	and his mother	and he cleaves	with his wife

2030.116	3937, 1340	259	25.	2030.126	8529	6414
cj, v Qal pf 3cp	prep, n ms	num		cj, v Qal impf 3mp	num, ps 3mp	adj
וְהָיוּ	לְבָשָׂר	אֶחָד		וַיִּהְיוּ	שְׁנֵיהֶם	עֲרוּמִּים
w^{e}hāyû	l^{e}vāsār	'echādh		wayyihyû	sh^{e}nêhem	‘ărûmmîm
and they become	flesh	one		and they were	the two of them	naked

119	828	3940	991.726	3:1	5357	2030.111	6415
art, n ms	cj, n fs, ps 3ms	cj, neg part	v Hithpolel impf 3mp		cj, art, n ms	v Qal pf 3ms	adj
הָאָדָם	וְאִשְׁתּוֹ	וְלֹא	יִתְבֹּשָׁשׁוּ		וְהַנָּחָשׁ	הָיָה	עָרוּם
hā’ādhām	w^{e}'ishtô	w^{e}lō'	yithbōshāshû		w^{e}hannāchāsh	hāyâh	‘ārûm
the man	and his wife	but not	they were ashamed		and the serpent	it was	subtle

4623, 3725	2516	7898	866	6449.111	3176	435	569.121
prep, adj	*n fs*	art, n ms	rel part	v Qal pf 3ms	pn	n mp	cj, v Qal impf 3ms
מִכֹּל	חַיַּת	הַשָּׂדֶה	אֲשֶׁר	עָשָׂה	יְהוָה	אֱלֹהִים	וַיֹּאמֶר
mikkōl	chayyath	hassādheh	'ăsher	‘āsāh	y^{e}hwāh	'ĕlōhîm	wayyō'mer
of all	the animals of	the field	which	He made	Yahweh	God	and he said

20. And Adam gave names to all cattle, and to the fowl of the air, and to every beast of the field: ... to all domestic animals, *Berkely Goodspeed.*

but for Adam there was not found an help meet for him: ... none proved to be the aid that would be fit for man, *Anchor* ... no one like himself as a help, *BB* ... no suitable partner was found, *REB* ... a helper comparable to him, *NKJV.*

21. And the LORD God caused a deep sleep to fall upon Adam, and he slept: ... threw the man into a stupor, *Fenton* ... trance, *NEB, Goodspeed.*

and he took one of his ribs, and closed up the flesh instead thereof: ... one of the bones from his side, *BB* ... filled up the place with flesh, *Berkeley* ... closed up the flesh at that spot, *Anchor.*

22. And the rib, which the LORD God had taken from man, made he a woman, and brought her unto the man: ... built up into a woman, *Goodspeed, REB.*

23. And Adam said, This is now bone of my bones, and flesh of my flesh: ... This is the proper step, *Young* ... here is one of my own kind, *Good News.*

she shall be called Woman, because she was taken out of Man: ... out of her man, *NAB.*

24. Therefore shall a man leave his father and his mother, and shall cleave unto his wife: and they shall be one flesh: ... be joined to his wife, *BB* ... attaches himself to his wife, *REB.*

25. And they were both naked, the man and his wife, and were not ashamed: ... felt no shame in each other's presence, *MLB.*

3:1. Now the serpent was more subtil than any beast of the field which the LORD God had made:

2:20. By the time he finished naming them all, Adam realized he was the only being in God's creation that did not have a partner corresponding to him. In other words, God let Adam become lonesome so he would be ready to receive the woman God was about to make.

2:21-22. God put Adam into a sleep of unconsciousness and took, not merely the bone of a rib, but a piece of Adam's side including skin, flesh, blood, nerves, and bone. From these He built a woman. When God created the man the word "formed" is the same word used of a potter forming a clay jar. But the word "build" here seems to mean God paid even more attention to the creation of the woman.

2:23. Adam received her with delight, recognizing that she was indeed created from his bones and flesh, and called her "woman" (Hebrew, *'ishshah*, also means "wife"), because she was taken out of man (Hebrew, *'ish*, "an individual male person," also means "husband."). As someone has said, God did not take the woman out of the man's feet to be stepped on as an inferior; nor out of his head to be put on a pedestal as a superior; but from his side close to his heart as an equal. She was to take her share of responsibility, and to love him and be loved by him.

2:24. Then Moses added God's application of this to Moses' own day. A man shall leave his father and mother and cleave unto (stick to, be glued to) his wife. The custom in Moses' day called for a man to bring his wife home where she became in effect a slave of her husband's mother. But Moses challenged the people to let couples have more of their own life. God wanted the family unit to be strong, with both love and loyalty continuing to seal the marriage bond.

2:25. The chapter concludes with the unashamed nakedness of Adam and his wife. They felt no disgrace because the human body was created by God and was part of everything that was very good (Gen. 1:31). The entire Old Testament considers every part of the body as beautiful and precious. This statement shows us that conditions were different in the beginning. Adam and Eve were in a state of innocence, as innocent as new born babies, and there was no sin yet to make them ashamed or to hinder the total openness of a perfect relationship with each other before God.

3:1. Now the question before us is: how will the man and woman respond to the goodness and love of God who created them with wonderful capabilities and put them in such a gorgeous garden? So God allowed a test. A serpent appears which is not identified here, but from its knowledge and what it says, it is obvious that it is more than an ordinary serpent. It was said to be different from all other creatures by its subtlety, that is, its shrewdness or cleverness. Revelation 12:9 and 20:2 clearly identify it and calls it "that old serpent, called the Devil and Satan."

The Bible does not tell us when Satan fell. Only that he did before Gen. 3:1 is certain. At the end of the sixth creation day, everything God creat-

420, 828	652	3706, 569.111	435	3940	404.126	4623, 3725
prep, art, n fs	cj	prep, v Qal pf 3ms	n mp	neg part	v Qal impf 3mp	prep, adj
אֶל־הָאִשָּׁה	אַף	כִּי־אָמַר	אֱלֹהִים	לֹא	תֹאכְלוּ	מִכֹּל
'el-hā'ishshāh	'aph	kî-'āmar	'ělōhîm	lō'	thō'kh^{e}lû	mikkōl
to the woman	indeed	so He has said	God	not	they will eat	from every

6320	1629		569.122	828	420, 5357	4623, 6780
n ms	art, n ms		cj, v Qal impf 3fs	art, n fs	prep, art, n ms	prep, *n ms*
עֵץ	הַגָּן	**2.**	וַתֹּאמֶר	הָאִשָּׁה	אֶל־הַנָּחָשׁ	מִפְּרִי
'ēts	haggān		wattō'mer	hā'ishshāh	'el-hannāchāsh	mipp^{e}rî
tree of	the garden		and she said	the woman	to the serpent	from the fruit of

6320, 1629	404.120		4623, 6780	6320	866
n ms, art, n ms	v Qal juss 1cp		cj, prep, *n ms*	art, *n ms*	rel part
עֵץ־הַגָּן	נֹאכֵל	**3.**	וּמִפְּרִי	הָעֵץ	אֲשֶׁר
'ēts-haggān	nō'khēl		ûmipp^{e}rî	hā'ēts	'ăsher
the trees of the garden	we may eat		but from fruit of	the tree of	which

904, 8761, 1629	569.111	435	3940	404.126	4623
prep, sub, art, n ms	v Qal pf 3ms	n mp	neg part	v Qal impf 3mp	prep, ps 3ms
בְּתוֹךְ־הַגָּן	אָמַר	אֱלֹהִים	לֹא	תֹאכְלוּ	מִמֶּנּוּ
b^{e}thôkh-haggān	'āmar	'ělōhîm	lō'	thō'kh^{e}lû	mimmennû
in the middle of the garden	He said	God	not	they will eat	from it

3940	5236.128	904	6678, 4322.128		569.121	5357
cj, neg part	v Qal impf 2mp	prep, ps 3ms	cj, v Qal impf 2mp		cj, v Qal impf 3ms	art, n ms
וְלֹא	תִגְּעוּ	בּוֹ	פֶּן־תְּמֻתוּן	**4.**	וַיֹּאמֶר	הַנָּחָשׁ
w^{e}lō'	thigg^{e}'û	bô	pen-t^{e}muthûn		wayyō'mer	hannāchāsh
and not	you will touch	it	otherwise you will die		and he said	the serpent

420, 828	3940, 4322.142	4322.128		3706	3156.151	435
prep, art, n fs	neg part, v Qal inf abs	v Qal impf 2mp		cj	v Qal act ptc ms	n mp
אֶל־הָאִשָּׁה	לֹא־מוֹת	תְּמֻתוּן	**5.**	כִּי	יֹדֵעַ	אֱלֹהִים
'el-hā'ishshāh	lō'-môth	t^{e}muthûn		kî	yōdhēa'	'ělōhîm
to the woman	not dying	you will die		because	One who knows	God

3706	904, 3219	404.141	4623	6741.216	6084
cj	prep, *n ms*	v Qal inf con, ps 2mp	prep, ps 3ms	cj, v Niphal pf 3cp	n fd, ps 2mp
כִּי	בְּיוֹם	אֲכָלְכֶם	מִמֶּנּוּ	וְנִפְקְחוּ	עֵינֵיכֶם
kî	b^{e}yôm	'ăkhāl^{e}khem	mimmennû	w^{e}niphqōchû	'ênêkhem
that	on the day of	your eating	from it	then they will be opened	your eyes

2030.117	3626, 435	3156.152	3005	7737		7495.122
cj, v Qal pf 2mp	prep, n mp	*v Qal act ptc mp*	adj	cj, adj		cj, v Qal impf 3fs
וִהְיִיתֶם	כֵּאלֹהִים	יֹדְעֵי	טוֹב	וָרָע	**6.**	וַתֵּרֶא
wihyîthem	kē'lōhîm	yōdh'ê	ṭôv	wārā'		wattēre'
and you will be	like God	knowers of	good	and evil		and she saw

828	3706	3005	6320	3937, 4120	3706	8707, 2000
art, n fs	cj	adj	art, n ms	prep, n ms	cj, cj	n fs, pers pron
הָאִשָּׁה	כִּי	טוֹב	הָעֵץ	לְמַאֲכָל	וְכִי	תַאֲוָה־הוּא
hā'ishshāh	kî	tov	hā'ēts	l^{e}ma'ăkhāl	w^{e}khî	tha'ăwāh-hû'
the woman	that	good	the tree	for food	and that	something pleasant it

3937, 6084	2629.255	6320	3937, 7959.541	4089.122	4623, 6780
prep, art, n fd	cj, v Niphal ptc ms	art, n ms	prep, v Hiphil inf con	cj, v Qal impf 3fs	prep, n ms, ps 3ms
לָעֵינַיִם	וְנֶחְמָד	הָעֵץ	לְהַשְׂכִּיל	וַתִּקַּח	מִפִּרְיוֹ
lā'ênayim	w^{e}nechmadh	hā'ēts	l^{e}hashkîl	wattiqqach	mippiryô
to the eyes	and something desirable	the tree	to make wise	and she took	from its fruit

more impudent, *Fenton* ... most cunning, *NAB* ... wiser, *BB* ... wiliest, *MLB*.

And he said unto the woman, Yea, hath God said, Ye shall not eat of every tree of the garden: ... Is it true that God has forbidden you, *REB* ... Did God really say, *NIV* ... has forbidden you to eat from any tree, *NEB*.

2. And the woman said unto the serpent, We may eat of the fruit of the trees of the garden: ... The woman interrupted the serpent, *Anchor* ... of the fruit of the trees we do eat, *Young*.

3. But of the fruit of the tree which is in the midst of the garden, God hath said, Ye shall not eat of it, neither shall ye touch it, lest ye die: ... it is only concerning, *Goodspeed* ... except for the tree in the middle, *NEB* ... If you take of it or put your hands on it, *BB*.

4. And the serpent said unto the woman, Ye shall not surely die: ... Of course you will not die, *REB* ... You would not die at all, *Goodspeed* ... snake said, *BB*.

5. For God doth know that in the day ye eat thereof, then your eyes shall be opened, and ye shall be as gods, knowing good and evil: ... the instant you eat it you will become like him, *LIVB* ... the moment you eat it, *NAB* ... you will be like God, *Darby*, *Fenton*.

6. And when the woman saw that the tree was good for food, and

---

ed was very good. So Satan must have sinned and fallen after Adam and Eve were created. Since angels were created to be servants and God's purpose was to make human beings His children, the creation of Adam and Eve may have stirred Satan to pride, conceit and jealousy that led to his fall (cf. 1 Tim. 3:6). Some wonder if angels were created before the world, but Gen. 1:1 does not seem to support this. Rather, the phrase "in the beginning God" points to God's preexistence. Furthermore, Heb. 1:14 indicates angels were created with humankind in mind.

Satan is a spirit being and since only God can create, Satan cannot make a physical form by his own power. He can only take possession of a creature God has made. He could not take possession of the man or the woman, because they had to choose to allow it, and they were still without sin. So he took possession of a serpent and that was all the woman saw. Since all God's creation was new to her, she was not surprised when the serpent spoke.

The serpent's temptation began with a question. (Satan still begins that way.) "Yea" (indeed, really) suggests surprise and astonishment. His question really denied the love of God and was intended to imply , "How could God keep any good thing from you if He loves you?" He also wanted to draw attention away from all the good things they could have and focus attention on the one thing they could not have. Satan still does this. He has not changed his basic methods, and we need to learn from this.

3:2-3. Adam probably told Eve of the command not to eat of the fruit of the tree of the knowledge of good and evil. She may have heard God herself repeat the command as they communed with Him in "the cool of the day" (verse 8). However, she added that they should not even touch it. The addition of not touching it perhaps was also implied by what God had said. God wants us to stay away from things forbidden in His Word.

3:4-5. The serpent then followed his question by a denial, "Ye shall not surely die." and added, "ye shall be as gods." Satan denied God's word of accountability and His purpose for humankind. God created them in His image. But Satan suggested God did not want them to be like Him, for He had forbidden them the one thing that God had known all along would make them like Him and enable them to live on a higher level of existence. That "knowing good and evil" would make them like God was another of Satan's lies, for God knows about evil but not through personal experience. By His very nature He is totally separate from all that is evil, and He hates it. Actually, they were like God in His image, but Satan tempted them to want more than was healthy for them.

3:6. The serpent did not have to force the woman to take the forbidden fruit. Once she gave her attention to it and spent some time contemplating it, it began to look good to her--good for food, to satisfy physical appetite. This is what the New Testament calls the lust of the flesh, the cravings of sinful persons for physical benefits and pleasures out of balance--pleasant to the eyes, the lust of the eyes that focuses on visual attraction despite its destructive results--and to be desired to make one wise--the pride of life that boasts of what a person has and does (1 John 2:16). Then she made a willful choice, took the fruit, ate it and gave some to her

404.122	5598.122	1612, 3937, 382	6196	404.121
cj, v Qal impf 3fs	cj, v Qal impf 3fs	cj, prep, n ms, ps 3fs	prep, ps 3fs	cj, v Qal impf 3ms
וַתֹּאכַל	וַתִּתֵּן	גַּם־לְאִישָׁהּ	עִמָּהּ	וַיֹּאכַל
wattō'khal	wattittēn	gam-l^{e}'îshāhh	'immāhh	wayyō'khal
and she ate	and she gave	also to her husband	with her	and he ate

7.	6741.227	6084	8529	3156.126	3706	6124
	cj, v Niphal impf 3fp	*n fd*	num, ps 3mp	cj, v Qal impf 3mp	cj	adj
	וַתִּפָּקַחְנָה	עֵינֵי	שְׁנֵיהֶם	וַיֵּדְעוּ	כִּי	עֵירֻמִּם
	wattippāqachnāh	'ênê	sh^{e}nêhem	wayyēdh'û	kî	'êrummim
	then they were opened	the eyes of	the two of them	and they knew	that	naked

2062	8944.126	6149	8711	6449.126	3937	2383
pers pron	cj, v Qal impf 3mp	*n ms*	n fs	cj, v Qal impf 3mp	prep, ps 3mp	n fp
הֵם	וַיִּתְפְּרוּ	עֲלֵה	תְאֵנָה	וַיַּעֲשׂוּ	לָהֶם	חֲגֹרֹת
hēm	wayyithp^{e}rû	'ălēh	th^{e}'ēnāh	wayya'ăsû	lāhem	chăghōrōth
they	and they sewed	leaves of	fig tree	and they made	for them	loincloths

8.	8471.126	881, 7249	3176	435	2050.751	904, 1629
	cj, v Qal impf 3mp	do, *n ms*	pn	n mp	v Hithpael ptc ms	prep, art, n ms
	וַיִּשְׁמְעוּ	אֶת־קוֹל	יְהוָה	אֱלֹהִים	מִתְהַלֵּךְ	בַּגָּן
	wayyishm^{e}'û	'eth-qôl	y^{e}hwāh	'ĕlōhîm	mithhallēkh	baggān
	and they heard	the sound of	Yahweh	God	walking	in the garden

3937, 7593	3219	2331.721	119	828	4623, 6681	3176
prep, *n fs*	art, n ms	cj, v Hithpael impf 3ms	art, n ms	cj, n fs, ps 3ms	prep, *n ms*	pn
לְרוּחַ	הַיּוֹם	וַיִּתְחַבֵּא	הָאָדָם	וְאִשְׁתּוֹ	מִפְּנֵי	יְהוָה
l^{e}rûach	hayyôm	wayyithchabbē'	hā'ādhām	w^{e}'ishtô	mipp^{e}nê	y^{e}hwāh
at the breeze of	the day	and he hid	the man	and his wife	from the face of	Yahweh

435	904, 8761	6320	1629	9.	7410.121	3176
n mp	prep, *sub*	*n ms*	art, n ms		cj, v Qal impf 3ms	pn
אֱלֹהִים	בְּתוֹךְ	עֵץ	הַגָּן		וַיִּקְרָא	יְהוָה
'ĕlōhîm	b^{e}thôkh	'ēts	haggān		wayyiqōrā'	y^{e}hwāh
God	in the middle of	the trees of	the garden		but He called	Yahweh

435	420, 119	569.121	3937	338	10.	569.121
n mp	prep, art, n ms	cj, v Qal impf 3ms	prep, ps 3ms	intrg, ps 2ms		cj, v Qal impf 3ms
אֱלֹהִים	אֶל־הָאָדָם	וַיֹּאמֶר	לוֹ	אַיֶּכָּה		וַיֹּאמֶר
'ĕlōhîm	'el-hā'ādhām	wayyō'mer	lô	'ayyekkāh		wayyō'mer
God	to the man	and He said	to him	where you		and he said

881, 7249	8471.115	904, 1629	3486.125	3706, 6124	609
do, n ms, ps 2ms	v Qal pf 1cs	prep, art, n ms	cj, v Qal impf 1cs	prep, adj	pers pron
אֶת־קֹלְךָ	שָׁמַעְתִּי	בַּגָּן	וָאִירָא	כִּי־עֵירֹם	אָנֹכִי
'eth-qōl^{e}khā	shāma'ättî	baggān	wa'îrā'	kî-'êrōm	'ānōkhî
your sound	I heard	in the garden	and I was afraid	because naked	I

2331.225	11.	569.121	4449	5222.511	3937	3706
cj, v Niphal impf 1cs		cj, v Qal impf 3ms	intrg	v Hiphil pf 3ms	prep, ps 2ms	cj
וָאֵחָבֵא		וַיֹּאמֶר	מִי	הִגִּיד	לְךָ	כִּי
wa'ēchāvē'		wayyō'mer	mî	higgîdh	l^{e}khā	kî
so I hid		and He said	who	he told	to you	that

6124	887	4623, 6320	866	6943.315	3937, 1153
adj	pers pron	intrg part, prep, art, n ms	rel part	v Piel pf 1cs, ps 2ms	prep, neg part
עֵירֹם	אַתָּה	הֲמִן־הָעֵץ	אֲשֶׁר	צִוִּיתִיךָ	לְבִלְתִּי
'êrōm	'āttāh	hămin-hā'ēts	'ăsher	tsiwwîthîkhā	l^{e}viltî
naked	you	did from the tree	which	I commanded you	to not

404.141, 4623 v Qal inf con, prep, ps 3ms אֱכָל־מִמֶּנּוּ 'ăkhāl-mimmennû to eat from it	404.113 v Qal pf 2ms אָכָלְתָּ 'ākhāl^ettā you ate	**12.**	569.121 cj, v Qal impf 3ms וַיֹּאמֶר wayyō'mer and he said	119 art, n ms הָאָדָם hā'ādhām the man	828 art, n fs הָאִשָּׁה hā'ishshāh the woman	866 rel part אֲשֶׁר 'ăsher whom

that it was pleasant to the eyes, and a tree to be desired to make one wise, she took of the fruit thereof, and did eat, and gave also unto her husband with her; and he did eat: ... desirable for gaining wisdom, *NIV* ... knowledge it could give, *REB* ... to give intelligence, *Darby* ... stimulating to the intellect, *Fenton.*

7. And the eyes of them both were opened, and they knew that they were naked: ... they were conscious, *BB* ... discovered they were naked, *NEB.*

and they sewed fig leaves together, and made themselves aprons: ... skirts, *MLB* ... coats of leaves, *BB* ... girdles, *Goodspeed.*

8. And they heard the voice of the LORD God walking in the garden in the cool of the day: ... heard the sound, *Goodspeed* ... moving about, *NAB.*

and Adam and his wife hid themselves from the presence of the LORD God amongst the trees of the garden: ... went to a secret place, *BB.*

9. And the LORD God called unto Adam, and said unto him, Where art thou?

10. And he said, I heard thy voice in the garden, and I was afraid, because I was naked; and I hid myself: ... kept myself from your eyes, *BB.*

11. And he said, Who told thee that thou wast naked? Hast thou eaten of the tree, whereof I commanded thee that thou shouldest not eat: ... who hath declared to thee, *Young* ... Who made you know, *Berkeley* ... Who gave you the knowledge, *BB.*

12. And the man said, The woman whom thou gavest to be with me, she gave me of the tree, and I did eat.

husband who was with her. He apparently was observing all this and became convinced that it was good, and he too made a willful choice. In fact Adam was more accountable, knowing what he was doing, while Eve was deceived (1 Tim. 2:14).

3:7. Their eyes were opened. That is, they now had knowledge of good and evil in their own experience instead of waiting for God's instructions. But it did not make them like God. Instead it filled them with guilt and shame--and they became painfully conscious of the fact they were naked. That is, they became aware they had nothing to hide their guilt. They were vulnerable to one another and to God. So they sewed (or twisted) the largest leaves available, fig leaves, to make coverings for themselves. The first effects of death (separation from God) were evident.

3:8. In the afternoon, when the cool on-shore breezes came through the garden, they heard the voice of Yahweh Elohim as He was walking in the garden. Some believe that Jesus would not appear in any physical form before the incarnation. But the uniqueness of incarnation is that Jesus identified with humankind totally from birth to death. And we will identify with Him in the rapture. It is logical that God would reveal Himself through the Son using some physical form or appearance, for He is the one Mediator between God and humankind (1 Tim. 2:15). So the two issues are not really related. Sin, however, had broken their fellowship with God, and their guilty consciences caused them to run and hide among the trees of the garden.

3:9-11. We can be sure that God knew what they had done for He is omniscient (all-knowing), but He wanted them to confess, so He called out to Adam. Adam's reply shows that sin and guilt bring fear. Again, God questioned him, demanding a confession of his guilt.

3:12. As is the selfish nature of one guilty of sin and not ready to admit responsibility, Adam tried to shift the blame. He implied the woman was responsible. But Adam was not simply shifting the blame to her, but like all unrepentant sinners, tried to put the blame on God as well, for God gave him the woman. He as much as said, "If you hadn't given me this woman it wouldn't have happened." God did not accept this, however, and put the responsibility back on Adam, as verse 17 shows. God questioned Adam first, for he was the one to whom God had first given the responsibility, and though he may not have been with her to hear the serpent's temptation, he was with her when she par-

5598.113	6200	2000	5598.112, 3937	4623, 6320	404.125
v Qal pf 2ms	prep, ps 1cs	pers pron	v Qal pf 3fs, prep, ps 1cs	prep, art, n ms	cj, v Qal impf 1cs
נָתַתָּה	עִמָּדִי	הִוא	נָתְנָה־לִּי	מִן־הָעֵץ	וָאֹכֵל
nāthattāh	'immādhî	hiw'	nāthnāh-lî	min-hā'ēts	wā'ōkhēl
You gave	with me	she	she gave to me	from the tree	and I ate

13.	569.121	3176	435	3937, 828	4242, 2148
	cj, v Qal impf 3ms	pn	n mp	prep, art, n fs	intrg part, dem pron
	וַיֹּאמֶר	יְהוָה	אֱלֹהִים	לָאִשָּׁה	מַה־זֹּאת
	wayyō'mer	y^{e}hwāh	'ĕlōhîm	lā'ishshāh	mah-zō'th
	and He said	Yahweh	God	to the woman	what this

6449.114	569.122	828	5357	5565.511	404.125
v Qal pf 2fs	cj, v Qal impf 3fs	art, n fs	art, n ms	v Hiphil pf 3ms, ps 1cs	cj, v Qal impf 1cs
עָשִׂית	וַתֹּאמֶר	הָאִשָּׁה	הַנָּחָשׁ	הִשִּׁיאַנִי	וָאֹכֵל
'āsîth	wattō'mer	hā'ishshāh	hannāchāsh	hishshî'anî	wā'ōkhēl
you have done	and she said	the woman	the serpent	he deceived me	and I ate

14.	569.121	3176	435	420, 5357	3706	6449.113
	cj, v Qal impf 3ms	pn	n mp	prep, art, n ms	cj	v Qal pf 2ms
	וַיֹּאמֶר	יְהֹוָה	אֱלֹהִים	אֶל־הַנָּחָשׁ	כִּי	עָשִׂיתָ
	wayyō'mer	y^{e}hōwāh	'ĕlōhîm	'el-hannāchāsh	kî	'āsîthā
	and He said	Yahweh	God	to the serpent	because	you did

2148	803.155	887	4623, 3725, 966	4623, 3725	2516	7898
dem pron	v Qal pass ptc ms	pers pron	prep, *adj*, art, n fs	cj, prep, adj	*n fs*	art, n ms
זֹּאת	אָרוּר	אַתָּה	מִכָּל־הַבְּהֵמָה	וּמִכֹּל	חַיַּת	הַשָּׂדֶה
zō'th	'ārûr	'attāh	mikkol-habb^{e}hēmāh	ûmikkōl	chayyath	hassādheh
this	cursed	you	more than all the animals	and more than all	the living things of	the field

6142, 1543	2050.123	6312	404.123	3725, 3219	2508
prep, n ms, ps 2ms	v Qal impf 2ms	cj, n ms	v Qal impf 2ms	adj, *n mp*	n mp, ps 2ms
עַל־גְּחֹנְךָ	תֵלֵךְ	וְעָפָר	תֹּאכַל	כָּל־יְמֵי	חַיֶּיךָ
'al-g^{e}chōn^{e}khā	thēlēkh	w^{e}'āphār	tō'khal	kāl-y^{e}mê	chayyêkhā
on your belly	you will crawl	and dust	you will eat	all the days of	your life

15.	343	8308.125	1033	1033	828	1033
	cj, n fs	v Qal impf 1cs	prep, ps 2ms	cj, prep	art, n fs	cj, prep
	וְאֵיבָה	אָשִׁית	בֵּינְךָ	וּבֵין	הָאִשָּׁה	וּבֵין
	w^{e}'êvāh	'āshîth	bên^{e}khā	ûvên	hā'ishshāh	ûvên
	and enmity	I will put	between you	and between	the woman	and between

2320	1033	2320	2000	8220.121	7513	887
n ms, ps 2ms	cj, prep	n ms, ps 3fs	pers pron	v Qal impf 3ms, ps 2ms	n ms	cj, pers pron
זַרְעֲךָ	וּבֵין	זַרְעָהּ	הוּא	יְשׁוּפְךָ	רֹאשׁ	וְאַתָּה
zar'ăkhā	ûvên	zar'āhh	hû'	y^{e}shûph^{e}khā	rō'sh	w^{e}'attāh
your seed	and between	her seed	he	he will crush you	head	and you

8220.123	6357	16.	420, 828	569.111	7528.542	7528.525
v Qal impf 2ms, ps 3ms	n ms		prep, art, n fs	v Qal pf 3ms	v Hiphil inf abs	v Hiphil impf 1cs
תְּשׁוּפֶנּוּ	עָקֵב		אֶל־הָאִשָּׁה	אָמַר	הַרְבָּה	אַרְבֶּה
t^{e}shûphennû	'āqēv		'el-hā'ishshāh	'āmar	harbāh	'arbeh
you will bruise him	heel		to the woman	He said	multiplying	I will multiply

6328	2116	904, 6325	3314.124	1158	420, 382
n ms, ps 2fs	cj, n ms, ps 2fs	prep, n	v Qal impf 2fs	n mp	cj, prep, n ms, ps 2fs
עִצְּבוֹנֵךְ	וְהֵרֹנֵךְ	בְּעֶצֶב	תֵּלְדִי	בָנִים	וְאֶל־אִישֵׁךְ
'itsts^{e}vônēkh	w^{e}hērōnēkh	b^{e}'etsev	tēl^{e}dhî	vānîm	w^{e}'el-'îshēkh
your labor pains	and your pregnancy	in pain	you will bear	children	and to your husband

13. And the LORD God said unto the woman, What is this that thou hast done? And the woman said, The serpent beguiled me, and I did eat: ... tricked by the deceit of the snake, *BB* ... misled me, *Goodspeed* ... caused me to forget, *Young* ... deceived me, *NASB*, *NIV*.

14. And the LORD God said unto the serpent, Because thou hast done this, thou art cursed above all cattle, and above every beast of the field: ... Banned shall you be, *Anchor* ... You will be punished, *Good News*.

upon thy belly shalt thou go, and dust shalt thou eat all the days of thy life: ... shall you crawl, *NCB* ... will go flat on the earth, *BB*.

15. And I will put enmity between thee and the woman, and between thy seed and her seed: ... cause antagonism, *Fenton* ... there will be war, *BB*.

it shall bruise thy head, and thou shalt bruise his heel: ... shall attack you and you attack them, *Goodspeed* ... crush your head and his heel, *Berkeley* ... strike your head and strike their heel, *Anchor*.

16. Unto the woman he said, I will greatly multiply thy sorrow and thy conception: ... pain in childbirth, *NASB* ... make great your distress, *NCB* ... increase your pregnancy troubles, *Berkeley*.

in sorrow thou shalt bring forth children; and thy desire shall be to thy husband: ... be devoted to, *Goodspeed* ... your urge shall be, *Anchor* ... be eager for, *NEB*.

and he shall rule over thee: ... will be your Master, *BB* ... will dominate you, *Berkeley*.

---

took, and he could have stopped her. The New Testament also makes it clear that it was Adam's sin that brought the curse on the human race and he was not deceived (Rom. 5:12).

3:13. The woman then tried to shift the blame to the serpent. The serpent beguiled or deceived her. Satan is still the great deceiver (2 Cor. 4:4). God did not accept this as an excuse either, as verse 16 shows.

3:14-15. God is a just God, so He proceeded to pronounce judgment on the serpent, the woman, and the man. First He put a curse on the serpent to cause it to crawl on the ground (snakes do have rudimentary legs that now do not develop, a fact that seems to fit the curse). God would also put enmity between the woman and the serpent. Though Adam and Eve had joined Satan and left God, God would restore them and separate them from Satan. The woman would then hate the serpent for what he had done to her. God would also put enmity between the seed or offspring of the serpent and the seed or offspring of the woman. The offspring of the serpent may refer to those who, like the Pharisees who opposed Jesus, have Satan as their "father" (John 8:44) in the sense that they are directed by him, whether they know it or not. Thus all unbelievers are the seed of the serpent until they are "born again" and become part of the family of God and are thus "in Christ" who is the true "Seed" of the woman (cf. Gal. 3:16).

In the midst of the judgment on the serpent God gave a promise that was good news. It is sometimes called the protevangelium or "pregospel." There would be a specific seed or offspring of the woman. "He" would crush the head of the same old serpent (the devil, Rev. 12:9) that tempted the woman, bringing total victory. But Satan would be able to bruise only His heel. Striking the heel would be only temporary. Thus the real victory would belong to the Seed of the woman who would crush the head of the serpent. This looks ahead to the Cross. There Satan did his worst to Jesus. But the cross became the means of our salvation and it, along with the resurrection of Jesus, assures us of the ultimate and final defeat of Satan (Rom. 16:20).

3:16. God's judgment on the woman was to increase her pain in childbearing. Her desire (impulse) would be toward her husband, and he would rule over her (not as a tyrant, but in the same sense that the sun rules the day, Gen. 1:16). This, of course, was not God's original intention, and now in Christ the negative aspects of this are removed and the husband and wife are restored to a healthy partnership. In Him there is neither male nor female (Rom. 8:1; Gal. 3:28). And in the marriage relationship the husband is to love the wife as Christ loved the Church and gave Himself for it (Eph. 6:25), and the wife is to respect the leadership of the husband.

3:17-19. Because Adam listened to his wife instead of obeying God, God put a curse on the ground (not on Adam). What had been pleasant work would now become toil, often unrewarding, often difficult because of the thorns and thistles. Sweat and toil would continue until the physical

9010	2000	5090.121, 904		3937, 120	569.111	3706
n fs, ps 2fs	cj, pers pron	v Qal impf 3ms, prep, ps 2fs	**17.**	cj, prep, pn	v Qal pf 3ms	cj
תְּשׁוּקָתֵךְ	וְהוּא	יִמְשָׁל־בָּךְ		וּלְאָדָם	אָמַר	כִּי
t^{e}shûqāthēkh	w^{e}hû'	yimshāl-bākh		ûl^{e}'ādhām	'āmar	kî
your desire	but he	he will rule over you		and to Adam	He said	because

8471.113	3937, 7249	828	404.122	4623, 6320	866
v Qal pf 2ms	prep, *n ms*	n fs, ps 2ms	cj, v Qal impf 2ms	prep, art, n ms	rel part
שָׁמַעְתָּ	לְקוֹל	אִשְׁתֶּךָ	וַתֹּאכַל	מִן־הָעֵץ	אֲשֶׁר
shāma'ättā	l^{e}qôl	'ishtekhā	wattō'khal	min-hā'ēts	'ăsher
you listened	to the voice of	your wife	and you ate	from the tree	which

6943.315	3937, 569.141	3940	404.123	4623	803.157
v Piel pf 1cs, ps 2ms	prep, v Qal inf con	neg part	v Qal impf 2ms	prep, ps 3ms	v Qal pass ptc fs
צִוִּיתִיךָ	לֵאמֹר	לֹא	תֹאכַל	מִמֶּנּוּ	אֲרוּרָה
tsiwwîthîkhā	lē'mōr	lō'	thō'khal	mimmennû	'ărûrāh
I commanded you	saying	not	you will eat	from it	cursed

124	904, 5877	904, 6328	404.123	3725	3219	2508
art, n fs	prep, prep, ps 2ms	prep, n ms	v Qal impf 2ms, ps 3fs	adj	*n mp*	n mp, ps 2ms
הָאֲדָמָה	בַּעֲבוּרֶךָ	בְּעִצָּבוֹן	תֹּאכְלֶנָּה	כֹּל	יְמֵי	חַיֶּיךָ
hā'ădhāmāh	ba'ăvûrekhā	b^{e}'itstsāvôn	tō'kh^{e}lennāh	kōl	yemê	chayyêkhā
the ground	on account of you	by hardship	you will eat from it	all	the days of	your life

	7259	1923	7048.522	3937	404.113	881, 6448
18.	cj, n ms	cj, n ms	v Hiphil impf 3fs	prep, ps 2ms	cj, v Qal pf 2ms	do, *n ms*
	וְקוֹץ	וְדַרְדַּר	תַּצְמִיחַ	לָךְ	וְאָכַלְתָּ	אֶת־עֵשֶׂב
	w^{e}qôts	w^{e}dhardar	tatsmîach	lākh	w^{e}'ākhaltā	'eth-'ēsev
	and thorns	and thistles	it will produce	for you	and you will eat	the plants of

7898		904, 2271	653	404.123	4035	5912
art, n ms	**19.**	prep, *n fs*	n mp, ps 2ms	v Qal impf 2ms	n ms	adv
הַשָּׂדֶה		בְּזֵעַת	אַפֶּיךָ	תֹּאכַל	לֶחֶם	עַד
hassādheh		b^{e}zē'ath	'appêkhā	tō'khal	lechem	'adh
the field		by the sweat of	your face	you will eat	bread	until

8178.141	420, 124	3706	4623	4089.413	3706, 6312
v Qal inf con, ps 2ms	prep, art, n fs	cj	prep, ps 3fs	v Pual pf 2ms	prep, n ms
שׁוּבְךָ	אֶל־הָאֲדָמָה	כִּי	מִמֶּנָּה	לֻקָּחְתָּ	כִּי־עָפָר
shûv^{e}khā	'el-hā'ădhāmāh	kî	mimmennāh	luqqāchättā	kî-'āphār
your returning	to the ground	because	from it	you were taken	because dust

887	420, 6312	8178.123		7410.121	119	8428
pers pron	cj, prep, n ms	v Qal impf 2ms	**20.**	cj, v Qal impf 3ms	art, n ms	*n ms*
אַתָּה	וְאֶל־עָפָר	תָּשׁוּב		וַיִּקְרָא	הָאָדָם	שֵׁם
'attāh	w^{e}'el-'āphār	tāshûv		wayyiqrā'	hā'ādhām	shēm
you	and to dust	you will return		and he called	the man	the name of

828	2428	3706	2000	2030.112	525	3706, 2508
n fs, ps 3ms	pn	cj	pers pron	v Qal pf 3fs	*n fs*	*adj*, adj
אִשְׁתּוֹ	חַוָּה	כִּי	הִוא	הָיְתָה	אֵם	כָּל־חָי
'ishtô	chawwāh	kî	hiw'	hāy^{e}thâh	'ēm	kol-chāy
his wife	Eve	because	she	she was	mother of	all living

	6449.121	3176	435	3937, 120	3937, 828	3930
21.	cj, v Qal impf 3ms	pn	n mp	prep, pn	cj, prep, n fs, ps 3ms	*n fp*
	וַיַּעַשׂ	יְהוָה	אֱלֹהִים	לְאָדָם	וּלְאִשְׁתּוֹ	כָּתְנוֹת
	wayya'as	y^{e}hwāh	'ĕlōhîm	l^{e}'ādhām	ûl^{e}'ishtô	kāthnôth
	and He made	Yahweh	God	for Adam	and for his wife	garments of

5997	3980.521		569.121	3176	435	2075
n ms	cj, v Hiphil impf 3ms, ps 3mp	22.	cj, v Qal impf 3ms	pn	n mp	intrj
עוֹר	וַיַּלְבִּשֵׁם		וַיֹּאמֶר	יְהוָה	אֱלֹהִים	הֵן
'ôr	wayyalbishēm		wayyō'mer	y^{e}hwāh	'ĕlōhîm	hēn
skins	and He clothed them		and He said	Yahweh	God	behold

119	2030.111	3626, 259	4623	3156.141	3005	7737II
art, n ms	v Qal pf 3ms	prep, num	prep, ps 1cp	v Qal inf con	adj	cj, adj
הָאָדָם	הָיָה	כְּאַחַד	מִמֶּנּוּ	לָדַעַת	טוֹב	וָרָע
hā'ādhām	hāyâh	k^{e}'achadh	mimmennû	lādha'ath	ṭôv	wārā'
the man	he has become	like one	of us	to know	good	and evil

6498	6678, 8365.121	3135	4089.111	1612	4623, 6320
cj, adv	cj, v Qal impf 3ms	n fs, ps 3ms	cj, v Qal pf 3ms	cj	prep, *n ms*
וְעַתָּה	פֶּן־יִשְׁלַח	יָדוֹ	וְלָקַח	גַּם	מֵעֵץ
w^{e}'attāh	pen-yishlach	yādhô	w^{e}lāqach	gam	mē'ēts
and now	otherwise he will reach out	his hand	and he will take	also	from the tree of

17. And unto Adam he said, Because thou hast hearkened unto the voice of thy wife, and hast eaten of the tree, of which I commanded thee, saying, Thou shalt not eat of it: ... Because you gave ear to, *BB* ... yielded to your wife's suggestion, *Berkeley.*

cursed is the ground for thy sake: in sorrow shalt thou eat of it all the days of thy life: ... condemned be the soil, *Anchor.* ... In suffering shall you gain, *Goodspeed* ... through painful toil, *NIV.*

18. Thorns also and thistles shall it bring forth to thee; and thou shalt eat the herb of the field: ... bramble, *Young* ... briars, *Fenton* ... waste plants, *BB.*

19. In the sweat of thy face shalt thou eat bread, till thou return unto the ground; for out of it wast thou taken: for dust thou art, and unto dust shalt thou return: ... With the hard work of your hands, *BB* ... must make a living, *Berkeley.*

20. And Adam called his wife's name Eve; because she was the mother of all living.

21. Unto Adam also and to his wife did the LORD God make coats of skins, and clothed them: ... tunics of skin, *NKJV* ... leather garments, *NAB.*

22. And the LORD God said, Behold, the man is become as one of us, to know good and evil: and now, lest he put forth his hand, and take also of the tree of life, and eat, and live for ever: ... suppose he

body in death would return to the ground. This does not mean that death is the end of the person. The Bible has much to say about future rewards and future judgment.

3:20. Up to this time Adam's wife was simply called the woman. Now Adam gave her the name Eve (Hebrew, *chawwah*, "life"). A change of name indicates a change in nature, character, or relationship. As "woman" she was potentially already the mother of all her descendants who would be physically alive. The only death they had known at this point was spiritual death. Thus, "living" here must mean spiritually alive. That is, she placed her faith in God and in His promise of Gen. 3:15, and was restored to spiritual life. Then she encouraged Adam to place his faith in the promise. Then he declared his faith in God's promise by giving his wife the new name, Eve.

3:21. Then God made garments of skins which were a better covering than the fig leaves they had twisted together. This God-given covering indicated His provision for their guilty shame and His acceptance of them. This also foreshadows future animal sacrifices and eventually, the sacrifice of Christ on the cross, in which His life-blood was given for our lives. It also shows that sacrifices were for the benefit of humankind. God did not need them, but Adam and Eve did.

3:22. Adam and Eve came to be like God knowing good and evil in this one respect ("like one of us" could foreshadow the truth about the Trinity). They were not like God in His divine nature, but in the increased possibilities of what they might do. If they stayed in the Garden of Eden and kept eating the fruit of the tree of life, which was not forbidden to them, they could keep eating and live forever. Possibly, something in the fruit counteracted decay and the effects of old age. But now God would not permit humankind to live forever on earth in a sinful condition.

2522	404.111	2030.111	3937, 5986	23.	8365.321
art, n mp	cj, v Qal pf 3ms	cj, v Qal pf 3ms	prep, n ms		cj, v Piel impf 3ms, ps 3ms
הַחַיִּים	וְאָכַל	וָחַי	לְעֹלָם		וַיְשַׁלְּחֵהוּ
hachayyîm	w^{e}'ākhal	wachay	l^{e}'ōlām		wayshall^{e}chēhû
the life	and he will eat	and he will live	for ever		so He drove him out

3176	435	4623, 1629, 5942	3937, 5856.141	881, 124	866
pn	n mp	prep, *n ms*, pn	prep, v Qal inf con	do, art, n fs	rel part
יְהוָה	אֱלֹהִים	מִגַּן־עֵדֶן	לַעֲבֹד	אֶת־הָאֲדָמָה	אֲשֶׁר
y^{e}hwāh	'ělōhîm	miggan-'ēdhen	la'ăvōdh	'eth-hā'ădhāmāh	'ăsher
Yahweh	God	from the garden of Eden	to cultivate	the ground	which

4089.411	4623, 8427	24.	1691.321	881, 119	8331.521
v Pual pf 3ms	prep, adv		cj, v Piel impf 3ms	do, art, n ms	cj, v Hiphil impf 3ms
לֻקַּח	מִשָּׁם		וַיְגָרֶשׁ	אֶת־הָאָדָם	וַיַּשְׁכֵּן
luqqach	mishshām		way^{e}ghāresh	'eth-hā'ādhām	wayyashkēn
he was taken	from there		and He drove	the man	and He positioned

4623, 7208	3937, 1629, 5942	881, 3872	881	3994	2820
prep, n ms	prep, *n ms*, pn	do, art, n mp	cj, do	*n ms*	art, n fs
מִקֶּדֶם	לְגַן־עֵדֶן	אֶת־הַכְּרֻבִים	וְאֵת	לַהַט	הַחֶרֶב
miqqedhem	l^{e}ghan-'ēdhen	'eth-hakk^{e}ruvîm	w^{e}'ēth	lahaṭ	hacherev
from the east	to the garden of Eden	the cherubim	and	the flame of	the sword

2089.753	3937, 8490.141	881, 1932	6320	2522
art, v Hithpael ptc fs	prep, v Qal inf con	do, *n ms*	*n ms*	art, n mp
הַמִּתְהַפֶּכֶת	לִשְׁמֹר	אֶת־דֶּרֶךְ	עֵץ	הַחַיִּים
hammithhappekheth	lishmōr	'eth-derekh	'ēts	hachayyîm
one that turns every direction	to guard	the way of	the tree of	the life

4:1	119	3156.111	882, 2428	828	2106.122
	cj, art, n s	v Qal pf 3ms	prep, pn	n fs, ps 3ms	cj, v Qal impf 3fs
	וְהָאָדָם	יָדַע	אֶת־חַוָּה	אִשְׁתּוֹ	וַתַּהַר
	w^{e}hā'ādhām	yādha'	'eth-chawwāh	'ishtô	wattahar
	and the man	he had relations	with Eve	his wife	and she conceived

3314.122	881, 7296	569.122	7353.115	382	882, 3176
cj, v Qal impf 3fs	do, pn	cj, v Qal impf 3fs	v Qal pf 1cs	n ms	prep, pn
וַתֵּלֶד	אֶת־קַיִן	וַתֹּאמֶר	קָנִיתִי	אִישׁ	אֶת־יְהוָה
wattēledh	'eth-qayin	wattō'mer	qānîthî	'îsh	'eth-y^{e}hwāh
and she gave birth	Cain	and she said	I have gotten	man	with the help of Yahweh

2.	3362.522	3937, 3314	881, 250	881, 1962	2030.121, 1962
	cj, v Hiphil impf 3fs	prep, v Qal inf con	do, n ms, ps 3ms	do, pn	cj, v Qal impf 3ms, pn
	וַתֹּסֶף	לָלֶדֶת	אֶת־אָחִיו	אֶת־הָבֶל	וַיְהִי־הֶבֶל
	wattōseph	lāledheth	'eth-'āchîw	'eth-hāvel	wayhî-hevel
	and she did again	to give birth	his brother	Abel	and Abel was

7749.151	6887	7296	2030.111	5856	124
v Qal act ptc ms	n fs	cj, pn	v Qal pf 3ms	*v Qal act ptc ms*	n fs
רֹעֵה	צֹאן	וְקַיִן	הָיָה	עֹבֵד	אֲדָמָה
rō'ēh	tsō'n	w^{e}qayin	hāyâh	'ōvēdh	'ădhāmāh
keeper of	sheep	but Cain	he was	cultivator of	ground

3.	2030.121	4623, 7377	3219	971.521	7296	4623, 6780
	cj, v Qal impf 3ms	prep, *n ms*	n mp	cj, v Hiphil impf 3ms	pn	prep, *n ms*
	וַיְהִי	מִקֵּץ	יָמִים	וַיָּבֵא	קַיִן	מִפְּרִי
	wayhî	miqqēts	yāmîm	wayyāvē'	qayin	mipp^{e}rî
	and it happened	after	days	and he brought	Cain	from the fruit of

were to reach out, *Goodspeed* ... he must not be allowed to reach out, *NIV*.

23. Therefore the LORD God sent him forth from the garden of Eden, to till the ground from whence he was taken: ... drove him out, *NEB* ... banished him, *REB* ... expelled him, *Goodspeed*.

24. So he drove out the man: ... cast him out, *NEB* ... sent the man out, *BB*.

and he placed at the east of the garden of Eden Cherubims, and a flaming sword which turned every way, to keep the way of the tree of life: ... put living creatures, *Good News* ... Divine Watchers, *Fenton* ... sword flashing back and forth, *NIV* ... which turned every direction, *NASB*.

4:1. And Adam knew Eve his wife: ... had relations with, *NASB* ... had connection with, *BB* ... had intercourse, *Good News*.

and she conceived, and bare Cain, and said, I have gotten a man from the LORD: ... brought into being, *REB* ... produced a man, *NRSV* ... have acquired a man, *Darby*.

2. And she again bare his brother Abel. And Abel was a keeper of sheep, but Cain was a tiller of the ground: ... cultivator of the soil, *Fenton* ... was a farmer, *BB*.

3. And in process of time it came to pass, that Cain brought of the fruit of the ground an offering unto the LORD: ... As time went on, *KJVII* ... during the harvest time, *Fenton* ... brought some produce as a gift, *NEB*.

4. And Abel, he also brought of the firstlings of his flock and of the fat thereof: ... brought of the best, *Fenton* ... brought the choicest, *REB*.

3:23. So God sent Adam out of the Garden of Eden to till the ground. The emphasis is on Adam's relation to the earth, not to God. All fallen humankind are earth creatures, needing to be born again, needing to be changed.

3:24. Adam did not go willingly. God had to drive him out. God knew Adam would want to return, so He placed cherubs (the Hebrew plural is cherubim) with a flaming sword that turned every way, flashing back and forth to prevent Adam (or humankind) from returning to the tree of life. This shows the universality of human fallenness and separation from God. All people have been born outside of Eden, and of fellowship with God. Through Christ, fellowship can be restored; only in the New Jerusalem will the fruit of the tree of life again be available (Rev. 22:2, 14). There it will be freely and continually accessible to the redeemed of the ages.

4:1. The word "know" (Heb., *yada'*) in the Bible is used of the closest personal relationship at whatever level is indicated in the context. Knowing God means knowing Him on the spiritual level in the closest personal way. Adam knew his wife by entering the closest personal relationship at the husband-wife level, a relationship of love, and Cain was born.

Cain (Heb. *Qayin*, "one gotten," "acquired one"), is similar to the root of the verb, "I brought forth." "From the LORD" (*'eth YHWH*) probably refers to her hope that Cain might be the "seed (offspring) of the woman" who would crush the old serpent's head. It thus refers to her faith in God's promise. (Heb. *'eth* here, means "with" or "with the help of." It is not the sign of the direct object here, for that would call for an *'eth* before "a man," Heb. *'ish* as well, and there is none there.)

4:2. Eve named her second son Abel (Heb. *Havel*, "vapor, breath, emptiness"), probably referring to her disappointment with life outside the Garden of Eden. (Some wish to connect Abel with the Akkadian word *ablu*, "son." But there are no real grounds for this.)

When Abel matured he became a keeper, literally, a "feeder" (a shepherd) of a flock (the Hebrew includes sheep and goats with the emphasis on sheep). Cain became a worker (cultivator) of the ground or soil, that is, a farmer. Evolutionists suppose that human beings started out as food gatherers and hunters and only later became shepherds and farmers. But it could very well be that people fell back into food gathering and hunting occupations later.

4:3. Cain apparently had a good harvest, with more than he needed. So he took some of what was left over and brought of (that is, some of) the fruit (produce) of the soil as an offering to the LORD. "Offering" (Heb., *minchah*, "gift, tribute", cf. 2 Chr. 26:8; 32:23) is not a sin offering (no sin offering was required before the Law was given at Mount Sinai; see Rom. 5:13). The same word is translated "meat offering" in Lev. 2:1, where "meat" is the old English word for food in general, and which was a vegetable offering under the Law.

124	4647	3937, 3176	4. 1962	971.511	1612, 2000
art, n fs	n fs	prep, pn	cj, pn	v Hiphil pf 3ms	cj, pers pron
הָאֲדָמָה	מִנְחָה	לַיהוָה	וְהֶבֶל	הֵבִיא	גַם־הוּא
hā'ădhāmāh	minchāh	lâhwāh	w^{e}hevel	hēvî'	gham-hû'
the ground	offering	to Yahweh	and Abel	he brought	also he

4623, 1111	6887	4623, 2561	8541.121	3176	420, 1962
prep, *n fp*	n fs, ps 3ms	cj, prep, n ms, ps 3fp	cj, v Qal impf 3ms	pn	prep, pn
מִבְּכֹרוֹת	צֹאנוֹ	וּמֵחֶלְבֵהֶן	וַיִּשַׁע	יְהוָה	אֶל־הֶבֶל
mibb^{e}khōrôth	tsō'nô	ûmēchel^{e}vēhen	wayyisha'	y^{e}hwāh	'el-hevel
from the first-born of	his sheep	and fat portions	and He looked at	Yahweh	to Abel

420, 4647	5. 420, 7296	420, 4647	3940	8541.111
cj, prep, n fs, ps 3ms	cj, prep, pn	cj, prep, n fs, ps 3ms	neg part	v Qal pf 3ms
וְאֶל־מִנְחָתוֹ	וְאֶל־קַיִן	וְאֶל־מִנְחָתוֹ	לֹא	שָׁעָה
w^{e}'el-minchāthô	w^{e}'el-qayin	w^{e}'el-minchāthô	lō'	shā'āh
and to his offering	but to Cain	and to his offering	not	He looked at

2835.121	3937, 7296	4108	5489.126	6686	6. 569.121
cj, v Qal impf 3ms	prep, pn	adv	cj, v Qal impf 3mp	n mp, ps 3ms	cj, v Qal impf 3ms
וַיִּחַר	לְקַיִן	מְאֹד	וַיִּפְּלוּ	פָּנָיו	וַיֹּאמֶר
wayyichar	l^{e}qayin	m^{e}'ōdh	wayyipp^{e}lû	pānâv	wayyō'mer
and he was angry	to Cain	very	and it fell	his face	and He said

3176	420, 7296	4066	2835.111	3937	4066	5849.116
pn	prep, pn	intrg	v Qal pf 3ms	prep, ps 2fs	intrg part	v Qal pf 3cp
יְהוָה	אֶל־קָיִן	לָמָּה	חָרָה	לָךְ	וְלָמָּה	נָפְלוּ
y^{e}hwāh	'el-qāyin	lāmmāh	chārāh	lākh	w^{e}lāmmāh	nāph^{e}lû
Yahweh	to Cain	why	it is hot	to you	and why	it fell

6686	7. 1950B, 3940	524, 3296.123	5558.141	524	3940
n mp, ps 2ms	intrg part, neg part	cj, v Qal impf 2ms	v Qal inf con	cj, cj	neg part
פָּנֶיךָ	הֲלוֹא	אִם־תֵּיטִיב	שְׂאֵת	וְאִם	לֹא
phānêkhā	hălô'	'im-têṯîv	s^{e}'ēth	w^{e}'im	lō'
your face	will not	if you do right	lifting up	but if	not

3296.123	3937, 6860	2496	7547.151	420	9010	887
v Qal impf 2ms	prep, art, n ms	n fs	v Qal act ptc ms	cj, prep, ps 2ms	n fs, ps 3ms	cj, pers pron
תֵיטִיב	לַפֶּתַח	חַטָּאת	רֹבֵץ	וְאֵלֶיךָ	תְּשׁוּקָתוֹ	וְאַתָּה
thêṯîv	lappethach	chaṯṯā'th	rōvēts	w^{e}'ēlêkhā	t^{e}shûqāthô	w^{e}'attāh
you do right	at the door	sin	crouching	and toward you	its desire	but you

5090.123, 904	8. 569.121	7296	420, 1962	250	2030.121
v Qal impf 2ms, prep, ps 3ms	cj, v Qal impf 3ms	pn	prep, pn	n ms, ps 3ms	cj, v Qal impf 3ms
תִּמְשָׁל־בּוֹ	וַיֹּאמֶר	קַיִן	אֶל־הֶבֶל	אָחִיו	וַיְהִי
timshāl-bô	wayyō'mer	qayin	'el-hevel	'āchîw	wayhî
you should rule over it	and he said	Cain	to Abel	his brother	and it was

904, 2030.141	904, 7898	7251.121	7296	420, 1962	250
prep, v Qal inf con, ps 3mp	prep, art, n ms	cj, v Qal impf 3ms	pn	prep, pn	n ms, ps 3ms
בִּהְיוֹתָם	בַּשָּׂדֶה	וַיָּקָם	קַיִן	אֶל־הֶבֶל	אָחִיו
bihyôthām	bassādheh	wayyāqām	qayin	'el-hevel	'āchîw
when they were	in the field	then he rose up	Cain	toward Abel	his brother

2103.121	9. 569.121	3176	420, 7296	338	1962
cj, v Qal impf 3ms, ps 3ms	cj, v Qal impf 3ms	pn	prep, pn	intrg part	pn
וַיַּהַרְגֵהוּ	וַיֹּאמֶר	יְהוָה	אֶל־קַיִן	אֵי	הֶבֶל
wayyahar^{e}ghēhû	wayyō'mer	y^{e}hwāh	'el-qayin	'ê	hevel
and he killed him	and He said	Yahweh	to Cain	where	Abel

And the LORD had respect unto Abel and to his offering: ... Lord approved of Abel, *Berkeley* ... Yahweh showed regard, *Anchor.*

5. But unto Cain and to his offering he had not respect: ... he hath not looked, *Young* ... He did not approve, *Berkeley.*

And Cain was very wroth, and his countenance fell: ... Cain resented this greatly, *Anchor* ... was furious and he glowered, *REB* ... very angry, *NEB.*

6. And the LORD said unto Cain, Why art thou wroth? and why is thy countenance fallen: ... resentful and crestfallen, *NAB* ... Why hast thou displeasure, *Young* ... Why are you resentful, *Anchor.*

7. If thou doest well, shalt thou not be accepted? and if thou doest not well, sin lieth at the door: ... sin is a demon crouching, *Anchor, REB* ... will be lurking, *Goodspeed.*

And unto thee shall be his desire, and thou shalt rule over him: ... you must master it, *NIV, NASB, NRSV* ... should conquer it, *Fenton.*

8. And Cain talked with Abel his brother: and it came to pass, when they were in the field, that Cain rose up against Abel his brother, and slew him: ... assaulted his brother, *Berkeley* ... attacked and murdered, *REB.*

9. And the LORD said unto Cain, Where is Abel thy brother? And he said, I know not: Am I my brother's keeper?

10. And he said, What hast thou done? the voice of thy brother's blood crieth unto me from the ground.

There is no indication that he brought the best or that he was wholeheartedly wanting to honor the Lord. He just brought "from" the fruit of the ground, whatever was available. He may have been looking for a reward for himself.

4:4. In contrast, Abel brought the firstborn and the "fat parts" of the flock. Giving the firstborn indicated he put God first. "Fat parts" is a Hebrew way of saying the very best of the best. The same word is translated "finest" (of the wheat) in Ps. 147:14.

The LORD looked with favor on Abel and his offering (Heb., minchah, as in Lev. 2). God's acceptance was first of Abel and then his offering. God has always wanted people, not just offerings. Even under the Law no one ever pleased God because of bringing the right sacrifices if they were not offered in the right spirit.

Abel presented his best through faith that expressed trust in God and a desire to obey Him (cf. Heb. 11:4). The Bible does not tell us how God showed He accepted Abel and his offering. Possibly, He did it by sending fire from heaven that consumed the offering, as He did in the case of the first offerings in the later Tabernacle and Temple (Lev. 9:24; 2 Chron. 7:1).

4:5. God did not accept Cain or his offering, which means Cain was without real faith or trust in the LORD. He revealed this attitude by flaming up in anger and by a crestfallen appearance, full of self-pity. If he truly wanted to please God, he would have humbled himself and asked how he could be accepted.

4:6. God did not ignore Cain. He asked him for an explanation of his attitude (his anger and his crestfallen appearance). God was more concerned about Cain than about his offering.

4:7. Cain still had an opportunity to do what was good and right. If he did God would accept him. But if he did not do what was good and right, sin was crouching at the door like a wild beast ready to spring. It was "at the door" because Cain's attitude brought him very close to sin. Sin was desiring or striving to get at Cain. But he could still reject the desire of sin and rule or take control over it. God was thus calling on Cain to repent of his wrong attitude and exercise self-discipline. But Cain would not worship God when He did not favor him. Cain put a higher priority on himself than on God.

4:8. An ancient copyist may have dropped out part of the sentence in the Hebrew here. The Greek Septuagint version, made about 200 years before the time of Christ, states "Cain said to Abel his brother, 'Let us go to the field.'" There Cain rose up against Abel and killed him. Thus, the results of the fall led to further sin and death--the first murder. The following verse indicates Cain buried Abel there.

4:9. God gave Cain an opportunity to repent by asking him where his brother was. But Cain tried to cover up his sin by lying about it, saying he did not know. One sin usually leads to another. He also showed his unbrotherly spirit by saying "Am I my brother's keeper?" "Keeper" includes the idea of guard and protector. He still was showing a wrong attitude.

250	569.121	3940	3156.115	1950B, 8490.151	250
n ms, ps 2ms	cj, v Qal impf 3ms	neg part	v Qal pf 1cs	intrg part, *v Qal act ptc ms*	n ms, ps 1cs
אָחִיךָ	וַיֹּאמֶר	לֹא	יָדַעְתִּי	הֲשֹׁמֵר	אָחִי
'āchîkhā	wayyō'mer	lō'	yādha'ttî	h^{e}shōmēr	'āchî
your brother	and he said	not	I know	am keeper of	my brother

609	**10.** 569.121	4242	6449.113	7249	1879
pers pron	cj, v Qal impf 3ms	intrg part	v Qal pf 2ms	*n ms*	*n mp*
אָנֹכִי	וַיֹּאמֶר	מֶה	עָשִׂיתָ	קוֹל	דְּמֵי
'ānōkhî	wayyō'mer	meh	'āsîthā	qôl	d^{e}mê
I	and He said	what	did you	the voice of	the blood of

250	7094.152	420	4623, 124	**11.** 6498	803.155
n ms, ps 2ms	v Qal act ptc mp	prep, ps 1cs	prep, art, n fs	cj, adv	v Qal pass ptc ms
אָחִיךָ	צֹעֲקִים	אֵלַי	מִן־הָאֲדָמָה	וְעַתָּה	אָרוּר
'āchîkhā	tsō'ăqim	'ēlay	min-hā'ădhāmāh	w^e'attāh	'ārûr
your brother	crying out	to Me	from the ground	and now	cursed one

887	4623, 124	866	6722.112	881, 6552	4089.141	881, 1879
pers pron	prep, art, n fs	rel part	v Qal pf 3fs	do, n ms, ps 3fs	prep, v Qal inf con	do, *n mp*
אָתָּה	מִן־הָאֲדָמָה	אֲשֶׁר	פָּצְתָה	אֶת־פִּיהָ	לָקַחַת	אֶת־דְּמֵי
'āttāh	min-hā'ădhāmāh	'āsher	pāts^{e}thāh	'eth-pîhā	lāqachath	'eth-d^{e}mê
you	from the ground	which	it has opened	its mouth	to receive	the blood of

250	4623, 3135	**12.** 3706	5856.123	881, 124	3940, 3362.522
n ms, ps 2ms	prep, n fp, ps 2ms	cj	v Qal impf 2ms	do, art, n fs	neg part, v Hiphil impf 3fs
אָחִיךָ	מִיָּדֶךָ	כִּי	תַעֲבֹד	אֶת־הָאֲדָמָה	לֹא־תֹסֵף
'āchîkhā	miyyādhekh	kî	tha'ăvōdh	'eth-hā'ădhāmāh	lō'-thōsēph
your brother	from your hands	when	you cultivate	the ground	it will not again

5598.141, 3699	3937	5309.151	5290.151	2030.123	904, 800
v Qal inf con, n ms, ps 3fs	prep, ps 2ms	v Qal act ptc ms	cj, v Qal act ptc ms	v Qal impf 2ms	prep, n fs
תֵּת־כֹּחָהּ	לָךְ	נָע	וָנָד	תִּהְיֶה	בָאָרֶץ
tēth-kōchāhh	lākh	nā'	wānādh	tihyeh	vā'ārets
give its strength	to you	wanderer	and vagabond	you will be	on the earth

13. 569.121	7296	420, 3176	1448	5988	4623, 5558.141
cj, v Qal impf 3ms	pn	prep, pn	adj	n ms, ps 1cs	prep, v Qal inf con
וַיֹּאמֶר	קָיִן	אֶל־יְהוָה	גָּדוֹל	עֲוֹנִי	מִנְּשֹׂא
wayyō'mer	qayin	'el-y^{e}hwāh	gādhôl	'ăônî	minn^{e}sô'
and he said	Cain	to Yahweh	great	my punishment	of bearing

14. 2075	1691.313	881	3219	4263, 6142	6686
intrj	v Piel pf 2ms	do, ps 1cs	art, n ms	prep, prep	*n mp*
הֵן	גֵּרַשְׁתָּ	אֹתִי	הַיּוֹם	מֵעַל	פְּנֵי
hēn	gērashtā	'ōthî	hayyôm	mē'al	p^{e}nê
behold	You have driven	me	today	from on	the surface of

124	4623, 6686	5846.225	2030.115	5309.151
art, n fs	cj, prep, n ms, ps 2ms	v Niphal impf 1cs	cj, v Qal pf 1cs	v Qal act ptc ms
הָאֲדָמָה	וּמִפָּנֶיךָ	אֶסָּתֵר	וְהָיִיתִי	נָע
hā'ădhāmāh	ûmippānêkhā	'essāthēr	w^{e}hāyîthî	nā'
the ground	and from your face	I will be hidden	and I have become	wanderer

5290.151	904, 800	2030.111	3725, 4834.151	2103.121
cj, v Qal act ptc ms	prep, art, n fs	cj, v Qal pf 3ms	*adj*, v Qal act ptc ms, ps 1cs	v Qal impf 3ms, ps 1cs
וָנָד	בָּאָרֶץ	וְהָיָה	כָל־מֹצְאִי	יַהַרְגֵנִי
wānādh	bā'ārets	w^{e}hāyāh	khol-mōts^{e}î	yahar^{e}ghēnî
and vagabond	on the earth	and it will be	any finder of me	he will kill me

15.

569.121	3937	3176	4062	3725, 2103	7296
cj, v Qal impf 3ms	prep, ps 3ms	pn	cj	*adj*, v Qal act ptc ms	pn
וַיֹּאמֶר	לוֹ	יְהוָה	לָכֵן	כָּל־הֹרֵג	קַיִן
wayyō'mer	lô	y^e^hwāh	lākhēn	kol-hōrēgh	qayin
and He said	to him	Yahweh	therefore	any killer	Cain

8094	5541.621	7947.121	3176	3937, 7296	225
num	v Hophal impf 3ms	cj, v Qal impf 3ms	pn	prep, pn	n ms
שִׁבְעָתַיִם	יֻקָּם	וַיָּשֶׂם	יְהוָה	לְקַיִן	אוֹת
shiv'āthayim	yuqqām	wayyāsem	y^e^hwāh	l^e^qayin	'ôth
seven times	he will suffer vengeance	and He put	Yahweh	for Cain	mark

11. And now art thou cursed from the earth, which hath opened her mouth to receive thy brother's blood from thy hand: ... under a curse and driven from the ground, *NIV* ... cursed more than the ground, *KJVII* ... will be banished, *REB*.

12. When thou tillest the ground, it shall not henceforth yield unto thee her strength: ... no longer give you its produce, *NAB* ... yield its crops, *NIV*.

a fugitive and a vagabond shalt thou be in the earth: ... vagrant and wanderer, *NASB* ... restless wanderer, *NIV*.

13. And Cain said unto the LORD, My punishment is greater than I can bear: ... too great to be borne, *Darby*.

14. Behold, thou hast driven me out this day from the face of the earth: ... banished me, *Anchor* ... away from the ground, *RSV*.

and from thy face shall I be hid: ... must avoid your presence, *NAB* ... deprived of your presence, *Fenton*.

and I shall be a fugitive and a vagabond in the earth; and it shall come to pass, that every one that findeth me shall slay me: ... in flight over the earth, *BB*.

15. And the LORD said unto him, Therefore whosoever slayeth Cain, vengeance shall be taken on him sevenfold: ... seven lives will be taken, *BB* ... shall be punished, *Fenton*.

4:10. "What hast thou done?" was the cry of God's broken heart, broken by Cain's attitude and sins as well as by Abel's violent death. From the ground where Abel's body was buried his blood was symbolically calling out, demanding justice.

4:11. Now a curse was put on Cain from the very ground that had received his brother's blood. God is concerned about justice for wrongdoing.

4:12. The ground would not yield it strength--that is, Cain would not have good crops and he would be forced to go from place to place. God further condemned him to be a fugitive continually, a restless wanderer, straying aimlessly, far from home and from the favored spot he formerly cultivated. Why a fugitive? Sin brings separation. We can be sure also that Adam and Eve did not wait until Cain and Abel were fully grown before having other children (see Gen. 5:4). Abel's other brothers and sisters would want to see justice done.

4:13. Cain's reply could be translated in three possible ways: "My punishment is greater than I can bear," "My guilt is more than I can bear," or, "My guilt is more than can be forgiven." The latter is more likely--because Cain was not confessing, but rather whining in self-pity.

4:14. Cain's self-pity is also seen as he complained about God's judgment on him that demanded he wander. He also recognized that his guilt would cause him to be hidden from God's face, that is, to be separated from God's presence. Without God's presence and blessing he was afraid that whoever (that is, of his brothers) would find him would kill him--to avenge Abel's death.

4:15. Possibly because there had been no human physical death before, God was merciful and promised that anyone killing Cain would suffer seven times the vengeance. Then God provided a sign (Heb., *'oth*) for Cain.

The Hebrew word probably does not mean that God put a mark on Cain. The Hebrew normally means a supernatural sign or miracle, as in Exodus 4:8. Possibly God gave something like fire from a rock. Thus God assured Cain that no one would kill him.

4:16. Cain left the presence of God, never to experience it again. He wandered east from Eden. "Nod" means "wandering," and the country was given that name because Cain wandered there.

3937, 1153	5409.541, 881	3725, 4834.151	16.	3428.121	7296
prep, neg part	v Hiphil inf con, do, ps 3ms	*adj*, v Qal act ptc ms, ps 3ms		cj, v Qal impf 3ms	pn
לְבִלְתִּי	הַכּוֹת־אֹתוֹ	כָּל־מֹצְאוֹ		וַיֵּצֵא	קַיִן
leviltî	hakôth-'ōthô	kol-mōts'ô		wayyētsē'	qayin
to not	to strike him down	any finder of him		and he went out	Cain

4623, 3937, 6686	3176	3553.121	904, 800, 5292	7209, 5942
prep, prep, *n mp*	pn	cj, v Qal impf 3ms	prep, *n fs*, pn	*n fs*, pn
מִלִּפְנֵי	יְהוָה	וַיֵּשֶׁב	בְּאֶרֶץ־נוֹד	קִדְמַת־עֵדֶן
milliphnê	yehwāh	wayyēshev	be'erets-nôdh	qidhmath-'ēdhen
from the presence of	Yahweh	and he dwelled	in the land of Nod	east of Eden

17.	3156	7296	882, 828	2106.122	3314.122
	cj, v Qal impf 3ms	pn	prep, n fs, ps 3ms	cj, v Qal impf 3fs	cj, v Qal impf 3fs
	וַיֵּדַע	קַיִן	אֶת־אִשְׁתּוֹ	וַתַּהַר	וַתֵּלֶד
	wayyēdha'	qayin	'eth-'ishtô	wattahar	wattēledh
	and he had relations	Cain	with his wife	and she conceived	and she gave birth

881, 2686	2030.121	1161.151	6111	7410.121	8428	6111
do, pn	cj, v Qal impf 3ms	*v Qal act ptc ms*	n fs	cj, v Qal impf 3ms	*n ms*	art, n fs
אֶת־חֲנוֹךְ	וַיְהִי	בֹּנֶה	עִיר	וַיִּקְרָא	שֵׁם	הָעִיר
'eth-chănôkh	wayhî	bōneh	'îr	wayyiqrā'	shēm	hā'îr
Enoch	and he was	builder of	city	and he called	the name of	the city

3626, 8428	1158	2686	18.	3314.221	3937, 2686	881, 6117
prep, *n ms*	n ms, ps 3ms	pn		cj, v Niphal impf 3ms	prep, pn	do, pn
כְּשֵׁם	בְּנוֹ	חֲנוֹךְ		וַיִּוָּלֵד	לַחֲנוֹךְ	אֶת־עִירָד
keshēm	benô	chănôkh		wayyiwwālēdh	lachnôkh	'eth-'îrādh
like the name of	his son	Enoch		and he was born	to Enoch	Irad

6117	3314.111	881, 4367	4367	3314.111	881, 5143
cj, pn	v Qal pf 3ms	do, pn	cj, pn	v Qal pf 3ms	do, pn
וְעִירָד	יָלַד	אֶת־מְחוּיָאֵל	וּמְחִיָּיאֵל	יָלַד	אֶת־מְתוּשָׁאֵל
we'îrādh	yāladh	'eth-mechûyā'ēl	ûmechîyyā'ēl	yāladh	'eth-methûshā'ēl
and Irad	he fathered	Mehujael	and Mehujael	he fathered	Methushael

5143	3314.111	881, 4069	19.	4089, 3937	4069	8530
cj, pn	v Qal pf 3ms	do, pn		cj, v Qal impf 3ms, prep, ps 3ms	pn	*num*
וּמְתוּשָׁאֵל	יָלַד	אֶת־לָמֶךְ		וַיִּקַּח־לוֹ	לֶמֶךְ	שְׁתֵּי
ûmethûshā'ēl	yāladh	'eth-lāmekh		wayyiqqach-lô	lemekh	shettê
and Methushael	he fathered	Lamech		and he took for him	Lamech	two

5571	8428	259	5919	8428	8529	7012
n fp	*n ms*	art, num	pn	cj, *n ms*	art, num	pn
נָשִׁים	שֵׁם	הָאַחַת	עָדָה	וְשֵׁם	הַשֵּׁנִית	צִלָּה
nāshîm	shēm	hā'achath	'ādhāh	weshēm	hashshēnîth	tsillāh
wives	the name of	the first	Adah	and the name of	the second	Zillah

20.	3314.122	5919	881, 3098	2000	2030.111	1
	cj, v Qal impf 3fs	pn	do, pn	pers pron	v Qal pf 3ms	*n ms*
	וַתֵּלֶד	עָדָה	אֶת־יָבָל	הוּא	הָיָה	אֲבִי
	wattēledh	'ādhāh	'eth-yāvāl	hû'	hāyâh	'ăvî
	and she gave birth	Adah	Jabal	he	he was	the father of

3553.151	164	4898	21.	8428	250	3209
v Qal act ptc ms	n ms	cj, n ms		cj, *n ms*	n ms, ps 3ms	pn
יֹשֵׁב	אֹהֶל	וּמִקְנֶה		וְשֵׁם	אָחִיו	יוּבָל
yōshēv	'ōhel	ûmiqōneh		weshēm	'āchîw	yûvāl
the dwellers of	tents	and cattle		and the name of	his brother	Jubal

2000	2030.111	1	3725, 8945.151	3780	5966		7012
pers pron	v Qal pf 3ms	*n ms*	*adj, v Qal act ptc ms*	n ms	cj, n ms		cj, pn
הוּא	הָיָה	אֲבִי	כָּל־תֹּפֵשׂ	כִּנּוֹר	וְעוּגָב	**22.**	וְצִלָּה
hû'	hāyâh	'ăvî	kol-tōphēs	kinnôr	w^{e}'ûghāv		w^{e}tsillāh
he	he was	the father of	all players of	lyre	and flute		and Zillah

And the LORD set a mark upon Cain, lest any finding him should kill him: ... a token, *Young, NCB* ... appointed a sign, *NASB*, ASV.

16. And Cain went out from the presence of the LORD, and dwelt in the land of Nod, on the east of Eden: ... land of Wandering, *Good News* ... land of exile, *Fenton.*

17. And Cain knew his wife; and she conceived, and bare Enoch: ... lay with his wife, *NIV* ... had relations, *NASB* ... had intercourse, *Goodspeed.*

and he builded a city, and called the name of the city, after the name of his son, Enoch.

18. And unto Enoch was born Irad: and Irad begat Mehujael: and Mehujael begat Methusael: and Methusael begat Lamech: ... became the father of, *NASB, NIV, BB.*

19. And Lamech took unto him two wives: the name of the one was Adah, and the name of the other Zillah: ... married two women, *NIV.*

20. And Adah bare Jabal: he was the father of such as dwell in tents, and of such as have cattle: ... originator of tent- dwellers, *Fenton* ... ancestor of herdsmen, *NEB* ... inhabiting tents and purchased possessions, *Young.*

21. And his brother's name was Jubal: he was the father of all such as handle the harp and organ: ... flute, *NCB* ... lyre and pipe, *Goodspeed* ... wind instruments, *Fenton.*

22. And Zillah, she also bare Tubalcain, an instructer of every artificer in brass and iron: and the sister of Tubalcain was Naamah: ... forger of every cutting instrument, ASV ... master of all copper-

---

4:17. Since God created only one man and one woman, it was necessary for brothers to marry sisters in order to continue the human race. There was nothing wrong with this in the beginning. Even in the time of Abraham, Sarah, his wife, was his half-sister (Gen. 20:12).

But as time passed, the effects of the fall multiplied. Mutations (gene changes), originally meant to bring additional variety, brought weaknesses, inherited diseases, and conditions that could be fatal if the genes for the weaknesses were received from both parents. That is, they were usually recessive so they would not show up in any of the children unless both parents carried the gene.

Thus, if close relatives married, defects would be more likely. It was probably for this reason that God forbade marriage between close relatives in the Law of Moses.

The son born to Cain was named Enoch (Heb. *Chanokh*), which can mean either "trained one" or "dedicated one." In this context Cain is not a worshiper of the Lord, so "trained one" is the proper meaning here. Cain also showed defiance by building a city which he named *Chanokh*. The city was probably not more than a small, walled citadel. But by building it Cain was saying, "I may have to wander, but my son Enoch will not have to." Thus, Enoch lived in a permanent settlement.

4:18. Five generations are named in this verse. No ages are given, and like most genealogies in the Bible, it is probably not complete. (Note that Matt. 1:8 leaves out 3 generations found in the Old Testament and in Ezra several names are left out found in First Chronicles.) This genealogy leads to Lamech who is the climax of Cain's line.

4:19. With Lamech we see dramatic evidence of moral breakdown in the line of Cain when Lamech took two wives. God's purpose was for a man to cleave or stick to his wife (2:24), letting nothing and no one come in between. No man can have that kind of relationship with two or more women. Adah probably means "bright ornament" or "adorned one." Zillah may mean "shaded or protected one." Their names show they were loved by their parents, cared about by God, and should not have been abused by Lamech.

4:20-22. Lamech's children were involved in the beginnings of a preflood civilization that seems to have ignored God. Jabal became the ancestor of those who lived in tents and had wealth in cattle. Jubal was the ancestor of musicians who play the harp (or lyre, similar in sound to a guitar) and flute, something that denotes the development of culture. There is nothing wrong with culture if it celebrates how God made us and the world. But if it is used to draw attention away from God it is wrong.

1612, 2026	3314.112	881, 8753	8753	4048.151	3725, 2896.151	5361
cj, pers pron	v Qal pf 3fs	do, pn	pn	v Qal act ptc ms	*adj, v Qal act ptc ms*	n ms
גַּם־הִוא	יָלְדָה	אֶת־תּוּבַל	קַיִן	לֹטֵשׁ	כָּל־חֹרֵשׁ	נְחֹשֶׁת
gham-hiw'	yāl^{e}dhāh	'eth-tûval	qayin	lōṭēsh	kol-chōrēsh	n^{e}chōsheth
also she	she gave birth	Tubal-	Cain	blacksmith	all craftsmen of	bronze

1298	269	8753	5462		569.121	4069
cj, n ms	cj, *n fs*	pn	pn	**23.**	cj, v Qal impf 3ms	pn
וּבַרְזֶל	וַאֲחוֹת	תּוּבַל־קַיִן	נַעֲמָה		וַיֹּאמֶר	לֶמֶךְ
ûvarzel	wa'ăchôth	tûval-qayin	na'ămāh		wayyō'mer	lemekh
and iron	and the sister of	Tubal-Cain	Naamah		and he said	Lamech

3937, 5571	5919	7012	8471.134	7249	5571	4069
prep, n fp, ps 3ms	pn	cj, pn	v Qal impv 2fp	n ms, ps 1cs	*n fp*	pn
לְנָשָׁיו	עָדָה	וְצִלָּה	שְׁמַעַן	קוֹלִי	נְשֵׁי	לֶמֶךְ
l^{e}nāshâv	'ādhāh	w^{e}tsillāh	sh^{e}ma'an	qôlî	n^{e}shê	lemekh
to his wives	Adah	and Zillah	hear	my voice	wives of	Lamech

237.534	571	3706	382	2103.111	3937, 6729	3315
v Hiphil impv 2fp	n fs, ps 1cs	cj	n ms	v Qal pf 1cs	prep, n ms, ps 1cs	cj, n ms
הַאֲזֵנָּה	אִמְרָתִי	כִּי	אִישׁ	הָרַגְתִּי	לְפִצְעִי	וְיֶלֶד
ha'ăzēnnāh	'imrāthî	kî	'îsh	hāragtî	l^{e}phits'î	w^{e}yeledh
listen to	my words	because	man	I have killed	for my wound	and a young one

3937, 2365		3706	8094	5541.621, 7296	4069	8124
prep, n fs, ps 1cs	**24.**	cj	num	v Hophal impf 3ms, pn	cj, pn	num
לְחַבֻּרָתִי		כִּי	שִׁבְעָתַיִם	יֻקַּם־קָיִן	וְלֶמֶךְ	שִׁבְעִים
l^{e}chabburāthî		kî	shiv'āthayim	yuqqam-qayin	w^{e}lemekh	shiv'îm
for my injury		if	seven times	Cain is avenged	then Lamech	seventy

8124		3156	120	5968	882, 828	3314.122
cj, num	**25.**	cj, v Qal impf 3ms	pn	adv	prep, n fs, ps 3ms	cj, v Qal impf 3fs
וְשִׁבְעָה		וַיֵּדַע	אָדָם	עוֹד	אֶת־אִשְׁתּוֹ	וַתֵּלֶד
w^{e}shiv'āh		wayyēdha'	'ādhām	'ôdh	'eth-'ishtô	wattēledh
and seven		and he had relations	Adam	again	with his wife	and she gave birth

1158	7410.122	881, 8428	8683	3706	8308, 3937	435
n ms	cj, v Qal impf 3fs	do, n ms, ps 3ms	pn	cj	v Qal pf 3ms, prep, ps 1cs	n mp
בֵּן	וַתִּקְרָא	אֶת־שְׁמוֹ	שֵׁת	כִּי	שָׁת־לִי	אֱלֹהִים
bēn	wattiqrā'	'eth-sh^{e}mô	shēth	kî	shoth-lî	'ĕlōhîm
son	and she called	his name	Seth	because	he has appointed for me	God

2320	311	8809	1962	3706	2103.111	7296		3937, 8683
n ms	adj	prep	pn	cj	v Qal pf 3ms, ps 3ms	pn	**26.**	cj, prep, pn
זֶרַע	אַחֵר	תַּחַת	הֶבֶל	כִּי	הֲרָגוֹ	קָיִן		וּלְשֵׁת
zera'	'achēr	tachath	hevel	kî	h^{e}rāghô	qāyin		ûlāshēth
seed	another	instead of	Abel	because	he killed him	Cain		and to Seth

1612, 2000	3314.411, 1158	7410.121	881, 8428	597	226	2591.611
cj, pers pron	v Pual pf 3ms, n ms	cj, v Qal impf 3ms	do, n ms, ps 3ms	pn	adv	v Hophal pf 3ms
גַּם־הוּא	יֻלַּד־בֵּן	וַיִּקְרָא	אֶת־שְׁמוֹ	אֱנוֹשׁ	אָז	הוּחַל
gam-hû'	yulladh-bēn	wayyiqrā'	'eth-sh^{e}mô	'ĕnôsh	'āz	hûchal
also he	son was born	and he called	his name	Enosh	then	he began

3937, 7410.141	904, 8428	3176		2172	5809	8765	119
prep, v Qal inf con	prep, *n ms*	pn	**5:1**	dem pron	*n ms*	*n fp*	pn
לִקְרֹא	בְּשֵׁם	יְהוָה		זֶה	סֵפֶר	תּוֹלְדֹת	אָדָם
liqrō'	b^{e}shēm	y^{e}hwāh		zeh	sēpher	tôl^{e}dhōth	'ādhām
to call	on the name of	Yahweh		this	the book of	the generations of	Adam

smiths and blacksmiths, *NEB* ... hammerer of every engraving tool, *KJVII*.

23. And Lamech said unto his wives, Adah and Zillah, Hear my voice; ye wives of Lamech, hearken unto my speech: for I have slain a man to my wounding, and a young man to my hurt: ... kill a man for wounding me, *Anchor*, *NEB* ... for striking, *RSV*, *NRSV*.

24. If Cain shall be avenged sevenfold, truly Lamech seventy and sevenfold: ... sevenfold protection, *Fenton* ... taken as punishment, *BB*.

25. And Adam knew his wife again; and she bare a son, and called his name Seth: For God, said she, hath appointed me another seed instead of Abel, whom Cain slew: ... another child, *Goodspeed* ... more offspring, *NAB* ... granted me other issue, *Anchor*.

26. And to Seth, to him also there was born a son; and he called his name Enos: then began men to call upon the name of the LORD: ... first made use of the name of the Lord in worship, *BB* ... beginning was made of preaching, *Young* ... name Yahweh was first invoked, *Anchor*.

5:1. This is the book of the generations of Adam: ... genealogy, *NKJV* ... list of the descendants, *Good News* ... written account of Adam's line, *NIV* ... the roll, *Berkeley*.

Tubal-cain (Tubal the smith) became an instructor (or hammerer, forger) of tools and weapons of bronze (or copper) and iron. Archaeologists have not found iron tools from before Noah's flood, but the Flood must have destroyed that early civilization. Also, iron rusts away rather quickly when moisture is present. Naamah means "pleasant" or "beautiful." A godless civilization may point to beautiful things but their materialism causes them drift further and further away from God.

4:23-24. Lamech showed the beginnings of another kind of moral breakdown in his use of violence. He would avenge himself (probably using his son's weapons). His defiance of God is also seen by the way he said he would avenge himself more than God promised to avenge Cain. He as much as said, "Now that I have my son's weapons I can take care of myself. I don't need God."

4:25. After dealing with Cain's line and the beginnings of corruption and violence, Genesis goes back to the beginning. The purpose is to show that in spite of the direction Cain's line was taking, there was still hope. To Adam and Eve, Seth (Heb. *Sheth*, cf. 1 Chr. 1:1, "appointed one" or "one given for a set purpose") was born as another seed instead of Abel. The term "seed" recalls the promise of Gen. 3:15--not that Seth was the Promised One, but through his line the Promised One would come. Seth was "instead of Abel" for Abel was the one accepted by God, so Eve believed Seth would also be accepted by God.

4:26. Seth's son Enos (Heb. *'Enosh*) means "mortal one." By this time people realized that everyone would die. Thus, the Hebrew *'enosh* became a term used for people from the angle of having weaknesses. But some of the people (apparently those in Seth's line) began to call upon the name of the LORD. The Hebrew uses the collective singular ("he began to call") and could mean they began to call down a blessing in the name of the Lord, implying that He is the Giver and Preserver of life. It can also mean they began to call themselves by the name of the LORD, and thus might be called the "sons of God." This could be in the same sense that God later called Israel "my son."

5:1-2. Chapter 5 gives us the line of Seth down to Noah. It begins a new section of the book with the word "generations" (Heb. *toledoth*). We are taken back in review to the creation of Adam and Eve in chapter one where God created them in His likeness, blessed them, and called their name Adam. Adam in the Hebrew thus became the word for humankind in general beside the specific name for the first man.

In this genealogy ages are given. We do not know, however, whether other people at the time lived as long as the ones named in Seth's chosen line. As in the case of other genealogies in the Bible, not every person in the line is named. For example, Matt. 1:8 leaves out 3 names given in the Old Testament. Ezra is called the "son" of Seraiah (Ezra 7:1), though Seriah was executed by Nebuchadnezzar in 586 B.C. about 128 years before Ezra came to Jerusalem.

The word "begat" is a general word and may mean that the one named as "begotten" was a son, a grandson, or a descendant a thousand years or more down the line. The Biblical Hebrew has no word for grandfather, great-grandfather, or ancestor, but

904, 3219	**1282.141**	**435**	**119**	**904, 1883**	**435**	**6449.111**	**881**
prep, *n ms*	v Qal inf con	n mp	n ms	prep, *n fs*	n mp	v Qal pf 3ms	do, ps 3ms
בְּיוֹם	בְּרֹא	אֱלֹהִים	אָדָם	בִּדְמוּת	אֱלֹהִים	עָשָׂה	אֹתוֹ
beyôm	berō'	'ĕlōhîm	'ādhām	bidhmûth	'ĕlōhîm	'āsāh	'ōthô
on the day of	creating	God	man	in the likeness of	God	He made	him

	2227	**5531**	**1282.111**	**1313.321**	**881**	**7410.121**
2.	n ms	cj, n fs	v Qal pf 3ms, ps 3mp	cj, v Piel impf 3ms	do, ps 3mp	cj, v Qal impf 3ms
	זָכָר	וּנְקֵבָה	בְּרָאָם	וַיְבָרֶךְ	אֹתָם	וַיִּקְרָא
	zākhār	ûnqēvāh	berā'ām	wayevārekh	'ōthām	wayyiqŏrā'
	male	and female	He created them	and He blessed	them	and He called

881, 8428	**119**	**904, 3219**	**1282.241**		**2513.121**	**120**	**8389**
do, n ms, ps 3mp	n ms	prep, *n ms*	v Niphal inf con, ps 3mp	**3.**	cj, v Qal impf 3ms	pn	num
אֶת־שְׁמָם	אָדָם	בְּיוֹם	הִבָּרְאָם		וַיְחִי	אָדָם	שְׁלֹשִׁים
'eth-shemām	'ādhām	beyôm	hibbār'ām		waychî	'ādhām	shelōshîm
their name	humankind	on the day of	their being created		and he lived	Adam	thirty

4109	**8523**	**3314.521**	**904, 1883**	**3626, 7021**	**7410.121**
cj, *num*	n fs	cj, v Hiphil impf 3ms	prep, n fs, ps 3ms	prep, n ms, ps 3ms	cj, v Qal impf 3ms
וּמְאַת	שָׁנָה	וַיּוֹלֶד	בִּדְמוּתוֹ	כְּצַלְמוֹ	וַיִּקְרָא
ûme'ath	shānāh	wayyôledh	bidhmûthô	ketsalmô	wayyiqŏrā'
and hundred of	years	when he fathered	in his likeness	according to his image	and he called

881, 8428	**8683**		**2030.126**	**3219, 120**	**311**	**3314.541**
do, n ms, ps 3ms	pn	**4.**	cj, v Qal impf 3mp	*n mp*, pn	*sub*	v Hiphil inf con, ps 3ms
אֶת־שְׁמוֹ	שֵׁת		וַיִּהְיוּ	יְמֵי־אָדָם	אַחֲרֵי	הוֹלִידוֹ
'eth-shemô	shēth		wayyihyû	yemê-'ādhām	'achrê	hôlîdhô
his name	Seth		and they were	the days of Adam	after	fathering him

881, 8683	**8470**	**4109**	**8523**	**3314.521**	**1158**	**1351**
do, pn	num	*num*	n fs	cj, v Hiphil impf 3ms	n mp	cj, n fp
אֶת־שֵׁת	שְׁמֹנֶה	מְאֹת	שָׁנָה	וַיּוֹלֶד	בָּנִים	וּבָנוֹת
'eth-shēth	shemōneh	mē'ōth	shānāh	wayyôledh	bānîm	ûvānôth
Seth	eight	hundreds of	years	and he fathered	sons	and daughters

	2030.126	**3725, 3219**	**120**	**866, 2513.111**	**9013**	**4109**	**8523**
5.	cj, v Qal impf 3mp	*adj, n mp*	pn	rel part, v Qal pf 3ms	num	*num*	n fs
	וַיִּהְיוּ	כָּל־יְמֵי	אָדָם	אֲשֶׁר־חַי	תְּשַׁע	מֵאוֹת	שָׁנָה
	wayyihyû	kol-yemê	'ādhām	'ăsher-chay	tesha'	mē'ôth	shānāh
	and they were	all the days of	Adam	which he lived	nine	hundreds of	years

8389	**8523**	**4322**		**2030.121, 8683**	**2675**	**8523**	**4109**
cj, num	n fs	cj, v Qal impf 3ms	**6.**	cj, v Qal impf 3ms, pn	num	n fp	cj, num
וּשְׁלֹשִׁים	שָׁנָה	וַיָּמֹת		וַיְחִי־שֵׁת	חָמֵשׁ	שָׁנִים	וּמְאַת
ûshelōshîm	shānāh	wayyāmōth		waychî-shēth	chāmēsh	shānîm	ûme'ath
and thirty	years	and he died		and Seth was	five	years	and hundred of

8523	**3314.521**	**881, 597**		**2030.121, 8683**	**311**	**3314.541**
n fs	cj, v Hiphil impf 3ms	do, pn	**7.**	cj, v Qal impf 3ms, pn	*sub*	v Hiphil inf con, ps 3ms
שָׁנָה	וַיּוֹלֶד	אֶת־אֱנוֹשׁ		וַיְחִי־שֵׁת	אַחֲרֵי	הוֹלִידוֹ
shānāh	wayyôledh	'eth-'ĕnôsh		waychî-shēth	'achrê	hôlîdhô
years	when he fathered	Enosh		and Seth was	after	fathering him

881, 597	**8124**	**8523**	**8470**	**4109**	**8523**	**3314.521**	**1158**
do, pn	num	n fp	cj, num	*num*	n fs	cj, v Hiphil impf 3ms	n mp
אֶת־אֱנוֹשׁ	שֶׁבַע	שָׁנִים	וּשְׁמֹנֶה	מֵאוֹת	שָׁנָה	וַיּוֹלֶד	בָּנִים
'eth-'ĕnôsh	sheva'	shānîm	ûshemōneh	mē'ôth	shānāh	wayyôledh	bānîm
Enosh	seven	years	and eight	hundreds of	years	and he fathered	sons

1351		2030.126	3725, 3219, 8683	8692	6462	8523	9013
cj, n fp	**8.**	cj, v Qal impf 3mp	*adj, n mp,* pn	num	num	n fs	cj, num
וּבָנוֹת		וַיִּהְיוּ	כָּל־יְמֵי־שֵׁת	שְׁתֵּים	עֶשְׂרֵה	שָׁנָה	וּתְשַׁע
ûvānôth		wayyihyû	kol-y^{e}mê-shēth	sh^{e}ttêm	ʻesrēh	shānāh	ûth^{e}shaʻ
and daughters		and they were	all the days of Seth	two	ten	years	and nine

4109	8523	4322		2513.121	597	9013	8523
num	n fs	cj, v Qal impf 3ms	**9.**	cj, v Qal impf 3ms	pn	num	n fs
מֵאוֹת	שָׁנָה	וַיָּמֹת		וַיְחִי	אֱנוֹשׁ	תִּשְׁעִים	שָׁנָה
mēʼôth	shānāh	wayyāmōth		waychî	ʼĕnôsh	tishʻîm	shānāh
hundreds of	years	and he died		and he lived	Enosh	ninety	years

In the day that God created man, in the likeness of God made he him: ... When God created humankind, *NRSV* ... making them to represent God, *Fenton* ... he made him in the likeness of God, *NAB* ... he made him in God's likeness, *Berkeley.*

2. Male and female created he them; and blessed them, and called their name Adam in the day when they were created: ... called them Mankind, *NKJV* ... named them Man, *NASB* ... named them Humankind, *NRSV* ... called them human, *Berkeley.*

3. And Adam lived an hundred and thirty years, and begat a son in his own likeness, after his image; and called his name Seth:

4. And the days of Adam after he had begotten Seth were eight hundred years: and he begat sons and daughters:

5. And all the days that Adam lived were nine hundred and thirty years: and he died.

6. And Seth lived an hundred and five years, and begat Enos:

7. And Seth lived after he begat Enos eight hundred and seven years, and begat sons and daughters:

8. And all the days of Seth were nine hundred and twelve years: and he died.

9. And Enos lived ninety years, and begat Cainan:

10. And Enos lived after he begat Cainan eight hundred and fifteen years, and begat sons and daughters:

uses the word "father" (Heb. *'ab*) for all of them. Similarly, it has no word for grandson, great-grandson, or descendant, but uses the word "son" or "seed" for all of them, just as Jesus is called "son of David, the son of Abraham" (Matt. 1:1), though there was about 1,000 years between each one.

All who are named in this Sethite line are spiritual giants. When we read that one of them "begat" the next one named, in most cases it usually means he had a son and thus became the ancestor of the next person named.

In each case they lived on and had other sons and daughters. This indicates that the ones named are key people in the line.

5:3-4. Adam was 130 years old when Seth was born. Seth is called a son in Adam's own likeness, that is, with the results of the fall and the tendency to sin being passed on to him. This points out he was in the image and likeness of God (see Gen. 9:6 which shows the image of God was still in humankind), but that he had the awesome privilege of passing on the image, now marred by the fall.

5:5. Adam lived 800 more years and fathered sons and daughters. Eve is not mentioned, but she was undoubtedly able to bear children during much of this time. Note the refrain that is repeated again and again in this chapter, "and he died." It calls attention the fact that all have sinned and the wages of sin is death (Rom. 3:23; 6:23).

5:6-8. Seth had other children in addition to Enosh and he lived 18 less years than Adam. Some have tried to shorten these years by making them months, but that would make Seth have children when he was eight years and nine months old. It is more likely that the atmosphere was free of pollution and the effects of the fall only gradually increased. It is a fact that the human heart could continue a thousand years if it were not for cholesterol and disease.

5:9-11. Kenan (Heb. *Qeynan*) means "flute player" or "hymn singer." The worship of Gen. 4:26 was still going on. From earliest times true worshipers have delighted to express their praise to God in music and song.

3314.521	881, 7300	**10.**	2513.121	597	311	3314.541
cj, v Hiphil impf 3ms	do, pn		cj, v Qal impf 3ms	pn	*sub*	v Hiphil inf con, ps 3ms
וַיּוֹלֶד	אֶת־קֵינָן		וַיְחִי	אֱנוֹשׁ	אַחֲרֵי	הוֹלִידוֹ
wayyôledh	'eth-qênān		waychî	'ĕnôsh	'achrê	hôlîdhô
when he fathered	Kenan		and he lived	Enosh	after	fathering him

881, 7300	2675	6462	8523	8470	4109	8523	3314.521
do, pn	num	num	n fs	cj, num	*num*	n fs	cj, v Hiphil impf 3ms
אֶת־קֵינָן	חֲמֵשׁ	עֶשְׂרֵה	שָׁנָה	וּשְׁמֹנֶה	מֵאוֹת	שָׁנָה	וַיּוֹלֶד
'eth-qênān	chămēsh	'esrēh	shānāh	ûshemōneh	mē'ôth	shānāh	wayyôledh
Kenan	five	ten	years	and eight	hundreds of	years	and he fathered

1158	1351	**11.**	2030.126	3725, 3219	597	2675	8523
n mp	cj, n fp		cj, v Qal impf 3mp	*adj, n mp*	pn	num	n fp
בָּנִים	וּבָנוֹת		וַיִּהְיוּ	כָּל־יְמֵי	אֱנוֹשׁ	חָמֵשׁ	שָׁנִים
bānîm	ûvānôth		wayyihyû	kol-yemê	'ĕnôsh	chāmēsh	shānîm
sons	and daughters		and they were	all the days of	Enosh	five	years

9013	4109	8523	4322	**12.**	2513.121	7300	8124
cj, num	*num*	n fs	cj, v Qal impf 3ms		cj, v Qal impf 3ms	pn	num
וּתְשַׁע	מֵאוֹת	שָׁנָה	וַיָּמֹת		וַיְחִי	קֵינָן	שִׁבְעִים
ûthesha'	mē'ôth	shānāh	wayyāmōth		waychî	qênān	shiv'îm
and nine	hundreds of	years	and he died		and he lived	Kenan	seventy

8523	3314.521	881, 4252	**13.**	2513.121	7300	311
n fs	cj, v Hiphil impf 3ms	do, pn		cj, v Qal impf 3ms	pn	*sub*
שָׁנָה	וַיּוֹלֶד	אֶת־מַהֲלַלְאֵל		וַיְחִי	קֵינָן	אַחֲרֵי
shānāh	wayyôledh	'eth-mahlal'ēl		waychî	qênān	'achrê
years	when he fathered	Mahalalel		and he lived	Kenan	after

3314.541	881, 4252	727	8523	8470	4109	8523
v Hiphil inf con, ps 3ms	do, pn	num	n fs	cj, num	*num*	n fs
הוֹלִידוֹ	אֶת־מַהֲלַלְאֵל	אַרְבָּעִים	שָׁנָה	וּשְׁמֹנֶה	מֵאוֹת	שָׁנָה
hôlîdhô	'eth-mahlal'ēl	'arbā'îm	shānāh	ûshemōneh	mē'ôth	shānāh
fathering him	Mahalalel	forty	years	and eight	hundreds of	years

3314.521	1158	1351	**14.**	2030.126	3725, 3219	7300	6460
cj, v Hiphil impf 3ms	n mp	cj, n fp		cj, v Qal impf 3mp	*adj, n mp*	pn	num
וַיּוֹלֶד	בָּנִים	וּבָנוֹת		וַיִּהְיוּ	כָּל־יְמֵי	קֵינָן	עֶשֶׂר
wayyôledh	bānîm	ûvānôth		wayyihyû	kol-yemê	qênān	'eser
and he fathered	sons	and daughters		and they were	all the days of	Kenan	ten

8523	9013	4109	8523	4322	**15.**	2513.121	4252
n fp	cj, num	*num*	n fs	cj, v Qal impf 3ms		cj, v Qal impf 3ms	pn
שָׁנִים	וּתְשַׁע	מֵאוֹת	שָׁנָה	וַיָּמֹת		וַיְחִי	מַהֲלַלְאֵל
shānîm	ûthesha'	mē'ôth	shānāh	wayyāmōth		waychî	mahlal'ēl
years	and nine	hundreds of	years	and he died		and he lived	Mahalalel

2675	8523	8676	8523	3314.521	881, 3496	**16.**	2513.121
num	n fp	cj, num	n fs	cj, v Hiphil impf 3ms	do, pn		cj, v Qal impf 3ms
חָמֵשׁ	שָׁנִים	וְשִׁשִּׁים	שָׁנָה	וַיּוֹלֶד	אֶת־יָרֶד		וַיְחִי
chāmēsh	shānîm	weshishshîm	shānāh	wayyôledh	'eth-yāredh		waychî
five	years	and sixty	years	when he fathered	Jared		and he lived

4252	311	3314.541	881, 3496	8389	8523	8470
pn	*sub*	v Hiphil inf con, ps 3ms	do, pn	num	n fs	cj, num
מַהֲלַלְאֵל	אַחֲרֵי	הוֹלִידוֹ	אֶת־יֶרֶד	שְׁלֹשִׁים	שָׁנָה	וּשְׁמֹנֶה
mahlal'ēl	'achrê	hôlîdhô	'eth-yeredh	sheloshîm	shānāh	ûshemōneh
Mahalalel	after	fathering him	Jared	thirty	years	and eight

4109	8523	3314.521	1158	1351		2030.126
num	n fs	cj, v Hiphil impf 3ms	n mp	cj, n fp	**17.**	cj, v Qal impf 3mp
מֵאוֹת	שָׁנָה	וַיּוֹלֶד	בָּנִים	וּבָנוֹת		וַיִּהְיוּ
mē'ôth	shānāh	wayyôledh	bānîm	ûvānôth		wayyihyû
hundreds of	years	and he fathered	sons	and daughters		and they were

3725, 3219	4252	2675	9013	8523	8470	4109	8523
adj, n mp	pn	num	cj, num	n fs	cj, num	*num*	n fs
כָּל־יְמֵי	מַהֲלַלְאֵל	חָמֵשׁ	וְתִשְׁעִים	שָׁנָה	וּשְׁמֹנֶה	מֵאוֹת	שָׁנָה
kol-y^{e}mê	mahlal'ēl	chāmēsh	w^{e}thish'îm	shānāh	ûsh^{e}mōneh	mē'ôth	shānāh
all the days of	Mahalalel	five	and ninety	years	and eight	hundreds of	years

4322		2030.121, 3496	8692	8676	8523	4109	8523
cj, v Qal impf 3ms	**18.**	cj, v Qal impf 3ms, pn	num	cj, num	n fs	cj, *num*	n fs
וַיָּמֹת		וַיְחִי־יֶרֶד	שְׁתַּיִם	וְשִׁשִּׁים	שָׁנָה	וּמְאַת	שָׁנָה
wayyāmōth		waychî-yeredh	sh^{e}ttayim	w^{e}shishshîm	shānāh	ûm^{e}'ath	shānāh
and he died		and Jared was	two	and sixty	years	and hundred of	years

3314.521	881, 2686		2030.121, 3496	311	3314.541	881, 2686
cj, v Hiphil impf 3ms	do, pn	**19.**	cj, v Qal impf 3ms, pn	*sub*	v Hiphil inf con, ps 3ms	do, pn
וַיּוֹלֶד	אֶת־חֲנוֹךְ		וַיְחִי־יֶרֶד	אַחֲרֵי	הוֹלִידוֹ	אֶת־חֲנוֹךְ
wayyôledh	'eth-chănôkh		waychî-yeredh	'achrê	hôlîdhô	'eth-chănôkh
when he fathered	Enoch		and Jared was	after	fathering him	Enoch

8470	4109	8523	3314.521	1158	1351		2030.126
num	*num*	n fs	cj, v Hiphil impf 3ms	n mp	cj, n fp	**20.**	cj, v Qal impf 3mp
שְׁמֹנֶה	מֵאוֹת	שָׁנָה	וַיּוֹלֶד	בָּנִים	וּבָנוֹת		וַיִּהְיוּ
sh^{e}mōneh	mē'ôth	shānāh	wayyôledh	bānîm	ûvānôth		wayyihyû
eight	hundreds of	years	and he fathered	sons	and daughters		and they were

11. And all the days of Enos were nine hundred and five years: and he died.

12. And Cainan lived seventy years, and begat Mahalaleel:

13. And Cainan lived after he begat Mahalaleel eight hundred and forty years, and begat sons and daughters:

14. And all the days of Cainan were nine hundred and ten years: and he died.

15. And Mahalaleel lived sixty and five years, and begat Jared:

16. And Mahalaleel lived after he begat Jared eight hundred and thirty years, and begat sons and daughters:

17. And all the days of Mahalaleel were eight hundred ninety and five years: and he died.

18. And Jared lived an hundred sixty and two years, and he begat Enoch:

19. And Jared lived after he begat Enoch eight hundred years, and begat sons and daughters:

20. And all the days of Jared were nine hundred sixty and two years: and he died.

21. And Enoch lived sixty and five years, and begat Methuselah:

22. And Enoch walked with God after he begat Methuselah three hundred years, and begat sons and daughters:

5:12-14. Mahlaleel (Heb. Mahalalel) means "the praise of God." He too was a worshiper of the Lord and a spiritual giant, as were all who are named in this chosen line.

5:15-17. Jared (Heb. Yared) means "one prostrating himself," that is, in regular habits of prayer to the true God. He was a real prayer warrior who spent much time on his face before the Lord. His example must have meant much to Enoch.

5:18-20. Enoch in this line seems to mean "dedicated one" or "consecrated one," rather than "trained one." He gave himself fully to the worship and service of the Lord.

5:21-24. Methuselah (Heb. *Methushelach*) probably means "man sent" or "messenger." Enoch is given special attention in verses 22 and 24.

3725, 3219, 3496	8692	8676	8523	9013	4109	8523	4322
adj, n mp, pn	num	cj, num	n fs	cj, num	*num*	n fs	cj, v Qal impf 3ms
כָּל־יְמֵי־יֶרֶד	שְׁתַּיִם	וְשִׁשִּׁים	שָׁנָה	וּתְשַׁע	מֵאוֹת	שָׁנָה	וַיָּמֹת
kol-y^{e}mê-yeredh	sh^{e}ttayim	w^{e}shishshîm	shānāh	ûth^{e}sha'	mē'ôth	shānāh	wayyāmōth
all the days of Jared	two	and sixty	years	and nine	hundreds of	years	and he died

21.	2513.121	2686	2675	8676	8523	3314.521	881, 5144
	cj, v Qal impf 3ms	pn	num	cj, num	n fs	cj, v Hiphil impf 3ms	do, pn
	וַיְחִי	חֲנוֹךְ	חָמֵשׁ	וְשִׁשִּׁים	שָׁנָה	וַיּוֹלֶד	אֶת־מְתוּשָׁלַח
	waychî	chănôkh	chāmēsh	w^{e}shishshîm	shānāh	wayyôledh	'eth-m^{e}thûshālach
	and he lived	Enoch	five	and sixty	years	when he fathered	Methuselah

22.	2050.721	2686	881, 435	311	3314.541	881, 5144
	cj, v Hithpael impf 3ms	pn	do, art, pn	*sub*	v Hiphil inf con, ps 3ms	do, pn
	וַיִּתְהַלֵּךְ	חֲנוֹךְ	אֶת־הָאֱלֹהִים	אַחֲרֵי	הוֹלִידוֹ	אֶת־מְתוּשֶׁלַח
	wayyithhallēkh	chănōkh	'eth-hā'ĕlōhîm	'achrê	hôlîdhô	'eth-m^{e}thûshelach
	and he walked	Enoch	God	after	fathering him	Methuselah

8421	4109	8523	3314.521	1158	1351	23.	2030.121
num	*num*	n fs	cj, v Hiphil impf 3ms	n mp	cj, n fp		cj, v Qal impf 3ms
שְׁלֹשׁ	מֵאוֹת	שָׁנָה	וַיּוֹלֶד	בָּנִים	וּבָנוֹת		וַיְהִי
sh^{e}lōsh	mē'ôth	shānāh	wayyôledh	bānîm	ûvānôth		wayhî
three	hundreds of	years	and he fathered	sons	and daughters		and he became

3725, 3219	2686	2675	8676	8523	8421	4109	8523
adj, n mp	pn	num	cj, num	n fs	cj, num	*num*	n fs
כָּל־יְמֵי	חֲנוֹךְ	חָמֵשׁ	וְשִׁשִּׁים	שָׁנָה	וּשְׁלֹשׁ	מֵאוֹת	שָׁנָה
kāl-y^{e}mê	chănôkh	chāmēsh	w^{e}shishshîm	shānāh	ûsh^{e}lōsh	mē'ôth	shānāh
all the days of	Enoch	five	and sixty	years	and three	hundreds of	years

24.	2050.721	2686	882, 435	375	3706, 4089	881
	cj, v Hithpael impf 3ms	pn	prep, art, pn	cj, sub, ps 3ms	prep, v Qal pf 3ms	do, ps 3ms
	וַיִּתְהַלֵּךְ	חֲנוֹךְ	אֶת־הָאֱלֹהִים	וְאֵינֶנּוּ	כִּי־לָקַח	אֹתוֹ
	wayyithhallēkh	chănôkh	'eth-hā'ĕlōhîm	w^{e}'ênennû	kî-lāqach	'ōthô
	and he walked	Enoch	with God	and there was not him	because He took	him

435	25.	2513.121	5144	8124	8470	8523	4109
n mp		cj, v Qal impf 3ms	pn	num	cj, num	n fs	cj, *num*
אֱלֹהִים		וַיְחִי	מְתוּשֶׁלַח	שֶׁבַע	וּשְׁמֹנִים	שָׁנָה	וּמְאַת
'ĕlōhîm		waychî	m^{e}thûshelach	sheva'	ûsh^{e}mōnîm	shānāh	ûm^{e}'ath
God		and he lived	Methuselah	seven	and eighty	years	and hundred of

8523	3314.521	881, 4069	26.	2513.121	5144	311
n fs	cj, v Hiphil impf 3ms	do, pn		cj, v Qal impf 3ms	pn	*sub*
שָׁנָה	וַיּוֹלֶד	אֶת־לָמֶךְ		וַיְחִי	מְתוּשֶׁלַח	אַחֲרֵי
shānāh	wayyôledh	'eth-lāmekh		waychî	m^{e}thûshelach	'achrê
years	when he fathered	Lamech		and he lived	Methuselah	after

3314.541	881, 4069	8692	8470	8523	8124	4109	8523
v Hiphil inf con, ps 3ms	do, pn	num	cj, num	n fs	cj, num	num	n fs
הוֹלִידוֹ	אֶת־לֶמֶךְ	שְׁתַּיִם	וּשְׁמוֹנִים	שָׁנָה	וּשְׁבַע	מֵאוֹת	שָׁנָה
hôlîdhô	'eth-lemekh	sh^{e}ttayim	sh^{e}mônîm	shānāh	ûsh^{e}va'	mē'ôth	shānāh
fathering him	Lamech	two	and eighty	years	and seven	hundreds of	years

3314.521	1158	1351	27.	2030.126	3725, 3219	5144
cj, v Hiphil impf 3ms	n mp	cj, n fp		cj, v Qal impf 3mp	*adj, n mp*	pn
וַיּוֹלֶד	בָּנִים	וּבָנוֹת		וַיִּהְיוּ	כָּל־יְמֵי	מְתוּשֶׁלַח
wayyôledh	bānîm	ûvānôth		wayyihyû	kāl-y^{e}mê	m^{e}thûshelach
and he fathered	sons	and daughters		and they were	all the days of	Methuselah

9013	8676	8523	9013	4109	8523	4322
num	cj, num	n fs	cj, num	*num*	n fs	cj, v Qal impf 3ms
תֵּשַׁע	וְשִׁשִּׁים	שָׁנָה	וּתְשַׁע	מֵאוֹת	שָׁנָה	וַיָּמֹת
tēsha'	w^{e}shishshîm	shānāh	ûth^{e}sha'	mē'ôth	shānāh	wayyāmōth
nine	and sixty	years	and nine	hundreds of	years	and he died

28.	2030.121, 4069	8692	8470	8523	4109	8523
	cj, v Qal impf 3ms, pn	num	cj, num	n fs	cj, *num*	n fs
	וַיְחִי־לֶמֶךְ	שְׁתַּיִם	וּשְׁמֹנִים	שָׁנָה	וּמְאַת	שָׁנָה
	waychî-lemekh	sh^{e}ttayim	ûsh^{e}mōnîm	shānāh	ûm^{e}'ath	shānāh
	and Lamech was	two	and eighty	years	and hundred of	years

3314.521	1158	29.	7410.121	881, 8428	5326	3937, 569.141
cj, v Hiphil impf 3ms	n ms		cj, v Qal impf 3ms	do, n ms, ps 3ms	pn	prep, v Qal inf con
וַיּוֹלֶד	בֵּן		וַיִּקְרָא	אֶת־שְׁמוֹ	נֹחַ	לֵאמֹר
wayyôledh	bēn		wayyiqōrā'	'eth-sh^{e}mô	nōach	lē'mōr
when he fathered	son		and he called	his name	Noah	saying

23. And all the days of Enoch were three hundred sixty and five years:

24. And Enoch walked with God: ... And Enoch walketh habitually with God, *Young* ... And Enoch went on in God's ways, *BB* ... And Hanok walked with God, *Fenton* ... He spent his life in fellowship with God, *Good News*.

and he was not; for God took him: ... and he was no more seene: for God tooke him away, *Geneva* ... then he disappeared, *Goodspeed* ... and he was not, for God took him, *Darby*.

25. And Methuselah lived an hundred eighty and seven years, and begat Lamech:

26. And Methuselah lived after he begat Lamech seven hundred eighty and two years, and begat sons and daughters:

27. And all the days of Methuselah were nine hundred sixty and nine years: and he died.

28. And Lamech lived an hundred eighty and two years, and begat a son:

29. And he called his name Noah, saying, This same shall comfort us: ... this child will bring us relief, *Good News* ... to bring us consolation, *Goodspeed* ... This one shall give us rest, *NASB* ... this boy will bring us relief, *REB*.

concerning our work and toil of our hands, because of the ground which the LORD hath cursed: ... the labor and painful toil of our hands, *NIV* ... our trouble and hard work, *BB* ... from our work, from the labor that has come upon us, *REB* ... concerning our work, and concerning the labour of our hands, *Young*.

Whereas the Bible says that others lived for a certain time after the next in the chosen line was born, these verses emphasize Enoch walked with God. The Hebrew form of the verb means he walked closely and continually with God. He lived every day in the presence of the Lord and in constant communion with Him. His faith and obedience, as well as his worship, were outstanding.

Only with Enoch is the phrase "and he died" missing. He did not die. Instead, "he was not" or, better, "he was absent," for suddenly, God took him, to heaven (cf. Heb.11:5).

What a great example of faith he was! He and Elijah are the only ones who were taken to heaven without dying.

5:25-27. The meaning of Lamech's name is uncertain. We can be sure, however, that he was quite different in his attitudes from the Lamech in Cain's line.

Methuselah's 969 years make him the oldest person named in the Bible. He apparently died just before Noah's flood. We must again recognize however, that as in the case of other Biblical genealogies, there may have been other persons between him and Lamech.

5:28-31. Noah (Heb. *Noach*) means "rest" or "relief." Lamech gave him that name as a wordplay on the Hebrew verb *nacham*, meaning "comfort."

The effects of the curse on the ground must have been getting worse. Lamech trusted that Noah would be able to intercede with God and bring relief from the toil that resulted from that curse. Lamech must have been a worshiper of the LORD as well.

2172	5341.321	4623, 4801	4623, 6328	3135	4623, 124
dem pron	v Piel impf 3ms, ps 1cp	prep, n mp, ps 1cp	cj, prep, *n ms*	n fp, ps 1cp	prep, art, n fs
זֶה	יְנַחֲמֵנוּ	מִמַּעֲשֵׂנוּ	וּמֵעִצְּבוֹן	יָדֵינוּ	מִן־הָאֲדָמָה
zeh	yenachmēnû	mimma'ăsēnû	ûmē'itstsevôn	yādhênû	min-hā'ădhāmāh
this	he will comfort us	from our work	and from the hardship of	our hands	from the ground

866	803.311	3176	**30.**	2030.121, 4069	311	3314.541
rel part	v Piel pf 3ms, ps 3fs	pn		cj, v Qal impf 3ms, pn	*sub*	v Hiphil inf con, ps 3ms
אֲשֶׁר	אֵרְרָהּ	יְהוָה		וַיְחִי־לֶמֶךְ	אַחֲרֵי	הוֹלִידוֹ
'ăsher	'ērrāhh	yehwāh		waychî-lemekh	'achrê	hôlîdhô
which	He has cursed it	Yahweh		and Lamech was	after	fathering him

881, 5326	2675	9013	8523	2675	4109	8523
do, pn	num	cj, num	n fs	cj, *num*	*num*	n fs
אֶת־נֹחַ	חָמֵשׁ	וְתִשְׁעִים	שָׁנָה	וַחֲמֵשׁ	מֵאֹת	שָׁנָה
'eth-nōach	chāmēsh	wethish'îm	shānāh	wachămēsh	mē'ōth	shānāh
Noah	five	and ninety	years	and five of	hundreds of	years

3314.521	1158	1351	**31.**	2030.121	3725, 3219, 4069	8124
cj, v Hiphil impf 3ms	n mp	cj, n fp		cj, v Qal impf 3ms	*adj, n mp*, pn	num
וַיּוֹלֶד	בָּנִים	וּבָנוֹת		וַיְהִי	כָּל־יְמֵי־לֶמֶךְ	שֶׁבַע
wayyôledh	bānîm	ûvānôth		wayhî	kol-yemê-lemekh	sheva'
and he fathered	sons	and daughters		and it was	all the days of Lamech	seven

8124	8523	8124	4109	8523	4322	**32.**	2030.121, 5326
cj, num	n fs	cj, *num*	*num*	n fs	cj, v Qal impf 3ms		cj, v Qal impf 3ms, pn
וְשִׁבְעִים	שָׁנָה	וּשְׁבַע	מֵאוֹת	שָׁנָה	וַיָּמֹת		וַיְהִי־נֹחַ
weshiv'îm	shānāh	ûsheva'	mē'ôth	shānāh	wayyāmōth		wayhî-nōach
and seventy	years	and seven of	hundreds of	years	and he died		and Noah was

1158, 2675	4109	8523	3314.521	5326	881, 8429	881, 2626	881, 3425
n ms, num	*num*	n fs	cj, v Hiphil impf 3ms	pn	do, pn	do, pn	cj, do, pn
בֶּן־חֲמֵשׁ	מֵאוֹת	שָׁנָה	וַיּוֹלֶד	נֹחַ	אֶת־שֵׁם	אֶת־חָם	וְאֶת־יָפֶת
ben-chămēsh	mē'ôth	shānāh	wayyôledh	nōach	'eth-shēm	'eth-chām	we'eth-yāpheth
son of five of	hundreds of	years	then he fathered	Noah	Shem	Ham	and Japheth

6:1	2030.121	3706, 2591.511	119	3937, 7525.141	6142, 6686	124
	cj, v Qal impf 3ms	prep, v Hiphil pf 3ms	art, n ms	prep, v Qal inf con	prep, *n mp*	art, n fs
	וַיְהִי	כִּי־הֵחֵל	הָאָדָם	לָרֹב	עַל־פְּנֵי	הָאֲדָמָה
	wayhî	kî-hēchēl	hā'ādhām	lārōv	'al-penê	hā'ădhāmāh
	and it was	that he began	the humankind	to multiply	on the surface of	the ground

1351	3314.416	3937	**2.**	7495.126	1158, 435	881, 1351
cj, n fp	v Pual pf 3cp	prep, ps 3mp		cj, v Qal impf 3mp	*n mp*, art, n mp	do, *n fp*
וּבָנוֹת	יֻלְּדוּ	לָהֶם		וַיִּרְאוּ	בְנֵי־הָאֱלֹהִים	אֶת־בְּנוֹת
ûvānôth	yulledhû	lāhem		wayyir'û	benê-hā'ĕlōhîm	'eth-benôth
and daughters	they were born	to them		and they saw	the sons of God	the daughters of

119	3706	3005	2078	4089.126	3937	5571	4623, 3725
art, n ms	cj	adj	pers pron	cj, v Qal impf 3mp	prep, ps 3mp	n fp	prep, adj
הָאָדָם	כִּי	טֹבֹת	הֵנָּה	וַיִּקְחוּ	לָהֶם	נָשִׁים	מִכֹּל
hā'ādhām	kî	ṭōvōth	hēnnāh	wayyiqchû	lāhem	nāshîm	mikkōl
the humankind	because	beautiful	they	and they took	for them	wives	from all

866	1013.116	**3.**	569.121	3176	3940, 1833.121	7593
rel part	v Qal pf 3cp		cj, v Qal impf 3ms	pn	neg part, v Qal impf 3ms	n fs, ps 1cs
אֲשֶׁר	בָּחָרוּ		וַיֹּאמֶר	יְהוָה	לֹא־יָדוֹן	רוּחִי
'ăsher	bāchārû		wayyō'mer	yehwāh	lō'-yādhôn	rûchî
which	they chose		and He said	Yahweh	it will not judge	my Spirit

30. And Lamech lived after he begat Noah five hundred ninety and five years, and begat sons and daughters:

31. And all the days of Lamech were seven hundred seventy and seven years: and he died.

32. And Noah was five hundred years old: and Noah begat Shem, Ham, and Japheth.

6:1. And it came to pass, when men began to multiply on the face of the earth and daughters were born unto them: ... the earth began to be populated, *Berkeley* ... when man began to grow numerous, *Goodspeed* ... The human race began to increase and to spread over the earth, *REB* ... when men were increasing on the earth, *BB.*

2. That the sons of God: ... The sons of the gods, *REB* ... the sons of heaven, *NAB* ... the supernatural beings, *Good News* ... the sons of the gods, *NEB.*

saw the daughters of men that they were fair: ... were beautiful, *NASB* ... admired their looks, *Berkeley* ... these girls were beautiful, *Good News.*

and they took them wives of all which they chose.

3. And the LORD said, My spirit shall not always strive with man: ... shall not remain in man forever, *NAB* ... My Spirit shall not call to man, *Fenton* ... My Spirit will not contend with man, *NIV* ... My Spirit shall not always plead with Man, *Darby.*

for that he also is flesh: ... because he is mortal flesh, *REB* ... is only flesh, *BB* ... hee is but flesh, *Geneva.*

yet his days: ... His lifetime, *NCB* ... the days of his life, *BB* ... their days, *NRSV*

shall be an hundred and twenty years.

5:32. Noah, at 500 years of age, had three sons. This may mean he had the first one at that time. Like the others in the chosen line, he may have had other children earlier, but these are mentioned by name because they survived the flood. Shem is named first, not because he was the oldest, but because the chosen line was continued through him.

Shem means "name," indicating they were dedicated worshipers of the LORD, upholding and exalting His name (cf. Gen. 4:26). Noah and his sons were probably the last in being true worshipers of God. Ham means "dark," probably in the sense of dark skin. Japheth means "fair," in the sense of light skin. Thus there were both light and dark skins in the family of Noah. Since everyone alive today is descended from Noah's family, the principles of heredity would cause us to expect that the human race today to be approximately one-fourth light skin and three-fourths dark skin. This is indeed the case.

6:1-3. In the background of Noah's flood the population of the world was increasing. Then the sons of God proceeded to look on the daughters of humankind and saw they were "good" (with reference to their appearance, thus, pleasing and desirable). They took wives, not on the basis of the spirituality or relation to God, but on what was physically pleasing to them.

Then "the LORD said, My spirit [the Holy Spirit] shall not always strive with man, for that he [humankind] also is flesh [with fleshly desires that come from the fallen human nature]." "Strive" has been interpreted as rule, judge, shield, abide in, or act in. Most likely, the meaning of "strive with" is "judge among." The Holy Spirit was probably using the word preached by people like Enoch and Noah to instruct and exhort people (2 Pet. 2:5), but the people were rejecting God's word. Thus, God determined to give him (humankind) 120 more years before the flood would bring His divine judgment. Some suppose the 120 years refer to the maximum life of individuals. However, the evidence is that the length of life was gradually shortened after the flood.

6:4. "Giants" (Heb. *nephilim*) here could mean "spiritual giants." Some suppose *nephilim* is derived from *naphal*, "to fall," but that is not a normal Hebrew construction. Rather, it could be from *pala'* and mean "wonderful ones," but it seems more likely that it is from *palal*, with the meaning "separated ones," meaning separated from the intermarriages verse 2 mentions and staying true to the LORD.

"Those days" are identified as the days when the sons of God came in to the daughters of humankind in general, the days before the flood. The Nephilim were also present after the flood. This means they went through the flood and thus the nephilim included Noah and his sons. Since the Hebrew has no noun "children" in verse 4 (notice that the word is in italics in KJV, which means the word was added by the KJV translators), "the same" also refers back to the nephilim, not the children of the intermarriages.

904, 119	3937, 5986	1343	2000	1340	2030.116	3219	4109
prep, n ms	prep, n ms	cj	pers pron	n ms	cj, v Qal pf 3cp	n mp, ps 3ms	num
בָּאָדָם	לְעֹלָם	בְּשַׁגַּם	הוּא	בָשָׂר	וְהָיוּ	יָמָיו	מֵאָה
vā’ādhām	le‘ōlām	beshaggam	hû’	vāsār	wehāyû	yāmâv	mē’āh
among humankind	forever	since	he	flesh	and they will be	his days	hundred

6465	8523		5485	2030.116	904, 800	904, 3219	2062
cj, num	n fs	**4.**	art, n mp	v Qal pf 3cp	prep, n fs	prep, art, n mp	art, dem pron
וְעֶשְׂרִים	שָׁנָה		הַנְּפִלִים	הָיוּ	בָאָרֶץ	בַּיָּמִים	הָהֵם
we‘esrîm	shānāh		hannephilîm	hāyû	vā’ārets	bayyāmîm	hāhēm
and twenty	years		the Nephilim	they were	on the earth	in the days	the those

1612	311, 3772	866	971.126	1158	435	420, 1351
cj, cj	*sub*, prep	rel part	v Qal impf 3mp	*n mp*	art, n mp	prep, *n fp*
וְגַם	אַחֲרֵי־כֵן	אֲשֶׁר	יָבֹאוּ	בְּנֵי	הָאֱלֹהִים	אֶל־בְּנוֹת
wegham	’achrê-khēn	’ăsher	yāvō’û	benê	hā’ĕlōhîm	’el-benôth
and also	afterward	when	they went	the sons of	God	to the daughters of

119	3314.116	3937	2065	1429	866	4623, 5986
art, n ms	cj, v Qal pf 3cp	prep, ps 3mp	pers pron	art, n mp	rel part	prep, n ms
הָאָדָם	וְיָלְדוּ	לָהֶם	הֵמָּה	הַגִּבֹּרִים	אֲשֶׁר	מֵעוֹלָם
hā’ādhām	weyāledhû	lāhem	hēmmāh	haggibbōrîm	’ăsher	mē‘ôlām
the humankind	and they bore	to them	they	the mighty ones	which	from ancient times

596	8428		7495.121	3176	3706	7521	7750	119
n mp	art, n ms	**5.**	cj, v Qal impf 3ms	pn	cj	adj	*n fs*	art, n ms
אַנְשֵׁי	הַשֵּׁם		וַיַּרְא	יְהוָה	כִּי	רַבָּה	רָעַת	הָאָדָם
’anshê	hashshēm		wayyar’	yehwāh	kî	rabbāh	rā‘ath	hā’ādhām
men of	the Name		and He saw	Yahweh	that	great	the evil of	the humankind

904, 800	3725, 3444	4422	3949	7828	7737	3725, 3219
prep, art, n fs	cj, *adj, n ms*	*n fp*	n ms, ps 3ms	adv	adj	*adj*, art, n ms
בָּאָרֶץ	וְכָל־יֵצֶר	מַחְשְׁבֹת	לִבּוֹ	רַק	רַע	כָּל־הַיּוֹם
bā’ārets	wekhol-yētser	machshebōth	libbô	raq	ra‘	kol-hayyôm
on the earth	and every form of	the thoughts of	his heart	only	evil	all the day

	5341.221	3176	3706, 6449.111	881, 119	904, 800
6.	cj, v Niphal impf 3ms	pn	prep, v Qal pf 3ms	do, art, n ms	prep, art, n fs
	וַיִּנָּחֶם	יְהוָה	כִּי־עָשָׂה	אֶת־הָאָדָם	בָּאָרֶץ
	wayyinnāchem	yehwāh	kî-‘āsāh	’eth-hā’ādhām	bā’ārets
	and He was grieved	Yahweh	that He made	the humankind	on the earth

6321.721	420, 3949		569.121	3176	4364.125	881, 119
cj, v Hithpael impf 3ms	prep, n ms, ps 3ms	**7.**	cj, v Qal impf 3ms	pn	v Qal impf 1cs	do, art, n ms
וַיִּתְעַצֵּב	אֶל־לִבּוֹ		וַיֹּאמֶר	יְהוָה	אֶמְחֶה	אֶת־הָאָדָם
wayyith‘atstsēv	’el-libbô		wayyō’mer	yehwāh	’emcheh	’eth-hā’ādhām
and He was distressed	toward his heart		and He said	Yahweh	I will wipe out	the humankind

866, 1282.115	4623, 6142	6686	124	4623, 119	5912, 966	5912, 7719
rel part, v Qal pf 1cs	prep, prep	*n mp*	art, n fs	prep, n ms	prep, n fs	prep n ms
אֲשֶׁר־בָּרָאתִי	מֵעַל	פְּנֵי	הָאֲדָמָה	מֵאָדָם	עַד־בְּהֵמָה	עַד־רֶמֶשׂ
’ăsher-bārā’thî	mē‘al	penê	hā’ădhāmāh	mē’ādhām	‘adh-behēmāh	‘adh-remes
which I created	on	the surface of	the ground	from humankind	unto animals	unto creeping things

5912, 5991	8452	3706	5341.215	3706	6449.115		5326
cj, prep, *n ms*	art, n md	cj	v Niphal pf 1cs	cj	v Qal pf 1cs, ps 3mp	**8.**	cj, pn
וְעַד־עוֹף	הַשָּׁמָיִם	כִּי	נִחַמְתִּי	כִּי	עֲשִׂיתִם		וְנֹחַ
we‘adh-‘ôph	hashshāmāyim	kî	nichamtî	kî	‘ăsîthim		wenōach
unto the birds of	the air	because	I am grieved	that	I made them		but Noah

4. There were giants: ... men of strength and size, *BB* ... Nephilim, *NASB* ... fallen ones, *Young*.

in the earth in those days and also after that: ... In those days, as well as afterward, *Goodspeed* ... and also afterward, *NRSV* ... in those days and even afterwards, *Young*.

when the sons of God came in unto the daughters of men, and they bare children to them, the same became mighty men: ... these were the heroes, *Darby* ... heroes, *REB* ... mighty men, *KJVII*.

which were of old, men of renown: ... famous men, *Good News* ... people of renown, *REB* ... men of renown, *NEB* ... the men of great name, *BB*.

5. And GOD saw that the wickedness of man was great in the earth, and that every imagination of the thoughts of his heart was only evil continually: ... every thought and inclination, *REB* ... no desire that his heart conceived was ever anything but evil, *NAB* ... every effort of the thought of his heart was to promote sin, *Fenton* ... intention of all human thinking produced nothing but evil, *Berkeley*.

6. And it repented the LORD that he had made man on the earth, and it grieved him at his heart: ... made Him sorrowful, *KJV* ... the Lord had sorrow, *BB* ... he was grieved to the heart, *Goodspeed* ... his heart was filled with pain, *NIV* ... hee was sory in his heart, *Geneva*.

7. And the LORD said, I will destroy man: ... I will wipe out, NAB ... I will sweep away, *Fenton* ... I will blot out, *NRSV* ... I shall wipe off, *REB*.

whom I have created from the face of the earth; both man, and beast, and the creeping thing, and the fowls of the air: ... man and beast, reptiles and birds, NEB ... all living things, *NKJV* ... from man to cattle, to creeping things, and to fowl of the heavens, *Darby*.

for it repenteth me that I have made them: ... for it is grief to Me that I have made them, *Berkeley* ... the LORD was sorry that He had made man, *NKJV* ... I have sorrow for having made them, *BB*.

The nephilim are then identified as mighty men of old and men of renown. "Mighty men" is usually used in a positive sense of strength that is admired and of God himself, and in some places is used of spiritually mighty men. "Men of renown" is literally "men of the Name." The phrase "the Name" in the Old Testament is only used of the name of God. This connects both the Nephilim and Noah with those worshipers of the Name of the Lord in Gen. 4:26.

Because "sons of" is used in a variety of ways in the Old Testament, often meaning "having the character of," and because the "sons of God" in Job 1:6 are angels, some teach that the sons of God in Gen. 6:2 are fallen angels. Some make a connection with 2 Peter and Jude. However, angels are spirit beings, and Jesus indicated that they do not marry (Mark 12:25). Furthermore, only God can create, so Satan would be unable to give fallen angels a physical body (as God sometimes has done for temporary appearances of good angels). Then, if they were fallen angels, they and their children would have perished in the flood, and it is hard to see why they would even be mentioned. The great emphasis here is on flesh (weak, frail, unregenerate human flesh) and on the Holy Spirit's ceasing to judge among humankind.

On the other hands, if the sons of God are the Sethite line, then some of them were nephilim, spiritual giants who kept themselves separate from the intermarriage mentioned in verse 4. Those actually named in the Sethite line in Genesis 5 were all spiritual giants. They all had other children, and must have had many descendants. Yet by the time of the flood, Noah and his sons were the only left who were still serving the Lord.

Now we can see a pattern. Chapter 4 shows how the Cainite line ended in immorality and violence. This spread among humankind in general. Chapter 5 shows how the godly Sethite line included spiritual giants, but because of the intermarriage with the daughters of humankind in general, the moral corruption and violence increased until only Noah is walking with God.

6:5. The LORD saw how great the wickedness had become. Evil filled the thoughts and imaginations of everyone's heart. (The Hebrew for "heart" includes the mind).

6:6. All this evil made God feel grieved that he had made humankind and he was "cut to the heart." God is not the unfeeling being imagined by the Greeks. He is a real person.

6:7. The LORD said He would blot out humankind, as well as the animals He had made for our benefit, because He was grieved that He had made them. The phrase "it repenteth me" (KJV) basically means, "I am grieved." In Numbers 23:19 we are told that God is not a man that he should

4834.111	2682	904, 6084	3176		431	8765	5326
v Qal pf 3ms	n ms	prep, *n fp*	pn		dem pron	*n fp*	pn
מָצָא	חֵן	בְּעֵינֵי	יְהוָה	**9.**	אֵלֶּה	תּוֹלְדֹת	נֹחַ
mātsā'	chēn	be'ênê	yehwāh		'ēlleh	tôledhōth	nōach
he found	favor	in the eyes of	Yahweh		these	the accounts of	Noah

5326	382	6926	8879	2030.111	904, 1810	882, 435
pn	n ms	adj	adj	v Qal pf 3ms	prep, n mp, ps 3ms	prep, art, pn
נֹחַ	אִישׁ	צַדִּיק	תָּמִים	הָיָה	בְּדֹרֹתָיו	אֶת־הָאֱלֹהִים
nōach	'îsh	tsaddîq	tāmîm	hāyâh	bedhōrōthâv	'eth-hā'ĕlōhîm
Noah	man	righteous	blameless	he was	among his contemporaries	with God

2050.711, 5326		3314.521	5326	8421	1158	881, 8429	881, 2626
v Hithpael pf 3ms, pn		cj, v Hiphil impf 3ms	pn	num	n mp	do, pn	do, pn
הִתְהַלֶּךְ־נֹחַ	**10.**	וַיּוֹלֶד	נֹחַ	שְׁלֹשָׁה	בָנִים	אֶת־שֵׁם	אֶת־חָם
hithhallekh-nōach		wayyôledh	nōach	shelōshāh	vānîm	'eth-shēm	'eth-chām
Noah walked		and he fathered	Noah	three	sons	Shem	Ham

881, 3425		8271.122	800	3937, 6686	435	4527.222
cj, do, pn		cj, v Qal impf 3fs	art, n fs	prep, *n mp*	art, n mp	cj, v Niphal impf 3fs
וְאֶת־יָפֶת	**11.**	וַתִּשָּׁחֵת	הָאָרֶץ	לִפְנֵי	הָאֱלֹהִים	וַתִּמָּלֵא
we'eth-yāpheth		wattishshāchēth	hā'ārets	liphnê	hā'ĕlōhîm	wattimmālē'
and Japheth		and it was corrupt	the earth	before	God	and it was filled with

800	2660		7495.121	435	881, 800	2079	8271.212
art, n fs	n ms		cj, v Qal impf 3ms	n mp	do, art, n fs	cj, intrj	v Niphal pf 3fs
הָאָרֶץ	חָמָס	**12.**	וַיַּרְא	אֱלֹהִים	אֶת־הָאָרֶץ	וְהִנֵּה	נִשְׁחָתָה
hā'ārets	chāmās		wayyar'	'ĕlōhîm	'eth-hā'ārets	wehinnēh	nishchāthāh
the earth	violence		and He saw	God	the earth	and behold	it was corrupt

3706, 8271.511	3725, 1340	881, 1932	6142, 800		569.121	435
prep, v Hiphil pf 3ms	*adj*, n ms	do, n ms, ps 3ms	prep, art, n fs		cj, v Qal impf 3ms	n mp
כִּי־הִשְׁחִית	כָּל־בָּשָׂר	אֶת־דַּרְכּוֹ	עַל־הָאָרֶץ	**13.**	וַיֹּאמֶר	אֱלֹהִים
kî-chishchîth	kol-bāsār	'eth-darkô	'al-hā'ārets		wayyō'mer	'ĕlōhîm
because it had corrupted	all flesh	its way	on the earth		and He said	God

3937, 5326	7377	3725, 1340	971.151	3937, 6686	3706, 4527.112	800
prep, pn	*n ms*	*adj*, n ms	v Qal act ptc ms	prep, n mp, ps 1cs	prep, v Qal pf 3fs	art, n fs
לְנֹחַ	קֵץ	כָּל־בָּשָׂר	בָּא	לְפָנַי	כִּי־מָלְאָה	הָאָרֶץ
lenōach	qēts	kol-bāsār	bā'	lephānay	kî-māle'āh	hā'ārets
to Noah	end of	all flesh	coming	before me	because it is filled	the earth

2660	4623, 6686	2079	8271.551	881, 800		6449.131
n ms	prep, n mp, ps 3mp	cj, intrj, ps 1cs	v Hiphil act ptc ms, ps 3mp	do, art, n fs		v Qal impv 2ms
חָמָס	מִפְּנֵיהֶם	וְהִנְנִי	מַשְׁחִיתָם	אֶת־הָאָרֶץ	**14.**	עֲשֵׂה
chāmās	mippenêhem	wehinnî	mashchîthām	'eth-hā'ārets		'ăsēh
violence	from their face	and behold I	about to destroy them	the earth		make

3937	8720	6320, 1656	7348	6449.123	882, 8720	3848.113
prep, ps 2ms	*n fs*	*n mp*, n ms	n mp	v Qal impf 2ms	prep, art, n fs	cj, v Qal pf 2ms
לְךָ	תֵּבַת	עֲצֵי־גֹפֶר	קִנִּים	תַּעֲשֶׂה	אֶת־הַתֵּבָה	וְכָפַרְתָּ
lekhā	tēvath	'ătsê-ghōpher	qinnîm	ta'ăseh	'eth-hattēvāh	wekhāphartā
for you	ark of	wood of gopher	rooms	you will make	with the ark	and you will cover

881	4623, 1041	4623, 2445	904, 3851		2172	866	6449.123
do, ps 3fs	prep, n ms	cj, prep, n ms	prep, art, n ms		cj, dem pron	rel part	v Qal impf 2ms
אֹתָהּ	מִבַּיִת	וּמִחוּץ	בַּכֹּפֶר	**15.**	וְזֶה	אֲשֶׁר	תַּעֲשֶׂה
'ōthāhh	mibbayith	ûmichûts	bakōpher		wezeh	'ăsher	ta'ăseh
it	from inside	and from outside	with pitch		and this	that	you will make

8. But Noah found grace in the eyes of the LORD: ... Noah, however, had won the LORD'S favour, *REB* ... Noah found favour in the presence of the EVER-LIVING, *Fenton* ... the LORD was pleased with Noah, *Good News* ... But Noah found favor, *ASV*.

9. These are the generations of Noah: Noah was a just man and perfect in his generations, and Noah walked with God: ... a good man and blameless, *NAB* ... an upright man and without sin, *BB* ... was a pious and exceedingly good man, *Goodspeed* ... Noah was a just and upright man in his time, *Geneva*.

10. And Noah begat three sons, Shem, Ham, and Japheth.

11. The earth also was corrupt before God: ... But the earth had grown corrupted in God's sight, *Berkeley* ... And the earth was evil in God's eyes, *BB* ... Now in God's sight, the earth was corrupt, *Goodspeed* ... earth corrupted itself in the presence of God, *Fenton*.

***and* the earth was filled with violence:** The Earth was full of crime, *Fenton* ... the earth was full of wrong-doing, *Goodspeed* ... earth was filled with cruelty, *Geneva* ... the earth was filled with lust for power, *Berkeley*.

12. And God looked upon the earth, and, behold, it was corrupt; for all flesh had corrupted his way upon the earth: ... since all mortals led depraved lives on earth, *NAB* ... the people were all living evil lives, *Good News* ... And God, looking on the earth, saw that it was evil, *BB* ... for every mortal on the earth had corrupted his life, *Goodspeed*.

13. And God said unto Noah, The end of all flesh is come before me: ... The end of all creatures of flesh is in my mind, *NCB* ... The loathsomeness of all mankind has become plain to me, *NEB* ... I have resolved on the extermination of all mortals, *Goodspeed* ... I decide to cut off all men from My sight, *Fenton*.

for the earth is filled with violence through them; and, behold, I will destroy them with the earth: ... the earth is full of lawlessness, *NAB* ... full of violence because of them, *NCB* ... from their presence, *Young*.

14. Make thee an ark of gopher wood; rooms shalt thou make in the ark and shalt pitch it within and without with pitch: ... Make thee an Arke of pine-trees, *Geneva*

---

repent. That is, when we repent we have to change our basic attitudes--sinful things we once loved we now hate. But God's attitude toward sin is always the same. His attitude toward genuine repentance, faith, and worship that is in the Spirit and in truth (John 4:23) is always the same. But people hurt God when they disobey and turn to evil. Hosea strongly illustrates this where Hosea's broken heart caused him to see how God's heart is broken over a backsliding, rebellious people.

6:8. Only Noah found grace (or favor) before the Lord. Verse 9 tells why. He was walking with the Lord as Enoch did, but instead of taking Noah to heaven, God left him here to continue the human race. Verse 9 identifies him further.

6:9. "These are the generations" indicates the beginning of the account of the flood. Noah is identified as just or righteous and perfect, meaning sound, mature, having integrity. He consistently responded to God in obedience and repented when he stumbled. Walking with God means he maintained a close relationship of faith, fellowship, and obedience.

6:10. The repetition of what we read in 5:32 draws attention to these sons being his immediate family, not just descendants (in contrast to the previous genealogy).

6:11. The result of the fall multiplied through the influence of the Cainite line, caused the whole earth to become corrupt and filled with violence. We see a similar increase in corruption and violence as we are approaching the judgments prophesied to follow the Rapture of the Church.

6:12. The earth was not only corrupt but people were working at making it more and more corrupt. That, too, will characterize the end of the Church Age--with people wanting to be open in their sin, wanting sinful lifestyles to be accepted, and encouraging others to partake of their sins.

6:13. The time came when God spoke to Noah about the coming end of all flesh (all humankind) because of the violence throughout the earth.

6:14. Because God wanted to save Noah, He gave him directions for building an ark, meaning "a vessel for floating." The same Hebrew word is used of the "ark of bulrushes" made for the baby Moses by his mother (Exo. 2:3).

A different word (Heb., 'aron) is used of the ark of the covenant--which was a gold-plated wooden box or chest (Exo. 37:1-2). Noah's ark would be made of gopher wood (gopher is the Hebrew for a common tree, possibly cypress), sealed with pitch inside and outside, with rooms (or nests) on three levels.

881	8421	4109	527	775	8720	2675	527
do, ps 3fs	num	num	n fs	n ms	art, n fs	num	n fs
אֹתָהּ	שְׁלֹשׁ	מֵאוֹת	אַמָּה	אֹרֶךְ	הַתֵּבָה	חֲמִשִּׁים	אַמָּה
'ōthāhh	shelōsh	mē'ōth	'ammāh	'ōrekh	hattēvāh	chămishshîm	'ammāh
it	three	hundreds of	cubits	the length of	the ark	fifty	cubits

7621	8389	527	7253	16.	6936	6449.123	3937, 8720
n ms, ps 3fs	cj, num	n fs	n fs, ps 3fs		n fs	v Qal impf 2ms	prep, art, n fs
רָחְבָּהּ	וּשְׁלֹשִׁים	אַמָּה	קוֹמָתָהּ		צֹהַר	תַּעֲשֶׂה	לַתֵּבָה
rāchbbāhh	ûshelōshîm	'ammāh	qômāthāhh		tsōhar	ta'ăseh	lattēvāh
its width	and thirty	cubits	its height		roof	you will make	for the ark

420, 527	3735.323	4623, 3937, 4762	6860	8720	904, 6917
cj, prep, n fs	v Piel impf 2ms, ps 3fs	prep, prep, adv	cj, n ms	art, n fs	prep, n ms, ps 3fs
וְאֶל־אַמָּה	תְּכַלֶנָּה	מִלְמַעְלָה	וּפֶתַח	הַתֵּבָה	בְּצִדָּהּ
we'el-'ammāh	tekhalennāh	milma'lāh	ûphethach	hattēvāh	betsiddāhh
and to a cubit	you will finish it	above	and the door of	the ark	in its side

7947.123	8812	8529	8389	6449.123	17.	603	2079
v Qal impf 2ms	adj	num	cj, num	v Qal impf 2ms		cj, pers pron	intrj, ps 1cs
תָּשִׂים	תַּחְתִּיִּם	שְׁנִיִּם	וּשְׁלִשִׁים	תַּעֲשֶׂהָ		וַאֲנִי	הִנְנִי
tāsîm	tachtiyyim	sheniyyim	ûshelishîm	ta'ăsehā		wa'ănî	hinnî
you will put	lower	second	and third	you will make		and I	behold I

971.551	881, 4138	4448	6142, 800	3937, 8271.341	3725, 1340	866, 904
v Hiphil ptc ms	do, art, n ms	n md	prep, art, n fs	prep, v Piel inf con	adj, n ms	rel part, prep, ps 3ms
מֵבִיא	אֶת־הַמַּבּוּל	מַיִם	עַל־הָאָרֶץ	לְשַׁחֵת	כָּל־בָּשָׂר	אֲשֶׁר־בּוֹ
mēvî'	'eth-hammabbûl	mayim	'al-hā'ārets	leshachēth	kol-bāsār	'ăsher-bô
about to bring	the flood of	waters	on the earth	to destroy	all flesh	which in it

7593	2508	4623, 8809	8452	3725	866, 904, 800	1510.121
n fs	n mp	prep, prep	art, n md	adj	rel part, prep, art, n fs	v Qal impf 3ms
רוּחַ	חַיִּים	מִתַּחַת	הַשָּׁמָיִם	כֹּל	אֲשֶׁר־בָּאָרֶץ	יִגְוָע
rûach	chayyîm	mittachath	hashshāmāyim	kōl	'ăsher-bā'ārets	yighwa'
the breath of	life	under	the heavens	all	that on the earth	it will die

18.	7251.515	881, 1311	882	971.113	420, 8720	887
	cj, v Hiphil pf 1cs	do, n fs, ps 1cs	prep, ps 2fs	cj, v Qal pf 2ms	prep, art, n fs	pers pron
	וַהֲקִמֹתִי	אֶת־בְּרִיתִי	אִתָּךְ	וּבָאתָ	אֶל־הַתֵּבָה	אַתָּה
	wahqimōthî	'eth-berîthî	'ittākh	ûvā'thā	'el-hattēvāh	'attāh
	but I will establish	my covenant	with you	and you will go	into the ark	you

1158	828	5571, 1158	882	19.	4623, 3725, 2508
cj, n mp, ps 2ms	cj, n fs, ps 2ms	cj, n fp, n mp, ps 2ms	prep, ps 2fs		cj, prep, adj, art, n ms
וּבָנֶיךָ	וְאִשְׁתְּךָ	וּנְשֵׁי־בָנֶיךָ	אִתָּךְ		וּמִכָּל־הָחַי
ûvānêkhā	we'ishttekhā	ûnshê-vānêkhā	'ittākh		ûmikkāl-hāchay
and your sons	and your wife	and the wives of your sons	with you		and from all living things

4623, 3725, 1340	8530	4623, 3725	971.523	420, 8720	3937, 2513.541	882
prep, adj, n ms	num	prep, adj	v Hiphil impf 2ms	prep, art, n fs	prep, v Hiphil inf con	prep, ps 2fs
מִכָּל־בָּשָׂר	שְׁנַיִם	מִכֹּל	תָּבִיא	אֶל־הַתֵּבָה	לְהַחֲיֹת	אִתָּךְ
mikkāl-bāsār	shenayim	mikkōl	tāvî'	'el-hattēvāh	lehachyōth	'ittākh
from all flesh	two	from every	you will bring	into the ark	to keep alive	with you

2227	5531	2030.126	20.	4623, 5991	3937, 4464	4623, 966
n ms	cj, n fs	v Qal impf 3mp		prep, art, n ms	prep, n ms, ps 3ms	cj, prep, art, n fs
זָכָר	וּנְקֵבָה	יִהְיוּ		מֵהָעוֹף	לְמִינֵהוּ	וּמִן־הַבְּהֵמָה
zākhār	ûneqēvāh	yihyû		mēhā'ôph	lemînēhû	ûmin-habbehēmāh
male	and female	they will be		from the birds	according to its kind	and from the animals

with ribs of cypress; cover it with reeds, *REB* ... Ark of pitch-pine, *Fenton* ... Make an ark of resin-wood; make it tight with fibre, *NCB* ... Make yourself an ark of oleander wood; make the ark with cabins, and smear it with bitumen, *Goodspeed.*

15. And this is the fashion which thou shalt make it of: The length of the ark shall be three hundred cubits, the breadth of it fifty cubits, and the height of it thirty cubits.

16. A window shalt thou make to the ark: ... put a window in the ark, *BB* ... make a ventilating-fan, fixed in a turret, *Fenton* ... A light shalt thou make to the ark, *ASV* ... Make a roof, *NRSV* ... Put an 18 inch window in the ark, *Berkeley.*

and in a cubit shalt thou finish it above; and the door of the ark shalt thou set in the side thereof; with lower, second, and third stories shalt thou make it: ... with bottom, second and third decks, *NAB* ... build three decks, lower, middle, and upper, *REB* ... make it with lower, second, and third decks, *NRSV* ... make it with lower, second and third stories, *KJVII.*

17. And, behold, I, even I, do bring a flood of waters upon the earth to destroy all flesh, wherein is the breath of life: ... I will send a great flow of waters over the earth, *BB* ... for I Myself will bring a downrush of waters upon the earth to sweep off all beings possessing the breath of life, *Fenton* ... I am bringing in the deluge of waters on the earth, *Young* ... I myself am about to bring a water-deluge, *Berkeley.*

from under heaven; and every thing that is in the earth shall die: ... all that is in the earth doth expire, *Young* ... everything on earth shall perish, *NAB* ... everything on earth will come to an end, *BB* ... All that are on the earth shall die, *NCB.*

18. But with thee will I establish my covenant: ... but with you I will make an agreement, *BB* ... Then I will establish My covenant with you, *Fenton* ... And I have established My covenant with thee, *Young* ... But I will establish my covenant with you, *NIV.*

and thou shalt come into the ark, thou, and thy sons, and thy wife, and thy sons' wives with thee: ... and you will enter the ark, *NIV.*

19. And of every living thing of all flesh, two of every sort: ... You must also have a pair of every kind of all living creatures, *Berkeley* ... You are to bring into the ark two of all living creatures, *NIV* ... Of every sort of living creature of all flesh you shall bring two, *NCB* ... of every living thing of all flesh, you shall bring two of every sort, *RSV.*

shalt thou bring into the ark, to keep them alive with thee; they shall be male and female.

20. Of fowls after their kind, and of cattle after their kind, of every creeping thing of the earth after his kind, two of every sort shall come unto thee, to keep them alive.

6:15. The older cubit, 22 1/2 inches long was probably used here. This would make the ark 562.5 feet (171 meters) long, 92.67 feet (28.5 meters) wide, and 56.25 feet (17 meters) high. These proportions would be like that of a large ocean liner today. However, there is no mention of a keel, so it must have been more like a seaworthy, flat-bottom barge. It is interesting to note that the account of the flood was preserved by many peoples in different parts of the world, but as time went on, most mixed it with heathen ideas. The Babylonian account describes the ark as a cube (which would roll on the water and kill everything inside). The biblical dimensions would also give plenty of room for all the varieties of animals and birds God wanted saved (most animals and birds are small).

6:16. Under the eaves of the overhanging roof was to be an opening for light an air 22.5 inches wide all around the ark. The three levels in the ark would have an 18.75 feet (5.67 meters) high ceiling.

6:17. The ark would be the only place where anyone could be saved from the flood which would totally destroy all humankind as well as all the land animals and birds remaining outside the ark. Some have proposed that the flood was only a local flood in the Near East, but the Bible's language seems too strong for that. The point is total judgment except for a new beginning with Noah and his family.

6:18. God established His covenant with Noah. This was a binding agreement God placed on Himself for the benefit of Noah and his family. But they had to respond in faith by going into the ark before there was any rain or any sign of a flood, in order for the covenant to be effective.

6:19-20. God commanded Noah to bring into the ark two of every kind of animal and bird, a male and female of each kind. Noah did not have to go out and look for them. They would come to him and he would only need to usher them into their rooms (or cages and nests). It is implied that God would bring the right representative of each kind of animal and bird.

Thus, there may have been some prehistoric animals and birds God did not see fit to preserve. Others may have already become extinct in the midst of the violence before the flood.

3937, 4464	**4623, 3725**	**7719**	**124**	**3937, 4464**	**8530**
prep, n ms, ps 3fs	prep, adj	*n ms*	art, n fs	prep, n ms, ps 3ms	num
לְמִינָהּ	מִכֹּל	רֶמֶשׂ	הָאֲדָמָה	לְמִינֵהוּ	שְׁנַיִם
l^{e}mînāhh	mikkōl	remes	hā'ădhāmāh	l^{e}mînēhû	sh^{e}nayim
according to its kind	from every	creeping thing of	the ground	according to its kind	two

4623, 3725	**971.126**	**420**	**3937, 2513.541**		**887**	**4089.131, 3937**
prep, adj	v Qal impf 3mp	prep, ps 2ms	prep, v Hiphil inf con	**21.**	cj, pers pron	v Qal impv 2ms, prep, ps 2ms
מִכֹּל	יָבֹאוּ	אֵלֶיךָ	לְהַחֲיוֹת		וְאַתָּה	קַח־לְךָ
mikkōl	yāvō'û	'ēlêkhā	l^{e}hachyôth		w^{e}'attāh	qach-l^{e}khā
from every	they will come	to you	to keep alive		and you	take for you

4623, 3725, 4120	**866**	**404.221**	**636.113**	**420**	**2030.111**	**3937**
prep, *adj*, n ms	rel part	v Niphal impf 3ms	cj, v Qal pf 2ms	prep, ps 2ms	cj, v Qal pf 3ms	prep, ps 2ms
מִכָּל־מַאֲכָל	אֲשֶׁר	יֵאָכֵל	וְאָסַפְתָּ	אֵלֶיךָ	וְהָיָה	לְךָ
mikkol-ma'ăkhol	'ăsher	yē'ākhēl	w^{e}'āsaphtā	'ēlêkhā	w^{e}hāyāh	l^{e}khā
from every food	which	it is eaten	and you will store	for you	and it will be	for you

3937	**3937, 408**		**6449.121**	**5326**	**3626, 3725**	**866**	**6943.311**
cj, prep, ps 3mp	prep, n fs	**22.**	cj, v Qal impf 3ms	pn	prep, adj	rel part	v Piel pf 3ms
וְלָהֶם	לְאָכְלָה		וַיַּעַשׂ	נֹחַ	כְּכֹל	אֲשֶׁר	צִוָּה
w^{e}lāhem	l^{e}'ākh^{e}lāh		wayya'as	nōach	k^{e}khōl	'ăsher	tsiwwāh
and for them	for food		and he made	Noah	according to all	which	He commanded

881	**435**	**3772**	**6449.111**		**569.121**	**3176**	**3937, 5326**
do, ps 3ms	n mp	adv	v Qal pf 3ms	**7:1**	cj, v Qal impf 3ms	pn	prep, pn
אֹתוֹ	אֱלֹהִים	כֵּן	עָשָׂה		וַיֹּאמֶר	יְהוָה	לְנֹחַ
'ōthô	'ĕlōhîm	kēn	'āsâh		wayyō'mer	y^{e}hwāh	l^{e}nōach
him	God	so	he did		and He said	Yahweh	to Noah

971.131, 887	**3725, 1041**	**420, 8720**	**3706, 881**	**7495.115**	**6926**
v Qal impv 2ms, pers pron	cj, *adj*, n ms, ps 2ms	prep, art, n fs	prep, do, ps 2ms	v Qal pf 1cs	adj
בֹּא־אַתָּה	וְכָל־בֵּיתְךָ	אֶל־הַתֵּבָה	כִּי־אֹתְךָ	רָאִיתִי	צַדִּיק
bō'-'attāh	w^{e}khol-bêth^{e}kh	'el-hattēvāh	kî-'ōth^{e}khā	rā'îthî	tsaddîq
you go	and all your household	into the ark	because you	I have seen	righteous

3937, 6686	**904, 1810**	**2172**		**4623, 3725**	**966**	**2999**
prep, n mp, ps 1cs	prep, art, n ms	art, dem pron	**2.**	prep, adj	art, n fs	art, adj
לְפָנַי	בַּדּוֹר	הַזֶּה		מִכֹּל	הַבְּהֵמָה	הַטְּהוֹרָה
l^{e}phānay	baddôr	hazzeh		mikkōl	habb^{e}hēmāh	hatt^{e}hôrāh
before me	in the generation	the this		from every	the animals	the clean

4089.123, 3937	**8124**	**8124**	**382**	**828**	**4623, 966**	**866**
v Qal impf 2ms, prep, ps 2ms	num	num	n ms	cj, n fs, ps 3ms	cj, prep, art, n fs	rel part
תִּקַּח־לְךָ	שִׁבְעָה	שִׁבְעָה	אִישׁ	וְאִשְׁתּוֹ	וּמִן־הַבְּהֵמָה	אֲשֶׁר
tiqqach-l^{e}khā	shiv'āh	shiv'āh	'îsh	w^{e}'ishtô	ûmin-habb^{e}hēmāh	'ăsher
you will take to you	seven	seven	male	and his mate	and from the animals	which

3940	**2999**	**2000**	**8530**	**382**	**828**		**1612**	**4623, 5991**	**8452**
neg part	adj	pers pron	num	n ms	cj, n fs, ps 3ms	**3.**	cj	prep, *n ms*	art, n md
לֹא	טְהֹרָה	הִוא	שְׁנַיִם	אִישׁ	וְאִשְׁתּוֹ		גַּם	מֵעוֹף	הַשָּׁמַיִם
lō'	t^{e}hōrāh	hiw'	sh^{e}nayim	'îsh	w^{e}'ishtô		gam	mē'ôph	hashshāmayim
not	clean	it	two	male	and his mate		also	from the birds of	the air

8124	**8124**	**2227**	**5531**	**3937, 2513.341**	**2320**	**6142, 6686**
num	num	n ms	cj, n fs	prep, v Piel inf con	n ms	prep, *n mp*
שִׁבְעָה	שִׁבְעָה	זָכָר	וּנְקֵבָה	לְחַיּוֹת	זֶרַע	עַל־פְּנֵי
shiv'āh	shiv'āh	zākhār	ûnqēvāh	l^{e}chayyôth	zera'	'al-p^{e}nê
seven	seven	male	and female	to keep alive	seed	on the surface of

3725, 800		3706	3937, 3219	5968	8124	609	4442.551	6142, 800
adj, art, n fs	**4.**	cj	prep, n mp	adv	num	pers pron	v Hiphil ptc ms	prep, art, n fs
כָּל־הָאָרֶץ		כִּי	לְיָמִים	עוֹד	שִׁבְעָה	אָנֹכִי	מַמְטִיר	עַל־הָאָרֶץ
khol-hā'ārets		kî	l^{e}yāmîm	'ôdh	shiv'āh	'ānōkhî	mamṭîr	'al-hā'ārets
all the earth		because	for days	yet	seven	I	maker of rain	on the earth

727	3219	727	4050	4364.115	881, 3725, 3462	866
num	n ms	cj, num	n ms	cj, v Qal pf 1cs	do, *adj*, art, n ms	rel part
אַרְבָּעִים	יוֹם	וְאַרְבָּעִים	לָיְלָה	וּמָחִיתִי	אֶת־כָּל־הַיְקוּם	אֲשֶׁר
'arbā'îm	yôm	w^{e}'arbā'îm	lāy^{e}lāh	ûmāchîthî	'eth-kol-hayqûm	'ăsher
forty	days	and forty	nights	and I will wipe out	every living thing	which

6449.115	4623, 6142	6686	124		6449.121	5326	3626, 3725
v Qal pf 1cs	prep, prep	*n mp*	art, n fs	**5.**	cj, v Qal impf 3ms	pn	prep, adj
עָשִׂיתִי	מֵעַל	פְּנֵי	הָאֲדָמָה		וַיַּעַשׂ	נֹחַ	כְּכֹל
'āsîthî	mē'al	p^{e}nê	hā'ădhāmāh		wayya'as	nōach	k^{e}khōl
I made	from on	the surface of	the ground		and he did	Noah	according to all

21. And take thou unto thee of all food that is eaten, and thou shalt gather it to thee; and it shall be for food for thee, and for them: ... all meate that is eaten, *Geneva* ... some of all food which is edible, *NASB* ... Collect and store enough suitable food, *Berkeley* ... See that you take and store every kind of food that can be eaten, *NEB*.

22. Thus did Noah; according to all that God commanded him, so did he: ... Exactly as God had commanded him, so Noah did, *NEB* ... Noah did everything that God commanded, *Good News* ... And Noah did so; he carried out God's orders, *Berkeley* ... Noah did everything just as God commanded him, *NIV*.

7:1. And the LORD said unto Noah, Come thou and all thy house into the ark; for thee have I seen righteous before me in this generation: ... you alone in this age have I found to be truly just, *NAB* ... upright, *BB* ... you alone are righteous, *NEB* ... the only one who does what is right, *Good News*.

2. Of every clean beast: ... each kind of ritually clean animal, *Good News* ... clean beasts, *Young* ... clean animal, *NIV*.

thou shalt take to thee by sevens, the male and his female: and of beasts that are not clean by two, the male and his female: ... a male and its mate, *NCB* ... male and female, *Fenton* ... pair of each kind, *Good News* ... the male and his female, *Geneva*.

3. Of fowls also of the air by sevens, the male and the female: ... a male and its mate, *NCB* ... male and female, *NEB* ... male and female, *RSV* ... a male and a female, *Young*.

to keep seed alive: ... to preserve, *Fenton* ... to ensure that life continues on earth, *NEB* ... to keep their kind alive, *NRSV* ... to keep various kinds alive, *NIV*.

upon the face of all the earth.

4. For yet seven days, and I will cause it to rain: ... Seven days from now I will bring rain down, *NAB* ... after seven more days, *NASB* ... For in yet seven days, *Darby* ... at the end of seven days, *Fenton*.

upon the earth forty days and

6:21. Noah was responsible to bring in a sufficient supply of food for himself and all the rest.

6:22. Noah obeyed. This shows he accepted God's covenant in faith and proceeded to build the ark, trusting God to guide and deliver him and his family. Hebrews 11:7 also shows he was moved by a godly fear that recognized and reverenced the holiness and justice of God.

7:1-3. When it was time for Noah to enter the ark, God acknowledged Noah's righteousness. Then God gave him an additional command to take seven pairs of clean animals and birds into the ark. They would be necessary in the future for food and for sacrifices (see Gen. 8:20; 9:3).

7:4-5. The command to enter the ark was given a week before the rain began to fall. God reemphasized that the destruction of all living things off the face of the earth, literally, from upon the face of the dry land. This indicates a universal flood, not just a local flood. Again Noah obeyed completely and fully, not leaving out anything God asked him to do.

866, 6943.311	3176	6.	5326	1158, 8666	4109	8523
rel part, v Piel pf 3ms, ps 3ms	pn		cj, pn	*n ms*, num	*num*	n fs
אֲשֶׁר־צִוָּהוּ	יְהוָה		וְנֹחַ	בֶּן־שֵׁשׁ	מֵאוֹת	שָׁנָה
'ăsher-tsiwwāhû	y^{e}hwāh		w^{e}nōach	ben-shēsh	mē'ôth	shānāh
which He commanded him	Yahweh		and Noah	son of six	hundreds of	years

4138	2030.111	4448	6142, 800	7.	971.121	5326	1158
cj, art, n ms	v Qal pf 3ms	n md	prep, art, n fs		cj, v Qal impf 3ms	pn	cj, n mp, ps 3ms
וְהַמַּבּוּל	הָיָה	מַיִם	עַל־הָאָרֶץ		וַיָּבֹא	נֹחַ	וּבָנָיו
w^{e}hammabbûl	hāyâh	mayim	'al-hā'ārets		wayyāvō'	nōach	ûvānâv
and the flood	it was	waters	on the earth		and he went	Noah	and his sons

828	5571, 1158	882	420, 8720	4623, 6681	4448	4138
cj, n fs, ps 3ms	cj, *n fp*, n mp, ps 3ms	prep, ps 3ms	prep, art, n fs	prep, *n ms*	*n mp*	art, n ms
וְאִשְׁתּוֹ	וּנְשֵׁי־בָנָיו	אִתּוֹ	אֶל־הַתֵּבָה	מִפְּנֵי	מֵי	הַמַּבּוּל
w^e'ishtô	ûnshê-vānâv	'ittô	'el-hattēvāh	mipp^{e}nê	mê	hammabbûl
and his wife	and the wives of his sons	with him	into the ark	before	the waters of	the flood

8.	4623, 966	2999	4623, 966	866	375	2999
	prep, art, n fs	art, adj	c, prep, art, n fs	rel part	sub, ps 3fs	adj
	מִן־הַבְּהֵמָה	הַטְּהוֹרָה	וּמִן־הַבְּהֵמָה	אֲשֶׁר	אֵינֶנָּה	טְהֹרָה
	min-habb^{e}hēmāh	hatt^{e}hôrāh	ûmin-habb^{e}hēmāh	'ăsher	'ênennāh	t^{e}hōrāh
	from the animals	the clean	and from the animals	which	it is not	clean

4623, 5991	3725	866, 7718.151	6142, 124	9.	8530	8530	971.116
cj, prep, art, n ms	cj, adj	rel part, v Qal act ptc ms	prep, art, n fs		num	num	v Qal pf 3cp
וּמִן־הָעוֹף	וְכֹל	אֲשֶׁר־רֹמֵשׂ	עַל־הָאֲדָמָה		שְׁנַיִם	שְׁנַיִם	בָּאוּ
ûmin-hā'ôph	w^{e}khōl	'ăsher-rōmēs	'al-hā'ădhāmāh		sh^{e}nayim	sh^{e}nayim	bā'û
and from the birds	and every	creeping thing	on the ground		two	two	they went

420, 5326	420, 8720	2227	5531	3626, 866	6943.311	435	881, 5326
prep, pn	prep, art, n fs	n ms	cj, n fs	prep, rel part	v Piel pf 3ms	n mp	do, pn
אֶל־נֹחַ	אֶל־הַתֵּבָה	זָכָר	וּנְקֵבָה	כַּאֲשֶׁר	צִוָּה	אֱלֹהִים	אֶת־נֹחַ
'el-nōach	'el-hattēvāh	zākhār	ûnqēvāh	ka'ăsher	tsiwwāh	'ĕlōhîm	'eth-nōach
to Noah	into the ark	male	and female	according to that	He commanded	God	Noah

10.	2030.121	3937, 8124	3219	4448	4138	2030.116	6142, 800
	cj, v Qal impf 3ms	prep, *num*	art, n mp	cj, *n mp*	art, n ms	v Qal pf 3cp	prep, art, n fs
	וַיְהִי	לְשִׁבְעַת	הַיָּמִים	וּמֵי	הַמַּבּוּל	הָיוּ	עַל־הָאָרֶץ
	wayhî	l^{e}shiv'ath	hayyāmîm	ûmê	hammabbûl	hāyû	'al-hā'ārets
	and it was	after seven of	the days	then the waters of	the flood	they were	above the earth

11.	904, 8523	8666, 4109	8523	3937, 2508, 5326	904, 2414	8529
	prep, *n fs*	num, *num*	n fs	prep, *n mp*, pn	prep, art, n ms	art, num
	בִּשְׁנַת	שֵׁשׁ־מֵאוֹת	שָׁנָה	לְחַיֵּי־נֹחַ	בַּחֹדֶשׁ	הַשֵּׁנִי
	bishnath	shēsh-mē'ôth	shānāh	l^{e}chayyê-nōach	bachōdhesh	hashshēnî
	in year of	six hundreds of	years	to the life of Noah	in the month	the second

904, 8124, 6461	3219	3937, 2414	904, 3219	2172	1260.216	3725, 4754
prep, num, num	n ms	prep, art, n ms	prep, art, n ms	art, dem pron	v Niphal pf 3cp	*adj, n mp*
בְּשִׁבְעָה־עָשָׂר	יוֹם	לַחֹדֶשׁ	בַּיּוֹם	הַזֶּה	נִבְקְעוּ	כָּל־מַעְיְנֹת
b^{e}shiv'āh-'āsār	yôm	lachōdhesh	bayyôm	hazzeh	nivqō'û	kol-ma'äynōth
on seven ten	day	to the month	on the day	the this	they burst open	all the springs of

8745	7521	724	8452	6858.116	12.	2030.121	1700
n fs	adj	cj, *n fp*	art, n md	v Niphal pf 3cp		cj, v Qal impf 3ms	art, n ms
תְּהוֹם	רַבָּה	וַאֲרֻבֹּת	הַשָּׁמַיִם	נִפְתָּחוּ		וַיְהִי	הַגֶּשֶׁם
t^{e}hôm	rabbāh	wa'ărubbōth	hashshāmayim	niphtāchû		wayhî	haggeshem
the deep	great	and the windows of	the heavens	they were opened		and it was	the rain

6142, 800	727	3219	727	4050		904, 6344	3219	2172
prep, art, n fs	num	n ms	cj, num	n ms	**13.**	prep, *n fs*	art, n ms	art, dem pron
עַל־הָאָרֶץ	אַרְבָּעִים	יוֹם	וְאַרְבָּעִים	לָיְלָה		בְּעֶצֶם	הַיּוֹם	הַזֶּה
'al-hā'ārets	'arbā'îm	yôm	we'arbā'îm	lāyelāh		be'etsem	hayyôm	hazzeh
on the earth	forty	days	and forty	nights		on the bone of	the day	the this

971.111	5326	8429, 2626	3425	1158, 5326	828	5326
v Qal pf 3ms	pn	cj, pn, cj, pn	cj, pn	*n mp*, pn	cj, *n fs*	pn
בָּא	נֹחַ	וְשֵׁם־וְחָם	וָיֶפֶת	בְּנֵי־נֹחַ	וְאֵשֶׁת	נֹחַ
bā'	nōach	weshēm-wechām	wāyepheth	benê-nōach	we'ēsheth	nōach
he went	Noah	and Shem and Ham	and Japheth	the sons of Noah	and the wife of	Noah

forty nights; and every living substance that I have made will I destroy from off the face of the earth: ... I will sweep away, *Fenton* ... and have wiped away all the substance, *Young* ... I will blot out, *NASB* ... every existing thing, *Berkeley*.

5. And Noah did according unto all that the LORD commanded him.

6. And Noah was six hundred years old when the flood of waters was upon the earth: ... the downrush of water, *Fenton* ... overwhelmed the earth, Berkeley ... when the floodwaters came, *NIV*.

7. And Noah went in, and his sons, and his wife, and his sons' wives with him, into the ark, because of the waters of the flood: ... entered the ark to escape, *NIV* ... to escape the flood, *REB* ... the flowing of the waters, *BB* ... the waters of the deluge, *Fenton*.

8. Of clean beasts, and of beasts that are not clean and of fowls, and of every thing that creepeth upon the earth,

9. There went in two and two unto Noah into the ark, the male and the female, as God had commanded Noah.

10. And it came to pass after seven days, that the waters of the flood were upon the earth: ... Seven days later the flood came, *Good News* ... towards the end of seven days the waters of the flood came, *NEB*.

11. In the six hundredth year of Noah's life, in the second month, the seventeenth day of the month, the same day were all the fountains of the great deep broken up: ... the fountains of the great abyss were all broken open, *Goodspeed* ... all the springs of the great deep burst out, *REB* ... all the fountains of the great deep came bursting through, *BB*.

and the windows of heaven were opened: ... floodgates, *NIV* ... and the net-work of the heavens, *Young* ... the great abyss burst forth, and the floodgates of the sky were opened, *NAB* ... the depths of the Great Ocean were heaved up and the belts in the heavens were broken, *Fenton* ... the sluices of heaven, *Berkeley*.

12. And the rain was upon the earth forty days and forty nights: ... And the rain fell, *NCB* ... the rains gushed down, *Berkeley* ... there was a downrush, *Fenton* ... the pour of rain, *Darby*.

13. In the selfsame day: ... At the close of that day, *Fenton* ... that was the day, *REB* ... on that very day, *NIV* ... This is the date, *Berkeley*.

entered Noah, and Shem, and Ham, and Japheth, the sons of Noah, and Noah's wife, and the three wives of his sons with them, into the ark;

7:6. Noah was 600 years old when the flood came. Thus, he had 100 years to prepare the ark (see Gen. 5:32). During that time, he was also a preacher of righteousness (2 Pet. 2:5). The people who heard him rejected his message and went their merry ways, never believing that God's judgment could come upon them.

7:7-10. Eight people entered the ark. Again it is implied that God caused the animals and birds to come to Noah and he and his sons escorted them to their places. This probably took 7 days.

7:11-12. The waters of the flood came from two sources, the clouds and the fountains of the great deep. There is definite evidence that much of the water now in the oceans was once in pockets in the earth's crust. Breaking up the fountains indicates violent earthquake action. The phrase "windows of heaven" indicates the clouds poured down rain. Some believe that there was still a cloud blanket around much of the earth before the flood, so there was much water to be released in the form of rain.

The rain lasted forty days and nights just as the LORD told Noah it would.

7:13-16. At the beginning of the 40 days of rain, Noah and his family entered the ark. The

8421	**5571, 1158**	**882**	**420, 8720**		**2065**	**3725, 2516**
cj, *num*	*n fp*, n mp, ps 3ms	prep, ps 3mp	prep, art, n fs	**14.**	pers pron	cj, adj, art, n fs
וּשְׁלֹשֶׁת	נְשֵׁי־בָנָיו	אִתָּם	אֶל־הַתֵּבָה		הֵמָּה	וְכָל־הַחַיָּה
ûshlōsheth	n^{e}shê-vānâv	'ittām	'el-hattēvāh		hēmmāh	w^{e}khol-hachayyāh
and the three of	the wives of his sons	with them	into the ark		they	and all the animals

3937, 4464	**3725, 966**	**3937, 4464**	**3725, 7719**
prep, n ms, ps 3fs	cj, *adj*, art, n fs	prep, n ms, ps 3fs	cj, *adj*, art, n ms
לְמִינָהּ	וְכָל־הַבְּהֵמָה	לְמִינָהּ	וְכָל־הָרֶמֶשׂ
l^{e}mînāhh	w^{e}khol-habb^{e}hēmāh	l^{e}mînāhh	w^{e}khol-hāremes
according to its kind	and all the beasts	according to its kind	and all the creeping things

7718.151	**6142, 800**	**3937, 4464**	**3725, 5991**	**3937, 4464**	**3725**
art, v Qal act ptc ms	prep, art, n fs	prep, n ms, ps 3ms	cj, *adj*, art, n ms	prep, n ms, ps 3ms	adj
הָרֹמֵשׂ	עַל־הָאָרֶץ	לְמִינֵהוּ	וְכָל־הָעוֹף	לְמִינֵהוּ	כֹּל
hārōmēs	'al-hā'ārets	l^{e}mînēhû	w^{e}khol-hā'ôph	l^{e}mînēhû	kōl
the creepers	on the earth	according to its kind	and all the birds	according to its kind	every

7109	**3725, 3796**		**971.126**	**420, 5326**	**420, 8720**	**8530**	**8530**
n fs	*adj*, n fs	**15.**	cj, v Qal impf 3mp	prep, pn	prep, art, n fs	num	num
צִפּוֹר	כָּל־כָּנָף		וַיָּבֹאוּ	אֶל־נֹחַ	אֶל־הַתֵּבָה	שְׁנַיִם	שְׁנַיִם
tsippôr	kol-kānāph		wayyāvō'û	'el-nōach	'el-hattēvāh	sh^{e}nayim	sh^{e}nayim
bird	every winged creature		and they went	to Noah	into the ark	two	two

4623, 3725, 1340	**866, 904**	**7593**	**2508**		**971.152**	**2227**
prep, adj, art, n ms	rel part, prep, ps 3ms	*n fs*	n mp	**16.**	cj, art, v Qal act ptc mp	n ms
מִכָּל־הַבָּשָׂר	אֲשֶׁר־בּוֹ	רוּחַ	חַיִּים		וְהַבָּאִים	זָכָר
mikkol-habbāsār	'ăsher-bô	rûach	chayyîm		w^{e}habbā'îm	zākhār
from all the flesh	which in it	the breath of	life		and the ones that entered	male

5531	**4623, 3725, 1340**	**971.116**	**3626, 866**	**6943.311**	**881**	**435**
cj, n fs	prep, *adj*, n ms	v Qal pf 3cp	prep, rel part	v Piel pf 3ms	do, ps 3ms	n mp
וּנְקֵבָה	מִכָּל־בָּשָׂר	בָּאוּ	כַּאֲשֶׁר	צִוָּה	אֹתוֹ	אֱלֹהִים
ûnqēvāh	mikkāl-bāsār	bā'û	ka'ăsher	tsiwwāh	'ōthô	'ĕlōhîm
and female	from all flesh	they went	according to that	He commanded	him	God

5646	**3176**	**1185**		**2030.121**	**4138**	**727**	**3219**
cj, v Qal impf 3ms	pn	prep, ps 3ms	**17.**	cj, v Qal impf 3ms	art, n ms	num	n ms
וַיִּסְגֹּר	יְהוָה	בַּעֲדוֹ		וַיְהִי	הַמַּבּוּל	אַרְבָּעִים	יוֹם
wayyisgōr	y^{e}hwāh	ba'ădhô		wayhî	hammabbûl	'arbā'îm	yôm
and He shut	Yahweh	behind him		and it was	the flood	forty	days

6142, 800	**7528.126**	**4448**	**5558.126**	**881, 8720**	**7597**
prep, art, n fs	cj, v Qal impf 3mp	art, n md	cj, v Qal impf 3mp	do, art, n fs	cj, v Qal impf 3fs
עַל־הָאָרֶץ	וַיִּרְבּוּ	הַמַּיִם	וַיִּשְׂאוּ	אֶת־הַתֵּבָה	וַתָּרָם
'al-hā'ārets	wayyirbû	hammayim	wayyish'û	'eth-hattēvāh	wattārām
on the earth	and they increased	the waters	and they lifted up	the ark	and it was high

4623, 6142	**800**		**1428.126**	**4448**	**7528.126**	**4108**
prep, prep	art, n fs	**18.**	cj, v Qal impf 3mp	art, n md	cj, v Qal impf 3mp	adv
מֵעַל	הָאָרֶץ		וַיִּגְבְּרוּ	הַמַּיִם	וַיִּרְבּוּ	מְאֹד
mē'al	hā'ārets		wayyighb^{e}rû	hammayim	wayyirbû	m^{e}'ōdh
above	the earth		and they were strong	the waters	and they increased	very

6142, 800	**2050.122**	**8720**	**6142, 6686**	**4448**		**4448**
prep, art, n fs	cj, v Qal impf 3fs	art, n fs	prep, *n mp*	art, n md	**19.**	cj, art, n mp
עַל־הָאָרֶץ	וַתֵּלֶךְ	הַתֵּבָה	עַל־פְּנֵי	הַמָּיִם		וְהַמַּיִם
'al-hā'ārets	wattēlekh	hattēvāh	'al-p^{e}nê	hammāyim		w^{e}hammayim
on the earth	but it went	the ark	on the surface of	the waters		and the waters

14. They, and every beast after his kind, and all the cattle after their kind, and every creeping thing that creepeth upon the earth after his kind: ... With them went every kind of animal, domestic and wild, *Good News* ... Wild animals of every kind, cattle of every kind, every kind of thing that creeps on the ground, *REB* ... together with every kind of wild beast, every kind of domestic animal, every kind of creeping thing of the earth, *NAB* ... every sort of beast and cattle, and every sort of thing which goes on the earth, *BB*.

and every fowl after his kind, every bird of every sort: ... all the various kinds of birds, *Goodspeed* ... even every bird of every feather, *Geneva* ... every bird of every sort, *KJVII* ... birds of every kind, *NEB*.

15. And they went in unto Noah into the ark, two and two of all flesh, wherein is the breath of life: ... in which is a living spirit, *Young* ... all creatures which have animal breath, *Fenton* ... that had life in them, *NEB* ... each kind of living being, *Good News*.

16. And they that went in, went in male and female of all flesh, as God had commanded him: and the LORD shut him in: ... Then the LORD closed the entrance, *Berkeley* ... Jehovah shut him in, *ASV* ... was shut by the Lord, *BB* ... Jehovah doth close it for him, *Young*.

17. And the flood was forty days upon the earth; and the waters increased: ... and the waters multiply, *Young* ... The waters mounted, *Berkeley* ... the waters swelled, *NEB* ... waters were increased, *BB*.

and bare up the ark and it was lift up above the earth: ... bore up, *KJVII* ... the water became deep enough for the boat to float, *Good News* ... was lifted up high over the earth, *BB* ... rose high above the earth, *RSV*.

18. And the waters prevailed: ... and the waters are mighty, *Young* ... The waters swelled, *NRSV* ... The swelling waters increased greatly, *NAB* ... the waters overcame everything, *BB*.

and were increased greatly upon the earth: ... and the waters swelled, *Fenton* ... multiply exceedingly, *Young* ... greatly increased, *NKJV* ... water became deeper, *Good News*.

and the ark went upon the face of the waters: ... the ark was resting on the face of the waters, *BB* ... and lifted up the Ark, and raised it from off the land, *Fenton* ... And the ark floated, *KJVII* ... the boat drifted on the surface, *Good News*.

19. And the waters prevailed exceedingly: ... And the waters have been very mighty, *Young* ... The waters also waxed strong, *Geneva* ... the waters rose over the earth, gaining the upper hand, *Berkeley* ... the water prevailed more and more, *NASB*.

upon the earth and all the high hills, that were under the whole heaven, were covered: ... until all the highest mountains everywhere were submerged, *NAB* ... And all the high hills that were under the whole heaven were covered, *KJVII* ... highest mountains everywhere under the heavens were covered, *NCB* ... all the high mountains that are under all the heavens were covered, *Darby*.

20. Fifteen cubits upward did the waters prevail; and the mountains were covered: ... to a depth of more than twenty feet, *NIV* ... covering them fifteen cubits deep, *RSV* ... More than 20 feet, *Berkeley* ... went 15 cubits higher, *BB*.

Hebrew uses the phrase "on bone of the day" to indicate that it was on the exact day that the rain began. The animals and birds all went into the ark with Noah and his family. The "kinds" here, as in Leviticus chapter 11, were probably superfamilies. So some of the varieties earlier in existence may not have entered the ark. That is, God probably brought a pair of elephants that would become the ancestors of African and Asian elephants, but He did not bring other types such as the hairy mammoth. It is quite possible that the 40 days of rain and the great earthquakes changed the shape of the continents (there is evidence that all the continents were once together in a super continent) and brought sudden freezing to the northern regions where the mammoths have been found quick-frozen with grass and buttercups still in their mouths.

7:17-20. The water level kept rising during the forty days causing the ark to float. Before the rains ended all the high hills were covered. It is quite possible the earth was much more level before the flood, thus there were no high mountains like Mount Everest. In fact, some mountains like the Sierra Nevadas are still rising (only a fraction of an inch a year now, but the initial thrust upward may have been very rapid).

The covering of the mountains also indicates a universal flood. Some scholars believe the flood was tidal and the waters washed over the mountains. They say the fact the ark came to rest on the side of a mountain instead of on a seashore bears this out. Others believe the sun may have attracted another planet from space and the planet came near enough to the earth to cause tremendous geologic changes before that planet (possibly Venus) went into orbit around the sun.

1428.116	4108	4108	6142, 800	3803.426	3725, 2098
v Qal pf 3cp	adv	adv	prep, art, n fs	cj, v Pual impf 3mp	*adj*, art, n mp
גָּבְרוּ	מְאֹד	מְאֹד	עַל־הָאָרֶץ	וַיְכֻסּוּ	כָּל־הֶהָרִים
gāv^{e}rû	m^{e}'ōdh	m^{e}'ōdh	'al-hā'ārets	way^{e}khussû	kol-hehārîm
they were strong	very	very	on the earth	and they were covered	all the mountains

1393	866, 8809	3725, 8452		2675	6462	527	4623, 3937, 4762
art, adj	rel part, prep	*adj*, art, n md	**20.**	num	num	n fs	prep, prep, adv
הַגְּבֹהִים	אֲשֶׁר־תַּחַת	כָּל־הַשָּׁמָיִם		חֲמֵשׁ	עֶשְׂרֵה	אַמָּה	מִלְמַעְלָה
hagg^{e}vōhîm	'ăsher-tachath	kol-hashshāmāyim		chămēsh	'esrēh	'ammāh	milma'ălāh
the high	which under	all the heavens		five	ten	cubits	above

1428.116	4448	3803.426	2098		1510.121	3725, 1340
v Qal pf 3cp	art, n md	cj, v Pual impf 3mp	art, n mp	**21.**	cj, v Qal impf 3ms	*adj*, n ms
גָּבְרוּ	הַמָּיִם	וַיְכֻסּוּ	הֶהָרִים		וַיִּגְוַע	כָּל־בָּשָׂר
gāv^{e}rû	hammāyim	way^{e}khussû	hehārîm		wayyighwa'	kol-bāsār
they were strong	the waters	and they were covered	the mountains		and it died	all flesh

7718.151	6142, 800	904, 5991	904, 966	904, 2516
art, v Qal act ptc ms	prep, art, n fs	prep, art, n ms	cj, prep, art, n fs	cj, prep, art, n fs
הָרֹמֵשׂ	עַל־הָאָרֶץ	בָּעוֹף	וּבַבְּהֵמָה	וּבַחַיָּה
hārōmēs	'al-hā'ārets	bā'ôph	ûvabb^{e}hēmāh	ûvachayyāh
the creeping things	on the earth	with the birds	and with the beasts	and with the animals

904, 3725, 8651	8650.151	6142, 800	3725	119
cj, prep, *adj*, art, n ms	art, v Qal act ptc ms	prep, art, n fs	cj, adj	art, n ms
וּבְכָל־הַשֶּׁרֶץ	הַשֹּׁרֵץ	עַל־הָאָרֶץ	וְכֹל	הָאָדָם
ûv^{e}khol-hashsherets	hashshōrēts	'al-hā'ārets	w^{e}khōl	hā'ādhām
and with all the swarming creatures	that which swarms	on the earth	and all	the humankind

	3725	866	5580, 7593	2508	904, 653	4623, 3725	866
22.	adj	rel part	*n fs, n fs*	n mp	prep, n mp, ps 3ms	prep, adj	rel part
	כֹּל	אֲשֶׁר	נִשְׁמַת־רוּחַ	חַיִּים	בְּאַפָּיו	מִכֹּל	אֲשֶׁר
	kōl	'ăsher	nishmath-rûach	chayyîm	b^{e}'appâv	mikkōl	'ăsher
	all	which	the breath of the spirit of	life	in its nostrils	of all	that

904, 2824	4322.116		4364.121	881, 3725, 3462	866	6142, 6686
prep, art, n fs	v Qal pf 3cp	**23.**	cj, v Qal impf 3ms	do, *adj*, art, n ms	rel part	prep, *n mp*
בֶּחָרָבָה	מֵתוּ		וַיִּמַח	אֶת־כָּל־הַיְקוּם	אֲשֶׁר	עַל־פְּנֵי
bechārāvāh	mēthû		wayyimach	'eth-kol-hayqûm	'ăsher	'al-p^{e}nê
on the dry land	they died		thus He wiped out	every living thing	which	on the surface of

124	4623, 119	5912, 966	5912, 7719	5912, 5991	8452
art, n fs	prep, n ms	prep, n fs	prep n ms	cj, prep, *n ms*	art, n md
הָאֲדָמָה	מֵאָדָם	עַד־בְּהֵמָה	עַד־רֶמֶשׂ	וְעַד־עוֹף	הַשָּׁמַיִם
hā'ădhāmāh	mē'ādhām	'adh-b^{e}hēmāh	'adh-remes	w^{e}'adh-'ôph	hashshāmayim
the ground	from humankind	unto animals	unto creeping things	and unto the birds of	the air

4364.526	4623, 800	8080.221	395, 5326	866	882
cj, v Hiphil impf 3mp	prep, art, n fs	cj, v Niphal impf 3ms	adj, pn	cj, rel part	prep, ps 3ms
וַיִּמָּחוּ	מִן־הָאָרֶץ	וַיִּשָּׁאֶר	אַךְ־נֹחַ	וַאֲשֶׁר	אִתּוֹ
wayyimmāchû	min-hā'ārets	wayishshā'er	'akh-nōach	wa'ăsher	'ittô
and they were wiped out	from the earth	and he remained	only Noah	and who	with him

904, 8720		1428.126	4448	6142, 800	2675	4109	3219
prep, art, n fs	**24.**	cj, v Qal impf 3mp	art, n md	prep, art, n fs	num	cj, *num*	n ms
בַּתֵּבָה		וַיִּגְבְּרוּ	הַמַּיִם	עַל־הָאָרֶץ	חֲמִשִּׁים	וּמְאַת	יוֹם
battēvāh		wayyighb^{e}rû	hammayim	'al-hā'ārets	chămishshîm	ûm'ath	yôm
on the ark		and they were strong	the waters	on the earth	fifty	and hundred of	days

8:1	**2226.121** cj, v Qal impf 3ms וַיִּזְכֹּר wayyizkōr then He remembered	**435** n mp אֱלֹהִים 'ĕlōhîm God	**881, 5326** do, pn אֶת־נֹחַ 'eth-nōach Noah	**881** cj, do וְאֵת w^{e}'ēth and	**3725, 2516** *adj*, art, n fs כָּל־הַחַיָּה kol-hachayyāh all the animals	**881, 3725, 966** cj, do, *adj*, art, n fs וְאֶת־כָּל־הַבְּהֵמָה w^{e}'eth-kol-habhēmāh and all the beasts

866 rel part אֲשֶׁר 'ăsher which	**882** prep, ps 3ms אִתּוֹ 'ittô with him	**904, 8720** prep, art, n fs בַּתֵּבָה battēvāh on the ark	**5882.521** cj, v Hiphil impf 3ms וַיַּעֲבֵר wayya'ăvēr and He caused to go over	**435** n mp אֱלֹהִים 'ĕlōhîm God	**7593** n fs רוּחַ rûach wind	**6142, 800** prep, art, n fs עַל־הָאָרֶץ 'al-hā'ārets on the earth

8322.126 cj, v Qal impf 3mp וַיָּשֹׁכּוּ wayyāshōkkû and they subsided	**4448** art, n md הַמָּיִם hammāyim the waters	**2.**	**5727.126** cj, v Qal impf 3mp וַיִּסָּכְרוּ wayyissākhrû and they closed	**4754** *n mp* מַעְיְנֹת ma'ăynōth the springs of	**8745** n fs תְּהוֹם t^{e}hôm the deep	**724** cj, *n fp* וַאֲרֻבֹּת wa'ărubbōth and the windows of

21. And all flesh died that moved upon the earth both of fowl, and of cattle, and of beast, and of every creeping thing that creepeth upon the earth, and every man: ... And destruction came on every living thing, *BB* ...

22. All in whose nostrils was the breath of life: ... all in whose nostrils is breath of a living spirit, *Young* ... the breath of the spirit of life, *NASB* ... the breath of the spirit of life, *ASV*.

of all that was in the dry land, died: ... Everything on dry land with the faintest breath of life in its nostrils died out, *NAB* ... came to its end, *BB*.

23. And every living substance was destroyedwhich was upon the face of the ground, both man, and cattle, and the creeping things, and the fowl of the heaven: ... God wiped out every living thing, *NEB* ... blotted out, *NASB* ... from man to beast, *Berkeley*.

and they were destroyed from the earth: and Noah only remained alive, and they that were with him in the ark: ... Noah and his company, *NEB* ... were kept from death, *BB* ... only Noah and those who were with him in the ark survived, *REB* ... Noah alone was left, and those that were with him in the ark, *Goodspeed*.

24. And the waters prevailed upon the earth an hundred and fifty days: ... maintained their crest, *NAB* ... For 150 days the waters dominated, *Berkeley*.

8:1. And God remembered Noah: ... God took thought, *REB* ... kept Noah in mind, *BB*.

and every living thing, and all the cattle: ... all the wild animals and all the domestic animals, *NRSV*.

that was with him in the ark: and God made a wind to pass over the earth, and the waters asswaged: ... the waters subsided, *KJVII* ... the waters went down, *BB* ... the waters receded, *NIV* ... the water started going down, *Good News* ... the waters ceased, *Geneva*.

7:21-23. These verses emphatically say every living person, land animal, and bird was destroyed and totally wiped out from the earth. Only Noah and those with him who had the faith to enter the ark were saved. Angels are not said to be included in the judgment.

7:24. The water remained high for 150 days. This strongly suggests it was more than a tidal flood.

8:1-2. When the Bible says God remembered, it does not mean God had forgotten. The Hebrew word means God proceeded to give His attention to a situation or a person, and that He was about to intervene either with blessing or judgment. Now God made a wind go over the earth. The fountains of the great deep had already closed, and the rain had also stopped.

8:3-4. The water level gradually fell after the end of the 150 days. Then 5 months after the flood began, the ark rested on one of the mountains of Ararat. Ararat (Akkadian, Urartu) was the ancient name of the whole country of Armenia. An ancient Jewish tradition says the ark rested on a mountain near the headwaters of the Tigris River. What is called Mount Ararat (or by the local people, Agri Dagi) today was not called this in ancient times. It seems more likely the old Jewish tradition is correct, because after Noah and his sons left the ark

8452	3727.221	1700	4623, 8452	3.	8178.126	4448
art, n md	cj, v Niphal impf 3ms	art, n ms	prep, art, n md		cj, v Qal impf 3mp	art, n md
הַשָּׁמָיִם	וַיִּכָּלֵא	הַגֶּשֶׁם	מִן־הַשָּׁמָיִם		וַיָּשֻׁבוּ	הַמַּיִם
hashshāmāyim	wayyikālē'	haggeshem	min-hashshāmāyim		wayyāshuvû	hammayim
the heavens	and it ended	the rain	from the heavens		and they returned	the waters

4623, 6142	800	2050.142	8178.142	2741.126	4448	4623, 7381
prep, prep	art, n fs	v Qal inf abs	cj, v Qal inf abs	cj, v Qal impf 3mp	art, n md	prep, *n ms*
מֵעַל	הָאָרֶץ	הָלוֹךְ	וָשׁוֹב	וַיַּחְסְרוּ	הַמַּיִם	מִקְֳצֵה
mē'al	hā'ārets	hālōkh	wāshôv	wayyachs^{e}rû	hammayim	miqŏtsēh
above	the earth	going	and returning	and they receded	the waters	after

2675	4109	3219	4.	5299.122	8720	904, 2414	8113
num	cj, *num*	n ms		cj, v Qal impf 3fs	art, n fs	prep, art, n ms	art, num
חֲמִשִּׁים	וּמְאַת	יוֹם		וַתָּנַח	הַתֵּבָה	בַּחֹדֶשׁ	הַשְּׁבִיעִי
chămishshîm	ûm^{e}'ath	yôm		wattānach	hattēvāh	bachōdhesh	hashsh^{e}vî'î
fifty	and hundred of	days		and it rested	the ark	in the month	the seventh

904, 8124, 6461	3219	3937, 2414	6142	2098	804	5.	4448
prep, num, num	n ms	prep, art, n ms	prep	*n mp*	pn		cj, art, n mp
בְּשִׁבְעָה־עָשָׂר	יוֹם	לַחֹדֶשׁ	עַל	הָרֵי	אֲרָרָט		וְהַמַּיִם
b^{e}shiv'āh-'āsār	yôm	lachōdhesh	'al	hārê	'ărārāṭ		w^{e}hammayim
on seven ten	day	to the month	on	the mountains of	Ararat		and the waters

2030.116	2050.142	2741.142	5912	2414	6455	904, 6455	904, 259
v Qal pf 3cp	v Qal inf abs	cj, v Qal inf abs	adv	art, n ms	art, num	prep, art, num	prep, num
הָיוּ	הָלוֹךְ	וְחָסוֹר	עַד	הַחֹדֶשׁ	הָעֲשִׂירִי	בָּעֲשִׂירִי	בְּאֶחָד
hāyû	hālôkh	w^{e}chāsôr	'adh	hachōdhesh	hā'ăsîrî	bā'ăsîrî	b^{e}'echādh
they were	going	and receding	until	the month	the tenth	on the tenth	on first

3937, 2414	7495.216	7513	2098	6.	2030.121	4623, 7377	727
prep, art, n ms	v Niphal pf 3cp	*n mp*	art, n mp		cj, v Qal impf 3ms	prep, *n ms*	num
לַחֹדֶשׁ	נִרְאוּ	רָאשֵׁי	הֶהָרִים		וַיְהִי	מִקֵּץ	אַרְבָּעִים
lachōdhesh	nir'û	rā'shê	hehārîm		wayhî	miqqēts	'arbā'îm
to the month	they were seen	the tops of	the mountains		and it was	after	forty

3219	6858.121	5326	881, 2574	8720	866	6449.111	7.	8365.321
n ms	cj, v Qal impf 3ms	pn	do, *n ms*	art, n fs	rel part	v Qal pf 3ms		cj, v Piel impf 3ms
יוֹם	וַיִּפְתַּח	נֹחַ	אֶת־חַלּוֹן	הַתֵּבָה	אֲשֶׁר	עָשָׂה		וַיְשַׁלַּח
yôm	wayyiphtach	nōach	'eth-challôn	hattēvāh	'ăsher	'āsāh		wayshallach
days	then he opened	Noah	the window of	the ark	which	he made		and he sent out

881, 6397	3428.121	3428.142	8178.142	5912, 3111	4448	4623, 6142
do, art, n ms	cj, v Qal impf 3ms	v Qal inf abs	cj, v Qal inf abs	prep, v Qal inf con	art, n md	prep, prep
אֶת־הָעֹרֵב	וַיֵּצֵא	יָצוֹא	וָשׁוֹב	עַד־יְבֹשֶׁת	הַמַּיִם	מֵעַל
'eth-hā'ōrēv	wayyētsē'	yātsô'	wāshôv	'adh-y^{e}vōsheth	hammayim	mē'al
the raven	and it went out	going out	and returning	until drying	the waters	from on

800	8.	8365.321	881, 3225	4623, 882	3937, 7495.141	1950B, 7327.116
art, n fs		cj, v Piel impf 3ms	do, art, n fs	prep, prep, ps 3ms	prep, v Qal inf con	intrg part, v Qal pf 3cp
הָאָרֶץ		וַיְשַׁלַּח	אֶת־הַיּוֹנָה	מֵאִתּוֹ	לִרְאוֹת	הֲקַלּוּ
hā'ārets		wayshallach	'eth-hayyônāh	mē'ittô	lir'ôth	hăqallû
the earth		and he sent	the dove	from him	to see	if they were abated

4448	4623, 6142	6686	124	9.	3940, 4834.112	3225	4638
art, n md	prep, prep	*n mp*	art, n fs		cj, neg part, v Qal pf 3fs	art, n fs	n ms
הַמַּיִם	מֵעַל	פְּנֵי	הָאֲדָמָה		וְלֹא־מָצְאָה	הַיּוֹנָה	מָנוֹחַ
hammayim	mē'al	p^{e}nê	hā'ădhāmāh		w^{e}lō'-māts'āh	hayyônāh	mānôach
the waters	from on	the surface of	the ground		but not it found	the dove	resting place

3937, 3834, 7559	8178.122	420	420, 8720	3706, 4448	6142, 6686
prep, *n fs*, n fs, ps 3fs	cj, v Qal impf 3fs	prep, ps 3ms	prep, art, n fs	prep, n md	prep, *n mp*
לְכַף־רַגְלָהּ	וַתָּשָׁב	אֵלָיו	אֶל־הַתֵּבָה	כִּי־מַיִם	עַל־פְּנֵי
l^{e}khaph-raghlāhh	wattāshāv	'ēlâv	'el-hattēvāh	kî-mayim	'al-p^{e}nê
for the sole of its foot	so it returned	to him	into the ark	because waters	on the surface of

3725, 800	8365.121	3135	4089.121	971.521	881
adj, art, n fs	cj, v Qal impf 3ms	n fs, ps 3ms	cj, v Qal impf 3ms, ps 3fs	cj, v Hiphil impf 3ms	do, ps 3fs
כָּל־הָאָרֶץ	וַיִּשְׁלַח	יָדוֹ	וַיִּקָּחֶהָ	וַיָּבֵא	אֹתָהּ
khol-hā'ārets	wayyishlach	yādhô	wayyiqqāchehā	wayyāvē'	'ōthāhh
all the earth	and he put out	his hand	and he took it	and he brought	it

420	420, 8720		3282.221	5968	8124	3219	313
prep, ps 3ms	prep, art, n fs	**10.**	cj, v Niphal impf 3ms	adv	*num*	n mp	*adv*
אֵלָיו	אֶל־הַתֵּבָה		וַיָּחֶל	עוֹד	שִׁבְעַת	יָמִים	אֲחֵרִים
'ēlâv	'el-hattēvāh		wayyāchel	'ôdh	shiv'ath	yāmîm	'ăchērîm
to him	into the ark		and he waited	again	seven	days	later

2. The fountains also of the deep: ... The springs of the deep, *REB* ... the outlets of water beneath the earth, *Good News*.

and the windows of heaven were stopped and the rain from heaven was restrained: ... the downpour was checked, *NEB* ... The fountains of the deep and the floodgates of the sky were closed, and the rain from the sky was restrained, *NASB* .

3. And the waters returned from off the earth continually: ... stayed the waters from going on to the earth, *Fenton* ... The waters steadily receded, *NCB* ... Steadily the waters moved back, *Berkeley* ... going and returning, *Geneva*.

and after the end of the hundred and fifty days the waters were abated: ... the waters had gone down, *KJVII* ... the waters had so diminished, *NAB* ... the waters were lower, *BB* ... it had abated, *REB*.

4. And the ark rested in the seventh month, on the seventeenth day of the month, upon the mountains of Ararat: ... And the ark resteth, *Young* ... the ark came to rest, *NIV* ... the ark grounded, *Berkeley* ... the ark rested, *NASB*.

5. And the waters decreased continually: ... the waters continued to abate, *RSV* ... going and decreasing, *Geneva* ... The waters continued to recede, *NCB*.

until the tenth month: in the tenth month, on the first day of the month, were the tops of the mountains seen: ... the heads, *Young* ... the mountains appeared, *NCB* ... the mountains became visible, *Goodspeed*.

6. And it came to pass at the end of forty days, that Noah opened the window of the ark which he had made: ... the hatch, *REV* ... the trap-door, *NEB* .

7. And he sent forth a raven, which went forth to and fro, until the waters were dried up from off the earth: ... wandered and turned about, *Fenton* ... kept flying back and forth, *NIV* ... going forth and returning, *Geneva*.

8. Also he sent forth a dove from him, to see if the waters were abated from off the face of the ground: ... had become low, *Darby* ... waters were diminished, *Geneva* ... waters had dried, *Goodspeed*, ... had gone down, *Good News*.

9. But the dove found no rest for the sole of her foot: ... found no roost, *Berkeley* ... no place to set her

they came down into the Tigris-Euphrates Valley. Archaeologists have found early settlements near the upper Tigris River.

8:5. By the 10th month, the tops of surrounding mountains or hills could be seen. It is possible new mountains arose and new ocean deeps were formed, allowing the water to go down. The deeps off Japan and the Philippines remain deep and not filled with silt, indicating they are geologically recent.

8:6-7. After forty more days Noah sent out a raven. Because it is a scavenger bird it did not come back but flew around until the waters dried up.

8:8-9. Next, Noah sent out a dove. It returned, for there was still water everywhere. Not being a scavenger, the dove needed a place to nest.

8:10-12. After another week the dove was sent out again and returned with an olive leaf as evidence that the waters had gone down and the valleys were becoming dry. In one more week the dove was sent out and did not return.

3362.121	8365.311	881, 3225	4623, 8720		971.122	420	3225
cj, v Qal impf 3ms	v Piel pf 3ms	do, art, n fs	prep, art, n fs	**11.**	cj, v Qal impf 3fs	prep, ps 3ms	art, n fs
וַיֹּסֶף	שִׁלַּח	אֶת־הַיּוֹנָה	מִן־הַתֵּבָה		וַתָּבֹא	אֵלָיו	הַיּוֹנָה
wayyōseph	shallach	'eth-hayyônāh	min-hattēvāh		wattāvō'	'ēlâv	hayyônāh
and he did again	he sent	the dove	from the ark		and it came	to him	the dove

3937, 6496	6394	2079	6149, 2215	3075	904, 6552
prep, *n fs*	n ms	cj, intrj	*n ms*, n ms	adj	prep, n ms, ps 3fs
לְעֵת	עֶרֶב	וְהִנֵּה	עֲלֵה־זַיִת	טָרָף	בְּפִיהָ
le'ēth	'erev	wehinnēh	'ălēh-zayith	ṭāraph	bephîhā
toward the time of	evening	and behold	leaf of olive tree	freshly plucked	in its mouth

3156	5326	3706, 7327.116	4448	4623, 6142	800		3282.221
cj, v Qal impf 3ms	pn	prep, v Qal pf 3cp	art, n md	prep, prep	art, n fs	**12.**	cj, v Niphal impf 3ms
וַיֵּדַע	נֹחַ	כִּי־קַלּוּ	הַמַּיִם	מֵעַל	הָאָרֶץ		וַיִּיָּחֶל
wayyēdha'	nōach	kî-qallû	hammayim	mē'al	hā'ārets		wayyiyyāchel
and he knew	Noah	that they were abated	the waters	from on	the earth		and he waited

5968	8124	3219	313	8365.321	881, 3225	3940, 3362.112
adv	*num*	n mp	adj	cj, v Piel impf 3ms	do, art, n fs	cj, neg part, v Qal pf 3fs
עוֹד	שִׁבְעַת	יָמִים	אֲחֵרִים	וַיְשַׁלַּח	אֶת־הַיּוֹנָה	וְלֹא־יָסְפָה
'ôdh	shiv'ath	yāmîm	'ăchērîm	wayshallach	'eth-hayyônāh	welō'-yāsephāh
again	seven	days	later	then he sent out	the dove	but not it did again

8178.141, 420	5968		2030.121	904, 259	8666, 4109	8523
v Qal inf con, prep, ps 3ms	adv	**13.**	cj, v Qal impf 3ms	prep, num	cj, num, *num*	n fs
שׁוּב־אֵלָיו	עוֹד		וַיְהִי	בְּאַחַת	וְשֵׁשׁ־מֵאוֹת	שָׁנָה
shûv-'ēlâv	'ôdh		wayhî	be'achath	weshēsh-mē'ôth	shānāh
to return to him	again		and it was	on first	and six hundreds of	years

904, 7518	904, 259	3937, 2414	2817.116	4448	4263, 6142	800
prep, art, adj	prep, num	prep, art, n ms	v Qal pf 3cp	art, n md	prep, prep	art, n fs
בָּרִאשׁוֹן	בְּאֶחָד	לַחֹדֶשׁ	חָרְבוּ	הַמַּיִם	מֵעַל	הָאָרֶץ
bāri'shôn	be'echādh	lachōdhesh	chārevû	hammayim	mē'al	hā'ārets
in the first	on first	to the month	they were dried up	the waters	from on	the earth

5681.521	5326	881, 4510	8720	7495.121	2079	2817.116
cj, v Hiphil impf 3ms	pn	do, *n ms*	art, n fs	cj, v Qal impf 3ms	cj, intrj	v Qal pf 3cp
וַיָּסַר	נֹחַ	אֶת־מִכְסֵה	הַתֵּבָה	וַיַּרְא	וְהִנֵּה	חָרְבוּ
wayyāsar	nōach	'eth-mikhsēh	hattēvāh	wayyar'	wehinnēh	chārevû
and he removed	Noah	the covering of	the ark	and he saw	and behold	they were dried up

6686	124		904, 2414	8529	904, 8124	6465	3219
n mp	art, n fs	**14.**	cj, prep, art, n ms	art, num	prep, num	cj, num	n ms
פְּנֵי	הָאֲדָמָה		וּבַחֹדֶשׁ	הַשֵּׁנִי	בְּשִׁבְעָה	וְעֶשְׂרִים	יוֹם
penê	hā'ădhāmāh		ûvachōdhesh	hashshēnî	beshiv'āh	we'esrîm	yôm
the surface of	the ground		and in the month	the second	on seven	and twenty	day

3937, 2414	3111.122	800		1744.321	435	420, 5326	3937, 569.141
prep, art, n ms	v Qal impf 3fs	art, n fs	**15.**	cj, v Piel impf 3ms	n mp	prep, pn	prep, v Qal inf con
לַחֹדֶשׁ	יָבְשָׁה	הָאָרֶץ		וַיְדַבֵּר	אֱלֹהִים	אֶל־נֹחַ	לֵאמֹר
lachōdhesh	yāvshāh	hā'ārets		waydhabbēr	'ĕlōhîm	'el-nōach	lē'mōr
to the month	it was dry	the earth		and He spoke	God	to Noah	saying

	3428.131	4623, 8720	887	828	1158	5571, 1158
16.	v Qal impv 2ms	prep, art, n fs	pers pron	cj, n fs, ps 2ms	cj, n mp, ps 2ms	cj, n fp, n mp, ps 2ms
	צֵא	מִן־הַתֵּבָה	אַתָּה	וְאִשְׁתְּךָ	וּבָנֶיךָ	וּנְשֵׁי־בָנֶיךָ
	tsē'	min-hattēvāh	'attāh	we'ishtekhā	ûvānêkhā	ûnshê-vānêkhā
	go out	from the ark	you	and your wife	and your sons	and wives of your sons

904, 966 cj, prep, art, n fs וּבַבְּהֵמָה ûvabbᵉhēmāh and with the beasts	904, 5991 prep, art, n ms בָּעוֹף bā'ôph with the birds	4623, 3725, 1340 prep, adj, n ms מִכָּל־בָּשָׂר mikkol-bāsār of all flesh	866, 882 rel part, prep, ps 2ms אֲשֶׁר־אִתְּךָ 'ăsher-'ittᵉkhā that with you	3725, 2516 adj, art, n fs כָּל־הַחַיָּה kol-hachayyāh all the living things	**17.**	882 prep, ps 2fs אִתָּךְ 'ittākh with you

882 prep, ps 2fs אִתָּךְ 'ittākh with you	3428.531 v Hiphil impv 2ms הַוְצֵא hawtsē' bring out	6142, 800 prep, art, n fs עַל־הָאָרֶץ 'al-hā'ārets on the earth	7718.151 art, v Qal act ptc ms הָרֹמֵשׂ hārōmēs the creepers	904, 3725, 7719 cj, prep, adj, art, n ms וּבְכָל־הָרֶמֶשׂ ûvᵉkhāl-hāremes and with all creeping things

foot, *RSV* ... found no place where she could settle, *NEB* ... could find no place to alight and perch, *NAB*.

and she returned unto him into the ark, for the waters were on the face of the whole earth: then he put forth his hand, and took her, and pulled her in unto him into the ark.

10. And he stayed yet other seven days; and again he sent forth the dove out of the ark;

11. And the dove came in to him in the evening: ... toward evening, *NASB* ... at eventide, *ASV* ... at dusk, *Fenton* ... about twilight, *Berkeley*.

and, lo, in her mouth was an olive leaf pluckt off: in its beak, *Good News* ... in its bill, *NAB* ... torn off, *Young* ... freshly picked, *NASB* ... freshly plucked, *NKJV* ... plucked off, *ASV*.

so Noah knew that the waters were abated from off the earth: ... the waters were draining, *Berkeley* ... subsided from the earth's surface, *REB* ... had receded, *NIV* ... had subsided still further, *NEB*.

12. And he stayed yet other seven days; and sent forth the dove; which returned not again unto him any more: ... this time it did not come back, *NAB* ... she returned no more to him, *Darby* ... did not come back to him, *BB* ... she never came back to him, *Goodspeed*.

13. And it came to pass in the six hundredth and first year, in the first month, the first day of the month, the waters were dried up from off the earth and Noah removed the covering of the ark: ... the surface of the ground was quite dry, *Goodspeed* ... the upper part of the ground was drie, *Geneva*.

and looked, and, behold, the face of the ground was dry: ... the earth was completely dry, *NIV* ... earth was dry, *NCB* ... the ground was dried up, *NASB* ... ground was drying up, *NAB*.

14. And in the second month, on the seven and twentieth day of the month, was the earth dried.

15. And God spake unto Noah, saying,

16. Go forth of the ark, thou, and thy wife, and thy sons, and thy sons' wives with thee.

17. Bring forth with thee every living thing that is with thee, of all flesh: ... wild and tame, *NAB* ... every animal of every sort, *Goodspeed* ... every living thing that is with you, *NAB*.

both of fowl, and of cattle, and of every creeping thing that creepeth upon the earth; that they may breed abundantly: ... all birds, quadrupeds, and all land reptiles, that they may breed freely, *Goodspeed* ... let them swarm, *NEB* ... and they have teemed in the earth, *Young* ... that they may abound on the earth, *NKJV*.

8:13. When it was certain that the ground was dry Noah took the roof off the ark. This is important to notice, for the roofless ark would certainly deteriorate and go to pieces in time. Thus, it is not likely that any remains of it are anywhere today. If it had been preserved, someone would have made a shrine of it. Expeditions to the modern Mount Ararat have not turned up anything certain, only speculation and questions.

8:14-19. Noah did not rush out of the ark as soon as he knew the ground was dry. Because he trusted God, he waited for God's direction. Then, after they were a year and 10 days in the ark, God told Noah to take his family and the animals and birds out of the ark. Noah undoubtedly let the smaller animals and birds out before he released the larger ones. God wanted all the animals and birds to breed abundantly.

This again implies a universal flood. If the flood were only local, they could have gone over the hills and brought in more animals and birds from the next valley.

8650.116	904, 800	6759.116	7528.116	6142, 800
cj, v Qal pf 3cp	prep, n fs	cj, v Qal pf 3cp	cj, v Qal pf 3cp	prep, art, n fs
וְשָׁרְצוּ	בָאָרֶץ	וּפָרוּ	וְרָבוּ	עַל־הָאָרֶץ
weshārtsû	vā'ārets	ûphārû	werāvû	'al-hā'ārets
and they will swarm	on the earth	and they will be fruitful	and they will multiply	on the earth

18.	3428.121	5326	1158	828	5571, 1158	882
	cj, v Qal impf 3ms	pn	cj, n mp, ps 3ms	cj, n fs, ps 3ms	cj, *n fp*, n mp, ps 3ms	prep, ps 3ms
	וַיֵּצֵא	נֹחַ	וּבָנָיו	וְאִשְׁתּוֹ	וּנְשֵׁי־בָנָיו	אִתּוֹ
	wayyētsē'	nōach	ûvāâv	we'ishtô	ûnshê-vānâv	'ittô
	and he went out	Noah	and his sons	and his wife	and the wives of his sons	with him

19.	3725, 2516	3725, 7719	3725, 5991	3725	7718.151	6142, 800
	adj, art, n fs	*adj*, art, n ms	cj, *adj*, art, n ms	adj	v Qal act ptc ms	prep, art, n fs
	כָּל־הַחַיָּה	כָּל־הָרֶמֶשׂ	וְכָל־הָעוֹף	כֹּל	רוֹמֵשׂ	עַל־הָאָרֶץ
	kol-hachayyāh	kol-hāremes	wekhol-hā'ôph	kōl	rômēs	'al-hā'ārets
	all the living things	all the creeping things	and all the birds	all	creepers	on the earth

3937, 5121	3428.116	4623, 8720	20.	1161.121	5326	4326	3937, 3176
prep, n fp, ps 3mp	v Qal pf 3cp	prep, art, n fs		cj, v Qal impf 3ms	pn	n ms	prep, pn
לְמִשְׁפְּחֹתֵיהֶם	יָצְאוּ	מִן־הַתֵּבָה		וַיִּבֶן	נֹחַ	מִזְבֵּחַ	לַיהוָה
lemishpechōthêhem	yāts'û	min-hattēvāh		wayyiven	nōach	mizbēach	lâhwāh
to their kind	they went out	from the ark		and he built	Noah	altar	to Yahweh

4089.121	4623, 3725	966	2999	4623, 3725	5991	2999
cj, v Qal impf 3ms	prep, adj	art, n fs	art, adj	cj, prep, adj	art, n ms	art, adj
וַיִּקַּח	מִכֹּל	הַבְּהֵמָה	הַטְּהֹרָה	וּמִכֹּל	הָעוֹף	הַטָּהֹר
wayyiqqach	mikkōl	habbehēmāh	hattehōrāh	ûmikkōl	hā'ôph	hattāhōr
and he took	from every	the animals	the clean	and from all	the birds	the clean

6148.521	6150	904, 4326	21.	7591.521	3176	881, 7666
cj, v Hiphil impf 3ms	n fp	prep, art, n ms		cj, v Hiphil impf 3ms	pn	do, *n ms*
וַיַּעַל	עֹלֹת	בַּמִּזְבֵּחַ		וַיָּרַח	יְהוָה	אֶת־רֵיחַ
wayya'al	'ōlōth	bammizbēach		wayyārach	yehwāh	'eth-rêach
and he caused to go up	burnt offerings	on the altar		and He smelled	Yahweh	the scent of

5394	569.121	3176	420, 3949	3940, 3362.525	3937, 7327.341	5968
art, adj	cj, v Qal impf 3ms	pn	prep, n ms, ps 3ms	neg part, v Hiphil impf 1cs	prep, v Piel inf con	adv
הַנִּיחֹחַ	וַיֹּאמֶר	יְהוָה	אֶל־לִבּוֹ	לֹא־אֹסִף	לְקַלֵּל	עוֹד
hannîchōach	wayyō'mer	yehwāh	'el-libbô	lō'-'ōsiph	leqallēl	'ôdh
the soothing	and He said	Yahweh	to his heart	not I will do again	to curse	again

881, 124	904, 5877	119	3706	3444	3949	119
do, art, n fs	prep, prep	art, n ms	cj	*n ms*	*n ms*	art, n ms
אֶת־הָאֲדָמָה	בַּעֲבוּר	הָאָדָם	כִּי	יֵצֶר	לֵב	הָאָדָם
'eth-hā'ădhāmāh	ba'ăvûr	hā'ādhām	kî	yētser	lēv	hā'ādhām
the ground	on account of	the humankind	because	the form of	the heart of	the humankind

7737	4623, 5474	3940, 3362.525	5968	3937, 5409.541	881, 3725, 2508
adj	prep, n mp, ps 3ms	cj, neg part, v Hiphil impf 1cs	adv	prep, v Hiphil inf con	do, *adj*, n ms
רַע	מִנְּעֻרָיו	וְלֹא־אֹסִף	עוֹד	לְהַכּוֹת	אֶת־כָּל־חַי
ra'	minne'urâv	welō'-'ōsiph	'ôdh	lehakkôth	'eth-kol-chay
evil	from his youth	and not I will do again	again	to strike down	all living creatures

3626, 866	6449.115	22.	5968	3725, 3219	800	2320	7392
prep, rel part	v Qal pf 1cs		adv	*adj, n mp*	art, n fs	n ms	cj, n ms
כַּאֲשֶׁר	עָשִׂיתִי		עֹד	כָּל־יְמֵי	הָאָרֶץ	זֶרַע	וְקָצִיר
ka'ăsher	'āsîthî		'ōdh	kol-yemê	hā'ārets	zera'	weqātsîr
like that	I have done		again	all the days of	the earth	seed	and harvest

7409	2627	7302	2886	3219	4050	3940	8139.126
cj, n ms	cj, n ms	cj, n ms	cj, n ms	cj, n ms	cj, n ms	neg part	v Qal impf 3mp
וְקֹר	וָחֹם	וְקַיִץ	וָחֹרֶף	וְיוֹם	וָלַיְלָה	לֹא	יִשְׁבֹּתוּ
weqōr	wāchōm	weqayits	wāchōreph	weyôm	wālaylāh	lō'	yishbōthû
and cold	and heat	and summer	and winter	and day	and night	not	they will not cease

	1313.321	435	881, 5326	881, 1158	569.121	3937	6759.133
9:1	cj, v Piel impf 3ms	n mp	do, pn	cj, do, n mp, ps 3ms	cj, v Qal impf 3ms	prep, ps 3mp	v Qal impv 2mp
	וַיְבָרֶךְ	אֱלֹהִים	אֶת־נֹחַ	וְאֶת־בָּנָיו	וַיֹּאמֶר	לָהֶם	פְּרוּ
	wayvārekh	'ĕlōhîm	'eth-nōach	we'eth-bānâv	wayyō'mer	lāhem	perû
	and He blessed	God	Noah	and his sons	and He said	to them	be fruitful

in the earth, and be fruitful and multiply upon the earth: ... be fertile, and be increased, *BB* ... increase in number, *NIV* ... increase over the earth, *Fenton* ... Let them be fruitful and multiply on the earth, *Berkeley.*

18. And Noah went forth, and his sons, and his wife, and his sons' wives with him:

19. Every beast, every creeping thing, and every fowl, and whatsoever creepeth upon the earth after their kinds went forth out of the ark: ... every living thing of every sort, *BB* ... everything that moves on the earth, *NIV* ... one kind after another, *NIV* ... by their families, *NASB.*

20. And Noah builded an altar unto the LORD; and took of every clean beast, and of every clean fowl: ... ritually clean, *REB* ... from every clean beast and from every clean bird, *Fenton.*

and offered burnt offerings on the altar: ... whole-offerings, *REB* ... holocausts, *NCB* ... burned them whole as a sacrifice, *Good News.*

21. And the LORD smelled a sweet savour: ... a sweet odor, *KJVII* ... soothing odour, *REB* ... the EVERLIVING perceived pleasant sweet perfume, *Fenton* ... smelled a savour of rest, *Geneva* ... discerned the pleasing fragrance, *Berkeley.*

and the LORD said in his heart, I will not again curse the ground any more for man's sake; for the imagination of man's heart is evil from his youth: ... Never again will I doom the earth, *NAB* ... I continue not to disesteem, *Young* ... I will not again curse the ground, *ASV* ... the desires, *NAB* ... thoughts, *BB* ... inclination of, *NCB* ... however evil their inclination, *REB* ... from his earliest days, *BB* ... from the start, *NAB.*

neither will I again smite any more every thing living as I have done: ... strike down, *NAB* ... never again will I send destruction, *BB.*

22. While the earth remaineth seedtime and harvest and cold and heat, and summer and winter and day and night shall not cease: ... as long as the earth lasts, *NAB* ... As long as the world exists, *Good News* ... sowing, *Fenton* ... the getting in of the grain, *BB.*

8:20. Noah's first thought was to honor God and rededicate himself to the LORD. His first act was to build an altar and offer burnt offerings. The Hebrew name for the burnt offering, *'olah*, comes from a root word meaning to go up, cause to go up, or exalt. Since it was completely burned, it represented a total exaltation of the LORD and a total dedication of the offerer to God. These were expressions of Noah's faith and love for the LORD.

8:21. Smelling the sweet savor is a way of saying that God accepted the offerings and was pleased with them. God purposed then in His heart, His inner being, never to curse the ground again because of what humankind does, although the imagination of every human being's heart (and mind) is evil (bad) from the time of youth to old age. God was speaking of fallen, unregenerate humankind. Nor would there be a world-wide destruction of human and animal life again, as there was in the flood.

8:22. God promised that the daily and annual cycles of nature would continue as long as the earth remains. There will never be another world-wide flood. That does not mean there will never be another world-wide judgment, however. The judgments of the great tribulation will affect a great deal of the world. But after the Millennium, Satan will be released for a short time.

Then after he is cast into the lake of fire, the Great White Throne will appear, the present heavens and earth will flee away, and no place will be found for them. They will go out of existence, for the very elements will be destroyed (cf. Ps. 102:25-26; Isa. 34:4; 51:6; 2 Peter 3:7,10,12). God will create new heavens and a new earth (Rev. 20:11; 21:1) and bring the New Jerusalem to the new earth.

7528.133	4527.133	881, 800		4307	2952	2030.121
cj, v Qal impv 2mp	cj, v Qal impv 2mp	do, art, n fs	**2.**	cj, n ms, ps 2mp	cj, n ms, ps 2mp	v Qal impf 3ms
וּרְבוּ	וּמִלְאוּ	אֶת־הָאָרֶץ		וּמוֹרַאֲכֶם	וְחִתְּכֶם	יִהְיֶה
ûrevû	ûmil'û	'eth-hā'ārets		ûmôra'ăkhem	wechittekhem	yihyeh
and multiply	and fill	the earth		and the fear of you	and the dread of you	it will be

6142	3725, 2516	800	6142	3725, 5991	8452	904, 3725	866
prep	*adj, n fs*	art, n fs	cj, prep	*adj, n ms*	art, n md	prep, adj	rel part
עַל	כָּל־חַיַּת	הָאָרֶץ	וְעַל	כָּל־עוֹף	הַשָּׁמָיִם	בְּכֹל	אֲשֶׁר
'al	kol-chayyath	hā'ārets	we'al	kol-'ôph	hashshāmāyim	bekhōl	'ăsher
on	every living thing of	the earth	and on	every bird of	the air	on all	which

7718.122	124	904, 3725, 1759	3328	904, 3135	5598.216
v Qal impf 3fs	art, n fs	cj, prep, *adj, n mp*	art, n ms	prep, n fs, ps 2mp	v Niphal pf 3cp
תִּרְמֹשׂ	הָאֲדָמָה	וּבְכָל־דְּגֵי	הַיָּם	בְּיֶדְכֶם	נִתָּנוּ
tirmōsh	hā'ădhāmāh	ûvekhol-deghê	hayyām	beyedhekhem	nittānû
it creeps	the ground	and on all the fish of	the sea	in your hand	they have been given

	3725, 7719	866	2000, 2513.111	3937	2030.121	3937, 403	3626, 3537
3.	*adj*, n ms	rel part	pers pron, v Qal pf 3ms	prep, ps 2mp	v Qal impf 3ms	prep, n fs	prep, *n ms*
	כָּל־רֶמֶשׂ	אֲשֶׁר	הוּא־חַי	לָכֶם	יִהְיֶה	לְאָכְלָה	כְּיֶרֶק
	kol-remes	'ăsher	hû'-chay	lākhem	yihyeh	le'ākhelāh	keyereq
	every creeping thing	which	it is living	to you	it will be	for food	like green thing of

6448	5595.115	3937	881, 3725		395	1340	904, 5497	1879
n ms	v Qal pf 1cs	prep, ps 2mp	do, n ms	**4.**	adv	n ms	prep, n fs, ps 3ms	n ms, ps 3ms
עֵשֶׂב	נָתַתִּי	לָכֶם	אֶת־כֹּל		אַךְ	בָּשָׂר	בְּנַפְשׁוֹ	דָמוֹ
'ēsev	nāthattî	lākhem	'eth-kōl		'akh	bāsār	benaphshô	dhāmô
plants	I have given	to you	everything		only	flesh	with its life	its blood

3940	404.128		395	881, 1879	3937, 5497	1938.125	4623, 3135
neg part	v Qal impf 2mp	**5.**	cj, adv	do, nn ms, ps 2mp	prep, n fp, ps 2mp	v Qal impf 1cs	prep, *n fs*
לֹא	תֹאכֵלוּ		וְאַךְ	אֶת־דִּמְכֶם	לְנַפְשֹׁתֵיכֶם	אֶדְרֹשׁ	מִיַּד
lō'	thō'khēlû		we'akh	'eth-dimkheme	lenaphshōthêkhem	'edhrōsh	miyyadh
not	you will eat		and surely	your blood	to your lives	I will demand	from the hand of

3725, 2516	1938.125	4623, 3135	119	4623, 3135	382
adj, n fs	v Qal impf 1cs, ps 1cp	cj, prep, *n fs*	art, n ms	prep, *n fs*	n ms
כָּל־חַיָּה	אֶדְרְשֶׁנּוּ	וּמִיַּד	הָאָדָם	מִיַּד	אִישׁ
kol-chayyāh	'edhreshennû	ûmiyyadh	hā'ādhām	miyyadh	'îsh
every living thing	I will demand of us	and from the hand of	the humankind	from the hand of	each

250	1938.125	881, 5497	119		8581.151	1879	119
n ms, ps 3ms	v Qal impf 1cs	do, *n fs*	art, n ms	**6.**	v Qal act ptc ms	*n ms*	art, n ms
אָחִיו	אֶדְרֹשׁ	אֶת־נֶפֶשׁ	הָאָדָם		שֹׁפֵךְ	דַּם	הָאָדָם
'āchîw	'edhrōsh	'eth-nephesh	hā'ādhām		shōphēkh	dam	hā'ādhām
his brother	I will demand	the life of	the humankind		the one who sheds	the blood of	the humankind

904, 119	1879	8581.221	3706	904, 7021	435	6449.111	881, 119
prep, art, n ms	n ms, ps 3ms	v Niphal impf 3ms	cj	prep, *n ms*	n mp	v Qal pf 3ms	do, art, n ms
בָּאָדָם	דָּמוֹ	יִשָּׁפֵךְ	כִּי	בְּצֶלֶם	אֱלֹהִים	עָשָׂה	אֶת־הָאָדָם
bā'ādhām	dāmô	yishshāphēkh	kî	betselem	'ělōhîm	'āsāh	'eth-hā'ādhām
by the humankind	his blood	it will be shed	for	in the image of	God	He made	the humankind

	894	6759.133	7528.133	8650.133	904, 800	7528.133, 904
7.	cj, pn	v Qal impv 2mp	cj, v Qal impv 2mp	v Qal impv 2mp	prep, n fs	cj, v Qal impv 2mp, prep, ps 3fs
	וְאַתֶּם	פְּרוּ	וּרְבוּ	שִׁרְצוּ	בָאָרֶץ	וּרְבוּ־בָהּ
	we'attem	perû	ûrevû	shirtsû	vā'ārets	ûrevû-vāhh
	and you	be fruitful	and multiply	swarm	on the earth	and multiply on it

9:1. And God blessed Noah and his sons, and said unto them, Be fruitful, and multiply, and replenish the earth: ... Be fertile and have increase, and make the earth full, *BB* ... fill the earth, *NEB* ... populate the earth, *Berkeley* ... Have many children so that your descendants will live all over the earth, *Good News.*

2. And the fear of you and the dread of you shall be upon every beast of the earth, and upon every fowl of the air, upon all that moveth upon the earth and upon all the fishes of the sea into your hand are they delivered: ... wherewith the ground teemeth, *ASV* ... and every bird of the sky, with all that swarm upon the ground, and all fish of the waters, *Fenton* ... delivered into your power, *Goodspeed.*

3. Every moving thing that liveth shall be meat for you even as the green herb have I given you all things: ... every living animal that moves, *Fenton* ... shall be food, *NASB* ... like the green herbage, *Fenton* ... all green plants, *NEB.*

4. But flesh with the life thereof, which is the blood thereof, shall ye not eat.

5. And surely your blood of your lives will I require: ... I shall demand satisfaction, *REB* ... I will require an account, *NCB* ... I will surely require a reckoning, *NRSV* ... for your lifeblood, *RSV* ... If anyone takes human life, he will be punished, *Good News.*

at the hand of every beast will I require it, and at the hand of man; at the hand of every man's brother will I require the life of man.

6. Whoso sheddeth man's blood, by man shall his blood be shed: for in the image of God made he man: ... God made humankind, *NRSV* ... he hath made man, *Darby* ... God made man His likeness, *Berkeley* ... made man in his own image, *Goodspeed.*

7. And you, be ye fruitful: ... Be fertile, *NAB* ... be fruitful, then, *REB* ... be fertile, *BB* .

and multiply; bring forth abundantly in the earth and multiply therein: ... abound on earth and subdue it, *NAB* ... increase in it, *KJV* ... rule over it, *REB* ... and rule over it, *NEB* ... swarm on the earth and multiply, *Darby.*

9:1. Isaiah 45:18 declares God did not create the earth in vain, that is, to be empty. He formed it to be inhabited. The fact God saved Noah and his family shows He had not changed his purpose. God confirmed His purpose again by giving Noah the same command to fill the earth He had given to Adam and Eve. But He did not give them the dominion over the animal world in the same way it was given to Adam before the fall.

9:2. Instead, fear and dread of humankind would be upon all animal life on land and in the sea, for they would be given into the hands of or under the power of human beings.

9:3. All animal life was now given as meat or food for people to eat. Adam and Eve were given only vegetables, grain, and fruit. But now the command to be vegetarians was lifted, and after the flood everyone was free to eat meat as well as the other food as God's gift.

9:4. Because the blood represented the life, they were to drain out the blood from slain animals and birds, respect it, and not eat it. This prepared the way for the importance of blood in the sacrifices and ultimately for the supreme sacrifice of Jesus who shed His precious blood on the cross.

9:5. God wanted them to recognize the killing of animals for food was not to cause them to minimize the importance of human blood representing human life. God would "demand an accounting from every animal" (NIV) that would become a killer of human beings. He would also demand an accounting from each person that killed a fellow human being.

9:6. The Hebrew has a participle in this particular passage. It means whoever becomes a habitual or repeated shedder of the blood of humankind, his (or her) blood will be shed by human beings. Because the flood had not changed fallen human nature, the violence preceding the flood would reappear. God wanted to guard the sanctity of human life because humankind (both male and female) were created in His image (1:26). He created them for himself, thus their lives were sacred to Him. Although the image was marred by the fall and by every individual's sin, the image remained, and it was, and is, valuable in God's sight. The Law of Moses commanded the death penalty for willful, premeditated murder (Exo. 21:12,14; 22:2; Num. 35:6-34; Deut. 19:1-13). The New Testament also recognizes the authority of civil government for punishment (Rom. 13:3-4).

9:7. Repetition of the command to be fruitful and multiply gives emphasis to God's desire to have many people who will gather around His throne and enjoy fellowship with Him throughout eternity (Rev. 5:9-10).

8.	569.121	435	420, 5326	420, 1158	882	3937, 569.141	**9.**	603
	cj, v Qal impf 3ms	n mp	prep, pn	cj, prep, n mp, ps 3ms	prep, ps 3ms	prep, v Qal inf con		cj, pers pron
	וַיֹּאמֶר	אֱלֹהִים	אֶל־נֹחַ	וְאֶל־בָּנָיו	אִתּוֹ	לֵאמֹר		וַאֲנִי
	wayyō'mer	'ĕlōhîm	'el-nōach	w^{e}'el-bānâv	'ittô	lē'mōr		wa'ănî
	and He said	God	to Noah	and to his sons	with him	saying		and I

2079	7251.551	881, 1311	882	882, 2320	313
intrj, ps 1cs	v Hiphil ptc ms	do, n fs, ps 1cs	prep, ps 2mp	cj, prep, n ms, ps 2mp	adv, ps 2mp
הִנְנִי	מֵקִים	אֶת־בְּרִיתִי	אִתְּכֶם	וְאֶת־זַרְעֲכֶם	אַחֲרֵיכֶם
hinnî	mēqîm	'eth-b^{e}rîthî	'itt^{e}khem	w^{e}'eth-zar'ăkhem	'achrêkhem
behold I	establishing	my covenant	with you	and with your seed	after you

10.	881	3725, 5497	2516	866	882	904, 5991	904, 966
	cj, do	*adj, n fs*	art, n fs	rel part	prep, ps 2mp	prep, art, n ms	prep, art, n fs
	וְאֵת	כָּל־נֶפֶשׁ	הַחַיָּה	אֲשֶׁר	אִתְּכֶם	בָּעוֹף	בַּבְּהֵמָה
	w^{e}'th	kol-nephesh	hachayyāh	'ăsher	'itt^{e}khem	bā'ôph	babb^{e}hēmāh
	and	every creature of	the living things	which	with you	with the birds	with the beasts

904, 3725, 2516	800	882	4623, 3725	3428.152	8720
cj, prep, *adj, n fs*	art, n fs	prep, ps 2mp	prep, adj	*v Qal act ptc mp*	art, n fs
וּבְכָל־חַיַּת	הָאָרֶץ	אִתְּכֶם	מִכֹּל	יֹצְאֵי	הַתֵּבָה
ûv^{e}khāl-chayyath	hā'ārets	'itt^{e}khem	mikkōl	yōts'ê	hattēvāh
and with every living thing of	the earth	with you	of all	those that came out of	the ark

3937, 3725	2516	800	**11.**	7251.515	881, 1311	882
prep, adj	*n fs*	art, n fs		cj, v Hiphil pf 1cs	do, n fs, ps 1cs	prep, ps 2mp
לְכֹל	חַיַּת	הָאָרֶץ		וַהֲקִמֹתִי	אֶת־בְּרִיתִי	אִתְּכֶם
l^{e}khōl	chayyath	hā'ārets		wahqimōthî	'eth-b^{e}rîthî	'itt^{e}khem
to every	living thing of	the earth		and I will establish	my covenant	with you

3940, 3901.221	3725, 1340	5968	4623, 4448	4138	3940, 2030.121
cj, neg part, v Niphal impf 3ms	*adj*, n ms	adv	prep, *n mp*	art, n ms	cj, neg part, v Qal impf 3ms
וְלֹא־יִכָּרֵת	כָּל־בָּשָׂר	עוֹד	מִמֵּי	הַמַּבּוּל	וְלֹא־יִהְיֶה
w^{e}lō'-yikkārēth	kol-bāsār	'ôdh	mimmê	hammabbûl	w^{e}lō'-yihyeh
and not it will be cut off	all flesh	again	by the waters of	the flood	and not it will be

5968	4138	3937, 8271.341	800	**12.**	569.121	435	2148
adv	n ms	prep, v Piel inf con	art, n fs		cj, v Qal impf 3ms	n mp	dem pron
עוֹד	מַבּוּל	לְשַׁחֵת	הָאָרֶץ		וַיֹּאמֶר	אֱלֹהִים	זֹאת
'ôdh	mabbûl	l^{e}shachēth	hā'ārets		wayyō'mer	'ĕlōhîm	zō'th
again	flood	to destroy	the earth		and He said	God	this

225, 1311	866, 603	5598.151	1033	1033	1033
n ms, art, n fs	rel part, pers pron	v Qal act ptc ms	prep, ps 1cs	cj, prep, ps 2mp	cj, prep
אוֹת־הַבְּרִית	אֲשֶׁר־אֲנִי	נֹתֵן	בֵּינִי	וּבֵינֵיכֶם	וּבֵין
'ôth-habb^{e}rîth	'ăsher-'ănî	nōthên	bênî	ûvênêkhem	ûvên
the sign of the covenant	which I	giving	between me	and between you	and between

3725, 5497	2516	866	882	3937, 1810	5986	**13.**	881, 7493
adj, n fs	n fs	rel part	prep, ps 2mp	prep, *n mp*	adv		do, n fs, ps 1cs
כָּל־נֶפֶשׁ	חַיָּה	אֲשֶׁר	אִתְּכֶם	לְדֹרֹת	עוֹלָם		אֶת־קַשְׁתִּי
kol-nephesh	chayyāh	'ăsher	'itt^{e}khem	l^{e}dhōrōth	'ôlām		'eth-qashtî
every creature of	living things	which	with you	for generations	forever		my bow

5595.115	904, 6281	2030.112	3937, 225	1311	1033	1033
v Qal pf 1cs	prep, art, n ms	cj, v Qal pf 3fs	prep, *n ms*	n fs	prep, ps 1cs	cj, prep
נָתַתִּי	בֶּעָנָן	וְהָיְתָה	לְאוֹת	בְּרִית	בֵּינִי	וּבֵין
nāthattî	be'ānān	w^{e}hāy^{e}thāh	l^{e}'ôth	b^{e}rîth	bênî	ûvên
I have given	in the clouds	and it will be	for sign of	covenant	between me	and between

800 art, n fs הָאָרֶץ hā'ārets the earth	**14.**	2030.111 cj, v Qal pf 3ms וְהָיָה w^{e}hāyāh and it will be	904, 6280.341 prep, v Piel inf con בְּעַנְנִי b^{e}'anănî with making appear	6281 n ms עָנָן 'ānān clouds	6142, 800 prep, art, n fs עַל־הָאָרֶץ 'al-hā'ārets above the earth	7495.212 cj, v Niphal pf 3fs וְנִרְאֲתָה w^{e}nir'ăthāh also it will be seen

7493 art, n fs הַקֶּשֶׁת haqqesheth the bow	904, 6281 prep, art, n ms בֶּעָנָן be'ānān in the clouds	**15.**	2226.115 cj, v Qal pf 1cs וְזָכַרְתִּי w^{e}zākhartî and I will remember	881, 1311 do, n fs, ps 1cs אֶת־בְּרִיתִי 'eth-b^{e}rîthî my covenant	866 rel part אֲשֶׁר 'ăsher which	1033 prep, ps 1cs בֵּינִי bênî between me

8. And God spake unto Noah, and to his sons with him, saying,

9. And I, behold, I establish my covenant with you: ... Take note! I Myself am establishing My covenant, *Berkeley* ... I will make my agreement, *BB* ... And I, Behold, I establish my covenant, *Darby.*

...**and with your seed after you:** ... with your descendants, *NASB* .

10. And with every living creature that is with you, of the fowl, of the cattle, and of every beast of the earthwith you; from all that go out of the ark, to every beast of the earth: ... the various tame and wild animals, *NAB* .

11. And I will establish my covenant with you: ... I shall sustain may covenant, *REB* ... I will establish my covenant, *NCB* ... I covenant with you, *Berkeley.*

neither shall all flesh be cut off: ... be eliminated, *Berkeley* ... be destroyed, *Goodspeed* ... be cut off, *ASV* ... to destroy, *NIV.*

any more by the waters of a flood; neither shall there any more be a flood: ... and henceforth there shall be no flood, *Darby* ... never again shall there be a flood, *NRSV* ... by waters of a deluge, *Fenton.*

to destroy the earth: ... to devastate the earth, *NAB* ... never again be a downrush to desolate the earth, *Fenton* ... to lay waste the earth, *NAB* ... to ravage the earth, *Goodspeed.*

12. And God said, This is the token of the covenant: ... This is the sign of the agreement, *BB* ... symbol, *Goodspeed* ... sign, *RSV* ... sign, *Darby.*

which I make between me and you and every living creature that is with you, for perpetual generations: ... endless generations, *Goodspeed* ... generations age-during, *Young* ... unto perpetual generations, *Geneva* ... for all ages, *NAB.*

13. I do set my bow in the cloud, and it shall be for a tokenof a covenant between me and the earth: ... symbol, *Goodspeed* ... sign, *RSV* ... sign, *Darby.*

14. And it shall come to pass, when I bring a cloud over the earth: ... When I collect My clouds above the earth, *Berkeley* ... When I cloud the sky, *NEB* ... when I bring a cloud, *NKJV.*

that the bow shall be seen in the cloud: ... rainbow, *NKJV* ... rainbow, *Goodspeed* ... bow, *NEB.*

15. And I will remember my covenant: ... And I will keep in mind the agreement, *BB* ... Then I

9:8-11. What God said to himself in 8:21-22, God now speaks to Noah and his sons, and puts it in the form of a covenant, a solemn, binding agreement. This kind of covenant is called a royal grant or royal command covenant. It is a monergistic covenant, that is, an unconditional, one-worker covenant. God would carry it out regardless of what anyone did. God called it "my" covenant and He made it for the benefit of all the descendants of Noah as well as all animal life. Never again would there be a world-wide flood to destroy the people and life on the earth.

9:12-17. As a sign that God would be faithful to keep His covenant for all generations to come, God set a rainbow in the clouds. This does not mean there had never been a rainbow before. There seems to be some evidence of rain before the flood. There could have been a rainbow even in the mists of the Garden of Eden.

But now God gives the rainbow a new significance. The rainbow would be a continual reminder of God's covenant promise to never send a flood to destroy all living creatures on the earth.

The repetition of the fact God established the covenant gives emphasis to it. The rainbow should also remind us we can trust God to be faithful to His promises and we can look to Him for mercy and grace.

1033	1033	3725, 5497	2516	904, 3725, 1340	3940, 2030.121
cj, prep, ps 2mp	cj, prep	*adj, n fs*	n fs	prep, *adj*, n ms	cj, neg part, v Qal impf 3ms
וּבֵינֵיכֶם	וּבֵין	כָּל־נֶפֶשׁ	חַיָּה	בְּכָל־בָּשָׂר	וְלֹא־יִהְיֶה
ûvênêkhem	ûvên	kol-nephesh	chayyāh	b^{e}khol-bāsār	w^{e}lō'-yihyeh
and between you	and between	all creatures of	living things	with all flesh	and not it will be

5968	4448	3937, 4138	3937, 8271.341	3725, 1340		2030.112	7493
adv	art, n md	prep, n ms	prep, v Piel inf con	*adj*, n ms	**16.**	cj, v Qal pf 3fs	art, n fs
עוֹד	הַמַּיִם	לְמַבּוּל	לְשַׁחֵת	כָּל־בָּשָׂר		וְהָיְתָה	הַקֶּשֶׁת
'ôdh	hammayim	l^{e}mabbûl	l^{e}shachēth	kol-bāsār		w^{e}hāy^{e}thāh	haqqesheth
again	the waters	for flood	to destroy	all flesh		and it will be	the bow

904, 6281	7495.115	3937, 2226.141	1311	5986	1033	435
prep, art, n ms	cj, v Qal pf 1cs, ps 3fs	prep, v Qal inf con	n fs	adv	prep	n mp
בֶּעָנָן	וּרְאִיתִיהָ	לִזְכֹּר	בְּרִית	עוֹלָם	בֵּין	אֱלֹהִים
be'ānān	ûr^{e}'îthîhā	lizkōr	b^{e}rîth	'ôlām	bên	'ĕlōhîm
in the clouds	and I will look at it	to remember	covenant	forever	between	God

1033	3725, 5497	2516	904, 3725, 1340	866	6142, 800
cj, prep	*adj, n fs*	n fs	prep, *adj*, n ms	rel part	prep, art, n fs
וּבֵין	כָּל־נֶפֶשׁ	חַיָּה	בְּכָל־בָּשָׂר	אֲשֶׁר	עַל־הָאָרֶץ
ûvên	kol-nephesh	chayyāh	b^{e}khol-bāsār	'ăsher	'al-hā'ārets
and between	all creatures of	living things	with all flesh	which	on the earth

	569.121	435	420, 5326	2148	225, 1311	866	7251.515
17.	cj, v Qal impf 3ms	n mp	prep, pn	dem pron	*n ms*, art, n fs	rel part	v Hiphil pf 1cs
	וַיֹּאמֶר	אֱלֹהִים	אֶל־נֹחַ	זֹאת	אוֹת־הַבְּרִית	אֲשֶׁר	הֲקִמֹתִי
	wayyō'mer	'ĕlōhîm	'el-nōach	zō'th	'ôth-habb^{e}rîth	'ăsher	h^{e}qimōthî
	and He said	God	to Noah	this	the sign of the covenant	which	I have established

1033	1033	3725, 1340	866	6142, 800		2030.126	1158, 5326
prep, ps 1cs	cj, prep	*adj*, n ms	rel part	prep, art, n fs	**18.**	cj, v Qal impf 3mp	*n mp*, pn
בֵּינִי	וּבֵין	כָּל־בָּשָׂר	אֲשֶׁר	עַל־הָאָרֶץ		וַיִּהְיוּ	בְנֵי־נֹחַ
bênî	ûvên	kol-bāsār	'ăsher	'al-hā'ārets		wayyihyû	b^{e}nê-nōach
between me	and between	all flesh	which	on the earth		and they were	the sons of Noah

3428.152	4623, 8720	8429	2626	3425	2626	2000	1
art, v Qal act ptc mp	prep, art, n fs	pn	cj, pn	cj, pn	cj, pn	pers pron	*n ms*
הַיֹּצְאִים	מִן־הַתֵּבָה	שֵׁם	וְחָם	וָיָפֶת	וְחָם	הוּא	אֲבִי
hayyōts'îm	min-hattēvāh	shēm	w^{e}chām	wāyāpheth	w^{e}chām	hû'	'ăvî
those who went out	from the ark	Shem	and Ham	and Japheth	and Ham	he	the father of

3791		8421	431	1158, 5326	4623, 431	5492.112
pn	**19.**	num	dem pron	*n mp*, pn	cj, prep, dem pron	v Qal pf 3fs
כְנָעַן		שְׁלֹשָׁה	אֵלֶּה	בְּנֵי־נֹחַ	וּמֵאֵלֶּה	נָפְצָה
kh^{e}nā'an		sh^{e}lōshāh	'ēlleh	b^{e}nê-nōach	ûmē'ēlleh	nāphtsāh
Caanan		three	these	sons of Noah	and from these	it was scattered

3725, 800		2591.521	5326	382	124	5378.121	3884
adj, art, n fs	**20.**	cj, v Hiphil impf 3ms	pn	*n ms*	art, n fs	cj, v Qal impf 3ms	n ms
כָל־הָאָרֶץ		וַיָּחֶל	נֹחַ	אִישׁ	הָאֲדָמָה	וַיִּטַּע	כָּרֶם
khol-hā'ārets		wayyāchel	nōach	'îsh	hā'ădhāmāh	wayyitta'	kārem
all the earth		and he began	Noah	the man of	the ground	and he planted	vineyard

	8685.121	4623, 3302	8335.121	1580.721	904, 8761
21.	cj, v Qal impf 3ms	prep, art, n ms	cj, v Qal impf 3ms	cj, v Hithpael impf 3ms	prep, *sub*
	וַיֵּשְׁתְּ	מִן־הַיַּיִן	וַיִּשְׁכָּר	וַיִּתְגַּל	בְּתוֹךְ
	wayyêsht	min-hayyayin	wayyishkār	wayyithgal	b^{e}thôkh
	and he drank	from the wine	and he became drunk	and he was uncovered	in the middle of

164		7495.121	2626	1	3791	881	6413
n ms, ps 3ms	**22.**	cj, v Qal impf 3ms	pn	*n ms*	pn	do	*n fs*
אָהֳלֹה		וַיַּרְא	חָם	אֲבִי	כְנָעַן	אֵת	עֶרְוַת
'āhlōh		wayyar'	chām	'ăvî	khᵉna'an	'ēth	'erwath
his tent		and he saw	Ham	the father of	Canaan		the nakedness of

1	5222.521	3937, 8530, 250	904, 2445		4089.121	8429
n ms, ps	cj, v Hiphil impf 3ms	prep, *num*, n mp, ps 3ms	prep, art, n ms	**23.**	cj, v Qal impf 3ms	pn
אָבִיו	וַיַּגֵּד	לִשְׁנֵי־אֶחָיו	בַּחוּץ		וַיִּקַּח	שֵׁם
'āvîw	wayyagēdh	lishnê-'echâv	bachûts		wayyiqqach	shēm
his father	and he told	to the two of his brothers	on the outside		and he took	Shem

shall remember the covenant, *REB* ... I shall remember My Covenant, *Fenton* ... Then I will remember the covenant, *NEB*.

which is between me and you and every living creature of all flesh; and the waters shall no more become a flood to destroy all flesh: a great flow of waters causing destruction, *BB* ... deluge, *Young* ... waters become a flood, *NIV* ... waters become a flood, *NEB* ... all mortal beings, *NAB* ... all life, *NIV* ... all creation, *REB* .

16. And the bow shall be in the cloud; and I will look upon it, that I may remember the everlasting covenant: ... recall the perpetual covenant, *NCB* ... remember the everlasting covenant, *RSV* ... recall the everlasting covenant ... *NAB* ... keep in mind the eternal agreement, *BB*.

between God and every living creature of all flesh that is upon the earth: ... every living creature of every sort, *Goodspeed* ... every living creature of all flesh, *KJVII* ... all animal life existing, *Fenton* ... living creatures of every kind, *REB*.

17. And God said unto Noah, This is the token of the covenant: ... symbol, *Goodspeed* ... sign, *RSV* ... sign, *NASB*.

which I have established between me and all flesh that is upon the earth: ... all life, *NIV* ... every living soul, *Darby* ... Me and all flesh, *Young* ... all that lives on earth, *NEB*.

18. And the sons of Noah, that went forth of the ark, were Shem, and Ham, and Japheth: and Ham is the father of Canaan.

19. These are the three sons of Noah: and of them was the whole earth overspread: ... their descendants spread over, *REB* ... was populated, *Berkeley*.

20. And Noah began to be an husbandman, and he planted a vineyard: ... a man of the soil, *NAB* ... the first tiller, *REB* ... Noah became a farmer, and he made a vine-garden, *BB* ... began to till the ground, NCB.

21. And he drank of the wine, and was drunken; and he was uncovered within his tent: ... was drunk. And he was uncovered, *KJVII* ... he became intoxicated, *Berkeley*.

22. And Ham, the father of Canaan, saw the nakedness of his father, and told his two brethren without: ... reported it, *Fenton* ... gave news of it, *BB* ... told, *NCB*.

9:18. The sons of Noah are named again with special attention to Ham as the father of Canaan. Genesis was written first for the benefit of the Israelites under Moses who were about to enter the land of Canaan, so this is emphasized for Israel's benefit.

9:19. In order to bring out the universality of the flood and Noah and his family being the only ones left, we are told that their descendants spread over or were dispersed over the whole earth. Chapter 10 deals with that more in detail.

9:20-21. Noah became a farmer and planted a vineyard. On one occasion he drank too much of the wine, and in his drunken state he lay uncovered inside his tent. Some writers have excused Noah by supposing that conditions before the flood were different, so that grape juice did not ferment Thus, Noah did not know he would become drunk. We cannot know that for sure.

Alcohol actually is a depressant and is chemically related to the ether used to put people to sleep. It dulls one's reactions and even one's conscience. So Noah was asleep in his tent. The Bible often warns against drunkenness. Proverbs 23:31 warns against even looking at wine when it is fermented.

9:22. Ham is again designated as the father of Canaan, probably because Canaan later shared in the same attitudes. Instead of showing honor to his father, Ham chose to look on his shameful condition and told his brothers about it, apparently in a disrespectful way.

9:23. Shem and Japheth had a different atti-

3425	881, 7980	7947.126	6142, 8327	8529	2050.126
cj, pn	do, art, n fs	cj, v Qal impf 3mp	prep, *n ms*	num, ps 3mp	cj, v Qal impf 3mp
וָיֶפֶת	אֶת־הַשִּׂמְלָה	וַיָּשִׂימוּ	עַל־שְׁכֶם	שְׁנֵיהֶם	וַיֵּלְכוּ
wāyepheth	'eth-hassimlāh	wayyāsîmû	'al-sh^{e}khem	sh^{e}nêhem	wayyēl^{e}khû
and Japheth	the garment	and they put	on the shoulders of	the two of them	and they walked

323	3803.326	881	6413	1	6686	323
adv	cj, v Piel impf 3mp	do	*n fs*	n ms, ps 3mp	cj, n mp, ps 3mp	adv
אֲחֹרַנִּית	וַיְכַסּוּ	אֵת	עֶרְוַת	אֲבִיהֶם	וּפְנֵיהֶם	אֲחֹרַנִּית
'ăchōrannîth	way^{e}khassû	'ēth	'erwath	'ăvîhem	ûphnêhem	'ăchōrannîth
backward	and they covered		the nakedness of	their father	and their faces	backward

6413	1	3940	7495.116	**24.**	3477.121	5326
cj, *n fs*	n ms, ps 3mp	neg part	v Qal pf 3cp		cj, v Qal impf 3ms	pn
וְעֶרְוַת	אֲבִיהֶם	לֹא	רָאוּ		וַיִּיקֶץ	נֹחַ
w^{e}'erwath	'ăvîhem	lō'	rā'û		wayyîqets	nōach
and the nakedness of	their father	not	they saw		and he awoke	Noah

4623, 3302	3156	881	866, 6449.111, 3937	1158	7278
prep, n ms, ps 3ms	cj, v Qal impf 3ms	do	rel part, v Qal pf 3ms, prep, ps 3ms	n ms, ps 3ms	art, adj
מִיֵּינוֹ	וַיֵּדַע	אֵת	אֲשֶׁר־עָשָׂה־לוֹ	בְּנוֹ	הַקָּטָן
miyyênô	wayyēdha'	'ēth	'ăsher-'āsāh-lô	b^{e}nô	haqqāṭān
from his wine	and he knew		what he did to him	his son	the younger

25.	569.121	803.155	3791	5860	5860	2030.121	3937, 250
	cj, v Qal impf 3ms	v Qal pass ptc ms	pn	*n ms*	n mp	v Qal impf 3ms	prep, n mp, ps 3ms
	וַיֹּאמֶר	אָרוּר	כְּנָעַן	עֶבֶד	עֲבָדִים	יִהְיֶה	לְאֶחָיו
	wayyō'mer	'ārûr	k^{e}nā'an	'evedh	'ăvādhîm	yihyeh	l^{e}'echâv
	and he said	cursed	Canaan	slave of	slaves	he will be	to his brothers

26.	569.121	1313.155	3176	435	8429	2030.121	3791
	cj, v Qal impf 3ms	v Qal pass ptc ms	pn	*n mp*	pn	cj, v Qal impf 3ms	pn
	וַיֹּאמֶר	בָּרוּךְ	יְהוָה	אֱלֹהֵי	שֵׁם	וִיהִי	כְנַעַן
	wayyō'mer	bārûkh	y^{e}hōwāh	'ĕlōhê	shēm	wîhî	kh^{e}na'an
	and he said	blessed be	Yahweh	the God of	Shem	and he will be	Canaan

5860	3937	**27.**	6853.521	435	3937, 3425	8331.121
n ms	prep, ps 3ms		v Hiphil impf 3ms	n mp	prep, pn	cj, v Qal impf 3ms
עֶבֶד	לָמוֹ		יַפְתְּ	אֱלֹהִים	לְיֶפֶת	וְיִשְׁכֹּן
'evedh	lāmô		yapht	'ĕlōhîm	l^{e}yepheth	w^{e}yishkōn
slave	to him		He will enlarge	God	to Japheth	and he will dwell

904, 164, 8429	2030.121	3791	5860	3937	**28.**	2030.121, 5326	313
prep, *n mp*, pn	cj, v Qal impf 3ms	pn	n ms	prep, ps 3ms		cj, v Qal impf 3ms, pn	adv
בְּאָהֳלֵי־שֵׁם	וִיהִי	כְנַעַן	עֶבֶד	לָמוֹ		וַיְחִי־נֹחַ	אַחַר
b^{e}'āhlê-shēm	wîhî	kh^{e}na'an	'evedh	lāmô		waychî-nōach	'achar
in the tents of Shem	and he will be	Canaan	slave	to him		and Noah was	after

4138	8421	4109	8523	2675	8523	**29.**	2030.126
art, n ms	num	*num*	n fs	cj, num	n fs		cj, v Qal impf 3mp
הַמַּבּוּל	שְׁלֹשׁ	מֵאוֹת	שָׁנָה	וַחֲמִשִּׁים	שָׁנָה		וַיִּהְיוּ
hammabbûl	sh^{e}lōsh	mē'ōth	shānāh	wachmishshîm	shānāh		wayyihyû
the flood	three	hundreds of	years	and fifty	years		and they were

3725, 3219, 5326	9013	4109	8523	2675	8523	4322
adj, n mp, pn	num	*num*	n fs	cj, num	n fs	cj, v Qal impf 3ms
כָּל־יְמֵי־נֹחַ	תְּשַׁע	מֵאוֹת	שָׁנָה	וַחֲמִשִּׁים	שָׁנָה	וַיָּמֹת
kol-y^{e}mê-nōach	t^{e}sha'	mē'ōth	shānāh	wachmishshîm	shānāh	wayyāmōth
all the days of Noah	nine	hundreds of	years	and fifty	years	and he died

23. And Shem and Japheth took a garment: ... shawl, *Fenton* ... a cloak, *NEB* ... a robe, *Berkeley* ... a garment, *NRSV*.

and laid it upon both their shoulders: ... and holding it on their backs, *NAB* ... laid it across their shoulders, *NIV* ... laid it on both their shoulders, *NRSV* ... they put on their shoulders, *Goodspeed*.

went backward, and covered the nakedness of their father; and their faces were backward: ... since their faces were turned the other way, *NAB* ... They kept their faces averted, *REB* ... keeping their faces turned the other way, *Berkeley* ... with their faces turned away, *BB*.

and they saw not their father's nakedness: ... they did not witness their father's shame, *Berkeley* ... did not see their father's nakedness, *NRSV* ... so that they might not see him unclothed, *BB* ... would not see their father's nakedness, *NIV*.

24. And Noah awoke from his wine: ... When Noah sobered up, *Good News* ... woke up from his wine, *Fenton* ... woke up from his drunken sleep, *NEB* ... awoke from his wine, *NIV*.

and knew what his younger son had done unto him: ... learned, *Darby* ... Noah saw what his youngest son had done, *BB* ... knew what, *Geneva* ... found out what, *NIV*.

25. And he said, Cursed be Canaan: ... He exclaimed, Cursed be Canaan, *Berkeley* ... A curse on Canaan!, *Good News* ... Cursed be Channan, *NCB*.

a servant of servants shall he be unto his brethren: ... the lowest of slaves, *NIV* ... a bondman of bondmen, *Darby* ... meanest of slaves, *NCB*.

26. And he said: ... He said moreover, *Geneva* ... He also said, *RSV* ... And he went on, *REB* ... He also said, *NASB*.

Blessed be the LORD God of Shem; and Canaan shall be his servant.

27. God shall enlarge Japheth: ... make Japheth great, *BB* ... May God make space for Japeth, *NRSV* ... May God expand Japheth, *Goodspeed* ... God doth give beauty to Japeth, *Young* ... God persuade Japeth, *Geneva*.

and he shall dwell in the tents of Shem; and Canaan shall be his servant: ... bondman, *Darby* ... slave, *REB* ... his slave, *NIV* ... his servant, *NKJV*.

28. And Noah lived after the flood three hundred and fifty years.

29. And all the days of Noah were nine hundred and fifty years: and he died.

---

tude. They took a garment or mantle in the form a large square piece of cloth, put it on their shoulders, and backed into the tent so they could cover Noah without looking at him.

9:24-25. When Noah awoke and learned what Ham had done he pronounced a curse on Canaan and prophesied that he would become a servant of servants to his brothers. The curse was placed on Canaan, not on Ham, probably because Canaan was the only son of Ham sharing in the same attitude.

By the time of Moses, the Canaanites had become an extremely immoral people, with the grossest kind of polytheistic religion, a cancer on the face of the human race. That is why the Israelites were commanded to drive them out.

Thus, the curse had nothing to do with black skin. It was not placed on the Egyptians or any of the other African descendants of Ham. Furthermore, although it is not stated, the curse was conditional. Canaanites who placed their faith in God could escape it. Rahab, a Canaanite and a prostitute, placed her faith in God and after a period of purification, was brought into Israel's camp. She married an Israelite, and became an ancestress of David and Jesus (Josh. 6:25; Matt. 1:5; Heb. 11:31).

9:26-27. Noah gave praise to the LORD (Yahweh) the God of Shem, for Shem's very name recognized and honored God. Then Noah prophesied that Canaan would be Shem's servant, a prophecy fulfilled when the Canaanites became servants of the Israelites.

Noah also prophesied that God would enlarge (provide ample space or territory for) Japheth and he would dwell in the tents of Shem, which implies he would share the blessings of Shem. (However, many believe the word "he" in verse 27 probably refers back to God, not to Japheth, so it would be God who would dwell in the tents of Shem, blessing his descendants.) The prophecy of servanthood is repeated to give emphasis to the future of the Canaanites and explain to the Israelites what Joshua was to lead them to do.

9:28-29. Noah lived 350 years after the flood. There is no evidence of any further drunkenness. He is remembered in Heb. 11:7 as an heir of the righteousness that comes by faith.

10:1							
	431	8765	1158, 5326	8429	2626	3425	3314.126
	cj, dem pron	*n fp*	*n mp*, pn	pn	pn	cj, pn	cj, v Qal impf 3mp
	וְאֵלֶּה	תּוֹלְדֹת	בְּנֵי־נֹחַ	שֵׁם	חָם	וָיָפֶת	וַיִּוָּלְדוּ
	we'ēlleh	tôledhōth	benê-nōach	shēm	chām	wāyāpheth	wayyiwwāledhû
	and these	the generations of	the sons of Noah	Shem	Ham	and Japheth	and they were born

3937	1158	313	4138	2.	1158	3425	1627	4170
prep, ps 3mp	n mp	adv	art, n ms		*n mp*	pn	pn	cj, pn
לָהֶם	בָּנִים	אַחַר	הַמַּבּוּל		בְּנֵי	יֶפֶת	גֹּמֶר	וּמָגוֹג
lāhem	bānîm	'achar	hammabbûl		benê	yepheth	gōmer	ûmāghôgh
to them	sons	after	the flood		the sons of	Japheth	Gomer	and Magog

4216	3222	8727	5084	8824	3.	1158	1627	840
cj, pn	cj, pn	cj, pn	cj, pn	cj, pn		cj, *n mp*	pn	pn
וּמָדַי	וְיָוָן	וְתֻבָל	וּמֶשֶׁךְ	וְתִירָס		וּבְנֵי	גֹּמֶר	אַשְׁכְּנַז
ûmādhay	weyāwān	wethuvāl	ûmeshekh	wethîrās		ûvnê	gōmer	'ashkenaz
and Madai	and Javan	and Tubal	and Meshech	and Tiras		and the sons of	Gomer	Ashkenaz

7670	8739	4.	1158	3222	478	8998	3923
cj, pn	cj, pn		cj, *n mp*	pn	pn	cj, pn	pn
וְרִיפַת	וְתֹגַרְמָה		וּבְנֵי	יָוָן	אֱלִישָׁה	וְתַרְשִׁישׁ	כִּתִּים
werîphath	wethōgharmāh		ûvnê	yawan	'ělîshāh	wetharshîsh	kittîm
and Riphath	and Togarmah		and the sons of	Javan	Elishah	and Tarshish	Kittim

1773	5.	4623, 431	6754.216	339	1504	904, 800
cj, pn		prep, dem pron	v Niphal pf 3cp	*n mp*	art, n mp	prep, n fp, ps 3mp
וְדֹדָנִים		מֵאֵלֶּה	נִפְרְדוּ	אִיֵּי	הַגּוֹיִם	בְּאַרְצֹתָם
wedhōdhānîm		mē'ēlleh	niphredhû	'iyyê	haggôyim	be'artsōthām
and Dodanim		from these	they were separated	the coastlands of	the nations	in their lands

382	3937, 4098	3937, 5121	904, 1504	6.	1158	2626	3688
n ms	prep, n ms, ps 3ms	prep, n fp, ps 3mp	prep, n mp, ps 3mp		cj, *n mp*	pn	pn
אִישׁ	לִלְשֹׁנוֹ	לְמִשְׁפְּחֹתָם	בְּגוֹיֵהֶם		וּבְנֵי	חָם	כּוּשׁ
'îsh	lilshōnô	lemishpechōtham	beghôyēhem		ûvnê	chām	kûsh
each	to his language	to their families	in their nations		and the sons of	Ham	Cush

4875	6559	3791	7.	1158	3688	5619	2434	5637
cj, pn	cj, pn	cj, pn		cj, *n mp*	pn	pn	cj, pn	cj, pn
וּמִצְרַיִם	וּפוּט	וּכְנָעַן		וּבְנֵי	כוּשׁ	סְבָא	וַחֲוִילָה	וְסַבְתָּה
ûmitsrayim	ûphût	ûkhenā'an		ûvnê	khûsh	sevā'	wachăwîlāh	wesavtāh
and Egypt	and Put	and Canaan		and the sons of	Cush	Seba	and Havilah	and Sabtah

7772	5638	1158	7772	8088	1771	8.	3688
cj, pn	cj, pn	cj, *n mp*	pn	pn	cj, pn		cj, pn
וְרַעְמָה	וְסַבְתְּכָא	וּבְנֵי	רַעְמָה	שְׁבָא	וּדְדָן		וְכוּשׁ
wera'ămāh	wesavtekhā'	ûvnê	ra'ămāh	shevā'	ûdhedhān		wekhûsh
and Raamah	and Sabteca	and the sons of	Raamah	Sheba	and Dedan		and Cush

10:1. Now these are the generations of the sons of Noah, Shem, Ham, and Japheth: and unto them were sons born after the flood.

2. The sons of Japheth; Gomer, and Magog, and Madai, and Javan, and Tubal, and Meshech, and Tiras.

3. And the sons of Gomer; Ashkenaz, and Riphath, and Togarmah.

4. And the sons of Javan; Elishah, and Tarshish, Kittim, and Dodanim.

5. By these were the isles of the

Gentiles: ... the maritime nations, *NAB* ... peoples of the coasts and islands, *REB* ... sealands, *BB* ... peoples of the coasts and islands, *NEB*.

divided in their lands; every one after his tongue: ... language, *NAB* ... each with its respective language, *Berkeley* ... according to his language, *NASB* ... each with its own language, *NIV*.

after their families, in their nations: ... clans, *NAB* ... family by family, nation by nation, *REB* ... the gentile tribes, *Fenton* ... different families and languages, *BB*.

6. And the sons of Ham; Cush, and Mizraim, and Phut, and Canaan.

7. And the sons of Cush; Seba, and Havilah, and Sabtah, and Raamah, and Sabtecha: and the sons of Raamah; Sheba, and Dedan.

8. And Cush begat Nimrod: he began to be a mighty one in the earth: ... despot, *Goodspeed* ... a mighty warrior, *NIV* ... powerful hunter, *Fenton* ... show himself a man of might, *NEB* ... first of the great men, *BB*.

9. He was a mighty hunter before the LORD: wherefore it is said,

---

10:1. This table of the nations descended from Noah's three sons is arranged to give most attention to those nations with whom the Israelites would have most contact. Thus the descendants of Japheth are briefly given first. Next, the descendants of Ham are given, with special attention to the Canaanites. Finally. the descendants of Shem are given in detail, which includes the Israelites.

Since the Israelites had little contact with the Negroid people of Africa or with the Mongoloid people of Asia, none of these are mentioned in the table, though it is probable that African people are descended from Ham and Asian people descended from Japheth. There is no intent of racism here--all descended from Noah. They are all part of the one human race. The names given in these lists are sometimes the heads or ancestors of nations, sometimes the names of nations or tribes. It is not a typical genealogy.

10:2. Gomer may be identified with the Gimirrai who settled in Cappadocia, called the Cimmerians by the Greeks. Magog is not further identified, except that Ezek. 38:15 identifies them as a people in the far north. Javan was probably the ancestor of the Ionian Greeks. Tubal's descendants, the Tabali, fought the Assyrians about 1100 B.C. Meshech's descendants, the Mushke, were in the territory east of Cappadocia and fought the Assyrians in the ninth century B.C. Tiras was probably the ancestor of the Tursenoi (Tyhrrenians) who became pirates in the Aegean region.

10:3. Ashkenaz was the ancestor of Ashkuz, the Scythians, who invaded the Middle East from the north and fought Assyrians, Persians, and Greeks. Josephus identified Riphath with the Paphligonians in the north. Togarmah probably settled in Tegaramah in southwestern Armenia.

10:4. Elishah or Alashia settled in Cyprus. Tarshish is associated with Sardinia and Tartessus in southern Spain near Gibraltar. Kittim also settled in Cyprus. Dodanim probably became the Dardanians of Troy, though 1 Chr. 1:7 calls them Rodanim, who settled in the island of Rhodes.

10:5. "Isles" includes both islands and coast lands. The descendants of Japheth were "divided," branched off, or spread out. The first thing mentioned as the basis for the division is language. This anticipates chapter 11 and the Tower of Babel. That is, chapter 10 tells where the descendants of Noah ended up in Moses' day. Then chapter 11 tells what brought about the scattering.

10:6. Some descendants of Cush may have settled in Kush in Yemen, and Kish near Babylon, then crossed the Red Sea and took Ethiopia (modern Sudan), which is called Cush later in the Bible.

Mizraim means "the double Egypt," referring to the fact that by about 2900 B.C. Upper Egypt along the Nile and Lower Egypt in the Delta were united as a double kingdom with a double crown for the Pharaoh.

Phut or Put settled in Cyrenaica, west of Egypt, though some may have gone to Somalia. Canaan became the ancestor of the Canaanites.

10:7. Seba or Sheba settled in northwest Arabia. Havilah "sandy" refers to a people of central or south Arabia. Sabtah settled in south Arabia and Raamah in southwest Arabia. People of Sheba and Raamah brought gold, spices, and gems to the markets of Tyre (Ezek. 27:22). Sabtecha probably was in south Arabia.

Sheba, descended from Raamah, was in southwest Arabia, in what is now part of Yemen. Many believe the Queen of Sheba came from this Sheba to visit Solomon, not from Ethiopia. Dedan was in Arabia near Edom (Isa. 21:13; Jer. 25:23; 49:8; Ezek. 25:13). Dedanites were a commercial people (Ezek. 27:15, 20; 38:13).

10:8. Nimrod ("rebel") may be associated with a city near Babylon named Kish. He became a mighty hero, a great leader, but a rebel against God.

3314.111	881, 5434	2000	2054.511	3937, 2030.141	1429	904, 800
v Qal pf 3ms	do, pn	pers pron	v Hiphil pf 3ms	prep, v Qal inf con	n ms	prep, art, n fs
יָלַד	אֶת־נִמְרֹד	הוּא	הֵחֵל	לִהְיוֹת	גִּבֹּר	בָּאָרֶץ
yāladh	'eth-nimrōdh	hû'	hēchēl	lihyôth	gibbōr	bā'ārets
he fathered	Nimrod	he	he began	to be	mighty man	on the earth

9.	2000, 2030.111	1429, 6987	3937, 6686	3176	6142, 3772	569.221
	pers pron, v Qal pf 3ms	*adj*, n ms	prep, *n mp*	pn	prep, adv	v Niphal impf 3ms
	הוּא־הָיָה	גִבֹּר־צַיִד	לִפְנֵי	יְהוָה	עַל־כֵּן	יֵאָמַר
	hû'-hāyāh	ghibbōr-tsayidh	liphnê	yehwāh	'al-kēn	yē'āmar
	he he was	mighty of hunting	before	Yahweh	therefore	it has been said

3626, 5434	1429	6987	3937, 6686	3176	10.	2030.122	7519
prep, pn	*adj*	n ms	prep, *n mp*	pn		cj, v Qal impf 3fs	*n fs*
כְּנִמְרֹד	גִּבּוֹר	צַיִד	לִפְנֵי	יְהוָה		וַתְּהִי	רֵאשִׁית
kenimrōdh	gibbôr	tsayidh	liphnê	yehwāh		wattehî	rē'shîth
like Nimrod	mighty of	hunting	before	Yahweh		and it was	the beginning of

4610	928	777	396	3761	904, 800	8534	11.	4623, 800
n fs, ps 3ms	pn	cj, pn	cj, pn	cj, pn	prep, *n fs*	pn		prep, art, n fs
מַמְלַכְתּוֹ	בָּבֶל	וְאֶרֶךְ	וְאַכַּד	וְכַלְנֵה	בְּאֶרֶץ	שִׁנְעָר		מִן־הָאָרֶץ
mamlakhtô	bavel	we'erekh	we'akkadh	wekhalnêh	be'erets	shin'ār		min-hā'ārets
his kingdom	Babel	and Erech	and Accad	and Calneh	in the land of	Shinar		from the land

2000	3428.111	831	1161.121	881, 5398	881, 7626	6111	881, 3745
art, dem pron	v Qal pf 3ms	pn	cj, v Qal impf 3ms	do, pn	cj, do, pn	n fs	cj, do, pn
הַהִוא	יָצָא	אַשּׁוּר	וַיִּבֶן	אֶת־נִינְוֵה	וְאֶת־רְחֹבֹת	עִיר	וְאֶת־כָּלַח
hahiw'	yātsâ'	'ashshûr	wayyiven	'eth-ninewēh	we'eth-rechōvōth	'îr	we'eth-kālach
the that	he went out	Assyria	and he built	Nineveh	and Rehoboth	city	and Calah

12.	881, 7735	1033	5398	1033	3745	2000	6111	1448
	cj, do, pn	prep	pn	cj, prep	pn	pers pron	art, n fs	art, adj
	וְאֶת־רֶסֶן	בֵּין	נִינְוֵה	וּבֵין	כָּלַח	הִוא	הָעִיר	הַגְּדֹלָה
	we'eth-resen	bên	nînewēh	ûvên	kālach	hiw'	hā'îr	haggedhōlāh
	and Resen	between	Nineveh	and between	Calah	it	the city	the great

13.	4875	3314.111	881, 4003	881, 6278	881, 3989	881, 5502
	cj, pn	v Qal pf 3ms	do, pn	cj, do, pn	cj, do, pn	cj, do, pn
	וּמִצְרַיִם	יָלַד	אֶת־לוּדִים	וְאֶת־עֲנָמִים	וְאֶת־לְהָבִים	וְאֶת־נַפְתֻּחִים
	ûmitsrayim	yāladh	'eth-lûdhîm	we'eth-'ănāmîm	we'eth-lehāvîm	we'eth-naphtuchîm
	and Egypt	he fathered	Ludim	and Anamim	and Lehabim	and Naphtuhim

14.	881, 6878	881, 3821	866	3428.116	4623, 8427	6674
	cj, do, pn	cj, do, pn	rel part	v Qal pf 3cp	prep, adv	pn
	וְאֶת־פַּתְרֻסִים	וְאֶת־כַּסְלֻחִים	אֲשֶׁר	יָצְאוּ	מִשָּׁם	פְּלִשְׁתִּים
	we'eth-pathrusîm	we'eth-kasluchîm	'ăsher	yāts'û	mishshām	pelishtîm
	and Pathrusim	and Casluhim	which	they went out	from there	Philistines

881, 3860	15.	3791	3314.111	881, 6991	1111	881, 2953
cj, do, pn		cj, pn	v Qal pf 3ms	do, pn	n ms, ps 3ms	cj, do, pn
וְאֶת־כַּפְתֹּרִים		וּכְנַעַן	יָלַד	אֶת־צִידֹן	בְּכֹרוֹ	וְאֶת־חֵת
we'eth-kaphtōrîm		ûkhena'an	yāladh	'eth-tsîdhōn	bekhōrô	we'eth-chēth
and Caphtorim		and Canaan	he fathered	Sidon	his firstborn	and Heth

16.	881, 3092	881, 578	881	1665	17.	881, 2433
	cj, do, art, pn	cj, do, art, pn	cj, do	art, pn		cj, do, art, pn
	וְאֶת־הַיְבוּסִי	וְאֶת־הָאֱמֹרִי	וְאֵת	הַגִּרְגָּשִׁי		וְאֶת־הַחִוִּי
	we'eth-hayvûsî	we'eth-hā'ĕmōrî	we'ēth	haggirgāshî		we'eth-hachiwwî
	and the Jebusites	and the Amorites	and	the Girgashites		and the Hivites

881, 6444	881, 5702	18.	881, 746	881, 7056	881, 2681
cj, do, art, pn	cj, do, art, pn		cj, do, art, pn	cj, do, art, pn	cj, do, art, pn
וְאֶת־הָעַרְקִי	וְאֶת־הַסִּינִי		וְאֶת־הָאַרְוָדִי	וְאֶת־הַצְּמָרִי	וְאֶת־הַחֲמָתִי
w^e'eth-ha'arqî	w^e'eth-hassînî		w^e'eth-hā'arwādhî	w^e'eth-hatsts^emārî	w^e'eth-hachmāthî
and the Arkites	and the Sinites		and the Arvadites	and the Zemarites	and the Hamathites

313	6571.216	5121	3793	19.	2030.121	1397
cj, adv	v Niphal pf 3cp	*n fp*	art, pn		cj, v Qal impf 3ms	*n ms*
וְאַחַר	נָפֹצוּ	מִשְׁפְּחוֹת	הַכְּנַעֲנִי		וַיְהִי	גְּבוּל
w^e'achar	nāphōtsû	mishp^echôth	hakk^ena'ănî		wayhî	g^evûl
and after	they were scattered	the families of	the Canaanites		and it was	the territory of

Even as Nimrod the mighty hunter before the LORD: ... a very great bowman, *BB* ... a hero in hunting, *Young* ... a great hunter, *Good News.*

10. And the beginning of his kingdom was Babel, and Erech, and Accad, and Calneh, in the land of Shinar.

11. Out of that land went forth Asshur, and builded Nineveh, and the city Rehoboth, and Calah: ... from that land he went forth into Assyria, *NASB.*

12. And Resen between Nineveh and Calah: the same is a great city.

13. And Mizraim begat Ludim, and Anamim, and Lehabim, and Naphtuhim,

14. And Pathrusim, and Casluhim, (out of whom came Philistim,) and Caphtorim.

15. And Canaan begat Sidon his firstborn, and Heth,

16. And the Jebusite, and the Amorite, and the Girgasite,

17. And the Hivite, and the Arkite, and the Sinite,

18. And the Arvadite, and the Zemarite, and the Hamathite: and afterward were the families of the Canaanites spread abroad.

19. And the border of the Canaanites was from Sidon, as thou comest to Gerar, unto Gaza; as thou goest, unto Sodom, and Gomorrah, and Admah, and Zeboim, even unto Lasha.

20. These are the sons of Ham,

10:9. Nimrod was vigorous in hunting before the LORD (Yahweh). The double "he" is for emphasis. This may mean he was such a great hunter that he set the standard, so others were compared with him. However, "before the LORD" may mean "in opposition to the LORD." Thus, some say Nimrod could have been one who hunted the lives of human beings drawing them away from the LORD.

10:10. Nimrod's kingdom or dominion, at first, included the cities of Babel (Babylon in the Old Testament is always Babel, but the Greeks liked to add endings, so they called it Babylon), Erech (about 100 miles southeast of Babylon), Accad (north of Babylon), and Calneh, probably near Kish. Shinar was the alluvial plain of Babylonia.

10:11-12. Asshur gave his name to the Assyrians (Assyria and Asshur are the same in Hebrew). He built Nineveh on the east bank of the Tigris River, Rehoboth ("wide places," a suburb of Nineveh), Calah (about 20 miles south of Nineveh), and Resen (a suburb of Nineveh). This complex of towns became the great city (greater Nineveh).

10:13-14. Ludim (*-im* is the Hebrew plural) probably settled in Libya. Their bowmen were hired by the armies of Egypt and Tyre (Jer. 46:9; Ezek. 27:10; 30:5). Anamim, Lehabim, and Naphtuhim were tribes bordering Egypt. Pathrusim settled in Pathros between Egypt and Cush (the modern Sudan). Casluhim became ancestors of the Philistim (Philistines). Caphtorim settle in Caphtor (Crete and its surrounding islands), as did the Philistines who came to Philistia from Caphtor (Amos 9:7).

10:15. Sidon gave his name to the oldest Canaanite city on the Mediterranean seacoast. It was important long before Tyre came to prominence. Heth was the ancestor of the Hittites who had a great empire in Asia Minor centered at Boghazkoi; 10,000 clay tablets with Hittite laws and customs have been discovered.

10:16-18. Canaan begat (became the ancestor of) all these Canaanite tribes. Jebusites occupied Jebus (Jerusalem). Amorites ("mountaineers" or "westerners") occupied the central highlands of Canaan. Some of them went out and conquered Syria and eventually Amorite kings reigned in Babylon from about 1794-1595 B.C. Girgashites probably lived near the Sea of Galilee. Hivites

3793	4623, 6991	971.141	1689	5912, 6017	971.141	5651
art, pn	prep, pn	v Qal inf con, ps 2ms	pn	prep, pn	v Qal inf con, ps 2ms	pn
הַכְּנַעֲנִי	מִצִּידֹן	בֹּאֲכָה	גְּרָרָה	עַד־עַזָּה	בֹּאֲכָה	סְדֹמָה
hakk^{e}na'ănî	mitstsîdhōn	bō'ākhāh	gh^{e}rārāh	'adh-'azzāh	bō'ākhāh	s^{e}dhōmāh
the Canaanites	from Sidon	to your going	Gerar	unto Gaza	to your going	Sodom

6244	126	6896	5912, 4104		431	1158, 2626	3937, 5121
cj, pn	cj, pn	cj, pn	prep, pn	**20.**	dem pron	*n mp*, pn	prep, n fp, ps 3mp
וַעֲמֹרָה	וְאַדְמָה	וּצְבֹיִם	עַד־לָשַׁע		אֵלֶּה	בְנֵי־חָם	לְמִשְׁפְּחֹתָם
wa'ămōrāh	w^{e}'adhmāh	ûts^{e}vōyim	'adh-lāsha'		'ēlleh	v^{e}nê-chām	l^{e}mishp^{e}chōtham
and Gomorrah	and Admah	and Zeboiim	until Lasha		these	the sons of Ham	to their families

3937, 4098	904, 800	904, 1504		3937, 8429	3314.411	1612, 2000
prep, n fp, ps 3mp	prep, n fp, ps 3mp	prep, n mp, ps 3mp	**21.**	cj, prep, pn	v Pual pf 3ms	cj, pers pron
לִלְשֹׁנֹתָם	בְּאַרְצֹתָם	בְּגוֹיֵהֶם		וּלְשֵׁם	יֻלַּד	גַּם־הוּא
lilshōnōthām	b^{e}'artsōthām	b^{e}ghôyēhem		ûlāshēm	yulladh	gam-hû'
to their languages	in their lands	in their nations		and to Shem	he was born	also he

1	3725, 1158, 5885	250	3425	1448		1158	8429
n ms	adj, *n mp*, pn	*n ms*	pn	art, adj	**22.**	*n mp*	pn
אֲבִי	כָּל־בְּנֵי־עֵבֶר	אֲחִי	יֶפֶת	הַגָּדוֹל		בְּנֵי	שֵׁם
'ăvî	kol-b^{e}nê-'ēver	'ăchî	yepheth	haggādhôl		b^{e}nê	shēm
the father of	all the sons of Eber	the brother of	Japheth	the great		the sons of	Shem

6082	831	799	4003	782		1158	782	5995
pn	cj, pn	cj, pn	cj, pn	cj, pn	**23.**	cj, *n mp*	pn	pn
עֵילָם	וְאַשּׁוּר	וְאַרְפַּכְשַׁד	וְלוּד	וַאֲרָם		וּבְנֵי	אֲרָם	עוּץ
'êlām	w^{e}'ashshûr	w^{e}'arpakhshadh	w^{e}lûdh	wa'ărām		ûvnê	'ărām	'ûts
Elam	and Asshur	and Arphaxad	and Lud	and Aram		and the sons of	Aram	Uz

2436	1714	5040		799	3314.111	881, 8369	8369
cj, pn	cj, pn	cj, pn	**24.**	cj, pn	v Qal pf 3ms	do, pn	cj, pn
וְחוּל	וְגֶתֶר	וָמַשׁ		וְאַרְפַּכְשַׁד	יָלַד	אֶת־שָׁלַח	וְשֶׁלַח
w^{e}chûl	w^{e}ghether	wāmash		w^{e}'arpakhshadh	yāladh	'eth-shālach	w^{e}shelach
and Hul	and Gether	and Mash		and Arphaxad	he fathered	Shelah	and Shelah

3314.111	881, 5885		3937, 5885	3314.411	8530	1158	8428	259
v Qal pf 3ms	do, pn	**25.**	cj, prep, pn	v Pual pf 3ms	*num*	n mp	*n ms*	art, num
יָלַד	אֶת־עֵבֶר		וּלְעֵבֶר	יֻלַּד	שְׁנֵי	בָנִים	שֵׁם	הָאֶחָד
yāladh	'eth-'ēver		ûlā'ēver	yulladh	sh^{e}nê	vānîm	shēm	hā'echādh
he fathered	Eber		and to Eber	they were born	two	sons	the name of	the first

6632	3706	904, 3219	6629.112	800	8428	250	3465
pn	cj	prep, n mp, ps 3ms	v Niphal pf 3fs	art, n fs	cj, *n ms*	n ms, ps 3ms	pn
פֶּלֶג	כִּי	בְיָמָיו	נִפְלְגָה	הָאָרֶץ	וְשֵׁם	אָחִיו	יָקְטָן
pelegh	kî	v^{e}yāmâv	niphl^{e}ghāh	hā'ārets	w^{e}shēm	'āchîw	yāqōṭān
Peleg	because	in his days	it was divided	the earth	and the name of	his brother	Joktan

	3465	3314.111	881, 492	881, 8419	881, 2801	881, 3506
26.	cj, pn	v Qal pf 3ms	do, pn	cj, do, pn	cj, do, pn	cj, do, pn
	וְיָקְטָן	יָלַד	אֶת־אַלְמוֹדָד	וְאֶת־שָׁלֶף	וְאֶת־חֲצַרְמָוֶת	וְאֶת־יָרַח
	weyāqōṭān	yāladh	'eth-'almôdhādh	w^{e}'eth-shāleph	w^{e}'eth-chătsarmāweth	w^{e}'eth-yārach
	and Joktan	he fathered	Almodad	and Sheleph	and Hazarmaveth	and Jerah

	881, 1982	881, 184	881, 1913		881, 5963	881, 39	881, 8088
27.	cj, do, pn	cj, do, pn	cj, do, pn	**28.**	cj, do, pn	cj, do, pn	cj, do, pn
	וְאֶת־הֲדוֹרָם	וְאֶת־אוּזָל	וְאֶת־דִּקְלָה		וְאֶת־עוֹבָל	וְאֶת־אֲבִימָאֵל	וְאֶת־שְׁבָא
	w^{e}'eth-h^{e}dhôrām	w^{e}'eth-'ûzāl	w^{e}'eth-diqōlāh		w^{e}'eth-'ôvāl	w^{e}'eth-'ăvîmā'ēl	w^{e}'eth-sh^{e}vā'
	and Hadoram	and Uzal	and Diklah		and Obal	and Abimael	and Sheba

29.						30.
881, 209	881, 2434	881, 3206	3725, 431	1158	3465	2030.121
cj, do, pn	cj, do, pn	cj, do, pn	*adj*, dem pron	*n mp*	pn	cj, v Qal impf 3ms
וְאֶת־אוֹפִר	וְאֶת־חֲוִילָה	וְאֶת־יוֹבָב	כָּל־אֵלֶּה	בְּנֵי	יָקְטָן	וַיְהִי
wᵉ'eth-'ôphir	wᵉ'eth-chăwîlāh	wᵉ'eth-yôvāv	kol-'ēlleh	bᵉnê	yāqṭān	wayhî
and Ophir	and Havilah	and Jobab	all these	the sons of	Joktan	and it was

4319	4623, 5042	971.141	5812	2098	7209
n ms, ps 3mp	prep, pn	v Qal inf con, ps 2ms	pn	*n ms*	art, n ms
מוֹשָׁבָם	מִמֵּשָׁא	בֹּאֲכָה	סְפָרָה	הַר	הַקֶּדֶם
môshāvām	mimmēshā'	bō'ăkhāh	sᵉphārāh	har	haqqedhem
their dwelling place	from Mesha	to your going	to Sephar	the mountain of	the East

after their families, after their tongues, in their countries, and in their nations.

21. Unto Shem also, the father of all the children of Eber, the brother of Japheth the elder, even to him were children born.

22. The children of Shem; Elam, and Asshur, and Arphaxad, and Lud, and Aram.

23. And the children of Aram; Uz, and Hul, and Gether, and Mash.

24. And Arphaxad begat Salah; and Salah begat Eber.

25. And unto Eber were born two sons: the name of one was Peleg; for in his days was the earth divided; and his brother's name was Joktan.

26. And Joktan begat Almodad, and Sheleph, and Hazarmaveth, and Jerah,

27. And Hadoram, and Uzal, and Diklah,

28. And Obal, and Abimael, and Sheba,

29. And Ophir, and Havilah, and Jobab: all these were the sons of Joktan.

30. And their dwelling was from Mesha, as thou goest unto Sephar a mount of the east.

("tent-villagers") lived in Shechem and Gibeon. Arkites probably lived about 80 miles north of Sidon. Sinites probably lived in southern Lebanon. Arvadites lived north of the Arkites on the seacoast and on the island of Aradus. They were the northernmost of the Canaanites tribes, about 105 miles north of Tyre. Zemarites lived on the coast south of Arvad. Hamathites lived on the Orontes River, about 250 miles north of Jerusalem.

10:19-20. The chief territory of the Canaanites initially was from Sidon on the north (120 miles north of Jerusalem) to Gerar on the south (about 8 miles south-southeast of Gaza, which was on the coast 50 miles southwest of Jerusalem), and included the five cities of the plain south of the Dead Sea and Lasha on the east side of the Dead Sea.

10:21. Shem is mentioned as the ancestor of all the children of Eber (verses 25-30), because Abraham and the Hebrews are identified as descendants of Eber. Eber (sometimes called Heber in KJV) means "one crossing over" or "one going to the region beyond" (the Euphrates River).

Japheth is also identified as the oldest of the three sons of Noah, which makes Shem the middle child, yet the chosen line of the Messiah came through Shem as is often seen in Genesis.

10:22. Elamites settled on the Persian Gulf east of Babylonia with Susa (Heb. *Shushan*) as their capital. Asshur was the ancestor of Assyrians. Arphaxad settled northeast of Nineveh. Lud fathered the Lydians in east Asia Minor. Aram's descendants occupied territory from Damascus to north of the Euphrates where Haran is located.

10:23. Uz settled southeast of Damascus. The locations of Hul and Gether are uncertain. Mash probably went into the desert east or southeast of Damascus.

10:24. Salah (or Shelah) was the ancestor of Eber. Eber was the ancestor of the Hebrews through Peleg and 13 Arabian tribes through Joktan.

10:25. Peleg ("division") was so named because in his days the earth was divided. "Divided" here means by languages, rather than the land being divided. Thus, the tower of Babel was built in his days (Gen. 11:7-9).

10:26-30. Prominent among the Arabian tribes descended from Joktan is Ophir, famous for its gold (Job 22:24; Ps. 45:9; Isa. 13:12). Most of the other Arabian tribes moved from place to place in the Arabian desert.

31.	431	1158, 8429	3937, 5121	3937, 4098	904, 800	3937, 1504
	dem pron	*n mp*, pn	prep, n fp, ps 3mp	prep, n fp, ps 3mp	prep, n fp, ps 3mp	prep, n mp, ps 3mp
	אֵלֶּה	בְנֵי־שֵׁם	לְמִשְׁפְּחֹתָם	לִלְשֹׁנֹתָם	בְּאַרְצֹתָם	לְגוֹיֵהֶם
	'ēlleh	v^{e}nê-shēm	l^{e}mishp^{e}chōtham	lilshōnōthām	b$^{e'}$artsōthām	l^{e}ghôyēhem
	these	the sons of Shem	to their families	to their languages	in their lands	to their nations

32.	431	5121	1158, 5326	3937, 8765	904, 1504	4623, 431
	dem pron	*n fp*	*n mp*, pn	prep, n fp, ps 3mp	prep, n mp, ps 3mp	cj, prep, dem pron
	אֵלֶּה	מִשְׁפְּחֹת	בְנֵי־נֹחַ	לְתוֹלְדֹתָם	בְּגוֹיֵהֶם	וּמֵאֵלֶּה
	'ēlleh	mishp^{e}chōth	b^{e}nê-nōach	l^{e}thôl^{e}dhōthām	b^{e}ghôyēhem	ûmē'ēlleh
	these	the families of	the sons of Noah	to their generations	in their nations	and from these

6754.216	1504	904, 800	313	4138	11:1	2030.121
v Niphal pf 3cp	art, n mp	prep, art, n fs	adv	art, n ms		cj, v Qal impf 3ms
נִפְרְדוּ	הַגּוֹיִם	בָּאָרֶץ	אַחַר	הַמַּבּוּל		וַיְהִי
niphr^{e}dhû	haggôyim	bā'ārets	'achar	hammabbûl		wayhî
they were separated	the nations	on the earth	after	the flood		and it was

3725, 800	8004	259	1745	259	2.	2030.121	904, 5450.141
adj, art, n fs	n fs	num	cj, n mp	n mp		cj, v Qal impf 3ms	prep, v Qal inf con, ps 3mp
כָל־הָאָרֶץ	שָׂפָה	אֶחָת	וּדְבָרִים	אֲחָדִים		וַיְהִי	בְּנָסְעָם
khol-hā'ārets	sāphāh	'echāth	ûdh^{e}vārîm	'ăchādhîm		wayhî	b^{e}nās̱'ām
all the earth	lip	one	and words	ones		and it was	in their pulling out

4623, 7208	4834.126	1262	904, 800	8534	3553.126	8427
prep, n ms	cj, v Qal impf 3mp	n fs	prep, *n fs*	pn	cj, v Qal impf 3mp	adv
מִקֶּדֶם	וַיִּמְצְאוּ	בִקְעָה	בְּאֶרֶץ	שִׁנְעָר	וַיֵּשְׁבוּ	שָׁם
miqqedhem	wayyimts$^{e'}$û	viqō'āh	b$^{e'}$erets	shin'ār	wayyēshvû	shām
from the East	then they found	plain	in the land of	Shinar	and they dwelled	there

3.	569.126	382	420, 7751	1957.131	3967.120	3973
	cj, v Qal impf 3mp	n ms	prep, n ms, ps 3ms	v Qal impv 2ms	v Qal impf 1cp	n fp
	וַיֹּאמְרוּ	אִישׁ	אֶל־רֵעֵהוּ	הָבָה	נִלְבְּנָה	לְבֵנִים
	wayyō'mrû	'îsh	'el-rē'ēhû	hāvāh	nilb^{e}nāh	l^{e}vēnîm
	and they said	each	to his friend	come	we will make bricks	bricks

8041.120	3937, 8044	2030.122	3937	3973	3937, 63	2668
cj, v Qal impf 1cp	prep, n fs	cj, v Qal impf 3fs	prep, ps 3mp	art, n fs	prep, n fs	cj, art, n ms
וְנִשְׂרְפָה	לִשְׂרֵפָה	וַתְּהִי	לָהֶם	הַלְּבֵנָה	לְאָבֶן	וְהַחֵמָר
w^{e}nisr^{e}phāh	lisrēphāh	watt^{e}hî	lāhem	hall^{e}vēnāh	l$^{e'}$āven	w^{e}hachēmār
and we will burn	for burning	and it was	for them	the brick	for stone	and the tar

2030.111	3937	3937, 2670	4.	569.126	1957.131	1161.120, 3937
v Qal pf 3ms	prep, ps 3mp	prep, art, n ms		cj, v Qal impf 3mp	v Qal impv 2ms	v Qal impf 1cp, prep, ps 1cp
הָיָה	לָהֶם	לַחֹמֶר		וַיֹּאמְרוּ	הָבָה	נִבְנֶה־לָּנוּ
hāyāh	lāhem	lachōmer		wayyō'mrû	hāvāh	nivneh-lānû
it was	for them	for the mortar		and they said	come	we will build for us

6111	4166	7513	904, 8452	6449.120, 3937	8428
n fs	cj, n ms	cj, n ms, ps 3ms	prep, art, n mp	cj, v Qal impf 1cp, prep, ps 1cp	n ms
עִיר	וּמִגְדָּל	וְרֹאשׁוֹ	בַשָּׁמַיִם	וְנַעֲשֶׂה־לָּנוּ	שֵׁם
'îr	ûmighdāl	w^{e}rō'shô	bashshāmayim	w^{e}na'ăseh-lānû	shēm
city	and tower	and its top	in the heavens	and we will make for us	name

6678, 6571.120	6142, 6686	3725, 800	5.	3495.121	3176
cj, v Qal impf 1cp	prep, *n mp*	*adj*, art, n fs		cj, v Qal impf 3ms	pn
פֶּן־נָפוּץ	עַל־פְּנֵי	כָל־הָאָרֶץ		וַיֵּרֶד	יְהוָה
pen-nāphûts	'al-p^{e}nê	khol-hā'ārets		wayyēredh	y^{e}hwāh
otherwise we will be scattered	over the surface of	all the earth		and He went down	Yahweh

31. These are the sons of Shem, after their families, after their tongues, in their lands, after their nations.

32. These are the families of the sons of Noah, after their generations, in their nations: and by these were the nations divided in the earth after the flood.

11:1. And the whole earth was of one language, and of one speech: ... used the same words, *REB* ... one language and few words, *RSV* ... the same language and the same words, *NASB* .

2. And it came to pass, as they journeyed: ... their wondering, *BB* ... migrating in the east, *NAB* ... migrating eastward, *NCB* ... journeyed in the east, *NEB*.

from the east, that they found a plain in the land of Shinar and they dwelt there: ... in the Bushland, *Fenton* ... valley in the land of Shinar, *NAB* .

3. And they said one to another, Go to, let us make brick, and burn them thoroughly: ... bake them hard, *NEB* ... let us mold bricks and thoroughly bake them, *Berkeley* ... burning them well, *BB*.

and they had brick for stone, and slime had they for morter: ... bitumen, *REB* ... sticky earth, *BB* ... asphalt, *Berkeley*.

4. And they said, Go to, let us build us a city and a tower, whose top may reach unto heaven: ... its head reaching the heavens, *Young* ... reach the sky, *Fenton* ... with its top in the sky, *NAB*.

and let us make us a name: ... we will make a Beacon, *Fenton* ... make ourselves famous, *Berkeley* ... make for ourselves a name, *NASB* ... make a great name for ourselves, *BB*.

lest we be scattered abroad upon the face of the whole earth: ... or we shall be dispersed, *REB* ... so that we may not be wanderers, *BB* ... scattered all over the face of the earth, *NAB*.

5. And the LORD came down to

10:31-32. By Moses' time the descendants of Noah were divided into families (including tribal units) and nations. The division first of all was by language, as chapter 11 shows.

11:1. The Bible does not always tell things in chronological order. It often finishes one account and then goes back and give further details about a particular aspect, just as chapter 2 went back to explain the details of the sixth of creation.

Chapter 10 finishes the account of Noah and his sons and tells where their descendants were scattered in Moses' day. Now, chapter 11 goes back and tells what initially brought about the scattering. and the condition of multiple languages and cultures, as Israel was experiencing and for which they needed an explanation.

The whole earth, all the descendants of Noah, continued to speak the same language, even the same types of words (not even dialectical differences had developed).

11:2. The phrase "from the east" (Heb. *miqqedem*) can also mean "in the east," "eastward" or "in ancient times." From the point of view of the Israelites, it probably means eastward or in the east. Shinar was the area occupied by the Sumerians about 3,000 B.C. (a dark Caucasoid people similar to the Dravidians of south India).

The Sumerian language was the first lingua franca (used internationally as a language of trade and governmental communication). The plain was in what was later Babylonia. They proceeded to settle there with the intention of staying.

11:3. In Egypt the Israelites lived in houses of sun-dried bricks, but the city buildings were built of stone. So Moses explained for their benefit that no stone was used in building this city in Shinar and the bricks were burned to make them hard and water-resistant, as bricks are today. The slime used for mortar was bitumen (asphalt, petroleum tar).

11:4. They encouraged one another to build a city for themselves with a high tower reaching toward heaven, and make a name for themselves in order to keep from being scattered in all directions. This was an expression of their pride and desire for self glory. It was also an expression of rebellion against God's command to go out and fill the earth. The city would be a permanent center to declare that they would not journey or wander away.

Josephus, the first century Jewish historian, supposed the high tower was intended as a refuge should there be another flood. But if that were the case, they should have built it on a mountain, not out in the plain. Rather, it was to be a rallying point for their forces and their patriotism.

The tower of Babel probably became a model for the later step pyramids which were sacred temple towers of Mesopotamia called ziggurats ("pinnacle," or "mountain top"), which were intended to give the appearance of a mountain on the flat plains of Babylonia. These later towers, as well as those

3937, 7495.141	881, 6111	881, 4166	866	1161.116	1158	119
prep, v Qal inf con	do, art, n fs	cj, do, art, n ms	rel part	v Qal pf 3cp	*n mp*	art, n ms
לִרְאֹת	אֶת־הָעִיר	וְאֶת־הַמִּגְדָּל	אֲשֶׁר	בָּנוּ	בְּנֵי	הָאָדָם
lir'ōth	'eth-hā'îr	w^{e}'eth-hammighdāl	'ăsher	bānû	b^{e}nê	hā'ādhām
to see	the city	and the tower	which	they built	the sons of	the humankind

6.	569.121	3176	2075	6194	259	8004	259	3937, 3725
	cj, v Qal impf 3ms	pn	intrj	n ms	num	cj, n fs	num	prep, adj, ps 3mp
	וַיֹּאמֶר	יְהוָה	הֵן	עַם	אֶחָד	וְשָׂפָה	אַחַת	לְכֻלָּם
	wayyō'mer	y^{e}hwāh	hēn	'am	'echādh	w^{e}sāphāh	'achath	l^{e}khullām
	and He said	Yahweh	behold	people	one	and lip	one	to all of them

2172	2591.541	3937, 6449.141	6498	3940, 1245.221	4623
cj, dem pron	v Hiphil inf con, ps 3mp	prep, v Qal inf con	cj, adv	neg part, v Niphal impf 3ms	prep, ps 3mp
וְזֶה	הַחִלָּם	לַעֲשׂוֹת	וְעַתָּה	לֹא־יִבָּצֵר	מֵהֶם
w^{e}zeh	hachillām	la'ăsôth	w^{e}'atāh	lō'-yibbātsēr	mēhem
and this	their beginning	to do	and now	not it will be inaccessible	from them

3725	866	2246.126	3937, 6449.141	7.	1957.131	3495.120
adj	rel part	v Qal impf 3mp	prep, v Qal inf con		v Qal impv 2ms	v Qal impf 1cp
כֹּל	אֲשֶׁר	יָזְמוּ	לַעֲשׂוֹת		הָבָה	נֵרְדָה
kōl	'ăsher	yāzmû	la'ăsôth		hāvāh	nērdhāh
all	which	they will plan	to do		come	we will go down

1140.120	8427	8004	866	3940	8471.126	382	8004
cj, v Qal impf 1cp	adv	n fs, ps 3mp	rel part	neg part	v Qal impf 3mp	n ms	*n fs*
וְנָבְלָה	שָׁם	שְׂפָתָם	אֲשֶׁר	לֹא	יִשְׁמְעוּ	אִישׁ	שְׂפַת
w^{e}nāvlāh	shām	s^{e}phāthām	'ăsher	lō'	yishm^{e}'û	'îsh	s^{e}phath
and we will mix up	there	their lip	that	not	they will hear	each	the lip of

7751	8.	6571.521	3176	881	4623, 8427	6142, 6686
n ms, ps 3ms		cj, v Hiphil impf 3ms	pn	do, ps 3mp	prep, adv	prep, *n mp*
רֵעֵהוּ		וַיָּפֶץ	יְהוָה	אֹתָם	מִשָּׁם	עַל־פְּנֵי
rē'ēhû		wayyāphets	y^{e}hwāh	'ōthām	mishshām	'al-p^{e}nê
his friend		and He scattered	Yahweh	them	from there	over the surface of

3725, 800	2403.126	3937, 1161.141	6111	9.	6142, 3772	7410.111
adj, art, n fs	cj, v Qal impf 3mp	prep, v Qal inf con	art, n fs		prep, adv	v Qal pf 3ms
כָל־הָאָרֶץ	וַיַּחְדְּלוּ	לִבְנֹת	הָעִיר		עַל־כֵּן	קָרָא
khol-hā'ārets	wayyachd^{e}lû	livnōth	hā'îr		'al-kēn	qārā'
all the earth	so they stopped	building	the city		therefore	he called

8428	928	3706, 8427	1140.111	3176	8004	3725, 800
n ms, ps 3fs	pn	cj, adv	v Qal pf 3ms	pn	*n fs*	*adj*, art, n fs
שְׁמָהּ	בָּבֶל	כִּי־שָׁם	בָּלַל	יְהוָה	שְׂפַת	כָּל־הָאָרֶץ
sh^{e}māhh	bavel	kî-shom	bālal	y^{e}hwāh	s^{e}phath	kol-hā'ārets
its name	Babel	because there	He mixed up	Yahweh	the lip of	all the earth

4623, 8427	6751.511	3176	6142, 6686	3725, 800	10.	431
cj, prep, adv	v Hiphil pf 3ms, ps 3mp	pn	prep, *n mp*	*adj*, art, n fs		dem pron
וּמִשָּׁם	הֱפִיצָם	יְהוָה	עַל־פְּנֵי	כָּל־הָאָרֶץ		אֵלֶּה
ûmishshom	hĕphîtsām	y^{e}hwāh	'al-p^{e}nê	kol-hā'ārets		'ēlleh
and from there	He mixed up them	Yahweh	over the surface of	all the earth		these

8765	8429	8429	1158, 4109	8523	3314.521	881, 799
n fp	pn	pn	*n ms, num*	n fs	cj, v Hiphil impf 3ms	do, pn
תּוֹלְדֹת	שֵׁם	שֵׁם	בֶּן־מְאַת	שָׁנָה	וַיּוֹלֶד	אֶת־אַרְפַּכְשָׁד
tôl^{e}dhōth	shēm	shēm	ben-m^{e}'ath	shānāh	wayyôledh	'eth-'arpakhshādh
the generations of	Shem	Shem	son of hundred of	years	when he fathered	Arphaxad

see the city and the tower, which the children of men builded: ... human beings, *Goodspeed* ... mortal men, *NEB.*

6. And the LORD said, Behold, the people is one, and they have all one language: ... and one pronunciation, *Young* ... speaking the same language, *NIV* ... all with one language, *Berkeley.*

and this they begin to do: and now nothing will be restrained from them, which they have imagined to do: ... nothing they have a mind to do will be beyond their reach, *NEB* ... dreamed of doing, *Young* ... nothing that they mediate doing, *Darby* ... nothing that they propose to do will now be impossible for them, *RSV* ... will be withheld from them, *NKJV.*

7. Go to, let us go down, and there confound their language that they may not understand one another's speech: ... confuse their speech, *Berkeley* ... mingle there their pronunciation, *Young* ... make such a babble of their language that they cannot comprehend, *Goodspeed.*

8. So the LORD scattered them abroad from thence upon the face of all the earth: and they left off to build the city: ... stopped building the city, *NASB* ... gave up building their town, *BB* ... left off building the city, *NEB.*

9. Therefore is the name of it called Babel; because the LORD did there confound the language of all the earth: and from thence did the LORD scatter them abroad upon the face of all the earth.

10. These are the generations of Shem: Shem was an hundred years old, and begat Arphaxad two years after the flood:

11. And Shem lived after he begat Arphaxad five hundred years, and begat sons and daughters.

---

pyramid towers in Egypt and Central America, were all temple towers. Babylonian ziggurats were centers for priests and priestesses who glorified immorality and lewd practices in the name of religion. It is no wonder that Babylon became a fit symbol for the "MOTHER OF HARLOTS" described in Revelation 17.

Two possibilities for the location of the tower have been suggested. One is Birs Nimrud, about 15 miles southwest of Babylon. It rose in great steps or stages to a height of over 150 feet. It did not have a peak until Nebuchadnezzar provided it with one. The other possibility is the great pyramid temple, *E-temenanaki*, in Babylon itself.

To make a name meant to make a reputation that would call for the loyalty of the people, and thus keep them settled in and around the city. Their exalting of their own name is in quite a contrast to those spiritual giants who called on and called themselves by the name of the LORD (Gen. 4:26).

11:5. The LORD came down to see, that is to give special attention to the city and the tower which the people were in the process of building.

11:6. God recognized that the people had lost the true unity that once caused them to join in the worship of the one true God. They were seeking to retain a false unity by human efforts.

This was but the beginning of their defiance. Their imagination was taking off in the wrong direction and would contribute to more and more defiance of God. God saw into their hearts, hearts that were "deceitful above all things, and desperately wicked" (Jer. 17:9).

11:7. People may ignore God's Word and plan, but He is still in control (Rom. 13:1; Dan. 4:17; 5:21). He may delay judgment because of His long-suffering love and mercy. Yet the time comes when He says it is enough. He saw what would happen if their evil, self-centered desires were left unchecked.

People who want to make a name for themselves will stop at nothing. So God determined to break up their false unity by confounding or confusing their language. Language is still a barrier, and people who cannot understand each other have difficulty trying to work together.

11:8. God probably worked through their minds and produced other languages. Linguists agree there are a number of basic languages which are not derived from each other. But whatever He did, it was effective and caused the people to scatter. Thus the building of the city was discontinued.

11:9. The name Babel is contracted from *balbel*, "confusion." Babel is also the Hebrew name for Babylon, so that the Israelites thought of this as the tower of Babylon. Later Babylonians rejected this meaning "confusion," split up the name arbitrarily, and put a case ending on it to make it Bab-ilu, "gate of god."

11:10-17. For the names of the descendants of Shem in these verses see the comments on Genesis 10:22-25. As in most biblical genealogies, key persons are listed, not every individual. The Greek

8523	313	4138		2513.121, 8429	311	3314.541
n md	adv	art, n ms	**11.**	cj, v Qal impf 3ms, pn	*sub*	v Hiphil inf con, ps 3ms
שְׁנָתַיִם	אַחַר	הַמַּבּוּל		וַיְחִי־שֵׁם	אַחֲרֵי	הוֹלִידוֹ
shenāthayim	'achar	hammabbûl		waychî-shēm	'achrê	hôlîdhô
two years	after	the flood		and he lived Shem	after	fathering him

881, 799	2675	4109	8523	3314.521	1158	1351
do, pn	num	*num*	n fs	cj, v Hiphil impf 3ms	n mp	cj, n fp
אֶת־אַרְפַּכְשָׁד	חֲמֵשׁ	מֵאוֹת	שָׁנָה	וַיּוֹלֶד	בָּנִים	וּבָנוֹת
'eth-'arpakhshādh	chămēsh	mē'ôth	shānāh	wayyôledh	bānîm	ûvānôth
Arphaxad	five	hundreds of	years	and he fathered	sons	and daughters

	799	2513.111	2675	8389	8523	3314.521	881, 8369
12.	cj, pn	v Qal pf 3ms	num	cj, num	n fs	cj, v Hiphil impf 3ms	do, pn
	וְאַרְפַּכְשַׁד	חַי	חָמֵשׁ	וּשְׁלֹשִׁים	שָׁנָה	וַיּוֹלֶד	אֶת־שָׁלַח
	we'arpakhshadh	chay	chāmēsh	ûshelōshîm	shānāh	wayyôledh	'eth-shālach
	and Arphaxad	he lived	five	and thirty	years	when he fathered	Shelah

	2513.121	799	311	3314.541	881, 8369	8421	8523
13.	cj, v Qal impf 3ms	pn	*sub*	v Hiphil inf con, ps 3ms	do, pn	num	n fp
	וַיְחִי	אַרְפַּכְשַׁד	אַחֲרֵי	הוֹלִידוֹ	אֶת־שֶׁלַח	שָׁלֹשׁ	שָׁנִים
	waychî	'arpakhshadh	'achrê	hôlîdhô	'eth-shelach	shālōsh	shānîm
	and he lived	Arphaxad	after	fathering him	Shelah	three	years

727	4109	8523	3314.521	1158	1351		8369
cj, num	num	n fs	cj, v Hiphil impf 3ms	n mp	cj, n fp	**14.**	cj, pn
וְאַרְבַּע	מֵאוֹת	שָׁנָה	וַיּוֹלֶד	בָּנִים	וּבָנוֹת		וְשֶׁלַח
we'arba'	mē'ôth	shānāh	wayyôledh	bānîm	ûvānôth		weshelach
and four	hundreds of	years	and he fathered	sons	and daughters		and Shelah

2513.111	8389	8523	3314.521	881, 5885		2513.121,8369
v Qal pf 3ms	num	n fs	cj, v Hiphil impf 3ms	do, pn	**15.**	cj, v Qal impf 3ms, pn
חַי	שְׁלֹשִׁים	שָׁנָה	וַיּוֹלֶד	אֶת־עֵבֶר		וַיְחִי־שֶׁלַח
chay	shelōshîm	shānāh	wayyôledh	'eth-'ēver		waychî-shelach
he lived	thirty	years	when he fathered	Eber		and he lived Shelah

311	3314.541	881, 5885	8421	8523	727	4109	8523
sub	v Hiphil inf con, ps 3ms	do, pn	num	n fp	cj, num	*num*	n fs
אַחֲרֵי	הוֹלִידוֹ	אֶת־עֵבֶר	שָׁלֹשׁ	שָׁנִים	וְאַרְבַּע	מֵאוֹת	שָׁנָה
'achrê	hôlîdhô	'eth-'ēver	shālōsh	shānîm	we'arba'	mē'ôth	shānāh
after	fathering him	Eber	three	years	and four	hundreds of	years

3314.521	1158	1351		2513.121, 5885	727	8389	8523
cj, v Hiphil impf 3ms	n mp	cj, n fp	**16.**	cj, v Qal impf 3ms, pn	num	cj, num	n fs
וַיּוֹלֶד	בָּנִים	וּבָנוֹת		וַיְחִי־עֵבֶר	אַרְבַּע	וּשְׁלֹשִׁים	שָׁנָה
wayyôledh	bānîm	ûvānôth		waychî-'ēver	'arba'	ûshelōshîm	shānāh
and he fathered	sons	and daughters		and he lived Eber	four	and thirty	years

3314.521	881, 6632		2513.121, 5885	311	3314.541	881, 6632
cj, v Hiphil impf 3ms	do, pn	**17.**	cj, v Qal impf 3ms, pn	*sub*	v Hiphil inf con, ps 3ms	do, pn
וַיּוֹלֶד	אֶת־פָּלֶג		וַיְחִי־עֵבֶר	אַחֲרֵי	הוֹלִידוֹ	אֶת־פֶּלֶג
wayyôledh	'eth-pālegh		waychî-'ēver	'achrê	hôlîdhô	'eth-pelegh
when he fathered	Peleg		and he lived Eber	after	fathering him	Peleg

8389	8523	727	4109	8523	3314.521	1158	1351
num	n fs	cj, num	*num*	n fs	cj, v Hiphil impf 3ms	n mp	cj, n fp
שְׁלֹשִׁים	שָׁנָה	וְאַרְבַּע	מֵאוֹת	שָׁנָה	וַיּוֹלֶד	בָּנִים	וּבָנוֹת
shelōshîm	shānāh	we'arba'	mē'ôth	shānāh	wayyôledh	bānîm	ûvānôth
thirty	years	and four	hundreds of	years	and he fathered	sons	and daughters

18.	2513.121, 6632	8389	8523	3314.521	881, 7754	**19.**	2513.121, 6632
	cj, v Qal impf 3ms, pn	num	n fs	cj, v Hiphil impf 3ms	do, pn		cj, v Qal impf 3ms, pn
	וַיְחִי־פֶלֶג	שְׁלֹשִׁים	שָׁנָה	וַיּוֹלֶד	אֶת־רְעוּ		וַיְחִי־פֶלֶג
	waychî-phelegh	sh^{e}lōshîm	shānāh	wayyôledh	'eth-r^{e}'û		waychî-phelegh
	and he lived Peleg	thirty	years	when he fathered	Reu		and he lived Peleg

311	3314.541	881, 7754	9013	8523	4109	8523
sub	v Hiphil inf con, ps 3ms	do, pn	num	n fp	cj, num	n fs
אַחֲרֵי	הוֹלִידוֹ	אֶת־רְעוּ	תֵּשַׁע	שָׁנִים	וּמָאתַיִם	שָׁנָה
'achrê	hôlîdhô	'eth-r^{e}'û	tēsha'	shānîm	ûmā'thayim	shānāh
after	fathering him	Reu	nine	years	and hundreds	years

3314.521	1158	1351	**20.**	2513.121	7754	8692	8389
cj, v Hiphil impf 3ms	n mp	cj, n fp		cj, v Qal impf 3ms	pn	num	cj, num
וַיּוֹלֶד	בָּנִים	וּבָנוֹת		וַיְחִי	רְעוּ	שְׁתַּיִם	וּשְׁלֹשִׁים
wayyôledh	bānîm	ûvānôth		waychî	r^{e}'û	sh^{e}ttayim	ûsh^{e}lōshîm
and he fathered	sons	and daughters		and he lived	Reu	two	and thirty

8523	3314.521	881, 8024	**21.**	2513.121	7754	311	3314.541
n fs	cj, v Hiphil impf 3ms	do, pn		cj, v Qal impf 3ms	pn	*sub*	v Hiphil inf con, ps 3ms
שָׁנָה	וַיּוֹלֶד	אֶת־שְׂרוּג		וַיְחִי	רְעוּ	אַחֲרֵי	הוֹלִידוֹ
shānāh	wayyôledh	'eth-s^{e}rûgh		waychî	r^{e}'û	'achrê	hôlîdhô
years	when he fathered	Serug		and he lived	Reu	after	fathering him

881, 8024	8124	8523	4109	8523	3314.521	1158	1158
do, pn	num	n fp	cj, num	n fs	cj, v Hiphil impf 3ms	n mp	cj, n fp
אֶת־שְׂרוּג	שֶׁבַע	שָׁנִים	וּמָאתַיִם	שָׁנָה	וַיּוֹלֶד	בָּנִים	וּבָנוֹת
'eth-s^{e}rûgh	sheva'	shānîm	ûmā'thayim	shānāh	wayyôledh	bānîm	ûvānôth
Serug	seven	years	and hundreds	years	and he fathered	sons	and daughters

22.	2513.121	8024	8389	8523	3314.521	881, 5331
	cj, v Qal impf 3ms	pn	num	n fs	cj, v Hiphil impf 3ms	do, pn
	וַיְחִי	שְׂרוּג	שְׁלֹשִׁים	שָׁנָה	וַיּוֹלֶד	אֶת־נָחוֹר
	waychî	s^{e}rûgh	sh^{e}lōshîm	shānāh	wayyôledh	'eth-nāchôr
	and he lived	Serug	thirty	years	when he fathered	Nahor

12. And Arphaxad lived five and thirty years, and begat Salah:

13. And Arphaxad lived after he begat Salah four hundred and three years, and begat sons and daughters.

14. And Salah lived thirty years, and begat Eber:

15. And Salah lived after he begat Eber four hundred and three years, and begat sons and daughters.

16. And Eber lived four and thirty years, and begat Peleg:

17. And Eber lived after he begat Peleg four hundred and thirty years, and begat sons and daughters.

18. And Peleg lived thirty years, and begat Reu:

19. And Peleg lived after he begat Reu two hundred and nine years, and begat sons and daughters.

20. And Reu lived two and thirty years, and begat Serug:

21. And Reu lived after he begat Serug two hundred and seven years, and begat sons and daughters.

22. And Serug lived thirty years,

Septuagint translation adds a name and says "Arphaxad begat Kenan who lived 130 years and begat Salah." Kenan is also included in the genealogy of Jesus (See Luke 3:36.)

11:18-20. Reu means "one exercising oversight--as a shepherd or a friend." He is called Ragau in Luke 3:35.

11:21-22. Serug may mean "shoot" or "branch." He is called Saruch in Luke 3:35.

11:23-24. Nahor means "breathing hard, snort-

	2513.121	8024	311	3314.541	881, 5331	4109	8523
23.	cj, v Qal impf 3ms	pn	*sub*	v Hiphil inf con, ps 3ms	do, pn	num	n fs
	וַיְחִי	שְׂרוּג	אַחֲרֵי	הוֹלִידוֹ	אֶת־נָחוֹר	מָאתַיִם	שָׁנָה
	waychî	s^{e}rûgh	'achrê	hôlîdhô	'eth-nāchôr	mā'thayim	shānāh
	and he lived	Serug	after	fathering him	Nahor	hundreds	years

3314.521	1158	1351		2513.121	5331	9013	6465
cj, v Hiphil impf 3ms	n mp	cj, n fp	**24.**	cj, v Qal impf 3ms	pn	num	cj, num
וַיּוֹלֶד	בָּנִים	וּבָנוֹת		וַיְחִי	נָחוֹר	תֵּשַׁע	וְעֶשְׂרִים
wayyôledh	bānîm	ûvānôth		waychî	nāchôr	tēsha'	w^{e}'esrîm
and he fathered	sons	and daughters		and he lived	Nahor	nine	and twenty

8523	3314.521	881, 8983		2513.121	5331	311	3314.541
n fs	cj, v Hiphil impf 3ms	do, pn	**25.**	cj, v Qal impf 3ms	pn	*sub*	v Hiphil inf con, ps 3ms
שָׁנָה	וַיּוֹלֶד	אֶת־תָּרַח		וַיְחִי	נָחוֹר	אַחֲרֵי	הוֹלִידוֹ
shānāh	wayyôledh	'eth-tārach		waychî	nāchôr	'achrê	hôlîdhô
years	when he fathered	Terah		and he lived	Nahor	after	fathering him

881, 8983	9013, 6462	8523	4109	8523	3314.521	1158
do, pn	num, num	n fs	cj, *num*	n fs	cj, v Hiphil impf 3ms	n mp
אֶת־תֶּרַח	תְּשַׁע־עֶשְׂרֵה	שָׁנָה	וּמְאַת	שָׁנָה	וַיּוֹלֶד	בָּנִים
'eth-terach	t^{e}sha'-'esrēh	shānāh	ûm^{e}'ath	shānāh	wayyôledh	bānîm
Terah	nine ten	years	and hundred of	years	and he fathered	sons

1351		2513.121, 8983	8124	8523	3314.521	881, 82	881, 5331
cj, n fp	**26.**	cj, v Qal impf 3ms, pn	num	n fs	cj, v Hiphil impf 3ms	do, pn	do, pn
וּבָנוֹת		וַיְחִי־תֶרַח	שִׁבְעִים	שָׁנָה	וַיּוֹלֶד	אֶת־אַבְרָם	אֶת־נָחוֹר
ûvānôth		waychî-therach	shiv'îm	shānāh	wayyôledh	'eth-'avrām	'eth-nāchôr
and daughters		and he lived Terah	seventy	years	when he fathered	Abram	Nahor

881, 2115		431	8765	8983	8983	3314.511	881, 82
cj, do, pn	**27.**	cj, dem pron	*n fp*	pn	pn	v Hiphil pf 3ms	do, pn
וְאֶת־הָרָן		וְאֵלֶּה	תּוֹלְדֹת	תֶּרַח	תֶּרַח	הוֹלִיד	אֶת־אַבְרָם
w^{e}'eth-hārān		w^{e}'ēlleh	tôl^{e}dhōth	terach	terach	hôlîdh	'eth-'avrām
and Haran		and these	the generations of	Terah	Terah	he fathered	Abram

881, 5331	881, 2115	2115	3314.511	881, 4013		4322.121	2115
do, pn	cj, do, pn	cj, pn	v Hiphil pf 3ms	do, pn	**28.**	cj, v Qal impf 3ms	pn
אֶת־נָחוֹר	וְאֶת־הָרָן	וְהָרָן	הוֹלִיד	אֶת־לוֹט		וַיָּמָת	הָרָן
'eth-nāchôr	w^{e}'eth-hārān	w^{e}hārān	hôlîdh	'eth-lôṯ		wayyāmāth	hārān
Nahor	and Haran	Haran	he fathered	Lot		and he died	Haran

6142, 6686	8983	1	904, 800	4274	904, 217	3908
prep, *n mp*	pn	n ms, ps	prep, *n fs*	n fs, ps 3ms	prep, pn	pn
עַל־פְּנֵי	תֶּרַח	אָבִיו	בְּאֶרֶץ	מוֹלַדְתּוֹ	בְּאוּר	כַּשְׂדִּים
'al-p^{e}nê	terach	'āvîw	b^{e}'erets	môladhtô	b^{e}'ûr	kasdîm
in the presence of	Terah	his father	in the land of	his relatives	in Ur of	the Chaldeans

	4089.121	82	5331	3937	5571	8428	828, 82	8030
29.	cj, v Qal impf 3ms	pn	cj, pn	prep, ps 3mp	n fp	*n ms*	*n fs*, pn	pn
	וַיִּקַּח	אַבְרָם	וְנָחוֹר	לָהֶם	נָשִׁים	שֵׁם	אֵשֶׁת־אַבְרָם	שָׂרָי
	wayyiqqach	'avrām	w^{e}nāchôr	lāhem	nāshîm	shēm	'ēsheth-'avrām	sārāy
	and he took	Abram	and Nahor	to them	wives	the name of	the wife of Abram	Sarai

8428	828, 5331	4575	1351, 2115	1, 4575	1
cj, *n ms*	*n fs*, pn	pn	*n fs*, pn	*n ms*, pn	cj, *n ms*
וְשֵׁם	אֵשֶׁת־נָחוֹר	מִלְכָּה	בַּת־הָרָן	אֲבִי־מִלְכָּה	וַאֲבִי
w^{e}shēm	'ēsheth-nāchôr	milkāh	bath-hārān	'ăvî-milkāh	wa'ăvî
and the name of	the wife of Nahor	Milcah	the daughter of Haran	the father of Milkah	and the father

3360 pn יִסְכָּה yis̱kāh Iscah	30.	2030.122 cj, v Qal impf 3fs וַתְּהִי watt^{e}hî and she was	8030 pn שָׂרַי sāray Sarai	6371 adj עֲקָרָה ʿăqārāh barren	375 sub אֵין 'ên there was not	3937 prep, ps 3fs לָהּ lāhh to her	2141 n ms וָלָד wālādh child

31.	4089.121 cj, v Qal impf 3ms וַיִּקַּח wayyiqqach and he took	8983 pn תֶּרַח terach Terah	881, 82 do, pn אֶת־אַבְרָם 'eth-'avrām Abram	1158 n ms, ps 3ms בְּנוֹ b^{e}nô his son	881, 4013 cj, do, pn וְאֶת־לוֹט w^e'eth-lôṯ and Lot	1158, 2115 *n ms*, pn בֶּן־הָרָן ben-hārān son of Haran	1158, 1158 *n ms*, n ms, ps 3ms בֶּן־בְּנוֹ ben-b^{e}nô son of his son

881 cj, do וְאֵת w^e'th and	8030 pn שָׂרַי sāray Sarai	3738 n fs, ps 3ms כַּלָּתוֹ kallāthô his daughter-in-law	828 *n fs* אֵשֶׁת 'ēsheth the wife of	82 pn אַבְרָם 'avrām Abram	1158 n ms, ps 3ms בְּנוֹ b^{e}nô his son	3428.126 cj, v Qal impf 3mp וַיֵּצְאוּ wayyēts'û and they went out

and begat Nahor:

23. And Serug lived after he begat Nahor two hundred years, and begat sons and daughters.

24. And Nahor lived nine and twenty years, and begat Terah:

25. And Nahor lived after he begat Terah an hundred and nineteen years, and begat sons and daughters.

26. And Terah lived seventy years, and begat Abram, Nahor, and Haran.

27. Now these are the generations of Terah: Terah begat Abram, Nahor, and Haran; and Haran begat Lot.

28. And Haran died before his father Terah in the land of his nativity, in Ur of the Chaldees.

29. And Abram and Nahor took them wives: the name of Abram's wife was Sarai; and the name of Nahor's wife, Milcah, the daughter of Haran, the father of Milcah, and the father of Iscah.

30. But Sarai was barren; she had no child.

31. And Terah took Abram his son, and Lot the son of Haran his son's son, and Sarai his daughter in law, his son Abram's wife; and they went forth with them from Ur of the Chaldees, to go into the land of Canaan; and they came unto Haran, and dwelt there.

ing." He is called Nachor in Luke 3:34.

11:25. Terah means "panting" or "ibex (wild goat)." He is called Tharah in Luke 3:34. Jewish tradition says he was an idol maker by trade. Joshua indicated that Israel's ancestors on the other side of the Euphrates did worship and serve idols (Josh. 24:2).

11:26-28. Abram means "exalted father." Nahor means "snoring, snorting." Haran means "high." Terah probably had the first of his sons when he was 70 years old. Abram was 75 when he entered Canaan after Terah died at 205 years of age. (See Gen. 12:4, cf. Acts 7:4). That means Terah was actually 130 when Abram was born. Haran was probably the oldest since he died before they left Ur of the Chaldees. Ur, 140 miles southeast of Babylon, was the center of a fertile, prosperous, civilized region; but was also a center of immoral devotion to the moon god, "Sin." There is some evidence, however, of another Ur north of Haran. Abram may have come from the northern Ur, which was occupied by Chaldeans about 2000 B.C. Both cities had a highly developed civilization. From either city it would take faith to leave its opportunities and culture. Lot, "concealment," was left an orphan, and the childless Abram took care of him.

11:29-30. Sarai meant "princess" in the Aramaic of her homeland. Later we learn that she and Abram had the same father but different mothers (Gen. 20:12). Milcah, "counsel," was the sister of Lot, so Nahor married his niece. There were no laws against marrying close relatives in those days. The barrenness of Sarah is mentioned because it would become a test of Abram's faith.

11:31-32. Acts 7:2-4 makes it clear that God appeared to Abram while he was still in the land of the Chaldees and told him to leave his country and his people. Because of the closeness of the extend-

971.126	3791	800	3937, 2050.141	3908	4623, 217	882
cj, v Qal impf 3mp	pn	*n fs*	prep, v Qal inf con	pn	prep, pn	prep, ps 3mp
וַיָּבֹאוּ	כְּנַעַן	אַרְצָה	לָלֶכֶת	כַּשְׂדִּים	מֵאוּר	אִתָּם
wayyābō'û	k^{e}na'an	'artsāh	lālekheth	kasdîm	mē'ûr	'ittām
and they went	Canaan	to the land of	to go	the Chaldeans	from Ur of	with them

8523	2675	3219, 8983	2030.126	32.	8427	3553.126	5912, 2115
n fp	num	*n mp*, pn	cj, v Qal impf 3mp		adv	cj, v Qal impf 3mp	prep, pn
שָׁנִים	חָמֵשׁ	יְמֵי־תֶרַח	וַיִּהְיוּ		שָׁם	וַיֵּשְׁבוּ	עַד־חָרָן
shānîm	chāmēsh	y^{e}mê-therach	wayyihyû		shām	wayyēshvû	'adh-chārān
years	five	the days of Terah	and they were		there	and they dwelled	to Haran

3176	569.121	12:1	904, 2115	8983	4322.121	8523	4109
pn	cj, v Qal impf 3ms		prep, pn	pn	cj, v Qal impf 3ms	n fs	cj, num
יְהוָה	וַיֹּאמֶר		בְּחָרָן	תָּרַח	וַיָּמָת	שָׁנָה	וּמָאתַיִם
y^{e}hwāh	wayyō'mer		b^{e}chārān	terach	wayyāmāth	shānāh	ûmā'thayim
Yahweh	and He said		in Haran	Terah	and he died	year	and hundreds

4623, 1041	4623, 4274	4623, 800	2050.131, 3937	420, 82
cj, prep, *n ms*	cj, prep, n fs, ps 2ms	prep, n fs, ps 2ms	v Qal impv 2ms, prep, ps 2ms	prep, pn
וּמִבֵּית	וּמִמּוֹלַדְתְּךָ	מֵאַרְצְךָ	לֶךְ־לְךָ	אֶל־אַבְרָם
ûmibêth	ûmimmôladt^{e}khā	mē'arts^{e}khā	lekh-l^{e}khā	'el-'avrām
and from the house of	and from your relatives	from your land	go for yourself	to Abram

3937, 1504	6449.125	2.	7495.525	866	420, 800	1
prep, n ms	cj, v Qal impf 1cs, 2ms		v Hiphil impf 1cs, ps 2ms	rel part	prep, art, n fs	n ms, ps 2ms
לְגוֹי	וְאֶעֶשְׂךָ		אַרְאֶךָּ	אֲשֶׁר	אֶל־הָאָרֶץ	אָבִיךָ
l^{e}ghôy	w^{e}'e'es^{e}khā		'ar'ekhā	'ăsher	'el-hā'ārets	'āvîkhā
nation	and I will make you		I will show you	which	to the land	your father

1318	2030.131	8428	1461.325	1313.325	1448
n fs	cj, v Qal impv 2ms	n ms, ps 2ms	cj, v Piel impf 1cs	cj, v Piel impf 1cs, ps 2ms	adj
בְּרָכָה	וֶהְיֵה	שְׁמֶךָ	וַאֲגַדְּלָה	וַאֲבָרֶכְךָ	גָּדוֹל
b^{e}rākhāh	wehyēh	sh^{e}mekhā	wa'ăghadd^{e}lāh	wa'ăvārekh^{e}khā	gādhôl
blessing	so become	your name	and I will make great	and I will bless you	great

1313.216	803.125	7327.351	1313.352	1313.325	3.
cj, v Niphal pf 3cp	v Qal impf 1cs	cj, v Piel ptc ms, ps 2ms	v Piel ptc mp, ps 2ms	cj, v Piel impf 1cs	
וְנִבְרְכוּ	אָאֹר	וּמְקַלֶּלְךָ	מְבָרְכֶיךָ	וַאֲבָרְכָה	
w^{e}nivr^{e}khû	'ā'ōr	ûm^{e}qallel^{e}khā	m^{e}vārăkhêkhā	wa'ăvārkhāh	
and they will be blessed	I will curse	and your curser	your blessers	and I will bless	

3626, 866	82	2050.121	4.	124	5121	3725	904
prep, rel part	pn	cj, v Qal impf 3ms		art, n fs	*n fp*	adj	prep, ps 2ms
כַּאֲשֶׁר	אַבְרָם	וַיֵּלֶךְ		הָאֲדָמָה	מִשְׁפְּחֹת	כֹּל	בְךָ
ka'ăsher	'avrām	wayyēlekh		hā'ădhāmāh	mishp^{e}chōth	kōl	v^{e}khā
according to that	Abram	and he went		the earth	the families of	all	by you

82	4013	882	2050.121	3176	420	1744.311
cj, pn	pn	prep, ps 3ms	cj, v Qal impf 3ms	pn	prep, ps 3ms	v Piel pf 3ms
וְאַבְרָם	לוֹט	אִתּוֹ	וַיֵּלֶךְ	יְהוָה	אֵלָיו	דִּבֶּר
w^{e}'avrām	lôṭ	'ittô	wayyēlekh	y^{e}hwāh	'ēlâv	dibber
and Abram	Lot	with him	and he went	Yahweh	to him	He spoke

4623, 2115	904, 3428.141	8523	8124	8523	1158, 2675
prep, pn	prep, v Qal inf con, ps 3ms	n fs	cj, num	n fp	*n ms*, num
מֵחָרָן	בְּצֵאתוֹ	שָׁנָה	וְשִׁבְעִים	שָׁנִים	בֶּן־חָמֵשׁ
mēchārān	b^{e}tsē'thô	shānāh	w^{e}shiv'îm	shānîm	ben-chāmēsh
from Haran	in his departing	years	and seventy	years	son of five

32. And the days of Terah were two hundred and five years: and Terah died in Haran.

12:1. Now the LORD had said unto Abram: ... Jehovah, *ASV* ... Yahweh, *Anchor* ... Ever-living, *Fenton.*

Get thee out of thy country, and from thy kindred, and from thy father's house: ... From your native land, *Anchor* ... Leave your land, and your relatives, *Berkeley* ... Depart from your native land and from the home of your forefathers, *Fenton* ... Go for thyself from the land, *Young* ... From your family, *BB* ... Kinsfolk, *NAB.*

unto a land that I will shew thee: ... Direct you, *Fenton* ... that I will guide you to, *LIVB* ... go to a country, *REB.*

2. And I will make of thee a great nation, and I will bless thee, and make thy name great; and thou shalt be a blessing: ... I will prosper and enable your name; and you shall be a benefactor, *Fenton* ... become the father of a great nation, *LIVB* ... that your name may be a blessing, *Anchor* ... Make your name famous, *MLB* ... Make your name so great that it will be used for blessings, *Goodspeed, NEB.*

3. And I will bless them that bless thee, and curse him that curseth thee: ... them who are good to you will I give blessing; him who does you wrong will I put my curse, *BB* ... Upon him who insults you, I will put my curse, *Berkeley, MLB* ... Bless those who benefit you, and punish those who injure you, *Fenton* ... Those that curse you, I will execrate, *NEB* ... And him who is disesteeming thee I curse, *Young.*

and in thee shall all families of the earth be blessed: ... You will become a name of blessing, *BB* ... shall bless themselves all the communities on earth, *Anchor; NAB* ... All nations of mankind shall become benefited from you, *Fenton* ... shall all the families of the earth invoke blessings on one another, *Goodspeed* ... Families of the earth shall bless themselves, *RSV* ... All the families on earth will pray to be blessed as you are blessed, *NEB.*

4. So Abram departed, as the LORD had spoken unto him; and Lot went with him: and Abram was seventy and five years old when he departed out of Haran: ... Went away, *NCB* ... Set out, *NEB* ... goeth on, *Young* ... Abram is a son of five and seventy years, *Good News.*

---

ed families in those days, and because Terah was still the family head, Terah took the initiative and took his family toward the Land of Canaan. However, when Terah came to Haran (Hebrew *Charran*, "Caravan route" or "mountaineer," not the same name as Abram's brother Haran), on the Balikh River, he found a city that was another headquarters for the worship of the moon god, Sin. Terah decided to settle there, and stayed there until he died at the age of 205.

12:1. After Terah died, God confirmed His command to Abram to leave his country and his relatives (cf. Acts 7:4). The Hebrew for "had said" indicates sequence, and probably means "proceeded to say" or "kept saying." This was not a sharp command, but the urging of a gracious invitation and a call to separation, not only from his old life and the idolatry that had taken over the world as a whole, but also separation to the worship and service of the Lord (cf. 2 Cor. 6:17-18).

Although Abram was moving toward Canaan, as Terah had started out doing, God did not identify it as the promised land at this point. Abram had to move trusting God daily for guidance (Heb. 11:8). But the fact God was going to show him "the land" is significant. The land is important in the covenant (solemn, binding agreement) God would make later with Abraham (his name at that point).

12:2-3. With the invitation God gave a threefold promise that involved personal blessings, national blessings, and universal blessings for all humankind. These blessings showed God still loved the world that had turned away from Him (John 3:16). The fulfillment would ultimately come through Jesus Christ (Acts 3:25; Gal. 3:8). God would also make Abram's descendants a great nation, not in a worldly sense (cf. Isa. 40:15,17), but as a special treasure to God, a holy nation (Exo. 19:5-6). The personal blessings for him would surely include spiritual blessings, and all God's blessings would magnify Abram's name, that is, make his reputation great. He would be famous.

God's purpose in this was to make it possible for Abram to be a blessing. In fact, the Hebrew phrase at the end of verse 2 is actually an imperative, a command. Abram had a responsibility to live in such a way that he would bless others. In fact, God purposed universal blessings to come in [by] Abraham to all the families of the earth, to all humankind. God wants His blessings to be a river that flows through us, not a dead sea that receives but never gives out. God's blessings bring His provision and power for our needs: physical, material, and above all, spiritual.

5.	4089.121	82	881, 8030	828	881, 4013	1158, 250
	cj, v Qal impf 3ms	pn	do, pn	n fs, ps 3ms	cj, do, pn	*n ms*, n ms, ps 3ms
	וַיִּקַּח	אַבְרָם	אֶת־שָׂרַי	אִשְׁתּוֹ	וְאֶת־לוֹט	בֶּן־אָחִיו
	wayyiqqach	'avrām	'eth-sāray	'ishtô	w^{e}'eth-lôṯ	ben-'āchîw
	and he took	Abram	Sarai	his wife	and Lot	the son of his brother

881, 3725, 7688	866	7697.116	881, 5497	866, 6449.116	904, 2115
cj, do, *adj*, n ms, ps 3mp	rel part	v Qal pf 3cp	cj, do, art, n fs	rel part, v Qal pf 3cp	prep, pn
וְאֶת־כָּל־רְכוּשָׁם	אֲשֶׁר	רָכָשׁוּ	וְאֶת־הַנֶּפֶשׁ	אֲשֶׁר־עָשׂוּ	בְחָרָן
w^{e}'eth-kol-r^{e}khûshām	'ăsher	rākhāshû	w^{e}'eth-hannephesh	'ăsher-'āsû	b^{e}chārān
and all their property	which	they gathered	and the people	which they acquired	in Haran

3428.126	3937, 2050.141	800	3791	971.126	800	3791
cj, v Qal impf 3mp	prep, v Qal inf con	*n fs*	pn	cj, v Qal impf 3mp	*n fs*	pn
וַיֵּצְאוּ	לָלֶכֶת	אַרְצָה	כְּנַעַן	וַיָּבֹאוּ	אַרְצָה	כְּנָעַן
wayyēts'û	lālekheth	'artsāh	k^{e}na'an	wayyābō'û	'artsāh	k^{e}nā'an
and they went out	to go	to the land of	Canaan	and they went	to the land of	Canaan

6.	5882.121	82	904, 800	5912	4887	8328	5912
	cj, v Qal impf 3ms	pn	prep, art, n fs	adv	*n ms*	pn	adv
	וַיַּעֲבֹר	אַבְרָם	בָּאָרֶץ	עַד	מְקוֹם	שְׁכֶם	עַד
	wayya'ăvōr	'avrām	bā'ārets	'adh	m^{e}qôm	sh^{e}khem	'adh
	and he passed through	Abram	in the land	until	the place of	Shechem	until

440	4310B	3793	226	904, 800	7.	7495.221	3176
n fs	pn	cj, art, pn	adv	prep, art, n fs		cj, v Niphal impf 3ms	pn
אֵלוֹן	מוֹרֶה	וְהַכְּנַעֲנִי	אָז	בָּאָרֶץ		וַיֵּרָא	יְהוָה
'ēlôn	môreh	w^{e}hakk^{e}na'ănî	'āz	bā'ārets		wayyērā'	y^{e}hwāh
the great tree of	Moreh	and the Canaanites	then	in the land		and He appeared	Yahweh

420, 82	569.121	3937, 2320	5598.125	881, 800	2148	1161.121
prep, pn	cj, v Qal impf 3ms	prep, n ms, ps 2ms	v Qal impf 1cs	do, art, n fs	art, dem pron	cj, v Qal impf 3ms
אֶל־אַבְרָם	וַיֹּאמֶר	לְזַרְעֲךָ	אֶתֵּן	אֶת־הָאָרֶץ	הַזֹּאת	וַיִּבֶן
'el-'avrām	wayyō'mer	l^{e}zar'ăkhā	'ettēn	'eth-hā'ārets	hazzō'th	wayyiven
to Abram	and He said	to your seed	I will give	the land	the this	and he built

8427	4326	3937, 3176	7495.255	420	8.	6514.521	4623, 8427
adv	n ms	prep, pn	v Niphal ptc ms	prep, ps 3ms		cj, v Hiphil impf 3ms	prep, adv
שָׁם	מִזְבֵּחַ	לַיהוָה	הַנִּרְאֶה	אֵלָיו		וַיַּעְתֵּק	מִשָּׁם
shām	mizbēach	lâhwāh	hannir'eh	'ēlâv		wayya'ăttēq	mishshām
there	altar	to Yahweh	the One seen	by him		and he moved on	from there

5. And Abram took Sarai his wife, and Lot his brother's son: ... Nephew, *Goodspeed.*

and all their substance that they had gathered, and the souls that they had gotten in Haran: ... Possessions that they had acquired and all the persons they had obtained, *NAB* ... all their goods and the servants which they had got, *BB* ... Property which he possessed, and the slaves which he had acquired, *Fenton* ... Property that they had accumulated, *Goodspeed* ... Dependents whom they had acquired, *NEB.*

and they went forth to go into the land of Canaan; and into the land of Canaan they came: ... Moved out to migrate, *MLB* ... went out, *Darby* ... started on their journey to Canaan, *NEB* ... departed, *NKJV* ... when they arrived there, *REB* ... when they had come to the land of Canaan, *NRSV.*

6. And Abram passed through the land unto the place of Sichem: ... Traveled as far as the site of Shechem, *Anchor* ... kept moving as far as the Shechem locality, *Berkeley* ... village of Shekhem, *Fenton* ... the sanctuary of Shechem, *Goodspeed, REB* ... sacred place at Shechem, *NCB.*

unto the plain of Moreh. And the Canaanite was then in the land: ... oak of Moreh, *ASV* ... Terebinth tree of Moreh, *REB* ... holy tree of Moreh, *BB* ... as far as Alon-Moreh, *Fenton* ... plain of Moreh, *Geneva.*

7. And the LORD appeared unto Abram, and said, Unto thy seed will I give this land: and there builded he an altar unto the LORD, who appeared unto him: ... I will give this land to your offspring, *Anchor* ... To your descendants, *NASB* ... to commemorate Jehovah's visit, *LIVB* ... who had let himself be seen by him, *BB*.

8. And he removed from thence unto a mountain on the east of Bethel, and pitched his tent, having Bethel on the west, and Hai on the east: ... country, *NRSV* ... to the hills, *Fenton* ... Mountain region, *NCB* ... went on toward the hills, *NIV* ... stretcheth out the tent, *Young*.

and there he builded an altar unto the LORD, and called upon the name of the LORD: ... gave worship to the name of the Lord, *BB* ... and invoked the Lord by name, *NRSV* ... Preacheth in the name of Jehovah, *Young* ... prayed to him, *LIVB*.

9. And Abram journeyed, going on still toward the south: ... Traveled

---

God recognized, however, not everyone would be willing to accept the blessings and promises coming through Abram. Many (the participle is plural) would put their faith in God, do the works of Abraham, and keep blessing (honoring and thanking) Abraham because of the promise. Thus, God would bless them. But a few (the participle is singular) would despise the promise and thus keep reviling, mocking, or making light of Abram, treating him (and his God) with contempt. God would curse them by putting them under His divine judgment. Note that this matter of blessing and cursing has to do with the Abraham and the promise. It does not mean we must approve everything the Jews do today. The Old Testament prophets did not do that in their day.

The blessing for all the families of the earth is central to the promise. It refers to God's plan to reverse the curse of Genesis 3 and all the effects of the fall. It is God's salvation promise, the gospel "preached before the gospel" to Abraham (Gal. 3:8). This promise of divine salvation-blessing is repeated five times in the Book of Genesis and becomes an important theme found throughout the entire Bible (Gen. 18:18; 22:18; 26:4; 28:14). It assures us God has a plan He will carry out to its ultimate consummation. Ultimately, the promise looks ahead to Jesus, for it is only through Him that we become Abraham's seed and heirs of the promise (Gal. 3:29; Eph. 2:13,19). Sometimes this means we too must leave all as Abraham did, but we do not lose when we do (Luke 18:29-30).

12:4-5. Probably about 2000 B.C., at the age of 75, Abram left with Sarai and Lot on a more than 300 mile journey to the land of Canaan with all the possessions they had acquired and with the "souls," that is, the people--their servants and slaves. Since Abram had 318 trained men with him, born in his household (14:14), there may have been about one thousand people in his entourage. As Abram journeyed on, he often dealt with kings and may have been considered a petty king himself. The mention of gold, silver, and spices in later chapters indicates he was at least a merchant prince, needing the protection of the trained and armed men with him. Archaeologists have discovered tablets at Ebla in northern Syria showing that a wealthy, educated, commercial society already existed in that part of the world before Abraham's time.

12:6-7. Abram's first stop was in the locality of Shechem about 35 miles north of Jerusalem. They camped by a great terebinth tree known as the teacher's tree (Moreh), since a prominent teacher probably once gathered his students under its shade. The Bible then draws attention to the fact that the Canaanites were in the land, showing that the land was occupied. The Canaanites had been living there for over one thousand years. Archaeologists have discovered that there were laws against foreigners buying property. Regarding this land, however, the LORD honored Abram's faith, appeared to him, and declared that He would give this land to Abram's descendants. It was not really the Canaanites' land, it was God's land, and He had the right to give it to whomever He willed. They were also a wicked, immoral people headed for judgment. Yet, it would take continued faith for Abram to keep obeying God and waiting. As long as Abram lived, the Canaanites were still in the land. He could have returned to Haran or to Ur (Heb. 11:13,15). Instead he expressed his faith by building an altar to the LORD signifying his dedication to God's will. Abram's faith kept pressing on in God, so that God was not ashamed to become known as the God of Abraham (Heb. 11:16).

12:8-9. Abram's next stop was in the central hill country between Bethel ("God's House," though Abram did not call it that, see Gen. 28:19) and Ai ("the heap of ruins," a village among some ruins) about ten miles north of Jerusalem. Again, he

2098	4623, 7208	3937, 1044	5371.121	164	1044	4623, 3328
art, n ms	prep, n ms	prep, pn	cj, v Qal impf 3ms	n ms, ps 3ms	pn	prep, n ms
הָהָרָה	מִקֶּדֶם	לְבֵית־אֵל	וַיֵּט	אָהֳלֹה	בֵּית־אֵל	מִיָּם
hāhārāh	miqqedhem	l^{e}vêth-'ēl	wayyēt̲	'āhlōh	bêth-'ēl	miyyām
to the mountain	of the east	to Bethel	and he spread out	his tent	Bethel	seaward

6069	4623, 7208	1161.121, 8427	4326	3937, 3176	7410.121	904, 8428
cj, art, pn	prep, n ms	cj, v Qal impf 3ms, adv	n ms	prep, pn	cj, v Qal impf 3ms	prep, *n ms*
וְהָעַי	מִקֶּדֶם	וַיִּבֶן־שָׁם	מִזְבֵּחַ	לַיהוָה	וַיִּקְרָא	בְּשֵׁם
w^{e}hā'â	miqqedhem	wayyiven-shām	mizbēach	lâhwāh	wayyiqōrā'	b^{e}shēm
and the Ai	of the east	and he built there	altar	to Yahweh	and he called	on the name of

3176		5450.121	82	2050.142	5450.142	5221
pn	**9.**	cj, v Qal impf 3ms	pn	v Qal inf abs	cj, v Qal inf abs	art, pn
יְהוָה		וַיִּסַּע	אַבְרָם	הָלוֹךְ	וְנָסוֹעַ	הַנֶּגְבָּה
y^{e}hwāh		wayyissa'	'avrām	hālôkh	w^{e}nāsôa'	hanneghbāh
Yahweh		and he pulled out	Abram	going	and pulling out	to the Negeb

	2030.121	7743	904, 800	3495.121	82	4875	3937, 1513.141
10.	cj, v Qal impf 3ms	n ms	prep, art, n fs	cj, v Qal impf 3ms	pn	pn	prep, v Qal inf con
	וַיְהִי	רָעָב	בָּאָרֶץ	וַיֵּרֶד	אַבְרָם	מִצְרַיְמָה	לָגוּר
	wayhî	rā'āv	bā'ārets	wayyēredh	'avrām	mitsraymāh	lāghûr
	and it was	famine	in the land	and he went down	Abram	to Egypt	to sojourn

8427	3706, 3633	7743	904, 800		2030.121	3626, 866
adv	prep, adj	art, n ms	prep, art, n fs	**11.**	cj, v Qal impf 3ms	prep, rel part
שָׁם	כִּי־כָבֵד	הָרָעָב	בָּאָרֶץ		וַיְהִי	כַּאֲשֶׁר
shām	kî-khāvēdh	hārā'āv	bā'ārets		wayhî	ka'ăsher
there	because heavy	the famine	in the land		and it was	according to that

7414.511	3937, 971.141	4875	569.121	420, 8030	828	2079, 5167
v Hiphil pf 3ms	prep, v Qal inf con	pn	cj, v Qal impf 3ms	prep, pn	n fs, ps 3ms	intrj, ptc
הִקְרִיב	לָבוֹא	מִצְרָיְמָה	וַיֹּאמֶר	אֶל־שָׂרַי	אִשְׁתּוֹ	הִנֵּה־נָא
hiqōrîv	lāvô'	mitsrāymāh	wayyō'mer	'el-sāray	'ishtô	hinnēh-nā'
he brought near	to go	to Egypt	and he said	to Sarai	his wife	behold please

3156.115	3706	828	3413, 4920	879		2030.111
v Qal pf 1cs	cj	n fs	*adj*, n ms	pers pron	**12.**	cj, v Qal pf 3ms
יָדַעְתִּי	כִּי	אִשָּׁה	יְפַת־מַרְאֶה	אָתְּ		וְהָיָה
yādha'ättî	kî	'ishshāh	y^{e}phath-mar'eh	'ätt		w^{e}hāyāh
I know	that	woman	beautiful of appearance	you		and it will be

3706, 7495.126	881	4875	569.116	828	2148
cj, v Qal impf 3mp	do, ps 2fs	art, pn	cj, v Qal pf 3cp	n fs, ps 3ms	dem pron
כִּי־יִרְאוּ	אֹתָךְ	הַמִּצְרִים	וְאָמְרוּ	אִשְׁתּוֹ	זֹאת
kî-yir'û	'ōthākh	hammitsrîm	w^{e}'āmrû	'ishtô	zō'th
that they will see	you	the Egyptians	and they will say	his wife	this

2103.116	881	881	2513.316		569.132, 5167	269
cj, v Qal pf 3cp	do, ps 1cs	cj, do, ps 2fs	v Piel pf 3cp	**13.**	v Qal impv 2fs, ptc	n fs, ps 1cs
וְהָרְגוּ	אֹתִי	וְאֹתָךְ	יְחַיּוּ		אִמְרִי־נָא	אֲחֹתִי
w^{e}hārghû	'ōthî	w^{e}'ōthākh	y^{e}chayyû		'imrî-nā'	'ăchōthî
and they will kill	me	and you	they will keep alive		say please	my sister

879	3937, 4775	3296.121, 3937	904, 5877	2513.112	5497
pers pron	prep, prep	v Qal impf 3ms, prep, ps 1cs	prep, prep, 2fs	cj, v Qal pf 3fs	n fs, ps 1cs
אָתְּ	לְמַעַן	יִיטַב־לִי	בַּעֲבוּרֵךְ	וְחָיְתָה	נַפְשִׁי
'ätt	l^{e}ma'an	yiyt̲av-lî	ba'ăvûrēkh	w^{e}chāy^{e}thāh	naphshî
you	so that	it will go well for me	on account of you	and it will live	my life

904, 1600 prep, n ms, ps 2fs בִּגְלָלֵךְ bighlālēkh on account of you	**14.**	2030.121 cj, v Qal impf 3ms וַיְהִי wayhî and it was	3626, 971.141 prep, v Qal inf con כְּבוֹא kᵉvô' as going	82 pn אַבְרָם 'avrām Abram	4875 pn מִצְרָיְמָה mitsrāymāh to Egypt	7495.126 cj, v Qal impf 3mp וַיִּרְאוּ wayyir'û and they saw

on, continuing toward the southland, *MLB* ... moved onward, *Darby* ... marched on his journey, and proceeded to the south, *Fenton* ... to the Negeb, *NCB* ... Journeyed by stages towards the Negeb, *NEB*.

10. And there was a famine in the land: ... famine was sore in the land, *RSV* ... famine in the land was severe, *NCB* ... famine visited the country, *Berkeley* ... there was little food to be had in the land, *BB* ... stricken by a famine, *REB*.

and Abram went down into Egypt to sojourn there; for the famine was grievous in the land: ... reside there, *Goodspeed* ... he lived as a stranger, *NCB* ... live there for a while, *NIV* ... to reside there as an alien, *NRSV*.

11. And it came to pass, when he was come near to enter into Egypt: ... as he was approaching Egypt, *Fenton* ... went down into Egypt, *BB* ... on the point of entering Egypt, *Goodspeed*.

that he said unto Sarai his wife, Behold now, I know that thou art a fair woman to look upon: ... what a beautiful woman you are, *Anchor* ... you are a good-looking woman, *Berkeley* ... beautiful woman to look upon, *KJVII* ... beautiful to behold, *NCB* ... beautiful countenance, *NKJV* ... beautiful in appearance, *Young*.

12. Therefore it shall come to pass, when the Egyptians shall see thee, that they shall say, This is his wife: ... I am certain that when the men of Egypt see you, *BB* ... I know that when the Egyptians see you and think, she is his wife, *REB* ... They will assume that you are my wife, *Good News*.

and they will kill me, but they will save thee alive: ... they will slay me, *Darby* ... Put me to death and keep you, *BB* ... they may murder me, *Fenton* ... but let you live, *Anchor* ... but will spare you, *MLB*.

13. Say, I pray thee, thou art my sister: that it may be well with me for thy sake; and my soul shall live because of thee: ... please, *Anchor* ... I beg you, *KJVII* ... favored on your account, *Berkeley* ... my life will be kept safe on your account, *BB* ... show respect to me, and my life may be saved by means of you, *Fenton* ... my life may be preserved, *Geneva*.

14. And it came to pass, that, when Abram was come into Egypt, the Egyptians beheld the woman that she was very fair: ... how very beautiful the woman was, *Anchor* ... how rarely beautiful a woman she was, *Berkeley* ... everyone spoke of her beauty, *LIVB*.

built an altar and called on the name of the LORD. "Called" often implies public worship, and it is evident that Abram's servants joined in the worship (cf. Gen. 24:12, 26-27). It was also a witness to Abram's Canaanite neighbors and let them know he was a friend of God (see 2 Chr. 20:6-7; Isa. 41:7-8; James 2:23).

Abram, as a tent dweller and a merchant, was always on the move. Each time he pulled up stakes, he went further south toward the Negev, the dry country south of Hebron.

12:10. Because of a severe famine Abram traveled to Egypt to live temporarily. He had a large entourage to feed, thus, staying in Canaan would mean they could starve. But he was moved by fear, not faith.

12:11-13. Egyptian custom would not allow a foreign prince and his entourage to live in Egypt without making a treaty. The custom also was for the foreign prince to give an acceptable daughter or a sister into the Pharaoh's harem to seal the treaty and guarantee the prince's good behavior while in Egypt. If no treaty was made, crossing the border into Egypt would be considered an invasion, an act of war.

Still moved by fear, Abram told Sarai to say she was his sister (see Gen. 20:11-12). Even at her age of 65, she was still very beautiful (she lived to be 137), and would be acceptable to Pharaoh. Abram reasoned if he didn't make a treaty they would attack and kill him, and take Sarai into Pharaoh's harem as a trophy of war--as was the custom. If he made the treaty she would also go into Pharaoh's harem, but at least he would stay alive and be able to take care of all those under him. He also expected he would be treated well because of her beauty.

4875 art, pn הַמִּצְרִים hammitsrîm the Egyptians	881, 828 do, art, n fs אֶת־הָאִשָּׁה 'eth-hā'ishshāh the woman	3706, 3414 cj, adj כִּי־יָפָה kî-yāphāh that beautiful	2000 pers pron הִוא hiw' she	4108 adv מְאֹד me'ōdh very	**15.**	7495.126 cj, v Qal impf 3mp וַיִּרְאוּ wayyir'û and they saw	881 do, ps 3fs אֹתָהּ 'ōthāhh her

8015 *n mp* שָׂרֵי sārê the officials of	6799 pn פַרְעֹה phar'ōh Pharaoh	2054.326 cj, v Piel impf 3mp וַיְהַלְלוּ wayhallû and they praised	881 do, ps 3fs אֹתָהּ 'ōthāhh her	420, 6799 prep, pn אֶל־פַּרְעֹה 'el-par'ōh to Pharaoh	4089.422 cj, v Pual impf 3fs וַתֻּקַּח wattuqqach and she was taken	828 art, n fs הָאִשָּׁה hā'ishshāh the woman

1041 *n ms* בֵּית bêth to the house of	6799 pn פַּרְעֹה par'ōh Pharaoh	**16.**	3937, 82 cj, prep, pn וּלְאַבְרָם ûlă'avrām and for Abram	3296.511 v Hiphil pf 3ms הֵיטִיב hêṭîv he made it go well	904, 5877 prep, prep, ps 3fs בַּעֲבוּרָהּ ba'ăvûrāhh on account of her

2030.121, 3937 cj, v Qal impf 3ms, prep, ps 3ms וַיְהִי־לוֹ wayhî-lô and it was to him	6887, 1267 n fs, cj, n ms צֹאן־וּבָקָר tsō'n-ûvāqār sheep and cattle	2645 cj, n mp וַחֲמֹרִים wachmōrîm and male donkeys	5860 cj, n mp וַעֲבָדִים wa'ăvādhîm and male servants	8569 cj, n fp וּשְׁפָחֹת ûshphāchōth and female slaves

888 cj, n fp וַאֲתֹנֹת wa'āthōnōth and female donkeys	1622 cj, n mp וּגְמַלִּים ûghemallîm and camels	**17.**	5236.321 cj, v Piel impf 3ms וַיְנַגַּע waynagga' but He afflicted	3176 pn יְהוָה yehwāh Yahweh	881, 6799 do, pn אֶת־פַּרְעֹה 'eth-par'ōh Pharaoh	5237 n mp נְגָעִים neghā'îm plagues

1448 adj גְּדֹלִים gedhōlîm great	881, 1041 cj, do, n ms, ps 3ms וְאֶת־בֵּיתוֹ we'eth-bêthô and his house	6142, 1745 prep, *n ms* עַל־דְּבַר 'al-devar over the matter of	8030 pn שָׂרַי sāray Sarai	828 *n fs* אֵשֶׁת 'ēsheth the wife of	82 pn אַבְרָם 'avrām Abram	**18.**	7410.121 cj, v Qal impf 3ms וַיִּקְרָא wayyiqŏrā' and he called	6799 pn פַרְעֹה phar'ōh Pharaoh

3937, 82 prep, pn לְאַבְרָם le'avrām to Abram	569.121 cj, v Qal impf 3ms וַיֹּאמֶר wayyō'mer and he said	4242, 2148 intrg part, dem pron מַה־זֹּאת mah-zō'th what this	6449.113 v Qal pf 2ms עָשִׂיתָ 'āsîthā you did	3937 prep, ps 1cs לִּי lî to me	4066 intrg לָמָּה lāmmāh why	3940, 5222.513 neg part, v Hiphil impf 2ms לֹא־הִגַּדְתָּ lō'-higgadhtā not you told me

3937 prep, ps 1cs לִּי lî to me	3706 cj כִּי kî that	828 n fs, ps 2ms אִשְׁתְּךָ 'ishtekhā your wife	2000 pers pron הִוא hiw' she	**19.**	4066 intrg לָמָה lāmāh why	569.113 v Qal pf 2ms אָמַרְתָּ 'āmartā you said	269 n fs, ps 1cs אֲחֹתִי 'ăchōthî my sister	2000 pers pron הִוא hiw' she

4089.125 cj, v Qal impf 1cs וָאֶקַּח wā'eqqach and I took	881 do, ps 3fs אֹתָהּ 'ōthāhh her	3937 prep, ps 1cs לִי lî for myself	3937, 828 prep, n fs לְאִשָּׁה le'ishshāh for wife	6498 cj, adv וְעַתָּה we'attāh and now	2079 intrj הִנֵּה hinnēh behold	828 n fs, ps 2ms אִשְׁתְּךָ 'ishtekhā your wife	4089.131 v Qal impv 2ms קַח qach take

2050.131 cj, v Qal impv 2ms וָלֵךְ wālēkh and go	**20.**	6943 cj, v Piel impf 3ms וַיְצַו waytsaw and he commanded	6142 prep, ps 3ms עָלָיו 'ālâv concerning him	6799 pn פַּרְעֹה par'ōh Pharaoh	596 n mp אֲנָשִׁים 'ănāshîm men	8365.316 cj, v Piel impf 3mp וַיְשַׁלְּחוּ wayshallechû and they sent

881 do, ps 3ms אֹתוֹ 'ōthô him	881, 828 cj, do, n fs, ps 3ms וְאֶת־אִשְׁתּוֹ we'eth-'ishtô and his wife	881, 3725, 866, 3937 cj, do, *adj*, rel part, prep, ps 3ms וְאֶת־כָּל־אֲשֶׁר־לוֹ we'eth-kol-'ăsher-lô and all which to him	**13:1**	6148.121 cj, v Qal impf 3ms וַיַּעַל wayya'al and he went up	82 pn אַבְרָם 'avrām Abram

4623, 4875 prep, pn מִמִּצְרַיִם mimmitsrayim from Egypt	2000 pers pron הוּא hû' he	828 cj, n fs, ps 3ms וְאִשְׁתּוֹ we'ishtô and his wife	3725, 866, 3937 cj, *adj*, rel part, prep, ps 3ms וְכָל־אֲשֶׁר־לוֹ wekhāl-'ăsher-lô and all which to him	4013 cj, pn וְלוֹט welôṭ and Lot	6196 prep, ps 3ms עִמּוֹ 'immô with him	5221 art, pn הַנֶּגְבָּה hanneghbāh to the Negeb

15. The princes also of Pharaoh saw her: ... nobles, *MLB* ... great men, *BB* ... officials, *NASB.*

and commended her before Pharaoh: ... said words in praise of her, *BB* ... sung her praises to Pharaoh, *REB, Fenton* ... praised her so highly, *Goodspeed* ... told the king how beautiful she was, *Good News.*

and the woman was taken into Pharaoh's house: ... household, *Goodspeed* ... palace, *MLB* ... into his harem, *LIVB.*

16. And he entreated Abram well for her sake: ... treated Abram generously, *Berkeley* ... It went very well with Abram, *NAB* ... He was good to Abram, *BB* ... he favored Abram, *Fenton*

and he had sheep, and oxen, and he asses, and menservants, and maidservants, and she asses, and camels: ... and he came to own male and female slaves, *Anchor* ... bondmen and bondwomen, *Darby* ... and he presented him with, *Fenton* ... came to possess, *NEB.*

17. And the LORD plagued Pharaoh and his house with great plagues because of Sarai Abram's wife: ... afflicted Pharaoh with extraordinary plagues, *Anchor* ... struck Pharaoh with serious diseases, *Goodspeed* ... sent great troubles, *BB*...severe plagues, *NAB* ... grave diseases, *NEB.*

18. And Pharaoh called Abram, and said, What is this that thou hast done unto me: ... see what you have done to me, *Anchor* ... what a way for you to treat me, *Goodspeed* ... how could you do this, *NCB.*

why didst thou not tell me that she was thy wife: ... why did you not inform me, *Fenton.*

19. Why saidst thou, She is my sister? so I might have taken her to me to wife: ... I took her to be my wife, *NASB* ... for I might have secured her as a wife for myself, *Fenton* ... and let me marry her, *NCB* ... I was about to take her to me as wife, *KJVII.*

now therefore behold thy wife, take her, and go thy way: ... take her and be gone, *Anchor* ... take her and get out, *Berkeley.*

20. And Pharaoh commanded his men concerning him: ... gave men

12:14-16. It happened as Abram said it would. Sarai was taken into Pharaoh's palace, and Abram was treated well on account of her. Abram's business prospered wonderfully, and he acquired additional sheep and cattle, donkeys, servants (slaves), and camels.

The camels were a rare addition. Camels were not available in large numbers in those days, though camel skeletons have been found in the Near East coming from before Abram's time. They apparently were not used in warfare until later (cf. Judges 6:5), but were used by wealthy traders like Abram.

12:17-18. God had His purpose for Abram and Sarai, and though they were not cooperating at the moment, God did not give up on them. He struck Pharaoh and his household with severe plagues. Somehow He let Pharaoh know the reason for these sicknesses. So Pharaoh went to Abram with a strong rebuke. Because Sarai was his half-sister, Abram's referring to her as his "sister" was not a simply a half-lie. It was a whole lie, since Abram intended to deceive.

Pharaoh took her to be his wife (one of his wives). This undoubtedly refers to a betrothal, so that no marriage was yet consummated. With a sharp command to take Sarai and go, Pharaoh then commanded Abram to get out of the country with everything and everyone belonging to him.

12:19-20. Pharaoh did not treat Abram harshly, however. He instructed his men to escort him, probably as a bodyguard, as far as the border. The plagues of verse 17 probably made him recognize that Abram's God is powerful and that God could bring further judgment on him (see Ps. 105:14-15).

2.	82	3633	4108	904, 4898	904, 3826B	904, 2174
	cj, pn	adj	adv	prep, art, n ms	prep, art, n ms	cj, prep, art, n ms
	וְאַבְרָם	כָּבֵד	מְאֹד	בַּמִּקְנֶה	בַּכֶּסֶף	וּבַזָּהָב
	we'avrām	kāvēdh	me'ōdh	bammiqōneh	bakkeseph	ûvazzāhāv
	and Abram	heavy	very	with the herds	with the silver	and with the gold

3.	2050.121	3937, 4702	4623, 5221	5912, 1044	5912, 4887	866, 2030.111
	cj, v Qal impf 3ms	prep, n mp, ps 3ms	prep, pn	cj, prep, pn	prep, art, n ms	rel part, v Qal pf 3ms
	וַיֵּלֶךְ	לְמַסָּעָיו	מִנֶּגֶב	וְעַד־בֵּית־אֵל	עַד־הַמָּקוֹם	אֲשֶׁר־הָיָה
	wayyēlekh	lemassā'âv	minneghev	we'adh-bêth-'ēl	'adh-hammāqôm	'ăsher-hāyâh
	and he went	to his pullings up	from Negeb	and unto Bethel	unto the place	that he was

8427	164	904, 8795	1033	1044	1033	6069	4.	420, 4887
adv	n ms, ps 3ms	prep, art, n fs	prep	pn	cj, prep	art, pn		prep, *n ms*
שָׁם	אָהֳלֹה	בַּתְּחִלָּה	בֵּין	בֵּית־אֵל	וּבֵין	הָעָי		אֶל־מְקוֹם
shām	'āhlōh	battechillāh	bên	bêth-'ēl	ûvên	hā'āy		'el-meqôm
there	his tent	in the beginning	between	Bethel	and between	the Ai		to the place of

4326	866, 6449.111	8427	904, 7518	7410.121	8427	82	904, 8428
art, n ms	rel part, v Qal pf 3ms	adv	prep, art, adj	cj, v Qal impf 3ms	adv	pn	prep, *n ms*
הַמִּזְבֵּחַ	אֲשֶׁר־עָשָׂה	שָׁם	בָּרִאשֹׁנָה	וַיִּקְרָא	שָׁם	אַבְרָם	בְּשֵׁם
hammizbēach	'ăsher-'āsāh	shām	bāri'shōnāh	wayyiqrā'	shām	'avrām	beshēm
the altar	which he made	there	at the first	and he called	there	Abram	on the name of

3176	5.	1613, 3937, 4013	2050.151	882, 82	2030.111	6887, 1267
pn		cj, cj, prep, pn	art, v Qal act ptc ms	do, prep	v Qal pf 3ms	n fs, cj, n ms
יְהוָה		וְגַם־לְלוֹט	הַהֹלֵךְ	אֶת־אַבְרָם	הָיָה	צֹאן־וּבָקָר
yehwāh		wegham-lelôt	hahōlēkh	'eth-'avrām	hāyâh	tsō'n-ûvāqār
Yahweh		and also to Lot	the one going	with Abram	it was	sheep and cattle

164	6.	3940, 5558.111	881	800	3937, 3553.141	3267
cj, n mp		cj, neg part, v Qal pf 3ms	do, ps 3mp	art, n fs	prep, v Qal inf con	adv
וְאֹהָלִים		וְלֹא־נָשָׂא	אֹתָם	הָאָרֶץ	לָשֶׁבֶת	יַחְדָּו
we'ōhālîm		welō'-nāsâ'	'ōthām	hā'ārets	lāsheveth	yachdāw
and tents		and it could not support	them	the land	for dwelling	together

3706, 2030.111	7688	7521	3940	3310.116	3937, 3553.141	3267
cj, v Qal pf 3ms	n ms, ps 3mp	adj	cj, neg part	v Qal pf 3cp	prep, v Qal inf con	adv
כִּי־הָיָה	רְכוּשָׁם	רָב	וְלֹא	יָכְלוּ	לָשֶׁבֶת	יַחְדָּו
kî-hāyâh	rekhûshām	rāv	welō'	yākehlû	lāsheveth	yachdāw
because it was	their property	much	and not	they were able	to dwell	together

7.	2030.121, 7663	1033	7749.152	4898, 82	1033	7749.152
	cj, v Qal impf 3ms, n ms	prep	*v Qal act ptc mp*	*n ms*, pn	cj, prep	*v Qal act ptc mp*
	וַיְהִי־רִיב	בֵּין	רֹעֵי	מִקְנֵה־אַבְרָם	וּבֵין	רֹעֵי
	wayhî-rîv	bên	rō'ê	miqōnēh-'avrām	ûvên	rō'ê
	and it was dispute	between	herdsmen of	herds of Abram	and between	herdsmen of

4898, 4013	3793	6773	226	3553.151	904, 800
n ms, pn	cj, art, pn	cj, art, pn	adv	v Qal act ptc ms	prep, art, n fs
מִקְנֵה־לוֹט	וְהַכְּנַעֲנִי	וְהַפְּרִזִּי	אָז	יֹשֵׁב	בָּאָרֶץ
miqōnēh-lôt	wehakkena'ănî	wehapperizzî	'āz	yōshēv	bā'ārets
herds of Lot	and the Canaanites	and the Perizzites	then	dwelling	in the land

8.	569.121	82	420, 4013	414, 5167	2030.122	4970	1033
	cj, v Qal impf 3ms	pn	prep, pn	neg part, part	v Qal impf 3fs	n fs	prep, ps 1cs
	וַיֹּאמֶר	אַבְרָם	אֶל־לוֹט	אַל־נָא	תְהִי	מְרִיבָה	בֵּינִי
	wayyō'mer	'avrām	'el-lôt	'al-nā'	thehî	merîvāh	bênî
	and he said	Abram	to Lot	not please	it will be	strife	between me

charge concerning him, *Young* ... ordered an escort for him, *Goodspeed* ... gave orders to his men, *NEB* ... under armed escort, *LIVB.*

and they sent him away, and his wife, and all that he had: ... brought him on the way, *ASV* ... conveyed him forth, *Geneva.*

13:1. And Abram went up out of Egypt, he, and his wife, and all that he had, and Lot with him, into the south: ... went up to the Negeb with all his possessions, *Anchor* ... Lot accompanied him to southern pastures, *Fenton* ... traveled north into the Negeb, *LIVB.*

2. And Abram was very rich in cattle, in silver, and in gold: ... extremely rich in livestock, in silver, and in gold, *MLB* ... had great wealth, *BB* ... Abram had become very wealthy, *NIV* ... Abram is exceedingly wealthy, *Young.*

3. And he went on his journeys from the south even to Bethel: ... from the Negeb he trekked by stages, *Berkeley* ... traveling on from the south, *BB* ... marched from the south, *Fenton* ... journeyed by stages to Bethel, *REB* ... he went from place to place, *NIV* ... then they continued northward, *LIVB.*

unto the place where his tent had been at the beginning, between Bethel and Hai: ... where his tent had been before, *BB* ... had at first been pitched, *Fenton* ... had formerly stood, *NAB* ... had been at the commencement, *Young.*

4. Unto the place of the altar, which he had made there at the first: ... the site of the altar, *Goodspeed* ... on the first occasion, *NEB* ... previously set up an altar, *REB.*

and there Abram called on the name of the LORD: ... gave worship to the name of the Lord, *BB* ... and there he invoked the Lord by name, *REB* ... preach in the name of Jehovah, *Young* ... there he again worshiped the Lord, *LIVB.*

5. And Lot also, which went with Abram, had flocks, and herds, and tents: ... possessed sheep, cattle, and camp-followers, *Fenton* ... who was moving about with Abram, *NIV* ... and many servants, *LIVB.*

6. And the land was not able to bear them, that they might dwell together: ... not able to support them, *NAB* ... land was not wide enough for the two of them, *BB* ... the land could not sustain them, *NASB* ... they could not settle in the same district, *REB* ... hath not suffered them to dwell together, *Young* ... too many animals for the available pasture, *LIVB.*

for their substance was great, so that they could not dwell together: ... their wealth was abundant, *Anchor* ... possessions so increased, *MLB* ... flocks were so great, *Fenton.*

7. And there was a strife between the herdmen of Abram's cattle and the herdmen of Lot's cattle: and the Canaanite and the Perizzite dwelled then in the land: ... there were quarrels between, *NEB* ... trouble arose accordingly, *Goodspeed* ... conflict developed, *Berkeley* ... there was an argument, *BB* ... a dispute accordingly took place, *Fenton* ... fights broke out despite the danger they all feared from the tribes of Canaanites and Perizzites, *Anchor.*

8. And Abram said unto Lot, Let there be no strife, I pray thee, between me and thee, and between my herdmen and thy herdmen; for we be brethren: ... let there be no disputing, *MLB* ... no contention, *Darby* ... no argument, *BB* ... no quarrel, *NEB* ... close relatives such as we are must present a united front, *LIVB* ... for we are kindred, *NRSV* ... kinsmen, *Anchor, MLB.*

13:1-2. Now we learn that Lot had been with Abram in Egypt and was with him and Sarai as they moved northward through the dry Negev. Abram was now much richer than when he left for Egypt, and his entourage much larger.

13:2-4. From the Negev he moved by stages, pitching tents for a while, then pulling up stakes and moving on until he came to the place between Bethel and Ai where he had built an altar before (Gen. 12:8). He built no altars in Egypt, but now that he was back in the promised land, his faith rose, and he again called on the name of the LORD, publicly worshiping Him and glorifying his holy name.

13:5-7. Egypt had one bad effect. Both Lot and Abram so increased their flocks and herds, as well as the tents for all the people, that the land could not support them. All the best places in the land were already occupied by Canaanites and Perizzites ("villagers" who had no walled cities and may have been the remnants of a people who preceded the Canaanites in the land). Thus, Abram had a hard time finding enough pasture and water all in one place, with the result that the herdsmen or shepherds of Abram and Lot began to quarrel over what was available.

13:8-9. Abram recognized that the continual controversy between the herdsmen could bring contention between him and Lot. He did not want that to happen, for they were "brothers," that is, close relatives. But, since there was not enough for all, he kindly suggested that they separate, each going a different way. Parting company would make it eas-

1033	1033	7749.152	1033	7749.152	3706, 596
cj, prep, ps 2ms	cj, prep	v Qal act ptc mp, ps 1cs	cj, prep	v Qal act ptc mp, ps 2ms	cj, n mp
וּבֵינֶךָ	וּבֵין	רֹעַי	וּבֵין	רֹעֶיךָ	כִּי־אֲנָשִׁים
ûvênêkhā	ûvên	rō‘ay	ûvên	rō‘êkhā	kî-’ănāshîm
and between you	and between	my herdsmen	and between	your herdsmen	because men

250	601		3940	3725, 800	3937, 6686	6754.231	5167
n mp	pers pron	**9.**	intrg part, neg part	*adj*, art, n fs	prep, n mp, ps 2ms	v Niphal impv 2ms	part
אַחִים	אֲנָחְנוּ		הֲלֹא	כָּל־הָאָרֶץ	לְפָנֶיךָ	הִפָּרֶד	נָא
’achîm	’ānāchănû		hălō’	khol-hā’ārets	l^{e}phānêkhā	hippāredh	nā’
brothers	we		is not	all the land	before you	separate	please

4623, 6142	524, 7972	3340.525	524, 3332	7973.525
prep, prep	cj, art, n ms	cj, v Hiphil impf 1cs	cj, cj, art, n fs	cj, v Hiphil impf 1cs
מֵעָלָי	אִם־הַשְּׂמֹאל	וְאֵימִנָה	וְאִם־הַיָּמִין	וְאַשְׂמְאִילָה
mē‘ālāy	’im-hass^{e}mō’l	w^{e}’êmināh	w^{e}’im-hayyāmîn	w^{e}’asm^{e}’îlāh
from me	if the left	then I will go to the right	and if the right	then I will go to the left

	5558.121, 4013	881, 6084	7495.121	881, 3725, 3724	3497	3706	3725
10.	cj, v Qal impf 3ms, pn	do, n fd, ps 3ms	cj, v Qal impf 3ms	do, *adj*, *n fs*	art, pn	cj	adj, ps 3fs
	וַיִּשָּׂא־לוֹט	אֶת־עֵינָיו	וַיַּרְא	אֶת־כָּל־כִּכַּר	הַיַּרְדֵּן	כִּי	כֻלָּהּ
	wayyissā’-lôṯ	’eth-‘ênâv	wayyar^{e}’	’eth-kol-kikkar	hayyardēn	kî	khullāhh
	and lifted up Lot	his eyes	and he saw	all the circle of	the Jordan	that	all it

5126	3937, 6686	8271.141	3176	881, 5651	881, 6244	3626, 1629, 3176
n ms	prep, *n mp*	v Qal inf con	pn	do, pn	cj, do, pn	prep, *n ms*, pn
מַשְׁקֶה	לִפְנֵי	שַׁחֵת	יְהוָה	אֶת־סְדֹם	וְאֶת־עֲמֹרָה	כְּגַן־יְהוָה
mashqeh	liphnê	shachēth	y^{e}hwāh	’eth-s̱^{e}dhōm	w^{e}’eth-‘ămōrāh	k^{e}ghan-y^{e}hwāh
watered	before	destroying	Yahweh	Sodom	and Gomorrah	like the garden of Yahweh

3626, 800	4875	971.141	7097		1013.121, 3937	4013	881
prep, *n fs*	pn	v Qal inf con, ps 2ms	pn	**11.**	cj, v Qal impf 3ms, prep, ps 3ms	pn	do
כְּאֶרֶץ	מִצְרַיִם	בֹּאֲכָה	צֹעַר		וַיִּבְחַר־לוֹ	לוֹט	אֵת
k^{e}’erets	mitsrayim	bō’ăkhāh	tsō‘ar		wayyivchar-lô	lôṯ	’ēth
like the land of	Egypt	in your going	to Zoar		and he chose for him	Lot	

3725, 3724	3497	5450.121	4013	4623, 7208	6754.126	382
adj, n fs	art, pn	cj, v Qal impf 3ms	pn	prep, n ms	cj, v Qal impf 3mp	n ms
כָּל־כִּכַּר	הַיַּרְדֵּן	וַיִּסַּע	לוֹט	מִקֶּדֶם	וַיִּפָּרְדוּ	אִישׁ
kol-kikkar	hayyardēn	wayyissa‘	lôṯ	miqqedhem	wayyippār^{e}dhû	’îsh
all the circle of	the Jordan	and he pulled out	Lot	from the east	and they separated	man

4623, 6142	250		82	3553.111	904, 800, 3791	4013	3553.111
prep, prep	n ms, ps 3ms	**12.**	pn	v Qal pf 3ms	prep, *n fs*, pn	cj, pn	v Qal pf 3ms
מֵעַל	אָחִיו		אַבְרָם	יָשַׁב	בְּאֶרֶץ־כְּנָעַן	וְלוֹט	יָשַׁב
mē‘al	’āchîw		’avrām	yāshav	b^{e}’erets-k^{e}nā‘an	w^{e}lôṯ	yāshav
from	his brother		Abram	he dwelled	in the land of Canaan	and Lot	he dwelled

904, 6111	3724	163.121	5912, 5651		596	5651	7737
prep, *n fp*	art, n fs	cj, v Qal impf 3ms	prep, pn	**13.**	cj, *n mp*	pn	adj
בְּעָרֵי	הַכִּכָּר	וַיֶּאֱהַל	עַד־סְדֹם		וְאַנְשֵׁי	סְדֹם	רָעִים
b^{e}‘ārê	hakkikkār	wayye’ĕhal	‘adh-s̱^{e}dhōm		w^{e}’anshê	s̱^{e}dhōm	rā‘îm
in the cities of	the circle	and he pitched his tent	toward Sodom		and men of	Sodom	evil

2491	3937, 3176	4108		3176	569.111	420, 82	311
cj, adj	prep, pn	adv	**14.**	cj, pn	v Qal pf 3ms	prep, pn	*sub*
וְחַטָּאִים	לַיהוָה	מְאֹד		וַיהוָה	אָמַר	אֶל־אַבְרָם	אַחֲרֵי
w^{e}chaṯṯā’îm	layhwāh	m^{e}’ōdh		wayhwāh	’āmar	’el-’avrām	’achrê
and sinners	against Yahweh	very		and Yahweh	He said	to Abram	after

9. Is not the whole land before thee? separate thyself, I pray thee, from me: ... Is not all the land open to you, *Anchor* ... the whole country is there in front of you, *REB*...withdraw from me, *NCB* ... let us part company, *REB.*

if thou wilt take the left hand, then I will go to the right; or if thou depart to the right hand, then I will go to the left: ... if you go north, I shall go south; if you go south, I shall go north, *REB* ... If you want that part over there to the east then I'll stay here in the western section. Or if you want the west, then I'll go over there to the east, *LIVB.*

10. And Lot lifted up his eyes: ... looked about, *NAB* ... took a good look, *Berkeley* ... looked out, *Goodspeed* ... looked around, *REB.*

and beheld all the plain of Jordan, that it was well watered every where: ... thoroughly watered was the whole Jordan Plain, *Anchor* ... well watered the whole Jordan district was, *Berkeley* ... valley of the Jordan, *NASB* ... whole region of the Jordan toward Segor, *NCB.*

before the LORD destroyed Sodom and Gomorrah: ... before the Lord had sent destruction, *BB* ... before the Lord swept away, *Fenton.*

even as the garden of the LORD, like the land of Egypt: ... as the garden of Jehovah, *Darby* ... like a garden of the Lord, from the land of Egypt to the valley of Zoar, *Fenton* ... like the Lord's own garden, *NAB.*

as thou comest unto Zoar: ... in the direction of Zoar, *RSV* ... like the garden of Eden, *LIVB* ... all the way to Zoar, *NEB.*

11. Then Lot chose him all the plain of Jordan; and Lot journeyed east: ... the whole valley of the Jordan pleased him, *Fenton* ... so Lot chose all the Jordan plain, *REB* ... Lot chose the Jordan valley to the east of them, *LIVB* ... took the road on the east side, *NEB.*

and they separated themselves the one from the other: ... they parted from each other, *Goodspeed* ... a man from his companion, *Young* ... they parted company, *REB.*

12. Abram dwelled in the land of Canaan, and Lot dwelled in the cities of the plain: ... Abram remained, and Lot settled amidst the cities of the plain, *Anchor* ... Lot went to the lowland towns, *BB* ... Lot hath dwelt in the cities of the circuit, and tenteth unto Sodom, *Young.*

and pitched his tent toward Sodom: ... extending his tents as far as Sodom, *Goodspeed, RSV* ... moved his tent as far as Sodom, *ASV.*

13. But the men of Sodom were wicked and sinners before the LORD exceedingly: ... flagrant *MLB* ... evil and great sinners, *BB* ... very wicked and sinful, *Fenton* ... in their wickedness had committed monstrous sins, *REB.*

14. And the LORD said unto Abram, after that Lot was separated from him, Lift up now thine

---

ier for them to find enough grass and water. Abram then told Lot to choose which direction he wanted to go. Abram did not have to do this. As the senior member of the group, he had the right to make that choice. Abram, who had been worshiping the LORD, now was acting in faith, trusting God. Like the LORD, he showed Lot grace, unmerited favor. He did it also in a humble, generous, unselfish way.

13:10-13. Lot chose the green fields of the well-watered "plain" ("circle" or "environs") of the Jordan. This district between Jericho and Zoar was a tropical area, 800 to 1200 feet below sea level, where crops could grow all year-round. Like the rich delta of the Nile area in Egypt, this well-watered land stretched to Zoar at the southeast end of the Dead Sea and reminded them of the garden of the LORD, the garden of Eden. Today, It no longer exists as a green, well-watered land. God's judgment on Sodom and Gomorrah brought a drastic change to the entire area.

Thus, Abram was left on the dry hillsides of central Canaan, and Lot settled among the five cities of the plain, pitching his tent near Sodom. Zoar may be mentioned because it was probably a center of heathen worship. A temple has been discovered in that area where the steps were warn down by thousands of feet--probably by people coming from all five cities. Lot failed to look at the green fields around Sodom through God's eyes, however. Sodom was a center of all kinds of wickedness that was evil in the sight of the Lord.

13:14-15. Abram did not lose anything by giving Lot the preference. After Lot moved away, the LORD told Abram to look in all directions, including the direction Lot went. All the land he could see in all directions God would give to Abram and his descendants forever, that is, for all time. Again, the promise of descendants and of the land are intertwined. As long as the promised land exists, it is still God's gift to them. Because of their sins God eventually scattered the Jews. His purpose did not change, however. He will yet uphold His holy

6754.241, 4013	4623, 6196	5558.131	5167	6084	7495.131	4623, 4887
v Niphal inf con, pn	prep, prep, ps 3ms	v Qal impv 2ms	part	n fd, ps 2ms	cj, v Qal impv 2ms	prep, art, n ms
הִפָּרֶד־לוֹט	מֵעִמּוֹ	שָׂא	נָא	עֵינֶיךָ	וּרְאֵה	מִן־הַמָּקוֹם
hippāredh-lôṭ	mē'immô	sā'	nā'	'ênêkhā	ûr'ēh	min-hammāqôm
separating Lot	from him	lift up	please	your eyes	and see	from the place

866, 887	8427	7103	5221	7209	3328		3706
rel part, pers pron	adv	n fs	cj, n ms	cj, n ms	cj, n ms	**15.**	cj
אֲשֶׁר־אַתָּה	שָׁם	צָפֹנָה	וָנֶגְבָּה	וָקֵדְמָה	וָיָמָּה		כִּי
'ăsher-'attāh	shām	tsāphōnāh	wāneghbāh	wāqēdhmāh	wāyāmmāh		kî
which you	there	northward	and southward	and eastward	and seaward		because

881, 3725, 800	866, 887	7495.151	3937	5598.125	3937, 2320
do, *adj*, art, n fs	rel part, pers pron	v Qal act ptc ms	prep, ps 2ms	v Qal impf 1cs, ps 3fs	cj, prep, n ms, ps 2ms
אֶת־כָּל־הָאָרֶץ	אֲשֶׁר־אַתָּה	רֹאֶה	לְךָ	אֶתְּנֶנָּה	וּלְזַרְעֲךָ
'eth-kol-hā'ārets	'ăsher-'attāh	rō'eh	lekhā	'ettenennāh	ûlăzar'ăkhā
all the land	which you	seeing	to you	I will give it	and to your seed

5912, 5986		7947.115	881, 2320	3626, 6312	800	866	524, 3310.121
prep, n ms	**16.**	cj, v Qal pf 1cs	do, n ms, ps 2ms	prep, *n ms*	art, n fs	rel part	cj, v Qal impf 3ms
עַד־עוֹלָם		וְשַׂמְתִּי	אֶת־זַרְעֲךָ	כַּעֲפַר	הָאָרֶץ	אֲשֶׁר	אִם־יוּכַל
'adh-'ôlām		wesamtî	'eth-zar'ăkhā	ka'ăphar	hā'ārets	'ăsher	'im-yûkhal
until forever		and I will make	your seed	like the dust of	the earth	which	if he can count

382	3937, 4630.141	881, 6312	800	1612	2320	4630.221
n ms	prep, v Qal inf con	do, *n ms*	art, n fs	cj	n ms, ps 2ms	v Niphal impf 3ms
אִישׁ	לִמְנוֹת	אֶת־עֲפַר	הָאָרֶץ	גַּם	זַרְעֲךָ	יִמָּנֶה
'îsh	limnôth	'eth-'ăphar	hā'ārets	gam	zar'ăkhā	yimmāneh
man	to count	the dust of	the earth	also	your seed	it will be counted

	7251.131	2050.731	904, 800	3937, 775	3937, 7621	3706
17.	v Qal impv 2ms	v Hithpael impv 2ms	prep, art, n fs	prep, n fs, ps 3fs	cj, prep, n ms, ps 3fs	cj
	קוּם	הִתְהַלֵּךְ	בָּאָרֶץ	לְאָרְכָּהּ	וּלְרָחְבָּהּ	כִּי
	qûm	hithhallēkh	bā'ārets	le'ārkāhh	ûlărāchăbbāhh	kî
	rise	walk	on the land	to its length	and to its width	because

3937	5598.125		163.121	82	971.121	3553.121
prep, ps 2ms	v Qal impf 1cs, ps 3fs	**18.**	cj, v Qal impf 3ms	pn	cj, v Qal impf 3ms	cj, v Qal impf 3ms
לְךָ	אֶתְּנֶנָּה		וַיֶּאֱהַל	אַבְרָם	וַיָּבֹא	וַיֵּשֶׁב
lekhā	'ettenennāh		wayye'ĕhal	'avrām	wayyāvō'	wayyēshev
to you	I will give it		and he pitched his tent	Abram	and he went	and he dwelled

904, 440	4613	866	904, 2367	1161.121, 8427	4326	3937, 3176
prep, *n fp*	pn	rel part	prep, pn	cj, v Qal impf 3ms, adv	n ms	prep, pn
בְּאֵלֹנֵי	מַמְרֵא	אֲשֶׁר	בְּחֶבְרוֹן	וַיִּבֶן־שָׁם	מִזְבֵּחַ	לַיהוָה
be'ēlōnê	mamrē'	'ăsher	bechevrôn	wayyiven-shām	mizbēach	layhwāh
by the great trees of	Mamre	which	by Hebron	and he built there	altar	to Yahweh

	2030.121	904, 3219	581	4567, 8534	769	4567	502
14:1	cj, v Qal impf 3ms	prep, *n mp*	pn	*n ms*, pn	pn	*n ms*	pn
	וַיְהִי	בִּימֵי	אַמְרָפֶל	מֶלֶךְ־שִׁנְעָר	אַרְיוֹךְ	מֶלֶךְ	אֶלָּסָר
	wayhî	bîmê	'amrāphel	melekh-shin'ār	'aryôkh	melekh	'ellāsār
	and it was	in the days of	Amraphel	king of Shinar	Arioch	king of	Ellasar

3660	4567	6082	8742	4567	1505B		6449.116	4560
pn	*n ms*	pn	cj, pn	*n ms*	pn	**2.**	v Qal pf 3cp	n fs
כְּדָרְלָעֹמֶר	מֶלֶךְ	עֵילָם	וְתִדְעָל	מֶלֶךְ	גּוֹיִם		עָשׂוּ	מִלְחָמָה
kedhārelā'ōmer	melekh	'êlām	wethidh'āl	melekh	gôyim		'āsû	milchāmāh
Chedorlaomer	king of	Elam	and Tidal	king of	Goiim		they waged	war

882, 1324	4567	5651	882, 1332	4567	6244	8518	4567
prep, pn	*n ms*	pn	cj, prep, pn	*n ms*	pn	pn	*n ms*
אֶת־בֶּרַע	מֶלֶךְ	סְדֹם	וְאֶת־בִּרְשַׁע	מֶלֶךְ	עֲמֹרָה	שִׁנְאָב	מֶלֶךְ
'eth-bera'	melekh	s^{e}dhōm	w^{e}'eth-birsha'	melekh	'ămōrāh	shin'āv	melekh
with Bera	king of	Sodom	and with Birsha	king of	Gomorrah	Shinab	king of

126	8432	4567	6913	4567	1145	2026, 7097		3725, 431
pn	cj, pn	*n ms*	pn	cj, *n ms*	pn	pers pron, pn	**3.**	*adj*, dem pron
אַדְמָה	וְשֶׁמְאֵבֶר	מֶלֶךְ	צְבֹיִים	וּמֶלֶךְ	בֶּלַע	הִיא־צֹעַר		כָּל־אֵלֶּה
'adhmāh	w^{e}shem'ēver	melekh	ts^{e}vōyîm	ûmelekh	bela'	hî'-tsō'ar		kol-'ēlleh
Admah	and Shemeber	king of	Zeboiim	and king of	Bela	it Zoar		all these

eyes, and look from the place where thou art northward, and southward, and eastward, and westward: ... after Lot had detached himself, *MLB* ... glance about you, *Anchor* ... look from where you stand, *Berkeley* ... a view northward, *Fenton* ... in every direction, *LIVB* ... gaze to the north, *NAB*.

15. For all the land which thou seest, to thee will I give it, and to thy seed for ever: ... to you and to your offspring forever, *NRSV* ... all the land you are viewing, *Berkeley* ... and to your race forever, *Fenton* ... your descendants for all time, *Goodspeed* ... to you and your posterity forever, *NCB*.

16. And I will make thy seed as the dust of the earth: so that if a man can number the dust of the earth, then shall thy seed also be numbered: ... I will make your descendants as countless, *NEB* ... if anyone is able to count the dust particles by number, *MLB* ... it will be as possible to count the dust of the earth as to count your descendants, *Goodspeed* ... only if the specks of dust on the ground could be counted, *REB*.

17. Arise, walk through the land in the length of it and in the breadth of it; for I will give it unto thee: ... traverse the land, *Berkeley* ... go through all the land from one end to the other, *BB* ... march through the land, inspect both its length and its breadth, *Fenton* ... set forth and walk about in the Lord, *NAB*.

18. Then Abram removed his tent, and came and dwelt in the plain of Mamre, which is in Hebron, and built there an altar unto the LORD: ... struck his camp, *Fenton* ... by the oaks of Mamre, *NASB* ... proceeded to settle near the terebinths of Mamre, *NAB* ... made his living-place by the holy tree of Mamre, *BB*.

14:1. And it came to pass in the days of Amraphel king of Shinar, Arioch king of Ellasar, Chedorlaomer king of Elam, and Tidal king of nations: ... it was now in the reign, *Fenton* ... in the time of, *NEB* ... King of Goiim, *ASV*.

2. That these made war with Bera king of Sodom, and with Birsha king of Gomorrah, Shinab king of Admah, and Shemeber king of

name not only by restoring Israel to the land, but also by restoring them spiritually, giving them a new heart, a new spirit, and putting His Spirit within them (Ezek. 20:41-42; 36:24-36; 37:11-14).

13:16. Though Abram had no son up to this time, God promised to make this descendants as the dust of the earth, innumerable.

13:17-18. Though Abram did not own any of the land, and could not buy any of it, God told him to walk through the length and width of the land, for God would give it all to him. That is, the land was Abram's in God's eyes, though his descendants would be the ones to possess it. Then Abram moved his tents from place to place, enjoying it as he thought of the future fulfillment. After a time, he settled by the great terebinth trees of Mamre (see Gen. 14:13) near Hebron. (The holm oak shown there to tourists today is not from Abram's time).

14:1-3. The four kings of Mesopotamia and Elam (east of Babylonia) were robber kings. Amraphel, the king of Shinar (Babylonia), was not Hammurabi as some once thought. Arioch (servant of the moon god Aku) ruled Ellasar (Larsa) and dominated Ur. Chedorlaomer ("servant of the god Logomar") king of Elam, and Tidal king of nations (Heb., *Goyim*, possibly a confederacy of Hittite cities), came down and conquered the five cities of the Jordan/Dead Sea plain. This is the first mention of war in the Bible, but not necessarily the first war. There is some evidence that these five cities were a well-known confederacy long before Abram's time. Bera ("gift" or "victor"), Birsha, Shinab ("the moon god, Sin, is father"), Shemeber ("the name is mighty"), and the unnamed king of Bela (a small city later called Zoar, Gen. 19:22) all joined forces in the Valley of Siddim ("valley" of fields or "salt

2357.116	420, 6231	7900	2000	3328	4556	4.	8692	6462
v Qal pf 3cp	prep, *n ms*	art, pn	pers pron	*n ms*	art, pn		num	num
חָבְרוּ	אֶל־עֵמֶק	הַשִּׂדִּים	הוּא	יָם	הַמֶּלַח		שְׁתֵּים	עֶשְׂרֵה
chāv^{e}rû	'el-'ēmeq	hassiddîm	hû'	yām	hammelach		sh^{e}têm	'esrēh
they joined	at the valley of	the Siddim	it	the Sea of	the Salt		two	ten

8523	5856.116	881, 3660	8421, 6462	8523	4937.116	5.	904, 727
n fs	v Qal pf 3cp	do, pn	cj, num, num	n fs	v Qal pf 3cp		cj, prep, num
שָׁנָה	עָבְדוּ	אֶת־כְּדָרְלָעֹמֶר	וּשְׁלֹשׁ־עֶשְׂרֵה	שָׁנָה	מָרָדוּ		וּבְאַרְבַּע
shānāh	'āv^{e}dhû	'eth-k^{e}dhār^{e}lā'ōmer	ûshlôsh-'esrēh	shānāh	mārādhû		ûb'arba'
years	they served	Chedorlaomer	but three ten	year	they rebelled		and in four

6462	8523	971.111	3660	4567	866	882	5409.526
num	n fs	v Qal pf 3ms	pn	cj, art, n mp	rel part	prep, ps 3ms	cj, v Hiphil impf 3mp
עֶשְׂרֵה	שָׁנָה	בָּא	כְּדָרְלָעֹמֶר	וְהַמְּלָכִים	אֲשֶׁר	אִתּוֹ	וַיַּכּוּ
'esrēh	shānāh	bā'	kh^{e}dhār^{e}lā'ōmer	w^{e}hamm^{e}lākhîm	'ăsher	'ittô	wayyakkû
ten	year	he came	Chedorlaomer	and the kings	who	with him	and they struck

881, 7788	904, 6494	7454	881, 2186	904, 2060	881	373	904, 8189
do, pn	prep, pn	pn	cj, do, art, pn	prep, pn	cj, do	art, pn	prep, pn
אֶת־רְפָאִים	בְּעַשְׁתְּרֹת	קַרְנַיִם	וְאֶת־הַזּוּזִים	בְּהָם	וְאֵת	הָאֵימִים	בְּשָׁוֵה
'eth-r^{e}phā'îm	b^{e}'asht^{e}rōth	qar nayim	w^{e}'eth-hazzûzîm	b^{e}hām	w^{e}'ēth	hā'êmîm	b^{e}shāwēh
Rephaim	in Ashteroth	Karnaim	and the Zuzim	in Ham	and	the Emim	in Shaveh

7445	6.	881, 2855	904, 2098	7990	5912	368	368	866
pn		cj, do, art, pn	prep, n ms, ps 3mp	pn	adv	pn	pn	rel part
קִרְיָתָיִם		וְאֶת־הַחֹרִי	בְּהַרְרָם	שֵׂעִיר	עַד	אֵיל	פָּארָן	אֲשֶׁר
qiryāthāyim		w^{e}'eth-hachōrî	b^{e}harrām	sē'îr	'adh	'êl	pā'rān	'ăsher
Kiriathaim		and the Horites	on their mountain	Seir	unto	El	Paran	which

6142, 4198	7.	8178.126	971.126	420, 6097	6097	2000	7229
prep, art, n ms		cj, v Qal impf 3mp	cj, v Qal impf 3mp	prep, pn	pn	pers pron	pn
עַל־הַמִּדְבָּר		וַיָּשֻׁבוּ	וַיָּבֹאוּ	אֶל־עֵין	מִשְׁפָּט	הִוא	קָדֵשׁ
'al-hammidhbār		wayyāshuvû	wayyābō'û	'el-'ên	mishpāṭ	hiw'	qādhēsh
in the wilderness		and they returned	and they went	to En	Mishpat	it	Kadesh

5409.526	881, 3725, 7898	6223	1612	881, 578	3553.151	904, 2790
cj, v Hiphil impf 3mp	do, *adj, n ms*	pn	cj, cj	do, art, pn	art, v Qal act ptc ms	prep, pn
וַיַּכּוּ	אֶת־כָּל־שְׂדֵה	הָעֲמָלֵקִי	וְגַם	אֶת־הָאֱמֹרִי	הַיֹּשֵׁב	בְּחַצְצֹן
wayyakû	'eth-kol-s^{e}dhēh	hā'ămālēqî	w^{e}gham	'eth-hā'ĕmōrî	hayyōshēv	b^{e}chatstsōn
and they struck	all the field of	the Amalekites	and also	the Amorites	the dwellers	in Hazazon

2790	8.	3428.121	4567, 5651	4567	6244	4567	126
pn		cj, v Qal impf 3ms	*n ms*, pn	cj, *n ms*	pn	cj, *n ms*	pn
תָּמָר		וַיֵּצֵא	מֶלֶךְ־סְדֹם	וּמֶלֶךְ	עֲמֹרָה	וּמֶלֶךְ	אַדְמָה
tāmār		wayyētsē'	melekh-s^{e}dhōm	ûmelekh	'ămōrāh	ûmelekh	'adhmāh
Tamar		and he went out	king of Sodom	and king of	Gomorrah	and king of	Admah

4567	6913	4567	1145	2000, 7097	6424.126	882
cj, *n ms*	pn	cj, *n ms*	pn	pers pron, pn	cj, v Qal impf 3mp	prep, ps 3mp
וּמֶלֶךְ	צְבֹיִים	וּמֶלֶךְ	בֶּלַע	הוּא־צֹעַר	וַיַּעַרְכוּ	אִתָּם
ûmelekh	ts^{e}vōyîm	ûmelekh	bela'	hiw'-tsō'ar	wayya'arkhû	'ittām
and king of	Zeboiim	and king of	Bela	it Zoar	and they joined	with them

4560	904, 6231	7900	9.	881	3660	4567	6082
n fs	prep, *n ms*	art, pn		do	pn	*n ms*	pn
מִלְחָמָה	בְּעֵמֶק	הַשִּׂדִּים		אֵת	כְּדָרְלָעֹמֶר	מֶלֶךְ	עֵילָם
milchāmāh	b^{e}'ēmeq	hassiddîm		'ēth	k^{e}dhār^{e}lā'ōmer	melekh	'êlām
war	in the valley of	the Siddim			Chedorlaomer	king of	Elam

Zeboiim, and the king of Bela, which is Zoar: ... waged war, *Fenton* ... went to war against, *NEB* ... King of Bala, which is, Segor, *NCB*.

3. All these were joined together: ... joined forces, *NAB* ... forces met, *Berkeley* ... all of whom had gathered in alliance, *Goodspeed* ... these came as allies, *NASB*.

in the vale of Siddim, which is the salt sea: ... Valley of Siddin, *KJVII* ... the Dead Sea, *NEB*.

4. Twelve years they served Chedorlaomer, and in the thirteenth year they rebelled: ... had been subject to, *Geneva* ... they were under the rule, *BB* ... they revolted, *Berkeley*.

5. And in the fourteenth year came Chedorlaomer, and the kings that were with him: ... Kings allied with him, *NIV* ... approached with the allied kings, *MLB* ... kings who were on his side, *BB*.

and smote the Rephaims in Ashteroth Karnaim: ... and defeated, *NCB* ... they conquered, *Berkeley* ... overcame, *BB* ... they crushed, *Goodspeed* ... and attacked, *NKJV* ... subdued, *NRSV*.

and the Zuzims in Ham, and the Emims in Shaveh Kiriathaim: ... at Ashteroth's Horn, *Fenton*.

6. And the Horites in their mount Seir: ... hill country of Seir, *NAB* ... Seir mountain range, *MLB* ... highlands of Seir, *Goodspeed* ... in their hill-country, *REB*.

unto Elparan, which is by the wilderness: ... penetrating as far as, *Goodspeed* ... driving them as far as El-Paran, *BB* ... as far as the pastures which adjoin the desert, *Fenton* ... near the desert, *Berkeley, NIV*.

7. And they returned: ... then they swung back, *Anchor* ... turning there, *Berkeley* ... retraining their steps, *Goodspeed* ... then they turned back, *NCB* ... on their way back, *NEB*.

and came to Enmishpat, which is Kadesh: ... well of Justice, *Fenton* ... to En-mesphat - that is, Cades, *NCB*.

and smote all the country of the Amalekites, and also the Amorites, that dwelt in Hazezontamar: ... subdued all the territory, *Anchor* ... and sacked the whole Amalekite region, *MLB* ... making waste all the country, *BB* ... ravaged all the country, *Goodspeed* ... the Amorites who inhabited the palm groves, *Fenton*.

8. And there went out the king of Sodom, and the king of Gomorrah, and the king of Admah, and the king of Zeboiim, and the king of Bela (the same is Zoar;) and they joined battle with them in the vale of Siddim: ... they set the battle in array against them, *ASV* ... marched forth and engaged them in battle, *Anchor* ... marched out in battle formation, *Berkeley* ... commenced hostilities in the valley, *Fenton* ... marched out and drew up their battle lines, *NIV*.

---

flats"), probably the area now covered by the southern third of the Dead Sea (which is always called the Salt Sea in the Bible). Silt carried in by the rivers raised the level of the Dead Sea a few feet since Abram's time, but currently, the southern portion is being drained.

14:4. Chedorlaomer was apparently the leading king of the four-king confederacy. Sodom and the other four cities of the plain served him, that is they were his subjects and sent him tribute or taxes every year for 12 years. But Elam was far away, and in the 13th year they rebelled, which means they sent no tribute, and paid no taxes.

14:5-7. Winning the war meant more war sooner or later, as it always does. (Only the coming of Jesus as the Prince of Peace will break this vicious cycle.) So Chedorlaomer and the three kings allied with him had to deal with the rebels.

On the way they had to fight and defeat the Rephaites ("giants," a tall people who were remnants of early inhabitants of Canaan) at Ashteroth Karnaim (named for the two-horned image of the goddess Astarte or Ishtar) about 20 miles east of the Sea of Galilee in Bashan.

Then they fought the Zuzites at Ham in Ammon, the Emites ("terrors") at Shaveh Kiriathaim in Moab, and the Horites (remnants of the ancient Hurrians who moved into the Middle East about 2400 B.C.) in Mount Seir (Edom). They continued south as far as El-paran ("the terebinth of Paran") on the border of the Sinai desert.

Then they circled back west to En-mishpat ("the well of judgment"), later called Kadesh ("holy"), an oasis about 70 miles southwest of the Dead Sea. They also conquered the territory that later belonged to the Amalekites, which extended from Beersheba to Mount Sinai and defeated the Amorites ("mountaineers," who dominated Palestine for a period beginning about 3,000 B.C.) at Hazezon-tamar ("sandy place of palms"), an oasis on the west side of the Dead Sea.

14:8-10. The king of Sodom and his allies set up battle lines in the valley of Siddim to try to stop Chedorlaomer and his allies, but they were forced to

8742	4567	1505B	581	4567	8534	769	4567
cj, pn	*n ms*	pn	cj, pn	*n ms*	pn	cj, pn	*n ms*
וְתִדְעָל	מֶלֶךְ	גּוֹיִם	וְאַמְרָפֶל	מֶלֶךְ	שִׁנְעָר	וְאַרְיוֹךְ	מֶלֶךְ
wethidh'āl	melekh	gôyim	we'amrāphel	melekh	shin'ār	we'aryôkh	melekh
and Tidal	king of	Goiim	and Amraphel	king of	Shinar	and Arioch	king of

502	727	4567	882, 2675		6231	7900	908	908
pn	num	n mp	prep, art, num	**10.**	cj, *n ms*	art, pn	n fp	*n fp*
אֶלָּסָר	אַרְבָּעָה	מְלָכִים	אֶת־הַחֲמִשָּׁה		וְעֵמֶק	הַשִּׂדִּים	בֶּאֱרֹת	בֶּאֱרֹת
'ellāsār	'arbā'āh	melākhîm	'eth-hachmishshāh		we'ēmeq	hasiddîm	be'ĕrōth	be'ĕrōth
Ellasar	four	kings	with the five		and the valley of	the Siddim	pits	pits of

2668	5308.126	4567, 5651	6244	5489.126, 8427	8080.256
n ms	cj, v Qal impf 3mp	*n ms*, pn	cj, pn	cj, v Qal impf 3mp, adv	cj, art, v Niphal ptc mp
חֵמָר	וַיָּנֻסוּ	מֶלֶךְ־סְדֹם	וַעֲמֹרָה	וַיִּפְּלוּ־שָׁמָּה	וְהַנִּשְׁאָרִים
chēmār	wayyānusû	melekh-sedhōm	wa'ămōrāh	wayyippelû-shāmmāh	wehannish'ārîm
tar	and they fled	king of Sodom	and Gomorrah	and they fell there	and the ones remaining

2098	5308.116		4089.126	881, 3725, 7688	5651	6244
n ms	v Qal pf 3cp	**11.**	cj, v Qal impf 3mp	do, *adj, n ms*	pn	cj, pn
הֶרָה	נָסוּ		וַיִּקְחוּ	אֶת־כָּל־רְכֻשׁ	סְדֹם	וַעֲמֹרָה
herāh	nāsû		wayyiqchû	'eth-kol-rekhush	sedhōm	wa'ămōrāh
to mountain	they fled		and they took	all the property of	Sodom	and Gomorrah

881, 3725, 408	2050.126		4089.126	881, 4013	881, 7688
cj, do, *adj*, n ms, ps 3mp	cj, v Qal impf 3mp	**12.**	cj, v Qal impf 3mp	do, pn	do, n ms, ps 3ms
וְאֶת־כָּל־אָכְלָם	וַיֵּלֵכוּ		וַיִּקְחוּ	אֶת־לוֹט	וְאֶת־רְכֻשׁוֹ
we'eth-kol-'ākhlām	wayyēlēkhû		wayyiqchû	'eth-lôt	we'eth-rekhushô
and all the food	and they went		and they took	Lot	and his property

1158, 250	82	2050.126	2000	3553.151	904, 5651		971.121
n ms, n ms	pn	cj, v Qal impf 3mp	cj, pers pron	v Qal act ptc ms	prep, pn	**13.**	cj, v Qal impf 3ms
בֶּן־אֲחִי	אַבְרָם	וַיֵּלֵכוּ	וְהוּא	יֹשֵׁב	בִּסְדֹם		וַיָּבֹא
ben-'ăchî	'avrām	wayyēlēkhû	wehû'	yōshēv	bisdhōm		wayyāvō'
the son of the brother of	Abram	and they went	and he	dweller	in Sodom		and he went

6654	5222.521	3937, 82	5888	2000	8331.151	904, 440
art, n ms	cj, v Hiphil impf 3ms	prep, pn	art, pn	cj, pers pron	v Qal act ptc ms	prep, *n fp*
הַפָּלִיט	וַיַּגֵּד	לְאַבְרָם	הָעִבְרִי	וְהוּא	שֹׁכֵן	בְּאֵלֹנֵי
happālît	wayyaggēdh	le'avrām	hā'ivrî	wehû'	shōkhēn	be'ēlōnê
the escaped one	and he told	to Abram	the Hebrew	and he	dweller	by the great trees of

4613	578	250	839	250	6293	2062	1196
pn	art, pn	*n ms*	pn	cj, *n ms*	pn	cj, pers pron	*n mp*
מַמְרֵא	הָאֱמֹרִי	אֲחִי	אֶשְׁכֹּל	וַאֲחִי	עָנֵר	וְהֵם	בַּעֲלֵי
mamrē'	hā'ĕmōrî	'ăchî	'eshkōl	wa'ăchî	'ānēr	wehēm	ba'ălê
Mamre	the Amorites	the brother of	Eshcol	and the brother of	Aner	and they	owners of

1311, 82		8471.121	82	3706	8091.211	250
n fs, pn	**14.**	cj, v Qal impf 3ms	pn	cj	v Niphal pf 3ms	n ms, ps 3ms
בְּרִית־אַבְרָם		וַיִּשְׁמַע	אַבְרָם	כִּי	נִשְׁבָּה	אָחִיו
berîth-'avrām		wayyishma'	'avrām	kî	nishbāh	'āchîw
covenant of Abram		when he heard	Abram	that	he was taken captive	his relative

7671.521	881, 2696	3320	1041	8470	6461	8421	4109
cj, v Hiphil impf 3ms	do, adj, ps 3ms	*adj*	n ms, ps 3ms	num	num	cj, num	num
וַיָּרֶק	אֶת־חֲנִיכָיו	יְלִידֵי	בֵּיתוֹ	שְׁמֹנָה	עָשָׂר	וּשְׁלֹשׁ	מֵאוֹת
wayyāreq	'eth-chănîkhâv	yelîdhê	vêthô	shemōnāh	'āsār	ûshelōsh	mē'ôth
then he poured out	his trained in war	born of	his house	eight	ten	and three	hundreds

9. With Chedorlaomer the king of Elam, and with Tidal king of nations, and Amraphel king of Shinar, and Arioch king of Ellasar; four kings with five: ... against Chedorlaomer, *Goodspeed* ... four kings against the five, *ASV.*

10. And the vale of Siddim was full of slimepits: ... one bitumen pit after another, *Anchor* ... tar pits, *Berkeley, NASB* ... pits of asphalt, *Darby* ... holes of sticky earth, *BB* ... petroleum pits, *Fenton.*

and the kings of Sodom and Gomorrah fled, and fell there: ... flung themselves into these in their flight, *Anchor* ... came to their end there, *BB* ... some of their men fell into them, *REB* ... some slipped into the pits, *LIVB.*

and they that remained fled to the mountain: ... the others escaped into the hills, *Anchor* ... but the rest got away, *BB* ... the residue fled, *Geneva* ... the survivors fled, *Goodspeed* ... the other three kings escaped to the mountains, *Good News.*

11. And they took all the goods of Sodom and Gomorrah, and all their victuals, and went their way: ... the invaders seized the possessions, *Anchor* ... the victors took the wealth and provisions, *Berkeley* ... captured the flocks and herds, *REB.*

12. And they took Lot, Abram's brother's son: ... they also captured Lot, *MLB* ... in addition they took Lot, *BB* ... they also carried off Lot, *NEB.*

who dwelt in Sodom, and his goods, and departed: ... with his possessions, *Anchor* ... and his chattels, *Fenton* ... had been living in Sodom, *Anchor, NCB.*

13. And there came one that had escaped, and told Abram the Hebrew: ... a fugitive brought the news, *REB* ... one who had got away from the fight, *BB* ... a fugitive came, *NASB* ... reported to Abram the Colonist, *Fenton.*

for he dwelt in the plain of Mamre the Amorite, brother of Eshcol, and brother of Aner: ... dwelt by the oaks of Mamre, *Darby* ... camping at the terebinths of Mamre, *Anchor* ... living by the holy tree of Mamre, *BB* ... settled at the oak woods, *Fenton* ... great trees of Mamre, *NIV.*

and these were confederate with Abram: ... who were allies of Abram, *Berkeley* ... who were friends of Abram, *BB* ... who were confederated chiefs, *Fenton* ... these had a covenant with Abram, *KJVII* ... these were in league with Abram, *NAB.*

14. And when Abram heard that his brother was taken captive: ... had been made a prisoner, *BB.*

he armed his trained servants: ... he led forth his trained men, *ASV* ... he called up his retainers, *Anchor* ... mustered his trained men, *Berkeley* ... mustered three hundred and eighteen of his retainers, *NAB.*

born in his own house, three hundred and eighteen, and pursued them unto Dan: ... his household slaves, *Goodspeed* ... of his own family, *Fenton* ... sons of his house, *BB* ... marched in pursuit, *Berkeley* ... as far as Dan, *ASV.*

15. And he divided himself against them, he and his servants, by night: ... deployed against the others, *Anchor* ... separating his forces by night, *BB* ... and overtook them in the night-time, *Fenton* ... with his slaves he fell upon them, *Goodspeed* ... formed parties against them, *NCB* ... surrounded the enemy by night, *REB.*

and smote them, and pursued them unto Hobah, which is on the left hand of Damascus: ... defeated them, *Anchor* ... he and his men defeated the enemy and chased them, *Berkeley* ... overcame them, putting them to flight, *BB* ... attacked them, *NEB* ... north of Damascus, *Goodspeed.*

---

flee. Some fell into tar or asphalt pits, others fled into the hills that flank the Dead Sea. (Asphalt lumps still float in the south end of the Dead Sea.)

14:11-12. Lot was no longer living in tents. The temptation of city living was too great. He had moved into Sodom, undoubtedly using part of his wealth to buy a fine house there. As a foreigner he was not required to join Sodom's army, but when the four kings looted the city, they took him captive and took all his possessions.

14:13. One of those who fled into the hills reported Lot's capture to Abram. Possibly because of the threat of the invasion by the four kings, Mamre, the owner of the great terebinth trees, his brother Eshcol, and Aner had joined in an alliance with Abram. Abram is identified as "the Hebrew," which may refer to his descent from Eber (Gen. 11:14-17), or may have identified him as an immigrant from the other side of the Euphrates River (since "Hebrew" is derived from the verb *'abar*, "to pass through, to cross over")..

14:14. Abram showed his concern for family and a sense of loyalty and responsibility by taking his 318 armed and trained men to courageously pursue the four kings, coming close to them at Dan. The Dan mentioned here is probably not the later Dan near the sources of the Jordan River, but another Dan in Gilead south of Damascus (Deut. 34:1).

7579.121	5912, 1896	**15.**	2606.221	6142	4050	2000	5860
cj, v Qal impf 3ms	prep, pn		cj, v Niphal impf 3ms	prep, ps 3mp	n ms	pers pron	cj, n mp, ps 3ms
וַיִּרְדֹּף	עַד־דָּן		וַיֵּחָלֵק	עֲלֵיהֶם	לַיְלָה	הוּא	וַעֲבָדָיו
wayyirdōph	ʻadh-dān		wayyēchālēq	ʻălêhem	laylāh	hû'	waʻăvādhâv
and he pursued	until Dan		and he divided	them	night	he	and his slaves

5409.521	7579.121	5912, 2421	866	4623, 7972	3937, 1894
cj, v Hiphil impf 3ms, ps 3mp	cj, v Qal impf 3ms, ps 3mp	prep, pn	rel part	prep, n ms	prep, pn
וַיַּכֵּם	וַיִּרְדְּפֵם	עַד־חוֹבָה	אֲשֶׁר	מִשְּׂמֹאל	לְדַמָּשֶׂק
wayyakkēm	wayyird^{e}phēm	ʻadh-chôvāh	'ăsher	miss^{e}mō'l	l^{e}dhammāseq
and he struck them	and he pursued them	until Hobah	which	from north	to Damascus

16.	8178.521	881	3725, 7688	1612	881, 4013	250
	cj, v Hiphil impf 3ms	do	*adj*, art, n ms	cj, cj	do, pn	n ms, ps 3ms
	וַיָּשֶׁב	אֵת	כָּל־הָרְכֻשׁ	וְגַם	אֶת־לוֹט	אָחִיו
	wayyāshev	'ēth	kol-hārkhush	w^{e}gham	'eth-lôṯ	'āchîw
	and he brought back		all the property	and also	Lot	his relative

7688	8178.511	1612	881, 5571	881, 6194	**17.**	3428.121
n ms	v Hiphil pf 3ms	cj, cj	do, art, n fp	cj, do, art, n ms		cj, v Qal impf 3ms
וּרְכֻשׁוֹ	הֵשִׁיב	וְגַם	אֶת־הַנָּשִׁים	וְאֶת־הָעָם		וַיֵּצֵא
ûrk^{e}hushô	hēshîv	w^{e}gham	'eth-hannāshîim	w^{e}'eth-hā'ām		wayyētsē'
and his property	he brought back	and also	the women	and the people		and he went out

4567, 5651	3937, 7410.141	311	8178.141	4623, 5409.541
n ms, pn	prep, v Qal inf con, ps 3ms	*sub*	v Qal inf con, ps 3ms	prep, v Hiphil inf con
מֶלֶךְ־סְדֹם	לִקְרָאתוֹ	אַחֲרֵי	שׁוּבוֹ	מֵהַכּוֹת
melekh-s^{e}dhōm	liqrā'thô	'achrê	shûvô	mēhakkôth
king of Sodom	to meet him	after	his returning	from striking

881, 3660	881, 4567	866	882	420, 6231	8189	2000	6231
do, pn	cj, do, art, n mp	rel part	prep, ps 3ms	prep, *n ms*	pn	pers pron	*n ms*
אֶת־כְּדָרְלָעֹמֶר	וְאֶת־הַמְּלָכִים	אֲשֶׁר	אִתּוֹ	אֶל־עֵמֶק	שָׁוֵה	הוּא	עֵמֶק
'eth-k^{e}dhār-lā'ōmer	w^{e}'eth-hamm^{e}lākhîm	'ăsher	'ittô	'el-ʻēmeq	shāwēh	hû'	ʻēmeq
Chedorlaomer	and the kings	which	with him	to the valley of	Shaveh	it	the valley of

4567	**18.**	4581	4567	8401	3428.511	4035	3302
art, n ms		cj, pn	*n ms*	pn	v Hiphil pf 3ms	n ms	cj, n ms
הַמֶּלֶךְ		וּמַלְכִּי־צֶדֶק	מֶלֶךְ	שָׁלֵם	הוֹצִיא	לֶחֶם	וָיָיִן
hammelekh		ûmalkî-tsedheq	melekh	shālēm	hôtsî'	lechem	wāyāyin
the king		and Melchizedek	king of	Salem	he brought out	bread	and wine

2000	3669	3937, 418	6169	**19.**	1313.321	569.121
cj, pers pron	n ms	prep, n ms	n ms		cj, v Piel impf 3ms, ps 3ms	cj, v Qal impf 3ms
וְהוּא	כֹהֵן	לְאֵל	עֶלְיוֹן		וַיְבָרְכֵהוּ	וַיֹּאמַר
w^{e}hû'	khōhēn	l^{e}'ēl	ʻelyôn		wayvār^{e}khēhû	wayyō'mar
and he	priest	to God	Most High		and he blessed him	and he said

1313.155	82	3937, 418	6169	7353.151	8452	800
v Qal pass ptc ms	pn	prep, n ms	n ms	*v Qal act ptc ms*	n md	cj, n fs
בָּרוּךְ	אַבְרָם	לְאֵל	עֶלְיוֹן	קֹנֵה	שָׁמַיִם	וָאָרֶץ
bārûkh	'avrām	l^{e}'ēl	ʻelyôn	qōnēh	shāmayim	wā'ārets
blessed be	Abram	to God	Most High	Creator of	heavens	and earth

20.	1313.155	418	6169	866, 4181.311	7141	904, 3135
	cj, v Qal pass ptc ms	n ms	n ms	rel part, v Piel pf 3ms	n mp, ps 2ms	prep, n fs, ps 2ms
	וּבָרוּךְ	אֵל	עֶלְיוֹן	אֲשֶׁר־מִגֵּן	צָרֶיךָ	בְּיָדֶךָ
	ûvārûkh	'ēl	ʻelyôn	'ăsher-miggēn	tsārêkhā	b^{e}yādhekhā
	and blessed be	God	Most High	who He delivered	your enemies	in your hand

5598.121, 3937 cj, v Qal impf 3ms, prep, ps 3ms וַיִּתֶּן־לוֹ wayyitten-lô and he gave to him	4804 n ms מַעֲשֵׂר ma'ăsēr tenth	4623, 3725 prep, adj מִכֹּל mikkōl from all	21.	569.121 cj, v Qal impf 3ms וַיֹּאמֶר wayyō'mer and he said	4567, 5651 *n ms*, pn מֶלֶךְ־סְדֹם melekh-sᵉdhōm king of Sodom	420, 82 prep, pn אֶל־אַבְרָם 'el-'avrām to Abram

16. And he brought back all the goods: ... he recovered all the possessions, *Anchor* ... he recaptured all the loot, *Berkeley* ... he brought back all the property, *Darby* ... he recovered all the substance, *Geneva* ... brought back all the flocks and herds, *NEB.*

and also brought again his brother Lot, and his goods, and the women also, and the people: ... and all his company, *REB*...the other captives, *NAB, NEB* ... together with the men, *Fenton* ... and other personnel, *Anchor.*

17. And the king of Sodom went out to meet him after his return from the slaughter of Chedorlaomer: ... met him to congratulate him, *Fenton* ... returned from his victory, *Anchor* ... from the defeat of, *Berkeley* ... returned from smiting, *BB.*

and of the kings that were with him: ... allied with him, *NIV* ... and his royal allies, *MLB* ... confederate kings, *NEB.*

at the valley of Shaveh, which is the king's dale: ... Vale of Shaveh, *ASV* ... Valley of Save, *NCB* ... Devil's Valley, *Fenton* ... King's Valley, *Darby* ... King's Vale, *ASV.*

18. And Melchizedek king of Salem brought forth bread and wine: and he was the priest of the most high God: ... king of Salem (Jerusalem), *LIVB* ... priest of El-Elyon, *Anchor* ... almighty God, *Fenton.*

19. And he blessed him, and said, Blessed be Abram of the most high God, possessor of heaven and earth: ... may the blessing ... be on Abram, *BB* ... creator of heaven and earth, *Goodspeed* ... maker of heaven and earth, *RSV.*

20. And blessed be the most high God, which hath delivered thine enemies into thy hand: ... and praised be El-Elyon, *Anchor* ... and you thank the Most High, *Fenton* ... who hath delivered thine adversaries into thine hand, *Young* ... delivered your foes to you, *Anchor* ... delivered your oppressors into your hand, *MLB.*

And he gave him tithes of all: ... he gave him a portion of everything, *Goodspeed* ... a tenth of all the spoil, *Fenton* ... a tenth of the goods, *BB* ... a tithe of all the booty, *NEB.*

14:15-16. Abram, as a wise commander, divided his forces for a surprise attack at night from two directions against the four kings. The attack was successful and the four kings and their armies fled. Abram pursued them as far as Hobah, probably about 80 miles northeast of Damascus. In their flight, they probably kept throwing away the goods they had captured. Thus, Abram was able to recover all the loot taken from Sodom as well as the people captured (including soldiers, Lot and his possessions).

14:17. News of the victory reached the king of Sodom and he went north to meet Abram in the King's Valley near Jerusalem. (*Shaveh* may be another word for "king.")

14:18. Melchizedek ("king of righteousness," cf. Heb. 7:2), king of Salem ("peace," or "at peace," an old name for Jerusalem) was a priest of *El Elyon*, "God Most High." Apparently he was a Canaanite who had somehow been given revelation of the true God. The Bible introduces him here without naming his father or mother and without giving his genealogy. In New Testament times Jewish priests had to prove their authority to be a priest by presenting a genealogy that would connect with the descendants of Aaron given in the Biblical record. But Melchizedek did not derive his priesthood from his father and mother. The Bible recognizes Melchizedek as a priest without any genealogical record mentioned in the Scriptures, which in Hebrews 7 means his authority was given directly by God Himself, just as Jesus was given authority later. Melchizedek brought out bread and wine as food and refreshment for the battle-weary men and as a victory celebration in the name of the Lord.

14:19-20. Melchizedek then proceeded to bless Abram, recognizing that *El Elyon* is the Creator of heaven and earth, and blessing or praising God Most High for giving Abram the victory over his enemies. That blessing was more than mere words, and we can be sure that Abram felt the presence of God as he responded by giving Melchizedek a tenth of everything. Tithing is recognition of God's provision and blessing.

5598.131, 3937	5497	7688	4089.131, 3937	22.	569.121
v Qal impv 2ms, prep, ps 1cs	art, n fs	cj, art, n ms	v Qal impv 2ms, prep, ps 2fs		cj, v Qal impf 3ms
תֶּן־לִי	הַנֶּפֶשׁ	וְהָרְכֻשׁ	קַח־לָךְ		וַיֹּאמֶר
ten-lî	hannephesh	w^{e}hār^{e}khush	qach-lākh		wayyō'mer
give to me	the people	and the property	take for you		and he said

82	420, 4567	5651	7597.515	3135	420, 3176	418	6169
pn	prep, *n ms*	pn	v Hiphil pf 1cs	n fs, ps 1cs	prep, pn	n ms	n ms
אַבְרָם	אֶל־מֶלֶךְ	סְדֹם	הֲרִימֹתִי	יָדִי	אֶל־יְהוָה	אֵל	עֶלְיוֹן
'avrām	'el-melekh	s^{e}dhōm	h^{e}rîmōthî	yādhî	'el-y^{e}hwāh	'ēl	'elyôn
Abram	to the king of	Sodom	I have raised	my hand	to Yahweh	God	Most High

7353.151	8452	800	23.	524, 4623, 2432	5912	8025, 5458
v Qal act ptc ms	n md	cj, n fs		cj, prep, n ms	cj, cj	*n ms*, n fs
קֹנֵה	שָׁמַיִם	וָאָרֶץ		אִם־מִחוּט	וְעַד	שְׂרוֹךְ־נַעַל
qōnēh	shāmayim	wā'ārets		'im-michûṯ	w^{e}'adh	s^{e}rôkh-na'al
Creator of	heavens	and earth		if from thread	and until	thong of sandal

524, 4089.125	4623, 3725, 866, 3937	3940	569.123	603	6483.515	881, 82
cj, cj, v Qal impf 1cs	prep, *adj*, rel part, prep, ps 2fs	cj, neg part	v Qal impf 2ms	pers pron	v Hiphil pf 1cs	do, pn
וְאִם־אֶקַּח	מִכָּל־אֲשֶׁר־לָךְ	וְלֹא	תֹאמַר	אֲנִי	הֶעֱשַׁרְתִּי	אֶת־אַבְרָם
w^{e}'im-'eqqach	mikkol-'ăsher-lākh	w^{e}lō'	thō'mar	'ănî	he'ĕshartî	'eth-'avrām
and if I take	from all which to you	and not	you will say	I	I made rich	Abram

24.	1146	7828	866	404.116	5470	2610	596	866
	cj	adv	rel part	v Qal pf 3cp	art, n mp	cj, *n ms*	art, n mp	rel part
	בִּלְעָדַי	רַק	אֲשֶׁר	אָכְלוּ	הַנְּעָרִים	וְחֵלֶק	הָאֲנָשִׁים	אֲשֶׁר
	bil'ādhay	raq	'ăsher	'ākh^{e}lû	hann^{e}'ārîm	w^{e}chēleq	hā'ănāshîm	'ăsher
	except	only	which	they ate	the young men	and the share of	the men	who

2050.116	882	6293	839	4613	2062	4089.126	2610
v Qal pf 3cp	prep, ps 1cs	pn	pn	cj, pn	pers pron	v Qal impf 3mp	n ms, ps 3mp
הָלְכוּ	אִתִּי	עָנֵר	אֶשְׁכֹּל	וּמַמְרֵא	הֵם	יִקְחוּ	חֶלְקָם
hāl^{e}khû	'ittî	'ānēr	'eshkōl	ûmamrē'	hēm	yiqchû	chelqām
they went	with me	Aner	Eshcol	and Mamre	they	they will take	their share

15:1	313	1745	431	2030.111	1745, 3176	420, 82	904, 4371
	adv	art, n mp	art, dem pron	v Qal pf 3ms	*n ms*, pn	prep, pn	prep, art, n ms
	אַחַר	הַדְּבָרִים	הָאֵלֶּה	הָיָה	דְבַר־יְהוָה	אֶל־אַבְרָם	בַּמַּחֲזֶה
	'achar	hadd^{e}vārîm	hā'ēlleh	hāyâh	dh^{e}var-y^{e}hwāh	'el-'avrām	bammachzeh
	after	the matters	the these	it was	the word of Yahweh	to Abram	in the vision

3937, 569.141	414, 3486.123	82	609	4182	3937	7964	7528.542
prep, v Qal inf con	adv, v Qal juss 2ms	pn	pers pron	n ms	prep, ps 2fs	n ms, ps 2ms	v Hiphil inf abs
לֵאמֹר	אַל־תִּירָא	אַבְרָם	אָנֹכִי	מָגֵן	לָךְ	שְׂכָרְךָ	הַרְבֵּה
lē'mōr	'al-tîrā'	'avrām	'ānōkhî	māghēn	lākh	s^{e}khār^{e}khā	harbēh
saying	do not fear	Abram	I	shield	to you	your reward	making great

4108	2.	569.121	82	112	3176	4242, 5598.123, 3937	609
adv		cj, v Qal impf 3ms	pn	n ms, ps 1cs	pn	intr part, v Qal impf 2ms, prep, ps 1cs	cj, pers pron
מְאֹד		וַיֹּאמֶר	אַבְרָם	אֲדֹנָי	יֱהוִה	מַה־תִּתֶּן־לִי	וְאָנֹכִי
m^{e}'ōdh		wayyō'mer	'avrām	'ădhōnāy	yěhwih	mah-titten-lî	w^{e}'ānōkhî
very		and he said	Abram	my Lord	Yahweh	what You will give to me	and I

2050.151	6423	1158, 5124	1041	2000	1894	466
v Qal act ptc ms	adj	cj, *n ms*, *n ms*	n ms, ps 1cs	pers pron	pn	pn
הוֹלֵךְ	עֲרִירִי	וּבֶן־מֶשֶׁק	בֵּיתִי	הוּא	דַּמֶּשֶׂק	אֱלִיעֶזֶר
hôlēkh	'ărîrî	ûven-mesheq	bêthî	hû'	dammeseq	'ĕlî'ezer
going	childless	and son of acquisition of	my house	he	Damascus	Eliezer

21. And the king of Sodom said unto Abram, Give me the persons, and take the goods to thyself: ... give me the souls, *Darby* ... give me the prisoners, *BB* ... you have given me my life, so take all the wealth, *Fenton* ... you can take the livestock, *REB* ... keep the property, *Anchor.*

22. And Abram said to the king of Sodom, I have lift up mine hand unto the LORD, the most high God, the possessor of heaven and earth: ... I have taken an oath to the Lord, *BB* ... I have sworn by uplifted hand, *Goodspeed* ... I have sworn to the Lord, *NAB* ... I raise my hand to the Lord God Most High, *NCB* ... Ever-Living God Almighty, *Fenton.*

23. That I will not take from a thread even to a shoelatchet: ... sandal strap, *Anchor* ... sandal-thong, *Darby* ... the cord of a shoe, *BB* ... shoestring, *Fenton.*

and that I will not take any thing that is thine, lest thou shouldest say, I have made Abram rich: ... nor aught that is thine, *ASV* ... that belongs to you, *Goodspeed.*

24. Save only that which the young men have eaten: ... what my men used up, *Anchor* ... young men who march with me have consumed, *MLB* ... which the fighting men have had, *BB* ... except what the soldiers have eaten, *Fenton* ... what my servants have used up, *NAB.*

and the portion of the men which went with me, Aner, Eshcol, and Mamre; let them take their portion: ... the men who accompanied me, *Goodspeed* ... part of the goods, *BB* ... their share, *Fenton.*

15:1. After these things the word of the LORD came unto Abram in a vision, saying: ... some time afterward, *Anchor* ... following these events, *MLB.*

Fear not, Abram: I am thy shield, and thy exceeding great reward: ... I am thy buckler, *Geneva* ... have no fear, Abram; I will keep you safe, and great will be your reward, *BB* ... your reward shall be very great, *Anchor* ... your reward is marvelously rich, *Berkeley* ... your abundant reward; I will greatly enrich you, *Fenton.*

2. And Abram said, Lord GOD,

14:21. The king of Sodom was so happy to retrieve the people who had been taken captive, and who would have been sold as slaves, he told Abram to keep all of the possessions of Sodom he had recovered.

14:22-24. In his response to the king of Sodom Abram identified El Elyon as the same God, the LORD (*Yahweh*), that he worshiped. He had solemnly promised God (raising his hand as in giving his oath) not to take even a thread or a sandal thong from the king of Sodom, so that the king of Sodom could never say he had made Abram rich.
What a difference this was from the situation in Egypt. There, Abram was acting in fear and accepted all kinds of gifts from Pharaoh. Now Abram was again acting in faith, had won a victory with the LORD's help, and had fellowship with another believer, Melchizedek. Faith is neither fearful nor greedy. Abram did let his allies take the share that was customary, however. Probably they divided a tenth among themselves (cf. 1 Sam. 8:15,17).

15:1. The events of chapters 13 and 14 lead to a monumental climax described in this chapter. The divine prophetic "vision" here includes the events of the entire chapter. It begins with the word of the LORD coming to Abram. "The word of the LORD," not war, would be the secret of real victory. It was night.

In the darkness Abram may have been thinking about the events of chapter 14. He had won the victory over the four kings by a stratagem. They had come back when the five kings rebelled. What if they would come back again and attack him? God told him not to be afraid. God emphatically said "I am your shield." God would be with him. His power would be sufficient to protect him. Also, Abram may have been thinking about his refusal to take any reward for defeating the four kings and restoring the captured people and property to Sodom. God emphatically said, "I am your very great reward." In other words, God was saying, forget about those things and be concerned with me! When we have the LORD we have enough.

15:2-3. This made Abram think of God's promise. He was not doubting that promise, but ancient documents show that if a man had no child, he could adopt a male servant or slave to be his heir. Abram had as his business manager or chief servant a slave named Eliezer ("God is my help") whom he had acquired in Damascus on his way to Canaan. Abram thought God could fulfill the promise through Eliezer, since legal inheritance was as important as natural inheritance in those days, as archaeological discoveries at Nuzu in Mesopotamia have shown. But this left Abram without personal satisfaction and it brought a question to his mind. What would God give him since He had not given him a child?

3. 569.121	82	2075	3937	3940	5598.113	2320	2079
cj, v Qal impf 3ms	pn	intrj	prep, ps 1cs	neg part	v Qal pf 2ms	n ms	cj, intrj
וַיֹּאמֶר	אַבְרָם	הֵן	לִי	לֹא	נָתַתָּה	זָרַע	וְהִנֵּה
wayyō'mer	'avrām	hēn	lî	lō'	nāthattāh	zāra'	w^{e}hinnēh
and he said	Abram	behold	to me	not	you gave	seed	and behold

1158, 1041	3542.151	881	**4.** 2079	1745, 3176	420	3937, 569.141
n ms, n ms, ps 1cs	v Qal act ptc ms	do, ps 1cs	cj, intrj	*n ms*, pn	prep, ps 3ms	prep, v Qal inf con
בֶּן־בֵּיתִי	יוֹרֵשׁ	אֹתִי	וְהִנֵּה	דְבַר־יְהוָה	אֵלָיו	לֵאמֹר
ven-bêthî	yôrēsh	'ōthî	w^{e}hinnēh	dh^{e}var-y^{e}hwāh	'ēlāv	lē'mōr
son of my house	heir	me	and behold	the word of Yahweh	to him	saying

3940	3542.121	2172	3706, 524	866	3428.121	4623, 4753
neg part	v Qal impf 3ms, ps 2ms	dem pron	cj, cj	rel part	v Qal impf 3ms	prep, n mp, ps 2ms
לֹא	יִירָשְׁךָ	זֶה	כִּי־אִם	אֲשֶׁר	יֵצֵא	מִמֵּעֶיךָ
lō'	yîrāsh^{e}khā	zeh	kî-'im	'ăsher	yētsē'	mimmē'êkhā
not	be your heir	this	but rather	who	he will go out	from your loins

2000	3542.121	**5.** 3428.521	881	2445	569.121
pers pron	v Qal impf 3ms	cj, v Hiphil impf 3ms	do, ps 3ms	art, n ms	cj, v Qal impf 3ms
הוּא	יִירָשֶׁךָ	וַיּוֹצֵא	אֹתוֹ	הַחוּצָה	וַיֹּאמֶר
hû'	yîrāshekhā	wayyôtsē'	'ōthô	hachûtsāh	wayyō'mer
he	he will be your heir	and He brought out	him	to the outside	and He said

5202.531, 5167	8452	5807.131	3676	524, 3310.123	3937, 5807.141
v Hiphil impv 2ms, ptc	art, n md	cj, v Qal impv 2ms	art, n mp	cj, v Qal impf 2ms	prep, v Qal inf con
הַבֶּט־נָא	הַשָּׁמַיְמָה	וּסְפֹר	הַכּוֹכָבִים	אִם־תּוּכַל	לִסְפֹּר
habbeṭ-nā'	hashshāmaymāh	ûs^{e}phōr	hakkôkhāvîm	'im-tûkhal	lispōr
look please	to the heavens	and count	the stars	if you are able	to count

881	569.121	3937	3662	2030.121	2320	**6.** 548.511
do, ps 3mp	cj, v Qal impf 3ms	prep, ps 3ms	adv	v Qal impf 3ms	n ms, ps 2ms	cj, v Hiphil pf 3ms
אֹתָם	וַיֹּאמֶר	לוֹ	כֹּה	יִהְיֶה	זַרְעֶךָ	וְהֶאֱמִן
'ōthām	wayyō'mer	lô	kōh	yihyeh	zar'ekhā	w^{e}he'ĕmin
them	and He said	to him	so	it will be	your seed	and he believed

904, 3176	2913.121	3937	6930	**7.** 569.121	420
prep, pn	cj, v Qal impf 3fs, ps 3fs	prep, ps 3ms	n fs	cj, v Qal impf 3ms	prep, ps 3ms
בַּיהוָה	וַיַּחְשְׁבֶהָ	לוֹ	צְדָקָה	וַיֹּאמֶר	אֵלָיו
bayhwāh	wayyachsh^{e}vehā	lô	ts^{e}dhāqāh	wayyō'mer	'ēlâv
in Yahweh	and He considered it	to him	righteousness	and He said	to him

603	3176	866	3428.515	4623, 217	3908	3937, 5598.141	3937
pers pron	pn	rel part	v Hiphil pf 1cs, ps 2ms	prep, pn	pn	prep, v Qal inf con	prep, ps 2ms
אֲנִי	יְהוָה	אֲשֶׁר	הוֹצֵאתִיךָ	מֵאוּר	כַּשְׂדִּים	לָתֶת	לְךָ
'ănî	y^{e}hwāh	'ăsher	hôtsē'thîkhā	mē'ûr	kasdîm	lātheth	l^{e}khā
I	Yahweh	who	I brought out you	from Ur of	the Chaldeans	to give	to you

881, 800	2148	3937, 3542.141	**8.** 569.121	112	3176
do, art, n fs	art, dem pron	prep, v Qal inf con, ps 3fs	cj, v Qal impf 3ms	n ms, ps 1cs	pn
אֶת־הָאָרֶץ	הַזֹּאת	לְרִשְׁתָּהּ	וַיֹּאמַר	אֲדֹנָי	יֱהוִה
'eth-hā'ārets	hazzō'th	l^{e}rishtāhh	wayyō'mar	'ădhōnāy	yĕhwih
the land	the this	to possess it	and he said	my Lord	Yahweh

904, 4242	3156.125	3706	3937.125	**9.** 569.121	420	4089.131
prep, art, intrg part	v Qal impf 1cs	cj	v Qal impf 1cs, ps 3fs	cj, v Qal impf 3ms	prep, ps 3ms	v Qal impv 2ms
בַּמָּה	אֵדַע	כִּי	אִירָשֶׁנָּה	וַיֹּאמֶר	אֵלָיו	קְחָה
bammāh	'ēdha'	kî	'îrāshennāh	wayyō'mer	'ēlâv	qōchāh
by the what	will I know	that	I will possess it	and He said	to him	take

what wilt thou give me, seeing I go childless: ... what good will your gifts be, *NAB* ... what good are all your blessings when I have no son, *LIVB* ... I am ending my life childless, *Berkeley*.

and the steward of my house is this Eliezer of Damascus: ... successor to my house is Dammesek Eliezer, *Anchor* ... my heir is this.

3. And Abram said, Behold, to me thou hast given no seed: ... granted me no offspring, *Anchor* ... no child, *BB* ... no posterity, *Goodspeed.*

and, lo, one born in my house is mine heir: ... one belonging to my household, *Berkeley* ... slave born in my house, *NCB* ... one of my servants will be my heir, *NAB*.

4. And, behold, the word of the LORD came unto him, saying, This shall not be thine heir: ... Yahweh's word came back to him in reply, *Anchor* ... the Lord's message to him was, *Berkeley* ... this man will not get the heritage, *BB*.

but he that shall come forth out of thine own bowels shall be thine heir: ... none but your own issue, *Anchor* ... born from your own body, *Goodspeed* ... your own son shall be your heir, *RSV.*

5. And he brought him forth abroad, and said: ... he took him outside, *Anchor* ... he conducted him outdoors, *MLB* ... he led him out, *Darby* ... he took him out into the open air, *BB*.

Look now toward heaven, and tell the stars, if thou be able to number them: ... let your eyes be lifted to heaven, *BB* ... look attentively, I pray thee, towards the heavens, *Young* ... look up at the sky and count the stars if you can, *Fenton*.

and he said unto him, So shall thy seed be: ... your posterity, *NCB* ... your descendants, *Goodspeed* ... race, *Fenton* ... offspring, *Anchor.*

6. And he believed in the LORD: ... he put his trust in Yahweh, *Anchor* ... he had faith in the Lord, *BB* ... he trusted the Lord, *Goodspeed.*

and he counted it to him for righteousness: ... credited it to him as an act of righteousness, *NAB* ... repaid to him in righteousness, *Fenton* ... credited the act to him as justice, *NCB* ... God considered him righteous on account of his faith, *LIVB*.

7. And he said unto him, I am the LORD that brought thee out of Ur of the Chaldees to give thee this land to inherit it: ... as a possession, *Anchor* ... occupy, *NEB* ... to take possession of it, *NIV.*

8. And he said, Lord GOD, whereby shall I know that I shall inherit it: ... in what way can I be assured it

---

15:4-5. God reassured Abram that the promises would be literally fulfilled by a child of Abram's own. Then, outside, God invited Abram to look at the clear night sky and see if he could count the stars. So great would the number of his descendants be!

Moses later pointed out that this applied to Israel and was already fulfilled in Israel as they were about to enter the Promised Land (Deut. 1:10; 10:22), though it also has an application to all who, by faith in Jesus, become heirs of the same promise (Gal. 3:29).

15:6. Notice that the Bible does not say Abram believed God's promise. He believed the LORD. He put his faith and trust in God recognizing Him as the kind of God we can trust, the faithful God who can be counted on to carry out His promise. The Hebrew for "believe" is related to the word "Amen," meaning "truly." It is related to the word for a faithful nurse (*'omeneth*) who can be trusted to take care of a child (Num. 11:12; Ruth 4:16; 2 Sam. 4:4), and to the word for a solid foundation (*'amna*) that will not collapse no matter what is built upon it.

Thus, by believing God Abram put himself in God's hands and determined to rest on God and His promise. This is the kind of faith that the New Testament recognizes as God-pleasing, saving faith (Rom. 4:3, 11, 20-21; Gal. 3:6; Heb. 11:7, 11-12). God credited this faith to Abram for righteousness. That is, God cleansed him of sin and guilt and made him acceptable to God.

In other words, Abram was saved by grace through faith, not by his good works. There is no other way of salvation anywhere in the Bible. But this did not condemn him to a life of inactivity. Good works always follow real faith. By the kind of active faith he had, which we place in God through Jesus, we become children of Abraham, heirs of the same promise (Gal. 3:7). Christians also have the promise that we shall do greater works (John 14:12).

15:7-8. God was about to confirm His promise of the Land by making a covenant (a solemn, binding agreement) for Abram's benefit. Covenants made by kings in those days began with the king identifying himself and giving a brief historical background. God always takes people where they are, so He began in a way that would help Abram

3937	5904	8420.457	6008	8420.457	356	8420.457	8782
prep, ps 1cs	n fs	v Pual ptc fs	cj, n fs	v Pual ptc fs	cj, n ms	v Pual ptc fs	cj, n fs
לִי	עֶגְלָה	מְשֻׁלֶּשֶׁת	וְעֵז	מְשֻׁלֶּשֶׁת	וְאַיִל	מְשֻׁלָּשׁ	וְתֹר
lî	‘eghlāh	meshullesheth	we‘ēz	meshullesheth	we’ayil	meshullāsh	wethōr
for Me	heifer	being three	and she-goat	being three	and ram	being three	and turtledove

1501		4089, 3937	881, 3725, 431	1363.321	881
cj, n ms	**10.**	cj, v Qal impf 3ms, prep, ps 3ms	do, *adj*, dem pron	cj, v Piel impf 3ms	do, ps 3mp
וְגוֹזָל		וַיִּקַּח־לוֹ	אֶת־כָּל־אֵלֶּה	וַיְבַתֵּר	אֹתָם
weghôzāl		wayyiqqach-lô	’eth-kol-’ēlleh	wayvattēr	’ōthām
and young bird		and he took for Him	all these	and he cut in two	them

904, 8761	5598.121	382, 1365	3937, 7410.141	7751	881, 7109	3940
prep, art, sub	cj, v Qal pf 3ms	n ms, n ms, ps 3ms	prep, v Qal inf con	n ms, ps 3ms	cj, do, art, n fs	neg part
בַּתָּוֶךְ	וַיִּתֵּן	אִישׁ־בִּתְרוֹ	לִקְרַאת	רֵעֵהוּ	וְאֶת־הַצִּפֹּר	לֹא
battāwekh	wayyittēn	’îsh-bithrô	liqōra’th	rē‘ēhû	we’eth-hatsippōr	lō’
in the middle	and he placed	each its piece	to be against	its companion	but the birds	not

1363.111		3495.121	6077	6142, 6538	5566.521	881
v Qal pf 3ms	**11.**	cj, v Qal impf 3ms	art, n ms	prep, art, n mp	cj, v Hiphil impf 3ms	do, ps 3mp
בָתָר		וַיֵּרֶד	הָעַיִט	עַל־הַפְּגָרִים	וַיַּשֵּׁב	אֹתָם
vāthār		wayyēredh	hā‘ayiṭ	‘al-happeghārîm	wayyashshēv	’ōthām
he cut in two		and they went down	the birds of prey	on the carcasses	but he made go	them

82		2030.121	8507	3937, 971.141	8976	5489.112	6142, 82
pn	**12.**	cj, v Qal impf 3ms	art, n ms	prep, v Qal inf con	cj, n fs	v Qal pf 3fs	prep, pn
אַבְרָם		וַיְהִי	הַשֶּׁמֶשׁ	לָבוֹא	וְתַרְדֵּמָה	נָפְלָה	עַל־אַבְרָם
’avrām		wayhî	hashshemesh	lāvô’	wethardēmāh	nāphelāh	‘al-’avrām
Abram		and it was	the sun	setting	and deep sleep	it fell	on Abram

2079	372	2934	1448	5489.153	6142		569.121	3937, 82
cj, intrj	n fs	n fs	adj	v Qal act ptc fs	prep, ps 3ms	**13.**	cj, v Qal impf 3ms	prep, pn
וְהִנֵּה	אֵימָה	חֲשֵׁכָה	גְדֹלָה	נֹפֶלֶת	עָלָיו		וַיֹּאמֶר	לְאַבְרָם
wehinnēh	’êmāh	chăshēkhāh	gedhōlāh	nōpheleth	‘ālâv		wayyō’mer	le’avrām
and behold	terror	darkness	great	falling	on him		and He said	to Abram

3156.142	3156.123	3706, 1658	2030.121	2320	904, 800	3940	3937
v Qal inf abs	v Qal impf 2ms	cj, n ms	v Qal impf 3ms	n ms, ps 2ms	prep, n fs	neg part	prep, ps 3mp
יָדֹעַ	תֵּדַע	כִּי־גֵר	יִהְיֶה	זַרְעֲךָ	בְּאֶרֶץ	לֹא	לָהֶם
yādhō‘a	tēdha‘	kî-ghēr	yihyeh	zar‘ăkhā	be’erets	lō’	lāhem
knowing	you will know	that stranger	he will be	your seed	in land	not	to them

5856.116	6257.316	881	727	4109	8523
cj, v Qal pf 3cp, ps 3mp	cj, v Piel pf 3cp	do, ps 3mp	num	*num*	n fs
וַעֲבָדוּם	וְעִנּוּ	אֹתָם	אַרְבַּע	מֵאוֹת	שָׁנָה
wa‘ăvādhûm	we‘innû	’ōthām	’arba‘	mē’ôth	shānāh
and they will serve them	and they will humble	them	four	hundreds of	years

	1612	881, 1504	866	5856.126	1833.151	609	311, 3772
14.	cj, cj	do, art, n ms	rel part	v Qal impf 3mp	v Qal act ptc ms	pers pron	cj, *sub*, adv
	וְגַם	אֶת־הַגּוֹי	אֲשֶׁר	יַעֲבֹדוּ	דָּן	אָנֹכִי	וְאַחֲרֵי־כֵן
	wegham	’eth-haggôy	’ăsher	ya‘ăvōdhû	don	’ānōkhî	we’achrê-khēn
	but also	the nation	which	they will serve	will judge	I	and afterward

3428.126	904, 7688	1448		887	971.123	420, 1
v Qal impf 3mp	prep, n ms	adj	**15.**	cj, pers pron	v Qal impf 2ms	prep, n mp, ps 2ms
יֵצְאוּ	בִּרְכֻשׁ	גָּדוֹל		וְאַתָּה	תָּבוֹא	אֶל־אֲבֹתֶיךָ
yēts’û	birekhush	gādhôl		we’attāh	tāvô’	’el-’ăvōthêkhā
they will come out	with property	great		and you	you will go	to your fathers

will be mine, *Berkeley* ... how may I be certain, *BB* ... how may I be sure that I shall occupy it, *NEB*.

9. And he said unto him, Take me an heifer of three years old: ... get me a three year old heifer, Berkeley ... take a young cow, *BB* ... procure a three year old heifer, *Goodspeed*.

and a she goat of three years old, and a ram of three years old, and a turtledove, and a young pigeon: ... and a fledgling, *NEB* ... and a young bird, *Young*.

10. And he took unto him all these and divided them in the midst: ... and slit them through the middle, *Anchor* ... cut them in halves, *Berkeley*.

and laid each piece one against another: ... and laid each half, *ASV* ... placing each half opposite the other, *Berkeley* ... opposite its corresponding piece, *NEB*.

but the birds divided he not: ... he did not cut the birds, *Anchor* ... did not halve the birds, *NEB*.

11. And when the fowls came down upon the carcasses Abram drove them away: ... the birds of prey came down, *ASV* ... swooped down, *Anchor* ... the vultures came down, *NKJV* ... Abram scared them away, *Darby*.

12. And when the sun was going down: ... sun was about to set, *Anchor* ... about sunset, *Berkeley*.

a deep sleep fell upon Abram: ... a trance fell upon Abram, *Goodspeed* ... a stupor fell on Abram, *Fenton* ... a heavy sleep, *Geneva*.

and, lo, an horror of great darkness fell upon him: ... a deep dark dread descended upon him, *Anchor* ... deep terrifying darkness enveloped him, *NAB* ... a horror of dense darkness, *Berkeley* ... a dark cloud of fear, *BB* ... great and terrible darkness oppressed him, *Fenton*.

13. And he said unto Abram, Know of a surety that thy seed shall be a stranger in a land that is not theirs: ... know with certainty that your descendants shall be aliens, *Berkeley* ... know assuredly that thy seed will be a sojourner, *Darby* ... know this, and be assured that your race will be foreigners, *Fenton* ... descendants shall be immigrants, *Goodspeed*.

and shall serve them; and they shall afflict them four hundred years: ... to be enslaved and oppressed, *Anchor* ... working for those who shall oppress them, *Berkeley* ... as servants to a people who will be cruel to them, *BB* ... enslaved and mistreated, *NIV*.

14. And also that nation, whom they shall serve, will I judge: ... I will bring judgment on the nation, *NRSV* ... I will punish the nation, *MLB*.

and afterward shall they come out with great substance: ... they shall leave with great wealth, *Anchor* ... come out with great property, *Darby* ... escape with great wealth, *Goodspeed* ... come out with many possessions, *NASB* ... go free with great possessions, *NCB*.

---

understand what He was doing. But Abram did not immediately understand. He wanted further assurance about the land. He had believed with respect to the promise of a son, but the promise of the land seemed even more impossible, since he did not have a big enough army to conquer it and the Canaanites would not sell it. The question in his heart and mind was "How shall I know?" This does not mean Abram doubted God. He just wanted God to give him further confirmation and assurance.

15:9-11. God asked Abram to bring a sacrifice. Abram spent the day getting the required animals and birds and arranging them, probably on a rock, with the animals cut in half. For a time nothing happened, but Abram waited in faith, driving away birds of prey (probably vultures) that were attracted by the carcasses.

15:12-14. At sundown, Abram fell into a deep sleep and felt terror as a great darkness enveloped him. In the midst of that darkness, the voice of the LORD assured him with respect to his question, "How shall I know?" Abram could surely know that his descendants would inherit the land, but not until they were enslaved and mistreated in a foreign land for (over) 400 years. (This is a round number, see Exod. 12:40 for 430 years as the exact number of years Israel was in Egypt.) God then would punish the nation that enslaved them and they would come out, not as slaves secretly trying to escape, but as victors going out boldly with great possessions.

15:15. Abram would not live to see the promise of the land fulfilled. He would simply have to accept the promise in faith. But he would enjoy a long life and go to his fathers in peace. This implies he would go to his godly fathers, like Enoch, who were in heaven in the presence of the LORD (Gen. 5:24; cf. Ps. 16:11; 17:15; 23:6; 49:15; 73:24, 26; Prov. 15:24).

15:16. Since Abram had his first child at 100 years of age, a generation here is 100 years (Gen. 21:5). Thus after the 400 years Abram's descendants would come back into the Promised Land.

904, 8361	7196.223	904, 7939	3009B	16.	1810	7536	8178.126
prep, n ms	v Niphal impf 2ms	prep, n fs	adj		cj, n ms	num	v Qal impf 3mp
בְּשָׁלוֹם	תִּקָּבֵר	בְּשֵׂיבָה	טוֹבָה		וְדוֹר	רְבִיעִי	יָשׁוּבוּ
beshālôm	tiqqāvēr	besêvāh	ṯôvāh		wedhôr	revî'î	yāshûvû
in peace	you will be buried	in old age	good		and generation	fourth	they will return

2078	3706	3940, 8400	5988	578	5912, 2077	17.	2030.121
pers pron	cj	neg part, adj	*n ms*	art, pn	cj, adv		cj, v Qal impf 3ms
הֵנָּה	כִּי	לֹא־שָׁלֵם	עֲוֹן	הָאֱמֹרִי	עַד־הֵנָּה		וַיְהִי
hēnnāh	kî	lō'-shālēm	'ăwōn	hā'ĕmōrî	'adh-hēnnāh		wayhî
they	because	not complete	the iniquity of	the Amorites	until now		and it was

8507	971.112	6161	2030.111	2079	8902	6476	4083
art, n ms	v Qal pf 3fs	cj, n fs	v Qal pf 3ms	cj, intrj	n ms	n ms	cj, n ms
הַשֶּׁמֶשׁ	בָּאָה	וַעֲלָטָה	הָיָה	וְהִנֵּה	תַנּוּר	עָשָׁן	וְלַפִּיד
hashshemesh	bā'āh	wa'ălāṯāh	hāyâh	wehinnēh	thannûr	'āshān	welappîdh
the sun	it set	and darkness	it was	and behold	fire pot	smoking	and torch

813	866	5882.111	1033	1536	431	18.	904, 3219	2000
n fs	rel part	v Qal pf 3ms	prep	art, n mp	art, dem pron		prep, art, n ms	art, dem pron
אֵשׁ	אֲשֶׁר	עָבַר	בֵּין	הַגְּזָרִים	הָאֵלֶּה		בַּיּוֹם	הַהוּא
'ēsh	'ăsher	'āvar	bên	haggezārîm	hā'ēlleh		bayyôm	hahû'
burning	which	it passed	between	the pieces	the these		in the day	the that

3901.111	3176	882, 82	1311	3937, 569.141	3937, 2320	5598.115
v Qal pf 3ms	pn	prep, pn	n fs	prep, v Qal inf con	prep, n ms, ps 2ms	v Qal pf 1cs
כָּרַת	יְהוָה	אֶת־אַבְרָם	בְּרִית	לֵאמֹר	לְזַרְעֲךָ	נָתַתִּי
kārath	yehwāh	'eth-'avrām	berîth	lē'mōr	lezar'ăkhā	nāthattî
He cut	Yahweh	with Abram	covenant	saying	to your seed	I have given

881, 800	2148	4623, 5282	4875	5912, 5282	1448	5282, 6828
do, art, n fs	art, dem pron	prep, *n ms*	pn	prep, art, n ms	art, adj	*n ms*, pn
אֶת־הָאָרֶץ	הַזֹּאת	מִנְּהַר	מִצְרַיִם	עַד־הַנָּהָר	הַגָּדֹל	נְהַר־פְּרָת
'eth-hā'ārets	hazzō'th	minnehar	mitsrayim	'adh-hannāhār	haggādhōl	nehar-perāth
the land	the this	from river of	Egypt	until the river	the great	river of Euphrates

19.	881, 7299	881, 7358	881	7220	20.	881, 2958
	do, art, pn	cj, do, art, pn	cj, do	art, pn		cj, do, art, pn
	אֶת־הַקֵּינִי	וְאֶת־הַקְּנִזִּי	וְאֵת	הַקַּדְמֹנִי		וְאֶת־הַחִתִּי
	'eth-haqqênî	we'eth-haqqenizzî	we'th	haqqadhmōnî		we'eth-hachittî
	the Kenites	and the Kenizzites	and	the Kadmonites		and the Hittites

881, 6773	881, 7788	21.	881, 578	881, 3793	881, 1665
cj, do, art, pn	cj, do, art, pn		cj, do, art, pn	cj, do, art, pn	cj, do, art, pn
וְאֶת־הַפְּרִזִּי	וְאֶת־הָרְפָאִים		וְאֶת־הָאֱמֹרִי	וְאֶת־הַכְּנַעֲנִי	וְאֶת־הַגִּרְגָּשִׁי
we'eth-happerizzî	we'eth-hārephā'îm		we'eth-hā'ĕmōrî	we'eth-hakkena'ănî	we'eth-haggirgāshî
and the Perizzites	and the Rephaim		and the Amorites	and the Canaanites	and the Girgashites

881, 3092	16:1	8030	828	82	3940	3314.112	3937
cj, do, art, pn		cj, pn	*n fs*	pn	neg part	v Qal pf 3fs	prep, ps 3ms
וְאֶת־הַיְבוּסִי		וְשָׂרַי	אֵשֶׁת	אַבְרָם	לֹא	יָלְדָה	לוֹ
we'eth-hayvûsî		wesāray	'ēsheth	'avrām	lō'	yāledhāh	lô
and the Jebusites		and Sarai	the wife of	Abram	not	she gave birth	to him

3937	8569	4874	8428	1972	2.	569.122	8030
cj, prep, ps 3fs	n fs	pn	cj, n ms, ps 3fs	pn		cj, v Qal impf 3fs	pn
וְלָהּ	שִׁפְחָה	מִצְרִית	וּשְׁמָהּ	הָגָר		וַתֹּאמֶר	שָׂרַי
welāhh	shiphchāh	mitsrîth	ûshemāhh	hāghār		watō'mer	sāray
and to her	female slave	Egyptian	and her name	Hagar		and she said	Sarai

15. And thou shalt go to thy fathers in peace: ... you shall join your forefathers, *Anchor* ... you shall go to your ancestors, *NRSV.*

thou shalt be buried in a good old age: ... with beautiful gray hairs, *Fenton* ... at the end of a long life.

16. But in the fourth generation they shall come hither again: ... in the fourth time span, *NAB* ... your descendants will come back, *NIV.*

for the iniquity of the Amorites is not yet full: ... not yet brim full, *Berkeley* ... not yet complete, *Goodspeed* ... will not have run its course, *Anchor* ... not reached its full measure, *NIV.*

17. And it came to pass, that, when the sun went down, and it was dark: ... sun had set and dense darkness had come, *Berkeley* ... after the sun set, followed by thick darkness, *Fenton.*

behold a smoking furnace, and a burning lamp that passed between those pieces: ... a smoking brazier, *NEB* ... smoking oven and a burning torch, *Berkeley* ... a blazing fire, *Fenton* ... a firebrand, *Geneva* ... went between the parts, *BB.*

18. In the same day the LORD made a covenant with Abram, saying: ... at that time, *Berkeley* ... made an agreement, *BB.*

Unto thy seed have I given this land, from the river of Egypt unto the great river, the river Euphrates: ... to your descendants I will give this country, *Berkeley* ... to your race, *Fenton* ... from the Wadi of Egypt, *NAB.*

19. The Kenites, and the Kenizzites, and the Kadmonites:

20. And the Hittites, and the Perizzites, and the Rephaims:

21. And the Amorites, and the Canaanites, and the Girgashites, and the Jebusites:

16:1. Now Sarai Abram's wife bare him no children: ... had given him no children, *BB, Fenton* ... hath not born to him, *Young.*

and she had an handmaid, an Egyptian, whose name was Hagar: ... maidservant, *Anchor* ... an Egyptian maid, *Berkeley, MLB* ... a servant, *BB* ... slave-girl, *NEB.*

The reason for the delay was the iniquity (sin and guilt) of the Amorites (the most important people of the central hill country of Canaan where Abram lived at this time) was not yet complete. God was allowing them a full measure before He would let the Israelites drive them out of the Land. Discoveries at the ancient Ugarit, north of Tyre and Sidon, have revealed Canaanite religion promoted child sacrifice, idolatry, prostitution in the name of religion, and all kinds of occultic and immoral practices. As the Book of Job teaches, Job's friends were wrong when they thought God immediately brings judgment on sinners. He is patient and longsuffering. But He is also just, and the judgment will eventually come.

15:17. After dark a smoking firepot (about 2 feet high) with a blazing torch or flame coming out of the top passed from one end of the sacrifice to the other in between the pieces. The Hebrew (except in the case of a marriage covenant) always speaks of cutting a covenant, that is, in the presence of a cut sacrifice. One way this was accomplished was by two people making the sacrifice. One would stand at each end. Then they would walk around or between the pieces of the sacrifice and exchange places (Jer. 34:18-19). By doing this each would solemnly promise to do his part, saying that if he did not, the other could cut him the way the sacrifice was cut. But Abram was off to the side. God in the symbol of fire went from one end to the other between the pieces, something Abram could not do. Thus, God covenanted to do the whole work of fulfilling the covenant. He would begin it. He would finish it. All Abram needed to do was accept it by faith. In fact, he could not help God fulfill it. He would not even live to see it fulfilled.

15:18-21. The content of the covenant God "cut" for Abram's benefit is given here. Ten nations are listed (cf. Gen. 10:15-18), for ten is the number of completeness and indicates the whole land would be given to Abram's descendants. The limits would be the river of Egypt on the south and the Euphrates on the north. "River" in both cases is the word for a river or canal with water in it all the year round. Some take the river of Egypt to be the insignificant *Wadi el-Arish* in northeastern Sinai, however, the Hebrew word for the wadi is different. The promised southern border is rather a branch of the Nile River in its delta. This promise was nearly fulfilled in Solomon's time (1 Ki. 8:65), but will have its complete fulfillment in the Millennium. The promise for the Messiah, however, is that He will rule from sea to sea and from the River (the Euphrates) to the ends of the earth (Zech. 9:10; Ps. 72:8). There will be no limits to His rule.

16:1-2. When Sarai was 75, she began to blame the LORD because she had no children. Ancient marriage contracts show it was the custom

420, 82	2079, 5167	6352.111	3176	4623, 3314.141	971.131, 5167
prep, pn	intrj, part	v Qal pf 3ms, ps 1cs	pn	prep, v Qal inf con	v Qal impv 2ms, ptc
אֶל־אַבְרָם	הִנֵּה־נָא	עֲצָרַנִי	יְהוָה	מִלֶּדֶת	בֹּא־נָא
'el-'avrām	hinnēh-nā'	'ătsāranî	y^{e}hwāh	milledheth	bō'-nā'
to Abram	behold please	he has kept me	Yahweh	from giving birth	go please

420, 8569	193	1161.225	4623	8471.121	82	3937, 7249
prep, n fs, ps 1cs	adv	v Niphal impf 1cs	prep, ps 3fs	cj, v Qal impf 3ms	pn	prep, *n ms*
אֶל־שִׁפְחָתִי	אוּלַי	אִבָּנֶה	מִמֶּנָּה	וַיִּשְׁמַע	אַבְרָם	לְקוֹל
'el-shiphchāthî	'ûlay	'ibbāneh	mimmĕnnāh	wayyishma'	'avrām	l^{e}qôl
to my female slave	perhaps	I will be built	from her	and he listened	Abram	to the voice of

8030		4089.122	8030	828	82	881, 1972	4874	8569
pn	**3.**	cj, v Qal impf 3fs	pn	*n fs*	pn	do, pn	art, pn	n fs, ps 3fs
שָׂרָי		וַתִּקַּח	שָׂרַי	אֵשֶׁת	אַבְרָם	אֶת־הָגָר	הַמִּצְרִית	שִׁפְחָתָהּ
sārāy		wattiqqach	sāray	'ēsheth	'avrām	'eth-hāghār	hammitsrîth	shiphchāthāhh
Sarai		and she took	Sarai	the wife of	Abram	Hagar	the Egyptian	her female slave

4623, 7377	6460	8523	3937, 3553.141	82	904, 800	3791	5598.122
prep, *n ms*	num	n fp	prep, v Qal inf con	pn	prep, *n fs*	pn	cj, v Qal impf 3fs
מִקֵּץ	עֶשֶׂר	שָׁנִים	לְשֶׁבֶת	אַבְרָם	בְּאֶרֶץ	כְּנָעַן	וַתִּתֵּן
miqqēts	'eser	shānîm	l^{e}sheveth	'avrām	b$^{e'}$erets	k^{e}nā'an	wattittēn
after	ten	years	dwelling	Abram	in the land of	Canaan	then she gave

881	3937, 82	382	3937	3937, 828		971.121	420, 1972
do, ps 3fs	prep, pn	n ms, ps 3fs	prep, ps 3ms	prep, n fs	**4.**	cj, v Qal impf 3ms	prep, pn
אֹתָהּ	לְאַבְרָם	אִישָׁהּ	לוֹ	לְאִשָּׁה		וַיָּבֹא	אֶל־הָגָר
'ōthāhh	l$^{e'}$avrām	'îshāhh	lô	l$^{e'}$ishshāh		wayyāvō'	'el-hāghār
her	to Abram	her husband	to him	for a wife		and he went	to Hagar

2106.122	7495.122	3706	2106.112	7327.122	1409
cj, v Qal impf 3fs	cj, v Qal impf 3fs	cj	v Qal pf 3fs	cj, v Qal impf 3fs	n fs, ps 3fs
וַתַּהַר	וַתֵּרֶא	כִּי	הָרָתָה	וַתֵּקַל	גְּבִרְתָּהּ
wattahar	wattēre'	kî	hārāthāh	wattēqal	g^{e}virtāhh
and she conceived	when she saw	that	she conceived	then she was belittled	her mistress

904, 6084		569.122	8030	420, 82	2660	6142	609
prep, n fd, ps 3fs	**5.**	cj, v Qal impf 3fs	pn	prep, pn	n ms, ps 1cs	prep, ps 2ms	pers pron
בְּעֵינֶיהָ		וַתֹּאמֶר	שָׂרַי	אֶל־אַבְרָם	חֲמָסִי	עָלֶיךָ	אָנֹכִי
b$^{e'}$ênêhā		wattō'mer	sāray	'el-'avrām	chămāsî	'ālêkhā	'ānōkhî
in her eyes		and she said	Sarai	to Abram	my wrong	on you	I

5598.115	8569	904, 2536	7495.122	3706	2106.112
v Qal pf 1cs	n fs, ps 1cs	prep, n ms, ps 2ms	cj, v Qal impf 3fs	cj	v Qal pf 3fs
נָתַתִּי	שִׁפְחָתִי	בְּחֵיקֶךָ	וַתֵּרֶא	כִּי	הָרָתָה
nāthattî	shiphchāthî	b^{e}chêqekh	wattēre'	kî	hārāthāh
I have given	my female slave	in your bosom	and she saw	that	she conceived

7327.125	904, 6084	8570.121	3176	1033	1033
cj, v Qal impf 1cs	prep, n fd, ps 3fs	v Qal impf 3ms	pn	prep, ps 1cs	cj, prep, ps 2ms
וָאֵקַל	בְּעֵינֶיהָ	יִשְׁפֹּט	יְהוָה	בֵּינִי	וּבֵינֶיךָ
wā'ēqal	b$^{e'}$ênêāh	yishpōṯ	y^{e}hwāh	bênî	ûvênêkh
and I was belittled	in her eyes	He will judge	Yahweh	between me	and between you

	569.121	82	420, 8030	2079	8569	904, 3135
6.	cj, v Qal impf 3ms	pn	prep, pn	intrj	n fs, ps 2fs	prep, n fs, ps 2fs
	וַיֹּאמֶר	אַבְרָם	אֶל־שָׂרַי	הִנֵּה	שִׁפְחָתֵךְ	בְּיָדֵךְ
	wayyō'mer	'avrām	'el-sāray	hinnēh	shiphchāthēkh	b^{e}yādhēkh
	and he said	Abram	to Sarai	behold	your female servant	in your hand

2. And Sarai said unto Abram, Behold now, the LORD hath restrained me from bearing: ... has prevented me from bearing, *Berkeley* ... has shut me up, *Darby* ... has not let me have children, *BB.*

I pray thee, go in unto my maid: ... suppose you marry my maid, *Goodspeed* ... have intercourse, then, with my maid, *NAB* ... take my slave-girl, *NEB, REB* ... go, sleep with my maidservant, *NIV.*

it may be that I may obtain children by her: ... maybe I shall reproduce through her, *Anchor* ... build up a family through her, *Berkeley, Goodspeed* ... shall be built up by her, *Darby* ... perhaps she will have a son for me, *Fenton* ... I shall receive a child, *Geneva.*

And Abram hearkened to the voice of Sarai: ... heeded Sarai's plea, *Anchor* ... did as Sarai said, *BB* ... listened, *Fenton, KJVII* ... obeyed, *Geneva* ... agreed to the suggestion, *Goodspeed.*

3. And Sarai Abram's wife took Hagar her maid the Egyptian after Abram had dwelt ten years in the land of Canaan: ... brought her slave-girl, *NEB* ... tenth year of Abram's residence, *Fenton.*

and gave her to her husband Abram to be his wife: ... as concubine, *Anchor* ... gave her in marriage, *Goodspeed.*

4. And he went in unto Hagar, and she conceived: ... he had intercourse with Hagar, *Goodspeed, NAB* ... he lay with Hagar, *NEB, REB* ... he slept with, *NIV.*

and when she saw that she had conceived: ... was pregnant, *Anchor, NIV* ... found herself with child, *MLB.*

her mistress was despised in her eyes: ... looked with disdain, *Goodspeed, NCB* ... she no longer had any respect, *BB* ... her mistress was lightly esteemed, *Darby, Young* ... looked down on her mistress, *Berkeley, MLB* ... looked upon her mistress with contempt, *Anchor.*

5. And Sarai said unto Abram, My wrong be upon thee: ... may the injury I suffer come home to you, *Berkeley, MLB* ... thou doeth me wrong, *Geneva* ... you are responsible for this outrage against me, *NAB* ... I am being wronged; you must do something about it, *REB.*

I have given my maid into thy bosom: ... I entrusted my maid, *Berkeley* ... put my maid in your lap, *Anchor* ... in your arms, *Goodspeed* ... to your embrace, *NAB, NCB.*

and when she saw that she had conceived, I was despised in her eyes: ... looking at me with contempt, *Anchor* ... lightly esteemed in her eyes, *Darby, Young* ... no longer had any respect for me, *BB.*

the LORD judge between me and thee: ... let the Lord do justice, *Berkeley, MLB* ... let the Ever-living decide, *Fenton.*

6. But Abram said unto Sarai, Behold, thy maid is in thy hand: ... your maid is in your power, *Berkeley* ... the woman, *BB.*

do to her as it pleaseth thee: ... whatever you consider right, *Fenton* ... what seems good, *NCB* ... whatever you think best, *NIV* ... as you like, *Anchor.*

---

for a wife who was unable to have children to give a female slave as a secondary wife to her husband in order for there to be an heir to carry on the line. Probably while in Egypt (Gen. 12:16) Sarai acquired an Egyptian slave named Hagar. Sarai decided that through Hagar she could have a child that would legally be hers. Abram listened to her, accepting her idea. His motive was probably good, for it came from a concern over God's promise (cf. Mal. 2:15). But he too was influenced by human custom. Instead of seeking God's way, he tried to help the LORD out by following worldly ways. See Galatians 4:29 for the New Testament evaluation of this.

16:3-4. After becoming Abram's wife, Hagar was soon pregnant. Though she was a secondary wife, or concubine, and a former slave, she became proud she was giving Abram a child and began to look down on Sarai as of no account. By her attitude and probably by her words, she began to make life miserable for Sarai.

16:5-6. To Sarai, Hagar's attitude was very wrong, and she put the blame on Abram for allowing it. He was responsible under God to be the leader of the family, and he should not have allowed this injustice. So Sarai called on the LORD to be the judge between her and Abram. But instead of dealing directly with Hagar, Abram told Sarai to do to her whatever she thought best. Sarai then went to the other extreme and proceeded to humiliate Hagar, trying to make her feel she was still her slave, harassing and mistreating her. This was too much for Hagar and she ran away.

16:7. The Angel of the LORD who found Hagar was more than an ordinary angel (*angel* means "messenger"). Many believe this was a preincarnate manifestation of the Second Person of the Trinity. As this passage progresses we find this

6449.132, 3937	3005	904, 6084	6257.322	8030	1300.122
v Qal impv 2fs, prep, ps 3fs	art, n ms	prep, n fd, ps 3fs	cj, v Piel impf 3fs, ps 3fs	pn	cj, v Qal impf 3fs
עֲשִׂי־לָהּ	הַטּוֹב	בְּעֵינָיִךְ	וַתְּעַנֶּהָ	שָׂרַי	וַתִּבְרַח
‘ăsî-lāhh	hattôv	beênāyikh	watte‘annehā	sāray	wattivrach
do to her	the good	in your eyes	and she humiliated her	Sarai	and she fled

4623, 6686	7.	4834.121	4534	3176	6142, 6084	4448
prep, n mp, ps 3fs		cj, v Qal impf 3ms, ps 3fs	*n ms*	pn	prep, *n fs*	art, n md
מִפָּנֶיהָ		וַיִּמְצָאָהּ	מַלְאַךְ	יְהוָה	עַל־עֵין	הַמַּיִם
mippānêhā		wayyimtsā’āhh	mal’akh	yehwāh	‘al-‘ên	hammayim
from her face		and he found her	the angel of	Yahweh	by the spring of	the waters

904, 4198	6142, 6084	904, 1932	8231	8.	569.121	1972	8569
prep, art, n ms	prep, art, n fs	prep, *n ms*	pn		cj, v Qal impf 3ms	pn	*n fs*
בַּמִּדְבָּר	עַל־הָעַיִן	בְּדֶרֶךְ	שׁוּר		וַיֹּאמַר	הָגָר	שִׁפְחַת
bammidbār	‘al-hā‘ayin	bedherekh	shûr		wayyō’mar	hāghār	shiphchath
in the wilderness	by the spring	on journey of	Shur		and he said	Hagar	female slave of

8030	338, 4623, 2172	971.114	590	2050.124	569.122	4623, 6681
pn	intrg, prep, dem pron	v Qal pf 2fs	cj, intrg	v Qal impf 2fs	cj, v Qal impf 3fs	prep, *n ms*
שָׂרַי	אֵי־מִזֶּה	בָאת	וְאָנָה	תֵלֵכִי	וַתֹּאמֶר	מִפְּנֵי
sāray	’ê-mizzeh	bā’th	weānāh	thēlēkhî	wattō’mer	mippenê
Sarai	where from this	you came	and where	you will go	and she said	from the presence of

8030	1409	609	1300.153	9.	569.121	3937	4534
pn	n fs, ps 1cs	pers pron	v Qal act ptc fs		cj, v Qal impf 3ms	prep, ps 3fs	*n ms*
שָׂרַי	גְּבִרְתִּי	אָנֹכִי	בֹּרַחַת		וַיֹּאמֶר	לָהּ	מַלְאַךְ
sāray	gevirtî	’ānōkhî	bōrachath		wayyō’mer	lāhh	mal’akh
Sarai	my mistress	I	one who flees		and he said	to her	the angel of

3176	8178.132	420, 1409	6257.732	8809	3135	10.	569.121
pn	v Qal impv 2fs	prep, n fs, ps 2fs	cj, v Hithpael impv 2fs	prep	n fp, ps 3fs		cj, v Qal impf 3ms
יְהוָה	שׁוּבִי	אֶל־גְּבִרְתֵּךְ	וְהִתְעַנִּי	תַּחַת	יָדֶיהָ		וַיֹּאמֶר
yehwāh	shûvî	’el-gevirtēkh	wehith‘annî	tachath	yādhêhā		wayyō’mer
Yahweh	return	to your mistress	and humble yourself	under	her hands		and he said

3937	4534	3176	7528.542	7528.525	881, 2320	3940
prep, ps 3fs	*n ms*	pn	v Hiphil inf abs	v Hiphil impf 1cs	do, n ms, ps 2fs	cj, neg part
לָהּ	מַלְאַךְ	יְהוָה	הַרְבָּה	אַרְבֶּה	אֶת־זַרְעֵךְ	וְלֹא
lāhh	mal’akh	yehwāh	harbāh	’arbeh	’eth-zar‘ēkh	welō’
to her	angel of	Yahweh	multiplying	I will multiply	your seed	and not

5807.221	4623, 7524	11.	569.121	3937	4534	3176	2079
v Niphal impf 3ms	prep, n ms		cj, v Qal impf 3ms	prep, ps 3fs	*n ms*	pn	intrj, ps 2fs
יִסָּפֵר	מֵרֹב		וַיֹּאמֶר	לָהּ	מַלְאַךְ	יְהוָה	הִנָּךְ
yissāphēr	mērōv		wayyō’mer	lāhh	mal’akh	yehwāh	hinnākh
they will be counted	for multitude		and he said	to her	angel of	Yahweh	behold you

2107	3314.153	1158	7410.112	8428	3579	3706, 8471.111
adj	cj, v Qal act ptc fs	n ms	cj, v Qal pf 3fs	n ms, ps 3ms	pn	cj, v Qal pf 3ms
הָרָה	וְיֹלַדְתְּ	בֵּן	וְקָרָאת	שְׁמוֹ	יִשְׁמָעֵאל	כִּי־שָׁמַע
hārāh	weyōladht	bēn	weqārā’th	shemô	yishmā‘ē’l	kî-shāma‘
pregnant	and bearing	son	and you will call	his name	Ishmael	because He heard

3176	420, 6271	12.	2000	2030.121	6751	119	3135
pn	prep, n ms, ps 2fs		cj, pers pron	v Qal impf 3ms	*n ms*	n ms	n fs, ps 3ms
יְהוָה	אֶל־עָנְיֵךְ		וְהוּא	יִהְיֶה	פֶּרֶא	אָדָם	יָדוֹ
yehwāh	’el-‘ānyēkh		wehû’	yihyeh	pere’	’ādhām	yādhô
Yahweh	to your affliction		and he	he will be	wild donkey of	man	his hand

And when Sarai dealt hardly with her she fled from her face: ... abused her so much, *Anchor* ... treated her harshly, *Berkeley* ... cruelly, *Goodspeed* ... humiliated her, *NCB*.

7. And the angel of the LORD found her: ... a messenger of the Ever-living, *Fenton* ... the Lord's messenger, *NAB*.

by a fountain of water in the wilderness, by the fountain in the way to Shur: ... springs of water in the desert, *Berkeley, MLB* ... in the waste land, *BB* ... well of waters, *Fenton*.

8. And he said, Hagar, Sarai's maid, whence camest thou? and whither wilt thou go: ... from where have you come and where are you going, *Anchor, BB* ... and what are you weeping for, *Fenton*.

she said, I flee from the face of my mistress Sarai: ... I am running away from my mistress, *Berkeley, Goodspeed* ... I am flying from the hand of, *Fenton*.

9. And the angel of the LORD said unto her, Return to thy mistress: ... go back to your mistress, *Berkeley, BB*.

and submit thyself under her hands: ... submit to abuse at her hand, *Anchor* ... humble yourself under her authority, *Berkeley, MLB*.

10. And the angel of the LORD said unto her, I will multiply thy seed exceedingly: ... I will greatly multiply they seed, *ASV* ... make your offspring numerous, *Anchor* ... greatly increase your descendants, *Berkeley*.

that it shall not be numbered for multitude: ... too many to count, *Anchor* ... beyond all counting, they will be so numerous, *Berkeley*.

11. And the angel of the LORD said unto her, Behold, thou art with child, and shalt bear a son, and shalt call his name Ishmael: ... give birth to a son, *Berkeley, BB* ... you are now pregnant, *NAB*.

because the LORD hath heard thy affliction: ... ears of the Lord were open to your sorrow, *BB* ... Yahweh has paid heed to your woes, *Anchor* ... thy tribulation, *Geneva* ... ill-treatment, *Goodspeed, NEB* ... humiliation, *NCB* ... misery, *NIV*.

12. And he will be a wild man his hand will be against every man, and every man's hand against him: ... wild colt of a man, *Anchor* ... a free man, *Fenton* ... wild donkey of a man, *NASB, NIV*.

and he shall dwell in the presence of all his brethren: ... live to the east of all his brothers, *NASB* ... dwell apart, opposing all his kinsmen, *NCB* ... he shall live at odds, *NEB* ... live in hostility toward, *NIV*.

13. And she called the name of the LORD that spake unto her, Thou God seest me: ... Thou art a God that seeth, *ASV* ... who reveals himself, *Darby* ... the God I saw, *Fenton* ... my beholder, *Young*.

for she said, Have I also here looked after him that seeth me?: ... have lived after he appeared to me, *Fenton* ... I have actually seen God, and am still alive, *Goodspeed*.

"angel" both distinguished from God and yet identified with Him. (This is also true in several other Old Testament references to the Angel of the Lord.) By this time Hagar was out in the desert at a spring by the road to Shur, that is, the road that would take her through the desert north of Sinai on the way to Egypt.

16:8. The Angel of the Lord addressed Hagar as the slave of Sarai and asked her where she came from and where she was going. She answered only his first question, for since she was running away, she really did not know where she was going.

16:9-10. The Angel told Hagar to go back to her mistress and take the humble place, submitting to her. Though Hagar was now a wife of Abram, she still was Sarai's servant. But the Angel added a promise, the kind of promise God had given Abram. Speaking in the first person the Angel spoke as God, promising her a multitude of descendants. God confirmed this promise to Abraham (Gen. 17:20), and it was indeed fulfilled (see Gen. 25:13-16).

16:11. The Angel further promised a son to be named Ishmael. Ishmael means "God hears." God had heard and responded to the mistreatment of Hagar. God recognized this was unjust, and He hates injustice no matter who is responsible for it.

16:12. The Angel prophesied that Ishmael would wander in the deserts like a wild donkey. He would be a man who loved the freedom of roaming the desert, but would be constantly in conflict with others. It is implied that he would also be a man of courage, but would be an aggressor full of hostility.

16:13. From these prophecies Hagar recognized that the Angel was the LORD (*Yahweh*), the God of Abram, and she said, "You are the God who sees me" (NIV). He is the God who cares, is concerned, and looks after me. What she said then can also be translated, "I have seen here the back of the one who sees me." Not even Moses was allowed to see God's face (Exo. 33:20-23).

904, 3725	3135	3725	904	6142. 6686	3725, 250
prep, art, adj	*n fs*	n ms	prep, ps 3ms	cj, prep, *n mp*	*adj*, n mp, ps 3ms
בַּכֹּל	וְיַד	כֹּל	בּוֹ	וְעַל־פְּנֵי	כָּל־אֶחָיו
vakkōl	w^{e}yadh	kōl	bô	w^{e}'al-p^{e}nê	khāl-'echâv
against everyone	and the hand of	everyone	against him	and against	all his brothers

8331.121		7410.122	8428, 3176	1744.151	420	887
v Qal impf 3ms	**13.**	cj, v Qal impf 3fs	*n ms*, pn	art, v Qal act ptc ms	prep, ps 3fs	pers pron
יִשְׁכֹּן		וַתִּקְרָא	שֵׁם־יְהוָה	הַדֹּבֵר	אֵלֶיהָ	אַתָּה
yishkōn		wattiqōrā'	shēm-y^{e}hwāh	haddōvēr	'ēlêhā	'attāh
he will live		and she called	the name of Yahweh	the One who spoke	to her	you

418	7503	3706	569.112	1612	2057	7495.115	311
n ms	n ms	cj	v Qal pf 3fs	intrg part, cj	adv	v Qal pf 1cs	*sub*
אֵל	רֳאִי	כִּי	אָמְרָה	הֲגַם	הֲלֹם	רָאִיתִי	אַחֲרֵי
'ēl	r^{e}'î	kî	'ām^{e}rāh	hăgham	hălōm	rā'îthî	'achrê
God of	seeing	because	she said	will also	here	I see	after

7495.151		6142, 3772	7410.111	3937, 908	915	915	915	2079
v Qal act ptc ms	**14.**	prep, adv	v Qal pf 3ms	prep, art, n ms	pn	pn	pn	intrj
רֹאִי		עַל־כֵּן	קָרָא	לַבְּאֵר	בְּאֵר	לַחַי	רֹאִי	הִנֵּה
rō'î		'al-kēn	qārā'	labb^{e}'ēr	b^{e}'ēr	lachay	rō'î	hinnēh
One who sees		therefore	he named	the well	Beer	Lahai	Roi	behold

1033, 7229	1033	1289		3314.122	1972	3937, 82	1158
prep, pn	cj, prep	pn	**15.**	cj, v Qal impf 3fs	pn	prep, pn	n ms
בֵּין־קָדֵשׁ	וּבֵין	בָּרֶד		וַתֵּלֶד	הָגָר	לְאַבְרָם	בֵּן
vên-qādhēsh	ûvên	bāredh		wattēledh	hāghār	l^{e}'avrām	bēn
between Kadesh	and between	Bered		and she gave birth	Hagar	for Abram	son

7410.121	82	8428, 1158	866, 3314.112	1972	3579
cj, v Qal impf 3ms	pn	*n ms*, n ms, ps 3ms	rel part, v Qal pf 3fs	pn	pn
וַיִּקְרָא	אַבְרָם	שֶׁם־בְּנוֹ	אֲשֶׁר־יָלְדָה	הָגָר	יִשְׁמָעֵאל
wayyiqōrā'	'avrām	shem-b^{e}nô	'ăsher-yāl^{e}dhāh	hāghār	yishmā'ē'l
and he called	Abram	the name of his son	whom she gave birth	Hagar	Ishmael

	82	1158, 8470	8523	8666	8523	904. 3314.141, 1972	881, 3579
16.	cj, pn	*n ms*, num	n fs	cj, num	n fp	prep, v Qal inf con, pn	do, pn
	וְאַבְרָם	בֶּן־שְׁמֹנִים	שָׁנָה	וְשֵׁשׁ	שָׁנִים	בְּלֶדֶת־הָגָר	אֶת־יִשְׁמָעֵאל
	w^{e}'avrām	ben-sh^{e}mōnîm	shānāh	w^{e}shēsh	shānîm	b^{e}ledheth-hāghār	'eth-yishmā'ē'l
	and Abram	son of eighty	years	and six	years	in giving birth Hagar	Ishmael

3937, 82		2030.121	82	1158, 9013	8523	9013	8523
prep, pn	**17:1**	cj, v Qal impf 3ms	pn	*n ms*, num	n fs	cj, num	n fp
לְאַבְרָם		וַיְהִי	אַבְרָם	בֶּן־תִּשְׁעִים	שָׁנָה	וְתֵשַׁע	שָׁנִים
l^{e}'avrām		wayhî	'avrām	ben-tish'îm	shānāh	w^{e}thēsha'	shānîm
for Abram		and he was	Abram	son of ninety	years	and nine	years

7495.221	3176	420, 82	569.121	420	603, 418	8163
cj, v Niphal impf 3ms	pn	prep, pn	cj, v Qal impf 3ms	prep, ps 3ms	pers pron, pn	pn
וַיֵּרָא	יְהוָה	אֶל־אַבְרָם	וַיֹּאמֶר	אֵלָיו	אֲנִי־אֵל	שַׁדַּי
wayyērā'	y^{e}hwāh	'el-'avrām	wayyō'mer	'ēlâv	'ănî-'ēl	shadday
and he appeared	Yahweh	to Abram	and He said	to him	I God	Almighty

2050.731	3937, 6686	2030.131	8879		5598.125	1311
v Hithpael impv 2ms	prep, n mp, ps 1cs	cj, v Qal impv 2ms	adj	**2.**	cj, v Qal impf 1cs	n fs, ps 1cs
הִתְהַלֵּךְ	לְפָנַי	וֶהְיֵה	תָמִים		וְאֶתְּנָה	בְרִיתִי
hithhallēkh	l^{e}phānay	wehyēh	thāmîm		w^{e}'ett^{e}nāh	v^{e}rîthî
walk	before Me	and be	blameless		and I will give	my covenant

1033	1033	7528.525	881	904, 4108	4108		5489
prep, ps 1cs	cj, prep, ps 2ms	cj, v Hiphil impf 1cs	do, ps 2ms	prep, adv	adv	**3.**	cj, v Qal impf 3ms
בֵּינִי	וּבֵינֶךָ	וְאַרְבֶּה	אוֹתְךָ	בִּמְאֹד	מְאֹד		וַיִּפֹּל
bênî	ûvênekhā	w^{e}'arbeh	'ôth^{e}khā	bim'ōdh	m^{e}'ōdh		wayyippōl
between Me	and between you	and I will multiply	you	by very	very		and he fell

82	6142, 6686	1744.321	882	435	3937, 569.141		603
pn	prep, n mp, ps 3ms	cj, v Piel impf 3ms	prep, ps 3ms	n mp	prep, v Qal inf con	**4.**	pers pron
אַבְרָם	עַל־פָּנָיו	וַיְדַבֵּר	אִתּוֹ	אֱלֹהִים	לֵאמֹר		אֲנִי
'avrām	'al-pānâv	waydhabbēr	'ittô	'ĕlōhîm	lē'mōr		'ănî
Abram	on his face	and He spoke	with him	God	saying		I

14. Wherefore the well was called Beerlahairoi; behold, it is between Kadesh and Bered: ... Well of the living One who sees me, *Berkeley* ... Well of the Vision of Life, *Fenton* ... Spring where one saw God and still lived, *Goodspeed.*

15. And Hagar bare Abram a son: and Abram called his son's name, which Hagar bare, Ishmael: ... gave birth to a son, *Fenton.*

16. And Abram was fourscore and six years old, when Hagar bare Ishmael to Abram: ... eighty-six years old, *BB.*

17:1. And when Abram was ninety years old and nine, the LORD appeared to Abram: ... 99 years old, *Anchor* ... ninety-six years old, *Fenton.*

and said unto him, I am the Almighty God: ... I am El Shaddai, *Anchor* ... I am God, Ruler of all, *BB* ... I am God all sufficient, *Geneva.*

walk before me, and be thou perfect: ... follow my ways and be blameless, *Anchor* ... live in my presence and be upright, *Berkeley* ... walk habitually before me, *Young.*

2. And I will make my covenant between me and thee, and will multiply thee exceedingly: ... make an agreement, *BB* ... confirm my covenant, *NIV* ... offspring will be greatly increased, *BB.*

3. And Abram fell on his face: and God talked with him, saying: ... threw himself on his face, *Anchor* ... went down on his face on the earth, *BB* ... prostrated himself, *NAB* ... bowed low, *REB.*

4. As for me, behold, my covenant is with thee: ... I now make a covenant with you, *Fenton.*

and thou shalt be a father of many nations: ... ancestor to many nations, *Berkeley* ... ancestor of a company of nations, *Goodspeed* ... father of a multitude of nations, *ASV* ... host of nations, *Anchor* ... nations without end, *BB.*

16:14. Because of this experience the well was given a name which means either "The well of the Living One who sees me," or "The well of the one who sees me and lives." In Moses' day the well was still there between Kadesh and Bered, a place west of Kadesh.

16:15-16. By the time Ishmael was born Abram was 86 years old. Hagar must have told him of the events at Beer-lahai-roi and of the prophecy given there, so He named the boy Ishmael.

17:1. Nothing is recorded of the 13 years after Ishmael was born. Then chapters 17-21 deal with the short time from Abram's age of 99 to 100. The central attention is on the events leading up to the birth of the promised son, Isaac. When Abram was 99 God appeared to him telling him I am "God Almighty" (Heb. *El Shaddai*). *Shaddai* comes from an old word meaning "mountain" and refers to His mighty power that is high, invincible, and unshakable. If Abram wanted to know God's power, he had to walk, that is live, close to the LORD and be "perfect," or blameless, that is. consistently responding to God in repentance and faith. He must be sincere and honest in his devotion and obedience to the LORD. Faith always calls for obedience if it is to be real (Rom. 1:5).

17:2. God calls the covenant between Him and Abram "my covenant." He gave it. He will confirm it. Abraham can depend on the promises that have been made and confirmed by it (Gen. 12:2-3; 13:14-16; 15:4-5). In chapter 15 the covenant confirmed the promise concerning the land. Now God was confirming He would greatly increase the numbers of Abram's descendants.

17:3-6. Abram fell flat on the ground, face down in an attitude of most humble worship and adoration before the LORD. God told him not only would he have many descendants but he would also

2079	1311	882	2030.113	3937, 1	2066	1504
intrj	n fs, ps 1cs	prep, ps 2fs	cj, v Qal pf 2ms	prep, *n ms*	*n ms*	n mp
הִנֵּה	בְרִיתִי	אִתָּךְ	וְהָיִיתָ	לְאַב	הֲמוֹן	גּוֹיִם
hinnēh	v^{e}rîthî	'ittākh	w^{e}hāyîthā	l^{e}'av	h^{e}môn	gôyim
behold	my covenant	with you	and you will be	for father of	multitude of	nations

5.	3940, 7410.221	5968	881, 8428	82	2030.111	8428
	cj, neg part, v Niphal impf 3ms	adv	do, n ms, ps 2ms	pn	cj, v Qal pf 3ms	n ms, ps 2ms
	וְלֹא־יִקָּרֵא	עוֹד	אֶת־שִׁמְךָ	אַבְרָם	וְהָיָה	שִׁמְךָ
	w^{e}lō'-yiqqārē'	'ôdh	'eth-shim^{e}khā	'avrām	w^{e}hāyāh	shim^{e}khā
	and not it will be called	again	your name	Abram	but it will be	your name

80	3706	1, 2066	1504	5598.115	**6.**	6759.515
pn	cj	*n ms, n ms*	n mp	v Qal pf 1cs, ps 2ms		cj, v Hiphil pf 1cs
אַבְרָהָם	כִּי	אַב־הֲמוֹן	גּוֹיִם	נְתַתִּיךָ		וְהִפְרֵתִי
'avrāhām	kî	'av-h^{e}môn	gôyim	n^{e}thattîkhā		w^{e}hiphrēthî
Abraham	because	father of multitude of	nations	I will make you		and I will make fruitful

881	904, 4108	4108	5598.115	3937, 1504	4567	4623
do, ps 2ms	prep, adv	adv	cj, v Qal pf 1cs, ps 2ms	prep, n mp	cj, n mp	prep, ps 2ms
אֹתְךָ	בִּמְאֹד	מְאֹד	וּנְתַתִּיךָ	לְגוֹיִם	וּמְלָכִים	מִמְּךָ
'ōth^{e}khā	bim'ōdh	m^{e}'ōdh	ûn^{e}thattîkhā	l^{e}ghôyim	ûm^{e}lākhîm	mimm^{e}khā
you	by very	very	and I will give you	for nations	and kings	from you

3428.116	**7.**	7251.515	881, 1311	1033	1033	1033
v Qal pf 3cp		cj, v Hiphil pf 1cs	do, n fs, ps 1cs	prep, ps 1cs	cj, prep, ps 2ms	cj, prep
יֵצֵאוּ		וַהֲקִמֹתִי	אֶת־בְּרִיתִי	בֵּינִי	וּבֵינְךָ	וּבֵין
yētsē'û		wahqimōthî	'eth-b^{e}rîthî	bênî	ûvênekhā	ûvên
they will go out		and I will establish	my covenant	between Me	and between you	and between

2320	313	3937, 1810	3937, 1311	5986	3937, 2030.141	3937
n ms, ps 2ms	adv, ps 2ms	prep, n mp, ps 3mp	prep, *n fs*	adv	prep, v Qal inf con	prep, ps 2ms
זַרְעֲךָ	אַחֲרֶיךָ	לְדֹרֹתָם	לִבְרִית	עוֹלָם	לִהְיוֹת	לְךָ
zar'ăkhā	'achrêkhā	l^{e}dhōrōthām	livrîth	'ôlām	lihyôth	l^{e}khā
your seed	after you	to their generations	for covenant of	forever	to be	to you

3937, 435	3937, 2320	313	**8.**	5598.115	3937	3937, 2320
prep n mp	cj, prep, n ms, ps 2ms	adv, ps 2ms		cj, v Qal pf 1cs	prep, ps 2ms	cj, prep, n ms, ps 2ms
לֵאלֹהִים	וּלְזַרְעֲךָ	אַחֲרֶיךָ		וְנָתַתִּי	לְךָ	וּלְזַרְעֲךָ
lē'lōhîm	ûlăzar'ăkhā	'achrêkhā		w^{e}nāthattî	l^{e}khā	ûlăzar'ăkhā
to God	and to your seed	after you		and I will give	to you	and to your seed

313	881	800	4175	881	3725, 800	3791	3937, 273
adv, ps 2ms	do	*n fs*	n mp, ps 2ms	do	*adj, n fs*	pn	prep, *n fs*
אַחֲרֶיךָ	אֵת	אֶרֶץ	מְגֻרֶיךָ	אֵת	כָּל־אֶרֶץ	כְּנַעַן	לַאֲחֻזַּת
'achrêkhā	'ēth	'erets	m^{e}ghurêkhā	'ēth	kol-'erets	k^{e}na'an	la'ăchuzzath
after you		the land of	your sojourning		all the land of	Canaan	for property of

5986	2030.115	3937	3937, 435	**9.**	569.121	435	420, 80
adv	cj, v Qal pf 1cs	prep, ps 3mp	prep n mp		cj, v Qal impf 3ms	n mp	prep, pn
עוֹלָם	וְהָיִיתִי	לָהֶם	לֵאלֹהִים		וַיֹּאמֶר	אֱלֹהִים	אֶל־אַבְרָהָם
'ôlām	w^{e}hāyîthî	lāhem	lē'lōhîm		wayyō'mer	'ĕlōhîm	'el-'avrāhām
forever	and I will be	to them	for God		and He said	God	to Abraham

887	881, 1311	8490.123	887	2320	313	3937, 1810
cj, pers pron	do, n fs, ps 1cs	v Qal impf 2ms	pers pron	cj, n ms, ps 2ms	adv, ps 2ms	prep, n mp, ps 3mp
וְאַתָּה	אֶת־בְּרִיתִי	תִשְׁמֹר	אַתָּה	וְזַרְעֲךָ	אַחֲרֶיךָ	לְדֹרֹתָם
w^{e}'attāh	'eth-b^{e}rîthî	thishmōr	'attāh	w^{e}zar'ăkhā	'achrêkhā	l^{e}dhōrōthām
and you	my covenant	you will keep	you	and your seed	after you	to their generations

5. Neither shall thy name any more be called Abram, but thy name shall be Abraham: ... shall no longer be Abram, *Berkeley.*

for a father of many nations have I made thee: ... host of nations, *Anchor, NAB* ... number of nations, *BB.*

6. And I will make thee exceeding fruitful: ... exceedingly fertile, *Anchor* ... more and more prolific, *Goodspeed* ... millions of descendants, *LIVB.*

and I will make nations of thee: ... nations will come from you, *BB* ... I will make nations and kingdoms proceed from you, *Fenton.*

and kings shall come out of thee: ... kings shall stem from you, *Anchor* ... shall spring, *Berkeley* ... will be your offspring, *BB* ... shall proceed of thee, *Geneva.*

7. And I will establish my covenant between me and thee: ... maintain the covenant, *Anchor* ... fulfill my covenant, *NEB.*

and thy seed after thee in their generations: ... throughout their generations, *ASV* ... your offspring to follow, through the ages, *Anchor* ... in their successive generations, *Berkeley* ... from generation to generation forever, *Fenton.*

to thy seed after thee: ... everlasting pact, *Anchor* ... eternal agreement, *BB* ... perpetual covenant, *Goodspeed* ... covenant age-during, *Young* ... I shall be your God, *REB.*

8. And I will give unto thee, and to thy seed after thee, the land wherein thou art a stranger: ... the land of thy sojourning, *ASV, NASB* ... in which you are living, *BB* ... where you are a foreigner, *Fenton* ... you are now only an immigrant, *Goodspeed* ... you are now aliens, *NEB.*

all the land of Canaan, for an everlasting possession; and I will be their God: ... the whole Canaanite country, *Berkeley* ... eternal heritage, *BB* ... permanent possession, *NAB* ... perpetual holding, *NRSV* ... possession for all time, *REB.*

9. And God said unto Abraham, Thou shalt keep my covenant: ... on your side, you are to keep the agreement, *BB* ... for your part, *Anchor* ... you must keep my covenant, *Berkeley.*

therefore, thou, and thy seed after thee in their generations: ... generations to come, *NIV* ... future generations, *Good News* ... respective generations, *Berkeley* ... throughout their generations, *ASV.*

10. This is my covenant, which ye shall keep, between me and you and thy seed after thee: ... which you must observe, *Berkeley.*

Every man child among you shall be circumcised: ... circumcise every male of them, *Fenton* ... circumcise yourselves, *NEB.*

---

be the father or ancestor of many nations. God confirmed this further by changing Abram' name to Abraham. Abram was a fairly common name in those days and means "exalted father" or "my father is exalted." To Terah, who was an idol worshiper, it probably meant "my [divine] father is exalted," referring to some heathen god as his "father." Thus, the name did not fit Abram's situation. But Abraham means "father of a multitude" and became a declaration of God's purpose and of His covenant with Abraham. God would accomplish this by making Abraham very prolific, so that not only populous nations but also kings would be among his descendants.

17:7. God declared that the covenant He established with Abraham was an everlasting covenant. He would continue to establish it with Abraham's descendants. God would be (and show Himself to be) Abraham's God and the God of Abraham's descendants for the generations to come. This implies God would guide them, help them, bless them, and protect them. He would always be with them to do this, though they would need to respond in faith and obedience in order to receive the benefits of this everlasting covenant.

17:8. God also confirmed the covenant promise of the land. The whole land of Canaan, not just a part, was to be their future possession. Abraham had to live there as a resident alien. But in God's eyes it belonged to Abraham's descendants who would worship the LORD as their God.

17:9. Abraham had a part. He could not bring about the possession of the land and would not see the crowds of descendants in the generations to come, but he must emphatically keep (guard and obey) God's covenant, and so must his descendants. Only by faith and obedience could they participate in the covenant. (See verse 1.)

17:10-13. The first act of obedience that would demonstrate participation in the covenant was the circumcision of every male person. This would be the sign in their bodies of the covenant. Abraham and all his household, including his servants and slaves, would need to be circumcised immediately.

10.	2148	1311	866	8490.123	1033	1033
	dem pron	n fs, ps 1cs	rel part	v Qal impf 2ms	prep, ps 1cs	cj, prep, ps 2mp
	זֹאת	בְּרִיתִי	אֲשֶׁר	תִּשְׁמְרוּ	בֵּינִי	וּבֵינֵיכֶם
	zō'th	b^{e}rîthî	'ăsher	tishm^{e}rû	bênî	ûvênêkhem
	this	my covenant	which	you will keep	between Me	and between you

1033	2320	313	4271.242	3937	3725, 2227
cj, prep	n ms, ps 2ms	adv, ps 2ms	v Niphal inf abs	prep, ps 2mp	adj, *n ms*
וּבֵין	זַרְעֲךָ	אַחֲרֶיךָ	הִמּוֹל	לָכֶם	כָּל־זָכָר
ûvên	zar'ăkhā	'achrêkhā	himmôl	lākhem	kol-zākhār
and between	your seed	after you	circumcising	to you	every male

11.	4271.217	881	1340	6428	2030.111	3937, 225
	cj, v Niphal pf 2mp	do	*n ms*	n fs, ps 2mp	cj, v Qal pf 3ms	prep, *n ms*
	וּנְמַלְתֶּם	אֵת	בְּשַׂר	עָרְלַתְכֶם	וְהָיָה	לְאוֹת
	ûn^{e}maltem	'ēth	b^{e}sar	'ārlath^{e}khem	w^{e}hāyāh	l$^{e'}$ôth
	you will be circumcised		the flesh of	your foreskins	and it will be	for sign of

1311	1033	1033	12.	1158, 8470	3219	4271.221
n fs	prep, ps 1cs	cj, prep, ps 2mp		cj, *n ms, num*	n mp	v Niphal impf 3ms
בְּרִית	בֵּינִי	וּבֵינֵיכֶם		וּבֶן־שְׁמֹנַת	יָמִים	יִמּוֹל
b^{e}rîth	bênî	ûvênêkhem		ûven-sh^{e}mōnath	yāmîm	yimmôl
covenant	between Me	and between you		and son of eight of	days	he will be circumcised

3937	3725, 2227	3937, 1810	3320	1041	4899, 3826B	4623, 3725
prep, ps 2mp	*adj*, n ms	prep, n mp, ps 2mp	*adj*	n ms	cj, *n fs*, n ms	prep, adj
לָכֶם	כָּל־זָכָר	לְדֹרֹתֵיכֶם	יְלִיד	בָּיִת	וּמִקְנַת־כֶּסֶף	מִכֹּל
lākhem	kāl-zākhār	l^{e}dhōrōthêkhem	y^{e}lîdh	bāyith	ûmiqônath-keseph	mikkōl
to you	every male	to your generations	born of	house	and purchase of silver	from every

1158, 5424	866	3940	4623, 2320	2000	13.	4271.242
n ms, n ms	rel part	neg part	prep, n ms, ps 2ms	pers pron		v Niphal inf abs
בֶּן־נֵכָר	אֲשֶׁר	לֹא	מִזַּרְעֲךָ	הוּא		הִמּוֹל
ben-nēkhār	'ăsher	lō'	mizzar'ăkhā	hû'		himmôl
son of foreign land	which	not	from your seed	he		circumcising

4271.221	3320	1041	4899	3826B	2030.112
v Niphal impf 3ms	*adj*	n ms, ps 2ms	cj, *n fs*	n ms, ps 2ms	cj, v Qal pf 3fs
יִמּוֹל	יְלִיד	בֵּיתְךָ	וּמִקְנַת	כַּסְפֶּךָ	וְהָיְתָה
yimmôl	y^{e}lîdh	bêth^{e}khā	ûmiqōnath	kaspekhā	w^{e}hāy^{e}thāh
he will be circumcised	born of	your house	and purchase of	your silver	and it will be

1311	904, 1340	3937, 1311	5986	14.	6427	2227
n fs, ps 1cs	prep, n ms, ps 2mp	prep, *n fs*	adv		cj, adj	n ms
בְרִיתִי	בִּבְשַׂרְכֶם	לִבְרִית	עוֹלָם		וְעָרֵל	זָכָר
v^{e}rîthî	bivsar^{e}khem	livrîth	'ôlām		w^{e}'ārēl	zākhār
my covenant	in your flesh	for covenant of	forever		and uncircumcised	male

866	3940, 4271.221	881, 1340	6428	3901.212	5497
rel part	neg part, v Niphal impf 3ms	do, *n ms*	n fs, ps 3ms	cj, v Niphal pf 3fs	art, n fs
אֲשֶׁר	לֹא־יִמּוֹל	אֶת־בְּשַׂר	עָרְלָתוֹ	וְנִכְרְתָה	הַנֶּפֶשׁ
'ăsher	lō'-yimmôl	'eth-b^{e}sar	'ārelāthô	w^{e}nikhr^{e}thāh	hannephesh
whom	not he has been circumcised	the flesh of	his foreskin	and then he will be cut off	the person

2000	4623, 6194	881, 1311	6815.511	15.	569.121	435
art, dem pron	prep, n mp, ps 3fs	do, n fs, ps 1cs	v Hiphil pf 3ms		cj, v Qal impf 3ms	n mp
הַהִוא	מֵעַמֶּיהָ	אֶת־בְּרִיתִי	הֵפַר		וַיֹּאמֶר	אֱלֹהִים
hahiw'	mē'ammêhā	'eth-b^{e}rîthî	hēphar		wayyō'mer	'ĕlōhîm
the that	from his people	my covenant	he has broken		and He said	God

420, 80	8030	828	3940, 7410.123	881, 8428	8030	3706
prep, pn	pn	n fs, ps 2ms	neg part, v Qal impf 2ms	do, n ms, ps 3fs	pn	cj
אֶל־אַבְרָהָם	שָׂרַי	אִשְׁתְּךָ	לֹא־תִקְרָא	אֶת־שְׁמָהּ	שָׂרָי	כִּי
'el-'avrāhām	sāray	'isht^{e}khā	lō'-thiqōrā'	'eth-sh^{e}māhh	sārāy	kî
to Abraham	Sarai	your wife	not you will call	her name	Sarai	because

8023	8428		1313.315	881	1612	5598.115	4623
pn	n ms, ps 3fs	**16.**	cj, v Piel pf 1cs	do, ps 3fs	cj, cj	v Qal pf 1cs	prep, ps 3fs
שָׂרָה	שְׁמָהּ		וּבֵרַכְתִּי	אֹתָהּ	וְגַם	נָתַתִּי	מִמֶּנָּה
sārāh	sh^{e}māhh		ûvērakhtî	'ōthāhh	w^{e}gham	nāthattî	mimmennāh
Sarah	her name		and I will bless	her	and also	I will give	from her

11. And ye shall circumcise the flesh of your foreskin: ... flesh of your private parts, *BB* ... foreskin of the body, *Fenton* ... foreskin of his penis shall be cut off, *LIVB.*

and it shall be a token of the covenant betwixt me and you: ... mark of the covenant, *Anchor* ... a covenant sign, *Berkeley* ... mark of the agreement, *BB* ... attestation of the covenant, *Fenton* ... symbol of the covenant, *Goodspeed*.

12. And he that is eight days old shall be circumcised among you: ... at the age of eight days, *Anchor* ... eight days after his birth, *Berkeley.*

every man child in your generations: ... from one generation to another, *BB* ... throughout your generations, *MLB, NRSV* ... in every generation, *NEB, REB.*

he that is born in the house: ... houseborn slaves, *Anchor* ... of your family circle, *Berkeley* ... every servant whose birth takes place in your house, *BB* ... born of the family, *Fenton.*

or bought with money of any stranger: ... acquired for money from any outsider, *Anchor* ... gave money to someone of another country, *BB* ... slaves bought from foreigners, *Good News* ... any stranger who is not of thy seed, *Darby.*

which is not of thy seed: ... who is not of your blood, *Anchor* ... not of your race, *Fenton.*

13. He that is born in thy house, and he that is bought with thy money, must needs be circumcised: and my covenant shall be in your flesh: ... marked on your flesh, *Anchor* ... my covenant in your body, *Fenton* ... a physical sign, *Good News* ... stand imprinted on your flesh, *Goodspeed.*

for an everlasting covenant: ... covenant age-during, *Young* ... everlasting bond, *Fenton* ... an agreement for all time, *BB* ... never-ending covenant, *Berkeley* ... perpetual covenant, *Goodspeed.*

14. And the uncircumcised man child whose flesh of his foreskin is not circumcised, that soul shall be cut off from his people; he hath broken my covenant: ... but the degraded male, *Fenton* ... cut off from his kin, *Anchor* ... eliminated from his people, *Berkeley* ... no longer be considered one of my people, *Good News.*

15. And God said unto Abraham, As for Sarai thy wife, thou shalt not call her name Sarai, but Sarah shall her name be.

From this point on and in all future generations, every male baby would need to be circumcised when eight days old. Any slave bought would also need to be circumcised. This was to be an everlasting covenant with the physical descendants of Abraham and their households. Thus, the servants and slaves were also brought into covenant relation with God and became part of His people.

17:14. There were to be no exceptions. Any male person who was not physically circumcised would be cut off from his people (implying judgment upon him, or at least separation from God's blessings, for disobedience to the covenant). From this it is clear that circumcision was a sign that they were to submit themselves to the LORD as their true King, serving and worshiping Him alone in humble dedication and consecration. (Some peoples in other parts of the world have practiced circumcision, but usually as a puberty rite, not as a covenant sign). But it was more than a sign. It symbolized the purification of life and called for a change of heart attitudes (Jer. 4:4; Deut. 10:16; 30:6).

17:15-16. God did not forget Abraham's wife. God confirmed her participation in the covenant blessings by changing her name from Sarai to Sarah. Sarai in Aramaic, spoken by her parents, meant princess. But in Canaan it was rather meaningless. Sarah in the Hebrew of Canaan means

3937	1158	1313.315	2030.112	3937, 1504	4567	6194
prep, ps 2ms	n ms	cj, v Piel pf 1cs, ps 3fs	cj, v Qal pf 3fs	prep, n mp	*n mp*	n mp
לְךָ	בֵּן	וּבֵרַכְתִּיהָ	וְהָיְתָה	לְגוֹיִם	מַלְכֵי	עַמִּים
l^{e}khā	bēn	ûvērakhtîhā	w^{e}hāy^{e}thāh	l^{e}ghôyim	malkhê	'ammîm
to you	son	and I will bless her	and she will be	for nations	kings of	peoples

4623	2030.126		5489	80	6142, 6686	6978.121
prep, ps 3fs	v Qal impf 3mp	**17.**	cj, v Qal impf 3ms	pn	prep, n mp, ps 3ms	cj, v Qal impf 3ms
מִמֶּנָּה	יִהְיוּ		וַיִּפֹּל	אַבְרָהָם	עַל־פָּנָיו	וַיִּצְחָק
mimmennāh	yihyû		wayyippōl	'avrāhām	'al-pānāv	wayyitschāq
from her	they will be		and he fell	Abraham	on his face	and he laughed

569.121	904, 3949	3937, 1158	4109, 8523	3314.221	524, 8023
cj, v Qal impf 3ms	prep, n ms, ps 3ms	intrg part, prep, *n ms*	num, n fs	v Niphal impf 3ms	cj, cj, pn
וַיֹּאמֶר	בְּלִבּוֹ	הַלְּבֶן	מֵאָה־שָׁנָה	יִוָּלֵד	וְאִם־שָׂרָה
wayyō'mer	b^{e}libbô	hall^{e}ven	mē'āh-shānāh	yiwwālēdh	w^{e}'im-sārāh
and he said	in his heart	will to a son of	hundred years	will he be born	and if Sarah

1351, 9013	8523	3314.122		569.121	80	420, 435
intrg part, *n fs*, num	n fs	v Qal impf 3fs	**18.**	cj, v Qal impf 3ms	pn	prep, art, n mp
הֲבַת־תִּשְׁעִים	שָׁנָה	תֵּלֵד		וַיֹּאמֶר	אַבְרָהָם	אֶל־הָאֱלֹהִים
h^{e}vath-tish'îm	shānāh	tēlēdh		wayyō'mer	'avrāhām	'el-hā'ĕlōhîm
daughter of ninety	years	will she give birth		and he said	Abraham	to God

4001	3579	2513.121	3937, 6686		569.121	435	61
cj	pn	v Qal impf 3ms	prep, n mp, ps 2ms	**19.**	cj, v Qal impf 3ms	n mp	adv
לוּ	יִשְׁמָעֵאל	יִחְיֶה	לְפָנֶיךָ		וַיֹּאמֶר	אֱלֹהִים	אֲבָל
lû	yishmā'ē'l	yichăyeh	l^{e}phānêkhā		wayyō'mer	'ĕlōhîm	'ăvāl
if only	Ishmael	he would live	before you		and He said	God	yes but

8023	828	3314.112	3937	1158	7410.113	881, 8428
pn	n fs, ps 2ms	v Qal pf 3fs	prep, ps 2ms	n ms	cj, v Qal pf 2ms	do, n ms, ps 3ms
שָׂרָה	אִשְׁתְּךָ	יֹלֶדֶת	לְךָ	בֵּן	וְקָרָאתָ	אֶת־שְׁמוֹ
sārāh	'isht^{e}khā	yōledeth	l^{e}khā	bēn	w^{e}qārā'thā	'eth-sh^{e}mô
Sarah	your wife	she will give birth	to you	son	and you will call	his name

3437	7251.515	881, 1311	882	3937, 1311	5986	3937, 2320
pn	cj, v Hiphil pf 1cs	do, n fs, ps 1cs	prep, ps 3ms	prep, *n fs*	adv	prep, n ms, ps 3ms
יִצְחָק	וַהֲקִמֹתִי	אֶת־בְּרִיתִי	אִתּוֹ	לִבְרִית	עוֹלָם	לְזַרְעוֹ
yitschāq	wahqimōthî	'eth-b^{e}rîthî	'ittô	livrîth	'ôlām	l^{e}zar'ô
Isaac	and I will establish	my covenant	with him	for covenant of	forever	to his seed

313		3937, 3579	8471.115	2079	1313.315	881
adv, ps 3ms	**20.**	cj, prep, pn	v Qal pf 1cs, ps 2ms	intrj	v Piel pf 1cs	do, ps 3ms
אַחֲרָיו		וּלְיִשְׁמָעֵאל	שְׁמַעְתִּיךָ	הִנֵּה	בֵּרַכְתִּי	אֹתוֹ
'achrâv		ûlăyishmā'ē'l	sh^{e}ma'ăttîkhā	hinnēh	bērakhtî	'ōthô
after him		and for Ishmael	I have heard you	behold	I will bless	him

6759.515	881	7528.515	881	904, 4108	4108	8530, 6461
cj, v Hiphil pf 1cs	do, ps 3ms	cj, v Hiphil pf 1cs	do, ps 3ms	prep, adv	adv	num, num
וְהִפְרֵיתִי	אֹתוֹ	וְהִרְבֵּיתִי	אֹתוֹ	בִּמְאֹד	מְאֹד	שְׁנֵים־עָשָׂר
w^{e}hiphrêthî	'ōthô	w^{e}hirbêthî	'ōthô	bim'ōdh	m^{e}'ōdh	sh^{e}nêm-'āsār
and I will make fruitful	him	and I will multiply	him	by very	very	two ten

5562	3314.521	5598.115	3937, 1504	1448		881, 1311
n mp	v Hiphil impf 3ms	cj, v Qal pf 1cs, ps 3ms	prep, n ms	adj	**21.**	cj, n fs, ps 1cs
נְשִׂיאִם	יוֹלִיד	וּנְתַתִּיו	לְגוֹי	גָּדוֹל		וְאֶת־בְּרִיתִי
n^{e}sî'im	yôlîdh	ûn^{e}thattîw	l^{e}ghôy	gādhôl		w^{e}'eth-b^{e}rîthî
chieftains	he will father	and I will make him	into nation	great		but my covenant

16. And I will bless her, and give thee a son also of her: ... I will give you a son by her, whom I will bless also, *Anchor* ... I will give her a blessing so that you will have a son by her, *BB.*

yea, I will bless her, and she shall be a mother of nations; kings of people shall be of her: ... she shall become nations, *Darby* ... rulers of people shall issue from him (Isaac), *NAB* ... kings of peoples shall spring, *Berkeley* ... rulers of peoples shall issue from her, *Anchor.*

17. Then Abraham fell upon his face: ... threw himself on his face, *Anchor* ... went down on his face, *BB* ... bowed down with his face touching the ground, *Good News* ... threw himself down in worship, LIVB ... prostrated himself, *NAB.*

and laughed, and said in his heart: ... and smiled as he said to himself, *Anchor* ... inside he was laughing in disbelief, LIVB.

shall a child be born unto him that is an hundred years old?: ... to a centenarian, *Berkeley* ... a son be born, *NEB.*

and shall Sarah, that is ninety years old, bear?: ... could Sarah give birth at 90, *Anchor.*

18. And Abraham said unto God, O that Ishmael might live before thee: ... Let but Ishmael thrive if you so will it, *Anchor* ... if only Ishmael's life might be your care, *BB* ... why not let Ishmael be my heir, *Good News* ... might live under your blessing, *NIV* ... might enjoy your special favor, *REB.*

19. And God said, Sarah thy wife shall bear thee a son indeed; and thou shalt call his name Isaac: ... Isaac (laughter), *Goodspeed.*

and I will establish my covenant with him for an everlasting covenant, and with his seed after him: ... fix my covenant, *Fenton* ... fulfill my covenant, *NEB* ... sustain my covenant, *Anchor* ... make my agreement with him forever, *BB* ... for his children after him, *Berkeley.*

20. And as for Ishmael, I have heard thee: ... I will heed you as regards Ishmael, *Anchor* ... I have given ear to your prayer, *BB* ... with reference to Ishmael, *Goodspeed.*

Behold, I have blessed him, and will make him fruitful, and will multiply him exceedingly: ... multiply him immensely, *Berkeley* ... fertile and exceedingly numerous, *Anchor* ... cause him to prosper and extend him very greatly, *Fenton.*

twelve princes shall he beget, and I will make him a great nation: ... father of twelve chiefs, *BB* ... ancestor to twelve princes, *Berkeley* ... bring twelve chieftains into being, *Anchor* ... twelve rulers, *NIV.*

21. But my covenant will I establish with Isaac, which Sarah shall

---

princess. So God restored her dignity by changing her name.

The change to a Hebrew form of the name also shows a complete break with the past. She would never return to her birthplace, for she was to focus her life on the promise of God. God further confirmed her participation in the covenant by promising that she herself would give Abraham a son and that she would be the mother of nations and kings.

17:17. The promise that Sarah would bear a son at first seemed impossible. He was old, and Sarah must have gone through the menopause by this time. He fell down in an attitude of worship and adoration, but at the same time he laughed. This may have involved a momentary feeling of doubt. Even the greatest of people of faith can have twinges of doubt, but they turn to the LORD and press on. On the other hand, God did not reprove him, so it may have been a joyous laughter at the thought of the miracle that would soon take place.

17:18. Part of Abraham's concern was for Ishmael. For 13 years Ishmael had been his only son. He had focused his hopes on Ishmael. He had trained him and he loved him. Ishmael had been sharing the good things God gave Abraham. But Abraham was not asking God to let Ishmael be the promised son. Rather, he wanted him to continue to live under God's blessing.

17:19. God emphatically repeats that Sarah will bear Abraham a son to be named Isaac, meaning "he laughs." The laughter, however, was to be a laughter of joy.

Throughout the Book of Genesis we see God, by His grace and foreknowledge, choosing individuals who would carry on the chosen line leading down to the fulfillment of the promise in Jesus Christ. (They were chosen for a ministry, not for salvation.) Thus the covenant, God's everlasting plan, would be established with Isaac and his descendants, not with Ishmael.

17:20. God also saw Abraham's concern for Ishmael and for Abraham's sake, He promised to bless him and multiply his descendants. Ishmael would have 12 sons who would become rulers and God would make him a great nation. This was fulfilled (Gen. 25:13-16).

7251.525	882, 3437	866	3314.122	3937	8023	3937, 4287
v Hiphil impf 1cs	prep, pn	rel part	v Qal impf 3fs	prep, ps 2ms	pn	prep, art, n ms
אָקִים	אֶת־יִצְחָק	אֲשֶׁר	תֵּלֵד	לְךָ	שָׂרָה	לַמּוֹעֵד
'āqîm	'eth-yitschāq	'ăsher	tēlēdh	l^{e}khā	sārāh	lammô'ēdh
I will establish	with Isaac	whom	she will give birth	to you	Sarah	at the set time

2172	904, 8523	311	**22.**	3735.321	3937, 1744.341	882
art, dem pron	prep, art, n fs	art, adj		cj, v Piel impf 3ms	prep, v Piel inf con	prep, ps 3ms
הַזֶּה	בַּשָּׁנָה	הָאַחֶרֶת		וַיְכַל	לְדַבֵּר	אִתּוֹ
hazzeh	bashshānāh	hā'achereth		waykhal	l^{e}dhabbēr	'ittô
the this	in the year	the next		and He finished	speaking	with him

6148.121	435	4623, 6142	80	**23.**	4089.121	80	881, 3579
cj, v Qal impf 3ms	n mp	prep, prep	pn		cj, v Qal impf 3ms	pn	do, pn
וַיַּעַל	אֱלֹהִים	מֵעַל	אַבְרָהָם		וַיִּקַּח	אַבְרָהָם	אֶת־יִשְׁמָעֵאל
wayya'al	'ĕlōhîm	mē'al	'avrāhām		wayyiqqach	'avrāhām	'eth-yishmā'ē'l
and He went up	God	from beside	Abraham		and he took	Abraham	Ishmael

1158	881	3725, 3320	1041	881	3725, 4899	3826B	3725, 2227
n ms, ps 3ms	cj, do	*adj, adj*	n ms, ps 3ms	cj, do	*adj, n fs*	n ms, ps 3ms	*adj*, n ms
בְּנוֹ	וְאֵת	כָּל־יְלִידֵי	בֵּיתוֹ	וְאֵת	כָּל־מִקְנַת	כַּסְפּוֹ	כָּל־זָכָר
b^{e}nô	w^{e}'ēth	kol-y^{e}lîdhê	vêthô	w^{e}'ēth	kāl-miqŏnath	kaspô	kol-zākhār
his son	and	all born of	his house	and	every purchase of	his silver	every male

904, 596	1041	80	4271.121	881, 1340	6428	904, 6344
prep, *n mp*	*n ms*	pn	cj, v Qal impf 3ms	do, *n ms*	n fs, ps 3mp	prep, *n fs*
בְּאַנְשֵׁי	בֵּית	אַבְרָהָם	וַיָּמָל	אֶת־בְּשַׂר	עָרְלָתָם	בְּעֶצֶם
b^{e}'anshê	bêth	'avrāhām	wayyāmāl	'eth-b^{e}sar	'ār^{e}lāthām	b^{e}'etsem
with men of	the house of	Abraham	and he circumcised	the flesh of	their foreskins	on the bone of

3219	2172	3626, 866	1744.311	882	435	**24.**	82
art, n ms	art, dem pron	prep, rel part	v Piel pf 3ms	prep, ps 3ms	n mp		cj, pn
הַיּוֹם	הַזֶּה	כַּאֲשֶׁר	דִּבֶּר	אִתּוֹ	אֱלֹהִים		וְאַבְרָהָם
hayyôm	hazzeh	ka'ăsher	dibber	'ittô	'ĕlōhîm		w^{e}'avrāhām
the day	the this	according to that	He spoke	with him	God		and Abraham

1158, 9013	9013	8523	904, 4271.241	1340	6428	**25.**	3579
n ms, num	cj, num	n fs	prep, v Niphal inf con, ps 3ms	*n ms*	n fs, ps 3ms		cj, pn
בֶּן־תִּשְׁעִים	וָתֵשַׁע	שָׁנָה	בְּהִמֹּלוֹ	בְּשַׂר	עָרְלָתוֹ		וְיִשְׁמָעֵאל
ben-tish'îm	wāthēsha'	shānāh	b^{e}himmōlô	b^{e}sar	'ār^{e}lāthô		w^{e}yishmā'ē'l
son of ninety	and nine	years	in his circumcising	the flesh of	his foreskin		and Ishmael

1158	1158, 8421	6462	8523	904, 4271.241	881	1340	6428
n ms, ps 3ms	*n ms*, num	num	n fs	prep, v Niphal inf con, ps 3ms	do	*n ms*	n fs, ps 3ms
בְּנוֹ	בֶּן־שְׁלֹשׁ	עֶשְׂרֵה	שָׁנָה	בְּהִמֹּלוֹ	אֵת	בְּשַׂר	עָרְלָתוֹ
b^{e}nô	ben-sh^{e}lōsh	'esrēh	shānāh	b^{e}himmōlô	'ēth	b^{e}sar	'ār^{e}lāthô
his son	son of three	ten	years	in his circumcising		the flesh of	his foreskin

26.	904, 6344	3219	2172	4271.255	80	3579	1158
	prep, *n fs*	art, n ms	art, dem pron	v Niphal ptc ms	pn	cj, pn	n ms, ps 3ms
	בְּעֶצֶם	הַיּוֹם	הַזֶּה	נִמּוֹל	אַבְרָהָם	וְיִשְׁמָעֵאל	בְּנוֹ
	b^{e}'etsem	hayyôm	hazzeh	nimmôl	'avrāhām	w^{e}yishmā'ē'l	b^{e}nô
	on the bone of	the day	the this	one circumcised	Abraham	and Ishmael	his son

27.	3725, 596	1041	3320	1041	4899, 3826B	4623, 882
	cj, adj, n mp	n ms, ps 3ms	*adj*	n ms	cj, *n fs*, n ms	prep, prep
	וְכָל־אַנְשֵׁי	בֵּיתוֹ	יְלִיד	בָּיִת	וּמִקְנַת־כֶּסֶף	מֵאֵת
	w^{e}khol-'anshê	vêthô	y^{e}lîdh	bāyith	ûmiqŏnath-keseph	mē'ēth
	and all the men of	his house	born of	house	and purchases of silver	from

1158, 5424	4271.216	882		7495.221	420	3176
n ms, n ms	v Niphal pf 3cp	prep, ps 3ms		cj, v Niphal impf 3ms	prep, ps 3ms	pn
בֶּן־נֵכָר	נִמֹּלוּ	אִתּוֹ	**18:1**	וַיֵּרָא	אֵלָיו	יְהוָה
ben-nēkhār	nimmōlû	'ittô		wayyērā'	'ēlâv	yehwāh
son of foreign land	they were circumcised	with him		and He appeared	to him	Yahweh

904, 440	4613	2000	3553.151	6860, 164	3626, 2627	3219
prep, *n fp*	pn	cj, pers pron	v Qal act ptc ms	*n ms*, art, n ms	prep, n ms	art, n ms
בְּאֵלֹנֵי	מַמְרֵא	וְהוּא	יֹשֵׁב	פֶּתַח־הָאֹהֶל	כְּחֹם	הַיּוֹם
be'ēlōnê	mamrē'	wehû'	yōshēv	pethach-hā'ōhel	kechōm	hayyôm
by the great trees of	Mamre	and he	sitting	door of the tent	as the heat	the day

bear unto thee at this set time in the next year: ... covenant I will maintain, *Anchor* ... at this appointed time, *Young* ... by this time next year, *Anchor* ... this season, *Berkeley*.

22. And he left off talking with him: ... he ceased to converse with him, *Fenton* ... as soon as he finished speaking with him, *Anchor*.

and God went up from Abraham: ... He ascended, *Berkeley* ... divine messenger went up, *Fenton* ... God was gone from Abraham, *Anchor*.

23. And Abraham took Ishmael his son, and all that were born in his house, and all that were bought with his money, every male among the men of Abraham's house; and circumcised the flesh of their foreskin in the selfsame day, as God had said unto him: ... from his communal group, *Berkeley* ... all his slaves, *Anchor*.

24. And Abraham was ninety years old and nine, when he was circumcised in the flesh of his foreskin: ... underwent circumcision, *BB*.

25. And Ishmael his son was thirteen years old, when he was circumcised in the flesh of his foreskin: ... underwent circumcision, *BB*.

26 In the selfsame day was Abraham circumcised, and Ishmael his son: ... on that very day, *BB*.

27. And all the men of his house, born in the house, and bought with money of the stranger, were circumcised with him: ... home-born, *Berkeley* ... all his retainers, *Anchor* ... bought with money of a foreigner, *ASV* ... from men of other lands, *BB* ... and foreigners were circumcised with him, *Fenton*.

18:1. And the LORD appeared unto him in the plains of Mamre: ... Oaks of Mamre, *ASV* ... Terebinths, *Anchor* ... holy tree, *BB* ... Oakwoods of Mamrah, *Fenton* ... great trees, *NIV*.

and he sat in the tent door: ... opening of his tent, *NEB* ... doorway, *BB* ... entrance, *Anchor*.

in the heat of the day: ... day was growing hot, *Anchor* ... middle of the day, *BB*.

2. And he lift up his eyes and

17:21. Again God promised to confirm His covenant with Isaac and for the third time God emphasized that Sarah would bear a son. God further specified the time. Isaac would be born twelve months from the time God was making this promise.

17:22. God must have seen faith rise in Abraham's heart and mind. This is confirmed in Romans 4:18-21 which compares Abraham's faith to a resurrection faith. That is, Sarah's womb was "dead" as far as her having any natural ability to have a child. But Abraham believed that out of that deadness God would bring life. We have the same kind of resurrection faith when we believe God raised Jesus from the dead, leaving His tomb empty.

After concluding the conversation God ascended to heaven.

17:23-27. That Abraham believed God and placed his faith in God's promise is shown by his obeying God's command immediately and completely without any hesitation. By this he declared that everything he had was dedicated to God and to God's service. Everyone in his household, including the slaves and Ishmael, were now to be recipients of the covenant blessings if they would continue to live in faith and obedience.

18:1. Abraham was enjoying the shade of his tent at its entrance one hot day when the LORD appeared to him. This begins a sequence that leads to the destruction of Sodom and the deliverance of Lot in chapter 19.

The emphasis is on how God dealt with Abraham and recognized him as a friend worthy of His confidence.

2. 5558.121	6084	7495.121	2079	8421	596	5507.256
cj, v Qal impf 3ms	n fp, ps 3ms	cj, v Qal impf 3ms	cj, intrj	num	n mp	v Niphal ptc mp
וַיִּשָּׂא	עֵינָיו	וַיַּרְא	וְהִנֵּה	שְׁלֹשָׁה	אֲנָשִׁים	נִצָּבִים
wayyissā'	‘ênâv	wayyar'	w^{e}hinnēh	sh^{e}lōshāh	'ănāshîm	nitstsāvîm
and he lifted up	his eyes	and he saw	and behold	three	men	standing

6142	7495.121	7608.121	3937, 7410.141	4623, 6860	164
prep, ps 3ms	cj, v Qal impf 3ms	cj, v Qal impf 3ms	prep, v Qal inf con, ps 3mp	prep, *n ms*	art, n ms
עָלָיו	וַיַּרְא	וַיָּרָץ	לִקְרָאתָם	מִפֶּתַח	הָאֹהֶל
‘ālâv	wayyar'	wayyārāts	liqrā'thām	mipethach	hā'ōhel
in front of him	and he saw	and he ran	to meet them	from the door of	the tent

8246.721	800	3. 569.121	112	524, 5167	4834.115	2682
cj, v Hithpalel impf 3ms	n fs	cj, v Qal impf 3ms	n ms, ps 1cs	cj, ptc	v Qal pf 1cs	n ms
וַיִּשְׁתַּחוּ	אָרְצָה	וַיֹּאמַר	אֲדֹנָי	אִם־נָא	מָצָאתִי	חֵן
wayyishtachû	'ārtsāh	wayyō'mar	'ădhōnāy	'im-nā'	mātsā'thî	chēn
and he bowed down	to the earth	and he said	my lord	if please	I have found	favor

904, 6084	414, 5167	5882.123	4623, 6142	5860	4. 4089.621, 5167
prep, n fd, ps 2ms	neg part, part	v Qal impf 2ms	prep, prep	n ms, ps 2ms	v Hophal impf 3ms, part
בְּעֵינֶיךָ	אַל־נָא	תַעֲבֹר	מֵעַל	עַבְדֶּךָ	יֻקַּח־נָא
b^{e}‘ênêkhā	'al-nā'	tha‘ăvōr	mē‘al	‘avdekhā	yuqqach-nā'
in your eyes	not please	you will pass	on from	your servant	it will be brought please

4746, 4448	7647.133	7559	8550.233	8809	6320	5. 4089.125
sub, n mp	cj, v Qal impv 2mp	n fd, ps 2mp	cj, v Niphal impv 2mp	prep	art, n ms	cj, v Qal impf 1cs
מְעַט־מַיִם	וְרַחֲצוּ	רַגְלֵיכֶם	וְהִשָּׁעֲנוּ	תַּחַת	הָעֵץ	וְאֶקְחָה
m^{e}‘aṭ-mayim	w^{e}rachtsû	raghlêkhem	w^{e}hishshā‘ănû	tachath	hā‘ēts	w^{e}eqōchāh
little water	and wash	your feet	and recline	under	the tree	and I will take

6846, 4035	5777.133	3949	313	5882.128	3706, 6142, 3772
n fs, n ms	cj, v Qal impv 2mp	n ms, ps 2mp	adv	v Qal impf 2mp	cj, prep, adv
פַּת־לֶחֶם	וְסַעֲדוּ	לִבְּכֶם	אַחַר	תַּעֲבֹרוּ	כִּי־עַל־כֵּן
phath-lechem	w^{e}sa‘ădhû	libb^{e}khem	'achar	ta‘ăvōrû	kî-‘al-kēn
morsel of bread	and strengthen	your heart	afterward	you may pass	since

5882.117	6142, 5860	569.126	3772	6449.123	3626, 866
v Qal pf 2mp	prep, n ms, ps 2mp	cj, v Qal impf 3mp	adv	v Qal impf 2ms	prep, rel part
עֲבַרְתֶּם	עַל־עַבְדְּכֶם	וַיֹּאמְרוּ	כֵּן	תַּעֲשֶׂה	כַּאֲשֶׁר
‘ăvartem	‘al-‘avd^{e}khem	wayyō'm^{e}rû	kēn	ta‘ăseh	ka'ăsher
you have passed	beside your servant	and they said	yes	you will make	according to that

1744.313	6. 4257.321	80	164	420, 8023	569.121
v Piel pf 2ms	cj, v Piel impf 3ms	pn	art, n ms	prep, pn	cj, v Qal impf 3ms
דִּבַּרְתָּ	וַיְמַהֵר	אַבְרָהָם	הָאֹהֱלָה	אֶל־שָׂרָה	וַיֹּאמֶר
dibbartā	waymahēr	'avrāhām	hā'ōhĕlāh	'el-sārāh	wayyō'mer
you have spoken	and he hurried	Abraham	to the tent	to Sarah	and he said

4257.332	8421	5613	7343	5755	4022.132	6449.132	5899
v Piel impv 2fs	*num*	*n fp*	n ms	n fs	v Qal impv 2fs	cj, v Qal impv 2fs	n fp
מַהֲרִי	שְׁלֹשׁ	סְאִים	קֶמַח	סֹלֶת	לוּשִׁי	וַעֲשִׂי	עֻגוֹת
mahrî	sh^{e}lōsh	s^{e}'îm	qemach	sōleth	lûshî	wa‘ăsî	‘ughôth
hurry	three of	measures of	flour	fine flour	knead	and make	bread cakes

7. 420, 1267	7608.111	80	4089.121	1158, 1267	7679	3005
cj, prep, art, n ms	v Qal pf 3ms	pn	cj, v Qal impf 3ms	*n ms*, n ms	adj	cj, adj
וְאֶל־הַבָּקָר	רָץ	אַבְרָהָם	וַיִּקַּח	בֶּן־בָּקָר	רַךְ	וָטוֹב
w^{e}el-habbāqār	rāts	'avrāhām	wayyiqqach	ben-bāqār	rakh	wāṭôv
and to the herd	he ran	Abraham	and he took	son of cow	tender	and good

looked: ... looking up, *Anchor* ... raised his eyes, *NCB.*

and, lo, three men stood by him: ... standing opposite him, *Berkeley* ... near him, *Darby* ... at a distance from him, *NCB* ... in front of him, *NEB, RSV.*

and when he saw them, he ran to meet them from the tent door: ... rushed from the entrance of the tent to greet them, *Anchor* ... moved quickly to them, *BB* ... called to him from the door of his tent, *Fenton.*

and bowed himself toward the ground: ... bowed himself to the earth, *ASV* ... went down on his face, *BB* ... bowing low, *REB.*

3. And said, My Lord, if now I have found favour in thy sight: ... my masters, *Fenton* ... if I may beg of you this favor, *Anchor* ... if I have grace in your eyes, *BB.*

pass not away, I pray thee, from thy servant: ... do not pass your servant by, *Berkeley, NASB* ... will you not come in to your servant, *Fenton* ... do not pass by my humble self without a visit, *NEB.*

4. Let a little water, I pray you, be fetched, and wash your feet: ... let us have a little water brought, *Berkeley* ... take a little water, *Fenton* ... bathe your feet, *Anchor.*

and rest yourselves under the tree: ... recline under the tree, *Berkeley* ... stretch yourselves out, *Goodspeed.*

5. And I will fetch a morsel of bread: ... get a bit of bread, *BB* ... bring you a little food, *NAB* ... get you something to eat, *NIV.*

and comfort ye your hearts after that ye shall pass on: ... strengthen ye your heart, *ASV* ... refresh your heart, *Fenton, NKJV* ... that ye may refresh yourselves, *Anchor* ... it will give you strength to continue your journey, *Good News.*

for therefore are ye come to your servant: ... this is why you have come, *BB* ... now that you have come right by, *Anchor* ... you will then have paid a visit, *Goodspeed.*

And they said, So do, as thou hast said: ... let it be so, *BB* ... thank you; we accept, *Good News* ... do as you propose, *Goodspeed.*

6. And Abraham hastened into the tent unto Sarah, and said: ... went quickly into the tent, *BB.*

Make ready quickly three measures of fine meal: ... quick, three seahs of the best flour, *Anchor* ... bring three pecks of fine flour, *Berkeley* ... three seahs of wheaten flour, *Darby* ... three measures of meal, *BB* ... choice flour, *NRSV.*

knead it, and make cakes upon the hearth: ... knead and make rolls, *Anchor* ... mix up some pancakes, *LIVB* ... make bread cakes, *NASB* ... make loaves, *NCB* ... bake some bread, *NIV.*

7. And Abraham ran unto the herd, and fetched a calf tender and good: ... picked out a tender and choice calf, *Anchor* ... took a young ox, soft and fat, *BB* ... took a fine, fat calf, *Fenton* ... picked out a bullock, tender and plump, *Goodspeed.*

and gave it unto a young man; and he hasted to dress it: ... gave it unto the servant, *ASV* ... to the attendant, *Darby* ... gave it to a boy who lost no time in preparing it, *Anchor* ... dressed it in short order, *Berkeley* ... quickly made it ready, *BB.*

8. And he took butter, and milk: ... curds and milk, *Anchor* ... and prepared veal, *Berkeley* ... thick and sweet milk, *Darby* ... cheese and milk, *Fenton.*

and the calf which he had dressed, and set it before them; and he stood by them under the tree, and they did eat: ... he stood opposite them, *Fenton* ... he served them himself, *Good News* ... he waited on them, *Goodspeed.*

18:2-5. Abraham's actions when he saw three strangers standing nearby shows the kind of person he was. He was sensitive to the needs of these strangers in the heat of the day and he showed them the best of oriental hospitality. His heart went out to them. He did not wait for them to come to him, but hurried out to them. He bowed low and addressed their leader respectfully as "my lord" and called himself "your servant." There is no indication at this point that he knew who they were. Hebrews 13:2 probably refers to this when it says "Do not forget to entertain strangers, for by so doing some people have entertained angels *without knowing it.*" (Italics mine.) Thus, he offered to give them water to wash their feet and give them something to eat, an offer they readily accepted.

18:6-8. Abraham asked Sarah to take about 22 quarts of flour and make flat cakes of bread which would be baked on hot stones. Then he had a servant select one of the best calves and prepare it. These along with milk and curds (the sour milk curds would be refreshing in the heat of the day) were fed to the strangers. As is still the Bedouin custom in that part of the world, Abraham did not eat with his guests, but stood nearby ready to serve them and respond to their wishes.

5598.121	420, 5470	4257.321	3937, 6449.141	881	**8.** 4089.121	2628
cj, v Qal pf 3ms	prep, art, n ms	cj, v Piel impf 3ms	prep, v Qal inf con	do, ps 3ms	cj, v Qal impf 3ms	n fs
וַיִּתֵּן	אֶל־הַנַּעַר	וַיְמַהֵר	לַעֲשׂוֹת	אֹתוֹ	וַיִּקַּח	חֶמְאָה
wayyittēn	'el-hanna'ar	waymahēr	la'ăsôth	'ōthô	wayyiqqach	chem'āh
and he gave	to the slave	and he hurried	to prepare	it	and he took	curds

2560	1158, 1267	866	6449.111	5598.121	3937, 6686
cj, n ms	cj, *n ms*, art, n ms	rel part	v Qal pf 3ms	cj, v Qal impf 3ms	prep, n mp, ps 3mp
וְחָלָב	וּבֶן־הַבָּקָר	אֲשֶׁר	עָשָׂה	וַיִּתֵּן	לִפְנֵיהֶם
wechālāv	ûven-habbāqār	'ăsher	'āsâh	wayyittēn	liphnêhem
and milk	and the son of the cow	which	he prepared	and he placed	before them

2000, 6198.151	6142	8809	6320	404.126	**9.** 569.126
cj, pers pron, v Qal act ptc ms	prep, ps 3mp	prep	art, n ms	cj, v Qal impf 3mp	cj, v Qal impf 3mp
וְהוּא־עֹמֵד	עֲלֵיהֶם	תַּחַת	הָעֵץ	וַיֹּאכֵלוּ	וַיֹּאמְרוּ
wehû'-'ōmēdh	'ălêhem	tachath	hā'ēts	wayyō'khēlû	wayyō'merû
and he standing	beside them	under	the tree	and they ate	and they said

420	347	8023	828	569.121	2079	904, 164
prep, ps 3ms	intrg	pn	n fs, ps 2ms	cj, v Qal impf 3ms	intrj	prep, art, n ms
אֵלָיו	אַיֵּה	שָׂרָה	אִשְׁתֶּךָ	וַיֹּאמֶר	הִנֵּה	בָאֹהֶל
'ēlâv	'ayyēh	sārāh	'ishtekhā	wayyō'mer	hinnēh	vā'ōhel
to him	where	Sarah	your wife	and he said	behold	in the tent

10. 569.121	8178.142	8178.125	420	3626, 6496	2516
cj, v Qal impf 3ms	v Qal inf abs	v Qal impf 1cs	prep, ps 2ms	prep, art, *n fs*	n fs
וַיֹּאמֶר	שׁוֹב	אָשׁוּב	אֵלֶיךָ	כָּעֵת	חַיָּה
wayyō'mer	shôv	'āshûv	'ēlêkhā	kā'ēth	chayyāh
and He said	returning	I will return	to you	according to the time of	life

2079, 1158	3937, 8023	828	8023	8471.153	6860	164	2000
cj, intrj, n ms	prep, pn	n fs, ps 2ms	cj, pn	v Qal act ptc fs	*n ms*	art, n ms	cj, pers pron
וְהִנֵּה־בֵן	לְשָׂרָה	אִשְׁתֶּךָ	וְשָׂרָה	שֹׁמַעַת	פֶּתַח	הָאֹהֶל	וְהוּא
wehinnēh-vēn	lesārāh	'ishtekhā	wesārāh	shōma'ath	pethach	hā'ōhel	wehû'
and behold son	to Sarah	your wife	and Sarah	listening	the door of	the tent	and it

313	**11.** 82	8023	2292	971.152	904, 3219	2403.111
adv, ps 3ms	cj, pn	cj, pn	adj	v Qal act ptc mp	prep, art, n mp	v Qal pf 3ms
אַחֲרָיו	וְאַבְרָהָם	וְשָׂרָה	זְקֵנִים	בָּאִים	בַּיָּמִים	חָדַל
'achrâv	we'avrāhām	wesārāh	zeqēnîm	bā'îm	bayyāmîm	chādhal
behind him	and Abraham	and Sarah	old	ones going	in the days	it stopped

3937, 2030.141	3937, 8023	758	3626, 5571	**12.** 6978.122	8023	904, 7419
prep, v Qal inf con	prep, pn	n ms	prep, art, n fp	cj, v Qal impf 3fs	pn	prep, n ms, ps 3fs
לִהְיוֹת	לְשָׂרָה	אֹרַח	כַּנָּשִׁים	וַתִּצְחַק	שָׂרָה	בְּקִרְבָּהּ
lihyôth	lesārāh	'ōrach	kannāshîm	wattitschaq	sārāh	beqirbāhh
to be	to Sarah	way	like the women	and she laughed	Sarah	within herself

3937, 569.141	311	1126.141	2030.112, 3937	5947	112	2290.111
prep, v Qal inf con	sub	v Qal inf con, ps 1cs	v Qal pf 3fs, prep, ps 1cs	n fs	cj, n ms, ps 1cs	v Qal pf 3ms
לֵאמֹר	אַחֲרֵי	בְלֹתִי	הָיְתָה־לִּי	עֶדְנָה	וַאדֹנִי	זָקֵן
lē'mōr	'achrê	velōthî	hāyethāh-lî	'edhnāh	wa'dhōnî	zāqēn
saying	after	my wearing out	will it be to me	pleasure	and my lord	he is old

13. 569.121	3176	420, 80	4066	2172	6978.112	8023
cj, v Qal impf 3ms	pn	prep, pn	intrg	dem pron	v Qal pf 3fs	pn
וַיֹּאמֶר	יְהוָה	אֶל־אַבְרָהָם	לָמָּה	זֶה	צָחֲקָה	שָׂרָה
wayyō'mer	yehwāh	'el-'avrāhām	lāmmāh	zeh	tsāchăqāh	sārāh
and He said	Yahweh	to Abraham	why	this	she laughed	Sarah

3937, 569.141	652	557	3314.125	603	2290.115
prep, v Qal inf con	intrg part, prep	cj	v Qal impf 1cs	cj, pers pron	v Qal pf 1cs
לֵאמֹר	הַאַף	אֻמְנָם	אֵלֵד	וַאֲנִי	זָקַנְתִּי
lē'mōr	ha'aph	'umnām	'ēlēdh	wa'ănî	zāqantî
saying	indeed	in fact	will I give birth	when I	I am old

14.

6623.121	4623, 3176	1745	3937, 4287	8178.125	420
intrg part, v Qal impf 3ms	prep, pn	n ms	prep, art, n ms	v Qal impf 1cs	prep, ps 2ms
הֲיִפָּלֵא	מֵיְהוָה	דָּבָר	לַמּוֹעֵד	אָשׁוּב	אֵלֶיךָ
h^{e}yippālē'	mēy^{e}hwāh	dāvār	lammô'ēdh	'āshûv	'ēlêkhā
is it too hard	for Yahweh	anything	to the set time	I will return	to you

9. And they said unto him, Where is Sarah thy wife? And he said, Behold, in the tent: ... they afterwards asked him, *Fenton.*

10. And he said, I will certainly return unto thee according to the time of life: ... the season cometh round, *ASV* ... life would be due, *Anchor* ... the reviving season, *Berkeley* ... the spring, *BB* ... this time next year, *NEB.*

and, lo, Sarah thy wife shall have a son. And Sarah heard it in the tent door, which was behind him: ... had been listening at the tent entrance, *Anchor* ... his words came to the ears of Sarah, *BB* ... hearkening, *Young* ... he was close beside it, *NEB.*

11. Now Abraham and Sarah were old and well stricken in age: ... advanced in years and feeble, *Fenton* ... far gone in days, *KJVII.*

and it ceased to be with Sarah after the manner of women: ... had stopped having a woman's periods, *Anchor* ... custom of women, *Berkeley* ... Sarah was past childbearing, *NASB.*

12. Therefore Sarah laughed within herself, saying, After I am waxed old: ... after I am wasted, *Fenton* ... that I am used up, *BB.*

shall I have pleasure, my lord being old also: ... withered as I am, am I still to know enjoyment and my husband so old, *Anchor* ... enjoyment for me, worn out as I am, *Berkeley* ... can I still enjoy sex, *Good News* ... can there be marriage pleasure for me, *Goodspeed.*

13. And the LORD said unto Abraham, Wherefore did Sarah laugh, saying, Shall I of a surety bear a child, which am old: ... why is this, that Sarah laughs, *Darby* ... shall I really give birth, old as I am, *Anchor* ... is it possible ... to give birth to a child, *BB* ... shall I suckle a child when I am old, *Fenton.*

14. Is any thing too hard for the LORD: ... anything too much for Yahweh, *Anchor* ... beyond the Lord's reach, *Berkeley* ... too marvelous for the Lord, *NAB* ... too wonderful, *NCB* ... impossible, *NEB* ... any wonder which the Lord is not able to do, *BB.*

18:9-10. It is obvious that Abraham had not told Sarah about God's promise that she should have a son. So when the three men called out asking where Sarah was, the purpose was undoubtedly to get her attention. Then, the One who was the leader, emphatically declared that when He returned this time the next year Sarah would have a son. Sarah was indeed listening as the LORD knew she would be.

18:11-12. Possibly, Abraham had not told Sarah because he knew she would have a hard time believing it. When Sarah heard it, she laughed to herself as she thought about her condition, not only old, passed menopause, but she felt like a worn-out garment. Her "lord" ("master, husband, cf. 1 Peter 3:6), whom she respected, was also old. Truly it seemed impossible, unbelievable that she would have the pleasure of bearing a child.

18:13-14. Now the Bible clearly identifies the One speaking to Abraham as the LORD (*Yahweh*), the one true God who had made the promises to Abraham. Though the LORD was speaking to Abraham, He knew Sarah was listening as He asked why Sarah laughed, and then asked if anything was too hard for the LORD. "Too hard," not only means too difficult, but also too extraordinary, too marvelous. He is able to do anything He wants or wills to do.

18:15. Sarah, suddenly realizing who was speaking, was overwhelmed with fear that God might bring judgment on her. She had only laughed within herself, so she lied and said she had not laughed. But the LORD said she did. However, in His grace, He did not punish her.

3626, 6496	2516	3937, 8023	1158		3703.322	8023
prep, art, *n fs*	n fs	cj, prep, pn	n ms		cj, v Piel impf 3fs	pn
כָּעֵת	חַיָּה	וּלְשָׂרָה	בֵן	**15.**	וַתְּכַחֵשׁ	שָׂרָה
kā'ēth	chayyāh	ûlāsārāh	vēn		wattekhachēsh	sārāh
according to the time of	life	and to Sarah	son		and she lied	Sarah

3937, 569.141	3940	6978.115	3706	3486.112	569.121	3940	3706
prep, v Qal inf con	neg part	v Qal pf 1cs	cj	v Qal pf 3fs	cj, v Qal impf 3ms	neg part	cj
לֵאמֹר	לֹא	צָחַקְתִּי	כִּי	יָרֵאָה	וַיֹּאמֶר	לֹא	כִּי
lē'mōr	lō'	tsāchaqtî	kî	yārē'āh	wayyō'mer	lō'	kî
saying	not	I laughed	because	she was afraid	but He said	no	rather

6978.114		7251.126	4623, 8427	596	8625.526
v Qal pf 2fs		cj, v Qal impf 3mp	prep, adv	art, n mp	cj, v Hiphil impf 3mp
צָחָקְתְּ	**16.**	וַיָּקֻמוּ	מִשָּׁם	הָאֲנָשִׁים	וַיַּשְׁקִפוּ
tsāchāqōte		wayyāqumû	mishshām	hā'ănāshîm	wayyashqiphû
you laughed		and they stood up	from there	the men	and they looked down

6142, 6686	5651	82	2050.151	6196	3937, 8365
prep, *n mp*	pn	cj, pn	v Qal act ptc ms	prep, ps 3mp	prep, v Piel inf con, ps 3mp
עַל־פְּנֵי	סְדֹם	וְאַבְרָהָם	הֹלֵךְ	עִמָּם	לְשַׁלְּחָם
'al-penê	sedhōm	we'avrāhām	hōlēkh	'immām	leshallechām
toward	Sodom	and Abraham	walking	with them	to send them

	3176	569.111	3803.351	603	4623, 80	866	603
	cj, pn	v Qal pf 3ms	intrg part, v Piel ptc ms	pers pron	prep, pn	rel part	pers pron
17.	וַיהוָה	אָמָר	הַמְכַסֶּה	אֲנִי	מֵאַבְרָהָם	אֲשֶׁר	אֲנִי
	wayhōwāh	'āmār	hamkhasseh	'ănî	mē'avrāhām	'ăsher	'ănî
	and Yahweh	He said	will hiding	I	from Abraham	which	I

6449.151		82	2030.142	2030.121	3937, 1504	1448	6335
v Qal act ptc ms		cj, pn	v Qal inf abs	v Qal impf 3ms	prep, n ms	adj	cj, adj
עֹשֶׂה	**18.**	וְאַבְרָהָם	הָיוֹ	יִהְיֶה	לְגוֹי	גָּדוֹל	וְעָצוּם
'ōseh		we'avrāhām	hāyô	yihyeh	leghôy	gādhôl	we'ātsûm
doing		since Abraham	being	he will be	for nation	great	and mighty

1313.216, 904	3725	1504	800		3706	3156.115
cj, v Niphal pf 3mp, prep, ps 3ms	adj	*n mp*	art, n fs		cj	v Qal pf 1cs, ps 3ms
וְנִבְרְכוּ־בוֹ	כֹּל	גּוֹיֵי	הָאָרֶץ	**19.**	כִּי	יְדַעְתִּיו
wenivrekhû-vô	kōl	gôyê	hā'ārets		kî	yedha'ătîw
and they will be blessed by him	all	the nations of	the earth		because	I have known him

3937, 4775	866	6943.321	881, 1158	881, 1041	313	8490.116
prep, prep	rel part	v Piel impf 3ms	do, n mp, ps 3ms	cj, do, n ms, ps 3ms	adv, ps 3ms	cj, v Qal pf 3cp
לְמַעַן	אֲשֶׁר	יְצַוֶּה	אֶת־בָּנָיו	וְאֶת־בֵּיתוֹ	אַחֲרָיו	וְשָׁמְרוּ
lema'an	'ăsher	yetsawweh	'eth-bānâv	we'eth-bêthô	'achrâv	weshāmerû
for	what	he will command	his sons	and his house	after him	and they will keep

1932	3176	3937, 6449.141	6930	5122	3937, 4775	971.541	3176
n ms	pn	prep, v Qal inf con	n fs	cj, n ms	prep, prep	v Hiphil inf con	pn
דֶּרֶךְ	יְהוָה	לַעֲשׂוֹת	צְדָקָה	וּמִשְׁפָּט	לְמַעַן	הָבִיא	יְהוָה
derekh	yehwāh	la'ăsôth	tsedhāqāh	ûmishepāṭ	lema'an	hāvî'	yehwāh
the way of	Yahweh	to do	righteousness	and justice	so that	to bring	Yahweh

6142, 80	881	866, 1744.311	6142		569.121	3176
prep, pn	do	rel part, v Piel pf 3ms	prep, ps 3ms		cj, v Qal impf 3ms	pn
עַל־אַבְרָהָם	אֵת	אֲשֶׁר־דִּבֶּר	עָלָיו	**20.**	וַיֹּאמֶר	יְהוָה
'al-'avrāhām	'ēth	'ăsher-dibber	'ālâv		wayyō'mer	yehwāh
on Abraham		what He has spoken	concerning him		and He said	Yahweh

At the time appointed I will return unto thee: ... at the set time, *ASV* ... when life is due, *Anchor* ... in the spring, *BB* ... at this time next year, *NASB* ... in due season, *NEB.*

according to the time of life, and Sarah shall have a son: ... when the season cometh round, *ASV* ... at the reviving season, *Berkeley* ... I will return to you the period of youth, *Fenton* ... the time for life to appear, *Goodspeed.*

15. Then Sarah denied, saying, I laughed not; for she was afraid. And he said, Nay; but thou didst laugh: ... Sarah dissembled, *Anchor, NAB* ... feeling afraid, *Berkeley* ... she was full of fear, *BB* ... Sarah lied because she was frightened, *NEB.*

16. And the men rose up from thence, and looked toward Sodom: ... got up to leave, *NIV* ... departed from there and faced toward Sodom, *Fenton* ... setting out from there, the men directed their steps toward Sodom, *Goodspeed* ... in the direction of Sodom, *BB* ... look on the face of Sodom, *Young.*

and Abraham went with them to bring them on the way: ... walking with them to see them off, *Anchor* ... to direct their way, *Berkeley* ... to conduct them, *Darby* ... to converse, *Fenton* ... escort them, *NCB.*

17. And the LORD said, Shall I hide from Abraham that thing which I do: ... am I hiding from Abraham what I am about to do, *Berkeley* ... am I to keep back from Abraham the knowledge of what I do, *BB* ... the Lord thought to himself, *NEB.*

18. Seeing that Abraham shall surely become a great and mighty nation: ... populous nation, *Anchor, NAB* ... powerful nation, *Goodspeed.*

and all the nations of the earth shall be blessed in him: ... nations of the world are to bless themselves through him, *Anchor* ... his name will be used ... as a blessing, *BB* ... nations of the earth will invoke blessings on one another, *Goodspeed* ... will pray to be blessed as he is blessed, *NEB.*

19. For I know him: ... I have singled him out, *Anchor* ... I have made him mine, *BB* ... I have instructed him, *Fenton* ... I will make it known to him, *Goodspeed* ... I have chosen him, *NASB* ... I have taken care of him on purpose, *NEB.*

that he will command his children and his household after him: ... instruct his sons and his future family, *Anchor* ... charge his children and his household, *Berkeley* ... give orders to his children and those of his line after him, *BB* ... command his sons and the sons of his house after him, *Fenton* ... sons and his posterity, *NAB.*

and they shall keep the way of the LORD: ... conform to the way of the Lord, *NEB, REB* ... keep to the path of, *Fenton.*

to do justice and judgment: ... righteousness and justice, *NASB* ... just and right, *Anchor* ... right and fair, *Berkeley* ... good and right, *BB.*

that the LORD may bring upon Abraham that which he hath spoken of him: ... may bestow on Abraham, *Berkeley* ... do to Abraham as he said, *BB* ... what he has promised to him, *Fenton* ... carry into effect for Abraham the promises he made, *NAB* ... thus I shall fulfill all that I have promised for him, *NEB.*

20. And the LORD said, Because the cry of Sodom and Gomorrah is great, and because their sin is very grievous: ... the outrage of Sodom and Gomorrah is so great, *Anchor* ... outcry is loud, *Berkeley* ... Sodom and Gomorrah shriek, *Fenton* ... terrible accusations, *Good News.*

18:16-19. Abraham was at an elevation of about 3,000 feet, and Sodom was about 1,200 feet below sea level, so the men were looking down as they looked toward Sodom. Abraham was escorting them on their way for a little while, probably about three miles to a point where the Dead Sea (and Sodom) would come into view.

Then the One identified as the LORD spoke, undoubtedly for Abraham's benefit. Why should He conceal from Abraham what He was about to do? Then He referred to the promise He had given to Abraham and declared that He had known him in a personal way.

The LORD also said He knew Abraham would command the sons or descendants and the household of the chosen line after him to do right and just deeds (according to the LORD's standards) so He might bring those promises to fulfillment that he had made for Abraham.

18:20-21. The outcry against Sodom and Gomorrah implies a cry for help from those who were oppressed, mistreated, and sinned against. The cities were heavily loaded with sin. The LORD purposed to go down and observe the situation to see if it was as bad as the cry for help indicated. If not He would know. This does not deny God's infinite knowledge of all things. God was telling Abraham He does not act on the basis of mere outcries and complaints. He enters into the situation so that He knows what is going on in a personal way.

2285	**5651**	**6244**	**3706, 7528.112**	**2492**	**3706**	**3632.112**
n fs	pn	cj, pn	cj, v Qal pf 3fs	cj, n fs, ps 3mp	cj	v Qal pf 3fs
זַעֲקַת	סְדֹם	וַעֲמֹרָה	כִּי־רָבָּה	וְחַטָּאתָם	כִּי	כָּבְדָה
za'ăqath	s^{e}dhōm	wa'ămōrāh	kî-rābbâh	w^{e}chattā'thām	kî	khāv^{e}dhāh
the outcry of	Sodom	and Gomorrah	it has become great	and their sin	that	it is heavy

4108	**21.**	**3495.125, 5167**	**7495.125**	**3626, 2285**	**971.153**	**420**
adv		v Qal impf 1cs, ptc	cj, v Qal impf 1cs	intrg part, prep, n fs, ps 3fs	art, v Qal act ptc fs	prep, ps 1cs
מְאֹד		אֵרְדָה־נָּא	וְאֶרְאֶה	הַכְּצַעֲקָתָהּ	הַבָּאָה	אֵלַי
m^{e}'ōdh		'ēr^{e}dhāh-nā'	w^{e}'erä'eh	hakk^{e}tsa'ăqāthāhh	habbā'āh	'ēlay
very		I will go down now	and I will see	whether like its outcry	coming	to Me

6449.116	**3735.111**	**524, 3940**	**3314.125**	**22.**	**6680.126**	**4623, 8427**
v Qal pf 3cp	v Qal pf 3ms	cj, cj, neg part	v Qal impf 1cs		cj, v Qal impf 3mp	prep, adv
עָשׂוּ	כָּלָה	וְאִם־לֹא	אֵדָעָה		וַיִּפְנוּ	מִשָּׁם
'āsû	kālāh	w^{e}'im-lō'	'ēdhā'āh		wayyiphnû	mishshām
they have done	is it complete	and if not	I will know		and they turned	from there

596	**2050.126**	**5651**	**82**	**5968**	**6198.151**	**3937, 6686**	**3176**
art, n mp	cj, v Qal impf 3mp	pn	cj, pn	adv, ps 3ms	v Qal act ptc ms	prep, *n mp*	pn
הָאֲנָשִׁים	וַיֵּלְכוּ	סְדֹמָה	וְאַבְרָהָם	עוֹדֶנּוּ	עֹמֵד	לִפְנֵי	יְהוָה
hā'ănāshîm	wayyēl^{e}khû	s^{e}dhōmāh	w^{e}'avrāhām	'ôdhennû	'ōmēdh	liphnê	y^{e}hwāh
the men	and they walked	to Sodom	and Abraham	still he	standing	before	Yahweh

23.	**5242.121**	**80**	**569.121**	**652**	**5793.123**	**6926**
	cj, v Qal impf 3ms	pn	cj, v Qal impf 3ms	intrg part, prep	v Qal impf 2ms	adj
	וַיִּגַּשׁ	אַבְרָהָם	וַיֹּאמַר	הַאַף	תִּסְפֶּה	צַדִּיק
	wayyiggash	'avrāhām	wayyō'mar	ha'aph	tispeh	tsaddîq
	and he drew near	Abraham	and he said	indeed	will You sweep away	righteous

6196, 7857	**24.**	**193**	**3552**	**2675**	**6926**	**904, 8761**	**6111**
prep, adj		adv	n ms	num	adj	prep, *sub*	art, n fs
עִם־רָשָׁע		אוּלַי	יֵשׁ	חֲמִשִּׁים	צַדִּיקִם	בְּתוֹךְ	הָעִיר
'im-rāshā'		'ûlay	yēsh	chămishshîm	tsaddîqim	b^{e}thôkh	hā'îr
with wicked		perhaps	there is	fifty	righteous	in the midst of	the city

652	**5793.123**	**3940, 5558.123**	**3937, 4887**	**3937, 4775**	**2675**
intrg part, prep	v Qal impf 2ms	cj, neg part, v Qal impf 2ms	prep, art, n ms	prep, prep	num
הַאַף	תִּסְפֶּה	וְלֹא־תִשָּׂא	לַמָּקוֹם	לְמַעַן	חֲמִשִּׁים
ha'aph	tispeh	w^{e}lō'-thissā'	lammāqôm	l^{e}ma'an	chămishshîm
indeed	will You sweep away	and will You not forgive	the place	for that	fifty

6926	**866**	**904, 7419**	**25.**	**2587**	**3937**	**4623, 6449.141**	**3626, 1745**
art, adj	rel part	prep, n ms, ps 3fs		intrj	prep, ps 2ms	prep, v Qal inf con	prep, art, n ms
הַצַּדִּיקִם	אֲשֶׁר	בְּקִרְבָּהּ		חָלִלָה	לְּךָ	מֵעֲשֹׂת	כַּדָּבָר
hatstsaddîqim	'ăsher	b^{e}qirbāhh		chālilāh	l^{e}khā	mē'ăshōth	kaddāvār
the righteous	who	within it		far be it	to You	from doing	like the thing

2172	**3937, 4322.541**	**6926**	**6196, 7857**	**2030.111**	**3626, 6926**
art, dem pron	prep, v Hiphil inf con	adj	prep, adj	cj, v Qal pf 3ms	prep, art, adj
הַזֶּה	לְהָמִית	צַדִּיק	עִם־רָשָׁע	וְהָיָה	כַּצַּדִּיק
hazzeh	l^{e}hāmîth	tsaddîq	'im-rāshā'	w^{e}hāyāh	khatstsaddîq
the this	to kill	righteous	with wicked	that it will be	as the righteous

3626, 7857	**2587**	**3937**	**8570.151**	**3725, 800**	**3940**	**6449.121**
prep, art, adj	intrj	prep, ps 2ms	intrg part, *v Qal act ptc ms*	*adj*, art, n fs	neg part	v Qal impf 3ms
כָּרָשָׁע	חָלִלָה	לָךְ	הֲשֹׁפֵט	כָּל־הָאָרֶץ	לֹא	יַעֲשֶׂה
kārāshā'	chālilāh	lākh	h^{e}shōphēt	kol-hā'ārets	lō'	ya'ăseh
as the wicked	far be it	to You	will the Judge of	all the earth	not	will He do

5122		569.121	3176	524, 4834.125	904, 5651	2675	6926
n ms	26.	cj, v Qal impf 3ms	pn	cj, v Qal impf 1cs	prep, pn	num	adj
מִשְׁפָּט		וַיֹּאמֶר	יְהוָה	אִם־אֶמְצָא	בִסְדֹם	חֲמִשִּׁים	צַדִּיקִם
mishpāṯ		wayyō'mer	y^ehwāh	'im-'emtsā'	vis^edhōm	chămishshîm	tsaddîqim
justice		and He said	Yahweh	if I find	in Sodom	fifty	righteous

904, 8761	6111	5558.115	3937, 3725, 4887	904, 5877
prep, *sub*	art, n fs	cj, v Qal pf 1cs	prep, *adj*, art, n ms	prep, art, prep, ps 3mp
בְּתוֹךְ	הָעִיר	וְנָשָׂאתִי	לְכָל־הַמָּקוֹם	בַּעֲבוּרָם
b^ethôkh	hā'îr	w^enāsā'thî	l^ekhol-hammāqôm	ba'ăvûrām
in the midst of	the city	then I will forgive	all the place	on account of them

21. I will go down now, and see whether they have done altogether according to the cry of it, which is come unto me: ... I will see what causes the shrieks, *Fenton* ... see whether their actions are at all like the outcry, *Anchor* ... see if their acts are as bad as they seem, *BB* ... their behaviors, *Berkeley.*

and if not, I will know: ... if they are not, I will see, *BB* ... I mean to find out, *NAB* ... I am resolved to know the truth, *NEB.*

22. And the men turned their faces from thence and went toward Sodom: ... from that place, *BB* ... turned away from there, *NASB.*

but Abraham stood yet before the LORD: ... stood firm, *Fenton* ... remained standing, *NCB* ... still waiting, *BB* ... Yahweh paused, *Anchor* ... Lord remained standing before Abraham, *Goodspeed.*

23. And Abraham drew near, and said, Wilt thou also destroy the righteous with the wicked: ... consume the righteous, *ASV* ... stamp out the innocent along with the guilty, *Anchor* ... wipe out the good too, with the bad, *Berkeley.*

24. Peradventure there be fifty righteous within the city: ... suppose, *Goodspeed* ... fifty who are innocent, *Anchor* ... fifty upright men, *BB.*

wilt thou also destroy and not spare the place for the fifty righteous that are therein: ... would you still level the place, *Anchor* ... wipe out and not pardon the community, *Berkeley* ... give the place to destruction, *BB* ... sweep it away, *Goodspeed* ... not forgive it, *NRSV.*

25. That be far from thee to do after this manner: ... far be it from you to do such a thing, *Anchor* ... let such a thing be far from you, *BB.*

to slay the righteous with the wicked: ... the innocent perish with the guilty, *Anchor* ... slay the good with the bad, *Berkeley* ... put the upright to death with the sinner, *BB.*

and that the righteous should be as the wicked: ... innocent and guilty fare alike, *Anchor* ... treat righteous and wicked alike, *Berkeley* ... the good would suffer with the bad, *NEB.*

that be far from thee: Shall not the Judge of all the earth do right: ... act with justice, *Anchor* ... deal justly, *Berkeley.*

26. And the LORD said, If I find in Sodom fifty righteous within the city: ... fifty who are innocent, *Anchor* ... fifty just men, *Fenton.*

then I will spare all the place for their sakes: ... I will forgive all the place, *Darby* ... I will have mercy, *BB* ... grant pardon to the whole

18:22-25. The two men who were with the LORD went on toward Sodom. Chapter 19:1 identifies them as angels. But Abraham faced the LORD and stepped up close to Him. Since 19:29 shows that God rescued Lot for Abraham's sake, we can be sure that concern for Lot was what prompted Abraham to try to persuade the LORD not to destroy Sodom. Because Abraham recognized the LORD as the Judge of all the earth who could be counted on to do right, he suggested that the LORD surely would not sweep away the righteous with the wicked. Abraham believed if there were 50 righteous in the city, God would surely spare it.

18:26-33. The LORD agreed to spare the whole city of Sodom if He found 50 righteous there. Abraham humbled himself before the LORD calling himself as nothing but dust and ashes, that is, insignificant in contrast to the greatness of God.

Then he proceeded to ask the LORD to lower the number by five, then by another five, then by a further ten, three times until God agreed to spare the city if there were only ten righteous present. His attitude was like that of Luke 11:8-10. God wants us to keep asking.

27.	6257.121	80	569.121	2079, 5167	3082.515	3937, 1744.341
	cj, v Qal impf 3ms	pn	cj, v Qal impf 3ms	intrj, part	v Hiphil pf 1cs	prep, v Piel inf con
	וַיַּעַן	אַבְרָהָם	וַיֹּאמַר	הִנֵּה־נָא	הוֹאַלְתִּי	לְדַבֵּר
	wayya'an	'avrāhām	wayyō'mar	hinnēh-nā'	hô'altî	l^{e}dhabbēr
	and he answered	Abraham	and he said	behold please	I have begun	to speak

420, 112	609	6312	684	28.	193	2741.126	2675	6926
prep, n mp, ps 1cs	cj, pers pron	n ms	cj, n ms		adv	v Qal impf 3mp	num	art, adj
אֶל־אֲדֹנָי	וְאָנֹכִי	עָפָר	וָאֵפֶר		אוּלַי	יַחְסְרוּן	חֲמִשִּׁים	הַצַּדִּיקִם
'el-'ădhōnāy	w^{e}'ānōkhî	'āphār	wā'ēpher		'ûlay	yachs^{e}rûn	chămishshîm	hatstsaddîqim
to my Lord	though I	dust	and ashes		perhaps	they lack	fifty	the righteous

2675	8271.523	904, 2675	881, 3725, 6111	569.121	3940
num	intrg part, v Hiphil impf 2ms	prep, art, num	do, *adj*, art, n fs	cj, v Qal impf 3ms	neg part
חֲמִשָּׁה	הֲתַשְׁחִית	בַּחֲמִשָּׁה	אֶת־כָּל־הָעִיר	וַיֹּאמֶר	לֹא
chămishshāh	h^{e}thashchîth	bachmishshāh	'eth-kol-hā'îr	wayyō'mer	lō'
five	will You wipe out	with the five	all the city	and He said	not

8271.525	524, 4834.125	8427	727	2675	29.	3362.121
v Hiphil impf 1cs	cj, v Qal impf 1cs	adv	num	cj, num		cj, v Qal impf 3ms
אַשְׁחִית	אִם־אֶמְצָא	שָׁם	אַרְבָּעִים	וַחֲמִשָּׁה		וַיֹּסֶף
'ashchîth	'im-'emtsā'	shām	'arbā'îm	wachmishshāh		wayyōseph
I will wipe out	if I find	there	forty	and five		and he continued

5968	3937, 1744.341	420	569.121	193	4834.226	8427	727
adv	prep, v Piel inf con	prep, ps 3ms	cj, v Qal impf 3ms	adv	v Niphal impf 3mp	adv	num
עוֹד	לְדַבֵּר	אֵלָיו	וַיֹּאמַר	אוּלַי	יִמָּצְאוּן	שָׁם	אַרְבָּעִים
'ôdh	l^{e}dhabbēr	'ēlâv	wayyō'mar	'ûlay	yimmāts'ûn	shom	'arbā'îm
again	to speak	to Him	and he said	perhaps	they are found	there	forty

569.121	3940	6449.125	904, 5877	727	30.	569.121	414, 5167
cj, v Qal impf 3ms	neg part	v Qal impf 1cs	prep, prep	art, num		cj, v Qal impf 3ms	neg part, part
וַיֹּאמֶר	לֹא	אֶעֱשֶׂה	בַּעֲבוּר	הָאַרְבָּעִים		וַיֹּאמֶר	אַל־נָא
wayyō'mer	lō'	'e'ĕseh	ba'ăvûr	hā'arbā'îm		wayyō'mer	'al-nā'
and He said	not	I will do	on account of	the forty		and he said	not please

2835.121	3937, 112	1744.325	193	4834.226	8427	8389
v Qal impf 3ms	prep, art, n mp	cj, v Piel impf 1cs	adv	v Niphal impf 3mp	adv	num
יִחַר	לַאדֹנָי	וַאֲדַבֵּרָה	אוּלַי	יִמָּצְאוּן	שָׁם	שְׁלֹשִׁים
yichar	la'dhōnāy	wa'ădhabbērāh	'ûlay	yimmāts'ûn	shom	sh^{e}lōshîm
it will be anger	to the Lord	and I will speak	perhaps	they are found	there	thirty

569.121	3940	6449.125	524, 4834.125	8427	8389	31.	569.121
cj, v Qal impf 3ms	neg part	v Qal impf 1cs	cj, v Qal impf 1cs	adv	num		cj, v Qal impf 3ms
וַיֹּאמֶר	לֹא	אֶעֱשֶׂה	אִם־אֶמְצָא	שָׁם	שְׁלֹשִׁים		וַיֹּאמֶר
wayyō'mer	lō'	'e'ĕseh	'im-'emtsā'	shom	sh^{e}lōshîm		wayyō'mer
and He said	not	I will do	if I find	there	thirty		and he said

2079, 5167	3082.515	3937, 1744.341	420, 112	193	4834.226	8427
intrj, part	v Hiphil pf 1cs	prep, v Piel inf con	prep, n ms, ps 1cs	adv	v Niphal impf 3mp	adv
הִנֵּה־נָא	הוֹאַלְתִּי	לְדַבֵּר	אֶל־אֲדֹנָי	אוּלַי	יִמָּצְאוּן	שָׁם
hinnēh-nā'	hô'altî	l^{e}dhabbēr	'el-'ădhōnāy	'ûlay	yimmāts'ûn	shom
behold please	I have begun	to speak	to my Lord	perhaps	they are found	there

6460	569.121	3940	8271.525	904, 5877	6460	32.	569.121
num	cj, v Qal impf 3ms	neg part	v Hiphil impf 1cs	prep, prep	art, num		cj, v Qal impf 3ms
עֶשְׂרִים	וַיֹּאמֶר	לֹא	אַשְׁחִית	בַּעֲבוּר	הָעֶשְׂרִים		וַיֹּאמֶר
'esrîm	wayyō'mer	lō'	'ashchîth	ba'ăvûr	hā'esrîm		wayyō'mer
twenty	and He said	not	I will wipe out	on account of	the twenty		and he said

414, 5167	2835.121	3937, 112	1744.325	395, 6718	193
neg part, part	v Qal impf 3ms	prep, art, n mp	cj, v Piel impf 1cs	adv, art, n fs	adv
אַל־נָא	יִחַר	לַאדֹנָי	וַאֲדַבְּרָה	אַךְ־הַפַּעַם	אוּלַי
'al-nā'	yichar	la'dhōnāy	wa'ădhabb^{e}rāh	'akh-happa'am	'ûlay
not please	it will be anger	to the Lord	and I will speak	only the time	perhaps

4834.226	8427	6463	569.121	3940	8271.525	904, 5877
v Niphal impf 3mp	adv	num	cj, v Qal impf 3ms	neg part	v Hiphil impf 1cs	prep, prep
יִמָּצְאוּן	שָׁם	עֲשָׂרָה	וַיֹּאמֶר	לֹא	אַשְׁחִית	בַּעֲבוּר
yimmāts'ûn	shom	'ăsārāh	wayyō'mer	lō'	'ashchîth	ba'ăvûr
they are found	there	ten	and He said	not	I will wipe out	on account of

6463	33. 2050.121	3176	3626, 866	3735.311	3937, 1744.341
art, num	cj, v Qal impf 3ms	pn	prep, rel part	v Piel pf 3ms	prep, v Piel inf con
הָעֲשָׂרָה	וַיֵּלֶךְ	יְהוָה	כַּאֲשֶׁר	כִּלָּה	לְדַבֵּר
hā'ăsārāh	wayyēlekh	y^{e}hwāh	ka'ăsher	killāh	l^{e}dhabbēr
the ten	and He went	Yahweh	when	He finished	speaking

place, *Berkeley* ... take off my hand, *Fenton* ... on their account, *Anchor*.

27. And Abraham answered and said, Behold now, I have taken upon me to speak unto the Lord, which am but dust and ashes: ... presuming to speak to the Lord, *Anchor* ... have undertaken to put my thoughts before the Lord, *BB* ... I am venturing to speak, *Goodspeed* ... now that I have been so bold as to speak to the Lord, *NIV*.

28. Peradventure there shall lack five of the fifty righteous: wilt thou destroy all the city for lack of five? And he said, If I find there forty and five, I will not destroy it: ... give up all the town to destruction because of these five, *BB* ... sweep away the whole city for want of five, *Fenton* ... on account of the five, *Darby*.

29. And he spake unto him yet again, and said, Peradventure there shall be forty found there. And he said, I will not do it for forty's sake: ... continued still to speak, *Fenton* ... but he persisted, and said, What if only forty are found there, *Anchor*. . . I will take no action, *Berkeley*.

30. And he said unto him, Oh let not the Lord be angry, and I will speak: Peradventure there shall thirty be found there. And he said, I will not do it, if I find thirty there: ... let not the Lord be impatient if I go on, *Anchor* ... let it not be, I pray thee, displeasing to the Lord, *Young*.

31. And he said, Behold now, I have taken upon me to speak unto the Lord: Peradventure there shall be twenty found there. And he said, I will not destroy it for twenty's sake: ... but he persisted, Again I presume to address the Lord, *Anchor* ... I have ventured to speak with the Lord, *Darby*.

32. And he said, Oh let not the Lord be angry, and I will speak yet but this once: Peradventure ten shall be found there. And he said, I will not destroy it for ten's sake: ... this last time, *Anchor* ... only one word more, *BB* ... I will not bring destruction, *Anchor*.

33. And the LORD went his way: ... he departed, *Anchor* ... then the Lord went to do what he had told to Abraham, *Fenton* ... Jehovah goeth on, *Young*.

as soon as he had left communing with Abraham: ... when his talk with Abraham was ended, *BB* ... finished speaking with Abraham, *Anchor* ... through talking, *Berkeley*.

and Abraham returned unto his place: ... went back home, *Anchor*.

Some Bible students have supposed that Abraham stopped with ten because there were ten in Lot's family, including Lot and his wife. The angels did ask Lot about sons-in-law, sons, and daughters (Gen. 19:12). So they suppose there must have been at least two sons and two married daughters beside the two unmarried daughters that are mentioned.

However, Lot went only to two sons-in-law who were pledged to marry his daughters. Therefore, no indication is made in the Bible that he had any children other than the two daughters.

He probably stopped with ten because he had been reducing the number by ten, and ten less would be zero. Perhaps he also thought Lot would have influenced at least a half dozen people toward righteousness. Nevertheless, God saw Abraham's concern over Lot.

420, 80	82	8178	3937, 4887		971.126	8530
prep, pn	cj, pn	v Qal pf 3ms	prep, n ms, ps 3ms		cj, v Qal impf 3mp	*num*
אֶל־אַבְרָהָם	וְאַבְרָהָם	שָׁב	לִמְקֹמוֹ	**19:1**	וַיָּבֹאוּ	שְׁנֵי
'el-'avrāhām	w^{e}'avrāhām	shāv	limqōmô		wayyābō'û	sh^{e}nê
to Abraham	and Abraham	he returned	to his place		and they went	the two

4534	5651	904, 6394	4013	3553.151	904, 8554, 5651	7495.121, 4013
art, n mp	pn	prep, art, n ms	cj, pn	v Qal act ptc ms	prep, *n ms*, pn	cj, v Qal impf 3ms, pn
הַמַּלְאָכִים	סְדֹמָה	בָּעֶרֶב	וְלוֹט	יֹשֵׁב	בְּשַׁעַר־סְדֹם	וַיַּרְא־לוֹט
hammal'ākhîm	s^{e}dhōmāh	bā'erev	w^{e}lôṯ	yōshēv	b^{e}sha'ar-s^{e}dhōm	wayyar'-lôṯ
the angels	to Sodom	in the evening	and Lot	sitting	in the gate of Sodom	and Lot saw

7251.121	3937, 7410.141	8246.721	653	800		569.121
cj, v Qal impf 3ms	prep, v Qal inf con, ps 3mp	cj, v Hithpalel impf 3ms	n md	n fs		cj, v Qal impf 3ms
וַיָּקָם	לִקְרָאתָם	וַיִּשְׁתַּחוּ	אַפַּיִם	אָרְצָה	**2.**	וַיֹּאמַר
wayyāqām	liqōrā'thām	wayyishtachû	'appayim	'ārtsāh		wayyō'mer
and he rose up	to meet them	and he bowed down	nostrils	to the earth		and he said

2079	5167, 112	5681.133	5167	420, 1041	5860	4053.133
intrj	part, n mp, ps 1cs	v Qal impv 2mp	part	prep, *n ms*	n ms, ps 2mp	cj, v Qal impv 2mp
הִנֶּה	נָּא־אֲדֹנַי	סוּרוּ	נָא	אֶל־בֵּית	עַבְדְּכֶם	וְלִינוּ
hinneh	nā'-'ădhōnay	sûrû	nā'	'el-bêth	'avd^{e}khem	w^{e}lînû
behold	please my lords	turn aside	please	to the house of	your servant	and spend the night

7647.133	7559	8326.517	2050.117	3937, 1932	569.126
cj, v Qal impv 2mp	n fd, ps 2mp	cj, v Hiphil pf 2mp	cj, v Qal pf 2mp	prep, n ms, ps 2mp	cj, v Qal impf 3mp
וְרַחֲצוּ	רַגְלֵיכֶם	וְהִשְׁכַּמְתֶּם	וַהֲלַכְתֶּם	לְדַרְכְּכֶם	וַיֹּאמְרוּ
w^{e}rachtsû	raghlêkhem	w^{e}hishkamtem	wahalakhtem	l^{e}dhark^{e}khem	wayyō'm^{e}rû
and wash	your feet	then you will rise early	and you will go	to your way	and they said

3940	3706	904, 7624	4053.120		6732.121, 904	4108
neg part	cj	prep, art, n fs	v Qal impf 1cp		cj, v Qal impf 3ms, prep, ps 3mp	adv
לֹּא	כִּי	בָרְחוֹב	נָלִין	**3.**	וַיִּפְצַר־בָּם	מְאֹד
lō'	kî	vārchôv	nālîn		wayyiphtsar-bām	m^{e}'ōdh
no	because	in the plaza	we will spend the night		but he insisted with them	very

5681.126	420	971.126	420, 1041	6449.121	3937	5136
cj, v Qal impf 3mp	prep, ps 3ms	cj, v Qal impf 3mp	prep, n fs, ps 3ms	cj, v Qal impf 3ms	prep, ps 3mp	n ms
וַיָּסֻרוּ	אֵלָיו	וַיָּבֹאוּ	אֶל־בֵּיתוֹ	וַיַּעַשׂ	לָהֶם	מִשְׁתֶּה
wayyāsurû	'ēlâv	wayyābō'û	'el-bêthô	wayya'as	lāhem	mishteh
so they turned aside	to him	and they went	to his house	and he made	for them	feast

4843	659.111	404.126		3071	8311.126	596
cj, n fp	v Qal pf 3ms	cj, v Qal impf 3mp		adv	v Qal impf 3mp	cj, *n mp*
וּמַצּוֹת	אָפָה	וַיֹּאכֵלוּ	**4.**	טֶרֶם	יִשְׁכָּבוּ	וְאַנְשֵׁי
ûmatstsôth	'āphāh	wayyō'khēlû		terem	yishkāvû	w^{e}'anshê
and unleavened bread	he baked	and they ate		before	they lay down	and the men of

6111	597	5651	5621.216	6142, 1041	4623, 5470	5912, 2293
art, n fs	*n mp*	pn	v Niphal pf 3cp	prep, art, n ms	prep, n ms	cj, prep, n ms
הָעִיר	אַנְשֵׁי	סְדֹם	נָסַבּוּ	עַל־הַבַּיִת	מִנַּעַר	וְעַד־זָקֵן
hā'îr	'anshê	s^{e}dhōm	nāsabbû	'al-habayith	minna'ar	w^{e}'adh-zāqēn
the city	the men of	Sodom	they surrounded	on the house	of young men	and until old men

3725, 6194	4623, 7381		7410.126	420, 4013	569.126	3937	347
adj, art, n ms	prep, n ms		cj, v Qal impf 3mp	prep, pn	cj, v Qal impf 3mp	prep, ps 3ms	intrg
כָּל־הָעָם	מִקָּצֶה	**5.**	וַיִּקְרְאוּ	אֶל־לוֹט	וַיֹּאמְרוּ	לוֹ	אַיֵּה
kol-hā'ām	miqqātseh		wayyiqōr'û	'el-lôṯ	wayyō'm^{e}rû	lô	'ayyēh
all the people	of last		and they called	to Lot	and they said	to him	where

19:1. And there came two angels to Sodom at even: ... two of the messengers, *Young* ... reached Sodom, *NAB* ... arrived at Sodom, *NIV* ... at nightfall, *BB*.

and Lot sat in the gate of Sodom: ... at the city gate, *Good News* ... gateway of the city, *NEB*.

and Lot seeing them rose up to meet them: ... noticed them, *MLB* ... seeth and riseth, *Young* ... to greet them, *Goodspeed* ... to invite them, *Fenton* ... came before them, *BB*.

and he bowed himself with his face toward the ground: ... falling prostrate, *NCB* ... bowed down, *Darby* ... bowed low, *NEB*.

2. And he said, Behold now, my lords: ... my good sirs, *Fenton* ... if you please, sirs, *Goodspeed* ... my masters, *Berkeley*.

turn in, I pray you, into your servant's house, and tarry all night: ... please come to my house, *Good News* ... stay overnight, *Berkeley* ... take your rest, *BB* ... spend the night, *REB*.

and wash your feet, and ye shall rise up early, and go on your ways: ... bathe your feet, *Anchor* ... let your feet be washed, *BB* ... quench your thirst, *Fenton* ... get up early to continue your journey, *NAB*.

And they said, Nay; but we will abide in the street all night: ... we will rest in the square, *Anchor* ... spend the night outdoors, *Berkeley* ... in the open place, *Darby* ... we must go farther, *Fenton* ... in the broadplace, *Young*.

3. And he pressed upon them greatly: ... made request more strongly, *BB* ... urged them, *ASV* ... pressed earnestly, *Geneva* ... insisted strongly, *NKJV*.

and they turned in unto him, and entered into his house: ... went over to his home, *Goodspeed* ... toward his place, *Anchor* ... went with him, *BB* ... accompanied him, *REB* ... turned with him, *Fenton*.

and he made them a feast: ... prepared a repast, *Anchor* ... got food ready for them, *BB* ... prepared a meal, *NEB* ... a banquet, *Young* ... dinner, *Berkeley*.

and did bake unleavened bread, and they did eat: ... baked flat cakes, *Anchor* ... unleavened cakes, *Darby* ... bread without yeast, *NIV* ... freshly baked unleavened bread, *LIVB* ... of which they took, *BB*.

4. But before they lay down: ... before they had gone to bed, *BB* ... had not yet retired, *NCB* ... it was not yet time for sleep, *Fenton*.

the men of the city, even the men of Sodom: ... townspeople to the last man, *Goodspeed*.

compassed the house round, both old and young: ... closed in on the house, *BB* ... from the youngest to the oldest, *Darby* ... against the house from young to aged, *Young*.

all the people from every quarter: ... all people from the extremity, *Young* ... from every part of town, *BB* ... all people from all quarters, *Geneva* ... everyone without exception, *NEB* ... in fact all the people of the neighborhood, *Fenton*.

5. And they called unto Lot, and said unto him: ... crying out, *BB* ... shouted, *Goodspeed*.

19:1-2. The two angels arrived that evening at the gate of Sodom to find Lot sitting by the gate, or in the gateway. Usually men congregated at the gate to talk and to hear the news from caravans or travelers going by.

Since the city gateway was also used as a place for legal matters to be settled, some have supposed that sitting in the gate implied Lot had achieved some official position. Sodom had its king, however, and it is clear from verse 9 that he was just a resident alien, not accepted as a citizen.

Though Lot was now living in this wicked city, he still had the same kind of courtesy, friendliness, and hospitality which characterized Abraham. So he bowed humbly before them and invited them to come to his house, wash their feet, and spend the night. At first, they refused and said they would spend the night in the open square or plaza just inside the gate.

19:3. Hebrews 13:2 probably also had Lot in mind because of his hospitality to the two angels. The meal was not as bountiful as the one Abraham prepared, but it was getting late, so Lot prepared a quick meal (with unleavened bread).

19:4-5. The angels appeared as young men, and the news that they were in Lot's house soon spread. Thus, before the angels could retire, all the men of Sodom surrounded Lot's house with the intention of sexually abusing what they thought were ordinary men.

That all the men without exception were involved in this demand is emphatic and shows the ten righteous whom Abraham hoped would be found were not. It also shows that homosexuality was not considered a sin by Sodom. Their consciences were seered.

But, in referring to this, Jude 7 calls it fornication (habitual immorality and perversion). The Bible strongly condemns it (Lev. 20:13; Deut. 23:17; Rom. 1:27; 1 Cor. 6:9; cf. 1 Tim. 1:8-10).

596	866, 971.116	420	4050	3428.531	420
art, n mp	rel part, v Qal pf 3cp	prep, ps 2ms	art, n ms	v Hiphil impv 2ms, ps 3mp	prep, ps 1cp
הָאֲנָשִׁים	אֲשֶׁר־בָּאוּ	אֵלֶיךָ	הַלָּיְלָה	הוֹצִיאֵם	אֵלֵינוּ
hā'anāshîm	'ăsher-bā'û	'ēlêkhā	hallāylāh	hôtsî'ēm	'ēlênû
the men	who came	to you	the night	bring them out	to us

3156.120	882		3428.121	420	4013	6860
cj, v Qal impf 1cp	prep, ps 3mp	**6.**	cj, v Qal impf 3ms	prep, ps 3mp	pn	art, n ms
וְנֵדְעָה	אֹתָם		וַיֵּצֵא	אֲלֵהֶם	לוֹט	הַפֶּתְחָה
w^{e}nēdh'āh	'ōthām		wayyētsē'	'ălēhem	lôṯ	happethchāh
and we will have relations	with them		and he went out	to them	Lot	at the door

1878	5646.111	313		569.121	414, 5167	250
cj, art, n fs	v Qal pf 3ms	adv, ps 3ms	**7.**	cj, v Qal impf 3ms	neg part, part	n mp, ps 1cs
וְהַדֶּלֶת	סָגַר	אַחֲרָיו		וַיֹּאמַר	אַל־נָא	אַחַי
w^{e}haddeleth	sāghar	'achrâv		wayyō'mar	'al-nā'	'achay
and the door	he shut	after him		and he said	not please	my brothers

7778.528		2079, 5167	3937	8530	1351	866
v Hiphil impf 2mp	**8.**	intrj, part	prep, ps 1cs	*num*	n fp	rel part
תָּרֵעוּ		הִנֵּה־נָא	לִי	שְׁתֵּי	בָנוֹת	אֲשֶׁר
tārē'û		hinnēh-nā'	lî	sh^{e}ttê	vānôth	'ăsher
you will act wickedly		behold please	to me	two	daughters	who

3940, 3156.116	382	3428.525, 5167	881	420	6449.133
neg part, v Qal pf 3cp	n ms	v Hiphil impf 1cs, part	do, ps 3fp	prep, ps 2mp	cj, v Qal impv 2mp
לֹא־יָדְעוּ	אִישׁ	אוֹצִיאָה־נָּא	אֶתְהֶן	אֲלֵיכֶם	וַעֲשׂוּ
lō'-yādh^{e}'û	'îsh	'ôtsî'āh-nā'	'ethhen	'ălêkhem	wa'ăsû
not they have had relations	man	I will bring out please	them	to you	and you do

3937	3626, 3005	904, 6084	7828	3937, 596	419	414, 6449.128
prep, ps 3fp	prep, art, adj	prep, n fd, ps 2mp	adv	prep, art, n mp	art, dem pron	adv, v Qal impf 2mp
לָהֶן	כַּטּוֹב	בְּעֵינֵיכֶם	רַק	לָאֲנָשִׁים	הָאֵל	אַל־תַּעֲשׂוּ
lāhen	kaṯṯôv	b^{e}'ênêkhem	raq	lā'ănāshîm	hā'ēl	'al-ta'ăsû
to them	according to the good	in your eyes	only	to the men	the these	not you will do

1745	3706, 6142, 3772	971.116	904, 7009	7264		569.126
n ms	cj, prep, adv	v Qal pf 3cp	prep, *n ms*	n fs, ps 1cs	**9.**	cj, v Qal impf 3mp
דָבָר	כִּי־עַל־כֵּן	בָּאוּ	בְּצֵל	קֹרָתִי		וַיֹּאמְרוּ
khāvār	kî-'al-kēn	bā'û	b^{e}tsēl	qōrāthî		wayyō'm^{e}rû
thing	since	they came	in the shadow of	my rafters		and they said

5242.131, 2042	569.126	259	971.111, 3937, 1513.141	8570.121	8570.142
v Qal impv 2ms, adv	cj, v Qal impf 3mp	art, num	v Qal pf 3ms, prep, v Qal inf con	cj, v Qal impf 3ms	v Qal inf abs
גֶּשׁ־הָלְאָה	וַיֹּאמְרוּ	הָאֶחָד	בָּא־לָגוּר	וַיִּשְׁפֹּט	שָׁפוֹט
gesh-hāl^{e}'āh	wayyō'm^{e}rû	hā'echādh	bā'-lāghûr	wayyishpōṯ	shāphôṯ
draw near to there	and they said	the one	he came to sojourn	and he will judge	judging

6498	7778.520	3937	4623	6732.126	904, 382	904, 4013
adv	v Hiphil impf 1cp	prep, ps 2ms	prep, ps 3mp	cj, v Qal impf 3mp	prep, art, n ms	prep, pn
עַתָּה	נָרַע	לְךָ	מֵהֶם	וַיִּפְצְרוּ	בָּאִישׁ	בְּלוֹט
'attāh	nāra'	l^{e}khā	mēhem	wayyiphts^{e}rû	vā'îsh	b^{e}lôṯ
now	we will do wickedly	to you	more than them	and they insisted	on the man	on Lot

4108	5242.126	3937, 8132.141	1878		8365.126	596
adv	cj, v Qal impf 3mp	prep, v Qal inf con	art, n fs	**10.**	cj, v Qal impf 3mp	art, n mp
מְאֹד	וַיִּגְּשׁוּ	לִשְׁבֹּר	הַדָּלֶת		וַיִּשְׁלְחוּ	הָאֲנָשִׁים
m^{e}'ōdh	wayyigg^{e}shû	lishbōr	haddāleth		wayyishl^{e}chû	hā'ănāshîm
very	and they drew near	to break down	the door		but they sent out	the men

Where are the men which came in to thee this night?: ... who came to your house, *BB* ... who entered, *NEB*.

bring them out unto us, that we may know them: ... know them carnally, *NKJV* ... have intimacies, *NAB* ... have relations with them, *NASB* ... have intercourse with them, *Goodspeed*, *NEB* ... may take our pleasure, *BB* ... rape them, *Berkeley* ... ravish them, *Fenton*.

6. And Lot went out at the door unto them: ... goeth out to them to the opening, *Young* ... met them outside at the entrance, *Anchor* ... went out to them to the porch, *Fenton* ... went out to them through the doorway, *NKJV*.

and shut the door after him: ... doors were closed behind him, *Fenton* ... closed the door behind him, *Berkeley*.

7. And said, I pray you, brethren, do not so wickedly: ... please, my friends, do not be so depraved, *Goodspeed* ... do not behave wickedly, *MLB* ... do not this evil, *BB* ... do not commit such wickedness, *Fenton* ... do not do this wicked thing, *NAB*.

8. Behold now, I have two daughters which have not known man: ... look here, I have two virgin daughters, *Berkeley* ... two unmarried daughters, *BB* ... have never had intercourse with man, *Goodspeed* ... relations with man, *NASB* ... never slept with a man, *NIV*.

let me, I pray you, bring them out unto you: ... I will send them out to you, *BB* ... I pray you, bring them out unto you, *Young* ... I'll surrender them to you, *LIVB*.

and do ye to them as is good in your eyes: ... as you please, *Anchor* ... as is good in your sight, *Darby* ... whatever seems good to you, *BB* ... as you wish, *NKJV*.

only unto these men do nothing; for therefore came they under the shadow of my roof: ... the shelter ... shade of my roof, *BB* ... as a protection from it, *Fenton* .

9. And they said, Stand back: ... out of the way, *Berkeley* ... give way, there, *BB* ... get out of the way, *Goodspeed*.

And they said again, This one fellow came in to sojourn: ... came here on sufferance, *Anchor* ... came as an immigrant, *Berkeley* ... from a strange country, *BB* ... came in as an alien, *NASB* ... came here a foreigner, *Fenton*.

and he will needs be a judge: ... now he would act as the master, *Anchor* ... keeps acting as a judge, *Berkeley* ... now he dares to give orders, *NAB*.

now will we deal worse with thee, than with them: ... now we'll be meaner to you than to them, *Anchor* ... treat you worse, *NAB* ... we do evil to thee, *Young*.

And they pressed sore upon the man, even Lot: ... pushing violently against Lot, *BB* ... they rushed to the man Lot with a vengeance, *Fenton* ... kept bringing pressure on Lot, *NIV*.

and came near to break the door: ... to get the door broken in, *BB* ... attempted to break the gates, *Fenton* ... tried to reach the door to break it in, *Goodspeed* ... smash the door, *NEB*.

10. But the men put forth their hand, and pulled Lot into the house to them: ... his guests, *NAB* ... the visitors, *NCB* ... two men inside, *NEB* ... but the men put out their hands and pulled Lot inside, *Anchor* ... thrust out their hands, *Berkeley*.

and shut to the door: ... closed the gates, *Fenton*.

19:6-8. Lot courageously faced the mob, shutting the door behind him to protect his guests. He called the men of Sodom "my brothers," and politely asked them not to do this wickedness. Apparently city dwellers did not have the same view of hospitality as did tent dwellers like Abraham and Lot (who was a tent dweller before moving to the city). Even today, desert tent dwellers feel obliged to protect visitors who come into their tent, and Lot felt that kind of obligation toward these men who had come under his roof. It does seem strange that Lot would offer to let them abuse his two virgin daughters, however. It may be that he thought he would shock the men, or perhaps he thought he had enough friends in the city who would not allow the daughters to be abused.

19:9. Though Lot lived in Sodom in order to enjoy its material advantages, he was "vexed" (tormented) with the filthy conversation (life-styles) of the wicked" and "with their unlawful (lawless, ungodly) deeds" (2 Pet. 2:7-8). In fact, he had spoken out against these things so often that the men of Sodom accused him of wanting to play the judge, even though he was a foreigner. They demanded he step aside, threatening to treat him worse than the two strangers. Lot tried to stop them, but they pushed forward intending to break down the door.

19:10-11. The two angels opened the door, pulled Lot in, shut the door, and struck all the men outside with a blindness or delusion that made them unable to find the door. They were able, however, to go back to their own houses.

881, 3135	971.526	881, 4013	420	1041	881, 1878	5646.116
do, n fs, ps 3mp	cj, v Hiphil impf 3mp	do, pn	prep, ps 3mp	art, n ms	cj, do, art, n fs	v Qal pf 3cp
אֶת־יָדָם	וַיָּבִיאוּ	אֶת־לוֹט	אֲלֵיהֶם	הַבָּיְתָה	וְאֶת־הַדֶּלֶת	סָגָרוּ
'eth-yādhām	wayyāvî'û	'eth-lôṯ	'ălêhem	habbāythāh	w^e'eth-haddeleth	sāghārû
their hand	and they brought	Lot	to them	to the house	and the door	they shut

11.	881, 596	866, 6860	1041	5409.516	904, 5770	4623, 7277
	cj, do, art, n mp	rel part, *n ms*	art, n ms	v Hiphil pf 3cp	prep, art, n mp	prep, adj
	וְאֶת־הָאֲנָשִׁים	אֲשֶׁר־פֶּתַח	הַבַּיִת	הִכּוּ	בַּסַּנְוֵרִים	מִקָּטֹן
	w^e'eth-hā'ănāshîm	'ăsher-pethach	habbayith	hikkû	bassanwērîm	miqqāṭōn
	and the men	who the door of	the house	they struck	with the blindness	from insignificant

5912, 1448	3942.126	3937, 4834.141	6860	**12.**	569.126	596
cj, prep, adj	cj, v Qal impf 3mp	prep, v Qal inf con	art, n ms		cj, v Qal impf 3mp	art, n mp
וְעַד־גָּדוֹל	וַיִּלְאוּ	לִמְצֹא	הַפָּתַח		וַיֹּאמְרוּ	הָאֲנָשִׁים
w^e'adh-gādhôl	wayyil'û	limtsō'	happāthach		wayyō'm^{e}rû	hā'ănāshîm
and until great	and they became tired	to find	the door		and they said	the men

420, 4013	5968	4449, 3937	6553	2968	1158	1351
prep, pn	adv	intrg, prep, ps 2ms	adv	n ms	cj, n mp, ps 2ms	cj, n fp, ps 2ms
אֶל־לוֹט	עֹד	מִי־לְךָ	פֹּה	חָתָן	וּבָנֶיךָ	וּבְנֹתֶיךָ
'el-lôṯ	'ōdh	mî-l^{e}khā	phōh	chāthān	ûvānêkhā	ûv^{e}nōthêkhā
to Lot	still	who to you	here	son-in-law	and your sons	and your daughters

3725	886, 3937	904, 6111	3428.531	4623, 4887	**13.**	3706, 8271.552
cj, adj	rel part, prep, ps 2ms	prep, art, n fs	v Hiphil impv 2ms	prep, art, n ms		cj, v Hiphil ptc mp
וְכֹל	אֲשֶׁר־לְךָ	בָּעִיר	הוֹצֵא	מִן־הַמָּקוֹם		כִּי־מַשְׁחִתִים
w^{e}khōl	'ăsher-l^{e}khā	bā'îr	hôtsē'	min-hammāqôm		kî-mashchithîm
and all	which to you	in the city	bring out	from the place		because destroyers

601	881, 4887	2172	3706, 1461.112	7095	881, 6686	3176
pers pron	do, art, n ms	art, dem pron	cj, v Qal pf 3fs	n fs, ps 3mp	do, *n mp*	pn
אֲנַחְנוּ	אֶת־הַמָּקוֹם	הַזֶּה	כִּי־גָדְלָה	צַעֲקָתָם	אֶת־פְּנֵי	יְהוָה
'ănachnû	'eth-hammāqôm	hazzeh	kî-ghādh^{e}lāh	tsa'ăqāthām	'eth-p^{e}nê	y^{e}hwāh
we	the place	the this	because it has become great	their outcry	before	Yahweh

8365.321	3176	3937, 8271.341	**14.**	3428.121	4013	1744.321
cj, v Piel impf 3ms, ps 1cp	pn	prep, v Piel inf con, ps 3fs		cj, v Qal impf 3ms	pn	cj, v Piel impf 3ms
וַיְשַׁלְּחֵנוּ	יְהוָה	לְשַׁחֲתָהּ		וַיֵּצֵא	לוֹט	וַיְדַבֵּר
wayshall^{e}chēnû	y^{e}hwāh	l^{e}shachthāhh		wayyētsē'	lôṯ	waydhabbēr
and He sent us	Yahweh	to wipe it out		and he went out	Lot	and he spoke

420, 2968	4089.152	1351	569.121	7251.133	3428.133
prep, n mp, ps 3ms	*v Qal act ptc mp*	n fp, ps 3ms	cj, v Qal impf 3ms	v Qal impv 2mp	v Qal impv 2mp
אֶל־חֲתָנָיו	לֹקְחֵי	בְּנֹתָיו	וַיֹּאמֶר	קוּמוּ	צְאוּ
'el-chăthānâv	lōqchê	v^{e}nōthâv	wayyō'mer	qûmû	ts^e'û
to his sons-in-law	the takers of	his daughters	and he said	rise	go out

4623, 4887	2172	3706, 8271.551	3176	881, 6111	2030.121	3626, 6978.351
prep, art, n ms	art, dem pron	cj, v Hiphil ptc ms	pn	do, art, n fs	cj, v Qal impf 3ms	prep, v Piel ptc ms
מִן־הַמָּקוֹם	הַזֶּה	כִּי־מַשְׁחִית	יְהוָה	אֶת־הָעִיר	וַיְהִי	כִּמְצַחֵק
min-hammāqôm	hazzeh	kî-mashchîth	y^{e}hwāh	'eth-hā'îr	wayhî	kimtsachēq
from the place	the this	because Destroyer	Yahweh	the city	but he was	like one joking

904, 6084	2968	**15.**	3765	8266	6148.111	211.526
prep, *n fp*	n mp, ps 3ms		cj, cj	art, n ms	v Qal pf 3ms	cj, v Hiphil impf 3mp
בְּעֵינֵי	חֲתָנָיו		וּכְמוֹ	הַשַּׁחַר	עָלָה	וַיָּאִיצוּ
b^e'ênê	chăthānâv		ûkh^{e}mô	hashshachar	'ālāh	wayyā'îtsû
in the eyes of	his sons-in-law		and when	the dawn	it went up	and they urged

11. And they smote the men that were at the door of the house with blindness, both small and great: ... then they struck with blindness, the men at the door, from small to big, *Berkeley* ... they smote with blinding light, *Anchor* ... from youngest to the oldest, *Fenton.*

so that they wearied themselves to find the door: ... were unable to reach the entrance, *Anchor* ... they wore themselves out trying to find the entrance, *MLB.*

12. And the men said unto Lot, Hast thou here any besides?: ... who else belongs to you, here, *Anchor* ... if there is anyone else belonging to you here, *Goodspeed.*

son in law, and thy sons, and thy daughters, and whatsoever thou hast in the city: ... relative, or son or daughter, *Fenton* ... or anyone, at all, that belongs to you, *Goodspeed* ... whatever you have in the city, *KJVII* ... get everyone you have in the city, *MLB.*

bring them out of this place: ... get everyone ... away from here, *MLB* ... take them away from it, *NAB* ... take them all out, *BB* ... away from here, *Berkeley.*

13. For we will destroy this place: ... for we are about to destroy this place, *Goodspeed* ... send destruction, *BB.*

because the cry of them is waxen great before the face of the LORD: ... a great outcry against them has come to the ears of the Lord, *BB* ... the Lord is aware of the great outcry against its citizens, *REB.*

and the LORD hath sent us to destroy it: ... for the Lord is at the point of wiping out the city, *Berkeley* ... the Lord has sent us to put an end to the town, *BB* ... to wipe it out, *MLB.*

14. And Lot went out, and spake unto his sons in law: ... spoke to his relatives, *Fenton* ... speak to his intended sons-in-law, *NCB* ... urged his sons-in-law, *REB.*

which married his daughters, and said: ... to the husbands of his daughters, *Fenton* ... contracted marriage, *NAB* ... pledged to marry, *NIV.*

Up, get you out of this place: ... leave this place, *Anchor* ... up and away from this place, *MLB* ... be quick, and leave this place, *NEB.*

for the LORD will destroy this city: ... is at the point of wiping out the city, *Berkeley* ... is about to send destruction on the town, *BB.*

But he seemed as one that mocked unto his sons in law: ... but the sons-in-law looked at him as if he were joking, *Anchor* ... he seemed to be as one who jested, *Berkeley* ... did not take him seriously, *NEB.*

15. And when the morning arose then the angels hastened Lot: ... did all in their power to make Lot go, *BB* ... angels urged Lot on, *NAB* ... hurried Lot along, *Berkeley.*

saying, Arise, take thy wife, and thy two daughters, which are here: ... bestir thyself, *Goodspeed* ... on your way, *NAB* ... Be quick, *NKJV* ... remove your wife, *Anchor* ... take away your wife, *Berkeley.*

lest thou be consumed in the iniquity of the city: ... swept away in the punishment of the city, *NAB* ... lest thou perish, *Darby* ... for fear that you come to destruction, *BB* ... for the crimes of this city are completed, *Fenton.*

16. And while he lingered: ... still he hesitated, *Anchor* ... while he was

---

19:12-13. The two angels are still called "men," for Lot did not yet recognize who they were. Now they declared that the LORD had sent them to destroy Sodom because of the wickedness of its people.

Since the word "angel" means messenger, they were telling Lot they were angels. They also urged Lot to get his family members and anyone else belonging to him out of the city before it was destroyed.

19:14. Lot went only to the men who were pledged to marry his two daughters. Marriages in those days were arranged by the parents, often for business or social advantage. That Lot was willing to turn his daughters over to men whom he knew were wicked shows that material prosperity had blinded him to the tragedy that could come to his family. He was distressed by the sins of Sodom so he did not partake of them himself. But this was not enough. His "playing the judge" had not influenced anyone to turn away from their lawlessness.

Perhaps he was so taken up with business and acquiring wealth, the people of Sodom did not really take his religion seriously. This seems evident when the men who were pledged to marry his daughters did not take his warning seriously but thought he was joking.

19:15-17. The angels were ready at dawn urging Lot to take his wife and daughters and leave, lest they be swept away in the judgment coming upon the city. Apparently, Lot himself did not take the angels seriously, or he may have hesitated because he was not given opportunity to load up all his possessions.

4534	904, 4013	3937, 569.141	7251.131	4089.131	881, 828	881, 8530
art, n mp	prep, pn	prep, v Qal inf con	v Qal impv 2ms	v Qal impv 2ms	do, n fs, ps 2ms	cj, do, *num*
הַמַּלְאָכִים	בְּלוֹט	לֵאמֹר	קוּם	קַח	אֶת־אִשְׁתְּךָ	וְאֶת־שְׁתֵּי
hammal'ākhîm	belôṯ	lē'mōr	qûm	qach	'eth-'ishtekhā	we'eth-shettê
the angels	with Lot	saying	rise	take	your wife	and the two of

1351	4834.258	6678, 5793.223	904, 5988	6111
n fp, ps 2ms	art, v Niphal ptc fp	cj, v Niphal impf 2ms	prep, art, *n ms*	art, n fs
בְּנֹתֶיךָ	הַנִּמְצָאֹת	פֶּן־תִּסָּפֶה	בַּעֲוֹן	הָעִיר
benōthêkhā	hannimtsā'ōth	pen-tissāpheh	ba'ăwôn	hā'îr
your daughters	the ones found	otherwise you will be swept away	in the punishment of	the city

16. 4244.721	2480.526	596	904, 3135	904, 3135, 828
cj, v Hithpalpel impf 3ms	cj, v Hiphil impf 3mp	art, n mp	prep, n fs, ps 3ms	cj, prep, *n fs*, n fs, ps 3ms
וַיִּתְמַהְמָהּ	וַיַּחֲזִקוּ	הָאֲנָשִׁים	בְּיָדוֹ	וּבְיַד־אִשְׁתּוֹ
wayyithmahmāhh	wayyachăziqû	hā'ănāshîm	beyādhô	ûveyadh-'ishtô
but he lingered	so they seized	the men	by his hand	and by the hand of his wife

904, 3135	8530	1351	904, 2655	3176	6142
cj, prep, *n fs*	*num*	n fp, ps 3ms	prep, *n fs*	pn	prep, ps 3ms
וּבְיַד	שְׁתֵּי	בְנֹתָיו	בְּחֶמְלַת	יְהוָה	עָלָיו
ûveyadh	shettê	venōthâv	bechemlath	yehwāh	'ālâv
and by the hand of	the two of	his daughters	with the compassion of	Yahweh	on him

3428.526	5299.526	4623, 2445	3937, 6111	17. 2030.121
cj, v Hiphil impf 3mp, ps 3ms	cj, v Hiphil impf 3mp, ps 3ms	prep, n ms	prep, art, n fs	cj, v Qal impf 3ms
וַיֹּצִאֻהוּ	וַיַּנִּחֻהוּ	מִחוּץ	לָעִיר	וַיְהִי
wayyōtsi'uhû	wayyannichuhû	michûts	lā'îr	wayhî
and they brought him out	and they set him	outside	of the city	and it was

3626, 3428.541	881	2445	569.121	4561.231	5912, 5497
prep, v Hiphil inf con, ps 3mp	do, ps 3mp	art, n ms	cj, v Qal impf 3ms	v Niphal impv 2ms	prep, n fs, ps 2ms
כְהוֹצִיאָם	אֹתָם	הַחוּצָה	וַיֹּאמֶר	הִמָּלֵט	עַל־נַפְשֶׁךָ
khehôtsî'ām	'ōthām	hachûtsāh	wayyō'mer	himmālēṭ	'al-naphshekhā
as they were bringing	them	to the outside	and he said	escape	concerning your life

414, 5202.523	313	414, 6198.123	904, 3725, 3724	2098
adv, v Hiphil juss 2ms	adv, ps 2ms	cj, adv, v Qal juss 2ms	prep, *adj*, art, n fs	art, n ms
אַל־תַּבִּיט	אַחֲרֶיךָ	וְאַל־תַּעֲמֹד	בְּכָל־הַכִּכָּר	הָהָרָה
'al-tabbîṭ	'achrêkhā	we'al-ta'ămōdh	bekhol-hakkikkār	hāhārāh
do not look	behind you	and do not stand	in all the circle	to the mountain

4561.231	6678, 5793.223	18. 569.121	4013	420
v Niphal impv 2ms	cj, v Niphal impf 2ms	cj, v Qal impf 3ms	pn	prep, ps 3mp
הִמָּלֵט	פֶּן־תִּסָּפֶה	וַיֹּאמֶר	לוֹט	אֲלֵהֶם
himmālēṭ	pen-tissāpheh	wayyō'mer	lôṭ	'ălēhem
escape	otherwise you will be swept away	and he said	Lot	to them

414, 5167	112	19. 2079, 5167	4834.111	5860	2682	904, 6084
neg part, part	n ms, ps 1cs	intrj, part	v Qal pf 3ms	n ms, ps 2ms	n ms	prep, n fd, ps 2ms
אַל־נָא	אֲדֹנָי	הִנֵּה־נָא	מָצָא	עַבְדְּךָ	חֵן	בְּעֵינֶיךָ
'al-nā'	'ădhōnāy	hinnēh-nā'	mātsâ'	'avdekhā	chēn	be'ênêkhā
not please	my lord	behold please	he found	your servant	favor	in your eyes

1461.523	2721	866	6449.113	6200	3937, 2513.541	881, 5497
cj, v Hiphil impf 2ms	n ms, ps 2ms	rel part	v Qal pf 2ms	prep, ps 1cs	prep, v Hiphil inf con	do, n fs, ps 1cs
וַתַּגְדֵּל	חַסְדְּךָ	אֲשֶׁר	עָשִׂיתָ	עִמָּדִי	לְהַחֲיוֹת	אֶת־נַפְשִׁי
wattaghdēl	hasdekhā	'ăsher	'āsîthā	'immādhî	lehachyôth	'eth-naphshî
and you made great	your mercy	which	you did	with me	to keep alive	my life

609	3940	3310.125	3937, 4561.241	2098	6678, 1740.122
cj, pers pron	neg part	v Qal impf 1cs	prep, v Niphal inf con	art, n ms	cj, v Qal impf 3fs, ps 1cs
וְאָנֹכִי	לֹא	אוּכַל	לְהִמָּלֵט	הָהָרָה	פֶּן־תִּדְבָּקַנִי
wᵉʼānōkhî	lōʼ	ʼûkhal	lᵉhimmālēṭ	hāhārāh	pen-tidhbāqanî
and I	not	I am able	to escape	to the mountain	otherwise it will fasten onto me

7750	4322.115		2079, 5167	6111	2148	7427	3937, 5308.141
art, n fs	cj, v Qal pf 1cs		intrj, part	art, n fs	art, dem pron	adj	prep, v Qal inf con
הָרָעָה	וָמַתִּי	**20.**	הִנֵּה־נָא	הָעִיר	הַזֹּאת	קְרֹבָה	לָנוּס
hārāʻāh	wāmattî		hinnēh-nāʼ	hāʻîr	hazzōʼth	qôrōvāh	lānûs
the disaster	and I will die		behold please	the city	the this	near	to flee

waiting, *BB* ... he prolonged the time, *Geneva* ... he delayed, *REB.*

the men laid hold upon his hand, and upon the hand of his wife, and upon the hand of his two daughters: ... so the men seized, *Anchor* ... the men took him, *BB* ... they grabbed his hand, *REB.*

the LORD being merciful unto him: ... because the Lord would spare them, *MLB* ... from the pity of the Lord towards him, *Fenton* ... for the compassion of the Lord was upon him, *NASB.*

and they brought him forth, and set him without the city: ... and led them to safety, outside the city, *NAB* ... brought them out, *Berkeley.*

17. And it came to pass, when they had brought them forth abroad, that he said: ... outside, *Anchor* ... when they had put them out, *BB.*

Escape for thy life; look not behind thee: ... go for your life, without looking back, *BB* ... flee for your life, *Anchor.*

neither stay thou in all the plain: ... do not stop anywhere in the valley, *Berkeley* ... waiting in the lowland, *BB* ... delay not in all the plain, *Fenton.*

escape to the mountain: ... go quickly, *BB* ... take flight, *Fenton* ... get off to the hills, *NAB.*

lest thou be consumed: ... you will be swept away, *NEB* ... you will come to destruction, *BB* ... so that you won't be killed, *Good News.*

18. And Lot said unto them, Oh, not so, my Lord: ... O no, please, my masters, *MLB* ... O, no, Sirs, *Goodspeed.*

19. Behold now, thy servant hath found grace in thy sight: ... let now your servant find favor in your sight, *Fenton* ... if you would but indulge your servant, *Anchor.*

and thou hast magnified thy mercy: ... thy loving kindness, *ASV* ... having shown so much kindness, *Anchor* ... goodness, *Darby* ... added to your unfailing care, *NEB.*

which thou hast shewed unto me in saving my life: ... to enliven my soul, *Fenton* ... in preserving my soul alive, *Darby* ... in keeping my life from destruction, *BB.*

and I cannot escape to the mountain: ... flee to the hills, *Anchor.*

lest some evil take me, and I die: ... calamity lay hold on me, *Darby* ... before evil overtakes me, and death, *BB* ... the disaster, *NAB* ... lest the evil cleave to me,*Young.*

The angels did not let him linger long. They grabbed his hands and the hands of his wife and daughters and hurried them out of the city. This was the LORD's mercy to them. They were not acting in faith or obedience, so bringing them out of the city was pure, unmerited grace. Then one of the angels commanded them to flee for their lives. Looking back, that is, in hesitation, with a desire to turn back, or stopping before they reached the mountains would mean that the judgment would sweep them away.

19:18-20. Now that Lot was convinced the angels were right, he should have been thankful to the LORD and showed faith and trust by obeying and fleeing to the mountains. Instead, he was overwhelmed by fear that he could not get to the mountains in time.

Though he recognized grace and covenant love were the reasons the angels had saved his life, he did not believe these were enough to keep him from dying in the coming disaster. So he begged to be allowed to flee to a small town that was closer. Since Zoar means "small," that became the name of the town.

19:21-22. The angel granted the request. No judgment would come on the little town. But Lot must hurry, for the angel could not do anything until Lot reached there. No doubt, if Lot had obeyed and fled to the mountains, the judgment would have been delayed until he reached them. (Cf. v. 29.)

8427	2026	4867	4561.225	5167	8427	3940	4867
adv	cj, pers pron	n ms	v Niphal impf 1cs	part	adv	intrg part, neg part	n ms
שָׁמָּה	וְהִיא	מִצְעָר	אִמָּלְטָה	נָּא	שָׁמָּה	הֲלֹא	מִצְעָר
shāmmāh	w^{e}hî'	mits'ār	'immālṯāh	nā'	shāmmāh	hălō'	mits'ār
to there	and it	a small one	I will escape	please	to there	is not	a small one

2000	2513.122	5497		569.121	420	2079	5558.115
pers pron	cj, v Qal impf 3fs	n fs, ps 1cs	**21.**	cj, v Qal impf 3ms	prep, ps 3ms	intrj	v Qal pf 1cs
הִוא	וּתְחִי	נַפְשִׁי		וַיֹּאמֶר	אֵלָיו	הִנֵּה	נָשָׂאתִי
hiw'	ûth^{e}chî	naphshî		wayyō'mer	'ēlâv	hinnēh	nāsā'thî
it	and it will live	my life		and he said	to him	behold	I will forgive

6686	1612	3937, 1745	2172	3937, 1153	2089.141	881, 6111	866
n mp, ps 2ms	cj	prep, art, n ms	art, dem pron	prep, neg part	v Qal inf con, ps 1cs	do, art, n fs	rel part
פָּנֶיךָ	גַּם	לַדָּבָר	הַזֶּה	לְבִלְתִּי	הָפְכִּי	אֶת־הָעִיר	אֲשֶׁר
phānêkhā	gam	laddāvār	hazzeh	l^{e}viltî	hāphkî	'eth-hā'îr	'ăsher
your face	also	for the thing	the this	for not	I am overturning	the city	which

1744.313		4257.331	4561.231	8427	3706	3940	3310.125
v Piel pf 2ms	**22.**	v Piel impv 2ms	v Niphal impv 2ms	adv	cj	neg part	v Qal impf 1cs
דִּבַּרְתָּ		מַהֵר	הִמָּלֵט	שָׁמָּה	כִּי	לֹא	אוּכַל
dibbartā		mahēr	himmālēṯ	shāmmāh	kî	lō'	'ûkhal
you have spoken		hurry	escape	to there	because	not	I am able

3937, 6449.141	1745	5912, 971.141	8427	6142, 3772	7410.111	8428, 6111
prep, v Qal inf con	n ms	prep, v Qal inf con, ps 2ms	adv	prep, adv	v Qal pf 3ms	*n ms*, art, n fs
לַעֲשׂוֹת	דָּבָר	עַד־בֹּאֲךָ	שָׁמָּה	עַל־כֵּן	קָרָא	שֵׁם־הָעִיר
la'ăsôth	dāvār	'adh-bō'ăkhā	shāmmāh	'al-kēn	qārā'	shēm-hā'îr
to do	anything	until you go	there	therefore	he called	the name of the city

6949		8507	3428.111	6142, 800	4013	971.151	6949
pn	**23.**	art, n ms	v Qal pf 3ms	prep, art, n fs	cj, pn	v Qal act ptc ms	pn
צוֹעַר		הַשֶּׁמֶשׁ	יָצָא	עַל־הָאָרֶץ	וְלוֹט	בָּא	צֹעֲרָה
tsô'ar		hashshemesh	yātsā'	'al-hā'ārets	w^{e}lôṯ	bā'	tsō'ărāh
Zoar		the sun	it rose	over the land	when Lot	coming	to Zoar

	3176	4442.511	6142, 5651	6142, 6244	1657	813	4623, 882
24.	cj, pn	v Hiphil pf 3ms	prep, pn	cj, prep, pn	n fs	cj, n fs	prep, prep
	וַיהוָה	הִמְטִיר	עַל־סְדֹם	וְעַל־עֲמֹרָה	גָּפְרִית	וָאֵשׁ	מֵאֵת
	wayhwāh	himṯîr	'al-s^{e}dhōm	w^{e}'al-'ămōrāh	gāph^{e}rîth	wā'ēsh	mē'ēth
	and Yahweh	he caused it to rain	on Sodom	and on Gomorrah	sulfur	and fire	from

3176	4623, 8452		2089.121	881, 6111	419	881	3725, 3724
pn	prep, art, n md	**25.**	cj, v Qal impf 3ms	do, art, n fp	art, dem pron	cj, do	*adj*, art, n fs
יְהוָה	מִן־הַשָּׁמָיִם		וַיַּהֲפֹךְ	אֶת־הֶעָרִים	הָאֵל	וְאֵת	כָּל־הַכִּכָּר
y^{e}hwāh	min-hashshāmāyim		wayyah^{e}phōkh	'eth-he'ārîm	hā'ēl	w^{e}'ēth	kol-hakkikkār
Yahweh	from the heavens		and he overturned	the cities	the these	and	all the circle

881	3725, 3553.152	6111	7049	124		5202.522
cj, do	*adj, v Qal act ptc mp*	art, n fp	cj, *n ms*	art, n fs	**26.**	cj, v Hiphil impf 3fs
וְאֵת	כָּל־יֹשְׁבֵי	הֶעָרִים	וְצֶמַח	הָאֲדָמָה		וַתַּבֵּט
w^{e}'ēth	kol-yōsh^{e}vê	he'ārîm	w^{e}tsemach	hā'ădhāmāh		wattabbēṯ
and	all the dwellers of	the cities	and the vegetation of	the ground		and she looked

828	4623, 313	2030.122	5518	4556		8326.521	80
n fs, ps 3ms	prep, adv, ps 3ms	cj, v Qal impf 3fs	*n ms*	n ms	**27.**	cj, v Hiphil impf 3ms	pn
אִשְׁתּוֹ	מֵאַחֲרָיו	וַתְּהִי	נְצִיב	מֶלַח		וַיַּשְׁכֵּם	אַבְרָהָם
'ishtô	mē'achărâv	watt^{e}hî	n^{e}tsîv	melach		wayyashkēm	'avrāhām
his wife	behind him	and she became	pillar of	salt		and he rose early	Abraham

20. Behold now, this city is near to flee unto: ... the town ahead is near enough to escape to, *Anchor* ... near enough for me to get to quickly, *REB.*

and it is a little one: ... and it is scarcely anything, *Anchor* ... is it not a trifle, *Fenton.*

Oh, let me escape thither, (is it not a little one?): ... let me flee there--it is a mere nothing, *Anchor* ... let me go there, *BB* ... save myself there, *NCB* ... it is very small, isn't it, *NIV.*

and my soul shall live: ... then my life will be spared, *NIV* ... so let me live, *NCB* ... my life will be preserved, *Fenton* ... may be safe, *BB.*

21. And he said unto him, See, I have accepted thee concerning this thing also: ... I am granting you this request, too, *Berkeley* ... I will accept your presence, *Fenton* ... I will also grant you the favor you now ask, *NAB* ... bear with you in this thing also, *Anchor.*

that I will not overthrow this city, for the which thou hast spoken: ... not to destroy this town, *Berkeley* ... will not send destruction, *BB.*

22. Haste thee, escape thither: ... make haste, seek safety there, *NCB* ... be quick, to escape there, *Fenton* ... go there quickly, *BB* ... hurry, flee there, *Anchor.*

for I cannot do any thing till thou be come thither: ... until you arrive there, *RSV* ... until you reach it, *Berkeley* ... till thine entering, *Young.*

Therefore the name of the city was called Zoar: ... this is how the town came to be called Zoar, *Anchor* ... for this reason, *BB.*

23. The sun was risen upon the earth when Lot entered into Zoar: ... just after sunrise, *MLB* ... sun was up, *BB.*

24. Then the LORD rained upon Sodom and upon Gomorrah brimstone and fire from the LORD out of heaven: ... poured down sulphur and fire, *NCB* ... sent fire and flaming smoke raining, *BB* ... sulphurous fire, *Anchor* ... lightning and fire from the skies, *Fenton.*

25. And he overthrew those cities: ... overturned, *MLB* ... overwhelmed, *Fenton* ... sent destruction on, *BB* ... devastating, *Goodspeed* ... utterly destroying them, *LIVB.*

and all the plain: ... the entire basin, *MLB* ... all the lowland, *BB* ... the valley, *RSV* ... the circuit, *Young* ... whole region, *NCB.*

and all the inhabitants of the cities: ... with the whole population of the towns, *Berkeley* ... all the people of the towns, *BB* ... everyone living there, *NEB.*

and that which grew upon the ground: ... vegetation, *Anchor* ... every green thing, *BB* ... plants of the soil, *NCB* ... produce of the land, *Fenton.*

26. But his wife looked back from behind him: ... glanced back, *Anchor* ... looked expectantly, *Young.*

and she became a pillar of salt: ... turned into, *NAB* ... transformed into, *Fenton.*

27. And Abraham gat up early in

19:23-25. By the time Lot reached Zoar, the sun was high in the sky. God caused burning brimstone (sulfur) to rain down out of the heavens on the cities of Sodom and Gomorrah. Because Abraham saw dense smoke rising from the whole area it is probable that the natural asphalt deposits of the area were also set on fire. The four cities, their inhabitants, and the vegetation in the area were all destroyed (cf. Deut. 29:23; Hos. 11:8).

Today, some believe a violent earthquake must have caused the disaster. But an earthquake can hardly account for the burning of the sulfur. The Bible emphatically attributes the judgment to the LORD. He probably used the layers of sulfur that was already there, along with the asphalt and salt also located there to bring the destruction. But the cause was supernatural, not natural. (There is nothing volcanic in the area.)

19:26. Lot's wife, as the custom was, walked behind Lot, but she kept looking back steadily, wistfully, and with desire (as the Hebrew indicates). Perhaps she could not believe anything could happen to the lovely home she had in Sodom. She had undoubtedly spent time and money decorating it and preparing for the weddings of her two daughters. Her heart was still back in Sodom, and the implication is that she kept trailing further and further behind Lot, so when he reached Zoar, she was closer to Sodom than to the little city.

That she became a pillar of salt probably means she was encrusted with salt, as she was also enveloped with the burning sulfur so that nothing but a pillar of salt was left. (See Luke 17:32 for the warning Jesus gave.)

19:27-28. One cannot see the Dead Sea from the place near Hebron where Abraham was staying, Because he believed the LORD's warning, he went to the place where he had stood before the LORD and

904, 1269	420, 4887	866, 6198.111	8427	881, 6686	3176	28.	8625.521
prep, art, n ms	prep, art, n ms	rel part, v Qal pf 3ms	adv	do, *n mp*	pn		cj, v Hiphil impf 3ms
בַּבֹּקֶר	אֶל־הַמָּקוֹם	אֲשֶׁר־עָמַד	שָׁם	אֶת־פְּנֵי	יְהוָה		וַיַּשְׁקֵף
babbōqer	'el-hammāqôm	'ăsher-'āmadh	shām	'eth-p^{e}nê	y^{e}hwāh		wayyashqēph
in the morning	to the place	where he stood	there	before	Yahweh		and he looked down

6142, 6686	5651	6244	6142, 3725, 6686	800	3724	7495.121
prep, *n mp*	pn	cj, pn	cj, prep, *adj, n mp*	*n fs*	art, n fs	cj, v Qal impf 3ms
עַל־פְּנֵי	סְדֹם	וַעֲמֹרָה	וְעַל־כָּל־פְּנֵי	אֶרֶץ	הַכִּכָּר	וַיַּרְא
'al-p^{e}nê	s^{e}dhōm	wa'ămōrāh	w^{e}'al-kol-p^{e}nê	'erets	hakkikkār	wayyar^{e}'
on	Sodom	and Gomorrah	and on all of	the land of	the circle	and he saw

2079	6148.111	7290	800	3626, 7290	3655	29.	2030.121
cj, intrj	v Qal pf 3ms	*n ms*	art, n fs	prep, *n ms*	art, n ms		cj, v Qal impf 3ms
וְהִנֵּה	עָלָה	קִיטֹר	הָאָרֶץ	כְּקִיטֹר	הַכִּבְשָׁן		וַיְהִי
w^{e}hinnēh	'ālāh	qîṭōr	hā'ārets	k^{e}qîṭōr	hakkivshān		wayhî
and behold	it went up	the smoke of	the land	like the smoke of	the furnace		and it was

904, 8271.341	435	881, 6111	3724	2226.121	435	881, 80
prep, v Piel inf con	n mp	do, *n fp*	art, n fs	cj, v Qal impf 3ms	n mp	do, pn
בְּשַׁחֵת	אֱלֹהִים	אֶת־עָרֵי	הַכִּכָּר	וַיִּזְכֹּר	אֱלֹהִים	אֶת־אַבְרָהָם
b^{e}shachēth	'ĕlōhîm	'eth-'ārê	hakkikkār	wayyizkōr	'ĕlōhîm	'eth-'avrāhām
in wiping out	God	the cities of	the circle	that He remembered	God	Abraham

8365.321	881, 4013	4623, 8761	2091	904, 2089.141	881, 6111
cj, v Piel impf 3ms	do, pn	prep, *sub*	art, n fs	prep, art, v Qal inf con	do, art, n fp
וַיְשַׁלַּח	אֶת־לוֹט	מִתּוֹךְ	הַהֲפֵכָה	בַּהֲפֹךְ	אֶת־הֶעָרִים
wayshallach	'eth-lôṯ	mittôkh	hah^{e}phēkhāh	bah^{e}phōkh	'eth-he'ārîm
and He sent out	Lot	from the midst of	the overturning	in the overturning	the cities

866, 3553.111	904	4013	30.	6148.121	4013	4623, 6949	3553.121
rel part, v Qal pf 3ms	prep, ps 3fp	pn		cj, v Qal impf 3ms	pn	prep, pn	cj, v Qal impf 3ms
אֲשֶׁר־יָשַׁב	בָּהֵן	לוֹט		וַיַּעַל	לוֹט	מִצּוֹעַר	וַיֵּשֶׁב
'ăsher-yāshav	bāhēn	lôṯ		wayya'al	lôṯ	mitstsô'ar	wayyēshev
which he dwelled	in them	Lot		and he went up	Lot	from Zoar	and he dwelled

904, 2098	8530	1351	6196	3706	3486.111	3937, 3553.141
prep, art, n ms	*num*	n fp, ps 3ms	prep, ps 3ms	cj	v Qal pf 3ms	prep, v Qal inf con
בָּהָר	וּשְׁתֵּי	בְנֹתָיו	עִמּוֹ	כִּי	יָרֵא	לָשֶׁבֶת
bāhār	ûsh^{e}ttê	v^{e}nōthâv	'immô	kî	yārē'	lāsheveth
on the mountain	and the two of	his daughters	with him	because	he was afraid	to dwell

904, 6949	3553.121	904, 4792	2000	8530	1351	31.	569.122
prep, pn	cj, v Qal impf 3ms	prep, art, n fs	pers pron	*num*	n fp, ps 3ms		cj, v Qal impf 3fs
בְּצוֹעַר	וַיֵּשֶׁב	בַּמְּעָרָה	הוּא	וּשְׁתֵּי	בְנֹתָיו		וַתֹּאמֶר
b^{e}tsô'ar	wayyēshev	bamm^{e}'ārāh	hû'	ûsh^{e}ttê	v^{e}nōthâv		wattō'mer
in Zoar	and he dwelled	in the cave	he	and the two of	his daughters		and she said

1106	420, 7089	1	2290.111	382	375	904, 800
art, n fs	prep, art, adj	n ms, ps 1cp	v Qal pf 3ms	cj, n ms	sub	prep, art, n fs
הַבְּכִירָה	אֶל־הַצְּעִירָה	אָבִינוּ	זָקֵן	וְאִישׁ	אֵין	בָּאָרֶץ
habb^{e}khîrāh	'el-hatsts^{e}'îrāh	'āvînû	zāqēn	w^{e}'îsh	'ên	bā'ārets
the older one	to the younger	our father	he is old	and man	there is not	in the land

3937, 971.141	6142	3626, 1932	3725, 800	32.	2050.131	8615.520
prep, v Qal inf con	prep, ps 1cp	prep, *n ms*	*adj*, art, n fs		v Qal impv 2ms	v Hiphil impf 1cp
לָבוֹא	עָלֵינוּ	כְּדֶרֶךְ	כָּל־הָאָרֶץ		לְכָה	נַשְׁקֶה
lāvô'	'ālênû	k^{e}dherekh	kol-hā'ārets		l^{e}khāh	nashqeh
to come	to us	like the way of	all the earth		come	we will give drink

the morning to the place where he stood before the LORD: ... hurried back, *Anchor* ... in the Lord's presence, *NAB* ... he had been talking to the Lord, *BB*.

28. And he looked toward Sodom and Gomorrah: ... looking in the direction, *BB* ... he gazed, *Goodspeed* ... looked upon the face of, *Young*.

and toward all the land of the plain: ... region of the valley, *Goodspeed* ... all the wide extent, *NEB* ... lowland, *BB*.

and beheld, and, lo, the smoke of the country went up: ... he saw a stench of smoke rise up, *Fenton* ... saw thick smoke rising high, *NEB* ... he could see only smoke, *Anchor* ... dense smoke, *NAB*.

as the smoke of a furnace: ... like the fumes from a kiln, *Goodspeed* ... of an oven, *BB* ... lime-kiln, *NEB*.

29. And it came to pass, when God destroyed the cities of the plain: ... and overthrew the cities amidst which Lot lived, *Anchor* ... when God wiped out the basin cities, *Berkeley* ... destruction on the towns of the lowland, *BB*.

that God remembered Abraham: ... God was mindful of, *Anchor* ... kept his word to, *BB* ... thought upon, *Geneva* ... heeded Abraham's plea, *LIVB*.

and sent Lot out of the midst of the overthrow: ... rescued Lot from the disaster, *NEB* ... beyond the reach of the destruction, *Fenton* ... safely away, *BB* ... out of the catastrophe, *MLB* ... removing Lot from the midst of the upheaval, *Anchor*.

when he overthrew the cities in the which Lot dwelt: ... devastated the cities, *Goodspeed* ... put an end to the towns, *BB* ... Lot had settled, *NRSV* ... amidst which Lot had lived, *Anchor*.

30. And Lot went up out of Zoar: ... went up from Segor, *NCB* ... left Zoar, *Goodspeed*.

and dwelt in the mountain: ... settled in the hills, *Fenton* ... live in the hills, *Goodspeed* ... stayed in the mountains, *NASB*.

and his two daughters with him: ... living there with his two daughters, *BB* ... accompanied by his two daughters, *Goodspeed* ... together with, *Berkeley*.

for he feared to dwell in Zoar: ... fearful of the people there, *LIVB*.

and he dwelt in a cave, he and his two daughters: ... lived with his two daughters in a cave, *Berkeley* ... in a hole in the rock, *BB* ... stayed in a cave, *NASB*.

31. And the firstborn said unto the younger, Our father is old: ... older daughter said to her sister, *BB* ... our father is aging, *Berkeley* ... will soon be too old for having children, *LIVB*.

and there is not a man in the earth to come in unto us: ... not a man in the land to marry us, *Berkeley* ... to be a husband to us, *BB* ... to unite with us, *NAB*.

after the manner of all the earth: ... in the usual way, *NEB* ... natural way, *BB* ... as others do all the world over, *Fenton* ... as is customary, *Goodspeed*.

32. Come, let us make our father drink wine: ... give our father much wine, *BB* ... drunk with wine, *Fenton* ... ply our father with, *REB*.

and we will lie with him: ... will go into his bed, *BB* ... cohabit, *Fenton* ... let us lie with him, *NASB*.

that we may preserve seed of our father: ... to perpetuate our family through our father, *MLB* ... preserve seed, *Geneva* ... preserve our lineage, *NKJV*.

---

sought Sodom's deliverance. He must have felt sorrow as he saw the dense smoke arising from that destruction.

19:29. But God had not forgotten what was really on Abraham's mind and in his heart when he petitioned Him for Sodom. Since God knows everything, He never forgets anything but the sins He has forgiven and put out of existence. When the Bible speaks of God remembering, it means God now breaks into the situation to do something about it. God sent His angels to bring Lot out of Sodom, not because Lot deserved it, but for Abraham's sake. Thus, although Sodom was not spared, the intent of Abraham's intercession was answered.

19:30. Lot, still moved by fear, took his daughters and went to live in a cave in the mountains of Moab on the east side of the Dead Sea. Zoar, though a small town, was as wicked as Sodom. It was a center of idolatrous worship for the whole area. Lot was probably afraid God would bring judgment on it too.

19:31-36. Family and preservation of the family line was important in ancient times. The area where Lot and his daughters were living was largely uninhabited at the time. Since Lot was old, and now poor since all their belongings were destroyed along with Sodom, Lot had neither the inclination nor the opportunity to make arrangements for his daughters to be married. The daughters had been in Sodom long enough to be influenced by the low

881, 1	3302	8311.120	6196	2513.320	4623, 1	2320
do, n ms, ps 1cp	n ms	cj, v Qal impf 1cp	prep, ps 3ms	cj, v Piel impf 1cp	prep, n ms, ps 1cp	n ms
אֶת־אָבִינוּ	יַיִן	וְנִשְׁכְּבָה	עִמּוֹ	וּנְחַיֶּה	מֵאָבִינוּ	זָרַע
'eth-'āvînû	yayin	w^{e}nishk^{e}vāh	'immô	ûn^{e}chayyeh	mē'āvînû	zāra'
our father	wine	and we will lie down	with him	and we will keep alive	from our father	seed

33.	8615.527	881, 1	3302	904, 4050	2000	971.122	1106
	cj, v Hiphil impf 3fp	do, n ms, ps 3fp	n ms	prep, art, n ms	dem pron	cj, v Qal impf 3fs	art, n fs
	וַתַּשְׁקֶיןָ	אֶת־אֲבִיהֶן	יַיִן	בַּלַּיְלָה	הוּא	וַתָּבֹא	הַבְּכִירָה
	wattashqênā	'eth-'ăvîhen	yayin	ballaylāh	hû'	wattāvō'	habb^{e}khîrāh
	and they gave drink	their father	wine	in the night	that	and she went	the older one

8311.122	882, 1	3940, 3314.111	904, 8311.141	904, 7251.141
cj, v Qal impf 3fs	prep, n ms, ps 3fs	cj, neg part, v Qal pf 3ms	prep, v Qal inf con, ps 3fs	cj, prep, v Qal inf con, ps 3fs
וַתִּשְׁכַּב	אֶת־אָבִיהָ	וְלֹא־יָדַע	בְּשִׁכְבָהּ	וּבְקוּמָהּ
wattishkav	'eth-'āvîhā	w^{e}lō'-yāda'	b^{e}shikh^{e}vāhh	ûv^{e}qûmāhh
and she lay down	with her father	and not he knew	in her lying down	or in her rising

34.	2030.121	4623, 4420	569.122	1106	420, 7089	2075, 8311.115
	cj, v Qal impf 3ms	prep, n fs	cj, v Qal impf 3fs	art, n fs	prep, art, adj	intrj, v Qal pf 1cs
	וַיְהִי	מִמָּחֳרָת	וַתֹּאמֶר	הַבְּכִירָה	אֶל־הַצְּעִירָה	הֵן־שָׁכַבְתִּי
	wayhî	mimmāchŏrāth	wattō'mer	habb^{e}khîrāh	'el-hatsts^{e}'îrāh	hēn-shākhavtî
	and it was	on the next day	and she said	the older one	to the younger	behold I lay down

582	882, 1	8615.520	3302	1612, 4050	971.132
adv	prep, n ms, ps 1cs	v Hiphil impf 1cp, ps 3ms	n ms	cj, art, n ms	cj, v Qal impv 2fs
אֶמֶשׁ	אֶת־אָבִי	נַשְׁקֶנּוּ	יַיִן	גַּם־הַלַּיְלָה	וּבֹאִי
'emesh	'eth-'āvî	nashqennû	yayin	gam-hallaylāh	ûvō'î
yesterday	with my father	we will give him drink	wine	also tonight	and go

8311.132	6196	2513.320	4623, 1	2320	35.	8615.527
v Qal impv 2fs	prep, ps 3ms	cj, v Piel impf 1cp	prep, n ms, ps 1cp	n ms		cj, v Hiphil impf 3fp
שִׁכְבִי	עִמּוֹ	וּנְחַיֶּה	מֵאָבִינוּ	זָרַע		וַתַּשְׁקֶיןָ
shikh^{e}vî	'immô	ûn^{e}chayyeh	mē'āvînû	zāra'		wattashqênā
lie down	with him	and we will keep alive	from our father	seed		and they gave drink

1612	904, 4050	2000	881, 1	3302	7251.122	7089
cj	prep, art, n ms	art, dem pron	do, n ms, ps 3fp	n ms	cj, v Qal impf 3fs	art, adj
גַּם	בַּלַּיְלָה	הַהוּא	אֶת־אֲבִיהֶן	יָיִן	וַתָּקָם	הַצְּעִירָה
gam	ballaylāh	hahû'	'eth-'ăvîhen	yāyin	wattāqām	hatsts^{e}'îrāh
also	in the night	the that	their father	wine	and she rose	the younger

8311.122	6196	3940, 3314.111	904, 8311.141	904, 7251.141
cj, v Qal impf 3fs	prep, ps 3ms	cj, neg part, v Qal pf 3ms	prep, v Qal inf con, ps 3fs	cj, prep, v Qal inf con, ps 3fs
וַתִּשְׁכַּב	עִמּוֹ	וְלֹא־יָדַע	בְּשִׁכְבָהּ	וּבְקֻמָהּ
wattishkav	'immô	w^{e}lō'-yāda'	b^{e}shikh^{e}vāhh	ûv^{e}qumāhh
and she lay	with him	and not he knew	in her lying	or in her rising

36.	2106.127	8530	1351, 4013	4623, 1	37.	3314.122
	cj, v Qal impf 3fp	*num*	*n fp*, pn	prep, n ms, ps 3fp		cj, v Qal impf 3fs
	וַתַּהֲרֶיןָ	שְׁתֵּי	בְנוֹת־לוֹט	מֵאֲבִיהֶן		וַתֵּלֶד
	wattahrênā	sh^{e}ttê	v^{e}nôth-lôṭ	mē'ăvîhen		wattēledh
	and they became pregnant	the two of	the daughters of Lot	from their father		and she gave birth

1106	1158	7410.122	8428	4262	2000	1, 4262	5912, 3219
art, n fs	n ms	cj, v Qal impf 3fs	n ms, ps 3ms	pn	pers pron	*n ms*, pn	prep, art, n ms
הַבְּכִירָה	בֵּן	וַתִּקְרָא	שְׁמוֹ	מוֹאָב	הוּא	אֲבִי־מוֹאָב	עַד־הַיּוֹם
habb^{e}khîrāh	bēn	wattiqŏrā'	sh^{e}mô	mô'āv	hû'	'ăvî-mô'āv	'adh-hayyôm
the older one	son	and she called	his name	Moab	he	the father of Moab	until today

38.	7089 cj, art, adj וְהַצְּעִירָה wehatstseʿîrāh and the younger	1612, 2026 cj, pers pron גַם־הִוא gham-hiw' also she	3314.112 v Qal pf 3fs יָלְדָה yāledhāh she gave birth	1158 n ms בֵּן bēn son	7410.122 cj, v Qal impf 3fs וַתִּקְרָא wattiqŏrā' and she called	8428 n ms, ps 3ms שְׁמוֹ shemô his name	1181B pn בֶּן־עַמִּי ben-ʿammî Ben-Ammi

2000 pers pron הוּא hû' he	1 *n ms* אֲבִי 'ăvî the father of	1158, 6205 *n mp*, pn בְנֵי־עַמּוֹן benê-ʿammôn the sons of Ammon	5912, 3219 prep, art, n ms עַד־הַיּוֹם ʿadh-hayyôm until today	20:1	5450.121 cj, v Qal impf 3ms וַיִּסַּע wayyissaʿ and he pulled out	4623, 8427 prep, adv מִשָּׁם mishshām from there

33. And they made their father drink wine that night: ... made their father drunk, *Fenton* ... plied their father, *NAB*.

and the firstborn went in, and lay with her father: ... went into his bed, *BB* ... had sexual intercourse with her father, *LIVB*.

and he perceived not when she lay down, nor when she arose: ... without his being aware, *Berkeley* ... was not conscious, *Anchor* ... did not know, *Darby* ... had no knowledge, *BB* ... did not notice, *KJVII* ... he was so drunk that he didn't know it, *Good News*.

34. And it came to pass on the morrow: ... next day, *Berkeley* ... next morning, *Anchor* ... on the day after, *BB* ... sometime afterward, *Fenton*.

that the firstborn said unto the younger, Behold, I lay yesternight with my father: ... last night, it was I, *Anchor* ... I was with my father, *BB* ... the other night, *Fenton*.

let us make him drink wine this night also: ... have him drink wine tonight as well, *Berkeley* ... we cause him to, *Young*.

and go thou in, and lie with him that we may preserve seed of our father: ... then you go in, *Berkeley* ... you sleep with him, *Good News*.

35. And they made their father drink wine that night also: and the younger arose, and lay with him; and he perceived not when she lay down, nor when she arose:

36. Thus were both the daughters of Lot with child by their father: ... conceived, *Berkeley* ... became pregnant, *NRSV*.

37. And the firstborn bare a son, and called his name Moab: ... older bore a son whom she called Moab, *Anchor* ... whom she named, *BB*.

the same is the father of the Moabites unto this day: ... he became the ancestor, *Berkeley* ... of the present day, *NCB* ... today, *Anchor*.

38. And the younger, she also bare a son, and called his name Benammi: ... whom she named, *Anchor* ... gave birth, *Fenton* ... the son of my kin, *NAB*.

the same is the father of the children of Ammon unto this day: ... he was the ancestor of Ammon, *Fenton* ... present day Ammonites, *Goodspeed* ... people of, *NKJV* ... sons of, *NASB* ... of this day, *Anchor*.

20:1. And Abraham journeyed from thence toward the south country: ... went on his way, *BB* ... removed quietly from thence, landward, *Fenton* ... journeyed by stages, *NEB* ... moved from Mamre, *Good News* ... for the region of the Negeb, *Goodspeed*.

moral standards of the city. So it is not strange that the older daughter suggested incest as the only way they could preserve the family line. They knew, however, Lot would not consent to this. But his righteous soul was not righteous enough to keep him from getting drunk. He was probably discouraged and depressed, making it easy for the daughters to suggest that wine would make him feel better. Then, the daughters in turn became pregnant through their father. What a tragic scene this was!

19:37-38. The consonants of Moab could read in the Hebrew "from [my] father." Ben-Ammi means "son of my people." Moses recognized them as the ancestors of the Moabites and Ammonites of "this day," that is, of Moses' day. Later, the Lord showed a concern for them as descendants of Lot (Deut. 2:9, 19), but they became enemies of Israel (1 Sam. 14:47; 2 Ki. 3:5; 2 Chr. 20:1, 22).

20:1-2. Like most tent-dwellers, Abraham did not stay too long in one place. During this same year while Abraham was 99 and Sarah 89, he moved south into the Negev desert, where he found enough grass and water between Kadesh and Shur to stay there for a while. Then he moved north to the territory belonging to the city of Gerar, about 16 miles northwest of Beersheba. Because he had

80	800	5221	3553.121	1033, 7229	1033	8231
pn	n fs	art, pn	cj, v Qal impf 3ms	prep, pn	cj, prep	pn
אַבְרָהָם	אַרְצָה	הַנֶּגֶב	וַיֵּשֶׁב	בֵּין־קָדֵשׁ	וּבֵין	שׁוּר
'avrāhām	'artsāh	hanneghev	wayyēshev	bên-qādhēsh	ûvên	shûr
Abraham	to the land of	the Negeb	and he dwelled	between Kadesh	and between	Shur

1513.121	904, 1689		569.121	80	420, 8023	828	269
cj, v Qal impf 3ms	prep, pn	**2.**	cj, v Qal impf 3ms	pn	prep, pn	n fs, ps 3ms	n fs, ps 1cs
וַיָּגָר	בִּגְרָר		וַיֹּאמֶר	אַבְרָהָם	אֶל־שָׂרָה	אִשְׁתּוֹ	אֲחֹתִי
wayyāghār	bigh^{e}rār		wayyō'mer	'avrāhām	'el-sārāh	'ishtô	'ăchōthî
and he sojourned	in Gerar		and he said	Abraham	about Sarah	his wife	my sister

2000	8365.121	40	4567	1689	4089.121	881, 8023
pers pron	cj, v Qal impf 3ms	pn	*n ms*	pn	cj, v Qal impf 3ms	do, pn
הִוא	וַיִּשְׁלַח	אֲבִימֶלֶךְ	מֶלֶךְ	גְּרָר	וַיִּקַּח	אֶת־שָׂרָה
hiw'	wayyishlach	'ăvîmelekh	melekh	g^{e}rār	wayyiqqach	'eth-sārāh
she	and he sent out	Abimelech	king of	Gerar	and he took	Sarah

	971.121	435	420, 40	904, 2573	4050I	569.121	3937
3.	cj, v Qal impf 3ms	n mp	prep, pn	prep, *n ms*	art, n ms	cj, v Qal impf 3ms	prep, ps 3ms
	וַיָּבֹא	אֱלֹהִים	אֶל־אֲבִימֶלֶךְ	בַּחֲלוֹם	הַלָּיְלָה	וַיֹּאמֶר	לוֹ
	wayyāvō'	'ĕlōhîm	'el-'ăvîmelekh	bachălôm	hallāylāh	wayyō'mer	lô
	and He came	God	to Abimelech	in the dream of	the night	and He said	to him

2079	4322.151	6142, 828	866, 4089.113	2026	1195.157
intrj, ps 2ms	v Qal act ptc ms	prep, art, n fs	rel part, v Qal pf 2ms	cj, pers pron	*v Qal pass ptc fs*
הִנְּךָ	מֵת	עַל־הָאִשָּׁה	אֲשֶׁר־לָקַחְתָּ	וְהִוא	בְּעֻלַת
hinn^{e}khā	mēth	'al-hā'ishshāh	'ăsher-lāqachtā	w^{e}hiw'	b^e'ulath
behold you	dead man	because of the woman	whom you have taken	for she	married woman of

1196		40	3940	7414.111	420	569.121	112
n ms	**4.**	cj, pn	neg part	v Qal pf 3ms	prep, ps 3fs	cj, v Qal impf 3ms	n ms, ps 1cs
בָּעַל		וַאֲבִימֶלֶךְ	לֹא	קָרַב	אֵלֶיהָ	וַיֹּאמַר	אֲדֹנָי
bā'al		wa'ăvîmelekh	lō'	qārav	'ēlêhā	wayyō'mar	'ădhōnāy
husband		and Abimelech	not	he drew near	to her	and he said	my Lord

1504	1612, 6926	2103		3940	2000	569.111, 3937
intrg part, n ms	cj, adj	v Qal impf 2ms	**5.**	intrg part, neg part	pers pron	v Qal pf 3ms, prep, ps 1cs
הֲגוֹי	גַּם־צַדִּיק	תַּהֲרֹג		הֲלֹא	הוּא	אָמַר־לִי
hăghôy	gam-tsaddîq	tahrōgh		hălō'	hû'	'āmar-lî
the people	also righteous	will You kill		did not	he	he say to me

269	2000	2000, 1612, 2026	569.112	250	2000	904, 8866, 3949
n fs, ps 1cs	pers pron	cj, pers pron, cj, pers pron	v Qal pf 3fs	n ms, ps 1cs	pers pron	prep, *n ms*, n ms, ps 1cs
אֲחֹתִי	הִוא	וְהִיא־גַם־הִוא	אָמְרָה	אָחִי	הוּא	בְּתָם־לְבָבִי
'ăchōthî	hiw'	w^{e}hî'-gham-hiw'	'ām^{e}rāh	'āchî	hû'	b^{e}thām-l^{e}vāvî
my sister	she	and she even she	she said	my brother	he	with integrity of my heart

904, 5539	3834	6449.115	2148		569.121	420	435
cj, prep, *n ms*	n fp, ps 1cs	v Qal pf 1cs	dem pron	**6.**	cj, v Qal impf 3ms	prep, ps 3ms	art, n mp
וּבְנִקְיֹן	כַּפַּי	עָשִׂיתִי	זֹאת		וַיֹּאמֶר	אֵלָיו	הָאֱלֹהִים
ûv^{e}niqôyōn	kappay	'āsîthî	zō'th		wayyō'mer	'ēlāv	hā'ĕlōhîm
and with the innocence of	my hands	I have done	this		and He said	to him	God

904, 2573	1612	609	3156.115	3706	904, 8866, 3949	6449.113
prep, art, n ms	cj	pers pron	v Qal pf 1cs	cj	prep, n ms, n ms, ps 2ms	v Qal pf 2ms
בַּחֲלֹם	גַּם	אָנֹכִי	יָדַעְתִּי	כִּי	בְּתָם־לְבָבְךָ	עָשִׂיתָ
bachlōm	gam	'ānōkhî	yādha'ttî	kî	b^{e}thām-l^{e}vāv^{e}khā	'āsîthā
in the dream	also	I	I know	that	in the integrity of your heart	you did

and dwelled between Kadesh and Shur: ... settled between Kadesh and the Wall, *REB* ... Cades and Sur, *NCB*.

and sojourned in Gerar: ... lived for a time, *Berkeley* ... resided, *Fenton* ... established himself as an immigrant, *Goodspeed* ... as an alien, *NEB*.

2. And Abraham said of Sarah his wife, She is my sister: ... about Sarah, his wife, *Berkeley* ... concerning Sarah, his wife, *Young*.

and Abimelech king of Gerar sent, and took Sarah: ... had Sarah brought to him, *Anchor* ... sent for Sarah, *Berkeley*.

3. But God came to Abimelech in a dream by night, and said to him: ... in a dream one night, *Anchor* ... in the night, *BB* ... God cometh in unto him, *Young*.

Behold, thou art but a dead man, for the woman which thou hast taken; for she is a man's wife: ... beware of death, *Fenton* ... you shall die, *REB* ... you are as good as dead, *NIV* ... you are due to die for she is a married woman, *Anchor* ... take notice you are about to die ... she has a husband, *Berkeley*.

4. But Abimelech had not come near her: and he said: ... had not touched her, *Berkeley* ... had not made advances to her, *Fenton* ... hadn't slept with her, *LIVB* ... had not approached her, *NCB*.

Lord, wilt thou slay also a righteous nation: ... slay one even though he be innocent, *Anchor* ... slay a plainly blameless people, *Berkeley* ... put to death an upright nation, *BB* ... one who is clearly innocent, *Goodspeed* ... Lord, I am innocent, *Good News*.

5. Said he not unto me, She is my sister: ... the fact is, *Anchor* ... did he not say to me, himself, *BB*.

and she, even she herself said, He is my brother: ... yea, and she, herself, *Geneva* ... didn't she also say, *NIV* ... yes, he is my brother, *LIVB* ... she said the same thing, *Good News*.

in the integrity of my heart and innocency of my hands have I done this: ... I did it in good faith, with clean hands, *NAB* ... with an upright heart, *BB* ... with an upright mind, *Geneva* ... a clean conscience and in all innocence, *NEB* ... I hadn't the slightest intention of doing anything wrong, *LIVB*.

6. And God said unto him in a dream: ... God answered him, *Anchor* ... by a dream, *Geneva* ... God replied in the dream, *REB*.

Yea, I know that thou didst this in the integrity of thy heart: ... yes, I know that you did this in good faith, *NAB* ... know very well you did this from an honest heart, *Berkeley* ... in purity of heart, *Goodspeed* ... in the sincerity, *KJVII* ... acted with clean conscience, *NEB*.

for I also withheld thee from sinning against me: ... I, myself kept you from sinning against me, *Anchor* ... restrained you, *Berkeley* ... warned you from sin, *Fenton* ... and furthermore, it was I, *Goodspeed* ... from committing a sin, *NEB*.

therefore suffered I thee not to touch her: ... for this reason, *Berkeley* ... which is why I would not let you touch her, *Anchor* ... I did not let you come near her, *BB* ... permit you to approach her, *Fenton* ... to come against her, *Young*.

7. Now therefore restore the man his wife: ... return the man's wife, *Anchor* ... give the man back his wife, *BB* ... return the woman to her husband now, *NEB*.

for he is a prophet: ... since he is one who speaks up, *Anchor* ... great teacher, *Fenton* ... as a spokesman, *NAB* ... he is inspired, *Young*.

---

moved into the territory of the city state of Gerar, he did the same thing that he did when he went to Egypt (see comments on Gen. 12:11-13). "Abimelech" was probably the title of the kings of Gerar, and means "my father is king." He came and claimed Sarah as a hostage to be his wife, as the custom was.

20:3. God's promise was that Sarah would bear Abraham a son. So God intervened to protect Sarah by coming to Abimelech in a dream and pronouncing judgment on him for taking a married woman.

20:4-5. Abimelech had not come near Sarah, so he knew he and his people were righteous and innocent with respect to Sarah. Surely God had no grounds to slay them. He probably knew about the destruction of Sodom and Gomorrah and thought that God's judgment on him would also mean the destruction of his city and people as well. Because Abraham said Sarah was his sister and Sarah had agreed, Abimelech claimed Sarah in the integrity of his heart and with clean hands (palms, open hands), that is, innocently.

20:6-7. Though Abimelech did not know it, God Himself was active in keeping him from sinning and did not let him touch Sarah. So Abimelech must not only return Sarah, but must let Abraham pray for him, lest he die. God also called Abraham a prophet, that is, a speaker for God. (Compare Exodus 7:1 and 4:16.) Thus, though Genesis does not mention the Holy Spirit's work in and through

Verse	Number	Parsing	Hebrew	Transliteration	Translation
	6142, 3772	prep, adv	עַל־כֵּן	'al-kēn	therefore
	4623, 2490.141, 3937	prep, v Qal inf con, prep, ps 1cs	מֵחֲטוֹ־לִי	mēchăṭô-lî	from sinning against Me
	881	do, ps 2ms	אוֹתְךָ	'ôthekhā	you
	1612, 609	cj, pers pron	גַּם־אָנֹכִי	gam-'ānōkhî	even I
	2910.125	cj, v Qal impf 1cs	וָאֶחְשֹׂךְ	wā'echsekh	so I held back
	2148	dem pron	זֹאת	zō'th	this
	828, 382	*n fs*, art, n ms	אֵשֶׁת־הָאִישׁ	'ēsheth-hā'îsh	the wife of the man
	8178.531	v Hiphil impv 2ms	הָשֵׁב	hāshēv	return
7.	6498	cj, adv	וְעַתָּה	we'attāh	and now
	420	prep, ps 3fs	אֵלֶיהָ	'ēlêhā	her
	3937, 5236.141	prep, v Qal inf con	לִנְגֹּעַ	lingōa'	to touch
	3940, 5598.115	neg part, v Qal pf 1cs, ps 2ms	לֹא־נְתַתִּיךָ	lō'-nethattîkhā	not I gave you
	524, 375	cj, cj, adv, ps 2ms	וְאִם־אֵינְךָ	we'im-'ênekhā	but if you are not
	2513.131	cj, v Qal impv 2ms	וֶחְיֵה	wechăyeh	and live
	1185	prep, ps 2ms	בַּעַדְךָ	ba'adhekhā	for you
	6663.721	cj, v Hithpael impf 3ms	וְיִתְפַּלֵּל	weyithpallēl	and he will pray
	2000	pers pron	הוּא	hû'	he
	3706, 5204	cj, n ms	כִּי־נָבִיא	kî-nāvî'	because prophet
	3725, 866, 3937	cj, *adj*, rel part, prep, ps 2ms	וְכָל־אֲשֶׁר־לָךְ	wekhol-'ăsher-lāk	and all who to you
	887	pers pron	אַתָּה	'attāh	you
	4322.123	v Qal impf 2ms	תָּמוּת	tāmûth	you will die
	3706, 4322.142	cj, v Qal inf abs	כִּי־מוֹת	kîmôth	that dying
	3156.131	v Qal impv 2ms	דַּע	da'	know
	8178.551	v Hiphil ptc ms	מֵשִׁיב	mēshîv	one who returns
	3937, 3725, 5860	prep, *adj*, n mp, ps 3ms	לְכָל־עֲבָדָיו	lekhol-'ăvādhâv	to all his slaves
	7410.121	cj, v Qal impf 3ms	וַיִּקְרָא	wayyiqrā'	and he called
	904, 1269	prep, art, n ms	בַּבֹּקֶר	babbōqer	in the morning
	40	pn	אֲבִימֶלֶךְ	'ăvîmelekh	Abimelech
8.	8326.521	cj, v Hiphil impf 3ms	וַיַּשְׁכֵּם	wayyashkēm	and he rose early
	4108	adv	מְאֹד	me'ōdh	very
	596	art, n mp	הָאֲנָשִׁים	hā'ănāshîm	the men
	3486.126	cj, v Qal impf 3mp	וַיִּירְאוּ	wayyîr'û	and they were afraid
	904, 238	prep, n fp, ps 3mp	בְּאָזְנֵיהֶם	be'āznêhem	in their ears
	431	art, dem pron	הָאֵלֶּה	hā'ēlleh	the these
	881, 3725, 1745	do, *adj*, art, n mp	אֶת־כָּל־הַדְּבָרִים	'eth-kol-haddevārîm	all the things
	1744.321	cj, v Piel impf 3ms	וַיְדַבֵּר	wayedhabbēr	and he spoke
	4242, 6449.113	intrg, v Qal pf 2ms	מֶה־עָשִׂיתָ	meh-'āsîthā	what you have done
	3937	prep, ps 3ms	לוֹ	lô	to him
	569.121	cj, v Qal impf 3ms	וַיֹּאמֶר	wayyō'mer	and he said
	3937, 80	prep, pn	לְאַבְרָהָם	le'avrāhām	Abraham
	40	pn	אֲבִימֶלֶךְ	'ăvîmelekh	Abimelech
9.	7410.121	cj, v Qal impf 3ms	וַיִּקְרָא	wayyiqrā'	and he called
	6142, 4608	cj, prep, n fs, ps 1cs	וְעַל־מַמְלַכְתִּי	we'al-mamlakhtî	and on my kingdom
	6142	prep, ps 1cs	עָלַי	'ālay	on me
	3706, 971.513	cj, v Hiphil pf 2ms	כִּי־הֵבֵאתָ	kî-hēvē'thā	that you have brought
	3937	prep, ps 2fs	לָךְ	lākh	against you
	4242, 2490.115	cj, intrg, v Qal pf 1cs	וּמֶה־חָטָאתִי	ûmeh-chāṭā'thî	and how have I sinned
	3937	prep, ps 1cs	לָנוּ	lānû	to us
10.	569.121	cj, v Qal impf 3ms	וַיֹּאמֶר	wayyō'mer	and he said
	6200	prep, ps 1cs	עִמָּדִי	'immādhî	against me
	6449.113	v Qal pf 2ms	עָשִׂיתָ	'āsîthā	you did
	3940, 6449.226	neg part, v Niphal impf 3mp	לֹא־יֵעָשׂוּ	lō'-yē'āsû	not should be done
	866	rel part	אֲשֶׁר	'ăsher	which
	4801	n mp	מַעֲשִׂים	ma'ăsîm	doings
	1448	adj	גְדֹלָה	gedhōlāh	great
	2494	n fs	חֲטָאָה	chăṭā'āh	sin
	2172	art, dem pron	הַזֶּה	hazzeh	the this
	881, 1745	do, art, n ms	אֶת־הַדָּבָר	'eth-haddāvār	the thing
	6449.113	v Qal pf 2ms	עָשִׂיתָ	'āsîthā	you did
	3706	cj	כִּי	kî	that
	7495.113	v Qal pf 2ms	רָאִיתָ	rā'îthā	have you seen
	4242	intrg	מָה	māh	what
	420, 80	prep, pn	אֶל־אַבְרָהָם	'el-'avrāhām	to Abraham
	40	pn	אֲבִימֶלֶךְ	'ăvîmelekh	Abimelech

11.	569.121 cj, v Qal impf 3ms וַיֹּאמֶר wayyō'mer and he said	80 pn אַבְרָהָם 'avrāhām Abraham	3706 cj כִּי kî because	569.115 v Qal pf 1cs אָמַרְתִּי 'āmartî I said	7828 adv רַק raq only	375, 3488 sub, *n fs* אֵין־יִרְאַת 'ên-yir'ath there is not fear of	435 n mp אֱלֹהִים 'ĕlōhîm God

904, 4887 prep, art, n ms בַּמָּקוֹם bammāqôm in the place	2172 art, dem pron הַזֶּה hazzeh the this	2103.116 cj, v Qal pf 3cp, ps 1cs וַהֲרָגוּנִי wahrāghûnî and they will kill me	6142, 1745 prep, *n ms* עַל־דְּבַר 'al-d^{e}var over the matter of	828 n fs, ps 1cs אִשְׁתִּי 'ishtî my wife	12.	1612, 557 cj, cj, intrj וְגַם־אָמְנָה w^{e}gham-'ām^{e}nāh and also really

and he shall pray for thee, and thou shalt live: ... will intercede for you, *Goodspeed* ... to save your life, *Anchor* ... you will survive, *MLB*.

and if thou restore her not: ... do not return her, *Berkeley* ... give her back, *REB*.

know thou that thou shalt surely die, thou, and all that are thine: ... death will come to you and all your house, *BB* ... you and all who belong to you shall die, *Goodspeed* ... doomed to die, *NEB*.

8. Therefore Abimelech rose early in the morning and called all his servants: ... all his attendants, *Anchor* ... called his ministers, *Fenton* ... summoning all his slaves, *Goodspeed* ... court officials, *NAB* ... hastily called a meeting of all the palace personnel, *LIVB*.

and told all these things in their ears: and the men were sore afraid: ... the people were deeply shocked, *Anchor* ... thoroughly frightened, *MLB* ... greatly afraid, *Darby* ... much terrified, *Goodspeed* ... horrified, *NAB*.

9. Then Abimelech called Abraham, and said unto him: ... summoned Abraham, *Goodspeed* ... sent for, *BB*.

What hast thou done unto us? and what have I offended thee: ... how could you do this, *NAB* ... why have you treated us like this, *NEB* ... in what have I sinned against thee, *Darby* ... what wrong have I done you, *BB*.

that thou hast brought on me and on my kingdom a great sin: ... that you should have brought such great guilt upon me and my kingdom, *Anchor* ... great danger for acts they have not done, *Fenton* ... monstrous guilt, *NAB*.

thou hast done deeds unto me that ought not to be done: ... behaved in an unforgivable manner, *Anchor* ... treated me in an unbecoming way, *MLB* ... done us a wrong, *Fenton* ... no one should be treated as you have treated me, *NCB*.

10. And Abimelech said unto Abraham, What sawest thou, that thou hast done this thing?: ... what then was your purpose, *Anchor* ... whatever possessed you, *Goodspeed* ... what were you afraid of, *NAB* ... what have you encountered, *NASB* ... what were you thinking of, *NRSV*.

11. And Abraham said, Because I thought, Surely the fear of God is not in this place and they will slay me for my wife's sake: ... they will kill me because of my wife, *NAS* ... they might put me to death, *BB* ... they will want my wife and will kill me to get her, *LIVB*.

12. And yet indeed she is my sister:

Abraham, it is clear that he was a man of the Spirit, as all the true prophets were (2 Pet. 1:21). True prophets were intercessors as well (cf. Num. 14:11-20; 1 Sam. 7:5; Amos 7:2,5)

20:8-10. The men of Abimelech's court (called "slaves" in the sense of his subjects, or as subordinate officials) were filled with fear when he told them. Then he had Abraham called in, scolded him for what he had done, and asked him what he saw or considered that caused him to do this.

20:11-13. Abraham, though he was called by God and led by the Holy Spirit, could still make decisions based on his own reasoning. God does not take away our free will when we choose to follow him and we can still make mistakes. The reaction of Abimelech and his men shows Abraham was wrong in thinking there was no fear of God in that place. However, Abraham knew the customs, and he also knew the low moral standards of that part of the world. Thus, he asked Sarah to show her love to him (the loyal love called for by the marriage covenant) by saying she was his sister whenever they came into a new place. Besides, as Abraham also explained, Sarah was his sister, that is, his half-sister. This had caused a problem only in Egypt and at Gerar.

269	1351, 1	2000	395	3940	1351, 525
n fs, ps 1cs	*n fs*, n ms, ps 1cs	pers pron	adv	neg part	*n fs*, n fs, ps 1cs
אֲחֹתִי	בַּת־אָבִי	הִוא	אַךְ	לֹא	בַּת־אִמִּי
'ăchōthî	vath-'āvî	hiw'	'akh	lō'	vath-'immî
my sister	the daughter of my father	she	only	not	the daughter of my mother

2030.122, 3937	3937, 828	**13.**	2030.121	3626, 866	8912.516
cj, v Qal impf 3fs, prep, ps 1cs	prep, n fs		cj, v Qal impf 3ms	prep, rel part	v Hiphil pf 3cp
וַתְּהִי־לִי	לְאִשָּׁה		וַיְהִי	כַּאֲשֶׁר	הִתְעוּ
watt^{e}hî-lî	l^{e}'ishshāh		wayhî	ka'ăsher	hith'û
and she became to me	for a wife		and it was	according to that	He caused to wander

881	435	4623, 1041	1	569.125	3937	2172	2721
do, ps 1cs	n mp	prep, *n ms*	n ms, ps 1cs	cj, v Qal impf 1cs	prep, ps 3fs	dem pron	n ms, ps 2fs
אֹתִי	אֱלֹהִים	מִבֵּית	אָבִי	וָאֹמַר	לָהּ	זֶה	חַסְדֵּךְ
'ōthî	'ĕlōhîm	mibbêth	'āvî	wā'ōmar	lāhh	zeh	chas̲dēkh
me	God	from house of	my father	and I said	to her	this	your mercy

866	6449.124	6200	420, 3725, 4887	866	971.120	8427
rel part	v Qal impf 2fs	prep, ps 1cs	prep, *adj*, art, n ms	rel part	Qal impf 1cp	adv
אֲשֶׁר	תַּעֲשִׂי	עִמָּדִי	אֶל־כָּל־הַמָּקוֹם	אֲשֶׁר	נָבוֹא	שָׁמָּה
'ăsher	ta'ăsî	'immādhî	'el-kol-hammāqôm	'ăsher	nāvô'	shāmmāh
which	you will do	with me	to all the places	which	we will come	to there

569.132, 3937	250	2000	**14.**	4089.121	40	6887	1267
v Qal impv 2fs, prep, ps 1cs	n ms, ps 1cs	pers pron		cj, v Qal impf 3ms	pn	n fs	cj, n ms
אִמְרִי־לִי	אָחִי	הוּא		וַיִּקַּח	אֲבִימֶלֶךְ	צֹאן	וּבָקָר
'imrî-lî	'āchî	hû'		wayyiqqach	'ăvîmelekh	tsō'n	ûvāqār
you will say about me	my brother	he		and he took	Abimelech	sheep	and cattle

5860	8568	5598.121	3937, 80	8178.521	3937	881
cj, n mp	cj, n fp	cj, v Qal pf 3ms	prep, pn	cj, v Hiphil impf 3ms	prep, ps 3ms	do
וַעֲבָדִים	וּשְׁפָחֹת	וַיִּתֵּן	לְאַבְרָהָם	וַיָּשֶׁב	לוֹ	אֵת
wa'ăvādhîm	ûsh^{e}phāchōth	wayyittēn	l^{e}'avrāhām	wayyāshev	lô	'ēth
and male slaves	and female slaves	and he gave	to Abraham	and he brought back	to him	

8023	828	**15.**	569.121	40	2079	800	3937, 6686
pn	n fs, ps 3ms		cj, v Qal impf 3ms	pn	intrj	n fs, ps 1cs	prep, n mp, ps 2ms
שָׂרָה	אִשְׁתּוֹ		וַיֹּאמֶר	אֲבִימֶלֶךְ	הִנֵּה	אַרְצִי	לְפָנֶיךָ
sārāh	'ishtô		wayyō'mer	'ăvîmelekh	hinnēh	'artsî	l^{e}phānêkhā
Sarah	his wife		and he said	Abimelech	behold	my land	before you

904, 3005	904, 6084	3553.131	**16.**	3937, 8023	569.111	2079	5595.115
prep, art, adj	prep, n fd, ps 2ms	v Qal impv 2ms		cj, prep, pn	v Qal pf 3ms	intrj	v Qal pf 1cs
בַּטּוֹב	בְּעֵינֶיךָ	שֵׁב		וּלְשָׂרָה	אָמַר	הִנֵּה	נָתַתִּי
bat̲tôv	b^{e}'ênêkhā	shēv		ûlăsārāh	'āmar	hinnēh	nāthattî
by the good	in your eyes	dwell		and to Sarah	he said	behold	I have given

512	3826B	3937, 250	2079	2000, 3937	3806	6084	3937, 3725
num	n ms	prep, n ms, ps 2fs	intrj	pers pron, prep, ps 2fs	*n fs*	n fd	prep, adj
אֶלֶף	כֶּסֶף	לְאָחִיךְ	הִנֵּה	הוּא־לָךְ	כְּסוּת	עֵינַיִם	לְכֹל
'eleph	kes̲eph	l^{e}'āchîkh	hinnēh	hû'-lākh	k^{e}s̲ûth	'ênayim	l^{e}khōl
thousand of	silver	to your brother	behold	it to you	covering of	eyes	to everyone

866	882	882	3725	3306.257	**17.**	6663.721	80
rel part	prep, ps 2fs	cj, prep	adj	cj, v Niphal ptc fs		cj, v Hithpael impf 3ms	pn
אֲשֶׁר	אִתָּךְ	וְאֵת	כֹּל	וְנֹכָחַת		וַיִּתְפַּלֵּל	אַבְרָהָם
'ăsher	'ittākh	w^{e}'ēth	kōl	w^{e}nōkhāchath		wayyithpallēl	'avrāhām
who	with you	and with	everyone	also you are being vindicated		and he prayed	Abraham

420, 435	7784.121	435	881, 40	881, 828	526
prep, art, n mp	cj, v Qal impf 3ms	n mp	do, pn	cj, do, n fs, ps 3ms	cj, n fp, ps 3ms
אֶל־הָאֱלֹהִים	וַיִּרְפָּא	אֱלֹהִים	אֶת־אֲבִימֶלֶךְ	וְאֶת־אִשְׁתּוֹ	וְאַמְהֹתָיו
'el-hā'ĕlōhîm	wayyirpā'	'ĕlōhîm	'eth-'ăvîmelekh	w^{e}'eth-'ishtô	w^{e}'amhōthâv
to God	and He healed	God	Abimelech	and his wife	and his female slaves

3314.126		3706, 6352.142	6352.111	3176	1185	3725, 7641
cj, v Qal impf 3mp	**18.**	cj, v Qal inf abs	v Qal pf 3ms	pn	prep	*adj*, n ms
וַיֵּלֵדוּ		כִּי־עָצֹר	עָצַר	יְהוָה	בְּעַד	כָּל־רֶחֶם
wayyēlēdhû		kî'ātsōr	'ātsar	y^{e}hwāh	b^{e}'adh	kol-rechem
and they bore children		because restraining	He restrained	Yahweh	behind	every womb

besides, she is, in truth, *Anchor* ... she actually is, *Berkeley.*

she is the daughter of my father, but not the daughter of my mother: ... the daughter-in-law of my father, but not of my mother, *Fenton* ... though not by the same mother, *NEB* ... at least a half-sister (we both have the same father), *LIVB.*

and she became my wife: ... was given to me for a wife, *Fenton* ... I married her, *Good News.*

13. And it came to pass when God caused me to wander from my father's house, that I said unto her: ... sent me wandering, *NAB* ... had me wander, *NIV* ... into foreign lands, *Good News.*

This is thy kindness which thou shalt shew unto me: ... I want you to do me this kindness, *Anchor* ... let this be the sign of your love, *BB* ... would you do me this favor, *NAB* ... there is a duty towards me which you must loyally fulfill, *REB.*

at every place whither we shall come, say of me, He is my brother: ... wherever we go, *Berkeley.*

14. And Abimelech took sheep, and oxen, and menservants, and womenservants: ... male and female slaves, *Anchor* ... made Abraham a present of flocks and herds, *Berkeley* ... bondmen and bondwomen, *Darby* ... sheep and beeves, *Geneva.*

and gave them unto Abraham, and restored him Sarah his wife: ... returned, *Berkeley* ... sendeth back to him, *Young.*

15. And Abimelech said, Behold, my land is before thee: ... here, my land is open to thee, *Anchor* ... at your disposal, *NAB.*

dwell where it pleaseth thee: ... settle, *Berkeley* ... take whatever place seems good to you, *BB* ... for your eyes, *Fenton* ... live wherever you like, *NIV.*

16. And unto Sarah he said, Behold, I have given thy brother a thousand pieces of silver: ... thousand worth, *Anchor* ... 1000 silver dollars, *Berkeley* ... a thousand gifts, *Fenton* ... shekels, *Goodspeed.*

behold, he is to thee a covering of the eyes, unto all that are with thee: ... so that your wrong may be put right, *BB* ... vaile of thine eyes, *Geneva* ... so that your own people may turn a blind eye on it all, *NEB* ... it is your exoneration, *NRSV.*

and with all other thus she was reproved: ... thou art righted, *ASV* ... you have been publicly vindicated, *Anchor* ... your name is totally cleared, *Berkeley* ... your honor has been preserved, *NAB* ... everyone will know that you have done no wrong, *Good News.*

17. So Abraham prayed unto God: ... interceded, *NEB* ... appealed for Abimelech to God, *Fenton.*

and God healed Abimelech, and his wife, and his maidservants and they bare children: ... restored full health to Abimelech, *Anchor* ... made Abimelech well again, *BB* ... made the wives of Abimelech fruitful, *Fenton* ... his slave girls, *KJVII.*

20:14-16. Not only did Abimelech return Sarah to Abraham, he showed his fear of God and his goodwill by giving Abraham gifts. He also gave Abraham permission to stay wherever he wanted in Gerar's territory (without any treaty or compensation). Then he informed Sarah that he was giving Abraham a thousand shekels weight (about 25 pounds) of silver as a compensation for the offense against Sarah, so that she was fully vindicated (as not having sinned)in the sight of everyone, and her household would recognize this.

20:17-18. The reason Abimelech needed prayer was because God had made it impossible for his wife and slave girls to become pregnant. So God answered Abraham's prayer and brought a healing or restoration to Abimelech and to them all. In all of this, God was faithfully watching over Sarah as the mother of the promised son, the one who would carry on the blessings of God's covenant.

3937, 1041	40	6142, 1745	8023	828	80		3176
prep, *n ms*	pn	prep, *n ms*	pn	*n fs*	pn		cj, pn
לְבֵית	אֲבִימֶלֶךְ	עַל־דְּבַר	שָׂרָה	אֵשֶׁת	אַבְרָהָם	**21:1**	וַיהוָה
levêth	'ăvîmelekh	'al-devar	sārāh	'ēsheth	'avrāhām		wayhwāh
to the house of	Abimelech	over the matter of	Sarah	the wife of	Abraham		and Yahweh

6734.111	882, 8023	3626, 866	569.111	6449.121	3176	3937, 8023
v Qal pf 3ms	prep, pn	prep, rel part	v Qal pf 3ms	cj, v Qal impf 3ms	pn	prep, pn
פָּקַד	אֶת־שָׂרָה	כַּאֲשֶׁר	אָמָר	וַיַּעַשׂ	יְהוָה	לְשָׂרָה
pāqadh	'eth-sārāh	ka'ăsher	'āmār	wayya'as	yehwāh	lesārāh
He intervened	with Sarah	according to that	He said	and He did	Yahweh	to Sarah

3626, 866	1744.311		2106.122	3314.122	8023	3937, 80
prep, rel part	v Piel pf 3ms		cj, v Qal impf 3fs	cj, v Qal impf 3fs	pn	prep, pn
כַּאֲשֶׁר	דִּבֵּר	**2.**	וַתַּהַר	וַתֵּלֶד	שָׂרָה	לְאַבְרָהָם
ka'ăsher	dibbēr		wattahar	wattēledh	sārāh	le'avrāhām
according to that	He spoke		and she conceived	and she gave birth	Sarah	to Abraham

1158	3937, 2295	3937, 4287	866, 1744.311	882	435		7410.121
n ms	prep, n mp, ps 3ms	prep, art, n ms	rel part, v Piel pf 3ms	prep, ps 3ms	n mp		cj, v Qal impf 3ms
בֵּן	לִזְקֻנָיו	לַמּוֹעֵד	אֲשֶׁר־דִּבֶּר	אֹתוֹ	אֱלֹהִים	**3.**	וַיִּקְרָא
bēn	lizqunāv	lammô'ēdh	'ăsher-dibber	'ōthô	'ĕlōhîm		wayyiqōrā'
son	to his old age	to the set time	which He spoke	with him	God		and he called

80	881, 8428 , 1158	3314.255, 3937	866, 3314.112, 3937	8023	3437
pn	do, *n ms*, n ms, ps 3ms	v Niphal ptc ms, prep	rel part, v Qal pf 3fs, prep, ps 3ms	pn	pn
אַבְרָהָם	אֶת־שֶׁם־בְּנוֹ	הַנּוֹלַד־לוֹ	אֲשֶׁר־יָלְדָה־לּוֹ	שָׂרָה	יִצְחָק
'avrāhām	'eth-shem-benô	hannôladh-lô	'ăsher-yāledāh-lô	sārāh	yitschāq
Abraham	the name of his son	the one born to him	whom she gave birth to him	Sarah	Isaac

	4271.121	80	881, 3437	1158	1158, 8470	3219
	cj, v Qal impf 3ms	pn	do, pn	n ms, ps 3ms	*n ms, num*	n mp
4.	וַיָּמָל	אַבְרָהָם	אֶת־יִצְחָק	בְּנוֹ	בֶּן־שְׁמֹנַת	יָמִים
	wayyāmāl	'avrāhām	'eth-yitschāq	benô	ben-shemōnath	yāmîm
	and he circumcised	Abraham	Isaac	his son	son of eight	days

3626, 866	6943.311	881	435		80	1158, 4109
prep, rel part	v Piel pf 3ms	do, ps 3ms	n mp		cj, pn	*n ms, num*
כַּאֲשֶׁר	צִוָּה	אֹתוֹ	אֱלֹהִים	**5.**	וְאַבְרָהָם	בֶּן־מְאַת
ka'ăsher	tsiwwāh	'ōthô	'ĕlōhîm		we'avrāhām	ben-me'ath
according to that	He commanded	him	God		and Abraham	son of hundred

8523	904, 3314.241	3937	881	3437	1158		569.122	8023
n fs	prep, v Niphal inf con	prep, ps 3ms	do	pn	n ms, ps 3ms		cj, v Qal impf 3fs	pn
שָׁנָה	בְּהִוָּלֶד	לוֹ	אֵת	יִצְחָק	בְּנוֹ	**6.**	וַתֹּאמֶר	שָׂרָה
shānāh	behiwwāledh	lô	'ēth	yitschāq	benô		wattō'mer	sārāh
years	in his being born	to him		Isaac	his son		and she said	Sarah

6979	6449.111	3937	435	3725, 8471.151	6978.121, 3937
n ms	v Qal pf 3ms	prep, ps 1cs	n mp	n ms, v Qal act ptc ms	v Qal impf 3ms, prep, ps 1cs
צְחֹק	עָשָׂה	לִי	אֱלֹהִים	כָּל־הַשֹּׁמֵעַ	יִצְחַק־לִי
tsechōq	'āsāh	lî	'ĕlōhîm	kol-hashshōmē'a	yitschaq-lî
laughter	He made	for me	God	everyone who hears	he will laugh for me

	569.122	4449	4589.311	3937, 80	3352.512	1158	8023
	cj, v Qal impf 3fs	intrg	v Piel pf 3ms	prep, pn	v Hiphil pf 3fs	n mp	pn
7.	וַתֹּאמֶר	מִי	מִלֵּל	לְאַבְרָהָם	הֵינִיקָה	בָנִים	שָׂרָה
	wattō'mer	mî	millēl	le'avrāhām	hênîqāh	vānîm	sārāh
	and she said	who	he would say	to Abraham	she will nurse	children	Sarah

3706, 3314.115	1158	3937, 2295		1461.121	3315
prep, v Qal pf 1cs	n ms	prep, n mp, ps 3ms		cj, v Qal impf 3ms	art, n ms
כִּי־יָלַדְתִּי	בֵן	לִזְקֻנָיו	**8.**	וַיִּגְדַּל	הַיֶּלֶד
kî-yāladhtî	vēn	lizqunâv		wayyighdal	hayyeledh
because I have given birth	son	to his old age		and he grew up	the child

1621.221	6449.121	80	5136	1448	904, 3219	1621.241
cj, v Niphal impf 3ms	cj, v Qal impf 3ms	pn	n ms	adj	prep, *n ms*	v Niphal inf con
וַיִּגָּמַל	וַיַּעַשׂ	אַבְרָהָם	מִשְׁתֶּה	גָדוֹל	בְּיוֹם	הִגָּמֵל
wayyiggāmal	wayya'as	'avrāhām	mishteh	ghādhôl	b^{e}yôm	higgāmēl
and he was weaned	and he made	Abraham	feast	great	on the day of	the weaning of

18. For the LORD had fast closed up all the wombs of the house of Abimelech: … completely closed, *MLB* … had kept all the women, *BB* … sterilized, *Fenton* … shut up, *Geneva* … had made barren, *REB.*

because of Sarah Abraham's wife: … on account of Sarah, *Berkeley* … for taking Abraham's wife, *LIVB.*

21:1. And the LORD visited Sarah as he had said: … dealt with, *NRSV* … was gracious, *NIV* … showed favor, *NEB.*

and the LORD did unto Sarah as he had spoken: … as he had undertaken, *BB* … promised, *NASB* … made good what he had said, *REB.*

2. For Sarah conceived, and bare Abraham a son in his old age: … became with child, *BB* … gave birth to a son, *Fenton* … became pregnant, *NAB.*

at the set time of which God had spoken to him: … appointed time, *Darby* … at the time named by God, *BB* … that God had indicated, *Goodspeed* … had promised, *NCB* … time foretold by God, *REB.*

3. And Abraham called the name of his son that was born unto him, whom Sarah bare to him, Isaac: … gave his newborn son, the name Isaac, *Anchor* … Isaac (meaning laughter), *LIVB.*

4. And Abraham circumcised his son Isaac being eight days old: … at the age of eight days, *Anchor* … made him undergo circumcision, *BB* … being a son of eight days, *Young.*

as God had commanded him: … in agreement with God's command, *Berkeley* … as God had said, *BB* … as God had instructed him, *Fenton* … as decreed by God, *REB.*

5. And Abraham was an hundred years old, when his son Isaac was born unto him: … when the birth of Isaac took place, *BB.*

6. And Sarah said, God hath made me to laugh: … God has brought me laughter, *Anchor* … has given me cause for laughing, *BB* … God has made a delight for me, *Fenton* … made me to rejoice, *Geneva* … made me a laughing-stock, *Goodspeed.*

so that all that hear will laugh with me: … everyone who hears, *NASB* … hears about this, *NIV* … will rejoice with me, *Anchor* … laugh over me, *RSV* … laugheth for me, *Young.*

7. And she said, Who would have said unto Abraham, that Sarah should have given children suck: … whoever would have ventured to tell Abraham, *Goodspeed* … who would have dreamed that I would

21:1-5. The birth of Isaac was brought about by divine intervention in a miraculous way. God was faithful as He promised and made it possible for Sarah to bear a son for Abraham when he was 100 and she was 90. The son was born at the exact time God promised. God's timing is always just right though it may not seem so beforehand.

Abraham named him Isaac "he laughs" as God had commanded (17:19). But we can be sure this spoke, not of the laugh of doubt or incredulity, but a laugh of joy that recognized the faithfulness of God. Then, in obedience to God and in recognition of the covenant, Abraham circumcised Isaac when he was 8 days old.

21:6-7. Not only did Sarah laugh with joy, she recognized everyone who would hear about it would laugh with her. No one would have told Abraham that Sarah would be able to nurse children in her old age. It had to be God. Thus, laughing with Sarah would be an expression of new faith in Him because of the fulfillment of His promise.

21:8. Mothers usually nursed children for 3 years or longer in those days. Then, when a boy was weaned he would be turned over to the father for training. Because Isaac was the son of promise, the heir of the covenant, the one who would carry on the line leading to salvation-blessing for all the nations of the world, Abraham made a big feast to honor him. Abraham realized the importance of Isaac in the plan of God.

881, 3437	9.	7495.122	8023	881, 1158, 1972	4874	866, 3314.112
do, pn		cj, v Qal impf 3fs	pn	do, n ms, pn	art, pn	rel part, v Qal pf 3fs
אֶת־יִצְחָק		וַתֵּרֶא	שָׂרָה	אֶת־בֶּן־הָגָר	הַמִּצְרִית	אֲשֶׁר־יָלְדָה
'eth-yitschāq		wattēre'	sārāh	'eth-ben-hāghār	hammitsrîth	'ăsher-yāl^{e}dhāh
Isaac		and she saw	Sarah	the son of Hagar	the Egyptian	whom she gave birth

3937, 80	6978.351	10.	569.122	3937, 80	1691.331	526
prep, pn	v Piel act ptc ms		cj, v Qal impf 3fs	prep, pn	v Piel impv 2ms	art, n fs
לְאַבְרָהָם	מְצַחֵק		וַתֹּאמֶר	לְאַבְרָהָם	גָּרֵשׁ	הָאָמָה
l^{e}'avrāhām	m^{e}tsachēq		wattō'mer	l^{e}'avrāhām	gārēsh	hā'āmāh
to Abraham	mocking		and she said	to Abraham	drive out	the female slave

2148	881, 1158	3706	3940	3542.121	1158, 526	2148
art, dem pron	cj, do, n ms, ps 3fs	cj	neg part	v Qal impf 3ms	n ms, art, n fs	art, dem pron
הַזֹּאת	וְאֶת־בְּנָהּ	כִּי	לֹא	יִירַשׁ	בֶּן־הָאָמָה	הַזֹּאת
hazzō'th	w^{e}'eth-b^{e}nāhh	kî	lō'	yîrash	ben-hā'āmāh	hazzō'th
the this	and her son	because	not	he will be an heir	the son of the female slave	the this

6196, 1158	6196, 3437	11.	7778.121	1745	4108	904, 6084	80
prep, n ms, ps 1cs	prep, pn		cj, v Qal impf 3ms	art, n ms	adv	prep, n fp	pn
עִם־בְּנִי	עִם־יִצְחָק		וַיֵּרַע	הַדָּבָר	מְאֹד	בְּעֵינֵי	אַבְרָהָם
'im-b^{e}nî	'im-yitschāq		wayyēra'	haddāvār	m^{e}'ōdh	b^{e}'ênê	'avrāhām
with my son	with Isaac		and it was evil	the matter	very	in the eyes of	Abraham

6142	180	1158	12.	569.121	435	420, 80	414, 7778.121
prep	n fs	n ms, ps 3ms		cj, v Qal impf 3ms	n mp	prep, pn	adv, v Qal impf 3ms
עַל	אוֹדֹת	בְּנוֹ		וַיֹּאמֶר	אֱלֹהִים	אֶל־אַבְרָהָם	אַל־יֵרַע
'al	'ôdhōth	b^{e}nô		wayyō'mer	'ĕlōhîm	'el-'avrāhām	'al-yēra'
on	the cause of	his son		and He said	God	to Abraham	not it will be evil

904, 6084	6142, 5470	6142, 526	3725	866	569.122
prep, n fd, ps 2ms	prep, art, n ms	cj, prep, n fs, ps 2ms	adj	rel part	v Qal impf 3fs
בְּעֵינֶיךָ	עַל־הַנַּעַר	וְעַל־אֲמָתֶךָ	כֹּל	אֲשֶׁר	תֹּאמַר
b^{e}'ênêkhā	'al-hana'ar	w^{e}'al-'ămāthekhā	kōl	'ăsher	tō'mar
in your eyes	concerning the boy	and concerning your female slave	all	which	she will say

420	8023	8471.131	904, 7249	3706	904, 3437	7410.221
prep, ps 2ms	pn	v Qal impv 2ms	prep, n ms, ps 3fs	cj	prep, pn	v Niphal impf 3ms
אֵלֶיךָ	שָׂרָה	שְׁמַע	בְּקֹלָהּ	כִּי	בְיִצְחָק	יִקָּרֵא
'ēlêkhā	sārāh	sh^{e}ma'	b^{e}qōlāhh	kî	v^{e}yitschāq	yiqqārē'
to you	Sarah	listen	by her voice	because	in Isaac	it will be called

3937	2320	13.	1612	881, 1158, 526	3937, 1504	7947.125
prep, ps 2ms	n ms		cj, cj	do, n ms, art, n fs	prep, n ms	v Qal impf 1cs, ps 3ms
לְךָ	זָרַע		וְגַם	אֶת־בֶּן־הָאָמָה	לְגוֹי	אֲשִׂימֶנּוּ
l^{e}khā	zāra'		w^{e}gham	'eth-ben-hā'āmāh	l^{e}ghôy	'ăsîmennû
to you	seed		and also	the son of the female slave	into nation	I will make him

3706	2320	2000	14.	8326.521	80	904, 1269
cj	n ms, ps 2ms	pers pron		cj, v Hiphil impf 3ms	pn	prep, art, n ms
כִּי	זַרְעֲךָ	הוּא		וַיַּשְׁכֵּם	אַבְרָהָם	בַּבֹּקֶר
kî	zar'ăkhā	hû'		wayyashkēm	'avrāhām	babbōqer
because	your seed	he		and he rose early	Abraham	in the morning

4089.121, 4035	2678	4448	5598.121	420, 1972	7947.151	6142, 8327
cj, v Qal impf 3ms, n ms	cj, n ms	n md	cj, v Qal impf 3ms	prep, pn	v Qal act ptc ms	prep, n ms, ps 3fs
וַיִּקַּח־לֶחֶם	וְחֵמַת	מַיִם	וַיִּתֵּן	אֶל־הָגָר	שָׂם	עַל־שִׁכְמָהּ
wayyiqqach-lechem	w^{e}chēmath	mayim	wayyittēn	'el-hāghār	sām	'al-shikhmāhh
and he took bread	and skin of	water	and he gave	to Hagar	putting	on her shoulder

have a baby, *LIVB* ... that Sarah might nurse children, *Anchor.*

for I have born him a son in his old age: ... I have given him a son, now when he is old, *BB* ... to his age, *Fenton* ... for his old age, *NEB.*

8. And the child grew, and was weaned: ... big enough, *Berkeley* ... old enough to be taken from the breast, *BB.*

and Abraham made a great feast the same day that Isaac was weaned: ... celebrated the weaning, *Fenton* ... a great banquet, *Young.*

9. And Sarah saw the son of Hagar the Egyptian, which she had born unto Abraham, mocking: ... playing with her son, *NCB* ... teasing *MLB* ... laughing at him, *NEB* ... scoffing, *NKJV.*

10. Wherefore she said unto Abraham: ... she turned on Abraham, *Anchor* ... told, *MLB* ... demanded of, *NAB.*

Cast out this bondwoman and her son: ... cast out that slave, *Anchor* ... expel this servant girl with her son, *MLB* ... get rid of this slave-girl, *Goodspeed.*

for the son of this bondwoman shall not be heir with my son, even with Isaac: ... no son of this slave is going to share inheritance, *Anchor* ... is not to have a part in the heritage, *BB* ... shall not be an inheritor, *Fenton* ... hath no possession with my son, *Young.*

11. And the thing was very grievous: ... the matter distressed Abraham, *Anchor* ... to Abraham the proposal seemed very wrong, *Berkeley* ... was vexed, *NEB* ... was very upset, *REB.*

in Abraham's sight because of his son: ... in Abraham's view, this speech was very bad, *Fenton* ... especially on account of his son Ishmael, *NAB* ... because it concerned his son, *NIV.*

12. And God said unto Abraham, Let it not be grievous in thy sight because of the lad, and because of thy bondwoman: ... do not be distressed about the boy or your slave-woman, *Anchor* ... consider it objectionable, *Berkeley* ... do not be vexed, *NEB* ... let it be displeasing, *NKJV* ... let it not be a grief, *BB.*

in all that Sarah hath said unto thee, hearken unto her voice: ... do whatever Sarah tells you, *Anchor* ... listen to, *Berkeley* ... follow Sarah's bidding, *Goodspeed* ... heed the demands of Sarah, *NAB.*

for in Isaac shall thy seed be called: ... that your line will be continued, *Anchor* ... your name shall be perpetuated, *MLB* ... your offspring will be reckoned, *NIV.*

13. And also of the son of the bondwoman will I make a nation because he is thy seed: ... of the son of your servant-woman, *BB* ... of your second-wife I will found a great nation, *Fenton* ... for a nation I set him, *Young* ... I will also give many children to the son, *Good News.*

21:9-10. Ishmael at this time was about 17 years old. Because he was Abraham's first son, he would legally have the right to a double portion of the inheritance. He therefore proceeded to mock Isaac again and again, probably with sarcastic laughter. (The Hebrew word is an intensive form of the word "laugh" and thus indicates a different kind of laughing here than the laugh of joy. He was not merely playing, as some versions translate it.) Ishmael may have thought that though Isaac would get the blessing he would get the property, so he was making fun of everything involved with God's promise. (See Gal. 4:29-30.) Sarah observed this with understanding and discernment. Sarah demanded Abraham to drive out Ishmael, for she saw that he was unworthy of sharing the inheritance with Isaac.

21:11-12. When Abraham stepped out of God's will to try to fulfill God's promise by becoming the father of Ishmael, it broke God's heart. Now Abraham's heart was broken, for Ishmael was indeed his son. He loved him and wanted God's best for him. It seemed very severe to him that Sarah wanted him to drive out Ishmael and thus disinherit him.

But this time Sarah had more spiritual insight than Abraham. God agreed with her. Isaac was the son of promise, the child of faith. He was given by God, chosen by God, and was the one through whom the blessing would come. God pointed Abraham away from his natural affections and desires. He must put his distress and displeasure aside. There was a greater fulfillment that could come only through Christ (Gal. 3:16). The New Testament points to Ishmael as an example of those who try to claim God's blessings through natural relationships and legalistic works, while Isaac is an example of those who claim the blessings of God's promise by faith alone (Gal. 4:21-31).

21:13. God then renewed the promise concerning Ishmael. He would not only survive, he would become a great nation, not because he deserved it, or because of the blessing, but for Abraham's sake, because he was Abraham's son.

881, 3315	8365.321	2050.122	8912.122	904, 4198	916
cj, do, art, n ms	cj, v Piel impf 3ms, ps 3fs	cj, v Qal impf 3fs	cj, v Qal impf 3fs	prep, *n ms*	pn
וְאֶת־הַיֶּלֶד	וַיְשַׁלְּחֶהָ	וַתֵּלֶךְ	וַתֵּתַע	בְּמִדְבַּר	בְּאֵר
w^{e}'eth-hayyeledh	wayshall^{e}chehā	wattēlekh	wattētha'	b^{e}midbar	b^{e}'ēr
and the boy	and he sent her	and she went	and she wandered	in the wilderness of	Beer

916		3735.126	4448	4623, 2678	8390.522	881, 3315	8809
pn	15.	cj, v Qal impf 3mp	art, n md	prep, art, n ms	cj, v Hiphil impf 3fs	do, art, n ms	prep
שָׁבַע		וַיִּכְלוּ	הַמַּיִם	מִן־הַחֵמֶת	וַתַּשְׁלֵךְ	אֶת־הַיֶּלֶד	תַּחַת
shāva'		wayyikhlû	hammayim	min-hachēmeth	wattashlēkh	'eth-hayyeledh	tachath
Sheba		and they ended	the waters	from the skin	and she threw	the boy	under

259	7944		2050.122	3553.122	3937	4623, 5224	7651.542
num	art, n mp	16.	cj, v Qal impf 3fs	cj, v Qal impf 3fs	prep, ps 3fs	prep, sub	v Hiphil inf abs
אַחַד	הַשִּׂיחִם		וַתֵּלֶךְ	וַתֵּשֶׁב	לָהּ	מִנֶּגֶד	הַרְחֵק
'achadh	hashshîchim		wattēlekh	wattēshev	lāhh	minneghedh	harchēq
one of	the bushes		and she went	and she sat	toward it	from opposite	going far off

3626, 3019.352	7493	3706	569.112	414, 7495.115	904, 4323	3315	3553.122
prep, v Pilpel ptc mp	n fs	cj	v Qal pf 3fs	adv, v Qal impf 1cs	prep, *n ms*	art, n ms	cj, v Qal impf 3fs
כִּמְטַחֲוֵי	קֶשֶׁת	כִּי	אָמְרָה	אַל־אֶרְאֶה	בְּמוֹת	הַיָּלֶד	וַתֵּשֶׁב
kimt̲achwê	qesheth	kî	'ām^{e}rāh	'al-'er'eh	b^{e}môth	hayyāledh	wattēshev
like archers	bow	because	she said	not I will look	on the death of	the boy	and she sat

4623, 5224	5558.122	881, 7249	1098.122		8471.121	435
prep, sub	cj, v Qal impf 3fs	do, n ms, ps 3fs	cj, v Qal impf 3fs	17.	cj, v Qal impf 3ms	n mp
מִנֶּגֶד	וַתִּשָּׂא	אֶת־קֹלָהּ	וַתֵּבְךְּ		וַיִּשְׁמַע	אֱלֹהִים
minneghedh	wattissā'	'eth-qōlāhh	wattēv^{e}kh		wayyishma'	'ělōhîm
opposite	and she lifted up	her voice	and she wept		and He heard	God

881, 7249	5470	7410.121	4534	435	420, 1972	4623, 8452
do, *n ms*	art, n ms	cj, v Qal impf 3ms	*n ms*	n mp	prep, pn	prep, art, n mp
אֶת־קוֹל	הַנַּעַר	וַיִּקְרָא	מַלְאַךְ	אֱלֹהִים	אֶל־הָגָר	מִן־הַשָּׁמַיִם
'eth-qôl	hanna'ar	wayyiqrā'	mal'akh	'ělōhîm	'el-hāghār	min-hashshāmayim
the voice of	the boy	and he called	the angel of	God	to Hagar	from the heavens

569.121	3937	4242, 3937	1972	414, 3486.124	3706, 8471.111	435
cj, v Qal impf 3ms	prep, ps 3fs	intrg, prep, ps 2fs	pn	adv, v Qal juss 2fs	cj, v Qal pf 3ms	n mp
וַיֹּאמֶר	לָהּ	מַה־לָּךְ	הָגָר	אַל־תִּירְאִי	כִּי־שָׁמַע	אֱלֹהִים
wayyō'mer	lāhh	mah-lākh	hāghār	'al-tîr'î	kî-shāma'	'ělōhîm
and he said	to her	what to you	Hagar	do not fear	because He listened	God

420, 7249	5470	904, 866	2000, 8427		7251.132	5558.132	881, 5470
prep, *n ms*	art, n ms	prep, rel part	pers pron, adv	18.	v Qal impv 2fs	v Qal impv 2fs	do, art, n ms
אֶל־קוֹל	הַנַּעַר	בַּאֲשֶׁר	הוּא־שָׁם		קוּמִי	שְׂאִי	אֶת־הַנַּעַר
'el-qôl	hanna'ar	ba'ăsher	hû'-shām		qûmî	s^{e}'î	'eth-hanna'ar
to the voice of	the boy	where	he there		arise	lift up	the boy

2480.532	882, 3135	904	3706, 3937, 1504	1448	7947.125
cj, v Hiphil impv 2fs	prep, n fs, ps 2fs	prep, ps 3ms	cj, prep, n ms	adj	v Qal impf 1cs, ps 3ms
וְהַחֲזִיקִי	אֶת־יָדֵךְ	בּוֹ	כִּי־לְגוֹי	גָּדוֹל	אֲשִׂימֶנּוּ
w^{e}hachzîqî	'eth-yādhēkh	bô	kî-l^{e}ghôy	gādhôl	'ăsîmennû
and take hold of	with your hand	him	because for nation	great	I will make him

	6741.121	435	881, 6084	7495.122	908	4448	2050.122
19.	cj, v Qal impf 3ms	n mp	do, n fd, ps 3fs	cj, v Qal impf 3fs	*n ms*	n mp	cj, v Qal impf 3fs
	וַיִּפְקַח	אֱלֹהִים	אֶת־עֵינֶיהָ	וַתֵּרֶא	בְּאֵר	מָיִם	וַתֵּלֶךְ
	wayyiphqach	'ělōhîm	'eth-'ênêhā	wattēre'	b^{e}'ēr	māyim	wattēlekh
	and He opened	God	her eyes	and she saw	well of	water	and she went

4527.322 cj, v Picl impf 3fs וַתְּמַלֵּא watt^e^mallē' and she filled	881, 2678 do, art, *n ms* אֶת־הַחֵמֶת 'eth-hachēmeth the skin of	4448 n md מַיִם mayim water	8615.522 cj, v Hiphil impf 3fs וַתַּשְׁקְ wattash^e^qô and she gave drink	881, 5470 do, art, n ms אֶת־הַנָּעַר 'eth-hannā'ar the boy	**20.**	2030.121 cj, v Qal impf 3ms וַיְהִי wayhî and He was

435 n mp אֱלֹהִים 'ĕlōhîm God	882, 5470 prep, art, n ms אֶת־הַנַּעַר 'eth-hanna'ar with the boy	1461.121 cj, v Qal impf 3ms וַיִּגְדָּל wayyighdāl and he grew up	3553.121 cj, v Qal impf 3ms וַיֵּשֶׁב wayyēshev and he dwelled	904, 4198 prep, art, n ms בַּמִּדְבָּר bammidbār in the wilderness	2030.121 cj, v Qal impf 3ms וַיְהִי wayhî and he became

14. And Abraham rose up early in the morning and took bread, and a bottle of water, and gave it unto Hagar: ... a skin of water, *Anchor* ... flask, *Darby.*

putting it on her shoulder, and the child, and sent her away: ... placed them on her back, *Anchor* ... also the lad and dismissed her, *MLB.*

and she departed, and wandered in the wilderness of Beersheba: ... went on her way, *NIV* ... roamed in the desert, *Berkeley* ... wasteland, *BB.*

15. And the water was spent in the bottle: ... water was used up, *Anchor* ... water was exhausted, *Darby* ... was gone, *KJVII.*

and she cast the child under one of the shrubs: ... left the child, *Anchor* ... put the youth, *Berkeley* ... throwing the child, *Goodspeed* ... under a tree, *BB* ... under a bush, *Fenton.*

16. And she went, and sat her down over against him a good way off, as it were a bowshot: ... at a distance, *Anchor* ... opposite him, *Berkeley* ... an arrow flight, *BB* ... two bowshots, *NEB.*

for she said, Let me not see the death of the child: ... not look on as the child dies, *Anchor* ... I must not see, *MLB* ... I cannot bear to see, *Goodspeed.*

And she sat over against him: ... as she sat there, *Berkeley* ... seating herself on the earth, *BB* ... rested on the other side, *Fenton* ... some way off, *Goodspeed.*

and lift up her voice, and wept: ... broke into sobs, *Anchor* ... gave way to bitter weeping, *BB.*

17. And God heard the voice of the lad and the angel of God called to Hagar out of heaven and said unto her, What aileth thee, Hagar: ... what troubles you, *NRSV* ... why are you weeping, *BB* ... what is the matter, *Fenton* ... what's wrong, *LIVB.*

fear not; for God hath heard the voice of the lad where he is: ... in his present plight, *Anchor* ... where you laid him, *NEB.*

18. Arise, lift up the lad, and hold him in thine hand for I will make him a great nation: ... come pick up the boy and comfort him, *Anchor* ... hold him by the hand, *Berkeley* ... take up the child in your arms, *NEB* ... great people, *Geneva.*

19. And God opened her eyes, and she saw a well of water: ... noticed a spring, *Berkeley* ... water-spring, *BB* ... well, full of water, *NEB.*

and she went, and filled the bottle with water, and gave the lad drink: ... let the boy drink, *Anchor* ... filled

21:14-16. With the prompt obedience of faith, Abraham gave Hagar food and a large goatskin full of water and sent her and Ishmael away. She did not know where to go so she simply wandered about in the wilderness near Beersheba until the water was gone. Ishmael was tired and probably dragging on his mother even though he was about 17 years old.

Women usually have more stamina and endurance than even young men. So she let him drop down under one of the bushes and went about a bowshot away where she sat down and began to sob. At this point she thought Ishmael would die and could not bear looking at him lying there.

21:17-19. God was faithful. Encouragement came to her by an angelic voice from heaven. Instead of fear, she needed to believe God heard the cries of the boy. Then she needed to show by an act of faith she believed God's promise that He would make him a great nation. In faith she must lift Ishmael up and take him firmly by the hand. As soon as she obeyed, God opened her eyes and she saw a well of water.

21:20-21. God continued to be faithful to His promise to Abraham concerning Ishmael. So God was with Ishmael whether he knew it or not. He lived in the desert of Paran in the north central part of the Sinai Peninsula and kept alive by hunting

7528.151	7494	**21.** 3553.121	904, 4198	368	4089.122, 3937
v Qal act ptc ms	n ms	cj, v Qal impf 3ms	prep, *n ms*	pn	cj, v Qal impf 3fs, prep, ps 3ms
רֹבֶה	קַשָּׁת	וַיֵּשֶׁב	בְּמִדְבַּר	פָּארָן	וַתִּקַּח־לוֹ
rōveh	qashshāth	wayyēshev	bemidbar	pā'rān	wattiqqach-lô
great one	archer	and he dwelled	in the wilderness of	Paran	and she took for him

525	828	4623, 800	4875	**22.** 2030.121	904, 6496	2000
n fs, ps 3ms	n fs	prep, *n fs*	pn	cj, v Qal impf 3ms	prep, art, n fs	art, dem pron
אִמּוֹ	אִשָּׁה	מֵאֶרֶץ	מִצְרָיִם	וַיְהִי	בָּעֵת	הַהִוא
'immô	'ishshāh	mē'erets	mitsrāyim	wayhî	bā'ēth	hahiw'
his mother	wife	from the land of	Egypt	and it was	in the time	the that

569.121	40	6612	8015, 6893	420, 80	3937, 569.141
cj, v Qal impf 3ms	pn	cj, pn	n ms, n ms, ps 3ms	prep, pn	prep, v Qal inf con
וַיֹּאמֶר	אֲבִימֶלֶךְ	וּפִיכֹל	שַׂר־צְבָאוֹ	אֶל־אַבְרָהָם	לֵאמֹר
wayyō'mer	'ăvîmelekh	ûphîkhōl	sar-tsevā'ô	'el-'avrāhām	lē'mōr
and he said	Abimelech	and Phicol	the commander of his army	to Abraham	saying

435	6196	904, 3725	866, 887	6449.151	**23.** 6498	8123.231, 3937
n mp	prep, ps 2ms	prep, adj	rel part, pers pron	v Qal act ptc ms	cj, adv	v Niphal impv 2ms, prep, ps 1cs
אֱלֹהִים	עִמְּךָ	בְּכֹל	אֲשֶׁר־אַתָּה	עֹשֶׂה	וְעַתָּה	הִשָּׁבְעָה־לִּי
'ĕlōhîm	'immekhā	bekhōl	'ăsher-'attāh	'ōseh	we'attāh	hishshāv'āh-lî
God	with you	with all	which you	doing	and now	swear to me

904, 435	2077	524, 8631.123	3937	3937, 5397	3937, 5408
prep, n mp	adv	cj, v Qal impf 2ms	prep, ps 1cs	cj, prep, n ms, ps 1cs	cj, prep, n ms, ps 1cs
בֵּאלֹהִים	הֵנָּה	אִם־תִּשְׁקֹר	לִי	וּלְנִינִי	וּלְנֶכְדִּי
vē'lōhîm	hēnnāh	'im-tishqōr	lî	ûlānînî	ûlănekhdî
by God	here	if you will deceive	me	or my offspring	or my descendants

3626, 2721	866, 6449.115	6196	6449.123	6200	6196, 800
prep, art, n ms	rel part, v Qal pf 1cs	prep, ps 2ms	v Qal impf 2ms	prep, ps 1cs	cj, prep, art, n fs
כַּחֶסֶד	אֲשֶׁר־עָשִׂיתִי	עִמְּךָ	תַּעֲשֶׂה	עִמָּדִי	וְעִם־הָאָרֶץ
kachesedh	'ăsher-'āsîthî	'immekhā	ta'ăseh	'immādhî	we'im-hā'ārets
like the favor	which I have done	for you	you will do	with me	and with the land

866, 1513.113	904	**24.** 569.121	80	609	8123.225
rel part, v Qal pf 2ms	prep, ps 3fs	cj, v Qal impf 3ms	pn	pers pron	v Niphal impf 1cs
אֲשֶׁר־גַּרְתָּה	בָּהּ	וַיֹּאמֶר	אַבְרָהָם	אָנֹכִי	אִשָּׁבֵעַ
'ăsher-gartāh	bāhh	wayyō'mer	'avrāhām	'ānōkhî	'ishshāvēa'
which you have sojourned	in it	and he said	Abraham	I	I will swear

25. 3306.511	80	881, 40	6142, 180	908	4448	866
cj, v Hiphil impf 3ms	pn	do, pn	prep, *n fp*	*n ms*	art, n md	rel part
וְהוֹכִחַ	אַבְרָהָם	אֶת־אֲבִימֶלֶךְ	עַל־אֹדוֹת	בְּאֵר	הַמַּיִם	אֲשֶׁר
wehôkhiach	'avrāhām	'eth-'ăvîmelekh	'al-'ōdhōth	be'ēr	hammayim	'ăsher
and he rebuked	Abraham	Abimelech	on account of	the well of	the water	which

1528.116	5860	40	**26.** 569.121	40	3940	3156.115	4449
v Qal pf 3cp	*n mp*	pn	cj, v Qal impf 3ms	pn	neg part	v Qal pf 1cs	intrg
גָּזְלוּ	עַבְדֵי	אֲבִימֶלֶךְ	וַיֹּאמֶר	אֲבִימֶלֶךְ	לֹא	יָדַעְתִּי	מִי
gāzlû	'avedhê	'ăvîmelekh	wayyō'mer	'ăvîmelekh	lō'	yādha'ăttî	mî
they took	the slaves of	Abimelech	and he said	Abimelech	not	I know	who

6449.111	881, 1745	2172	1612, 887	3940, 5222.513	3937	1612
v Qal pf 3ms	do, art, n ms	art, dem pron	cj, cj, pers pron	neg part, v Hiphil impf 2ms	prep, ps 1cs	cj, cj
עָשָׂה	אֶת־הַדָּבָר	הַזֶּה	וְגַם־אַתָּה	לֹא־הִגַּדְתָּ	לִי	וְגַם
'āsāh	'eth-haddāvār	hazzeh	wegham-'attāh	lō'-higgadhtā	lî	wegham
he did	the thing	the this	and also you	not you told	me	and also

609	3940	8471.115	1153	3219		4089.121	80	6887
pers pron	neg part	v Qal pf 1cs	*adj*	art, n ms	**27.**	cj, v Qal impf 3ms	pn	n fs
אָנֹכִי	לֹא	שָׁמַעְתִּי	בִּלְתִּי	הַיּוֹם		וַיִּקַּח	אַבְרָהָם	צֹאן
'ānōkhî	lō'	shāma'ättî	biltî	hayyôm		wayyiqqach	'avrāhām	tsō'n
I	not	I heard	except	today		and he took	Abraham	sheep

1267	5598.121	3937, 40	3901.126	8529	1311
cj, n ms	cj, v Qal impf 3ms	prep, pn	cj, v Qal impf 3mp	num, ps 3mp	n fs
וּבָקָר	וַיִּתֵּן	לַאֲבִימֶלֶךְ	וַיִּכְרְתוּ	שְׁנֵיהֶם	בְּרִית
ûvāqār	wayyittēn	la'ăvîmelekh	wayyikhrethû	shenêhem	berîth
and cattle	and he gave	to Abimelech	and they cut	the two of them	covenant

the flask, *Darby* ... causeth the youth to drink, *Young*.

20. And God was with the lad and he grew and dwelt in the wilderness and became an archer: ... a skilled bowman, *Anchor* ... an expert bowman, *NCB* ... mighty archer, *Fenton*.

21. And he dwelt in the wilderness of Paran and his mother took him a wife out of the land of Egypt: ... chose a wife for him, *NCB* ... found him a wife, *NEB* ... arranged a marriage, *LIVB*.

22. And it came to pass at that time that Abimelech and Phichol the chief captain of his host spake unto Abraham, saying: ... his general, *Berkeley* ... captain of his army, *BB*.

God is with thee in all that thou doest: ... in everything that you undertake, *Anchor* ... it is evident that God helps you, *LIVB*.

23. Now therefore swear unto me here by God: ... give me your oath, *BB* ... make a vow, *Good News*.

that thou wilt not deal falsely with me, nor with my son, nor with my son's son: ... never be false nor to my descendants, *Goodspeed* ... nor with my progeny, *NAB* ... not lie to me or to my successor, *Young*.

but according to the kindness that I have done unto thee: ... as I have acted, *Anchor* ... as I have shown you fellowship, *Berkeley* ... as I have been good to you, *BB*.

thou shalt do unto me, and to the land wherein thou hast sojourned: ... so you must keep faith with me, *REB* ... me and the land in which you are an immigrant, *Berkeley* ... this land where you have been living, *BB* ... where you have been forgiven, *Fenton* ... and to the country you have come to live as an alien, *NEB*.

24. And Abraham said, I will swear: ... I will give you my oath, *BB* ... all right, I swear to it, *LIVB*.

25. And Abraham reproved Abimelech because of a well of water: ... reproached Abimelech, *Anchor* ... complained, *Berkeley* ... rebuked, *Geneva*.

which Abimelech's servants had violently taken away: ... had seized, *Anchor* ... taken by force, *BB* ... stolen, *Fenton*.

26. And Abimelech said, I wot not who hath done this thing: ... I have no idea who did this, *Anchor* ... I did not myself know of that matter, *Fenton* ... who is responsible, *LIVB*.

neither didst thou tell me, neither yet heard I of it, but to day: ... you

with bows and arrows. Parents arranged marriages in those days, and Hagar was able to get a wife for him from Egypt.

21:22-24. We now go back to the time shortly after Ishmael was sent away. Abimelech and the commander of his army recognized God was blessing Abraham and may have been afraid Abraham would become too powerful. Or they may have heard how Abraham rescued Lot from the four kings, and they did not want Abraham to turn against them.

What Abimelech wanted was a new treaty guaranteeing that Abraham would continue to show the same kind of covenant faithfulness he had enjoyed since living as a resident alien in Abimelech's territory. Abimelech wanted this confirmed by swearing before God to do so. Abraham agreed to do this.

21:25-26. At the same time Abraham reproved Abimelech because his servants had seized a well Abraham (or his servants) dug. Abimelech quickly apologized. His servants had done this without his knowledge.

21:27. Abraham then brought sheep and cattle to Abimelech and the two men "cut" a covenant, a solemn binding agreement or treaty sealed by a sacrifice. What follows indicates that some of the sheep and cattle were used in the sacrifice before God to confirm the treaty along with Abraham's oath that he would keep it.

28.	5507.521	80	881, 8124	3652	6887	3937, 940
	cj, v Hiphil impf 3ms	pn	do, num	*n fp*	art, n fs	prep, n ms, ps 3fp
	וַיַּצֵּב	אַבְרָהָם	אֶת־שֶׁבַע	כִּבְשֹׂת	הַצֹּאן	לְבַדְּהֶן
	wayyatstsēv	'avrāhām	'eth-sheva'	kivsōth	hatstsō'n	l^{e}vadd^{e}hen
	and he set	Abraham	seven	female lambs	the sheep	by themselves

29.	569.121	40	420, 80	4242	2078	8124	3652
	cj, v Qal impf 3ms	pn	prep, pn	intrg	pers pron	num	n fp
	וַיֹּאמֶר	אֲבִימֶלֶךְ	אֶל־אַבְרָהָם	מָה	הֵנָּה	שֶׁבַע	כְּבָשֹׂת
	wayyō'mer	'ăvîmelekh	'el-'avrāhām	māh	hēnnāh	sheva'	k^{e}vāsōth
	and he said	Abimelech	to Abraham	what	they	seven	female lambs

431	866	5507.513	3937, 940	30.	569.121	3706	881, 8124
art, dem pron	rel part	v Hiphil pf 2ms	prep, n ms ps 3fp		cj, v Qal impf 3ms	cj	do, num
הָאֵלֶּה	אֲשֶׁר	הִצַּבְתָּ	לְבַדָּנָה		וַיֹּאמֶר	כִּי	אֶת־שֶׁבַע
hā'ēlleh	'ăsher	hitstsavtā	l^{e}vaddānāh		wayyō'mer	kî	'eth-sheva'
the these	which	you have set	by themselves		and he said	because	seven

3652	4089.123	4623, 3135	904, 5877	2030.123, 3937	3937, 5921
n fp	v Qal impf 2ms	prep, n fs, ps 1cs	prep, prep	v Qal impf 2ms, prep, ps 1cs	prep, n fs
כְּבָשֹׂת	תִּקַּח	מִיָּדִי	בַּעֲבוּר	תִּהְיֶה־לִּי	לְעֵדָה
k^{e}vāsōth	tiqqach	miyyādhî	ba'ăvûr	tihyeh-lî	l^{e}'ēdhāh
female lambs	you will take	from my hand	on account of	you will be to me	witness

3706	2763.115	881, 908	2148	31.	6142, 3772	7410.111	3937, 4887
cj	v Qal pf 1cs	do, art, n fs	art, dem pron		prep, adv	v Qal pf 3ms	prep, art, n ms
כִּי	חָפַרְתִּי	אֶת־הַבְּאֵר	הַזֹּאת		עַל־כֵּן	קָרָא	לַמָּקוֹם
kî	chāphartî	'eth-habb^{e}'ēr	hazzō'th		'al-kēn	qārā'	lammāqôm
because	I dug	the well	the this		therefore	he named	the place

2000	916	916	3706	8427	8123.216	8530
art, dem pron	pn	pn	cj	adv	v Niphal pf 3cp	num, ps 3mp
הַהוּא	בְּאֵר	שָׁבַע	כִּי	שָׁם	נִשְׁבְּעוּ	שְׁנֵיהֶם
hahû'	b^{e}'ēr	shāva'	kî	shām	nishb^{e}'û	sh^{e}nêhem
the that	Beer	Sheba	because	there	they swore	the two of them

32.	3901.126	1311	904, 916	916	7251.121	40	6612
	cj, v Qal impf 3mp	n fs	prep, pn	pn	cj, v Qal impf 3ms	pn	cj, pn
	וַיִּכְרְתוּ	בְרִית	בִּבְאֵר	שָׁבַע	וַיָּקָם	אֲבִימֶלֶךְ	וּפִיכֹל
	wayyikhr^{e}thû	v^{e}rîth	biv'ēr	shāva'	wayyāqām	'ăvîmelekh	ûphîkhōl
	and they cut	covenant	in Beer	Sheba	and he rose up	Abimelech	and Phicol

8015, 6893	8178.126	420, 800	6674	33.	5378.121	842
n ms, n ms, ps 3ms	cj, v Qal impf 3mp	prep, *n fs*	pn		cj, v Qal impf 3ms	n ms
שַׂר־צְבָאוֹ	וַיָּשֻׁבוּ	אֶל־אֶרֶץ	פְּלִשְׁתִּים		וַיִּטַּע	אֶשֶׁל
sar-ts^{e}vā'ô	wayyāshuvû	'el-'erets	p^{e}lishtîm		wayyitta'	'ēshel
the head of his army	and they returned	to the land of	the Philistines		and he planted	tamarisk

904, 916	916	7410.121, 8427	904, 8428	3176	418	5986	34.	1513.121
prep, pn	pn	cj, v Qal impf 3ms, adv	prep, *n ms*	pn	n ms	adj		cj, v Qal impf 3ms
בִּבְאֵר	שָׁבַע	וַיִּקְרָא־שָׁם	בְּשֵׁם	יְהוָה	אֵל	עוֹלָם		וַיָּגָר
biv'ēr	shāva'	wayyiqŏrā'-shām	b^{e}shēm	y^{e}hwāh	'ēl	'ôlām		wayyāghār
in Beer	Sheba	and he called there	on the name of	Yahweh	God	Eternal		and he sojourned

80	904, 800	6674	3219	7521	22:1	2030.121	313	1745
pn	prep, *n fs*	pn	n mp	adj		cj, v Qal impf 3ms	adv	art, n mp
אַבְרָהָם	בְּאֶרֶץ	פְּלִשְׁתִּים	יָמִים	רַבִּים		וַיְהִי	אַחַר	הַדְּבָרִים
'avrāhām	b^{e}'erets	p^{e}lishtîm	yāmîm	rabbîm		wayhî	'achar	hadd^{e}vārîm
Abraham	in the land of	the Philistines	days	many		and it was	after	the matters

never gave me word of it, and I had no knowledge of it, *BB* ... you never mentioned it nor did I hear it from anyone else, *REB* ... even thou didst not declare to me, *Young* ... until this moment, *Anchor* ... until now, *NAB*.

27. And Abraham took sheep and oxen, and gave them unto Abimelech: ... presented sheep and cattle, *Berkeley* ... sheep and beeves, *Geneva*.

and both of them made a covenant: ... the two of them concluded a pact, *Anchor* ... made an agreement, *BB* ... entered into a treaty, *Fenton* ... as sacrifices to seal their pact, *LIVB*.

28. And Abraham set seven ewe lambs of the flock by themselves: ... from the flock, *Anchor, Berkeley* ... on one side, by themselves, *BB* ... apart, *RSV*.

29. And Abimelech said unto Abraham, What mean these seven ewe lambs which thou hast set by themselves: ... what about those, *MLB* ... which you have put on one side, *BB* ... the significance, *Goodspeed* ... what is the purpose, *NAB* ... why he had done so, *REB*.

30. And he said, For these seven ewe lambs shalt thou take of my hand: ... you will accept the seven ewe-lambs from me, *Anchor* ... they are my gift to you, *LIVB*.

that they may be a witness unto me, that I have digged this well: ... this well was dug by me, *Anchor* ... I have made this water-hole, *BB* ... that this well is mine, *LIVB*.

31. Wherefore he called that place Beersheba: ... this is why, *NAB* ... therefore named, *Berkeley* ... well of the oath, *Fenton*.

because there they sware both of them: ... meaning that two of them swore an oath, *Anchor*.

32. Thus they made a covenant at Beersheba: ... upon the conclusion of the pact, *Anchor* ... made an agreement, *BB* ... extend into a treaty at Bersabee, *NCB*.

then Abimelech rose up, and Phichol the chief captain of his host and they returned into the land of the Philistines: ... and his general, *Berkeley* ... commander of his army, *NCB* ... returned at once, *NEB* ... returned home again, *LIVB*.

33. And Abraham planted a grove in Beersheba: ... after planting a holy tree, *BB* ... they also planted Tamarisk trees, *Fenton* ... planted a stripe of ground, *NEB* ... planted a tamarisk tree, *NASB*.

and called there on the name of the LORD, the everlasting God: ... invoked the name of Yahweh, the eternal God, *Anchor* ... gave worship to the name of the Lord, *BB* ... Ever-living, *Fenton* ... and preacheth there, *Young*.

34. And Abraham sojourned in the Philistines' land many days: ... resided in Philistine country many years, *Anchor* ... lived as a stranger, many a day, *Berkeley* ... as in a strange country, *BB* ... a long season, *Geneva* ... as an alien, *NRSV*.

22:1. And it came to pass after these things, that God did tempt Abraham and said unto him, Abraham and he said, Behold,

---

21:28-30. In the dry area from Beersheba southward the rainfall is only about five inches a year, so water is important. Abraham wanted to be sure Abimelech's servants would not take away the good well he had dug, so he set aside seven female lambs as a witness that he dug the well. The special gift to Abimelech of these lambs was something unusual, so Abimelech asked what they meant.

21:31. Beersheba, 28 miles southwest of Hebron, can mean either "well of seven" or "well of [the] oath." As is often the case in the Bible a word or a name with two meanings is given because both are in mind. Thus, the name referred both to the seven lambs and to the oath the two men swore.

21:32. The territory of Abimelech is called the land of the Philistines here for the first time. The main body of the Philistines who established their cities in the south coastal plain of Canaan did not arrive until later.

It is probably that these earlier Philistines were Minoan merchants who established a trading colony in the area of Gerar. Abimelech was not as aggressive as the later Philistines, since he was willing to make this treaty and allow Abraham to live in his territory.

21:33-34. Abraham planted a tamarisk tree; a tree that is loaded with beautiful pink blossoms in the spring. This is still about the only tree that does well in the area of Beersheba. Then he called on the name of the LORD (*Yahweh*) and identified Him as the Eternal God. He thus declared that *Yahweh* is different from the gods of the pagans. The pagans believed the Ir gods were born at some point and could die. Abraham continued to call on the Eternal God there and lived a long time at Beersheba.

22:1-2. God tested Abraham's faith many times. It was a test to leave his homeland, to live among the Canaanites, to face famine, to separate from Lot, to have the birth of Isaac delayed 25 years after coming to Canaan, and to give up Ishmael.

431	435	5441.311	881, 80	569.121	420	80
art, dem pron	cj, art, n mp	v Piel pf 3ms	do, pn	cj, v Qal impf 3ms	prep, ps 3ms	pn
הָאֵלֶּה	וְהָאֱלֹהִים	נִסָּה	אֶת־אַבְרָהָם	וַיֹּאמֶר	אֵלָיו	אַבְרָהָם
hā'ēlleh	w^{e}hā'ĕlōhîm	nissāh	'eth-'avrāhām	wayyō'mer	'ēlâv	'avrāhām
the these	and God	He tested	Abraham	and He said	to him	Abraham

569.121	2079		569.121	4089.131, 5167	881, 1158	881, 3279
cj, v Qal impf 3ms	intrj, ps 1cs	**2.**	cj, v Qal impf 3ms	v Qal impv 2ms, part	do, n ms, ps 2ms	do, sub, ps 2ms
וַיֹּאמֶר	הִנֵּנִי		וַיֹּאמֶר	קַח־נָא	אֶת־בִּנְךָ	אֶת־יְחִידְךָ
wayyō'mer	hinnēnî		wayyō'mer	qach-nā'	'eth-bin^{e}khā	'eth-yechîdh^{e}khā
and he said	behold I		and He said	take please	your son	your only

866, 154.113	881, 3437	2050.131, 3937	420, 800	4974
rel part, v Qal pf 2ms	do, pn	cj, v Qal impv 2ms, prep, ps 2ms	prep, *n fs*	art, pn
אֲשֶׁר־אָהַבְתָּ	אֶת־יִצְחָק	וְלֶךְ־לְךָ	אֶל־אֶרֶץ	הַמֹּרִיָּה
'ăsher-'āhav^{e}tā	'eth-yitschāq	w^{e}lekh-l^{e}khā	'el-'erets	hammōriyyāh
whom you love	Isaac	and go for yourself	to the land of	the Moriah

6148.531	8427	3937, 6150	6142	259	2098	866
cj, v Hiphil impv 2ms, ps 3ms	adv	prep, n fs	prep	*num*	art, n mp	rel part
וְהַעֲלֵהוּ	שָׁם	לְעֹלָה	עַל	אַחַד	הֶהָרִים	אֲשֶׁר
w^{e}ha'ălēhû	shām	l^{e}'ōlāh	'al	'achadh	hehārîm	'ăsher
and cause him to go up	there	for burnt offering	on	one of	the mountains	which

569.125	420		8326.521	80	904, 1269	2372.121
v Qal impf 1cs	prep, ps 2ms	**3.**	cj, v Hiphil impf 3ms	pn	prep, art, n ms	cj, v Qal impf 3ms
אֹמַר	אֵלֶיךָ		וַיַּשְׁכֵּם	אַבְרָהָם	בַּבֹּקֶר	וַיַּחֲבֹשׁ
'ōmar	'ēlêkhā		wayyashkēm	'avrāhām	babbōqer	wayyachvōsh
I will say	to you		and he rose early	Abraham	in the morning	and he saddled

881, 2645	4089.121	881, 8530	5470	882	881	3437	1158
do, n ms, ps 3ms	cj, v Qal impf 3ms	do, *num*	n mp, ps 3ms	prep, ps 3ms	cj, do	pn	n ms, ps 3ms
אֶת־חֲמֹרוֹ	וַיִּקַּח	אֶת־שְׁנֵי	נְעָרָיו	אִתּוֹ	וְאֵת	יִצְחָק	בְּנוֹ
'eth-chămōrô	wayyiqqach	'eth-sh^{e}nê	n^{e}'ārâv	'ittô	w^{e}'ēth	yitschāq	b^{e}nô
his donkey	and he took	two of	his young men	with him	and	Isaac	his son

1260.321	6320	6150	7251.121	2050.121	420, 4887
cj, v Piel impf 3ms	*n mp*	n fs	cj, v Qal impf 3ms	cj, v Qal impf 3ms	prep, art, n ms
וַיְבַקַּע	עֲצֵי	עֹלָה	וַיָּקָם	וַיֵּלֶךְ	אֶל־הַמָּקוֹם
way^{e}vaqqa'	'ătsê	'ōlāh	wayyāqām	wayyēlekh	'el-hammāqôm
and he split	wood of	burnt offering	and he rose up	and he went	to the place

866, 569.111, 3937	435		904, 3219	8389	5558.121	80
rel part, v Qal pf 3ms, prep, ps 3ms	art, n mp	**4.**	prep, art, n ms	art, num	cj, v Qal impf 3ms	pn
אֲשֶׁר־אָמַר־לוֹ	הָאֱלֹהִים		בַּיּוֹם	הַשְּׁלִישִׁי	וַיִּשָּׂא	אַבְרָהָם
'ăsher-'āmar-lô	hā'ĕlōhîm		bayyôm	hashsh^{e}lîshî	wayyissā'	'avrāhām
where He said to him	God		on the day	the third	and he lifted up	Abraham

881, 6084	7495.121	881, 4887	4623, 7632		569.121	80
do, n fd, ps 3ms	cj, v Qal impf 3ms	do, art, n ms	prep, adj	**5.**	cj, v Qal impf 3ms	pn
אֶת־עֵינָיו	וַיַּרְא	אֶת־הַמָּקוֹם	מֵרָחֹק		וַיֹּאמֶר	אַבְרָהָם
'eth-'ênâv	wayyar^{e}'	'eth-hammāqôm	mērāchōq		wayyō'mer	'avrāhām
his eyes	and he saw	the place	from far		and he said	Abraham

420, 5470	3553.133, 3937	6553	6196, 2645	603	5470
prep, n mp, ps 3ms	v Qal impv 2mp, prep, ps 2mp	adv	prep, art, n ms	cj, pers pron	cj, art, n ms
אֶל־נְעָרָיו	שְׁבוּ־לָכֶם	פֹּה	עִם־הַחֲמוֹר	וַאֲנִי	וְהַנַּעַר
'el-n^{e}'ārâv	sh^{e}vû-lākhem	pōh	'im-hachmôr	wa'ănî	w^{e}hanna'ar
to his young men	stay by yourselves	here	with the donkey	and I	and the boy

here I am: ... some time afterwards, *Anchor* ... prove Abraham, *Geneva* ... tested, *KJVII* ... put Abraham to the test, *NCB* ... God tested Abraham's faith and obedience, *LIVB*.

2. And he said, Take now thy son, thine only son Isaac, whom thou lovest: ... take I pray thee, *Young* ... your peculiar one, *Fenton* ... your one and only, *REB* ... your beloved one, *Anchor* ... your dearly loved, *BB* ... whom you love so much, *LIVB*.

and get thee into the land of Moriah: ... betake yourself to the region of, *MLB* ... go for thyself, *Young* ... to the land of vision, *Fenton* ... district of Moria, *NCB*.

and offer him there for a burnt offering: ... sacrifice him there, *NIV* ... cause him to ascend there, *Young* ... offer him up, *Anchor* ... as a burnt sacrifice, *Berkeley* ... as a holocaust, *NAB*.

upon one of the mountains which I will tell thee of: ... on one of the heights, *REB* ... summits, *MLB* ... one of the hills, which I will point out, *Fenton* ... shall designate, *Goodspeed* ... I will tell you about, *NIV*.

3. And Abraham rose up early in the morning: ... early next morning, *Berkeley* ... when Abraham woke in the morning, *Fenton*.

and saddled his ass, and took two of his young men with him, and Isaac his son: ... made ready his ass, *BB* ... saddled his donkey and selected two young men, *Berkeley* ... two youths, *Fenton* ... two servants, *Geneva* ... two of his servant boys along with his son Isaac, *Anchor*.

and clave the wood for the burnt offering: ... having first slit some wood, *Anchor* ... when he had cut enough wood, *NIV* ... for a sacrifice, *Fenton* ... for the holocaust, *NCB*.

and rose up, and went unto the place of which God had told him: ... to the location, *Berkeley* ... place in the distance, *NRSV* ... God had indicated, *Anchor* ... God had given him word, *BB* ... for the sanctuary God had designated, *Goodspeed*.

4. Then on the third day Abraham lifted up his eyes and saw the place afar off: ... in the distance saw the place, *Darby* ... a long way off, *BB* ... looked up, *MLB* ... saw the shrine, *REB* ... sighted the place from afar, *Anchor*.

5. And Abraham said unto his young men, Abide ye here with the ass: ... you stay here, *KJVII* ... stay here yourselves with the donkey, *Berkeley* ... keep here, *BB* ... to his attendants, *Fenton* ... to his servants, *Goodspeed*.

and I and the lad will go yonder and worship: ... I and the child, *Geneva* ... I and the youth, *Young* ... go on and give worship, *BB* ... to

---

All of these tests led up to the hardest test of all, a test that would reveal what God had done in Abraham. God struck right at Abraham's heart as he asked for his son, his "only" son, whom he loved and who had brought joy as the one fulfilling the promise. "Only" means only in the sense of unique, one-of-kind, and special. Isaac was Abraham's only hope for the fulfillment of God's salvation-promise. Hebrews 11:17 refers to this by the Greek word *monogenes*, the same word used of Jesus in John 3:16. Isaac representing Abraham's "only" son whom he loved thus became a type of God's "only" Son who is also called His "beloved" Son (Matt. 3:17).

Abraham was asked to sacrifice him as a burnt offering on a mountain in the land of Moriah that God would tell him of when he arrived. The land or region of Moriah was the area around Jerusalem (2 Chron. 3:1). The burnt offering is literally "an ascent," because it went up completely in smoke as a type or illustration of complete surrender to God and complete exaltation of Him. Abraham, of course, had no written Scriptures.

The Canaanites believed that the greatest way they could please a god was to offer a firstborn son as a sacrifice to the god. Abraham did not know the one true God did not want human sacrifices. So the test was very real.

22:3-4. Abraham did not consult with anyone about this. He simply obeyed God, trusting Him (like the psalmist in Ps. 119:60). The very next morning he took his donkey, two personal servants, and Isaac.

After cutting the wood for the burnt offering, they started for the land of Moriah, about 50 miles away. On the third day, Abraham saw the place in the distance God told him of. The mountains around Jerusalem come into view clearly at a distance of about 3 miles.

22:5. It took faith for Abraham to tell the servants that he and Isaac would go and worship and would come back to them.

22:6. It is interesting that just as God's Son bore a wooden cross on his back on the way to his death, so Isaac, the son of promise, bore the wood for his impending sacrifice. Isaac was probably about 20 years old at this time. Abraham carried a large knife and a container full of live coals.

2050.120	5912, 3662	8246.720	8178.120	420		4089.121
v Qal impf 1cp	prep, adv	cj, v Hithpalpel impf 1cp	cj, v Qal impf 1cp	prep, ps 2mp	**6.**	cj, v Qal impf 3ms
נֵלְכָה	עַד־כֹּה	וְנִשְׁתַּחֲוֶה	וְנָשׁוּבָה	אֲלֵיכֶם		וַיִּקַּח
nēl^{e}khāh	ʻadh-kōh	w^{e}nishtachweh	w^{e}nāshûvāh	ʼălêkhem		wayyiqqach
we will go	until so	and we will worship	then we will return	to you		and he took

80	881, 6320	6150	7947.121	6142, 3437	1158	4089.121
pn	do, *n mp*	art, n fs	cj, v Qal impf 3ms	prep, pn	n ms, ps 3ms	cj, v Qal impf 3ms
אַבְרָהָם	אֶת־עֲצֵי	הָעֹלָה	וַיָּשֶׂם	עַל־יִצְחָק	בְּנוֹ	וַיִּקַּח
ʼavrāhām	ʼeth-ʻătsê	hāʻōlāh	wayyāsem	ʻal-yitschāq	b^{e}nô	wayyiqqach
Abraham	the wood of	the burnt offering	and he put	on Isaac	his son	and he took

904, 3135	881, 813	881, 4121	2050.126	8530	3267
prep, n fs, ps 3ms	do, art, n fs	cj, do, art, n fs	cj, v Qal impf 3mp	num, ps 3mp	adv
בְּיָדוֹ	אֶת־הָאֵשׁ	וְאֶת־הַמַּאֲכֶלֶת	וַיֵּלְכוּ	שְׁנֵיהֶם	יַחְדָּו
b^{e}yādhô	ʼeth-hāʼēsh	w^{e}ʼeth-hammaʼăkheleth	wayyēl^{e}khû	sh^{e}nêhem	yachdāw
in his hand	the fire	and the knife	and they walked	the two of them	together

	569.121	3437	420, 80	1	569.121	1	569.121
7.	cj, v Qal impf 3ms	pn	prep, pn	n ms, ps	cj, v Qal impf 3ms	n ms, ps 1cs	cj, v Qal impf 3ms
	וַיֹּאמֶר	יִצְחָק	אֶל־אַבְרָהָם	אָבִיו	וַיֹּאמֶר	אָבִי	וַיֹּאמֶר
	wayyōʼmer	yitschāq	ʼel-ʼavrāhām	ʼāvîw	wayyōʼmer	ʼāvî	wayyōʼmer
	and he said	Isaac	to Abraham	his father	and he said	my father	and he said

2079	1158	569.121	2079	813	6320	347	7902
intrj, ps 1cs	n ms, ps 1cs	cj, v Qal impf 3ms	intrj	art, n fs	cj, art, n mp	cj, adv	art, n ms
הִנֶּנִּי	בְּנִי	וַיֹּאמֶר	הִנֵּה	הָאֵשׁ	וְהָעֵצִים	וְאַיֵּה	הַשֶּׂה
hinnennî	v^{e}nî	wayyōʼmer	hinnēh	hāʼēsh	w^{e}hāʻētsîm	w^{e}ʼayyēh	hasseh
behold I	my son	and he said	behold	the fire	and the wood	but where	the lamb

3937, 6150		569.121	80	435	7495.121, 3937	7902
prep, n fs	**8.**	cj, v Qal impf 3ms	pn	n mp	v Qal impf 3ms, prep, ps 3ms	art, n ms
לְעֹלָה		וַיֹּאמֶר	אַבְרָהָם	אֱלֹהִים	יִרְאֶה־לּוֹ	הַשֶּׂה
l^{e}ʻōlāh		wayyōʼmer	ʼavrāhām	ʼĕlōhîm	yirʼeh-lô	hasseh
for burnt offering		and he said	Abraham	God	He will provide for himself	the lamb

3937, 6150	1158	2050.126	8530	3267		971.126
prep, n fs	n ms, ps 1cs	cj, v Qal impf 3mp	num, ps 3mp	adv	**9.**	cj, v Qal impf 3mp
לְעֹלָה	בְּנִי	וַיֵּלְכוּ	שְׁנֵיהֶם	יַחְדָּו		וַיָּבֹאוּ
l^{e}ʻōlāh	b^{e}nî	wayyēl^{e}khû	sh^{e}nêhem	yachdāw		wayyāvōʼû
for burnt offering	my son	and they walked	the two of them	together		and they went

420, 4887	866	569.111, 3937	435	1161.121	8427	80
prep, art, n ms	rel part	v Qal pf 3ms, prep, ps 3ms	art, n mp	cj, v Qal impf 3ms	adv	pn
אֶל־הַמָּקוֹם	אֲשֶׁר	אָמַר־לוֹ	הָאֱלֹהִים	וַיִּבֶן	שָׁם	אַבְרָהָם
ʼel-hammāqôm	ʼăsher	ʼāmar-lô	hāʼĕlōhîm	wayyiven	shām	ʼavrāhām
to the place	where	he said to him	God	and he built	there	Abraham

881, 4326	6424.121	881, 6320	6361.121	881, 3437	1158
do, art, n ms	cj, v Qal impf 3ms	do, art, n mp	cj, v Qal impf 3ms	do, pn	n ms, ps 3ms
אֶת־הַמִּזְבֵּחַ	וַיַּעֲרֹךְ	אֶת־הָעֵצִים	וַיַּעֲקֹד	אֶת־יִצְחָק	בְּנוֹ
ʼeth-hammizbēach	wayyaʻărōkh	ʼeth-hāētsîm	wayyaʻăqōdh	ʼeth-yitschāq	b^{e}nô
the altar	and he laid in order	the wood	and he bound	Isaac	his son

7947.121	881	6142, 4326	4623, 4762	3937, 6320		8365.121
cj, v Qal impf 3ms	do, ps 3ms	prep, art, n ms	prep, prep	prep, art, n mp	**10.**	cj, v Qal impf 3ms
וַיָּשֶׂם	אֹתוֹ	עַל־הַמִּזְבֵּחַ	מִמַּעַל	לָעֵצִים		וַיִּשְׁלַח
wayyāsem	ʼōthô	ʻal-hammizbēach	mimmaʻal	lāʻētsîm		wayyishlach
and he put	him	on the altar	upon	the wood		and he put out

perform our devotion, *Goodspeed* ... and where we have worshipped, *NEB*.

and come again to you: ... come back, *Anchor* ... turn back, *Young*.

6. And Abraham took the wood of the burnt offering: ... accordingly took the wood for the sacrifice, *Fenton* ... placed the wood, *LIVB* ... for the holocaust, *NAB*.

and laid it upon Isaac his son: ... on his son's back, *BB* ... shoulders, *NAB* ... Abraham made Isaac carry the wood, *Good News*.

and he took the fire in his hand, and a knife: ... live coals, *Good News* ... the firestone and the cleaver he carried, *Anchor* ... torch and a knife, *MLB* ... the knife and the flint for striking a fire, *LIVB*.

and they went both of them together: ... the two walked off, *Anchor* ... went on, *BB* ... walked along, *Good News*.

7. And Isaac spake unto Abraham his father: ... Isaac broke the silence, *Anchor*.

and said, My father: and he said, Here am I, my son: ... yes, my son, *Goodspeed* ... what is it, my son, *REB*.

And he said, Behold the fire and the wood: ... there is the firestone and the wood, *Anchor* ... we have wood and fire here, *BB*.

but where is the lamb for a burnt offering: ... where is the sheep, *Anchor* ... where is the young beast for the sacrifice, *NEB*.

8. And Abraham said, My son, God will provide himself a lamb for a burnt offering: ... God will see to the sheep, *Anchor* ... God will see to it my son, *LIVB*.

so they went both of them together: ... walked on, together, *Berkeley* ... proceeded on their way, together, *Goodspeed* ... continued going forward, *NAB*.

9. And they came to the place which God had told him of: ... the spot of which God had told him, *Berkeley* ... sanctuary designated to him, *Goodspeed* ... spoken of, *Anchor* ... given him knowledge, *BB* ... commanded him, *Fenton*.

and Abraham built an altar there, and laid the wood in order: ... laid out the wood, *Anchor* ... arranged, *Fenton* ... piled, *Darby* ... put the wood in place, *BB* ... couched the wood, *Geneva*.

and bound Isaac his son: ... tied up his son, *NAB* ... having made tight the bands round Isaac, *BB*.

and laid him on the altar upon the wood: ... on top of the wood, *Fenton* ... above the wood, *Young*.

10. And Abraham stretched forth his hand: ... put out his hand, *Anchor* ... reached out, *Berkeley*.

and took the knife to slay his son: ... to slaughter his son, *Darby* ... put his son to death, *BB* ... to kill, *Geneva* ... to plunge it into his son, *LIVB*.

11. And the angel of the LORD called unto him out of heaven: ... angel of Jehovah, *ASV* ... the Lord's messenger, *NAB* ... but at that moment, the angel of God shouted to him, *LIVB* ... from the heavens, *Darby* ... from the skies, *Fenton*.

and said, Abraham, Abraham: and he said, Here am I: ... yes, Lord, *NAB*.

22:7-8. Isaac saw something was missing. There was no lamb for the burnt offering. As far as Abraham knew at that point, Isaac was to be the "lamb." But he emphatically answered that God himself would see to (look out for, provide) the lamb. The sacrificial lamb would be God's choice.

22:9. When they reached the top of the mountain (possibly what was later the temple hill, or the hill just to the north now known as Gordon's Calvary) Abraham built an altar, using field stones which were plentiful there, and still are plentiful in that land. Then he arranged the wood on the altar, tied up Isaac, and laid him on the wood.

He must have explained God's command to Isaac; Isaac must have submitted with faith in God and confidence in his father. A 20-year-old young man surely could have resisted a 120-year-old father if he wanted to. In his submission to Abraham, he was like Jesus who "committed [gave, entrusted] himself to him that judgeth righteously" (1 Pet. 2:23).

22:10. When Abraham took the knife and raised it, he expected to plunge it into the heart of Isaac, set fire to the wood and see Isaac reduced to a pile of ashes. But he also believed that out of the pile of ashes God would raise up Isaac, for God had promised to establish His covenant with Isaac (17:19) and had said, "in Isaac shall thy seed be called" (21:12). This truly was resurrection faith (Heb. 11:19).

22:11-12. When Abraham took the knife his surrender was complete. God had all of Abraham's heart. His faith and consecration had been demonstrated in a new way, and the angel of the LORD

80	881, 3135	4089.121	881, 4121	3937, 8250.141	881, 1158
pn	do, n fs, ps 3ms	cj, v Qal impf 3ms	do, art, n fs	prep, v Qal inf con	do, n ms, ps 3ms
אַבְרָהָם	אֶת־יָדוֹ	וַיִּקַּח	אֶת־הַמַּאֲכֶלֶת	לִשְׁחֹט	אֶת־בְּנוֹ
'avrāhām	'eth-yādhô	wayyiqqach	'eth-hamma'ăkheleth	lishchōṯ	'eth-b^{e}nô
Abraham	his hand	and he took	the knife	to slaughter	his son

	7410.121	420	4534	3176	4623, 8452	569.121
11.	cj, v Qal impf 3ms	prep, ps 3ms	*n ms*	pn	prep, art, n mp	cj, v Qal impf 3ms
	וַיִּקְרָא	אֵלָיו	מַלְאַךְ	יְהוָה	מִן־הַשָּׁמַיִם	וַיֹּאמֶר
	wayyiqŏrā'	'ēlâv	mal'akh	y^{e}hwāh	min-hashshāmayim	wayyō'mer
	and He called	to him	the angel of	Yahweh	from the heavens	and He said

80	80	569.121	2079		569.121	414, 8365.123
pn	pn	cj, v Qal impf 3ms	intrj, ps 1cs	**12.**	cj, v Qal impf 3ms	adv, v Qal impf 2ms
אַבְרָהָם	אַבְרָהָם	וַיֹּאמֶר	הִנֵּנִי		וַיֹּאמֶר	אַל־תִּשְׁלַח
'avrāhām	'avrāhām	wayyō'mer	hinnēnî		wayyō'mer	'al-tishlach
Abraham	Abraham	and he said	behold I		and He said	not you will put out

3135	420, 5470	414, 6449.123	3937	4114	3706	6498	3156.115
n fs, ps 2ms	prep, art, n ms	cj, adv, v Qal impf 2ms	prep, ps 3ms	indef pron	cj	adv	v Qal pf 1cs
יָדְךָ	אֶל־הַנַּעַר	וְאַל־תַּעַשׂ	לוֹ	מְאוּמָּה	כִּי	עַתָּה	יָדַעְתִּי
yadh^{e}khā	'el-hanna'ar	w^e'al-ta'as	lô	m^e'ûmmāh	kî	'attāh	yādha'ättî
your hand	to the boy	and not you will do	to him	anything	because	now	I know

3706, 3486.151	435	887	3940	2910.113	881, 1158	881, 3279
cj, *v Qal act ptc ms*	n mp	pers pron	cj, neg part	v Qal pf 2ms	do, n ms, ps 2ms	do, adj, ps 2ms
כִּי־יְרֵא	אֱלֹהִים	אַתָּה	וְלֹא	חָשַׂכְתָּ	אֶת־בִּנְךָ	אֶת־יְחִידְךָ
kî-y^{e}rē'	'ĕlōhîm	'attāh	w^{e}lō'	chāsakhtā	'eth-bin^{e}khā	'eth-yechîdh^{e}khā
that one who fears	God	you	and not	you have withheld	your son	your only

4623		5558.121	80	881, 6084	7495.121	2079, 356
prep, ps 1cs	**13.**	cj, v Qal impf 3ms	pn	do, n fd, ps 3ms	cj, v Qal impf 3ms	cj, intrj, n ms
מִמֶּנִּי		וַיִּשָּׂא	אַבְרָהָם	אֶת־עֵינָיו	וַיַּרְא	וְהִנֵּה־אַיִל
mimmennî		wayyissā'	'avrāhām	'eth-'ênâv	wayyar'	w^{e}hinnēh-'ayil
from Me		and he lifted up	Abraham	his eyes	and he saw	and behold ram

313	270.255	904, 5625	904, 7451	2050.121	80	4089.121
adv	v Niphal ptc ms	prep, art, n ms	prep, n fd, ps 3ms	cj, v Qal impf 3ms	pn	cj, v Qal impf 3ms
אַחַר	נֶאֱחַז	בַּסְּבַךְ	בְּקַרְנָיו	וַיֵּלֶךְ	אַבְרָהָם	וַיִּקַּח
'achar	ne'ĕchaz	bass^{e}vakh	b^{e}qarnâv	wayyēlekh	'avrāhām	wayyiqqach
behind	being caught	in the thicket	by his horns	and he went	Abraham	and he took

881, 356	6148.521	3937, 6150	8809	1158
do, art, n ms	cj, v Hiphil impf 3ms, ps 3ms	prep, n fs	prep	n ms, ps 3ms
אֶת־הָאַיִל	וַיַּעֲלֵהוּ	לְעֹלָה	תַּחַת	בְּנוֹ
'eth-hā'ayil	wayya'ălēhû	l^e'ōlāh	tachath	b^{e}nô
the ram	and he caused it to go up	for burnt offering	instead of	his son

	7410.121	80	8428, 4887	2000	3176	7495.121	866
14.	cj, v Qal impf 3ms	pn	*n ms*, art, n ms	art, dem pron	pn	v Qal impf 3ms	rel part
	וַיִּקְרָא	אַבְרָהָם	שֵׁם־הַמָּקוֹם	הַהוּא	יְהוָה	יִרְאֶה	אֲשֶׁר
	wayyiqŏrā'	'avrāhām	shēm-hammāqôm	hahû'	y^{e}hwāh	yir'eh	'ăsher
	and he called	Abraham	the name of the place	the that	Yahweh	He will see	which

569.221	3219	904, 2098	3176	7495.221		7410.121	4534
v Niphal impf 3ms	art, n ms	prep, *n ms*	pn	v Niphal impf 3ms	**15.**	cj, v Qal impf 3ms	*n ms*
יֵאָמֵר	הַיּוֹם	בְּהַר	יְהוָה	יֵרָאֶה		וַיִּקְרָא	מַלְאַךְ
yē'āmēr	hayyôm	b^{e}har	y^{e}hwāh	yērā'eh		wayyiqŏrā'	mal'akh
it is said	today	on the mountain of	Yahweh	He provided		and He called	the angel of

12. And he said, Lay not thine hand upon the lad: ... do not lay hands, *Goodspeed* ... against the lad, *Darby* ... against the young man, *Fenton* ... put not forth thy hand unto the youth, *Young*.

neither do thou any thing unto him: ... nor do the least thing to him, *NAB* ... nor do to him what you intended, *Fenton* ... do nothing of the sort, *Goodspeed* ... do not touch him, *NEB* ... don't hurt the lad in any way, *LIVB*.

for now I know that thou fearest God: ... now I know how dedicated you are to God, *Anchor* ... I know that you revere God, *Berkeley* ... I am certain that the fear of God is in your heart, *BB* ... you are a God-fearing man, *NEB* ... God is first in your life, *LIVB*.

seeing thou hast not withheld thy son, thine only son from me: ... not held back your only one, *MLB* ... kept back your special one, *Fenton* ... spared, *Geneva* ... your own beloved son, *Anchor*.

13. And Abraham lifted up his eyes, and looked and behold behind him: ... as Abraham looked up, his eye fell upon, *Anchor* ... Abraham raised his eyes, and there behind him, *Berkeley* ... as Abraham looked about, he spied, *NCB* ... looked around, *REB* ... Abraham noticed, *LIVB*.

a ram caught in a thicket by his horns: ... a ram snagged, *Anchor* ... entangled, *Berkeley* ... a sheep fixed in the brushwood, *BB* ... a goat caught in a bush, *Fenton* ... seized in a thicket, *Young*.

and Abraham went and took the ram: ... took the sheep, *BB* ... took the goat, *Fenton* ... seized the ram, *REB*.

and offered him up for a burnt offering: ... causeth it to ascend, *Young* ... offered it for a sacrifice, *Berkeley* ... as a holocaust, *NAB*.

in the stead of his son: ... in place of, *BB* ... on the altar, *LIVB*.

14. And Abraham called the name of that place Jehovah-jireh: ... named that site Yahweh-Yireh, *Anchor* ... that sanctuary, *Goodspeed* ... the Lord will provide, *NKJV* ... named that shrine, *REB*.

as it is said to this day: ... hence the present saying, *Anchor* ... so that, to this day, it is said, *Berkeley* ... today interpreted, *Goodspeed* ... and it still goes by that name, *LIVB*.

In the mount of the LORD it shall be seen: ... on Yahweh's mountain there is vision, *Anchor* ... in the mountain, the Lord is seen, *BB* ... at the hill of the Lord, *Goodspeed* ... the Lord will see, *NAB* ... provision shall be made, *NCB*.

15. And the angel of the LORD called unto Abraham out of heaven the second time: ... Yahweh's Angel, *Anchor* ... Angel of Jehovah, *Darby* ... the messenger of the Ever-living, *Fenton* ... from the heavens, *Young*.

16. And said, By myself have I

---

stopped him with an urgent call. God set his seal of approval once more on Abraham's faith and marked him out as a man who truly feared God with a reverential awe. He would return to God the love and confidence God showed him and entrusted to him. God chose Abraham to do a work for Him. Abraham chose God as the One he would serve and obey.

22:13. Isaac, though he was a good and obedient son, could not have died in place of anyone else. Isaac was still a sinner, as all of us are (Rom. 3:23), and he could only have died for his own sins. Thus, God provided a ram to be offered in Isaac's place.

This added a picture of substitutionary sacrifice which meant the saving of Isaac's life. It also made the experience a more complete type of the sufferings, atoning death and resurrection of Jesus. Isaac was *a* promised son. Jesus is *the* promised Son. God the Father gave Him willingly out of a loving heart that was broken for our sins (John 3:16; see also how this idea of God's broken heart is developed in the book of Hosea.

22:14. When Abraham called that place "Jehovah-jireh," (Heb. *Yahweh Yireh*; Jehovah is a non-biblical name made up of the Latin consonant of *Yahweh* combined with the vowels taken from the Hebrew word for LORD. The Latin used a "j" for a consonantal "y") "The LORD will see to [and provide]," he showed he understood something of God's plan of redemption. God would see the need of sinners and provide a substitute who would die the death we deserve. This was one of the times, surely a most significant time, that Abraham saw Christ's day and was glad (John 8:56). This test drew him closer to God and made him appreciate God's promises more than ever. Tests can drive us away from God or cause us to draw near to Him.

22:15-18. Again Abraham heard the voice of the Angel of the LORD who told him that the LORD had sworn by himself that because Abraham had not withheld his only son, God would indeed keep the promise He had made concerning His blessing on Abraham's descendants and their victories that would enable them to possess the "gate" of their

3176	420, 80	8529	4623, 8452		569.121	904
pn	prep, pn	num	prep, art, n md	16.	cj, v Qal impf 3ms	prep, ps 1cs
יְהוָה	אֶל־אַבְרָהָם	שֵׁנִית	מִן־הַשָּׁמָיִם		וַיֹּאמֶר	בִּי
y^{e}hwāh	'el-'avrāhām	shēnîth	min-hashshāmāyim		wayyō'mer	bî
Yahweh	to Abraham	second	from the heavens		and He said	by myself

8123.215	5177, 3156	3706	3391	866	6449.113	881, 1745	2172
v Niphal pf 1cs	*n ms*, pn	cj	cj	rel part	v Qal pf 2ms	do, art, n ms	art, dem pron
נִשְׁבַּעְתִּי	נְאֻם־יְהוָה	כִּי	יַעַן	אֲשֶׁר	עָשִׂיתָ	אֶת־הַדָּבָר	הַזֶּה
nishba'ättî	n^{e}'um-y^{e}hwāh	kî	ya'an	'ăsher	'āsîthā	'eth-haddāvār	hazzeh
I have sworn	declaration of Yahweh	for	because	which	you did	the thing	the this

3940	2910.113	881, 1158	881, 3279		3706, 1313.342	1313.325
cj, neg part	v Qal pf 2ms	do, n ms, ps 2ms	do, adj, ps 2ms	17.	cj, v Piel inf abs	v Piel impf 1cs, ps 2ms
וְלֹא	חָשַׂכְתָּ	אֶת־בִּנְךָ	אֶת־יְחִידְךָ		כִּי־בָרֵךְ	אֲבָרֶכְךָ
w^{e}lō'	chāsakhtā	'eth-binkhā	'eth-y^{e}chîdekhā		kî-vārēkh	'ăvārekh^{e}khā
and not	you have withheld	your son	your only		because blessing	I will bless you

7528.542	7528.525	881, 2320	3626, 3676	8452	3626, 2437	866
cj, v Hiphil inf abs	v Hiphil impf 1cs	do, n ms, ps 2ms	prep, *n mp*	art, n md	cj, prep, n ms	rel part
וְהַרְבָּה	אַרְבֶּה	אֶת־זַרְעֲךָ	כְּכוֹכְבֵי	הַשָּׁמַיִם	וְכַחוֹל	אֲשֶׁר
w^{e}harbāh	'arbeh	'eth-zar'ăkhā	kh^{e}khôkh^{e}vê	hashshāmayim	w^{e}khachôl	'ăsher
and multiplying	I will multiply	your seed	like the stars of	the heavens	and like the sand	which

6142, 8004	3328	3542.121	2320	881	8554	342.152
prep, *n fs*	art, n ms	cj, v Qal impf 3ms	n ms, ps 2ms	do	*n ms*	v Qal act ptc mp, ps 3ms
עַל־שְׂפַת	הַיָּם	וְיִרַשׁ	זַרְעֲךָ	אֵת	שַׁעַר	אֹיְבָיו
'al-s^{e}phath	hayyām	w^{e}yirash	zar'ăkhā	'ēth	sha'ar	'ōy^{e}vâv
on shore of	the sea	and he will take possession of	your seed		the gate of	his enemies

	1313.716	904, 2320	3725	1504	800	6358	866
18.	cj, v Hithpael pf 3cp	prep, n ms, ps 2ms	adj	*n mp*	art, n fs	cj	rel part
	וְהִתְבָּרְכוּ	בְזַרְעֲךָ	כֹּל	גּוֹיֵי	הָאָרֶץ	עֵקֶב	אֲשֶׁר
	w^{e}hithbār^{e}khû	b^{e}zar'ăkhā	kōl	gôyê	hā'ārets	'ēqev	'ăsher
	and they will be blessed	by your seed	all	the nations of	the earth	because	that

8471.113	904, 7249		8178.121	80	420, 5470	7251.126
v Qal pf 2ms	prep, n ms, ps 1cs	19.	cj, v Qal impf 3ms	pn	prep, n mp, ps 3ms	cj, v Qal impf 3mp
שָׁמַעְתָּ	בְּקֹלִי		וַיָּשָׁב	אַבְרָהָם	אֶל־נְעָרָיו	וַיָּקֻמוּ
shāma'ättā	b^{e}qōlî		wayyāshāv	'avrāhām	'el-n^{e}'ārāv	wayyāqumû
you listened	by my voice		and he returned	Abraham	to his young men	and they rose up

2050.126	3267	420, 916	916	3553.121	80	904, 916	916
cj, v Qal impf 3mp	adv	prep, pn	pn	cj, v Qal impf 3ms	pn	prep, pn	pn
וַיֵּלְכוּ	יַחְדָּו	אֶל־בְּאֵר	שָׁבַע	וַיֵּשֶׁב	אַבְרָהָם	בִּבְאֵר	שָׁבַע
wayyēl^{e}khû	yachdāw	'el-b^{e}'ēr	shāva'	wayyēshev	'avrāhām	biv'ēr	shāva'
and they walked	together	to Beer	Sheba	and he dwelled	Abraham	in Beer	Sheba

	2030.121	311	1745	431	5222.621	3937, 80
20.	cj, v Qal impf 3ms	sub	art, n mp	art, dem pron	cj, v Hophal impf 3ms	prep, pn
	וַיְהִי	אַחֲרֵי	הַדְּבָרִים	הָאֵלֶּה	וַיֻּגַּד	לְאַבְרָהָם
	wayhî	'achrê	hadd^{e}värîm	hā'ēlleh	wayyuggadh	l^{e}'avrāhām
	and it was	after	the matters	the these	and it was told	to Abraham

3937, 569.141	2079	3314.112	4575	1612, 2026	1158	3937, 5331	250
prep, v Qal inf con	intrj	v Qal pf 3fs	pn	cj, pers pron	n mp	prep, pn	n ms, ps 2ms
לֵאמֹר	הִנֵּה	יָלְדָה	מִלְכָּה	גַם־הִוא	בָּנִים	לְנָחוֹר	אָחִיךָ
lē'mōr	hinnēh	yāl^{e}dhāh	milkāh	gham-hiw'	bānîm	l^{e}nāchôr	'āchîkh
saying	behold	she gave birth	Milcah	also she	sons	to Nahor	your brother

21.

881, 5995	1111	881, 974	250	881, 7340	1	782
do, pn	n ms, ps 3ms	cj, do, pn	n ms, ps 3ms	cj, do, pn	n ms	pn
אֶת־עוּץ	בְּכֹרוֹ	וְאֶת־בּוּז	אָחִיו	וְאֶת־קְמוּאֵל	אֲבִי	אֲרָם
'eth-'ûts	b^{e}khōrô	w^{e}'eth-bûz	'āchîw	w^{e}'eth-qᵒmû'ēl	'ăvî	'ărām
Uz	his firstborn	and Buz	his brother	and Kemuel	the father of	Aram

22.

881, 3906	881, 2467	881, 6639	881, 3155	881	1357	**23.** 1357
cj, do, pn	cj, do, pn	cj, do, pn	cj, do, pn	cj, do	pn	cj, pn
וְאֶת־כֶּשֶׂד	וְאֶת־חֲזוֹ	וְאֶת־פִּלְדָּשׁ	וְאֶת־יִדְלָף	וְאֵת	בְּתוּאֵל	וּבְתוּאֵל
w^{e}'eth-kesedh	w^{e}'eth-chăzô	w^{e}'eth-pildāsh	w^{e}'eth-yidhlāph	w^{e}ēth	b^{e}thû'ēl	ûv^{e}thû'ēl
and Chesed	and Hazo	and Pildash	and Jidlaph	and	Bethuel	and Bethuel

3314.111	881, 7549	8470	431	3314.112	4575	3937, 5331	250
v Qal pf 3ms	do, pn	num	dem pron	v Qal pf 3fs	pn	prep, pn	*n ms*
יָלַד	אֶת־רִבְקָה	שְׁמֹנָה	אֵלֶּה	יָלְדָה	מִלְכָּה	לְנָחוֹר	אֲחִי
yāladh	'eth-rivqāh	sh^{e}mōnāh	'ēlleh	yāldhāh	milkāh	l^{e}nāchôr	'ăchî
he fathered	Rebekah	eight	these	she gave birth	Milcah	to Nahor	the brother of

sworn, saith the LORD for because thou hast done this thing: ... I have taken an oath by my name, *BB* ... because you have obeyed me, *LIVB.*

and hast not withheld thy son, thine only son: ... did not withhold your beloved son from me, *Anchor* ... have not held back your only one, *Berkeley* ... your dearly loved, *BB* ... your special son, *Fenton* ... not spared, *Geneva.*

17. That in blessing I will bless thee: ... I will therefore, bestow my blessing upon you, *Anchor* ... I will bless you beyond words, *MLB* ... I will richly bless thee, *Darby* ... certainly give you my blessing, *BB.*

and in multiplying I will multiply thy seed: ... will greatly multiply, *Berkeley* ... descendants, *NKJV.*

as the stars of the heaven: ... numerous as, *Anchor* ... so as to compare with, *MLB* ... as countless, *NAB.*

and as the sand which is upon the sea shore and thy seed shall possess the gate of his enemies: ... shall take over, *Anchor* ... take the land of those against them, *BB* ... take possession of the cities, *Goodspeed.*

18. And in thy seed shall all the nations of the earth be blessed because thou hast obeyed my voice: ... shall bless themselves, *Darby* ... will be a blessing, *BB* ... I will benefit all, *Fenton* ... shall invoke blessings on one another, *Goodspeed* ... wish to be blessed as your descendants, *REB.*

19. So Abraham returned unto his young men and they rose up and went together to Beersheba and Abraham dwelt at Beersheba: ... and they left together, *Anchor* ... where Abraham made his home, *Berkeley* ... lived at, *KJVII* ... remained, *REB.*

20. And it came to pass after these things that it was told Abraham: ... word reached Abraham, *Anchor* ... this news came to, *MLB* ... a message was delivered, *Fenton.*

saying, Behold, Milcah, she hath also born children unto thy brother Nahor: ... the wife of his brother, Nahor, *BB* ... your sister, *Fenton* ... Milcah is also a mother, *NIV.*

21. Huz his firstborn, and Buz his brother, and Kemuel the father of Aram: ... Kemuel the ancestor of the Aramians, *Goodspeed.*

22. And Chesed, and Hazo, and Pildash, and Jidlaph, and Bethuel:

enemies (that is, their cities). Then, through one of his offspring, salvation-blessing would come to all the nations of the earth. (Though a different form of the verb for bless is used, the meaning is still "be blessed," not "bless themselves," as some would take it. See Acts 3:25; Gal. 3:8.) Hebrews 6:13-18 shows God's oath and God's promise are two unchangeable things in which God it is impossible for God to lie. This gives us a hope as well, a hope that is an anchor for the soul (Heb. 6:19).

22:19. Abraham returned with Isaac as he believed he would. How his heart must have rejoiced as he returned to Beersheba with his faith in God vindicated and Isaac by his side. Abraham then made his home in Beersheba and probably spent most of his old age there. From time to time, however, he may have visited Mamre, near Hebron, where he had stayed earlier.

22:20-24. Abraham's brother Nahor must have heard where Abraham was and sent the news that his wife had eight sons and his concubine four more. Significantly, a son, Bethuel, is mentioned as

80		6637	8428	7501	3314.122	1612, 2000
pn	24.	cj, n fs, ps 3ms	cj, n ms, ps 3fs	pn	cj, v Qal impf 3fs	cj, pers pron
אַבְרָהָם		וּפִילַגְשׁוֹ	וּשְׁמָהּ	רְאוּמָה	וַתֵּלֶד	גַּם־הוּא
'avrāhām		ûphîlaghshô	ûshmāhh	re'ûmāh	wattēledh	gam-hiw'
Abraham		and his concubine	and her name	Reumah	and she gave birth	also she

881, 2985	881, 1545	881, 8808	881, 4757		2030.126	2508	8023
do, pn	cj, do, pn	cj, do, pn	cj, do, pn	23:1	cj, v Qal impf 3mp	*n mp*	pn
אֶת־טֶבַח	וְאֶת־גַּחַם	וְאֶת־תַּחַשׁ	וְאֶת־מַעֲכָה		וַיִּהְיוּ	חַיֵּי	שָׂרָה
'eth-ṯevach	we'eth-gacham	we'eth-tachash	we'eth-ma'ăkhāh		wayyihyû	chayyê	sārāh
Tebah	and Gaham	and Tahash	and Maacah		and it was	the life of	Sarah

4109	8523	6465	8523	8124	8523	8523	2508	8023
num	n fs	cj, num	n fs	cj, num	n fp	n fp	*n mp*	pn
מֵאָה	שָׁנָה	וְעֶשְׂרִים	שָׁנָה	וְשֶׁבַע	שָׁנִים	שְׁנֵי	חַיֵּי	שָׂרָה
mē'āh	shānāh	we'esrîm	shānāh	wesheva'	shānîm	shenê	chayyê	sārāh
hundred	years	and twenty	years	and seven	years	the years of	the life of	Sarah

	4322.122	8023	904, 7442	7442	2000	2367	904, 800	3791
2.	cj, v Qal impf 3fs	pn	prep, pn	pn	pers pron	pn	prep, *n fs*	pn
	וַתָּמָת	שָׂרָה	בְּקִרְיַת	אַרְבַּע	הִוא	חֶבְרוֹן	בְּאֶרֶץ	כְּנָעַן
	wattāmāth	sārāh	beqiryath	'arba'	hiw'	chevrôn	be'erets	kenā'an
	and she died	Sarah	in Kiriath	Arba	it	Hebron	in the land of	Canaan

971.121	80	3937, 5792.141	3937, 8023	3937, 1098.141		7251.121
cj, v Qal impf 3ms	pn	prep, v Qal inf con	prep, pn	cj, prep, v Qal inf con, ps 3fs	3.	cj, v Qal impf 3ms
וַיָּבֹא	אַבְרָהָם	לִסְפֹּד	לְשָׂרָה	וְלִבְכֹּתָהּ		וַיָּקָם
wayyāvō'	'avrāhām	lispōdh	lesārāh	welivkōthāhh		wayyāqām
and he went	Abraham	to mourn	to Sarah	and to weep for her		and he rose up

80	4623, 6142	6686	4322.151	1744.321	420, 1158, 2953
pn	prep, prep	*n mp*	v Qal act ptc ms, ps 3ms	cj, v Piel impf 3ms	prep, n mp, pn
אַבְרָהָם	מֵעַל	פְּנֵי	מֵתוֹ	וַיְדַבֵּר	אֶל־בְּנֵי־חֵת
'avrāhām	mē'al	penê	mēthô	waydhabbēr	'el-benê-chēth
Abraham	from beside	the face of	his dead one	and he spoke	to the sons of Heth

3937, 569.141		1658, 8785	609	6196	5598.133	3937
prep, v Qal inf con	4.	n ms, cj, n ms	pers pron	prep, ps 2mp	v Qal impv 2mp	prep, ps 1cs
לֵאמֹר		גֵּר־וְתוֹשָׁב	אָנֹכִי	עִמָּכֶם	תְּנוּ	לִי
lē'mōr		gēr-wethôshāv	'ānōkhî	'immākhem	tenû	lî
saying		sojourner and alien	I	among you	give	to me

273, 7197	6196	7196.125	4322.151	4623, 3937, 6686
n fs, n ms	prep, ps 2mp	cj, v Qal impf 1cs	v Qal act ptc ms, ps 1cs	prep, prep, n mp, ps 1cs
אֲחֻזַּת־קֶבֶר	עִמָּכֶם	וְאֶקְבְּרָה	מֵתִי	מִלְּפָנָי
'ăchuzzath-qever	'immākhem	we'eqŏbberāh	mēthî	millephānāy
property of tomb	among you	and I will bury	my dead one	from my face

	6257.126	1158, 2953	881, 80	3937, 569.141	3937		8471.131
5.	cj, v Qal impf 3mp	n mp, pn	do, pn	prep, v Qal inf con	prep, ps 3ms	6.	v Qal impv 2ms, ps 1cp
	וַיַּעֲנוּ	בְנֵי־חֵת	אֶת־אַבְרָהָם	לֵאמֹר	לוֹ		שְׁמָעֵנוּ
	wayya'ănû	venê-chēth	'eth-'avrāhām	lē'mōr	lô		shemā'ēnû
	and they answered	the sons of Heth	Abraham	saying	to him		hear us

112	5562	435	887	904, 8761	904, 4144	7197
n ms, ps 1cs	*n ms*	n mp	pers pron	prep, n ms, ps 1cp	prep, *n ms*	n mp, ps 1cp
אֲדֹנִי	נְשִׂיא	אֱלֹהִים	אַתָּה	בְּתוֹכֵנוּ	בְּמִבְחַר	קְבָרֵינוּ
'ădhōnî	nesî'	'ĕlōhîm	'attāh	bethôkhēnû	bemivchar	qŏvārênû
my master	prince of	God	you	in our midst	in best one of	our tombs

7196.131 v Qal impv 2ms קְבֹר qŏvōr bury	881, 4322.151 do, v Qal act ptc ms, ps 2ms אֶת־מֵתֶךָ 'eth-mēthekhā your dead one	382 n ms אִישׁ 'îsh each	4623 prep, ps 1cp מִמֶּנּוּ mimmennû from us	881, 7197 do, n ms, ps 3ms אֶת־קִבְרוֹ 'eth-qivrô his tomb	3940, 3727.121 neg part, v Qal impf 3ms לֹא־יִכְלֶה lō'-yikhleh not he will withhold

4623 prep, ps 2ms מִמְּךָ mimm^{e}khā from you	4623, 7196.141 prep, v Qal inf con מִקְּבֹר miqq^{e}vōr from burying	4322.151 v Qal act ptc ms, ps 2ms מֵתֶךָ mēthekhā your dead one	7.	7251.121 cj, v Qal impf 3ms וַיָּקָם wayyāqām and he rose up	80 pn אַבְרָהָם 'avrāhām Abraham	8246.721 cj, v Hithpalel impf 3ms וַיִּשְׁתַּחוּ wayyishtachû and he bowed down

3937, 6194, 800 prep, *n ms*, art, n fs לְעַם־הָאָרֶץ l^e'am-hā'ārets to the people of the land	3937, 1158, 2953 prep, *n mp*, pn לִבְנֵי־חֵת livnê-chēth to the sons of Heth	8.	1744.321 cj, v Piel impf 3ms וַיְדַבֵּר way^{e}dhabbēr and he spoke	882 prep, ps 3mp אִתָּם 'ittām with them	3937, 569.141 prep, v Qal inf con לֵאמֹר lē'mōr saying	524, 3552 cj, sub אִם־יֵשׁ 'im-yēsh if there is

23. And Bethuel begat Rebekah: these eight Milcah did bear to Nahor, Abraham's brother: ... fathered, *KJVII.*

24. And his concubine, whose name was Reumah, she bare also Tebah, and Gaham, and Thahash, and Maachah: ... and his servant, *BB* ... his second wife, *Fenton* ... his consort, *Goodspeed.*

23:1. And Sarah was an hundred and seven and twenty years old: these were the years of the life of Sarah: ... Sarah lived to be, *NIV* ... the span of Sarah's life, *Anchor.*

2. And Sarah died in Kirjatharba; the same is Hebron in the land of Canaan: and Abraham came to mourn for Sarah, and to weep for her: ... proceeded to mourn and to bewail her, *Anchor* ... performed the customary mourning rite, *NAB* ... went into his house, weeping and sorrowing, *BB.*

3. And Abraham stood up from before his dead and spake unto the sons of Heth, saying: ... rose from beside his dead wife, *NIV* ... the sight of his corpse, *Geneva* ... the presence of his dead, *Young.*

4. I am a stranger and a sojourner with you: ... foreigner and wanderer, *Fenton* ... immigrant, *Berkeley* ... serf, *Goodspeed* ... alien and settler, *NCB* ... I am living among you as one from a strange country, *BB.*

give me a possession of a burying-place with you, that I may bury my dead out of my sight: ... a sepulcher, *Darby* ... grave, *Fenton* ... my own burial ground, *Berkeley.*

5. And the children of Heth answered Abraham, saying unto him,

6. Hear us, my lord thou art a mighty prince among us: ... great chief, *BB* ... godlike prince among us, *Berkeley* ... elect of God, *Anchor.*

in the choice of our sepulchres bury thy dead: ... burial sites, *NAB* ... best of our resting places, *BB* ... choose from our tombs, *Fenton.*

none of us shall withhold from thee his sepulchre but that thou mayest bury thy dead: ... refuse you, *Berkeley* ... deny you, *NEB* ... withhold from you, *NKJV.*

7. And Abraham stood up, and

the father of Rebekah. This helps prepare us for the events of chapter 24.

23:1-2. Since Sarah was 90 at the birth of Isaac, he was 37 and Abraham 137 when she died. Kirjath-arba, "City of Arba (the hero of the Anakim, Josh. 14:15)," is the old name of Hebron. The Anakim also thought of it as "City of Four," because Anak and his three sons lived there (Judg. 1:10,20). Abraham must have moved into this territory temporarily. Now he went to her dead body, beat his breast, and wept and wailed over her, not merely as the custom was, but in genuine grief.

23:3-4. Because it was the custom to bury on the same day, Abraham went immediately to the Hittites, who controlled the territory of Hebron at the time, and asked them to sell some land for a burial site. These Hittites were descendants of Heth, Canaan, and Ham (Gen. 10:15). Some suggest they may have been related to the northern Hittites who had a great empire in Asia Minor until about 1200 B.C. Abraham recognized that as an alien and a stranger he had no right to buy property, so he approached them with a sincere humility. (See also Heb. 11:13-16 for further insight into Abraham's view of himself as and alien and stranger.)

23:5-16. What follows in these verses is the

881, 5497	3937, 7196.141	881, 4322.151	4623, 3937, 6686	8471.133
do, n fs, ps 2mp	prep, v Qal inf con	do, v Qal act ptc ms, ps 1cs	prep, prep, n mp	v Qal impv 2mp, ps 1cs
אֶת־נַפְשְׁכֶם	לִקְבֹּר	אֶת־מֵתִי	מִלְּפָנָי	שְׁמָעוּנִי
'eth-naphshekhem	liqöbbör	'eth-mēthî	millephānay	shemā'ûnî
your willingness	to bury	my dead one	beside me	hear me

6534.133, 3937	904, 6317	1158, 6982		5598.121, 3937	881, 4792
cj, v Qal impv 2mp, prep, ps 1cs	prep, pn	*n ms*, pn	**9.**	cj, v Qal impf 3ms, prep, ps 1cs	do, *n fs*
וּפִגְעוּ־לִי	בְּעֶפְרוֹן	בֶּן־צֹחַר		וְיִתֶּן־לִי	אֶת־מְעָרַת
ûphigh'û-lî	be'ephrôn	ben- tsōchar		weyitten-lî	'eth-me'ārath
and meet for me	with Ephron	the son of Zohar		and give to me	the cave of

4512	866, 3937	866	904, 7381	7898	904, 3826B	4529
art, pn	rel part, prep, ps 3ms	rel part	prep, *n ms*	n ms, ps 3ms	prep, n ms	adj
הַמַּכְפֵּלָה	אֲשֶׁר־לוֹ	אֲשֶׁר	בִּקְצֵה	שָׂדֵהוּ	בְּכֶסֶף	מָלֵא
hammakhpēlāh	'ăsher-lô	'ăsher	biqötsēh	sādēhû	bekheseph	mālē'
the Machpelah	which to him	which	by the end of	his field	with silver	full

5598.121	3937	904, 8761	3937, 273, 7197		6317	3553.151
v Qal impf 3ms, ps 3fs	prep, ps 1cs	prep, sub, ps 2mp	prep, *n fs*, n ms	**10.**	cj, pn	v Qal act ptc ms
יִתְּנֶנָּה	לִי	בְּתוֹכְכֶם	לַאֲחֻזַּת־קָבֶר		וְעֶפְרוֹן	יֹשֵׁב
yittennennāh	lî	bethôkhekhem	la'ăchuzzath-qāver		we'ephrôn	yōshēv
he will give it	to me	in your midst	for property of tomb		and Ephron	sitting

904, 8761	1158, 2953	6257.121	6317	2958	881, 80	904, 238
prep, *sub*	*n mp*, pn	cj, v Qal impf 3ms	pn	art, pn	do, pn	prep, *n fp*
בְּתוֹךְ	בְּנֵי־חֵת	וַיַּעַן	עֶפְרוֹן	הַחִתִּי	אֶת־אַבְרָהָם	בְּאָזְנֵי
bethôkh	benê-chēth	wayya'an	'ephrôn	hachittî	'eth-'avrāhām	be'āznê
in the midst of	the sons of Heth	and he answered	Ephron	the Hittite	Abraham	in the ears of

1158, 2953	3937, 3725	971.152	8554, 6111	3937, 569.141		3940, 112
n mp, pn	prep, adj	*v Qal act ptc mp*	*n ms*, n fs, ps 3ms	prep, v Qal inf con	**11.**	neg part, n ms, ps 1cs
בְנֵי־חֵת	לְכֹל	בָּאֵי	שַׁעַר־עִירוֹ	לֵאמֹר		לֹא־אֲדֹנִי
vênê-chēth	lekhōl	bā'ê	sha'ar-'îrô	lē'mōr		lō'-'ădhōnî
the sons of Heth	to all	going into	the gate of his city	saying		no my lord

8471.131	7898	5598.115	3937	4792	866, 904	3937
v Qal impv 2ms, ps 1cs	art, n ms	v Qal pf 1cs	prep, ps 2fs	cj, art, n fs	rel part, prep, ps 3ms	prep, ps 2ms
שְׁמָעֵנִי	הַשָּׂדֶה	נָתַתִּי	לָךְ	וְהַמְּעָרָה	אֲשֶׁר־בּוֹ	לְךָ
shemā'ênî	hassādeh	nāthattî	lākh	wehamme'ārāh	'ăsher-bô	lekhā
hear me	the field	I have given	to you	and the cave	which on it	to you

5598.115	3937, 6084	1158, 6194	5598.115	3937	7196.131
v Qal pf 1cs, ps 3fs	prep, *n fd*	*n mp*, n ms, ps 1cs	v Qal pf 1cs, ps 3fs	prep, ps 2ms	v Qal impv 2ms
נְתַתִּיהָ	לְעֵינֵי	בְנֵי־עַמִּי	נְתַתִּיהָ	לָךְ	קְבֹר
nethattîhā	le'ênê	venê-'ammî	nethattîhā	lākh	qővōr
I have given it	in the eyes of	the sons of my people	I have given it	to you	bury

4322.151		8246.721	80	3937, 6686	6194	800
v Qal act ptc ms, ps 2ms	**12.**	cj, v Hithpalel impf 3ms	pn	prep, *n mp*	*n ms*	art, n fs
מֵתֶךָ		וַיִּשְׁתַּחוּ	אַבְרָהָם	לִפְנֵי	עַם	הָאָרֶץ
mēthekhā		wayyishtachû	'avrāhām	liphnê	'am	hā'ārets
your dead one		and he bowed down	Abraham	before	the people of	the land

	1744.321	420, 6317	904, 238	6194, 800	3937, 569.141	395	524, 887
13.	cj, v Piel impf 3ms	prep, pn	prep, *n fp*	*n ms*, art, n fs	prep, v Qal inf con	adv	cj, pers pron
	וַיְדַבֵּר	אֶל־עֶפְרוֹן	בְּאָזְנֵי	עַם־הָאָרֶץ	לֵאמֹר	אַךְ	אִם־אַתָּה
	wayedhabbēr	'el-'ephrôn	be'āznê	'am-hā'ārets	lē'mōr	'akh	'im-'attāh
	and he spoke	to Ephron	in the ears of	the people of the land	saying	only	if you

4001	8471.131	5598.115	3826B	7898	4089.131	4623
part	v Qal impv 2ms, ps 1cs	v Qal pf 1cs	*n ms*	art, n ms	v Qal impv 2ms	prep, ps 1cs
לוּ	שְׁמָעֵנִי	נָתַתִּי	כֶּסֶף	הַשָּׂדֶה	קַח	מִמֶּנִּי
lû	shemā'ēnî	nāthattî	keseph	hassādeh	qach	mimmennî
if only	listen to me	I have given	the silver of	the field	take	from me

7196.125	881, 4322.151	8427		6257.121	6317	881, 80
cj, v Qal impf 1cs	do, v Qal act ptc ms, ps 1cs	adv	**14.**	cj, v Qal impf 3ms	pn	do, pn
וְאֶקְבְּרָה	אֶת־מֵתִי	שָׁמָּה		וַיַּעַן	עֶפְרוֹן	אֶת־אַבְרָהָם
we'eqōberāh	'eth-mēthî	shāmmāh		wayya'an	'ephrôn	'eth-'avrāhām
then I will bury	my dead one	there		and he answered	Ephron	Abraham

3937, 569.141	3937		112	8471.131	800	727	4109
prep, v Qal inf con	prep, ps 3ms	**15.**	n ms, ps 1cs	v Qal impv 2ms, ps 1cs	*n fs*	*num*	*num*
לֵאמֹר	לוֹ		אֲדֹנִי	שְׁמָעֵנִי	אֶרֶץ	אַרְבַּע	מְאֹת
lē'mōr	lô		'ădhōnî	shemā'ēnî	'erets	'arba'	mē'ōth
saying	to him		my master	hear me	land of	four	hundreds of

bowed himself to the people of the land even to the children of Heth: ... natives, *Goodspeed* ... local citizens, *NAB* ... that region, *REB.*

8. And he communed with them, saying: ... addressed them, *Fenton* ... pleaded with them, *Anchor.*

If it be your mind that I should bury my dead out of my sight: ... if you really wish me to remove my dead for burial, *Anchor* ... if you are willing, *Berkeley* ... proper burial, *NEB* ... consent, *Goodspeed.*

hear me, and intreat for me to Ephron the son of Zohar: ... intercede for me with Ephron, *Anchor.*

9. That he may give me the cave of Machpelah: ... that he sell me, *Anchor* ... the hollow in the rock named Machpelah, *BB.*

which he hath which is in the end of his field for as much money as it is worth he shall give it me for a possession of a buryingplace amongst you: ... let him sell it to me at full price, *Anchor* ... for a burial site, *NASB.*

10. And Ephron dwelt among the children of Heth: ... Ephron was on hand, *Anchor* ... sitting in the midst of the children of Heth, *ASV.*

and Ephron the Hittite answered Abraham in the audience of the children of Heth, even of all that went in at the gate of his city, saying: ... all who sat on the council of that town, *Anchor* ... of all those who came into his town, *BB.*

11. Nay, my lord, hear me: ... not at all, sir, *Goodspeed* ... hear me out, *Anchor* ... Listen to me, *Berkeley.*

the field give I thee, and the cave that is therein, I give it thee in the presence of the sons of my people give I it thee bury thy dead: ... I will make you a present of the field and the cave as well, *Goodspeed* ... my kinsmen, *Anchor* ... with my people witnessing, *Berkeley.*

12. And Abraham bowed down himself before the people of the land.

13. And he spake unto Ephron in the audience of the people of the land, saying, But if thou wilt give it, I pray thee, hear me: I will give thee money for the field; take it of me, and I will bury my dead there: ... I will pay, *Anchor* ... Accept my payment, *Good News.*

14. And Ephron answered Abraham, saying unto him,

record of the kind of polite, indirect, oriental bargaining common among people of that day. The Hittites call Abraham not only a prince (a word used of a minor king or the chief of a tribe), but God's prince, and offer him the choicest of their tombs to bury his dead. Abraham then bowed down and said that since they were willing to let him bury his dead, then let them intercede with Ephron to give him (that is, sell him) the cave of Machpelah at the end of his field for the full amount of silver that it was worth. Ephron was now among the crowd who had come to the gate of the city where legal proceedings usually took place. He politely said he had given the field and the cave. This was a way of saying that the field had to go with the cave.

Abraham knew this was only politeness, so he bowed down again and insisted on paying the full price. Ephron, with the same kind of politeness as before named a high price, about 160 ounces of silver. Abraham did not argue or try to get the price reduced. Immediately he proceeded to weigh it out to him using the shekel weight that was common among the merchants of that day and acceptable to everyone.

8621, 3826B	**1033**	**1033**	**4242, 2000**	**881, 4322.151**	**7196.131**
n ms, n ms	prep, ps 1cs	cj, prep, ps 2ms	intrg, pers pron	cj, do, v Qal act ptc ms, ps 2ms	v Qal impv 2ms
שֶׁקֶל־כֶּסֶף	בֵּינִי	וּבֵינְךָ	מַה־הִוא	וְאֶת־מֵתְךָ	קְבֹר
sheqel-keseph	bênî	ûvên^{e}khā	mah-hiw'	w^{e}'eth-mēth^{e}khā	qŏvōr
shekels of silver	between me	and between you	what it	now your dead one	bury

16.

8471.121	**80**	**420, 6317**	**8620.121**	**80**	**3937, 6317**
cj, v Qal impf 3ms	pn	prep, pn	cj, v Qal impf 3ms	pn	prep, pn
וַיִּשְׁמַע	אַבְרָהָם	אֶל־עֶפְרוֹן	וַיִּשְׁקֹל	אַבְרָהָם	לְעֶפְרֹן
wayyishma'	'avrāhām	'el-'ephrôn	wayyishqōl	'avrāhām	l^{e}'ephrōn
and he listening	Abraham	to Ephron	and he weighed	Abraham	for Ephron

881, 3826B	**866**	**1744.311**	**904, 238**	**1158, 2953**	**727**	**4109**	**8621**
do, art, n ms	rel part	v Piel pf 3ms	prep, *n fp*	*n mp*, pn	*num*	*num*	*n ms*
אֶת־הַכֶּסֶף	אֲשֶׁר	דִּבֶּר	בְּאָזְנֵי	בְנֵי־חֵת	אַרְבַּע	מֵאוֹת	שֶׁקֶל
'eth-hakeseph	'ăsher	dibber	b^{e}'āznê	v^{e}nê-chēth	'arba'	mē'ôth	sheqel
the silver	which	he spoke	in the ears of	the sons of Heth	four	hundreds of	shekels of

3826B	**5882.151**	**3937, 5692.151**		**7251.121**	**7898**	**6317**
n ms	v Qal act ptc ms	prep, art, v Qal act ptc ms	**17.**	cj, v Qal impf 3ms	*n ms*	pn
כֶּסֶף	עֹבֵר	לַסֹּחֵר		וַיָּקָם	שְׂדֵה	עֶפְרוֹן
keseph	'ōvēr	lassōchēr		wayyāqām	s^{e}dhēh	'ephrôn
silver	which passes over	to the merchant		and it became	the field of	Ephron

866	**904, 4512**	**866**	**3937, 6686**	**4613**	**7898**	**4792**
rel part	prep, art, pn	rel part	prep, *n mp*	pn	art, n ms	cj, art, n fs
אֲשֶׁר	בַּמַּכְפֵּלָה	אֲשֶׁר	לִפְנֵי	מַמְרֵא	הַשָּׂדֶה	וְהַמְּעָרָה
'ăsher	bammakhpēlāh	'ăsher	liphnê	mamrē'	hassādeh	w^{e}hamm^{e}'ārāh
which	in the Machpelah	which	facing	Mamre	the field	and the cave

866, 904	**3725, 6320**	**866**	**904, 7898**	**866**	**904, 3725, 1397**	**5623**
rel part, prep, ps 3ms	cj, *adj*, art, n ms	rel part	prep, art, n ms	rel part	prep, *adj*, n ms, ps 3ms	adv
אֲשֶׁר־בּוֹ	וְכָל־הָעֵץ	אֲשֶׁר	בַּשָּׂדֶה	אֲשֶׁר	בְּכָל־גְּבֻלוֹ	סָבִיב
'ăsher-bô	w^{e}khol-hā'ēts	'ăsher	bassādheh	'ăsher	b^{e}khol-g^{e}vulô	sāvîv
which on it	and all the trees	which	in the field	which	on all its area	all around

18.

3937, 80	**3937, 4899**	**3937, 6084**	**1158, 2953**	**904, 3725**	**971.152**	**8554, 6111**
prep, pn	prep, n fs	prep, *n fd*	*n mp*, pn	prep, adj	*v Qal act ptc mp*	*n ms*, n fs, ps 3ms
לְאַבְרָהָם	לְמִקְנָה	לְעֵינֵי	בְנֵי־חֵת	בְּכֹל	בָּאֵי	שַׁעַר־עִירוֹ
l^{e}avrāhām	l^{e}miqnāh	l^{e}'ênê	v^{e}nê-chēth	b^{e}khōl	bā'ê	sha'ar-'îrô
to Abraham	for property	in the eyes of	the sons of Heth	with all	going into	the gate of his city

19.

313, 3772	**7196.111**	**80**	**881, 8023**	**828**	**420, 4792**	**7898**
cj, adv, cj	v Qal pf 3ms	pn	do, pn	n fs, ps 3ms	prep, *n fs*	*n ms*
וְאַחֲרֵי־כֵן	קָבַר	אַבְרָהָם	אֶת־שָׂרָה	אִשְׁתּוֹ	אֶל־מְעָרַת	שְׂדֵה
w^{e}'achrê-khēn	qāvar	'avrāhām	'eth-sārāh	'ishtô	'el-m^{e}'ārath	s^{e}dhēh
and afterward	he buried	Abraham	Sarah	his wife	in the cave of	the field of

4512	**6142, 6686**	**4613**	**2000**	**2367**	**904, 800**	**3791**
art, pn	prep, *n mp*	pn	pers pron	pn	prep, *n fs*	pn
הַמַּכְפֵּלָה	עַל־פְּנֵי	מַמְרֵא	הִוא	חֶבְרוֹן	בְּאֶרֶץ	כְּנָעַן
hammakhpēlāh	'al-p^{e}nê	mamrē'	hiw'	chevrôn	b^{e}'erets	k^{e}nā'an
the Machpelah	facing	Mamre	it	Hebron	in the land of	Canaan

20.

7251.121	**7898**	**4792**	**866, 904**	**3937, 80**	**3937, 273, 7197**
cj, v Qal impf 3ms	art, n ms	cj, art, n fs	rel part, prep, ps 3ms	prep, pn	prep, *n fs*, n ms
וַיָּקָם	הַשָּׂדֶה	וְהַמְּעָרָה	אֲשֶׁר־בּוֹ	לְאַבְרָהָם	לַאֲחֻזַּת־קָבֶר
wayyāqām	hassādeh	w^{e}hamm^{e}'ārāh	'ăsher-bô	l^{e}'avrāhām	la'ăchuzzath-qāver
and it became	the field	and the cave	which on it	to Abraham	for property of tomb

15. My lord, hearken unto me: ... pray hear me, my lord, *Anchor* ... listen to me, Sir, *Berkeley* ... my lord, give ear to me, *BB*.

the land is worth four hundred shekels of silver: ... the land is worth 1,000 dollars, *Berkeley* ... for four hundred shekels of money, *Fenton* ... land worth only four hundred pieces of silver, *Good News* ... the land is worth two hundred and sixty dollars, *MLB*.

what is that betwixt me and thee: ... what is that between you and me as long as you can bury your dead, *NAB* ... but what is that between friends, *LIV* ... what does that amount to between me and you, *Berkeley*.

bury therefore thy dead: ... you may bury your dead there, *REB* ... bury your wife in it, *Good News* ... then you can bury your dead, *Anchor*.

16. And Abraham hearkened unto Ephron: ... complied with Ephron's request, *Anchor* ... understood Ephron, *Berkeley* ... took note of the price fixed by Ephron, *BB* ... accepted Ephron's terms, *Goodspeed* ... closed the bargain with him, *REB*.

and Abraham weighed to Ephron the silver: ... weighed out to Ephron the silver that he spoke of, *Anchor* ... the silver he had stipulated, *Berkeley* ... the money which he had agreed upon, *Fenton*.

which he had named in the audience of the sons of Heth: ... sight of, *Fenton* ... in the hearing of the children of Heth, *Anchor*.

four hundred shekels of silver: ... 1,000 dollars, *Berkeley* ... two hundred and sixty dollars, *Fenton*.

current money with the merchant: ... of commercial standard, *Goodspeed* ... which passes with the merchant, *KJVII* ... according to the weights current among the merchants, *RSV* ... standard recognized by merchants, *NEB*.

17. And the field of Ephron, which was in Machpelah, which was before Mamre: ... this secured Ephron's field, *Berkeley* ... thus he bought the field, *Fenton* ... and established, *Young*.

the field, and the cave which was therein: ... with the hollow in the rock, *BB*.

and all the trees that were in the field, that were in all the borders round about: ... to its surrounding boundaries, *Berkeley* ... with all the hedge around it, *Fenton* ... within all the confines of its border, *NASB*.

were made sure: ... was made over, *RSV* ... was conveyed, *NAB*.

18. Unto Abraham for a possession: ... to Abraham as his property, *Goodspeed* ... for a possession, *ASV* ... were legally conveyed, *Berkeley* ... by purchase, *NAB*.

in the presence of the children of Heth: ... witnessed by all the Hittites, *Berkeley* ... his fellow citizens, *NCB*.

before all that went in at the gate of his city: ... all who sat on the council of that town, *Anchor* ... who were entering, *Berkeley* ... who came into town, *BB* ... all who were there at the meeting, *Good News*.

19. And after this Abraham buried Sarah his wife in the cave of the field of Machpelah before Mamre: the same is Hebron in the land of Canaan: ... put Sarah to rest in the hollow rock, *BB*.

20. And the field, and the cave that is therein were made sure unto Abraham for a possession: ... legally conveyed, *MLB* ... were assured, *Darby* ... handed over, *BB* ... passed from the possession of the Hittites, *Goodspeed* ... were deeded to Abraham, *NKJV*.

of a buryingplace by the sons of Heth: ... for a cemetery, *Berkeley* ... a sepulchre, *Darby* ... as his property, *BB* ... property for a burial site, *NKJV*.

24:1. And Abraham was old: ... Abraham however grew old, *Fenton* ... Abraham had now reached a ripe old age, *NAB*.

and well stricken in age: ... advanced in years, *Fenton* ... far gone in age, *KJVII* ... was now a very old man, *LIVB*.

23:17-20. The Hebrew of verses 17 and 20 literally says the field "went up" to Abraham. This is a figure of speech which simply means the property changed hands and now belongs to Abraham.

The field and everything in it was now Abraham's as a burial site, and all the people at the gate of the city were witnesses to the transaction, which made it official and a matter of record. This was a final cutting off of ties with his old homeland. Abraham now had property in Canaan, even though it was to be used only as a burial site. Abraham then buried Sarah there. Later Abraham, Isaac, Rebekah, Jacob, and Leah were buried there (25:9; 35:27,29; 49:31; 50:13).

Mamre was about two miles north of ancient Hebron, which was on a hill to the west of the modern Hebron. A Christian church was built over the traditional site of the cave of Machpelah. This was later converted into a mosque, and the modern city of Hebron grew up around it.

4623, 882	1158, 2953		80	2290.111	971.151	904, 3219
prep, prep	*n mp*, pn	**24:1**	cj, pn	v Qal pf 3ms	v Qal act ptc ms	prep, art, n mp
מֵאֵת	בְּנֵי־חֵת		וְאַבְרָהָם	זָקֵן	בָּא	בַּיָּמִים
mē'ēth	b^{e}nê-chēth		w^{e}'avrāhām	zāqēn	bā'	bayyāmîm
from	the sons of Heth		now Abraham	he was old	one coming	in the days

3176	1313.311	881, 80	904, 3725		569.121	80
cj, pn	v Piel pf 3ms	do, pn	prep, art, n ms	**2.**	cj, v Qal impf 3ms	pn
וַיהוָה	בֵּרַךְ	אֶת־אַבְרָהָם	בַּכֹּל		וַיֹּאמֶר	אַבְרָהָם
wayhwāh	bērakh	'eth-'avrāhām	bakkōl		wayyō'mer	'avrāhām
and Yahweh	He blessed	Abraham	in everything		and he said	Abraham

420, 5860	2292	1041	5090.151	904, 3725, 866, 3937	7947.131, 5167
prep, n ms, ps 3ms	*adj*	n ms, ps 3ms	art, v Qal act ptc ms	prep, *adj*, rel part, prep, ps 3ms	v Qal impv 2ms, part
אֶל־עַבְדּוֹ	זְקַן	בֵּיתוֹ	הַמֹּשֵׁל	בְּכָל־אֲשֶׁר־לוֹ	שִׂים־נָא
'el-'avdô	z^{e}qan	bêthô	hammōshēl	b^{e}khol-'ăsher-lô	sîm-nā'
to his slave	the oldest of	his house	the steward	over all which to him	put please

3135	8809	3525		8123.525	904, 3176	435
n fs, ps 2ms	prep	n fs, ps 1cs	**3.**	cj, v Hiphil impf 1cs, ps 2ms	prep, pn	*n mp*
יָדְךָ	תַּחַת	יְרֵכִי		וְאַשְׁבִּיעֲךָ	בַּיהוָה	אֱלֹהֵי
yadh^{e}khā	tachath	y^{e}rēkhî		w^{e}'ashbî'ăkhā	bayhwāh	'ĕlōhê
your hand	under	my loins		and I will make you swear	by Yahweh	the God of

8452	435	800	866	3940, 4089.123	828	3937, 1158
art, n md	cj, *n mp*	art, n fs	rel part	neg part, v Qal impf 2ms	n fs	prep, n ms, ps 1cs
הַשָּׁמַיִם	וֵאלֹהֵי	הָאָרֶץ	אֲשֶׁר	לֹא־תִקַּח	אִשָּׁה	לִבְנִי
hashshāmayim	wē'lōhê	hā'ārets	'ăsher	lō'-thiqqach	'ishshāh	livnî
the heavens	and the God of	the earth	that	not you will take	wife	for my son

4623, 1351	3793	866	609	3553.151	904, 7419		3706
prep, *n fp*	art, pn	rel part	pers pron	v Qal act ptc ms	prep, n ms, ps 3ms	**4.**	cj
מִבְּנוֹת	הַכְּנַעֲנִי	אֲשֶׁר	אָנֹכִי	יוֹשֵׁב	בְּקִרְבּוֹ		כִּי
mibb^{e}nôth	hakk^{e}na'ănî	'ăsher	'ānōkhî	yôshēv	b^{e}qirbô		kî
from the daughters of	the Canaanites	where	I	dwelling	in their midst		because

420, 800	420, 4274	2050.123	4089.113	828	3937, 1158	3937, 3437
prep, n fs, ps 1cs	cj, prep, n fs, ps 1cs	v Qal impf 2ms	cj, v Qal pf 2ms	n fs	prep, n ms, ps 1cs	prep, pn
אֶל־אַרְצִי	וְאֶל־מוֹלַדְתִּי	תֵּלֵךְ	וְלָקַחְתָּ	אִשָּׁה	לִבְנִי	לְיִצְחָק
'el-'artsî	w^{e}'eth-môladhtî	tēlēkh	w^{e}lāqachtā	'ishshāh	livnî	l^{e}yitschāq
to my land	and to my family	you will go	and you will take	wife	for my son	for Isaac

	569.121	420	5860	193	3940, 13.122	828
5.	cj, v Qal impf 3ms	prep, ps 3ms	art, n ms	adv	neg part, v Qal impf 3fs	art, n fs
	וַיֹּאמֶר	אֵלָיו	הָעֶבֶד	אוּלַי	לֹא־תֹאבֶה	הָאִשָּׁה
	wayyō'mer	'ēlâv	hā'evedh	'ûlay	lō'-thō'veh	hā'ishshāh
	and he said	to him	the slave	perhaps	not she is not willing	the woman

3937, 2050.141	313	420, 800	2148	8178.542	8178.525
prep, v Qal inf con	adv, ps 1cs	prep, art, n fs	art, dem pron	intrg part, v Hiphil inf abs	v Hiphil impf 1cs
לָלֶכֶת	אַחֲרָי	אֶל־הָאָרֶץ	הַזֹּאת	הֶהָשֵׁב	אָשִׁיב
lālekheth	'achray	'el-hā'ārets	hazzō'th	hehāshēv	'āshîv
to go	after me	to the land	the this	returning	will I return

881, 1158	420, 800	866, 3428.113	4623, 8427		569.121	420
do, n ms, ps 2ms	prep, art, n fs	rel part, v Qal pf 2ms	prep, adv	**6.**	cj, v Qal impf 3ms	prep, ps 3ms
אֶת־בִּנְךָ	אֶל־הָאָרֶץ	אֲשֶׁר־יָצָאתָ	מִשָּׁם		וַיֹּאמֶר	אֵלָיו
'eth-bin^{e}khā	'el-hā'ārets	'ăsher-yātsā'thā	mishshām		wayyō'mer	'ēlâv
your son	to the land	which you came out	from there		and he said	to him

80	8490.231	3937	6678, 8178.523	881, 1158	8427
pn	v Niphal impv 2ms	prep, ps 2ms	cj, v Hiphil impf 2ms	do, n ms, ps 1cs	adv
אַבְרָהָם	הִשָּׁמֶר	לְךָ	פֶּן־תָּשִׁיב	אֶת־בְּנִי	שָׁמָּה
'avrāhām	hishshāmer	l^{e}khā	pen-tāshîv	'eth-b^{e}nî	shāmmāh
Abraham	be careful	for yourself	that not you will return	my son	there

7.

3176	435	8452	866	4089.111	4623, 1041	1
pn	*n mp*	art, n md	rel part	v Qal pf 3ms, ps 1cs	prep, *n ms*	n ms, ps 1cs
יְהוָה	אֱלֹהֵי	הַשָּׁמַיִם	אֲשֶׁר	לְקָחַנִי	מִבֵּית	אָבִי
y^{e}hwāh	'ĕlōhê	hashshāmayim	'ăsher	l^{e}qāchanî	mibbêth	'āvî
Yahweh	the God of	the heavens	who	He took me	from the house of	my father

and the LORD had blessed Abraham in all things: ... Yahweh had blessed, *Anchor* ... blessed of God in every way, *Berkeley* ... the Lord had prospered Abraham, *Fenton.*

2. And Abraham said unto his eldest servant of his house: ... senior servant of his household, *NAB* ... oldest slave, *Fenton* ... oldest slave of his household, *Fenton* ... who had been longest in his service, *REB.*

that ruled over all that he had: ... who had charge of all his possessions, *Anchor* ... steward over all he had, *Fenton.*

Put, I pray thee, thy hand under my thigh: ... kindly place your hand, *Berkeley* ... between my thighs, *Good News* ... under my leg, *BB.*

3. And I will make thee swear by the LORD, the God of heaven, and the God of the earth: ... that I may adjure you, *NCB* ... make you swear by Yahweh, *Anchor* ... take an oath to me by the Ever-living the God of Heaven, *Fenton* ... I want you to swear by the Lord, *RSV.*

that thou shalt not take a wife unto my son of the daughters of the Canaanites:. . . get my son a wife from the daughters, *MLB* ... take a wife for my son from the women, *NEB* ... that you will not marry my son to a daughter of the Canaanites, *Goodspeed.*

among whom I dwell: ... among whom I am living, *Berkeley* ... among whom I reside, *Fenton.*

4. But thou shalt go unto my country and to my kindred and take a wife unto my son Isaac: ... my own land, *Goodspeed* ... my relatives, *NASB* ... my old family, *Fenton.*

5. And the servant said unto him Peradventure the woman will not be willing to follow me unto this land: ... what if the woman refuses, *Anchor* ... is not willing, *Berkeley* ... will not come, *BB.*

must I needs bring thy son again unto the land from whence thou camest: ... must I then bring thy son again in any case, *Darby* ... then shall I take Isaac there, *LIVB.*

6. And Abraham said unto him Beware thou that thou bring not my son thither again: ... on no account are you to take my son back there, *Anchor* ... take care that you do not let my son go back to that land, *BB* ... never take my son back there for any reason, *NAB.*

7. The LORD God of heaven: ... Yahweh God of heaven, *Anchor* ... Jehovah, *Young* ... the Ever-living, the God of heaven, *Fenton* ... it was the Lord, *Goodspeed.*

24:1. Isaac was 40 when he married Rebekah (Gen. 25:20). Thus, the aged Abraham was 140, but was in good health and was blessed by God in his business as a merchant prince. Since it was customary for parents to arrange the marriages of their children (often through go-betweens), he now felt Isaac should have a wife before he got any older.

24:2-4. Abraham then called in his "oldest" slave, not oldest in years, but the one who had the seniority, the chief servant who was his steward or business manager, possibly Eliezer of Damascus (15:2). Abraham asked him to swear that he would not get a wife for Isaac from the Canaanites, but would go and get a wife for him from his own relatives in western Mesopotamia. By putting his hand under Abraham's thigh (pointing to procreation), the slave would be indicating that the oath had to do with carrying on the chosen line, the line of God's promise. Swearing by the LORD as the God of heaven and earth recognized Him as the one true God, the all-powerful Creator, as well as the covenant-keeping God.

24:5-6. The slave was afraid the woman would not be willing to go so far from her home and asked whether he should take Isaac there (that is, to live there), if that were the case. Abraham's answer was very emphatic. He must not let that happen.

24:7-9. Abraham was confident the God of

4623, 800	4274	866	1744.311, 3937	866	8123.211, 3937
cj, prep, *n fs*	n fs, ps 1cs	cj, rel part	v Piel pf 3ms, prep, ps 1cs	cj, rel part	v Niphal pf 3ms, prep, ps 1cs
וּמֵאֶרֶץ	מוֹלַדְתִּי	וַאֲשֶׁר	דִּבֶּר־לִי	וַאֲשֶׁר	נִשְׁבַּע־לִי
ûmē'erets	môladhtî	wa'ăsher	dibber-lî	wa'ăsher	nishba'-lî
and from the land of	my family	and who	He spoke to me	and who	He swore to me

3937, 569.141	3937, 2320	5598.125	881, 800	2148	2000	8365.121
prep, v Qal inf con	prep, n ms, ps 2ms	v Qal impf 1cs	do, art, n fs	art, dem pron	pers pron	v Qal impf 3ms
לֵאמֹר	לְזַרְעֲךָ	אֶתֵּן	אֶת־הָאָרֶץ	הַזֹּאת	הוּא	יִשְׁלַח
lē'mōr	l^{e}zar'ăkhā	'ettēn	'eth-hā'ārets	hazzō'th	hû'	yishlach
saying	to your seed	I will give	the land	the this	He	He will send

4534	3937, 6686	4089.113	828	3937, 1158	4623, 8427
n ms, ps 3ms	prep, n mp, ps 2ms	cj, v Qal pf 2ms	n fs	prep, n ms, ps 1cs	prep, adv
מַלְאָכוֹ	לְפָנֶיךָ	וְלָקַחְתָּ	אִשָּׁה	לִבְנִי	מִשָּׁם
mal'ākhô	l^{e}phānêkhā	w^{e}lāqachtā	'ishshāh	livnî	mishshām
his angel	before you	and you will take	wife	for my son	from there

	524, 3940	13.122	828	3937, 2050.141	313	5536.213
8.	cj, cj, neg part	v Qal impf 3fs	art, n fs	prep, v Qal inf con	adv, ps 2ms	cj, v Niphal pf 2ms
	וְאִם־לֹא	תֹאבֶה	הָאִשָּׁה	לָלֶכֶת	אַחֲרֶיךָ	וְנִקִּיתָ
	w^{e}'im-lō'	thō'veh	hā'ishshāh	lālekheth	'achrêkhā	w^{e}niqqîthā
	and if not	she is willing	the woman	to go	after you	then you will be exempt

4623, 8095	2148	7828	881, 1158	3940	8178.123	8427
prep, n fs, ps 1cs	dem pron	adv	do, n ms, ps 1cs	neg part	v Hiphil impf 2ms	adv
מִשְּׁבֻעָתִי	זֹאת	רַק	אֶת־בְּנִי	לֹא	תָשֵׁב	שָׁמָּה
mishsh^{e}vu'āthî	zō'th	raq	'eth-b^{e}nî	lō'	thāshēv	shāmmāh
from my oath	this	only	my son	not	you will return	to there

	7947.121	5860	881, 3135	8809	3525	80	112
9.	cj, v Qal impf 3ms	art, n ms	do, n fs, ps 3ms	prep	*n fs*	pn	n ms, ps 3ms
	וַיָּשֶׂם	הָעֶבֶד	אֶת־יָדוֹ	תַּחַת	יֶרֶךְ	אַבְרָהָם	אֲדֹנָיו
	wayyāsem	hā'evedh	'eth-yādhô	tachath	yerekh	'avrāhām	'ădhōnâv
	so he put	the slave	his hand	under	the loins of	Abraham	his master

8123.221	3937	6142, 1745	2172		4089.121	5860	6463
cj, v Niphal impf 3ms	prep, ps 3ms	prep, art, n ms	art, dem pron	**10.**	cj, v Qal impf 3ms	art, n ms	num
וַיִּשָּׁבַע	לוֹ	עַל־הַדָּבָר	הַזֶּה		וַיִּקַּח	הָעֶבֶד	עֲשָׂרָה
wayyishshāva'	lô	'al-haddāvār	hazzeh		wayyiqqach	hā'evedh	'ăsārāh
and he swore	to him	on the matter	the this		and he took	the slave	ten

1622	4623, 1622	112	2050.121	3725, 3008	112
n mp	prep, *n mp*	n ms, ps 3ms	cj, v Qal impf 3ms	cj, *adj, n ms*	n ms, ps 3ms
גְמַלִּים	מִגְּמַלֵּי	אֲדֹנָיו	וַיֵּלֶךְ	וְכָל־טוּב	אֲדֹנָיו
g^{e}mallîm	migg^{e}mallê	'ădhōnâv	wayyēlekh	w^{e}khol-ṭûv	'ădhōnâv
camels	from the camels of	his master	and he went	and all the best things of	his master

904, 3135	7251.121	2050.121	420, 782	5282	420, 6111	5331
prep, n fs, ps 3ms	cj, v Qal impf 3ms	cj, v Qal impf 3ms	prep, pn	n md	prep, *n fs*	pn
בְּיָדוֹ	וַיָּקָם	וַיֵּלֶךְ	אֶל־אֲרַם	נַהֲרַיִם	אֶל־עִיר	נָחוֹר
b^{e}yādhô	wayyāqām	wayyēlekh	'el-'ăram	nah^{e}rayim	'el-'îr	nāchôr
in his hand	and he rose up	and he went	to Aram of	two rivers	to the city of	Nahor

	1313.521	1622	4623, 2445	3937, 6111	420, 908	4448
11.	cj, v Hiphil impf 3ms	art, n mp	prep, n ms	prep, art, n fs	prep, *n fs*	art, n md
	וַיַּבְרֵךְ	הַגְּמַלִּים	מִחוּץ	לָעִיר	אֶל־בְּאֵר	הַמָּיִם
	wayyavrēkh	hagg^{e}mallîm	michûts	lā'îr	'el-b^{e}'ēr	hammāyim
	and he made kneel down	the camels	outside	the city	at the well of	the waters

3937, 6496	6394	3937, 6496	3428.142	8056.154		569.121
prep, *n fs*	n ms	prep, *n fs*	v Qal inf con	art, v Qal act ptc fp	**12.**	cj, v Qal impf 3ms
לְעֵת	עֶרֶב	לְעֵת	צֵאת	הַשֹּׁאֲבֹת		וַיֹּאמַר
l^{e}'ēth	'erev	l^{e}'ēth	tsē'th	hashshō'ăvōth		wayyō'mar
toward time of	evening	toward time of	going out	the drawing ones		and He said

3176	435	112	80	7424.531, 5167	3937, 6686	3219
pn	*n mp*	n ms, ps 1cs	pn	v Hiphil impv 2ms, part	prep, n mp, ps 1cs	art, n ms
יְהוָה	אֱלֹהֵי	אֲדֹנִי	אַבְרָהָם	הַקְרֵה־נָא	לְפָנַי	הַיּוֹם
y^{e}hwāh	'ĕlōhê	'ădhōnî	'avrāhām	haqŏrēh-nā'	l^{e}phānay	hayyôm
Yahweh	God of	my master	Abraham	cause to happen please	before me	today

which took me from my father's house and from the land of my kindred, and which spake unto me: ... father's household, *NIV* ... land of my birth, *Anchor* ... nativity, *Darby.*

and that sware unto me, saying: ... who solemnly promised, *Anchor* ... made oath to me, *Berkeley* ... confirmed by oath the promise, *NAB.*

Unto thy seed will I give this land: ... your offspring, *Anchor* ... country to your race, *Fenton* ... your descendants, *Goodspeed.*

he shall send his angel before thee: ... he will send his angel ahead, *Berkeley* ... messenger before, *NAB.*

and thou shalt take a wife unto my son from thence: ... and you will bring a wife for my son from there, *Fenton.*

8. And if the woman will not be willing to follow thee: ... should the woman still refuse, *Anchor* ... if the woman will not come, *BB.*

then thou shalt be clear from this my oath: ... you shall then be absolved, *Anchor* ... you shall be free, *Fenton* ... you are released from this oath, *Berkeley.*

only bring not my son thither again: ... but you must not take my son back there, *Anchor.*

9. And the servant put his hand under the thigh of Abraham his master and sware to him concerning that matter: ... and swore to him in this undertaking, *NAB* ... an oath in those terms, *NEB.*

10. And the servant took ten camels of the camels of his master and departed for all the goods of his master were in his hand: ... having all good things of his master's, *ASV* ... all sorts of his master's treasures, *Berkeley.*

and he arose, and went to Mesopotamia unto the city of Nahor: ... Aram Naharaim, *Geneva* ... Aram between the Rivers, *Fenton* ... to Nahor's town, *Berkeley* ... city where Nahor lived, *NEB.*

11. And he made his camels to kneel down without the city by a well of water at the time of the evening: ... he made the camels take their rest outside the town, *BB* ... it being close to evening, *Anchor.*

even the time that women go out to draw water: ... by the water-spring, *BB.*

12. And he said, O LORD God of my master Abraham: ... O Yahweh, God of my master, Abraham, *Anchor* ... Ever-living God, *Fenton.*

---

heaven, who brought him out of that land and confirmed His promise with His oath, would be faithful to give Abraham's descendants the land of Canaan. He was sure that God would send his angel to prepare the situation and make it possible for the slave to get a wife for Isaac. However, to settle the slave's question, Abraham said that if the woman was not willing to come, then the slave would be released from the oath. This satisfied the slave, and he swore the oath as Abraham asked.

24:10-11. That Abraham had more than ten camels, in a day when camels were not common, was an evidence of his wealth. Such a caravan could be counted on to impress his relatives. The slave also took all sorts of the best and most valuable things of his master with him and went to Mesopotamia (literally, "Aram of the two rivers"). This was in the western part of Mesopotamia, and the two rivers were the Balikh and the Khabur, tributaries of the Euphrates River.

The city of Haran was on the Balikh River about a 700 mile journey north-northeast of Beersheba. Nearby was the city of Nahor. Arriving there, the slave made the camels kneel down by the well outside the city. The custom was for women to come out and draw water, and they would wait until the heat of the day was over to do so.

24:12-14. The slave recognized the LORD as the God of Abraham, because Abraham introduced him to the LORD. But in this prayer he was also rec-

6449.131, 2721	6196	112	80		2079	609	5507.255
cj, v Qal impv 2ms, n ms	prep	n ms, ps 1cs	pn	13.	intrj	pers pron	v Niphal pass ptc ms
וַעֲשֵׂה־חֶסֶד	עִם	אֲדֹנִי	אַבְרָהָם		הִנֵּה	אָנֹכִי	נִצָּב
wa'ăsēh-chesedh	'im	'ădhōnî	'avrāhām		hinnēh	'ānōkhî	nitstsāv
and show favor	with	my master	Abraham		behold	I	standing

6142. 6084	4448	1351	596	6111	3428.154	3937, 8056.141
prep, *n fs*	art, n md	*n fp*	*n mp*	art, n fs	v Qal act ptc fp	prep, v Qal inf con
עַל־עֵין	הַמָּיִם	וּבְנוֹת	אַנְשֵׁי	הָעִיר	יֹצְאֹת	לִשְׁאֹב
'al-'ên	hammāyim	ûvenôth	'anshê	hā'îr	yōtse'ōth	lish'ōv
beside the spring of	the waters	and the daughters of	the men of	the city	going out	to draw

4448		2030.111	5472	866	569.125	420	5371.532, 5167
n mp	14.	cj, v Qal pf 3ms	art, n fs	rel part	v Qal impf 1cs	prep, ps 3fs	v Hiphil impv 2fs, part
מָיִם		וְהָיָה	הַנַּעֲרָ	אֲשֶׁר	אֹמַר	אֵלֶיהָ	הַטִּי־נָא
māyim		wehāyāh	hanna'ărā	'ăsher	'ōmar	'ēlêhā	hattî-nā'
water		and it will be	the young woman	whom	I will say	to her	put down please

3656	8685.125	569.112	8685.131	1612, 1622	8615.525	881
n fs, ps 2fs	cj, v Qal impf 1cs	cj, v Qal pf 3fs	v Qal impv 2ms	cj, cj, n mp, ps 2ms	v Hiphil impf 1cs	do, ps 3fs
כַדֵּךְ	וְאֶשְׁתֶּה	וְאָמְרָה	שְׁתֵה	וְגַם־גְּמַלֶּיךָ	אַשְׁקֶה	אֹתָהּ
khaddēkh	we'eshteh	we'āmrāh	shethēh	wegham-gemallêkhā	'ashqeh	'ōthāhh
your jar	and I will drink	and she will say	drink	and also your camels	I will water	she

3306.513	3937, 5860	3937, 3437	904	3156.125	3706, 6449.113
v Hiphil pf 2ms	prep, n ms, ps 2ms	prep, pn	cj, prep, ps 3fs	v Qal impf 1cs	cj, v Qal pf 2ms
הֹכַחְתָּ	לְעַבְדְּךָ	לְיִצְחָק	וּבָהּ	אֵדַע	כִּי־עָשִׂיתָ
hōkhachtā	le'avdekhā	leyitschāq	ûvāhh	'ēdha'	kî-'āsîthā
you have determined	for your servant	for Isaac	and by it	I will know	that You have shown

2721	6196, 112		2030.121, 2000	3071	3735.311	3937, 1744.341
n ms	prep, n ms, ps 1cs	15.	cj, v Qal impf 3ms, pers pron	adv	v Piel pf 3ms	prep, v Piel inf con
חֶסֶד	עִם־אֲדֹנִי		וַיְהִי־הוּא	טֶרֶם	כִּלָּה	לְדַבֵּר
chesedh	'im-'ădhōnî		wayhî-hû'	terem	killāh	ledhabbēr
favor	with my master		and it happened that	not yet	he finished	speaking

2079	7549	3428.153	866	3314.412	3937, 1357	1158, 4575
cj, intrj	pn	v Qal act ptc fs	rel part	v Pual pf 3fs	prep, pn	*n ms*, pn
וְהִנֵּה	רִבְקָה	יֹצֵאת	אֲשֶׁר	יֻלְּדָה	לִבְתוּאֵל	בֶּן־מִלְכָּה
wehinnēh	rivqāh	yōtsē'th	'ăsher	yulledhāh	livthû'ēl	ben-milkāh
and behold	Rebekah	coming out	who	she was born	to Bethuel	the son of Milcah

828	5331	250	80	3656	6142, 8327		5472
n fs	pn	*n ms*	pn	cj, n fs, ps 3fs	prep, n ms, ps 3fs	16.	cj, art, n fs
אֵשֶׁת	נָחוֹר	אֲחִי	אַבְרָהָם	וְכַדָּהּ	עַל־שִׁכְמָהּ		וְהַנַּעֲרָ
'ēsheth	nāchôr	'ăchî	'avrāhām	wekhaddāhh	'al-shikhmāhh		wehanna'ărā
the wife of	Nahor	the brother of	Abraham	and her jar	on her shoulder		and the young girl

3005	4920	4108	1359	382	3940	3156.112
adj	n ms	adv	n fs	cj, n ms	neg part	v Qal pf 3fs
טֹבַת	מַרְאֶה	מְאֹד	בְּתוּלָה	וְאִישׁ	לֹא	יְדָעָהּ
tōvath	mar'eh	me'ōdh	bethûlāh	we'îsh	lō'	yedhā'āhh
beautiful of	appearance	very	virgin	and man	not	she had ever had relations with

3495.122	6084	4527.322	3656	6148.122		7608.121
cj, v Qal impf 3fs	art, n fs	cj, v Piel impf 3fs	n fs, ps 3fs	cj, v Qal impf 3fs	17.	cj, v Qal impf 3ms
וַתֵּרֶד	הָעַיְנָה	וַתְּמַלֵּא	כַדָּהּ	וַתָּעַל		וַיָּרָץ
wattēredh	hā'aynāh	wattemallē'	khaddāhh	wattā'al		wayyārāts
and she went down	to the spring	and she filled	her jar	and she went up		and he ran

5860	3937, 7410.141	569.121	1613.532	5167	4746, 4448	4623, 3656
art, n ms	prep, v Qal inf con, ps 3fs	cj, v Qal impf 3ms	v Hiphil impv 2fs, ps 1cs	part	*sub*, n mp	prep, n fs, ps 2fs
הָעֶבֶד	לִקְרָאתָהּ	וַיֹּאמֶר	הַגְמִיאִינִי	נָא	מְעַט־מַיִם	מִכַּדֵּךְ
hā'evedh	liqŏrā'thāhh	wayyō'mer	haghmî'înî	nā'	m^{e}'aṭ-mayim	mikkaddēkh
the slave	to meet her	and he said	give me drink	please	little water	from your jar

18.

569.122	8685.131	112	4257.322	3495.522	3656
cj, v Qal impf 3fs	v Qal impv 2ms	n ms, ps 1cs	cj, v Piel impf 3fs	cj, v Hiphil impf 3fs	n fs, ps 3fs
וַתֹּאמֶר	שְׁתֵה	אֲדֹנִי	וַתְּמַהֵר	וַתֹּרֶד	כַּדָּהּ
wattō'mer	sh^{e}thēh	'ădhōnî	watt^{e}mahēr	wattōredh	kaddāhh
and she said	drink	my master	and she hurried	and she put down	her jar

I pray thee, send me good speed this day: ... grant me a propitious sign this day, *Anchor* ... prosper me, I pray, *MLB* ... give me success, *Goodspeed* ... let it turn out favorably, *NAB.*

and shew kindness unto my master Abraham: ... deal thus graciously with my master, *Anchor* ... show steadfast love, *NRSV.*

13. Behold, I stand here by the well of water and the daughters of the men of the city come out to draw water: ... girls of the village, *LIVB* ... the young women of the city, *Good News.*

14. And let it come to pass, that the damsel to whom I shall say: ... that the maiden, *Darby* ... when the girl, *Fenton.*

Let down thy pitcher, I pray thee, that I may drink: ... please lower your jug that I may drink, *Anchor* ... let down your vessel and give me a drink, *BB* ... hand me your jar, and I will drink, *Fenton.*

and she shall say, Drink, and I will give thy camels drink also: ... here is a drink for you and let me give water to your camels, *BB* ... drink, and I'll water your camels too, *NIV.*

let the same be she that thou hast appointed for thy servant Isaac: ... may she be the one marked out by you, *BB* ... you have decreed, *Anchor* ... thou hast designated, *Berkeley* ... let your servant take her to Isaac, *Fenton.*

and thereby shall I know that thou hast shewed kindness unto my master: ... by this I shall be assured that thou wilt really be gracious to my master, *Goodspeed* ... that you have shown your favor, *NCB* ... that thou hast kept faith with my master, *NEB* ... you have shown steadfast love, *RSV.*

15. And it came to pass, before he had done speaking, that, behold, Rebekah came out, who was born to Bethuel, son of Milcah, the wife of Nahor, Abraham's brother with her pitcher upon her shoulder: he had not yet finished, *NCB* ... before he had finished praying silently, *NEB.*

16. And the damsel was very fair to look upon: ... the girl was very beautiful, *Anchor* ... exceptionally good looking, *Berkeley.*

a virgin, neither had any man known her: ... no man had had relations, *NASB* ... intercourse, *NEB* ... lain with her, *NIV* ... a virgin undefiled, *NCB.*

and she went down to the well, and filled her pitcher, and came up: ... she went down to the spring and filled her jug, *Anchor* ... jar, *NIV.*

17. And the servant ran to meet her, and said: ... the steward was delighted, *Fenton* ... hurried to meet her, *REB.*

Let me, I pray thee, drink a little water of thy pitcher: ... please let me have a little sip of water from your jug, *Anchor* ... from your jar, *NASB.*

ognizing Him as his God. He asked for success and for God to show covenant love to Abraham. Then he asked God to confirm His choice for Isaac by a test. The girl must volunteer to draw water for ten thirsty camels. The slave knew the kind of hospitality that characterized Abraham, so the test would also show that she was the kind of woman who would fit into Abraham's family.

24:15-16. The answer was already on the way. God had indeed sent His angel to prepare the situation. Rebekah came out, went down a series of steps to the spring that fed the well, and filled her water jar. Not only was she from Abraham's relatives, she was beautiful in face and form, and was a virgin. Her name meaning "noose" was a figurative term for a fascinating beauty that traps and entrances.

24:17-21. The slave then put Rebekah to the test by asking her for a drink. She responded in the way he had prayed she would, and kept pouring water for the camels until they were satisfied. The servant watched without saying a word. He wanted the LORD to provide the answer without any interference on his part.

6142, 3135	8615.522		3735.322	3937, 8615.541	569.122
prep, n fs, ps 3fs	cj, v Hiphil impf 3fs, ps 3ms	**19.**	cj, v Piel impf 3fs	prep, v Hiphil inf con, ps 3ms	cj, v Qal impf 3fs
עַל־יָדָהּ	וַתַּשְׁקֵהוּ		וַתְּכַל	לְהַשְׁקֹתוֹ	וַתֹּאמֶר
'al-yādhāhh	wattashqēhû		watt^{e}khal	l^{e}hashqōthô	wattō'mer
on her hand	and she gave him a drink		when she finished	giving him a drink	then she said

1612	3937, 1622	8056.125	5912	524, 3735.316	3937, 8685.141
cj	prep, n mp, ps 2ms	v Qal impf 1cs	adv	adv, v Piel pf 3cp	prep, v Qal inf con
גַּם	לִגְמַלֶּיךָ	אֶשְׁאָב	עַד	אִם־כִּלּוּ	לִשְׁתֹּת
gam	lighmallêkhā	'esh'āv	'adh	'im-killû	lishtōth
also	for your camels	I will draw	until	they have finished	drinking

	4257.322	6408.322	3656	420, 8633	7608.122	5968
20.	cj, v Piel impf 3fs	cj, v Piel impf 3fs	n fs, ps 3fs	prep, art, n fs	cj, v Qal impf 3fs	adv
	וַתְּמַהֵר	וַתְּעַר	כַּדָּהּ	אֶל־הַשֹּׁקֶת	וַתָּרָץ	עוֹד
	watt^{e}mahēr	watt^{e}'ar	kaddāhh	'el-hashshōqeth	wattārāts	'ôdh
	and she hurried	and she emptied out	her jar	into the trough	and she ran	again

420, 908	3937, 8056.141	8056.122	3937, 3725, 1622		382	8059.751
prep, art n fs	prep, v Qal inf con	cj, v Qal impf 3fs	prep, *adj*, n mp, ps 3ms	**21.**	cj, art, n ms	v Hithpael ptc ms
אֶל־הַבְּאֵר	לִשְׁאֹב	וַתִּשְׁאַב	לְכָל־גְּמַלָּיו		וְהָאִישׁ	מִשְׁתָּאֵה
'el-habb^{e}'ēr	lish'ōv	wattish'av	l^{e}khol-g^{e}mallāyw		w^{e}hā'îsh	mishtā'ēh
to the well	to draw	and she drew	for all his camels		and the man	he was debating

3937	2896.551	3156.141	7014.511	3176	1932	524, 3940
prep, ps 3fs	v Hiphil ptc ms	v Qal inf con	intrg part, v Hiphil pf 3ms	pn	n ms, ps 3ms	cj, adv
לָהּ	מַחֲרִישׁ	לָדַעַת	הַהִצְלִיחַ	יְהוָה	דַּרְכּוֹ	אִם־לֹא
lāhh	machrîsh	lādha'ath	hahitslîach	y^{e}hwāh	darkô	'im-lō'
about her	being silent	to determine	if He had made successful	Yahweh	his journey	or not

	2030.121	3626, 866	3735.316	1622	3937, 8685.141	4089.121
22.	cj, v Qal impf 3ms	prep, rel part	v Piel pf 3cp	art, n mp	prep, v Qal inf con	cj, v Qal impf 3ms
	וַיְהִי	כַּאֲשֶׁר	כִּלּוּ	הַגְּמַלִּים	לִשְׁתּוֹת	וַיִּקַּח
	wayhî	ka'ăsher	killû	hagg^{e}mallîm	lishtôth	wayyiqqach
	and it was	according to that	they finished	the camels	drinking	then he took

382	5321	2174	1261	4623, 8621	8530	7050	6142, 3135
art, n ms	*n ms*	n ms	*num*	prep, n ms, ps 3ms	cj, *num*	n mp	prep, n fd, ps 3fs
הָאִישׁ	נֶזֶם	זָהָב	בֶּקַע	מִשְׁקָלוֹ	וּשְׁנֵי	צְמִידִים	עַל־יָדֶיהָ
hā'îsh	nezem	zāhāv	beqa'	mishqālô	ûsh^{e}nê	ts^{e}mîdhîm	'al-yādhêhā
the man	ring	gold	half of	shekel	and two	bracelets	on her hands

6463	2174	4623, 8621		569.121	1351, 4449	879	5222.532
num	n ms	prep, n ms, ps 3mp	**23.**	cj, v Qal impf 3ms	*n fs*, interr	pers pron	v Hiphil impv 2fs
עֲשָׂרָה	זָהָב	מִשְׁקָלָם		וַיֹּאמֶר	בַּת־מִי	אַתְּ	הַגִּידִי
'ăsārāh	zāhāv	mishqālām		wayyō'mer	bath-mî	'att^{e}	haggîdhî
ten	gold	shekels		and he said	daughter of whom	you	tell

5167	3937	3552	904, 1041, 1	4887	3937	3937, 4053.141
part	prep, ps 1cs	intrg part, sub	prep, *n ms*, n ms, ps 2fs	n ms	prep, ps 1cp	prep, v Qal inf con
נָא	לִי	הֲיֵשׁ	בֵּית־אָבִיךְ	מָקוֹם	לָנוּ	לָלִין
nā'	lî	h^{e}yēsh	bêth-'āvîkh	māqôm	lānû	lālîn
please	to me	is there	in the house of your father	place	for us	to spend the night

	569.122	420	1351, 1357	609	1158, 4575	866
24.	cj, v Qal impf 3fs	prep, ps 3ms	*n fs*, pn	pers pron	*n ms*, pn	rel part
	וַתֹּאמֶר	אֵלָיו	בַּת־בְּתוּאֵל	אָנֹכִי	בֶּן־מִלְכָּה	אֲשֶׁר
	wattō'mer	'ēlāv	bath-b^{e}thû'ēl	'ānōkhî	ben-milkāh	'ăsher
	and she said	to him	the daughter of Bethuel	I	the son of Milcah	whom

3314.112 v Qal pf 3fs יָלְדָה yāledhāh she gave birth	3937, 5331 prep, pn לְנָחוֹר lenāchôr for Nahor	**25.**	569.122 cj, v Qal impf 3fs וַתֹּאמֶר wattō'mer and she said	420 prep, ps 3ms אֵלָיו 'ēlâv to him	1612, 8730 cj, n ms גַּם־תֶּבֶן gam-teven both straw	1612, 4706 cj, n ms גַּם־מִסְפּוֹא gam-mispô' and fodder	7521 adj רַב rav much

6196 prep, ps 1cp עִמָּנוּ 'immānû with us	1612, 4887 cj, n ms גַּם־מָקוֹם gam-māqôm and place	3937, 4053.141 prep, v Qal inf con לָלוּן lālûn to spend the night	**26.**	7199.121 cj, v Qal impf 3ms וַיִּקֹּד wayyiqqōdh and he bowed down	382 art, n ms הָאִישׁ hā'îsh the man	8246.721 cj, v Hithpalel impf 3ms וַיִּשְׁתַּחוּ wayyishtachû and he worshiped

18. And she said, Drink, my lord: and she hasted, and let down her pitcher upon her hand, and gave him drink: ... lowering the jug onto her hand, *NAB* ... jar, *RSV*.

19. And when she had done giving him drink, she said, I will draw water for thy camels also, until they have done drinking: ... when she had let him drink his fill, *Anchor* ... was through quenching his thirst, *MLB*.

20. And she hasted, and emptied her pitcher into the trough: ... she hastened, *NKJV* ... went quickly to the spring, *BB*. . . emptied her jar, *RSV* ... jug, *Anchor*.

and ran again unto the well to draw water and drew for all his camels: ... ran back to the well to draw anew, *Anchor* ... hurried again, *REB*.

21. And the man wondering at her held his peace: ... stood gaping at her, *Anchor* ... looked steadfastly on her, holding his peace, *ASV*.

to wit whether the LORD had made his journey prosperous or not: ... not daring to speak until he learned whether Yahweh had made his errand successful or not, *Anchor* ... a good outcome, *BB*.

22. And it came to pass, as the camels had done drinking that the man took a golden earring of half a shekel weight: ... took a brooch of gold, *Fenton* ... a gold nose-ring, *BB* ... a quarter ounce, *Berkeley* ... took out a gold ring, *Anchor*.

and two bracelets for her hands of ten shekels weight of gold: ... two ornaments for her arms, *BB* ... two five-ounce golden bracelets for her wrists, *Berkeley* ... two gold bands for her arms, *Anchor*.

23. And said, Whose daughter art thou? Tell me, I pray thee is there room in thy father's house for us to lodge in?: ... to spend the night, *Anchor* ... stay overnight, *NCB*.

24. And she said unto him, I am the daughter of Bethuel the son of Milcah, which she bare unto Nahor.

25. She said moreover unto him, We have both straw and provender enough and room to lodge in: ... plenty of straw and feed in our house, *Anchor* ... a great store of dry grass and cattle-food, *BB*.

26. And the man bowed down his head, and worshipped the LORD: ... the man stooped, *Darby* ... with bent head, *BB* ... bowed in homage to, *Anchor*.

27. And he said, Blessed be the LORD God of my master Abraham: ... praised be the Lord God, *Berkeley* ... praised be Yahweh, *Anchor*.

who hath not left destitute my master of his mercy and his truth: ... not withdrawn his loving-kindness and his faithfulness, *Darby* ... his steadfast kindness, *Anchor* ... has given a sign that he is good and true, *BB* ... has not forgotten, *Fenton* ... has not failed, *Berkeley*.

I being in the way, the LORD led me to the house of my master's brethren: ... straight to, *Anchor* ... kinfolk, *Berkeley* ... relatives, *NIV*.

24:22-23. The slave, as a token of appreciation, took out a gold nose ring weighing about 1/5 ounce (5.69 grams), and two gold bracelets weighing about 4 ounces, and gave them to her. Then he asked who her father was and if there was room for him and the camels to spend the night.

24:24-25. Rebekah's response was positive. She was actually Abraham's grandniece, and they had fodder for the camels and room for the man.

24:26-27. The servant recognized this as a marvelous demonstration of God's divine providence. He did not wait for the Sabbath to express his thanks. He bowed down to the ground and worshiped the LORD right where he was. He blessed, that is, praised and thanked God for not forsaking His covenant love and lasting faithfulness, and for leading him right to his master's relatives.

24:28-31. Rebekah ran to her mother's household (her father probably had other wives). Her brother Laban saw the nose ring (which was usual-

3937, 3176		569.121	1313.155	3176	435	112	80
prep, pn	**27.**	cj, v Qal impf 3ms	v Qal pass ptc ms	pn	*n mp*	n ms, ps 1cs	pn
לַיהוָה		וַיֹּאמֶר	בָּרוּךְ	יְהוָה	אֱלֹהֵי	אֲדֹנִי	אַבְרָהָם
layhwāh		wayyō'mer	bārûkh	y^{e}hwāh	'ělōhê	'ădhōnî	'avrāhām
Yahweh		and he said	blessed be	Yahweh	the God of	my master	Abraham

866	3940, 6013.111	2721	583	4623, 6196	112	609
rel part	neg part, v Qal pf 3ms	n ms, ps 3ms	cj, n fs, ps 3ms	prep, prep	n ms, ps 1cs	pers pron
אֲשֶׁר	לֹא־עָזַב	חַסְדּוֹ	וַאֲמִתּוֹ	מֵעִם	אֲדֹנִי	אָנֹכִי
'ăsher	lō'-'āzav	chasdô	wa'ămittô	mē'im	'ădhōnî	'ānōkhî
who	not He has forsaken	his steadfast love	or his reliability	for	my master	I

904, 1932	5328.111	3176	1041	250	112		7608.122
prep, art, n ms	v Qal pf 3ms, ps 1cs	pn	*n ms*	*n mp*	n ms, ps 1cs	**28.**	cj, v Qal impf 3fs
בַּדֶּרֶךְ	נָחַנִי	יְהוָה	בֵּית	אֲחֵי	אֲדֹנִי		וַתָּרָץ
badderekh	nāchanî	y^{e}hwāh	bêth	'ăchê	'ădhōnî		wattārāts
on the journey	He has guided me	Yahweh	to the house of	the relatives of	my master		and she ran

5472	5222.522	3937, 1041	525	3626, 1745	431
art, n fs	cj, v Hiphil impf 3fs	prep, *n ms*	n fs, ps 3fs	prep, art, n mp	art, dem pron
הַנַּעֲרָ	וַתַּגֵּד	לְבֵית	אִמָּהּ	כַּדְּבָרִים	הָאֵלֶּה
hanna'ărā	wattaggēdh	l^{e}vêth	'immāhh	kadd^{e}vārîm	hā'ēlleh
the young woman	and she told	to the house of	her mother	about the things	the these

	3937, 7549	250	8428	3969	7608.121	3969	420, 382
29.	cj, prep, pn	n ms	cj, n ms, ps 3ms	pn	cj, v Qal impf 3ms	pn	prep, art, n ms
	וּלְרִבְקָה	אָח	וּשְׁמוֹ	לָבָן	וַיָּרָץ	לָבָן	אֶל־הָאִישׁ
	ûlārivqāh	'āch	ûsh^{e}mô	lāvān	wayyārāts	lāvān	'el-hā'îsh
	and to Rebekah	brother	and his name	Laban	and he ran	Laban	to the man

2445	420, 6084		2030.121	3626, 7495.141	881, 5321	881, 7050
art, n ms	prep, art, n fs	**30.**	cj, v Qal impf 3ms	prep, v Qal inf con	do, art, n ms	cj, do, art, n mp
הַחוּצָה	אֶל־הָעָיִן		וַיְהִי	כִּרְאֹת	אֶת־הַנֶּזֶם	וְאֶת־הַצְּמִדִים
hachûtsāh	'el-hā'āyin		wayhî	kir'ōth	'eth-hannezem	w^{e}'eth-hatsts^{e}midhîm
outside	to the spring		and it was	when seeing	the ring	and the bracelets

6142, 3135	269	3626, 8471.141	881, 1745	7549	269	3937, 569.141
prep, *n fd*	n fs, ps 3ms	cj, v Qal inf con, ps 3ms	do, *n mp*	pn	n fs, ps 3ms	prep, v Qal inf con
עַל־יְדֵי	אֲחֹתוֹ	וּכְשָׁמְעוֹ	אֶת־דִּבְרֵי	רִבְקָה	אֲחֹתוֹ	לֵאמֹר
'al-y^{e}dhê	'ăchōthô	ûkh^{e}shām'ô	'eth-divrê	rivqāh	'ăchōthô	l^{e}mōr
on the hands of	his sister	and when hearing	the words of	Rebekah	his sister	saying

3662, 1744.311	420	382	971.121	420, 382	2079	6198.151
adv, v Piel pf 3ms	prep, ps 1cs	art, n ms	cj, Qal impf 3ms	prep, art, n ms	cj, intrj	v Qal act ptc ms
כֹּה־דִבֶּר	אֵלַי	הָאִישׁ	וַיָּבֹא	אֶל־הָאִישׁ	וְהִנֵּה	עֹמֵד
kōh-dhiber	'ēlay	hā'îsh	wayyāvō'	'el-hā'îsh	w^{e}hinnēh	'ōmēdh
thus he spoke	to me	the man	then he went	to the man	and behold	standing

6142, 1622	6142, 6084		569.121	971.131	1313.155	3176
prep, art, n mp	prep, art, n fs	**31.**	cj, v Qal impf 3ms	v Qal impv 2ms	*v Qal pass ptc ms*	pn
עַל־הַגְּמַלִּים	עַל־הָעָיִן		וַיֹּאמֶר	בּוֹא	בְּרוּךְ	יְהוָה
'al-hagg^{e}mallîm	'al-hā'āyin		wayyō'mer	bô'	b^{e}rûkh	y^{e}hwāh
beside the camels	beside the spring		and he said	come	blessed of	Yahweh

4066	6198.123	904, 2445	609	6680.315	1041	4887
intrg	v Qal impf 2ms	prep, art, n ms	cj, pers pron	v Piel pf 1cs	art, noun ms	cj, n ms
לָמָּה	תַעֲמֹד	בַּחוּץ	וְאָנֹכִי	פִּנִּיתִי	הַבַּיִת	וּמָקוֹם
lāmmāh	ta'ămōdh	bachûts	w^{e}'ānōkhî	pinnîthî	habbayith	ûmāqôm
why	you are standing	outside	when I	I have cleared	the house	and place

3937, 1622		971.121	382	1041	6858.321	1622
prep, art, n mp	**32.**	cj, v Qal impf 3ms	art, n ms	art, n fs	cj, v Piel impf 3ms	art, n mp
לַגְּמַלִּים		וַיָּבֹא	הָאִישׁ	הַבַּיְתָה	וַיְפַתַּח	הַגְּמַלִּים
lagg^{e}mallîm		wayyāvō'	hā'îsh	habbay^{e}thāh	way^{e}phattach	hagg^{e}mallîm
for the camels		and he went	the man	to the house	and he unloaded	the camels

5598.121	8730	4706	3937, 1622	4448	3937, 7647.141	7559
cj, v Qal perf 3ms	n ms	cj, n ms	prep, art, n mp	cj, n mp	prep, v Qal inf con	n fd, ps 3ms
וַיִּתֵּן	תֶּבֶן	וּמִסְפּוֹא	לַגְּמַלִּים	וּמַיִם	לִרְחֹץ	רַגְלָיו
wayyittēn	teven	ûmispô'	lagg^{e}mallîm	ûmayim	lirchōts	raghlâv
and he gave	straw	and fodder	to the camels	and water	to wash	his feet

28. And the damsel ran: ... the girl went at a run, *Anchor* ... young person runneth, *Young.*

and told them of her mother's house these things: ... and took the news to her mother's house, *BB* ... gave an account, *Goodspeed* ... to spread the news, *Anchor* ... tell everything, *Berkeley.*

29. And Rebekah had a brother, and his name was Laban: and Laban ran out unto the man, unto the well: ... unto the fountain, *ASV* ... at the spring, *Anchor.*

30. And it came to pass, when he saw the earring and bracelets upon his sister's hands: ... having noticed the nose-ring, *Anchor* ... bands on his sister's arms, *Anchor* ... bracelets, *Berkeley* ... ornaments, *BB* ... brooches, *Fenton.*

and when he heard the words of Rebekah his sister, saying, Thus spake the man unto me: ... heard his sister Rebekah repeat what the man said to her, *Berkeley* ... Rebekah's account, *REB.*

that he came unto the man and, behold, he stood by the camels at the well: ... sitting by the camels near the spring, *NCB.*

31. And he said, Come in, thou blessed of the LORD; wherefore standest thou without?: ... come in, you whom the Lord has blessed, *REB* ... why do you remain outside, *Anchor* ... stay outdoors, *NCB.*

for I have prepared the house, and room for the camels: ... I have gotten the house ready and a place for the camels, *Berkeley* ... I offer you a house and a stable, *Fenton.*

32. And the man came into the house: ... entered the house, *Fenton* ... went inside, *NAB* ... bringeth in the man, *Young.*

and he ungirded his camels: ... unloaded the camels, *Fenton* ... unharnessed, *Goodspeed* ... unsaddled, *Geneva* ... took the cords off, *BB* ... looseth, *Young.*

and gave straw and provender for the camels: ... provided straw and fodder, *Berkeley* ... gave them grass and food, *BB* ... straw to bed down the camels, *LIVB.*

and water to wash his feet and the men's feet that were with him: ... for the man himself, *NCB* ... water was brought to bathe his feet, *NAB.*

33. And there was set meat before him to eat: ... when food was set before him, *Anchor* ... also placed food before them, *Fenton* ... then supper was served, *LIVB.*

but he said, I will not eat, until I have told mine errand: ... delivered my message, *Fenton* ... made known my business, *Darby* ... my business clear, *BB* ... told my tale, *Anchor.*

And he said, Speak on: ... do so, *BB* ... tell it, *MLB* ... let us hear it, *NEB.*

34. And he said, I am Abraham's servant: ... I am Abraham's slave, *Goodspeed.*

35. And the LORD hath blessed my master greatly and he is become great: ... abundantly, *NAB* ... man of power, *NEB* ... wealthy, *NAB* ...

ly put in a pierced left nostril) and the bracelets, and heard what Abraham's slave had said, including, probably, his prayer and praise to the LORD, the God of Abraham. So he concluded that Abraham's slave was blessed of the LORD and he hurried out to invite the slave to come and bring his camels.

24:32. The provision for the camels was generous, and they were taken care of first. Another important courtesy was water to wash the feet of Abraham's slave and of the men who were with him. For the first time, we are told that Abraham's slave did not manage the ten camels all by himself.

24:33-48. Abraham's slave refused food until he could tell them what he had to say. Then he proceeded to tell the whole story from the time Abraham asked him to swear an oath not to take a wife for Isaac from the Canaanites, to the time God answered his prayer and he bowed and worshiped God for leading him to the granddaughter of Abraham's brother.

7559	596	866	882		7947.621	3937, 6686
cj, *n fd*	art, n mp	rel part	prep, ps 3ms	**33.**	cj, v Hophal impf 3ms	prep, n mp, ps 3ms
וְרַגְלֵי	הָאֲנָשִׁים	אֲשֶׁר	אִתּוֹ		וַיִּישַׂם	לְפָנָיו
weraghlê	hā'ănāshîm	'ăsher	'ittô		wayysām	lephānâv
and the feet of	the men	who	with him		and it was set	before him

3937, 404	569.121	3940	404.125	5912	524, 1744.315	1745
prep, v Qal inf con	cj, v Qal impf 3ms	neg part	v Qal impf 1cs	adv	adv, v Piel pf 1cs	n mp, ps 1cs
לֶאֱכֹל	וַיֹּאמֶר	לֹא	אֹכַל	עַד	אִם־דִּבַּרְתִּי	דְּבָרָי
le'ĕkhōl	wayyō'mer	lō'	'ōkhal	'adh	'im-dibbartî	devāray
to eat	and he said	not	I will eat	until	I have spoken	my words

569.121	1744.331		569.121	5860	80	609		3176
cj, v Qal impf 3ms	v Piel impv 2ms	**34.**	cj, v Qal impf 3ms	*n ms*	pn	pers pron	**35.**	cj, pn
וַיֹּאמֶר	דַּבֵּר		וַיֹּאמַר	עֶבֶד	אַבְרָהָם	אָנֹכִי		וַיהוָה
wayyō'mer	dabbēr		wayyō'mar	'evedh	'avrāhām	'ānōkhî		wayhwāh
and he said	speak		and he said	the slave of	Abraham	I		and Yahweh

1313.311	881, 112	4108	1461.121	5598.121, 3937	6887	1267
v Piel pf 3ms	do, n ms, ps 1cs	adv	cj, v Qal impf 3ms	cj, v Qal impf 3ms, prep, ps 3ms	n fs	cj, n ms
בֵּרַךְ	אֶת־אֲדֹנִי	מְאֹד	וַיִּגְדָּל	וַיִּתֶּן־לוֹ	צֹאן	וּבָקָר
bērakh	'eth-'ădhōnî	me'ōdh	wayyighdāl	wayyitten-lô	tsō'n	ûvāqār
He blessed	my master	very	and he became great	and He gave to him	sheep	and cattle

3826B	2174	5860	8569	1622	2645
cj, n ms	cj, n ms	cj, n mp	cj, n fp	cj, n mp	cj, n mp
וְכֶסֶף	וְזָהָב	וַעֲבָדִם	וּשְׁפָחֹת	וּגְמַלִּים	וַחֲמֹרִים
wekheseph	wezāhāv	wa'ăvādhim	ûshephāchōth	ûghmallîm	wachmōrîm
and silver	and gold	and male slaves	and female slaves	and camels	and donkeys

	3314.122	8023	828	112	1158	3937, 112	311
36.	cj, v Qal impf 3fs	pn	*n fs*	n ms, ps 1cs	n ms	prep, n ms, ps 1cs	*sub*
	וַתֵּלֶד	שָׂרָה	אֵשֶׁת	אֲדֹנִי	בֵן	לַאדֹנִי	אַחֲרֵי
	wattēledh	sārāh	'ēsheth	'ădhōnî	vēn	la'dhōnî	'achrê
	and she gave birth	Sarah	the wife of	my master	son	for my master	after

2294	5598.121, 3937	881, 3725, 866, 3937		8123.521
n fs, ps 3fs	cj, v Qal impf 3ms, prep, ps 3ms	do, *adj*, rel part, prep, ps 3ms	**37.**	cj, v Hiphil impf 3ms, ps 1cs
זִקְנָתָהּ	וַיִּתֶּן־לוֹ	אֶת־כָּל־אֲשֶׁר־לוֹ		וַיַּשְׁבִּעֵנִי
ziqōnāthāhh	wayyitten-lô	'eth-kol-'ăsher-lô		wayyashbi'ēnî
her growing old	and he gave to him	all which to him		and he made me swear

112	3937, 569.141	3940, 4089.123	828	3937, 1158	4623, 1351
n ms, ps 1cs	prep, v Qal inf con	neg part, v Qal impf 2ms	n fs	prep, n ms, ps 1cs	prep, *n fp*
אֲדֹנִי	לֵאמֹר	לֹא־תִקַּח	אִשָּׁה	לִבְנִי	מִבְּנוֹת
'ădhōnî	lē'mōr	lō'-tiqqach	'ishshāh	livnî	mibbenôth
my master	saying	not you will take	wife	for my son	from the daughters of

3793	866	609	3553.151	904, 800		524, 3940
art, pn	rel part	pers pron	v Qal act ptc ms	prep, n fs, ps 3ms	**38.**	conj, adv
הַכְּנַעֲנִי	אֲשֶׁר	אָנֹכִי	יֹשֵׁב	בְּאַרְצוֹ		אִם־לֹא
hakkena'ănî	'ăsher	'ānōkhî	yōshēv	be'artsô		'im-lō'
the Canaanites	where	I	dwelling	in their land		but rather

420, 1041, 1	2050.123	420, 5121	4089.113	828	3937, 1158
prep, *n ms*, n ms, ps 1cs	v Qal impf 2ms	cj, prep, n fs, ps 1cs	cj, v Qal pf 2ms	n fs	prep, n ms, ps 1cs
אֶל־בֵּית־אָבִי	תֵּלֵךְ	וְאֶל־מִשְׁפַּחְתִּי	וְלָקַחְתָּ	אִשָּׁה	לִבְנִי
'el-bêth-'āvî	tēlēkh	we'eth-mishpachtî	welāqachtā	'ishshāh	livnî
to house of my father	you will go	and to my family	and you will take	wife	for my son

39.	569.125	420, 112	193	3940, 2050.122	828	313
	cj, v Qal impf 1cs	prep, n ms, ps 1cs	adv	neg part, v Qal impf 3fs	art, n fs	adv, ps 1cs
	וָאֹמַר	אֶל־אֲדֹנִי	אֻלַי	לֹא־תֵלֵךְ	הָאִשָּׁה	אַחֲרָי
	wā'ōmar	'el-'ădhōnî	'ulay	lō'-thēlēkh	hā'ishshāh	'achrāy
	and I said	to my master	perhaps	not she will go	the woman	after me

40.	569.121	420	3176	866, 2050.715	3937, 6686	8365.121
	cj, v Qal impf 3ms	prep, ps 1cs	pn	rel part, v Hithpael pf 1cs	prep, n mp, ps 3ms	v Qal impf 3ms
	וַיֹּאמֶר	אֵלָי	יְהוָה	אֲשֶׁר־הִתְהַלַּכְתִּי	לְפָנָיו	יִשְׁלַח
	wayyō'mer	'ēlāy	y^{e}hwāh	'ăsher-hithhallachtî	l^{e}phānâv	yishlach
	and He said	to me	Yahweh	whom I walk	before him	He will send

4534	882	7014.511	1932	4089.113	828
n ms, ps 3ms	prep, ps 2fs	cj, v Hiphil pf 3ms	n ms, ps 2ms	cj, v Qal pf 2ms	n fs
מַלְאָכוֹ	אִתָּךְ	וְהִצְלִיחַ	דַּרְכֶּךָ	וְלָקַחְתָּ	אִשָּׁה
mal'ākhô	'ittākh	w^{e}hitslîach	darkekhā	w^{e}lāqachtā	'ishshāh
his angel	with you	and He will make successful	your journey	and you will take	wife

3937, 1158	4623, 5121	4623, 1041	1	41.	226	5536.223
prep, n ms, ps 1cs	prep, n fs, ps 1cs	cj, prep, *n ms*	n ms, ps 1cs		adv	v Niphal impf 2ms
לִבְנִי	מִמִּשְׁפַּחְתִּי	וּמִבֵּית	אָבִי		אָז	תִּנָּקֶה
livnî	mimmishpachtî	ûmibêth	'āvî		'āz	tinnāqeh
for my son	from my family	and from the house of	my father		then	you will be exempt

4623, 427	3706	971.123	420, 5121	524, 3940	5598.126	3937
prep, n fs, ps 1 cs	cj	v Qal impf 2ms	prep, n fs, ps 1cs	cj, cj, neg part	v Qal impf 3mp	prep, ps 2fs
מֵאָלָתִי	כִּי	תָבוֹא	אֶל־מִשְׁפַּחְתִּי	וְאִם־לֹא	יִתְּנוּ	לָךְ
mē'ālāthî	kî	thāvô'	'el-mishpachtî	w^{e}'im-lō'	yitt^{e}nû	lākh
from my oath	because	you went	to my family	even if not	they will give	to you

2030.113	5538	4623, 427	42.	971.125	3219	420, 6084
cj, v Qal pf 2ms	adj	prep, n fs, ps 1 cs		cj, v Qal impf 1cs	art, n ms	prep, art, n fs
וְהָיִיתָ	נָקִי	מֵאָלָתִי		וָאָבֹא	הַיּוֹם	אֶל־הָעָיִן
w^{e}hāyîthā	nāqî	mē'ālāthî		wā'āvō'	hayyôm	'el-hā'āyin
still you will be	exempt	from my oath		so I came	today	to the spring

become rich, *NASB* ... who has prospered, *Anchor.*

and he hath given him flocks, and herds, and silver, and gold, and menservants, and maidservants, and camels, and asses: ... and donkeys, *NRSV.*

36. And Sarah my master's wife bare a son to my master when she was old: ... hath been aged, *Young* ... after reaching old age, *Anchor.*

and unto him hath he given all that he hath: ... to him he is leaving everything, *Goodspeed* ... given him all his property, *NCB.*

37. And my master made me swear, saying: ... pledged me, *Fenton* ... put me under oath, *Anchor* ... adjured, *NCB* ... procure, *NAB.*

Thou shalt not take a wife to my son of the daughters of the Canaanites, in whose land I dwell: ... secure no wife, *Berkeley* ... not obtain a wife for my son, *Anchor* ... not to marry one of the local girls, *LIVB.*

38. But thou shalt go unto my father's house, and to my kindred, and take a wife unto my son: ... my father's family, *Anchor* ... relatives, *Berkeley.*

39. And I said unto my master, Peradventure the woman will not follow me: ... suppose I can't find a girl who will come, *LIVB* ... what if the woman refuses, *Anchor.*

40. And he said unto me, The LORD, before whom I walk: ... walk habitually, *Young.*

will send his angel with thee, and prosper thy way; and thou shalt take a wife for my son of my kindred, and of my father's house: ... render your trip successful, *Berkeley* ... prosper your way, *Darby.*

41. Then shalt thou be clear from this my oath when thou comest to my kindred: and if they give not thee one, thou shalt be clear from my oath: ... clan, *NIV* ... if they refuse, *Goodspeed* ... released from my ban, *Anchor* ... discharged, *Geneva* ... acquitted, *Young.*

569.125 cj, v Qal impf 1cs וָאֹמַר wā'ōmar and I said	**3176** pn יְהוָה y^{e}hwāh Yahweh	**435** *n mp* אֱלֹהֵי 'ĕlōhê God of	**112** n ms, ps 1cs אֲדֹנִי 'ădhōnî my master	**80** pn אַבְרָהָם 'avrāhām Abraham	**524, 3552, 5167** cj, n ms, ps 2ms, part אִם־יֶשְׁךָ־נָּא 'im-yesh^{e}khā-nā' if You will be please

7014.551 *v Hiphil ptc ms* מַצְלִיחַ matslîach One who brings success of	**1932** n ms, ps 1cs דַּרְכִּי darkî my journey	**866** rel part אֲשֶׁר 'ăsher which	**609** pers pron אָנֹכִי 'ānōkhî I	**2050.151** v Qal act ptc ms הֹלֵךְ hōlēkh one going	**6142** prep, ps 3fs עָלֶיהָ 'ālêhā on it	**43.**	**2079** intrj הִנֵּה hinnēh behold

609 pers pron אָנֹכִי 'ānōkhî I	**5507.255** v Niphal ptc ms נִצָּב nitstsāv standing	**6142. 6084** prep, *n fs* עַל־עֵין 'al-'ên beside the spring of	**4448** art, n md הַמָּיִם hammāyim the waters	**2030.111** cj, v Qal pf 3ms וְהָיָה w^{e}hāyāh and it was	**6183** art, n fs הָעַלְמָה hā'almāh the young woman

3428.153 art, v Qal act ptc fs הַיֹּצֵאת hayyōtsē'th the one coming out	**3937, 8056.141** prep, v Qal inf con לִשְׁאֹב lish'ōv to draw	**569.115** cj, v Qal impf 1cs וְאָמַרְתִּי w^{e}'āmartî and I will say	**420** prep, ps 3fs אֵלֶיהָ 'ēlêhā to her	**8615.532, 5167** v Hiphil impv 2fs, ps 1cs, part הַשְׁקִינִי־נָא hashqînî-nā' give me a drink please

4746, 4448 *sub*, n mp מְעַט־מַיִם m^{e}'aṯ-mayim little water	**4623, 3656** prep, n fs, ps 2fs מִכַּדֵּךְ mikkaddēkh from your jar	**44.**	**569.112** cj, v Qal pf 3fs וְאָמְרָה w^{e}'ām^{e}rāh and she will say	**420** prep, ps 1cs אֵלַי 'ēlay to me	**1612, 887** cj, pers pron גַּם־אַתָּה gam-'attāh both you	**8685.131** v Qal impv 2ms שְׁתֵה sh^{e}thēh drink	**1612** cj, cj וְגַם w^{e}gham and also

3937, 1622 prep, n mp, ps 2ms לִגְמַלֶּיךָ lighmallêkhā for your camels	**8056.125** v Qal impf 1cs אֶשְׁאָב 'esh'āv I will draw	**2000** pers pron הִוא hiw' she	**828** art, n fs הָאִשָּׁה hā'ishshāh the woman	**866, 3306.511** rel part, v Hiphil pf 3ms אֲשֶׁר־הֹכִיחַ 'ăsher-hōkhîach which You have determined	**3176** pn יְהוָה y^{e}hwāh Yahweh

3937, 1158, 112 prep, *n ms*, n ms, ps 1cs לְבֶן־אֲדֹנִי l^{e}ven-'ădhōnî for son of my master	**45.**	**603** pers pron אֲנִי 'ănî I	**3071** adv טֶרֶם ṯerem not yet	**3735.325** v Piel impf 1cs אֲכַלֶּה 'ăkhalleh I had finished	**3937, 1744.341** prep, v Piel inf con לְדַבֵּר l^{e}dhabbēr speaking	**420, 3949** prep, n ms, ps 1cs אֶל־לִבִּי 'el-libbî to my heart

2079 cj, intrj וְהִנֵּה w^{e}hinnēh and behold	**7549** pn רִבְקָה rivqāh Rebekah	**3428.153** v Qal act ptc fs יֹצֵאת yōtsē'th coming out	**3656** cj, n fs, ps 3fs וְכַדָּהּ w^{e}khaddāhh and her jar	**6142, 8327** prep, n ms, ps 3fs עַל־שִׁכְמָהּ 'al-shikhmāhh on her shoulder	**3495.122** cj, v Qal impf 3fs וַתֵּרֶד wattēredh and she went down	**6084** art, n fs הָעַיְנָה hā'aynāh to the spring

8056.122 cj, v Qal impf 3fs וַתִּשְׁאָב wattish'āv and she drew	**569.125** cj, v Qal impf 1cs וָאֹמַר wā'ōmar and I said	**420** prep, ps 3fs אֵלֶיהָ 'ēlêhā to her	**8615.532** v Hiphil impv 2fs, ps 1cs הַשְׁקִינִי hashqînî give me a drink	**5167** part נָא nā' please	**46.**	**4257.322** cj, v Piel impf 3fs וַתְּמַהֵר watt^{e}mahēr and she hurried

3495.522 cj, v Hiphil impf 3fs וַתּוֹרֶד wattôredh and she put down	**3656** n fs, ps 3fs כַּדָּהּ kaddāhh her jar	**4623, 6142** prep, prep, ps 3fs מֵעָלֶיהָ mē'ālêhā from on her	**569.122** cj, v Qal impf 3fs וַתֹּאמֶר wattō'mer and she said	**8685.131** v Qal impv 2ms שְׁתֵה sh^{e}thēh drink	**1612, 1622** cj, cj, n mp, ps 2ms וְגַם־גְּמַלֶּיךָ w^{e}gham-g^{e}mallêkhā and also your camels

8615.525	8685.125	1612	1622	8615.512		8068.125	881
v Hiphil impf 1cs	cj, v Qal impf 1cs	cj, cj	art, n mp	v Hiphil pf 3fs	**47.**	cj, v Qal impf 1cs	do, ps 3fs
אַשְׁקֶה	וָאֵשְׁתְּ	וְגַם	הַגְּמַלִּים	הִשְׁקָתָה		וָאֶשְׁאַל	אֹתָהּ
'ashqeh	wā'ēsht^{e}	w^{e}gham	hagg^{e}mallîm	hishqāthāh		wā'esh'al	'ōthāhh
I will water	and I drank	and also	the camels	she watered		and I asked	her

569.125	1351, 4449	879	569.122	1351, 1357	1158, 5331	866
cj, v Qal impf 1cs	*n fs*, interr	pers pron	cj, v Qal impf 3fs	*n fs*, pn	*n ms*, pn	rel part
וָאֹמַר	בַּת־מִי	אַתְּ	וַתֹּאמֶר	בַּת־בְּתוּאֵל	בֶּן־נָחוֹר	אֲשֶׁר
wā'ōmar	bath-mî	'att^{e}	wattō'mer	bath-b^{e}thû'ēl	ben-nāchôr	'ăsher
and I said	daughter of who	you	and she said	the daughter of Bethuel	the son of Nahor	whom

3314.112, 3937	4575	7947.525	5321	6142, 653	7050
v Qal pf 3fs, prep, ps 3ms	pn	cj, v Hiphil impf 1cs	art, n ms	prep, n ms, ps 3fs	cj, art, n mp
יָלְדָה־לּוֹ	מִלְכָּה	וָאָשִׂם	הַנֶּזֶם	עַל־אַפָּהּ	וְהַצְּמִידִים
yāl^{e}dhāh-lô	milkāh	wā'āsim	hannezem	'al-'appāhh	w^{e}hatsts^{e}mîdhîm
she gave birth for him	Milcah	and I put	the ring	on her nose	and the bracelets

6142, 3135		7199.125	8246.725	3937, 3176	1313.325	881, 3176
prep, n fd, ps 3fs	**48.**	cj, v Qal impf 1cs	cj, v Hithpalpel impf 1cs	prep, pn	cj, v Piel impf 1cs	do, pn
עַל־יָדֶיהָ		וָאֶקֹּד	וָאֶשְׁתַּחֲוֶה	לַיהוָה	וָאֲבָרֵךְ	אֶת־יְהוָה
'al-yādhêhā		wā'eqqōdh	wā'eshtachweh	layhwāh	wā'ăvārēkh	'eth-y^{e}hwāh
on her hands		and I bowed	and I worshiped	Yahweh	and I blessed	Yahweh

435	112	80	866	5328.511	904, 1932	583
n mp	n ms, ps 1cs	pn	rel part	v Hiphil pf 3ms, ps 1cs	prep, *n ms*	n fs
אֱלֹהֵי	אֲדֹנִי	אַבְרָהָם	אֲשֶׁר	הִנְחַנִי	בְּדֶרֶךְ	אֱמֶת
'ĕlōhê	'ădhōnî	'avrāhām	'ăsher	hinchanî	b^{e}dherekh	'ĕmeth
the God of	my master	Abraham	who	He guided me	on journey of	reliability

42. And I came this day unto the well, and said, O LORD God of my master Abraham, if now thou do prosper my way which I go: ... planning to make my mission a success, *LIVB* ... lend success, *Anchor.*

43. Behold, I stand by the well of water: ... spring, *REB* ... fountain, *Young.*

and it shall come to pass, that when the virgin cometh forth to draw water: ... maiden, *NIV* ... young woman, *NRSV* ... girl, *MLB.*

and I say to her, Give me, I pray thee, a little water of thy pitcher to drink: ... jar, *REB.*

44. And she say to me, Both drink thou, and I will also draw for thy camels: let the same be the woman whom the LORD hath appointed out for my master's son: ... designated, *MLB* ... intends, *NEB* ... decided, *Young* ... selected, *LIVB.*

45. And before I had done speaking in mine heart: ... speech had not come to an end, *Fenton* ... saying this in my mind, *Anchor* ... not yet finished planning, *NCB* ... praying silently, *NEB* ... my meditation, *Goodspeed.*

behold, Rebekah came forth with her pitcher on her shoulder and she went down unto the well, and drew water, and I said unto her, Let me drink, I pray thee: ... jug, *Anchor* ... jar, *NASB* ... bucket, *Fenton* ... vessel from her arm, *BB.*

46. And she made haste: ... straight away, *BB* ... quickly, *Fenton* ... she hurried, *KJVII.*

and let down her pitcher from her shoulder, and said, Drink, and I will give thy camels drink also: so I drank, and she made the camels drink also:

47. And I asked her, and said: ... inquired, *Anchor* ... questioning, *BB.*

Whose daughter art thou? And she said, The daughter of Bethuel, Nahor's son, whom Milcah bare unto him: ... my girl, who are you, *Fenton.*

and I put the earring upon her face: ... ring on her nose, *Darby* ... abillement, *Geneva.*

and the bracelets upon her hands: ... wrists, *Berkeley* ... on her arms, *NRSV* ... bands, *Anchor* ... ornaments, *BB.*

48. And I bowed down my head, and worshipped the LORD, and blessed the LORD God of my master Abraham: ... stooped, *Berkeley* ... bent head, *BB* ... bow and due obeisance, *Young* ... prostrated myself, *Goodspeed.*

which had led me in the right way to take my master's brother's daughter unto his son: ... in the way of truth, *NKJV.*

4089.141	881, 1351, 250	112	3937, 1158		6498	524, 3552
prep, v Qal inf con	do, *n fs*, *n ms*, ps 1cs	n ms, ps 1cs	prep, n ms, ps 3ms	**49.**	cj, adv	cj, n ms, ps 2mp
לָקַחַת	אֶת־בַּת־אֲחִי	אֲדֹנִי	לִבְנוֹ		וְעַתָּה	אִם־יֶשְׁכֶם
lāqachath	'eth-bath-'ăchî	'ădhōnî	livnô		w^{e}‘attāh	'im-yeshkhem
to take	the daughter of the brother of	my master	for his son		and now	if there is

6449.152	2721	583	882, 112	5222.533	3937	524, 3940
v Qal act ptc mp	n ms	cj, n fs	prep, n ms, ps 1cs	v Hiphil impv 2mp	prep, ps 1cs	cj, cj, neg part
עֹשִׂים	חֶסֶד	וֶאֱמֶת	אֶת־אֲדֹנִי	הַגִּידוּ	לִי	וְאִם־לֹא
‘ōsîm	chesedh	we'ĕmeth	'eth-'ădhōnî	haggîdhû	lî	w^{e}'im-lō'
one who does	loyalty	and reliability	with my master	tell	to me	and if not

5222.533	3937	6680.125	6142, 3332	173	6142, 7972		6257.121
v Hiphil impv 2mp	prep, ps 1cs	cj, Qal impf 1cs	prep, n fs	cj	prep, n ms	**50.**	cj, v Qal impf 3ms
הַגִּידוּ	לִי	וְאֶפְנֶה	עַל־יָמִין	אוֹ	עַל־שְׂמֹאל		וַיַּעַן
haggîdhû	lî	w^{e}'ephneh	‘al-yāmîn	'ô	‘al-s^{e}mō'l		wayya‘an
tell	to me	and I will turn	on right	or	on left		and he answered

3969	1357	569.126	4623, 3176	3428.111	1745	3940	3310.120
pn	cj, pn	cj, v Qal impf 3mp	prep, pn	v Qal pf 3ms	art, n ms	neg part	v Qal impf 1cp
לָבָן	וּבְתוּאֵל	וַיֹּאמְרוּ	מֵיְהוָה	יָצָא	הַדָּבָר	לֹא	נוּכַל
lāvān	ûv^{e}thû'ēl	wayyō'mrû	mēy^{e}hwāh	yātsā'	haddāvār	lō'	nûkhal
Laban	then Bethuel	and they said	from Yahweh	it went out	the thing	not	we are able

1744.341	420	7737	173, 3005		2079, 7549	3937, 6686	4089.131
v Piel inf con	prep, ps 2ms	adj	cj, adj	**51.**	intrj, pn	prep, n mp, ps 2ms	v Qal impv 2ms
דַּבֵּר	אֵלֶיךָ	רַע	אוֹ־טוֹב		הִנֵּה־רִבְקָה	לְפָנֶיךָ	קַח
dabbēr	'ēlêkhā	ra‘	'ô-ṯôv		hinnēh-rivqāh	l^{e}phānêkhā	qach
to speak	to you	bad	or good		behold Rebekah	before you	take

2050.131	2030.122	828	3937, 1158, 112	3626, 866	1744.311
cj, v Qal impv 2ms	cj, v Qal impf 3fs	n fs	prep, n ms, n ms, ps 2ms	prep, rel part	v Piel pf 3ms
וָלֵךְ	וּתְהִי	אִשָּׁה	לְבֶן־אֲדֹנֶיךָ	כַּאֲשֶׁר	דִּבֶּר
wālēkh	ûth^{e}hî	'ishshāh	l^{e}ven-'ădhōnêkhā	ka'ăsher	dibber
and go	and she will be	wife	for the son of your master	according to that	He spoke

3176		2030.121	3626, 866	8471.111	5860	80	881, 1745
pn	**52.**	cj, v Qal impf 3ms	prep, rel part	v Qal pf 3ms	*n ms*	pn	do, n mp, ps 3mp
יְהוָה		וַיְהִי	כַּאֲשֶׁר	שָׁמַע	עֶבֶד	אַבְרָהָם	אֶת־דִּבְרֵיהֶם
y^{e}hwāh		wayhî	ka'ăsher	shāma‘	‘evedh	'avrāhām	'eth-divrêhem
Yahweh		and it was	when	he heard	the slave of	Abraham	their words

8246.721	800	3937, 3176		3428.521	5860	3747, 3826B
cj, v Hithpalel impf 3ms	n fs	prep, pn	**53.**	cj, v Hiphil impf 3ms	art, n ms	*n mp*, n ms
וַיִּשְׁתַּחוּ	אַרְצָה	לַיהוָה		וַיּוֹצֵא	הָעֶבֶד	כְּלֵי־כֶסֶף
wayyishtachû	'artsāh	layhwāh		wayyôtsē'	hā‘evedh	k^{e}lê-kheseph
then he bowed down	to the earth	to Yahweh		and he brought out	the slave	ornaments of silver

3747	2174	933	5598.121	3937, 7549	4162	5598.111
cj, *n mp*	n ms	cj, n mp	cj, v Qal pf 3ms	prep, pn	cj, n fp	v Qal pf 3ms
וּכְלֵי	זָהָב	וּבְגָדִים	וַיִּתֵּן	לְרִבְקָה	וּמִגְדָּנֹת	נָתַן
ûkh^{e}lê	zāhāv	ûv^{e}ghādhîm	wayyittēn	l^{e}rivqāh	ûmighdānōth	nāthan
and ornaments of	gold	and clothes	and he gave	to Rebekah	and expensive gifts	he gave

3937, 250	3937, 525		404.126	8685.126	2000	596
prep, n ms, ps 3fs	cj, prep, n fs, ps 3fs	**54.**	cj, v Qal impf 3mp	cj, v Qal impf 3mp	pers pron	cj, art, n mp
לְאָחִיהָ	וּלְאִמָּהּ		וַיֹּאכְלוּ	וַיִּשְׁתּוּ	הוּא	וְהָאֲנָשִׁים
l^{e}'āchîhā	ûlă'immāhh		wayyō'khlû	wayyishtû	hû'	w^{e}hā'ănāshîm
to her brother	and to her mother		and they ate	and they drank	he	and the men

569.121 cj, v Qal impf 3ms וַיֹּאמֶר wayyō'mer and he said	904, 1269 prep, art, n ms בַבֹּקֶר vabbōqer in the morning	7251.126 cj, v Qal impf 3mp וַיָּקוּמוּ wayyāqûmû and they arose	4053 cj, v Qal impf 3mp וַיָּלִינוּ wayyālînû and they spent the night	866, 6196 rel part, prep, ps 3ms אֲשֶׁר־עִמּוֹ 'ăsher-'immô who with him

525 cj, n fs, ps 3fs וְאִמָּהּ w^{e}'immāhh and her mother	250 n ms, ps 3fs אָחִיהָ 'āchîhā her brother	569.121 cj, v Qal impf 3ms וַיֹּאמֶר wayyō'mer and he said	55.	3937, 112 prep, n ms, ps 1cs לַאדֹנִי la'dhōnî to my master	8365.333 v Piel impv 2mp, ps 1cs שַׁלְּחֻנִי shall^{e}chunî send me

49. And now if ye will deal kindly and truly with my master, tell me: ... if you mean to treat my master with true loyalty, *Anchor* ... whether my master can depend on your favor, *NCB* ... will you or won't you be kind to my master, *LIVB*.

and if not, tell me; that I may turn to the right hand, or to the left: ... if not, I will turn elsewhere, *NEB* ... that I may proceed, *Anchor* ... can determine my course, *NCB* ... proceed accordingly, *NAB* ... and I will decide what to do, *Good News*.

50. Then Laban and Bethuel answered and said: ... Laban and his household, *NAB*.

The thing proceedeth from the LORD: ... this matter stems from Yahweh, *Anchor*.

we cannot speak unto thee bad or good: ... it is not for us to say yes or no, *BB* ... to make a decision, *Good News* ... adversely or favorably, *Goodspeed* ... either good or ill, *Fenton* ... neither disapprove or approve, *Anchor*.

51. Behold, Rebekah is before thee: ... ready for you, *NAB* ... at your call, *Anchor* ... present, *Berkeley*.

take her, and go, and let her be thy master's son's wife: ... let her marry your master's son, *Berkeley* ... she shall be the wife of, *NEB* ... she is a wife to thy lord's son, *Young*.

as the LORD hath spoken: ... in agreement with the Lord's message, *MLB*.

52. And it came to pass, that, when Abraham's servant heard their words, he worshipped the LORD, bowing himself to the earth: ... he bowed to the ground, *Anchor* ... prostrated himself, *REB*.

53. And the servant brought forth jewels of silver, and jewels of gold, and raiment, and gave them to Rebekah: ... gold articles and clothing, *Darby* ... ornaments, *Fenton* ... garments, *Young*.

he gave also to her brother and to her mother precious things: ... he gave jewelry too, *Berkeley* ... things of value, *BB* ... treasures, *Fenton* ... costly presents, *NCB*.

54. And they did eat and drink, he and the men that were with him, and tarried all night: ... stayed overnight, *NCB* ... lodged, *Darby* ... retired for the night, *Goodspeed* ... spent the night, *REB*.

and they rose up in the morning, and he said, Send me away unto my master: ... give me leave to return, *NAB* ... to go back, *REB*.

55. And her brother and her mother said, Let the damsel abide with us a few days, at the least ten; after that she shall go: ... a short while, *NAB* ... a week or ten days, *BB* ... at least ten days, *Geneva* ... let the girl stay with us a few days, *Berkeley* ... a day or two, *Fenton*.

24:49. Abraham's slave concluded by asking them to respond to God's covenant love and faithfulness by showing the same kind of love and faithfulness to Abraham.

24:50-51. Rebekah's father and brother recognized the decision was not theirs. The LORD had already decided Rebekah was the one for Isaac. That they could not say anything bad or good, means there was nothing more to be said.

24:52-54. Again, Abraham's slave bowed and worshiped the LORD immediately, right where he was. Then he proceeded to give a variety of expensive gifts to Rebekah and also to her brother and her mother (as compensation for the loss of her presence and service and as proof to them that Rebekah would be well cared for). Not until after that, did he and the men with him have their meal and retire for the night.

24:55-56. Abraham's slave was ready to go now that the LORD had answered his prayer. But Laban and Rebekah's mother knew they would probably never see her again, so they wanted her to stay for about ten days more. Possibly they wanted to allow relatives and friends to give her farewell

3553.122 v Qal impf 3fs תֵּשֵׁב tēshēv she will dwell	5472 art, n fs הַנַּעַר hanna'ărā the young woman	882 prep, ps 1cp אִתָּנוּ 'ittānû with us	3219 n mp יָמִים yāmîm days	173 cj אוֹ 'ô or	6452 num עָשׂוֹר 'āsôr ten	313 adv אַחַר 'achar afterward	2050.123 v Qal impf 3fs תֵּלֵךְ tēlēkh she will go

56.	569.121 cj, v Qal impf 3ms וַיֹּאמֶר wayyō'mer and he said	420 prep, ps 3mp אֲלֵהֶם 'ălēhem to them	420, 310.328 adv, v Piel juss 2mp אַל־תְּאַחֲרוּ 'al-t^{e}'achrû do not delay	881 do, ps 1cs אֹתִי 'ōthî me	3176 cj, pn וַיהוָה wayhwāh and Yahweh	7014.511 v Hiphil pf 3ms הִצְלִיחַ hitslîach He has made successful

1932 n ms, ps 1cs דַּרְכִּי darkî my journey	8365.333 v Piel impv 2mp, ps 1cs שַׁלְּחוּנִי shall^{e}chûnî send me	2050.125 cj, v Qal impf 1cs וְאֵלְכָה w^{e}'ēl^{e}khāh and I will go	3937, 112 prep, n ms, ps 1cs לַאדֹנִי la'dhōnî to my master	**57.**	569.126 cj, v Qal impf 3mp וַיֹּאמְרוּ wayyō'mrû and they said	7410.120 v Qal impf 1cp נִקְרָא niqōrā' we will call

3937, 5472 prep, art, n fs לַנַּעֲרָ lanna'ărā the young woman	8068.120 cj, v Qal impf 1cp וְנִשְׁאֲלָה w^{e}nish'ălāh and we will ask	881, 6552 do, n ms, ps 3fs אֶת־פִּיהָ 'eth-pîhā her mouth	**58.**	7410.126 cj, v Qal impf 3mp וַיִּקְרְאוּ wayyiqōr'û and they called	3937, 7549 prep, pn לְרִבְקָה l^{e}rivqāh Rebekah	569.126 cj, v Qal impf 3mp וַיֹּאמְרוּ wayyō'mrû and they said

420 prep, ps 3fs אֵלֶיהָ 'ēlêhā to her	2050.124 intrg part, v Qal impf 2fs הֲתֵלְכִי h^{e}thēl^{e}khî will you go	6196, 382 prep, art, n ms עִם־הָאִישׁ 'im-hā'îsh with the man	2172 art, dem pron הַזֶּה hazzeh the this	569.122 cj, v Qal impf 3fs וַתֹּאמֶר wattō'mer and she said	2050.125 v Qal impf 1cs אֵלֵךְ 'ēlēkh I will go

59.	8365.316 cj, v Piel impf 3cp וַיְשַׁלְּחוּ wayshall^{e}chû and they sent	881, 7549 do, pn אֶת־רִבְקָה 'eth-rivqāh Rebekah	269 n fs, ps 3mp אֲחֹתָם 'ăchōthām their sister	881, 3352.553 cj, do, v Hiphil part fs, ps 3fs וְאֶת־מֵנִקְתָּהּ w^{e}'eth-mēniqōttāhh and her nurse	881, 5860 cj, do, *n ms* וְאֶת־עֶבֶד w^{e}'eth-'evedh and the slave of	80 pn אַבְרָהָם 'avrāhām Abraham

881, 596 cj, do, n mp, ps 3ms וְאֶת־אֲנָשָׁיו w;'eth-'ănāshâv and his men	**60.**	1313.326 cj, v Piel impf 3mp וַיְבָרְכוּ wayvār^{e}khû and they blessed	881, 7549 do, pn אֶת־רִבְקָה 'eth-rivqāh Rebekah	569.126 cj, v Qal impf 3mp וַיֹּאמְרוּ wayyō'mrû and they said	3937 prep, ps 3fs לָהּ lāhh to her	269 n fs, ps 1cp אֲחֹתֵנוּ 'ăchōthēnû our sister	879 pers pron אַתְּ 'att^{e} you

2030.132 v Qal impv 2fs הֲיִי h^{e}yî be	3937, 512 prep, *num pl* לְאַלְפֵי l^{e}alphê for thousands of	7526 n fs רְבָבָה r^{e}vāvāh a great number	3542.121 cj, v Qal impf 3ms וְיִירַשׁ w^{e}yîrash and may he take possession of	2320 n ms, ps 2fs זַרְעֵךְ zar'ēkh your seed	881 do אֵת 'ēth

8554 *n ms* שַׁעַר sha'ar the gate of	7983.152 v Qal act part mp, ps 3ms שֹׂנְאָיו sōn^{e}'âv ones who hate him	**61.**	7251.122 cj, v Qal impf 3fs וַתָּקָם wattāqām and she rose	7549 pn רִבְקָה rivqāh Rebekah	5472 cj, n fp, ps 3fs וְנַעֲרֹתֶיהָ w^{e}na'ărōthêhā and her young women

7680.127 cj, v Qal impf 3fp וַתִּרְכַּבְנָה wattirkavnāh and they rode	6142, 1622 prep, art, n mp עַל־הַגְּמַלִּים 'al-hagg^{e}mallîm on the camels	2050.127 cj, v Qal impf 3fp וַתֵּלַכְנָה wattēlakhnāh and they went	311 *sub* אַחֲרֵי 'achrê after	382 art, n ms הָאִישׁ hā'îsh the man	4089.121 cj, v Qal impf 3ms וַיִּקַּח wayyiqqach and he took	5860 art, n ms הָעֶבֶד hā'evedh the slave

881, 7549	2050.121		3437	971.111	4623, 971.141	915	915	915
do, pn	cj, v Qal impf 3ms	**62.**	cj, pn	v Qal pf 3ms	prep, v Qal inf con	pr	pn	pn
אֶת־רִבְקָה	וַיֵּלַךְ		וְיִצְחָק	בָּא	מִבּוֹא	בְּאֵר	לַחַי	רֹאִי
'eth-rivqāh	wayyēlakh		w^{e}yitschāq	bā'	mibbô'	b^{e}'ēr	lachay	rō'î
Rebekah	and he went		and Isaac	he came	from going to	Beer	Lahai	Roi

2000	3553.151	904, 800	5221		3428.121	3437	3937, 7910.141
cj, pers pron	v Qal act ptc ms	prep, *n fs*	art, pn	**63.**	cj, v Qal impf 3ms	pn	prep, v Qal inf con
וְהוּא	יוֹשֵׁב	בְּאֶרֶץ	הַנֶּגֶב		וַיֵּצֵא	יִצְחָק	לָשׂוּחַ
w^{e}hû'	yôshēv	b^{e}'erets	hanneghev		wayyētsē'	yitschāq	lāsûach
and he	dwelling	in the land of	the Negeb		and he went out	Isaac	to pray

904, 7898	3937, 6680.141	6394	5558.121	6084	7495.121	2079
prep, art, n ms	prep, v Qal inf con	n ms	cj, v Qal impf 3ms	n fp, ps 3ms	cj, v Qal impf 3ms	cj, intrj
בַּשָּׂדֶה	לִפְנוֹת	עָרֶב	וַיִּשָּׂא	עֵינָיו	וַיַּרְא	וְהִנֵּה
bassādheh	liphnôth	'ārev	wayyissā'	'ênâv	wayyar^{e}'	w^{e}hinnēh
in the field	toward turning of	evening	and he lifted up	his eyes	and he saw	and behold

56. And he said unto them, Hinder me not, seeing the LORD hath prospered my way; send me away that I may go to my master: ... do not detain me, *Anchor* ... delay, *NRSV* ... if not, I will go, *Fenton.*

57. And they said, We will call the damsel, and enquire at her mouth: ... ask her consent, *Geneva* ... call the girl and ask her own mind, *Anchor* ... ask her personally, *Berkeley* ... let her make the decision, *BB* ... consult her, *NASB.*

58. And they called Rebekah, and said unto her, Wilt thou go with this man? And she said, I will go: ... are you ready to go, *BB* ... do you wish to go, *NAB.*

59. And they sent away Rebekah their sister, and her nurse, and Abraham's servant, and his men: ... they saw their sister Rebekah off with her nurse, *Berkeley.*

60. And they blessed Rebekah, and said unto her, Thou art our sister, be thou the mother of thousands of millions: ... grow into thousands of myriads, *NRSV* ... mother of myriads, *NEB* ... thousands of tens of thousands, *Darby* ... increase to thousands, *Fenton.*

and let thy seed possess the gate of those which hate them: ... offspring, *NIV* ... sons, *REB* ... descendants, *RSV* ... overcome all your enemies, *LIVB.*

61. And Rebekah arose, and her damsels, and they rode upon the camels, and followed the man: ... and her maids, *Anchor* ... servant women, *BB* ... young women, *KJVII* ... companions, *REB* ... mounted camels, *NCB.*

and the servant took Rebekah, and went his way: ... slave got Rebekah and departed, *NKJV* ... servant obtained and took his course, *MLB* ... and goeth, *Young.*

62. And Isaac came from the way of the well Lahairoi: ... had moved from the neighborhood of, *Goodspeed* ... had come back from the vicinity, *Anchor* ... from the waste land, *BB* ... a trip to the well, *Berkeley.*

parties as well. But Abraham's slave insisted they dismiss him at once to go to his master. What the LORD had done also called for obedience.

24:57-58. Laban and Rebekah's mother then did something that was very unusual in those days. Ordinarily a girl simply had to submit to whatever marriage arrangements were made for her. But Rebekah was to become part of God's chosen family, and it was important that she be given the opportunity to choose in a way that would express her faith. So she was called in, and asked if she was ready. She made the choice to go at once.

24:59-61. Rebekah's nurse is later identified as Deborah (35:8), meaning "honey-bee." Before sending Rebekah away, Laban and her mother pronounced a blessing over her, indicating their wishes for the success and victories of her progeny, something that was in line with God's promise to Abraham. Rebekah also took other slave girls with her, indicating that her family, too, was prosperous.

24:62-63. Isaac had been down to Beer Lahairoi ("The Well of the Living One Who Sees Me") about 50 miles southwest of Beersheba and was living in the Negev desert south of Beersheba. After a busy day, he went out into the open country to meditate or to pray, as the Jewish Targums (early Aramaic translations and commentaries) say. We can be sure he wanted to be alone with God, and

1622	971.152		5558.122	7549	881, 6084	7495.122	881, 3437
n mp	v Qal act ptc mp	64.	cj, v Qal impf 3fs	pn	do, n fd, ps 3fs	cj, v Qal impf 3fs	do, pn
גְמַלִּים	בָּאִים		וַתִּשָּׂא	רִבְקָה	אֶת־עֵינֶיהָ	וַתֵּרֶא	אֶת־יִצְחָק
gemallîm	bā'îm		wattissā'	rivqāh	'eth-'ênêhā	wattēre'	'eth-yitschāq
camels	coming		and she lifted up	Rebekah	her eyes	and she saw	Isaac

5489.122	4263, 6142	1622		569.122	420, 5860	4449, 382
cj, v Qal impf 3fs	prep, prep	art, n ms	65.	cj, v Qal impf 3fs	prep, art, n ms	intrg, art, n ms
וַתִּפֹּל	מֵעַל	הַגָּמָל		וַתֹּאמֶר	אֶל־הָעֶבֶד	מִי־הָאִישׁ
wattippōl	mē'al	haggāmāl		wattō'mer	'el--hā'evedh	mî-hā'îsh
and she fell	from upon	the camel		and she said	to the slave	who the man

2045	2050.151	904, 7898	3937, 7410.141	569.121	5860	2000
dem pron	art, v Qal act ptc ms	prep, art, n ms	prep, v Qal inf con, ps 1cp	cj, v Qal impf 3ms	art, n ms	pers pron
הַלָּזֶה	הַהֹלֵךְ	בַּשָּׂדֶה	לִקְרָאתֵנוּ	וַיֹּאמֶר	הָעֶבֶד	הוּא
hallāzeh	hahōlēkh	bassādheh	liqōrā'thēnû	wayyō'mer	hā'evedh	hû'
this	the one coming	in the field	to meet us	and he said	the slave	he

112	4089.122	7086	3803.722		5807.321	5860	3937, 3437
n ms, ps 1cs	cj, v Qal impf 3fs	art, n ms	cj, v Hithpael impf 3fs	66.	cj, v Piel impf 3ms	art, n ms	prep, pn
אֲדֹנִי	וַתִּקַּח	הַצָּעִיף	וַתִּתְכָּס		וַיְסַפֵּר	הָעֶבֶד	לְיִצְחָק
'ădhōnî	wattiqqach	hatstsā'îph	wattithkās		waysappēr	hā'evedh	leyitschāq
my master	and she took	the veil	and covered herself		and he reported	the slave	to Isaac

881	3725, 1745	866	6449.111		971.521	3437	164	8023
do	*adj*, art, n mp	rel part	v Qal pf 3ms	67.	cj, v Hiphil impf 3ms, ps 3fs	pn	art, n ms	pn
אֵת	כָּל־הַדְּבָרִים	אֲשֶׁר	עָשָׂה		וַיְבִאֶהָ	יִצְחָק	הָאֹהֱלָה	שָׂרָה
'ēth	kol-haddevārîm	'ăsher	'āsāh		wayvi'ehā	yitschāq	hā'ōhĕlāh	sārāh
	all the things	that	he did		and he brought her	Isaac	to the tent of	Sarah

525	4089.121	881, 7549	2030.122, 3937	3937, 828	154.121
n fs, ps 3ms	cj, v Qal impf 3ms	do, pn	cj, v Qal impf 3fs, prep, ps 3ms	prep, n fs	cj, v Qal impf 3ms, ps 3fs
אִמּוֹ	וַיִּקַּח	אֶת־רִבְקָה	וַתְּהִי־לוֹ	לְאִשָּׁה	וַיֶּאֱהָבֶהָ
'immô	wayyiqqach	'eth-rivqāh	wattehî-lô	le'ishshāh	wayye'ĕhāvehā
his mother	and he took	Rebekah	and she was to him	for a wife	and he loved her

5341.221	3437	311	525		3362.121	80
cj, v Niphal impf 3ms	pn	*sub*	n fs, ps 3ms	25:1	cj, v Qal impf 3ms	pn
וַיִּנָּחֵם	יִצְחָק	אַחֲרֵי	אִמּוֹ		וַיֹּסֶף	אַבְרָהָם
wayyinnāchēm	yitschāq	'achrê	'immô		wayyōseph	'avrāhām
and he was comforted	Isaac	after	his mother		and he did again	Abraham

4089.121	828	8428	7271		3314.122	3937	881, 2260
cj, v Qal impf 3ms	n fs	cj, n ms, ps 3fs	pn	2.	cj, v Qal impf 3fs	prep, ps 3ms	do, pn
וַיִּקַּח	אִשָּׁה	וּשְׁמָהּ	קְטוּרָה		וַתֵּלֶד	לוֹ	אֶת־זִמְרָן
wayyiqqach	'ishshāh	ûshemāhh	qōṭûrāh		wattēledh	lô	'eth-zimrān
and he took	wife	and her name	Keturah		and she gave birth	for him	Zimran

881, 3484	881, 4232	881, 4220	881, 3559	881, 8191		3484	3314.111
cj, do, pn	cj, do, pn	cj, do, pn	cj, do, pn	cj, do, pn	3.	cj, pn	v Qal pf 3ms
וְאֶת־יָקְשָׁן	וְאֶת־מְדָן	וְאֶת־מִדְיָן	וְאֶת־יִשְׁבָּק	וְאֶת־שׁוּחַ		וְיָקְשָׁן	יָלַד
we'eth-yāqōshān	we'eth-medhān	we'eth-midhyān	we'eth-yishbāq	we'eth-shûach		weyāqōshān	yāladh
and Jokshan	and Medan	and Midian	and Ishbak	and Shuah		and Jokshan	he fathered

881, 8088	881, 1771	1158	1771	2030.116	833	4047
do, pn	cj, do, pn	cj, *n mp*	pn	v Qal pf 3cp	pn	cj, pn
אֶת־שְׁבָא	וְאֶת־דְּדָן	וּבְנֵי	דְדָן	הָיוּ	אַשּׁוּרִם	וּלְטוּשִׁים
'eth-shevā'	we'eth-dedhān	ûvnê	dhedhān	hāyû	'ashshûrim	ûlăṭûshîm
Sheba	and Dedan	and the sons of	Dedan	they were	Asshurim	and Letushim

3948 cj, pn וּלְאֻמִּים ûlā'ummîm and Leummim	**4.**	1158 cj, *n mp* וּבְנֵי ûvnê and the sons of	4220 pn מִדְיָן midhyān Midian	6108 pn עֵיפָה 'êphāh Ephah	6313 cj, pn וָעֵפֶר wā'ēpher and Epher	2699 cj, pn וַחֲנֹךְ wachnōkh and Hanoch	26 cj, pn וַאֲבִידָע wa'ăvîdhā' and Abida

425 cj, pn וְאֶלְדָּעָה w^{e}'eldā'āh and Eldaah	3725, 431 *adj*, dem pron כָּל־אֵלֶּה kol-'ēlleh all these	1158 *n mp* בְּנֵי b^{e}nê the sons of	7271 pn קְטוּרָה qōṭûrāh Keturah	**5.**	5598.121 cj, v Qal perf 3ms וַיִּתֵּן wayyittēn and he gave	80 pn אַבְרָהָם 'avrāhām Abraham	881, 3725, 866, 3937 do, adj, rel part, prep, ps 3ms אֶת־כָּל־אֲשֶׁר־לוֹ 'eth-kol-'ăsher-lô all which to him

for he dwelt in the south country: ... region of the Negeb, *NEB* ... district of, *NCB.*

63. And Isaac went out to meditate in the field: ... to pray, *Geneva* ... was out walking, *Anchor* ... went wandering out, *BB* ... to think things over, *KJVII.*

at the eventide and he lifted up his eyes, and saw, and, behold, the camels were coming: ... twilight, *Berkeley* ... evening was near, *BB.*

64. And Rebekah lifted up her eyes, and when she saw Isaac: ... Rebekah noticed, *Anchor* ... Rebekah, too, was looking about, *NAB.*

she lighted off the camel: ... slid down from, *MLB* ... sprang off, *Darby* ... dismounted, *NCB.*

65. For she had said unto the servant, What man is this that walketh in the field to meet us? And the servant had said, It is my master: therefore she took a veil, and covered herself: ... scarf and covered her face, *Goodspeed.*

66. And the servant told Isaac all things that he had done: ... gave Isaac the story, *BB* ... recounteth, *Young.*

67. And Isaac brought her into his mother Sarah's tent: ... conducted her inside, *MLB* ... into his tent, *BB.*

and took Rebekah, and she became his wife and he loved her: and Isaac was comforted after his mother's death: ... and in his love for her, found solace, *NAB* ... consolation, Berkeley.

25:1. Then again Abraham took a wife, and her name was Keturah: ... another wife, *Anchor* ... married another, *Berkeley.*

2. And she bare him Zimran, and Jokshan, and Medan, and Midian, and Ishbak, and Shuah: ... bore him, *Fenton* ... became the mother of, *BB.*

3. And Jokshan begat Sheba, and Dedan. And the sons of Dedan were Asshurim, and Letushim, and Leummim: ... became the father, *BB* ... fathered, *KJVII.*

4. And the sons of Midian; Ephah, and Epher, and Hanoch, and Abida, and Eldaah. All these were the children of Keturah: ... sons, *Darby* ... offspring, *BB* ... descendants, *Fenton.*

5. And Abraham gave all that he

---

talk to Him about the coming marriage. Surely if Abraham's slave prayed with such faith and confidence, Abraham's son was praying too. Then, as he looked up from bowing before the LORD, he saw camels coming.

24:64-65. When Rebekah saw Isaac she became so excited she practically fell off the camel. She was in a hurry to get down and approach Isaac with humility and proper dress. After Abraham's servant confirmed it was Isaac coming, she quickly enveloped herself in a wedding veil that covered her face and body.

24:66-67. After the slave told Isaac all he had done, Isaac brought Rebekah into Sarah's tent--giving her a place of honor. Then the marriage ceremony took place. She became a good wife to Isaac and he loved her. Arranged marriages can have love grow after marriage. Truly, love must grow after marriage if it is to be what God wants it to be (Eph. 5:25). Isaac's being comforted by her after his mother's death, shows he did not make comparisons with his mother and let Rebekah be the queen of the home.

25:1-4. Now that Isaac was married Abraham was alone. Probably, with the promise of Genesis 17:4 in mind, he proceeded to take another wife, Keturah (a name related to the word for incense). She, like Hagar, was a secondary wife or concubine (1 Chr. 1:32). She bore Abraham six sons. These became ancestors of tribes that lived in the area east of the Dead Sea and in Arabia. The Midianites later joined with the Ishmaelites, and Midian's territory was primarily on the east side of the Gulf of Aqaba.

25:5-6. Abraham made Isaac his heir.

3937, 3437	6.	3937, 1158	6637	866	3937, 80	5598.111	80
prep, pn		cj, prep, *n mp*	art, n fp	rel part	prep, pn	v Qal pf 3ms	pn
לְיִצְחָק		וְלִבְנֵי	הַפִּילַגְשִׁים	אֲשֶׁר	לְאַבְרָהָם	נָתַן	אַבְרָהָם
leyitschāq		welivnê	happîlaghshîm	'ăsher	le'avrāhām	nāthan	'avrāhām
to Isaac		and to the sons of	the concubines	who	to Abraham	he gave	Abraham

5150	8365.321	4263, 6142	3437	1158	904, 5968	2508	7209
n fp	cj, v Piel impf 3ms, ps 3mp	prep, prep	pn	n ms, ps 3ms	prep, adv, ps 3ms	n ms	adv
מַתָּנֹת	וַיְשַׁלְּחֵם	מֵעַל	יִצְחָק	בְּנוֹ	בְּעוֹדֶנּוּ	חַי	קֵדְמָה
mattānōth	wayshallechēm	mē'al	yitschāq	benô	be'ôdhennû	chay	qēdehmāh
gifts	and he sent them	from	Isaac	his son	while still	living	eastward

420, 800	7208	7.	431	3219	8523, 2508	80	866, 2513.111
prep, *n fs*	n ms		cj, dem pron	*n mp*	*n fp, n mp*	pn	rel part, v Qal pf 3ms
אֶל־אֶרֶץ	קֶדֶם		וְאֵלֶּה	יְמֵי	שְׁנֵי־חַיֵּי	אַבְרָהָם	אֲשֶׁר־חָי
'el-'erets	qedhem		we'ēlleh	yemê	shenê-chayyê	'avrāhām	'ăsher-chāy
to the land of	the East		and these	the days of	the years of life of	Abraham	which he lived

4109	8523	8124	8523	2675	8523	8.	1510.121	4322.121
num	n fs	cj, num	n fs	cj, num	noun fp		cj, v Qal impf 3ms	cj, v Qal impf 3ms
מְאַת	שָׁנָה	וְשִׁבְעִים	שָׁנָה	וְחָמֵשׁ	שָׁנִים		וַיִּגְוַע	וַיָּמָת
me'ath	shānāh	weshiv'îm	shānāh	wechāmēsh	shānîm		wayyighwa'	wayyāmāth
hundred of	year	and seventy	year	and five	years		and he expired	and he died

80	904, 7939	3009B	2290.111	7884	636.221	420, 6194
pn	prep, n fs	adj	v Qal pf 3ms	cj, adj	cj, v Niphal impf 3ms	prep, n mp, ps 3ms
אַבְרָהָם	בְּשֵׂיבָה	טוֹבָה	זָקֵן	וְשָׂבֵעַ	וַיֵּאָסֶף	אֶל־עַמָּיו
'avrāhām	besêvāh	ṯôvāh	zāqēn	wesāvēa'	wayyē'āseph	'el-'ammâv
Abraham	in old age	good	he was old	and satisfied	and he was gathered	to his people

9.	7196.126	881	3437	3579	1158	420, 4792	4512
	cj, v Qal impf 3mp	do, ps 3ms	pn	cj, pn	n mp, ps 3ms	prep, *n fs*	art, pn
	וַיִּקְבְּרוּ	אֹתוֹ	יִצְחָק	וְיִשְׁמָעֵאל	בָּנָיו	אֶל־מְעָרַת	הַמַּכְפֵּלָה
	wayyiqōberû	'ōthô	yitschāq	weyishmā'ē'l	bānâv	'el-me'ārath	hammakhpēlāh
	and they buried	him	Isaac	and Ishmael	his sons	in the cave of	the Machpelah

420, 7898	6317	1158, 6982	2958	866	6142, 6686	4613
prep, *n ms*	pn	*n ms*, pn	art, pn	rel part	prep, *n mp*	pn
אֶל־שְׂדֵה	עֶפְרֹן	בֶּן־צֹחַר	הַחִתִּי	אֲשֶׁר	עַל־פְּנֵי	מַמְרֵא
'el-sedhēh	'ephrōn	ben- tsōchar	hachittî	'ăsher	'al-penê	mamrē'
in the field of	Ephron	the son of Zohar	the Hittite	which	facing	Mamre

10.	7898	866, 7353.111	80	4623, 881	1158, 2953	8427	7196.411
	art, n ms	rel part, v Qal pf 3ms	pn	prep, do	*n mp*, pn	adv	v Pual pf 3ms
	הַשָּׂדֶה	אֲשֶׁר־קָנָה	אַבְרָהָם	מֵאֵת	בְּנֵי־חֵת	שָׁמָּה	קֻבַּר
	hassādeh	'ăsher-qānâh	'avrāhām	mē'ēth	benê-chēth	shāmmāh	qubbar
	the field	which he bought	Abraham	from	the sons of Heth	there	he was buried

80	8023	828	11.	2030.121	311	4322.142	80
pn	cj, pn	n fs, ps 3ms		cj, v Qal impf 3ms	*sub*	Qal inf abs	pn
אַבְרָהָם	וְשָׂרָה	אִשְׁתּוֹ		וַיְהִי	אַחֲרֵי	מוֹת	אַבְרָהָם
'avrāhām	wesārāh	'ishtô		wayhî	'achrê	môth	'avrāhām
Abraham	and Sarah	his wife		and it was	after	dying	Abraham

1325.321	435	881, 3437	1158	3553.121	3437	6196, 915	915
cj, v Piel impf 3ms	n mp	do, pn	n ms, ps 3ms	cj, v Qal impf 3ms	pn	prep, pn	pr noun
וַיְבָרֶךְ	אֱלֹהִים	אֶת־יִצְחָק	בְּנוֹ	וַיֵּשֶׁב	יִצְחָק	עִם־בְּאֵר	לַחַי
wayevārekh	'ĕlōhîm	'eth-yitschāq	benô	wayyēshev	yitschāq	'im-be'ēr	lachay
and He blessed	God	Isaac	his son	and he dwelled	Isaac	at Beer	Lahai

915	12. 431	8765	3579	1158, 80	866	3314.112
pn	cj, dem pron	*n fp*	pn	*n ms*, pn	rel part	v Qal pf 3fs
רֹאִי	וְאֵלֶּה	תֹּלְדֹת	יִשְׁמָעֵאל	בֶּן־אַבְרָהָם	אֲשֶׁר	יָלְדָה
rōʼî	wᵉʼēlleh	tōlᵉdhōth	yishmāʻēʼl	ben-ʼavrāhām	ʼăsher	yālᵉdhāh
Roi	and these	the descendants of	Ishmael	the son of Abraham	which	she gave birth

1972	4874	8569	8023	3937, 80	13. 431	8428	1158
pn	art, pn	*n fs*	pn	prep, pn	cj, dem pron	*n mp*	*n mp*
הָגָר	הַמִּצְרִית	שִׁפְחַת	שָׂרָה	לְאַבְרָהָם	וְאֵלֶּה	שְׁמוֹת	בְּנֵי
hāghār	hammitsrîth	shiphchath	sārāh	lᵉʼavrāhām	wᵉʼēlleh	shᵉmôth	bᵉnê
Hagar	the Egyptian	the female slave of	Sarah	for Abraham	and these	the names of	the sons of

had unto Isaac: ... deeded, *Anchor* ... left all that was with him, *Fenton.*

6. But unto the sons of the concubines: ... sons by concubinage, *Anchor* ... children of his concubines, *Berkeley* ... sons of his other women, *BB* ... secondary wives, *Fenton* ... by consorts, *Goodspeed.*

which Abraham had, Abraham gave gifts: ... made grants while he was still living, *NAB* ... presents, *Berkeley* ... offerings, *BB* ... fortunes, *Fenton.*

and sent them away from Isaac his son, while he yet lived, eastward, unto the east country: ... sent them out of Isaac's way, *Berkeley* ... so that they might not interfere with his son Isaac, *Goodspeed.*

7. And these are the days of the years of Abraham's life which he lived, an hundred threescore and fifteen years:

8. Then Abraham gave up the ghost, and died in a good old age: ... had breathed his last, *NAB* ... expired, *Darby* ... came to his death, *BB* ... yielded the spirit, *Geneva* ... at a ripe old age, *Berkeley.*

an old man, and full of years; and was gathered to his people: ... grey-headed, and satisfied, *Fenton* ... kin, *Anchor* ... forefathers, *REB.*

9. And his sons Isaac and Ishmael buried him in the cave of Machpelah: ... in the hollow rock, *BB* ... cave of Makphelah on the estate of, *Fenton.*

in the field of Ephron the son of Zohar the Hittite, which is before Mamre:

10. The field which Abraham purchased of the sons of Heth: there was Abraham buried, and Sarah his wife:

11. And it came to pass after the death of Abraham, that God blessed his son Isaac; and Isaac dwelt by the well Lahairoi: ... God poured out rich blessings, *LIVB* ... resided at the Well of Vision, *Fenton* ... settled close by, *REB* ... who then lived near, *NIV* ... Well of the Living One, my Beholder, *Young.*

12. Now these are the generations of Ishmael, Abraham's son, whom Hagar the Egyptian, Sarah's handmaid, bare unto Abraham: ... maid, *Berkeley* ... bondwoman, *Darby* ... slave, *NCB* ... servant, *BB.*

13. And these are the names of the sons of Ishmael, by their names, according to their generations: the

Ordinarily Isaac was only entitled to a double portion of the inheritance, with the rest divided up among the other sons of Abraham. But because Isaac was the only one to carry on the chosen line, he inherited everything after Abraham died. However, Abraham was good to the sons of his concubines (Hagar and Keturah), and while he was still alive, he wisely gave them rich gifts and sent them away from Isaac to the land of the east, that is, to Arabia.

25:7-8. Abraham lived 100 years in the promised land, but all he actually owned of it was a burial plot. His was a good old age, and after a life that brought fulfillment and blessing, he died a natural death, apparently without pain. He simply breathed his last and went to be with his people. In this case, since he was a godly man, he would join the spiritual giants of the Sethite line and Enoch in heaven where he would enjoy the presence of God.

25:9-11. Ishmael must have prospered by this time. He forgot the past, and although he had no inheritance with Isaac, he joined him to bury Abraham in the cave of Machpelah where Sarah was buried. Verse 11 ends this section of Genesis with a note that God continued to bless Isaac.

25:12-17. This brief section gives the names of the sons of Ishmael who became tribal rulers as God had promised. Then it tells of the death of Ishmael and where his descendants settled, indicating they gave their names to the villages and encampments where they lived. Their territory was extended from Shur, east of the Red Sea, to Havilah,

3579	904, 8428	3937, 8765	1111	3579	5207	7223
pn	prep, n mp, ps 3mp	prep, n fp, ps 3mp	n ms	pn	pn	cj, pn
יִשְׁמָעֵאל	בִּשְׁמֹתָם	לְתוֹלְדֹתָם	בְּכֹר	יִשְׁמָעֵאל	נְבָיֹת	וְקֵדָר
yishmā'ē'l	bishmōthām	lethôledhōthām	bekhōr	yishmā'ē'l	nevāyōth	weqēdhār
Ishmael	with their names	to their genealogies	the first-born of	Ishmael	Nebaioth	and Kedar

107	4155	14.	5108	1799	5016	15.	2396	8815
cj, pn	cj, pn		cj, pn	cj, pn	cj, pn		pn	cj, pn
וְאַדְבְּאֵל	וּמִבְשָׂם		וּמִשְׁמָע	וְדוּמָה	וּמַשָּׂא		חֲדַד	וְתֵימָא
we'adhbe'ēl	ûmivsām		ûmishmā'	wedhûmāh	ûmassā'		chădhadh	wethêmā'
and Adbeel	and Mibsam		and Mishma	and Dumah	and Massa		Hadad	and Tema

3301	5487	7214	16.	431	2062	1158	3579	431
pn	pn	cj, pn		dem pron	pers pron	n mp	pn	cj, dem pron
יְטוּר	נָפִישׁ	וָקֵדְמָה		אֵלֶּה	הֵם	בְּנֵי	יִשְׁמָעֵאל	וְאֵלֶּה
yeṭûr	nāphîsh	wāqēdhmāh		'ēlleh	hēm	benê	yishmā'ē'l	we'ēlleh
Jetur	Naphish	and Kedemah		these	they	the sons of	Ishmael	and these

8428	904, 2793	904, 3029	8530, 6461	5562	3937, 531
n mp, ps 3mp	prep, n mp, ps 3mp	cj, prep, n fp, ps 3mp	num pl, num	n mp	prep, n fp, ps 3mp
שְׁמֹתָם	בְּחַצְרֵיהֶם	וּבְטִירֹתָם	שְׁנֵים־עָשָׂר	נְשִׂיאִם	לְאֻמֹּתָם
shemōthām	bechatsrêhem	ûveṭîrōthām	shenêm- 'āsār	nesî'im	le'ummōthām
their names	by their villages	and by their encampments	two ten	chieftains	to their tribes

17.	431	8523	2508	3579	4109	8523	8389	8523	8124
	cj, dem pron	n fp	n mp	pn	num	n fs	cj, num	n fs	cj, num
	וְאֵלֶּה	שְׁנֵי	חַיֵּי	יִשְׁמָעֵאל	מְאַת	שָׁנָה	וּשְׁלֹשִׁים	שָׁנָה	וְשֶׁבַע
	we'ēlleh	shenê	chayyê	yishmā'ē'l	me'ath	shānāh	ûshelōshîm	shānāh	wesheva'
	and these	the years of	the life of	Ishmael	hundred of	years	and thirty	years	and seven

8523	1510.121	4322.121	636.221	420, 6194	18.	8331.126
n fp	cj, v Qal impf 3ms	cj, v Qal impf 3ms	cj, v Niphal impf 3ms	prep, n mp, ps 3ms		cj, v Qal impf 3mp
שָׁנִים	וַיִּגְוַע	וַיָּמָת	וַיֵּאָסֶף	אֶל־עַמָּיו		וַיִּשְׁכְּנוּ
shānîm	wayyighwa'	wayyāmāth	wayyē'āseph	'el-'ammâv		wayyishkenû
years	and he expired	and he died	and he was gathered	to his people		and they dwelled

4623, 2434	5912, 8231	866	6142, 6686	4875	971.141	831
prep, pn	prep, pn	rel part	prep, n mp	pn	v Qal inf con, ps 2ms	pn
מֵחֲוִילָה	עַד־שׁוּר	אֲשֶׁר	עַל־פְּנֵי	מִצְרַיִם	בֹּאֲכָה	אַשּׁוּרָה
mēchăwîlāh	'adh-shûr	'ăsher	'al-penê	mitsrayim	bō'ăkhāh	'ashshûrāh
from Havilah	until Shur	which	opposite	Egypt	in your going	to Assyria

6142, 6686	3725, 250	5489.111	19.	431	8765	3437
prep, n mp	adj, n mp, ps 3ms	v Qal pf 3ms		cj, dem pron	n fp	pn
עַל־פְּנֵי	כָל־אֶחָיו	נָפָל		וְאֵלֶּה	תּוֹלְדֹת	יִצְחָק
'al-penê	khol-'echâv	nāphâl		we'ēlleh	tôledhōth	yitschāq
in the presence of	all his relatives	he went down		and these	the generations of	Isaac

1158, 80	80	3314.511	881, 3437	20.	2030.121	3437	1158, 727
n ms, pn	pn	v Hiphil pf 3ms	do, pn		cj, v Qal impf 3ms	pn	n ms, num
בֶּן־אַבְרָהָם	אַבְרָהָם	הוֹלִיד	אֶת־יִצְחָק		וַיְהִי	יִצְחָק	בֶּן־אַרְבָּעִים
ben-'avrāhām	'avrāhām	hôlîdh	'eth-yitschāq		wayhî	yitschāq	ben-ēarbā'îm
the son of Abraham	Abraham	he fathered	Isaac		when he was	Isaac	son of forty

8523	904, 4089.141	881, 7549	1351, 1357	784	4623, 6549	782
n fs	prep, v Qal inf con, ps 3ms	do, pn	n fs, pn	art, pn	prep, pn	pn
שָׁנָה	בְּקַחְתּוֹ	אֶת־רִבְקָה	בַּת־בְּתוּאֵל	הָאֲרַמִּי	מִפַּדַּן	אֲרָם
shānāh	beqachtô	'eth-rivqāh	bath-bethû'ēl	hā'ărammî	mippaddan	'ărām
years	in his taking	Rebekah	the daughter of Bethuel	the Aramean	from Paddan	Aram

269	3969	784	3937	3937, 828		6518.121	3437	3937, 3176
n fs	pn	art, pn	prep, ps 3ms	prep, noun fs	21.	cj, v Qal impf 3ms	pn	prep, pn
אֲחוֹת	לָבָן	הָאֲרַמִּי	לוֹ	לְאִשָּׁה		וַיֶּעְתַּר	יִצְחָק	לַיהוָה
'ăchôth	lāvān	hā'ărammî	lô	l^{e}'ishshāh		wayye'ăttar	yitschāq	layhwāh
the sister of	Laban	the Aramean	to him	for a wife		and he prayed	Isaac	to Yahweh

3937, 5415	828	3706	6371	2000	6518.221	3937	3176
prep, *sub*	n fs, ps 3ms	cj	adj	pers pron	cj, v Niphal impf 3m	prep, ps 3ms	pn
לְנֹכַח	אִשְׁתּוֹ	כִּי	עֲקָרָה	הִוא	וַיֵּעָתֶר	לוֹ	יְהוָה
l^{e}nōkhach	'ishtô	kî	'ăqārāh	hiw'	wayyē'āther	lô	y^{e}hwāh
for	his wife	because	barren	she	and He granted a request	to him	Yahweh

firstborn of Ishmael, Nebajoth; and Kedar, and Adbeel, and Mibsam:

14. And Mishma, and Dumah, and Massa:

15. Hadar, and Tema, Jetur, Naphish, and Kedemah:

16. These are the sons of Ishmael, and these are their names, by their towns, and by their castles: ... by their villages, and by their encampments, *ASV* ... hamlets, *Darby* ... towers, *Fenton* ... tent-circles, *BB.*

twelve princes according to their nations: ... twelve chieftains of as many tribal groups, *Anchor* ... with their clans, *Berkeley.*

17. And these are the years of the life of Ishmael, an hundred and thirty and seven years: and he gave up the ghost and died; and was gathered unto his people: ... when he had breathed his last and died, *NKJV.*

18. And they dwelt from Havilah unto Shur, that is before Egypt, as thou goest toward Assyria: ... Ishmael's sons inhabited the land, *NEB.*

and he died in the presence of all his brethren: ... laying him with all his relatives, *Fenton* ... each made forays against his various kinsmen, *Anchor* ... in defiance of all his relatives, *NAS* ... in conflict with, *NCB.*

19. And these are the generations of Isaac, Abraham's son: Abraham begat Isaac: ... these are the records of, *NASB* ... family history, *NCB* ... genealogy, *NKJV* ... table of descendants, *NEB* ... account of, *REB.*

20. And Isaac was forty years old when he took Rebekah to wife, the daughter of Bethuel the Syrian of Padanaram, the sister to Laban the Syrian:

21. And Isaac intreated the LORD for his wife, because she was barren: ... prayed the Lord on behalf of, *Berkeley* ... pleaded with Yahweh, *Anchor* ... appealed, *NEB.*

and the LORD was intreated of him, and Rebekah his wife conceived: ... Yahweh responded, *Anchor* ... yielded to his entreaty, *Goodspeed* ... became with child, *BB* ... pregnant, *NIV.*

22. And the children struggled together within her: ... struggle together in her breast, *Fenton* ... clashed inside her, *Anchor* ... fighting together, *BB* ... within her body, jostled each other, *Berkeley.*

and she said, If it be so, why am I thus?: ... if all is well, why am I this way, *NKJV* ... if this be so, why am I pregnant, *NCB* ... on whose side am I to be, *Goodspeed* ... if this is how it is to be, why do I go on living, *Anchor* ... I can't endure this, *LIVB.*

And she went to enquire of the LORD: ... put the question to the Lord, *BB* ... finally, she inquired of Yahweh, *Anchor* ... went off to consult, *Goodspeed* ... seek guidance, *NEB.*

which was probably in central Arabia. This was east of where their brothers settled. No more is said about them because they did not carry on the chosen line.

25:19-20. Here a new section of Genesis begins that goes through chapter 36 and deals with the next step in the chosen line. It centers its attention on Jacob, the one who carries on the line. Padan Aram ("plain of Aram") is another name for Aram Naharaim.

Aram is the Hebrew word usually translated "Syria," but today, Syria is usually applied to the area around Damascus, south of Padan Aram.

25:21. Because Rebekah was barren, Isaac kept praying for her for 20 years (see v. 26). This delay was a test to his faith as well as Rebekah's.

It was another test to Abraham too, for he lived for 35 years after Isaac was married. Isaac did not give up, neither did he try to help the LORD out as his father, Abraham, did. Finally, his faith was rewarded and his prayer was answered by God's divine grace.

2106.122	7549	828		7827.726	1158	904, 7419
cj, v Qal impf 3fs	pn	n fs, ps 3ms	**22.**	cj, v Hithpoel impf 3mp	art, n mp	prep, n ms, ps 3fs
וַתַּהַר	רִבְקָה	אִשְׁתּוֹ		וַיִּתְרֹצְצוּ	הַבָּנִים	בְּקִרְבָּהּ
wattahar	rivqāh	'ishtô		wayyithrōts^{e}tsû	habbānîm	b^{e}qirbāhh
and she conceived	Rebekah	his wife		and they struggled	the sons	within her

569.122	524, 3772	4066	2172	609	2050.122	3937, 1938	882, 3176
cj, v Qal impf 3fs	cj, adv	intrg	dem pron	pers pron	cj, v Qal impf 3fs	prep, v Qal inf con	prep, pn
וַתֹּאמֶר	אִם־כֵּן	לָמָּה	זֶּה	אָנֹכִי	וַתֵּלֶךְ	לִדְרֹשׁ	אֶת־יְהוָה
wattō'mer	'im-kēn	lāmmāh	zeh	'ānōkhî	wattēlekh	lidhrōsh	'eth-y^{e}hwāh
and she said	if so	why	this	I	and she went	to inquire	of Yahweh

	569.121	3176	3937	8530	1504	904, 1027	8530	3948
23.	cj, v Qal impf 3ms	pn	prep, ps 3fs	*num*	n mp	prep, n fs, ps 2fs	cj, *num*	n mp
	וַיֹּאמֶר	יְהוָה	לָהּ	שְׁנֵי	גֹיִים	בְּבִטְנֵךְ	וּשְׁנֵי	לְאֻמִּים
	wayyō'mer	y^{e}hwāh	lāhh	sh^{e}nê	ghōyîm	b^{e}viṭnēkh	ûshnê	l^{e}'ummîm
	and He said	Yahweh	to her	two	nations	in your womb	and two	peoples

4623, 4753	6754.226	3947	4623, 3947	563.121	7521
prep, n mp, ps 2fs	v Niphal impf 3mp	cj, n ms	prep, n ms	v Qal impf 3ms	cj, adj
מִמֵּעַיִךְ	יִפָּרֵדוּ	וּלְאֹם	מִלְאֹם	יֶאֱמָץ	וְרַב
mimmē'ayikh	yippārēdhû	ûlă'ōm	mil'ōm	ye'ĕmāts	w^{e}rav
from your inward parts	they will divide	and people	from people	he will be stronger	and elder

5856.121	7087		4527.126	3219	3937, 3314	2079	8751
v Qal impf 3ms	adj	**24.**	cj, v Qal impf 3mp	n mp, ps 3fs	prep, v Qal inf con	cj, intrj	n mp
יַעֲבֹד	צָעִיר		וַיִּמְלְאוּ	יָמֶיהָ	לָלֶדֶת	וְהִנֵּה	תוֹמִם
ya'ăvōdh	tsā'îr		wayyiml^{e}'û	yāmêhā	lāledheth	w^{e}hinnēh	thômim
he will serve	younger		and they were complete	her days	to give birth	and behold	twins

904, 1027		3428.121	7518	127	3725	3626, 152	7998
prep, n fs, ps 3fs	**25.**	cj, v Qal impf 3ms	art, adj	adj	adj, ps 3ms	prep, *n fs*	n ms
בְּבִטְנָהּ		וַיֵּצֵא	הָרִאשׁוֹן	אַדְמוֹנִי	כֻּלּוֹ	כְּאַדֶּרֶת	שֵׂעָר
b^{e}viṭnāhh		wayyētsē'	hāri'shôn	'adhmônî	kullô	k^{e}'addereth	sē'ār
in her womb		and he came out	the first	reddish	all of him	like garment of	hair

7410.126	8428	6451		313, 3772	3428.111	250	3135
cj, v Qal impf 3mp	n ms, ps 3ms	pn	**26.**	cj, adv, cj	v Qal pf 3ms	n ms, ps 3ms	cj, n fs, ps 3ms
וַיִּקְרְאוּ	שְׁמוֹ	עֵשָׂו		וְאַחֲרֵי־כֵן	יָצָא	אָחִיו	וְיָדוֹ
wayyiqŏr'û	sh^{e}mô	'ēsāw		w^{e}'achrê-khēn	yātsā'	'āchîw	w^{e}yādhô
so they called	his name	Esau		and afterward	he came out	his brother	and his hand

270.153	904, 6357	6451	7410.121	8428	3399	3437
v Qal act part fs	prep, *n ms*	pn	cj, v Qal impf 3ms	n ms, ps 3ms	pn	cj, pn
אֹחֶזֶת	בַּעֲקֵב	עֵשָׂו	וַיִּקְרָא	שְׁמוֹ	יַעֲקֹב	וְיִצְחָק
'ōchezeth	ba'ăqēv	'ēsāw	wayyiqŏrā'	sh^{e}mô	ya'ăqōv	w^{e}yitschāq
it was taking hold	on the heel of	Esau	so he called	his name	Jacob	and Isaac

1158, 8666	8523	904, 3314.141	881		1461.126	5470	2030.121
n ms, num	n fs	prep, v Qal inf con	do, ps 3mp	**27.**	cj, v Qal impf 3mp	art, n mp	cj, v Qal impf 3ms
בֶּן־שִׁשִּׁים	שָׁנָה	בְּלֶדֶת	אֹתָם		וַיִּגְדְּלוּ	הַנְּעָרִים	וַיְהִי
ben-shishshîm	shānāh	b^{e}ledheth	'ōthām		wayyighd^{e}lû	hann^{e}'ārîm	wayhî
son of sixty	years	when fathering of	them		and they grew up	the boys	and he became

6451	382	3156.151	6987	382	7898	3399	382	8865	3553.151
pn	n ms	v Qal act ptc ms	n ms	*n ms*	n ms	cj, pn	n ms	adj	*v Qal act ptc ms*
עֵשָׂו	אִישׁ	יֹדֵעַ	צַיִד	אִישׁ	שָׂדֶה	וְיַעֲקֹב	אִישׁ	תָּם	יֹשֵׁב
'ēsāw	'îsh	yōdhēa'	tsayidh	'îsh	sādheh	w^{e}ya'ăqōv	'îsh	tām	yōshēv
Esau	man	one who knows	hunting	man of	field	but Jacob	man	mature	dweller of

23. And the LORD said unto her, Two nations are in thy womb, and two manner of people shall be separated from thy bowels: ... two peoples born of you shall be divided, *NRSV* ... have been hostile ever since conception in you, *Goodspeed* ... two peoples shall stem from your body, *NCB* ... are quarreling while within you, *NASB*.

and the one people shall be stronger than the other people: ... one people shall master the other, *Goodspeed*.

and the elder shall serve the younger: ... one people shall surpass the other, *Anchor*.

24. And when her days to be delivered were fulfilled: ... days are fulfilled, *Young* ... for her to give birth, *NKJV* ... her time had come, *REB*.

behold, there were twins in her womb: ... twin boys, *NIV* ... in her body, *BB*.

25. And the first came out red: ... red as a hairy robe, *Young* ... first one emerged reddish, *Anchor*.

all over like an hairy garment; and they called his name Esau: ... hairy mantle, *NAB* ... hairs like a cloak, *REB* ... rough as a garment, *Geneva* ... robe of hair, *BB* ... so covered with red hair, *LIVB*.

26. And after that came his brother out, and his hand took hold on Esau's heel; and his name was called Jacob: and Isaac was threescore years old when she bare them: ... holding on tightly to, *Good News* ... grasping, *NEB* ... gripping Esau's foot, *BB*.

27. And the boys grew: ... as the boys matured, *MLB* ... came to full growth, *BB*.

and Esau was a cunning hunter, a man of the field: ... expert bowman, *BB* ... skilled hunter, *Anchor*.

and Jacob was a plain man, dwelling in tents: ... a retiring man, *Anchor* ... quiet, *ASV* ... homely, *Darby*.

28. And Isaac loved Esau, because he did eat of his venison: ... he had a taste for, *NASB* ... favoured Esau because he kept him supplied with, *REB* ... venison was his meat, *Geneva* ... preferred, *NAB*.

but Rebekah loved Jacob: ... Rebekah was fonder of Jacob, *Anchor* ... preferred, *NCB*.

25:22-23. Because twins were pushing each other around in an unusual way in her womb, Rebekah sought the LORD in prayer and worship. She knew God's promise, and wanted to know what God had planned. The two nations God told her about are the Edomites and Israelites. From her womb, that is, from the time of their birth, they would be separated, divided, even hostile, for they would have nothing in common, and the elder people (descended from the one born first) would serve the people descended from the younger son. This had a fulfillment when the Edomites were made subject to King David (2 Sam. 8:13-14). See also Malachi 1:2-3; and Romans 9:11. Again, we see that the chosen line was not merely one of natural inheritance, for neither Abraham, Isaac, nor Jacob were firstborn sons, but God gave them the place of "firstborn" in His eyes. In each case the ones carrying on the line eventually responded to God's grace by their faith.

25:24-25. The first to be born came out reddish (or reddish-brown), so that he was later called Edom ("Red"). But because his whole body was covered like a robe of hair, they named him Esau ("hairy one").

25:26. The second son came out holding tight to Esau's heel, which he grasped before he himself came out (Hos. 12:3). So they named him Jacob, meaning "Heel-catcher," from the Hebrew root *`akev*, "heel." Later on Esau connected it with a similar root, *`akav*, meaning to cheat or deceive (27:36).

25:27. When the boys grew up, Esau became a skillful hunter, a man of the field, that is, of the open country (outside of the cultivated areas) where he loved to roam. In the Hebrew, a beast of the field means a wild animal. A plant of the field means a wild plant. Thus, Esau was a wild, undisciplined man who lived a wild life seeking sport and adventure. In contrast to him, Jacob was a quiet (or mature) man. The Hebrew *tam* also means he was sensible, diligent, dutiful, and peaceful. He could be counted on to carry out the duties of life. He was also a characteristic, or we might say, an ideal tent dweller. He was orderly, paid attention to business, and was everything a tent dweller ought to be.

25:28. Isaac was a godly man, but he developed a love for Esau's wild game. This became a blind spot that made him prefer Esau. Rebekah, however, preferred Jacob. What mother would not prefer a son that was always there when she needed him, a son who could be counted on to keep the business of these tent dwellers going smoothly and prosperously! Moreover, Rebekah had made a

164		154.121	3437	881, 6451	3706, 6987	904, 6552	7549
n mp	**28.**	cj, v Qal impf 3ms	pn	do, pn	cj, n ms	prep, n ms, ps 3ms	cj, pn
אֹהָלִים		וַיֶּאֱהַב	יִצְחָק	אֶת־עֵשָׂו	כִּי־צַיִד	בְּפִיו	וְרִבְקָה
'ōhālîm		wayye'ĕhav	yitschāq	'eth-'ēsāw	kî-tsayidh	b^{e}phîw	w^{e}rivqāh
tents		and he loved	Isaac	Esau	because game	in his mouth	but Rebekah

154.153	881, 3399		2202.521	3399	5318	971.121
v Qal act ptc fs	do, pn	**29.**	cj, v Hiphil impf 3ms	pn	n ms	cj, v Qal impf 3ms
אֹהֶבֶת	אֶת־יַעֲקֹב		וַיָּזֶד	יַעֲקֹב	נָזִיד	וַיָּבֹא
'ōheveth	'eth-ya'ăqōv		wayyāzedh	ya'ăqōv	nāzîdh	wayyāvō'
one who loves	Jacob		and he boiled	Jacob	something boiled	and he came

6451	4623, 7898	2000	6106		569.121	6451	420, 3399	4080.531
pn	prep, art, n ms	cj, pers pron	adj	**30.**	cj, v Qal impf 3ms	pn	prep, pn	v Hiphil impv 2ms, pf 1cs
עֵשָׂו	מִן־הַשָּׂדֶה	וְהוּא	עָיֵף		וַיֹּאמֶר	עֵשָׂו	אֶל־יַעֲקֹב	הַלְעִיטֵנִי
'ēsāw	min-hassādheh	w^{e}hû'	'āyēph		wayyō'mer	'ēsāw	'el-ya'ăqōv	hal'îṭēnî
Esau	from the field	and he	faint		and he said	Esau	to Jacob	let me eat quickly

5167	4623, 121	121	2172	3706	6106	609	6142, 3772	7410.111, 8428
part	prep, art, adj	art, adj	art, dem pron	cj	adj	pers pron	prep, adv	v Qal pf 3ms, n ms, ps 3ms
נָא	מִן־הָאָדֹם	הָאָדֹם	הַזֶּה	כִּי	עָיֵף	אָנֹכִי	עַל־כֵּן	קָרָא־שְׁמוֹ
nā'	min-hā'ādhōm	hā'ādhōm	hazzeh	kî	'āyēph	'ānōkhî	'al-kēn	qārā'-sh^{e}mô
please	from the red	the red	the this	because	faint	I	therefore	he called his name

110		569.121	3399	4513.131	3626, 3219	881, 1112	3937
pn	**31.**	cj, v Qal impf 3ms	pn	v Qal impv 2ms	prep, art, n ms	do, n fs, ps 2ms	prep, ps 1cs
אֱדוֹם		וַיֹּאמֶר	יַעֲקֹב	מִכְרָה	כַיּוֹם	אֶת־בְּכֹרָתְךָ	לִי
'ĕdhôm		wayyō'mer	ya'ăqōv	mikhrāh	khayyôm	'eth-b^{e}khōrāth^{e}khā	lî
Edom		and he said	Jacob	sell	today	your birthright	to me

	569.121	6451	2079	609	2050.151	3937, 4322.141	4066, 2172
32.	cj, v Qal impf 3ms	pn	intrj	pers pron	v Qal act ptc ms	prep, v Qal inf con	cj, intrg, dem pron
	וַיֹּאמֶר	עֵשָׂו	הִנֵּה	אָנֹכִי	הוֹלֵךְ	לָמוּת	וְלָמָּה־זֶּה
	wayyō'mer	'ēsāw	hinnēh	'ānōkhî	hôlēkh	lāmûth	w^{e}lāmmāh-zeh
	and he said	Esau	behold	I	going	to die	and for what this

3937	1112		569.121	3399	8123.231	3937	3626, 3219
prep, ps 1cs	n fs	**33.**	cj, v Qal impf 3ms	pn	v Niphal impv 2ms	prep, ps 1cs	prep, n ms
לִי	בְּכֹרָה		וַיֹּאמֶר	יַעֲקֹב	הִשָּׁבְעָה	לִי	כַּיּוֹם
lî	b^{e}khōrāh		wayyō'mer	ya'ăqōv	hishshāv^{e}'āh	lî	kiyyôm
to me	birthright		and he said	Jacob	swear	to me	today

8123.221	3937	4513.121	881, 1112	3937, 3399		3399	5598.111
cj, v Niphal impf 3ms	prep, ps 3ms	cj, v Qal impf 3ms	do, n fs, ps 3ms	prep, pn	**34.**	cj, pn	v Qal pf 3ms
וַיִּשָּׁבַע	לוֹ	וַיִּמְכֹּר	אֶת־בְּכֹרָתוֹ	לְיַעֲקֹב		וְיַעֲקֹב	נָתַן
wayyishshāva'	lô	wayyimkōr	'eth-b^{e}khōrāthô	l^{e}ya'ăqōv		w^{e}ya'ăqōv	nāthan
and he swore	to him	and he sold	his birthright	to Jacob		and Jacob	he gave

3937, 6451	4035	5318	5958	404.121	8685.121	7251.121
prep, pn	n ms	cj, *n ms*	n fp	cj, v Qal impf 3ms	cj, v Qal impf 3ms	cj, v Qal impf 3ms
לְעֵשָׂו	לֶחֶם	וּנְזִיד	עֲדָשִׁים	וַיֹּאכַל	וַיֵּשְׁתְּ	וַיָּקָם
l^{e}'ēsāw	lechem	ûn^{e}zîdh	'ădhāshîm	wayyō'khal	wayyēsht	wayyāqām
to Esau	bread	and boiled	lentils	and he ate	and he drank	and he rose up

2050.121	995.121	6451	881, 1112		2030.121	7743
cj, v Qal impf 3ms	cj, v Qal impf 3ms	pn	do, art, n fs	**26:1**	cj, v Qal impf 3ms	n ms
וַיֵּלַךְ	וַיִּבֶז	עֵשָׂו	אֶת־הַבְּכֹרָה		וַיְהִי	רָעָב
wayyēlakh	wayyivez	'ēsāw	'eth-habb^{e}khōrāh		wayhî	rā'āv
and he went	and he despised	Esau	the birthright		and it was	famine

904, 800	4623, 3937, 940	7743	7518	866	2030.111	904, 3219	80
prep, art, n fs	prep, prep, n ms	art, n ms	art, adj	rel part	v Qal pf 3ms	prep, *n mp*	pn
בָּאָרֶץ	מִלְּבַד	הָרָעָב	הָרִאשׁוֹן	אֲשֶׁר	הָיָה	בִּימֵי	אַבְרָהָם
bā'ārets	mill^{e}vadh	hārā'āv	hāri'shôn	'ăsher	hāyāh	bîmê	'avrāhām
in the land	besides	the famine	the former	which	it was	in the days of	Abraham

2050.121	3437	420, 40	4567, 6674	1689		7495.221	420
cj, v Qal impf 3ms	pn	prep, pn	*n ms*, pn	pn		cj, v Niphal impf 3ms	prep, ps 3ms
וַיֵּלֶךְ	יִצְחָק	אֶל־אֲבִימֶלֶךְ	מֶלֶךְ־פְּלִשְׁתִּים	גְּרָרָה	**2.**	וַיֵּרָא	אֵלָיו
wayyēlekh	yitschāq	'el-'ăvîmmelekh	melekh-p^{e}lishtîm	g^{e}rārāh		wayyērā'	'ēlāv
and he went	Isaac	to Abimelech	king of the Philistines	to Gerar		and he appeared	to him

29. And Jacob sod pottage: ... cooking a stew, *NAB* ... cooked a dish, *Darby* ... boiling porridge, *Fenton* ... a broth, *NEB.*

and Esau came from the field, and he was faint: ... famished, *NASB* ... exhausted, *Fenton* ... weary, *NKJV* ... great need of food, *BB.*

30. And Esau said to Jacob, Feed me, I pray thee, with that same red pottage; for I am faint: ... give me a swallow of that red stuff, for I am famished, *Anchor* ... some of that red, that red there, *Berkeley* ... let me gulp down ... I'm starving, *NAB.*

therefore was his name called Edom: ... red soup, *Fenton* ... red stuff, *LIVB.*

31. And Jacob said, Sell me this day thy birthright: ... first give me your birthright in exchange, *NCB* ... trade, *LIVB* ... not till you sell me your rights as the first-born, *REB.*

32. And Esau said, Behold, I am at the point to die: and what profit shall this birthright do to me?: ... here I am at the point of death, *Anchor* ... I am dying, *MLB* ... death's door, *NEB.*

33. And Jacob said, Swear to me this day: ... give me your oath, *Goodspeed* ... vow, *Good News.*

and he sware unto him: and he sold his birthright unto Jacob: ... thus, handing over, *BB* ... sold his birthright under oath, *NAB.*

34. Then Jacob gave Esau bread and pottage of lentiles; and he did eat and drink, and rose up, and went his way thus Esau despised his birthright: ... lightly did Esau esteem, *Berkeley* ... misprize, *Anchor* ... condemned, *Geneva* ... showed how little he valued, *NEB.*

26:1. And there was a famine in the land, beside the first famine that was in the days of Abraham: ... a famine visited the land, *Berkeley* ... a great need, *BB* ... distinct from the

choice for God and she saw in Jacob a concern for spiritual things as well. He needed to be changed, but he was the kind of person God could work with.

25:29-30. Esau came in from a day of hunting to find Jacob boiling something (not until v. 34 does the Bible state it was lentils). Because he was famished Esau asked excitedly and repeatedly for some of "that red." This was another reason that he was later called Edom ("Red").

25:31-34. Jacob stopped him and demanded that before anything else, Esau must sell him his birthright. Esau replied that he was "a going to die" person. That is, he was always in danger of death because he lived as a hunter. He did not know whether the birthright would do him any good or not. (Others later followed his example. See Isaiah 22:13.) Then Jacob demanded that he swear an oath. So Esau did so and sold his birthright. This satisfied Jacob and he gave Esau bread and the lentil stew he wanted. In doing this, Esau despised his birthright. This was very serious. The birthright normally included a double portion of the inheritance, as well as family leadership in worship and in war. But in this chosen line, the birthright included the promise and blessing given to Abraham (Gen. 28:4) as well as the privilege of carrying on the line that would bring salvation-blessing to the whole world. Jacob knew this and wanted the relation with God the covenant blessings promised. But Esau had no concern for God or spiritual things. Hebrews 12:16 calls him "profane," that is, "godless," not in the sense of atheistic, but simply "secular," leaving God out of his life, his plans, his thinking. Actually, Jacob did not need to buy the birthright. If he had simply trusted the Lord, God would have given it to him. The important point, however, is that Jacob valued the birthright, Esau did not.

26:1. This verse is like a title for this chapter, the only chapter where Isaac is prominent. Because Isaac had some experiences similar to Abraham's, the Bible is very careful to point out that this famine was different from the earlier one in Abraham's time (Gen. 12:10). Abimelech ("my father is king")

3176	569.121	414, 3495.123	4875	8331.131	904, 800	866
pn	cj, v Qal impf 3ms	adv, v Qal impf 2ms	pn	v Qal impv 2ms	prep, art, n fs	rel part
יְהוָה	וַיֹּאמֶר	אַל־תֵּרֵד	מִצְרָיְמָה	שְׁכֹן	בָּאָרֶץ	אֲשֶׁר
y^{e}hwāh	wayyō'mer	'al-tērēdh	mitsrāy^{e}māh	sh^{e}khōn	bā'ārets	'ăsher
Yahweh	and he said	not you will go down	to Egypt	dwell	in the land	which

569.125	420	3.	1513.131	904, 800	2148	2030.125	6196
v Qal impf 1cs	prep, ps 2ms		v Qal impv 2ms	prep, art, n fs	art, dem pron	cj, v Qal impf 1cs	prep, ps 2ms
אֹמַר	אֵלֶיךָ		גּוּר	בָּאָרֶץ	הַזֹּאת	וְאֶהְיֶה	עִמְּךָ
'ōmar	'ēlêkhā		gûr	bā'ārets	hazzō'th	w^{e}'ehyeh	'imm^{e}khā
I will say	to you		sojourn	in the land	the this	and I will be	with you

1313.125	3706, 3937	3937, 2320	5598.125	881, 3725, 800	419
cj, v Qal impf 1cs, ps 2ms	prep, prep, ps 2ms	cj, prep, n ms, ps 2ms	v Qal impf 1cs	do, *adj*, art, n fp	art, dem pron
וַאֲבָרְכֶךָּ	כִּי־לְךָ	וּלְזַרְעֲךָ	אֶתֵּן	אֶת־כָּל־הָאֲרָצֹת	הָאֵל
wa'ăvārkhekhā	kî-l^{e}khā	ûlăzar'ăkhā	'ettēn	'eth-kol-hā'ărātsōth	hā'ēl
and I will bless you	because to you	and to your seed	I will give	all the lands	the these

7251.515	881, 8095	866	8123.215	3937, 80	1
cj, v Hiphil perf 1cs	do, art, n fs	rel part	v Niphal pf 1cs	prep, pn	n ms, ps 2ms
וַהֲקִמֹתִי	אֶת־הַשְּׁבֻעָה	אֲשֶׁר	נִשְׁבַּעְתִּי	לְאַבְרָהָם	אָבִיךָ
wahqimōthî	'eth-hashsh^{e}vu'āh	'ăsher	nishba'ttî	l^{e}'avrāhām	'āvîkhā
and I will establish	the oath	which	I have sworn	to Abraham	your father

4.	7528.515	881, 2320	3626, 3676	8452	5598.115	3937, 2320
	cj, v Hiphil perf 1cs	do, n ms, ps 2ms	prep, *n mp*	art, n md	cj, v Qal pf 1cs	prep, n ms, ps 2ms
	וְהִרְבֵּיתִי	אֶת־זַרְעֲךָ	כְּכוֹכְבֵי	הַשָּׁמַיִם	וְנָתַתִּי	לְזַרְעֲךָ
	w^{e}hirbêthî	'eth-zar'ăkhā	kh^{e}khôkh^{e}vê	hashshāmayim	w^{e}nāthattî	l^{e}zar'ăkhā
	and I will multiply	your seed	like the stars of	the heavens	and I will give	to your seed

881	3725, 800	419	1313.716	904, 2320	3725	1504	800
do	*adj*, art, n fp	art, dem pron	cj, v Hithpael pf 3cp	prep, n ms, ps 2ms	adj	*n mp*	art, n fs
אֵת	כָּל־הָאֲרָצֹת	הָאֵל	וְהִתְבָּרְכוּ	בְזַרְעֲךָ	כֹּל	גּוֹיֵי	הָאָרֶץ
'ēth	kol-hā'ărātsōth	hā'ēl	w^{e}hithbār^{e}khû	b^{e}zar'ăkhā	kōl	gôyê	hā'ārets
	all the lands	the these	and they will be blessed	by your seed	all	the nations of	the earth

5.	6358	866, 8471.111	80	904, 7249	8490.121	5111
	cj	rel part, v Qal pf 3ms	pn	prep, n ms, ps 1cs	cj, v Qal impf 3ms	n fs, ps 1cs
	עֵקֶב	אֲשֶׁר־שָׁמַע	אַבְרָהָם	בְּקֹלִי	וַיִּשְׁמֹר	מִשְׁמַרְתִּי
	'ēqev	'ăsher-shāma'	'avrāhām	b^{e}qōlî	wayyishmōr	mishmartî
	because	that he listened	Abraham	by my voice	and he kept	my charge

4851	2807	8784	6.	3553.121	3437	904, 1689
n fp, ps 1cs	n fp, ps 1cs	cj, n fp, ps 1cs		cj, v Qal impf 3ms	pn	prep, pn
מִצְוֹתַי	חֻקּוֹתַי	וְתוֹרֹתָי		וַיֵּשֶׁב	יִצְחָק	בִּגְרָר
mitswōthay	chuqqôthay	w^{e}thôrōthāy		wayyēshev	yitschāq	bighrār
my commandments	my statutes	and my laws		and he dwelled	Isaac	in Gerar

7.	8068.126	596	4887	3937, 828	569.121	269	2000
	cj, v Qal impf 3mp	*n mp*	art, n ms	prep, n fs, ps 3ms	cj, v Qal impf 3ms	n fs, ps 1cs	pers pron
	וַיִּשְׁאֲלוּ	אַנְשֵׁי	הַמָּקוֹם	לְאִשְׁתּוֹ	וַיֹּאמֶר	אֲחֹתִי	הִוא
	wayyish'ălû	'anshê	hammāqôm	l^{e}'ishtô	wayyō'mer	'ăchōthî	hiw'
	and they asked	the men of	the place	about his wife	and he said	my sister	she

3706	3486.111	3937, 569.141	828	6678, 2103.126	596	4887
cj	v Qal pf 3ms	prep, v Qal inf con	n fs, ps 1cs	adv, v Qal impf 3mp, ps 1cs	*n mp*	art, n ms
כִּי	יָרֵא	לֵאמֹר	אִשְׁתִּי	פֶּן־יַהַרְגֻנִי	אַנְשֵׁי	הַמָּקוֹם
kî	yārē'	lē'mōr	'ishtî	pen-yaharghunî	'anshê	hammāqôm
because	he was afraid	to say	my wife	otherwise they will kill me	the men of	the place

earlier one, *NAB* ... aside from the previous, *Anchor*.

And Isaac went unto Abimelech king of the Philistines unto Gerar: ... so Isaac moved, *Berkeley*.

2. And the LORD appeared unto him, and said: ... Yahweh, *Anchor* ... Ever-Living, *Fenton*.

Go not down into Egypt; dwell in the land which I shall tell thee of: ... remain in the land which I indicate, *Berkeley* ... tabernacle, *Young*.

3. Sojourn in this land, and I will be with thee: ... live as an immigrant in this land, *MLB* ... establish yourself, *Goodspeed* ... reside as a stranger, *NCB* ... as an alien, *NRSV*.

and will bless thee; for unto thee, and unto thy seed, I will give all these countries, and I will perform the oath which I sware unto Abraham thy father: ... offspring, *Anchor* ... you and your race, *Fenton* ... descendants I will give all this territory, *Berkeley*.

4. And I will make thy seed to multiply as the stars of heaven: ... descendants as numerous, *Anchor* ... offspring as countless, *Berkeley* ... increase your race, *Fenton*.

and will give unto thy seed all these countries; and in thy seed shall all the nations of the earth be blessed: ... through your heir, *Fenton* ... will invoke blessings on one another through, *Goodspeed* ... so that all nations shall bless themselves by your offspring, *Anchor* ... will pray to be blessed as they are blessed, *NEB* ... will wish, *REB*.

5. Because that Abraham obeyed my voice, and kept my charge, my commandments, my statutes, and my laws: ... obeyed me and kept all my laws and commands, *Good News* ... kept my requirements, *NIV* ... heeded my call and kept my mandate, *Anchor*.

6. And Isaac dwelt in Gerar: ... went on living in Gerar, *BB*.

7. And the men of the place asked him of his wife; and he said, She is my sister: ... he would not admit that she was his wife, *Good News*.

for he feared to say, She is my wife; lest, said he, the men of the place should kill me for Rebekah: ... slay me on account of, *Anchor* ... murder him, *Fenton* ... in case they killed him, *NEB* ... kill him to get her, *LIVB*.

because she was fair to look upon: ... since she is so beautiful, *BB* ... fair in countenance, *Darby* ... good-looking, *Goodspeed* ... attractive in appearance, *NRSV*.

---

also is a different Abimelech from the one Abraham knew (20:2). This royal title undoubtedly had been passed on to the son or grandson of the earlier Abimelech.

26:2. The famine was a test of Isaac's faith. Lest he follow Abraham's example, the LORD warned him not to go to Egypt (as Abraham did, Gen. 12:15), but to live wherever He told him to live. This does not mean he would have to stay in one place. God would give him guidance as he moved about. God wanted him to follow in the good footsteps of Abraham and live a life of faith, trust, and obedience. This meant he must trust God for himself in a personal way.

26:3-4. Isaac was to continue to live as a resident alien in the promised land. But he would not be alone. God promised to be with him and to bless him. Then God reconfirmed the promise and the oath given to Abraham. To Isaac and his descendants God promised to give all these lands, that is, the lands of the various Canaanite tribes. The promises of descendants as numerous as the stars in the sky (that is, the visible stars), and that all nations (*goyim*, a word often translated Gentiles) would be blessed through his descendants (actually, through one of his descendants, our Lord Jesus Christ, see Gal. 3:16) were also confirmed. The Hebrew (v. 4) means "be blessed," not "bless themselves."

26:5-6. The reason Isaac could inherit the promise and enjoy God's presence and blessing was because Abraham obeyed God, fulfilled the obligations God put on him, and kept the requirements, commandments, rules, and instructions God gave him. These would include the moral codes and customs God allowed Abraham to follow. God told Isaac this to let him know that if he wanted to continue to enjoy God's salvation-blessing and presence he needed to continue in the same sort of faith and obedience to all the various aspects of God's instructions to him. He did not yet have a written law. But he had the example of Abraham, and we can be sure that Abraham trained him well. (See Gen. 18:19.) Now, however, Isaac had to trust God for himself. He began well. He did not go to Egypt but stayed where he was in Gerar. Then, because of the famine, he may have lost much of the wealth he inherited from Abraham.

26:7-9. Isaac unwisely followed Abraham's example in Gerar. There are many parallels between the experiences of Abraham and Isaac, but

6142, 7549	3706, 3009B	4920	2000		2030.121	3706
prep, pn	conj, adj	n ms	pers pron	**8.**	cj, v Qal impf 3ms	cj
עַל־רִבְקָה	כִּי־טוֹבַת	מַרְאֶה	הִוא		וַיְהִי	כִּי
'al-rivqāh	kî-ṭôvath	mar'eh	hiw'		wayhî	kî
over Rebekah	because beautiful	appearance	she		and it was	that

773.116, 3937	8427	3219	8625.521	40	4567	6674
v Qal pf 3cp, prep, ps 3ms	adv	art, n mp	cj, v Hiphil impf 3ms	pn	*n ms*	pn
אָרְכוּ־לוֹ	שָׁם	הַיָּמִים	וַיַּשְׁקֵף	אֲבִימֶלֶךְ	מֶלֶךְ	פְּלִשְׁתִּים
'ār^{e}khû-lô	shām	hayyāmîm	wayyashqēph	'ăvîmelekh	melekh	p^{e}lishtîm
they were long to him	there	the days	and he looked down	Abimelech	king of	Philistines

1185	2574	7495.121	2079	3437	6978	881	7549	828
prep	art, n ms	cj, v Qal impf 3ms	cj, intrj	pn	v Piel part ms	do	pn	n fs, ps 3ms
בְּעַד	הַחַלּוֹן	וַיַּרְא	וְהִנֵּה	יִצְחָק	מְצַחֵק	אֵת	רִבְקָה	אִשְׁתּוֹ
b^{e}'adh	hachallôn	wayyar'	w^{e}hinnēh	yitschāq	m^{e}tsachēq	'ēth	rivqāh	'ishtô
through	the window	and he saw	and behold	Isaac	fondling		Rebekah	his wife

	7410.121	40	3937, 3437	569.121	395	2079	828	2000
9.	cj, v Qal impf 3ms	pn	prep, pn	cj, v Qal impf 3ms	adv	intrj	n fs, ps 2ms	pers pron
	וַיִּקְרָא	אֲבִימֶלֶךְ	לְיִצְחָק	וַיֹּאמֶר	אַךְ	הִנֵּה	אִשְׁתְּךָ	הִוא
	wayyiqŏrā'	'ăvîmelekh	l^{e}yitschāq	wayyō'mer	'akh	hinnēh	'isht^{e}khā	hiw'
	and he called	Abimelech	for Isaac	and he said	only	behold	your wife	she

351	569.113	269	2000	569.121	420	3437	3706	569.115
cj, intrg	v Qal pf 2ms	n fs, ps 1cs	pers pron	cj, v Qal impf 3ms	prep, ps 3ms	pn	cj	v Qal pf 1cs
וְאֵיךְ	אָמַרְתָּ	אֲחֹתִי	הִוא	וַיֹּאמֶר	אֵלָיו	יִצְחָק	כִּי	אָמַרְתִּי
w^{e}'êkh	'āmartā	'ăchōthî	hiw'	wayyō'mer	'ēlâv	yitschāq	kî	'āmartî
and how	you said	my sister	she	and he said	to him	Isaac	because	I said

6678, 4322.125	6142		569.121	40	4242, 2148	6449.113
adv, v Qal impf 1cs	prep, ps 3fs	**10.**	cj, v Qal impf 3ms	pn	intrg, dem pron	v Qal pf 2ms
פֶּן־אָמוּת	עָלֶיהָ		וַיֹּאמֶר	אֲבִימֶלֶךְ	מַה־זֹּאת	עָשִׂיתָ
pen-'āmûth	'ālêhā		wayyō'mer	'ăvîmelekh	mah-zō'th	'āsîthā
otherwise I will die	over her		and he said	Abimelech	what this	you did

3937	3626, 4746	8311.111	259	6194	882, 828	971.513
prep, ps 1cs	prep, sub	v Qal pf 3ms	*num*	art, n ms	prep, n fs, ps 2ms	cj, v Hiphil pf 2ms
לָּנוּ	כִּמְעַט	שָׁכַב	אַחַד	הָעָם	אֶת־אִשְׁתֶּךָ	וְהֵבֵאתָ
lānû	kim'aṭ	shākhav	'achadh	hā'ām	'eth-'ishtekhā	w^{e}hēvē'thā
to us	for little	he would have laid	one of	the people	with your wife	and you brought

6142	844		6943	40	881, 3725, 6194	3937, 569.141
prep, ps 1cp	n ms	**11.**	cj, v Piel impf 3ms	pn	do, *adj*, art, n ms	prep, v Qal inf con
עָלֵינוּ	אָשָׁם		וַיְצַו	אֲבִימֶלֶךְ	אֶת־כָּל־הָעָם	לֵאמֹר
'ālênû	'āshām		waytsaw	'ăvîmelekh	'eth-kol-hā'ām	lē'mōr
to us	guilt		and he commanded	Abimelech	all the people	saying

5236	904, 382	2172	904, 828	4322.142	4322.621
art, v Qal act part ms	prep, n ms	art, dem pron	cj, prep, n fs, ps 3ms	v Qal inf abs	v Hophal impf 3ms
הַנֹּגֵעַ	בָּאִישׁ	הַזֶּה	וּבְאִשְׁתּוֹ	מוֹת	יוּמָת
hannōghēa'	bā'îsh	hazzeh	ûv^{e}'ishtô	môth	yûmāth
the one who touches	the man	the this	or his wife	dying	he will be put to death

	2319.121	3437	904, 800	2000	4834.121	904, 8523	2000
12.	cj, v Qal impf 3ms	pn	prep, art, n fs	art, dem pron	cj, v Qal impf 3ms	prep, art, fs	art, dem pron
	וַיִּזְרַע	יִצְחָק	בָּאָרֶץ	הַהִוא	וַיִּמְצָא	בַּשָּׁנָה	הַהִוא
	wayyizra'	yitschāq	bā'ārets	hahiw'	wayyimtsā'	bashshānāh	hahiw'
	and he sowed	Isaac	in the land	the that	and he found	in the year	the that

4109	8555	1313.321	3176	13.	1461.121	382
num	n mp	cj, v Piel impf 3ms, ps 3ms	pn		cj, v Qal impf 3ms	art, n ms
מֵאָה	שְׁעָרִים	וַיְבָרְכֵהוּ	יְהוָה		וַיִּגְדַּל	הָאִישׁ
mēʼāh	sh^{e}ʻārîm	way^{e}vār^{e}khēhû	y^{e}hwāh		wayyighdal	hāʼîsh
hundred	measures	and he blessed him	Yahweh		and he became great	the man

2050.121	2050.142	1462	5912	3706, 1461.111	4108
cj, v Qal impf 3ms	v Qal inf abs	cj, adj	adv	cj, v Qal pf 3ms	adv
וַיֵּלֶךְ	הָלוֹךְ	וְגָדֵל	עַד	כִּי־גָדַל	מְאֹד
wayyēlekh	hālôkh	w^{e}ghādhēl	ʻadh	kî-ghādhal	m^{e}ʼōdh
and he went	going	and becoming great	until	that he had become great	very

8. And it came to pass, when he had been there a long time: ... considerable, *NEB* ... when the days have been prolonged, *Young* ... sometime later, *LIVB.*

that Abimelech king of the Philistines looked out at a window, and saw: ... happened to look, *NCB* ... looked down from, *REB.*

and, behold, Isaac was sporting with Rebekah his wife: ... fondling, *Goodspeed* ... caressing, *NASB* ... laughing together, *NEB* ... showing endearment, *NKJV.*

9. And Abimelech called Isaac, and said, Behold, of a surety she is thy wife: ... see here, she really is, *Berkeley* ... then she is your wife, *Anchor* ... it is clear that she is, *BB* ... quite obviously, *NKJV.*

and how saidst thou, She is my sister? And Isaac said unto him, Because I said, Lest I die for her: ... cost me my life, *Berkeley* ... I thought I might lose my life, *Anchor.*

10. And Abimelech said, What is this thou hast done unto us?: ... Abimelech retorted, *MLB* ... what a way to treat us, *Goodspeed* ... how could you do this to us, *NAB.*

one of the people might lightly have lien with thy wife: ... might have lain, *ASV* ... slept, *NIV* ... it would have taken very little, *NAB.*

and thou shouldest have brought guiltiness upon us: ... brought a trespass on us, *Darby* ... sin would have been ours, *BB* ... made us incur guilt, *REB* ... been responsible for our guilt, *Good News.*

11. And Abimelech charged all his people, saying: ... warned all his people, *NCB* ... threatened, *NEB* ... issued orders, *Anchor.*

He that toucheth this man or his wife shall surely be put to death: ... molests, *NAB* ... cometh against, *Young* ... executed, *Berkeley.*

12. Then Isaac sowed in that land, and received in the same year an hundredfold: and the LORD blessed him: ... hundredfold by estimation, *Geneva* ... obtained that year one hundred measures of barley, *Goodspeed* ... got in the same year fruit a hundred times much, *BB* ... prospered him, *Fenton.*

13. And the man waxed great, and went forward, and grew until he became very great: ... continually

there are also distinct differences. Because Rebekah was so beautiful Isaac was afraid to say she was his wife lest someone kill him in order to take her captive, so he told the men of Gerar she was his sister, but he kept her with him instead of letting Abimelech take her into his harem.

One day, after Isaac had been there a long time, Abimelech looked out a small, latticework-covered window and saw Isaac caressing her in a tender, most loving way. This was not a quick kiss, such as a brother might give a sister, but was long, lingering, and obviously expressing desire, for Isaac loved her dearly (24:67). It is no wonder that Abimelech immediately summoned Isaac and wanted to know why Isaac said Rebekah was his sister.

Isaac, like Abraham, had become concerned over himself. He let fear dominate his words and actions, and he forgot God's promise to be with him and bless him. Once again we see the Bible does not whitewash its heroes. It lets us learn from their mistakes as well as from their victories.

26:10. Abimelech sharply reproved Isaac for this. One of the men of Gerar could easily have raped Rebekah and brought guilt (and punishment) on the people of Gerar. In the minds of these Philistines, raping a married woman was considered much worse than enticing a virgin and raping her, for then there could be a marriage and compensation to the woman's family.

26:11. Abimelech then gave strict orders that anyone who touches, that is, harms or hurts Isaac or Rebekah would definitely be put to death.

26:12. Isaac was not changing his way of living here. It was not unusual for nomadic tent dwellers to stop for a season and plant a crop. This is done even today. The hundredfold return was

14.	**2030.121, 3937**	**4898, 6887**	**4898**	**1267**	**5866**	**7521**
	cj, v Qal impf 3ms, prep, ps 3ms	*n ms*, n fs	cj, *n ms*	n ms	cj, n fs	adj
	וַיְהִי־לוֹ	מִקְנֵה־צֹאן	וּמִקְנֵה	בָקָר	וַעֲבֻדָּה	רַבָּה
	wayhî-lô	miqŏnēh-tsō'n	ûmiqŏnēh	vāqār	wa'ăvuddāh	rabbāh
	and it was to him	livestock of flocks	and livestock of	herds	and slaves	many

7353.126	**881**	**6674**	**15.**	**3725, 908**	**866**	**2763.116**	**5860**
cj, v Qal impf 3mp	do, ps 3ms	pn		cj, *adj*, art, n fp	rel part	v Qal pf 3cp	*n mp*
וַיְקַנְאוּ	אֹתוֹ	פְּלִשְׁתִּים		וְכָל־הַבְּאֵרֹת	אֲשֶׁר	חָפְרוּ	עַבְדֵי
wayqan'û	'ōthô	p^{e}lishtîm		w^{e}khol-habb^{e}'ērōth	'ăsher	chāph^{e}rû	'av^{e}dhê
and they envied	him	Philistines		and all the wells	which	they dug	the slaves of

1	**904, 3219**	**80**	**1**	**5845.316**	**6674**	**4527.326**
n ms, ps	prep, *n mp*	pn	n ms, ps	v Piel pf 3cp, ps 3mp	pn	cj, v Piel impf 3mp, ps 3mp
אָבִיו	בִּימֵי	אַבְרָהָם	אָבִיו	סִתְּמוּם	פְּלִשְׁתִּים	וַיְמַלְאוּם
'āvîw	bîmê	'avrāhām	'āvîw	sitt^{e}mûm	p^{e}lishtîm	waymal'ûm
his father	in the days of	Abraham	his father	they stopped them up	Philistines	and they filled them with

6312	**16.**	**569.121**	**40**	**420, 3437**	**2050.131**	**4623, 6196**
n ms		cj, v Qal impf 3ms	pn	prep, pn	v Qal impv 2ms	prep, prep, ps 1cp
עָפָר		וַיֹּאמֶר	אֲבִימֶלֶךְ	אֶל־יִצְחָק	לֵךְ	מֵעִמָּנוּ
'āphār		wayyō'mer	'ăvîmelekh	'el-yitschāq	lēkh	mē'immānû
dirt		and he said	Abimelech	to Isaac	go	from us

3706, 6343.113	**4623**	**4108**	**17.**	**2050.121**	**4623, 8427**	**3437**
cj, v Qal pf 2ms	prep, ps 3mp	adv		cj, v Qal impf 3ms	prep, adv	pn
כִּי־עָצַמְתָּ	מִמֶּנּוּ	מְאֹד		וַיֵּלֶךְ	מִשָּׁם	יִצְחָק
kî-'ātsamtā	mimmennû	m^{e}'ōdh		wayyēlekh	mishshām	yitschāq
because you are mightier	than us	very		and he went	from there	Isaac

2684.121	**904, 5337, 1689**	**3553.121**	**8427**	**18.**	**8178.121**	**3437**
cj, v Qal impf 3ms	prep, *n ms*, pn	cj, v Qal impf 3ms	adv		cj, v Qal impf 3ms	pn
וַיִּחַן	בְּנַחַל־גְּרָר	וַיֵּשֶׁב	שָׁם		וַיָּשָׁב	יִצְחָק
wayyichan	b^{e}nachal-g^{e}rār	wayyēshev	shām		wayyāshāv	yitschāq
and he camped	in the valley of Gerar	and he dwelled	there		and he returned	Isaac

2763.121	**881, 908**	**4448**	**866**	**2763.116**	**904, 3219**	**80**	**1**
cj, v Qal impf 3ms	do, *n fp*	art, n md	rel part	v Qal pf 3cp	prep, *n mp*	pn	n ms, ps
וַיַּחְפֹּר	אֶת־בְּאֵרֹת	הַמַּיִם	אֲשֶׁר	חָפְרוּ	בִּימֵי	אַבְרָהָם	אָבִיו
wayyachpōr	'eth-b^{e}'ērōth	hammayim	'ăsher	chāph^{e}rû	bîmê	'avrāhām	'āvîw
and he dug	the wells of	the water	which	they dug	in the days of	Abraham	his father

5845.326	**6674**	**311**	**4322.142**	**80**	**7410.121**
cj, v Piel impf 3mp, ps 3mp	pn	*sub*	v Qal inf abs	pn	cj, v Qal impf 3ms
וַיְסַתְּמוּם	פְּלִשְׁתִּים	אַחֲרֵי	מוֹת	אַבְרָהָם	וַיִּקְרָא
waysatt^{e}mûm	p^{e}lishtîm	'achrê	môth	'avrāhām	wayyiqŏrā'
and they stopped them up	Philistines	after	dying	Abraham	and he called

3937	**8428**	**3626, 8428**	**866, 7410.111**	**3937**	**1**	**19.**	**2763.126**
prep, ps 3fp	n mp	prep, art, n mp	rel part, v Qal pf 3ms	prep, ps 3fp	n ms, ps		cj, v Qal impf 3mp
לָהֶן	שֵׁמוֹת	כַּשֵּׁמֹת	אֲשֶׁר־קָרָא	לָהֶן	אָבִיו		וַיַּחְפְּרוּ
lāhen	shēmôth	kashshēmôth	'ăsher-qārā'	lāhen	'āvîw		wayyachp^{e}rû
them	names	like the names	which he called	them	his father		and they dug

5860, 3437	**904, 5337**	**4834.126, 8427**	**908**	**4448**	**2508**	**20.**	**7662.126**
n mp, pn	prep, art, n ms	cj, v Qal impf 3mp, adv	*n ms*	n md	adj		cj, v Qal impf 3mp
עַבְדֵי־יִצְחָק	בַּנָּחַל	וַיִּמְצְאוּ־שָׁם	בְּאֵר	מַיִם	חַיִּים		וַיָּרִיבוּ
'av^{e}dhê-yitschāq	bannāchal	wayyimts^{e}'û-shām	b^{e}'ēr	mayim	chayyîm		wayyārîvû
the slaves of Isaac	in the valley	and they found there	well of	water	flowing		and they argued

7749.152	1689	6196, 7749.152	3437	3937, 569.141	3937	4448
v Qal act ptc mp	pn	prep, *v Qal act part mp*	pn	prep, v Qal inf con	prep, ps 1cp	art, n md
רֹעֵי	גְּרָר	עִם־רֹעֵי	יִצְחָק	לֵאמֹר	לָנוּ	הַמָּיִם
rōʻê	gherār	ʻim-rōʻê	yitschāq	lēʼmōr	lānû	hammāyim
the herdsmen of	Gerar	with the herdsmen of	Isaac	saying	to us	the waters

7410.121	8428, 908	6457	3706	6479.716	6196		2763.126
cj, v Qal impf 3ms	*n ms*, art, n fs	pn	cj	v Hithpael pf 3cp	prep, ps 3ms	**21.**	cj, v Qal impf 3mp
וַיִּקְרָא	שֵׁם־הַבְּאֵר	עֵשֶׂק	כִּי	הִתְעַשְּׂקוּ	עִמּוֹ		וַיַּחְפְּרוּ
wayyiqōrāʼ	shēm-habbeʼēr	ʻēseq	kî	hithʻasseqû	ʻimmô		wayyachperû
so he called	the name of the well	Esek	because	they quarrelled	with him		and they dug

greater, *Darby* ... increasing more and more, *BB* ... grew richer all the time, *Anchor* ... became very rich indeed, *Goodspeed* ... became very prosperous, *NKJV.*

14. For he had possession of flocks, and possession of herds, and great store of servants: ... many slaves, *REB* ... great household, *RSV* ... large retinue, *Anchor* ... many beasts for plowing, *NCB* ... working-animals, *Goodspeed.*

and the Philistines envied him: ... jealous of him, *LIVB* ... vented their spite on him, *Goodspeed.*

15. For all the wells which his father's servants had digged in the days of Abraham his father, the Philistines had stopped them, and filled them with earth.

16. And Abimelech said unto Isaac, Go from us; for thou art much mightier than we: ... leave our midst, *Goodspeed* ... move away from us, *MLB* ... you are more powerful, *Berkeley* ... you have become too big for us by far, *Anchor.*

17. And Isaac departed thence, and pitched his tent in the valley of Gerar, and dwelt there: ... camped, *ASV* ... made the Wadi Gerar his regular campsite, *NAB* ... where he remained, *Anchor.*

18. And Isaac digged again the wells of water, which they had digged in the days of Abraham his father: ... water-wells he reopened, *MLB* ... cleared out, *Fenton.*

for the Philistines had stopped them after the death of Abraham: and he called their names after the names by which his father had called them: ... Philistines had choked them, *Berkeley.*

19. And Isaac's servants digged in the valley, and found there a well of springing water: ... digging in the Wadi, *Anchor* ... made holes in the valley, *BB* ... living water, *Young* ... struck a spring of running water, *Berkeley.*

20. And the herdmen of Gerar did strive with Isaac's herdmen, saying, The water is ours: ... had a fight, *BB* ... disputed, *NIV* ... quarreled, *NASB* ... challenged, *NAB.*

and he called the name of the well Esek; because they strove with him: ... Strife, *Fenton* ... Quarrel, *Good News* ... Argument, *LIVB.*

unusual for that area, and most unusual in the year of the famine. Thus, it was a happy surprise to Isaac. It demonstrated that the LORD, the covenant-keeping God, was indeed blessing him.

26:13-15. Isaac kept growing greater in wealth and possessions until he grew wealthy. This was further evidence of God's blessing (Prov. 10:22). Especially noticeable was the great increase in flocks of sheep and goats, herds of cattle, as well as the enlarged retinue of servants and slaves needed to take care of them. This made the Philistines of Gerar envious. They expressed their jealousy by spitefully filling up with dirt all the wells Abraham's servants had dug when Abraham lived in the area of Gerar. Their purpose was to drive Isaac away.

26:16. Abimelech then stated their purpose by demanding that Isaac move away, for he had become too powerful for them. That is, they were afraid Isaac would soon have more people with him, along with his great wealth, and would try to conquer the territory.

26:17-18. Isaac moved to the southeast, but not very far. He encamped in the dry stream bed that ran through the rather narrow valley (wadi, arroyo) that was still part of the territory claimed by Gerar. Then he dug out and reopened the wells Abraham had dug in that area and kept the names that Abraham gave them. Water was a prime essential, and keeping the older names showed Isaac's respect for his father.

26:19-21. Isaac's servants then dug a new well that turned out to be a well of living, that is, flowing water, possibly an artesian well that poured out

908	311	7662.126	1612, 6142	7410.121	8428	7933
n ms	adj	cj, v Qal impf 3mp	cj, prep, ps 3fs	cj, v Qal impf 3ms	n ms, ps 3fs	pn
בְּאֵר	אַחֶרֶת	וַיָּרִיבוּ	גַּם־עָלֶיהָ	וַיִּקְרָא	שְׁמָהּ	שִׂטְנָה
b^{e}'ēr	'achereth	wayyārîvû	gam-'ālêhā	wayyiqōrā'	sh^{e}māhh	siṭnāh
well	another	and they argued	also over it	so he called	its name	Sitnah

	6514.521	4623, 8427	2763.121	908	311	3940	7662.116	6142
22.	cj, v Hiphil impf 3ms	prep, adv	cj, v Qal impf 3ms	n ms	adj	cj, neg part	v Qal pf 3cp	prep, ps 3fs
	וַיַּעְתֵּק	מִשָּׁם	וַיַּחְפֹּר	בְּאֵר	אַחֶרֶת	וְלֹא	רָבוּ	עָלֶיהָ
	wayya'ăttēq	mishshām	wayyachpōr	b^{e}'ar	'achereth	w^{e}lō'	rāvû	'ālêhā
	and he moved on	from there	and he dug	well	another	and not	they argued	over it

7410.121	8428	7626	569.121	3706, 6498	7620.511	3176
cj, v Qal impf 3ms	n ms, ps 3fs	pn	cj, v Qal impf 3ms	cj, adv	v Hiphil pf 3ms	pn
וַיִּקְרָא	שְׁמָהּ	רְחֹבוֹת	וַיֹּאמֶר	כִּי־עַתָּה	הִרְחִיב	יְהוָה
wayyiqōrā'	sh^{e}māhh	r^{e}chōvôth	wayyō'mer	kî-'attāh	hirchîv	y^{e}hwāh
so he called	its name	Rehoboth	and he said	because now	He made it wide	Yahweh

3937	6759.119	904, 800		6148.121	4623, 8427	916	916
prep, ps 1cp	cj, v Qal pf 1cp	prep, n fs	23.	cj, v Qal impf 3ms	prep, adv	pn	pn
לָנוּ	וּפָרִינוּ	בָאָרֶץ		וַיַּעַל	מִשָּׁם	בְּאֵר	שָׁבַע
lānû	ûphārînû	vā'ārets		wayya'al	mishshām	b^{e}'ēr	shāva'
for us	now we will be fruitful	in the land		and he went up	from there	to Beer	Sheba

	7495.221	420	3176	904, 4050	2000	569.121	609
24.	cj, v Niphal impf 3ms	prep, ps 3ms	pn	prep, art, n ms	art, dem pron	cj, v Qal impf 3ms	pers pron
	וַיֵּרָא	אֵלָיו	יְהוָה	בַּלַּיְלָה	הַהוּא	וַיֹּאמֶר	אָנֹכִי
	wayyērā'	'ēlāv	y^{e}hwāh	ballaylāh	hahû'	wayyō'mer	'ānōkhî
	and He appeared	to him	Yahweh	in the night	the that	and He said	I

435	80	1	414, 3486.123	3706, 882	609	1313.315
n mp	pn	n ms, ps 2ms	adv, v Qal juss 2ms	cj, prep, ps 2ms	pers pron	cj, v Piel pf 1cs, ps 2ms
אֱלֹהֵי	אַבְרָהָם	אָבִיךָ	אַל־תִּירָא	כִּי־אִתְּךָ	אָנֹכִי	וּבֵרַכְתִּיךָ
'ělōhê	'avrāhām	'āvîkhā	'al-tîrā'	kî-'itt^{e}khā	'ānōkhî	ûvērakhtîkhā
the God of	Abraham	your father	do not fear	because with you	I	and I will bless you

7528.115	881, 2320	904, 5877	80	5860		1161.121
cj, v Hiphil pf 1cs	do, n ms, ps 2ms	prep, prep	pn	n ms, ps 1cs	25.	cj, v Qal impf 3ms
וְהִרְבֵּיתִי	אֶת־זַרְעֲךָ	בַּעֲבוּר	אַבְרָהָם	עַבְדִּי		וַיִּבֶן
w^{e}hirbêthî	'eth-zar'ăkhā	ba'ăvûr	'avrāhām	'avdî		wayyiven
and I will multiply	your seed	on account of	Abraham	my servant		and he built

8427	4326	7410.121	904, 8428	3176	5371.121, 8427	164
adv	n ms	cj, v Qal impf 3ms	prep, *n ms*	pn	cj, v Qal impf 3ms, adv	n ms, ps 3ms
שָׁם	מִזְבֵּחַ	וַיִּקְרָא	בְּשֵׁם	יְהוָה	וַיֶּט־שָׁם	אָהֳלוֹ
shām	mizbēach	wayyiqōrā'	b^{e}shēm	y^{e}hwāh	wayyeṭ-shām	'āhlô
there	altar	and he called	on the name of	Yahweh	and he spread out there	his tent

3868.126, 8427	5860, 3437	908		40	2050.111	420	4623, 1689
cj, v Qal impf 3mp, adv	*n mp*, pn	n ms	26.	cj, pn	v Qal pf 3ms	prep, ps 3ms	prep, pn
וַיִּכְרוּ־שָׁם	עַבְדֵי־יִצְחָק	בְּאֵר		וַאֲבִימֶלֶךְ	הָלַךְ	אֵלָיו	מִגְּרָר
wayyikhrû-shām	'av^{e}dhê-yitschāq	b^{e}'ēr		wa'ăvîmelekh	hālakh	'ēlāv	migg^{e}rār
and they dug there	the slaves of Isaac	well		and Abimelech	he went	to him	from Gerar

277	4992	6612	8015, 6893		569.121	420
cj, pn	n ms, ps 3ms	cj, pn	*n ms*, n ms, ps 3ms	27.	cj, v Qal impf 3ms	prep, ps 3mp
וַאֲחֻזַּת	מֵרֵעֵהוּ	וּפִיכֹל	שַׂר־צְבָאוֹ		וַיֹּאמֶר	אֲלֵהֶם
wa'ăchuzzath	mērē'ēhû	ûphîkhōl	sar-ts^{e}vā'ô		wayyō'mer	'ălēhem
and Ahuzzath	his friend	and Phicol	the commander of his army		and he said	to them

21. And they digged another well, and strove for that also: and he called the name of it Sitnah: ... contention, *Anchor* ... quarrel arose, *REB* ... hatred, *Young* ... enmity, *Good News*.

22. And he removed from thence, and digged another well: ... moving on from there, *Anchor* ... abandoning that one, *LIVB*.

and for that they strove not: ... no contention, *Anchor* ... no fighting, *BB* ... dispute, *REB* ... local residents finally left him alone, *LIVB*.

and he called the name of it Rehoboth: ... room enough, *Fenton* ... enlargements, *Young* ... freedom, *Good News*.

and he said, For now the LORD hath made room for us: ... this time Yahweh has granted us room, *Anchor* ... ample room, *NAB* ... plenty, *NEB*.

and we shall be fruitful in the land: ... increase upon the earth, *Geneva* ... we shall prosper, *NCB* ... flourish, *NIV* ... become more numerous, *REB*.

23. And he went up from thence to Beersheba: ... the well of oath, *Fenton* ... Bersabee, *NCB*.

24. And the LORD appeared unto him the same night, and said: ... in a vision, *BB*.

I am the God of Abraham thy father: fear not, for I am with thee: ... fear nothing, *NEB*.

and will bless thee, and multiply thy seed for my servant Abraham's sake: ... increase your offspring, *Anchor* ... descendants numerous, *Goodspeed* ... increase your race, *Fenton*.

25. And he builded an altar there, and called upon the name of the LORD: ... preacheth in the name of Jehovah, *Young* ... invoked the Lord by name, *NAB*.

and pitched his tent there: and there Isaac's servants digged a well: ... made camp, *Berkeley* ... stretcheth out there his tent, *Young* ... slaves dug, *Goodspeed*.

26. Then Abimelech went to him from Gerar, and Ahuzzath one of his friends: ... with his chief herdsman, *Fenton* ... counselor, *NAB* ... one of his ministers, *Goodspeed* ... adviser, *NASB*.

and Phichol the chief captain of his army: ... chief of his troops, *Anchor* ... captain of his host, *Darby* ... general, *Berkeley*.

27. And Isaac said unto them, Wherefore come ye to me, seeing ye hate me: ... you have been unfriendly, *Anchor* ... when you are my enemies, *Fenton* ... hostile to me,

---

wonderful fresh water. When the herdsmen of Gerar saw this, they claimed it. Isaac saw that a well that produced strife could never bring blessing, so he gave them the well but named it Esek, "dispute," a name derived from the verb *`asak*, meaning to quarrel. Isaac's servants then dug another well. When the herdsmen of Gerar argued over it, claiming it also, Isaac named the well Sitnah, "accusation," or "hostile opposition," a strong word from the same root word as Satan, who is the adversary, the accuser.

26:22. Hoping for peace, and God's blessing, Isaac moved on quite a bit further to a broad, open valley. This time there was no opposition or dispute when his servants dug another well. So he called it Rehoboth, "wide open spaces," signifying plenty of room and implying security and comfort. There he honored God for making this possible so that they could prosper in the land as he promised (26:4). Rehoboth was southwest of Beersheba, probably about 40 miles from Gerar.

26:23-24. Isaac remained a pilgrim and an alien in the promised land with no settled dwelling place. After a time he went up to Beersheba, which was about 15 miles from Gerar. The night after he arrived the LORD appeared to him telling him not to be afraid, which may mean to stop being afraid. It may be that the hostile opposition of men of Gerar and Abimelech's demand that he leave them caused a little fear to arise. If their envy and enmity increased they might attack him. But God assured Isaac again that He would bless him and multiply the number of his descendants for Abraham's sake. That is, Isaac was living under the promise and salvation-blessing given to Abraham, who is here called God's servant because he did God's will.

26:25. Isaac responded by building an altar. These altars built by God's people before the Law was given to Moses were all altars for burnt offerings. They expressed total consecration to God and total exaltation of God. It thus involved submission to God's will and a recognition of God's faithfulness to His promises. Calling on the name of the LORD indicated public worship with his family, servants, and slaves taking part. Then he pitched his tent (actually, tents, the Hebrew word is collective), and his slaves proceeded to dig another well.

26:26-27. About that time Abimelech went up to Beersheba with Ahuzzath ("Possession"), a close friend and confidential adviser, and Phicol ("mouth

3437	4211	971.117	420	894	7983.117	881	8365.328
pn	intrg	v Qal pf 2mp	prep, ps 1cs	cj, pers pron	v Qal pf 2mp	do, ps 1cs	cj, v Piel impf 2mp, ps 1cs
יִצְחָק	מַדּוּעַ	בָּאתֶם	אֵלָי	וְאַתֶּם	שְׂנֵאתֶם	אֹתִי	וַתְּשַׁלְּחוּנִי
yitschāq	maddû'a	bā'them	'ēlāy	w^{e}'attem	s^{e}nē'them	'ōthî	watt^{e}shall^{e}chûnî
Isaac	why	you came	to me	and you	you hated	me	and you sent me

4623, 882	28.	569.126	7495.142	7495.119	3706, 2030.111	3176	6196
prep, prep, ps 2mp		cj, v Qal impf 3mp	v Qal inf abs	v Qal pf 1cp	cj, v Qal pf 3ms	pn	prep, ps 2fs
מֵאִתְּכֶם		וַיֹּאמְרוּ	רָאוֹ	רָאִינוּ	כִּי־הָיָה	יְהוָה	עִמָּךְ
mē'itt^{e}khem		wayyō'mrû	rā'ô	rā'înû	kî-hāyāh	y^{e}hwāh	'immāk
from you		and they said	seeing	we have seen	that He is	Yahweh	with you

569.120	2030.122	5167	427	1033	1033	1033
cj, v Qal impf 1cp	v Qal juss 3fs	part	n fs	prep, ps 1cp	prep, ps 1cp	cj, prep, ps 2ms
וַנֹּאמֶר	תְּהִי	נָא	אָלָה	בֵּינוֹתֵינוּ	בֵּינֵינוּ	וּבֵינֶךָ
wannō'mer	t^{e}hî	nā'	'ālāh	bênôthênû	bênênû	ûvênekhā
so we are saying	let it be	please	oath	between us	between us	and between you

3901.212	1311	6196	29.	524, 6449.123	6196	7750	3626, 866	3940
cj, v Niphal pf 3fs	n fs	prep, ps 2fs		cj, v Qal impf 2ms	prep, ps 1cp	n fs	prep, rel part	neg part
וְנִכְרְתָה	בְרִית	עִמָּךְ		אִם־תַּעֲשֵׂה	עִמָּנוּ	רָעָה	כַּאֲשֶׁר	לֹא
w^{e}nikhr^{e}thāh	v^{e}rîth	'immāk		'im-ta'ăseh	'immānû	rā'āh	ka'ăsher	lō'
and it will be cut	covenant	with you		if you will do	with us	evil	like that	not

5236.119	3626, 866	6449.119	6196	7828, 3005	8365.320
v Qal pf 1cp, ps 2ms	cj, prep, rel part	v Qal pf 1cp	prep, ps 2ms	adv, adj	cj, v Piel impf 1cp, ps 2ms
נְגַעֲנוּךָ	וְכַאֲשֶׁר	עָשִׂינוּ	עִמְּךָ	רַק־טוֹב	וַנְּשַׁלֵּחֲךָ
n^{e}gha'ănûkhā	w^{e}kha'ăsher	'āsînû	'imm^{e}khā	raq-ṭôv	wann^{e}shallēchăkhā
we touched you	and like which	we have done	with you	only good	and we sent you out

904, 8361	887	6498	1313.155	3176	30.	6449.121	3937	5136
prep, n ms	pers pron	adv	*v Qal pass ptc ms*	pn		cj, v Qal impf 3ms	prep, ps 3mp	n ms
בְּשָׁלוֹם	אַתָּה	עַתָּה	בְּרוּךְ	יְהוָה		וַיַּעַשׂ	לָהֶם	מִשְׁתֶּה
b^{e}shālôm	'attāh	'attāh	b^{e}rûkh	y^{e}hwāh		wayya'as	lāhem	mishteh
in peace	you	now	blessed of	Yahweh		and he made	for them	feast

404.126	8685.126	31.	8326.526	904, 1269	8123.226	382
cj, v Qal impf 3mp	cj, v Qal impf 3mp		cj, v Hiphil impf 3mp	prep, art, n ms	cj, v Niphal impf 3mp	n ms
וַיֹּאכְלוּ	וַיִּשְׁתּוּ		וַיַּשְׁכִּימוּ	בַבֹּקֶר	וַיִּשָּׁבְעוּ	אִישׁ
wayyō'kh^{e}lû	wayyishtû		wayyashkîmû	vabbōqer	wayyishshāv'û	'îsh
and they ate	and they drank		and they rose early	in the morning	and they swore	man

3937, 250	8365.321	3437	2050.126	4623, 882	904, 8361
prep, n ms, ps 3ms	cj, v Piel impf 3ms, ps 3mp	pn	cj, v Qal impf 3mp	prep, prep, ps 3ms	prep, n ms
לְאָחִיו	וַיְשַׁלְּחֵם	יִצְחָק	וַיֵּלְכוּ	מֵאִתּוֹ	בְּשָׁלוֹם
l^{e}'āchîw	wayshall^{e}chēm	yitschāq	wayyēl^{e}khû	mē'ittô	b^{e}shālôm
to his brother	and he sent them	Isaac	and they went	from him	in safety

32.	2030.121	904, 3219	2000	971.126	5860	3437	5222.526
	cj, v Qal impf 3ms	prep, art, n ms	art, dem pron	cj, v Qal impf 3mp	*n mp*	pn	cj, v Hiphil impf 3mp
	וַיְהִי	בַּיּוֹם	הַהוּא	וַיָּבֹאוּ	עַבְדֵי	יִצְחָק	וַיַּגִּדוּ
	wayhî	bayyôm	hahû'	wayyāvō'û	'av^{e}dhê	yitschāq	wayyaggidhû
	and it was	in the day	the that	that they came	the slaves of	Isaac	and they reported

3937	6142, 180	908	866	2763.116	569.126	3937	4834.119
prep, ps 3ms	prep, *n fp*	art, n fs	rel part	v Qal pf 3cp	cj, v Qal impf 3mp	prep, ps 3ms	v Qal pf 1cp
לוֹ	עַל־אֹדוֹת	הַבְּאֵר	אֲשֶׁר	חָפְרוּ	וַיֹּאמְרוּ	לוֹ	מָצָאנוּ
lô	'al-'ōdhôth	habb^{e}'ēr	'ăsher	chāphārû	wayyō'mrû	lô	mātsā'nû
to him	on account of	the well	which	they dug	and they said	to him	we found

NIV ... ill-disposed towards me, *REB* ... this is obviously no friendly visit, *LIVB*.

and have sent me away from you?: ... driven me away, *Darby* ... made me leave your country, *Good News* ... since you kicked me out in a most uncivil way, *LIVB*.

28. And they said, We saw certainly that the LORD was with thee: ... we saw plainly that Jehovah was with thee, *ASV* ... we are convinced that, *NAB* ... we are terribly afraid, because God is with you, *Fenton*.

and we said, Let there be now an oath betwixt us, even betwixt us and thee: ... sworn treaty, *Anchor* ... a sworn agreement, *NAB*.

and let us make a covenant with thee: ... let us conclude a pact, *Anchor* ... be an understanding, *Fenton* ... that will bind us, *NEB*.

29. That thou wilt do us no hurt, as we have not touched thee: ... you shall not be hostile to us, *Anchor* ... do us no damage, *BB* ... will not do wrong to us, *Fenton* ... swear that you will do us no harm, *NEB* ... do not evil with us, *Young*.

and as we have done unto thee nothing but good: ... just as we have not molested you, *NAB* ... we have not attacked, *NEB* ... always treated you well, *NIV* ... always ready to do you a good turn, *REB*.

and have sent thee away in peace: ... and let you go amicably, *Goodspeed*.

thou art now the blessed of the LORD: ... you are the blessed of the Ever-Living, *Fenton* ... henceforth Yahweh's blessing upon you, *Anchor* ... now the Lord has prospered you, *REB*.

30. And he made them a feast, and they did eat and drink: ... he then prepared a banquet, *Berkeley* ... swore each to his brother, *Fenton* ... exchanged oaths, *REB* ... ate and drank in preparation for the treaty ceremonies, *LIVB*.

31. And they rose up betimes in the morning, and sware one to another: ... each man made his promise and sealed it with a vow, *Good News* ... took solemn oaths to seal a non-aggression pact, *LIVB*.

and Isaac sent them away, and they departed from him in peace: ... bid them farewell, *MLB* ... sent them happily home again, *LIVB*.

32. And it came to pass the same day, that Isaac's servants came, and told him concerning the well which they had digged: ... slaves, *NEB* ... come and declare to him concerning the circumstances of the well, *Young*.

and said unto him, We have found water: ... come to water, *BB* ... reached water, *NAB*.

33. And he called it Shebah: therefore the name of the city is Beersheba unto this day: ... village by the well is called satisfaction, *Fenton* ... well of the oath, *Young* ... Vow, *Good News*.

---

of all"), the title of his chief army officer who was probably also his prime minister.

Isaac remembered how they hated him and drove him away from Gerar, though there was no hatred or ill will on his part—so he was suspicious about their reason for coming and challenged them to tell him.

26:28-29. Their answer put emphasis on the fact they had really seen that the LORD was with Isaac. They wanted an oath (not the ordinary word for an oath but a "curse oath," a solemn agreement sworn to by Isaac and Abimelech, each calling down a curse on the one who would break it). Along with the oath they wanted to cut a covenant with Isaac that he would not do anything bad to them (which may mean cause God's judgment to come on them).

Then they reminded Isaac that when he lived in the territory of Gerar they did not touch (hurt, harm) him, but only treated him well and dismissed him in peace (that is, without making any further demands on him).

26:30-31. As an expression of good will and as a celebration of the covenant Isaac provided a great feast for them. Sharing a meal was a further expression of friendship. Then early the next morning they confirmed their covenant or treaty by swearing to each other that they would keep it.

Isaac then let them go, and they went away in peace, that is, in a spirit of goodwill. Isaac was a peacemaker when he let the men of Gerar have the wells and moved on. He is still a peacemaker here. We too are to be peacemakers and as far as we are able, we are to promote peace (Matt. 5:9; Rom. 12:18; Heb. 12:14). However, the real peacemaker was the LORD. As Proverbs 16:7 says, "When a man's ways are pleasing to the LORD, he makes even his enemies live at peace with him."

26:32. Isaac's slaves who were digging a new well then came to him and reported that they had found water. Only those who live on the edge of a desert can understand their excitement.

26:33. Isaac called the well Shibah, meaning "oath" or "seven," probably because seven animals were sacrificed when the covenant was "cut." Then the oath further confirmed it. Shibah also carries

4448	33.	7410.121	881	8127	6142, 3772	8428, 6111	915	915
n mp		cj, v Qal impf 3ms	do, ps 3fs	pn	prep, adv	*n ms*, art, n fs	pn	pn
מָיִם		וַיִּקְרָא	אֹתָהּ	שִׁבְעָה	עַל־כֵּן	שֵׁם־הָעִיר	בְּאֵר	שֶׁבַע
māyim		wayyiqōrā'	'ōthāhh	shiveʻāh	'al-kēn	shēm-hā'îr	beʼēr	sheva'
waters		and he called	it	Shibah	therefore	the name of the city	Beer	Sheba

5912	3219	2172	34.	2030.121	6451	1158, 727	8523	4089.121
adv	art, n ms	art, dem pron		cj, v Qal impf 3ms	pn	*n ms*, num	n fs	cj, v Qal impf 3ms
עַד	הַיּוֹם	הַזֶּה		וַיְהִי	עֵשָׂו	בֶּן־אַרְבָּעִים	שָׁנָה	וַיִּקַּח
'adh	hayyôm	hazzeh		wayhî	'ēsāw	ben-'arbā'îm	shānāh	wayyiqqach
until	the day	the this		and he was	Esau	son of forty	years	and he took

828	881, 3175	1351, 914	2958	881, 1338	1351, 362	2958
n fs	do, pn	*n fs*, pn	art, pn	cj, do, pn	*n fs*, pn	art, pn
אִשָּׁה	אֶת־יְהוּדִית	בַּת־בְּאֵרִי	הַחִתִּי	וְאֶת־בָּשְׂמַת	בַּת־אֵילֹן	הַחִתִּי
'ishshāh	'eth-yehûdhîth	bath-beʼērî	hachittî	weʼeth-bāsemath	bath-'êlōn	hachittî
wife	Judith	the daughter of Beeri	the Hittite	and Basemath	the daughter of Elon	the Hittite

35.	2030.127	4948	7593	3937, 3437	3937, 7549	27:1	2030.121
	cj, v Qal impf 3fp	*n fs*	n fs	prep, pn	cj, prep, pn		cj, v Qal impf 3ms
	וַתִּהְיֶיןָ	מֹרַת	רוּחַ	לְיִצְחָק	וּלְרִבְקָה		וַיְהִי
	wattiheyênā	mōrath	rûach	leyitschāq	ûlārivqāh		wayhî
	and they were	bitterness of	spirit	to Isaac	and to Rebekah		and it was

3706, 2290.111	3437	3663.127	6084	4623, 7495.141	7410.121	881, 6451
cj, v Qal pf 3ms	pn	cj, v Qal impf 3fp	n fp, ps 3ms	prep, v Qal inf con	cj, v Qal impf 3ms	do, pn
כִּי־זָקֵן	יִצְחָק	וַתִּכְהֶיןָ	עֵינָיו	מֵרְאֹת	וַיִּקְרָא	אֶת־עֵשָׂו
kî-zāqēn	yitschāq	wattikhhênā	'ênāv	mēreʼōth	wayyiqōrā'	'eth-'ēsāw
that he was old	Isaac	and they were dim	his eyes	from seeing	and he called	Esau

1158	1448	569.121	420	1158	569.121	420	2079
n ms, ps 3ms	art, adj	cj, v Qal impf 3ms	prep, ps 3ms	n ms, ps 1cs	cj, v Qal impf 3ms	prep, ps 3ms	intrj, ps 1cs
בְּנוֹ	הַגָּדֹל	וַיֹּאמֶר	אֵלָיו	בְּנִי	וַיֹּאמֶר	אֵלָיו	הִנֵּנִי
benô	haggādhōl	wayyō'mer	'ēlāv	benî	wayyō'mer	'ēlāv	hinnēnî
his son	the older	and he said	to him	my son	and he said	to him	behold I

2.	569.121	2079, 5167	2290.115	3940	3156.115	3219	4323	3.	6498
	cj, v Qal impf 3ms	intrj, part	v Qal pf 1cs	neg part	v Qal pf 1cs	*n ms*	n ms, ps 1cs		cj, adv
	וַיֹּאמֶר	הִנֵּה־נָא	זָקַנְתִּי	לֹא	יָדַעְתִּי	יוֹם	מוֹתִי		וְעַתָּה
	wayyō'mer	hinnēh-nā'	zāqantî	lō'	yādha'ttî	yôm	môthî		we'attāh
	and he said	behold please	I am old	not	I know	the day of	my death		and now

5558.131, 5167	3747	8851	7493	3428.131	7898	6942.131
v Qal impv 2ms, part	n mp, ps 2ms	n ms, ps 2ms	cj, n fs, ps 2ms	cj, v Qal impv 2ms	art, n ms	cj, v Qal impv 2ms
שָׂא־נָא	כֵּלֶיךָ	תֶּלְיְךָ	וְקַשְׁתֶּךָ	וְצֵא	הַשָּׂדֶה	וְצוּדָה
sā'-nā'	khēlêkhā	telyekhā	weqashtekhā	wetsē'	hassādeh	wetsûdhāh
lift up please	your weapons	your quiver	and your bow	and go out	to the field	and hunt

3937	6987	4.	6449.131, 3937	4440	3626, 866	154.115
prep, ps 1cs	n ms		cj, v Qal impv 2ms, prep, ps 1cs	n mp	prep, rel part	v Qal pf 1cs
לִּי	צָיִדָה		וַעֲשֵׂה־לִי	מַטְעַמִּים	כַּאֲשֶׁר	אָהַבְתִּי
lî	tsāyidāh		wa'ăsēh-lî	maṭ'ammîm	ka'ăsher	'āhavtî
for me	game		and make for me	delicious food	like that	I love

971.531	3937	404.125	904, 5877	1313.322	5497	904, 3071
cj, v Hiphil impv 2ms	prep, ps 1cs	cj, v Qal impf 1cs	prep, prep	v Piel impf 3fs, ps 2ms	n fs, ps 1cs	prep, adv
וְהָבִיאָה	לִּי	וְאֹכֵלָה	בַּעֲבוּר	תְּבָרֶכְךָ	נַפְשִׁי	בְּטֶרֶם
wehāvî'āh	lî	weʼōkhēlāh	ba'ăvûr	tevārekhekhā	naphshî	beṭerem
and bring	to me	and I will eat	on account of	it will bless you	my soul	before

34. And Esau was forty years old when he took to wife Judith the daughter of Beeri the Hittite, and Bashemath the daughter of Elon the Hittite:

35. Which were a grief of mind unto Isaac and to Rebekah: ... became a source of embitterment, *NAB* ... great distress, *Berkeley* ... bitter wind, *Fenton* ... bitterness of spirit, *Young*.

27:1. And it came to pass: ... one day, *Goodspeed* ... it came about, *NASB*.

that when Isaac was old: ... was aging, *Berkeley*.

and his eyes were dim, so that he could not see: ... his eyesight had faded away, *Anchor* ... had become clouded, *BB* ... had failed him, *NAB* ... had become blind, *Good News* ... so weak, *NIV*.

he called Esau his eldest son, and said unto him, My son: ... sent for, *BB* ... called for, *NIV*.

and he said unto him, Behold, here am I: ... yes, father, *NAB*.

2. And he said, Behold now, I am old: ... as you see, I am so old, *NAB* ... look here, I am growing old, *Berkeley* ... I am an old man, *Goodspeed*.

I know not the day of my death: ... there is no telling when I may die, *Anchor* ... my death may take place at any time, *BB* ... may die soon, *Good News* ... expect to die most any day, *LIVB*.

3. Now therefore take, I pray thee, thy weapons: ... take your hunting outfit, *MLB* ... take your gear, *NAB* ... your spear, *Fenton* ... thine instruments, *Geneva*.

thy quiver and thy bow: ... your arrow-case and your bow, *Berkeley* ... arrows, *BB*.

and go out to the field: ... to the country, *Anchor* ... in the open country, *MLB* ... into the fields, *Goodspeed*.

and take me some venison: ... hunt game, *Berkeley* ... get meat, *BB* ... wild game, *NIV* ... hunt some venison, *Anchor* ... hunt provision, *Young*.

4. And make me savoury meat: ... prepare me a tasty dish, *MLB* ... prepare it as a festive dish, *Anchor* ... food, good to the taste, *BB* ... appetizing dish, *NAB* ... tasteful things, *Young*.

such as I love: ... the way I like, *Anchor* ... the kind I am fond of, *Berkeley* ... such as is pleasing to me, *BB*.

---

another meaning, "Fortunate." This was another reason for calling the place Beersheba.

26:34. When Esau reached the age of 40, the same age as Isaac was when he married, Esau took two wives. He was still "a man of the field," a rather wild, uncontrolled person. Instead of letting his parents arrange the marriage, he did this on his own (though he may have used go-betweens).

Both wives were Hittites, short, stocky, pagan, Aryan people with thick lips, large noses, and receding foreheads. Their religion and culture had been contaminated with Canaanite corruption (cf. 28:7). Judith ("from Jehud") was from a town at the foothills west of Jerusalem (Josh. 19:45). Basemath means "fragrance." See 35:2-3 for more wives of Esau.

26:35. Esau brought his wives home, and left them much of the time while he was out hunting. They apparently brought with them their pagan ways and attitudes. Thus they became a source of bitterness of spirit (including mental anguish and grief) to Isaac and Rebekah. Most probably, they rejected the worship of the true God. Esau made a mistake in not following the example of Abraham and Isaac when seeking a wife.

27:1. By the time Isaac was 137 years of age he was blind and felt the weakness of old age. Though he actually lived 43 more years, Ishmael had died 14 years earlier at the age of 137 (25:17), so he was afraid he might die soon. The Bible does not tell us whether or not he knew Esau sold his birthright. But it is evident Isaac wanted Esau to carry on the blessing of Abraham. Though Jacob was now 77, Isaac had made no arrangements for a marriage for him. He evidently did not intend to do so since he wanted Esau to carry on the chosen line. So he called for Esau with this in mind.

27:2-4. Isaac was as much concerned about his own fleshly appetite as he was about God's promise and salvation-blessing. So he asked Esau to go out into the open country, hunt and prepare some of the wild game he loved. He wanted him to make it tasty by flavoring it with nuts, raisins, and spices. After enjoying the meal he would give Esau the blessing he had in his heart before he died.

Such oral blessings had legal force in those days (as archaeological discoveries at Nuzu have shown). Moreover, in this chosen family, they had prophetic force. Notice, however, that Isaac at this point did not recognize the grace of God. He was treating the blessing as a bargain between himself and Esau. He did not seek God about this. In fact,

4322.125	**5.** 7549	8471.153	904, 1744.341	3437	420, 6451	1158
v Qal impf 1cs	cj, pn	Qal act part fs	prep, v Piel inf con	pn	prep, pn	n ms, ps 3ms
אָמוּת	וְרִבְקָה	שֹׁמַעַת	בְּדַבֵּר	יִצְחָק	אֶל־עֵשָׂו	בְּנוֹ
'āmûth	w^{e}rivqāh	shōma'ath	b^{e}dhabbēr	yitschāq	'el-'ēsāw	b^{e}nô
I will die	and Rebekah	listener	in speaking	Isaac	to Esau	his son

2050.121	6451	7898	3937, 6942.141	6987	3937, 971.541	**6.** 7549
cj, v Qal impf 3ms	pn	art, n ms	prep, v Qal inf con	n ms	prep, v Hiphil inf con	cj, pn
וַיֵּלֶךְ	עֵשָׂו	הַשָּׂדֶה	לָצוּד	צַיִד	לְהָבִיא	וְרִבְקָה
wayyēlekh	'ēsāw	hassādeh	lātsûdh	tsayidh	l^{e}hāvî'	w^{e}rivqāh
and he went	Esau	to the field	to hunt	game	to bring	and Rebekah

569.112	420, 3399	1158	3937, 569.141	2079	8471.115	881, 1
v Qal pf 3fs	prep, pn	n ms, ps 3fs	prep, v Qal inf con	intrj	v Qal pf 1cs	do, n ms, ps 2ms
אָמְרָה	אֶל־יַעֲקֹב	בְּנָהּ	לֵאמֹר	הִנֵּה	שָׁמַעְתִּי	אֶת־אָבִיךָ
'ām^{e}rāh	'el-ya'ăqōv	b^{e}nāhh	lē'mōr	hinnēh	shāma'ttî	'eth-'āvîkhā
she said	to Jacob	her son	saying	behold	I heard	your father

1744.351	420, 6451	250	3937, 569.141	**7.** 971.531	3937	6987
v Piel part ms	prep, pn	n ms, ps 2ms	prep, v Qal inf con	v Hiphil impv 2ms	prep, ps 1cs	n ms
מְדַבֵּר	אֶל־עֵשָׂו	אָחִיךָ	לֵאמֹר	הָבִיאָה	לִּי	צַיִד
m^{e}dhabbēr	'el-'ēsāw	'āchîkhā	lē'mōr	hāvî'āh	lî	tsayidh
speaking	to Esau	your brother	saying	bring	to me	game

6449.131, 3937	4440	404.125	1313.325	3937, 6686	3176
cj, v Qal impv 2ms, prep, ps 1cs	n mp	cj, v Qal impf 1cs	cj, v Piel impf 1cs, ps 2ms	prep, *n mp*	pn
וַעֲשֵׂה־לִי	מַטְעַמִּים	וְאֹכֵלָה	וַאֲבָרֶכְכָה	לִפְנֵי	יְהוָה
wa'ăsēh-lî	maṭ'ammîm	w^{e}'ōkhēlāh	wa'ăvārekh^{e}khāh	liphnê	y^{e}hwāh
and make for me	delicious food	and I will eat	and I will bless you	before	Yahweh

3937, 6686	4323	**8.** 6498	1158	8471.131	904, 7249	3937, 866	603
prep, *n mp*	n ms, ps 1cs	cj, adv	n ms, ps 1cs	v Qal impv 2ms	prep, n ms, ps 1cs	prep, rel part	pers pron
לִפְנֵי	מוֹתִי	וְעַתָּה	בְנִי	שְׁמַע	בְּקֹלִי	לַאֲשֶׁר	אֲנִי
liphnê	môthî	w^{e}'attāh	v^{e}nî	sh^{e}ma'	b^{e}qōlî	la'ăsher	'ănî
before	my death	and now	my son	listen	by my voice	to what	I

6943.353	881	**9.** 2050.131, 5167	420, 6887	4089.131, 3937	4623, 8427
v Piel act part fs	do, ps 2fs	v Qal impv 2ms, part	prep, art, n fs	cj, v Qal impv 2ms, prep, ps 1cs	prep, adv
מְצַוָּה	אֹתָךְ	לֶךְ־נָא	אֶל־הַצֹּאן	וְקַח־לִי	מִשָּׁם
m^{e}tsawwāh	'ōthākh	lekh-nā'	'el-hatstsō'n	w^{e}qach-lî	mishshām
commanding	you	go please	to the flock	and take for me	from there

8530	1454	6008	3005	6449.125	881	4440	3937, 1
num	*n mp*	n fp	adj	cj, v Qal impf 1cs	do, ps 3mp	n mp	prep, n ms, ps 2ms
שְׁנֵי	גְּדָיֵי	עִזִּים	טֹבִים	וְאֶעֱשֶׂה	אֹתָם	מַטְעַמִּים	לְאָבִיךָ
sh^{e}nê	g^{e}dhāyê	'izzîm	ṭōvîm	w^{e}'e'ĕseh	'ōthām	maṭ'ammîm	l^{e}'āvîkhā
two	kids of	she-goats	good	and I will make	them	delicious food	for your father

3626, 866	154.111	**10.** 971.513	3937, 1	404.111	904, 5877
prep, rel part	v Qal pf 3ms	cj, v Hiphil pf 2ms	prep, n ms, ps 2ms	cj, v Qal pf 3ms	prep, prep
כַּאֲשֶׁר	אָהֵב	וְהֵבֵאתָ	לְאָבִיךָ	וְאָכָל	בַּעֲבֻר
ka'ăsher	'āhēv	w^{e}hēvē'thā	l^{e}'āvîkhā	w^{e}'ākhāl	ba'ăvûr
like that	he has loved	and you will bring	to your father	and he will eat	on account of

866	1313.321	3937, 6686	4323	**11.** 569.121	3399	420, 7549
rel part	v Piel impf 3ms, ps 2ms	prep, *n mp*	n ms, ps 3ms	cj, v Qal impf 3ms	pn	prep, pn
אֲשֶׁר	יְבָרֶכְךָ	לִפְנֵי	מוֹתוֹ	וַיֹּאמֶר	יַעֲקֹב	אֶל־רִבְקָה
'ăsher	y^{e}vārekh^{e}khā	liphnê	môthô	wayyō'mer	ya'ăqōv	'el-rivqāh
that	he will bless you	before	his death	and he said	Jacob	to Rebekah

and bring it to me, that I may eat that my soul may bless thee before I die: ... that I may give you my very own blessing, *Anchor* ... special blessing, *NAB* ... final blessing, *Good News* ... put it before me before death comes to me, *BB.*

5. And Rebekah heard when Isaac spake to Esau his son: ... Rebekah had been listening, *REB* ... was eavesdropping, *MLB* ... in Rebekah's hearing, *BB.*

And Esau went to the field: ... had gone off to the country, *Anchor* ... went out, *BB.*

to hunt for venison, and to bring it: ... hunting game to bring in, *Berkeley* ... hunt venison for his father, *Anchor* ... went out to get meat, *BB* ... for deer meat, *KJVII* ... to hunt provision, *Young.*

6. And Rebekah spake unto Jacob her son, saying: ... told her son, *Berkeley* ... called her son, *LIVB.*

Behold, I heard thy father speak unto Esau thy brother, saying: ... in my hearing, *BB* ... I just overheard, *Anchor* ... telling your brother, *MLB.*

7. Bring me venison: ... bring me game, *Berkeley* ... go out and get some roe's meat, *BB* ... bring me provision, *Young* ... bring me an animal, *Good News.*

and make me savoury meat, that I may eat: ... prepare it for me as a festive dish, *Anchor* ... prepare me a tasty dish, *Goodspeed* ... make me a good meal that I may be full, *BB* ... an appetizing dish, *NAB* ... tasteful things, *Young.*

and bless thee before the LORD before my death: ... in the Lord's presence, *MLB* ... with Yahweh's approval, *Anchor* ... before Jehovah, *Young* ... in the sight of the Lord, *NCB.*

8. Now therefore, my son, obey my voice: ... listen carefully, *NIV* ... hearken to my voice, *Darby* ... listen to me, *NEB* ... obey my word, *RSV.*

according to that which I command thee: ... do what I tell you, *NIV* ... to my instructions, *Anchor* ... to what I order you, *Berkeley* ... do what I say, *BB* ... in the charge that I shall give you, *Goodspeed.*

9. Go now to the flock: ... go, I pray thee, *Darby* ... get thee now to the flock, *Geneva.*

and fetch me from thence two good kids of the goats: ... from there choice kids, *Anchor* ... get me fat young kids, *BB* ... pick me fine kids, *NEB.*

and I will make them savoury meat for thy father: ... make of them a meal, *BB* ... pleasant food, *Fenton* ... appetizing dish, *NAB* ... a festive dish, *Anchor* ... savory food, *NRSV.*

such as he loveth: ... to your father's taste, *BB* ... the way he likes, *Anchor* ... your father likes so much, *Good News.*

10. And thou shalt bring it to thy father: ... take it to your father, *Anchor* ... carry it, *Fenton* ... take them into your father, *NEB.*

that he may eat: ... so he can eat, *Berkeley* ... he may have a good meal, *BB* ... and he will eat them, *NEB* ... when he will eat, *Fenton.*

and that he may bless thee before his death: ... give you the blessing, *MLB* ... to the intent, *Geneva* ... instead of Esau, *LIVB.*

---

he was almost putting himself in the place of God. Let Esau bring him an offering and he would give Esau the blessing! Earlier Esau had not been concerned about the birthright or blessing. But now that Isaac seemed about to die, Esau saw the material part of the blessing as something worth having.

27:5-7. Rebekah was close by, possibly hidden behind a curtain, and overheard Isaac's whole plot. She no doubt remembered what the LORD had told her before her children were born—that the elder would serve the younger (25:23). Probably Isaac knew about this too, for she surely would have told him. Yet, he may have blocked this out of his mind because of his preference for Esau. Thus, Rebekah must have felt it would be useless to try to change his mind. Therefore, (without trusting God or praying), she decided something had to be done immediately and came up with a desperate plan. As soon as Esau was gone she told Jacob about it, adding that Isaac would do this before the LORD, that is, in His presence. Isaac may not have had the LORD in mind at this point. But Rebekah recognized that what was done in relation to the covenant promise God gave Abraham would be before the LORD and would thus be a true blessing.

27:8-10. Rebekah had enough spiritual insight to realize that Jacob would be God's choice as well as hers. But she went about gaining the blessing in a deceitful, underhanded, manipulative way. She probably felt justified, because this was a family problem, and Isaac had decided what to do without consulting his wife. Since he was doing something in an underhanded way, so could she. Young goats would have a similar taste to wild game. Rebekah had lived long enough with Isaac to know how to prepare what he would consider delicious food. So she commanded Jacob to bring the goats.

27:11-13. Jacob questioned his mother's com-

525	2075	6451	250	382	7997	609	382	2607
n fs, ps 3ms	intrj	pn	n ms, ps 1cs	n ms	adj	cj, pers pron	n ms	adj
אִמּוֹ	הֵן	עֵשָׂו	אָחִי	אִישׁ	שָׂעִר	וְאָנֹכִי	אִישׁ	חָלָק
'immô	hēn	'ēsāw	'āchî	'îsh	sā'ir	we'ānōkhî	'îsh	chālāq
his mother	behold	Esau	my brother	man	hairy	but I	man	smooth

12.	193	5135.121	1	2030.115	904, 6084	3626, 8924.351
	adv	v Qal impf 3ms, ps 1cs	n ms, ps 1cs	cj, v Qal pf 1cs	prep, n fd, ps 3ms	prep, v Pilpel ptc ms
	אוּלַי	יְמֻשֵּׁנִי	אָבִי	וְהָיִיתִי	בְּעֵינָיו	כִּמְתַעְתֵּעַ
	'ûlay	yemushshēnî	'āvî	wehāyîthî	be'ênâv	kimetha'ttēa'
	perhaps	he will feel me	my father	and I will be	in his eyes	like mocker

971.515	6142	7329	3940	1318	13.	569.122	3937
cj, v Hiphil pf 1cs	prep, ps 1cs	n fs	cj, neg part	n fs		cj, v Qal impf 3fs	prep, ps 3ms
וְהֵבֵאתִי	עָלַי	קְלָלָה	וְלֹא	בְרָכָה		וַתֹּאמֶר	לוֹ
wehēvē'thî	'ālay	qǒlālāh	welō'	verākhāh		wattō'mer	lô
and I will have brought	on me	curse	and not	blessing		and she said	to him

525	6142	7329	1158	395	8471.131	904, 7249	2050.131
n fs, ps 3ms	prep, ps 1cs	n fs, ps 2ms	n ms, ps 1cs	adv	v Qal impv 2ms	prep, n ms, ps 1cs	cj, v Qal impv 2ms
אִמּוֹ	עָלַי	קִלְלָתְךָ	בְּנִי	אַךְ	שְׁמַע	בְּקֹלִי	וְלֵךְ
'immô	'ālay	qillāthekhā	benî	'akh	shema'	beqōlî	welēkh
his mother	on me	your curse	my son	only	listen	by my voice	and go

4089.131, 3937	14.	2050.121	4089.121	971.521	3937, 525
v Qal impv 2ms, prep, ps 1cs		cj, v Qal impf 3ms	cj, v Qal impf 3ms	cj, v Hiphil impf 3ms	prep, n fs, ps 3ms
קַח־לִי		וַיֵּלֶךְ	וַיִּקַּח	וַיָּבֵא	לְאִמּוֹ
qach-lî		wayyēlekh	wayyiqqach	wayyāvē'	le'immô
take for me		and he went	and he took	and he brought	to his mother

6449.122	525	4440	3626, 866	154.111	1	15.	4089.122
cj, v Qal impf 3fs	n fs, ps 3ms	n mp	prep, rel part	v Qal pf 3ms	n ms, ps		cj, v Qal impf 3fs
וַתַּעַשׂ	אִמּוֹ	מַטְעַמִּים	כַּאֲשֶׁר	אָהֵב	אָבִיו		וַתִּקַּח
watta'as	'immô	maṭ'ammîm	ka'ăsher	'āhēv	'āvîw		wattiqach
and she made	his mother	delicious food	like that	he loved	his father		and she took

7549	881, 933	6451	1158	1448	2632	866	882	904, 1041
pn	do, *n mp*	pn	n ms, ps 3fs	art, adj	art, n fp	rel part	prep, ps 3fs	prep, art, n ms
רִבְקָה	אֶת־בִּגְדֵי	עֵשָׂו	בְּנָהּ	הַגָּדֹל	הַחֲמֻדֹת	אֲשֶׁר	אִתָּהּ	בַּבָּיִת
rivqāh	'eth-bighedhê	'ēsāw	benāhh	haggādhōl	hachmudhōth	'ăsher	'ittāhh	babbāyith
Rebekah	the clothes of	Esau	her son	the older	the best ones	which	with her	in the house

3980.522	881, 3399	1158	7278	16.	881	5997	1454	6008
cj, v Hiphil impf 3fs	do, pn	n ms, ps 3fs	art, adj		cj, do	*n mp*	*n mp*	art, n fp
וַתַּלְבֵּשׁ	אֶת־יַעֲקֹב	בְּנָהּ	הַקָּטָן		וְאֵת	עֹרֹת	גְּדָיֵי	הָעִזִּים
wattalbēsh	'eth-ya'ăqōv	benāhh	haqqāṭān		we'ēth	'ōrōth	gedhāyê	hā'izzîm
and she clothed	Jacob	her son	the younger		and	the skins of	the kids of	the goats

3980.512	6142, 3135	6142	2613	6939	17.	5598.122
v Hiphil pf 3fs	prep, n fd, ps 3ms	cj, prep	*n fs*	n mp, ps 3ms		cj, v Qal impf 3fs
הִלְבִּישָׁה	עַל־יָדָיו	וְעַל	חֶלְקַת	צַוָּארָיו		וַתִּתֵּן
hilbîshāh	'al-yādhâv	we'al	chelqath	tsawwā'râv		wattittēn
she clothed	on his hands	and on	the smooth part of	his neck		and she gave

881, 4440	881, 4035	866	6449.112	904, 3135	3399	1158
do, art, n mp	cj, do, art, n ms	rel part	v Qal pf 3fs	prep, *n fs*	pn	n ms, ps 3fs
אֶת־הַמַּטְעַמִּים	וְאֶת־הַלֶּחֶם	אֲשֶׁר	עָשָׂתָה	בְּיַד	יַעֲקֹב	בְּנָהּ
'eth-hammaṭ'ammîm	we'eth-hallechem	'ăsher	'āsāthāh	beyadh	ya'ăqōv	benāhh
the delicious food	and the bread	which	she made	in the hand of	Jacob	her son

18.

971.121	420, 1	569.121	1	569.121	2079	4449
cj, v Qal impf 3ms	prep, n ms, ps 3ms	cj, v Qal impf 3ms	n ms, ps 1cs	cj, v Qal impf 3ms	intrj, ps 1cs	intrg
וַיָּבֹא	אֶל־אָבִיו	וַיֹּאמֶר	אָבִי	וַיֹּאמֶר	הִנֶּנִּי	מִי
wayyāvō'	'el-'āvîw	wayyō'mer	'āvî	wayyō'mer	hinnennî	mî
and he went	to his father	and he said	my father	and he said	behold I	who

887	1158	**19.** 569.121	3399	420, 1	609	6451	1111
pers pron	n ms, ps 1cs	cj, v Qal impf 3ms	pn	prep, n ms, ps 3ms	pers pron	pn	n ms, ps 2ms
אַתָּה	בְּנִי	וַיֹּאמֶר	יַעֲקֹב	אֶל־אָבִיו	אָנֹכִי	עֵשָׂו	בְּכֹרֶךָ
'attāh	b^{e}nî	wayyō'mer	ya'ăqōv	'el-'āvîw	'ānōkhî	'ēsāw	b^{e}khōrekhā
you	my son	and he said	Jacob	to his father	I	Esau	your firstborn

11. And Jacob said to Rebekah his mother, Behold, Esau my brother is a hairy man and I am a smooth man: ... is covered with hair, *BB* ... is rough, *Geneva* ... I am smooth-skinned, *NAB*.

12. My father peradventure will feel me: ... suppose my father feels me, *NEB* ... if by chance, my father puts his hand on me, *BB* ... if my father touches me, *NCB*.

and I shall seem to him as a deceiver: ... like an impious person, *Goodspeed* ... a mocker, *Berkeley* ... that I am tricking him, *BB* ... like a swindler, *Fenton*.

and I shall bring a curse upon me, and not a blessing: ... put a curse on me in place of, *BB* ... bring down a curse rather than, *NIV* ... brought upon me disesteem, *Young*.

13. And his mother said unto him, Upon me be thy curse, my son: ... I will take your curse, *Berkeley* ... let any curse against you be my concern, *Anchor* ... fall on me, *REB*.

only obey my voice: ... just do as I say, *NAB* ... do as I tell you, *Fenton* ... listen to me, *NCB* ... obey my word, *NRSV* ... hearken, *Young*.

and go fetch me them: ... go and get them, *BB* ... get me the kids, *NAB* ... get the goats, *LIVB*.

14. And he went, and fetched and brought them to his mother, and his mother made savoury meat: ... savory food, *ASV* ... appetizing dish, *NAB*.

such as his father loved: ... as his father liked, *Berkeley* ... just the way his father liked it, *NIV*.

15. And Rebekah took goodly raiment of her eldest son Esau: ... the best clothes, *NCB* ... choicest clothes, *MLB*.

which were with her in the house: ... at home, *Berkeley* ... she kept by her, *NEB*.

and put them upon Jacob her younger son: ... and dressed Jacob, *MLB* ... clothed, *Geneva*.

16. And she put the skins of the kids of the goats: ... goatskins, *NIV* ... hairy skin of the goats, *LIVB*.

upon his hands and upon the smooth of his neck: ... she covered up his hands, *Anchor* ... hairless parts, *NAB* ... smooth part, *Fenton* ... smooth nape, *REB*.

17. And she gave the savoury meat and the bread: ... delicious meat, *MLB* ... savoury dishes, *Darby* ... dainties, *Fenton* ... festive dish, *Anchor* ... tasty dish, *Goodspeed*.

which she had prepared: ... she had baked, *Berkeley* ... made ready, *BB*.

into the hand of her son Jacob: ... handed to her son, *NIV*.

18. And he came unto his father: ... went to his father, *NCB* ... bringing them to, *NAB* ... carried the platter of

mand, not because he thought it was wrong, but because he was afraid he would be caught in this deception and bring down a curse upon himself. All blind Isaac would have to do was touch his arm and he would know that this was not Esau. But Rebekah had a well-thought-out plan. She knew what she was doing. So she said she would take any curse intended for him on herself (implying that she did not believe there would be one). Then she demanded that Jacob bring her the goats.

27:14-17. Jacob obeyed, and Rebekah began to carry out her daring plan. She fixed delicious food just the way she knew Isaac would like it. She put Esau's best outer garments on Jacob, and covered the smooth part of his neck and his hands (the Hebrew word for hand, *yad*, includes the forearms up to the elbows) with goatskin from goats that had very fine hair. so close to human hair that people used it to make wigs. Then she sent him to Isaac with thin, flat loaves of home-made bread and delicious food.

27:18-20. Jacob came in to Isaac's tent, called himself Esau, and invited his father to rise from his bed and sit down to a delicious meal. Isaac was sur-

6449.115	3626, 866	1744.313	420	7251.131, 5167	3553.131	404.131
v Qal pf 1cs	prep, rel part	v Piel pf 2ms	prep, ps 1cs	v Qal impv 2ms, part	v Qal impv 2ms	cj, v Qal impv 2ms
עָשִׂיתִי	כַּאֲשֶׁר	דִּבַּרְתָּ	אֵלָי	קוּם־נָא	שְׁבָה	וְאָכְלָה
'āsîthî	ka'ăsher	dibbartā	'ēlāy	qûm-nā'	sh^{e}vāh	w^{e}'ākh^{e}lāh
I have made	like that	you have spoken	to me	arise please	sit down	and eat

4623, 6987	904, 5877	1313.322	5497	20.	569.121	3437
prep, n ms, ps 1cs	prep, prep	v Piel impf 3fs, ps 1cs	n fs, ps 2ms		cj, v Qal impf 3ms	pn
מִצֵּידִי	בַּעֲבוּר	תְּבָרְכַנִּי	נַפְשֶׁךָ		וַיֹּאמֶר	יִצְחָק
mitstsêdhî	ba'ăvûr	t^{e}vār^{e}khannî	naphshekhā		wayyō'mer	yitschāq
from my game	on account of	it will bless me	your soul		and he said	Isaac

420, 1158	4242, 2172	4257.313	3937, 4834.141	1158	569.121	3706
prep, n ms, ps 3ms	intrg, dem pron	v Piel pf 2ms	prep, Qal inf con	n ms, ps 1cs	cj, v Qal impf 3ms	cj
אֶל־בְּנוֹ	מַה־זֶּה	מִהַרְתָּ	לִמְצֹא	בְּנִי	וַיֹּאמֶר	כִּי
'el-b^{e}nô	mah-zeh	mihartā	limtsō'	b^{e}nî	wayyō'mer	kî
to his son	what this	you have done quickly	to find	my son	and he said	because

7424.511	3176	435	3937, 6686	21.	569.121	3437	420, 3399
v Hiphil pf 3ms	pn	n mp, ps 2ms	prep, n mp, ps 1cs		cj, v Qal impf 3ms	pn	prep, pn
הִקְרָה	יְהוָה	אֱלֹהֶיךָ	לְפָנָי		וַיֹּאמֶר	יִצְחָק	אֶל־יַעֲקֹב
hiqrāh	y^{e}hwāh	'ĕlōhêkhā	l^{e}phānāy		wayyō'mer	yitschāq	'el-ya'ăqōv
He caused to encounter	Yahweh	your God	before me		and he said	Isaac	to Jacob

5242.131, 5167	4318.125	1158	887	2172	1158	6451
v Qal impv 2ms, part	cj, v Qal impf 1cs, ps 2ms	n ms, ps 1cs	intrg part, pers pron	dem pron	n ms, ps 1cs	pn
גְּשָׁה־נָּא	וַאֲמֻשְׁךָ	בְּנִי	הַאַתָּה	זֶה	בְּנִי	עֵשָׂו
g^{e}shāh-nā'	wa'ămushkhā	b^{e}nî	ha'attāh	zeh	b^{e}nî	'ēsāw
come near please	and I will feel you	my son	are you	this	my son	Esau

524, 3940	22.	5242.121	3399	420, 3437	1	5135.121
cj, adv		cj, v Qal impf 3ms	pn	prep, pn	n ms, ps	cj, v Qal impf 3ms, ps 3ms
אִם־לֹא		וַיִּגַּשׁ	יַעֲקֹב	אֶל־יִצְחָק	אָבִיו	וַיְמֻשֵּׁהוּ
'im-lō'		wayyiggash	ya'ăqōv	'el-yitschāq	'āvîw	waymushshēhû
or not		and he drew near	Jacob	to Isaac	his father	and he felt him

569.121	7317	7249	3399	3135	3135	6451	23.	3940
cj, v Qal impf 3ms	art, n ms	*n ms*	pn	cj, art, n fd	*n fd*	pn		cj, neg part
וַיֹּאמֶר	הַקֹּל	קוֹל	יַעֲקֹב	וְהַיָּדַיִם	יְדֵי	עֵשָׂו		וְלֹא
wayyō'mer	haqqōl	qôl	ya'ăqōv	w^{e}hayyādayim	y^{e}dhê	'ēsāw		w^{e}lō'
and he said	the voice	the voice of	Jacob	but the hands	the hands of	Esau		and not

5421.511	3706, 2030.116	3135	3626, 3135	6451	250	7997
v Hiphil pf 3ms, ps 3ms	cj, v Qal pf 3cp	n fd	prep, *n fd*	pn	n ms, ps 3ms	adj
הִכִּירוֹ	כִּי־הָיוּ	יָדָיו	כִּידֵי	עֵשָׂו	אָחִיו	שְׂעִרֹת
hikkîrô	kî-hāyû	yādhâv	kîdhê	'ēsāw	'āchîw	s^{e}'irōth
he recognized	because they were	his hands	like the hands of	Esau	his brother	hairy

1313.321	24.	569.121	887	2172	1158	6451	569.121
cj, v Piel impf 3ms, ps 3ms		cj, v Qal impf 3ms	pers pron	dem pron	n ms, ps 1cs	pn	cj, v Qal impf 3ms
וַיְבָרְכֵהוּ		וַיֹּאמֶר	אַתָּה	זֶה	בְּנִי	עֵשָׂו	וַיֹּאמֶר
wayvārākhēhû		wayyō'mer	'attāh	zeh	b^{e}nî	'ēsāw	wayyō'mer
and he blessed him		and he said	you	this	my son	Esau	and he said

603	25.	569.121	5242.531	3937	404.125	4623, 6987	1158
pers pron		cj, v Qal impf 3ms	v Hiphil impv 2ms	prep, ps 1cs	cj, v Qal impf 1cs	prep, *n ms*	n ms, ps 1cs
אָנִי		וַיֹּאמֶר	הַגִּשָׁה	לִי	וְאֹכְלָה	מִצֵּיד	בְּנִי
'ānî		wayyō'mer	haggishāh	lî	w^{e}'ōkh^{e}lāh	mitstsêdh	b^{e}nî
I		and he said	bring near	to me	and I will eat	from the game of	my son

food into the room where his father was lying, *LIVB*.

and said, My father: and he said, Here am I: ... yes, my son, *REB*.

who art thou, my son?: ... which one of my sons, *Anchor* ... who is it, *NIV* ... which are you, *REB*.

19. And Jacob said unto his father, I am Esau thy firstborn: ... told his father, *Berkeley* ... your oldest, *BB*.

I have done according as thou badest me: ... I did as you told me, *NAB* ... as you asked me, *KJVII* ... as thou hast spoken, *Young* ... as thou didst say to me, *Darby*.

Arise, I pray thee, sit and eat of my venison: ... come now, be seated, and take of my meat, *BB* ... of my game, *Berkeley* ... of my deer-meat, *KJVII* ... turn and eat, *Fenton*.

that thy soul may bless me: ... that you may give me your very own blessing, *Anchor* ... special blessing, *NAB* ... may heartily give, *MLB*.

20. And Isaac said unto his son, How is it that thou hast found it so quickly, my son?: ... succeeded so quickly, *Anchor* ... so quick in meeting with it, *Fenton* ... what is this that you have found so quickly, *NEB* ... hasted to find, *Young*.

And he said, Because the LORD thy God brought it to me: ... made things go well for me, *Anchor* ... brought it direct to me, *Berkeley* ... put it in my way, *Darby* ... let me come upon it, *NCB* ... gave me success, *NIV*.

21. And Isaac said unto Jacob, Come near, I pray thee: ... come up close, *Goodspeed* ... come closer, *NAB* ... come nigh, *Young* ... come over here, *LIVB*.

that I may feel thee, my son: ... I may stroke you, *MLB* ... put my hand on you, *BB* ... that I may touch you, *NCB*.

whether thou be my very son Esau or not: ... to be sure, *REB* ... are you really Esau, *Good News* ... truly, *KJVII*.

22. And Jacob went near unto Isaac his father: ... moved up, *Anchor* ... moved closer, *MLB* ... approached, *Fenton*.

and he felt him, and said: ... stroked him, *Berkeley* ... put his hands on, *BB* ... touched him, *NIV*.

The voice is Jacob's voice, but the hands are the hands of Esau: ... were hairy, *NKJV*.

23. And he discerned him not: ... not make out who he was, *BB* ... had not identified, *Anchor* ... did not detect, *Fenton* ... knew him not, *Geneva* ... did not recognize, *NASB*.

because his hands were hairy, as his brother Esau's hands: ... wrists, *Berkeley* ... covered with hair, *BB* ... were rough, *Geneva*.

so he blessed him: ... gave him a blessing, *BB* ... he was thankful, *Fenton* ... was about to give him his blessing, *Good News*.

24. And he said, Art thou my very son Esau?: ... thou art he, *Young* ... are you really, *Darby*.

And he said, I am: ... Of course, *Anchor* ... it is I, *Darby* ... certainly, *NAB*.

25. And he said, Bring it near to me: ... serve it to me, *Anchor* ... put it before me, *BB* ... serve me your game, *NAB* ... some of the meat, *Good News*.

and I will eat of my son's venison: ... game, *NASB* ... meat, *BB* ... deer meat, *KJVII* ... provision, *Young*.

that my soul may bless thee: ... I may personally bless you, *Berkeley* ... give you my very own blessing, *Anchor* ... with all my heart, *LIVB*.

And he brought it near to him, and he did eat: ... he served it to him, *Anchor* ... put it before him, and he took it, *BB* ... presented it, *Fenton* ... set it before him, *NCB*.

and he brought him wine, and he drank: ... had a drink, *BB* ... which he drank, *NCB*.

26. And his father Isaac said unto him, Come near now, and kiss me, my son: ... come closer, *Anchor* ... come here, *NIV* ... give me a kiss, *BB* ... give me a drink, *Fenton*.

---

prised that he had found wild game so quickly. Jacob then added blasphemy to his deceit by saying that the LORD, Isaac's God, had directed him. This may have aroused Isaac's suspicions, since there is no record of Esau mentioning the name of the LORD.

27:21-24. However, it was Jacob's voice that nearly gave him away. But it may be that the voices of Esau and Jacob were similar and had been mistaken before. To reassure himself, Isaac asked Jacob to come closer and let Isaac touch him.

The hairy skin was enough to convince Isaac, so he proceeded to bless him. But to be sure, he asked, "Is this you, my son, Esau?" Jacob affirmed that he was, and Isaac was satisfied.

27:25-26. After eating the delicious food, Isaac drank wine that Jacob brought him. Then, with emphasis, he asked Jacob to kiss him. Such a kiss was meant to be a token, not only of affection, but of loyalty. Jacob made it a perfidious token of treachery.

27:27. The smell of the open country was on

3937, 4775	1313.322	5497	5242.521, 3937	404.121	971.521
prep, prep	v Piel impf 3fs, ps 2ms	n fs, ps 1cs	cj, v Hiphil impf 3ms, prep, ps 3ms	cj, v Qal impf 3ms	cj, v Hiphil impf 3ms
לְמַעַן	תְּבָרֶכְךָ	נַפְשִׁי	וַיַּגֶּשׁ־לוֹ	וַיֹּאכַל	וַיָּבֵא
l^{e}ma'an	t^{e}vārekh^{e}khā	naphshî	wayyaggesh-lô	wayyō'khal	wayyāvē'
so that	it will bless you	my soul	and he brought near to him	and he ate	and he brought

3937	3302	8685.121		569.121	420	3437	1
prep, ps 3ms	n ms	cj, v Qal impf 3ms	**26.**	cj, v Qal impf 3ms	prep, ps 3ms	pn	n ms, ps
לוֹ	יַיִן	וַיֵּשְׁתְּ		וַיֹּאמֶר	אֵלָיו	יִצְחָק	אָבִיו
lô	yayin	wayyēsht		wayyō'mer	'ēlâv	yitschāq	'āvîw
to him	wine	and he drank		and he said	to him	Isaac	his father

5242.131, 5167	5583.131, 3937	1158		5242.121	5583.121, 3937
v Qal impv 2ms, part	cj, v Qal impv 2ms, prep, ps 1cs	n ms, ps 1cs	**27.**	cj, v Qal impf 3ms	cj, v Qal impf 3ms, prep, ps 3ms
גְּשָׁה־נָּא	וּשְׁקָה־לִּי	בְּנִי		וַיִּגַּשׁ	וַיִּשַּׁק־לוֹ
g^{e}shāh-nā'	ûshqāh-lî	b^{e}nî		wayyiggash	wayyishshaq-lô
come near please	and kiss me	my son		and he drew near	and he kissed him

7591.521	881, 7666	933	1313.321	569.121
cj, v Hiphil impf 3ms	do, *n ms*	n mp, ps 3ms	cj, v Piel impf 3ms, ps 3ms	cj, v Qal impf 3ms
וַיָּרַח	אֶת־רֵיחַ	בְּגָדָיו	וַיְבָרְכֵהוּ	וַיֹּאמֶר
wayyārach	'eth-rêach	b^{e}ghādhâv	wayvār^{e}khēhû	wayyō'mer
and he smelled	the scent of	his clothes	and he blessed him	and he said

7495.131	7666	1158	3626, 7666	7898	866	1313.311	3176
v Qal impv 2ms	*n ms*	n ms, ps 1cs	prep, *n ms*	n ms	rel part	v Piel pf 3ms, ps 3ms	pn
רְאֵה	רֵיחַ	בְּנִי	כְּרֵיחַ	שָׂדֶה	אֲשֶׁר	בֵּרְכוֹ	יְהוָה
r^e'ēh	rêach	b^{e}nî	k^{e}rêach	sādheh	'ăsher	bēr^{e}khô	y^{e}hwāh
see	the smell of	my son	like smell of	field	which	He blessed him	Yahweh

	5598.121, 3937	435	4623, 3030	8452	4623, 8468
28.	cj, v Qal impf 3ms, prep, ps 2ms	art, n mp	prep, n ms	art, n md	cj, prep, *n mp*
	וְיִתֶּן־לְךָ	הָאֱלֹהִים	מִטַּל	הַשָּׁמַיִם	וּמִשְׁמַנֵּי
	w^{e}yitten-l^{e}khā	hā'ĕlōhîm	mittal	hashshāmayim	ûmishmannê
	and He will give to you	God	from the dew of	the heavens	and from the fat of

800	7524	1765	8822		5856.126	6194
art, n fs	cj, *n ms*	n ms	cj, n ms	**29.**	v Qal impf 3mp, ps 2ms	n mp
הָאָרֶץ	וְרֹב	דָּגָן	וְתִירֹשׁ		יַעַבְדוּךָ	עַמִּים
hā'ārets	w^{e}rōv	dāghān	w^{e}thîrōsh		ya'avdûkhā	'ammîm
the land	and abundance of	grain	and wine		they will serve you	peoples

8246.726	3937	3948	2030.131	1408	3937, 250
cj, v Hithpalel impf 3mp	prep, ps 2ms	n mp	v Qal impv 2ms	n ms	prep, n mp, ps 2ms
וְיִשְׁתַּחֲוֻ	לְךָ	לְאֻמִּים	הֱוֵה	גְבִיר	לְאַחֶיךָ
w^{e}yishtachăwu	l^{e}khā	l^e'ummîm	hĕwēh	gh^{e}vîr	l^e'achêkhā
and they will bow down	to you	peoples	be	master	to your brothers

8246.726	3937	1158	525	803.152	803.155
cj, v Hithpalel impf 3mp	prep, ps 2ms	*n mp*	n fs, ps 2ms	v Qal act ptc mp, ps 2ms	v Qal pass ptc ms
וְיִשְׁתַּחֲווּ	לְךָ	בְּנֵי	אִמֶּךָ	אֹרְרֶיךָ	אָרוּר
w^{e}yishtachăwû	l^{e}khā	b^{e}nê	'immekhā	'ōr^{e}rêkhā	'ārûr
and they will bow down	to you	the sons of	your mother	ones who curse you	cursed

1313.352	1313.155		2030.121	3626, 866	3735.311	3437
cj, v Piel ptc mp, ps 2ms	v Qal pass ptc ms	**30.**	cj, v Qal impf 3ms	prep, rel part	v Piel pf 3ms	pn
וּמְבָרְכֶיךָ	בָּרוּךְ		וַיְהִי	כַּאֲשֶׁר	כִּלָּה	יִצְחָק
ûm^{e}vār^{e}khêkhā	bārûkh		wayhî	ka'ăsher	killāh	yitschāq
and ones who bless you	blessed		and it was	when	he finished	Isaac

27. And he came near, and kissed him: ... went to him, *NIV* ... he went up, *Goodspeed* ... gave him a kiss, *BB* ... gave him a drink, *Fenton.*

and he smelled the smell of his raiment: ... sniffed the smell of his clothes, *Anchor* ... the savour, *Geneva* ... fragrance, *NCB* ... caught the smell, *NIV* ... his garments, *NRSV.*

and blessed him, and said: ... gave him a blessing, *Fenton.*

See, the smell of my son is as the smell of a field: ... fragrance of my son is like the fragrance, *Young* ... like the smell of open country, *REB* ... pleasant smell of my son, *Good News.*

which the LORD hath blessed: ... Yahweh has blessed, *Anchor* ... Jehovah, *Darby* ... on which the blessing of the Lord has come, *BB* ... blessed by the Lord, *NEB.*

28. Therefore God give thee of the dew of heaven: ... of heaven's dew, *Goodspeed* ... dew from the skies, *Fenton* ... plenty of rain for your crops, *LIVB.*

and the fatness of the earth: ... fertility of the earth, *NAB* ... good things of the earth, *BB* ... earth's riches, *Anchor* ... fruitfulness, *NCB.*

and plenty of corn and wine: ... abundance of new grain, *Anchor* ... increase and possession, *Fenton* ... wheat and wine, *Geneva* ... new wine, *NIV* ... in full measure, *BB.*

29. Let people serve thee: ... be your servants, *Geneva* ... slaves, *LIVB* ... may nations serve thee, *Berkeley.*

and nations bow down to thee: ... pay homage, *NAB* ... go down before you, *BB* ... a multitude of mighty peoples, *Fenton* ... races, *Darby.*

be lord over thy brethren: ... be your brother's master, *Anchor* ... master over your kinsmen, *MLB* ... your brothers shall also pay tribute, *Fenton* ... ruler over, *KJVII.*

and let thy mother's sons bow down to thee: ... prostrate themselves, *Berkeley* ... go down before you, *BB* ... honour thee, *Geneva* ... mother's descendants, *Good News.*

cursed be every one that curseth thee: ... a curse be on, *BB* ... if any curses you he shall be cursed, *Fenton.*

and blessed be he that blesseth thee: ... if any blesses you, *Fenton* ... who give you a blessing, *BB.*

30. And it came to pass, as soon as Isaac had made an end of blessing Jacob: ... Isaac had hardly finished, *Berkeley* ... had come to the end of, *BB* ... right after Isaac had finished, *Anchor* ... had pronounced, *NCB.*

and Jacob was yet scarce gone out from the presence of Isaac his father: ... had but just left, *Berkeley* ... no sooner left his father, *Anchor* ... had not long gone away, *BB* ... is only just going out, *Young.*

that Esau his brother came in from his hunting: ... from the field, *BB* ... with his venison, *Fenton* ... returned, *NCB* ... Esau arrives, *LIVB.*

31. And he also had made savoury meat and brought it unto his father, and said unto his father: ... made ready a meal, *BB* ... prepared a festive dish, *Anchor* ... also had made dainties, *Fenton* ... appetizing dish, *NAB.*

Let my father arise: ... sit up, *Goodspeed* ... get up, *BB* ... come, father, *REB.*

and eat of his son's venison: ... game, *Berkeley* ... take of his son's meat, *BB* ... deer meat, *KJVII* ... provision, *Young* ... game I have for you, *REB.*

that thy soul may bless me: ... personally bless me, *Berkeley* ... give me his very own blessing, *Anchor* ... your special blessing, *NAB.*

Esau's clothes, and Isaac went into a rhapsody about it as the smell of a field the LORD has blessed, as Rebekah foresaw he would.

27:28-29. Isaac now recognized that the blessing was really God's blessing and God would have to give it. However, Isaac did not repeat all the blessing that God had covenanted for Abraham and his descendants. Isaac knew Esau was not interested in the spiritual part of the blessing. So he spoke only of material blessings, of heaven's dew (heavy dew or night mist that came off the Mediterranean during the rainless summer was a blessing), of rich harvests of grain and new wine (fresh grape juice, the same Hebrew word is used in Isa. 65:8 of juice still in the grapes), of victory over nations (something that will have its final fulfillment when Jesus comes to establish His millennial kingdom), and lordship over his brothers and the sons of his mother. Of course, Rebekah only had one other son. But in the Hebrew, "brothers" often includes other close relatives, and "sons" includes grandsons and descendants.

27:30-33. When Esau came in from the hunt and brought food to Isaac, Isaac was shocked and trembled violently. He also declared that the one who had first come with the food would indeed be blessed. The blessing was legal and prophetic, and he could not take it back. More important, Isaac

3937, 1313.341	881, 3399	2030.121	395	3428.142	3428.111	3399	4623, 882
prep, v Piel inf con	do, pn	cj, v Qal impf 3ms	adv	v Qal inf abs	v Qal pf 3ms	pn	prep, prep
לְבָרֵךְ	אֶת־יַעֲקֹב	וַיְהִי	אַךְ	יָצֹא	יָצָא	יַעֲקֹב	מֵאֵת
lᵉvārēkh	'eth-ya'ăqōv	wayhî	'akh	yātsō'	yātsā'	ya'ăqōv	mē'ēth
to bless	Jacob	and it was	only	going out	he went out	Jacob	from

6686	3437	1	6451	250	971.111	4623, 6987
n mp	pn	n ms, ps	cj, pn	n ms, ps 3ms	v Qal pf 3ms	prep, n ms, ps 3ms
פְּנֵי	יִצְחָק	אָבִיו	וְעֵשָׂו	אָחִיו	בָּא	מִצֵּידוֹ
pᵉnê	yitschāq	'āvîw	wᵉ'ēsāw	'āchîw	bā'	mitstsêdhô
the presence of	Isaac	his father	and Esau	his brother	he came	from his hunting

	6449.121	1612, 2000	4440	971.521	3937, 1	569.121
31.	cj, v Qal impf 3ms	cj, pers pron	n mp	cj, v Hiphil impf 3ms	prep, n ms, ps 3ms	cj, v Qal impf 3ms
	וַיַּעַשׂ	גַּם־הוּא	מַטְעַמִּים	וַיָּבֵא	לְאָבִיו	וַיֹּאמֶר
	wayya'as	gam-hû'	maṭ'ammîm	wayyāvē'	lᵉ'āvîw	wayyō'mer
	and he made	also he	delicious food	and he brought	to his father	and he said

3937, 1	7251.121	1	404.121	4623, 6987	1158	904, 5877
prep, n ms, ps 3ms	v Qal juss 3ms	n ms, ps 1cs	cj, v Qal impf 3ms	prep, n ms	n ms, ps 3ms	prep, prep
לְאָבִיו	יָקֻם	אָבִי	וְיֹאכַל	מִצֵּיד	בְּנוֹ	בַּעֲבֻר
lᵉ'āvîw	yāqum	'āvî	wᵉyō'khal	mitstsêdh	bᵉnô	ba'ăvûr
to his father	let him arise	my father	and let him eat	from the game of	his son	on account of

1313.322	5497		569.121	3937	3437	1	4449, 887
v Piel impf 3fs, ps 1cs	n fs, ps 2ms	**32.**	cj, v Qal impf 3ms	prep, ps 3ms	pn	n ms, ps	intrg, pers pron
תְּבָרְכַנִּי	נַפְשֶׁךָ		וַיֹּאמֶר	לוֹ	יִצְחָק	אָבִיו	מִי־אָתָּה
tᵉvārᵉkhannî	naphshekhā		wayyō'mer	lô	yitschāq	'āvîw	mî-'āttāh
it will bless me	your soul		and he said	to him	Isaac	his father	who you

569.121	603	1158	1111	6451		2829.121	3437	2832
cj, v Qal impf 3ms	pers pron	n ms, ps 2ms	n ms, ps 2ms	pn	**33.**	cj, v Qal impf 3ms	pn	n fs
וַיֹּאמֶר	אֲנִי	בִּנְךָ	בְּכֹרְךָ	עֵשָׂו		וַיֶּחֱרַד	יִצְחָק	חֲרָדָה
wayyō'mer	'ănî	binᵉkhā	vᵉkhōrᵉkhā	'ēsāw		wayyechĕradh	yitschāq	chărādhāh
and he said	I	your son	your firstborn	Esau		and he trembled	Isaac	trembling

1462	5912, 4108	569.121	4449, 660	2000	6942, 6987	971.521
adv	prep, adv	cj, v Qal impf 3ms	intrg, cj	pers pron	art, v Qal act part ms, n ms	cj, v Hiphil impf 3ms
גְּדֹלָה	עַד־מְאֹד	וַיֹּאמֶר	מִי־אֵפוֹא	הוּא	הַצָּד־צַיִד	וַיָּבֵא
gᵉdhōlāh	'adh-mᵉ'ōdh	wayyō'mer	mî-'ēphô'	hû'	hatstsādh-tsayidh	wayyāvē'
greatly	until very	and he said	who then	he	the hunter of game	and he brought

3937	404.125	4623, 3725	904, 3071	971.123	1313.325
prep, ps 1cs	cj, v Qal impf 1cs	prep, prep	prep, adv	v Qal impf 2ms	cj, v Piel impf 1cs, ps 3ms
לִי	וָאֹכַל	מִכֹּל	בְּטֶרֶם	תָּבוֹא	וָאֲבָרְכֵהוּ
lî	wā'ōkhal	mikkōl	bᵉṭerem	tāvô'	wā'ăvārᵉkhēhû
to me	and I ate	from all	before	you came	and I blessed him

1612, 1313.155	2030.121		3626, 8471.141	6451	881, 1745	1
cj, v Qal pass ptc ms	v Qal impf 3ms	**34.**	prep, v Qal inf con	pn	do, *n mp*	n ms, ps
גַּם־בָּרוּךְ	יִהְיֶה		כִּשְׁמֹעַ	עֵשָׂו	אֶת־דִּבְרֵי	אָבִיו
gam-bārûkh	yihyeh		kishmōa'	'ēsāw	'eth-divrê	'āvîw
also blessed	he will be		as hearing	Esau	the words of	his father

7094.121	7095	1462	4914	5912, 4108	569.121	3937, 1
cj, v Qal impf 3ms	n fs	adj	cj, adj	prep, adv	cj, v Qal impf 3ms	prep, n ms, ps 3ms
וַיִּצְעַק	צְעָקָה	גְּדֹלָה	וּמָרָה	עַד־מְאֹד	וַיֹּאמֶר	לְאָבִיו
wayyits'aq	tsᵉ'āqāh	gᵉdhōlāh	ûmārāh	'adh-mᵉ'ōdh	wayyō'mer	lᵉ'āvîw
and he cried out	cry	great	and bitter	until very	and he said	to his father

1313.331	1622, 603	1	**35.** 569.121	971.111	250	
v Piel impv 2ms, ps 1cs	cj, pers pron	n ms, ps 1cs	cj, v Qal impf 3ms	v Qal pf 3ms	n ms, ps 2ms	
בָּרְכֵנִי	גַּם־אָנִי	אָבִי	וַיֹּאמֶר	בָּא	אָחִיךָ	
bār^{e}khēnî	gham-'ānî	'āvî	wayyō'mer	bā'	'āchîkhā	
bless me	also I	my father	and he said	he came in	your brother	

904, 4983	4089.121	1318	**36.** 569.121	3706	7410.111	8428
prep, n fs	cj, v Qal impf 3ms	n fs, ps 2ms	cj, v Qal impf 3ms	intrg part, cj	v Qal pf 3ms	n ms, ps 3ms
בְּמִרְמָה	וַיִּקַּח	בִּרְכָתֶךָ	וַיֹּאמֶר	הֲכִי	קָרָא	שְׁמוֹ
b^{e}mirmāh	wayyiqqach	bir^{e}khāthekhā	wayyō'mer	h^{e}khî	qārā'	sh^{e}mô
with deceit	and he took	your blessing	and he said	it's true isn't it	he called	his name

32. And Isaac his father said unto him, Who art thou?: ... who are you, *BB* ... who is it, *LIVB.*

And he said, I am thy son, thy firstborn Esau: ... I am your oldest son, Esau, *BB* ... your elder son, *REB* ... why, your son Esau, your first-born, *Anchor.*

33. And Isaac trembled very exceedingly: ... in great fear, *BB* ... was terrified, *Fenton* ... seized with a violent fit of trembling, *Anchor* ... very greatly agitated, *NEB* ... greatly disturbed, *NCB.*

and said, Who? where is he that hath taken venison, and brought it me: ... who was it then, *Berkeley* ... who and where, *Geneva* ... who hunted deer, *KJVII* ... who got meat, *BB* ... that hunted game, *NASB.*

and I have eaten of all before thou camest: ... I finished eating it just before you came, *NAB* ... I took it all, *BB* ... I ate heartily of it, *Goodspeed.*

and have blessed him?: ... gave him a blessing, *BB* ... my final blessing, *Good News.*

Yea, and he shall be blessed: ... now he must remain blessed, *NAB* ... his it will be, *BB* ... the blessing will stand, *NEB* ... indeed blessed, *NIV* ... it is his forever, *Good News.*

34. And when Esau heard the words of his father: ... on hearing his father's words, *Goodspeed* ... the speech of, *Fenton* ... the voice of, *KJVII* ... what his father said, *NEB.*

he cried with a great and exceeding bitter cry: ... wailed with a most loud cry, *MLB* ... burst into sobbing of the most violent and bitter kind, *Anchor* ... lamented loudly and bitterly, *REB* ... out of measure, *Geneva.*

and said unto his father, Bless me, even me also, O my father: ... begged, *NAB* ... pleading, *Berkeley* ... give a blessing to me, *BB.*

35. And he said, Thy brother came with subtilty: ... by a ruse, *NAB* ... with guile, *RSV* ... with pretence, *MLB* ... with deceit, *KJVII* ... under false colors, *Goodspeed.*

and hath taken away thy blessing: ... carried off, *NAB* ... stole, *Fenton* ... received, *NCB.*

36. And he said, Is not he rightly named Jacob?: ... not called Jacob for nothing, *REB* ... true to his name,

was basically a spiritual person, and his eyes were now opened to the fact that God had overruled and Esau was not God's choice. Thus he recognized that giving the blessing to Jacob was the will of God. Part of Isaac's reason for trembling may have been the memory of Esau's unsanctified life, heathen wives, and lack of spiritual desires that made him unfit to carry on the chosen line and receive the salvation-blessing of Abraham.

27:34-35. Esau responded with loud and bitter wailing. Then he begged his father for a blessing. But Isaac refused, because he had already given Esau's blessing to Jacob. The New Testament refers to this, saying that Esau was rejected and could not bring about any repentance ("change of mind") on the part of Isaac "though he sought the blessing with tears" (Heb. 12:17). It is clear from this that Esau did not repent or change his mind and attitudes toward God. He simply wanted Isaac to change his mind and bless him anyway. By this time, Esau felt that the material side of the blessing would be worth something. But even though Isaac recognized that Jacob took the blessing with deceit, it was indeed his.

27:36. Esau then drew attention to the other meaning of Jacob, the deceiver. Jacob had supplanted and outwitted him by trickery. Jacob took his birthright (Heb., *bekhorah*) and now his blessing (Heb., *berakhah*, note the word play).

Esau mistakenly thought he could have the blessing without the birthright. In this family, and in God's plan, the two were intertwined, however. Both had to do with God's promise to Abraham, a promise that could only be claimed by grace

3399	6356.121	2172	6718	881, 1112	4089.111	2079	6498
pn	cj, v Qal impf 3ms, ps 1cs	dem pron	n fd	do, n fs, ps 1cs	v Qal pf 3ms	cj, intrj	adv
יַעֲקֹב	וַיַּעְקְבֵנִי	זֶה	פַעֲמַיִם	אֶת־בְּכֹרָתִי	לָקָח	וְהִנֵּה	עַתָּה
ya'ăqōv	wayya'āqŏvēnî	zeh	pha'ămayim	'eth-b^{e}khōrāthî	lāqāch	w^{e}hinnēh	'attāh
Jacob	and he deceived me	there	two times	my birthright	he took	and behold	now

4089.111	1318	569.121	3940, 702.113	3937	1318
v Qal pf 3ms	n fs, ps 1cs	cj, v Qal impf 3ms	intrg part, neg part, v Qal pf 2ms	prep, ps 1cs	n fs
לָקָח	בִּרְכָתִי	וַיֹּאמַר	הֲלֹא־אָצַלְתָּ	לִּי	בְּרָכָה
lāqach	bir^{e}khāthî	wayyō'mar	hălō'-'ātsaltā	lî	b^{e}rākhāh
he took	my blessing	and he said	have you not reserved	for me	blessing

37.	6257.121	3437	569.121	3937, 6451	2075	1408	7947.115
	cj, v Qal impf 3ms	pn	cj, v Qal impf 3ms	prep, pn	intrj	n ms	v Qal pf 1cs, ps 3ms
	וַיַּעַן	יִצְחָק	וַיֹּאמֶר	לְעֵשָׂו	הֵן	גְּבִיר	שַׂמְתִּיו
	wayya'an	yitschāq	wayyōmer	l^e'ēsāw	hēn	g^{e}vîr	samtîw
	and he answered	Isaac	and he said	to Esau	behold	master	I put him

3937	881, 3725, 250	5598.115	3937	3937, 5860	1765	8822
prep, ps 2fs	cj, do, *adj*, n mp, ps 3ms	v Qal pf 1cs	prep, ps 3ms	prep, n mp	cj, n ms	cj, n ms
לָךְ	וְאֶת־כָּל־אֶחָיו	נָתַתִּי	לוֹ	לַעֲבָדִים	וְדָגָן	וְתִירשׁ
lākh	w^e'eth-kol-'echāyw	nāthattî	lô	la'ăvādhîm	w^{e}dhāghān	w^{e}thîrōsh
for you	and all his brothers	I have given	to him	slaves	and grain	and wine

5759.115	3937	660	4242	6449.125	1158	38.	569.121
v Qal pf 1cs, ps 3ms	cj, prep, ps 2ms	adv	intrg	v Qal impf 1cs	n ms, ps 1cs		cj, v Qal impf 3ms
סְמַכְתִּיו	וּלְכָה	אֵפוֹא	מָה	אֶעֱשֶׂה	בְּנִי		וַיֹּאמֶר
s^{e}makhtîw	ûlākhāh	'ēphô'	māh	'e'ĕseh	b^{e}nî		wayyō'mer
I have sustained him	and for you	then	what	I will do	my son		and he said

6451	420, 1	1318	259	2000, 3937	1	1313.331
pn	prep, n ms, ps 3ms	intrg part, n fs	num	dem pron, prep, ps 2ms	n ms, ps 1cs	v Piel impv 2ms, ps 1cs
עֵשָׂו	אֶל־אָבִיו	הַבְרָכָה	אַחַת	הִוא־לְךָ	אָבִי	בָּרְכֵנִי
'ēsāw	'el-'āvîw	havrākhāh	'achath	hiw'-l^{e}khā	'āvî	bār^{e}khēnî
Esau	to his father	is blessing	one	that to you	my father	bless me

1622, 603	1	5558.121	6451	7249	1098.121	39.	6257.121
cj, pers pron	n ms, ps 1cs	cj, v Qal impf 3ms	pn	n ms, ps 3ms	cj, v Qal impf 3ms		cj, v Qal impf 3ms
גַּם־אָנִי	אָבִי	וַיִּשָּׂא	עֵשָׂו	קֹלוֹ	וַיֵּבְךְּ		וַיַּעַן
gham-'ānî	'āvî	wayyissā'	'ēsāw	qōlô	wayyēv^{e}kh		wayya'an
also I	my father	and he lifted up	Esau	his voice	and he wept		and he answered

3437	1	569.121	420	2079	4623, 8468	800	2030.121
pn	n ms, ps	cj, v Qal impf 3ms	prep, ps 3ms	intrj	prep, *n mp*	art, n fs	v Qal impf 3ms
יִצְחָק	אָבִיו	וַיֹּאמֶר	אֵלָיו	הִנֵּה	מִשְׁמַנֵּי	הָאָרֶץ	יִהְיֶה
yitschāq	'āvîw	wayyō'mer	'ēlāv	hinnēh	mishmannê	hā'ārets	yihyeh
Isaac	his father	and he said	to him	behold	away from the fat of	the land	it will be

4319	4623, 3030	8452	4623, 6142	40.	6142, 2820	2513.123
n ms, ps 2ms	cj, prep, *n ms*	art, n md	prep, prep		cj, prep, n fs, ps 2ms	v Qal impf 2ms
מוֹשָׁבֶךָ	וּמִטַּל	הַשָּׁמַיִם	מֵעָל		וְעַל־חַרְבְּךָ	תִחְיֶה
môshāvekhā	ûmittal	hashshāmayim	mē'āl		w^e'al-charb^{e}khā	thichăyeh
your dwelling	and away from the dew of	the heavens	above		and with your sword	you will live

881, 250	5856.123	2030.111	3626, 866	7586.523	6811.113
cj, do, n ms, ps 2ms	v Qal impf 2ms	cj, v Qal perf 3ms	prep, rel part	v Hiphil impf 2ms	cj, v Qal pf 2ms
וְאֶת־אָחִיךָ	תַּעֲבֹד	וְהָיָה	כַּאֲשֶׁר	תָּרִיד	וּפָרַקְתָּ
w^e'eth-'āchîkhā	ta'ăvōdh	w^{e}hāyāh	ka'ăsher	tārîdh	ûphāraqŏttā
and your brother	you will serve	but it will be	when	you become restless	then you will pull off

NCB ... is it because he is named, *BB* ... was he not well-named, *Berkeley*.

for he hath supplanted me these two times: ... that he should cheat me twice, *Anchor* ... tricked me twice, *Fenton* ... got the better of me, *Goodspeed* ... twice now he has over-reached me, *Berkeley* ... take me by the heel, *Young*.

he took away my birthright: ... robbed me, *MLB* ... stole, *Goodspeed* ... my right as the first-born, *NEB*.

and, behold, now he hath taken away my blessing: ... gotten away with, *Anchor* ... stolen, *Goodspeed*.

And he said, Hast thou not reserved a blessing for me?: ... haven't you saved, *NAB* ... left for me, *Fenton* ... even one, *LIVB*.

37. And Isaac answered and said unto Esau, Behold, I have made him thy lord: ... I have already made him master over you, *Anchor* ... appointed him, *NAB* ... your ruler, *KJVII* ... a mighty one, *Young*.

and all his brethren have I given to him for servants: ... all his kinsmen his slaves, *Anchor* ... kinsfolk, *MLB* ... relatives, *NIV* ... under him, *REB*.

and with corn and wine have I sustained him: ... endowed him with increase and possession, *Fenton* ... braced him with new grain and wine, *Anchor* ... supplied him, *Darby* ... provided, *Berkeley* ... furnished, *Geneva*.

and what shall I do now unto thee, my son?: ... what then am I to do for you, *BB* ... where now, my son, is there anything I can do, *Fenton* ... now as for you then, *NASB* ... what is there left, *NEB* ... so what can I possibly, *NIV*.

38. And Esau said unto his father: ... pleaded with, *Berkeley* ... urged his father, *NAB*.

Hast thou but one blessing, my father?: ... have you just that one blessing, *Anchor* ... is that your only, *Berkeley* ... not one blessing, *LIVB*.

bless me, even me also, O my father: ... bless me, too, *Anchor* ... give a blessing to me, *BB*.

And Esau lifted up his voice, and wept: ... cried loudly, *Berkeley* ... was overcome with weeping, *BB* ... cried bitterly, *NEB* ... he began to cry, *Good News*.

39. And Isaac his father answered and said unto him: ... responded to him, *MLB* ... spoke up, *Anchor* ... complied, *Goodspeed* ... finally, Isaac spoke again, *NAB*.

Behold, thy dwelling shall be the fatness of the earth: ... home shall be far from the earth's riches, *Anchor* ... far from the fertile places, *BB* ... without the fruitfulness, *NCB* ... away from the fat of the earth, *Goodspeed*.

and of the dew of heaven from above: ... far from the dew of heaven on high, *BB* ... away from the dew, *Goodspeed* ... without the dew, *NCB*.

40. And by thy sword shalt thou live: ... you will sustain yourself by your sword, *Berkeley* ... will you get your living, *BB* ... by thy word, *Geneva* ... hew your way with your sword, *LIVB*.

and shalt serve thy brother: ... will be your brother's servant, *Geneva* ... brother's slave, *Good News*.

and it shall come to pass when thou shalt have the dominion: ... when you strenuously exert your power, *Berkeley* ... as you grow restive, *Anchor* ... when your power is increased, *BB* ... when thou shalt get the mastery, *Geneva* ... when thou rovest about, *Darby*.

---

through faith. Esau did not understand this, and asked whether Isaac had reserved a blessing for him.

27:37-38. Isaac reminded Esau of what was included in the blessing given to Jacob, and questioned whether there was anything else that could be given to Esau. But Esau kept insisting that there surely could be one blessing left for him, and again he wept loudly.

27:39-40. Isaac did not change his mind about giving Esau a blessing. Instead, he gave a prophecy. Esau would not participate in the blessing of the earth's richness and the dew of heaven as Jacob would. He would live away from fertile places. This implies he would live in a dry and barren land—as Edom on the whole actually was. He would live in continuous conflict, always having to defend himself. He, that is, his descendants in Edom would serve his brother, that is Israel. But the time would come when Edom would be restless and break free (see 1 Ki. 11:14-15; 2 Ki. 8:20-21). This prophecy of future freedom was in a sense a blessing, so that Heb. 11:20 could say "By faith Isaac blessed Jacob and Esau in regard to their future."

27:41. Esau could not forgive Jacob and his animosity grew until he began making threats (when among his friends) that as soon as Isaac died and the days of mourning were over, he would kill Jacob. He may have been a little self-righteous in thinking he would spare his father's feelings by waiting until after Isaac died.

6144	4263, 6142	6939		7929.121	6451	881, 3399
n ms, ps 3ms	prep, prep	n ms, ps 2ms	**41.**	cj, v Qal impf 3ms	pn	do, pn
עֻלּוֹ	מֵעַל	צַוָּארֶךָ		וַיִּשְׂטֹם	עֵשָׂו	אֶת־יַעֲקֹב
'ullô	mē'al	tsawwā'rekhā		wayyisṭōm	'ēsāw	'eth-ya'ăqōv
his yoke	from on	your neck		and he hated	Esau	Jacob

6142, 1318	866	1313.311	1	569.121	6451
prep, art, n fs	rel part	v Piel pf 3ms, ps 3ms	n ms, ps	cj, v Qal impf 3ms	pn
עַל־הַבְּרָכָה	אֲשֶׁר	בֵּרְכוֹ	אָבִיו	וַיֹּאמֶר	עֵשָׂו
'al-habb^{e}rākhāh	'ăsher	bēr^{e}khô	'āvîw	wayyō'mer	'ēsāw
concerning the blessing	which	he blessed him	his father	and he said	Esau

904, 3949	7414.126	3219	60	1	2103.125
prep, n ms, ps 3ms	v Qal impf 3mp	*n mp*	*n ms*	n ms, ps 1cs	cj, v Qal impf 1cs
בְּלִבּוֹ	יִקְרְבוּ	יְמֵי	אֵבֶל	אָבִי	וְאַהַרְגָה
b^{e}libbô	yiqŏr^{e}vû	y^{e}mê	'ēvel	'āvî	w^{e}'ahar^{e}ghāh
in his heart	they are approaching	the days of	the mourning rites of	my father	then I will kill

881, 3399	250		5222.621	3937, 7549	881, 1745	6451	1158
do, pn	n ms, ps 1cs	**42.**	cj, v Hophal impf 3ms	prep, pn	do, *n mp*	pn	n ms, ps 3fs
אֶת־יַעֲקֹב	אָחִי		וַיֻּגַּד	לְרִבְקָה	אֶת־דִּבְרֵי	עֵשָׂו	בְּנָהּ
'eth-ya'ăqōv	'āchî		wayyuggadh	l^{e}rivqāh	'eth-divrê	'ēsāw	b^{e}nāhh
Jacob	my brother		and it was told	to Rebekah	the words of	Esau	her son

1448	8365.122	7410.122	3937, 3399	1158	7278	569.122
art, adj	cj, v Qal impf 3fs	cj, v Qal impf 3fs	prep, pn	n ms, ps 3fs	art, adj	cj, v Qal impf 3fs
הַגָּדֹל	וַתִּשְׁלַח	וַתִּקְרָא	לְיַעֲקֹב	בְּנָהּ	הַקָּטָן	וַתֹּאמֶר
haggādhōl	wattishlach	wattiqŏrā'	l^{e}ya'ăqōv	b^{e}nāhh	haqqāṭān	wattō'mer
the older	so she sent	and she called	to Jacob	her son	the younger	and she said

420	2079	6451	250	5341.751	3937	3937, 2103.141
prep, ps 3ms	intrj	pn	n ms, ps 2ms	v Hithpael part ms	prep, ps 2ms	prep, v Qal inf con, ps 2ms
אֵלָיו	הִנֵּה	עֵשָׂו	אָחִיךָ	מִתְנַחֵם	לְךָ	לְהָרְגֶךָ
'ēlâv	hinnēh	'ēsāw	'āchîkhā	mithnachēm	l^{e}khā	l^{e}hār^{e}ghekhā
to him	behold	Esau	your brother	comforting himself	about you	to kill you

	6498	1158	8471.131	904, 7249	7251.131	1300.131, 3937
43.	cj, adv	n ms, ps 1cs	v Qal impv 2ms	prep, n ms, ps 1cs	cj, v Qal impv 2ms	v Qal impv 2ms, prep, ps 2ms
	וְעַתָּה	בְנִי	שְׁמַע	בְּקֹלִי	וְקוּם	בְּרַח־לְךָ
	w^{e}'attāh	v^{e}nî	sh^{e}ma'	b^{e}qōlî	w^{e}qûm	b^{e}rach-l^{e}khā
	and now	my son	listen	by my voice	and arise	flee for yourself

420, 3969	250	2877		3553.113	6196	3219	259	5912
prep, pn	n ms, ps 1cs	pn	**44.**	cj, v Qal pf 2ms	prep, ps 3ms	n mp	n mp	adv
אֶל־לָבָן	אָחִי	חָרָנָה		וְיָשַׁבְתָּ	עִמּוֹ	יָמִים	אֲחָדִים	עַד
'el-lāvān	'āchî	chārānāh		w^{e}yāshavtā	'immô	yāmîm	'ăchādhîm	'adh
to Laban	my brother	to Haran		and you will dwell	with him	days	ones	until

866, 8178.122	2635	250		5912, 8178.141	653, 250	4623
rel part, v Qal impf 3fs	*n fs*	n ms, ps 2ms	**45.**	adv, v Qal inf con	*n ms*, n ms, ps 2ms	prep, ps 2ms
אֲשֶׁר־תָּשׁוּב	חֲמַת	אָחִיךָ		עַד־שׁוּב	אַף־אָחִיךָ	מִמְּךָ
'ăsher-tāshûv	chămath	'āchîkhā		'adh-shûv	'aph-'āchîkhā	mimm^{e}khā
that it turns	the anger of	your brother		until turning	the anger of your brother	from you

8319.111	881	866, 6449.113	3937	8365.115	4089.115
cj, v Qal pf 3ms	do	rel part, v Qal pf 2ms	prep, ps 3ms	cj, v Qal pf 1cs	cj, v Qal pf 1cs, ps 2ms
וְשָׁכַח	אֵת	אֲשֶׁר־עָשִׂיתָ	לוֹ	וְשָׁלַחְתִּי	וּלְקַחְתִּיךָ
w^{e}shākhach	'ēth	'ăsher-'āsîthā	lô	w^{e}shālachtî	ûlăqachtîkhā
and he has forgotten		what you have done	to him	then I will send	and I will get you

4623, 8427 prep, adv מִשָּׁם mishshām from there	4066 intrg לָמָה lāmāh why	8323.125 v Qal impf 1cs אֶשְׁכַּל 'eshkal should I be bereaved	1612, 8530 cj, num pl, ps 2mp גַּם־שְׁנֵיכֶם gam-sh^{e}nêkhem also two of you	3219 n ms יוֹם yôm day	259 num אֶחָד 'echādh one	**46.**	569.122 cj, v Qal impf 3fs וַתֹּאמֶר wattō'mer and she said

7549 pn רִבְקָה rivqāh Rebekah	420, 3437 prep, pn אֶל־יִצְחָק 'el-yitschāq to Isaac	7258.115 v Qal pf 1cs קַצְתִּי qatstî I am disgusted	908, 2508 prep, n mp, ps 1cs בְחַיַּי v^{e}chayyay with my life	4623, 6681 prep, *n ms* מִפְּנֵי mipp^{e}nê because of	1351 *n fp* בְּנוֹת b^{e}nôth the daughters of	2953 pn חֵת chēth Heth	524, 4089.151 cj, v Qal act ptc ms אִם־לֹקֵחַ 'im-lōqēach if taking

that thou shalt break his yoke from off thy neck: ... throw off, *NAB* ... shake, *NCB* ... break away from his control, *Good News.*

41. And Esau hated Jacob: ... harbored a grudge, *Anchor* ... nurtured a grudge, *Berkeley* ... full of hate, *BB.*

because of the blessing wherewith his father blessed him: ... had bestowed on him, *Goodspeed* ... had given him, *NEB.*

and Esau said in his heart: ... said to himself, *Goodspeed* ... under his breath, *MLB* ... he thought, *Good News.*

The days of mourning for my father are at hand: ... days of weeping are near, *BB* ... is not far off, *Berkeley.*

then will I slay my brother Jacob: ... put to death, *BB* ... I will kill, *Anchor.*

42. And these words of Esau her elder son were told to Rebekah: ... sentiments reached Rebekah, *Berkeley* ... was informed of the designs, *Goodspeed* ... got news of, *NAB.*

and she sent and called Jacob her younger son, and said unto him, Behold, thy brother Esau, as touching thee, doth comfort himself purposing to kill thee: ... consoling himself, *Berkeley* ... threatening to take revenge, *Goodspeed* ... to settle accounts with you, *NAB* ... planning to get even, *Good News.*

43. Now therefore, my son, obey my voice: ... listen to my request, *Anchor* ... hearken to, *Young* ... do what I say, *NIV* ... listen to me, *REB.*

and arise, flee thou to Laban my brother to Haran: ... get ready, *Berkeley* ... go quickly, *BB* ... slip away at once, *NEB* ... be off, *REB.*

44. And tarry with him a few days: ... stay with him a while, *Anchor* ... some days, *Darby* ... a few days, *KJVII.*

until thy brother's fury turn away: ... anger subsided, *Anchor* ... blown over, *Berkeley* ... fierceness swaged, *Geneva* ... anger cools, *REB.*

45. Until thy brother's anger turn away from thee: ... he is no longer angry, *NIV* ... the rage of your brother against you has passed, *Fenton* ... wrath against you relents, *NCB* ... when it has died down, *REB.*

and he forget that which thou hast done to him: ... memory of what you have done to him is past, *BB.*

then I will send, and fetch thee from thence: ... send word, *BB* ... for you to bring you back, *Anchor.*

why should I be deprived also of you both in one day?: ... be taken from me, *BB* ... let me not be bereft, *Anchor* ... at the same time, *MLB* ... on the same day, *Goodspeed.*

27:42-45. When Rebekah heard about Esau's threats, she called Jacob in and told him how Esau was scheming revenge. She was afraid that if Esau killed Jacob, Esau would have to be put to death, so she would lose both her sons. So she commanded Jacob to flee for his life to her brother Laban in Haran and stay with him a few days until the heat of Esau's anger would subside. She thought time would heal Esau's wounds and he would forget. Then she would send for Jacob and she would enjoy having him home again. What she did not know was that she would die before Jacob returned.

Actually, all four who were involved in the schemes of this chapter suffered. Esau lost the blessing. Esau's delicious food never tasted good to Isaac again. Now that his spiritual eyes were opened, he never had the same fellowship with his favorite son Esau. Rebekah never saw her favorite son again. Jacob had to flee alone with nothing but what he could carry on his back. He would have to work hard, be deceived by his future father-in-law, and by his own sons.

27:46. To get Isaac to let Jacob go, Rebekah complained about Esau's Hittite wives and their disgusting behavior. This was a legitimate complaint, as Isaac well knew (26:35). If Jacob married a woman like them, Rebekah would be extremely disappointed with her life.

3399	828	4623, 1351, 2953	3626, 431	4623, 1351	800	4066
pn	n fs	prep, *n fp*, pn	prep, dem pron	prep, *n fp*	art, n fs	intrg
יַעֲקֹב	אִשָּׁה	מִבְּנוֹת־חֵת	כָּאֵלֶּה	מִבְּנוֹת	הָאָרֶץ	לָמָּה
ya'ăqōv	'ishshāh	mibbenôth-chēth	kā'ēlleh	mibbenôth	hā'ārets	lāmmāh
Jacob	wife	from the daughters of Heth	like these	from the daughters of	the land	what

3937	2508		7410.121	3437	420, 3399	1313.321	881
prep, ps 1cs	n mp	**28:1**	cj, v Qal impf 3ms	pn	prep, pn	cj, v Piel impf 3ms	do, ps 3ms
לִי	חַיִּים		וַיִּקְרָא	יִצְחָק	אֶל־יַעֲקֹב	וַיְבָרֶךְ	אֹתוֹ
lî	chayyîm		wayyiqrā'	yitschāq	'el-ya'ăqōv	wayevārekh	'ōthô
to me	life		and he called	Isaac	to Jacob	and he blessed	him

6943.321	569.121	3937	3940, 4089.123	828	4623, 1351
cj, v Piel impf 3ms, ps 3ms	cj, v Qal impf 3ms	prep, ps 3ms	neg part, v Qal impf 2ms	n fs	prep, *n fp*
וַיְצַוֵּהוּ	וַיֹּאמֶר	לוֹ	לֹא־תִקַּח	אִשָּׁה	מִבְּנוֹת
waytsawwēhû	wayyō'mer	lô	lō'-thiqqach	'ishshāh	mibbenôth
and he commanded him	and he said	to him	not you will take	wife	from the daughters of

3791		7251.131	2050.131	6549	782	904, 1041	1357	1
pn	**2.**	v Qal impv 2ms	v Qal impv 2ms	pn	pn	*n ms*	pn	*n ms*
כְּנָעַן		קוּם	לֵךְ	פַּדֶּנָה	אֲרָם	בֵּיתָה	בְתוּאֵל	אֲבִי
kenā'an		qûm	lēkh	paddenāh	'ărām	bêthāh	vethû'ēl	'ăvî
Canaan		rise	go	to Paddan	Aram	to the house of	Bethuel	the father of

525	4089.131, 3937	4623, 8427	828	4623, 1351	3969	250
n fs, ps 2ms	cj, v Qal impv 2ms, prep, ps 2ms	prep, adv	n fs	prep, *n fp*	pn	*n ms*
אִמֶּךָ	וְקַח־לְךָ	מִשָּׁם	אִשָּׁה	מִבְּנוֹת	לָבָן	אֲחִי
'immekhā	weqach-lekhā	mishshām	'ishshāh	mibbenôth	lāvān	'ăchî
your mother	and take for you	from there	wife	from the daughters of	Laban	the brother of

525		418	8163	1313.321	881	6759.521
n fs, ps 2ms	**3**	cj, n ms	pn	v Piel impf 3ms	do, ps 2ms	cj, v Hiphil impf 3ms, ps 2ms
אִמֶּךָ		וְאֵל	שַׁדַּי	יְבָרֵךְ	אֹתְךָ	וְיַפְרְךָ
'immekhā		we'ēl	shadday	yevārēkh	'ōthekhā	weyaphrekhā
your mother		and God	Almighty	He will bless	you	and He will make you fruitful

7528.521	2030.113	3937, 7235	6194		5598.121, 3937
cj, v Hiphil impf 3ms, ps 2ms	cj, v Qal pf 2ms	prep, *n ms*	n mp	**4.**	cj, v Qal impf 3ms, prep, ps 2ms
וְיַרְבֶּךָ	וְהָיִיתָ	לִקְהַל	עַמִּים		וְיִתֶּן־לְךָ
weyarbekhā	wehāyîthā	liqhal	'ammîm		weyitten-lekhā
and He will multiply you	and you will be	company of	peoples		and He will give to you

881, 1318	80	3937	3937, 2320	882	3937, 3542
do, *n fs*	pn	prep, ps 2ms	cj, prep, n ms, ps 2ms	prep, ps 2fs	prep, v Qal inf con, ps 2ms
אֶת־בִּרְכַּת	אַבְרָהָם	לְךָ	וּלְזַרְעֲךָ	אִתָּךְ	לְרִשְׁתְּךָ
'eth-birkath	'avrāhām	lekhā	ûlăzar'ăkhā	'ittākh	lerishtekhā
the blessing of	Abraham	to you	and to your seed	with you	for your taking possession of

881, 800	4175	866, 5598.111	435	3937, 80		8365.121	3437
do, *n fs*	n mp, ps 2ms	rel part, v Qal pf 3ms	n mp	prep, pn	**5.**	cj, v Qal impf 3ms	pn
אֶת־אֶרֶץ	מְגֻרֶיךָ	אֲשֶׁר־נָתַן	אֱלֹהִים	לְאַבְרָהָם		וַיִּשְׁלַח	יִצְחָק
'eth-'erets	meghurêkhā	'ăsher-nāthan	'ĕlōhîm	le'avrāhām		wayyishlach	yitschāq
the land of	your sojourning	which He gave	God	to Abraham		and he sent out	Isaac

881, 3399	2050.121	6549	782	420, 3969	1158, 1357	784
do, pn	cj, v Qal impf 3ms	pn	pn	prep, pn	*n ms*, pn	art, pn
אֶת־יַעֲקֹב	וַיֵּלֶךְ	פַּדֶּנָה	אֲרָם	אֶל־לָבָן	בֶּן־בְּתוּאֵל	הָאֲרַמִּי
'eth-ya'ăqōv	wayyēlekh	paddenāh	'ărām	'el-lāvān	ben-bethû'ēl	hā'ărammî
Jacob	and he went	to Paddan	Aram	to Laban	the son of Bethuel	the Aramean

46. And Rebekah said to Isaac: ... to Isaac Rebekah complained, *Berkeley.*

I am weary of my life because of the daughters of Heth: ... I am disgusted of life on account of the Hittite women, *Anchor* ... the presence of those Hittite women wears me down so, *Berkeley.*

if Jacob take a wife of the daughters of Heth: ... marries one of the Hittite girls, *Berkeley* ... marry a Hittite woman, *Anchor* ... from among the women of this land, *NIV.*

such as these which are of the daughters of the land: ... women of this land, *BB* ... such girls as they are, *Fenton* ... Hittite woman, *NCB.*

what good shall my life do me?: ... my life will not be worth living, *NIV* ... why should I live, *Fenton* ... what would life mean to me, *NCB* ... I might as well die, *Good News.*

28:1. And Isaac called Jacob, and blessed him, and charged him, and said unto him: ... sent for Jacob, greeted him, and enjoined him, *Anchor* ... commanded him, *Fenton* ... gave him instructions, *NEB.*

Thou shalt not take a wife of the daughters of Canaan: ... must not marry one of these women of Canaan, *NEB* ... you are not to marry a Canaanite woman, *Anchor.*

2. Arise, go to Padanaram, to the house of Bethuel thy mother's father: ... get ready, *Berkeley* ... go instead to Mesopotamia, *Good News.*

and take thee a wife from thence of the daughters of Laban thy mother's brother: ... choose there a wife for yourself from among the daughters of your uncle Laban, *Anchor* ... procure a wife, *Goodspeed* ... there find a wife, *NEB.*

3. And God Almighty bless thee: ... may El Shaddai, *Anchor* ... God all sufficient, *Geneva.*

and make thee fruitful, and multiply thee: ... make you prolific, *MLB* ... fertile and numerous, *Anchor* ... increase your descendants, *NEB* ... increase your numbers, *NIV.*

that thou mayest be a multitude of people: ... company of peoples, *ASV* ... assembly of tribes, *Anchor* ... association, *MLB* ... host of nations, *NEB* ... community, *NIV.*

4. And give thee the blessing of Abraham: ... extend to you, *Anchor* ... the blessing he bestowed on Abraham, *Berkeley* ... vouchsafed to Abraham, *Goodspeed.*

to thee, and to thy seed with thee: ... to you and your race with you, *Fenton* ... your offspring, *Anchor* ... your descendants, *NAB.*

that thou mayest inherit the land wherein thou art a stranger: ... of thy sojournings, *ASV* ... your wanderings, *BB* ... of your strangerhood, *Fenton* ... in which you are now only an immigrant, *Goodspeed* ... gain possession of the land where you are staying, *NAB.*

which God gave unto Abraham: ... land that God gave, *NRSV* ... which God assigned to, *REB.*

5. And Isaac sent away Jacob: and he went to Padanaram unto Laban, son of Bethuel the Syrian, the brother of Rebekah, Jacob's and Esau's mother: ... Bethuel the Aramaean, *Anchor.*

6. When Esau saw that Isaac had blessed Jacob, and sent him away to Padanaram: ... given Jacob his blessing, *BB* ... when Esau discovered, *Goodspeed* ... Esau noted, *NAB* ... learned, *NCB.*

to take him a wife from thence: ... to get a wife for himself there, *BB* ... to take himself a wife from there to comfort him, *Fenton* ... to marry there, *NCB.*

28:1-2. Isaac understood Rebekah's concern. So he called Jacob in, and of his own free will, proceeded to give him a better blessing than he gave before. With the blessing, he commanded him not to take a Canaanite wife. Jacob must go to Paddan Aram ("the field, plain, or garden of Aram," the same as Aram of the Two Rivers, see 24:10). There, from the household of Bethuel ("Dweller in God") he should take a daughter of Laban ("White") as his wife. Isaac recognized Rebekah as a good wife. Surely her brother's daughter would make a good wife for Jacob. Marrying cousins was common in those days. The Law of Moses did not prohibit it either (cf. Lev. 18:6-18). Today, however, this kind of family inbreeding is usually weakening and is probably not wise.

28:3-4. Isaac recognized that God Almighty would have to be the one who would bless Jacob. In contrast to the previous blessing (27:28-29), Isaac now looked for God to give Jacob the full salvation-blessing of Abraham, not only with respect to his posterity, but also with respect to the promised land. Isaac's faith was now renewed with respect to God's faithfulness to His promise, for he acknowledged Jacob as the rightful heir and expected that Jacob's descendants would be an assembly (religious congregation) of peoples and would possess the land. This must have encouraged Jacob to have a renewed faith in God.

28:5. Note in this formal report Rebekah is identified as the mother of Jacob and Esau. Jacob is mentioned first now because they acknowledge that

250	7549	525	3399	6451		7495.121	6451	3706, 1313.311
n ms	pn	*n fs*	pn	cj, pn	**6.**	cj, v Qal impf 3ms	pn	cj, v Piel pf 3ms
אֲחִי	רִבְקָה	אֵם	יַעֲקֹב	וְעֵשָׂו		וַיַּרְא	עֵשָׂו	כִּי־בֵרַךְ
'ăchî	rivqāh	'ēm	ya'ăqōv	we'ēsāw		wayyare'	'ēsāw	kî-vērakh
the brother of	Rebekah	the mother of	Jacob	and Esau		and he saw	Esau	that he blessed

3437	881, 3399	8365.311	881	6549	782	3937, 4089.141, 3937
pn	do, pn	cj, v Piel pf 3ms	do, ps 3ms	pn	pn	prep, v Qal inf con, prep, ps 3ms
יִצְחָק	אֶת־יַעֲקֹב	וְשִׁלַּח	אֹתוֹ	פַּדֶּנָה	אֲרָם	לָקַחַת־לוֹ
yitschāq	'eth-ya'ăqōv	weshillach	'ōthô	paddenāh	'ărām	lāqachath-lô
Isaac	Jacob	and he sent	him	to Paddan	Aram	to take for him

4623, 8427	828	904, 1313.341	881	6943.321	6142	3937, 569.141
prep, adv	n fs	prep, v Piel inf con, 3ms	do, ps 3ms	cj, v Piel impf 3ms	prep, ps 3ms	prep, v Qal inf con
מִשָּׁם	אִשָּׁה	בְּבָרְכוֹ	אֹתוֹ	וַיְצַו	עָלָיו	לֵאמֹר
mishshām	'ishshāh	bevārekhô	'ōthô	waytsaw	'ālâv	lē'mōr
from there	wife	with his blessing	him	and he commanded	him	saying

3940, 4089.123	828	4623, 1351	3791		8471.121	3399	420, 1
neg part, v Qal impf 2ms	n fs	prep, *n fp*	pn	**7.**	cj, v Qal impf 3ms	pn	prep, n ms, ps 3ms
לֹא־תִקַּח	אִשָּׁה	מִבְּנוֹת	כְּנָעַן		וַיִּשְׁמַע	יַעֲקֹב	אֶל־אָבִיו
lō'-thiqqach	'ishshāh	mibbenôth	kenā'an		wayyishma'	ya'ăqōv	'el-'āvîw
not you will take	wife	from the daughters of	Canaan		and he listened	Jacob	to his father

420, 525	2050.121	6549	782		7495.121	6451	3706	7737
cj, prep, n fs, ps 3ms	cj, v Qal impf 3ms	pn	pn	**8.**	cj, v Qal impf 3ms	pn	cj	adj
וְאֶל־אִמּוֹ	וַיֵּלֶךְ	פַּדֶּנָה	אֲרָם		וַיַּרְא	עֵשָׂו	כִּי	רָעוֹת
we'el-'immô	wayyēlekh	paddenāh	'ărām		wayyar'	'ēsāw	kî	rā'ôth
and to his mother	and he went	to Paddan	Aram		and he saw	Esau	that	evil

1351	3791	904, 6084	3437	1		2050.121	6451	420, 3579
n fp	pn	prep, *n fp*	pn	n ms, ps	**9.**	cj, v Qal impf 3ms	pn	prep, pn
בְּנוֹת	כְּנָעַן	בְּעֵינֵי	יִצְחָק	אָבִיו		וַיֵּלֶךְ	עֵשָׂו	אֶל־יִשְׁמָעֵאל
benôth	kenā'an	be'ênê	yitschāq	'āvîw		wayyēlekh	'ēsāw	'el-yishmā'ē'l
the daughters of	Canaan	in the eyes of	Isaac	his father		so he went	Esau	to Ishmael

4089.121	881, 4395	1351, 3579	1158, 80	269	5207
cj, v Qal impf 3ms	do, pn	*n fs*, pn	*n ms*, pn	*n fs*	pn
וַיִּקַּח	אֶת־מָחֲלַת	בַּת־יִשְׁמָעֵאל	בֶּן־אַבְרָהָם	אֲחוֹת	נְבָיוֹת
wayyiqqach	'eth-māchălath	bath-yishmā'ē'l	ben-'avrāhām	'ăchôth	nevāyôth
and he took	Mahalath	the daughter of Ishmael	the son of Abraham	the sister of	Nebaioth

6142, 5571	3937	3937, 828		3428.121	3399	4623, 916	916
prep, n fp, ps 3ms	prep, ps 3ms	prep, n fs	**10.**	cj, v Qal impf 3ms	pn	prep, pn	pr noun
עַל־נָשָׁיו	לוֹ	לְאִשָּׁה		וַיֵּצֵא	יַעֲקֹב	מִבְּאֵר	שָׁבַע
'al-nāshâv	lô	le'ishshāh		wayyētsē'	ya'ăqōv	mibbe'ēr	shāva'
beside his wives	to him	for a wife		and he went out	Jacob	from Beer	Sheba

2050.121	2877		6534.121	904, 4887	4053.121	8427
cj, v Qal impf 3ms	pn	**11.**	cj, v Qal impf 3ms	prep, art, n ms	cj, v Qal impf 3ms	adv
וַיֵּלֶךְ	חָרָנָה		וַיִּפְגַּע	בַּמָּקוֹם	וַיָּלֶן	שָׁם
wayyēlekh	chārānāh		wayyiphga'	bammāqôm	wayyālen	shām
and he went	to Haran		and he reached	the place	and he spent the night	there

3706, 971.111	8507	4089.121	4623, 63	4887	7947.121	4924
cj, v Qal pf 3ms	art, n ms	cj, v Qal impf 3ms	prep, *n fp*	art, n ms	cj, v Qal impf 3ms	n fp, ps 3ms
כִּי־בָא	הַשֶּׁמֶשׁ	וַיִּקַּח	מֵאַבְנֵי	הַמָּקוֹם	וַיָּשֶׂם	מְרַאֲשֹׁתָיו
kî-vā'	hashshemesh	wayyiqqach	mē'avnê	hammāqôm	wayyāsem	mera'ăshōthâv
because it set	the sun	and he took	from the stones of	the place	and he put	his pillow

and that as he blessed him he gave him a charge, saying: ... had ordered him saying, *Fenton* ... gave him a command, *KJVII* ... he had forbidden him, *NEB.*

Thou shalt not take a wife of the daughters of Canaan: ... you shall not marry a Canaanite woman, *Anchor* ... the girls of Canan, *Fenton.*

7. And that Jacob obeyed his father and his mother, and was gone to Padanaram: ... Jacob had done as his father and mother said, *BB* ... had listened to the voice of his father and mother, *Fenton* ... departed for Phaddam-Aram in obedience, *NCB* ... hearkeneth unto his father, *Young.*

8. And Esau seeing that the daughters of Canaan pleased not Isaac his father: ... daughters of Canaan are evil in the eyes, *Young* ... Isaac disliked Canaanite women, *Goodspeed* ... did not approve of, *Good News* ... realized how much the Canaanite women displeased his father, *Anchor.*

9. Then went Esau unto Ishmael, and took unto the wives which he had: ... besides the wives that he had, *ASV* ... in addition to the wives he had, *Anchor.*

Mahalath the daughter of Ishmael Abraham's son, the sister of Nebajoth, to be his wife: ... took to wife, *Anchor* ... married Mahalath, *NIV* ... to be his wife, *NRSV* ... married two additional wives, *LIVB.*

10. And Jacob went out from Beersheba, and went toward Haran: ... as he traveled toward Haran, *MLB* ... set out for Haran, *Anchor* ... set out from the Well of the Oath, *Fenton* ... proceeded toward Haran, *NAB.*

11. And he lighted upon a certain place: ... a certain place, *BB* ... arrived at a place, *Fenton* ... reaching a certain sanctuary, *Goodspeed* ... came upon a certain shrine, *NAB.*

and tarried there all night: ... stopped there for the night, *NAB* ... spent the night, *NASB* ... and lodged there, *Darby* ... made it his resting-place for the night, *BB.*

because the sun was set; and he took of the stones of that place: ... took one of the stones, *ASV* ... resting his head on a stone, *Good News.*

and put them for his pillows: ... put it under his head, *ASV* ... made pillows, *KJVII* ... found a rock for a headrest, *LIVB* ... made it a pillow for his head, *NEB.*

and lay down in that place to sleep: ... lay down on that spot, *Anchor* ... lay down in that sanctuary, *Goodspeed* ... went to sleep there, *NCB.*

---

the birthright is his. This verse emphasizes the importance of Jacob's going to Paddan-Aram to Laban. Because he would be outside the promised land he would have to trust God to bring him back and give him and his descendants the promised salvation-blessing and the promised land. He would also have to learn the hard way that he did not deserve God's blessings and that they were his by God's pure grace.

28:6-9. When Esau learn of Jacob's departure, he finally realized how displeasing his Hittite-Canaanite wives were to Isaac. Apparently, he had not known how they acted toward Isaac and Rebekah when he was not around (which was all too often). But he did understand the real problem their Canaanite ways caused. He thought it was because they were not relatives. Since Jacob was sent to get a wife from a relative, Esau jumped to the conclusion that he could please his father by marrying a relative. Perhaps he also thought this would bring a blessing from Isaac. Esau never did see the spiritual issues involved, nor his own spiritual lack. So he went to Ishmael's home or family (Ishmael himself had been dead about 14 years) and married Mahalath ("sickness," also called Basemath, "fragrance," in Gen. 36:3), a daughter of Ishmael and his Egyptian wife. This, we can be sure, only compounded the problem. It shows also that Esau had no spiritual perception and did not realize that Ishmael had been dropped from the chosen line (the line that would bring redemption through Christ).

28:10. This verse introduces a new section dealing with Jacob' journey of about 465 miles to Haran and the events there. It was a hard journey, yet he was willing to leave all the material blessings behind in order to find a wife who would be pleasing to his parents and to God. God, however, would take Jacob through many lessons to get him to understand the ways of the LORD. God did not give up on him, for Jacob had a desire, a hope, and a faith in God's promise that meant God could work on him and change him.

28:11. Bethel is about 60 or 70 miles by road from Beersheba, over rough, mountainous country. Thus, it is probable that Jacob came to this place on the third night after leaving home. Traveling alone, he was used to sleeping on the ground. All that area is limestone country, so there were plenty of stones in the field. He used one of them as a pillow

8311.121	904, 4887	2000	**12.**	2593.121	2079	5746
cj, v Qal impf 3ms	prep, art, n ms	art, dem pron		cj, v Qal impf 3ms	cj, intrj	n ms
וַיִּשְׁכַּב	בַּמָּקוֹם	הַהוּא		וַיַּחֲלֹם	וְהִנֵּה	סֻלָּם
wayyishkav	bammāqôm	hahû'		wayyachlōm	wehinnēh	sullām
and he lay down	in the place	the that		and he dreamed	and behold	ladder

5507.655	800	7513	5236.551	8452	2079	4534
v Hophal part ms	n fs	cj, n ms, ps 3ms	v Hiphil ptc ms	art, n mp	cj, intrj	*n mp*
מֻצָּב	אַרְצָה	וְרֹאשׁוֹ	מַגִּיעַ	הַשָּׁמָיְמָה	וְהִנֵּה	מַלְאֲכֵי
mutstsāv	'artsāh	werō'shô	maggîa'	hashshāmāyemāh	wehinnēh	mal'ăkhê
it was set up	to the earth	and its top	reaching	to the heavens	and behold	the angels of

435	6148.152	3495.152	904	**13.**	2079	3176	5507.255	6142
n mp	v Qal act part mp	cj, v Qal act part mp	prep, ps 3ms		cj, intrj	pn	v Niphal ptc ms	prep, ps 3ms
אֱלֹהִים	עֹלִים	וְיֹרְדִים	בּוֹ		וְהִנֵּה	יְהוָה	נִצָּב	עָלָיו
'ĕlōhîm	'ōlîm	weyōredhîm	bô		wehinnēh	yehwāh	nitstsāv	'ālâv
God	going up	and going down	on it		and behold	Yahweh	standing	above it

569.121	603	3176	435	80	1	435	3437
cj, v Qal impf 3ms	pers pron	pn	n mp	pn	n ms, ps 2ms	cj, *n mp*	pn
וַיֹּאמַר	אֲנִי	יְהוָה	אֱלֹהֵי	אַבְרָהָם	אָבִיךָ	וֵאלֹהֵי	יִצְחָק
wayyō'mar	'ănî	yehwāh	'ĕlōhê	'avrāhām	'āvîkhā	wē'lōhê	yitschāq
and He said	I	Yahweh	the God of	Abraham	your father	and the God of	Isaac

800	866	887	8311.151	6142	3937	5598.125	3937, 2320
art, n fs	rel part	pers pron	v Qal act ptc ms	prep, ps 3fs	prep, ps 2ms	v Qal impf 1cs, ps 3fs	cj, prep, n ms, ps 2ms
הָאָרֶץ	אֲשֶׁר	אַתָּה	שֹׁכֵב	עָלֶיהָ	לְךָ	אֶתְּנֶנָּה	וּלְזַרְעֶךָ
hā'ārets	'ăsher	'attāh	shōchēv	'ālêhā	lekhā	'etennennāh	ûlazar'ekhā
the land	which	you	lying	on	to you	I will give it	and to your seed

14.	2030.111	2320	3626, 6312	800	6805.113	3328
	cj, v Qal pf 3ms	n ms, ps 2ms	prep, *n ms*	art, n fs	cj, v Qal pf 2ms	n ms
	וְהָיָה	זַרְעֲךָ	כַּעֲפַר	הָאָרֶץ	וּפָרַצְתָּ	יָמָּה
	wehāyāh	zar'ăkhā	ka'ăphar	hā'ārets	ûphāratstā	yāmmāh
	and it will be	your seed	like the dust of	the earth	and you will overflow	westward

7209	7103	5221	1313.216	904	3725, 5121
cj, n ms	cj, n fs	cj, n ms	cj, v Niphal pf 3cp	prep, ps 2ms	*adj, n fp*
וָקֵדְמָה	וְצָפֹנָה	וָנֶגְבָּה	וְנִבְרְכוּ	בְךָ	כָּל־מִשְׁפְּחֹת
wāqēdhemāh	wetsāphōnāh	wāneghbāh	wenivrekhû	vekhā	kol-mishpechōth
and eastward	and northward	and southward	and they will be blessed	in you	all the families of

124	904, 2320	**15.**	2079	609	6196	8490.115	904, 3725
art, n fs	cj, prep, n ms, ps 2ms		cj, intrj	pers pron	prep, ps 2fs	cj, v Qal pf 1cs, ps 2ms	prep, adj
הָאֲדָמָה	וּבְזַרְעֶךָ		וְהִנֵּה	אָנֹכִי	עִמָּךְ	וּשְׁמַרְתִּיךָ	בְּכֹל
hā'ădhāmāh	ûvezar'ekhā		wehinnēh	'ānōkhî	'immāk	ûshemartîkhā	bekhōl
the earth	and in your seed		and behold	I	with you	and I will protect you	in all

866, 2050.123	8178.515	420, 124	2148	3706	3940
rel part, v Qal impf 2ms	cj, v Hiphil pf 1cs, ps 2ms	prep, art, n fs	art, dem pron	cj	neg part
אֲשֶׁר־תֵּלֵךְ	וַהֲשִׁבֹתִיךָ	אֶל־הָאֲדָמָה	הַזֹּאת	כִּי	לֹא
'ăsher-tēlēkh	wahashivōthîkhā	'el-hā'ădhāmāh	hazzō'th	kî	lō'
where you will go	and I will bring you back	to the land	the this	because	not

6321.125	5912	866	524, 6449.115	881	866, 1744.315	3937
v Qal impf 1cs, ps 2ms	adv	rel part	cj, v Qal pf 1cs	do	rel part, v Piel pf 1cs	prep, ps 2fs
אֶעֱזָבְךָ	עַד	אֲשֶׁר	אִם־עָשִׂיתִי	אֵת	אֲשֶׁר־דִּבַּרְתִּי	לָךְ
'e'ĕzāvekhā	'adh	'ăsher	'im-'āshîthî	'ēth	'ăsher-dibbartî	lākh
I will leave you	until	that	when I have done		what I have spoken	to you

12. And he dreamed, and behold a ladder set up on the earth: ... foot standing on the ground, *Fenton* ... he saw steps stretching from earth to heaven, *BB* ... stairway rested on the ground, *NAB* ... dreamt that he saw a ladder, *NEB.*

and the top of it reached to heaven: ... reaching to the sky, *Anchor* ... head reaching to the heavens, *Fenton.*

And behold the angels of God ascending and descending on it: ... messengers of God, *Young* ... going up and down on it, *Anchor.*

13. And, behold, the LORD stood above it, and said, I am the LORD God of Abraham thy father, and the God of Isaac: ... Jehovah stood above it, *ASV* ... he saw the Lord by his side, *BB* ... Lord stood over him, *Goodspeed* ... standing beside him, *NAB* ... Jehovah is standing upon it, *Young.*

the land whereon thou liest, to thee will I give it, and to thy seed: ... ground on which you are resting, *Anchor* ... land on which you are sleeping, *BB* ... which you now lie upon, *Fenton* ... your offspring, *NRSV* ... your race, *Fenton.*

14. And thy seed shall be as the dust of the earth: ... as numerous as the specks of dust, *Good News* ... plentiful as the dust, *NAB* ... countless as the dust, *NEB.*

and thou shalt spread abroad to the west, and to the east, and to the north, and to the south: ... west and east, north and south, *Fenton* ... you will enlarge westward and eastward, northward and southward, *Berkeley* ... covering all the land, *BB* ... extend their territory in all directions, *Good News* ... shall spread, *Goodspeed.*

and in thee and in thy seed shall all the families of the earth be blessed: ... communities of the earth shall bless themselves by you, *Anchor* ... will be a name of blessing, *BB* ... nations of the world shall be benefited by you and your heir, *Fenton* ... all races of the earth will invoke blessings on one another, *Goodspeed* ... pray to be blessed as you are blessed, *NEB.*

15. And, behold, I am with thee, and will keep thee in all places whither thou goest: ... be assured also that I am with you, *Fenton* ... whithersoever thou goest, *ASV* ... protect you wherever you go, *NCB* ... watch over you, *MLB* ... guard you, *Fenton.*

and will bring thee again into this land: ... bring you back to this country, *Berkeley* ... guiding you back again, *BB* ... give you a quiet return to this country, *Fenton* ... have caused thee to turn back unto this ground, *Young.*

for I will not leave thee, until I have done that which I have spoken to thee of: ... I shall not forsake you, *Berkeley* ... not give you up, *BB* ... everything I have mentioned to you, *MLB* ... accomplished what I have promised to you, *Fenton* ... till I fulfill my promise, *NCB.*

("head-place") and fell asleep, no doubt feeling alone and forsaken, having left everything he held dear behind. He may have been feeling at this point that "the way of the transgressor is hard" (Cf. Proverbs 13:5.)

28:12. In a dream Jacob saw a broad, high staircase (more likely than a ladder with rungs) reaching up to heaven. Many angels were on the staircase, some ascending and others descending at the same time. The word angel means "messenger," so the fact they were both ascending and descending meant uninterrupted, continuous communication with God was available. They were first ascending, coming to God from Jacob. Thus, they had been with Jacob even though he did not know it. Then they were descending. God wanted to give His message to Jacob. Jacob had to flee from home, but he was not leaving the God of Abraham and Isaac behind. God was concerned over him and was still accessible. Jesus used this as an illustration of the fact that we have access to God through Him (John 1:51; cf. John 14:6; Acts 4:12). He is the one Mediator between God and humankind (1 Tim. 2:5), and through Him heaven is always standing open to us.

28:13-14. At the top of the staircase the LORD took a stand to reveal His purpose. After declaring who He is, He confirmed the promise of the land, the multiplied offspring, and the salvation-blessing to all the families on earth, just as He had to Abraham and to Isaac. Jacob indeed was the next in the chosen line. His offspring would break out like an overflowing flood, bursting through all barriers and spreading out in all directions.

28:15. God further promised He would be with Jacob, protecting him wherever he might go. This was a great encouragement. The pagans looked at their gods as having power in certain localities. The true God is over all. God also promised to bring him back to the promised land. Jacob could be sure God would never leave him or forsake him until the promise was fulfilled. Thus God declared His faithfulness (cf. Heb. 13:5). With heaven open, this also implied forgiveness. Jesus alone is the ladder that

16.	3477.121	3399	4623, 8524	569.121	409	3552	3176
	cj, v Qal impf 3ms	pn	prep, n fs, ps 3ms	cj, v Qal impf 3ms	intrj	sub	pn
	וַיִּיקַץ	יַעֲקֹב	מִשְּׁנָתוֹ	וַיֹּאמֶר	אָכֵן	יֵשׁ	יְהוָה
	wayyîqats	ya'ăqōv	mishshenāthô	wayyō'mer	'ākhēn	yēsh	yehwāh
	and he woke up	Jacob	from his sleep	and he said	truly	He is	Yahweh

904, 4887	2172	609	3940	3156.115	17.	3486.121	569.121
prep, art, n ms	art, dem pron	cj, pers pron	neg part	v Qal pf 1cs		cj, v Qal impf 3ms	cj, v Qal impf 3ms
בַּמָּקוֹם	הַזֶּה	וְאָנֹכִי	לֹא	יָדָעְתִּי		וַיִּירָא	וַיֹּאמַר
bammāqôm	hazzeh	we'ānōkhî	lō'	yādhā'ättî		wayyîrā'	wayyō'mar
in the place	the this	and I	not	I knew		and he was afraid	and he said

4242, 3486.255	4887	2172	375	2172	3706	524, 1041	435
intrg, v Niphal ptc ms	art, n ms	art, dem pron	*sub*	dem pron	cj	cj, *n fs*	n mp
מַה־נּוֹרָא	הַמָּקוֹם	הַזֶּה	אֵין	זֶה	כִּי	אִם־בֵּית	אֱלֹהִים
mah-nôrā'	hammāqôm	hazzeh	'ên	zeh	kî	'im-bêth	'ĕlōhîm
what a awesome thing	the place	the this	nothing	this	that	than the house of	God

2172	8554	8452	18.	8326.521	3399	904, 1269	4089.121
cj, dem pron	*n ms*	art, n md		cj, v Hiphil impf 3ms	pn	prep, art, n ms	cj, v Qal impf 3ms
וְזֶה	שַׁעַר	הַשָּׁמָיִם		וַיַּשְׁכֵּם	יַעֲקֹב	בַּבֹּקֶר	וַיִּקַּח
wezeh	sha'ar	hashshāmāyim		wayyashkēm	ya'ăqōv	babbōqer	wayyiqqach
and this	the gate of	the heavens		and he rose early	Jacob	in the morning	and he took

881, 63	866, 7947.111	4924	7947.121	881	4838	3441.121	8467
do, art, n fs	rel part, v Qal pf 3ms	n fp, ps 3ms	cj, v Qal impf 3ms	do, ps 3fs	n fs	cj, v Qal impf 3ms	n ms
אֶת־הָאֶבֶן	אֲשֶׁר־שָׂם	מְרַאֲשֹׁתָיו	וַיָּשֶׂם	אֹתָהּ	מַצֵּבָה	וַיִּצֹק	שֶׁמֶן
'eth-hā'even	'ăsher-shām	mera'ăshōthāv	wayyāsem	'ōthāhh	matstsēvāh	wayyitsōq	shemen
the stone	which he put	his pillow	and he set	it	memorial	and he poured	olive oil

6142, 7513	19.	7410.121	881, 8428, 4887	2000	1044	195	4007
prep, n ms, ps 3fs		cj, v Qal impf 3ms	do, *n ms*, art, n ms	art, dem pron	pn	cj, cj	pn
עַל־רֹאשָׁהּ		וַיִּקְרָא	אֶת־שֵׁם־הַמָּקוֹם	הַהוּא	בֵּית־אֵל	וְאוּלָם	לוּז
'al-rō'shāhh		wayyiqōrā'	'eth-shēm-hammāqôm	hahû'	bêth-'ēl	we'ûlām	lûz
on its top		and he called	the name of the place	the that	Bethel	and however	Luz

8428, 6111	3937, 7518	20.	5265.121	3399	5266	3937, 569.141	524, 2030.121
n ms, art, n fs	prep, art, adj		v Qal impf 3ms	pn	n ms	prep, v Qal inf con	cj, v Qal impf 3ms
שֵׁם־הָעִיר	לָרִאשֹׁנָה		וַיִּדַּר	יַעֲקֹב	נֶדֶר	לֵאמֹר	אִם־יִהְיֶה
shēm-hā'îr	lāri'shōnāh		wayyiddar	ya'ăqōv	nedher	lē'mōr	'im-yihyeh
the name of the city	at the first		and he made a vow	Jacob	vow	saying	if he will be

435	6200	8490.111	904, 1932	2172	866	609	2050.151
n mp	prep, ps 1cs	cj, v Qal pf 3ms, ps 1cs	prep, art, n ms	art, dem pron	rel part	pers pron	v Qal act ptc ms
אֱלֹהִים	עִמָּדִי	וּשְׁמָרַנִי	בַּדֶּרֶךְ	הַזֶּה	אֲשֶׁר	אָנֹכִי	הוֹלֵךְ
'ĕlōhîm	'immādhî	ûshemāranî	badderekh	hazzeh	'ăsher	'ānōkhî	hôlēkh
God	with me	and he will protect me	on the journey	the this	which	I	going

5598.111, 3937	4035	3937, 404	933	3937, 3980.141	21.	8178.115
cj, v Qal pf 3ms, prep, ps 1cs	n ms	prep, v Qal inf con	cj, n ms	prep, v Qal inf con		cj, v Qal pf 1cs
וְנָתַן־לִי	לֶחֶם	לֶאֱכֹל	וּבֶגֶד	לִלְבֹּשׁ		וְשַׁבְתִּי
wenāthan-lî	lechem	le'ĕkhōl	ûveghedh	lilbōsh		weshavtî
and he will give to me	bread	to eat	and clothes	to wear		then I will return

904, 8361	420, 1041	1	2030.111	3176	3937	3937, 435	22.	63
prep, n ms	prep, *n ms*	n ms, ps 1cs	cj, v Qal pf 3ms	pn	prep, ps 1cs	prep n mp		cj, art, n fs
בְשָׁלוֹם	אֶל־בֵּית	אָבִי	וְהָיָה	יְהוָה	לִי	לֵאלֹהִים		וְהָאֶבֶן
veshālôm	'el-bêth	'āvî	wehāyāh	yehwāh	lî	lē'lōhîm		wehā'even
in peace	to the house of	my father	and He will be	Yahweh	to me	God		and the stone

16. And Jacob awaked out of his sleep: ... when Jacob awoke, *MLB.*

and he said, Surely the LORD is in this place; and I knew it not: ... abides in this site, but I was not aware, *Anchor* ... I was not conscious of it, *BB.*

17. And he was afraid, and said: ... reverently he continued, *NCB* ... in solemn wonder he cried out, *NAB* ... he exclaimed in terror, *LIVB* ... he was awe-struck, *Goodspeed* ... shaken, he exclaimed, *Anchor.*

How dreadful is this place: ... how awesome is this place, *NASB* ... this is a holy place, *BB* ... how fearful, *Geneva.*

this is none other but the house of God, and this is the gate of heaven: ... the abode of God, and that is the gateway to heaven, *Anchor* ... entrance, *LIVB* ... doorway, *BB* ... gate of the sky, *Goodspeed.*

18. And Jacob rose up early in the morning, and took the stone that he had put for his pillows: ... put under his head, *ASV* ... on which he had laid his head, *NEB.*

and set it up for a pillar: ... for a memorial pillar, *Berkeley* ... a memorial stone, *NAB* ... as a sacred pillar, *NEB* ... standing pillar, *Young.*

and poured oil upon the top of it: ... on its top, *Anchor* ... put oil, *BB* ... poured olive oil on it, *Good News.*

19. And he called the name of that place Beth-el: ... gave that place the name, *BB* ... named that site, *Anchor* ... God's House, *Fenton* ... name of that sanctuary, *Goodspeed.*

but the name of that city was called Luz at the first: ... former name of that town had been Luz, *Anchor* ... previously called Luz, *Berkeley* ... Andam-loz was its former name, *Fenton* ... earlier name, *NEB.*

20. And Jacob vowed a vow, saying: ... took an oath, *BB* ... made a vow, *NIV.*

If God will be with me, and will keep me in this way that I go: ... remains with me, protecting me on this journey, *NAB* ... accompanies me, and watches over me, *Berkeley* ... keep me safe, *BB* ... guard me in the way that I now go, *Fenton.*

and will give me bread to eat, and raiment to put on: ... food to eat and clothes to wear, *Berkeley* ... garment to put on, *BB.*

21. So that I come again to my father's house in peace: ... come home safely, *Goodspeed* ... return to my father's house in safety, *NASB* ... safe return, *NCB.*

then shall the LORD be my God: ... then I will take the Lord to be my God, *BB.*

22. And this stone, which I have set for a pillar: ... erected for a memorial pillar, *Berkeley* ... set up as a sacred pillar, *Goodspeed* ... as a memorial stone, *NAB.*

shall be God's house: ... House of God, *Fenton* ... God's abode, *Anchor* ... will be the place that you are worshipped, *Good News.*

and of all that thou shalt give me I will surely give the tenth unto thee: ... without fail allot a tenth part, *NEB* ... give to thee a portion of everything, *Goodspeed* ... will without fail give thee a tithe, *Berkeley* ... always set aside a tenth, *Anchor.*

---

ascends into heaven (John 3:13). Through Him alone do we have access to the Father and forgiveness (John 14:6).

28:16-17. When Jacob awoke he was overwhelmed with holy awe and reverence. When he went to sleep, he had no idea that the LORD would reveal himself by His covenant-keeping name of Yahweh there. Now he felt that the place was awesome, awe-inspiring, the house of God, the very gate of heaven. He still sensed the presence of God and recognized that God had given him access to heaven there. For us every place is the gate of heaven. God is always accessible to us through our Lord Jesus Christ (John 1:51).

28:18. Jacob took the ordinary piece of limestone that was his pillow and set it up as monument, a memorial to mark the spot where God appeared to him, and probably as a pledge of a future altar. (Some have tried to identify Jacob's pillow with the stone of Scone under the throne where British sovereigns are crowned, however the stone of Scone is Scottish sandstone, and all the stone around Bethel are limestone.) Jacob had no animals with him that he could offer as a sacrifice. But, as was the custom, he carried oil for cooking and for anointing his face. He took oil and poured it on the stone as a form of offering and as a symbol of his dedication, consecration, and gratitude to the LORD as well as a recognition of the grace that God had promised.

28:19. Jacob called the place Bethel, "House of God," though the nearby city was called Luz, "almond tree." It is about 10 miles north of Jerusalem.

28:20-22. Jacob's vow is not a bargain with God here. God had already promised to be with him and bring him back. "If" can mean "truly," or "since." Jacob by this spontaneous vow expressed gratitude, faith, and confidence, not doubt, as he

2148	866, 7947.115	4838	2030.121	1041	435	3725	866
art, dem pron	rel part, v Qal pf 1cs	n fs	v Qal impf 3ms	n ms	n mp	cj, adj	rel part
הַזֹּאת	אֲשֶׁר־שַׂמְתִּי	מַצֵּבָה	יִהְיֶה	בֵּית	אֱלֹהִים	וְכֹל	אֲשֶׁר
hazzō'th	'ăsher-samtî	matstsēvāh	yihyeh	bêth	'ĕlōhîm	wekhōl	'ăsher
the this	which I have set	memorial	it will be	the house of	God	and all	which

5598.123, 3937	6458.342	6458.325	3937		5558.121
v Qal impf 2ms, prep, ps 1cs	v Piel inf abs	v Piel impf 1cs, ps 3ms	prep, ps 2fs	**29:1**	cj, v Qal impf 3ms
תִּתֶּן־לִי	עַשֵּׂר	אֲעַשְּׂרֶנּוּ	לָךְ		וַיִּשָּׂא
titten-lî	'assēr	'ă'asserennû	lākh		wayyissā'
You will give to me	giving a tenth	I will give a tenth of it	to You		and he lifted up

3399	7559	2050.121	800	1158, 7208		7495.121	2079
pn	n fd, ps 3ms	cj, v Qal impf 3ms	n fs	n mp, n ms	**2.**	cj, v Qal impf 3ms	cj, intrj
יַעֲקֹב	רַגְלָיו	וַיֵּלֶךְ	אַרְצָה	בְנֵי־קֶדֶם		וַיַּרְא	וְהִנֵּה
ya'ăqōv	raghlâv	wayyēlekh	'artsāh	venê-qedhem		wayyar'	wehinnēh
Jacob	his feet	and he went	to the land of	the sons of the East		and he saw	and behold

908	904, 7898	2079, 8427	8421	5953, 6887	7547.152	6142	3706
n fs	prep, art, n ms	cj, intrj, adv	num	n mp, n fs	v Qal act ptc mp	prep, ps 3fs	cj
בְאֵר	בַּשָּׂדֶה	וְהִנֵּה־שָׁם	שְׁלֹשָׁה	עֶדְרֵי־צֹאן	רֹבְצִים	עָלֶיהָ	כִּי
ve'ēr	bassādheh	wehinnēh-shām	shelōshāh	'edrê-tsō'n	rōvetsîm	'ālêhā	kî
well	in the field	and behold there	three	flocks of sheep	lying	beside it	because

4623, 908	2000	8615.526	5953	63	1448	6142, 6552
prep, art, n fs	art, dem pron	v Hiphil impf 3mp	art, n mp	cj, art, n fs	adj	prep, n ms
מִן־הַבְּאֵר	הַהִוא	יַשְׁקוּ	הָעֲדָרִים	וְהָאֶבֶן	גְּדֹלָה	עַל־פִּי
min-habbe'ēr	hahiw'	yashqû	hā'ădhārîm	wehā'even	gedhōlāh	'al-pî
from the well	the that	they watered	the flocks	and the stone	large	on the mouth of

908		636.216, 8427	3725, 5953	1597.116	881, 63	4263, 6142
art, n fs	**3.**	cj, v Niphal pf 3cp, adv	adj, art, n mp	cj, v Qal pf 3cp	do, art, n fs	prep, prep
הַבְּאֵר		וְנֶאֶסְפוּ־שָׁמָּה	כָל־הָעֲדָרִים	וְגָלֲלוּ	אֶת־הָאֶבֶן	מֵעַל
habbe'ēr		wene'esphû-shāmmāh	kol-hā'ădhārîm	weghāllû	'eth-hā'even	mē'al
the well		and they gathered there	all the flocks	and they rolled	the stone	from

6552	908	8615.516	881, 6887	8178.516	881, 63	6142, 6552
n ms	art, n fs	cj, v Hiphil pf 3cp	do, art, n fs	cj, v Hiphil pf 3cp	do, art, n fs	prep, n ms
פִּי	הַבְּאֵר	וְהִשְׁקוּ	אֶת־הַצֹּאן	וְהֵשִׁיבוּ	אֶת־הָאֶבֶן	עַל־פִּי
pî	habbe'ēr	wehishqû	'eth-hatstsō'n	wehēshîvû	'eth-hā'even	'al-pî
the mouth of	the well	and they watered	the sheep	then they put back	the stone	on the mouth of

908	3937, 4887		569.121	3937	3399	250	4623, 376
art, n fs	prep, n ms, ps 3fs	**4.**	cj, v Qal impf 3ms	prep, ps 3mp	pn	n mp, ps 1cs	prep, adv
הַבְּאֵר	לִמְקֹמָהּ		וַיֹּאמֶר	לָהֶם	יַעֲקֹב	אַחַי	מֵאַיִן
habbe'ēr	limqōmāhh		wayyō'mer	lāhem	ya'ăqōv	'achay	mē'ayin
the well	to its place		and he said	to them	Jacob	my brothers	from where

894	569.126	4623, 2115	601		569.121	3937	3156.117
pers pron	cj, v Qal impf 3mp	prep, pn	pers pron	**5.**	cj, v Qal impf 3ms	prep, ps 3mp	intrg part, v Qal pf 2mp
אַתֶּם	וַיֹּאמְרוּ	מֵחָרָן	אֲנָחְנוּ		וַיֹּאמֶר	לָהֶם	הַיְדַעְתֶּם
'attem	wayyō'mrû	mēchārān	'ănachănû		wayyō'mer	lāhem	hayedha'ättem
you	and they said	from Haran	we		and he said	to them	do you know

881, 3969	1158, 5331	569.126	3156.116		569.121	3937	8361
do, pn	n ms, pn	cj, v Qal impf 3mp	v Qal pf 3cp	**6.**	cj, v Qal impf 3ms	prep, ps 3mp	intrg part, n ms
אֶת־לָבָן	בֶּן־נָחוֹר	וַיֹּאמְרוּ	יָדָעְנוּ		וַיֹּאמֶר	לָהֶם	הֲשָׁלוֹם
'eth-lāvān	ben-nāchôr	wayyō'mrû	yādhā'ānû		wayyō'mer	lāhem	heshālôm
Laban	the son of Nahor	and they said	we know		and he said	to them	is health

29:1. Then Jacob went on his journey: ... traveled on, *Berkeley* ... resumed his journey, *Anchor* ... arose on to his feet, *Fenton* ... lift up his feet, *Geneva.*

and came into the land of the people of the east: ... sons of the East, *Fenton* ... land of the Easterners, *Anchor* ... East country, *Geneva* ... land of the Kedemites, *Goodspeed* ... eastern tribes, *NEB.*

2. And he looked, and behold a well in the field: ... looking around, *Goodspeed* ... there before his eyes, *Anchor* ... a water-hole in a field, *BB* ... in the open country, *Berkeley.*

and, lo, there were three flocks of sheep lying by it: ... three droves of a flock crouching by it, *Young* ... droves of sheep huddled beside it, *Anchor* ... by the side of it, *BB.*

for out of that well they watered the flocks: ... they regularly watered, *Anchor* ... there they got water for the sheep, *BB.*

and a great stone was upon the well's mouth: ... mouth of the water-hole, *BB* ... stone on the mouth of the well was large, *NASB* ... over its mouth was a huge stone, *NEB.*

3. And thither were all the flocks gathered: ... when all the shepherds had assembled there together, *Anchor* ... flocks had collected there, *Fenton* ... all the herdsmen used to gather there, *NEB* ... come together there, *BB.*

and they rolled the stone from the well's mouth: ... shepherds would roll the stone away, *NIV* ... could they roll the stone from the mouth of the well, *Anchor* ... men would roll the stone, *Berkeley* ... stone had been rolled away, *BB.*

and watered the sheep: ... they would give the sheep water, *BB* ... the flocks were watered, *NCB.*

and put the stone again upon the well's mouth in his place: ... return the stone to its place, *NIV* ... replace the stone over the well, *REB.*

4. And Jacob said unto them, My brethren, whence be ye?: ... my friends, *NEB* ... he asked them, *Fenton* ... said to the herdmen, *BB* ... went over to the shepherds and asked them where they lived, *LIVB* ... where are you from, *Anchor.*

And they said, Of Haran are we: ... we are from Haran, *Anchor.*

5. And he said unto them, Know ye Laban the son of Nahor?: ... Laban of Nahor's family, *Berkeley* ... have you any knowledge of, *BB* ... if they knew Laban the grandson of Nahor, *NEB* ... Laban, Nahor's grandson, *NIV.*

And they said, We know him: ... we do, *Anchor* ... we have known, *Young.*

6. And he said unto them, Is he well? And they said, He is well: ... is it well with him, *ASV* ... is he in good health, *Geneva* ... hath he peace, *Young.*

and, behold, Rachel his daughter cometh with the sheep: ... here comes his daughter Rachel with his flock, *NCB* ... arriving with the flock, *Anchor.*

---

appropriated the promise and expressed his purpose to continue to worship the one true God. Since God would take care of him, provide for him, and bring him back to the promised land, and since the LORD would show Himself to be God to him, then this stone would be a house of Elohim, that is, a sacred place for God, a place where he would expect God to manifest Himself. He did not think of God as being in the stone, nor did he worship the stone itself. He worshiped God.

Later Jacob built an altar there (35:1-7). Further, in response to God's blessing, the least Jacob could do would be to give Him a tenth or tithe of all God would give to him. By this too he would be dedicating his life to God, recognizing Him as his Lord and King, as well as the true source of all that he was and had.

29:1-3. After three or four weeks of uneventful travel on foot, Jacob crossed the Euphrates River. Now he was in the territory we call Mesopotamia, a land that stretched east to the Persian Gulf, so that its people are called eastern here. Jacob then continued north for two or three days, and saw a well in a field with a large stone over it to prevent pollution and to keep anything or anyone from falling into it. Three flocks of sheep were lying near it. Strangely, no one was doing anything about getting water from the well for them.

29:4-6. Jacob called the young shepherds "brothers," since his mother was from the same area. Jacob undoubtedly spoke in their Aramaic language, since it was also the trade language in Canaan as well as his mother's native language. His polite inquiry let him know he was near Haran. In his next question he called Laban the son of Nahor, though he was the grandson. In Hebrew and Aramaic there is no separate word for grandson. "Son" means any descendant down the line. In typical oriental style Jacob then asked about Laban's health. At that very time, Rachel was seen in the distance coming with her father's flock of sheep.

3937	569.126	8361	2079	7637	1351	971.153	6196, 6887
prep, ps 3ms	cj, v Qal impf 3mp	n ms	cj, intrj	pn	n fs, ps 3ms	v Qal ptc 2fs	prep, art, n fs
לוֹ	וַיֹּאמְרוּ	שָׁלוֹם	וְהִנֵּה	רָחֵל	בִּתּוֹ	בָּאָה	עִם־הַצֹּאן
lô	wayyō'mrû	shālôm	w^{e}hinnēh	rāchēl	bittô	bā'āh	'im-hatstsō'n
to him	and they said	health	and behold	Rachel	his daughter	coming	with the sheep

7.	569.121	2075	5968	3219	1448	3940, 6496	636.241	4898
	cj, v Qal impf 3ms	intrj	adv	art, n ms	adj	neg part, *n fs*	v Niphal inf con	art, n ms
	וַיֹּאמֶר	הֵן	עוֹד	הַיּוֹם	גָּדוֹל	לֹא־עֵת	הֵאָסֵף	הַמִּקְנֶה
	wayyō'mer	hēn	'ôdh	hayyôm	gādhôl	lō'-'ēth	hē'āsēph	hammiqōneh
	and he said	behold	still	the day	great	not the time of	the gathering of	the flock

8615.533	6887	2050.133	7749.133	8.	569.126	3940	3310.120
v Hiphil impv 2mp	art, n fs	cj, v Qal impv 2mp	v Qal impv 2mp		cj, v Qal impf 3mp	neg part	v Qal impf 1cp
הַשְׁקוּ	הַצֹּאן	וּלְכוּ	רְעוּ		וַיֹּאמְרוּ	לֹא	נוּכַל
hashqû	hatstsō'n	ûlǎkhû	r^{e}'û		wayyō'mrû	lō'	nûkhal
water	the sheep	and go	pasture		and they said	not	we are able

5912	866	636.226	3725, 5953	1597.116	881, 63	4263, 6142	6552
adv	rel part	v Niphal impf 3mp	*adj*, art, n mp	cj, v Qal pf 3cp	do, art, n fs	prep, prep	*n ms*
עַד	אֲשֶׁר	יֵאָסְפוּ	כָּל־הָעֲדָרִים	וְגָלֲלוּ	אֶת־הָאֶבֶן	מֵעַל	פִּי
'adh	'ăsher	yē'ās^{e}phû	kol-hā'ădhārîm	w^{e}ghāllû	'eth-hā'even	mē'al	pî
until	that	they are gathered	all the flocks	and they have rolled	the stone	from	the mouth of

908	8615.519	6887	9.	5968	1744.351	6196	7637
art, n fs	cj, v Hiphil pf 1cp	art, n fs		adv, ps 3ms	v Piel ptc ms	prep, ps 3mp	cj, pn
הַבְּאֵר	וְהִשְׁקִינוּ	הַצֹּאן		עוֹדֶנּוּ	מְדַבֵּר	עִמָּם	וְרָחֵל
habb^{e}'ēr	w^{e}hishqînû	hatstsō'n		'ôdhennû	m^{e}dhabbēr	'immām	w^{e}rāchēl
the well	then we will water	the sheep		still he	speaking	with them	and Rachel

971.112	6196, 6887	866	3937, 1	3706	7749.153	2000
v Qal pf 3fs	prep, art, n fs	rel part	prep, n ms, ps 3fs	cj	v Qal act ptc 3fs	pers pron
בָּאָה	עִם־הַצֹּאן	אֲשֶׁר	לְאָבִיהָ	כִּי	רֹעָה	הִוא
bā'āh	'im-hatstsō'n	'ăsher	l^{e}'āvîhā	kî	rō'āh	hiw'
she came	with the sheep	which	to her father	because	shepherdess	she

10.	2030.121	3626, 866	7495.111	3399	881, 7637	1351, 3969	250
	cj, v Qal impf 3ms	prep, rel part	v Qal pf 3ms	pn	do, pn	*n fs*, pn	*n ms*
	וַיְהִי	כַּאֲשֶׁר	רָאָה	יַעֲקֹב	אֶת־רָחֵל	בַּת־לָבָן	אֲחִי
	wayhî	ka'ăsher	rā'āh	ya'ăqōv	'eth-rāchēl	bath-lāvān	'ăchî
	and it was	when	he saw	Jacob	Rachel	the daughter of Laban	the brother of

525	881, 6887	3969	250	525	5242.121	3399
n fs, ps 3ms	cj, do, *n fs*	pn	*n ms*	n fs, ps 3ms	cj, v Qal impf 3ms	pn
אִמּוֹ	וְאֶת־צֹאן	לָבָן	אֲחִי	אִמּוֹ	וַיִּגַּשׁ	יַעֲקֹב
'immô	w^{e}'eth-tsō'n	lāvān	'ăchî	'immô	wayyiggash	ya'ăqōv
his mother	and the flocks of	Laban	the brother of	his mother	and he drew near	Jacob

1597.521	881, 63	4263, 6142	6552	908	8615.521	881, 6887
cj, v Hiphil impf 3ms	do, art, n fs	prep, prep	n ms	art, n fs	cj, v Hiphil impf 3ms	do, n fs
וַיָּגֶל	אֶת־הָאֶבֶן	מֵעַל	פִּי	הַבְּאֵר	וַיַּשְׁקְ	אֶת־צֹאן
wayyāghel	'eth-hā'even	mē'al	pî	habb^{e}'ēr	wayyash^{e}qǒ	'eth-tsō'n
and he rolled	the stone	from	the mouth of	the well	and he watered	the flocks of

3969	250	525	11.	5583.121	3399	3937, 7637	5558.121
pn	n ms	n fs, ps 3ms		cj, v Qal impf 3ms	pn	prep, pn	cj, v Qal impf 3ms
לָבָן	אֲחִי	אִמּוֹ		וַיִּשַּׁק	יַעֲקֹב	לְרָחֵל	וַיִּשָּׂא
lāvān	'ăchî	'immô		wayyishshaq	ya'ăqōv	l^{e}rāchēl	wayyissā'
Laban	the brother of	his mother		and he kissed	Jacob	Rachel	and he lifted up

881, 7249	1098.121		5222.521	3399	3937, 7637	3706	250
do, n ms, ps 3ms	cj, v Qal impf 3ms	**12.**	cj, v Hiphil impf 3ms	pn	prep, pn	cj	*n ms*
אֶת־קֹלוֹ	וַיֵּבְךְּ		וַיַּגֵּד	יַעֲקֹב	לְרָחֵל	כִּי	אֲחִי
'eth-qōlô	wayyēvekh		wayyaggēdh	ya'ăqōv	lerāchēl	kî	'ăchî
his voice	and he wept		and he told	Jacob	Rachel	that	the brother of

1	2000	3706	1158, 7549	2000	7608.122	5222.522
n ms, ps 3fs	pers pron	cj, cj	*n ms*, pn	pers pron	cj, v Qal impf 3fs	cj, v Hiphil impf 3fs
אָבִיהָ	הוּא	וְכִי	בֶּן־רִבְקָה	הוּא	וַתָּרָץ	וַתַּגֵּד
'āvîhā	hû'	wekhî	ben-rivqāh	hû'	wattārāts	wattaggēdh
her father	he	and that	the son of Rebekah	he	and she ran	and she told

7. And he said, Lo, it is yet high day: ... the day is still in its prime, *Berkeley* ... the sun is still high, *BB* ... day has still long to run, *Goodspeed* ... there is still much daylight left, *NAB* ... day is still great, *Young*.

neither is it time that the cattle should be gathered together: ... the time for folding the sheep has not yet come, *NEB* ... not yet time for penning the sheep, *REB* ... livestock to be gathered, *NASB* ... round up the animals, *Anchor* ... bring in the livestock, *Berkeley*.

water ye the sheep, and go and feed them: ... why don't you water them and go on grazing, *Anchor* ... water ye the flock, and go, delight yourselves, *Young* ... go and give them their food, *BB* ... continue pasturing them, *NAB* ... lead them back to pasture, *NCB*.

8. And they said, We cannot, until all the flocks be gathered together: ... flocks are collected, *Fenton* ... all the shepherds are gathered together, *Anchor* ... all the shepherds assemble, *Goodspeed* ... until all the shepherds are here to roll the stone away, *NAB*.

and till they roll the stone from the well's mouth; then we water the sheep: ... water the droves, *Anchor*.

9. And while he yet spake with them: ... conversing with them, *Berkeley* ... talking with them, *Anchor* ... speaking with them, *NKJV* ... as this conversation was going on, *LIVB*.

Rachel came with her father's sheep: ... arrived with her father's flocks, *NCB*.

for she kept them: ... she was a shepherdess, *Anchor* ... she took care of them, *BB* ... she shepherded them, *Fenton* ... she was the one who tended them, *NAB* ... her custom to tend them, *NCB*.

10. And it came to pass, when Jacob saw Rachel the daughter of Laban his mother's brother: ... as soon as Jacob saw Rachel, *Anchor*.

and the sheep of Laban his mother's brother: ... with the sheep of his uncle Laban, *Berkeley* ... coming with Laban's sheep, *BB* ... with the flock, *NCB*.

that Jacob went near, and rolled the stone from the well's mouth: ... stepped up, *Berkeley* ... stepped forward, *NEB*.

and watered the flock of Laban his mother's brother: ... he got water for Laban's flock, *BB* ... watered his uncle's sheep, *NAB*.

11. And Jacob kissed Rachel, and lifted up his voice, and wept: ... burst into tears, *Anchor* ... wept audibly, *Berkeley* ... lifted up his voice in weeping, *Goodspeed* ... wept aloud, *NCB*.

29:7-8. Jacob knew the shepherding business, and he wanted to know why the sheep were lying around without being watered. They needed to go where they could graze. The shepherds explained that they could not do so until all the flocks were there and the stone rolled away. This suggests that the shepherds were young boys and needed several to roll the stone away.

29:9-10. Ordinarily a daughter would not be herding sheep, but at this point Laban had no sons, though he had sons later. As the younger daughter, Rachel was assigned to that task. As soon as Rachel came Jacob removed the stone from the well and watered Laban's sheep.

29:11. Then Jacob kissed Rachel's hand (as is meant when the Hebrew verb is not followed by the accusative) and wept for joy. Meeting Rachel in this way could be no coincidence. He had come to the right place and found the right person. God was with him as He promised.

29:12-13. As soon as Rachel knew Jacob was a son of Rebekah, she ran and told her father. Laban than ran to meet Jacob, hugged and kissed him repeatedly, and brought him to his house. There Jacob told the news about his parents, his journey and the events at the well.

3937, 1	13.	2030.121	3626, 8471.141	3969	881, 8475	3399	1158, 269
prep, n ms, ps 3fs		cj, v Qal impf 3ms	prep, v Qal inf con	pn	do, *n ms*	pn	*n ms*, n fs, ps 3ms
לְאָבִיהָ		וַיְהִי	כִּשְׁמֹעַ	לָבָן	אֶת־שֵׁמַע	יַעֲקֹב	בֶּן־אֲחֹתוֹ
l^{e}'āvîhā		wayhî	khishmōa'	lāvān	'eth-shēma'	ya'ăqōv	ben-'ăchōthô
her father		and it was	when hearing	Laban	the news of	Jacob	the son of his sister

7608.121	3937, 7410.141	2354.321, 3937	5583.321, 3937
cj, v Qal impf 3ms	prep, v Qal inf con, ps 3ms	cj, v Piel impf 3ms, prep, ps 3ms	cj, v Piel impf 3ms, prep, ps 3ms
וַיָּרָץ	לִקְרָאתוֹ	וַיְחַבֶּק־לוֹ	וַיְנַשֶּׁק־לוֹ
wayyārāts	liqrā'thô	way^{e}chabbeq-lô	waynashsheq-lô
then he ran	to meet him	and he hugged him	and he kissed him

971.521	420, 1041	5807.321	3937, 3969	881	3725, 1745	431
cj, v Hiphil impf 3ms, ps 3ms	prep, n fs, ps 3ms	cj, v Piel impf 3ms	prep, pn	do	*adj*, art, n mp	art, dem pron
וַיְבִיאֵהוּ	אֶל־בֵּיתוֹ	וַיְסַפֵּר	לְלָבָן	אֵת	כָּל־הַדְּבָרִים	הָאֵלֶּה
way^{e}vî'ēhû	'el-bêthô	waysappēr	l^{e}lāvān	'ēth	kol-hadd^{e}vārîm	hā'ēlleh
and he brought him	to his house	and he reported	to Laban		all the things	the these

14.	569.121	3937	3969	395	6344	1340	887	3553.121
	cj, v Qal impf 3ms	prep, ps 3ms	pn	adv	n fs, ps 1cs	cj, n ms, ps 1cs	pers pron	cj, v Qal impf 3ms
	וַיֹּאמֶר	לוֹ	לָבָן	אַךְ	עַצְמִי	וּבְשָׂרִי	אָתָּה	וַיֵּשֶׁב
	wayyō'mer	lô	lāvān	'akh	'atsmî	ûv^{e}sārî	'āttāh	wayyēshev
	and he said	to him	Laban	surely	my bone	and my flesh	you	and he dwelled

6196	2414	3219	15.	569.121	3969	3937, 3399	3706, 250
prep, ps 3ms	*n ms*	n mp		cj, v Qal impf 3ms	pn	prep, pn	intrg part, cj, n ms
עִמּוֹ	חֹדֶשׁ	יָמִים		וַיֹּאמֶר	לָבָן	לְיַעֲקֹב	הֲכִי־אָחִי
'immô	chōdhesh	yāmîm		wayyō'mer	lāvān	l^{e}ya'ăqōv	h^{e}khî-'āchî
with him	month of	days		and he said	Laban	to Jacob	because my relative

887	5856.113	2703	5222.531	3937	4242, 5032
pers pron	cj, v Qal pf 2ms, ps 1cs	adv	v Hiphil impv 2ms	prep, ps 1cs	intrg, n fs, ps 2ms
אַתָּה	וַעֲבַדְתַּנִי	חִנָּם	הַגִּידָה	לִּי	מַה־מַּשְׂכֻּרְתֶּךָ
'attāh	wa'ăvadhtanî	chinnām	haggîdhāh	lî	mah-maskurtekhā
you	then will you serve me	for nothing	tell	to me	what your wages

16.	3937, 3969	8530	1351	8428	1448	3943	8428	7278
	cj, prep, pn	*num*	n fp	*n ms*	art, adj	pn	cj, *n ms*	art, adj
	וּלְלָבָן	שְׁתֵּי	בָנוֹת	שֵׁם	הַגְּדֹלָה	לֵאָה	וְשֵׁם	הַקְּטַנָּה
	ûlălāvān	sh^{e}ttê	vānôth	shēm	hagg^{e}dhōlāh	lē'āh	w^{e}shēm	haqq^{e}tannāh
	and to Laban	two	daughters	the name of	the older	Leah	and the name of	the younger

7637	17.	6084	3943	7679	7637	2030.112	3413, 8717
pn		cj, *n fd*	pn	adj	cj, pn	v Qal pf 3fs	adj, *n ms*
רָחֵל		וְעֵינֵי	לֵאָה	רַכּוֹת	וְרָחֵל	הָיְתָה	יְפַת־תֹּאַר
rāchēl		w^{e}'ênê	lē'āh	rakkôth	w^{e}rāchēl	hāy^{e}thâh	y^{e}phath-tō'ar
Rachel		and the eyes of	Leah	weak	but Rachel	she was	beautiful of form

3413	4920	18.	154.121	3399	881, 7637	569.121
cj, *adj*	n ms		cj, v Qal impf 3ms	pn	do, pn	cj, v Qal impf 3ms
וִיפַת	מַרְאֶה		וַיֶּאֱהַב	יַעֲקֹב	אֶת־רָחֵל	וַיֹּאמֶר
wîphath	mar'eh		wayye'ĕhav	ya'ăqōv	'eth-rāchēl	wayyō'mer
and beautiful of	appearance		and he loved	Jacob	Rachel	and he said

5856.125	8124	8523	904, 7637	1351	7278
v Qal impf 1cs, ps 2ms	num	n fp	prep, pn	n fs, ps 2ms	art, adj
אֶעֱבָדְךָ	שֶׁבַע	שָׁנִים	בְּרָחֵל	בִּתְּךָ	הַקְּטַנָּה
'e'ĕvādh^{e}khā	sheva'	shānîm	b^{e}rāchēl	bitt^{e}khā	haqq^{e}tannāh
I will serve you	seven	years	for Rachel	your daughter	the younger

12. And Jacob told Rachel that he was her father's brother, and that he was Rebekah's son: ... father's nephew, *Berkeley* ... father's relation, *BB* ... kinsman, *Anchor* ... relative of your father's, *Fenton.*

and she ran and told her father: ... hastened to tell, *NCB* ... reported it to her father, *Fenton* ... went running to give her father news of it, *BB.*

13. And it came to pass, when Laban heard the tidings of Jacob his sister's son: ... hearing news of Jacob, *BB* ... heard the report, *Fenton.*

that he ran to meet him: ... hastened to meet him, *NCB* ... hurried out, *NAB* ... ran to invite him, *Fenton* ... came running, *BB* ... rushed out to greet him, *Anchor.*

and embraced him, and kissed him: ... took Jacob in his arms, *BB* ... hugged him, *Good News* ... received him with embraces and kisses, *NCB.*

and brought him to his house: ... took him to his house, *Anchor* ... made him come into his house, *BB* ... brought him to his dwelling, *NCB* ... welcomed him to his home, *NEB.*

And he told Laban all these things: ... recounted to Laban everything that had happened, *Anchor* ... all the particulars, *Berkeley* ... gave him news of everything, *BB* ... related to Laban all these events, *Fenton* ... told Laban his whole story, *Goodspeed.*

14. And Laban said to him, Surely thou art my bone and my flesh: ... flesh and blood, *Anchor.*

And he abode with him the space of a month: ... he kept Jacob with him, *BB* ... stayed five days with him, *Fenton* ... a month's time, *Anchor* ... dwelleth with him a month of days, *Young.*

15. And Laban said unto Jacob, Because thou art my brother: ... near kin to me, *Berkeley* ... you are my relative, *Fenton.*

shouldest thou therefore serve me for nought?: ... should you serve me for nothing, *Anchor* ... be my servant for nothing, *BB* ... work for me, *NEB.*

tell me, what shall thy wages be?: ... what is your payment to be, *BB* ... inform me what wages I shall pay you, *Fenton* ... what wage you would settle for, *REB* ... what is thy hire, *Young.*

16. And Laban had two daughters: the name of the elder was Leah, and the name of the younger was Rachel.

17. Leah was tender eyed: ... had no sparkle, *Berkeley* ... were timid, *Fenton* ... had lovely eyes, *NAB* ... weak eyes, *Goodspeed* ... dull-eyed, *NEB.*

but Rachel was beautiful and well favoured: ... beautiful in both face and figure, *REB* ... beautiful form and beautiful countenance, *Darby* ... lovely of form and face, *Berkeley* ... those of Rachel perfect in form and beautiful to see, *Fenton* ... well formed and beautiful, *NAB.*

18. And Jacob loved Rachel: ... was in love with, *BB* ... had fallen in love, *Goodspeed.*

and said, I will serve thee seven years for Rachel thy younger daughter: ... I will be your servant, *BB.*

19. And Laban said, It is better that I give her to thee: ... for you to have her, *BB* ... she shall be yours, *Fenton.*

than that I should give her to another man: ... give her to an outsider, *Anchor* ... than to anyone else, *Goodspeed* ... some other man, *NIV.*

abide with me: ... remain, *Anchor*

29:14-15. By saying Jacob was his own bone and flesh, Laban was welcoming Jacob into the family. (They considered the flesh to contain the blood, so this expression corresponds to the English way of saying "you are my own flesh and blood.") Jacob then stayed with Laban for a month. Since he knew the shepherding business, we can be sure he did not sit and do nothing. Apparently he worked so hard, that at the end of the month Laban felt he could not take advantage of Jacob's being a "brother," that is, a relative. His hard work deserved wages, so Laban asked him to state what he wanted.

29:16-17. Laban had an older daughter, Leah ("wild cow") whose eyes were weak or delicate. This does not mean she had poor vision, but they lacked the deep lustrous color common among brown-eyed people. An Egyptian Christian pointed out to me that on the ancient monuments the evil eye is always pictured as blue. He suggested that Leah's eyes were blue and, though they were pretty, that drew away from all her other qualities. On the other hand, Rachel ("ewe") was beautiful in face and form.

29:18. Jacob came with nothing. He had no dowry to offer, no gifts such as the servant of Abraham brought when he came for a wife for Isaac. He probably did not need to offer seven years of hard labor to obtain Rachel as his wife, but he did so to show how much he loved her and how much he valued her.

	569.121	3969	3005	5598.141	881	3937	4623, 5598.141
19.	cj, v Qal impf 3ms	pn	adj	v Qal inf con, ps 1cs	do, ps 3fs	prep, ps 2fs	prep, v Qal inf con, ps 1cs
	וַיֹּאמֶר	לָבָן	טוֹב	תִּתִּי	אֹתָהּ	לָךְ	מִתִּתִּי
	wayyō'mer	lāvān	ṯôv	tittî	'ōthāhh	lākh	mittittî
	and he said	Laban	better	my giving	her	to you	than my giving

881	3937, 382	311	3553.131	6200		5856.121	3399	904, 7637
do, ps 3fs	prep, n ms	adj	v Qal impv 2ms	prep, ps 1cs	**20.**	cj, v Qal impf 3ms	pn	prep, pn
אֹתָהּ	לְאִישׁ	אַחֵר	שְׁבָה	עִמָּדִי		וַיַּעֲבֹד	יַעֲקֹב	בְּרָחֵל
'ōthāhh	le'îsh	'achēr	shevāh	'immādhî		wayya'ăvōdh	ya'ăqōv	berāchēl
her	to man	another	stay	with me		so he served	Jacob	for Rachel

8124	8523	2030.126	904, 6084	3626, 3219	259	904, 154.141	881
num	n fp	cj, v Qal impf 3mp	prep, n fd, ps 3ms	prep, n mp	n mp	prep, v Qal inf con, ps 3ms	do, ps 3fs
שֶׁבַע	שָׁנִים	וַיִּהְיוּ	בְּעֵינָיו	כְּיָמִים	אֲחָדִים	בְּאַהֲבָתוֹ	אֹתָהּ
sheva'	shānîm	wayyihyû	ve'ênâv	keyāmîm	'ăchādhîm	be'ahevāthô	'ōthāhh
seven	years	and they were	in his eyes	like days	ones	in his loving	her

	569.121	3399	420, 3969	1957.131	881, 828	3706	4527.116
21.	cj, v Qal impf 3ms	pn	prep, pn	v Qal impv 2ms	do, n fs, ps 1cs	cj	v Qal pf 3cp
	וַיֹּאמֶר	יַעֲקֹב	אֶל־לָבָן	הָבָה	אֶת־אִשְׁתִּי	כִּי	מָלְאוּ
	wayyō'mer	ya'ăqōv	'el-lāvān	hāvâh	'eth-'ishtî	kî	māle'û
	and he said	Jacob	to Laban	give	my wife	because	they are complete

3219	971.125	420		636.121	3969	881, 3725, 596	4887
n mp, ps 1cs	cj, v Qal impf 1cs	prep, ps 3fs	**22.**	cj, v Qal impf 3ms	pn	do, *adj, n mp*	art, n ms
יָמָי	וְאָבוֹאָה	אֵלֶיהָ		וַיֶּאֱסֹף	לָבָן	אֶת־כָּל־אַנְשֵׁי	הַמָּקוֹם
yāmāy	we'āvô'āh	'ēlêhā		wayye'ěsōph	lāvān	'eth-kol-'anshê	hammāqôm
my days	and I will go in	to her		and he gathered	Laban	all the men of	the place

6449.121	5136		2030.121	904, 6394	4089.121	881, 3943
cj, v Qal impf 3ms	n ms	**23.**	cj, v Qal impf 3ms	prep, art, n ms	cj, v Qal impf 3ms	do, pn
וַיַּעַשׂ	מִשְׁתֶּה		וַיְהִי	בָעֶרֶב	וַיִּקַּח	אֶת־לֵאָה
wayya'as	mishteh		wayhî	vā'erev	wayyiqqach	'eth-lē'āh
and he made	feast		and it was	in the evening	that he took	Leah

1351	971.521	881	420	971.121	420		5598.121
n fs, ps 3ms	cj, v Hiphil impf 3ms	do, ps 3fs	prep, ps 3ms	cj, v Qal impf 3ms	prep, ps 3fs	**24.**	cj, v Qal impf 3ms
בִּתּוֹ	וַיָּבֵא	אֹתָהּ	אֵלָיו	וַיָּבֹא	אֵלֶיהָ		וַיִּתֵּן
vittô	wayyāvē'	'ōthāhh	'ēlâv	wayyāvō'	'ēlêhā		wayyittēn
his daughter	and he brought	her	to him	and he went in	to her		and he gave

3969	3937	881, 2238	8569	3937, 3943	1351	8569
pn	prep, ps 3fs	do, pn	n fs, ps 3ms	prep, pn	n fs, ps 3ms	n fs
לָבָן	לָהּ	אֶת־זִלְפָּה	שִׁפְחָתוֹ	לְלֵאָה	בִּתּוֹ	שִׁפְחָה
lāvān	lāhh	'eth-zilpāh	shiphchāthô	lelē'āh	vittô	shiphchāh
Laban	to her	Zilpah	his female slave	to Leah	his daughter	female slave

	2030.121	904, 1269	2079, 2000	3943	569.121	420, 3969
25.	cj, v Qal impf 3ms	prep, art, n ms	cj, intrj, pers pron	pn	cj, v Qal impf 3ms	prep, pn
	וַיְהִי	בַבֹּקֶר	וְהִנֵּה־הִוא	לֵאָה	וַיֹּאמֶר	אֶל־לָבָן
	wayhî	vabbōqer	wehinnēh-hiw'	lē'āh	wayyō'mer	'el-lāvān
	and it was	in the morning	and behold she	Leah	and he said	to Laban

4242, 2148	6449.113	3937	3940	904, 7637	5856.115	6196	4066
intrg part, dem pron	v Qal pf 2ms	prep, ps 1cs	intrg part, neg part	prep, pn	v Qal pf 1cs	prep, ps 2fs	cj, intrg
מַה־זֹּאת	עָשִׂיתָ	לִּי	הֲלֹא	בְרָחֵל	עָבַדְתִּי	עִמָּךְ	וְלָמָּה
mah-zō'th	'āsîthā	lî	hălō'	verāchēl	'āvadhtî	'immākh	welāmmāh
what this	you did	to me	was it not	for Rachel	I served	with you	and why

you stay with me, *Berkeley* ... go on living with me, *BB* ... after you have stayed with me, *Fenton*.

20. And Jacob served seven years for Rachel: ... did seven year's work, *BB* ... waited for Rachel seven years, *Fenton*.

and they seemed unto him but a few days: ... in his eyes as single days, *Darby* ... only a very little time, *BB* ... like a single day, *Fenton*.

for the love he had to her: ... because of his love for her, *BB* ... he loved her, *NEB*.

21. And Jacob said unto Laban, Give me my wife for my days are fulfilled: ... term is completed, *Anchor* ... time is up, *Berkeley* ... time has come, *NCB* ... served my time, *NEB* ... fulfilled by contract, *LIVB*.

that I may go in unto her: ... I want to lie with her, *NIV* ... we may sleep together, *NEB* ... consummate my marriage, *NAB* ... that I may have her, *BB* ... unite with her, *Anchor*.

22. And Laban gathered together all the men of the place: ... invited all the people, *Berkeley* ... collected all the men, *Fenton* ... all the local inhabitants, *Anchor*.

and made a feast: ... served a banquet, *Berkeley* ... held a wedding feast, *REB*.

23. And it came to pass in the evening: ... when it was dark, *Fenton* ... when the evening was come, *Geneva* ... in the course of the evening, *Goodspeed* ... at nightfall, *NAB*.

that he took Leah his daughter, and brought her to him: ... and gave her to him, *BB*.

and he went in unto her: ... lay with her, *NIV* ... slept with her, *NEB* ... had relations with her, *NCB* ... consummated the marriage, *NAB* ... cohabited with her, *Anchor*.

24. And Laban gave unto his daughter Leah Zilpah his maid for an handmaid: ... assigned his maidservant, *Anchor* ... to be her waiting-woman, *BB* ... to be her servant, *Fenton* ... slave girl, *Good News*.

25. And it came to pass, that in the morning, behold, it was Leah: ... came morning, *Anchor* ... and so it was in the morning, *Berkeley* ... when it was morning he discovered it was Leah, *Fenton* ... Jacob was amazed, *NAB* ... Jacob saw that it was Leah, *BB*.

and he said to Laban, What is this thou hast done unto me?: ... how could you do this to me, *NAB* ... why then hast thou deceived me, *Darby* ... is this the way to treat me, *Berkeley* ... why did you do this to me, *Anchor*.

did not I serve with thee for Rachel?: ... have I not worked with you for Rachel, *Berkeley* ... was I not working for you so that I might have Rachel, *BB*.

wherefore then hast thou beguiled me?: ... played this trick on me, *REB* ... why have you deceived me, *NEB* ... why did you dupe me, *NAB* ... have you been false to me, *BB* ... have you cheated me, *Berkeley*.

29:19-20. Laban recognized what a good worker Jacob was and said it was better for him to give Rachel to Jacob than to some other man. Since Laban still had no sons, Jacob could be the heir and carry on the family line.

Tablets discovered at the ruins of Nuzu show that a son-in-law would be adopted and treated as a son in such a case. So Jacob worked like a slave for Laban for 7 years. But they seemed like only a few days, so great was his love for Rachel. What affection, what tender love this must have been!

29:21-23. At the end of the 7 years God began to put Jacob through a discipline that would teach him many lessons. Jacob asked for his wife without naming her. Because of the betrothal agreement (v. 18), he could speak of Rachel as his wife. However, the fact that he did not name her gave Laban an opportunity to substitute Leah for Rachel.

After a wedding feast enjoyed by the whole community, Laban brought Leah to Jacob. She was probably about the same size as Rachel and wore the wedding veil that covered the whole body. Thus, in the darkness of his tent Jacob did not realize he was being tricked. But through this treachery, he surely came to understand how Esau must have felt when he lost the blessing.

29:24. Laban also gave his slave girl Zilpah ("dignity, nearness, intimacy") to Leah to be her own personal servant. He must have arranged this before he brought Leah to Jacob.

Since marriages were usually arranged in those days, Leah would be expected to obey her father. But it may be that she wanted Zilpah as her servant. She was probably attracted to Jacob as well.

29:25-26. Jacob was shocked in the morning when he awoke and Leah was there beside him. He confronted Laban and asked the reason for this deception.

Laban's answer may have had to do with a local custom. However, it is also possible that his answer was also a deception since the feast was indeed made for Rachel.

7700.313		569.121	3969	3940, 6449.221	3772	904, 4887
v Piel pf 2ms, ps 1cs	**26.**	cj, v Qal impf 3ms	pn	neg part, v Niphil impf 3ms	adv	prep, n ms, ps 1cp
רִמִּיתָנִי		וַיֹּאמֶר	לָבָן	לֹא־יֵעָשֶׂה	כֵן	בִּמְקוֹמֵנוּ
rimmîthānî		wayyō'mer	lāvān	lō'-yē'āseh	khēn	bimqômēnû
have you deceived me		and he said	Laban	not it is done	so	in our place

3937, 5598.141	7089	3937, 6686	1106		4527.331	8094	2148
prep, v Qal inf con	art, adj	prep, *n mp*	art, n fs	**27.**	v Piel impv 2ms	*n ms*	dem pron
לָתֵת	הַצְּעִירָה	לִפְנֵי	הַבְּכִירָה		מַלֵּא	שְׁבֻעַ	זֹאת
lāthēth	hatsts^{e}'îrāh	liphnê	habb^{e}khîrāh		mallē'	sh^{e}vua'	zō'th
to give	the younger	before	the older		complete	the week of	this one

5598.120	3937	1612, 881, 2148	904, 5865	866	5856.123	6200
cj, v Qal impf 1cp	prep, ps 2ms	cj, do, dem pron	prep, n fs	rel part	v Qal impf 2ms	prep, ps 1cs
וְנִתְּנָה	לְךָ	גַּם־אֶת־זֹאת	בַּעֲבֹדָה	אֲשֶׁר	תַּעֲבֹד	עִמָּדִי
w^{e}nitt^{e}nāh	l^{e}khā	gam-'eth-zō'th	ba'ăvōdhāh	'ăsher	ta'ăvōdh	'immādhî
then we will give	to you	also this	for work	which	you will serve	with me

5968	8124, 8523	311		6449.121	3399	3772	4527.321	8094
adv	num, n fp	adj	**28.**	cj, v Qal impf 3ms	pn	adv	cj, v Piel impf 3ms	*n ms*
עוֹד	שֶׁבַע־שָׁנִים	אֲחֵרוֹת		וַיַּעַשׂ	יַעֲקֹב	כֵּן	וַיְמַלֵּא	שְׁבֻעַ
'ôdh	sheva'-shānîm	'ăchērôth		wayya'as	ya'ăqōv	kēn	waymallē'	sh^{e}vua'
again	seven years	another		and he did	Jacob	so	and he completed	the week of

2148	5598.121, 3937	881, 7637	1351	3937	3937, 828
dem pron	cj, v Qal impf 3ms, prep, ps 3ms	do, pn	n fs, ps 3ms	prep, ps 3ms	prep, n fs
זֹאת	וַיִּתֶּן־לוֹ	אֶת־רָחֵל	בִּתּוֹ	לוֹ	לְאִשָּׁה
zō'th	wayyitten-lô	'eth-rāchēl	bittô	lô	l^{e}'ishshāh
this one	and he gave to him	Rachel	his daughter	to him	for a wife

	5598.121	3969	3937, 7637	1351	881, 1131	8569	3937
29.	cj, v Qal impf 3ms	pn	prep, pn	n fs, ps 3ms	do, pn	n fs, ps 3ms	prep, ps 3fs
	וַיִּתֵּן	לָבָן	לְרָחֵל	בִּתּוֹ	אֶת־בִּלְהָה	שִׁפְחָתוֹ	לָהּ
	wayyittēn	lāvān	l^{e}rāchēl	bittô	'eth-bilhāh	shiphchāthô	lāhh
	and he gave	Laban	to Rachel	his daughter	Bilhah	his female slave	to her

3937, 8569		971.121	1612	420, 7637	154.121	1612, 881, 7637
prep, n fs	**30.**	cj, v Qal impf 3ms	cj	prep, pn	cj, v Qal impf 3ms	cj, do, pn
לְשִׁפְחָה		וַיָּבֹא	גַּם	אֶל־רָחֵל	וַיֶּאֱהַב	גַּם־אֶת־רָחֵל
l^{e}shiphchāh		wayyāvō'	gam	'el-rāchēl	wayye'ĕhav	gam-'eth-rāchēl
for female slave		and he went in	also	to Rachel	and he loved	also Rachel

4623, 3943	5856.121	6196	5968	8124, 8523	311		7495.121
prep, pn	cj, v Qal impf 3ms	prep, ps 3ms	adv	num, n fp	adj	**31.**	cj, v Qal impf 3ms
מִלֵּאָה	וַיַּעֲבֹד	עִמּוֹ	עוֹד	שֶׁבַע־שָׁנִים	אֲחֵרוֹת		וַיַּרְא
millē'āh	wayya'ăvōdh	'immô	'ôdh	sheva'-shānîm	'ăchērôth		wayyar^{e}'
more than Leah	and he served	with him	again	seven years	another		and he saw

3176	3706, 7983.157	3943	6858.121	881, 7641	7637	6371
pn	cj, v Qal pass ptc fs	pn	cj, v Qal impf 3ms	do, n ms, ps 3fs	cj, pn	adj
יְהוָה	כִּי־שְׂנוּאָה	לֵאָה	וַיִּפְתַּח	אֶת־רַחְמָהּ	וְרָחֵל	עֲקָרָה
y^{e}hwāh	kî-sh^{e}nû'āh	lē'āh	wayyiphtach	'eth-rachmāhh	w^{e}rāchēl	'ăqārāh
Yahweh	that one hated	Leah	and he opened	her womb	but Rachel	barren

	2106.122	3943	3314.122	1158	7410.122	8428	7498
32.	cj, v Qal impf 3fs	pn	cj, v Qal impf 3fs	n ms	cj, v Qal impf 3fs	n ms, ps 3ms	pn
	וַתַּהַר	לֵאָה	וַתֵּלֶד	בֵּן	וַתִּקְרָא	שְׁמוֹ	רְאוּבֵן
	wattahar	lē'āh	wattēledh	bēn	wattiqrā'	sh^{e}mô	r^{e}'ûvēn
	and she conceived	Leah	and she gave birth	son	and she called	his name	Reuben

26. And Laban said, It must not be so done in our country: ... it is not the practice, *Anchor* ... not our custom, *Fenton* ... not the manner of this place, *Geneva* ... not customary, *Goodspeed* ... it is not right, *NEB.*

to give the younger before the firstborn: ... the younger daughter be married before the older, *BB* ... to marry off the younger, *Anchor.*

27. Fulfil her week: ... let the week of the bride-feast come to its end, *BB* ... finish the week's festivities, *Goodspeed* ... complete the week of this one's nuptials, *NCB* ... complete this one's week, *Berkeley* ... count the seven for this, *Fenton.*

and we will give thee this also: ... younger shall be given you, *NEB* ... I will give you Rachel, *Good News* ... give you that one too, *Anchor* ... give thee the other also, *ASV* ... in addition, *BB.*

for the service which thou shalt serve with me yet seven other years: ... in exchange for your remaining in my service another seven years, *Anchor* ... further seven year's work. *NEB.*

28. And Jacob did so, and fulfilled her week: ... Jacob agreed and waited until the first bride's week was ended, *Anchor* ... completed the seven days, *NEB* ... finished the bridal week, *NAB* ... fulfilled her seven years, *Geneva* ... finished her week's festivities, *Goodspeed.*

and he gave him Rachel his daughter to wife also: ... gave him his daughter Rachel in marriage, *Goodspeed.*

29. And Laban gave to Rachel his daughter Bilhah his handmaid to be her maid: ... assigned his maidservant, *Anchor* ... to be her waiting-woman, *BB* ... slave girl, *Good News.*

30. And he went in also unto Rachel: ... lay with Rachel, *NIV* ... slept with Rachel also, *NEB* ... consummated the marriage, *NAB* ... had intercourse with Rachel, *Good News* ... cohabited with her also, *Anchor.*

and he loved also Rachel more than Leah: ... he loved her rather than Leah, *NEB* ... loved Rachel completely, *Fenton* ... love for her was greater than his love for Leah, *BB.*

and served with him yet seven other years: ... worked for him, *Berkeley* ... went on working, *BB* ... stayed in service with Laban seven more years, *Anchor.*

31. And when the LORD saw that Leah was hated: ... disliked, *NCB* ... despised, *Geneva* ... slighted, *Berkeley* ... unloved, *Anchor.*

he opened her womb: ... made her pregnant, *Goodspeed* ... made her fruitful, *Geneva* ... gave her a child, *BB* ... gave her fertility, *Berkeley* ... unclosed her womb, *Anchor.*

but Rachel was barren: ... sterile, *Berkeley* ... had no children, *BB* ... was childless, *Fenton* ... remained barren, *NAB.*

32. And Leah conceived, and bare a son: ... was with child and gave birth to a son, *BB* ... became pregnant, *NIV.*

and she called his name Reuben: ... whom she named, *Anchor* ... whom she gave the name, *BB* ... Behold a Son, *Goodspeed.*

for she said, Surely the LORD hath looked upon my affliction: ... seen my humiliation, *NEB* ... has had regard for my misery, *NCB* ... looked upon my tribulation, *Geneva* ... seen my sorrow, *BB* ... my distress, *Anchor.*

now therefore my husband will love me: ... have love for me, *BB* ... surely my husband will love me now, *NIV.*

29:27-28. Laban was exacting a high price for Rachel. After one week of customary festivities, there would be another wedding and Jacob would have two wives. But he would have to work like a slave for Laban for another seven years.

29:29. Laban then gave his slave girl Bilhah ("simple, stupid," or perhaps "terror") to be a personal servant to Rachel. Bilhah was evidently not as highly regarded by Laban as Zilpah was.

29:30. Rachel was Jacob's choice, so he loved her more than Leah. It must have been hard for Jacob to have to work like a slave for Laban for another seven years. But he did it—faithfully and well, we can be sure.

29:31. God saw Jacob's lack of love for Leah as being in the same category as hatred. (Hatred in that culture seems to have referred to rejection from being in first place in one's life.)

God had not forgotten His promise to multiply the descendants of Abraham and Jacob. But He chose to give Leah the privilege of being the mother of Jacob's first four sons, including Judah, the ancestor of David and Jesus. Rachel, however, was barren.

29:32. Reuben means "See, a son!" in the Hebrew it also has a similar sound to the Hebrew for "He (the LORD) looked (with concern) on my misery." She recognized the grace of the God of Abraham, Isaac, and Jacob. She hoped also that Jacob would recognize the LORD's hand in this and her bearing a son would not only raise her in Jacob's esteem but also cause him to love her.

3706	569.112	3706, 7495.111	3176	904, 6271	3706	6498	154.121
cj	v Qal pf 3fs	cj, v Qal pf 3ms	pn	prep, n ms, ps 1cs	cj	adv	v Qal impf 3ms, ps 1cs
כִּי	אָמְרָה	כִּי־רָאָה	יְהוָה	בְּעָנְיִי	כִּי	עַתָּה	יֶאֱהָבַנִי
kî	'āmerāh	kî-rā'āh	yehwāh	be'ānеyî	kî	'attāh	ye'ěhāvanî
because	she said	because he looked	Yahweh	on my misery	that	now	he will love me

382		2106.122	5968	3314.122	1158	569.122
n ms, ps 1cs	33.	cj, v Qal impf 3fs	adv	cj, v Qal impf 3fs	n ms	cj, v Qal impf 3fs
אִישִׁי		וַתַּהַר	עוֹד	וַתֵּלֶד	בֵּן	וַתֹּאמֶר
'îshî		wattahar	'ôdh	wattēledh	bēn	wattō'mer
my husband		and she conceived	again	and she gave birth	son	and she said

3706, 8471.111	3176	3706, 7983.157	609	5598.121, 3937	1612, 881, 2172
cj, v Qal pf 3ms	pn	cj, v Qal pass ptc fs	pers pron	cj, v Qal impf 3ms, prep, ps 1cs	cj, do, dem pron
כִּי־שָׁמַע	יְהוָה	כִּי־שְׂנוּאָה	אָנֹכִי	וַיִּתֶּן־לִי	גַּם־אֶת־זֶה
kî-shāma'	yehwāh	kî-senû'āh	'ānōkhî	wayyitten-lî	gam-'eth-zeh
because he heard	Yahweh	that one hated	I	now he is giving to me	also this

7410.122	8428	8482		2106.122	5968	3314.122	1158
cj, v Qal impf 3fs	n ms, ps 3ms	pn	34.	cj, v Qal impf 3fs	adv	cj, v Qal impf 3fs	n ms
וַתִּקְרָא	שְׁמוֹ	שִׁמְעוֹן		וַתַּהַר	עוֹד	וַתֵּלֶד	בֵּן
wattiqōrā'	shemô	shim'ôn		wattahar	'ôdh	wattēledh	bēn
and she called	his name	Simeon		and she conceived	again	and she gave birth	son

569.122	6498	6718	4004.221	382	420
cj, v Qal impf 3fs	adv	art, n fs	v Niphal impf 3ms	n ms, ps 1cs	prep, ps 1cs
וַתֹּאמֶר	עַתָּה	הַפַּעַם	יִלָּוֶה	אִישִׁי	אֵלַי
wattō'mer	'attāh	happa'am	yillāweh	îshî	'ēlay
and she said	now	this time	he will become attached	my husband	to me

3706, 3314.115	3937	8421	1158	6142, 3772	7410.111, 8428
prep, v Qal pf 1cs	prep, ps 3ms	num	n mp	prep, adv	v Qal pf 3ms, n ms, ps 3ms
כִּי־יָלַדְתִּי	לוֹ	שְׁלֹשָׁה	בָנִים	עַל־כֵּן	קָרָא־שְׁמוֹ
kî-yāladhtî	lô	shelōshāh	vānîm	'al-kēn	qārā'-shemô
because I have given birth	to him	three	sons	therefore	he called his name

4015		2106.122	5968	3314.122	1158	569.122	6718
pn	35.	cj, v Qal impf 3fs	adv	cj, v Qal impf 3fs	n ms	cj, v Qal impf 3fs	art, n fs
לֵוִי		וַתַּהַר	עוֹד	וַתֵּלֶד	בֵּן	וַתֹּאמֶר	הַפַּעַם
lēwî		wattahar	'ôdh	wattēledh	bēn	wattō'mer	happa'am
Levi		and she conceived	again	and she gave birth	son	and she said	this time

3142.525	881, 3176	6142, 3772	7410.112	8428	3171	6198.122
v Hiphil impf 1cs	do, pn	prep, adv	v Qal pf 3fs	n ms, ps 3ms	pn	cj, v Qal impf 3fs
אוֹדֶה	אֶת־יְהוָה	עַל־כֵּן	קָרְאָה	שְׁמוֹ	יְהוּדָה	וַתַּעֲמֹד
'ôdheh	'eth-yehwāh	'al-kēn	qāre'āh	shemô	yehûdhāh	watta'ămōdh
I will praise	Yahweh	therefore	she called	his name	Judah	and she stood still

4623, 3314.141		7495.122	7637	3706	3940	3314.112	3937, 3399
prep, v Qal inf con	30:1	cj, v Qal impf 3fs	pn	cj	neg part	v Qal pf 3fs	prep, pn
מִלֶּדֶת		וַתֵּרֶא	רָחֵל	כִּי	לֹא	יָלְדָה	לְיַעֲקֹב
milledheth		wattēre'	rāchēl	kî	lō'	yāledhāh	leya'ăqōv
bearing children		and she saw	Rachel	that	not	she gave birth	for Jacob

7349.322	7637	904, 269	569.122	420, 3399	1957.131, 3937
cj, v Piel impf 3fs	pn	prep, n fs, ps 3fs	cj, v Qal impf 3fs	prep, pn	v Qal impv 2ms, prep, ps 1cs
וַתְּקַנֵּא	רָחֵל	בַּאֲחֹתָהּ	וַתֹּאמֶר	אֶל־יַעֲקֹב	הָבָה־לִּי
watteqannē'	rāchēl	ba'ăchōthāhh	wattō'mer	'el-ya'ăqōv	hāvāh-lî
and she envied	Rachel	because of her sister	and she said	to Jacob	give to me

1158 n mp בָּנִים vānîm children	524, 375 cj, cj, n ms וְאִם־אַיִן w^{e}'im-'ayin or if not	4322.153 v Qal act ptc fs מֵתָה mēthāh dead woman	609 pers pron אָנֹכִי 'ānōkhî I	**2.**	2835.121, 653 cj, v Qal impf 3ms, *n ms* וַיִּחַר־אַף wayyichar-'aph and it became hot the nose of	3399 pn יַעֲקֹב ya'ăqōv Jacob

904, 7637 prep, pn בְּרָחֵל b^{e}rāchēl against Rachel	569.121 cj, v Qal impf 3ms וַיֹּאמֶר wayyō'mer and he said	8809 intrg part, prep הֲתַחַת h^{e}thachath am instead of	435 n mp אֱלֹהִים 'ĕlōhîm God	609 pers pron אָנֹכִי 'ānōkhî I	866, 4661.111 rel part, v Qal pf 3ms אֲשֶׁר־מָנַע 'ăsher-māna' who He withheld	4623 prep, ps 3fs מִמֵּךְ mimmēkh from you

33. And she conceived again, and bare a son and said, Because the LORD hath heard that I was hated: ... it has come to the Lord's ears, *BB* ... has heard that he hates me, *Fenton* ... unloved, *Anchor* ... slighted, *Berkeley* ... disliked, *NCB.*

he hath therefore given me this son also: ... in addition, *BB.*

and she called his name Simeon: ... gave him the name, *BB* ... Hearing, *Goodspeed.*

34. And she conceived again, and bare a son and said, Now this time will my husband be joined unto me: ... will grow attached to me, *Berkeley* ... will cling to me, *Fenton* ... surely be united, *NEB* ... keep me company, *Geneva* ... feel affection for me, *LIVB.*

because I have born him three sons: ... given him three sons, *BB.*

therefore was his name called Levi: ... Attachment, *Goodspeed.*

35. And she conceived again, and bare a son and she said, Now will I praise the LORD: ... this time will I praise Jehovah, *ASV* ... let me praise Yahweh, *Anchor* ... this time I will give grateful praise, *NAB.*

therefore she called his name Judah: ... he was named, *BB* ... Praise, *Goodspeed.*

and left bearing: ... she had no more children for a time, *BB* ... ceased to bear children, *Fenton* ... stopped bearing children, *Goodspeed* ... quit bearing, *KJVII* ... for a while she bore no more children, *REB.*

30:1. And when Rachel saw that she bare Jacob no children: ... was not bearing children, *Goodspeed* ... she had no children, *BB* ... had failed to bear, *Anchor.*

Rachel envied her sister: ... became jealous, *NASB* ... full of envy, *BB* ... became envious, *Anchor.*

and said unto Jacob, Give me children, or else I die: ... I will not go on living, *BB* ... if there is none--I die, *Young.*

29:33. Leah must have cried out again and again to the LORD because she was the one disdained and unloved. Because the LORD heard her, she honored Him by naming her second son, Simeon, meaning "hearing," or "one who hears."

29:34. Leah longed for love, but she would be happy if Jacob would show some attachment to her instead of disdaining her, or just putting up with her. So she named her third son, Levi, meaning "joined, accompanying, attachment." Thus the Aaronic priestly line and the Levites who ministered in the music and worship of the Temple were descended from Leah.

29:35. With the birth of her fourth son, Leah turned all her attention to the LORD and named the son, Judah, meaning "Let Him (God) be praised!" Thus she became the ancestress of David and of our Lord Jesus Christ. Then she stopped having children. Since she was not barren, this probably means she stopped insisting on her physical rights as a wife and let Jacob give all his attention to Rachel. Judah's name eventually became the name of all the descendants of Jacob (Jew, Hebrew, *Yehudim*, means people of Judah, Hebrew, *Yehudah*).

30:1-2. Rachel, however was not satisfied with Jacob's love and attention. She wanted sons. The sight of Leah's sons filled her with jealousy. The biblical account here probably goes back to the time after Leah had one or two sons. In her desperation she demanded that Jacob give her sons, lest she die (of shame and grief).

This made Jacob explode with justifiable anger. He was not in the place of God. Only He can give children. In his opinion, God had kept her from having children. But there is no mention of his praying for Rachel to have a son as Isaac did for Rebekah when she was barren (25:21).

6780, 1027	3.	569.122	2079	526	1131	971.131	420
n ms, n fs		cj, v Qal impf 3fs	intrj	n fs, ps 1cs	pn	v Qal impv 2ms	prep, ps 3fs
פְּרִי־בָטֶן		וַתֹּאמֶר	הִנֵּה	אֲמָתִי	בִלְהָה	בֹּא	אֵלֶיהָ
p^{e}rî-vāṭen		wattō'mer	hinnēh	'ămāthî	vilhāh	bō'	'ēlêhā
fruit of womb		and she said	behold	my female slave	Bilhah	go in	to her

3314.122	6142, 1314	1161.225	1612, 609	4623
cj, v Qal impf 3fs	prep, n fp, ps 1cs	cj, v Niphal impf 1cs	cj, pers pron	prep, ps 3fs
וְתֵלֵד	עַל־בִּרְכַּי	וְאִבָּנֶה	גַּם־אָנֹכִי	מִמֶּנָּה
w^{e}thēlēdh	'al-birkay	w^{e}'ibbāneh	gham-'ānōkhî	mimmennāh
and she will give birth	on my knees	and I will be built	also I	from her

4.	5598.122, 3937	881, 1131	8569	3937, 828	971.121	420
	cj, v Qal impf 3fs, prep, ps 3ms	do, pn	n fs, ps 3fs	prep, n fs	cj, v Qal impf 3ms	prep, ps 3fs
	וַתִּתֶּן־לוֹ	אֶת־בִּלְהָה	שִׁפְחָתָהּ	לְאִשָּׁה	וַיָּבֹא	אֵלֶיהָ
	wattitten-lô	'eth-bilhāh	shiphchāthāhh	l^{e}'ishshāh	wayyāvō'	'ēlêhā
	and she gave to him	Bilhah	her female slave	for a wife	and he went in	to her

3399	5.	2106.122	1131	3314.122	3937, 3399	1158	6.	569.122
pn		cj, v Qal impf 3fs	pn	cj, v Qal impf 3fs	prep, pn	n ms		cj, v Qal impf 3fs
יַעֲקֹב		וַתַּהַר	בִּלְהָה	וַתֵּלֶד	לְיַעֲקֹב	בֵּן		וַתֹּאמֶר
ya'ăqōv		wattahar	bilhāh	wattēledh	l^{e}ya'ăqōv	bēn		wattō'mer
Jacob		and she conceived	Bilhah	and she gave birth	for Jacob	son		and she said

7637	1833.111	435	1612	8471.111	904, 7249	5598.121, 3937
pn	v Qal pf 3ms, ps 1cs	n mp	cj, cj	v Qal pf 3ms	prep, n ms, ps 1cs	cj, v Qal impf 3ms, prep, ps 1cs
רָחֵל	דָּנַנִּי	אֱלֹהִים	וְגַם	שָׁמַע	בְּקֹלִי	וַיִּתֶּן־לִי
rāchēl	dānannî	'ĕlōhîm	w^{e}gham	shāma'	b^{e}qōlî	wayyitten-lî
Rachel	He judged me	God	but also	he heard	my voice	and he is giving to me

1158	6142, 3772	7410.112	8428	1896	7.	2106.122	5968	3314.122
n ms	prep, adv	v Qal pf 3fs	n ms, ps 3ms	pn		cj, v Qal impf 3fs	adv	cj, v Qal impf 3fs
בֵּן	עַל־כֵּן	קָרְאָה	שְׁמוֹ	דָּן		וַתַּהַר	עוֹד	וַתֵּלֶד
bēn	'al-kēn	qār^{e}'āh	sh^{e}mô	dān		wattahar	'ôdh	wattēledh
son	therefore	she called	his name	Dan		and she conceived	again	and she gave birth

1131	8569	7637	1158	8529	3937, 3399	8.	569.122	7637
pn	*n fs*	pn	n ms	num	prep, pn		cj, v Qal impf 3fs	pn
בִּלְהָה	שִׁפְחַת	רָחֵל	בֵּן	שֵׁנִי	לְיַעֲקֹב		וַתֹּאמֶר	רָחֵל
bilhāh	shiphchath	rāchēl	bēn	shēnî	l^{e}ya'ăqōv		wattō'mer	rāchēl
Bilhah	the female slave of	Rachel	son	second	for Jacob		and she said	Rachel

5501	435	6871	6196, 269	1612, 3310.115	7410.122	8428
n mp	n mp	v Niphal pf 1cs	prep, n fs, ps 1cs	cj, v Qal pf 1cs	cj, v Qal impf 3fs	n ms, ps 3ms
נַפְתּוּלֵי	אֱלֹהִים	נִפְתַּלְתִּי	עִם־אֲחֹתִי	גַּם־יָכֹלְתִּי	וַתִּקְרָא	שְׁמוֹ
naphtûlê	'ĕlōhîm	niphtaltî	'im-'ăchōthî	gam-yākhōl^{e}tî	wattiqōrā'	sh^{e}mô
the wrestlings of	God	I have wrestled	with my sister	also I have won	and she called	his name

5503	9.	7495.122	3943	3706	6198.112	4623, 3314.141	4089.122
pn		cj, v Qal impf 3fs	pn	cj	v Qal pf 3fs	prep, v Qal inf con	cj, v Qal impf 3fs
נַפְתָּלִי		וַתֵּרֶא	לֵאָה	כִּי	עָמְדָה	מִלֶּדֶת	וַתִּקַּח
naphtālî		wattēre'	lē'āh	kî	'ām^{e}dhāh	milledheth	wattiqqach
Naphtali		and she saw	Leah	that	she stopped	from bearing children	and she took

881, 2238	8569	5598.122	881	3937, 3399	3937, 828	10.	3314.122
do, pn	n fs, ps 3fs	cj, v Qal impf 3fs	do, ps 3fs	prep, pn	prep, n fs		cj, v Qal impf 3fs
אֶת־זִלְפָּה	שִׁפְחָתָהּ	וַתִּתֵּן	אֹתָהּ	לְיַעֲקֹב	לְאִשָּׁה		וַתֵּלֶד
'eth-zilpāh	shiphchāthāhh	wattittēn	'ōthāhh	l^{e}ya'ăqōv	l^{e}'ishshāh		wattēledh
Zilpah	her female slave	and she gave	her	to Jacob	for a wife		and she gave birth

2. And Jacob's anger was kindled against Rachel: ... anger was aroused, *NKJV* ... blazed with anger, *Goodspeed* ... anger fired at Rachel, *Fenton* ... anger rose hotly, *Berkeley* ... became impatient, *NCB*.

and he said, Am I in God's stead: ... I can't take the place of God, *Good News* ... am I in the position of God, *Anchor* ... am I taking God's place, *Berkeley*.

who hath withheld from thee the fruit of the womb?: ... deprived you of fertility, *Berkeley* ... kept your body from having fruit, *BB* ... hold back from you the fruit of your body, *Fenton* ... who has made you barren, *NCB* ... denied you children, *NEB*.

3. And she said, Behold my maid Bilhah, go in unto her: ... lie with her, *NEB* ... have intercourse with her, *Goodspeed* ... sleep with her, *NIV* ... consider my maid, *Berkeley* ... cohabit with her, *Anchor*.

and she shall bear upon my knees: ... sons to be laid upon my knees, *REB* ... bear children for my knees, *Goodspeed* ... she can have a child for me, *Good News* ... give birth on my knees, *Anchor* ... at my knee, *Fenton*.

that I may also have children by her: ... reproduce through her, *Anchor* ... through her I will rear a family, *Berkeley* ... be built up by her, *Darby* ... build up a family, *Goodspeed* ... I too may have offspring, *NAB*.

4. And she gave him Bilhah her handmaid to wife: ... as a consort, *NAB* ... in marriage, *Goodspeed* ... her servant, *Fenton* ... as concubine, *Anchor*.

and Jacob went in unto her: ... slept with her, *NIV* ... lay with her, *NEB* ... had relations, *NCB* ... had intercourse, *Good News*.

5. And Bilhah conceived, and bare Jacob a son: ... became with child, *BB* ... became pregnant, *NIV*.

6. And Rachel said, God hath judged me: ... has pronounced judgment in my favor, *NCB* ... brought judgment on me, *Goodspeed* ... given sentence on my side, *Geneva* ... done me justice, *Berkeley* ... vindicated me, *Anchor*.

and hath also heard my voice: ... has heard my prayer, *NCB* ... given ear to my voice, *BB* ... has heeded my plea, *Anchor*.

and hath given me a son: therefore called she his name Dan: ... He Brought Judgment, *Goodspeed*.

7. And Bilhah Rachel's maid conceived again, and bare Jacob a second son: ... became pregnant again, *Good News*.

8. And Rachel said, With great wrestlings have I wrestled with my sister: ... a fateful contest waged I, *Anchor* ... wrestlings of God have I wrestled, *Darby* ... I struggled with God; I also struggled with my sister, *Fenton* ... I have used a clever device against my sister, *NCB* ... it was a clever trick that I played my sister, *Goodspeed*.

and I have prevailed: ... I have won out, *Berkeley* ... I have overcome her, *BB* ... have gotten the upper hand, *Geneva* ... I succeeded, too, *Goodspeed*.

and she called his name Naphtali: ... Trick, *Goodspeed*.

9. When Leah saw that she had left bearing: ... would have no more children, *BB* ... ceased to bear, *Fenton* ... bearing no more children, *NEB* ... stopped bearing, *NKJV*.

she took Zilpah her maid, and gave her Jacob to wife: ... as concubine, *Anchor* ... her attendant, *Fenton* ... as a consort, *NAB* ... in marriage, *Goodspeed*.

10. And Zilpah Leah's maid bare Jacob a son: ... gave birth, *BB* ... the servant of Leah, *Fenton*.

11. And Leah said, A troop cometh: and she called his name Gad: ... I am fortunate, *Berkeley* ... it has gone well for me, *BB* ... what good luck, *NAB* ... a company cometh, *Geneva* ... how propitious, *Anchor*.

30:3. Rachel then gave her servant Bilhah to Jacob as a wife, that is, as a secondary wife or concubine. She wanted Bilhah to bear children on her (Rachel's) knees, which was a way of saying that she would adopt the children and they would be considered hers. Thus, through Bilhah she could build a family.

30:4-6. When Bilhah bore Jacob a son, Rachel claimed him as her own. She believed that God, as her Judge, had vindicated her through Bilhah, that is had taken away the reproach of her childlessness. So she named the boy Dan, meaning "judge," "vindicator" or "he has vindicated."

30:7-8. Rachel considered her relationship with her sister to be like a wrestling match. But she was not wrestling simply with her sister. She was wrestling with God for His mercy. When Bilhah gave her a second son by Jacob, she felt she had won a victory in her struggle with Leah and with God. So she named the boy Naphtali, "my wrestling" or "my struggle."

30:9-11. Leah was not one to give up. She continued the struggle by giving Jacob her servant Zilpah as a (secondary) wife, that is, as a concubine.

2238	8569	3943	3937, 3399	1158	**11.**	569.122	3943	904, 1439
pn	*n fs*	pn	prep, pn	n ms		cj, v Qal impf 3fs	pn	prep, n ms
זִלְפָּה	שִׁפְחַת	לֵאָה	לְיַעֲקֹב	בֵּן		וַתֹּאמֶר	לֵאָה	בְּגָד
zilpāh	shiphchath	lē'āh	l^{e}ya‘ăqōv	bēn		wattō'mer	lē'āh	b^{e}ghādh
Zilpah	the female slave of	Leah	for Jacob	son		and she said	Leah	by good fortune

7410.122	881, 8428	1440	**12.**	3314.122	2238	8569	3943
cj, v Qal impf 3fs	do, n ms, ps 3ms	pn		cj, v Qal impf 3fs	pn	*n fs*	pn
וַתִּקְרָא	אֶת־שְׁמוֹ	גָּד		וַתֵּלֶד	זִלְפָּה	שִׁפְחַת	לֵאָה
wattiqrā'	'eth-sh^{e}mô	gādh		wattēledh	zilpāh	shiphchath	lē'āh
and she called	his name	Gad		and she gave birth	Zilpah	the female slave of	Leah

1158	8529	3937, 3399	**13.**	569.122	3943	904, 865	3706
n ms	num	prep, pn		cj, v Qal impf 3fs	pn	prep, n ms, ps 1cs	cj
בֵּן	שֵׁנִי	לְיַעֲקֹב		וַתֹּאמֶר	לֵאָה	בְּאָשְׁרִי	כִּי
bēn	shēnî	l^{e}ya‘ăqōv		wattō'mer	lē'āh	b^{e}'āsh^{e}rî	kî
son	second	for Jacob		and she said	Leah	in my good fortune	that

861.316	1351	7410.122	881, 8428	862	**14.**	2050.121
v Piel pf 3cp, ps 1cs	n fp	cj, v Qal impf 3fs	do, n ms, ps 3ms	pn		cj, v Qal impf 3ms
אִשְּׁרוּנִי	בָּנוֹת	וַתִּקְרָא	אֶת־שְׁמוֹ	אָשֵׁר		וַיֵּלֶךְ
'ishsh^{e}rûnî	bānôth	wattiqrā'	'eth-sh^{e}mô	'āshēr		wayyēlekh
they will call me fortunate	daughters	and she called	his name	Asher		and he went

7498	904, 3219	7392, 2498	4834.121	1786	904, 7898	971.521
pn	prep, *n mp*	*n ms*, n fp	cj, v Qal impf 3ms	n mp	prep, art, n ms	cj, v Hiphil impf 3ms
רְאוּבֵן	בִּימֵי	קְצִיר־חִטִּים	וַיִּמְצָא	דוּדָאִים	בַּשָּׂדֶה	וַיָּבֵא
r^{e}'ûvēn	bîmê	qǭtsîr-chiṯṯîm	wayyimtsā'	dhûdhā'îm	bassādheh	wayyāvē'
Reuben	in the days of	the harvest of wheat	and he found	mandrakes	in the field	and he brought

881	420, 3943	525	569.122	7637	420, 3943	5598.132, 5167	3937
do, ps 3mp	prep, pn	n fs, ps 3ms	cj, v Qal impf 3fs	pn	prep, pn	v Qal impv 2fs, part	prep, ps 1cs
אֹתָם	אֶל־לֵאָה	אִמּוֹ	וַתֹּאמֶר	רָחֵל	אֶל־לֵאָה	תְּנִי־נָא	לִי
'ōthām	'el-lē'āh	'immô	wattō'mer	rāchēl	'el-lē'āh	t^{e}nî-nā'	lî
them	to Leah	his mother	and she said	Rachel	to Leah	give please	to me

4623, 1786	1158	**15.**	569.122	3937	4746	4089.141
prep, *n mp*	n ms, ps 2fs		cj, v Qal impf 3fs	prep, ps 3fs	intrg part, *sub*	v Qal inf con, ps 2fs
מִדּוּדָאֵי	בְּנֵךְ		וַתֹּאמֶר	לָהּ	הַמְעַט	קַחְתֵּךְ
middûdhā'ê	b^{e}nēkh		wattō'mer	lāhh	ham‘aṯ	qachtēkh
from the mandrakes of	your son		and she said	to her	is small thing	your taking

881, 382	4089.114	1612	881, 1786	1158	569.122	7637	4062
do, n ms, ps 1cs	cj, v Qal pf 2fs	cj	do, *n mp*	n ms, ps 1cs	cj, v Qal impf 3fs	pn	cj
אֶת־אִישִׁי	וְלָקַחַת	גַּם	אֶת־דּוּדָאֵי	בְּנִי	וַתֹּאמֶר	רָחֵל	לָכֵן
'eth-'îshî	w^{e}lāqachath	gam	'eth-dûdhā'ê	b^{e}nî	wattō'mer	rāchēl	lākhēn
my husband	and will you take	also	the mandrakes of	my son	and she said	Rachel	therefore

8311.121	6196	4050	8809	1786	1158	**16.**	971.121
v Qal impf 3ms	prep, ps 2fs	art, n ms	prep	*n mp*	n ms, ps 2fs		cj, v Qal impf 3ms
יִשְׁכַּב	עִמָּךְ	הַלַּיְלָה	תַּחַת	דוּדָאֵי	בְנֵךְ		וַיָּבֹא
yishkav	‘immākh	hallaylāh	tachath	dûdhā'ê	v^{e}nēkh		wayyāvō'
he will lie	with you	tonight	for	the mandrakes of	your son		and he came

3399	4623, 7898	904, 6394	3428.122	3943	3937, 7410.141	569.122
pn	prep, art, n ms	prep, art, n ms	cj, v Qal impf 3fs	pn	prep, v Qal inf con, ps 3ms	cj, v Qal impf 3fs
יַעֲקֹב	מִן־הַשָּׂדֶה	בָּעֶרֶב	וַתֵּצֵא	לֵאָה	לִקְרָאתוֹ	וַתֹּאמֶר
ya‘ăqōv	min-hassādheh	bā‘erev	wattētsē'	lē'āh	liqrā'thô	wattō'mer
Jacob	from the field	in the evening	and she went out	Leah	to meet him	and she said

420	971.123	3706	7963.142	7963.115	904, 1786	1158
prep, ps 1cs	v Qal impf 2ms	cj	v Qal inf abs	v Qal pf 1cs, ps 2ms	prep, *n mp*	n ms, ps 1cs
אֵלַי	תָּבוֹא	כִּי	שָׂכֹר	שְׂכַרְתִּיךָ	בְּדוּדָאֵי	בְּנִי
'ēlay	tāvô'	kî	sākhōr	s^{e}khartîkhā	b^{e}dhûdhā'ê	b^{e}nî
to me	you will go in	because	hiring	I hired you	with the mandrakes of	my son

8311.121	6196	904, 4050	2000		8471.121	435	420, 3943
cj, v Qal impf 3ms	prep, ps 3fs	prep, art, n ms	pers pron		cj, v Qal impf 3ms	n mp	prep, pn
וַיִּשְׁכַּב	עִמָּהּ	בַּלַּיְלָה	הוּא	**17.**	וַיִּשְׁמַע	אֱלֹהִים	אֶל־לֵאָה
wayyishkav	'immāhh	ballaylāh	hû'		wayyishma'	'ĕlōhîm	'el-lē'āh
and he lay	with her	in the night	that		and He listened	God	to Leah

12. And Zilpah Leah's maid bare Jacob a second son: ... handmaid, *ASV* ... attendant of Leah, *Fenton.*

13. And Leah said, Happy am I: ... how fortunate, *Anchor* ... to my happiness, *Berkeley* ... I am blessed, *Fenton* ... what good fortune, *NAB* ... what happiness, *NCB.*

for the daughters will call me blessed: and she called his name Asher: ... will call me happy, *ASV* ... will consider me fortunate, *Anchor* ... will give witness to my joy, *BB.*

14. And Reuben went in the days of wheat harvest: ... at the time of the wheat harvest, *Anchor* ... grain-cutting, *BB.*

and found mandrakes in the field: ... found May-apples, *Berkeley* ... love-fruits, *BB* ... love apples, *Young* ... mandrake plants, *NIV.*

and brought them unto his mother Leah. Then Rachel said to Leah, Give me, I pray thee, of thy son's mandrakes.

15. And she said unto her, Is it a small matter that thou hast taken my husband?: ... was it not enough, *Anchor* ... trifle, *Berkeley* ... is it a trivial matter, *NCB.*

and wouldest thou take away my son's mandrakes also?: ... should also take my son's mandrakes, *Anchor* ... take the apples of my son, *Fenton.*

And Rachel said, Therefore he shall lie with thee to night for thy son's mandrakes: ... in return for, *Anchor* ... he shall sleep with you tonight in exchange, *Fenton.*

16. And Jacob came out of the field in the evening: ... came in from the field, *Berkeley* ... from the country, *NEB.*

and Leah went out to meet him, and said, Thou must come in unto me: ... sleep with me tonight, *NEB* ... come home with me, *Berkeley* ... stay with me, *Anchor.*

for surely I have hired thee with my son's mandrakes: ... I have bargained for you, *NCB* ... bought and paid for thee, *Geneva* ... given my son's love-fruits as a price, *BB.*

And he lay with her that night: ... went in to her, *BB* ... so sleep with me tonight, *Fenton.*

17. And God hearkened unto Leah and she conceived, and bare Jacob the fifth son: ... listened to Leah, *KJVII* ... Lord heard Leah, *Berkeley* ... heeded Leah, *Anchor.*

18. And Leah said, God hath given me my hire: ... granted me my reward, *Anchor* ... made payment to me, *BB* ... has paid me wages, *Fenton.*

When Zilpah bore a son to Jacob, Leah considered it good fortune, and named the boy Gad, meaning "good fortune, fortunate." Gad can also mean "a troop," though Leah did not have that meaning in mind.

30:12-13. Zilpah's second son made Leah happy and caused her to believe other women would call her happy. So she named the boy Asher, meaning "happy" or "fortunate."

30:14. The wheat harvest in that part of Canaan would have been in May. The mandrake plants (Atropa Mandragora officianarum) Reuben found, and brought to his mother, are in the nightshade family. They have a large forked root which was considered to have properties that would promote conception. Probably because she hoped they might help, Rachel asked Leah for some of the mandrakes.

30:15. From Leah's accusation it becomes clear that Rachel had preempted Jacob, probably persuading him not to sleep with Leah. That was bad enough. Giving Rachel mandrakes would add to the problem. But Leah gave them to her on condition that she could sleep with Jacob.

30:16-18. Leah met Jacob with the news of her bargain with Rachel. But there was more than bargaining here. Leah must have spent time in prayer, for she gave God credit, and she believed God had

2106.122	3314.122	3937, 3399	1158	2653		569.122	3943
cj, v Qal impf 3fs	cj, v Qal impf 3fs	prep, pn	n ms	num	18.	cj, v Qal impf 3fs	pn
וַתַּהַר	וַתֵּלֶד	לְיַעֲקֹב	בֵּן	חֲמִישִׁי		וַתֹּאמֶר	לֵאָה
wattahar	wattēledh	l^{e}ya‘ăqōv	bēn	chămîshî		wattō'mer	lē'āh
and she conceived	and she gave birth	for Jacob	son	fifth		and she said	Leah

5598.111	435	7964	866, 5598.115	8569	3937, 382	7410.122
v Qal pf 3ms	n mp	n ms, ps 1cs	rel part, v Qal pf 1cs	n fs, ps 1cs	prep, n ms, ps 1cs	cj, v Qal impf 3fs
נָתַן	אֱלֹהִים	שְׂכָרִי	אֲשֶׁר־נָתַתִּי	שִׁפְחָתִי	לְאִישִׁי	וַתִּקְרָא
nāthan	'ĕlōhîm	s^{e}khārî	'ăsher-nāthattî	shiphchāthî	l^{e}'îshî	wattiqōrā'
He gave	God	my wages	because I gave	my female slave	to my husband	and she called

8428	3551		2106.122	5968	3943	3314.122	1158, 8676
n ms, ps 3ms	pn	19.	cj, v Qal impf 3fs	adv	pn	cj, v Qal impf 3fs	n ms, num
שְׁמוֹ	יִשָּׂכָר		וַתַּהַר	עוֹד	לֵאָה	וַתֵּלֶד	בֵּן־שִׁשִּׁי
sh^{e}mô	yissākhār		wattahar	‘ôdh	lē'āh	wattēledh	bēn-shishshî
his name	Issachar		and she conceived	again	Leah	and she gave birth	son sixth

3937, 3399		569.122	3943	2149.111	435	881	2150	3005
prep, pn	20.	cj, v Qal impf 3fs	pn	v Qal pf 3ms, ps 1cs	n mp	do, ps 1cs	n ms	adj
לְיַעֲקֹב		וַתֹּאמֶר	לֵאָה	זְבָדַנִי	אֱלֹהִים	אֹתִי	זֵבֶד	טוֹב
l^{e}ya‘ăqōv		wattō'mer	lē'āh	z^{e}vādhanî	'ĕlōhîm	'ōthî	zēvedh	ṯôv
for Jacob		and she said	Leah	He has given a gift	God	me	gift	good

6718	2165.121	382	3706, 3314.115	3937	8666	1158
art, n fs	v Qal impf 3ms, ps 1cs	n ms, ps 1cs	prep, v Qal pf 1cs	prep, ps 3ms	num	n mp
הַפַּעַם	יִזְבְּלֵנִי	אִישִׁי	כִּי־יָלַדְתִּי	לוֹ	שִׁשָּׁה	בָנִים
happa‘am	yizb^{e}lēnî	'îshî	kî-yāladhtî	lô	shishshāh	vānîm
this time	he will exalt me	my husband	because I have given birth	for him	six	sons

7410.122	881, 8428	2157		313	3314.112	1351	7410.122
cj, v Qal impf 3fs	do, n ms, ps 3ms	pn	21.	cj, adv	v Qal pf 3fs	n fs	cj, v Qal impf 3fs
וַתִּקְרָא	אֶת־שְׁמוֹ	זְבֻלוּן		וְאַחַר	יָלְדָה	בַּת	וַתִּקְרָא
wattiqōrā'	'eth-sh^{e}mô	z^{e}vulûn		w^{e}'achar	yāl^{e}dhāh	bath	wattiqōrā'
and she called	his name	Zebulun		and afterward	she gave birth	daughter	and she called

881, 8428	1839		2226.121	435	881, 7637	8471.121	420
do, n ms, ps 3fs	pn	22.	cj, v Qal impf 3ms	n mp	do, pn	cj, v Qal impf 3ms	prep, ps 3fs
אֶת־שְׁמָהּ	דִּינָה		וַיִּזְכֹּר	אֱלֹהִים	אֶת־רָחֵל	וַיִּשְׁמַע	אֵלֶיהָ
'eth-sh^{e}māhh	dînāh		wayyizkōr	'ĕlōhîm	'eth-rāchēl	wayyishma‘	'ēlêhā
her name	Dinah		then He remembered	God	Rachel	and He listened	to her

435	6858.121	881, 7641		2106.122	3314.122	1158
n mp	cj, v Qal impf 3ms	do, n ms, ps 3fs	23.	cj, v Qal impf 3fs	cj, v Qal impf 3fs	n ms
אֱלֹהִים	וַיִּפְתַּח	אֶת־רַחְמָהּ		וַתַּהַר	וַתֵּלֶד	בֵּן
'ĕlōhîm	wayyiphtach	'eth-rachmāhh		wattahar	wattēledh	bēn
God	and He opened	her womb		and she conceived	and she gave birth	son

569.122	636.111	435	881, 2887		7410.122	881, 8428
cj, v Qal impf 3fs	v Qal pf 3ms	n mp	do, n fs, ps 1cs	24.	cj, v Qal impf 3fs	do, n ms, ps 3ms
וַתֹּאמֶר	אָסַף	אֱלֹהִים	אֶת־חֶרְפָּתִי		וַתִּקְרָא	אֶת־שְׁמוֹ
wattō'mer	'āsaph	'ĕlōhîm	'eth-cherpāthî		wattiqōrā'	'eth-sh^{e}mô
and she said	He has taken away	God	my disgrace		and she called	his name

3231	3937, 569.141	3362.521	3176	3937	1158	311		2030.121
pn	prep, v Qal inf con	v Hiphil impf 3ms	pn	prep, ps 1cs	n ms	adj	25.	cj, v Qal impf 3ms
יוֹסֵף	לֵאמֹר	יֹסֵף	יְהוָה	לִי	בֵּן	אַחֵר		וַיְהִי
yôsēph	lē'mōr	yōsēph	y^{e}hwāh	lî	bēn	'achēr		wayhî
Joseph	saying	He will add	Yahweh	to me	son	another		and it was

3626, 866	3314.112	7637	881, 3231	569.121	3399	420, 3969
prep, rel part	v Qal pf 3fs	pn	do, pn	cj, v Qal impf 3ms	pn	prep, pn
כַּאֲשֶׁר	יָלְדָה	רָחֵל	אֶת־יוֹסֵף	וַיֹּאמֶר	יַעֲקֹב	אֶל־לָבָן
ka'ăsher	yāl^{e}dhāh	rāchēl	'eth-yôsēph	wayyō'mer	ya'ăqōv	'el-lāvān
when	she gave birth	Rachel	Joseph	and he said	Jacob	to Laban

8365.131	2050.125	420, 4887	3937, 800		5598.131	881, 5571
v Piel impv 2ms, ps 1cs	cj, v Qal impf 1cs	prep, n ms, ps 1cs	cj, prep, n fs, ps 1cs	**26.**	v Qal impv 2ms	do, n fp, ps 1cs
שַׁלְּחֵנִי	וְאֵלְכָה	אֶל־מְקוֹמִי	וּלְאַרְצִי		תְּנָה	אֶת־נָשַׁי
shall^{e}chēnî	w^e'ēl^{e}khāh	'el-m^{e}qômî	ûlă'artsî		t^{e}nāh	'eth-nāshay
send me	and I will go	to my place	and to my land		give	my wives

because I have given my maiden to my husband: and she called his name Issachar: ... handmaid, *ASV* ... servant-girl, *BB* ... gave my slave, *Good News* ... maidservant, *NAB.*

19. And Leah conceived again, and bare Jacob the sixth son: ... became with child, *BB* ... became pregnant again, *Good News.*

20. And Leah said, God hath endued me with a good dowry: ... endowed me with a good endowment, *NKJV* ... made me a magnificent present, *Goodspeed* ... a good bride-price, *BB* ... has given me a precious gift, *Anchor* ... a rich dowry, *Berkeley.*

now will my husband dwell with me, because I have born him six sons: and she called his name Zebulun: ... will honor me like a princess, *REB* ... treat me in princely style, *NEB* ... stay with me now, *Goodspeed* ... bring me presents, *Anchor* ... live with me, *Berkeley.*

21. And afterwards she bare a daughter, and called her name Dinah: ... lastly, she bore a daughter, *Anchor.*

22. And God remembered Rachel: ... gave thought to Rachel, *BB* ... Rachel's plight, *LIVB.*

and God hearkened to her: ... heard her prayer, *NEB* ... answered her prayer, *Good News* ... listened to her, *Darby* ... heeded her, *Anchor.*

and opened her womb: ... gave her a child, *NEB* ... made her pregnant, *Goodspeed* ... fertile, *Berkeley.*

23. And she conceived, and bare a son; and said, God hath taken away my reproach: ... hath gathered up my reproach, *Young* ... taken away my humiliation, *REB* ... removed the dark slur against my name, *LIVB* ... taken away my rebuke, *Geneva* ... removed my disgrace, *NAB.*

24. And she called his name Joseph; and said, The LORD shall add to me another son: ... the Ever-Living has added to me another son, *Fenton* ... may the Lord give me another son, *Good News.*

25. And it came to pass, when Rachel had born Joseph: ... after the birth of Joseph, *BB* ... when Rachel had born Joseph, *Fenton* ... had given birth to, *Goodspeed.*

rewarded her for giving Zilpah to Jacob. So she named the boy Issachar, meaning "he is a reward," or "he will bring a reward."

30:19-20. Leah said her sixth son was a good gift from God. She hoped that six sons would be enough to cause Jacob to exalt her, that is give her the place of honor that the primary wife ought to have. So she named the boy Zebulun, probably meaning "honor" or "exalted dwelling."

30:21. Leah's next child was Jacob's only girl. Dinah, meaning "justice" or "vindication." She was later raped by Shechem (Gen. 34:2).

30:22-24. When God remembers it does not mean He had forgotten. Rather it means that it was God's time and He actively entered the situation to do something about it. This intervention was to answer Rachel's prayers that He had been listening to the entire time of Leah's childbearing years. God, not the mandrakes, made it possible for Rachel to have a son. Barrenness was considered a disgrace. Now that disgrace was removed by the birth of a son. But she was not satisfied, since Leah had six sons. So she named the boy Joseph, meaning "may He [God] add," and she asked for another son. Unfortunately, the fulfillment of that prayer would cause her death (35:16-19).

30:25-26. Rachel gave birth to Joseph at the end of the fourteen years of Jacob's slave labor to Laban. Jacob now had eleven sons and a daughter, all born during the last seven years. Now that he had fulfilled his bargain, he asked Laban to dismiss him and let him go home with his wives and children. It seems that Laban, as head of the extended family, still had the legal right to his daughters and grandchildren and would have to acknowledge that Jacob had done the work he had bargained to do.

881, 3315	866	5856.115	881	904	2050.125	3706	887
cj, do, n mp, ps 1cs	rel part	v Qal pf 1cs	do, ps 2ms	prep, ps 3fp	cj, v Qal impf 1cs	cj	pers pron
וְאֶת־יְלָדַי	אֲשֶׁר	עָבַדְתִּי	אֹתְךָ	בָּהֵן	וְאֵלֵכָה	כִּי	אַתָּה
w^{e}'eth-y^{e}lādhay	'ăsher	'āvadhtî	'ōth^{e}khā	bāhēn	w^{e}'ēlēkhāh	kî	'attāh
and my children	which	I served	you	for them	and I will go	because	you

3156.113	881, 5865	866	5856.115		569.121	420	3969
v Qal pf 2ms	do, n fs, ps 1cs	rel part	v Qal pf 1cs, ps 2ms	**27.**	cj, v Qal impf 3ms	prep, ps 3ms	pn
יָדַעְתָּ	אֶת־עֲבֹדָתִי	אֲשֶׁר	עֲבַדְתִּיךָ		וַיֹּאמֶר	אֵלָיו	לָבָן
yādha'ättā	'eth-'ăvōdhāthî	'ăsher	'ăvadtîkhā		wayyō'mer	'ēlāv	lāvān
you know	my work	which	I have served you		and he said	to him	Laban

524, 5167	4834.115	2682	904, 6084	5355.315	1313.321
cj, part	v Qal pf 1cs	n ms	prep, n fd, ps 2ms	v Piel pf 1cs	cj, v Piel impf 3ms, ps 1cs
אִם־נָא	מָצָאתִי	חֵן	בְּעֵינֶיךָ	נִחַשְׁתִּי	וַיְבָרְכֵנִי
'im-nā'	mātsā'thî	chēn	b^{e}'ênêkhā	nichashtî	wayvār^{e}khēnî
if please	I have found	favor	in your eyes	I learned by divination	that He has blessed me

3176	904, 1600		569.121	5529.131	7964	6142
pn	prep, n ms, ps 2ms	**28.**	cj, v Qal impf 3ms	v Qal impv 2ms	n ms, ps 2ms	prep, ps 1cs
יְהוָה	בִּגְלָלֶךָ		וַיֹּאמַר	נָקְבָה	שְׂכָרְךָ	עָלַי
y^{e}hwāh	bighlālekhā		wayyō'mar	nāqŏvāh	s^{e}khār^{e}khā	'ālay
Yahweh	on account of you		and he said	name	your wages	on me

5598.125		569.121	420	887	3156.113	881	866
cj, v Qal impf 1cs	**29.**	cj, v Qal impf 3ms	prep, ps 3ms	pers pron	v Qal pf 2ms	do	rel part
וְאֶתֵּנָה		וַיֹּאמֶר	אֵלָיו	אַתָּה	יָדַעְתָּ	אֵת	אֲשֶׁר
w^{e}'ettēnāh		wayyō'mer	'ēlâv	'attāh	yādha'ättā	'ēth	'ăsher
and I will give		and he said	to him	you	you know		that

5856.115	881	866, 2030.111	4898	882		3706	4746
v Qal pf 1cs, ps 2ms	cj, do	rel part, Qal perf 3ms	n ms, ps 2ms	prep, ps 1cs	**30.**	cj	sub
עֲבַדְתִּיךָ	וְאֵת	אֲשֶׁר־הָיָה	מִקְנְךָ	אִתִּי		כִּי	מְעַט
'ăvadtîkhā	w^{e}ēth	'ăsher-hāyāh	miqōn^{e}khā	'ittî		kî	m^{e}'at
I have served you	and	how it was	your livestock	with me		because	little

866, 2030.111	3937	3937, 6686	6805.121	3937, 7525.141	1313.321
rel part, v Qal pf 3ms	prep, ps 2ms	prep, n mp, ps 1cs	cj, v Qal impf 3ms	prep, v Qal inf con	cj, v Piel impf 3ms
אֲשֶׁר־הָיָה	לְךָ	לְפָנַי	וַיִּפְרֹץ	לָרֹב	וַיְבָרֶךְ
'ăsher-hāyāh	l^{e}khā	l^{e}phānay	wayyiphrōts	lārōv	way^{e}vārekh
which it was	to you	before me	and he increased	to multiply	and he blessed

3176	881	3937, 7559	6498	5146	6449.125	1612, 609
pn	do, ps 2ms	prep, n fs, ps 1cs	cj, adv	intrg	v Qal impf 1cs	cj, pers pron
יְהוָה	אֹתְךָ	לְרַגְלִי	וְעַתָּה	מָתַי	אֶעֱשֶׂה	גַּם־אָנֹכִי
y^{e}hwāh	'ōth^{e}khā	l^{e}raghlî	w^{e}'attāh	māthay	'e'ĕseh	gham-'ānōkhî
Yahweh	you	at my foot	and now	when	will I do	also I

3937, 1041		569.121	4242	5598.125, 3937	569.121	3399
prep, n ms, ps 1cs	**31.**	cj, v Qal impf 3ms	intrg	v Qal impf 1cs, prep, ps 2ms	cj, v Qal impf 3ms	pn
לְבֵיתִי		וַיֹּאמֶר	מָה	אֶתֶּן־לָךְ	וַיֹּאמֶר	יַעֲקֹב
l^{e}vêthî		wayyō'mer	māh	'etten-lākhā	wayyō'mer	ya'ăqōv
for my household		and he said	what	will I give to you	and he said	Jacob

3940, 5598.123, 3937	4114	524, 6449.123, 3937	1745	2172
neg part, v Qal impf 2ms, prep, ps 1cs	indef pron	cj, v Qal impf 2ms, prep, ps 1cs	art, n ms	art, dem pron
לֹא־תִתֶּן־לִי	מְאוּמָה	אִם־תַּעֲשֶׂה־לִי	הַדָּבָר	הַזֶּה
lō'-thitten-lî	m^{e}'ûmāh	'im-ta'ăseh-lî	haddāvār	hazzeh
not you will give to me	anything	if you will do for me	the thing	the this

that Jacob said unto Laban, Send me away, that I may go unto mine own place, and to my country: ... let me return to my own home, *NCB* ... let me go, *Goodspeed* ... move on to my own community, *Berkeley* ... go to my own homeland, *Anchor.*

26. Give me my wives and my children, for whom I have served thee, and let me go: ... for whom I have worked, *Goodspeed* ... I have been your servant, *BB* ... that I may depart, *Anchor* ... I will be on my way, *NIV.*

for thou knowest my service which I have done thee: ... you know how much my service has done for you, *Anchor* ... what service I have rendered you, *Berkeley* ... knowledge of all the work I have done for you, *BB* ... the wages for which I have served, *Fenton.*

27. And Laban said unto him, I pray thee, if I have found favour in thine eyes, tarry: for: ... if I have found grace, *Young* ... stay if you care enough for me, *Berkeley* ... if you will let me say so, do not go away, *BB.*

I have learned by experience: ... I have learned by divination, *NIV* ... I have discovered, *Darby* ... I have learned from the omens, *Goodspeed* ... I have observed diligently, *Young* ... seen by the signs, *BB.*

that the LORD hath blessed me for thy sake: ... I have become prosperous and the Lord has blessed me through you, *REB* ... the Lord has been good to me because of you, *BB* ... Yahweh has blessed me on account of you, *Anchor.*

28. And he said, Appoint me thy wages, and I will give it: ... say then what your payment is to be and I will give it, *BB* ... name any wages you want from me, and I will pay, *Anchor* ... what I owe you in wages, *NEB.*

29. And he said unto him, Thou knowest how I have served thee: ... you know what my service has meant to you, *Anchor* ... you know how I have worked for you, *NIV* ... you have seen what I have done for you, *BB* ... you know what work I did for you, *NAB.*

and how thy cattle was with me: ... how thy cattle have fared, *ASV* ... how your livestock has fared under my care, *NIV* ... what thy cattle has become, *Berkeley* ... your cattle have done well under my care, *BB* ... herds have prospered under my care, *REB.*

30. For it was little which thou hadst before I came: ... before I came you had little, *BB* ... for they were small that were with you before me, *Fenton* ... you had only a few when I came, *NEB* ... it is little which thou hast had at my appearance, *Young.*

and it is now increased unto a multitude: ... has broadened into a great many, *Berkeley* ... greatly increased, *BB* ... expanded into a great deal, *Goodspeed* ... increased beyond measure, *NEB* ... grown into very much, *NAB.*

and the LORD hath blessed thee since my coming: ... blessed thee whithersoever I turned, *ASV* ... given you a blessing in everything I have done, *BB* ... blessed you for my actions, *Anchor* ... at my every step, *NCB* ... from the time I came, *Darby.*

and now when shall I provide for mine own house also?: ... when should I provide for my own family, *LIVB* ... yet have I gained even a house of my own, *Fenton* ... when shall I travel for mine own house, also, *Geneva* ... when am I to make provision, *Goodspeed.*

31. And he said, What shall I give thee?: ... what wages do you want, *LIVB* ... what should I pay you, *Anchor.*

And Jacob said, Thou shalt not give me any thing: ... not give me aught, *ASV* ... need not pay me anything outright, *Anchor* ... pay me nothing, *Berkeley* ... I don't want any wages, *Good News* ... give me nothing at all, *NCB.*

if thou wilt do this thing for me: ... if you will agree with me on this, *Berkeley* ... if you agree to the proposal, *NCB* ... if you will do what I suggest, *REB.*

30:27-28. Though Laban talked about the LORD, he did not understand who He is. Laban was still involved in heathen practices such as divination (including such things as fortune telling). These were strictly forbidden when God gave Moses the Law (Lev. 19:26; Deut. 18:10-14). They caused people to trust in evil or demonic forces instead of trusting God.

However, God must have overruled here and caused Laban to realize that it was the LORD who was blessing him with material blessings on account of Jacob. God was using Jacob to be a blessing. So Laban wanted Jacob to continue working for him and asked him to name his wages.

30:29-30. Jacob again reminded Laban how hard he had worked for him and how the LORD had blessed and multiplied the little Laban had when Jacob first came. Now it was time for Jacob to do something for his own household.

30:31-34. When Laban asked what he should give Jacob, Jacob said he does not want him to give anything. That is, he was not asking for Laban to divide his flock and give Jacob part. Rather, let him take as wages the future speckled and spotted young

8178.125	7749.125	6887	8490.125		5882.125
v Qal impf 1cs	v Qal impf 1cs	n fs, ps 2ms	v Qal impf 1cs	**32.**	v Qal impf 1cs
אָשׁוּבָה	אֶרְעֶה	צֹאנְךָ	אֶשְׁמֹר		אֶעֱבֹר
'āshûvāh	'er'eh	tsō'nekhā	'eshmōr		'e'ĕvōr
I will do again	I will shepherd	your flock	I will keep		I will pass through

904, 3725, 6887	3219	5681.542	4623, 8427	3725, 7902	5532
prep, *adj*, n fs, ps 2ms	art, n ms	v Hiphil inf abs	prep, adv	*adj*, n ms	adj
בְּכָל־צֹאנְךָ	הַיּוֹם	הָסֵר	מִשָּׁם	כָּל־שֶׂה	נָקֹד
bekhol-tsō'nekhā	hayyôm	hāsēr	mishshām	kol-seh	nāqōdh
among all your flocks	today	removing	from there	every young	speckled

3032.155	3725, 7902, 2439	904, 3904	3032.155	5532
cj, v Qal pass ptc ms	cj, *adj*, n ms, adj	prep, art, n mp	cj, v Qal pass ptc ms	cj, adj
וְטָלוּא	וְכָל־שֶׂה־חוּם	בַּכְּשָׂבִים	וְטָלוּא	וְנָקֹד
wetālû'	wekhol-seh-chûm	bakkesāvîm	wetālû'	wenāqōdh
and spotted one	and every young one darkened	among the lambs	and spotted ones	speckled

904, 6008	2030.111	7964		6257.112, 904	6930	904, 3219
prep, art, n fp	cj, v Qal pf 3ms	n ms, ps 1cs	**33.**	cj, v Qal pf 3fs, prep, ps 1cs	n fs, ps 1cs	prep, n ms
בָּעִזִּים	וְהָיָה	שְׂכָרִי		וְעָנְתָה־בִּי	צִדְקָתִי	בְּיוֹם
bā'izzîm	wehāyāh	sekhārî		we'ānethāh-bî	tsidhqāthî	beyôm
among the goats	and it will be	my wages		and it will answer for me	my honesty	on day

4417	3706, 971.123	6142, 7964	3937, 6686	3725	866, 375	5532
adv	cj, v Qal impf 2ms	prep, n ms, ps 1cs	prep, n mp, ps 2ms	adj	rel part, sub, ps 3ms	adj
מָחָר	כִּי־תָבוֹא	עַל־שְׂכָרִי	לְפָנֶיךָ	כֹּל	אֲשֶׁר־אֵינֶנּוּ	נָקֹד
māchār	kî-thāvō'	'al-shekhārî	lephānêkhā	kōl	'ăsher-'ênennû	nāqōdh
next day	that you will come	about my wages	before you	all	which it is not	speckled

3032.155	904, 6008	2439	904, 3904	1630.155	2000
cj, v Qal pass ptc ms	prep, art, n fp	cj, adj	prep, art, n mp	v Qal pass ptc ms	pers pron
וְטָלוּא	בָּעִזִּים	וְחוּם	בַּכְּשָׂבִים	גָּנוּב	הוּא
wetālû'	bā'izzîm	wechûm	bakkesāvîm	gānûv	hû'
and spotted ones	among the goats	and darkened ones	among the lambs	stolen	it

882		569.121	3969	2075	4001	2030.121	3626, 1745
prep, ps 1cs	**34.**	cj, v Qal impf 3ms	pn	intrj	cj	v Qal juss 3ms	prep, n mp, ps 2ms
אִתִּי		וַיֹּאמֶר	לָבָן	הֵן	לוּ	יְהִי	כִדְבָרֶךָ
'ittî		wayyō'mer	lāvān	hēn	lû	yehî	khidhvārekhā
with me		and he said	Laban	behold	if only	let it be	like your words

	5681.521	904, 3219	2000	881, 8825	6362	3032.157
35.	cj, v Hiphil impf 3ms	prep, art, n ms	art, dem pron	do, art, n mp	art, adj	cj, art, v Qal pass ptc mp
	וַיָּסַר	בַּיּוֹם	הַהוּא	אֶת־הַתְּיָשִׁים	הָעֲקֻדִּים	וְהַטְּלֻאִים
	wayyāsar	bayyôm	hahû'	'eth-hattevāshîm	hā'ăquddîm	wehattelu'îm
	and he removed	in the day	the that	the he-goats	streaked	and the spotted ones

881	3725, 6008	5532	3032.158	3725	866, 3968	904
cj, do	*adj*, art, n fp	art, adj	cj, art, v Qal pass ptc fp	adj	rel part, adj	prep, ps 3ms
וְאֵת	כָּל־הָעִזִּים	הַנְּקֻדּוֹת	וְהַטְּלֻאֹת	כֹּל	אֲשֶׁר־לָבָן	בּוֹ
we'ēth	kol-hā'izzîm	hannequddôth	wehattelu'ōth	kōl	'ăsher-lāvān	bô
and	all of the she-goats	the speckled	and the spotted ones	all	which white	on it

3725, 2439	904, 3904	5598.121	904, 3135, 1158		7947.121
cj, *adj*, adj	prep, art, n mp	cj, v Qal pf 3ms	prep, *n fs*, n mp, ps 3ms	**36.**	cj, v Qal impf 3ms
וְכָל־חוּם	בַּכְּשָׂבִים	וַיִּתֵּן	בְּיַד־בָּנָיו		וַיָּשֶׂם
wekhol-chûm	bakkesāvîm	wayyittēn	beyadh-bānâv		wayyāsem
and all darkened ones	among the lambs	and he placed	in the hand of his sons		and he put

I will again feed and keep thy flock: ... take up the care of your flock, *BB* ... pasture and tend your flock, *Anchor* ... conduct your sheep and guard them, *Fenton* ... I turn back; I have delight; thy flock I watch, *Young*.

32. I will pass through all thy flock to day: ... go over all your sheep today counting, *Fenton* ... I will inspect all your livestock, *Berkeley* ... go through your entire flock today, *Anchor*.

removing from thence all the speckled and spotted cattle: ... separate from them, *Berkeley* ... marked or colored, *BB* ... with little spots and great spots, *Geneva* ... remove from it every dark animal, *NAB*.

and all the brown cattle among the sheep: ... every black one among the sheep, *ASV* ... every animal that is dark-colored, *Anchor* ... every black lamb, *NEB* ... all of the black sheep among the lambs, *KJVII*.

and the spotted and speckled among the goats: ... in the rams, *Fenton* ... great spotted and little spotted, *Geneva* ... brindled and spotted, *NEB*.

and of such shall be my hire: ... these will compose my wages, *Berkeley* ... they alone shall be my wages, *Anchor* ... these will be my payment, *BB*.

33. So shall my righteousness answer for me in time to come: ... let your own view of my honesty be used as an argument against me, *Anchor* ... my fairness will testify for me in the days ahead, *Berkeley* ... you will be able to put my honour to the test, *BB* ... you shall assign them justly to me from to-day forward, *Fenton* ... I will stand self-condemned before you, *NCB*.

when it shall come for my hire before thy face: ... when you examine my wages, *Berkeley* ... as my wages for you, *Fenton* ... when it shall come for my reward, *Geneva* ... concerning my wages, *NASB* ... setting my wages, *NEB*.

every one that is not speckled and spotted among the goats: ... marked or coloured, *BB* ... hath not little or great spots, *Geneva*.

and brown among the sheep: ... black among the sheep, *ASV* ... any sheep that is not dis-colored, *Anchor* ... any that are not black, *Berkeley*.

that shall be counted stolen with me: ... if found with me, shall be counted stolen, *ASV* ... got there by theft, *Anchor* ... consider them stolen, *Berkeley* ... you may take me for a thief, *BB*.

34. And Laban said, Behold, I would it might be according to thy word: ... let it be as you say, *Anchor* ... I am agreeable to your proposition, *Berkeley* ... it shall be exactly as you say, *Fenton*.

35. And he removed that day the he goats that were ringstraked and spotted: ... streaked and spotted, *NAB* ... set apart then and there, *Berkeley* ... banded or coloured, *BB* ... partly coloured and with great spots, *Geneva* ... striped and brindled, *NEB*.

and all the she goats that were speckled and spotted: ... marked or coloured, *BB* ... with little and great spots, *Geneva* ... spotted and brindled, *NEB*.

and every one that had some white in it: ... all that had any white on them, *NEB* ... from all that were white, *Fenton* ... or had white marks, *BB* ... every one that had a touch of white, *Anchor*.

and all the brown among the sheep: ... all the black ones among the sheep, *ASV* ... fully dark-colored sheep, *NAB* ... every black lamb, *Berkeley* ... every ram that was black, *NEB*.

and gave them into the hand of his sons: ... left them in the charge of, *Anchor* ... put them in the keeping of, *Geneva* ... handing them over to his sons, *Goodspeed*.

36. And he set three days' journey betwixt himself and Jacob: ... distance of three days journey, *NASB*.

---

of the sheep and goats and the dark colored young of the sheep. Normally the sheep in that part of the world in those days were white and the goats black. Those that Jacob asked for would normally be in a small minority. It would also be easy to determine which were Jacob's and which were Laban's. Thus Laban thought this would be a good deal for him, a cheap price for Jacob's knowledge and skilled care for his flock. Laban agreed without hesitation.

30:35-36. Laban shows his own selfish, crafty nature as well as his distrust of Jacob, when, without letting Jacob know, Laban himself separated out all the goats that were not solid white or black and all the dark colored lambs and put them in the care of the young sons that he now had. Then he showed further distrust by putting a distance of three days journey between his sons and Jacob. Jacob was left to continue to shepherd the remainder of Laban's flock.

30:37-39. In order to understand what Jacob did here it is necessary to take into account Jacob's dream recorded in Genesis 31:10-12. The sticks or stakes that Jacob peeled were fairly long, such as were used as a staff for travelers or shepherds (Gen. 32:11; 1 Sam. 17:40). Jacob used them to make a fence around the watering troughs. Then he fenced

1932	8421	3219	1033	1033	3399	3399	7749.151
n ms	*num*	n mp	prep, ps 3ms	cj, prep	pn	cj, pn	v Qal act ptc ms
דֶּרֶךְ	שְׁלֹשֶׁת	יָמִים	בֵּינוֹ	וּבֵין	יַעֲקֹב	וְיַעֲקֹב	רֹעֶה
derekh	sh^{e}lōsheth	yāmîm	bênô	ûvên	ya'ăqōv	w^{e}ya'ăqōv	rō'eh
journey of	three	days	between him	and between	Jacob	and Jacob	shepherding

881, 6887	3969	3613.258		4089, 3937	3399	4894	3974
do, *n fs*	pn	art, v Niphal ptc fp	**37.**	cj, v Qal impf 3ms, prep, ps 3ms	pn	*n fs*	n ms
אֶת־צֹאן	לָבָן	הַנּוֹתָרֹת		וַיִּקַּח־לוֹ	יַעֲקֹב	מַקַּל	לִבְנֶה
'eth-tsō'n	lāvān	hannôthārōth		wayyiqqach-lô	ya'ăqōv	maqqal	livneh
the flocks of	Laban	the remainder		and he took for him	Jacob	sticks of	storax tree

4026	4006	6432	6732.321	904	6726	3968	4421
adj	cj, n ms	cj, n ms	cj, v Piel impf 3ms	prep, ps 3fp	n fp	adj	*n ms*
לַח	וְלוּז	וְעַרְמוֹן	וַיְפַצֵּל	בָּהֵן	פְּצָלוֹת	לְבָנוֹת	מַחְשֹׂף
lach	w^{e}lûz	w^{e}'armôn	way^{e}phatstsēl	bāhen	p^{e}tsālôth	l^{e}vānôth	machsōph
fresh	and almond tree	and plane tree	and he peeled	on them	peelings	white	exposing

3968	866	6142, 4894		3431.521	881, 4894	866	6732.111
art, adj	rel part	prep, art, n fp	**38.**	cj, v Hiphil impf 3ms	do, art, n fp	rel part	v Piel pf 3ms
הַלָּבָן	אֲשֶׁר	עַל־הַמַּקְלוֹת		וַיַּצֵּג	אֶת־הַמַּקְלוֹת	אֲשֶׁר	פִּצֵּל
hallāvān	'ăsher	'al-hammaqŏlôth		wayyatstsēgh	'eth-hammaqŏlôth	'ăsher	pitstsēl
the white	which	on the sticks		and he placed	the sticks	which	he peeled

904, 7584	904, 8633	4448	866	971.127	6887	3937, 8685.141
prep, art n mp	prep, *n fp*	art, n md	rel part	v Qal impf 3fp	art, n fs	prep, v Qal inf con
בָּרְהָטִים	בְּשִׁקֲתוֹת	הַמָּיִם	אֲשֶׁר	תָּבֹאןָ	הַצֹּאן	לִשְׁתּוֹת
bār^{e}hāṭîm	b^{e}shiqŏthôth	hammāyim	'āsher	tāvō'nā	hatstsō'n	lishtôth
by the troughs	by the troughs of	the waters	where	they came	the sheep	to drink

3937, 5415	6887	2657.127	904, 971.141	3937, 8685.141
prep, prep	art, n fs	cj, v Qal impf 3fp	prep, v Qal inf con, ps 3fp	prep, v Qal inf con
לְנֹכַח	הַצֹּאן	וַיֵּחַמְנָה	בְּבֹאָן	לִשְׁתּוֹת
l^{e}nōkhach	hatstsō'n	wayyēchamnāh	b^{e}vō'ān	lishtôth
in front of	the sheep	when they were in heat	in their coming	to drink

	2657.126	6887	420, 4894	3314.127	6887	6362
39.	cj, v Qal impf 3mp	art, n fs	prep, art, n fp	cj, v Qal impf 3fp	art, n fs	adj
	וַיֶּחֱמוּ	הַצֹּאן	אֶל־הַמַּקְלוֹת	וַתֵּלַדְןָ	הַצֹּאן	עֲקֻדִּים
	wayyechĕmû	hatstsō'n	'el-hammaqŏlôth	wattēladh^{e}nā	hatstsō'n	'ăquddîm
	and they were in heat	the flocks	toward the sticks	and they gave birth	the flocks	streaked

5532	3032.156		3904	6754.511	3399	5598.121	6686
adj	cj, v Qal pass ptc mp	**40.**	cj, art, n mp	v Hiphil pf 3ms	pn	cj, v Qal pf 3ms	*n mp*
נְקֻדִּים	וּטְלֻאִים		וְהַכְּשָׂבִים	הִפְרִיד	יַעֲקֹב	וַיִּתֵּן	פְּנֵי
n^{e}quddîm	ût^{e}lu'îm		w^{e}hakk^{e}sāvîm	hiphrîdh	ya'ăqōv	wayyittēn	p^{e}nê
speckled	and spotted ones		and the lambs	he separated	Jacob	and he placed	before

6887	420, 6362	3725, 2439	904, 6887	3969	8701.121, 3937
art, n fs	prep, adj	cj, *adj*, adj	prep, *n fs*	pn	cj, v Qal impf 3ms, prep, ps 3ms
הַצֹּאן	אֶל־עָקֹד	וְכָל־חוּם	בְּצֹאן	לָבָן	וַיָּשֶׁת־לוֹ
hatstsō'n	'el-'āqōdh	w^{e}khol-chûm	b^{e}tsō'n	lāvān	wayyāsheth-lô
the sheep	toward streaked ones	and all darkened ones	among the flocks of	Laban	and he put for himself

5953	3937, 940	3940	8701.111	6142, 6887	3969		2030.111
n mp	prep, n ms, ps 3ms	cj, neg part	v Qal pf 3ms, ps 3mp	prep, *n fs*	pn	**41.**	cj, v Qal pf 3ms
עֲדָרִים	לְבַדּוֹ	וְלֹא	שָׁתָם	עַל־צֹאן	לָבָן		וְהָיָה
'ădhārîm	l^{e}vaddô	w^{e}lō'	shāthām	'al-tsō'n	lāvān		w^{e}hāyāh
flocks	by themselves	and not	he put them	beside the flocks of	Laban		and it was

904, 3725, 3285.341	6887	7489.458	7947.111	3399	881, 4894
prep, *adj*, v Piel inf con	art, n fs	art, v Pual ptc fp	cj, v Qal pf 3ms	pn	do, art, n fp
בְּכָל־יַחֵם	הַצֹּאן	הַמְקֻשָּׁרוֹת	וְשָׂם	יַעֲקֹב	אֶת־הַמַּקְלוֹת
b^{e}khol-yachēm	hatstsō'n	hamqushshārôth	w^{e}sām	ya'ăqōv	'eth-hammaqōlôth
during all the breeding of	the sheep	the stronger ones	then he put	Jacob	the sticks

3937, 6084	6887	904, 7584	3937, 3285.341	904, 4894	42.	904, 6063.541
prep, *n fd*	art, n fs	prep, art n mp	prep, v Piel inf con, ps 3fs	prep, art, n fp		cj, prep, v Hiphil inf con
לְעֵינֵי	הַצֹּאן	בָּרְהָטִים	לְיַחְמֵנָּה	בַּמַּקְלוֹת		וּבְהַעֲטִיף
l^{e}'ênê	hatstsō'n	bārhāṭîm	l^{e}yachămennāh	bammaqōlôth		ûv^{e}ha'ăṭîph
to the eyes of	the flock	by the troughs	for their breeding	by the sticks		but by the weak of

and Jacob fed the rest of Laban's flocks: ... went about pasturing, *Anchor* ... shepherded the other sheep, *Fenton* ... remained in charge of the rest, *Goodspeed* ... tending Laban's flocks that remained, *NEB.*

37. And Jacob took him rods of green poplar: ... fresh shoots of poplar, *NAB* ... young branches of trees, *BB* ... young wands of willow, *Fenton.*

and of the hazel and chestnut tree: ... and of the almond and of the plane-tree, *ASV* ... and maple, *Darby.*

and pilled white strakes in them: ... peeled white stripes in them, *NCB* ... cutting off the skin, *BB* ... peeled off strips of bark, *NEB.*

and made the white appear which was in the rods: ... laying bare the white of the shoots, *Anchor* ... peeling off the bark down to the white core, *NAB* ... exposing the white of the rods, *NEB.*

38. And he set the rods which he had pilled: ... peeled, *Anchor* ... banded sticks, *BB.*

before the flocks in the gutters in the watering troughs: ... the water-receptacles, *Anchor* ... in the troughs at the watering-places, *Darby* ... fixed the peeled rods upright in the troughs, *NEB.*

when the flocks came to drink: ... came to get water, *BB* ... came to be watered, *NCB.*

that they should conceive when they came to drink: ... since they mated, *Anchor* ... they bred, MLB ... they were in heat, *Geneva.*

39. And the flocks conceived before the rods: ... they felt a longing for the rods, *NEB* ... were in heat, *Geneva* ... mated, *Anchor.*

and brought forth cattle ringstraked, speckled, and spotted: ... flocks lambed striped, *MLB* ... marked with bands of colour, *BB* ... partly colour and with small and great spots, *Geneva.*

40. And Jacob did separate the lambs: ... the ewes Jacob kept apart, *Anchor* ... as for the rams, Jacob divided them, *NEB.*

and set the faces of the flocks toward the ringstraked: ... made the animals face the streaked, *Anchor* ... striped, *Berkeley* ... turned the faces of the flock, *Geneva* ... let the ewes run only with such of the rams as were striped and black, *NEB.*

and all the brown in the flock of Laban: ... and all the black in the flock, *ASV* ... fully dark-colored animals, *Anchor.*

and he put his own flocks by themselves: ... he put his own droves apart, *ASV* ... he produced special flocks for himself, *Anchor* ... made himself separate flocks, *Darby.*

and put them not unto Laban's cattle: ... did not put them with Laban's flock, *Darby* ... not adding them to, *Anchor.*

41. And it came to pass, whensoever the stronger cattle did conceive: ... whenever the more vigorous were in heat, *REB* ... hardier ewes were breeding, *Goodspeed* ... when any of the strong sheep were hot for union, *Fenton* ... sturdier animals were mating, *Anchor.*

---

up the strong females when they were in heat and allowed only the males that had the markings he wanted to mate with them.

This would produce an increase in the first generation and probably about fifty percent would have the markings in the second generation. The peeling of the sticks was done so that Laban would not know what was really happening.

30:40. Jacob then made a separate flock for himself so they would not be mixed with Laban's flock. By this time, Jacob had learned that Laban could not be trusted. This mutual distrust was evident between them until they parted at Mizpah (Gen. 31:44-55).

30:41-42. Jacob fenced up the strong animals of Laban's flock only. He let the weak one mate without doing so. Thus the best of those born went into Jacob's flock.

6887	3940	7947.121	2030.111	6063.156	3937, 3969	7489.156
art, n fs	neg part	v Qal impf 3ms	cj, v Qal pf 3ms	art, v Qal pass ptc mp	prep, pn	cj, art, v Qal pass ptc mp
הַצֹּאן	לֹא	יָשִׂים	וְהָיָה	הָעֲטֻפִים	לְלָבָן	וְהַקְּשֻׁרִים
hatstsō'n	lō'	yasîm	wehāyāh	hā'ăṭuphîm	lelāvān	wehaqqeshurîm
the flock	not	he put	and it was	the weaker ones	to Laban	and the stronger ones

3937, 3399		6805.121	382	4108	4108	2030.121, 3937	6887
prep, pn	**43.**	cj, v Qal impf 3ms	art, n ms	adv	adv	cj, v Qal impf 3ms, prep, ps 3ms	*n fs*
לְיַעֲקֹב		וַיִּפְרֹץ	הָאִישׁ	מְאֹד	מְאֹד	וַיְהִי־לוֹ	צֹאן
leya'ăqōv		wayyiphrōts	hā'îsh	me'ōdh	me'ōdh	wayhî-lô	tsō'n
to Jacob		and he increased	the man	very	very	and it was to him	flocks

7521	8569	5860	1622	2645		8471.121
adj	cj, n fp	cj, n mp	cj, n mp	cj, n mp	**31:1**	cj, v Qal impf 3ms
רַבּוֹת	וּשְׁפָחוֹת	וַעֲבָדִים	וּגְמַלִּים	וַחֲמֹרִים		וַיִּשְׁמַע
rabbôth	ûshephāchôth	wa'ăvādhîm	ûghemallîm	wahmōrîm		wayyishma'
great	and female slaves	and male slaves	and camels	and donkeys		and he heard

881, 1745	1158, 3969	3937, 569.141	4089.111	3399	881	3725, 866	3937, 1
do, *n mp*	*n mp*, pn	prep, v Qal inf con	v Qal pf 3ms	pn	do	adj, rel part	prep, n ms, ps 1cp
אֶת־דִּבְרֵי	בְנֵי־לָבָן	לֵאמֹר	לָקַח	יַעֲקֹב	אֵת	כָּל־אֲשֶׁר	לְאָבִינוּ
'eth-divrê	venê-lāvān	lē'mōr	lāqach	ya'ăqōv	'ēth	kol-'ăsher	le'āvînû
the words of	the sons of Laban	saying	he took	Jacob		all which	to our father

4623, 866	3937, 1	6449.111	881	3725, 3638	2172		7495.121
cj, prep, rel part	prep, n ms, ps 1cp	v Qal pf 3ms	do	*adj*, art, n ms	art, dem pron	**2.**	cj, v Qal impf 3ms
וּמֵאֲשֶׁר	לְאָבִינוּ	עָשָׂה	אֵת	כָּל־הַכָּבֹד	הַזֶּה		וַיַּרְא
ûmē'ăsher	le'āvînû	'āsāh	'ēth	kol-hakkāvōdh	hazzeh		wayyar'
and from what	to our father	he made		all the wealth	the this		and he saw

3399	881, 6686	3969	2079	375	6196	3626, 8873	8425
pn	do, *n mp*	pn	cj, intrj	sub, ps 3ms	prep, ps 3ms	prep, adv	adv
יַעֲקֹב	אֶת־פְּנֵי	לָבָן	וְהִנֵּה	אֵינֶנּוּ	עִמּוֹ	כִּתְמוֹל	שִׁלְשׁוֹם
ya'ăqōv	'eth-penê	lāvān	wehinnēh	'ênennû	'immô	kithmôl	shilshôm
Jacob	the face of	Laban	and behold	it was not	with him	like yesterday	three days ago

	569.121	3176	420, 3399	8178.131	420, 800	1	3937, 4274
3.	cj, v Qal impf 3ms	pn	prep, pn	v Qal impv 2ms	prep, *n fs*	n mp, ps 2ms	cj, prep, n fs,ps 2ms
	וַיֹּאמֶר	יְהוָה	אֶל־יַעֲקֹב	שׁוּב	אֶל־אֶרֶץ	אֲבוֹתֶיךָ	וּלְמוֹלַדְתֶּךָ
	wayyō'mer	yehwāh	'el-ya'ăqōv	shûv	'el-'erets	'ăvôthêkhā	ûlămôladhtekhā
	and he said	Yahweh	to Jacob	return	to the land of	your fathers	and to your relatives

2030.125	6196		8365.121	3399	7410.121	3937, 7637	3937, 3943
cj, v Qal impf 1cs	prep, ps 2fs	**4.**	cj, v Qal impf 3ms	pn	cj, v Qal impf 3ms	prep, pn	cj, prep, pn
וְאֶהְיֶה	עִמָּךְ		וַיִּשְׁלַח	יַעֲקֹב	וַיִּקְרָא	לְרָחֵל	וּלְלֵאָה
we'ehyeh	'immāk		wayyishlach	ya'ăqōv	wayyiqrā'	lerāchēl	ûlălē'āh
and I will be	with you		and he sent	Jacob	and he called	Rachel	and Leah

7898	420, 6887		569.121	3937	7495.151	609	881, 6686
art, n ms	prep, n fs, ps 3ms	**5.**	cj, v Qal impf 3ms	prep, ps 3fp	v Qal act ptc ms	pers pron	do, *n mp*
הַשָּׂדֶה	אֶל־צֹאנוֹ		וַיֹּאמֶר	לָהֶן	רֹאֶה	אָנֹכִי	אֶת־פְּנֵי
hassādeh	'el-tsō'nô		wayyō'mer	lāhen	rō'eh	'ānōkhî	'eth-penê
to the field	to his flock		and he said	to them	seeing	I	the face of

1	3706, 375	420	3626, 8873	8425	435	1
n ms, ps 2fp	cj, sub, ps 3ms	prep, ps 1cs	prep, adv	adv	cj, *n mp*	n ms, ps 1cs
אֲבִיכֶן	כִּי־אֵינֶנּוּ	אֵלַי	כִּתְמֹל	שִׁלְשֹׁם	וֵאלֹהֵי	אָבִי
'ăvîkhen	kî-'ênennû	'ēlay	kithmōl	shilshōm	wē'lōhê	'āvî
your father	that it is not	to me	like yesterday	three days ago	and the God of	my father

that Jacob laid the rods before the eyes of the cattle in the gutters: ... in full view of the animals, *Anchor* ... when they saw the sticks, *BB*.

that they might conceive among the rods: ... to inflame them among the wands, *Fenton* ... might breed, *Berkeley* ... mated, *NAB* ... they would long for the rods, *NEB*.

42. But when the cattle were feeble, he put them not in: ... weaker herds he did not place them, *MLB* ... but not so in the case of the weaker ones, *NCB* ... did not put the sticks before them, *BB*.

so the feebler were Laban's, and the stronger Jacob's: ... weaker fell to Laban and the stronger to Jacob, *MLB* ... Laban had all the weak animals, and Jacob all the healthy ones, *Good News*.

43. And the man increased exceedingly: ... exceedingly prosperous, *Anchor* ... grew richer and richer, *MLB* ... wealth was greatly increased, *BB*.

and had much cattle, and maidservants, and menservants, and camels, and asses: ... and had large flocks, *ASV* ... male and female servants, camels and donkeys, *MLB*.

31:1. And he heard the words of Laban's sons, saying: ... heard the sons of Laban talking, *Fenton* ... it came to the ears of Jacob, *BB* ... learned of the things that Laban's sons were saying, *Anchor*.

Jacob hath taken away all that was our father's: ... will take all that our father has, *Fenton* ... has taken everything our father owned, *NIV* ... everything that belonged, *NAB*.

and of that which was our father's hath he gotten all this glory: ... he has built up all this wealth out of what should be our father's, *Anchor* ... in this way he has got all this wealth, *BB* ... from what our father possessed he has made all his wealth, *Fenton* ... of our father's goods hath he gotten all his honour, *Geneva*.

2. And Jacob beheld the countenance of Laban: ... seeth the face of Laban, *Young* ... consequently watched the face of Laban, *Fenton* ... saw that Laban's feelings for him, *BB* ... noticed that Laban's manner toward him, *Anchor*.

and, behold, it was not toward him as before: ... was not so well disposed to him as he had once been, *REB* ... did not regard him with favor as before, *RSV* ... was not with him as formerly, *Fenton*.

3. And the LORD said unto Jacob: ... the Ever-living said, *Fenton* ... Jehovah said, *Darby* ... also the Lord told, *Berkeley* ... Yahweh told Jacob, *Anchor*.

Return unto the land of thy fathers, and to thy kindred; and I will be with thee: ... go back to the land of your fathers and to your kinsfolk, *Berkeley* ... where you were born, *NAB* ... to your relatives, *NIV* ... and your birth, *Fenton*.

4. And Jacob sent and called Rachel and Leah: ... sent word to, *Good News* ... to meet him where he was, *NAB* ... sent to fetch, *NEB*.

to the field unto his flock: ... to the field where his flocks were, *Berkeley* ... in the field to his sheep, *Fenton* ... to his flocks out in the country, *NEB*.

5. And said unto them, I see your father's countenance, that it is not toward me as before; but the God of my father hath been with me: ... I see that the face of your father is not with me as formerly, *Fenton* ... father's attitude is not what it used to be, *NAB* ... manner toward me is not the same as in the past, *Anchor* ... not as well disposed, *NEB*.

6. And ye know that with all my power I have served your father:

30:43. All this took place during a six year period (Gen. 31:41). With the great increase of Jacob's flocks, he was able to obtain male and female slaves, camels, and donkeys. He was now a rich man. Truly God was fulfilling His promise.

31:1-2. Jacob's increasing prosperity stirred up jealousy on the part of Laban's sons. They recognized that all Jacob's wealth and abundance came from what had been their father's. What they disregarded, was the fact that during the first 14 years, Jacob worked like a slave to build up Laban's wealth. Laban's attitude also changed, shown by dark looks instead of smiles. He had been willing to use Jacob as long as it was to his advantage, but he was not happy to see Jacob's prosperity above his own. The situation became more uncomfortable for Jacob. Now, it was definitely time to leave.

31:3. The LORD then confirmed that Jacob should leave. Telling Jacob to go back to the land of his fathers was a reminder of the promise of the land given to Abraham. Going back to his relatives might not be that easy, for they included Esau who had threatened to kill Jacob. But God promised to be with him. That meant Jacob need not fear.

31:4-5. Jacob needed to be sure that Rachel and Leah would be willing to leave their home city and go with him. So he sent for them to come out to the country fields where he was shepherding his flocks and where he could speak to them without anyone overhearing. He began by pointing out the change in Laban's attitude caused by the fact that the God of Isaac (and Abraham) was with Jacob.

2030.111	6200		897	3156.118	3706	904, 3725, 3699
v Qal pf 3ms	prep, ps 1cs	**6.**	cj, pers pron	v Qal pf 2fp	cj	prep, *adj*, n ms, ps 1cs
הָיָה	עִמָּדִי		וְאַתֵּנָה	יְדַעְתֶּן	כִּי	בְּכָל־כֹּחִי
hāyāh	ʻimmādhî		w^{e}ʼattēnāh	y^{e}dhaʻătten	kî	b^{e}khol-kōchî
He was	with me		and you	you know	that	with all my strength

5856.115	881, 1		1	8853.511	904	2599.511
v Qal pf 1cs	do, n ms, ps 2fp	**7.**	cj, n ms, ps 2fp	v Hiphil pf 3ms	prep, ps 1cs	cj, v Hiphil pf 3ms
עָבַדְתִּי	אֶת־אֲבִיכֶן		וַאֲבִיכֶן	הֵתֶל	בִּי	וְהֶחֱלִף
ʻāvadhtî	ʼeth-ʼăvîkhen		waʼăvîkhen	hēthel	bî	w^{e}hechĕliph
I served	your father		yet your father	he cheated	me	and he changed

881, 5032	6467	4634	3940, 5598.111	435	3937, 7778.541	6200
do, n fs, ps 1cs	*num*	n mp	cj, neg part, v Qal pf 3ms, ps 3ms	n mp	prep, v Hiphil inf con	prep, ps 1cs
אֶת־מַשְׂכֻּרְתִּי	עֲשֶׂרֶת	מֹנִים	וְלֹא־נְתָנוֹ	אֱלֹהִים	לְהָרַע	עִמָּדִי
ʼeth-maskurtî	ʻăsereth	mōnîm	w^{e}lōʼ-n^{e}thānô	ʼĕlōhîm	l^{e}hāraʻ	ʻimmādhî
my wages	ten	times	but not He gave him	God	to harm	me

	524, 3662	569.121	5532	2030.121	7964	3314.116
8.	cj, adv	v Qal impf 3ms	adj	v Qal impf 3ms	n ms, ps 2ms	cj, v Qal pf 3cp
	אִם־כֹּה	יֹאמַר	נְקֻדִּים	יִהְיֶה	שְׂכָרֶךָ	וְיָלְדוּ
	ʼim-kōh	yōʼmar	n^{e}quddîm	yihyeh	s^{e}khārekhā	w^{e}yāl^{e}dhû
	if so	he said	speckled	it will be	your wages	then they bore

3725, 6887	5532	524, 3662	569.121	6362	2030.121	7964
adj, art, n fs	adj	cj, cj, adv	v Qal impf 3ms	adj	v Qal impf 3ms	n ms, ps 2ms
כָל־הַצֹּאן	נְקֻדִּים	וְאִם־כֹּה	יֹאמַר	עֲקֻדִּים	יִהְיֶה	שְׂכָרֶךָ
khol-hatstsōʼn	n^{e}quddîm	w^{e}ʼim-kōh	yōʼmar	ʻăquddîm	yihyeh	s^{e}khārekhā
all the flock	speckled	and if so	he said	streaked	it will be	your wages

3314.116	3725, 6887	6362		5522.521	435	881, 4898
cj, v Qal pf 3cp	*adj*, art, n fs	adj	**9.**	cj, v Hiphil impf 3ms	n mp	do, n ms
וְיָלְדוּ	כָל־הַצֹּאן	עֲקֻדִּים		וַיַּצֵּל	אֱלֹהִים	אֶת־מִקְנֵה
w^{e}yāl^{e}dhû	khol-hatstsōʼn	ʻăquddîm		wayyatstsēl	ʼĕlōhîm	ʼeth-miqōnēh
then they bore	all the flock	streaked		and He has taken away	God	the livestock of

1	5598.121, 3937		2030.121	904, 6496	3285.341	6887
n ms, ps 2mp	cj, v Qal impf 3ms, prep, ps 1cs	**10.**	cj, v Qal impf 3ms	prep, *n fs*	v Piel inf con	art, n fs
אֲבִיכֶם	וַיִּתֶּן־לִי		וַיְהִי	בְּעֵת	יַחֵם	הַצֹּאן
ʼăvîkhem	wayyitten-lî		wayhî	b^{e}ʻēth	yachēm	hatstsōʼn
your father	and He has given to me		and it was	in the time of	the mating of	the flocks

5558.125	6084	7495.125	904, 2573	2079	6500	6148.152
cj, v Qal impf 1cs	n fd, ps 1cs	cj, v Qal impf 1cs	prep, n ms	cj, intrj	art, n mp	art, v Qal act ptc mp
וָאֶשָּׂא	עֵינַי	וָאֵרֶא	בַּחֲלוֹם	וְהִנֵּה	הָעַתֻּדִים	הָעֹלִים
wāʼessāʼ	ʻênay	wāʼēreʼ	bachlôm	w^{e}hinnēh	hāʻattudhîm	hāʻōlîm
that I lifted up	my eyes	and I saw	in dream	and behold	the he-goats	going up

6142, 6887	6362	5532	1288		569.121	420	4534
prep, art, n fs	adj	adj	cj, adj	**11.**	cj, v Qal impf 3ms	prep, ps 1cs	*n ms*
עַל־הַצֹּאן	עֲקֻדִּים	נְקֻדִּים	וּבְרֻדִּים		וַיֹּאמֶר	אֵלַי	מַלְאַךְ
ʻal-hatstsōʼn	ʻăquddîm	n^{e}quddîm	ûvruddîm		wayyōʼmer	ʼēlay	malʼakh
on the flock	streaked	speckled	and mottled		and he said	to me	the angel of

435	904, 2573	3399	569.125	2079		569.121	5558.131, 5167
art, n mp	prep, n ms	pn	cj, v Qal impf 1cs	intrj, ps 1cs	**12.**	cj, v Qal impf 3ms	v Qal impv 2ms, part
הָאֱלֹהִים	בַּחֲלוֹם	יַעֲקֹב	וָאֹמַר	הִנֵּנִי		וַיֹּאמֶר	שָׂא־נָא
hāʼĕlōhîm	bachlôm	yaʻăqōv	wāʼōmar	hinnēnî		wayyōʼmer	sāʼ-nāʼ
God	in dream	Jacob	and I said	behold I		and He said	lift up please

6084	7495.131	3725, 6500	6148.152	6142, 6887	6362	5532
n fd, ps 2ms	cj, v Qal impv 2ms	*adj*, art, n mp	art, v Qal act ptc mp	prep, art, n fs	adj	adj
עֵינֶיךָ	וּרְאֵה	כָּל־הָעַתֻּדִים	הָעֹלִים	עַל־הַצֹּאן	עֲקֻדִּים	נְקֻדִּים
'ênêkhā	ûr^{e}'ēh	kol-hā'attudhîm	hā'ōlîm	'al-hatstsō'n	'ăquddîm	n^{e}quddîm
your eyes	and see	all the he-goats	going up	on the flock	streaked	speckled

1288	3706	7495.115	881	3725, 866	3969	6449.151	3937
cj, adj	cj	v Qal pf 1cs	do	adj, rel part	pn	v Qal act ptc ms	prep, ps 2ms
וּבְרֻדִּים	כִּי	רָאִיתִי	אֵת	כָּל־אֲשֶׁר	לָבָן	עֹשֶׂה	לָּךְ
ûv^{e}ruddîm	kî	rā'îthî	'ēth	kol-'ăsher	lāvān	'ōseh	lākh
and mottled	because	I have seen		all which	Laban	doing	to you

to the best of my ability, *Goodspeed* ... with all my strength, *NASB* ... with all my might, *NKJV.*

7. And your father hath deceived me: ... has cheated me, *Goodspeed* ... played upon me, *Young* ... mocked me, *Darby* ... not kept faith with me, *BB.*

and changed my wages ten times: ... changed my hire, *Young* ... made changes in my payment, *BB* ... has broken his wage contract with me again and again, *LIVB.*

but God suffered him not to hurt me: ... has not allowed him to do me any harm, *Goodspeed* ... to do evil with me, *Young* ... kept him from doing me damage, *BB.*

8. If he said thus, The speckled shall be thy wages: ... spotted animals will be your pay, *NCB* ... those which have marks are yours, *BB.*

then all the cattle bare speckled: ... all the sheep had speckled lambs, *Goodspeed* ... all the flock bore spotted, *RSV.*

and if he said thus, The ringstraked shall be thy hire; then bare all the cattle ringstraked: ... striped animals are to be your wage, *Goodspeed* ... streaked animals, *Anchor* ... banded ones are to be yours, *BB* ... partly coloured shall be thy reward, *Geneva.*

9. Thus God hath taken away the cattle of your father, and given them to me: ... reclaimed your father's livestock, *NAB* ... your father's property, *NEB.*

10. And it came to pass at the time that the cattle conceived: ... breeding season, *NAB* ... flocks were in heat, *REB* ... in mating season, *RSV.*

that I lifted up mine eyes, and saw in a dream: ... suddenly saw in a dream, *Anchor.*

and, behold, the rams which leaped upon the cattle: ... male goats which were mating, *NASB* ... he-goats mounting the flocks, *NEB.*

were ringstraked, speckled, and grisled: ... partly coloured with little and great spots, *Geneva* ... banded and marked and coloured, *BB* ... striped and spotted and dappled, *NEB* ... striped, speckled, and mottled, *Goodspeed.*

11. And the angel of God spake unto me in a dream, saying: ... said to me in a dream, *Goodspeed* ... God's messenger called to me, *NAB.*

Jacob: And I said, Here am I: ... at once! I answered, *Anchor.*

12. And he said, Lift up now thine eyes, and see: ... raise your eyes and look, *Goodspeed* ... note well, *NAB* ... look and take note, *NCB* ... see what is happening, *REB.*

31:6-9. Jacob reminded them that he had put everything he had into working for Laban. From what Jacob says, it is clear that the statement in Genesis 30:32 is a summary statement, and that Laban allowed only one of these markings at a time to be Jacob's wages. Then when animals with that marking multiplied, Laban would change to another. Thus, it was always Laban's intention to cheat Jacob by giving him what he thought would be a small number of the young of his flocks. "Ten" is probably the number of completion. That is, Jacob means Laban had cheated him long enough.

31:10-12. The laws of heredity were unknown until the Austrian botanist, Gregor Mendel, made his experiments in the latter part of the nineteenth century. Even then, no one paid attention until about 1900. But God knew the laws of heredity from the beginning. So He gave Jacob directions that would enable him to take advantage of those laws in breeding his flocks. Laban had mistreated Jacob long enough. What Laban had done to Jacob in cheating him had not escaped God's notice. Now He was doing something to help compensate Jacob for the long years of hard work.

31:13. Jacob now jumps to the recent word of the LORD given in verse 3 and adds something else that God told him. The angel of God identified himself as the God who had revealed himself to

13.	609	418	1044	866	5066.113	8427	4838	866
	pers pron	art, n ms	pn	rel part	v Qal pf 2ms	adv	n fs	rel part
	אָנֹכִי	הָאֵל	בֵּית־אֵל	אֲשֶׁר	מָשַׁחְתָּ	שָּׁם	מַצֵּבָה	אֲשֶׁר
	'ānōkhî	hā'ēl	bêth-'ēl	'ăsher	māshach^{e}ttā	shām	matstsēvāh	'ăsher
	I	the God of	Bethel	where	you anointed	there	memorial	where

5265.131	3937	8427	5266	6498	7251.131	3428.131	4263, 800
v Qal impv 2ms	prep, ps 1cs	adv	n ms	adv	v Qal impv 2ms	v Qal impv 2ms	prep, art, n fs
נָדַרְתָּ	לִּי	שָּׁם	נֶדֶר	עַתָּה	קוּם	צֵא	מִן־הָאָרֶץ
nādhar^{e}ttā	lî	shām	nedher	'attāh	qûm	tsē'	min-hā'ārets
you made a vow	to Me	there	vow	now	rise	go out	from the land

2148	8178.131	420, 800	4274	14.	6257.122	7637	3943
art, dem pron	cj, v Qal impv 2ms	prep, *n fs*	n fs, ps 2ms		cj, v Qal impf 3fs	pn	cj, pn
הַזֹּאת	וְשׁוּב	אֶל־אֶרֶץ	מוֹלַדְתֶּךָ		וַתַּעַן	רָחֵל	וְלֵאָה
hazzō'th	w^{e}shûv	'el-'erets	môladhtekhā		watta'an	rāchēl	w^{e}lē'āh
the this	and return	to the land of	your birth		and she answered	Rachel	and Leah

569.127	3937	5968	3937	2610	5338	904, 1041
cj, v Qal impf 3fp	prep, ps 3ms	intrg part, adv	prep, ps 1cp	n ms	cj, n fs	prep, *n ms*
וַתֹּאמַרְנָה	לוֹ	הַעוֹד	לָנוּ	חֵלֶק	וְנַחֲלָה	בְּבֵית
wattō'marnāh	lô	ha'ôdh	lānû	chēleq	w^{e}nachlāh	b^{e}vêth
and they said	to him	is still	to us	allotment	and inheritance	in the house of

1	15.	3940	5425	2913.219	3937	3706	4513.111
n ms, ps 1cp		intrg part, neg part	n fp	v Niphal pf 1cp	prep, ps 3ms	cj	v Qal pf 3ms, ps 1cs
אָבִינוּ		הֲלוֹא	נָכְרִיּוֹת	נֶחְשַׁבְנוּ	לוֹ	כִּי	מְכָרָנוּ
'āvînû		h^{e}lô'	nākh^{e}riyyôth	nechshavnû	lô	kî	m^{e}khārānû
our father		are not	foreigners	we are considered	to him	because	he sold us

404.121	1612, 404.142	881, 3826B	16.	3706	3725, 6484	866	5522.511
cj, v Qal impf 3ms	cj, v Qal inf abs	do, n ms, ps 1cp		cj	*adj*, art, n ms	rel part	v Hiphil pf 3ms
וַיֹּאכַל	גַּם־אָכוֹל	אֶת־כַּסְפֵּנוּ		כִּי	כָל־הָעֹשֶׁר	אֲשֶׁר	הִצִּיל
wayyō'khal	gam-'ākhôl	'eth-kaspēnû		kî	khol-hā'ōsher	'ăsher	hitstsîl
and he ate	also consuming	our silver		because	all the wealth	which	He took away

435	4623, 1	3937	2000	3937, 1158	6498	3725	866
n mp	prep, n ms, ps 1cp	prep, ps 1cp	pers pron	cj, prep, n mp, ps 1cp	cj, adv	adj	rel part
אֱלֹהִים	מֵאָבִינוּ	לָנוּ	הוּא	וּלְבָנֵינוּ	וְעַתָּה	כֹּל	אֲשֶׁר
'ĕlōhîm	mē'āvînû	lānû	hû'	ûlāvānênû	w^{e}'attāh	kōl	'ăsher
God	from our father	for us	it	and for our children	and now	all	which

569.111	435	420	6449.131	17.	7251.121	3399	5558.121
v Qal pf 3ms	n mp	prep, ps 2ms	v Qal impv 2ms		cj, v Qal impf 3ms	pn	cj, v Qal impf 3ms
אָמַר	אֱלֹהִים	אֵלֶיךָ	עֲשֵׂה		וַיָּקָם	יַעֲקֹב	וַיִּשָּׂא
'āmar	'ĕlōhîm	'ēlêkhā	'ăsēh		wayyāqām	ya'ăqōv	wayyissā'
He said	God	to you	do		and he rose up	Jacob	and he lifted up

881, 1158	881, 5571	6142, 1622	18.	5268.121	881, 3725, 4898
do, n mp, ps 3ms	cj, do, n fp, ps 3ms	prep, art, n mp		cj, v Qal impf 3ms	do, *adj*, n ms, ps 3ms
אֶת־בָּנָיו	וְאֶת־נָשָׁיו	עַל־הַגְּמַלִּים		וַיִּנְהַג	אֶת־כָּל־מִקְנֵהוּ
'eth-bānâv	w^{e}'eth-nāshâv	'al-hagg^{e}mallîm		wayyinhagh	'eth-kol-miqōnēhû
his sons	his wives	on the camels		and he drove away	all of his livestock

881, 3725, 7688	866	7697.111	4898	7359	866	7697.111
cj, do, *adj*, n ms, ps 3ms	rel part	v Qal pf 3ms	*n ms*	n ms, ps 3ms	rel part	v Qal pf 3ms
וְאֶת־כָּל־רְכֻשׁוֹ	אֲשֶׁר	רָכָשׁ	מִקְנֵה	קִנְיָנוֹ	אֲשֶׁר	רָכַשׁ
w^{e}'eth-kol-r^{e}khushô	'ăsher	rākhāsh	miqōnēh	qinyānô	'ăsher	rākhash
and all of his property	which	he acquired	the livestock of	his property	which	he acquired

all the rams which leap upon the cattle: ... male goats which are mating, *NASB* ... he-goats mounting the flocks, *NEB.*

are ringstraked, speckled, and grisled: for I have seen all that Laban doeth unto thee: ... has been doing to you, *Goodspeed* ... have noted all the things, *Anchor.*

13. I am the God of Bethel: ... of the House of God, *Fenton* ... who appeared to you, *Goodspeed.*

where thou anointedst the pillar: ... anointed a sacred pillar, *Goodspeed* ... a memorial stone, *NAB* ... a standing pillar, *Young* ... a stele, *Anchor* ... you put oil on, *BB.*

and where thou vowedst a vow unto me: ... made a vow, *NAB* ... took an oath, *BB.*

now arise, get thee out from this land: ... leave, *NAB* ... this country at once, *NEB* ... go forth from, *RSV.*

and return unto the land of thy kindred: ... land of your birth, *Goodspeed* ... of your kin, *NCB* ... go back to your native land, *NIV.*

14. And Rachel and Leah answered and said unto him, Is there yet any portion or inheritance for us in our father's house?: ... what part or heritage is there for us, *BB* ... what share or legacy, *Berkeley* ... our father's estate, *NIV.*

15. Are we not counted of him strangers?: ... foreigners by him, *Goodspeed* ... outsiders, *NAB.*

for he hath sold us, and hath quite devoured also our money: ... has enjoyed our dowry, *Goodspeed* ... consumed, *NASB* ... spent on himself the money, *NEB.*

16. For all the riches which God hath taken from our father: ... all the property, *Goodspeed* ... all the wealth that God reclaimed, *NAB* ... God has stripped, *Fenton.*

that is ours, and our children's: ... really belongs to us, *NAB.*

now then, whatsoever God hath said unto thee, do: ... do everything that God has said, *NEB* ... do what God told you, *Goodspeed.*

17. Then Jacob rose up, and set his sons and his wives upon camels;

18. And he carried away all his cattle: ... livestock, *NKJV* ... drove all his livestock ahead of him, *NIV* ... sending on before him,*BB* ... collected the whole of his herds, *Fenton.*

and all his goods which he had gotten: ... all the movable property, *Berkeley* ... all his substance, *Young* ... possessions, *NKJV* ... he had acquired, *Goodspeed.*

the cattle of his getting, which he had gotten in Padanaram: ... herds of his possession which he had accumulated, *Berkeley* ... acquired by trading, *Fenton* ... stock he had obtained, *NCB* ... livestock, *NKJV.*

for to go to Isaac his father in the land of Canaan: ... in order to go to Isaac, *KJVII* ... to trek to his father, *Berkeley* ... he made ready to go, *BB.*

Jacob at Bethel. Then He reminded Jacob of his worship at Bethel and of his vow. Jacob must leave at once and return to the land where he was born. It seems also that the LORD (Yahweh), God, and the angel of God are all identified in this passage. Many believe that this angel of God was another preincarnate manifestation of Christ.

31:14-16. Rachel and Leah also felt the change in the attitude of their father and brothers. Now that Laban had sons, they no longer had any inheritance from their father. They were treating them like foreigners. The silver (money) that Laban completely used up could refer to a price paid for them, however, Jacob paid no money for them. Thus, it probably refers to money that should have been theirs. Thus God was just in allowing Jacob to accumulate wealth, and it truly belonged to Jacob and his family. So Rachel and Leah were made willing to encourage Jacob to obey God.

31:17-19. Jacob lost no time putting his children and wives on camels and gathering everything together to set out in haste for Isaac and Canaan. He would have put the material goods on donkeys, and had servants drive his flocks ahead of him. Laban had gone to shear his sheep when Jacob loaded up everything he had accumulated.

Rachel had a reason for stealing the teraphim. These were small idols (like figurines) considered the family gods and were kept on a god-shelf, probably in the corner of the main room of the house. When there was any question about the inheritance, the person who had the teraphim was considered to have the right to the double portion of the primary heir. When Jacob first came, he was welcomed into the family and adopted as the heir, since Laban had no sons at the time. But Laban had sons born shortly after, and that normally would invalidate Jacob's claim unless he possessed the teraphim. Rachel felt Jacob deserved more than he was getting, so she stole them for his benefit, and for the benefit of Jacob's family. There is no evidence she wanted to worship these images.

904, 6549	782	3937, 971.141	420, 3437	1	800	3791		3969
prep, pn	pn	prep, v Qal inf con	prep, pn	n ms, ps	*n fs*	pn		cj, pn
בְּפַדַּן	אֲרָם	לָבוֹא	אֶל־יִצְחָק	אָבִיו	אַרְצָה	כְּנָעַן	**19.**	וְלָבָן
bephaddan	'ărām	lāvô'	'el-yitschāq	'āvîw	'artsāh	kenā'an		welāvān
in Paddan	Aram	to go	to Isaac	his father	to the land of	Canaan		and Laban

2050.111	3937, 1525.141	881, 6887	1630.122	7637	881, 8994	866
v Qal pf 3ms	prep, v Qal inf con	do, n fs, ps 3ms	cj, v Qal impf 3fs	pn	do, art, n mp	rel part
הָלַךְ	לִגְזֹז	אֶת־צֹאנוֹ	וַתִּגְנֹב	רָחֵל	אֶת־הַתְּרָפִים	אֲשֶׁר
hālakh	lighzōz	'eth-tsō'nô	wattighnōv	rāchēl	'eth-hatterāphîm	'ăsher
he went	to shear	his sheep	and she stole	Rachel	the idols	which

3937, 1		1630.121	3399	881, 3949	3969	784	6142, 1136
prep, n ms, ps 3fs		cj, v Qal impf 3ms	pn	do, *n ms*	pn	art, pn	prep, neg part
לְאָבִיהָ	**20.**	וַיִּגְנֹב	יַעֲקֹב	אֶת־לֵב	לָבָן	הָאֲרַמִּי	עַל־בְּלִי
le'āvîhā		wayyighnōv	ya'ăqōv	'eth-lēv	lāvān	hā'ărammî	'al-belî
to her father		and he stole	Jacob	the heart of	Laban	the Aramean	for not

5222.511	3937	3706	1300.151	2000		1300.121	2000
v Hiphil pf 3ms	prep, ps 3ms	cj	v Qal act ptc ms	pers pron		cj, v Qal impf 3ms	pers pron
הִגִּיד	לוֹ	כִּי	בֹרֵחַ	הוּא	**21.**	וַיִּבְרַח	הוּא
higgîdh	lô	kî	vōrēach	hû'		wayyivrach	hû'
he told	him	that	about to flee	he		and he fled	he

3725, 866, 3937	7251.121	5882.121	881, 5282	7947.121	881, 6686
cj, adj, rel part, prep, ps 3ms	cj, v Qal impf 3ms	cj, v Qal impf 3ms	do, art, n ms	cj, v Qal impf 3ms	do, n mp, ps 3ms
וְכָל־אֲשֶׁר־לוֹ	וַיָּקָם	וַיַּעֲבֹר	אֶת־הַנָּהָר	וַיָּשֶׂם	אֶת־פָּנָיו
wekhol-'ăsher-lô	wayyāqām	wayya'ăvōr	'eth-hannāhār	wayyāsem	'eth-pānâv
and all which to him	and he rose up	and he passed over	the river	and he set	his face

2098	1609		5222.621	3937, 3969	904, 3219	8389
n ms	art, pn		cj, v Hophal impf 3ms	prep, pn	prep, art, n ms	art, num
הַר	הַגִּלְעָד	**22.**	וַיֻּגַּד	לְלָבָן	בַּיּוֹם	הַשְּׁלִישִׁי
har	haggil'ādh		wayyuggadh	lelāvān	bayyôm	hashshelîshî
toward the mountain of	the Gilead		and it was told	to Laban	in the day	the third

3706	1300.111	3399		4089.121	881, 250	6196	7579.121
cj	v Qal pf 3ms	pn		cj, v Qal impf 3ms	do, n ms, ps 3ms	prep, ps 3ms	cj, v Qal impf 3ms
כִּי	בָרַח	יַעֲקֹב	**23.**	וַיִּקַּח	אֶת־אֶחָיו	עִמּוֹ	וַיִּרְדֹּף
kî	vārach	ya'ăqōv		wayyiqqach	'eth-'echâv	'immô	wayyirdōph
that	he had fled	Jacob		and he took	his relatives	with him	and he pursued

313	1932	8124	3219	1740.521	881	904, 2098
adv, ps 3ms	*n ms*	*num*	n mp	cj, v Hiphil impf 3ms	do, ps 3ms	prep, *n ms*
אַחֲרָיו	דֶּרֶךְ	שִׁבְעַת	יָמִים	וַיַּדְבֵּק	אֹתוֹ	בְּהַר
'achrâv	derekh	shiv'ath	yāmîm	wayyadhbēq	'ōthô	behar
after him	journey of	seven	days	and he caught up with	him	in the mountain of

1609		971.121	435	420, 3969	784	904, 2573	4050I
art, pn		cj, v Qal impf 3ms	n mp	prep, pn	art, pn	prep, art, *n ms*	art, n ms
הַגִּלְעָד	**24.**	וַיָּבֹא	אֱלֹהִים	אֶל־לָבָן	הָאֲרַמִּי	בַּחֲלֹם	הַלָּיְלָה
haggil'ādh		wayyāvō'	'ĕlōhîm	'el-lāvān	hā'ărammî	bachlōm	hallāyelāh
the Gilead		but he came	God	to Laban	the Aramean	in the dream of	the night

569.121	3937	8490.231	3937	6678, 1744.323	6196, 3399	4623, 3005
cj, v Qal impf 3ms	prep, ps 3ms	v Niphal impv 2ms	prep, ps 2ms	cj, v Piel impf 2ms	prep, pn	prep, adj
וַיֹּאמֶר	לוֹ	הִשָּׁמֶר	לְךָ	פֶּן־תְּדַבֵּר	עִם־יַעֲקֹב	מִטּוֹב
wayyō'mer	lô	hishshāmer	lekhā	pen-tedhabbēr	'im-ya'ăqōv	mittôv
and he said	to him	be careful	for yourself	for fear that you speak	with Jacob	good

5912, 7737		5560.521	3969	881, 3399	3399	8965.111	881, 164
cj, adj	**25.**	cj, v Hiphil impf 3ms	pn	do, pn	cj, pn	v Qal pf 3ms	do, n ms, ps 3ms
עַד־רָע		וַיַּשֵּׂג	לָבָן	אֶת־יַעֲקֹב	וְיַעֲקֹב	תָּקַע	אֶת־אָהֳלוֹ
'adh-rā'		wayyassēgh	lāvān	'eth-ya'ăqōv	w^{e}ya'ăqōv	tāqa'	'eth-'āhlô
or evil		and he caught up	Laban	with Jacob	and Jacob	he pitched	his tent

904, 2098	3969	8965.111	881, 250	904, 2098	1609
prep, art, n ms	cj, pn	v Qal pf 3ms	do, n ms, ps 3ms	prep, *n ms*	art, pn
בָּהָר	וְלָבָן	תָּקַע	אֶת־אֶחָיו	בְּהַר	הַגִּלְעָד
bāhār	w^{e}lāvān	tāqa'	'eth-'echâv	b^{e}har	haggil'ādh
on the mountain	and Laban	he pitched	with his relatives	on the mountain of	the Gilead

19. And Laban went to shear his sheep: ... had gone away, *NAB* ... to see to the cutting of the wool of his sheep, *BB.*

and Rachel had stolen the images that were her father's: ... stole the household gods, *Goodspeed* ... idols, *NAB* ... stealeth the teraphim, *Young* ... household images, *Anchor.*

20. And Jacob stole away unawares to Laban the Syrian: ... outwitted Laban, *Goodspeed* ... stole away the heart, *KJVII* ... hoodwinked Laban, *NAB* ... lulled the mind, *Anchor* ... got the best of, *Berkeley.*

in that he told him not that he fled: ... that he was going to flee, *Goodspeed* ... of his intended flight, *NAB* ... keeping his departure secret, *NEB* ... without giving news of his flight, *BB.*

21. So he fled with all that he had: ... all that he possessed, *REB* ... thus he made his escape, *NAB* ... with all that belonged to him, *Goodspeed.*

and he rose up, and passed over the river: ... starting forth, he crossed the River, *Goodspeed* ... soon was over the Euphrates, *REB.*

and set his face toward the mount Gilead: ... the highlands of Gilead, *Goodspeed* ... headed for the mountains, *NKJV* ... was on the way to the hill-country, *REB* ... turned toward the Gilead mountain range, *Berkeley.*

22. And it was told Laban on the third day that Jacob was fled: ... three days later, *Goodspeed* ... word came to Laban, *NAB* ... it was reported that Jacob had fled, *Fenton.*

23. And he took his brethren with him, and pursued after him seven days' journey: ... a distance of seven days, *Anchor* ... went in pursuit, *Berkeley.*

and they overtook him in the mount Gilead: ... caught up with him in the hill country, *NAB* ... followed close after him, *RSV.*

24. And God came to Laban the Syrian in a dream by night, and said unto him, Take heed that thou speak not to Jacob either good or bad: ... guard yourself in what you do to Jacob for either good or ill, *Fenton* ... not to press matters, *Anchor* ... not to threaten, *NAB.*

25. Then Laban overtook Jacob: ... caught up with Jacob, *LIVB* ... came up with, *Goodspeed.*

Now Jacob had pitched his tent in the mount: ... having pitched his tent on mount Mizpeh, *Goodspeed*

31:20-21. That Jacob stole the heart of Laban by not telling him he was running away is a Hebrew way of saying he deceived or tricked Laban. It seems that unless he had Laban's permission, Jacob would be treated like a runaway slave. Jacob went south, crossed the Euphrates River and headed for the hill country of Gilead on the east side of the Jordan River.

31:22-23. As soon as Laban heard the news he called his relatives and they pursued Jacob. Jacob probably went as fast as he could with all he had, but Laban caught up with him in seven days. By that time, Jacob was in the hill country of Gilead, which meant he traveled about 30 miles a day, which was unusual for such a company of people.

31:24. Before Laban actually caught up with Jacob, God warned him in a dream to be careful not to say good or bad to Jacob. That is, he must not entice Jacob to return by giving him a good offer and he must not say anything bitter or make any threats against Jacob for leaving.

31:25. Gilead means "rough country," and its mountainous terrain is spectacular in many places. It is quite a change from Bashan ("smooth land") south of Damascus. Both Jacob and Laban set up tents on a mountainside.

31:26-28. Laban reproached Jacob for deceiving him and running off secretly. He could not believe his daughters would want to go of their own accord, so he accused Jacob of carrying them off like captives taken by the sword in a war. He also said that Jacob missed having a joyous going-away

26.	569.121	3969	3937, 3399	4242	6449.113	1630.123	881, 3949
	cj, v Qal impf 3ms	pn	prep, pn	intrg	v Qal pf 2ms	cj, v Qal impf 2ms	do, n ms ps 1cs
	וַיֹּאמֶר	לָבָן	לְיַעֲקֹב	מֶה	עָשִׂיתָ	וַתִּגְנֹב	אֶת־לְבָבִי
	wayyō'mer	lāvān	leya'ăqōv	meh	‘āsîthā	wattighnōv	'eth-levāvî
	and he said	Laban	to Jacob	what	have you done	now you have stolen	my heart

5268.323	881, 1351	3626, 8091.158	2820	27.	4066	2331.213
cj, v Piel impf 2ms	do, n fp, ps 1cs	prep, *v Qal pass ptc fp*	n fs		intrg	v Niphal pf 2ms
וַתְּנַהֵג	אֶת־בְּנֹתַי	כִּשְׁבֻיוֹת	חָרֶב		לָמָּה	נַחְבֵּאתָ
wattenahēgh	'eth-benōthay	kishvuyôth	chārev		lāmmāh	nachbē'thā
and you carried off	my daughters	like the captives of	the sword		why	you hid

3937, 1300.141	1630.123	881	3940, 5222.513	3937	8365.325
prep, v Qal inf con	cj, v Qal impf 2ms	do, ps 1cs	cj, neg part, v Hiphil pf 2ms	prep, ps 1cs	cj, v Piel impf 1cs, ps 2ms
לִבְרֹחַ	וַתִּגְנֹב	אֹתִי	וְלֹא־הִגַּדְתָּ	לִּי	וָאֲשַׁלֵּחֲךָ
livrōach	wattighnōv	'ōthî	welō'-higgadhtā	lî	wā'ăshallēchăkhā
to flee	and you stole	me	and not you told	me	and I would have sent you

904, 7977	904, 8302	904, 8929	904, 3780	28.	3940	5389.113
prep, n fs	cj, prep, n mp	prep, n ms	cj, prep, n ms		cj, neg part	v Qal pf 2ms, ps 1cs
בְּשִׂמְחָה	וּבְשִׁרִים	בְּתֹף	וּבְכִנּוֹר		וְלֹא	נְטַשְׁתַּנִי
besimchāh	ûveshirîm	bethōph	ûvekhinnôr		welō'	netashtanî
with rejoicing	and with songs	with tambourine	and with lyre		and not	you gave me a chance

3937, 5583.341	3937, 1158	3937, 1351	6498	5721.513	6449.141
prep, v Piel inf con	prep, n mp, ps 1cs	cj, prep, n fp, ps 1cs	adv	v Hiphil pf 2ms	v Qal inf con
לְנַשֵּׁק	לְבָנַי	וְלִבְנֹתָי	עַתָּה	הִסְכַּלְתָּ	עֲשׂוֹ
lenashshēq	levānay	welivnōthāy	‘attāh	hiskaltā	‘āsô
to kiss	my sons	and my daughters	now	you have acted foolishly	doing

29.	3552, 3937, 417	3135	3937, 6449.141	6196	7737	435	1
	sub, prep, n ms	n fs, ps 1cs	prep, v Qal inf con	prep, ps 2mp	adj	cj, *n mp*	n ms, ps 2mp
	יֶשׁ־לְאֵל	יָדִי	לַעֲשׂוֹת	עִמָּכֶם	רָע	וֵאלֹהֵי	אֲבִיכֶם
	yesh-le'ēl	yādhî	la‘ăsôth	‘immākhem	rā‘	we'lōhê	'ăvîkhem
	there is to the power of	my hand	to do	among you	harm	but the God of	your father

582	569.111	420	3937, 569.141	8490.231	3937	4623, 1744.341
adv	v Qal pf 3ms	prep, ps 1cs	prep, v Qal inf con	v Niphal impv 2ms	prep, ps 2ms	prep, v Piel inf con
אֶמֶשׁ	אָמַר	אֵלַי	לֵאמֹר	הִשָּׁמֶר	לְךָ	מִדַּבֵּר
'emesh	'āmar	'ēlay	lē'mōr	hishshāmer	lekhā	middabbēr
yesterday	He said	to me	saying	be careful	for yourself	speaking

6196, 3399	4623, 3005	5912, 7737	30.	6498	2050.142	2050.113	3706, 3826.242
prep, pn	prep, adj	cj, adj		cj, adv	v Qal inf abs	v Qal pf 2ms	cj, v Niphal inf abs
עִם־יַעֲקֹב	מִטּוֹב	עַד־רָע		וְעַתָּה	הָלֹךְ	הָלַכְתָּ	כִּי־נִכְסֹף
‘im-ya‘ăqōv	mittôv	‘adh-rā‘		we‘attāh	hālōkh	hālakhettā	kî-nikhsōph
with Jacob	good	or evil		and now	going	you went	because longing

3826.213	3937, 1041	1	4066	1630.113	881, 435	31.	6257.121
v Niphal pf 2ms	prep, *n ms*	n ms, ps 2ms	intrg	v Qal pf 2ms	do, n mp, ps 1cs		cj, v Qal impf 3ms
נִכְסַפְתָּה	לְבֵית	אָבִיךָ	לָמָּה	גָנַבְתָּ	אֶת־אֱלֹהָי		וַיַּעַן
nikhsaphtāh	levêth	'āvîkh	lāmmāh	ghānavtā	'eth-'ĕlōhāy		wayya‘an
you longed	for the house of	your father	why	have you stolen	my gods		and he answered

3399	569.121	3937, 3969	3706	3486.115	3706	569.115
pn	cj, v Qal impf 3ms	prep, pn	cj	v Qal pf 1cs	cj	v Qal pf 1cs
יַעֲקֹב	וַיֹּאמֶר	לְלָבָן	כִּי	יָרֵאתִי	כִּי	אָמַרְתִּי
ya‘ăqōv	wayyō'mer	lelāvān	kî	yārē'thî	kî	'āmartî
Jacob	and he said	to Laban	because	I was afraid	because	I said

... pitched in the highlands, *NAB* ... hill country, *NASB* ... mountains, *NKJV* ... on the Height, *Anchor.*

and Laban with his brethren pitched in the mount of Gilead: ... fellow-tribesmen, *Goodspeed* ... relatives, *NIV* ... camped, *Berkeley.*

26. And Laban said to Jacob, What hast thou done: ... what did you mean, *Anchor* ... what have you done, *NKJV* ... why have you acted so, *NCB.*

that thou hast stolen away unawares to me: ... stolen away my heart, *KJVII* ... deceiving me, *NASB* ... outwitting me, *Goodspeed* ... lulling my mind, *Anchor* ... take advantage of me, *Berkeley.*

and carried away my daughters, as captives taken with the sword?: ... like prisoners of war, *Goodspeed* ... like war captives, *NAB.*

27. Wherefore didst thou flee away secretly: ... hidden thyself, *Young* ... flee so furtively, *Anchor* ... make a secret of your flight, *BB.*

and steal away from me; and didst not tell me: ... should have told me, *NAB* ... did not let me know, *NCB.*

that I might have sent thee away with mirth, and with songs, with tabret, and with harp?: ... with tambourine and lyre, *Goodspeed* ... merry singing, *NAB* ... rejoicing and song, *NCB* ... songs and the music of tambourines, *NEB* ... joy and singing to the music, *NIV.*

28. And hast not suffered me to kiss my sons and my daughters?: ... did not allow me, *Goodspeed* ... a parting kiss to my daughters and grandchildren, *NAB* ... my children, and your children, *Fenton.*

thou hast now done foolishly in so doing: ... what you have now done is a senseless thing, *NAB* ... in this you were at fault, *NEB.*

29. It is in the power of my hand to do you hurt: ... to do you harm, *Goodspeed* ... an injury, *NEB* ... damage, *BB.*

but the God of your father spake unto me yesternight, saying: ... spoke to me last night, *KJVII* ... told me last night, *Berkeley.*

Take thou heed that thou speak not to Jacob either good or bad: ... take care to say nothing to Jacob, *Goodspeed* ... not to threaten Jacob with any harm, *NAB* ... take care not to press matters, *Anchor* ... guard yourself in dealing with Jacob, *Fenton.*

30. And now, though thou wouldest needs be gone: ... so go your journey, *Fenton* ... even though you had to go, *NRSV* ... you have indeed gone away, *NASB* ... and now you have gone, *KJVII.*

because thou sore longedst after thy father's house: ... you were desperately homesick, *NAB* ... longed so much for your father's home, *NCB* ... homesick and pining for, *NEB* ... been very desirous, *Young* ... your heart's desire, *BB.*

yet wherefore hast thou stolen my gods?: ... why did you steal my gods, *Goodspeed.*

31. And Jacob answered and said to Laban, Because I was afraid: ... I was frightened, *NAB* ... I fled because I feared, *Berkeley.*

for I said, Peradventure thou wouldest take by force thy daughters from me: ... he will certainly steal his daughters from me, *Fenton* ... take violently away, *Young* ... I thought you would take, *NEB.*

32. With whomsoever thou findest thy gods, let him not live: ... if you find anyone who has your gods, *NIV* ... find your gods in anyone's possession, *NCB* ... the one you find them with shall not remain alive, *NAB.*

---

celebration with tambourines and lyres (small, hand-held instruments similar to harps).

Laban was incensed also that he didn't even have an opportunity to give a fervent kiss to his daughters and grandchildren. This, Laban said, was foolish on Jacob's part and frustrating to Laban. Thus Laban acted as if he was totally innocent of doing anything to cause Jacob to leave and that Jacob was wrong.

31:29. Laban then told Jacob he had the power to harm him, implying that he and his relatives were carrying weapons and outnumbered Jacob. He also implied he would have harmed Jacob if God had not warned him in that dream.

31:30. Laban recognized that Jacob's longing to return to Isaac's household was legitimate. It was customary for sons to bring their wives home. But there was something that was not right. Apparently Laban thought Jacob had left in such a hurry because he stole the family gods.

31:31-32. Jacob said the only reason he fled was because he was afraid Laban would tear away his daughters, that is, take them from Jacob by force. But he did not take the teraphim. He let Laban, accompanied by his relatives, search, and if anyone had the teraphim they would be turned over to Laban for him to put to death, and anything else that they found that belonged to Laban they should take. It was a good thing at this point that Jacob did not know Rachel had the teraphim.

6678, 1528.123	881, 1351	4623, 6196		6196	866	4834.123
cj, v Qal impf 2ms	do, n fp, ps 2ms	prep, prep, ps 1cs	**32.**	prep	rel part	v Qal impf 2ms
פֶּן־תִּגְזֹל	אֶת־בְּנוֹתֶיךָ	מֵעִמִּי		עִם	אֲשֶׁר	תִּמְצָא
pen-tighzōl	'eth-b^{e}nōthêkhā	mē'immî		'im	'ăsher	timtsā'
otherwise you will take away	your daughters	from me		with	whom	you will find

881, 435	3940	2513.121	5224	250	5421.531, 3937	4242
do, n mp, ps 2ms	neg part	v Qal impf 3ms	prep	n mp, ps 1cp	v Hiphil impv 2ms, prep, ps 2ms	intrg
אֶת־אֱלֹהֶיךָ	לֹא	יִחְיֶה	נֶגֶד	אַחֵינוּ	הַכֶּר־לְךָ	מָה
'eth-'ĕlōhêkhā	lō'	yichăyeh	neghedh	'achênû	hakker-l^{e}khā	māh
your gods	not	he will live	in front of	our relatives	recognize for yourself	what

6200	4089.131, 3937	3940, 3156.111	3399	3706	7637	1630.112
prep, ps 1cs	cj, v Qal impv 2ms, prep, ps 2ms	cj, neg part, v Qal pf 3ms	pn	cj	pn	v Qal pf 3fs, ps 3mp
עִמָּדִי	וְקַח־לָךְ	וְלֹא־יָדַע	יַעֲקֹב	כִּי	רָחֵל	גְּנָבָתַם
'immādhî	w^{e}qach-lākh	w^{e}lō'-yāda'	ya'ăqōv	kî	rāchēl	g^{e}nāvātham
with me	and take for yourself	and not he knew	Jacob	that	Rachel	she stole them

	971.121	3969	904, 164	3399	904, 164	3943	904, 164	8530
33.	cj, v Qal impf 3ms	pn	prep, *n ms*	pn	cj, prep, *n ms*	pn	cj, prep, *n ms*	*num*
	וַיָּבֹא	לָבָן	בְּאֹהֶל	יַעֲקֹב	וּבְאֹהֶל	לֵאָה	וּבְאֹהֶל	שְׁתֵּי
	wayyāvō'	lāvān	b^{e}'ōhel	ya'ăqōv	ûv^{e}'ōhel	lē'āh	ûv^{e}'ōhel	sh^{e}ttê
	and he went	Laban	in the tent of	Jacob	and in the tent of	Leah	and in the tent of	the two of

526	3940	4834.111	3428.121	4623, 164	3943	971.121
art, n fp	cj, neg part	v Qal pf 3ms	cj, v Qal impf 3ms	prep, *n ms*	pn	cj, v Qal impf 3ms
הָאֲמָהֹת	וְלֹא	מָצָא	וַיֵּצֵא	מֵאֹהֶל	לֵאָה	וַיָּבֹא
hā'ămāhōth	w^{e}lō'	mātsā'	wayyētsē'	mē'ōhel	lē'āh	wayyāvō'
the female slaves	and not	he found	and he went out	from the tent of	Leah	and he went

904, 164	7637		7637	4089.112	881, 8994	7947.122
prep, *n ms*	pn	**34.**	cj, pn	v Qal pf 3fs	do, art, n mp	cj, v Qal impf 3fs, ps 3mp
בְּאֹהֶל	רָחֵל		וְרָחֵל	לָקְחָה	אֶת־הַתְּרָפִים	וַתְּשִׂמֵם
b^{e}'ōhel	rāchēl		w^{e}rāchēl	lāqōchāh	'eth-hatt^{e}rāphîm	watt^{e}simēm
in the tent of	Rachel		and Rachel	she had taken	the idols	and she put them

3863	1622	3553.122	6142	5135.321	3969	881, 3725, 164
prep, *n ms*	art, n ms	cj, v Qal impf 3fs	prep, ps 3mp	cj, v Piel impf 3ms	pn	do, *adj*, art, n ms
בְּכַר	הַגָּמָל	וַתֵּשֶׁב	עֲלֵיהֶם	וַיְמַשֵּׁשׁ	לָבָן	אֶת־כָּל־הָאֹהֶל
b^{e}khar	haggāmāl	wattēshev	'ălêhem	waymashshēsh	lāvān	'eth-kol-hā'ōhel
in the saddle-bag of	the camel	and she sat	on them	and he felt	Laban	all of the tent

3940	4834.111		569.122	420, 1	414, 2835.121	904, 6084
cj, neg part	v Qal pf 3ms	**35.**	cj, v Qal impf 3fs	prep, n ms, ps 3fs	adv, v Qal impf 3ms	prep, *n fp*
וְלֹא	מָצָא		וַתֹּאמֶר	אֶל־אָבִיהָ	אַל־יִחַר	בְּעֵינֵי
w^{e}lō'	mātsā'		wattō'mer	'el-'āvîhā	'al-yichar	b^{e}'ênê
but not	he found		and she said	to her father	let it not be anger	in the eyes of

112	3706	3940	3310.125	3937, 7251.141	4623, 6686	3706, 1932
n ms, ps 1cs	cj	neg part	v Qal impf 1cs	prep, v Qal inf con	prep, n mp, ps 2ms	cj, *n ms*
אֲדֹנִי	כִּי	לוֹא	אוּכַל	לָקוּם	מִפָּנֶיךָ	כִּי־דֶרֶךְ
'ădhōnî	kî	lô'	'ûkhal	lāqûm	mippānêkhā	kî-dherek
my master	because	not	I am able	to rise	before you	because the way of

5571	3937	2769.321	3940	4834.111	881, 8994		2835.121
n fp	prep, ps 1cs	cj, v Piel impf 3ms	cj, neg part	v Qal pf 3ms	do, art, n mp	**36.**	cj, v Qal impf 3ms
נָשִׁים	לִי	וַיְחַפֵּשׂ	וְלֹא	מָצָא	אֶת־הַתְּרָפִים		וַיִּחַר
nāshîm	lî	waychappēs	w^{e}lō'	mātsâ'	'eth-hatt^{e}rāphîm		wayyichar
women	to me	and he searched	and not	he found	the idols		then it was anger

before our brethren: ... in the presence of our tribesmen, *Goodspeed* ... with my kinsmen looking on, *NAB* ... let our kinsmen be witnesses, *NEB* ... presence of our relatives, *NIV* ... under supervision of, *Berkeley.*

discern thou what is thine with me, and take it to thee: ... choose what is yours, KJVII ... identify anything here as belonging to you, *NAB* ... point out what is yours among my belongings, *NASB* ... see for yourself whether there is anything of yours, *NIV* ... make a search, *Berkeley.*

For Jacob knew not that Rachel had stolen them: ... had no idea, *NAB* ... had appropriated them, *Anchor* ... had purloined them, *Berkeley* ... had no knowledge that Rachel had taken them, *BB.*

33. And Laban went into Jacob's tent, and into Leah's tent: ... the tent of Jacob, *Goodspeed* ... searched Jacob's tent, *NAB* ... went through, *NCB* ... went round, *Fenton.*

and into the two maidservants' tents: ... tent of the two maids, *NASB* ... through those of both the maids, *NCB* ... two slave-girls, *NEB* ... two servant-women, *BB* ... of the two mothers, *Fenton.*

but he found them not: ... found nothing, *Goodspeed* ... did not find them, *KJVII* ... without finding them, *NCB.*

Then went he out of Leah's tent, and entered into Rachel's tent: ... leaving Leah's tent, he went into Rachel's, *Goodspeed.*

34. Now Rachel had taken the images: ... the household gods, *Goodspeed* ... the idols, *NAB* ... hath taken the teraphim, *Young.*

and put them in the camel's furniture: ... camel's saddle, *KJVII* ... cushion, *NAB* ... camel-bag, *NEB* ... camels' basket, *BB* ... litter, *Geneva.*

and sat upon them: ... seated herself, *NAB* ... was sitting on them, *NCB* ... sat on top of them, *Anchor.*

And Laban searched all the tent: ... felt all over the tent, *Goodspeed* ... rummaged through the rest of her tent, *NAB* ... explored all the tent, *Darby* ... combed through, *Anchor* ... searched through everything, *NIV.*

but found them not: ... did not come across them, *BB* ... to no avail, *Anchor* ... found nothing, *NEB.*

35. And she said to her father, Let it not displease my lord that I cannot rise up before thee: ... let it not be an occasion of anger in the eyes of my lord, *Darby* ... I hope my master does not object to my being unable to get up, *Berkeley* ... do not take it amiss, sir, *NEB* ... do not feel offended, *NAB.*

for the custom of women is upon me: ... customary way of a woman, *Berkeley* ... common lot of women, *NEB* ... I am having my periods, *NCB* ... woman's period is upon me, *NAB* ... ailment common to women, *Goodspeed.*

And he searched, but found not the images: ... did not find the household gods, *Goodspeed* ... his idols, *NAB* ... hath not found the teraphim, *Young.*

36. And Jacob was wroth, and chode with Laban: ... angrily Jacob reprimanded Laban, *Berkeley* ... was wroth, and chode with, *ASV* ... he expostulated with, *NEB* ... remonstrated with, *NCB* ... contended with, *NASB.*

and Jacob answered and said to Laban, What is my trespass?: ... what is my crime, *NIV* ... what have I done wrong, *NEB* ... what is my transgression, *NASB* ... what is my misdemeanor, *Berkeley.*

what is my sin: ... what is my offence, *NEB* ... what sin have I committed, *NIV* ... what is my misdeed, *Goodspeed* ... what is my guilt, *Anchor* ... what have I offended, *Geneva.*

that thou hast so hotly pursued after me?: ... come after me with such a passion, *BB* ... thou hast burned after me, *Young* ... hunt me down, *NIV* ... in hot pursuit, *NEB* ... you should have come raging, *Goodspeed.*

37. Whereas thou hast searched all my stuff: ... explored all my baggage, *Darby* ... felt all my vessels, *Young* ... searched through all my goods, *NIV* ... ransacked, *NAB.*

31:33-35. The search for the teraphim focused on the tents of Jacob's wives and concubines, for they were the ones who would have had access to the room where the teraphim were kept. Rachel had hidden them in her camel saddle, which with its carpet covers made a comfortable seat. (Some believe a palanquin rather than a saddle is meant—a curtained compartment usually tied on to the saddle, but this would be more likely to invite a search.) Laban accepted Rachel's excuse that she was having her period and went on with the search in other places.

31:36-37. Jacob was angry and called for a judgment scene. He knew he was innocent and he felt the suspicions of his father-in-law were unfair and unjustified. He also felt Laban had made up the story of stolen teraphim as an excuse to search Jacob's possessions. If Laban found anything that belonged to him, he should set it before all the relatives and let them judge what to do.

3937, 3399	7662.121	904, 3969	6257.121	3399	569.121	3937, 3969
prep, pn	cj, v Qal impf 3ms	prep, pn	cj, v Qal impf 3ms	pn	cj, v Qal impf 3ms	prep, pn
לְיַעֲקֹב	וַיָּרֶב	בְּלָבָן	וַיַּעַן	יַעֲקֹב	וַיֹּאמֶר	לְלָבָן
l^{e}ya'ăqōv	wayyārev	b^{e}lāvān	wayya'an	ya'ăqōv	wayyō'mer	l^{e}lāvān
to Jacob	and he brought charges	against Laban	and he answered	Jacob	and he said	to Laban

4242, 6840	4242	2490.115	3706	1875.113	313		3706, 5135.313
intrg, n ms, ps 1cs	intrg	v Qal pf 1cs	cj	v Qal pf 2ms	adv, ps 1cs	**37.**	cj, v Piel pf 2ms
מַה־פִּשְׁעִי	מַה	חָטָּאתִי	כִּי	דָלַקְתָּ	אַחֲרָי		כִּי־מִשַּׁשְׁתָּ
mah-pish'î	mah	chattā'thî	kî	dhālaqōttā	'achrāy		kî-mishshashtā
what my crime	how	have I sinned	that	you hotly pursued	after me		because you felt

881, 3725, 3747	4242, 4834.113	4623, 3725	3747, 1041	7947.131
do, *adj*, n mp, ps 1cs	intrg, v Qal pf 2ms	prep, prep	*n mp*, n ms, ps 2ms	v Qal impv 2ms
אֶת־כָּל־כֵּלַי	מַה־מָּצָאתָ	מִכֹּל	כְּלֵי־בֵיתֶךָ	שִׂים
'eth-kol-kēlay	mah-mātsā'thā	mikkōl	k^{e}lê-vêthekhā	sîm
all my belongings	what have you found	of all	the belongings of your house	put

3662	5224	250	250	3306.526	1033	8530
adv	prep	n mp, ps 1cs	cj, n mp, ps 2ms	cj, v Hiphil impf 3mp	prep	num, ps 1cp
כֹּה	נֶגֶד	אַחַי	וְאַחֶיךָ	וְיוֹכִיחוּ	בֵּין	שְׁנֵינוּ
kōh	neghedh	'achay	w^{e}'achêkhā	w^{e}yôkhîchû	bên	sh^{e}nênû
here	in front of	my relatives	and your relatives	and they will arbitrate	between	the two of us

	2172	6465	8523	609	6196	7636	6008	3940
38.	dem pron	num	n fs	pers pron	prep, ps 2fs	n fp, ps 2ms	cj, n fp, ps 2ms	neg part
	זֶה	עֶשְׂרִים	שָׁנָה	אָנֹכִי	עִמָּךְ	רְחֵלֶיךָ	וְעִזֶּיךָ	לֹא
	zeh	'esrîm	shānāh	'ānōkhî	'immāk	r^{e}chēlêkhā	w^{e}'izzêkhā	lō'
	these	twenty	years	I	with you	your ewes	and your she-goats	not

8323.316	356	6887	3940	404.115		3076
v Piel pf 3cp	cj, *n mp*	n fs, ps 2ms	neg part	v Qal pf 1cs	**39.**	n fs
שִׁכֵּלוּ	וְאֵילֵי	צֹאנְךָ	לֹא	אָכָלְתִּי		טְרֵפָה
shikkēlû	w^{e}'êlê	tsō'n^{e}khā	lō'	'ākhāltî		t^{e}rēphāh
they have miscarried	and the rams of	your flock	not	I have eaten		what is torn

3940, 971.515	420	609	2490.325	4623, 3135	1272.323
neg part, v Hiphil pf 1cs	prep, ps 2ms	pers pron	v Piel impf 1cs, ps 3fs	prep, n fs, ps 1cs	v Piel impf 2ms, ps 3fs
לֹא־הֵבֵאתִי	אֵלֶיךָ	אָנֹכִי	אֲחַטֶּנָּה	מִיָּדִי	תְּבַקְשֶׁנָּה
lō'-hēvē'thî	'ēlêkhā	'ānōkhî	'ăchattennāh	miyyādhî	t^{e}vaqōshennāh
not I brought	to you	I	I made up for it	from my hand	you sought for it

1630.157	3219	1630.157	4050		2030.115	904, 3219	404.111
v Qal pass ptc fs	n ms	cj, v Qal pass ptc fs	n ms	**40.**	v Qal pf 1cs	prep, art, n ms	v Qal pf 3ms, ps1cs
גְּנֻבְתִי	יוֹם	וּגְנֻבְתִי	לָיְלָה		הָיִיתִי	בַיּוֹם	אֲכָלַנִי
g^{e}nuv^{e}thî	yôm	ûgh^{e}nuv^{e}thî	lāy^{e}lāh		hāyîthî	vayyôm	'ăkhālanî
one stolen of	day	or one stolen of	night		I was	in the day	it consumed me

2821	7430	904, 4050	5252.122	8524	4623, 6084		2172, 3937
n ms	cj, n ms	prep, art, n ms	cj, v Qal impf 3fs	n fs, ps 1cs	prep, n fd, ps 1cs	**41.**	dem pron, prep, ps 1cs
חֹרֶב	וְקֶרַח	בַּלָּיְלָה	וַתִּדַּד	שְׁנָתִי	מֵעֵינָי		זֶה־לִּי
chōrev	w^{e}qerach	ballāy^{e}lāh	wattiddadh	sh^{e}nāthî	mē'ênāy		zeh-lî
heat	and frost	in the night	and it fled	my sleep	from my eyes		this to me

6465	8523	904, 1041	5856.115	727, 6462	8523	904, 8530
num	n fs	prep, n ms, ps 2ms	v Qal pf 1cs, ps 2ms	num, num	n fs	prep, *num*
עֶשְׂרִים	שָׁנָה	בְּבֵיתֶךָ	עֲבַדְתִּיךָ	אַרְבַּע־עֶשְׂרֵה	שָׁנָה	בִּשְׁתֵּי
'esrîm	shānāh	b^{e}vêthekhā	'ăvadtîkhā	'arba'-'esrēh	shānāh	bishtê
twenty	years	in your household	I have served you	four ten	year	for the two of

what hast thou found of all thy household stuff?: ... what have you seen which is yours, *BB* ... which of all your utensils have you discovered, *Berkeley* ... what household article of yours have you found, *NCB* ... have you found a single object, *NAB.*

set it here: ... produce it here, *NAB* ... put it out here, *NCB* ... make it clear now, *BB* ... put everything I stole out here in front of us, *LIVB.*

before my brethren and thy brethren: ... in the sight of my tribesmen and yours, *Goodspeed* ... your kinsmen and mine, *NAB* ... relatives, *NIV* ... companions, *Anchor* ... my people and your people, *BB.*

that they may judge betwixt us both: ... they may divide the issue between us two, *Goodspeed* ... let them decide, *NAB* ... they may be judges, *BB.*

38. This twenty years have I been with thee: ... that I was under you, *NAB.*

thy ewes and thy she goats have not cast their *Young*: ... have never miscarried, *NEB* ... have had Young without loss, *BB* ... I have not lost a sheep or a goat of yours, *Fenton* ... have not failed to reproduce, *Good News.*

and the rams of thy flock have I not eaten: ... never feasted on a ram, *NAB* ... not one of your he-goats have I taken for food, *BB.*

39. That which was torn of beasts: ... animals torn by wild beasts, *NIV* ... the body of any animal mangled, *NEB* ... the prey of beasts, *Anchor* ... wounded, *BB* ... maimed, *Fenton.*

I brought not unto thee: ... I never reported to you, *Goodspeed.*

I bare the loss of it: ... I bore the loss myself, *NEB* ... I repay it, *Young* ... I myself made good the loss, *Anchor* ... I personally replaced it, *Berkeley.*

of my hand didst thou require it: ... you held me responsible, *Goodspeed* ... you exacted it at my hand, *KJVII* ... you claimed compensation from me, *NEB* ... demanded payment from me, *NIV* ... thou dost seek it, *Young.*

whether stolen by day, or stolen by night: ... for anything stolen, *NEB* ... I have been deceived by day, and I have been deceived by night, *Young* ... snatched by day, *Anchor* ... carried off, *Berkeley* ... whatever was taken by thieves, *BB.*

40. Thus I was: ... this was my condition, *BB* ... as for me personally, *Berkeley* ... this was my situation, *NIV* ... this was the way of it, *REB* ... so it was with me, *KJVII.*

in the day the drought consumed me: ... heat wear me out in the daytime, *Goodspeed* ... how often the scorching heat ravaged me, *NAB* ... heat wasted me, *NCB.*

and the frost by night: ... cold at night, *Goodspeed* ... bitter cold, *BB.*

and my sleep departed from mine eyes: ... me eyes never rested, *Fenton* ... wander doth my sleep, *Young* ... sleep deserted me, *NEB* ... sleep fled from my eyes, *ASV* ... I got no sleep, *REB.*

41. Thus have I been twenty years in thy house: ... this is to me twenty years in thy house:, *Young* ... it was like this for the twenty years, *NIV* ... spent in your household, *NAB* ... a member of your household, *Goodspeed.*

I served thee fourteen years for thy two daughters: ... I slaved fourteen years, *NAB* ... worked for you fourteen years to win, *NEB.*

and six years for thy cattle: ... sheep, *Goodspeed* ... flocks, *KJVII.*

and thou hast changed my wages ten times: ... time after time, *NAB* ... changest my hire, *Young* ... time and again, *Anchor* ... was my payment changed, *BB* ... you cheated me over my wages ten times, *Fenton.*

42. Except the God of my father: ... if my ancestral God, *NAB.*

the God of Abraham, and the fear of Isaac: ... awe of Isaac, *Goodspeed* ... Awesome One of Isaac, *NAB* ... reverence of Isaac, *Berkeley* ... worshipped of Isaac, *Fenton.*

had been with me: ... had not been on my side, *NRSV* ... had not favored me, *NCB.*

surely thou hadst sent me away

31:38-40. Jacob defended his faithful and skillful care of Laban's flocks. He even bore losses that were really not his fault and for which he was not legally responsible (as the law code of Hammurabi coming from this general period shows).

The 20 years of his service were not easy, for he was out in the heat of the day and in the cold of the night, often without sleep.

31:41-42. Laban had not been fair in changing Jacob's wages, but God was with Jacob, saw his hard work, and overruled Laban's intention to send Jacob away with nothing. The dream God gave Laban was a deserved rebuke. When Jacob called God the "fear" of Isaac, he meant Isaac stood in awe of the true God. Some, however, take the word "fear" to have the meaning of trembling with joy, or it may speak of a close relationship with God.

1351	8666	8523	904, 6887	2599.523	881, 5032	6467	4634
n fp, ps 2ms	cj, num	n fp	prep, n fs, ps 2ms	cj, v Hiphil impf 2ms	do, n fs, ps 1cs	num	n mp
בְּנֹתֶיךָ	וְשֵׁשׁ	שָׁנִים	בְּצֹאנֶךָ	וַתַּחֲלֵף	אֶת־מַשְׂכֻּרְתִּי	עֲשֶׂרֶת	מֹנִים
benōthêkhā	weshēsh	shānîm	betsō'nekhā	wattachlēph	'eth-maskurtî	'ăsereth	mōnîm
your daughters	and six	years	for your flock	and you changed	my wages	ten	times

42.	4020	435	1	435	80	6586	3437	2030.111
	cj	*n mp*	n ms, ps 1cs	*n mp*	pn	cj, *n ms*	pn	v Qal pf 3ms
	לוּלֵי	אֱלֹהֵי	אָבִי	אֱלֹהֵי	אַבְרָהָם	וּפַחַד	יִצְחָק	הָיָה
	lûlê	'ĕlōhê	'āvî	'ĕlōhê	'avrāhām	ûphachadh	yitschāq	hāyāh
	if not	the God of	my father	the God of	Abraham	and the fear of	Isaac	it was

3937	3706	6498	7674	8365.313	882, 6271	881, 3127
prep, ps 1cs	intrj	adv	adv	v Piel pf 2ms, ps 1cs	prep, n ms, ps 1cs	cj, do, n ms
לִי	כִּי	עַתָּה	רֵיקָם	שִׁלַּחְתָּנִי	אֶת־עָנְיִי	וְאֶת־יְגִיעַ
lî	kî	'attāh	rêqām	shillachtānî	'eth-'āneyî	we'eth-yeghîa'
to me	truly	now	empty-handed	you would send me	with my misery	and with the labor of

3834	7495.111	435	3306.521	582	43.	6257.121	3969	569.121
n fp, ps 1cs	v Qal pf 3ms	n mp	v Hiphil impf 3ms	adv		cj, v Qal impf 3ms	pn	cj, v Qal impf 3ms
כַּפַּי	רָאָה	אֱלֹהִים	וַיּוֹכַח	אָמֶשׁ		וַיַּעַן	לָבָן	וַיֹּאמֶר
kappay	rā'āh	'ĕlōhîm	wayyôkhach	'āmesh		wayya'an	lāvān	wayyō'mer
my hands	He saw	God	but He rebuked	yesterday		and he answered	Laban	and he said

420, 3399	1351	1351	1158	1158	6887	6887
prep, pn	art, n fp	n fp	cj, art, n mp	n mp	cj, art, n fs	n fs
אֶל־יַעֲקֹב	הַבָּנוֹת	בְּנֹתַי	וְהַבָּנִים	בָּנַי	וְהַצֹּאן	צֹאנִי
'el-ya'ăqōv	habbānôth	benōthay	wehabbānîm	bānay	wehatstsō'n	tsō'nî
to Jacob	the daughters	my daughters	and the children	my children	and the flock	my flocks

3725	866, 887	7495.151	3937, 2000	3937, 1351	4242, 6449.125
cj, adj	rel part, pers pron	v Qal act ptc ms	prep, ps 1cs, pers pron	cj, prep, n fp, ps 1cs	intrg, v Qal impf 1cs
וְכֹל	אֲשֶׁר־אַתָּה	רֹאֶה	לִי־הוּא	וְלִבְנֹתַי	מָה־אֶעֱשֶׂה
wekhōl	'ăsher-'attāh	rō'eh	lî-hû'	welivnōthay	māh-'e'ĕseh
and all	which you	seeing	to me it	and to my daughters	what will I do

3937, 431	3219	173	3937, 1158	866	3314.116	44.	6498
prep, dem pron	art, n ms	cj	prep, n mp, ps 3fp	rel part	v Qal pf 3cp		cj, adv
לָאֵלֶּה	הַיּוֹם	אוֹ	לִבְנֵיהֶן	אֲשֶׁר	יָלָדוּ		וְעַתָּה
lā'ēlleh	hayyôm	'ô	livnêhen	'ăsher	yālādû		we'attāh
for these	today	or	for their children	whom	they gave birth		and now

2050.131	3901.120	1311	603	887	2030.111	3937, 5915
v Qal impv 2ms	v Qal impf 1cp	n fs	pers pron	cj, pers pron	cj, v Qal pf 3ms	prep, n ms
לְכָה	נִכְרְתָה	בְרִית	אֲנִי	וָאָתָּה	וְהָיָה	לְעֵד
lekhāh	nikhrethāh	verîth	'ănî	wā'āttāh	wehāyāh	le'ēdh
come	we will cut	covenant	I	and you	and it will be	witness

1033	1033	45.	4089.121	3399	63	7597.521	4838
prep, ps 1cs	cj, prep, ps 2ms		cj, v Qal impf 3ms	pn	n fs	cj, v Hiphil impf 3ms, ps 3fs	n fs
בֵּינִי	וּבֵינֶךָ		וַיִּקַּח	יַעֲקֹב	אָבֶן	וַיְרִימֶהָ	מַצֵּבָה
bênî	ûvênekhā		wayyiqqach	ya'ăqōv	'āven	wayrîmehā	matstsēvāh
between me	and between you		and he took	Jacob	stone	and he set it	memorial

46.	569.121	3399	3937, 250	4092.133	63	4089.126	63
	cj, v Qal impf 3ms	pn	prep, n mp, ps 3ms	v Qal impv 2mp	n fp	cj, v Qal impf 3mp	n fp
	וַיֹּאמֶר	יַעֲקֹב	לְאֶחָיו	לִקְטוּ	אֲבָנִים	וַיִּקְחוּ	אֲבָנִים
	wayyō'mer	ya'ăqōv	le'echâv	liqṭû	'ăvānîm	wayyiqchû	'ăvānîm
	and he said	Jacob	to his relatives	gather	stones	and they took	stones

6449.126, 1569 cj, v Qal impf 3mp, n ms וַיַּעֲשׂוּ־גָל wayya'ăsû-ghāl and they made heap	404.126 cj, v Qal impf 3mp וַיֹּאכְלוּ wayyō'kh^e^lû and they ate	8427 adv שָׁם shām there	6142, 1569 prep, art, n ms עַל־הַגָּל 'al-haggāl beside the heap	**47.**	7410.121, 3937 cj, v Qal impf 3ms, prep, ps 3ms וַיִּקְרָא־לוֹ wayyiqŏrā'-lô and he named it	3969 pn לָבָן lāvān Laban

A3134 pn יְגַר y^e^ghar Jegar	A7905 pn שָׂהֲדוּתָא sāh^e^dhûthā' Sahadutha	3399 cj, pn וְיַעֲקֹב w^e^ya'ăqōv but Jacob	7410.111 v Qal pf 3ms קָרָא qārā' he named	3937 prep, ps 3ms לוֹ lô it	1608 pn גַּלְעֵד gal'ēdh Galeed	**48.**	569.121 cj, v Qal impf 3ms וַיֹּאמֶר wayyō'mer and he said	3969 pn לָבָן lāvān Laban

now empty: ... empty-handed, *NEB* ... dismissed me, *Berkeley* ... nothing in my hands, *BB.*

God hath seen mine affliction: ... saw my suffering, *Goodspeed* ... plight, *NAB* ... hardships, *NEB* ... misery, *Berkeley* ... weary feat, *Fenton* ... tribulation, *Geneva.*

and the labour of my hands: ... fruits of my toil, *NAB* ... manual labor, *Berkeley* ... work I have done, *Good News.*

and rebuked thee yesternight: ... last night he gave judgment, *NAB* ... pronounced sentence, *NCB* ... reproveth, *Young* ... kept you back, *BB* ... defended me, *Fenton.*

43. And Laban answered and said unto Jacob: These daughters are my daughters, and these children are my children: ... the women are mine, their children are mine, *NAB* ... the women are my daughters, the children are my children, *NIV.*

and these cattle are my cattle and all that thou seest is mine: ... and these flocks are my flocks, *KJVII* ... everything you see belongs to me, *NAB.*

and what can I do this day unto these my daughters: ... I will now do something for them, *NAB* ... what am I to do now, *REB* ... what now may I do for my daughters, *BB.*

or unto their children which they have born?: ... or to their sons, *Young.*

44. Now therefore come thou, let us make a covenant, I and thou: ... you and I, *KJVII* ... we will make a pact, *NAB* ... an agreement, *NEB* ... a settlement, *Fenton.*

and let it be for a witness between me and thee: ... the Lord shall be a witness, *NAB* ... let there be a witness, *REB.*

45. And Jacob took a stone and set it up for a pillar: ... chose a great stone, *NEB* ... as a memorial stone, *NAB* ... sacred pillar, *NEB* ... lifteth it up for a standing pillar, *Young.*

46. And Jacob said unto his brethren, Gather stones: ... kinsmen, *NAB* ... relatives, *NIV* ... companions, *Anchor* ... father-in-law, *Fenton.*

and they took stones, and made an heap: ... and made a mound, *NAB* ... took them and made a cairn, *NEB* ... piled them in a heap, *NIV.*

and they did eat there upon the heap: ... the had a meal, *NAB* ... there beside the cairn they ate together, *REB* ... broke bread there over the mound, *Anchor.*

47. And Laban called it Jegarsahadutha: ... the heap of witnesses, *Fenton.*

but Jacob called it Galeed: ... the heap of evidence, *Fenton.*

48. And Laban said, This heap is a witness between me and thee this day: ... this mound shall be a witness from now on, *NAB* ... this cairn is witness today, *NEB* ... this pile of rocks will be a reminder, *Good News.*

Therefore was the name of it called Galeed: ... it was named, *NEB.*

31:43-44. Laban still refused to accept the fact that Jacob had earned what he had. Laban claimed Jacob's family and all Jacob had. As the head of the extended family he felt he had that right. Yet, because of the warning God gave him, he could do nothing about it, so he asked Jacob to make a covenant as a witness between them. Apparently he felt that Jacob might grow stronger and come back to take revenge for what Laban had done to him.

31:45-47. Jacob set up a stone as a memorial pillar and his relatives piled stones in a heap. These would mark the boundaries between Laban on the north and Jacob on the south. Laban gave the heap of stones a name in Aramaic (his native language) meaning "witness heap." Jacob gave it the same name in Hebrew.

31:48-50. The witness heap was also called Mizpah, "watchtower," because of what the suspicious Laban said. He meant, "I do not trust you Jacob, and since I won't be here to watch you, may

1569	2172	5915	1033	1033	3219	6142, 3772
art, n ms	art, dem pron	n ms	prep, ps 1cs	cj, prep, ps 2ms	art, n ms	prep, adv
הַגַּל	הַזֶּה	עֵד	בֵּינִי	וּבֵינֶךָ	הַיּוֹם	עַל־כֵּן
haggal	hazzeh	'ēdh	bênî	ûvênekhā	hayyôm	'al-kēn
the heap	the this	witness	between me	and between you	today	therefore

7410.111, 8428	1608	49.	4870	866	569.111	7099.121	3176
v Qal pf 3ms, n ms, ps 3ms	pn		cj, art, pn	rel part	v Qal pf 3ms	v Qal impf 3ms	pn
קָרָא־שְׁמוֹ	גַּלְעֵד		וְהַמִּצְפָּה	אֲשֶׁר	אָמַר	יִצֶף	יְהוָה
qārā'-shemô	gal'ēdh		wehammitspāh	'ăsher	'āmar	yitseph	yehwāh
he called its name	Galeed		and Mizpah	where	he said	He will watch	Yahweh

1033	1033	3706	5846.220	382	4623, 4991
prep, ps 1cs	cj, prep, ps 2ms	cj	v Niphal impf 1cp	n ms	prep, n ms, ps 3ms
בֵּינִי	וּבֵינֶךָ	כִּי	נִסָּתֵר	אִישׁ	מֵרֵעֵהוּ
bênî	ûvênekhā	kî	nissāthēr	'îsh	mērē'ēhû
between me	and between you	because	we will be hidden	one	from his friend

50.	524, 6257.323	881, 1351	524, 4089.223	5571	6142, 1351	375
	cj, v Piel impf 2ms	do, n fp, ps 1cs	cj, cj, v Qal impf 2ms	n fp	prep, n fp, ps 1cs	*sub*
	אִם־תְּעַנֶּה	אֶת־בְּנֹתַי	וְאִם־תִּקַּח	נָשִׁים	עַל־בְּנֹתַי	אֵין
	'im-te'anneh	'eth-benōthay	we'im-tiqqach	nāshîm	'al-benōthay	'ên
	if you treat badly	my daughters	or if you take	wives	beside my daughters	there is not

382	6196	7495.131	435	5915	1033	1033
n ms	prep, ps 1cp	v Qal impv 2ms	n mp	n ms	prep, ps 1cs	cj, prep, ps 2ms
אִישׁ	עִמָּנוּ	רְאֵה	אֱלֹהִים	עֵד	בֵּינִי	וּבֵינֶךָ
'îsh	'immānû	re'ēh	'ĕlōhîm	'ēdh	bênî	ûvênekhā
man	with us	see	God	witness	between me	and between you

51.	569.121	3969	3937, 3399	2079	1569	2172	2079	4838
	cj, v Qal impf 3ms	pn	prep, pn	intrj	art, n ms	art, dem pron	cj, intrj	art, n fs
	וַיֹּאמֶר	לָבָן	לְיַעֲקֹב	הִנֵּה	הַגַּל	הַזֶּה	וְהִנֵּה	הַמַּצֵּבָה
	wayyō'mer	lāvān	leya'ăqōv	hinnēh	haggal	hazzeh	wehinnēh	hamatstsēvāh
	and he said	Laban	to Jacob	behold	the heap	the this	and behold	the memorial

866	3498.115	1033	1033	52.	5915	1569	2172	5921
rel part	v Qal pf 1cs	prep, ps 1cs	cj, prep, ps 2ms		n ms	art, n ms	art, dem pron	cj, n fs
אֲשֶׁר	יָרִיתִי	בֵּינִי	וּבֵינֶךָ		עֵד	הַגַּל	הַזֶּה	וְעֵדָה
'ăsher	yārîthî	bênî	ûvênekhā		'ēdh	haggal	hazzeh	we'ēdhāh
which	I raised	between me	and between you		witness	the heap	the this	and witness

4838	524, 603	3940, 5882.125	420	881, 1569	2172	524, 887
art, fs	cj, pers pron	neg part, v Qal impf 1cs	prep, ps 2ms	do, art, n ms	art, dem pron	cj, cj, pers pron
הַמַּצֵּבָה	אִם־אָנִי	לֹא־אֶעֱבֹר	אֵלֶיךָ	אֶת־הַגַּל	הַזֶּה	וְאִם־אַתָּה
hammatstsēvāh	'im-'ānî	lō'-'e'ĕvōr	'ēlêkhā	'eth-haggal	hazzeh	we'im-'attāh
the memorial	that I	not I will pass beyond	to you	the heap	the this	and that you

3940, 5882.123	420	881, 1569	2172	881, 4838	2148	3937, 7750
neg part, v Qal impf 2ms	prep, ps 1cs	do, art, n ms	art, dem pron	cj, do, art, n fs	art, dem pron	prep, n fs
לֹא־תַעֲבֹר	אֵלַי	אֶת־הַגַּל	הַזֶּה	וְאֶת־הַמַּצֵּבָה	הַזֹּאת	לְרָעָה
lō'-tha'ăvōr	'ēlay	'eth-haggal	hazzeh	we'eth-hammatstsēvāh	hazzō'th	lerā'āh
not you will pass beyond	to me	the heap	the this	and the memorial	the this	for evil

53.	435	80	435	5331	8570.126	1033	435
	n mp	pn	cj, *n mp*	pn	v Qal impf 3mp	prep, ps 1cp	*n mp*
	אֱלֹהֵי	אַבְרָהָם	וֵאלֹהֵי	נָחוֹר	יִשְׁפְּטוּ	בֵּינֵינוּ	אֱלֹהֵי
	'ĕlōhê	'avrāhām	wē'lōhê	nāchôr	yishpetû	vênênû	'ĕlōhê
	the God of	Abraham	and the gods of	Nahor	they will judge	between us	the gods of

49. And Mizpah; for he said, The LORD watch between me and thee: ... and the pillar Mizpah, *NRSV* ... a watch-tower, *Fenton* ... may Yahweh keep watch, *Anchor* ... let Jehovah watch, *Darby* ... let the Ever-living watch, *Fenton.*

when we are absent one from another: ... out of each others sight, *NAB* ... away from each other, *NCB* ... for we are hidden on from another, *Young* ... when we are unable to see one another's doing, *BB* ... to keep each from evil, *Fenton.*

50. If thou shalt afflict my daughters: ... mistreat, *NAB, NIV* ... ill-treat, *NEB* ... cruel, *BB* ... grieve, *Fenton.*

or if thou shalt take other wives beside my daughters: ... or marry others besides them, *NCB* ... in addition to, *NRSV.*

no man is with us: ... even though no one else is about, *NAB* ... when no one is there to see, *NEB* ... though no one is there as a witness, *REB* ... although no person is present, *Berkeley* ... when we are not together, *Fenton.*

see, God is witness betwixt me and thee: ... remember, *NCB.*

51. And Laban said to Jacob, Behold this heap, and behold this pillar: ... here is this mound, *NAB* ... here is the memorial stone, *NAB* ... here is this cairn, *NEB.*

which I have cast betwixt me and thee: ... set up, *NAB, NEB* ... placed, *NKJV* ... erected, *Anchor.*

52. This heap be witness, and this pillar be witness: ... this pillar is a memorial, *KJVII* ... mound shall be witness, and this memorial stone, *NAB* ... this stele, *Anchor.*

that I will not pass over this heap to thee: ... with hostile intent, neither may I pass beyond this mound into your territory, *NAB* ... I for my part will not pass beyond this cairn, *NEB* ... I am not to cross to you past this mound, *Anchor.*

and that thou shalt not pass over this heap and this pillar unto me, for harm: ... nor may you pass beyond it, *NAB* ... you for your part shall not pass beyond this cairn ... to attack, *Good News* ... with hostile intent, *Anchor* ... for evil, *Young* ... to do injury, *NEB* ... for any evil purpose; *BB.*

53. The God of Abraham, and the God of Nahor, the God of their father, judge betwixt us: ... maintain justice, *NAB* ... (the gods of their father), *NCB* ... (their respective ancestral deities), *Anchor* ... and the God of their father, *Geneva* ... maintain order, *Anchor.*

And Jacob sware by the fear of his father Isaac: ... swore by the fear of Isaac, *KJVII* ... took the oath by the Awesome One of Isaac, *NAB* ... swore by him whom his father Isaac revered, *NCB* ... swore this oath in the name of the Fear of Isaac, *NEB* ... swore by the reverence of his father, *Berkeley* ... swore by the Worshipped of his father, *Fenton.*

54. Then Jacob offered sacrifice upon the mount: ... on the mountain, *NAB* ... in the highlands, *NCB* ... he slaughtered an animal for sacrifice there in the hill-country, *NEB* ... on the height, *NRSV* ... mountainside, *Berkeley* ... on the heap, *Fenton.*

and called his brethren to eat bread: ... invited his kinsmen to share in the meal, *NAB* ... invited his kinsmen to take food, *NCB* ... summoned his kinsmen to the feast, *REB* ... invited his relatives to a meal, *NIV* ... invited his companions to partake of the meal, *Anchor.*

and they did eat bread: ... when they had eaten, *NAB* ... so they ate together, *NEB.*

and tarried all night in the mount: ... passed the night on the mountain, *NAB* ... spent the night in the highlands, *NCB* ... stayed all night on the mountain, *NKJV* . . lodge in the mount, *Young* ... rested on the heap, *Fenton.*

---

the LORD keep watch." Laban wanted God to punish Jacob if he mistreated Laban's daughters or took any additional wives. Actually, Laban had not been that concerned about his daughters or solicitous for their welfare (cf. 31:15). This was pretense on his part.

31:51-52. Either Laban set up another heap and pillar to mark the line of separation between him and Jacob or he simply took Jacob's over as if he was the one responsible for setting it up.

The covenant involved Laban's not going south of the line marked by the memorial pillar and witness heap to harm or steal from Jacob, while Jacob would not go north of it to act against Laban.

31:53. Laban added an oath to the covenant, calling on the God of Abraham, and the gods of Nahor, the gods of their father to judge between Jacob and Laban. Laban was still a polytheist, as evidenced by his household gods that Rachel took. Thus, *Elohe* is better translated "gods of" when referring to Laban's gods and the gods of Nahor. Terah, Abraham's father, was actually an idol-maker, according to Jewish tradition. But Jacob ignored the gods of Nahor and took his oath only in the name of the one true God who was the "Fear" of, or "the One Reverenced" by, Isaac.

1	8123.221	3399	904, 6586	1	3437		2159.121	3399
n ms, ps 3mp	cj, v Niphal impf 3ms	pn	prep, *n ms*	n ms, ps	pn	**54.**	cj, v Qal impf 3ms	pn
אֲבִיהֶם	וַיִּשָּׁבַע	יַעֲקֹב	בְּפַחַד	אָבִיו	יִצְחָק		וַיִּזְבַּח	יַעֲקֹב
'ăvîhem	wayyishshāva'	ya'ăqōv	b^{e}phachadh	'āvîw	yitschāq		wayyizbach	ya'ăqōv
their father	and he swore	Jacob	by the fear of	his father	Isaac		and he slaughtered	Jacob

2160	904, 2098	7410.121	3937, 250	3937, 404.141, 4035	404.126
n ms	prep, art, n ms	cj, v Qal impf 3ms	prep, n mp, ps 3ms	prep, v Qal inf con, n ms	cj, v Qal impf 3mp
זֶבַח	בָּהָר	וַיִּקְרָא	לְאֶחָיו	לֶאֱכָל־לָחֶם	וַיֹּאכְלוּ
zevach	bāhār	wayyiqrā'	l^{e}'echâv	le'ĕkhāl-lāchem	wayyō'kh^{e}lû
sacrifice	on the mountain	and he called	to his relatives	to eat bread	and they ate

4035	4053	904, 2098		8326.521	3969	904, 1269
n ms	cj, v Qal impf 3mp	prep, art, n ms	**55.**	cj, v Hiphil impf 3ms	pn	prep, art, n ms
לֶחֶם	וַיָּלִינוּ	בָּהָר		וַיַּשְׁכֵּם	לָבָן	בַּבֹּקֶר
lechem	wayyālînû	bāhār		wayyashkēm	lāvān	babbōqer
bread	and they spent the night	on the mountain		and he rose early	Laban	in the morning

5583.321	3937, 1158	3937, 1351	1313.321	881	2050.121
cj, v Piel impf 3ms	prep, n mp, ps 3ms	cj, prep, n fp, ps 3ms	cj, v Piel impf 3ms	do, ps 3mp	cj, v Qal impf 3ms
וַיְנַשֵּׁק	לְבָנָיו	וְלִבְנוֹתָיו	וַיְבָרֶךְ	אֶתְהֶם	וַיֵּלֶךְ
waynashshēq	l^{e}vānâv	w^{e}livnôthâv	way^{e}vārekh	'ethhem	wayyēlekh
and he kissed	his sons	and his daughters	and he blessed	them	and he went

8178.121	3969	3937, 4887		3399	2050.111	3937, 1932
cj, v Qal impf 3ms	pn	prep, n ms, ps 3ms	**32:1**	cj, pn	v Qal pf 3ms	prep, n ms, ps 3ms
וַיָּשָׁב	לָבָן	לִמְקֹמוֹ		וְיַעֲקֹב	הָלַךְ	לְדַרְכּוֹ
wayyāshāv	lāvān	limqōmô		w^{e}ya'ăqōv	hālakh	l^{e}dharkô
and he returned	Laban	to his place		and Jacob	he went	to his way

6534.126, 904	4534	435		569.121	3399	3626, 866
cj, v Qal impf 3mp, prep, ps 3ms	*n mp*	n mp	**2.**	cj, v Qal impf 3ms	pn	prep, rel part
וַיִּפְגְּעוּ־בוֹ	מַלְאֲכֵי	אֱלֹהִים		וַיֹּאמֶר	יַעֲקֹב	כַּאֲשֶׁר
wayyiphg^{e}'û-vô	mal'ăkhê	'ĕlōhîm		wayyō'mer	ya'ăqōv	ka'ăsher
and they met on it	the angels of	God		and he said	Jacob	when

7495.111	4402	435	2172	7410.121	8428, 4887	2000
v Qal pf 3ms, ps 3mp	*n ms*	n mp	dem pron	cj, v Qal impf 3ms	*n ms*, art, n ms	art, dem pron
רָאָם	מַחֲנֵה	אֱלֹהִים	זֶה	וַיִּקְרָא	שֵׁם־הַמָּקוֹם	הַהוּא
rā'ām	machnēh	'ĕlōhîm	zeh	wayyiqrā'	shēm-hammāqôm	hahû'
he saw them	army of	God	this	and he called	the name of the place	the that

4404		8365.121	3399	4534	3937, 6686	420, 6451	250
pn	**3.**	cj, v Qal impf 3ms	pn	n mp	prep, n mp, ps 3ms	prep, pn	n ms, ps 3ms
מַחֲנָיִם		וַיִּשְׁלַח	יַעֲקֹב	מַלְאָכִים	לְפָנָיו	אֶל־עֵשָׂו	אָחִיו
machnāyim		wayyishlach	ya'ăqōv	mal'ākhîm	l^{e}phānâv	'el-'ēsāw	'āchîw
Mahanaim		and he sent out	Jacob	messengers	before him	to Esau	his brother

800	7990	7898	110		6943	881	3937, 569.141	3662
n fs	pn	*n ms*	pn	**4.**	cj, v Piel impf 3ms	do, ps 3mp	prep, v Qal inf con	adv
אַרְצָה	שֵׂעִיר	שְׂדֵה	אֱדוֹם		וַיְצַו	אֹתָם	לֵאמֹר	כֹּה
'artsāh	sē'îr	s^{e}dhēh	'ĕdhôm		waytsaw	'ōthām	lē'mōr	kōh
to the land of	Seir	the field of	Edom		and he commanded	them	saying	thus

569.128	3937, 112	3937, 6451	3662	569.111	5860	3399	6196, 3969
v Qal impf 2mp	prep, n ms, ps 1cs	prep, pn	adv	v Qal pf 3ms	n ms, ps 2ms	pn	prep, pn
תֹאמְרוּן	לַאדֹנִי	לְעֵשָׂו	כֹּה	אָמַר	עַבְדְּךָ	יַעֲקֹב	עִם־לָבָן
thōēm^{e}rûn	la'dhōnî	l^{e}'ēsāw	kōh	'āmar	'avdh^{e}khā	ya'ăqōv	'im-lāvān
you will say	to my master	to Esau	thus	he says	your servant	Jacob	with Laban

55. And early in the morning Laban rose up: ... early the next morning, *NAB.*

and kissed his sons and his daughters: ... kissed his grandchildren and his daughters good-bye, *NAB* ... kissed his daughters and their children, *NEB.*

and blessed them: ... bade them farewell, *NCB* ... gave them his blessing, *REB.*

and Laban departed, and returned unto his place: ... set out on his journey back home, *NAB* ... returned to his home, *NCB* ... went home again, *NEB* ... back to his country, *BB.*

32:1. And Jacob went on his way: ... resumed his journey, *NCB* ... continued his journey, *NEB* ... resumed his trek, *Berkeley.*

and the angels of God met him: ... encountered him, *Goodspeed* ... God's messengers encountered, *NAB* ... and was met by angels of God, *NEB* ... came face to face with, *BB* ... messenger of God, *Fenton.*

2. And when Jacob saw them, he said: ... as soon as he saw them, *Goodspeed.*

This is God's host: ... encampment, *NAB* ... the company of God, *REB* ... camp of God, *NIV* ... God's army, *RSV* ... what a glorious encampment of God this place is, *Fenton.*

and he called the name of that place Mahanaim: ... (camps), *Goodspeed* ... two camps, *Young* ... the encampment, *Fenton.*

3. And Jacob sent messengers before him to Esau his brother: ... ahead of him, *REB* ... before his face, *Darby.*

unto the land of Seir, the country of Edom: ... region of Seir, *NCB* ... district of Seir, *NEB* ... Edomite territory, *REB* ... the field of Edom, *Young* ... Seir range, *Berkeley.*

4. And he commanded them, saying: ... with this message, *NAB* ... this is what he told them to say, *NEB* ... he instructed them, *NIV* ... charging them, *Berkeley* ... gave them orders, *BB.*

Thus shall ye speak unto my lord Esau: ... this is what you are to say, *NIV* ... thus shall ye say, *ASV* ... you must say to my master Esau, *Berkeley.*

Thy servant Jacob saith thus: ... thus says your servant Jacob, *Goodspeed* ... speaks as follows, *NAB* ... sends you this message, *NCB* ... I, Jacob, your obedient servant, *Good News.*

I have sojourned with Laban: ... I have lived with, *KJVII* ... been staying with, *NAB* ... been dwelling with, *NCB* ... lived with Laban as an alien, *NRSV* ... living as a stranger, *Berkeley.*

and stayed there until now: ... stayed right up to now, *Goodspeed* ... been detained there until now, *NAB* ... remained there till now, *NIV* ... and I tarry there until now, *Young* ... been held up there until now, *Anchor.*

5. And I have oxen, and asses, flocks: ... cattle, *NAB* ... donkeys, *NASB* ... sheep, *NEB.*

and menservants, and womenservants: ... male and female slaves, *NEB* ... male and female servants, *NAB* ... bondmen and bondwomen, *Darby* ... serving men and women, *Fenton.*

and I have sent to tell my lord: ... I am sending my lord this information, *NAB* ... I am sending word, *NCB* ... I am sending this message, *NIV* ... and I send to declare, *Young* ... I have sent to give my lord news of these things, *BB.*

that I may find grace in thy sight: ... hope of finding favor, *Goodspeed* ... may win your favor, *REB* ... find favor in your eyes, *NIV.*

31:54-55. Offering a sacrifice was part of making (cutting) a covenant (except for the marriage covenant, which was a covenant before the community). Their eating together was a way of expressing their acceptance of the covenant. Thus satisfied, Laban was ready to return home. So he kissed his grandchildren first, then his daughters, pronounced some kind of blessing on them, and left.

32:1-2. As Jacob moved south, the angels of God met him, probably the same angels he saw in his dream at Bethel (chapter 28). This manifestation caused him to call the place Mahanaim, meaning two camps or encampments, God's and his, recognizing that the angels had been there with him all the time even though he could not see them.

32:3-5. Jacob's mind did not dwell on God, however. He remembered Esau's threat to kill him, and he knew how some people nurse a grudge. Now he was coming near Esau's territory, so he tried to do something on his own to appease him. He sent messengers in advance with a humble message calling himself Esau's servant or slave and calling Esau lord or master. He wanted Esau to know that he was not intending to claim the prophecy that the older son would serve the younger. The mention of his wealth was probably intended to imply that he no longer wanted anything from Esau. All he wanted was to find favor in Esau's eyes.

1513.115	310.125	5912, 6498		2030.121, 3937	8228	2645
v Qal pf 1cs	cj, v Qal impf 1cs	prep, adv	**5.**	cj, v Qal impf 3ms, prep, ps 1cs	n ms	cj, n ms
גַּרְתִּי	וָאֵחַר	עַד־עָתָּה		וַיְהִי־לִי	שׁוֹר	וַחֲמוֹר
gartî	wā'ēchar	'adh-'āttāh		wayhî-lî	shôr	wachmôr
I have sojourned	and I delayed	until now		and it is to me	cattle	and donkeys

6687	5860	8569	8365.125	3937, 5222.541	3937, 112
n fs	cj, n ms	cj, n fs	cj, v Qal impf 1cs	prep, v Hiphil inf con	prep, n ms, ps 1cs
צֹאן	וְעֶבֶד	וְשִׁפְחָה	וָאֶשְׁלְחָה	לְהַגִּיד	לַאדֹנִי
tsō'n	w^{e}'eved	w^{e}shiphchāh	wā'eshl^{e}chāh	l^{e}haggîdh	la'dhōnî
flocks	and male slaves	and female slaves	and I sent	to report	to my master

3937, 4834.141, 2682	904, 6084		8178.126	4534	420, 3399	3937, 569.141
prep, v Qal inf con, n ms	prep, n fd, ps 2ms	**6.**	cj, v Qal impf 3mp	art, n mp	prep, pn	prep, v Qal inf con
לִמְצֹא־חֵן	בְּעֵינֶיךָ		וַיָּשֻׁבוּ	הַמַּלְאָכִים	אֶל־יַעֲקֹב	לֵאמֹר
limtsō'-chēn	b^{e}'ênêkhā		wayyāshuvû	hammal'ākhîm	'el-ya'ăqōv	lē'mōr
to find favor	in your eyes		and they returned	the messengers	to Jacob	saying

971.119	420, 250	420, 6451	1612	2050.151	3937, 7410.141
v Qal pf 1cp	prep, n ms, ps 2ms	prep, pn	cj, cj	v Qal act ptc ms	prep, v Qal inf con, pf 2ms
בָּאנוּ	אֶל־אָחִיךָ	אֶל־עֵשָׂו	וְגַם	הֹלֵךְ	לִקְרָאתְךָ
bā'nû	'el-'āchîkhā	'el-'ēsāw	w^{e}gham	hōlēkh	liqrā'th^{e}khā
we went	to your brother	to Esau	and also	coming	to meet you

727, 4109	382	6196		3486.121	3399	4108	7173.121
cj, num, num	n ms	prep, ps 3ms	**7.**	cj, v Qal impf 3ms	pn	adv	cj, v Qal impf 3ms
וְאַרְבַּע־מֵאוֹת	אִישׁ	עִמּוֹ		וַיִּירָא	יַעֲקֹב	מְאֹד	וַיֵּצֶר
w^{e}'arba'-mē'ôth	'îsh	'immô		wayyîrā'	ya'ăqōv	m^{e}'ōdh	wayyētser
and four hundred	men	with him		and he was afraid	Jacob	very	and he became anxious

3937	2779.121	881, 6194	866, 882	881, 6887	881, 1267
prep, ps 3ms	v Qal impf 3ms	do, art, n ms	rel part, prep, ps 3ms	cj, do, art, n fs	cj, do, art, n ms
לוֹ	וַיַּחַץ	אֶת־הָעָם	אֲשֶׁר־אִתּוֹ	וְאֶת־הַצֹּאן	וְאֶת־הַבָּקָר
lô	wayyachats	'eth-hā'ām	'ăsher-'ittô	w^{e}'eth-hatstsō'n	w^{e}'eth-habbāqār
for himself	so he divided	the people	who with him	and the flocks	and the cattle

1622	3937, 8530	4402		569.121	524, 971.121	6451	420, 4402	259
cj, art, n mp	prep, *num*	n mp	**8.**	cj, v Qal impf 3ms	cj, v Qal impf 3ms	pn	prep, art, n ms	art, num
וְהַגְּמַלִּים	לִשְׁנֵי	מַחֲנוֹת		וַיֹּאמֶר	אִם־יָבוֹא	עֵשָׂו	אֶל־הַמַּחֲנֶה	הָאַחַת
w^{e}hagg^{e}mallîm	lishnê	machnôth		wayyō'mer	'im-yāvō'	'ēsāw	'el-hammachneh	hā'achath
and the camels	into two	camps		and he said	if he comes	Esau	to the camp	the one

5409.511	2030.111	4402	8080.255	3937, 6656		569.121
cj, v Hiphil pf 3ms, ps 3ms	cj, v Qal pf 3ms	art, n ms	art, v Niphal ptc ms	prep, n fs	**9.**	cj, v Qal impf 3ms
וְהִכָּהוּ	וְהָיָה	הַמַּחֲנֶה	הַנִּשְׁאָר	לִפְלֵיטָה		וַיֹּאמֶר
w^{e}hikkāhû	w^{e}hāyāh	hammachneh	hannish'ār	liphlêṭāh		wayyō'mer
and he strikes it down	then it will be	the camp	the one left	to escape		and he said

3399	435	1	80	435	1	3437
pn	*n mp*	n ms, ps 1cs	pn	cj, *n mp*	n ms, ps 1cs	pn
יַעֲקֹב	אֱלֹהֵי	אָבִי	אַבְרָהָם	וֵאלֹהֵי	אָבִי	יִצְחָק
ya'ăqōv	'ĕlōhê	'āvî	'avrāhām	wē'lōhê	'āvî	yitschāq
Jacob	the God of	my father	Abraham	and the God of	my father	Isaac

3176	569.151	420	8178.131	3937, 800	3937, 4274
pn	art, v Qal act ptc ms	prep, ps 1cs	v Qal impv 2ms	prep, n fs, ps 2ms	cj, prep, n fs, ps 2ms
יְהוָה	הָאֹמֵר	אֵלַי	שׁוּב	לְאַרְצְךָ	וּלְמוֹלַדְתְּךָ
y^{e}hwāh	hā'ōmēr	'ēlay	shûv	l^{e}'arts^{e}khā	ûlāmôladht^{e}khā
Yahweh	the One who says	to me	return	to your land	and to your relatives

3296.525	6196		7275	4623, 3725	2721
cj, v Hiphil impf 1cs	prep, ps 2fs	**10.**	v Qal pf 1cs	prep, prep	art, n mp
וְאֵיטִיבָה	עִמָּךְ		קָטֹנְתִּי	מִכֹּל	הַחֲסָדִים
w^{e}'êṭivāh	'immāk		qāṭōntî	mikkōl	hachṣādhîm
and I will cause it to go well	with you		I am insignificant	from all	the steadfast love

4623, 3725, 583	866	6449.113	882, 5860	3706	904, 4894
cj, prep, *adj*, art, n fs	rel part	v Qal pf 2ms	prep, n ms, ps 2ms	cj	prep, n ms, ps 1cs
וּמִכָּל־הָאֱמֶת	אֲשֶׁר	עָשִׂיתָ	אֶת־עַבְדֶּךָ	כִּי	בְמַקְלִי
ûmikkol-hā'ĕmeth	'ăsher	'āsîthā	'eth-'avdekhā	kî	v^{e}maqōlî
and from all the faithfulness	which	you did	with your servant	for	with my staff

6. And the messengers returned to Jacob, saying: ... when the servants came back, *BB.*

We came to thy brother Esau: ... we reached your brother, *NAB* ... we met your brother, *NEB* ... we went to your brother, *REB* ... we arrived at, *Berkeley* ... we have seen your brother, *BB.*

and also he cometh to meet thee: ... he was on his way to meet you, *Goodspeed* ... already on the way to meet you, *REB* ... coming to call upon you, *Fenton* ... he also cometh against thee, *Geneva.*

and four hundred men with him: ... accompanied by, *NAB.*

7. Then Jacob was greatly afraid and distressed: ... very much terrified, *Goodspeed* ... fear and anxiety, *NCB* ... feareth exceedingly, *Young* ... greatly alarmed, *Berkeley* ... great fear and trouble of mind, *BB.*

and he divided the people that was with him, and the flocks, and herds, and the camels, into two bands: ... companies, *NASB* ... camps, *NAB* ... groups, *NIV.*

8. And said, If Esau come to the one company, and smite it: ... attack and overwhelm one camp, *NAB* ... come to the one troop, *Darby* ... and destroys it, *NRSV* ... and strike it, *KJVII* ... and attack it, *Anchor* ... assails it, *Fenton.*

then the other company which is left shall escape: ... remaining camp may still survive, *NAB* ... the other will be saved, *NCB* ... would survive, *NEB* ... there will be the other to fly to, *Fenton.*

9. And Jacob said, O God of my father Abraham, and God of my father Isaac, the LORD which saidst unto me: ... who didst say to me, *Goodspeed* ... you told me, O Lord, *NAB* ... at whose bidding, *NEB* ... Yahweh, *Anchor.*

Return unto thy country, and to thy kindred: ... land of thy birth, *Fenton* ... relatives, *NASB* ... kin, *NCB* ... native land, *Anchor* ... and your family, *BB.*

and I will deal well with thee: ... be good to you, *NAB* ... didst promise me prosperity, *NEB* ... treat you kindly, *Berkeley.*

10. I am not worthy of the least of all the mercies: ... I do not deserve all the acts of kindness, *Goodspeed* ... I am unworthy of, *NAB* ... true and steadfast love, *REB* ... I am too small, *Darby* ... I am less than nothing in comparison, *BB.*

and of all the truth: ... fidelity, *Goodspeed* ... faithfulness, *NASB* ... constant solicitude, *NCB* ... all the support, *Fenton.*

which thou hast shewed unto thy servant: ... you have loyally performed for your servant, *NAB* ... thou hast rendered, *Berkeley.*

for with my staff I passed over this Jordan: ... I owned nothing but the staff in my hand, *REB* ... with only my stick, *BB* ... passed over this torrent, *Fenton.*

and now I am become two bands: ... two companies, *Goodspeed* ... grown into two camps, *NCB* ... groups, *NIV* ... troops, *Darby* ... armies, *BB.*

11. Deliver me, I pray thee, from the hand of my brother, from the hand of Esau: ... save me, I beseech

32:6. The messengers returned with terrible news. Esau's response was to get 400 men together, undoubtedly armed, and start out to meet Jacob.

32:7-8. The news terrified Jacob and overwhelmed him with anguish. He was sure Esau intended to destroy him. So he divided the people and animals into two "camps." He forgot that Mahanaim was God's camp and his. Now he was trusting in two camps of his own, hoping one of them would escape Esau's wrath.

32:9-10. Finally, Jacob decided to pray. He reminded the LORD that He told him to go back and promised to prosper him. He confessed his unworthiness of God's acts of love and faithfulness that had indeed prospered him so that he now had enough to divide into two camps.

5882.115	881, 3497	2172	6498	2030.115	3937, 8530	4402
v Qal pf 1cs	do, art, pn	art, dem pron	cj, adv	v Qal pf 1cs	prep, *num*	n mp
עָבַרְתִּי	אֶת־הַיַּרְדֵּן	הַזֶּה	וְעַתָּה	הָיִיתִי	לִשְׁנֵי	מַחֲנוֹת
ʿāvartî	'eth-hayyardēn	hazzeh	weʿattāh	hāyîthî	lishnê	machnôth
I passed over	the Jordan	the this	and now	I am	into two	camps

11.	5522.531	5167	4623, 3135	250	4623, 3135	6451
	v Hiphil impv 2ms, sp 1cs	part	prep, *n fs*	n ms, ps 1cs	prep, *n fs*	pn
	הַצִּילֵנִי	נָא	מִיַּד	אָחִי	מִיַּד	עֵשָׂו
	hatstsîlēnî	nā'	miyyadh	'āchî	miyyadh	ʿēsāw
	rescue me	please	from the hand of	my brother	from the hand of	Esau

3706, 3486.151	609	881	6678, 971.121	5409.511
cj, v Qal act ptc ms	pers pron	do, ps 3ms	cj, v Qal impf 3ms	cj, v Hiphil pf 3ms, ps 1cs
כִּי־יָרֵא	אָנֹכִי	אֹתוֹ	פֶּן־יָבוֹא	וְהִכַּנִי
kî-yārē'	'ānōkhî	'ōthô	pen-yāvô'	wehikkanî
because fearing	I	him	otherwise he will come	and he will strike me down

525	6142, 1158	12.	887	569.113	3296.542	3296.525
n fs	prep, n mp		cj, pers pron	v Qal pf 2ms	v Hiphil inf abs	v Hiphil impf 1cs
אֵם	עַל־בָּנִים		וְאַתָּה	אָמַרְתָּ	הֵיטֵב	אֵיטִיב
'ēm	ʿal-bānîm		we'attāh	'āmartā	hêtēv	'êtîv
mother	upon the children		and You	You said	causing to go well	I will cause it to go well

6196	7947.115	881, 2320	3626, 2437	3328	866	3940, 5807.221
prep, ps 2fs	cj, v Qal pf 1cs	do, n ms, ps 2ms	prep, *n ms*	art, n ms	rel part	neg part, v Niphal impf 3ms
עִמָּךְ	וְשַׂמְתִּי	אֶת־זַרְעֲךָ	כְּחוֹל	הַיָּם	אֲשֶׁר	לֹא־יִסָּפֵר
ʿimmāk	wesamtî	'eth-zarʿăkhā	kechôl	hayyām	'ăsher	lō'-yissāphēr
with you	and I will make	your seed	like the sand of	the sea	which	not it will be counted

4623, 7524	13.	4053.121	8427	904, 4050	2000	4089.121
prep, n ms		cj, v Qal impf 3ms	adv	prep, art, n ms	art, dem pron	cj, v Qal impf 3ms
מֵרֹב		וַיָּלֶן	שָׁם	בַּלַּיְלָה	הַהוּא	וַיִּקַּח
mērōv		wayyālen	shām	ballayelāh	hahû'	wayyiqqach
for multitude		and he spent the night	there	in the night	the that	and he took

4623, 971.151	904, 3135	4647	3937, 6451	250	14.	6008	4109
prep, art, v Qal act ptc ms	prep, n fs, ps 3ms	n fs	prep, pn	n ms, ps 3ms		n fp	num
מִן־הַבָּא	בְיָדוֹ	מִנְחָה	לְעֵשָׂו	אָחִיו		עִזִּים	מָאתַיִם
min-habbā'	veyādhô	minchāh	leʿēsāw	'āchîw		ʿizzîm	mā'thayim
from that which went	in his hand	gift	to Esau	his brother		she-goats	hundreds

8825	6465	7636	4109	356	6465	15.	1622	3352.554
cj, n mp	num	n fp	num	cj, n mp	num		n fp	v Hiphil ptc fp
וּתְיָשִׁים	עֶשְׂרִים	רְחֵלִים	מָאתַיִם	וְאֵילִים	עֶשְׂרִים		גְּמַלִּים	מֵינִיקוֹת
ûtheyāshîm	ʿesrîm	rechēlîm	mā'thayim	we'êlîm	ʿesrîm		gemallîm	mênîqôth
and he-goats	twenty	ewes	hundreds	and rams	twenty		camels	nursing

1158	8421	6760	727	6749	6463	888	6465
cj, n mp, ps 3mp	num	n fp	num	cj, n mp	num	n fp	num
וּבְנֵיהֶם	שְׁלֹשִׁים	פָּרוֹת	אַרְבָּעִים	וּפָרִים	עֲשָׂרָה	אֲתֹנֹת	עֶשְׂרִים
ûvenêhem	shelōshîm	pārôth	'arbāʿîm	ûphārîm	ʿăsārāh	'ăthōnōth	ʿesrîm
and their young	thirty	cows	forty	and bulls	ten	female donkeys	twenty

6114	6463	16.	5598.121	904, 3135, 5860	5953	5953	3937, 940
cj, n mp	num		cj, v Qal pf 3ms	prep, *n fs*, n mp, ps 3ms	n ms	n ms	prep, n ms, ps 3ms
וַעְיָרִם	עֲשָׂרָה		וַיִּתֵּן	בְּיַד־עֲבָדָיו	עֵדֶר	עֵדֶר	לְבַדּוֹ
waʿăyārim	ʿăsārāh		wayyittēn	beyadh-ʿăvādhâv	ʿēdher	ʿēdher	levaddô
and male donkeys	ten		and he gave	in the hand of his slaves	herd	herd	each separately

569.121	420, 5860	5882.133	3937, 6686	7592	7947.133	1033
cj, v Qal impf 3ms	prep, n mp, ps 3ms	v Qal impv 2mp	prep, n mp, ps 1cs	cj, n ms	v Qal impf 2mp	prep
וַיֹּאמֶר	אֶל־עֲבָדָיו	עִבְרוּ	לְפָנַי	וְרֶוַח	תָּשִׂימוּ	בֵּין
wayyō'mer	'el-'ăvādhâv	'ivrû	lephānay	werewach	tāsîmû	bên
and he said	to his slaves	pass on	before me	and space	put	between

5953	1033	5953		6943	881, 7518	3937, 569.141	3706
n ms	cj, prep	n ms	**17.**	cj, v Piel impf 3ms	do, art, adj	prep, v Qal inf con	cj
עֵדֶר	וּבֵין	עֵדֶר		וַיְצַו	אֶת־הָרִאשׁוֹן	לֵאמֹר	כִּי
'ēdher	ûvên	'ēdher		waytsaw	'eth-hāri'shôn	lē'mōr	kî
herd	and between	herd		and he commanded	the first	saying	when

6539.121	6451	250	8068.111	3937, 569.141	3937, 4449, 887	590
v Qal impf 3ms, ps 2ms	pn	n ms, ps 1cs	cj, v Qal pf 3ms, ps 2ms	prep, v Qal inf con	prep, intrg, pers pron	cj, intrg
יִפְגָּשְׁךָ	עֵשָׂו	אָחִי	וּשְׁאֵלְךָ	לֵאמֹר	לְמִי־אַתָּה	וְאָנָה
yiphgāshekhā	'ēsāw	'āchî	wish'ēlekhā	lē'mōr	lemî-'attāh	we'ānāh
he meets you	Esau	my brother	and he asks you	saying	to whom you	and where

thee, from the power of, *Goodspeed* ... be my saviour from the hand, *BB* ... grant me a deliverance, *Fenton.*

for I fear him, lest he will come and smite me: ... attack me, *NASB* ... kill me, *NCB* ... destroy me, *NEB* ... strike us down, *Anchor* ... slay me, *Goodspeed.*

and the mother with the children: ... and all my family, *NCB* ... sparing neither mother nor child, *REB* ... mother and children alike, *Anchor.*

12. And thou saidst, I will surely do thee good: ... prosper you, *NASB* ... treat you well, *NKJV* ... unfailingly deal kindly with you, *Berkeley.*

and make thy seed as the sand of the sea: ... descendants, *NAB* ... offspring, *NRSV* ... race, *Fenton.*

which cannot be numbered for multitude: ... too numerous to count, *NCB* ... for quantity, *Fenton.*

13. And he lodged there that same night: ... put up his tent, *BB* ... spent the night, *NASB* ... stayed there, *Goodspeed.*

and took of that which came to his hand a present for Esau his brother: ... chose a gift from the herds he had with him, *REB* ... selected a gift, *NIV.*

14. Two hundred she goats, and twenty he goats: ... female goats and twenty male goats, *NASB.*

two hundred ewes, and twenty rams: ... females and twenty males from the sheep, *BB.*

15. Thirty milch camels with their colts, forty kine: ... milk camels, *KJVII* ... female camels, *NIV* ... suckling camels and their young oncs, *Young* ... forty cows, *Goodspeed.*

and ten bulls, twenty she asses, and ten foals: ... he-asses, *Goodspeed* ... female donkeys and ten male donkeys, *NASB.*

16. And he delivered them into the hand of his servants: ... entrusted to his servants, *Berkeley* ... into the care of, *NEB* ... putting them in charge of his slaves, *Goodspeed.*

every drove by themselves; and said unto his servants: ... in separate droves, *NAB* ... put each herd separately, *NEB.*

Pass over before me: ... proceed ahead of me, *Goodspeed* ... drive ahead, *Berkeley.*

and put a space betwixt drove and drove: ... between the herds, *NIV* ... distance, *NKJV.*

17. And he commanded the foremost, saying: ... he charged the leaders, *NCB* ... to the servant in the lead he gave this instruction, *NAB* ... to the leader he gave this order, *Goodspeed.*

32:11-12. Jacob then prayed that God would save him from the hand, that is, the power, of Esau. He had no way of defending himself against 400 armed men. So he confessed his fear that Esau might kill him and also the mothers (wives and concubines) upon the children—a picture of mothers in front of the children to shield them and thus falling on the children when killed. Then he concluded his prayer by reminding God of His promise given to his forefathers and confirmed to him (cf. 22:17).

32:13-19. It was a good prayer, a noble prayer, but too short and too hasty. With the prayer said, instead of trusting God, Jacob again tried to manipulate the situation himself. He carefully selected a number of animals as a gift for Esau, divided them up into a number of herds and put each herd in the

2050.123	3937, 4449	431	3937, 6686		569.113	3937, 5860
v Qal impf 2ms	cj, intrg	dem pron	prep, n mp, ps 2ms		cj, v Qal pf 2ms	prep, n ms, ps 2ms
תֵּלֵךְ	וּלְמִי	אֵלֶּה	לְפָנֶיךָ	**18.**	וְאָמַרְתָּ	לְעַבְדְּךָ
thēlēkh	ûlămî	'ēlleh	lephānêkhā		we'āmartā	le'avdekhā
are you going	and to whom	these	before you		and you will say	to your servant

3937, 3399	4647	2000	8365.157	3937, 112	3937, 6451	2079	1612, 2000
prep, pn	n fs	pers pron	v Qal pass ptc fs	prep, n ms, ps 1cs	prep, pn	cj, intrj	cj, pers pron
לְיַעֲקֹב	מִנְחָה	הִוא	שְׁלוּחָה	לַאדֹנִי	לְעֵשָׂו	וְהִנֵּה	גַם־הוּא
leya'ăqōv	minchāh	hiw'	shelûchāh	la'dhōnî	le'ēsāw	wehinnēh	gham-hû'
to Jacob	gift	it	being sent	to my master	to Esau	and behold	also he

313		6943	1612	881, 8529	1612	881, 8389	1612
adv, ps 1cp		cj, v Piel impf 3ms	cj	do, art, num	cj	do, art, num	cj
אַחֲרֵינוּ	**19.**	וַיְצַו	גַּם	אֶת־הַשֵּׁנִי	גַּם	אֶת־הַשְּׁלִישִׁי	גַּם
'achrênû		waytsaw	gam	'eth-hashshēnî	gam	'eth-hashshelîshî	gam
behind us		and he commanded	also	the second	also	the third	also

881, 3725, 2050.152	311	5953	3937, 569.141	3626, 1745	2172
do, *adj*, art, v Qal act ptc mp	*sub*	art, n mp	prep, v Qal inf con	prep, art, n ms	art, dem pron
אֶת־כָּל־הַהֹלְכִים	אַחֲרֵי	הָעֲדָרִים	לֵאמֹר	כַּדָּבָר	הַזֶּה
'eth-kol-hahōlekhîm	'achrê	hā'ădhārîm	lē'mōr	kaddāvār	hazzeh
all the ones going	following	the flocks	saying	like the thing	the this

1744.328	420, 6451	904, 4834.152	881		569.117	1612
v Piel impf 2mp	prep, pn	prep, v Qal act ptc mp, ps 2mp	do, ps 3ms		cj, v Qal pf 2mp	cj
תְּדַבְּרוּן	אֶל־עֵשָׂו	בְּמֹצַאֲכֶם	אֹתוֹ	**20.**	וַאֲמַרְתֶּם	גַּם
tedhabberûn	'el-'ēsāw	bemōtsa'ăkhem	'ōthô		wa'ămartem	gam
you will speak	to Esau	in your finding	him		and you will say	also

2079	5860	3399	313	3706, 569.111	3848.325	6686	904, 4647
intrj	n ms, ps 2ms	pn	adv, ps 1cp	prep, v Qal pf 3ms	v Piel impf 1cs	n mp, ps 3ms	prep, art, n fs
הִנֵּה	עַבְדְּךָ	יַעֲקֹב	אַחֲרֵינוּ	כִּי־אָמַר	אֲכַפְּרָה	פָנָיו	בַּמִּנְחָה
hinnēh	'avdekhā	ya'ăqōv	'achrênû	kî-'āmar	'ăkhapperāh	phānâv	bamminchāh
behold	your servant	Jacob	behind us	because he said	I will appease	his face	with the gift

2050.153	3937, 6686	311, 3772	7495.125	6686	193	5558.121
art, v Qal act ptc fs	prep, n mp, ps 1cs	cj, *sub*, cj	v Qal impf 1cs	n mp, ps 3ms	adv	v Qal impf 3ms
הַהֹלֶכֶת	לְפָנָי	וְאַחֲרֵי־כֵן	אֶרְאֶה	פָנָיו	אוּלַי	יִשָּׂא
hahōlekheth	lephānāy	we'achrê-khēn	'er'eh	phānâv	'ûlay	yissā'
the one going	before me	and afterward	I will see	his face	perhaps	he will lift up

6686		5882.122	4647	6142, 6686	2000	4053.111
n mp, ps 1cs		cj, v Qal impf 3fs	art, n fs	prep, n mp, ps 3ms	cj, pers pron	v Qal pf 3ms
פָנָי	**21.**	וַתַּעֲבֹר	הַמִּנְחָה	עַל־פָּנָיו	וְהוּא	לָן
phānāy		watta'ăvōr	hamminchāh	'al-pānâv	wehû'	lān
my face		and it passed on	the gift	before him	and he	he spent the night

904, 4050, 2000	904, 4402		7251.121	904, 4050	2000	4089.121
prep, art, n ms, art, pers pron	prep, art, n ms		cj, v Qal impf 3ms	prep, art, n ms	pers pron	cj, v Qal impf 3ms
בַּלַּיְלָה־הַהוּא	בַּמַּחֲנֶה	**22.**	וַיָּקָם	בַּלַּיְלָה	הוּא	וַיִּקַּח
ballaylāh-hahû'	bammachneh		wayyāqām	ballaylāh	hû'	wayyiqqach
in the night the that	in the camp		and he rose up	in the night	that	and he took

881, 8530	5571	881, 8530	8569	881, 259	6461	3315
do, *num*	n fp, ps 3ms	cj, do, *num*	n fp, ps 3ms	cj, do, num	num	n mp, ps 3ms
אֶת־שְׁתֵּי	נָשָׁיו	וְאֶת־שְׁתֵּי	שִׁפְחֹתָיו	וְאֶת־אַחַד	עָשָׂר	יְלָדָיו
'eth-shettê	nāshâv	we'eth-shettê	shiphchōthâv	we'eth-'achadh	'āsār	yelādhâv
the two of	his wives	and the two of	his female slaves	and one	ten	his children

5882.521 cj, v Hiphil impf 3ms	881 do	4722 n ms	3108 pn	23.	4089.121 cj, v Qal impf 3ms, ps 3mp	5882.521 cj, v Hiphil impf 3ms, ps 3mp
וַיַּעֲבֹר	אֵת	מַעֲבַר	יַבֹּק		וַיִּקָּחֵם	וַיַּעֲבִרֵם
wayya'ăvōr	'ēth	ma'ăvar	yabbōq		wayyiqqāchēm	wayya'ăvirēm
and he sent over		the ford of	Jabbok		and he took them	and he sent them over

881, 5337 do, art, n ms	5882.521 cj, v Hiphil impf 3ms	881, 866, 3937 do, rel part, prep, ps 3ms	24.	3613.221 cj, v Niphal impf 3ms	3399 pn	3937, 940 prep, n ms, ps 3ms
אֶת־הַנָּחַל	וַיַּעֲבֵר	אֶת־אֲשֶׁר־לוֹ		וַיִּוָּתֵר	יַעֲקֹב	לְבַדּוֹ
'eth-hannāchal	wayya'ăvēr	'eth-'ăsher-lô		wayyiwwāthēr	ya'ăqōv	lᵉvaddô
the stream	and he sent over	which to him		but he remained	Jacob	by himself

When Esau my brother meeteth thee, and asketh thee, saying, Whose art thou?: ... to whom do you belong, *KJVII* ... whose man are you, *Anchor* ... servant, *BB*.

and whither goest thou?: ... where are you going, *NRSV*.

and whose are these before thee?: ... to whom do these animals belong, *Goodspeed* ... who owns these beasts you are driving, *NEB* ... who is the owner, *Anchor*.

18. Then thou shalt say, They be thy servant Jacob's: ... belong to your brother Jacob, *NAB*.

it is a present sent unto my lord Esau: and, behold, also he is behind us: ... they are a gift, *NIV* ... dispatched, *Anchor* ... an offering, *BB*.

19. And so commanded he the second, and the third: ... he gave the same orders to the second, *Goodspeed* ... similar instructions, *NAB* ... charged the second, *NCB*.

and all that followed the droves, saying: ... to all the others who were driving the droves, *Goodspeed* ... followed the herds, *NIV* ... were in charge of the herds, *Good News*.

On this manner shall ye speak unto Esau, when ye find him: ... give this same message to Esau, when you meet him, *Goodspeed*.

20. And say ye moreover, Behold, thy servant Jacob is behind us. For he said, I will appease him with the present that goeth before me: ... pacify him, *NIV* ... with gifts that precede me, *NAB* ... I will take away his wrath by the offering, *BB*.

and afterward I will see his face: ... when he does see me, *Goodspeed* ... when I face him, *NAB* ... when I come into his presence, *NEB* ... when I meet him personally, *Berkeley*.

peradventure he will accept of me: ... I will have grace in his eyes, *BB* ... perhaps he will accept me, *KJVII* ... forgive me, *NAB* ... be kind to me, *NCB*.

21. So went the present over before him: ... so the gifts went on ahead, *NAB* ... so the servants with the offerings went on in front, *BB*.

and himself lodged that night in the company: ... spent that night in the camp, *NASB* ... stayed at Mahaneh, *REB* ... remained, *Anchor* ... took his rest in the tents, *BB*.

22. And he rose up that night, and took his two wives, and his two womenservants, and his eleven sons, and passed over the ford Jabbok: ... sent them across, *Goodspeed* ... crossed the ford, *NAB* ... forded the Jaboc, *NCB*.

23. And he took them, and sent them over the brook: ... across the stream, *NAB* ... the gorge, *NEB* ...

charge of a servant. Then he sent them on ahead with a distance in between each one. Thus, every few miles Esau would meet another servant with another present from Jacob. Each would politely call Jacob slave, and call Esau lord or master.

32:20-21. Jacob hoped these gifts would appease or pacify Esau (literally, "cover his face," so that he would not look on Jacob with anger). Actually, if Esau were still as bitter as before, such an attempt to appease him would probably have only infuriated him more.

32:22-23. That night Jacob could not rest, so he took his wives, concubines, and children to the ford of the Jabbok River (a tributary of the Jordan about half way between the Sea of Galilee and the Dead Sea) and sent them across, came back, and sent the rest of his possessions across. He probably came back again to be sure everyone had gone across.

32:24-25. While all alone in the dark, a man grabbed Jacob and wrestled with him until dawn. (Hosea 12:4 calls this man "an angel," but Jacob only saw him as a man at first.)

When the man saw he could not make Jacob give up, he touched the socket of his hip and dislocated it. With his hip out of joint, Jacob could not effectively wrestle any more, all he could do was prevent his adversary from escaping.

74.221	382	6196	5912	6148.141	8266		7495.121	3706
cj, v Niphal impf 3ms	n ms	prep, ps 3ms	adv	v Qal inf con	art, n ms	**25.**	cj, v Qal impf 3ms	cj
וַיֵּאָבֵק	אִישׁ	עִמּוֹ	עַד	עֲלוֹת	הַשָּׁחַר		וַיַּרְא	כִּי
wayyē'āvēq	'îsh	'immô	'adh	'ălôth	hashshāchar		wayyar'	kî
and he wrestled	man	with him	until	rising of	the dawn		and he saw	that

3940	3310.111	3937	5236.121	904, 3834, 3525	3475.122
neg part	v Qal pf 3ms	prep, ps 3ms	cj, v Qal impf 3ms	prep, *n fs*, n fs, ps 3ms	cj, v Qal impf 3fs
לֹא	יָכֹל	לוֹ	וַיִּגַּע	בְּכַף־יְרֵכוֹ	וַתֵּקַע
lō'	yākhōl	lô	wayyigga'	b^{e}khaph-y^{e}rēkhô	wattēqa'
not	he was able	against him	so he touched	in the socket of his hip	and it was dislocated

3834, 3525	3399	904, 74.241	6196		569.121	8365.331
n fs, n fs	pn	prep, v Niphal inf con, ps 3ms	prep, ps 3ms	**26.**	cj, v Qal impf 3ms	v Piel impv 2ms, ps 1cs
כַּף־יֶרֶךְ	יַעֲקֹב	בְּהֵאָבְקוֹ	עִמּוֹ		וַיֹּאמֶר	שַׁלְּחֵנִי
kaph-yerekh	ya'ăqōv	b^{e}hē'āv^{e}qô	'immô		wayyō'mer	shall^{e}chēnî
the hip socket of	Jacob	in his wrestling	with him		and he said	release me

3706	6148.111	8266	569.121	3940	8365.325	3706
cj	v Qal pf 3ms	art, n ms	cj, v Qal impf 3ms	neg part	v Piel impf 1cs, pf 2ms	cj
כִּי	עָלָה	הַשָּׁחַר	וַיֹּאמֶר	לֹא	אֲשַׁלֵּחֲךָ	כִּי
kî	'ālâh	hashshāchar	wayyō'mer	lō'	'ăshallēchăkhā	kî
because	it is rising	the dawn	and he said	not	I will release you	except

524, 1313.313		569.121	420	4242, 8428	569.121	3399
cj, v Piel pf 2ms, ps 1cs	**27.**	cj, v Qal impf 3ms	prep, ps 3ms	intrg, n ms, ps 2ms	cj, v Qal impf 3ms	pn
אִם־בֵּרַכְתָּנִי		וַיֹּאמֶר	אֵלָיו	מַה־שְּׁמֶךָ	וַיֹּאמֶר	יַעֲקֹב
'im-bērakhtānî		wayyō'mer	'ēlâv	mah-sh^{e}mekhā	wayyō'mer	ya'ăqōv
if you bless me		and he said	to him	what your name	and he said	Jacob

	569.121	3940	3399	569.221	5968	8428	3706	524, 3547
28.	cj, v Qal impf 3ms	neg part	pn	v Niphal impf 3ms	adv	n ms, ps 2ms	cj	cj, pn
	וַיֹּאמֶר	לֹא	יַעֲקֹב	יֵאָמֵר	עוֹד	שִׁמְךָ	כִּי	אִם־יִשְׂרָאֵל
	wayyō'mer	lō'	ya'ăqōv	yē'āmēr	'ôdh	shim^{e}khā	kî	'im-yisrā'ēl
	and he said	not	Jacob	it will be said	again	your name	because	rather Israel

3706, 8021	6196, 435	6196, 596	3310.123		8068.121	3399
cj, v Qal pf 2ms	cj, n mp	cj, cj, n mp	cj, v Qal impf 2ms	**29.**	cj, v Qal impf 3ms	pn
כִּי־שָׂרִיתָ	עִם־אֱלֹהִים	וְעִם־אֲנָשִׁים	וַתּוּכָל		וַיִּשְׁאַל	יַעֲקֹב
kî-sārîthā	'im-'ĕlōhîm	w^e'im-'ănāshîm	wattûkhāl		wayyish'al	ya'ăqōv
because you contended	with God	and with men	and you prevailed		and he asked	Jacob

569.121	5222.531, 5167	8428	569.121	4066	2172	8068.123
cj, v Qal impf 3ms	v Hiphil impv 2ms, part	n ms, ps 2ms	cj, v Qal impf 3ms	intrg	dem pron	v Qal impf 2ms
וַיֹּאמֶר	הַגִּידָה־נָּא	שְׁמֶךָ	וַיֹּאמֶר	לָמָּה	זֶּה	תִּשְׁאַל
wayyō'mer	haggîdhāh-nā'	sh^{e}mekhā	wayyō'mer	lāmmāh	zeh	tish'al
and he said	tell please	your name	and he said	why	this	you are asking

3937, 8428	1313.321	881	8427		7410.121	3399	8428
prep, n ms, ps 1cs	cj, v Piel impf 3ms	do, ps 3ms	adv	**30.**	cj, v Qal impf 3ms	pn	*n ms*
לִשְׁמִי	וַיְבָרֶךְ	אֹתוֹ	שָׁם		וַיִּקְרָא	יַעֲקֹב	שֵׁם
lishmî	way^{e}vārekh	'ōthô	shām		wayyiqrā'	ya'ăqōv	shēm
for my name	and he blessed	him	there		and he called	Jacob	the name of

4887	6684	3706, 7495.115	435	6686	420, 6686	5522.222	5497
art, n ms	pn	cj, v Qal pf 1cs	n mp	n mp	prep, n mp	cj, v Niphal impf 3fs	n fs, ps 1cs
הַמָּקוֹם	פְּנִיאֵל	כִּי־רָאִיתִי	אֱלֹהִים	פָּנִים	אֶל־פָּנִים	וַתִּנָּצֵל	נַפְשִׁי
hammāqôm	p^{e}nî'ēl	kî-rā'îthî	'ĕlōhîm	pānîm	'el-pānîm	wattinnātsēl	naphshî
the place	Peniel	because I saw	God	face	to face	and it was spared	my life

the wadi, *REB* ... over the river, *Darby.*

and sent over that he had: ... with everything that belonged to him, *NCB* ... brought over all his possessions, *NAB* ... sent across whatever he had, *NASB* ... all who were with him, *Fenton.*

24. And Jacob was left alone: ... was left behind all alone, *Goodspeed* ... remained behind, *NCB* ... was by himself, *BB.*

and there wrestled a man with him: ... someone wrestled with him, *NCB* ... a man was fighting, *BB.*

until the breaking of the day: ... break of dawn, *NAB* ... ascending of the dawn, *Young* ... rising of the dawn, *Darby* ... departure of the darkness, *Fenton.*

25. And when he saw that he prevailed not against him: ... not winning the struggle, *Good News* ... not equal to him, *Fenton* ... could not get the better of, *REB* ... overpower him, *NIV* ... overcome Jacob, *NCB.*

he touched the hollow of his thigh: ... socket, *NASB* ... struck Jacob's hip at its socket, *NAB* ... joint of his thigh, *Darby* ... gave him a blow in the hollow part of his leg, *BB.*

and the hollow of Jacob's thigh was out of joint, as he wrestled with him: ... socket of Jacob's thigh was dislocated, *NASB* ... the hip socket was wrenched, *Anchor* ... was strained, *ASV* ... his leg was damaged, *BB.*

26. And he said, Let me go, for the day breaketh. And he said, I will not let thee go, except thou bless me: ... it is daybreak, *NIV* ... send me away, for the dawn hath ascended, *Young* ... dawn is near, *BB* ... the darkness is going, *Fenton.*

27. And he said unto him, What is thy name? And he said, Jacob.

28. And he said, Thy name shall be called no more Jacob, but Israel: ... no longer Jacob, but Israel (wrestler with God), *Goodspeed* ... no longer spoken of as, *NAB* ... name shall no longer be, *NEB.*

for as a prince hast thou power with God and with men: ... you have wrestled with God and man, *Goodspeed* ... because you have contended with divine and human beings, *NAB* ... you have striven, *Anchor* ... struggled with, *NKJV.*

and hast prevailed: ... have been the victor, *Goodspeed* ... have triumphed, *NCB* ... have overcome, *NIV* ... you have won, *Berkeley* ... been equal to it, *Fenton.*

29. And Jacob asked him, and said, Tell me, I pray thee, thy name: ... please tell me your name, *NASB.*

And he said, Wherefore is it that thou dost ask after my name?: ... why is it that you ask, *Goodspeed* ... why should you want to know my name, *NAB* ... you must not ask my name, *Anchor* ... why do you inquire after my name, *Berkeley.*

And he blessed him there: ... he bade him farewell, *NAB* ... gave him his blessing, *NEB.*

30. And Jacob called the name of the place Peniel: ... (face of God), *Goodspeed.*

for I have seen God face to face, and my life is preserved: ... I have seen a heavenly being, *NCB* ... life has been spared, *NAB* ... is delivered, *Young* ... still I am living, *BB.*

31. And as he passed over Penuel the sun rose upon him: ... at sunrise, as he left Penuel, *NAB* ... the sun came up, *BB* ... as he crossed over, *NASB.*

and he halted upon his thigh: ... limping because of his thigh, *NCB* ...

32:26. Jacob refused to let go because by this time he realized this was not an ordinary man. There must have been something different, something very powerful, about that touch that dislocated his hip. This person could bless him, and Jacob wanted his blessing.

32:27. Jacob was about to meet Esau. Giving his name here was a confession that he was Jacob, the supplanter, the deceiver, just as Esau said he was.

32:28. Giving a new name in Bible times meant either a change in nature or a change in relationship. Jacob was to become Israel, "he struggles with God," or "God's fighter." It also came to mean God's prince. The root verb means to struggle or strive with determination, and then to rule. The emphasis here is on Jacob's contending with God and with men and on the fact Jacob prevailed. The name Israel was later given to the people descended from Jacob. It is a title of victory and speaks of contending for the faith with power from God. Jacob did not always act like Israel, however, and God had to deal with him again later and confirm his new name.

32:29-30. The response to Jacob's question implies he ought to know who the one is that he had struggled with. Jacob understood, so he named the place Peniel, "the face of God" (another form of the same word is Penuel). He recognized that this one was God manifest in the flesh. Many believe this means the one who actually wrestled with Jacob was a preincarnate manifestation of Christ.

31.	2311.121, 3937	8507	3626, 866	5882.111	881, 6683	2000
	cj, v Qal impf 3ms, prep, ps 3ms	art, n ms	prep, rel part	v Qal pf 3ms	do, pn	cj, pers pron
	וַיִּזְרַח־לוֹ	הַשֶּׁמֶשׁ	כַּאֲשֶׁר	עָבַר	אֶת־פְּנוּאֵל	וְהוּא
	wayyizrach-lô	hashshemesh	ka'ăsher	‘āvar	'eth-p^{e}nû'ēl	w^{e}hû'
	and it rose on him	the sun	when	he passed	Penuel	and he

7027	6142, 3525	32.	6142, 3772	3940, 404.126	1158, 3547	881, 1552
v Qal act ptc ms	prep, n fs, ps 3ms		prep, adv	neg part, v Qal impf 3mp	*n mp*, pn	do, *n ms*
צֹלֵעַ	עַל־יְרֵכוֹ		עַל־כֵּן	לֹא־יֹאכְלוּ	בְנֵי־יִשְׂרָאֵל	אֶת־גִּיד
tsōlēa‘	‘al-y^{e}rēkhô		‘al-kēn	lō'-yō'kh^{e}lû	v^{e}nê-yisrā'ēl	'eth-gîdh
limping	because of his hip		therefore	not they eat	the sons of Israel	the sinew of

5568	866	6142, 3834	3525	5912	3219	2172	3706	5236.111
art, n ms	rel part	prep, *n fs*	art, n fs	adv	art, n ms	art, dem pron	cj	v Qal pf 3ms
הַנָּשֶׁה	אֲשֶׁר	עַל־כַּף	הַיָּרֵךְ	עַד	הַיּוֹם	הַזֶּה	כִּי	נָגַע
hannāsheh	'ăsher	‘al-kaph	hayyārēkh	‘adh	hayyôm	hazzeh	kî	nāgha‘
the hip	which	on the socket of	the hip	until	the day	the this	because	he touched

904, 3834, 3525	3399	904, 1552	5568	33:1	5558.121	3399	6084
prep, *n fs*, n fs	pn	prep, *n ms*	art, n ms		cj, v Qal impf 3ms	pn	n fp, ps 3ms
בְּכַף־יֶרֶךְ	יַעֲקֹב	בְּגִיד	הַנָּשֶׁה		וַיִּשָּׂא	יַעֲקֹב	עֵינָיו
b^{e}khaph-yerekh	ya‘ăqōv	b^{e}ghîdh	hannāsheh		wayyissā'	ya‘ăqōv	‘ênâv
on the hip socket of	Jacob	on the sinew of	the hip		and he lifted up	Jacob	his eyes

7495.121	2079	6451	971.151	6196	727	4109	382
cj, v Qal impf 3ms	cj, intrj	pn	v Qal act ptc ms	cj, prep, ps 3ms	num	*num*	n ms
וַיַּרְא	וְהִנֵּה	עֵשָׂו	בָּא	וְעִמּוֹ	אַרְבַּע	מֵאוֹת	אִישׁ
wayyar^{e}'	w^{e}hinnēh	‘ēsāw	bā'	w^{e}‘immô	'arba‘	mē'ôth	'îsh
and he saw	and behold	Esau	coming	and with him	four	hundred	men

2779.121	881, 3315	6142, 3943	6142, 7637	6142	8530
v Qal impf 3ms	do, art, n mp	prep, pn	cj, prep, pn	cj, prep	*num*
וַיַּחַץ	אֶת־הַיְלָדִים	עַל־לֵאָה	וְעַל־רָחֵל	וְעַל	שְׁתֵּי
wayyachats	'eth-haylādhîm	‘al-lē'āh	w^{e}‘al-rāchēl	w^{e}‘al	sh^{e}ttê
and he divided	the children	in front of Leah	and in front of Rachel	and in front of	the two of

8569	2.	7947.121	881, 8569	881, 3315	7518	881, 3943
art, n fp		cj, v Qal impf 3ms	do, art, n fp	cj, do, n mp, ps 3fp	adj	cj, do, pn
הַשְּׁפָחוֹת		וַיָּשֶׂם	אֶת־הַשְּׁפָחוֹת	וְאֶת־יַלְדֵיהֶן	רִאשֹׁנָה	וְאֶת־לֵאָה
hashsh^{e}phāchôth		wayyāsem	'eth-hashsh^{e}phāchôth	w^{e}'eth-yal^{e}dhêhen	ri'shōnāh	w^{e}'eth-lē'āh
the female slaves		and he put	the female slaves	and their children	first	and Leah

3315	313	881, 7637	881, 3231	313	3.	2000	5882.111
cj, n mp, 3fs	adv	cj, do, pn	cj, do, pn	adv		cj, pers pron	v Qal pf 3ms
וִילָדֶיהָ	אַחֲרֹנִים	וְאֶת־רָחֵל	וְאֶת־יוֹסֵף	אַחֲרֹנִים		וְהוּא	עָבַר
wîlādhêhā	'achrōnîm	w^{e}'eth-rāchēl	w^{e}'eth-yôs̱ēph	'achrōnîm		w^{e}hû'	‘āvar
and her children	behind	and Rachel	and Joseph	behind		and he	he passed on

3937, 6686	8246.721	800	8124	6718	5912, 5242.141
prep, n mp, ps 3mp	cj, v Hithpalel impf 3ms	n fs	num	n fp	prep, v Qal inf con, ps 3ms
לִפְנֵיהֶם	וַיִּשְׁתַּחוּ	אַרְצָה	שֶׁבַע	פְּעָמִים	עַד־גִּשְׁתּוֹ
liphnêhem	wayyishtachû	'artsāh	sheva‘	p^{e}‘āmîm	‘adh-gishtô
before them	and he bowed down	to the ground	seven	times	until his drawing near

5912, 250	4.	7608.121	6451	3937, 7410.141	2354.321
prep, n ms, ps 3ms		cj, v Qal impf 3ms	pn	prep, v Qal inf con, ps 3ms	cj, v Piel impf 3ms, ps 3ms
עַד־אָחִיו		וַיָּרָץ	עֵשָׂו	לִקְרָאתוֹ	וַיְחַבְּקֵהוּ
‘adh-'āchîw		wayyārāts	‘ēsāw	liqŏrā'thô	waychabb^{e}qēhû
to his brother		and he ran	Esau	to meet him	and he embraced him

5489.121	6142, 6939	5583.121	1098.126		5558.121
cj, v Qal impf 3ms	prep, n ms, ps 3ms	cj, v Qal impf 3ms, ps 3ms	cj, v Qal impf 3mp		cj, v Qal impf 3ms
וַיִּפֹּל	עַל־צַוָּארוֹ	וַיִּשָּׁקֵהוּ	וַיִּבְכּוּ	5.	וַיִּשָּׂא
wayyippōl	'al-tsawwā'rô	wayyishshāqēhû	wayyivkû		wayyissā'
and he fell	on his neck	and he kissed him	and they wept		and he lifted up

881, 6084	7495.121	881, 5571	881, 3315	569.121	4449, 431
do, n fd, ps 3ms	cj, v Qal impf 3ms	do, art, n fp	cj, do, art, n mp	cj, v Qal impf 3ms	intrg, dem pron
אֶת־עֵינָיו	וַיַּרְא	אֶת־הַנָּשִׁים	וְאֶת־הַיְלָדִים	וַיֹּאמֶר	מִי־אֵלֶּה
'eth-'ênâv	wayyar^e'	'eth-hannāshîm	w^e'eth-haylādhîm	wayyō'mer	mî-'ēlleh
his eyes	and he saw	the women	and the children	and he said	who these

limping along because of his hip, *NAB* ... went with unequal steps because of his damaged leg, *BB.*

32. Therefore the children of Israel eat not of the sinew which shrank: ... the hip muscle, *Goodspeed* ... sciatic muscle, *NAB* ... sinew of the nerve, *NEB* ... tendon attached to the socket, *NIV* ... sinew-nerve from the foot to the thigh, *Fenton.*

which is upon the hollow of the thigh, unto this day: because he touched the hollow of Jacob's thigh in the sinew that shrank: ... on the socket of the thigh, *NCB* . . .on the hip socket, *NAB.*

33:1. And Jacob lifted up his eyes, and looked, and, behold, Esau came: ... Esau approached, *Fenton* ... Jacob saw Esau coming, *Anchor.*

and with him four hundred men: ... with his men, *BB* ... accompanied by, *Berkeley.*

And he divided the children unto Leah, and unto Rachel: ... distributed, *Darby* ... separated, *Fenton* ... arranged, *LIVB* ... apportioned, *Berkeley.*

and unto the two handmaids: ... women-servants, *BB* ... two second wives, *Anchor* ... slave-girls, *REB* ... concubines, *Good News.*

2. And he put the handmaids and their children foremost: ... first, *Anchor* ... in front, *Berkeley.*

and Leah and her children after: ... behind them, *Berkeley* ... next, *NASB.*

and Rachel and Joseph hindermost: ... in the rear, *Goodspeed* ... at the back, *BB* ... last, *NASB* ... behind, *Fenton.*

3. And he passed over before them, and bowed himself to the ground seven times, until he came near to his brother: ... next to his brother, *Anchor* ... until he reached, *NCB* ... came close, *Berkeley.*

4. And Esau ran to meet him: ... came running up to him, *BB* ... had rushed out to meet him, *Anchor.*

and embraced him, and fell on his neck, and kissed him: ... hugged him, and flung himself on, *Anchor* ... threw his arms around him, *Berkeley.*

and they wept: ... were overcome with weeping, *BB* ... and they both cried, *MLB* ... as he wept, *NAB.*

5. And he lifted up his eyes, and saw the women and the children; and said, Who are those with thee?: ... what relation are these to you, *Goodspeed* ... what are these to thee, *Young.*

And he said, The children which God hath graciously given thy servant: ... whom God has favored, *Anchor* ... to whom God in his mercy, *BB* ... bestowed, *Goodspeed.*

32:31-32. Jacob went on his way, limping because of his hip. We are not told whether this was a permanent disability or whether it lasted only a short period of time. His limp reminded him of his encounter with God. The later Israelites, however, made it a rule not to eat the sciatic muscle of slaughtered animals as a reminder to them as well. They were Israelites, not Jacobites, because God in His divine providence touched Jacob and changed his name.

33:1-3 When Esau and his 400 men came in sight Jacob distributed his wives and children in an order that if anything happened, the maidservants and their children would get the brunt of it while Rachel and Joseph in the rear would be in the most protected position. But this time, Jacob went on ahead to be the first to meet Esau. Nearing Esau, he bowed down so his forehead touched the ground. Then he went on a few steps and bowed again. Bowing seven times indicated a completeness of humility and was customarily done before kings.

33:4. What a wonderful change Jacob saw in Esau as Esau ran to meet him, hugged and kissed him. It was a very emotional encounter as both wept. Esau's hatred was replaced with generosity and love.

33:5-7. As Jacob responded to Esau and presented his wives and children he gave God the cred-

3937	569.121	3315	886, 2706.111	435	881, 5860
prep, ps 2ms	cj, v Qal impf 3ms	art, n mp	rel part, v Qal pf 3ms	n mp	do, n ms, ps 2ms
לָךְ	וַיֹּאמַר	הַיְלָדִים	אֲשֶׁר־חָנַן	אֱלֹהִים	אֶת־עַבְדֶּךָ
lākh	wayyō'mar	haylādhîm	'ăsher-chānan	'ĕlōhîm	'eth-'avdekhā
to you	and he said	the children	which He graciously gave	God	your servant

6.	5242.127	8569	2078	3315	8246.727
	cj, v Qal impf 3fp	art, n fp	pers pron	cj, n mp, ps 3fp	cj, v Hithpalel impf 3fp
	וַתִּגַּשְׁןָ	הַשְּׁפָחוֹת	הֵנָּה	וְיַלְדֵיהֶן	וַתִּשְׁתַּחֲוֶיןָ
	wattiggash^{e}nā	hashsh^{e}phāchôth	hēnnāh	w^{e}yal^{e}dhêhen	wattishtachwênā
	and they drew near	the female slaves	they	and their children	and they bowed down

7.	5242.122	1612, 3943	3315	8246.726	313
	cj, v Qal impf 3fs	cj, pn	cj, n mp, 3fs	cj, v Hithpalel impf 3mp	cj, adv
	וַתִּגַּשׁ	גַּם־לֵאָה	וִילָדֶיהָ	וַיִּשְׁתַּחֲווּ	וְאַחַר
	wattiggash	gam-lē'āh	wîlādhêhā	wayyishtachwû	w^{e}'achar
	and she drew near	also Leah	and her children	and they bowed down	and afterward

5242.211	3231	7637	8246.726	8.	569.121	4449	3937
v Niphal pf 3ms	pn	cj, pn	cj, v Hithpalel impf 3mp		cj, v Qal impf 3ms	intrg	prep, ps 2ms
נִגַּשׁ	יוֹסֵף	וְרָחֵל	וַיִּשְׁתַּחֲווּ		וַיֹּאמֶר	מִי	לְךָ
niggash	yôsēph	w^{e}rāchēl	wayyishtachwû		wayyō'mer	mî	l^{e}khā
he came near	Joseph	and Rachel	and they bowed down		and he said	who	to you

3725, 4402	2172	866	6539.115	569.121	3937, 4834.141, 2682	904, 6084
adj, art, n ms	art, dem pron	rel part	v Qal pf 1cs	cj, v Qal impf 3ms	prep, v Qal inf con, n ms	prep, *n fp*
כָּל־הַמַּחֲנֶה	הַזֶּה	אֲשֶׁר	פָּגָשְׁתִּי	וַיֹּאמֶר	לִמְצֹא־חֵן	בְּעֵינֵי
kol-hammachneh	hazzeh	'ăsher	pāghāshtî	wayyō'mer	limtsō'-chēn	b^{e}'ênê
all the company	the this	which	I met	and he said	to find favor	in the eyes of

112	9.	569.121	6451	3552, 3937	7521	250	2030.121
n ms, ps 1cs		cj, v Qal impf 3ms	pn	sub, prep, ps 1cs	adj	n ms, ps 1cs	v Qal juss 3ms
אֲדֹנִי		וַיֹּאמֶר	עֵשָׂו	יֶשׁ־לִי	רָב	אָחִי	יְהִי
'ădhōnî		wayyō'mer	'ēsāw	yesh-lî	rāv	'āchî	y^{e}hî
my master		and he said	Esau	there is to me	much	my brother	let it be

3937	866, 3937	10.	569.121	3399	414, 5167	524, 5167	4834.115
prep, ps 2ms	rel part, prep, ps 2fs		cj, v Qal impf 3ms	pn	neg part, part	cj, part	v Qal pf 1cs
לְךָ	אֲשֶׁר־לָךְ		וַיֹּאמֶר	יַעֲקֹב	אַל־נָא	אִם־נָא	מָצָאתִי
l^{e}khā	'ăsher-lākh		wayyō'mer	ya'ăqōv	'al-nā'	'im-nā'	mātsā'thî
for you	which to yourself		and he said	Jacob	no please	if please	I have found

2682	904, 6084	4089.113	4647	4623, 3135	3706	6142, 3772
n ms	prep, n fd, ps 2ms	cj, v Qal pf 2ms	n fs, ps 1cs	prep, n fs, ps 1cs	cj	prep, adv
חֵן	בְּעֵינֶיךָ	וְלָקַחְתָּ	מִנְחָתִי	מִיָּדִי	כִּי	עַל־כֵּן
chēn	b^{e}'ênêkhā	w^{e}lāqachtā	minchāthî	miyyādhî	kî	'al-kēn
favor	in your eyes	then you will take	my gift	from my hand	because	thus

7495.115	6686	3626, 7495.141	6686	435	7813.123
v Qal pf 1cs	n mp, ps 2ms	prep, v Qal inf con	*n mp*	n mp	cj, v Qal impf 2ms, ps 1cs
רָאִיתִי	פָּנֶיךָ	כִּרְאֹת	פְּנֵי	אֱלֹהִים	וַתִּרְצֵנִי
rā'îthî	phānêkhā	kir'ōth	p^{e}nê	'ĕlōhîm	wattirtsēnî
I have seen	your face	like seeing	the face of	God	and you received me favorably

11.	4089.131, 5167	881, 1318	866	971.612	3937	3706, 2706.111
	v Qal impv 2ms, part	do, n fs, ps 1cs	rel part	v Hophal pf 3fs	prep, ps 2ms	cj, v Qal pf 3ms, ps 1cs
	קַח־נָא	אֶת־בִּרְכָתִי	אֲשֶׁר	הֻבָאת	לָךְ	כִּי־חַנַּנִי
	qach-nā'	'eth-birkhāthî	'ăsher	huvā'th	lākh	kî-channanî
	take please	my blessing	which	it was brought	to you	because He was gracious

435	3706	3552, 3937, 3725	6732.121, 904	4089.121
n mp	cj, cj	sub, prep, ps 1cs, adj	cj, v Qal impf 3ms, prep, ps 3ms	cj, v Qal impf 3ms
אֱלֹהִים	וְכִי	יֶשׁ־לִי־כֹל	וַיִּפְצַר־בּוֹ	וַיִּקָּח
'ělōhîm	wekhî	yesh-lî-khōl	wayyiphtsar-bô	wayyiqqāch
God	and because	there is to me everything	and he urged him	and he took

12.	569.121	5450.120	2050.120	2050.125	3937, 5224
	cj, v Qal impf 3ms	v Qal impf 1cp	cj, v Qal impf 1cp	cj, v Qal impf 1cs	prep, prep, ps 2ms
	וַיֹּאמֶר	נִסְעָה	וְנֵלֵכָה	וְאֵלְכָה	לְנֶגְדֶּךָ
	wayyō'mer	nis'āh	wenēlēkhāh	we'ēlekhāh	leneghdekhā
	and he said	we will pull out	and we will go	and I will go	before you

6. Then the handmaidens came near, they and their children, and they bowed themselves: ... bowed low, *NAB* ... went down on their faces, *BB*.

7. And Leah also with her children came near, and bowed themselves: ... bowed to the ground, *Berkeley*.

and after came Joseph near and Rachel, and they bowed themselves: ... bowed deeply, *MLB* ... they did the same, *BB* ... did reverence, *Geneva*.

8. And he said, What meanest thou by all this drove which I met?: ... what did you want with all that train that I came across, *Anchor* ... what did you intend, *NAB* ... by all this company, *ASV* ... all those herds, *BB* ... all this camp, *Fenton*.

And he said, These are to find grace in the sight of my lord: ... to find favor, *ASV* ... gain my master's favor, *Berkeley*.

9. And Esau said, I have enough, my brother; keep that thou hast unto thyself: ... you should keep what you have, *ASV* ... let what you have remain yours, *MLB*.

10. And Jacob said, Nay, I pray thee: ... no, please, urged Jacob, *Berkeley* ... on no account, *NEB* ... no, I beg of you, *Anchor*.

if now I have found grace in thy sight: ... if now I have found favor in your eyes, *NASB* ... if you will do me the favor, *Anchor*.

then receive my present at my hand: ... please accept this present from me, *Anchor* ... take them as a sign of my love, *BB*.

for therefore I have seen thy face, as though I had seen the face of God: ... being in your presence is like being in God's presence, *Berkeley* ... I have come before you as before God, *NCB* ... I was as frightened of you as though approaching God, *LIVB*.

and thou wast pleased with me: ... thou hast received me with pleasure, *Darby* ... favorably, *Goodspeed* ... you have been pleased with me, *MLB* ... accepted me, *Geneva* ... so kindly, *NAB*.

11. Take, I pray thee, my blessing that is brought to thee: ... accept, then, from me, the bounty that is offered you, *Anchor* ... my gift, *ASV*.

because God hath dealt graciously with me: ... God has treated me lavishly, *MLB* ... been generous with me, *NAB*.

and because I have enough: ... everything, *Darby* ... plenty, *NASB* ... all I want, *NEB* ... all I need, *NIV*.

And he urged him, and he took it: ... so at his strong request, *BB* ... he pressed him until he took them, *Fenton* ... because Jacob insisted, Esau accepted it, *NIV*.

12. And he said, Let us take our journey, and let us go: ... let us

it for giving them to him by His grace—His undeserved favor. Each of them bowed down humbly.

33:8-9. When Esau asked about the gifts sent ahead to him, Jacob confessed they were meant to seek Esau's favor. Esau replied that he had much (plenty, an abundance, enough). This reply may have been oriental politeness, but it was typical of Esau. In this entire interchange between Jacob and Esau, Jacob keeps giving God the credit, the praise and the honor. Esau never mentions God once. "I" have enough—this is the statement of a person who thinks he does not need God. That is another reason for calling Esau a "profane" (that is, a secular) person (Heb. 13:16). Esau was not an atheist; he simply left God out of his life. Then he called Jacob his brother, and told him to keep the gifts for himself.

33:10-11. Jacob insisted that Esau keep the gift (*minchah*, a gift or offering for a king or for God; the same word is used in Genesis 4:3-4 and Leviticus 2:1-15). Behind the hug, the kiss, and the tears of Esau, Jacob saw the face of the one true God, the God who had blessed him and given him everything he needed. In verse 11 Jacob calls this gift or offering, "my blessing." Since Jacob continued to insist, Esau accepted the gifts and Jacob

13.	569.121	420	112	3156.151	3706, 3315	7679	6887
	cj, v Qal impf 3ms	prep, ps 3ms	n ms, ps 1cs	v Qal act ptc ms	cj, art, n mp	adj	cj, art, n fs
	וַיֹּאמֶר	אֵלָיו	אֲדֹנִי	יֹדֵעַ	כִּי־הַיְלָדִים	רַכִּים	וְהַצֹּאן
	wayyō'mer	'ēlâv	'ădhōnî	yōdhēa'	kî-haylādhîm	rakkîm	w^{e}hatstsō'n
	and he said	to him	my master	knowing	that the children	weak	and the flock

1267	5980.154	6142	1909.116	3219	259
cj, art, n fs	v Qal act ptc fp	prep, ps 1cs	cj, v Qal pf 3cp, ps 3mp	n ms	num
וְהַבָּקָר	עָלוֹת	עָלָי	וּדְפָקוּם	יוֹם	אֶחָד
w^{e}habbāqār	'ālôth	'ālāy	ûdh^{e}phāqûm	yôm	'echādh
and the herd	nursing	concerning me	if they are driven hard	day	one

4322.116	3725, 6887	14.	5882.121, 5167	112	3937, 6686	5860
cj, v Qal pf 3cp	*adj*, art, n fs		v Qal impf 3ms, part	n ms, ps 1cs	prep, *n mp*	n ms, ps 3ms
וָמֵתוּ	כָּל־הַצֹּאן		יַעֲבָר־נָא	אֲדֹנִי	לִפְנֵי	עַבְדּוֹ
wāmēthû	kol-hatstsō'n		ya'ăvār-nā'	'ădhōnî	liphnê	'avdô
then they will die	all the flocks		he will pass on please	my master	before	his servant

603	5273.725	3937, 330	3937, 7559	4536	866, 3937, 6686
cj, pers pron	v Hithpael impf 1cs	prep, sub, ps 1cs	prep, *n fs*	art, n fs	rel part, prep, n mp, ps 1cs
וַאֲנִי	אֶתְנָהֲלָה	לְאִטִּי	לְרֶגֶל	הַמְּלָאכָה	אֲשֶׁר־לְפָנַי
wa'ănî	'ethnāh^{e}lāh	l^{e}'ittî	l^{e}reghel	hamm^{e}lā'khāh	'ăsher-l^{e}phānay
and I	I will move	at my slowness	at the pace of	the group	which before me

3937, 7559	3315	5912	866, 971.125	420, 112	7990
cj, prep, n fs	art, n mp	adv	rel part, v Qal impf 1cs	prep, n ms, ps 1cs	pn
וּלְרֶגֶל	הַיְלָדִים	עַד	אֲשֶׁר־אָבֹא	אֶל־אֲדֹנִי	שֵׂעִירָה
ûlăreghel	haylādhîm	'adh	'ăsher-'āvō'	'el-'ădhōnî	sē'îrāh
and at the pace of	the children	until	that I come	to my master	to Seir

15.	569.121	6451	3431.525, 5167	6196	4623, 6194	866
	cj, v Qal impf 3ms	pn	v Hiphil impf 1cs, part	prep, ps 2ms	prep, art, n ms	rel part
	וַיֹּאמֶר	עֵשָׂו	אַצִּיגָה־נָּא	עִמְּךָ	מִן־הָעָם	אֲשֶׁר
	wayyō'mer	'ēsāw	'atstsighāh-nā'	'imm^{e}khā	min-hā'ām	'ăsher
	and he said	Esau	I will place please	with you	from the people	which

882	569.121	4066	2172	4834.125, 2682	904, 6084	112
prep, ps 1cs	cj, v Qal impf 3ms	intrg	dem pron	v Qal juss 1cs, n ms	prep, *n fp*	n ms, ps 1cs
אִתִּי	וַיֹּאמֶר	לָמָּה	זֶּה	אֶמְצָא־חֵן	בְּעֵינֵי	אֲדֹנִי
'ittî	wayyō'mer	lāmmāh	zeh	'em^{e}tsā'-chēn	b^{e}'ênê	'ădhōnî
with me	and he said	why	this	may I find favor	in the eyes of	my master

16.	8178.121	904, 3219	2000	6451	3937, 1932	7990	17.	3399
	cj, v Qal impf 3ms	prep, art, n ms	art, dem pron	pn	prep, n ms, ps 3ms	pn		cj, pn
	וַיָּשָׁב	בַּיּוֹם	הַהוּא	עֵשָׂו	לְדַרְכּוֹ	שֵׂעִירָה		וְיַעֲקֹב
	wayyāshāv	bayyôm	hahû'	'ēsāw	l^{e}dharkô	sē'îrāh		w^{e}ya'ăqōv
	and he returned	on the day	the that	Esau	to his way	to Seir		but Jacob

5450.111	5713	1161.121	3937	1041	3937, 4898	6449.111
v Qal pf 3ms	pn	cj, v Qal impf 3ms	prep, ps 3ms	n ms	cj, prep, n ms, ps 3ms	v Qal pf 3ms
נָסַע	סֻכֹּתָה	וַיִּבֶן	לוֹ	בָּיִת	וּלְמִקְנֵהוּ	עָשָׂה
nāsa'	sukkōthāh	wayyiven	lô	bāyith	ûlămiqōnēhû	'āsâh
he pulled out	to Succoth	and he built	for him	house	and for his livestock	he made

5712	6142, 3772	7410.111	8428, 4887	5713	18.	971.121	3399
n fp	prep, adv	v Qal pf 3ms	*n ms*, art, n ms	pn		cj, v Qal impf 3ms	pn
סֻכֹּת	עַל־כֵּן	קָרָא	שֵׁם־הַמָּקוֹם	סֻכּוֹת		וַיָּבֹא	יַעֲקֹב
sukkōth	'al-kēn	qārā'	shēm-hammāqôm	sukkôth		wayyāvō'	ya'ăqōv
shelters	therefore	he called	the name of the place	Succoth		and he went	Jacob

break camp and travel on together, *MLB* ... I will rise up and travel and we will go along together, *Fenton* ... let us set out on our way, *Goodspeed.*

and I will go before thee: ... I will go in front, *BB* ... alongside, *Goodspeed* ... at your pace, *NEB* ... accompany you, *Berkeley.*

13. And he said unto him, My lord knoweth that the children are tender: ... frail, *Anchor* ... small, *BB* ... many, *Fenton* ... weak, *NKJV.*

and the flocks and herds with young are with me: ... are giving suck, *Berkeley* ... suckling sheep and kine are with me, *Darby* ... are nursing, much to my encumbrance, *Anchor* ... sheep and cattle with me are breeding, *Fenton* ... which are nursing are a care to me, *NASB.*

and if men should overdrive them one day, all the flock will die: ... one day's overdriving will be the destruction of all the flock, *BB* ... drive them a single day, then all the sheep will die, *Fenton* ... if they are driven hard one day, *NASB* ... my beasts will die, *REB.*

14. Let my lord, I pray thee, pass over before his servant: ... please let my master go in advance, *MLB.*

and I will lead on softly: ... drive on at my ease, *Darby* ... move on slowly, at my leisure, *MLB* ... go by easy stages, *NEB* ... I lead on gently, *Young.*

according as the cattle that goeth before me: ... to the pace of the cattle, *Darby* ... adjusting ourselves to the pace that suits the endurance of the livestock, *MLB* ... according to the foot of the work, *Young* ... at the pace of the children and livestock, *NEB.*

and the children be able to endure, until I come unto my lord unto Seir: ... to the pace of the children, *Darby* ... foot of the children, *Young* ... until I join my Lord, *NAB.*

15. And Esau said, Let me now leave with thee some of the folk that are with me: ... detail some of my men to escort you, *NEB* ... put at your disposal some of the men, *Anchor* ... I should like to assign some of my men, *Berkeley* ... leave with you some of the troops accompanying me, *Goodspeed.*

And he said, What needeth it? let me find grace in the sight of my lord: ... but why do that, *NIV* ... what for, *Anchor* ... it is enough that I enjoy your favor, *MLB.*

16. So Esau returned that day on his way unto Seir.

17. And Jacob journeyed to Succoth, and built him an house: ... pitched his tent, *Fenton* ... where he established quarters for himself, *MLB.*

and made booths for his cattle: ... stalls for his livestock, *Anchor* ... tents, *BB* ... making an encampment, *Fenton* ... sheds, *Goodspeed* ... shelters, *REB.*

therefore the name of the place is called Succoth: ... place came to be named Succoth (sheds), *Goodspeed.*

18. And Jacob came to Shalem, a city of Shechem, which is in the land of Canaan, when he came from Padanaram: ... Jacob came in peace, *ASV* ... went quietly to the village, *Fenton* ... arrived safely, *NAB.*

and pitched his tent before the city: ... encamped within sight of the city, *Anchor* ... to the east of it, *NEB* ... camped before the city, *RSV* ... in front, *KJVII.*

19. And he bought a parcel of a field, where he had spread his tent: ... the plot of ground, *Anchor* ...

---

was satisfied. Again, God was faithful to His promise.

33:12-14. Jacob refused Esau's offer to accompany him on his way because Esau's 400 men would be anxious to get back home, and would want to push on faster than Jacob could go with his flocks and children. There is no record that Jacob actually went to visit Esau in Seir (Edom), though he may have. Some Jewish rabbis say the final fulfillment will be in the days of the Messiah (what we call the Millennium).

33:15. Jacob also refused Esau's offer to leave some of his men with them. Perhaps Esau thought Jacob needed protection and his men could act as guards. But Jacob was just happy to find favor in Esau's eyes. The fear of Esau had been in the back of his mind for 20 years. Now he was relieved because all of those fears had been unnecessary.

33:16-17. After Esau left, going south toward Seir, the mountainous country south of the Dead Sea, Jacob went west toward the Jordan about five miles and built a house and made shelters for his livestock, calling the place Succoth ("shelters").

33:18. We are not told how long Jacob stayed at Succoth. The name implies something temporary, though the building of a house probably means he stayed there a few years. Then he crossed the Jordan River and came peacefully (safely and unharmed) to the city of Shechem, 31 miles north of Jerusalem, and camped near the city. (Jacob's well is still there.) This was the culmination of his journey from Paddan Aram, for he was now back in the promised land, Canaan. God had fulfilled His promise of Genesis 28:15.

8400	6111	8328	866	904, 800	3791	904, 971.141	4623, 6549
adv	*n fs*	pn	rel part	prep, *n fs*	pn	prep, v Qal inf con, ps 3ms	prep, pn
שָׁלֵם	עִיר	שְׁכֶם	אֲשֶׁר	בְּאֶרֶץ	כְּנַעַן	בְּבֹאוֹ	מִפַּדַּן
shālēm	ʻîr	shekhem	'ăsher	be'erets	kena'an	bevō'ô	mippaddan
safely	to the city of	Shechem	which	in the land of	Canaan	on his going	from Paddan

782	2684.121	882, 6686	6111		7353.121	881, 2614	7898
pn	cj, v Qal impf 3ms	prep, *n mp*	art, n fs	**19.**	cj, v Qal impf 3ms	do, *n fs*	art, n ms
אֲרָם	וַיִּחַן	אֶת־פְּנֵי	הָעִיר		וַיִּקֶן	אֶת־חֶלְקַת	הַשָּׂדֶה
'ărām	wayyichan	'eth-penê	hā'îr		wayyiqen	'eth-chelqath	hassādeh
Aram	and he camped	by	the city		and he bought	the piece of	the field

866	5371.111, 8427	164	4623, 3135	1158, 2647	1	8328
rel part	v Qal pf 3ms, adv	n ms, ps 3ms	prep, n fs	*n mp*, pn	*n ms*	pn
אֲשֶׁר	נָטָה־שָׁם	אָהֳלוֹ	מִיַּד	בְּנֵי־חֲמוֹר	אֲבִי	שְׁכֶם
'ăsher	nāṭāh-shām	'āhelô	miyyadh	benê-chămôr	'ăvî	shekhem
where	he pitched there	his tent	from the hand	the sons of Hamor	the father of	Shechem

904, 4109	7473		5507.521, 8427	4326	7410.121, 3937	418
prep, *num*	n fs	**20.**	cj, v Hiphil impf 3ms, adv	n ms	cj, v Qal impf 3ms, prep, ps 3ms	n ms
בְּמֵאָה	קְשִׂיטָה		וַיַּצֶּב־שָׁם	מִזְבֵּחַ	וַיִּקְרָא־לוֹ	אֵל
bemē'āh	qŏsîṭāh		wayyatstsev-shām	mizbēach	wayyiqōrā'-lô	'ēl
with hundred	weights		and he set up there	altar	and he called to him	God

435	3547		3428.122	1839	1351, 3943	866	3314.112
n mp	pn	**34:1**	cj, v Qal impf 3fs	pn	*n fs*, pn	rel part	v Qal pf 3fs
אֱלֹהֵי	יִשְׂרָאֵל		וַתֵּצֵא	דִּינָה	בַּת־לֵאָה	אֲשֶׁר	יָלְדָה
'ĕlōhê	yisrā'ēl		wattētsē'	dhînāh	bath-lē'āh	'ăsher	yāledhāh
the God of	Israel		and she went out	Dinah	the daughter of Leah	whom	she gave birth

3937, 3399	3937, 7495.141	904, 1351	800		7495.121	881	8328
prep, pn	prep, v Qal inf con	prep, n fp	art, n fs	**2.**	cj, v Qal impf 3ms	do, ps 3fs	pn
לְיַעֲקֹב	לִרְאוֹת	בִּבְנוֹת	הָאָרֶץ		וַיַּרְא	אֹתָהּ	שְׁכֶם
leya'ăqōv	lir'ôth	bivnôth	hā'ārets		wayyare'	'ōthāhh	shekhem
for Jacob	to see	the daughters of	the land		and he saw	her	Shechem

1158, 2647	2433	5562	800	4089.121	881	8311.121
n ms, pn	art, pn	*n ms*	art, n fs	cj, v Qal impf 3ms	do, ps 3fs	cj, v Qal impf 3ms
בֶּן־חֲמוֹר	הַחִוִּי	נְשִׂיא	הָאָרֶץ	וַיִּקַּח	אֹתָהּ	וַיִּשְׁכַּב
ben-chămôr	hachiwwî	nesî'	hā'ārets	wayyiqqach	'ōthāhh	wayyishkav
son of Hamor	the Hivite	the prince of	the land	and he took	her	and he lay down

882	6257.321		1740.122	5497	904, 1839	1351, 3399
prep, ps 3fs	cj, v Piel impf 3ms, ps 3fs	**3.**	cj, v Qal impf 3fs	n fs, ps 3ms	prep, pn	*n fs*, pn
אִתָּהּ	וַיְעַנֶּהָ		וַתִּדְבַּק	נַפְשׁוֹ	בְּדִינָה	בַּת־יַעֲקֹב
'ōthāhh	way'annehā		wattidhbaq	naphshô	bedhînāh	bath-ya'ăqōv
with her	and he violated her		and it clung	his soul	with Dinah	the daughter of Jacob

154.121	881, 5472	1744.321	6142, 3949	5472		569.121
cj, v Qal impf 3ms	do, art, n fs	cj, v Piel impf 3ms	prep, *n ms*	art, n fs	**4.**	cj, v Qal impf 3ms
וַיֶּאֱהַב	אֶת־הַנַּעֲרָ	וַיְדַבֵּר	עַל־לֵב	הַנַּעֲרָ		וַיֹּאמֶר
wayye'ĕhav	'eth-hanna'ărā	waydhabbēr	'al-lēv	hanna'ărā		wayyō'mer
and he loved	the young woman	and he spoke	to the heart of	the young woman		and he said

8328	420, 2647	1	3937, 569.141	4089.131, 3937	881, 3316	2148
pn	prep, pn	n ms, ps	prep, v Qal inf con	v Qal impv 2ms, prep, ps 1cs	do, art, n fs	art, dem pron
שְׁכֶם	אֶל־חֲמוֹר	אָבִיו	לֵאמֹר	קַח־לִי	אֶת־הַיַּלְדָּה	הַזֹּאת
shekhem	'el-chămôr	'āvîw	lē'mōr	qach-lî	'eth-hayyaldāh	hazzō'th
Shechem	to Hamor	his father	saying	take for me	the girl	the this

3937, 828		3399	8471.111	3706	3041.311	881, 1839	1351	1158
prep, n fs	5.	cj, pn	v Qal pf 3ms	cj	v Piel pf 3ms	do, pn	n fs, ps 3ms	cj, n mp, ps 3ms
לְאִשָּׁה		וְיַעֲקֹב	שָׁמַע	כִּי	טִמֵּא	אֶת־דִּינָה	בִתּוֹ	וּבָנָיו
l^{e}'ishshāh		w^{e}ya'ăqōv	shāma'	kî	ṭimmē'	'eth-dînāh	vittô	ûvānâv
for a wife		and Jacob	he heard	that	he defiled	Dinah	his daughter	and his sons

2030.116	882, 4898	904, 7898	2896.511	3399	5912, 971.141
v Qal pf 3cp	prep, n ms, ps 3ms	prep, art, n ms	cj, v Hiphil pf 3ms	pn	prep, v Qal inf con, ps 3mp
הָיוּ	אֶת־מִקְנֵהוּ	בַּשָּׂדֶה	וְהֶחֱרִשׁ	יַעֲקֹב	עַד־בֹּאָם
hāyû	'eth-miqōnēhû	bassādheh	w^{e}hechĕrish	ya'ăqōv	'adh-bō'ām
they were	with his livestock	in the field	and he kept silent	Jacob	until their coming

bought the lot, *Berkeley* ... strip of country, *NEB.*

at the hand of the children of Hamor, Shechem's father, for an hundred pieces of money: ... two hundred dollars, *MLB* ... sheep, *REB* ... pieces of silver, *NIV* ... kesitahs, *Darby.*

20. And he erected there an altar, and called it Elelohe-Israel: ... also built an altar there and called on God, *Fenton* ... a memorial pillar, *NCB.*

34:1. And Dinah the daughter of Leah, which she bare unto Jacob: ... Leah's daughter, *Berkeley* ... daughter of Jacob and Leah, *Good News* ... whom Leah had borne to Jacob, *Anchor.*

went out to see the daughters of the land: ... to visit, *Anchor* ... get acquainted with the girls of the community, *Berkeley* ... to present herself among, *NCB* ... of the country, *Fenton* ... some of the Canaanite women, *Good News.*

2. And when Shechem the son of Hamor the Hivite, prince of the country: ... head of the region, *Anchor* ... local chief, *MLB* ... lord of, *Geneva* ... ruler of that area, *NIV.*

saw her, he took her: ... laid eyes on her, *Berkeley* ... seized her, *Anchor.*

and lay with her, and defiled her: ... ravished, *Goodspeed* ... violated and disgraced, *Fenton* ... raped her, *Good News* ... slept with her by force, *Anchor.*

3. And his soul clave unto Dinah the daughter of Jacob, and he loved the damsel: ... passionately in love, *MLB* ... being deeply attracted, *Anchor* ... deeply attached, *REB* ... fell deeply in love, *LIVB* ... remained true, *NEB.*

and spake kindly unto the damsel: ... sought to win her affection, *REB* ... talked to the girl in endearing terms, *MLB* ... said comforting words, *BB* ... to the girl's heart, *Fenton* ... spoke tenderly, *NASB.*

4. And Shechem spake unto his father Hamor, saying, Get me this damsel to wife: ... take me this girl as wife, *Darby* ... get this girl for me in marriage, *Goodspeed* ... this young woman, *NKJV* ... this maiden, *ASV.*

5. And Jacob heard that he had defiled Dinah his daughter: now his sons were with his cattle in the field: ... with his livestock, *Anchor* ... his herd, *Berkeley* ... at the fold, *Fenton* ... in the open country, *NEB.*

and Jacob held his peace until they were come: ... took no action, *Goodspeed* ... kept quiet, *MLB* ... said nothing, *NEB* ... was silent, *KJVII* ... held his peace, *NAB.*

33:19. Jacob then bought property outside the cultivated area around Shechem for a hundred "kasitahs." A kasitah was an old weight used for measuring the amount of silver (silver pieces or coins were not used until about the fifth century B.C. when they were introduced by the Persians). What the kasitah weighed is not known. The Septuagint and other ancient versions indicate is was in the form of a lamb. The property was purchased from Hamor the father of Shechem.

33:20. The name of Jacob's altar, "God, the God of Israel," or "Powerful is the God is Israel." By this Jacob testified publicly that the God of Abraham and Isaac was truly his God. (See 28:21.)

34:1-2. Dinah was innocently going to see the young women that lived in the land (seeking their friendship is implied). But Shechem seized her and forcibly raped her. His father is identified as a Hivite and as the chief or a minor king over that part of the country.

34:3-5. Shechem did not push her away. His inner self felt joined to her, and he loved her and spoke to her heart, that is spoke tender, loving words to her. Since marriages were arranged, Shechem asked his father to negotiate the wedding.

When Jacob heard about how Dinah was raped, but he said nothing until his sons returned from the fields with their flocks.

6.	3428.121	2647	1, 8328	420, 3399	3937, 1744.341	882
	cj, v Qal impf 3ms	pn	*n ms*, pn	prep, pn	prep, v Piel inf con	prep, ps 3ms
	וַיֵּצֵא	חֲמוֹר	אֲבִי־שְׁכֶם	אֶל־יַעֲקֹב	לְדַבֵּר	אִתּוֹ
	wayyētsē'	chămôr	'ăvî-sh^{e}khem	'el-ya'ăqōv	l^{e}dhabbēr	'ittô
	and he went out	Hamor	the father of Shechem	to Jacob	to speak	with him

7.	1158	3399	971.116	4623, 7898	3626, 8471.141	6321.726
	cj, *n mp*	pn	v Qal pf 3cp	prep, art, n ms	prep, v Qal inf con, ps 3mp	cj, v Hithpael impf 3mp
	וּבְנֵי	יַעֲקֹב	בָּאוּ	מִן־הַשָּׂדֶה	כְּשָׁמְעָם	וַיִּתְעַצְּבוּ
	ûv^{e}nê	ya'ăqōv	bā'û	min-hassādheh	k^{e}shām^e'ām	wayyith'atsts^{e}vû
	and the sons of	Jacob	they went	from the field	when their hearing	and it was hot to them

596	2835.121	3937	4108	3706, 5214	6449.111	904, 3547
art, n mp	cj, v Qal impf 3ms	prep, ps 3mp	adv	cj, n fs	v Qal pf 3ms	prep, pn
הָאֲנָשִׁים	וַיִּחַר	לָהֶם	מְאֹד	כִּי־נְבָלָה	עָשָׂה	בְיִשְׂרָאֵל
hā'ănāshîm	wayyichar	lāhem	m^e'ōdh	kî-n^{e}vālāh	'āsâh	v^{e}yisrā'ēl
the men	and it was anger	to them	very	because foolishness	he did	with Israel

3937, 8311.141	881, 1351, 3399	3772	3940	6449.221	8.	1744.321
prep, v Qal inf con	do, *n fs*, pn	cj, adv	neg part	v Niphal impf 3ms		cj, v Piel impf 3ms
לִשְׁכַּב	אֶת־בַּת־יַעֲקֹב	וְכֵן	לֹא	יֵעָשֶׂה		וַיְדַבֵּר
lishkav	'eth-bath-ya'ăqōv	w^{e}khēn	lō'	yē'āseh		way^{e}dhabbēr
to lie	with the daughter of Jacob	for so	not	it was done		and he spoke

2647	882	3937, 569.141	8328	1158	2945.112	5497
pn	prep, ps 3mp	prep, v Qal inf con	pn	n ms, ps 1cs	v Qal pf 3fs	n fs, ps 3ms
חֲמוֹר	אִתָּם	לֵאמֹר	שְׁכֶם	בְּנִי	חָשְׁקָה	נַפְשׁוֹ
chămôr	'ittām	lē'mōr	sh^{e}khem	b^{e}nî	chāsh^{e}qāh	naphshô
Hamor	with them	saying	Shechem	my son	it is attached	his soul

904, 1351	5598.133	5167	881	3937	3937, 828	9.	2967.733
prep, n fs, ps 2mp	v Qal impv 2mp	part	do, ps 3fs	prep, ps 3ms	prep, n fs		cj, v Hithpael impv 2mp
בְּבִתְּכֶם	תְּנוּ	נָא	אֹתָהּ	לוֹ	לְאִשָּׁה		וְהִתְחַתְּנוּ
b^{e}vitt^{e}khem	t^{e}nû	nā'	'ōthāhh	lô	l^e'ishshāh		w^{e}hithchatt^{e}nû
with your daughter	give	please	her	to him	for a wife		and intermarry

882	1351	5598.128, 3937	881, 1351	4089.128	3937
prep, ps 1cp	n fp, ps 2mp	v Qal impf 2mp, prep, ps 1cp	cj, do, n fp, ps 1cp	v Qal impf 2mp	prep, ps 2mp
אֹתָנוּ	בְּנֹתֵיכֶם	תִּתְּנוּ־לָנוּ	וְאֶת־בְּנֹתֵינוּ	תִּקְחוּ	לָכֶם
'ōthānû	b^{e}nōthêkhem	titt^{e}nû-lānû	w^e'eth-b^{e}nōthênû	tiqŏchû	lākhem
with us	your daughters	you will give to us	and our daughters	you will take	for yourselves

10.	882	3553.128	800	2030.122	3937, 6686	3553.133
	cj, prep, ps 1cp	v Qal impf 2mp	cj, art, n fs	v Qal impf 3fs	prep, n mp, ps 2mp	v Qal impv 2mp
	וְאִתָּנוּ	תֵּשֵׁבוּ	וְהָאָרֶץ	תִּהְיֶה	לִפְנֵיכֶם	שְׁבוּ
	w^e'ittānû	tēshēvû	w^{e}hā'ārets	tihyeh	liphnêkhem	sh^{e}vû
	and with us	you will dwell	and the land	it will be	before you	dwell

5692.133	270.233	904	11.	569.121	8328	420, 1
cj, v Qal impv 2mp, ps 3fs	cj, v Niphal impv 2mp	prep, ps 3fs		cj, v Qal impf 3ms	pn	prep, n ms, ps 3fs
וּסְחָרוּהָ	וְהֵאָחֲזוּ	בָּהּ		וַיֹּאמֶר	שְׁכֶם	אֶל־אָבִיהָ
ûs̱^{e}chārûhā	w^{e}hē'āchăzû	bāhh		wayyō'mer	sh^{e}khem	'el-'āvîhā
and move about in it	and be settled	in it		and he said	Shechem	to her father

420, 250	4834.125, 2682	904, 6084	866	569.128	420
cj, prep, n mp, ps 3fs	v Qal impf 1cs, n ms	prep, n fd, ps 2mp	cj, rel part	v Qal impf 2mp	prep, ps 1cs
וְאֶל־אַחֶיהָ	אֶמְצָא־חֵן	בְּעֵינֵיכֶם	וַאֲשֶׁר	תֹּאמְרוּ	אֵלַי
w^e'el-'achêhā	'emtsā'-chēn	b^e'ênêkhem	wa'ăsher	tō'm^{e}rû	'ēlay
and to her brothers	I will find favor	in your eyes	and whatever	you will say	to me

6. And Hamor the father of Shechem went out unto Jacob to commune with him: ... to make arrangements, *Anchor* ... to talk, *Berkeley* ... discuss the matter, *NAB.*

7. And the sons of Jacob came out of the field when they heard it: ... just as Jacob's sons, *Anchor* ... on hearing of it, *Berkeley* ... as soon as they heard the news, *Goodspeed.*

and the men were grieved, and they were very wroth: ... very displeasing, *Young* ... aroused, *NCB* ... furious, *Good News* ... disgusted and angry, *Berkeley* ... shocked and seething with anger, *Anchor.*

because he had wrought folly in Israel: ... such a shameful deed, *MLB* ... disgraceful, *Darby* ... villeny, *Geneva* ... had committed a crime, *NCB* ... outrage, *Anchor.*

in lying with Jacob's daughter: ... violating, *Fenton* ... raping, *Good News* ... sleeping with, *Anchor.*

which thing ought not to be done: ... and so it is not done, *Young* ... an intolerable crime, *NCB.*

8. And Hamor communed with them, saying: ... addressed them, *Anchor* ... conversed, *Berkeley* ... spoke, *Darby* ... appealed, *NAB* ... in these terms, *NEB.*

The soul of my son Shechem longeth for your daughter: ... is in love with, *NEB* ... full of desire, *BB* ... affections are centered, *MLB* ... has his heart set, *Anchor.*

I pray you give her him to wife: ... I beg of you, *Berkeley* ... please, *KJVII* ... in marriage, *Goodspeed* ... let him marry her, *Good News.*

9. And make ye marriages with us: ... intermarry with us, *NIV* ... let our two peoples be joined together, *BB* ... give your girls to us, *Fenton* ... let us ally ourselves, *NEB* ... make affinity, *Geneva.*

and give your daughters unto us, and take our daughters unto you: ... intermarriage between our people and yours, *Good News* ... in exchange, *NEB* ... marrying ours, *Goodspeed* ... for yourselves, *Anchor.*

10. And ye shall dwell with us: ... you can thus live among us, *Anchor* ... settle among us, *NIV* ... go on living with us, *BB* ... make your home with us, *Goodspeed* ... stay here in our country, *Good News.*

and the land shall be before you: ... live any where you wish, *Good News* ... at your disposal, *Goodspeed* ... will be yours, *NCB* ... shall be open to you, *Anchor.*

dwell and trade ye therein: ... move about freely, *REB* ... make your home in it, *MLB* ... travel about, *Fenton* ... do your business in it, *Geneva.*

and get you possessions therein: ... acquire land of your own, *REB* ... possess it, *Fenton* ... acquire holdings, *Anchor* ... property, *Berkeley.*

11. And Shechem said unto her father and unto her brethren: ... addressed himself, *Anchor* ... appealed to, *NAB.*

Let me find grace in your eyes: ... do me this favor, *NAB* ... let me have your consent, *MLB* ... let me find favour in your eyes, *Darby* ... if you will give ear to my request, *BB.*

and what ye shall say unto me I will give: ... I will pay whatever you say, *Anchor* ... pay the sum you name, *Berkeley* ... whatever ye shall appoint me, *Geneva* ... that you demand of me, *Goodspeed.*

12. Ask me never so much dowry and gift: ... put your price and dowry as high as you want to, *Berkeley* ... a bridal payment ever so high, *Anchor* ... impose on me very much, *Darby* ... however great you make the bride-price, *BB* . . .ask of me abundantly, *Geneva.*

and I will give according as ye shall say unto me: ... will pay whatever you say, *Anchor* ... I will meet your demands, *MLB.*

34:6-7. By the time Hamor came to talk with Jacob about getting Dinah as a wife for his son, someone had already carried the news to Dinah's brothers and they had hurried back. The eleven brothers had only one sister, and they were very protective of her. So they were deeply hurt, outraged, and became very hot with anger because of this senseless, immoral offense, something that should not have been done against Israel, who had bought property from them and become their neighbor.

34:8-10. Not only did Hamor declare Shechem's love for Dinah, he invited Jacob's sons to intermarry with his people, live and move about freely (as citizens rather than resident aliens) and settle in the land.

To accept this invitation would mean that the Israelites would be absorbed by the Canaanites and lose their identity. This invitation seemed cordial, but to Hamor it meant he and his people would gain Israel's blessings and wealth (see verse 23). It was also contrary to God's will for His people.

34:11-12. Shechem then spoke up and offered to give as big a dowry and gift as they wished. This was unusual because the amount of the dowry was usually a set amount. Shechem's generous offer may have indicated the guilt felt over his misconduct, but there was also an element of greed.

5598.125		7528.533	6142	4108	4258	5150	5598.125
v Qal impf 1cs	**12.**	v Hiphil impv 2mp	prep, ps 1cs	adv	n ms	cj, n ms	cj, v Qal impf 1cs
אֶתֵּן		הַרְבּוּ	עָלַי	מְאֹד	מֹהַר	וּמַתָּן	וְאֶתְּנָה
'ettēn		harbû	'ālay	m^{e}'ōdh	mōhar	ûmattān	w^{e}'ett^{e}nāh
I will give		make great	on me	very	dowry	and gift	and I will give

3626, 866	569.128	420	5598.133, 3937	881, 5472	3937, 828
prep, rel part	v Qal impf 2mp	prep, ps 1cs	cj, v Qal impv 2mp, prep, ps 1cs	do, art, n fs	prep, n fs
כַּאֲשֶׁר	תֹּאמְרוּ	אֵלָי	וּתְנוּ־לִי	אֶת־הַנַּעֲרָ	לְאִשָּׁה
ka'ăsher	tō'm^{e}rû	'ēlāy	ûth^{e}nû-lî	'eth-hanna'ărā	l^{e}'ishshāh
according to that	you will say	to me	and give to me	the young woman	for a wife

	6257.126	1158, 3399	881, 8328	881, 2647	1	904, 4983
13.	cj, v Qal impf 3mp	*n mp*, pn	do, pn	cj, do, pn	n ms, ps	prep, n fs
	וַיַּעֲנוּ	בְנֵי־יַעֲקֹב	אֶת־שְׁכֶם	וְאֶת־חֲמוֹר	אָבִיו	בְּמִרְמָה
	wayya'ănû	v^{e}nê-ya'ăqōv	'eth-sh^{e}khem	w^{e}'eth-chămôr	'āvîw	b^{e}mirmāh
	and they answered	the sons of Jacob	Shechem	and Hamor	his father	with deceit

1744.326	866	3041.311	881	1839	269		569.126
cj, v Piel impf 3mp	cj	v Piel pf 3ms	do	pn	n fs, ps 3mp	**14.**	cj, v Qal impf 3mp
וַיְדַבֵּרוּ	אֲשֶׁר	טִמֵּא	אֵת	דִּינָה	אֲחֹתָם		וַיֹּאמְרוּ
way^{e}dhabbērû	'ăsher	ṯimmē'	'ēth	dînāh	'ăchōthām		wayyō'm^{e}rû
and they spoke	because	he defiled		Dinah	their sister		and they said

420	3940	3310.120	3937, 6449.141	1745	2172	3937, 5598.141
prep, ps 3mp	neg part	v Qal impf 1cp	prep, v Qal inf con	art, n ms	art, dem pron	prep, v Qal inf con
אֲלֵיהֶם	לֹא	נוּכַל	לַעֲשׂוֹת	הַדָּבָר	הַזֶּה	לָתֵת
'ălêhem	lō'	nûkhal	la'ăsôth	haddāvār	hazzeh	lāthēth
to them	not	we are able	to do	the thing	the this	to give

881, 269	3937, 382	866, 3937	6428	3706, 2887	2000	3937
do, n fs, ps 1cp	prep, n ms	rel part, prep, ps 3ms	n fs	cj, n fs	pers pron	prep, ps 1cp
אֶת־אֲחֹתֵנוּ	לְאִישׁ	אֲשֶׁר־לוֹ	עָרְלָה	כִּי־חֶרְפָּה	הִוא	לָנוּ
'eth-'ăchōthēnû	l^{e}'îsh	'ăsher-lô	'ār^{e}lāh	kî-cherpāh	hiw'	lānû
our sister	to man	which to him	foreskin	because disgrace	it	for us

	395, 904, 2148	224.220	3937	524	2030.128	3765
15.	adv, prep, dem pron	v Niphal impf 1cp	prep, ps 2mp	cj	v Qal impf 2mp	prep, ps 1cp
	אַךְ־בְּזֹאת	נֵאוֹת	לָכֶם	אִם	תִּהְיוּ	כָמֹנוּ
	'akh-b^{e}zō'th	nē'ôth	lākhem	'im	tihyû	khāmōnû
	only with this	we will consent	to you	if	you will be	just like us

3937, 4271.241	3937	3725, 2227		5598.129	881, 1351	3937
prep, v Niphal inf con	prep, ps 2mp	*adj*, n ms	**16.**	cj, v Qal pf 1cp	do, n fp, ps 1cp	prep, ps 2mp
לְהִמֹּל	לָכֶם	כָּל־זָכָר		וְנָתַנּוּ	אֶת־בְּנֹתֵינוּ	לָכֶם
l^{e}himmōl	lākhem	kol-zākhār		w^{e}nāthannû	'eth-b^{e}nōthênû	lākhem
to be circumcised	to you	every male		and we will give	our daughters	to you

881, 1351	4089.120, 3937	3553.119	882	2030.119	3937, 6194
cj, do, n fp, ps 2mp	v Qal impf 1cp, prep, ps 1cp	cj, v Qal pf 1cp	prep, ps 2mp	cj, v Qal pf 1cp	prep, n ms
וְאֶת־בְּנֹתֵיכֶם	נִקַּח־לָנוּ	וְיָשַׁבְנוּ	אִתְּכֶם	וְהָיִינוּ	לְעָם
w^{e}'eth-b^{e}nōthêkhem	niqqach-lānû	w^{e}yāshavnû	'itt^{e}khem	w^{e}hāyînû	l^{e}'am
and your daughters	we will take for us	and we will dwell	with you	and we will be	people

259		524, 3940	8471.128	420	3937, 4271.241	4089.119
num	**17.**	cj, cj, neg part	v Qal impf 2mp	prep, ps 1cp	prep, v Niphal inf con	cj, v Qal pf 1cp
אֶחָד		וְאִם־לֹא	תִשְׁמְעוּ	אֵלֵינוּ	לְהִמּוֹל	וְלָקַחְנוּ
'echādh		w^{e}'im-lō'	thishm^{e}'û	'ēlênû	l^{e}himmôl	w^{e}lāqachnû
one		and if not	you will listen	to us	to be circumcised	then we will take

881, 1351	2050.119	18.	3296.126	1745	904, 6084	2647
do, n fs, ps 1cp	cj, v Qal pf 1cp		cj, v Qal impf 3mp	n mp, ps 3mp	prep, *n fp*	pn
אֶת־בִּתֵּנוּ	וְהָלָכְנוּ		וַיִּיטְבוּ	דִבְרֵיהֶם	בְּעֵינֵי	חֲמוֹר
'eth-bittēnû	wehālākhenû		wayyîtevû	dhivrêhem	be'ênê	chămôr
our daughter	and we will go		and they pleased	their words	in the eyes of	Hamor

904, 6084	8328	1158, 2647	19.	3940, 310.311	5470
cj, prep, *n fd*	pn	*n ms*, pn		cj, neg part, v Piel pf 3ms	art, n ms
וּבְעֵינֵי	שְׁכֶם	בֶּן־חֲמוֹר		וְלֹא־אֵחַר	הַנַּעַר
ûve'ênê	shekhem	ben-chămôr		welō'-'ēchar	hanna'ar
and in the eyes of	Shechem	the son of Hamor		and not he delayed	the young man

3937, 6449.141	1745	3706	2759.111	904, 1351, 3399	2000	3632.255
prep, v Qal inf con	art, n ms	cj	v Qal pf 3ms	prep, *n fs*, pn	cj, pers pron	v Niphal ptc ms
לַעֲשׂוֹת	הַדָּבָר	כִּי	חָפֵץ	בְּבַת־יַעֲקֹב	וְהוּא	נִכְבָּד
la'ăsôth	haddāvār	kî	chāphēts	bevath-ya'ăqōv	wehû'	nikhbādh
to do	the thing	because	he was delighted	with the daughter of Jacob	and he	honored

but give me the damsel to wife: ... let me marry her, *Good News* ... young woman, *NKJV.*

13. And the sons of Jacob answered Shechem and Hamor his father deceitfully: ... with guile, *Anchor* ... laying a trap for them, *NEB.*

and said, because he had defiled Dinah their sister: ... he had dishonored, *MLB* ... has corrupted, *Fenton* ... had violated, *Goodspeed.*

14. And they said unto them, We cannot do this thing, to give our sister to one that is uncircumcised; for that were a reproach unto us: ... a cause of shame, *BB* ... a disgrace among us, *Anchor.*

15. But in this will we consent unto you: ... on one condition, *Anchor* ... yet, if you will agree with us, *Fenton* ... will we accede to your requests, *Goodspeed.*

If ye will be as we be, that every male of you be circumcised: ... if every male among you become like us, *BB* ... follow our example, *NEB.*

16. Then will we give our daughters unto you, and we will take your daughters to us: ... in marriage, *Goodspeed* ... marry your daughters, *Berkeley* ... for ourselves, *NASB.*

and we will dwell with you: ... settle among you, *MLB* ... go on living with you, *BB* ... reside, *Fenton* ... make our home, *Goodspeed.*

and we will become one people: ... be one kindred, *Anchor* ... a single people, *Goodspeed.*

17. But if ye will not hearken unto us, to be circumcised: ... if you do not agree to our terms, *Anchor* ... not listen, *KJVII* ... do not comply, *NAB* ... if you refuse, *NCB* ... if you will not undergo circumcision, *BB.*

then will we take our daughter: ... our sister, *NIV* ... the girl, *NEB.*

and we will be gone: ... move away, *MLB* ... depart, *Geneva* ... be on our way, *LIVB.*

18. And their words pleased Hamor, and Shechem Hamor's son: ... suggestion appealed to, *Berkeley* ... request seemed fair, *Anchor* ... were good in the eyes, *Darby* ... proposal was agreeable, *Goodspeed.*

19. And the young man deferred not to do the thing: ... the youth lost no time, *Anchor* ... without delay, *Berkeley* ... without loss of time, *BB* ... did not hesitate, *KJVII.*

because he had delight in Jacob's daughter: ... he was in love with, *Goodspeed* ... so strong was his desire, *Anchor* ... had an affection, *Fenton* ... his heart was taken, *NEB* ... heart had been captured, *REB.*

34:13-17. The sons of Jacob are now the deceivers. They declared that to give their sister to an uncircumcised man would be a disgrace, so they demanded that all the males of the city of Shechem be circumcised. Then Jacob and his sons would settle among them and become one people with them. Otherwise they would take Dinah and leave.

34:18-19. Hamor and Shechem were pleased. Shechem was the most honored son of Hamor, that is, he was the "crown prince," the heir who would become the next chief or petty king of the region. Without delay, he went to do what had been asked.

34:20-22. Hamor went to the city gate where town business would be carried on and told the men how peaceable (friendly) the sons of Jacob were and how they should let them live in the land, for it was a broad land (with plenty of room for them), so let them move about freely (carry on their business), and intermarry. The one condition for absorbing them would be for all the males to be circumcised.

4623, 3725	1041	1		971.121	2647	8328	1158
prep, prep	*n ms*	n ms, ps	**20.**	cj, v Qal impf 3ms	pn	cj, pn	n ms, ps 3ms
מִכֹּל	בֵּית	אָבִיו		וַיָּבֹא	חֲמוֹר	וּשְׁכֶם	בְּנוֹ
mikkōl	bêth	'āvîw		wayyāvō'	chămôr	ûsh^{e}khem	b^{e}nô
above all	the house of	his father		and he went	Hamor	and Shechem	his son

420, 8554	6111	1744.326	420, 596	6111	3937, 569.141		596
prep, *n ms*	n fs, ps 3mp	cj, v Piel impf 3mp	prep, *n mp*	n fs, ps 3mp	prep, v Qal inf con	**21.**	art, n mp
אֶל־שַׁעַר	עִירָם	וַיְדַבְּרוּ	אֶל־אַנְשֵׁי	עִירָם	לֵאמֹר		הָאֲנָשִׁים
'el-sha'ar	'îrām	way^{e}dhabb^{e}rû	'el-'anshê	'îrām	lē'mōr		hā'ănāshîm
to the gate of	their city	and they spoke	to the men of	their city	saying		the men

431	8400	2062	882	3553.126	904, 800	5692.126
art, dem pron	adj	pers pron	prep, ps 1cp	cj, v Qal impf 3mp	prep, n fs	cj, v Qal impf 3mp
הָאֵלֶּה	שְׁלֵמִים	הֵם	אִתָּנוּ	וְיֵשְׁבוּ	בָאָרֶץ	וְיִסְחֲרוּ
hā'ēlleh	sh^{e}lēmîm	hēm	'ittānû	w^{e}yēsh^{e}vû	vā'ārets	w^{e}yischărû
the these	peaceable	they	with us	and they will dwell	in the land	and they will move about

881	800	2079	7622, 3135	3937, 6686	881, 1351
do, ps 3fs	cj, art, n fs	intrj	*adj*, n fd	prep, n mp, ps 3mp	do, n fp, ps 3mp
אֹתָהּ	וְהָאָרֶץ	הִנֵּה	רַחֲבַת־יָדַיִם	לִפְנֵיהֶם	אֶת־בְּנֹתָם
'ōthāhh	w^{e}hā'ārets	hinnēh	rach^{e}vath-yādhayim	liphnêhem	'eth-b^{e}nōthām
it	for the land	behold	wide of hands	before them	their daughters

4089.120, 3937	3937, 5571	881, 1351	5598.120	3937		395, 904, 2148
v Qal impf 1cp, prep, ps 1cp	prep, n fp	cj, do, n fp, ps 1cp	v Qal impf 1cp	prep, ps 3mp	**22.**	adv, prep, dem pron
נִקַּח־לָנוּ	לְנָשִׁים	וְאֶת־בְּנֹתֵינוּ	נִתֵּן	לָהֶם		אַךְ־בְּזֹאת
niqqach-lānû	l^{e}nāshîm	w^{e}'eth-b^{e}nōthênû	nittēn	lāhem		'akh-b^{e}zō'th
we will take for us	for wives	and our daughters	we will give	to them		only with this

224.226	3937	596	3937, 3553.141	882	3937, 2030.141	3937, 6194
v Niphal impf 3mp	prep, ps 1cp	art, n mp	prep, v Qal inf con	prep, ps 1cp	prep, v Qal inf con	prep, n ms
יֵאֹתוּ	לָנוּ	הָאֲנָשִׁים	לָשֶׁבֶת	אִתָּנוּ	לִהְיוֹת	לְעָם
yē'ōthû	lānû	hā'ănāshîm	lāsheveth	'ittānû	lihyôth	l^{e}'am
they will consent	to us	the men	for dwelling	with us	to be	people

259	904, 4271.241	3937	3725, 2227	3626, 866	2062	4271.256
num	prep, v Niphal inf con	prep, ps 1cp	adj, *n ms*	prep, rel part	pers pron	v Niphal ptc mp
אֶחָד	בְּהִמּוֹל	לָנוּ	כָּל־זָכָר	כַּאֲשֶׁר	הֵם	נִמֹּלִים
'echādh	b^{e}himmôl	lānû	kol-zākhār	ka'ăsher	hēm	nimmōlîm
one	with being circumcised	for us	every male	like that	they	circumcised

	4898	7359	3725, 866	3940	3937	2062
23.	n ms, ps3mp	cj, n ms, ps 3mp	cj, *adj*, n fs, ps 3mp	intrg part, neg part	prep, ps 1cp	pers pron
	מִקְנֵהֶם	וְקִנְיָנָם	וְכָל־בְּהֶמְתָּם	הֲלוֹא	לָנוּ	הֵם
	miqŏnēhem	w^{e}qinyānām	w^{e}khol-b^{e}hemtām	h^{e}lô'	lānû	hēm
	their livestock	and their property	and all their beasts	will not	to us	they

395	224.220	3937	3553.126	882		8471.126
adv	v Niphal impf 1cp	prep, ps 3mp	cj, v Qal impf 3mp	prep, ps 1cp	**24.**	cj, v Qal impf 3mp
אַךְ	נֵאוֹתָה	לָהֶם	וְיֵשְׁבוּ	אִתָּנוּ		וַיִּשְׁמְעוּ
'akh	nē'ôthāh	lāhem	w^{e}yēsh^{e}vû	'ittānû		wayyishm^{e}'û
only	may we agree	to them	and they will dwell	with us		and they listened

420, 2647	420, 8328	1158	3725, 3428.152	8554	6111
prep, pn	cj, prep, pn	n ms, ps 3ms	*adj*, v Qal act ptc mp	*n ms*	n fs, ps 3ms
אֶל־חֲמוֹר	וְאֶל־שְׁכֶם	בְּנוֹ	כָּל־יֹצְאֵי	שַׁעַר	עִירוֹ
'el-chămôr	w^{e}'el-sh^{e}khem	b^{e}nô	kol-yōts^{e}'ê	sha'ar	'îrô
to Hamor	and to Shechem	his son	all going out	to the gate of	his city

4271.226	**3725, 2227**	**3725, 3428.152**	**8554**	**6111**
cj, v Niphal impf 3mp	*adj*, n ms	*adj*, v Qal act ptc mp	*n ms*	n fs, ps 3ms
וַיִּמֹּלוּ	כָּל־זָכָר	כָּל־יֹצְאֵי	שַׁעַר	עִירוֹ
wayyimmōlû	kāl-zākhār	kāl-yōts'ê	sa'ar	'îrô
and they were circumcised	every male	all going out	to the gate of	his city

25.	**2030.121**	**904, 3219**	**8389**	**904, 2030.141**	**3628.152**	**4089.126**
	cj, v Qal impf 3ms	prep, art, n ms	art, num	prep, v Qal inf con, ps 3mp	v Qal act ptc mp	cj, v Qal impf 3mp
	וַיְהִי	בַּיּוֹם	הַשְּׁלִישִׁי	בִּהְיוֹתָם	כֹּאֲבִים	וַיִּקְחוּ
	wayhî	vayyôm	hashsh^{e}lîshî	bihyôthām	kō'ăvîm	wayyiqŏchû
	and it was	in the day	the third	when they were	ones in pain	and they took

8530, 1158, 3399	**8482**	**4015**	**250**	**1839**	**382**	**2820**	**971.126**
num, n mp, pn	pn	cj, pn	*n mp*	pn	n ms	n fs, ps 3ms	cj, v Qal impf 3mp
שְׁנֵי־בְנֵי־יַעֲקֹב	שִׁמְעוֹן	וְלֵוִי	אֲחֵי	דִינָה	אִישׁ	חַרְבּוֹ	וַיָּבֹאוּ
sh^{e}nê-v^{e}nê-ya'ăqōv	shim'ôn	w^{e}lēwî	'ăchê	dhînāh	'îsh	charbô	wayyābō'û
two of sons of Jacob	Simeon	and Levi	the brothers of	Dinah	each	his sword	and they went

6142, 6111	**1020**	**2103.126**	**3725, 2227**	**26.**	**881, 2647**	**881, 8328**	**1158**
prep, art, n fs	adv	cj, v Qal impf 3mp	adj, *n ms*		cj, do, pn	cj, do, pn	n ms, ps 3ms
עַל־הָעִיר	בֶּטַח	וַיַּהַרְגוּ	כָּל־זָכָר		וְאֶת־חֲמוֹר	וְאֶת־שְׁכֶם	בְּנוֹ
'al-hā'îr	betach	wayyaharghû	kāl-zākhār		w^{e}'eth-chămôr	w^{e}'eth-sh^{e}khem	b^{e}nô
against the city	safely	and they killed	every male		and Hamor	and Shechem	his son

and he was more honourable than all the house of his father: ... most distinguished, *NCB* ... held high rank, *MLB* ... respected, *Anchor.*

20. And Hamor and Shechem his son came unto the gate of their city: ... went to their Town Council, *NAB* ... meeting place, *BB.*

and communed with the men of their city, saying: ... talked it over , *MLB* ... presented the matter, *NAB.*

21. These men are peaceable with us: ... in harmony with us, *Berkeley* ... at peace with us, *BB* ... friendly toward us, *NIV.*

therefore let them dwell in the land: ... go on living in this country, *BB* ... make their home, *Goodspeed* ... settle, *Anchor* ... stay, *Berkeley.*

and trade therein: ... do business, *Berkeley* ... engage in trade, *Goodspeed.*

for the land, behold, it is large enough for them; let us take their daughters to us for wives, and let us give them our daughters: ... there is ample room, *NAB* ... spacious enough, *Goodspeed* ... plenty of room, *NIV.*

22. Only herein will the men consent unto us for to dwell with us, to be one people, if every male among us be circumcised, as they are circumcised: ... on one condition, *Anchor* ... unite, *Fenton* ... living with us, *BB* ... mixing with us, *MLB.*

23. Shall not their cattle and their substance and every beast of theirs be ours?: ... livestock, *Anchor* ... be to our advantage, *NCB.*

only let us consent unto them, and they will dwell with us: ... let us give in to them, *NAB* ... accept their condition, *Berkeley.*

24. And unto Hamor and unto Shechem his son hearkened all that went out of the gate of his city: ... gave ear, *BB* ... listened, *Fenton.*

and every male was circumcised, all that went out of the gate of his city: ... underwent circumcision, *BB* ... every single one, *NEB.*

25. And it came to pass on the third day, when they were sore: ... while they were still in pain, *REB* ... before the wounds were well, *BB* ... while they were still ailing, *Anchor.*

that two of the sons of Jacob, Simeon and Levi, Dinah's brethren: ... full brothers, *NAB.*

34:23-24. Shechem then stirred their greed. Circumcision was a small price to pay to make the wealth of the sons of Israel theirs. So they agreed. They were circumcised, and Shechem took Dinah home as his wife.

34:25-26. Simeon and Levi, who were full brothers of Dinah, waited through the next day, then on the following day (counting the day of the circumcision as the first day) they took swords (possibly including servants with swords) and killed all the males, including Hamor and Shechem. They were still in pain and in their houses completely unsuspecting. Simeon and Levi then took Dinah from Shechem's house.

2103.116	3937, 6686, 2820	4089.126	881, 1839	4623, 1041	8328
v Qal pf 3cp	prep, *n mp*, n fs	cj, v Qal impf 3mp	do, pn	prep, *n ms*	pn
הָרְגוּ	לְפִי־חָרֶב	וַיִּקְחוּ	אֶת־דִּינָה	מִבֵּית	שְׁכֶם
hārghû	lephî-chārev	wayyiqōchû	'eth-dînāh	mibbêth	shekhem
they killed	with the edge of the sword	and they took	Dinah	from the house of	Shechem

3428.126		1158	3399	971.116	6142, 2592	997.126	6111
cj, v Qal impf 3mp	**27.**	*n mp*	pn	v Qal pf 3cp	prep, art, n mp	cj, v Qal impf 3mp	art, n fs
וַיֵּצֵאוּ		בְּנֵי	יַעֲקֹב	בָּאוּ	עַל־הַחֲלָלִים	וַיָּבֹזּוּ	הָעִיר
wayyētsē'û		bene	ya'ăqōv	bā'û	'al-hachlālîm	wayyāvōzzû	hā'îr
and they went out		the sons of	Jacob	they came	upon the slain	and they plundered	the city

866	3041.316	269		881, 6887	881, 1267	881, 2645
rel part	v Piel pf 3cp	n fs, ps 3mp	**28.**	do, n fs, ps 3mp	cj, do, n ms, ps 3mp	cj, do, n mp, ps 3mp
אֲשֶׁר	טִמְּאוּ	אֲחוֹתָם		אֶת־צֹאנָם	וְאֶת־בְּקָרָם	וְאֶת־חֲמֹרֵיהֶם
'ăsher	timme'û	'ăchôthām		'eth-tsō'nām	we'eth-beqārām	we'eth-chămōrêhhem
who	they defiled	their sister		their flocks	and their herds	and their donkeys

881	866, 904, 6111	881, 866	904, 7898	4089.116		881, 3725, 2524
cj, do	rel part, prep, art, n fs	cj, do, rel part	prep, art, n ms	v Qal pf 3cp	**29.**	cj, do, *adj*, n ms, ps 3ms
וְאֵת	אֲשֶׁר־בָּעִיר	וְאֶת־אֲשֶׁר	בַּשָּׂדֶה	לָקָחוּ		וְאֶת־כָּל־חֵילָם
we'ēth	'ăsher-bā'îr	we'eth-'ăsher	bassādheh	lāqāchû		we'eth-kol-chêlām
and	what in the city	and what	in the field	they took		and all their wealth

881, 3725, 3054	881, 5571	8091.116	997.126	881
cj, do, *adj*, n fp, ps 3mp	cj, do, n fp, ps 3mp	v Qal pf 3cp	cj, v Qal impf 3mp	cj, do
וְאֶת־כָּל־טַפָּם	וְאֶת־נְשֵׁיהֶם	שָׁבוּ	וַיָּבֹזּוּ	וְאֵת
we'eth-kol-tappām	weth-neshêhem	shāvû	wayyāvōzzû	we'ēth
and all their small children	and their women	they captured	and they plundered	and

3725, 866	904, 1041		569.121	3399	420, 8482	420, 4015
adj, rel part	prep, art, n ms	**30.**	cj, v Qal impf 3ms	pn	prep, pn	cj, prep, pn
כָּל־אֲשֶׁר	בַּבָּיִת		וַיֹּאמֶר	יַעֲקֹב	אֶל־שִׁמְעוֹן	וְאֶל־לֵוִי
kol-'ăsher	babbāyith		wayyō'mer	ya'ăqōv	'el-shim'ôn	we'el-lēwî
all which	in the house		and he said	Jacob	to Simeon	and to Levi

6138.117	881	3937, 919.541	904, 3553.151	800	904, 3793
v Qal pf 2mp	do, ps 1cs	prep, v Hiphil inf con, ps 1cs	prep, *v Qal act ptc ms*	art, n fs	prep, art, pn
עֲכַרְתֶּם	אֹתִי	לְהַבְאִישֵׁנִי	בְּיֹשֵׁב	הָאָרֶץ	בַּכְּנַעֲנִי
'ăkhartem	'ōthî	lehav'îshēnî	beyōshēv	hā'ārets	bakkena'ănî
you have troubled	me	to make me stink	with the dwellers of	the land	with the Canaanites

904, 6773	603	5139	4709	636.216	6142
cj, prep, art, pn	cj, pers pron	n mp	n ms	cj, v Niphal pf 3cp	prep, ps 1cs
וּבַפְּרִזִּי	וַאֲנִי	מְתֵי	מִסְפָּר	וְנֶאֶסְפוּ	עָלַי
ûvapperizzî	wa'ănî	methê	mispār	wene'esephû	'ālay
and with the Perizzites	and I	men of	number	and they will unite muster	against me

5409.516	8436.215	603	1041		569.126
cj, v Hiphil pf 3cp, ps 1cs	cj, v Niphal pf 1cs	pers pron	cj, n ms, ps 1cs	**31.**	cj, v Qal impf 3mp
וְהִכּוּנִי	וְנִשְׁמַדְתִּי	אֲנִי	וּבֵיתִי		וַיֹּאמְרוּ
wehikkûnî	wenishmadhtî	'ănî	ûvêthî		wayyō'merû
and they will strike me down	and I will be destroyed	I	and my household		and they said

3626, 2265.153	6449.121	881, 269		569.121	435	420, 3399
intrg part, prep, v Qal act ptc fs	v Qal impf 3ms	do, n fs, ps 1cp	**35:1**	cj, v Qal impf 3ms	n mp	prep, pn
הַכְזוֹנָה	יַעֲשֶׂה	אֶת־אֲחוֹתֵנוּ		וַיֹּאמֶר	אֱלֹהִים	אֶל־יַעֲקֹב
hakhzōnāh	ya'ăseh	'eth-'ăchôthēnû		wayyō'mer	'ĕlōhîm	'el-ya'ăqōv
like a prostitute	will he make	our sister		and He said	God	to Jacob

took each man his sword: ... either of them, *Geneva* ... armed themselves, *NEB.*

and came upon the city boldly: ... advanced against the city unopposed, *Anchor* ... by surprise, *BB* ... without any trouble, *NAB.*

and slew all the males: ... massacred, *NAB* ... put to the sword, *MLB* ... put all the males to death, *BB.*

26. And they slew Hamor and Shechem his son with the edge of the sword: ... including Hamor and his son Shechem, *Berkeley* ... put to death, *BB* ... cut down, *REB* ... by the mouth of the sword, *Young.*

and took Dinah out of Shechem's house and went out: ... removed, *Anchor* ... rescued, *LIVB* ... went their way, *Geneva* ... left, *Berkeley.*

27. The sons of Jacob came upon the slain: ... came upon the dead, *Geneva* ... followed up the slaughter, *NAB.*

and spoiled the city: ... plundered the city, *Anchor* ... made waste, *BB* ... sacked the city, *NCB* ... looted, *NASB.*

because they had defiled their sister: ... they had ravished, *Berkeley* ... of what had been done, *BB* ... violated, *Goodspeed* ... to avenge their sister's dishonour, *NEB.*

28. They took their sheep, and their oxen, and their asses: ... seized their flocks, and herds, and donkeys, *NIV* ... confiscated, *LIVB.*

and that which was in the city, and that which was in the field: ... all their moveable property, *MLB* ... everything else of theirs, *NIV* ... inside the city and outside in the open country, *NEB.*

29. And all their wealth: ... possessions, *Anchor* ... goods, *Darby.*

and all their little ones, and their wives took they captive, and spoiled even all that was in the house: ... plundered, *Anchor* ... looted, *NCB* ... and made them waste, *BB.*

30. And Jacob said to Simeon and Levi, Ye have troubled me: ... shocked me, *Berkeley* ... made trouble for me, *BB* ... are a sorrow to me, *Fenton.*

to make me to stink among the inhabitants of the land, among the Canaanites and the Perizzites: ... making me obnoxious, *Anchor* ... given me a bad name, *BB* ... loathsome, *NCB* ... bad odor, *REB.*

and I being few in number: ... I have so few men, *NAB* ... small in number, *BB* ... since we are few, *MLB* ... with our ranks so meager, *Anchor.*

they shall gather themselves together against me, and slay me: ... combine, *REB* ... join forces, *NIV* ... band together, *Good News* ... unite against me, *NAB* ... outnumber me, *Fenton* ... smite, *ASV* ... make war, *BB...* crush, *LIVB.*

and I shall be destroyed, I and my house: ... wiped out with all my people, *Anchor* ... and my family, *MLB* ... household, *NRSV.*

31. And they said, Should he deal with our sister as with an harlot?: ... like a prostitute, *Berkeley* ... as a loose woman, *BB* ... should our sister be treated like a whore, *NRSV* ... should he abuse our sister, *Geneva.*

35:1. And God said unto Jacob, Arise, go up to Bethel: ... move up to Bethel, *Berkeley* ... go up now, *REB* ... proceed to, *Anchor.*

and dwell there: and make there an altar unto God: ... and settle there, *NAB* ... reside, *Fenton* ... make your living place there, *BB.*

that appeared unto thee when thou fleddest from the face of Esau thy brother: ... who appeared to you in your flight from your brother Esau, *Fenton.*

2. Then Jacob said unto his household, and to all that were with him, Put away the strange gods that are among you: ... throw away, *Fenton* ... rid yourself of, *Anchor.*

34:27-29. The sons of Jacob then came and looted the city because of their sister's being defiled. They carried off all their wealth and captured their women and children making them slaves. They considered this plunder as the spoils of war. Most slaves in ancient times were captives taken in war.

34:30-31. Jacob was not pleased. He told Simeon and Levi that they had cut him off from the people of the land by making him a stench to the Canaanites and Perizzites. He and has household would be destroyed if they jointed forces against him. But Jacob's sons did not confess any sin. They felt justified because Shechem had treated their sister like a prostitute. Later Jacob rebuked them further (see 49:5-7).

35:1. When Jacob arrived near Shechem and set up an altar declaring that the one true God was his God, he fulfilled part of his promise to God (Gen. 28:21-22), but he delayed fulfilling the other part, for he did not go immediately back to Bethel. So God reminded him and commanded him to go up to Bethel (Shechem is about 1,880 feet above sea level; Bethel is about 2,890 feet above sea level). He must live there for a time and build an altar to the God who appeared to him there.

7251.131	6148.131	1044	3553.131, 8427	6449.131, 8427	4326	3937, 418
v Qal impv 2ms	v Qal impv 2ms	pn	cj, v Qal impv 2ms, adv	cj, v Qal impv 2ms, adv	n ms	prep, art, n ms
קוּם	עֲלֵה	בֵית־אֵל	וְשֵׁב־שָׁם	וַעֲשֵׂה־שָׁם	מִזְבֵּחַ	לָאֵל
qûm	‘ălēh	vêth-’ēl	w^{e}shev-shām	wa‘ăsēh-shām	mizbēach	lā’ēl
rise	go up	to Bethel	and dwell there	and make there	altar	to God

7495.255	420	904, 1300.141	4623, 6681	6451	250
v Niphal ptc ms	prep, ps 2ms	prep, v Qal inf con, ps 2ms	prep, *n ms*	pn	n ms, ps 2ms
הַנִּרְאֶה	אֵלֶיךָ	בְּבָרְחֲךָ	מִפְּנֵי	עֵשָׂו	אָחִיךָ
hannir’eh	’ēlêkhā	b^{e}vārchăkhā	mipp^{e}nê	‘ēsāw	’āchîkhā
the One appearing	to you	in your fleeing	from the face of	Esau	your brother

	569.121	3399	420, 1041	420	3725, 866	6196	5681.533
2.	cj, v Qal impf 3ms	pn	prep, n fs, ps 3ms	cj, prep	adj, rel part	prep, ps 3ms	v Hiphil impv 2mp
	וַיֹּאמֶר	יַעֲקֹב	אֶל־בֵּיתוֹ	וְאֶל	כָּל־אֲשֶׁר	עִמּוֹ	הָסִרוּ
	wayyō’mer	ya‘ăqōv	’el-bêthô	w^{e}’el	kol-’ăsher	‘immô	hāsirû
	and he said	Jacob	to his household	and to	all who	with him	get rid of

881, 435	5424	866	904, 8761	3000.533	2599.533
do, *n mp*	art, n ms	rel part	prep, n ms, ps 2mp	cj, v Hiphil impv 2mp	cj, v Hiphil impv 2mp
אֶת־אֱלֹהֵי	הַנֵּכָר	אֲשֶׁר	בְּתֹכְכֶם	וְהִטַּהֲרוּ	וְהַחֲלִיפוּ
’eth-’ĕlōhê	hannēkhār	’āsher	b^{e}thōkh^{e}khem	w^{e}hiṯṯahrû	w^{e}hachlîphû
the gods of	the foreign land	which	in your midst	and purify yourselves	and change

7980		7251.120	6148.120	1044	6449.125. 8427	4326
n fp, ps 2mp	**3.**	cj, v Qal impf 1cp	cj, v Qal impf 1cp	pn	cj, v Qal impf 1cs, adv	n ms
שִׂמְלֹתֵיכֶם		וְנָקוּמָה	וְנַעֲלֶה	בֵּית־אֵל	וְאֶעֱשֶׂה־שָּׁם	מִזְבֵּחַ
simlōthêkhem		w^{e}nāqûmāh	w^{e}na‘ăleh	bêth-’ēl	w^{e}’e‘ĕseh-shām	mizbēach
your clothes		and we will arise	and we will go up	to Bethel	and I will make there	altar

3937, 418	6257.151	881	904, 3219	7150	2030.121	6200
prep, art, n ms	art, v Qal act ptc ms	do, ps 1cs	prep, *n ms*	n fs, ps 1cs	cj, v Qal impf 3ms	prep, ps 1cs
לָאֵל	הָעֹנֶה	אֹתִי	בְּיוֹם	צָרָתִי	וַיְהִי	עִמָּדִי
lā’ēl	hā‘ōneh	’ōthî	b^{e}yôm	tsārāthî	wayhî	‘immādhî
to God	the One who answered	me	on the day of	my distress	and He was	with me

904, 1932	866	2050.115		5598.126	420, 3399	881	3725, 435
prep, art, n ms	rel part	v Qal pf 1cs	**4.**	cj, v Qal impf 3mp	prep, pn	do	*adj, n mp*
בַּדֶּרֶךְ	אֲשֶׁר	הָלָכְתִּי		וַיִּתְּנוּ	אֶל־יַעֲקֹב	אֵת	כָּל־אֱלֹהֵי
badderekh	’ăsher	hālākhtî		wayitt^{e}nû	’el-ya‘ăqōv	’ēth	kol-’ĕlōhê
on the journey	which	I went		and they gave	to Jacob		all the gods of

5424	866	904, 3135	881, 5321	866	904, 238	3045.121
art, n ms	rel part	prep, n fs, ps 3mp	cj, do, art, n mp	rel part	prep, n fp, ps 3mp	cj, v Qal impf 3ms
הַנֵּכָר	אֲשֶׁר	בְּיָדָם	וְאֶת־הַנְּזָמִים	אֲשֶׁר	בְּאָזְנֵיהֶם	וַיִּטְמֹן
hannēkhār	’ăsher	b^{e}yādhām	w^{e}’eth-hann^{e}zāmîm	’ăsher	b^{e}’āz^{e}nêhem	wayyiṯmōn
the foreign land	which	in their hand	and the rings	which	in their ears	and he hid

881	3399	8809	428	866	6196, 8328		5450.126
do, ps 3mp	pn	prep	art, n fs	rel part	prep, pn	**5.**	cj, v Qal impf 3mp
אֹתָם	יַעֲקֹב	תַּחַת	הָאֵלָה	אֲשֶׁר	עִם־שְׁכֶם		וַיִּסָּעוּ
’ōthām	ya‘ăqōv	tachath	hā’ēlāh	’ăsher	‘im-sh^{e}khem		wayyissā‘û
them	Jacob	under	the large tree	which	near Shechem		and they pulled out

2030.121	2955	435	6142, 6111	866	5623	3940	7579.116
cj, v Qal impf 3ms	*n fs*	n mp	prep, art, n fp	rel part	prep, ps 3mp	cj, neg part	v Qal pf 3cp
וַיְהִי	חִתַּת	אֱלֹהִים	עַל־הֶעָרִים	אֲשֶׁר	סְבִיבֹתֵיהֶם	וְלֹא	רָדְפוּ
wayhî	chittath	’ĕlōhîm	‘al-he‘ārîm	’ăsher	s^{e}vîvōthêhem	w^{e}lō’	rādh^{e}phû
and it was	the terror of	God	on the cities	which	all around them	and not	they pursued

311	1158	3399		971.121	3399	4007	866	904, 800
sub	*n mp*	pn		cj, v Qal impf 3ms	pn	pn	rel part	prep, *n fs*
אַחֲרֵי	בְּנֵי	יַעֲקֹב	**6.**	וַיָּבֹא	יַעֲקֹב	לוּזָה	אֲשֶׁר	בְּאֶרֶץ
'achrê	b^{e}nê	ya'ăqōv		wayyāvō'	ya'ăqōv	lûzāh	'ăsher	b^{e}'erets
after	the sons of	Jacob		and he went	Jacob	to Luz	which	in the land of

3791	2000	1044	2000	3725, 6194	866, 6196		1161.121
pn	pers pron	pn	pers pron	cj, adj, art, n ms	rel part, prep, ps 3ms		cj, v Qal impf 3ms
כְּנַעַן	הִוא	בֵּית־אֵל	הוּא	וְכָל־הָעָם	אֲשֶׁר־עִמּוֹ	**7.**	וַיִּבֶן
k^{e}na'an	hiw'	bêth-'ēl	hû'	w^{e}khol-hā'ām	'ăsher-'immô		wayyiven
Canaan	it	Bethel	he	and all the people	who with him		and he built

8427	4326	7410.121	3937, 4887	418	1044	3706	8427	1580.216
adv	n ms	cj, v Qal impf 3ms	prep, art, n ms	pn	pn	cj	adv	v Niphal pf 3cp
שָׁם	מִזְבֵּחַ	וַיִּקְרָא	לַמָּקוֹם	אֵל	בֵּית־אֵל	כִּי	שָׁם	נִגְלוּ
shām	mizbēach	wayyiqōrā'	lammāqôm	'ēl	bêth-'ēl	kî	shām	nighlû
there	altar	and he named	the place	El	Bethel	because	there	He was revealed

and be clean, and change your garments: ... purify yourselves and change your clothes, *NIV* ... put on fresh clothes, *REB* ... see your clothes are mended, *NEB*.

3. And let us arise, and go up to Bethel; and I will make there an altar unto God, who answered me in the day of my distress: ... who pitied me, *Fenton* ... who is answering me, *Young*.

and was with me in the way which I went: ... wherever I have gone, *NASB* ... kept me company on my journey, *Berkeley*.

4. And they gave unto Jacob all the strange gods which were in their hand, and all their earrings which were in their ears: ... they handed over, *REB*.

and Jacob hid them under the oak which was by Shechem: ... put them under the holy tree, *BB* ... buried beneath the terebinth, *Berkeley* ... at the foot, *Goodspeed* ... under, *NCB*.

5. And they journeyed: and the terror of God was upon the cities that were round about them, and they did not pursue after the sons of Jacob: ... they broke camp, *Berkeley* ... towns round about were panic-stricken, *NEB* ... terror from God was upon their neighbors, *Fenton*. ... they made no attack on, *BB*.

6. So Jacob came to Luz, which is in the land of Canaan, that is, Bethel, he and all the people that were with him.

7. And he built there an altar, and called the place El bethel: ... called the house of God Bethel, *Fenton* ... called the place the God of Beth-el, *Geneva* ... named the place Bethel, *NCB*.

because there God appeared unto him: ... revealed Himself to him, *NASB* ... he had the vision of God, *BB* ... was revealed unto him, *ASV*.

when he fled from the face of his brother: ... fleeing from his brother, *NCB*.

35:2-3. Jacob then commanded everyone with him to get rid of the foreign gods, the idols that many of them (not just Rachel) had brought with them. Also, there probably were idols among the spoils taken from Shechem. To come into the presence of a holy God, they must purify themselves and change their clothes.

This would indicate putting off the old way of life as they came before God. It meant also a new trust in God and in God alone. Then at Bethel, Jacob would build an altar to the God who had answered his cry of distress when he fled from Esau and who had fulfilled His promise to protect, provide and be with him.

35:4. When Jacob buried the idols whatever Rachel hoped to gain by stealing the teraphim (the family gods) was put aside as well. He also buried the earrings under the terebinth tree. Only free persons wore earrings. By giving them up they were humbling themselves as servants of the LORD.

35:5. When Jacob set out in obedience to God, God made a supernatural terror or shattering dismay fall on all neighboring cities, so that none pursued him. There is no evidence that Jacob ever returned to Shechem.

35:6-7. Bethel is about 20 miles south of Shechem. The city was still called Luz. Jacob went to the place where God had appeared to him, built the altar, and called the place El Bethel ("the God of God's House"). That is, he was not just coming back to God's house, but to the one true God who manifested himself at God's house.

420	435	904, 1300.141	4623, 6681	250		4322.122	1732
prep, ps 3ms	art, n mp	prep, v Qal inf con, ps 3ms	prep, *n ms*	n ms, ps 3ms	**8.**	cj, v Qal impf 3fs	pn
אֵלָיו	הָאֱלֹהִים	בְּבָרְחוֹ	מִפְּנֵי	אָחִיו		וַתָּמָת	דְּבֹרָה
'ēlâv	hā'ělōhîm	bevārchô	mippenê	'āchîw		wattāmāth	devōrāh
to him	God	in his fleeing	from the face of	his brother		and she died	Deborah

3352.553	7549	7196.222	4263, 8809	3937, 1044	8809	441
v Hiphil ptc fs	pn	cj, v Niphal impf 3fs	prep, prep	prep, pn	prep	art, n ms
מֵינֶקֶת	רִבְקָה	וַתִּקָּבֵר	מִתַּחַת	לְבֵית־אֵל	תַּחַת	הָאַלּוֹן
mêneqeth	rivqāh	wattiqqāvēr	mittachath	levêth-'ēl	tachath	hā'allôn
the nurse of	Rebekah	and she was buried	below	Bethel	under	the large tree

7410.121	8428	442	1103		7495.221	435	420, 3399	5968
cj, v Qal impf 3ms	n ms, ps 3ms	pn	pn	**9.**	cj, v Niphal impf 3ms	n mp	prep, pn	adv
וַיִּקְרָא	שְׁמוֹ	אַלּוֹן	בָּכוּת		וַיֵּרָא	אֱלֹהִים	אֶל־יַעֲקֹב	עוֹד
wayyiqōrā'	shemô	'allôn	bākhûth		wayyērā'	'ělōhîm	'el-ya'ăqōv	'ôdh
and he called	its name	Allon	Bacuth		and He appeared	God	to Jacob	again

904, 971.141	4623, 6549	782	1313.321	881		569.121, 3937
prep, v Qal inf con, ps 3ms	prep, pn	pn	cj, v Piel impf 3ms	do, ps 3ms	**10.**	cj, v Qal impf 3ms, prep, ps 3ms
בְּבֹאוֹ	מִפַּדַּן	אֲרָם	וַיְבָרֶךְ	אֹתוֹ		וַיֹּאמֶר־לוֹ
bevō'ô	mippaddan	'ărām	wayevārekh	'ōthô		wayyō'mer-lô
in his going	from Paddan	Aram	and He blessed	him		and He said to him

435	8428	3399	3940, 7410.221	8428	5968	3399	3706
n mp	n ms, ps 2ms	pn	neg part, v Niphal impf 3ms	n ms, ps 2ms	adv	pn	cj
אֱלֹהִים	שִׁמְךָ	יַעֲקֹב	לֹא־יִקָּרֵא	שִׁמְךָ	עוֹד	יַעֲקֹב	כִּי
'ělōhîm	shimekhā	ya'ăqōv	lō'-yiqqārē'	shimekhā	'ôdh	ya'ăqōv	kî
God	your name	Jacob	not it will be called	your name	again	Jacob	because

524, 3547	2030.121	8428	7410.121	881, 8428	3547
cj, pn	v Qal impf 3ms	n ms, ps 2ms	cj, v Qal impf 3ms	do, n ms, ps 3ms	pn
אִם־יִשְׂרָאֵל	יִהְיֶה	שְׁמֶךָ	וַיִּקְרָא	אֶת־שְׁמוֹ	יִשְׂרָאֵל
'im-yisrā'ēl	yihyeh	shemekhā	wayyiqōrā'	'eth-shemô	yisrā'ēl
rather Israel	it will be	your name	and He called	his name	Israel

	569.121	3937	435	603	418	8163	6759.131	7528.131
11.	cj, v Qal impf 3ms	prep, ps 3ms	n mp	pers pron	n ms	pn	v Qal impv 2ms	cj, v Qal impv 2ms
	וַיֹּאמֶר	לוֹ	אֱלֹהִים	אֲנִי	אֵל	שַׁדַּי	פְּרֵה	וּרְבֵה
	wayyō'mer	lô	'ělōhîm	'ănî	'ēl	shadday	perēh	ûrevēh
	and He said	to him	God	I	God	Almighty	be fruitful	and multiply

1504	7235	1504	2030.121	4623	4567	4623, 2604
n ms	cj, *n ms*	n mp	v Qal impf 3ms	prep, ps 2fs	cj, n mp	prep, n fd, ps 2ms
גּוֹי	וּקְהַל	גּוֹיִם	יִהְיֶה	מִמֵּךְ	וּמְלָכִים	מֵחֲלָצֶיךָ
gôy	ûqōhal	gôyim	yihyeh	mimmekh	ûmelākhîm	mēchălātsêkhā
nation	and company of	nations	it will be	from yourself	and kings	from your loins

3428.116		881, 800	866	5598.115	3937, 80	3937, 3437	3937
v Qal pf 3cp	**12.**	cj, do, art, n fs	rel part	v Qal pf 1cs	prep, pn	cj, prep, pn	prep, ps 2ms
יֵצֵאוּ		וְאֶת־הָאָרֶץ	אֲשֶׁר	נָתַתִּי	לְאַבְרָהָם	וּלְיִצְחָק	לְךָ
yētsē'û		we'eth-hā'ārets	'ăsher	nāthattî	le'avrāhām	ûlăyitschāq	lekhā
they will go out		and the land	which	I have given	to Abraham	and to Isaac	to you

5598.125	3937, 2320	313	5598.125	881, 800		6148.121
v Qal impf 1cs, ps 3fs	cj, prep, n ms, ps 2ms	adv, ps 2ms	v Qal impf 1cs	do, art, n fs	**13.**	cj, v Qal impf 3ms
אֶתְּנֶנָּה	וּלְזַרְעֲךָ	אַחֲרֶיךָ	אֶתֵּן	אֶת־הָאָרֶץ		וַיַּעַל
'ettenennāh	ûlăzar'ăkhā	'achrêkhā	'ettēn	'eth-hā'ārets		wayya'al
I will give it	and to your seed	after you	I will give	the land		and he went up

4623, 6142	435	904, 4887	866, 1744.311	882		5507.521
prep, prep, ps 3ms	n mp	prep, art, n ms	rel part, v Piel pf 3ms	prep, ps 3ms	**14.**	cj, v Hiphil impf 3ms
מֵעָלָיו	אֱלֹהִים	בַּמָּקוֹם	אֲשֶׁר־דִּבֶּר	אִתּוֹ		וַיַּצֵּב
mēʻālāv	'ĕlōhîm	bammāqôm	'ăsher-dibber	'ittô		wayyatstsēv
from beside him	God	in the place	where He had spoken	with him		and he set

3399	4838	904, 4887	866, 1744.311	882	4838	63
pn	n fs	prep, art, n ms	rel part, v Piel pf 3ms	prep, ps 3ms	*n fs*	n fs
יַעֲקֹב	מַצֵּבָה	בַּמָּקוֹם	אֲשֶׁר־דִּבֶּר	אִתּוֹ	מַצֶּבֶת	אָבֶן
ya'ăqōv	matstsēvāh	bammāqôm	'ăsher-dibber	'ittô	matstseveth	'āven
Jacob	memorial	on the place	where he had spoken	with him	memorial of	stone

8. But Deborah Rebekah's nurse died, and she was buried beneath Bethel under an oak: ... between Bethel and Alon, *Fenton* ... under the holy tree, *BB.*

and the name of it was called Allonbachuth: ... so it came to be named the Oak of Weeping, *Young.*

9. And God appeared unto Jacob again, when he came out of Padanaram, and blessed him.

10. And God said unto him, Thy name is Jacob: thy name shall not be called any more Jacob: ... shall not henceforth be called, *Darby.*

but Israel shall be thy name: and he called his name Israel: ... so he was called Israel, *NRSV* ... came to be named, *Goodspeed.*

11. And God said unto him, I am God Almighty: ... I am God all sufficient, *Geneva* ... the Ruler of all, *BB* ... El Shaddai, *Anchor.*

be fruitful and multiply; a nation and a company of nations shall be of thee: ... have increase, *BB* ... an assembly of nations, *Fenton* ... nations shall stem from you, *NAB* ... community of nations will come from you, *NIV.*

and kings shall come out of thy loins: ... proceed from, *Young* ... will come from your body, *NIV.*

12. And the land which I gave Abraham and Isaac, to thee I will give it, and to thy seed after thee will I give the land: ... the same land will I give to you and your race, *Fenton.*

13. And God went up from him in the place where he talked with him: ... then God departed, *NCB* ... then the Divine Messenger went up from him, *Fenton.*

14. And Jacob set up a pillar in the place where he talked with him, even a pillar of stone: ... erected a sacred pillar, *Goodspeed* ... a memorial stone, *Berkeley* ... a stele of stone, *Anchor* ... a standing pillar, *Young.*

and he poured a drink offering thereon, and he poured oil thereon: ... poured a libation on it, *NCB* ... anointed it with oil, *Goodspeed* ... poureth on it an oblation, *Young.*

15. And Jacob called the name of the place where God spake with him, Bethel: ... God's House, *Fenton.*

35:8. The mention of the death of Rebekah's nurse Deborah ("honeybee") shows how highly she was regarded. The great oak tree in the valley south of Bethel was called the oak of weeping because of the grief they felt.

35:9-10. The mention of the return from Paddan Aram draws attention again to the fulfillment of God's promise to bring Jacob back (28:15). God was faithful, and showed that faithfulness further by appearing to Jacob, blessing him, and confirming that his name would be Israel. Perhaps this was necessary because Jacob was not consistently acting in accordance with the name Israel.

35:11-13. God identified himself as God Almighty (El Shaddai, where *Shad* is an old word meaning "mountain" and signifying power and permanence). God then reconfirmed to Jacob that he was the heir of the promise given to Abraham and confirmed to Isaac. His physical descendants would include a nation, a community or congregation of nations (probably referring to the twelve tribes of Israel), and kings.

Though Jacob was still a resident alien in the promised land, it was really his according to God's promise and would become the actual possession of his descendants. Then God ascended visibly (to heaven, as in 17:22). This was a real visit, not just a dream or vision.

35:14-15. Again Jacob set up a stone as a memorial pillar as he had done over 20 years before. This time he poured a drink offering of wine or grape juice on it as well as oil. Again Moses notes that Jacob called the place where God talked with him, "God's house."

5445.521	6142	5447	3441.121	6142	8467		7410.121
cj, v Hiphil impf 3ms	prep, ps 3fs	n ms	cj, v Qal impf 3ms	prep, ps 3fs	n ms	**15.**	cj, v Qal impf 3ms
וַיַּסֵּךְ	עָלֶיהָ	נֶסֶךְ	וַיִּצֹק	עָלֶיהָ	שָׁמֶן		וַיִּקְרָא
wayyassēkh	ʿālêhā	nesekh	wayyitsōq	ʿālêhā	shāmen		wayyiqōrā'
and he poured out	on it	drink offering	and he poured	on it	olive oil		and he called

3399	881, 8428	4887	866	1744.311	882	8427	435	1044
pn	do, *n ms*	art, n ms	rel part	v Piel pf 3ms	prep, ps 3ms	adv	n mp	pn
יַעֲקֹב	אֶת־שֵׁם	הַמָּקוֹם	אֲשֶׁר	דִּבֶּר	אִתּוֹ	שָׁם	אֱלֹהִים	בֵּית־אֵל
ya'ăqōv	'eth-shēm	hammāqôm	'ăsher	dibber	'ittô	shām	'ĕlōhîm	bêth-'ēl
Jacob	the name of	the place	where	he spoke	with Him	there	God	Bethel

	5450.126	4623, 1044	1044	2030.121, 5968	3650, 800	3937, 971.141
16.	cj, v Qal impf 3mp	prep, pn	pn	cj, v Qal impf 3ms, adv	*n fs*, art, n fs	prep, v Qal inf con
	וַיִּסְעוּ	מִבֵּית	אֵל	וַיְהִי־עוֹד	כִּבְרַת־הָאָרֶץ	לָבוֹא
	wayyis'û	mibbēth	'ēl	wayhî-'ôdh	kivrath-hā'ārets	lāvô'
	and they pulled out	from Beth	El	and it was still	distance of the land	to go

693	3314.122	7637	7481.322	904, 3314.141
pn	cj, v Qal impf 3fs	pn	cj, v Piel impf 3fs	prep, v Qal inf con, ps 3fs
אֶפְרָתָה	וַתֵּלֶד	רָחֵל	וַתְּקַשׁ	בְּלִדְתָּהּ
'ephrāthāh	wattēledh	rāchēl	watteqash	belidhtāhh
to Ephrathah	and she gave birth	Rachel	and she was in hard labor	in her giving birth

	2030.121	904, 7481.541	904, 3314.141	569.122	3937
17.	cj, v Qal impf 3ms	prep, v Hiphil inf con, ps 3fs	prep, v Qal inf con, ps 3fs	cj, v Qal impf 3fs	prep, ps 3fs
	וַיְהִי	בְּהַקְשֹׁתָהּ	בְּלִדְתָּהּ	וַתֹּאמֶר	לָהּ
	wayhî	vehaqōshōthāhh	belidhtāhh	wattō'mer	lāhh
	and it was	in her difficult laboring	in her giving birth	and she said	to her

3314.353	414, 3486.124	3706, 1612, 2172	3937	1158		2030.121
art, v Piel ptc fs	adv, Qal juss 2fs	cj, cj, dem pron	prep, ps 2fs	n ms	**18.**	cj, v Qal impf 3ms
הַמְיַלֶּדֶת	אַל־תִּירְאִי	כִּי־גַם־זֶה	לָךְ	בֵן		וַיְהִי
hamyalledheth	'al-tîr'î	kî-gham-zeh	lākh	bēn		wayhî
the midwife	do not fear	because also this	to you	son		and it was

904, 3428.141	5497	3706	4322.153	7410.122	8428	1160
prep, v Qal inf con	n fs, ps 3fs	cj	v Qal act ptc fs	cj, v Qal impf 3fs	n ms, ps 3ms	pn
בְּצֵאת	נַפְשָׁהּ	כִּי	מֵתָה	וַתִּקְרָא	שְׁמוֹ	בֶּן־אוֹנִי
betsē'th	naphshāhh	kî	mēthāh	wattiqōrā'	shemô	ben-'ônî
in going out	her soul	because	dying woman	and she called	his name	Ben-Oni

1	7410.111, 3937	1175		4322.122	7637	7196.222
cj, n ms, ps 3ms	v Qal pf 3ms, prep, ps 3ms	pn	**19.**	cj, v Qal impf 3fs	pn	cj, v Niphal impf 3fs
וְאָבִיו	קָרָא־לוֹ	בִנְיָמִין		וַתָּמָת	רָחֵל	וַתִּקָּבֵר
we'āvîw	qārā'-lô	vinyāmîn		wattāmāth	rāchēl	wattiqqāvēr
but his father	he named him	Benjamin		and she died	Rachel	and she was buried

904, 1932	693	2000	1074	1074		5507.521	3399	4838
prep, *n ms*	pn	pers pron	pn	pn	**20.**	cj, v Hiphil impf 3ms	pn	n fs
בְּדֶרֶךְ	אֶפְרָתָה	הִוא	בֵּית	לָחֶם		וַיַּצֵּב	יַעֲקֹב	מַצֵּבָה
bedherekh	'ephrāthāh	hiw'	bêth	lāchem		wayyatstsēv	ya'ăqōv	matstsēvāh
on the way	to Ephrathah	that	Beth	lehem		and he set	Jacob	memorial

6142, 7185	2000	4838	7185, 7637	5912, 3219		5450.121
prep, n fs, ps 3fs	pers pron	*n fs*	*n fs*, pn	prep, art, n ms	**21.**	cj, v Qal impf 3ms
עַל־קְבֻרָתָהּ	הִוא	מַצֶּבֶת	קְבֻרַת־רָחֵל	עַד־הַיּוֹם		וַיִּסַּע
'al-qŏvurāthāhh	hiw'	matstseveth	qŏvurath-rāchēl	'adh-hayyôm		wayyissa'
on her tomb	it	the memorial of	the tomb of Rachel	until today		and he pulled out

3547	5371.121	164	4623, 2042	3937, 4167, 5955	22.	2030.121
pn	cj, v Qal impf 3ms	n ms, ps 3ms	prep, adv	prep, pn, pn		cj, v Qal impf 3ms
יִשְׂרָאֵל	וַיֵּט	אָהֳלֹה	מֵהָלְאָה	לְמִגְדַּל־עֵדֶר		וַיְהִי
yisrā'ēl	wayyēṯ	'āh^{e}lōh	mēhāl^{e}'āh	l^{e}migdal-'ēdher		wayhî
Israel	and he spread out	his tent	from beyond	to Migdal-Eder		and it was

904, 8331.141	3547	904, 800	2000	2050.121	7498	8311.121
prep, v Qal inf con	pn	prep, art, n fs	art, dem pron	cj, v Qal impf 3ms	pn	cj, v Qal impf 3ms
בִּשְׁכֹּן	יִשְׂרָאֵל	בָּאָרֶץ	הַהִוא	וַיֵּלֶךְ	רְאוּבֵן	וַיִּשְׁכַּב
bishkōn	yisrā'ēl	bā'ārets	hahiw'	wayyēlekh	r^{e}'ûvēn	wayyishkav
in dwelling	Israel	in the land	the that	and he went	Reuben	and he lay down

16. And they journeyed from Bethel; and there was but a little way to come to Ephrath: ... moved from Bethel, *Berkeley* ... afterwards marched from there, *Fenton* ... half a days journey of ground, *Geneva* ... yet a Kibrath of land before, *Young*.

and Rachel travailed, and she had hard labour: ... amid great pain, *NCB* ... felt the birth pangs, *Berkeley* ... suffered severe labor, *REB* ... the childing went hard with her, *Darby* ... the travailing was in peril, *Geneva*.

17. And it came to pass, when she was in hard labour, that the midwife said unto her: ... the woman who was helping her said, *BB*.

Fear not; thou shalt have this son also: ... don't be afraid for you have another son, *NIV* ... this time too you have a son, *NASB* ... be not downhearted, for this child is a son, *Fenton*.

18. And it came to pass, as her soul was in departing, (for she died) that she called his name Benoni: but his father called him Benjamin: ... Son of my Anguish, *Fenton* ... with her last breath, *Berkeley* ... then as she was about to yield up the ghost, *Geneva*.

19. And Rachel died, and was buried in the way to Ephrath, which is Bethlehem: ... on the Ephrath or Bethlehem road, *MLB* ... buried on the road, *NAB* ... at Ephrath, which is near Bethlehem, *Fenton*.

20. And Jacob set a pillar upon her grave: that is the pillar of Rachel's grave unto this day: ... erected a memorial over her grave, *NCB* ... erected a pillar, *Darby*.

21. And Israel journeyed, and spread his tent beyond the tower of Edar: ... on the other side of Migdal-eder, *NEB* ... put up his tents on the other side of the tower of the flock, *BB* ... at the encampment of, *Fenton*.

22. And it came to pass, when Israel dwelt in that land: ... in that district, *REB*.

that Reuben went and lay with Bilhah his father's concubine: ... consort, *Goodspeed* ... had connection with Bilhah his father's servant woman, *BB*.

and Israel heard it. Now the sons of Jacob were twelve: ... he was greatly offended, *NAB*.

35:16. Jacob did not stay at Bethel but moved on toward Ephrath, or Ephrathah, (Bethlehem—"House of Bread" or "Breadville," see v. 19) about 16 miles to the south. He was still living in the areas not settled by Canaanites, and had to move on seeking grass for his flocks. On the way Rachel was in hard labor.

35:17-18. In Rachel's increasingly hard labor, the midwife tried to encourage her by telling her to stop being afraid, for she was giving birth to a son. But she knew she was dying and with her last breath she named the son Ben-oni, "son of my sorrow."

Jacob, however, did not want his son to feel guilty for the death of his mother, so he changed the name to Benjamin, "son of my right hand." He wanted the boy to feel he loved him and that he was fortunate to have him.

35:19-20. Rachel was buried where she died. Jacob set up a stone memorial pillar over her grave. Moses notes that the memorial pillar was still there in his day. The building on the road to Bethlehem that is known as Rachel's tomb was built later.

35:21. Jacob is called Israel here. He must have been acting in God's will when he moved on to his next stop beyond (south of) Migdol Eder ("the watch tower of the flock," that is, for shepherds).

35:22. Reuben, Jacob's oldest son, had been influenced too much by Canaanite morals. He raped Bilhah, his father's concubine. She probably did not tell Jacob herself, but he heard of it (see 49:4). This is something to keep in mind as a reason why the chosen line did not continue through Reuben.

882, 1131	6637	1	8471.121	3547	2030.126	1158, 3399
prep, pn	*n fs*	n ms, ps	cj, v Qal impf 3ms	pn	cj, v Qal impf 3mp	*n mp*, pn
אֶת־בִּלְהָה	פִּילֶגֶשׁ	אָבִיו	וַיִּשְׁמַע	יִשְׂרָאֵל	וַיִּהְיוּ	בְנֵי־יַעֲקֹב
'eth-bilhāh	pîleghesh	'āvîw	wayyishma'	yisrā'ēl	wayyihyû	v^{e}nê-ya'ăqōv
with Bilhah	the concubine of	his father	and he heard	Israel	and they were	the sons of Jacob

8530	6461		1158	3943	1111	3399	7498	8482	4015
num	num	**23.**	*n mp*	pn	*n ms*	pn	pn	cj, pn	cj, pn
שְׁנֵים	עָשָׂר		בְּנֵי	לֵאָה	בְּכוֹר	יַעֲקֹב	רְאוּבֵן	וְשִׁמְעוֹן	וְלֵוִי
sh^{e}nêm	'āsār		b^{e}nê	lē'āh	b^{e}khôr	ya'ăqōv	r^{e}'ûvēn	w^{e}shim'ôn	w^{e}lēwî
two	ten		the sons of	Leah	the firstborn of	Jacob	Reuben	and Simeon	and Levi

3171	3551	2157		1158	7637	3231	1175
cj, pn	cj, pn	cj, pn	**24.**	*n mp*	pn	pn	cj, pn
וִיהוּדָה	וְיִשָּׂשכָר	וּזְבֻלוּן		בְּנֵי	רָחֵל	יוֹסֵף	וּבִנְיָמִן
wîhûdhāh	w^{e}yissākhār	ûz^{e}vulûn		b^{e}nê	rāchēl	yôsēph	ûvinyāmin
and Judah	and Issachar	and Zebulun		the sons of	Rachel	Joseph	and Benjamin

	1158	1131	8569	7637	1896	5503		1158
25.	cj, *n mp*	pn	*n fs*	pn	pn	cj, pn	**26.**	cj, *n mp*
	וּבְנֵי	בִלְהָה	שִׁפְחַת	רָחֵל	דָּן	וְנַפְתָּלִי		וּבְנֵי
	ûv^{e}nê	vilhāh	shiphchath	rāchēl	dān	w^{e}naphtālî		ûv^{e}nê
	and the sons of	Bilhah	the female slave of	Rachel	Dan	and Naphtali		and the sons of

2238	8569	3943	1440	862	431	1158	3399	866
pn	*n fs*	pn	pn	cj, pn	dem pron	*n mp*	pn	rel part
זִלְפָּה	שִׁפְחַת	לֵאָה	גָּד	וְאָשֵׁר	אֵלֶּה	בְּנֵי	יַעֲקֹב	אֲשֶׁר
zilpāh	shiphchath	lē'āh	gādh	w^{e}'āshēr	'ēlleh	b^{e}nê	ya'ăqōv	'ăsher
Zilpah	the female slave of	Leah	Gad	and Asher	these	the sons of	Jacob	which

3314.411, 3937	904, 6549	782		971.121	3399	420, 3437	1
v Pual pf 3ms, prep, ps 3ms	prep, pn	pn	**27.**	cj, v Qal impf 3ms	pn	prep, pn	n ms, ps
יֻלַּד־לוֹ	בְּפַדַּן	אֲרָם		וַיָּבֹא	יַעֲקֹב	אֶל־יִצְחָק	אָבִיו
yulladh-lô	b^{e}phaddan	'ărām		wayyāvō'	ya'ăqōv	'el-yitschāq	'āvîw
they were born to him	in Paddan	Aram		and he went	Jacob	to Isaac	his father

4613	7442	7442	2000	2367	866, 1513.111, 8427	80	3437
pn	pn	art, pn	pers pron	pn	rel part, v Qal pf 3ms, adv	pn	cj, pn
מַמְרֵא	קִרְיַת	הָאַרְבַּע	הִוא	חֶבְרוֹן	אֲשֶׁר־גָּר־שָׁם	אַבְרָהָם	וְיִצְחָק
mamrē'	qiryath	hā'arba'	hiw'	hevrôn	'ăsher-gār-shām	'avrāhām	w^{e}yitschāq
to Mamre	Kiriath	Arba	that	Hebron	where he sojourned there	Abraham	and Isaac

	2030.126	3219	3437	4109	8523	8470	8523		1510.121
28.	cj, v Qal impf 3mp	*n mp*	pn	*num*	n fs	cj, num	n fs	**29.**	cj, v Qal impf 3ms
	וַיִּהְיוּ	יְמֵי	יִצְחָק	מְאַת	שָׁנָה	וּשְׁמֹנִים	שָׁנָה		וַיִּגְוַע
	wayyihyû	yemê	yitschāq	m^{e}'ath	shānāh	ûsh^{e}mōnîm	shānāh		wayyighwa'
	and they were	the days of	Isaac	hundred of	years	and eighty	years		and he expired

3437	4322.121	636.221	420, 6194	2292	7884	3219
pn	cj, v Qal impf 3ms	cj, v Niphal impf 3ms	prep, n mp, ps 3ms	adj	cj, *adj*	n mp
יִצְחָק	וַיָּמָת	וַיֵּאָסֶף	אֶל־עַמָּיו	זָקֵן	וּשְׂבַע	יָמִים
yitschāq	wayyāmāth	wayyē'āseph	'el-'ammâv	zāqēn	ûs^{e}va'	yāmîm
Isaac	and he died	and he was gathered	to his people	old	and full of	days

7196.126	881	6451	3399	1158		431	8765
cj, v Qal impf 3mp	do, ps 3ms	pn	cj, pn	n mp, ps 3ms	**36:1**	cj, dem pron	*n fp*
וַיִּקְבְּרוּ	אֹתוֹ	עֵשָׂו	וְיַעֲקֹב	בָּנָיו		וְאֵלֶּה	תֹּלְדוֹת
wayyiqŏb^{e}rû	'ōthô	'ēsāw	w^{e}ya'ăqōv	bānâv		w^{e}'ēlleh	tōl^{e}dhōth
and they buried	him	Esau	and Jacob	his sons		and these	the descendants of

6451	2000	110		6451	4089.111	881, 5571	4623, 1351	3791	881, 5919
pn	pers pron	pn	**2.**	pn	v Qal pf 3ms	do, n fp, ps 3ms	prep, *n fp*	pn	do, pn
עֵשָׂו	הוּא	אֱדוֹם		עֵשָׂו	לָקַח	אֶת־נָשָׁיו	מִבְּנוֹת	כְּנָעַן	אֶת־עָדָה
'ēsāw	hû'	'ĕdhôm		'ēsāw	lāqach	'eth-nāshâv	mibb^{e}nôth	k^{e}nā'an	'eth-'ādhāh
Esau	that	Edom		Esau	he took	his wives	from the daughters of	Canaan	Adah

1351, 362	2958	881, 170	1351, 6261	1351, 6912
n fs, pn	art, pn	cj, do, pn	*n fs*, pn	*n fs*, pn
בַּת־אֵילוֹן	הַחִתִּי	וְאֶת־אָהֳלִיבָמָה	בַּת־עֲנָה	בַּת־צִבְעוֹן
bath-'êlôn	hachitî	w^{e}'eth-'āh^{e}lîvāmāh	bath-'ănāh	bath-tsiv'ôn
the daughter of Elon	the Hittite	and Oholibamah	the daughter of Anah	the daughter of Zibeon

23. The sons of Leah; Reuben, Jacob's firstborn, and Simeon, and Levi, and Judah, and Issachar, and Zebulun:

24. The sons of Rachel; Joseph, and Benjamin:

25. And the sons of Bilhah, Rachel's handmaid; Dan, and Naphtali: ... slave girl, *NEB.*

26. And the sons of Zilpah, Leah's handmaid; Gad, and Asher: these are the sons of Jacob, which were born to him in Padanaram.

27. And Jacob came unto Isaac his father unto Mamre, unto the city of Arbah, which is Hebron: ... suburban to Kiriath-Arba, *Berkeley.*

where Abraham and Isaac sojourned: ... had settled as immigrants, *Goodspeed* ... resided as aliens, *NRSV* ... pilgrimaged, *MLB* ... stayed, *NIV.*

28. And the days of Isaac were an hundred and fourscore years: ... one hundred and eighty years, *KJVII.*

29. And Isaac gave up the ghost, and died: ... gave up the spirit, *KJVII* ... expired and died, *Darby.*

and was gathered unto his people: ... was added to his people, *Fenton* ... taken to his kinsmen, *NAB.*

being old and full of days: and his sons Esau and Jacob buried him: ... of ripe age, *NASB* ... aged and satisfied with life, *Berkeley* ... at a very great age, *REB.*

36:1. Now these are the generations of Esau, who is Edom: ... this is the genealogy of Esau, *NKJV* ... the line of, *Anchor* ... the account of, *NIV* ... births of, *Young.*

2. Esau took his wives of the daughters of Canaan: ... from the women, *NIV* ... chose his wives, *Anchor* ... married the Canaanite women, *NCB.*

Adah the daughter of Elon the Hittite, and Aholibamah the daughter of Anah the daughter of Zibeon the Hivite: ... the granddaughter, *NAB* ... the son of Zibeon, *Berkeley.*

35:23-26. Jacob's 12 sons are listed her just before another geneology. The list ends with a summary statement which does not include Benjamin. He was born in Canaan, while the others were born in the plain of Aram north of the Euphrates River.

35:27. Jacob finally came home to Isaac who was still living in Mamre near Hebron, which was still called Kiriath Arba "the village of Arba," the same place where Abraham as well as Isaac often stayed. Isaac was 168 years old at this time. He lived 12 more years (until 10 years after Joseph was sold by his brothers).

35:28-29. Isaac had a full and long life of 180 years, five years longer than Abraham lived. When he died he was gathered to his people, that is, his soul went to be in paradise with Abraham and his other godly ancestors. Then Esau came and helped Jacob bury him. This marks the end of the Jacob narrative that began in 25:19. The Joseph narrative which begins in 37:2 when Joseph was seventeen years old, actually goes back to begin when Isaac was still alive.

36:1. This verse is the title of the chapter. The chapter deals with the progeny of Esau, that is of Edom. It gives a little information about Esau and then gives the names of his descendants, as well as those of Horites who joined with Esau.

After this Esau is dropped out of the record, for the chosen line did not continue through him. The chapter was important to the later Israelites in Moses' day, however, for the Edomites were their close neighbors.

36:2-3. The names of Esau's wives given here are different from those listed in 26:34 and 28:9. Some suggest that later copyists made mistakes. It is more likely that the wives had more than one name, or that Esau married additional wives.

36:4-5. Esau had five sons born in Canaan.

2433		881, 1338	1351, 3579	269	5207		3314.122
art, pn	3.	cj, do, pn	*n fs*, pn	*n fs*	pn	4.	cj, v Qal impf 3fs
הַחִוִּי		וְאֶת־בָּשְׂמַת	בַּת־יִשְׁמָעֵאל	אֲחוֹת	נְבָיוֹת		וַתֵּלֶד
hachiwwî		we'eth-bāsemath	bath-yishmā'ē'l	'ăchôth	nevāyôth		wattēledh
the Hivite		and Basemath	the daughter of Ishmael	the sister of	Nebaioth		and she gave birth

5919	3937, 6451	881, 469	1338	3314.112	881, 7756		170
pn	prep, pn	do, pn	cj, pn	v Qal pf 3fs	do, pn	5.	cj, pn
עָדָה	לְעֵשָׂו	אֶת־אֱלִיפָז	וּבָשְׂמַת	יָלְדָה	אֶת־רְעוּאֵל		וְאָהֳלִיבָמָה
'ādhāh	le'ēsāw	'eth-'ĕlîphāz	ûvāsemath	yāledhāh	'eth-re'û'ēl		we'āhelîvāmāh
Adah	for Esau	Eliphaz	and Basemath	she gave birth	Reuel		and Oholibamah

3314.112	881, 3383	881, 3390	881, 7432	431	1158	6451	866
v Qal pf 3fs	do, pn	cj, do, pn	cj, do, pn	dem pron	*n mp*	pn	rel part
יָלְדָה	אֶת־יְעִישׁ	וְאֶת־יַעְלָם	וְאֶת־קֹרַח	אֵלֶּה	בְּנֵי	עֵשָׂו	אֲשֶׁר
yāledhāh	'eth-ye'yyōsh	we'eth-ya'ălām	we'eth-qōrach	'ēlleh	benê	'ēsāw	'ăsher
she gave birth	Jeush	and Jalam	and Korah	these	the sons of	Esau	which

3314.416, 3937	904, 800	3791		4089.121	6451	881, 5571
v Pual pf 3cp, prep, ps 3ms	prep, *n fs*	pn	6.	cj, v Qal impf 3ms	pn	do, n fp, ps 3ms
יֻלְּדוּ־לוֹ	בְּאֶרֶץ	כְּנָעַן		וַיִּקַּח	עֵשָׂו	אֶת־נָשָׁיו
yullédhû-lô	be'erets	kenā'an		wayyiqqach	'ēsāw	'eth-nāshâv
they were born to him	in the land of	Canaan		and he took	Esau	his wives

881, 1158	881, 1351	881, 3725, 5497	1041	881, 4898
cj, do, n mp, ps 3ms	cj, do, n fs, ps 3ms	cj, do, *adj*, *n fp*	n ms, ps 3ms	cj, do, n ms, ps 3ms
וְאֶת־בָּנָיו	וְאֶת־בְּנֹתָיו	וְאֶת־כָּל־נַפְשׁוֹת	בֵּיתוֹ	וְאֶת־מִקְנֵהוּ
we'eth-bānâv	we'eth-benōthâv	we'eth-kol-naphshôth	bêthô	we'eth-miqōnēhû
and his sons	and his daughters	and all the souls of	his household	and his livestock

881, 3725, 966	881	3725, 7359	866	7697.111	904, 800	3791
cj, do, *adj*, n fs, ps 3ms	cj, do	*adj*, n ms, ps 3ms	rel part	v Qal pf 3ms	prep, *n fs*	pn
וְאֶת־כָּל־בְּהֶמְתּוֹ	וְאֵת	כָּל־קִנְיָנוֹ	אֲשֶׁר	רָכַשׁ	בְּאֶרֶץ	כְּנָעַן
we'eth-kol-behemtô	we'ēth	kol-qinyānô	'ăsher	rākhash	be'erets	kenā'an
and all his beasts	and	all his property	which	he acquired	in the land of	Canaan

2050.121	420, 800	4623, 6681	3399	250		3706, 2030.111	7688
cj, v Qal impf 3ms	prep, n fs	prep, *n ms*	pn	n ms, ps 3ms	7.	cj, v Qal pf 3ms	n ms, ps 3mp
וַיֵּלֶךְ	אֶל־אֶרֶץ	מִפְּנֵי	יַעֲקֹב	אָחִיו		כִּי־הָיָה	רְכוּשָׁם
wayyēlekh	'el-'erets	mippenê	ya'ăqōv	'āchîw		kî-hāyāh	rekhûshām
and he went	to land	away from	Jacob	his brother		because it was	their property

7521	4623, 3553.141	3267	3940	3310.112	800	4175
adj	prep, v Qal inf con	adv	cj, neg part	v Qal pf 3fs	*n fs*	n mp, ps 3mp
רָב	מִשֶּׁבֶת	יַחְדָּו	וְלֹא	יָכְלָה	אֶרֶץ	מְגוּרֵיהֶם
rāv	mishsheveth	yachdāw	welō'	yākhelāh	'erets	meghûrêhem
great	for dwelling	together	and not	it was able	the land of	their sojournings

3937, 5558.141	881	4623, 6681	4898		3553.121	6451
prep, v Qal inf con	do, ps 3mp	prep, *n ms*	n mp, ps 3mp	8.	cj, v Qal impf 3ms	pn
לָשֵׂאת	אֹתָם	מִפְּנֵי	מִקְנֵיהֶם		וַיֵּשֶׁב	עֵשָׂו
lāshē'th	'ōthām	mippenê	miqōnêhem		wayyēshev	'ēsāw
to support	them	on account of	their livestock		and he dwelled	Esau

904, 2098	7990	6451	2000	110		431	8765	6451
prep, *n ms*	pn	pn	pers pron	pn	9.	cj, dem pron	*n fp*	pn
בְּהַר	שֵׂעִיר	עֵשָׂו	הוּא	אֱדוֹם		וְאֵלֶּה	תֹּלְדוֹת	עֵשָׂו
behar	sē'îr	'ēsāw	hû'	'ĕdhôm		we'elleh	tōledhôth	'ēsāw
on the mountain of	Seir	Esau	he	Edom		and these	the descendants of	Esau

1	110	904, 2098	7990		431	8428	1158, 6451
n ms	pn	prep, *n ms*	pn	**10.**	dem pron	*n mp*	*n mp*, pn
אֲבִי	אֱדוֹם	בְּהַר	שֵׂעִיר		אֵלֶּה	שְׁמוֹת	בְּנֵי־עֵשָׂו
'ăvî	'ĕdhôm	behar	sē'îr		'ēlleh	shemôth	benê-'ēsāw
the father of	Edom	on the mountain of	Seir		these	the names of	the sons of Esau

469	1158, 5919	828	6451	7756	1158, 1338	828	6451
pn	*n ms*, pn	*n fs*	pn	pn	*n ms*, pn	*n fs*	pn
אֱלִיפַז	בֶּן־עָדָה	אֵשֶׁת	עֵשָׂו	רְעוּאֵל	בֶּן־בָּשְׂמַת	אֵשֶׁת	עֵשָׂו
'ĕlîphaz	ben-'ādhāh	'ēsheth	'ēsāw	re'û'ēl	ben-bāsemath	'ēsheth	'ēsāw
Eliphaz	son of Adah	the wife of	Esau	Reuel	the son of Basemath	the wife of	Esau

	2030.126	1158	469	8817	200	7101	1651	7357
11.	cj, v Qal impf 3mp	*n mp*	pn	pn	pn	pn	cj, pn	cj, pn
	וַיִּהְיוּ	בְּנֵי	אֱלִיפָז	תֵּימָן	אוֹמָר	צְפוֹ	וְגַעְתָּם	וּקְנַז
	wayyihyû	benê	'ĕlîphāz	têmān	'ômār	tsephô	wegha'ăttām	ûqŏnaz
	and they were	the sons of	Eliphaz	Teman	Omar	Zepho	and Gatam	and Kenaz

	8885	2030.112	6637	3937, 469	1158, 6451	3314.122	3937, 469
12.	cj, pn	v Qal pf 3fs	n fs	prep, pn	*n ms*, pn	cj, v Qal impf 3fs	prep, pn
	וְתִמְנַע	הָיְתָה	פִּילֶגֶשׁ	לֶאֱלִיפַז	בֶּן־עֵשָׂו	וַתֵּלֶד	לֶאֱלִיפַז
	wethimna'	hāyethāh	phîleghesh	le'ĕlîphaz	ben-'ēsāw	wattēledh	le'ĕlîphaz
	and Timna	she was	concubine	to Eliphaz	the son of Esau	and she gave birth	for Eliphaz

3. And Bashemath Ishmael's daughter, sister of Nebajoth.

4. And Adah bare to Esau Eliphaz; and Bashemath bare Reuel;

5. And Aholibamah bare Jeush, and Jaalam, and Korah: these are the sons of Esau, which were born unto him in the land of Canaan.

6. And Esau took his wives, and his sons, and his daughters, and all the persons of his house, and his cattle, and all his beasts, and all his substance, which he had got in the land of Canaan: ... all his possessions, *ASV* ... beasts of burden and all his moveable property, *MLB* ... all the chattels that he had acquired, *NEB*.

and went into the country from the face of his brother Jacob: ... a land away from his brother, *ASV* ... some distance from, *NIV*.

7. For their riches were more than that they might dwell together: ... for their property was too great, *Darby* ... so much stock, *REB*.

and the land wherein they were strangers: ... immigrants, *Berkeley* ... land of their sojournings, *ASV*.

could not bear them because of their cattle: ... support, *Goodspeed* ... land was not wide enough, *BB*.

8. Thus dwelt Esau in mount Seir: Esau is Edom: ... settled in the highlands, *NCB* ... hill country, *NIV*.

9. And these are the generations of Esau the father of the Edomites in mount Seir: ... ancestors of, *Berkeley*.

10. These are the names of Esau's sons; Eliphaz the son of Adah the wife of Esau, Reuel the son of Bashemath the wife of Esau.

11. And the sons of Eliphaz were Teman, Omar, Zepho, and Gatam, and Kenaz.

12. And Timna was concubine to Eliphaz Esau's son; and she bare to Eliphaz Amalek: these were the sons of Adah Esau's wife: ... was secondary wife to, *Fenton* ... a consort of, *Goodspeed* ... had connection with a woman, *BB*.

Eliphaz may mean "pure gold." Reuel means "friend of God." Jeush may mean "helper." Korah may mean "baldness."

36:6-8. Esau had accumulated considerable livestock. Since Esau and Jacob lived in between the towns and cities of Canaan, and since the southern part of Canaan where they were had little rainfall and insufficient grass for all their flocks, it was necessary for one of them to move on. Esau chose to move south of the Dead Sea to the hill country of Seir ("Shaggy," covered with brushwood). Esau`s other name, Edom ("Red"), is mentioned, because that is the name later given to the country.

36:9. This verse begins the account of Esau's descendants.

36:10-14. These are Esau's sons and grandsons. Some Jewish rabbis identify Eliphaz with the first of Job's three friends. His concubine Timna was a Horite (v. 22).

36:15-19. These are Esau's descendants who

881, 6222	431	1158	5919	828	6451	**13.**	431	1158	7756
do, pn	dem pron	*n mp*	pn	*n fs*	pn		cj, dem pron	*n mp*	pn
אֶת־עֲמָלֵק	אֵלֶּה	בְּנֵי	עָדָה	אֵשֶׁת	עֵשָׂו		וְאֵלֶּה	בְּנֵי	רְעוּאֵל
'eth-'ămālēq	'ēlleh	b^{e}nê	'ādhāh	'ēsheth	'ēsāw		w^{e}'ēlleh	b^{e}nê	r^{e}'û'ēl
Amalek	these	the sons of	Adah	the wife of	Esau		and these	the sons of	Reuel

5370	2313	8440	4329	431	2030.116	1158	1338
pn	cj, pn	pn	cj, pn	dem pron	v Qal pf 3cp	*n mp*	pn
נַחַת	וָזֶרַח	שַׁמָּה	וּמִזָּה	אֵלֶּה	הָיוּ	בְּנֵי	בָשְׂמַת
nachath	wāzerach	shammāh	ûmizzāh	'ēlleh	hāyû	b^{e}nê	vās^{e}math
Nahath	and Zerah	Shammah	and Mizzah	these	they were	the sons of	Basemath

828	6451	**14.**	431	2030.116	1158	170	1351, 6261
n fs	pn		cj, dem pron	v Qal pf 3cp	*n mp*	pn	*n fs*, pn
אֵשֶׁת	עֵשָׂו		וְאֵלֶּה	הָיוּ	בְּנֵי	אָהֳלִיבָמָה	בַת־עֲנָה
'ēsheth	'ēsāw		w^{e}'ēlleh	hāyû	b^{e}nê	'āh^{e}lîvāmāh	vath-'ănāh
the wife of	Esau		and these	they were	the sons of	Oholibamah	the daughter of Anah

1351, 6912	828	6451	3314.122	3937, 6451	881, 3383	881, 3390
n fs, pn	*n fs*	pn	cj, v Qal impf 3fs	prep, pn	do, pn	cj, do, pn
בַּת־צִבְעוֹן	אֵשֶׁת	עֵשָׂו	וַתֵּלֶד	לְעֵשָׂו	אֶת־יְעִישׁ	וְאֶת־יַעְלָם
bath-tsiv'ôn	'ēsheth	'ēsāw	wattēledh	l^{e}'ēsāw	'eth-y^{e}'yyôsh	w^{e}'eth-ya'ălām
the daughter of Zibeon	the wife of	Esau	and she gave birth	for Esau	Jeush	and Jalam

881, 7432	**15.**	431	444	1158, 6451	1158	469	1111
cj, do, pn		dem pron	*n mp*	*n mp*, pn	*n mp*	pn	*n ms*
וְאֶת־קֹרַח		אֵלֶּה	אַלּוּפֵי	בְנֵי־עֵשָׂו	בְּנֵי	אֱלִיפַז	בְּכוֹר
w^{e}'eth-qōrach		'ēlleh	'allûphê	v^{e}nê-'ēsāw	b^{e}nê	'ĕlîphaz	b^{e}khôr
and Korah		these	the chieftains of	the sons of Esau	the sons of	Eliphaz	the firstborn of

6451	444	8817	444	200	444	7101	444	7357
pn	n ms	pn	n ms	pn	n ms	pn	n ms	pn
עֵשָׂו	אַלּוּף	תֵּימָן	אַלּוּף	אוֹמָר	אַלּוּף	צְפוֹ	אַלּוּף	קְנַז
'ēsāw	'allûph	têmān	'allûph	'ômār	'allûph	ts^{e}phô	'allûph	qŏnaz
Esau	chieftain	Teman	chieftain	Omar	chieftain	Zepho	chieftain	Kenaz

16.	444	7432	444	1651	444	6222	431	444	469
	n ms	pn	n ms	pn	n ms	pn	dem pron	*n mp*	pn
	אַלּוּף	קֹרַח	אַלּוּף	גַּעְתָּם	אַלּוּף	עֲמָלֵק	אֵלֶּה	אַלּוּפֵי	אֱלִיפַז
	'allûph	qōrach	'allûph	ga'ăttām	'allûph	'ămālēq	'ēlleh	'allûphê	'ĕlîphaz
	chieftain	Korah	chieftain	Gatam	chieftain	Amalek	these	the chieftains of	Eliphaz

904, 800	110	431	1158	5919	**17.**	431	1158	7756	1158, 6451
prep, *n fs*	pn	dem pron	*n mp*	pn		cj, dem pron	*n mp*	pn	*n ms*, pn
בְּאֶרֶץ	אֱדוֹם	אֵלֶּה	בְּנֵי	עָדָה		וְאֵלֶּה	בְּנֵי	רְעוּאֵל	בֶּן־עֵשָׂו
b^{e}'erets	'ĕdhôm	'ēlleh	b^{e}nê	'ādhāh		w^{e}'ēlleh	b^{e}nê	r^{e}'û'ēl	ben-'ēsāw
in the land of	Edom	these	the sons of	Adah		and these	the sons of	Reuel	the son of Esau

444	5370	444	2313	444	8440	444	4329	431
n ms	pn	n ms	pn	n ms	pn	n ms	pn	dem pron
אַלּוּף	נַחַת	אַלּוּף	זֶרַח	אַלּוּף	שַׁמָּה	אַלּוּף	מִזָּה	אֵלֶּה
'allûph	nachath	'allûph	zerach	'allûph	shammāh	'allûph	mizzāh	'ēlleh
chieftain	Nahath	chieftain	Zerah	chieftain	Shammah	chieftain	Mizzah	these

444	7756	904, 800	110	431	1158	1338	828	6451
n mp	pn	prep, *n fs*	pn	dem pron	*n mp*	pn	*n fs*	pn
אַלּוּפֵי	רְעוּאֵל	בְּאֶרֶץ	אֱדוֹם	אֵלֶּה	בְּנֵי	בָשְׂמַת	אֵשֶׁת	עֵשָׂו
'allûphê	r^{e}'û'ēl	b^{e}'erets	'ĕdhôm	'ēlleh	b^{e}nê	vās^{e}math	'ēsheth	'ēsāw
the chieftains of	Reuel	in the land of	Edom	these	the sons of	Basemath	the wife of	Esau

18.	431	1158	170	828	6451	444	3383	444	3390
	cj, dem pron	*n mp*	pn	*n fs*	pn	n ms	pn	n ms	pn
	וְאֵלֶּה	בְּנֵי	אָהֳלִיבָמָה	אֵשֶׁת	עֵשָׂו	אַלּוּף	יְעוּשׁ	אַלּוּף	יַעְלָם
	we'ēlleh	bené	'āhlîvāmāh	'ēsheth	'ēsāw	'allûph	ye'ûsh	'allûph	ya'ălām
	and these	the sons of	Oholibamah	the wife of	Esau	chieftain	Jeush	chieftain	Jalam

444	7432	431	444	170	1351, 6261	828	6451
n ms	pn	dem pron	*n mp*	pn	*n fs*, pn	*n fs*	pn
אַלּוּף	קֹרַח	אֵלֶּה	אַלּוּפֵי	אָהֳלִיבָמָה	בַּת־עֲנָה	אֵשֶׁת	עֵשָׂו
'allûph	qōrach	'ēlleh	'allûphê	'āhelîvāmāh	bath-'ănāh	'ēsheth	'ēsāw
chieftain	Korah	these	the chieftains of	Oholibamah	the daughter of Anah	the wife of	Esau

19.	431	1158, 6451	431	444	2000	110	20.	431
	dem pron	*n mp*, pn	cj, dem pron	n mp, ps 3mp	pers pron	pn		dem pron
	אֵלֶּה	בְנֵי־עֵשָׂו	וְאֵלֶּה	אַלּוּפֵיהֶם	הוּא	אֱדוֹם		אֵלֶּה
	'ēlleh	venê-'ēsāw	we'ēlleh	'allûphêhem	hû'	'ĕdhôm		'ēlleh
	these	the sons of Esau	and these	their chieftains	that	Edom		these

1158, 7990	2855	3553.152	800	4014	8185	6912
n mp, pn	art, pn	*v Qal act ptc mp*	art, *n fs*	pn	cj, pn	cj, pn
בְנֵי־שֵׂעִיר	הַחֹרִי	יֹשְׁבֵי	הָאָרֶץ	לוֹטָן	וְשׁוֹבָל	וְצִבְעוֹן
venê-sē'îr	hachōrî	yōshevê	hā'ārets	lôṭān	weshôvāl	wetsiv'ôn
the sons of Seir	the Horites	the ones dwelling	the land of	Lotan	and Shobal	and Zibeon

6261	21.	1844	710	1846	431	444	2855
cj, pn		cj, pn	cj, pn	cj, pn	dem pron	*n mp*	art, pn
וַעֲנָה		וְדִשׁוֹן	וְאֵצֶר	וְדִישָׁן	אֵלֶּה	אַלּוּפֵי	הַחֹרִי
wa'ănāh		wedhishôn	we'ētser	wedhîshān	'ēlleh	'allûphê	hachōrî
and Anah		and Dishon	and Ezer	and Dishan	these	the chieftains of	the Horites

13. And these are the sons of Reuel; Nahath, and Zerah, Shammah, and Mizzah: these were the sons of Bashemath Esau's wife.

14. And these were the sons of Aholibamah, the daughter of Anah the daughter of Zibeon, Esau's wife: and she bare to Esau Jeush, and Jaalam, and Korah: ... the grand-daughter of Zibeon, *NAB.*

15. These were dukes of the sons of Esau: the sons of Eliphaz the first-born son of Esau; duke Teman, duke Omar, duke Zepho, duke Kenaz: ... chief, *Young* ... clans, *NAB* ... the chieftains, *Goodspeed* ... the princes, *KJVII.*

16. Duke Korah, duke Gatam, and duke Amalek: these are the dukes that came of Eliphaz in the land of Edom; these were the sons of Adah: ... descendants, *Berkeley.*

17. And these are the sons of Reuel Esau's son; duke Nahath, duke Zerah, duke Shammah, duke Mizzah: these are the dukes that came of Reuel in the land of Edom: these are the sons of Bashemath Esau's wife.

18. And these are the sons of Aholibamah Esau's wife; duke Jeush, duke Jaalam, duke Korah: these were the dukes that came of Aholibamah the daughter of Anah, Esau's wife.

19. These are the sons of Esau, who is Edom, and these are their dukes.

20. These are the sons of Seir the Horite, who inhabited the land; Lotan, and Shobal, and Zibeon, and Anah: ... living in that country, *BB* ... original settlers on that land, *NAB* ... inhabited the country, *Fenton* ... occupants of the land, *Anchor.*

21. And Dishon, and Ezer, and Dishan: these are the dukes of the Horites, the children of Seir in the land of Edom: ... chiefs of the rock-dwellers, *MLB.*

became tribal chiefs. Teman ("on the right hand") settled in the north part of Edom. His descendants became known for their wisdom (Jer. 49:7). Zepho was also called Zephi ("watch"). The descendants of Amalek later settled around Kadesh Barnea.

36:20-28. These are the descendants of Seir the Horite, who gave his name to the region. The Horites were remnants of the old Hurrian Empire that once dominated the Middle East. They were rather disorganized and Esau came in, brought them together, gave them leadership, and united with them with his people. They intermarried and

1158	7990	904, 800	110	22.	2030.126	1158, 4014	2855	2036
n mp	pn	prep, *n fs*	pn		cj, v Qal impf 3mp	*n mp*, pn	pn	cj, pn
בְּנֵי	שֵׂעִיר	בְּאֶרֶץ	אֱדוֹם		וַיִּהְיוּ	בְנֵי־לוֹטָן	חֹרִי	וְהֵימָם
benê	sē'îr	be'erets	'ĕdhôm		wayyihyû	venê-lôṭān	chōrî	wehêmām
the sons of	Seir	in the land of	Edom		and they were	the sons of Lotan	Hori	and Hemam

269	4014	8885	23.	431	1158	8185	6157	4651
cj, *n fs*	pn	pn		cj, dem pron	*n mp*	pn	pn	cj ,pn
וַאֲחוֹת	לוֹטָן	תִּמְנָע		וְאֵלֶּה	בְּנֵי	שׁוֹבָל	עַלְוָן	וּמָנַחַת
wa'ăchôth	lôṭān	timnā'		we'ēlleh	benê	shôvāl	'alwān	ûmānachath
and the sister of	Lotan	Timna		and these	the sons of	Shobal	Alvan	and Manahath

6072	8564	206	24.	431	1158, 6912	346	6261	2000
cj, pn	pn	cj, pn		cj, dem pron	*n mp*, pn	cj, pn	cj, pn	pers pron
וְעֵיבָל	שְׁפוֹ	וְאוֹנָם		וְאֵלֶּה	בְנֵי־צִבְעוֹן	וְאַיָּה	וַעֲנָה	הוּא
we'êvāl	shephô	we'ônām		we'ēlleh	venê-tsiv'ôn	we'ayyāh	wa'ănāh	hû'
and Ebal	Shepho	and Onam		and these	the sons of Zibeon	and Aiah	and Anah	he

6261	866	4834.111	881, 3339	904, 4198	904, 7749.141	881, 2645
pn	rel part	v Qal pf 3ms	do, art, n mp	prep, art, n ms	prep, v Qal inf con, ps 3ms	do, art, n mp
עֲנָה	אֲשֶׁר	מָצָא	אֶת־הַיֵּמִם	בַּמִּדְבָּר	בִּרְעֹתוֹ	אֶת־הַחֲמֹרִים
'ănāh	'ăsher	mātsā'	'eth-hayyēmim	bammidbār	bir'ōthô	'eth-hachmōrîm
Anah	which	he found	the hot springs	in the wilderness	in his tending	the donkeys

3937, 6912	1	25.	431	1158, 6261	1844	170
prep, pn	n ms, ps		cj, dem pron	*n mp*, pn	pn	cj, pn
לְצִבְעוֹן	אָבִיו		וְאֵלֶּה	בְנֵי־עֲנָה	דִּשֹׁן	וְאָהֳלִיבָמָה
letsiv'ôn	'āvîw		we'ēlleh	venê-'ănāh	dishōn	we'āhelîvāmāh
to Zibeon	his father		and these	the children of Anah	Dishon	and Oholibamah

1351, 6261	26.	431	1158	1844	2633	819	3622	3892
n fs, pn		cj, dem pron	*n mp*	pn	pn	cj, pn	cj, pn	cj, pn
בַּת־עֲנָה		וְאֵלֶּה	בְּנֵי	דִּישׁוֹן	חֶמְדָּן	וְאֶשְׁבָּן	וְיִתְרָן	וּכְרָן
bath-'ănāh		we'ēlleh	benê	dhîshôn	chemdān	we'eshbān	weyithrān	ûkherān
the daughter of Anah		and these	the sons of	Dishon	Hemdan	and Eshban	and Ithran	Cheran

27.	431	1158, 710	1132	2273	6368	28.	431	1158, 1846
	dem pron	*n mp*, pn	pn	cj, pn	cj, pn		dem pron	*n mp*, pn
	אֵלֶּה	בְּנֵי־אֵצֶר	בִּלְהָן	וְזַעֲוָן	וַעֲקָן		אֵלֶּה	בְנֵי־דִישָׁן
	'ēlleh	benê-'ētser	bilhān	weza'ăwān	wa'ăqān		'ēlleh	venê-dhîshān
	these	the sons of Ezer	Bilhan	and Zaavan	and Akan		these	the sons of Dishan

5995	788	29.	431	444	2855	444	4014	444
pn	cj, pn		dem pron	*n mp*	art, pn	n ms	pn	n ms
עוּץ	וַאֲרָן		אֵלֶּה	אַלּוּפֵי	הַחֹרִי	אַלּוּף	לוֹטָן	אַלּוּף
'ûts	wa'ărān		'ēlleh	'allûphê	hachōrî	'allûph	lôṭān	'allûph
Uz	and Aran		these	the chieftains of	the Horites	chieftain	Lotan	chieftain

8185	444	6912	444	6261	30.	444	1844	444	710
pn	n ms	pn	n ms	pn		n ms	pn	n ms	pn
שׁוֹבָל	אַלּוּף	צִבְעוֹן	אַלּוּף	עֲנָה		אַלּוּף	דִּשֹׁן	אַלּוּף	אֵצֶר
shôvāl	'allûph	tsiv'ôn	'allûph	'ănāh		'allûph	dishōn	'allûph	'ētser
Shobal	chieftain	Zibeon	chieftain	Anah		chieftain	Dishon	chieftain	Ezer

444	1846	431	444	2855	3937, 444	904, 800	7990
n ms	pn	dem pron	*n mp*	art, pn	prep, n mp, ps 3mp	prep, *n fs*	pn
אַלּוּף	דִּישָׁן	אֵלֶּה	אַלּוּפֵי	הַחֹרִי	לְאַלֻּפֵיהֶם	בְּאֶרֶץ	שֵׂעִיר
'allûph	dîshān	'ēlleh	'allûphê	hachōrî	le'alluphêhem	be'erets	sē'îr
chieftain	Dishan	these	the chieftains of	the Horites	to their chieftain	in the land of	Seir

31.	431	4567	866	4566.116	904, 800	110	3937, 6686
	cj, dem pron	art, n mp	rel part	v Qal pf 3cp	prep, *n fs*	pn	prep, *n mp*
	וְאֵלֶּה	הַמְּלָכִים	אֲשֶׁר	מָלְכוּ	בְּאֶרֶץ	אֱדוֹם	לִפְנֵי
	w^{e}'ēlleh	hamm^{e}lākhîm	'āsher	māl^{e}khû	b^{e}'erets	'ĕdhôm	liphnê
	and these	the kings	who	they reigned	in the land of	Edom	before

4566.141, 4567	3937, 1158	3547	32.	4566.121	904, 110	1145	1158, 1189
v Qal inf con, n ms	prep, *n mp*	pn		cj, v Qal impf 3ms	prep, pn	pn	*n ms*, pn
מְלָךְ־מֶלֶךְ	לִבְנֵי	יִשְׂרָאֵל		וַיִּמְלֹךְ	בֶּאֱדוֹם	בֶּלַע	בֶּן־בְּעוֹר
m^{e}lākh-melekh	livnê	yisrā'ēl		wayyimlōkh	be'ĕdhôm	bela'	ben-b^{e}'ôr
reigning of king	to the sons of	Israel		and he reigned	in Edom	Bela	the son of Beor

8428	6111	1899	33.	4322.121	1145	4566.121	8809
cj, *n ms*	n fs, ps 3ms	pn		cj, v Qal impf 3ms	pn	cj, v Qal impf 3ms	prep, ps 3ms
וְשֵׁם	עִירוֹ	דִּנְהָבָה		וַיָּמָת	בָּלַע	וַיִּמְלֹךְ	תַּחְתָּיו
w^{e}shēm	'îrô	dinhāvāh		wayyāmāth	bāla'	wayyimlōkh	tachtâv
and the name of	his city	Dinhabah		and he died	Bela	and he reigned	instead of him

3206	1158, 2313	4623, 1249	34.	4322.121	3206	4566.121
pn	*n ms*, pn	prep, pn		cj, v Qal impf 3ms	pn	cj, v Qal impf 3ms
יוֹבָב	בֶּן־זֶרַח	מִבָּצְרָה		וַיָּמָת	יוֹבָב	וַיִּמְלֹךְ
yôvāv	ben-zerach	mibbāts^{e}rāh		wayyāmāth	yôvāv	wayyimlōkh
Jobab	the son of Zerah	from Bozrah		and he died	Jobab	and he reigned

22. And the children of Lotan were Hori and Hemam; and Lotan's sister was Timna: ... Lotan was the ancestor of the clans of Hori and Hemam, *Good News.*

23. And the children of Shobal were these; Alvan, and Manahath, and Ebal, Shepho, and Onam: ... descendants, *NAB* ... these are the sons of, *Darby.*

24. And these are the children of Zibeon; both Ajah, and Anah: ... Zibeon's sons, *Goodspeed.*

this was that Anah that found the mules in the wilderness, as he fed the asses of Zibeon his father: ... Anah that found the warm springs, *NRSV* ... found water in the desert while he was pasturing the asses, *NAB* ... water-springs in the waste-land, *BB* ... hot springs, *NCB.*

25. And the children of Anah were these; Dishon, and Aholibamah the daughter of Anah.

26. And these are the children of Dishon; Hemdan, and Eshban, and Ithran, and Cheran.

27. The children of Ezer are these; Bilhan, and Zaavan, and Akan.

28. The children of Dishan are these; Uz, and Aran.

29. These are the dukes that came of the Horites; duke Lotan, duke Shobal, duke Zibeon, duke Anah: ... chiefs of the Horites, *Fenton* ... the Horite chiefs, *BB* ... chiefs of the rockdwellers, *Berkeley.*

30. Duke Dishon, duke Ezer, duke Dishan: these are the dukes that came of Hori: among their dukes in the land of Seir.

31. And these are the kings that reigned in the land of Edom, before there reigned any king over the children of Israel: ... over the sons of Israel, *NAB.*

32. And Bela the son of Beor reigned in Edom: and the name of his city was Dinhabah: ... with Dinhabah as his capital, *Berkeley* ... name of his chief town was, *BB* ... name of his capital was, *Goodspeed.*

33. And Bela died, and Jobab the son of Zerah of Bozrah reigned in his stead: ... succeeded to the throne, *Goodspeed* ... became king in his place, *NASB.*

together they became the Edomites. The Hebrew of verse 24 is uncertain, but "hot springs" are probably what Anah found. Hot springs are still found southeast of the Dead Sea in Edomite territory. Some Jewish commentators said Anah found mules, others said he found vipers. But these ideas may have been the result of Jewish prejudice against the Edomites.

36:29-31. The tribal chiefs among the Horites were few. The phrase, "before any Israelite king reigned" may have been added by Moses in view of God's promise (35:11) and his prophecy of kings to come (Deut. 38:36).

36:32-39. These verses contain a list of the Edomite kings with some of their relatives, cities they built and outstanding historical events.

8809	2938	4623, 800	8818		4322.121	2938
prep, ps 3ms	pn	prep, *n fs*	pn		cj, v Qal impf 3ms	pn
תַּחְתָּיו	חֻשָׁם	מֵאֶרֶץ	הַתֵּימָנִי	**35.**	וַיָּמָת	חֻשָׁם
tachtâv	chushām	mē'erets	hattêmānî		wayyāmāth	chushām
instead of him	Husham	from the land of	the Temanites		and he died	Husham

4566.121	8809	1976	1158, 946	5409.551	881, 4220	904, 7898
cj, v Qal impf 3ms	prep, ps 3ms	pn	*n ms*, pn	art, v Hiphil ptc ms	do, pn	prep, *n ms*
וַיִּמְלֹךְ	תַּחְתָּיו	הֲדַד	בֶּן־בְּדַד	הַמַּכֶּה	אֶת־מִדְיָן	בִּשְׂדֵה
wayyimlōkh	tachtâv	h^{e}dhadh	ben-b^{e}dhadh	hammakkeh	'eth-midhyān	bisdhēh
and he reigned	instead of him	Hadad	the son of Bedad	the one who struck	Midian	in the field of

4262	8428	6111	5978		4322.121	1976	4566.121
pn	cj, *n ms*	n fs, ps 3ms	pn		cj, v Qal impf 3ms	pn	cj, v Qal impf 3ms
מוֹאָב	וְשֵׁם	עִירוֹ	עֲוִית	**36.**	וַיָּמָת	הֲדָד	וַיִּמְלֹךְ
mô'āv	w^{e}shēm	'îrô	'ăwîth		wayyāmāth	h^{e}dhādh	wayyimlōkh
Moab	and the name of	his city	Avith		and he died	Hadad	and he reigned

8809	7979	4623, 5038		4322.121	7979	4566.121
prep, ps 3ms	pn	prep, pn		cj, v Qal impf 3ms	pn	cj, v Qal impf 3ms
תַּחְתָּיו	שַׂמְלָה	מִמַּשְׂרֵקָה	**37.**	וַיָּמָת	שַׂמְלָה	וַיִּמְלֹךְ
tachtâv	samlāh	mimmasrēqāh		wayyāmāth	samlāh	wayyimlōkh
instead of him	Samlah	from Masrekah		and he died	Samlah	and he reigned

8809	8062	4623, 7626	5282		4322.121	8062	4566.121
prep, ps 3ms	pn	prep, *pn*	art, n ms		cj, v Qal impf 3ms	pn	cj, v Qal impf 3ms
תַּחְתָּיו	שָׁאוּל	מֵרְחֹבוֹת	הַנָּהָר	**38.**	וַיָּמָת	שָׁאוּל	וַיִּמְלֹךְ
tachtâv	shā'ûl	mēr^{e}chōnôth	hannāhār		wayyāmāth	shā'ûl	wayyimlōkh
instead of him	Shaul	from Rehoboth of	the River		and he died	Shaul	and he reigned

8809	1204	1204	1158, 6129		4322.121	1204	1204
prep, ps 3ms	n ms	pn	*n ms*, pn		cj, v Qal impf 3ms	n ms	pn
תַּחְתָּיו	בַּעַל	חָנָן	בֶּן־עַכְבּוֹר	**39.**	וַיָּמָת	בַּעַל	חָנָן
tachtâv	ba'al	chānān	ben-'akhbôr		wayyāmāth	ba'al	chānān
instead of him	lord	Hanan	the son of Achbor		and he died	lord	Hanan

1158, 6129	4566.121	8809	1993	8428	6111	6710
n ms, pn	cj, v Qal impf 3ms	prep, ps 3ms	pn	cj, *n ms*	n fs, ps 3ms	pn
בֶּן־עַכְבּוֹר	וַיִּמְלֹךְ	תַּחְתָּיו	הֲדַר	וְשֵׁם	עִירוֹ	פָּעוּ
ben-'akhbôr	wayyimlōkh	tachtâv	h^{e}dhar	w^{e}shēm	'îrô	pā'û
the son of Achbor	and he reigned	instead of him	Hadar	and the name of	his city	Pau

8428	828	4247	1351, 4445	1351	4454	4454
cj, *n ms*	n fs, ps 3ms	pn	*n fs*, pn	*n fs*	pn	pn
וְשֵׁם	אִשְׁתּוֹ	מְהֵיטַבְאֵל	בַּת־מַטְרֵד	בַּת	מֵי	זָהָב
w^{e}shēm	'ishtô	m^{e}hêtav'ēl	bath-matrēdh	bath	mê	zāhāv
and the name of	his wife	Mehetabel	the daughter of Matred	the daughter of	Me	Zehab

	431	8428	444	6451	3937, 5121	3937, 4887
	cj, dem pron	*n mp*	*n mp*	pn	prep, n fp, ps 3mp	prep, n mp, ps 3mp
40.	וְאֵלֶּה	שְׁמוֹת	אַלּוּפֵי	עֵשָׂו	לְמִשְׁפְּחֹתָם	לִמְקֹמֹתָם
	w^{e}'ēlleh	sh^{e}môth	'allûphê	'ēsāw	l^{e}mishp^{e}chōtham	limqōmōthām
	and these	the names of	the chieftains of	Esau	to their families	to their places

904, 8428	444	8885	444	6154	444	3625		444
prep, n mp, ps 3mp	n ms	pn	n ms	pn	n ms	pn		n ms
בִּשְׁמֹתָם	אַלּוּף	תִּמְנָע	אַלּוּף	עַלְוָה	אַלּוּף	יְתֵת	**41.**	אַלּוּף
bishmōthām	'allûph	timnā'	'allûph	'alwāh	'allûph	y^{e}thēth		'allûph
by their names	chieftain	Timna	chieftain	Alvah	chieftain	Jetheth		chieftain

170	444	429	444	6616		444	7357	444	8817
pn	n ms	pn	n ms	pn	**42.**	n ms	pn	n ms	pn
אָהֳלִיבָמָה	אַלּוּף	אֵלָה	אַלּוּף	פִּינֹן		אַלּוּף	קְנַז	אַלּוּף	תֵּימָן
'āhelîvāmāh	'allûph	'ēlāh	'allûph	pînōn		'allûph	qŏnaz	'allûph	têmān
Oholibamah	chieftain	Elah	chieftain	Pinon		chieftain	Kenaz	chieftain	Teman

444	4153		444	4164	444	6123	431	444	110
n ms	pn	**43.**	n ms	pn	n ms	pn	dem pron	*n mp*	pn
אַלּוּף	מִבְצָר		אַלּוּף	מַגְדִּיאֵל	אַלּוּף	עִירָם	אֵלֶּה	אַלּוּפֵי	אֱדוֹם
'allûph	mivtsār		'allûph	magdî'ēl	'allûph	'îrām	'ēlleh	'allûphê	'ĕdhôm
chieftain	Mibzar		chieftain	Magdiel	chieftain	Iram	these	the chieftains of	Edom

3937, 4319	904, 800	273	2000	6451	1	110
prep, n mp, ps 3mp	prep, *n fs*	n fs, ps 3mp	pers pron	pn	*n ms*	pn
לְמֹשְׁבֹתָם	בְּאֶרֶץ	אֲחֻזָּתָם	הוּא	עֵשָׂו	אֲבִי	אֱדוֹם
lemōshevōthām	be'erets	'ăchuzzāthām	hû'	'ēsāw	'ăvî	'ĕdhôm
to their dwellings	in the land of	their property	that	Esau	the father of	Edom

	3553.121	3399	904, 800	4175	1	904, 800	3791
37:1	cj, v Qal impf 3ms	pn	prep, *n fs*	*n mp*	n ms, ps	prep, *n fs*	pn
	וַיֵּשֶׁב	יַעֲקֹב	בְּאֶרֶץ	מְגוּרֵי	אָבִיו	בְּאֶרֶץ	כְּנָעַן
	wayyēshev	ya'ăqōv	be'erets	meghûrê	'āvîw	be'erets	kenā'an
	and he dwelled	Jacob	in the land of	the sojournings of	his father	in the land of	Canaan

34. And Jobab died, and Husham of the land of Temani reigned in his stead: ... from the land of the Temanites, *Berkeley.*

35. And Husham died, and Hadad the son of Bedad, who smote Midian in the field of Moab, reigned in his stead: and the name of his city was Avith: ... who defeated the Midianites in the land of Moab, *Berkeley* ... defeated Midian, *NASB.*

36. And Hadad died, and Samlah of Masrekah reigned in his stead.

37. And Samlah died, and Saul of Rehoboth by the river reigned in his stead: ... on the River, *NAB* ... Euphrates river, *NASB.*

38. And Saul died, and Baalhanan the son of Achbor reigned in his stead.

39. And Baalhanan the son of Achbor died, and Hadar reigned in his stead: and the name of his city was Pau; and his wife's name was Mehetabel, the daughter of Matred, the daughter of Mezahab:. . . capital being Peor, *Goodspeed.*

40. And these are the names of the dukes that came of Esau, according to their families, after their places, by their names; duke Timnah, duke Alvah, duke Jetheth: ... individually according to their subdivisions and localities, *NAB* ... sub-tribes, *LIVB.*

41. Duke Aholibamah, duke Elah, duke Pinon,

42. Duke Kenaz, duke Teman, duke Mibzar,

43. Duke Magdiel, duke Iram: these be the dukes of Edom, according to their habitations in the land of their possession: he is Esau the father of the Edomites: ... settlements in their territorial holdings, *NIV* ... land which they possessed, *NEB* ... places in their heritage, *BB* ... in reference to their dwellings, *Young* ... land they ruled, *Berkeley.*

37:1. And Jacob dwelt wherein his father was a stranger, in the land of Canaan.

Bela ("destruction, devouring") was the first king. Husham means "haste." The name Hadad (vv. 35-36, 39) is the name of the Syrian storm god. Baal-hanan (v. 38) means "Baal is favorable." Another form of the name is Hannibal. Samlah means "garment, tunic." Shaul means "asked for." Baal-Hanan means "Baal is favorable."

36:40-43. This is a list of later tribal or clan chiefs of Edom who were descended from Esau. They gave their names to the regions where they lived. The concluding statement ends the account of Esau and his progeny.

Esau was the ancestor of the Edomites, who eventually became Idumaeans, and included Herod the Great. But he had no part in the chosen line of God's promise.

	431	8765	3399	3231	1158, 8124, 6462	8523	2030.111
2.	dem pron	*n fp*	pn	pn	*n ms*, num, num	n fs	v Qal pf 3ms
	אֵלֶּה	תֹּלְדוֹת	יַעֲקֹב	יוֹסֵף	בֶּן־שְׁבַע־עֶשְׂרֵה	שָׁנָה	הָיָה
	'ēlleh	tōl^{e}dhōth	ya'ăqōv	yôsēph	ben-sh^{e}va'-'esrēh	shānāh	hāyāh
	these	the descendants of	Jacob	Joseph	son of seven ten	year	he was

7449.151	882, 250	904, 6887	2000	5470	882, 1158	1131
v Qal act ptc ms	prep, n ms, ps 3ms	prep, art, n fs	cj, pers pron	n ms	prep, *n mp*	pn
רֹעֶה	אֶת־אֶחָיו	בַּצֹּאן	וְהוּא	נַעַר	אֶת־בְּנֵי	בִלְהָה
rō'eh	'eth-'echâv	batstsō'n	w^{e}hû'	na'ar	'eth-b^{e}nê	vilhāh
shepherd	with his brothers	with the flock	and he	servant	with the sons of	Bilhah

882, 1158	2238	5571	1	971.521	3231	881, 1745
cj, do, *n mp*	pn	*n fp*	n ms, ps	cj, v Hiphil impf 3ms	pn	do, n fs, ps 3mp
וְאֶת־בְּנֵי	זִלְפָּה	נְשֵׁי	אָבִיו	וַיָּבֵא	יוֹסֵף	אֶת־דִּבָּתָם
w^{e}'eth-b^{e}nê	zilpāh	n^{e}shê	'āvîw	wayyāvē'	yôsēph	'eth-dibbāthām
and with the sons of	Zilpah	the wives of	his father	and he brought	Joseph	word of them

7737	420, 1		3547	154.111	881, 3231	4623, 3725, 1158
adj	prep, n ms, ps 3mp	**3.**	cj, pn	v Qal pf 3ms	do, pn	prep, *adj*, n mp, ps 3ms
רָעָה	אֶל־אֲבִיהֶם		וְיִשְׂרָאֵל	אָהַב	אֶת־יוֹסֵף	מִכָּל־בָּנָיו
rā'āh	'el-'ăvîhem		w^{e}yisrā'ēl	'āhav	'eth-yôsēph	mikkol-bānâv
evil	to their father		and Israel	he loved	Joseph	more than all of his sons

3706, 1158, 2295	2000	3937	6449.111	3937	3930
prep, *n ms*, n mp	pers pron	prep, ps 3ms	cj, v Qal pf 3ms	prep, ps 3ms	*n fs*
כִּי־בֶן־זְקֻנִים	הוּא	לוֹ	וְעָשָׂה	לוֹ	כְּתֹנֶת
kî-ven-z^{e}qunîm	hû'	lô	w^{e}'āsāh	lô	k^{e}thōneth
because son of old age	he	to him	and he made	for him	tunic with sleeves of

6692		7495.126	250	3706, 881	154.111	1
n mp	**4.**	cj, v Qal impf 3mp	n mp, ps 3ms	cj, do, ps 3ms	v Qal pf 3ms	n ms, ps 3mp
פַּסִּים		וַיִּרְאוּ	אֶחָיו	כִּי־אֹתוֹ	אָהַב	אֲבִיהֶם
passîm		wayyir'û	'echâv	kî-'ōthô	'āhav	'ăvîhem
long tunic		and they saw	his brothers	that him	he loved	their father

4623, 3725, 250	7983.126	881	3940	3310.116	1744.341
prep, *adj*, n mp, ps 3ms	cj, v Qal impf 3mp	do, ps 3ms	cj, neg part	v Qal pf 3cp	v Piel inf con, ps 3ms
מִכָּל־אֶחָיו	וַיִּשְׂנְאוּ	אֹתוֹ	וְלֹא	יָכְלוּ	דַּבְּרוֹ
mikkol-'echâv	wayyisn^{e}'û	'ōthô	w^{e}lō'	yākh^{e}lû	dabb^{e}rô
more than all his brothers	and they hated	him	and not	they were able	to speak of him

3937, 8361		2593.121	3231	2573	5222.521	3937, 250
prep, n ms	**5.**	cj, v Qal impf 3ms	pn	n ms	cj, v Hiphil impf 3ms	prep, n mp, ps 3ms
לְשָׁלֹם		וַיַּחֲלֹם	יוֹסֵף	חֲלוֹם	וַיַּגֵּד	לְאֶחָיו
l^{e}shālōm		wayyachlōm	yôsēph	chălôm	wayyaggēdh	l^{e}'echâv
peaceably		and he dreamed	Joseph	dream	and he told	to his brothers

3362.526	5968	7983.141	881		569.121	420	8471.133, 5167
cj, v Hiphil impf 3mp	adv	v Qal inf con	do, ps 3ms	**6.**	cj, v Qal impf 3ms	prep, ps 3mp	v Qal impv 2mp, part
וַיּוֹסִפוּ	עוֹד	שְׂנֹא	אֹתוֹ		וַיֹּאמֶר	אֲלֵיהֶם	שִׁמְעוּ־נָא
wayyôsiphû	'ôdh	s^{e}nō'	'ōthô		wayyō'mer	'ălêhem	shim'û-nā'
and they did more	again	to hate	him		and he said	to them	listen please

2573	2172	866	2593.115		2079	601	487.352	491
art, n ms	art, dem pron	rel part	v Qal pf 1cs	**7.**	cj, intrj	pers pron	v Piel ptc mp	n fp
הַחֲלוֹם	הַזֶּה	אֲשֶׁר	חָלַמְתִּי		וְהִנֵּה	אֲנַחְנוּ	מְאַלְּמִים	אֲלֻמִּים
hachlôm	hazzeh	'ăsher	chālāmtî		w^{e}hinnēh	'ănachnû	m^{e}'all^{e}mîm	'ălummîm
the dream	the this	which	I dreamed		and behold	we	ones binding	sheaves

2. These are the generations of Jacob: ... These are births of Jacob, *Young*: ... These are the progeny of Jacob, *Fenton*: ... This is the account of Jacob, *NIV* ... the story of the descendants of Jacob, *NEB*.

Joseph, being seventeen years old, was feeding the flock with his brethren; and the lad was with the sons of Bilhah, and with the sons of Zilpah, his father's wives: ... hath been enjoying himself with his brethren, *Young*: ... his father's concubines, *Good News*: ... he was an assistant to the sons of, *NASB*.

and Joseph brought unto his father their evil report: ... and he told tales about them to their father, *REB*.

3. Now Israel loved Joseph more than all his children, because he was the son of his old age: and he made him a coat of many colours: ... ornamented tunic, *Anchor* ... long coat reaching to his feet, *Berkeley*.

4. And when his brethren saw that their father loved him more than all his brethren, they hated him, and could not speak peaceably unto him: ... and would not let him be in peace, *Fenton*.

5. And Joseph dreamed a dream, and he told it his brethren and they hated him yet the more: ... Once Joseph had a dream, which he told to his brothers, *NASB*.

6. And he said unto them, Hear, I pray you, this dream which I have dreamed: ... Let me give you the story of my dream, *BB*.

7. For, behold, we were binding sheaves in the field, and, lo, my sheaf arose, and also stood upright; and, behold, your sheaves stood round about: ... formed a ring around my sheaf, *Anchor, NASB*.

and made obeisance to my sheaf: ... and went down on the earth before mine, *BB*.

8. And his brethren said to him, Shalt thou indeed reign over us? or shalt thou indeed have dominion over us? And they hated him yet the more for his dreams, and for his words: ... domineer us, *Berkeley*

37:1-2. The account now returns to Jacob in Canaan, where Isaac was still a resident alien (without recognized property rights) and was about 170 years old at this time. The "toledoth" or the narrative of Jacob's progeny (descendants) is the 10th and final main heading of Genesis. The account centers on Joseph who is now 17 years old. At this time, the sons of Leah were the keepers of the flocks, and the sons of the concubines were the servants working under them. Joseph, though he was the son of a primary wife, was put with the sons of the concubines. He had to do the hardest work and wait on the sons of Leah. His position was perhaps because of his youth.

Joseph brought a report of evil to Jacob about what his brothers were doing, which had to do with their participation in Canaanite practices, probably including Canaanite immorality and idolatry, as the next chapter indicates. Joseph must have already developed a concern for the true worship of God and for spiritual and moral values. From what Joseph says later on, it seems he must have spoken about this to his brothers first. But they had forgotten Bethel where Jacob called for purification, and were yielding to the pressure of the pagan ways and morals around them.

37:3-4. Favoritism shouldn't be shown in families, but it often is. Jacob loved Joseph more than his brothers because he was a son of his old age. That is, he was the baby of the family, even though Benjamin was born after him. Some see this love, however, as making Joseph a type of Jesus, the Beloved of His Father (Matt. 3:17).

To show his love, Jacob made him a long-sleeved, richly-decorated, possibly many-colored, shirt-like tunic reaching to the ankles. This was something crown princes wore. Virgin daughters of kings wore a similar tunic, probably with different decorations (2 Sam. 13:18-19). What a contrast this was to the plain, sleeveless, short tunics his brothers wore while working!

Joseph, of course, could not go out in the fields and work wearing such a tunic, so he was kept home. All this special treatment must have made Joseph's brothers think their father intended to give Joseph the birthright, making him the leader and priest of the family. They became so full of hate and jealousy that they could not speak calmly or say a good word to him.

37:5. Joseph's dreams were revelations from God. Joseph, however, was young, inexperienced, and unwise. He was neither humble nor modest while announcing his dreams. Telling the dreams only made his brothers hate him more. Yet, in God's providence, the dreams and the telling of them had important effects.

37:6-7. The meaning of this dream was obvious. The sheaves of the brothers bowing down respectfully before Joseph's sheaf while his sheaf remained standing could only mean that Joseph's royal tunic had a future significance. He would rule over his brothers.

904, 8761	7898	2079	7251.112	491	1612, 5507.212	2079
prep, *sub*	art, n ms	cj, intrj	v Qal pf 3fs	n fs, ps 1cs	cj, cj, v Niphal pf 3fs	cj, intrj
בְּתוֹךְ	הַשָּׂדֶה	וְהִנֵּה	קָמָה	אֲלֻמָּתִי	וְגַם־נִצָּבָה	וְהִנֵּה
b^{e}thôkh	hassādeh	w^{e}hinnēh	qāmāh	'ălummāthî	w^{e}gham-nitstsāvāh	w^{e}hinnēh
in the middle of	the field	and behold	it rose up	my sheaf	and remained it standing	and behold

5621.127	491	8246.727	3937, 491		569.126
v Qal impf 3fp	n fp, ps 2mp	cj, v Hithpalel impf 3fp	prep, n fs, ps 1cs	**8.**	cj, v Qal impf 3mp
תְּסֻבֶּינָה	אֲלֻמֹּתֵיכֶם	וַתִּשְׁתַּחֲוֶיןָ	לַאֲלֻמָּתִי		וַיֹּאמְרוּ
th^{e}subbênāh	'ălummōthêkhem	wattishtachwênā	la'ălummāthî		wayyō'm^{e}rû
they surrounded	your sheaves	and they bowed down	to my sheaf		and they said

3937	250	4566.142	4566.123	6142	524, 5090.142	5090.123
prep, ps 3ms	n mp, ps 3ms	intrg part, v Qal inf abs	v Qal impf 2ms	prep, ps 1cp	cj, v Qal inf abs	v Qal impf 2ms
לוֹ	אֶחָיו	הֲמָלֹךְ	תִּמְלֹךְ	עָלֵינוּ	אִם־מָשׁוֹל	תִּמְשֹׁל
lô	'echâv	h^{e}mālōkh	timlōkh	'ālênû	'im-māshôl	timshōl
to him	his brothers	reigning	will you reign	over us	indeed ruling	will you rule

904	3362.526	5968	7983.141	881	6142, 2573
prep, ps 1cp	cj, v Hiphil impf 3mp	adv	v Qal inf con	do, ps 3ms	prep, n mp, ps 3ms
בָּנוּ	וַיּוֹסִפוּ	עוֹד	שְׂנֹא	אֹתוֹ	עַל־חֲלֹמֹתָיו
bānû	wayyôsiphû	'ôdh	s^{e}nō'	'ōthô	'al-chălōmōthâv
among us	and they more did	again	to hate	him	because of his dreams

6142, 1745		2593.121	5968	2573	311	5807.321	881
cj, prep, n mp, ps 3ms	**9.**	cj, v Qal impf 3ms	adv	n ms	adj	cj, v Piel impf 3ms	do, ps 3ms
וְעַל־דְּבָרָיו		וַיַּחֲלֹם	עוֹד	חֲלוֹם	אַחֵר	וַיְסַפֵּר	אֹתוֹ
w^{e}'al-d^{e}vārâv		wayyachlōm	'ôdh	chălôm	'achēr	waysappēr	'ōthô
and because of his words		and he dreamed	again	dream	another	and he reported	it

3937, 250	569.121	2079	2593.115	2573	5968	2079	8507
prep, n mp, ps 3ms	cj, v Qal impf 3ms	intrj	v Qal pf 1cs	n ms	adv	cj, intrj	art, n ms
לְאֶחָיו	וַיֹּאמֶר	הִנֵּה	חָלַמְתִּי	חֲלוֹם	עוֹד	וְהִנֵּה	הַשֶּׁמֶשׁ
l^{e}'echâv	wayyō'mer	hinnēh	chālamtî	chălôm	'ôdh	w^{e}hinnēh	hashshemesh
to his brothers	and he said	behold	I dreamed	dream	again	and behold	the sun

3507	259	6461	3676	8246.752	3937
cj, art, n ms	cj, num	num	n mp	v Hithpael ptc mp	prep, ps 1cs
וְהַיָּרֵחַ	וְאַחַד	עָשָׂר	כּוֹכָבִים	מִשְׁתַּחֲוִים	לִי
w^{e}hayyārēach	w^{e}'achadh	'āsār	kôkhāvîm	mishtachwîm	lî
and the moon	and one	ten	stars	ones bowing down	to me

	5807.321	420, 1	420, 250	1647.121, 904	1
10.	cj, v Piel impf 3ms	prep, n ms, ps 3ms	cj, prep, n mp, ps 3ms	cj, v Qal impf 3ms, prep, ps 3ms	n ms, ps
	וַיְסַפֵּר	אֶל־אָבִיו	וְאֶל־אֶחָיו	וַיִּגְעַר־בּוֹ	אָבִיו
	waysappēr	'el-'āvîw	w^{e}'el-'echâv	wayyigh'ar-bô	'āvîw
	and he reported	to his father	and to his brothers	and he rebuked him	his father

569.121	3937	4242	2573	2172	866	2593.113
cj, v Qal impf 3ms	prep, ps 3ms	intrg	art, n ms	art, dem pron	rel part	v Qal pf 2ms
וַיֹּאמֶר	לוֹ	מָה	הַחֲלוֹם	הַזֶּה	אֲשֶׁר	חָלָמְתָּ
wayyō'mer	lô	māh	hachlôm	hazzeh	'ăsher	chālām^{e}ttā
and he said	to him	what	the dream	the this	which	you dreamed

971.142	971.120	603	525	250	3937, 8246.741
intrg part, v Qal inf abs	v Qal impf 1cp	pers pron	cj, n fs, ps 2ms	cj, n mp, ps 2ms	prep, v Hithpalpel inf con
הֲבוֹא	נָבוֹא	אֲנִי	וְאִמְּךָ	וְאַחֶיךָ	לְהִשְׁתַּחֲוֺת
h^{e}vô'	nāvô'	'ănî	w^{e}'imm^{e}khā	w^{e}'achêkhā	l^{e}hishtachwôth
coming	will we come	I	and your mother	and your brothers	to bow down

3937 prep, ps 2ms לְךָ l^{e}kha to you	800 n fs אַרְצָה 'ārtsāh to the earth	**11.**	7349.326, 904 cj, v Piel impf 3mp, prep, ps 3ms וַיְקַנְאוּ־בוֹ wayqan'û-vô and they were jealous of him	250 n mp, ps 3ms אֶחָיו 'echâv his brothers	1 cj, n ms, ps 3ms וְאָבִיו w^{e}'āvîw but his father	8490.111 v Qal pf 3ms שָׁמַר shāmar he kept
881, 1745 do, art, n ms אֶת־הַדָּבָר 'eth-haddāvār the matter	**12.**	2050.126 cj, v Qal impf 3mp וַיֵּלְכוּ wayyēl^{e}khû and they went	250 n mp, ps 3ms אֶחָיו 'echâv his brothers	3937, 7749.141 prep, v Qal inf con לִרְעוֹת lir'ôth to shepherd	881, 6887 do, *n fs* אֶת־צֹאן 'eth-tsō'n the flocks of	1 n ms, ps 3mp אֲבִיהֶם 'ǎvîhem their father
904, 8328 prep, pn בִּשְׁכֶם bishkhem by Shechem	**13.**	569.121 cj, v Qal impf 3ms וַיֹּאמֶר wayyō'mer and he said	3547 pn יִשְׂרָאֵל yisrā'ēl Israel	420, 3231 prep, pn אֶל־יוֹסֵף 'el-yôsēph to Joseph	3940 intrg part, neg part הֲלוֹא h^{e}lô' are not	250 n mp, ps 2ms אַחֶיךָ 'achêkhā your brothers

and lord it over us, *NEB* ... be our master, *Anchor.*

9. And he dreamed yet another dream, and told it his brethren, and said, Behold, I have dreamed a dream more; and, behold, the sun and the moon and the eleven stars made obeisance to me: ... which he told to his father and his brothers, *NEB* ... came and did homage to me, *Fenton.*

10 And he told it to his father, and to his brethren: and his father rebuked him: ... took him to task, *NEB, REB* ... reproved him, *NASB, Fenton, NCB* ... protesting, *BB.*

and said unto him, What is this dream that thou hast dreamed? Shall I and thy mother and thy brethren indeed come to bow down ourselves to thee to the earth?: ... bow down to the ground before you, *NIV, NRSV.*

11. And his brethren envied him: ... wrought up against him, *NASB* ... resentful, *Berkeley* ... jealous, *NEB* ... zealous against him, Young **but his father observed the saying** ... did not forget, *NEB* ... kept the matter in mind, *NKJV* ... kept the saying in mind, *NASB, RSV, ASV.*

12. And his brethren went to feed their father's flock in Shechem: ... take care of, *Good News* ... keep watch, *BB.*

13. And Israel said unto Joseph, Do not thy brethren feed the flock in Shechem? And he said to him, Here am I: ... with the flock, *BB* ...

37:8. Joseph's brothers rejected the idea. Their reply was sarcastic. Surely, this young brother could not possibly reign over them or even rule among them. So they hated him more, not only because of his prophetic dreams, but because of his words. That is, the way Joseph told the dream exuded his self-importance.

37:9. A second dream emphasized the same theme, except this time the sun. moon, and 11 stars included Benjamin, Jacob, and Leah. They were bowing down repeatedly to him. He reported this in detail, probably with relish, to his brothers.

37:10. Then he told the details of the dream again to his father with his brothers present. In those days, family respect was great. Neither parents, nor older brothers would ever bow down to young children. Jacob probably felt righteously indignant and sharply rebuked Joseph, probably even yelling at him, as the Hebrew may mean. His words imply that in no way would Jacob and Leah or the brothers ever bow down to Joseph. Here Leah is called Joseph's mother. After the death of Rachel, Leah became the mother of all of Jacob's children.

37:11. The dream only stirred the jealousy of Joseph's brothers, but his father kept the matter in mind. This means he kept thinking it over and did not forget it. God had given dreams to Jacob, and those dreams were fulfilled. Though nothing in Joseph's dreams specifically indicated they were from God, the fact that he had two dreams with the same theme surely meant they were significant.

37:12. It is still common for Bedouin shepherds in that land to move northward as the summer progresses, for there is more rain and better water supply the further north one travels. Joseph's brothers took Jacob's flocks to the area of Shechem, about 50 miles north of Hebron. The ruins of Shechem are just southeast of the modern town of Nablus.

7749.152	904, 8328	2050.131	8365.125	420	569.121
v Qal act ptc mp	prep, pn	v Qal impv 2ms	cj, v Qal impf 1cs, ps 2ms	prep, ps 3mp	cj, v Qal impf 3ms
רֹעִים	בִּשְׁכֶם	לְכָה	וְאֶשְׁלָחֲךָ	אֲלֵיהֶם	וַיֹּאמֶר
rō'îm	bishkhem	l^{e}khāh	w^{e}'eshlāchăkhā	'ălêhem	wayyō'mer
shepherding	by Shechem	go	and I will send you	to them	and he said

3937	2079		569.121	3937	2050.131, 5167	7495.131	881, 8361
prep, ps 3ms	intrj, ps 1cs	**14.**	cj, v Qal impf 3ms	prep, ps 3ms	v Qal impv 2ms, part	v Qal impv 2ms	do, *n ms*
לוֹ	הִנֵּנִי		וַיֹּאמֶר	לוֹ	לֶךְ־נָא	רְאֵה	אֶת־שְׁלוֹם
lô	hinnēnî		wayyō'mer	lô	lekh-nā'	r^{e}'ēh	'eth-sh^{e}lôm
to him	behold I		and he said	to him	go please	see	the welfare of

250	881, 8361	6887	8178.531	1745	8365.121
n mp, ps 2ms	cj, do, *n ms*	art, n fs	cj, v Hiphil impv 2ms, ps 1cs	n ms	cj, v Qal impf 3ms, ps 3ms
אַחֶיךָ	וְאֶת־שְׁלוֹם	הַצֹּאן	וַהֲשִׁבֵנִי	דָּבָר	וַיִּשְׁלָחֵהוּ
'achêkhā	w^{e}'eth-sh^{e}lôm	hatstsō'n	wahshivēnî	dāvār	wayyishlāchēhû
your brothers	and welfare of	the flocks	and bring me	word	and he sent him

4623, 6231	2367	971.121	8328		4834.121	382	2079
prep, *n ms*	pn	cj, v Qal impf 3ms	pn	**15.**	cj, v Qal impf 3ms, ps 3ms	n ms	cj, intrj
מֵעֵמֶק	חֶבְרוֹן	וַיָּבֹא	שְׁכֶמָה		וַיִּמְצָאֵהוּ	אִישׁ	וְהִנֵּה
mē'ēmeq	chevrôn	wayyāvō'	sh^{e}khemāh		wayyimtsā'ēhû	'îsh	w^{e}hinnēh
from the valley of	Hebron	and he went	to Shechem		and he found him	man	and behold

8912.151	904, 7898	8068.121	382	3937, 569.141	4242, 1272.323
v Qal act ptc ms	prep, art, n ms	cj, v Qal impf 3ms, ps 3ms	art, n ms	prep, v Qal inf con	intrg, v Piel impf 2ms
תֹעֶה	בַּשָּׂדֶה	וַיִּשְׁאָלֵהוּ	הָאִישׁ	לֵאמֹר	מַה־תְּבַקֵּשׁ
thō'eh	bassādheh	wayyish'ālēhû	hā'îsh	lē'mōr	mah-t^{e}vaqqēsh
wandering	in the field	and he asked him	the man	saying	what you are seeking

	569.121	881, 250	609	1272.351	5222.531, 5167	3937
16.	cj, v Qal impf 3ms	do, n mp, ps 1cs	pers pron	v Piel ptc ms	v Hiphil impv 2ms, part	prep, ps 1cs
	וַיֹּאמֶר	אֶת־אַחַי	אָנֹכִי	מְבַקֵּשׁ	הַגִּידָה־נָּא	לִי
	wayyō'mer	'eth-'achay	'ānōkhî	m^{e}vaqqēsh	haggîdhāh-nā'	lî
	and he said	my brothers	I	seeking	tell please	to me

381	2062	7749.152		569.121	382	5450.116	4623, 2172
adv	pers pron	v Qal act ptc mp	**17.**	cj, v Qal impf 3ms	art, n ms	v Qal pf 3cp	prep, dem pron
אֵיפֹה	הֵם	רֹעִים		וַיֹּאמֶר	הָאִישׁ	נָסְעוּ	מִזֶּה
'êphōh	hēm	rō'îm		wayyō'mer	hā'îsh	nās^{e}'û	mizzeh
where	they	shepherding		and he said	the man	they pulled out	from this

3706	8471.115	569.152	2050.120	1948	2050.121	3231	313
cj	v Qal pf 1cs	v Qal act ptc mp	v Qal impf 1cp	pn	cj, v Qal impf 3ms	pn	adv
כִּי	שָׁמַעְתִּי	אֹמְרִים	נֵלְכָה	דֹּתָיְנָה	וַיֵּלֶךְ	יוֹסֵף	אַחַר
kî	shāma'ätî	'ōm^{e}rîm	nēl^{e}khāh	dōthāy^{e}nāh	wayyēlekh	yôsēph	'achar
because	I heard	ones saying	we will go	to Dothan	and he went	Joseph	after

250	4834.121	904, 1948		7495.126	881	4623, 7632
n mp, ps 3ms	cj, v Qal impf 3ms, ps 3mp	prep, pn	**18.**	cj, v Qal impf 3mp	do, ps 3ms	prep, adj
אֶחָיו	וַיִּמְצָאֵם	בְּדֹתָן		וַיִּרְאוּ	אֹתוֹ	מֵרָחֹק
'echâv	wayyimtsā'ēm	b^{e}dhōthān		wayyir'û	'ōthô	mērāchōq
his brothers	and he found them	in Dothan		and they saw	him	from far

904, 3071	7414.121	420	5417.726	881	3937, 4322.541
cj, prep, adv	v Qal impf 3ms	prep, ps 3mp	cj, v Hithpael impf 3mp	do, ps 3ms	prep, v Hiphil inf con, ps 3ms
וּבְטֶרֶם	יִקְרַב	אֲלֵיהֶם	וַיִּתְנַכְּלוּ	אֹתוֹ	לַהֲמִיתוֹ
ûv^{e}terem	yiqŏrav	'ălêhem	wayyithnakk^{e}lû	'ōthô	lahmîthô
and before	he came near	to them	and they conspired against	him	to kill him

19.

569.126	382	420, 250	2079	1196	2573	2045	971.151
cj, v Qal impf 3mp	n ms	prep, n ms, ps 3ms	intrj	*n ms*	art, n mp	pron	v Qal act ptc ms
וַיֹּאמְרוּ	אִישׁ	אֶל־אָחִיו	הִנֵּה	בַּעַל	הַחֲלֹמוֹת	הַלָּזֶה	בָּא
wayyō'm^{e}rû	'îsh	'el-'āchîw	hinnēh	ba'al	hachlōmôth	hallāzeh	bā'
and they said	each	to his brother	behold	the lord of	the dreams	this	coming

20.

6498	2050.133	2103.120	8390.120	904, 259
cj, adv	v Qal impv 2mp	cj, v Qal impf 1cp, ps 3ms	cj, v Qal impf 1cp, ps 3ms	prep, *num*
וְעַתָּה	לְכוּ	וְנַהַרְגֵהוּ	וְנַשְׁלִכֵהוּ	בְּאַחַד
w^{e}'attāh	l^{e}khû	w^{e}nahargēhû	w^{e}nashlikhēhû	b^{e}'achadh
and now	come	and we will kill him	and we will throw him down	in one of

come, and I will send thee unto them.

14. And he said to him, Go, I pray thee, see whether it be well with thy brethren, and well with the flocks; and bring me word again. So he sent him out of the vale of Hebron, and he came to Shechem: ... They had gone, however, from the vale of Hebron, and removed to Shekhem, *Fenton.*

15. And a certain man found him, and, behold, he was wandering in the field: and the man asked him, saying, What seekest thou?: ... wandering in the country, *Darby* ... wandering in an open country, *REB* ... meandering, *Berkeley.*

16. And he said, I seek my brethren: tell me, I pray thee, where they feed their flocks: ... herding the flock, *REB.*

17. And the man said, They are departed hence; for I heard them say, Let us go to Dothan. And Joseph went after his brethren, and found them in Dothan: ... Let us go to the Two Wells, *Fenton.*

18. And when they saw him afar off, even before he came near unto them, they conspired against him to slay him: ... plotted, *NAB.*

19. And they said one to another, Behold, this dreamer cometh: ... that master dreamer, *NAB* ... master of dreams, *Berkeley* ... My Lord, the Dreamer, *Fenton.*

20. Come now therefore, and let us slay him, and cast him into some pit: ... cistern, *NAB, NCB, RSV* ... holes, *BB.*

and we will say, Some evil beast hath devoured him: and we shall see what will become of his

37:13-14. Jacob is called Israel here. The name may indicate that what he was doing was in the plan of God, though he did not know it at the time. Some see Israel's sending Joseph to his brothers as a parallel of the Heavenly Father sending Jesus to the nation of Israel. Jacob's concern over the health and welfare of his sons and his flocks was commendable. Jacob wanted Joseph to bring a full report, but he did not realize the depth of the brothers' hatred.

37:15-16. Arriving at Shechem, Joseph did not find his brothers. A man saw him wandering around in the open country around Shechem and asked him what he was looking for. Joseph politely asked the man to tell him where his brothers were shepherding.

37:17. The man told Joseph he heard them say they were going to Dothan. Dothan ("twin wells") is 12 miles north of Shechem on a hill surrounded by a flat, fertile valley. Shepherds from the Hebron area still come to Dothan and stop there to enjoy its wonderful water supply. I have seen caravans and camel trains stop there also. Joseph found his brothers there.

37:18. When the brothers saw Joseph in the distance, they probably recognized him easily by the long-sleeved, fancy tunic he was wearing. It reminded them of the dreams and perhaps of Joseph's superior airs, and of his condemnation of their sins. Immediately they made him the object of a knavish, crafty, murderous conspiracy. Because of the hatred of Joseph, they were already murderers in their hearts (1 John 3:15).

37:19-20. With contemptuous mockery of the dreams God had given Joseph, they called him the "master" or lord of dreams. They may have meant this one who in his dreams is master or lord over us. They planned to murder him and throw him down into one of the cisterns which caught the runoff from the rains and were commonly located at the bottom of the hills. These cisterns had narrow mouths covered by a large rock and were pear-shaped, so it would be impossible to climb out of them. The brothers would say some evil wild animal had eaten him. Then they would see what would become of his dreams. They were still being sarcastic. Notice that God was not considered in any of their plans.

4242, 2030.126	7495.120	404.112	7750	2516	569.120	988
intrg, v Qal impf 3mp	cj, v Qal impf 1cp	v Qal pf 3fs, ps 3ms	n fs	n fs	cj, v Qal impf 1cp	art, n mp
מַה־יִּהְיוּ	וְנִרְאֶה	אֲכָלָתְהוּ	רָעָה	חַיָּה	וְאָמַרְנוּ	הַבֹּרוֹת
mah-yihyû	w^{e}nir'eh	'ăkhālāth^{e}hû	rā'āh	chayyāh	w^{e}'āmarnû	habbōrôth
what they will become	and we will see	it ate him	evil	animal	and we will say	the cisterns

569.121	4623, 3135	5522.521	7498	8471.121		2573
cj, v Qal impf 3ms	prep, n fs, ps 3mp	cj, v Hiphil impf 3ms, ps 3ms	pn	cj, v Qal impf 3ms		n mp, ps 3ms
וַיֹּאמֶר	מִיָּדָם	וַיַּצִּלֵהוּ	רְאוּבֵן	וַיִּשְׁמַע	**21.**	חֲלֹמֹתָיו
wayyō'mer	miyyādhām	wayyatstsilēhû	r^{e}'ûvēn	wayyishma'		chălōmōthâv
and he said	from their hand	and he rescued him	Reuben	and he heard		his dreams

7498	420	569.121		5497	5409.520	3940
pn	prep, ps 3mp	cj, v Qal impf 3ms		n fs	v Hiphil impf 1cp, ps 3ms	neg part
רְאוּבֵן	אֲלֵהֶם	וַיֹּאמֶר	**22.**	נָפֶשׁ	נַכֶּנּוּ	לֹא
r^{e}'ûvēn	'ălēhem	wayyō'mer		nāphesh	nakkennû	lō'
Reuben	to them	and he said		life	we will strike down	not

866	2172	420, 988	881	8390.533	414, 8581.128, 1879
rel part	art, dem pron	prep, art, n ms	do, ps 3ms	v Hiphil impv 2mp	adv, v Qal impf 2mp, n ms
אֲשֶׁר	הַזֶּה	אֶל־הַבּוֹר	אֹתוֹ	הַשְׁלִיכוּ	אַל־תִּשְׁפְּכוּ־דָם
'ăsher	hazzeh	'el-habbôr	'ōthô	hashlîkhû	'al-tishp^{e}khû-dhām
which	the this	into the cistern	him	throw down	do not shed blood

881	5522.541	3937, 4775	420, 8365.128, 904	3135	904, 4198
do, ps 3ms	v Hiphil inf con	prep, prep	adv, v Qal juss 2mp, prep, ps 3ms	cj, n fs	prep, art, n ms
אֹתוֹ	הַצִּיל	לְמַעַן	אַל־תִּשְׁלְחוּ־בוֹ	וְיָד	בַּמִּדְבָּר
'ōthô	hatstsîl	l^{e}ma'an	'al-tishl^{e}chû-vô	w^{e}yādh	bammidhbār
him	to rescue	in order	do not put forth on him	but hand	in the wilderness

3626, 866, 971.111	2030.121		420, 1	3937, 8178.541	4623, 3135
prep, rel part, v Qal pf 3ms	cj, v Qal impf 3ms		prep, n ms, ps 3ms	prep, v Hiphil inf con, ps 3ms	prep, n fs, ps 3mp
כַּאֲשֶׁר־בָּא	וַיְהִי	**23.**	אֶל־אָבִיו	לַהֲשִׁיבוֹ	מִיָּדָם
ka'ăsher-bā'	wayhî		'el-'āvîw	lahshîvô	miyyādhām
when he came	and it was		to his father	to bring him back	from their hand

881, 3930	881, 3930	881, 3231	6838.526	420, 250	3231
do, *n fs*	do, n fs, ps 3ms	do, pn	cj, v Hiphil impf 3mp	prep, n ms, ps 3ms	pn
אֶת־כְּתֹנֶת	אֶת־כֻּתָּנְתּוֹ	אֶת־יוֹסֵף	וַיַּפְשִׁיטוּ	אֶל־אֶחָיו	יוֹסֵף
'eth-k^{e}thōneth	'eth-kuttāntô	'eth-yôsēph	wayyaphshîṭû	'el-'echâv	yôsēph
the tunic with sleeves of	his tunic	Joseph	that they stripped off	to his brothers	Joseph

881	8390.526	4089.126		6142	866	6692
do, ps 3ms	v Hiphil impf 3mp	cj, v Qal impf 3mp, ps 3ms		prep, ps 3ms	rel part	art, n mp
אֹתוֹ	וַיַּשְׁלִכוּ	וַיִּקָּחֻהוּ	**24.**	עָלָיו	אֲשֶׁר	הַפַּסִּים
'ōthô	wayyashlikhû	wayyiqqāchuhû		'ālâv	'ăsher	happassîm
him	and they threw down	and they took him		on him	which	the long tunic

3553.126		4448	904	375	7673	988	988
cj, v Qal impf 3cp		n mp	prep, ps 3ms	*sub*	adj	cj, art, n ms	art, n ms
וַיֵּשְׁבוּ	**25.**	מָיִם	בּוֹ	אֵין	רֵק	וְהַבּוֹר	הַבֹּרָה
wayyēsh^{e}vû		māyim	bô	'ên	rēq	w^{e}habbôr	habbōrāh
and they sat down		waters	in it	there was not	empty	and the cistern	to the cistern

759	2079	7495.126	6084	5558.126	3937, 404.141, 4035
n fs	cj, intrj	cj, v Qal impf 3mp	n fd, ps 3mp	cj, v Qal impf 3mp	prep, v Qal inf con, n ms
אֹרְחַת	וְהִנֵּה	וַיִּרְאוּ	עֵינֵיהֶם	וַיִּשְׂאוּ	לֶאֱכָל־לֶחֶם
'ōr^{e}chath	w^{e}hinnēh	wayyir'û	'ênêhem	wayyis'û	le'ĕkhāl-lechem
the caravan of	and behold	and they saw	their eyes	and they lifted up	to eat bread

3580	971.153	4623, 1609	1622	5558.152	5407	7159
pn	v Qal act ptc fs	prep, pn	cj, n mp, ps 3mp	v Qal act ptc mp	n fs	cj, n ms
יִשְׁמְעֵאלִים	בָּאָה	מִגִּלְעָד	וּגְמַלֵּיהֶם	נֹשְׂאִים	נְכֹאת	וּצְרִי
yishm^{e}'ē'lîm	bā'āh	miggil'ādh	ûgh^{e}mallêhem	nōs^{e}'îm	n^{e}khō'th	ût^{e}srî
Ishmaelites	coming	from Gilead	and their camels	bearing	spices	and balm

4045	2050.152	3937, 3495.541	4875		569.121	3171	420, 250
cj, n ms	v Qal act ptc mp	prep, v Hiphil inf con	pn	**26.**	cj, v Qal impf 3ms	pn	prep, n ms, ps 3ms
וָלֹט	הוֹלְכִים	לְהוֹרִיד	מִצְרָיְמָה		וַיֹּאמֶר	יְהוּדָה	אֶל־אֶחָיו
wālōṯ	hôl^{e}khîm	l^{e}hôrîdh	mitsrāymāh		wayyō'mer	y^{e}hûdhāh	'el-'echâv
and myrrh	going	to go down	to Egypt		and he said	Judah	to his brothers

dreams: ... wild, *Anchor, NEB* ... ferocious, *NIV* ... and we see what his dreams are, *Young.*

21. And Reuben heard it, and he delivered him out of their hands; and said, Let us not kill him: ... tried to save (rescue) him, *Goodspeed, NIV* ... smite the life, *Young.*

22. And Reuben said unto them, Shed no blood, : ... do not put him to a voilent death, *BB,*

but cast him into this pit that is in the wilderness: ... desert-pit, Berkeley,... in the desert, *NIV, NASB, Anchor.*

and lay no hand upon him; that he might rid him out of their hands, to deliver him to his father again. ...do not do him injury, *REB* ... they should not stab him, *Fenton* ... restore him, *Goodspeed, NASB, RSV.*

23. And it came to pass, when Joseph was come unto his brethren, that they stript Joseph out of his coat, his coat of many colours that was on him: ... ornamented tunic, *Anchor* ... long sleeved robe, *NEB, Fenton* ... long tunic, *NASB, NCB* ... coat, the princely robe, *Berkeley* ... long robe with (full) sleeves, *REB, RSV, NRSV* ... tunic of many colors, *NKJV* ... richly ornamented robe, *NIV.*

24. And they took him, and cast him into a pit: and the pit was empty, there was no water in it: ... cistern, *NCB, NASB, REB* ... hole, *BB* ... empty well, *Fenton.*

25. And they sat down to eat bread: and they lifted up their eyes and looked, and, behold, a company of Ishmeelites came from Gilead with their camels bearing spicery and balm and myrrh, going to carry it down to Egypt: ... with spices and perfumes, *BB* ... camels carrying gum, balm, and resin, *NRSV* ... and laudanum (ladanum), *Goodspeed, Anchor* ... tragacanth, and galsam, and ladanum, *Darby* ... tragacanth, *REB, NEB* ... nuts, *Fenton.*

37:21-22. Reuben was not in on the conspiracy. When he heard about it, he rescued Joseph in advance by saying strongly "We will not take life," and adding, "Let us not shed blood."

Then, as the elder brother, he commanded them to throw Joseph in a nearby cistern in the wilderness (that is, in the uninhabited area between towns), without putting a hand on him, that is to harm him physically.

Reuben, as the oldest of the brothers, also must have had an understanding of how his father would feel. His secret purpose was to rescue Joseph and take him back to his father, but that would not have been a step toward the fulfillment of Joseph's dreams.

37:23-24. As soon as Joseph arrived, his brothers stripped off the hated long tunic and threw him into the cistern. Fortunately, it was far enough along in the rainless summer, so the cistern was dry. Genesis 42:21 lets us know that Joseph did not take this calmly. He begged them to let him live, but they turned a deaf ear and had no mercy.

37:25. Since bread was part of every meal, eating bread means to eat a meal. Thus, while the brothers were enjoying a meal, they saw an Ishmaelite caravan coming from Gilead, the rugged hills east of the Jordan River. The caravan was heading for Egypt. Their camels were carrying spices (probably gum tragacanth, from a bush in the pea family), balm (mastic, a resin from the mastic tree, *Pistacia lenticus*), and Myrrh (*labdanum*, a soft gum resin from the rockrose, *Cistus*). These gums and resins were used by Egyptians for embalming or for medicine.

37:26-27. Judah took the leadership here and suggested there would be no profit in killing Joseph and concealing his blood. He realized that throwing Joseph in the cistern made them just as guilty of murder as if they had killed him outright. He urged the brothers to sell Joseph to the Ishmaelites. He was their brother, their own flesh, and they should not be guilty of killing him. If they sold him to the Ishmaelites, they would not be guilty of laying a hand on him. The brothers listened (and agreed).

4242, 1240	3706	2103.120	881, 250	3803.319	881, 1879		2050.133
intrg, n ms	cj	v Qal impf 1cp	do, n ms, ps 1cp	cj, v Piel pf 1cp	do, n ms, ps 3ms	**27.**	v Qal impv 2mp
מַה־בֶּצַע	כִּי	נַהֲרֹג	אֶת־אָחִינוּ	וְכִסִּינוּ	אֶת־דָּמוֹ		לְכוּ
mah-betsa‘	kî	nahrōgh	'eth-'āchînû	wekhissînû	'eth-dāmô		lekhû
what profit	that	we kill	our brother	and we conceal	his blood		come

4513.120	3937, 3580	3135	414, 2030.122, 904	3706, 250
cj, v Qal impf 1cp, ps 3ms	prep, art, pn	cj, n fs, ps 1cp	adv, v Qal impf 3fs, prep, ps 3ms	cj, n ms, ps 1cp
וְנִמְכְּרֶנּוּ	לַיִּשְׁמְעֵאלִים	וְיָדֵנוּ	אַל־תְּהִי־בוֹ	כִּי־אָחִינוּ
wenimkerennû	layyishme‘ē'lîm	weyādhēnû	'al-tehî-vô	kî-'āchînû
and we will sell him	to the Ishmaelites	but our hand	not it will be on him	because our brother

1340	2000	8471.126	250		5882.126	596	4226
n ms, ps 1cp	pers pron	cj, v Qal impf 3mp	n mp, ps 3ms	**28.**	cj, v Qal impf 3mp	n mp	pn
בְשָׂרֵנוּ	הוּא	וַיִּשְׁמְעוּ	אֶחָיו		וַיַּעַבְרוּ	אֲנָשִׁים	מִדְיָנִים
vesārēnû	hû'	wayyishme‘û	'echâv		wayya‘avrû	'ănāshîm	midhyānîm
our flesh	he	and they listened	his brothers		and they passed by	men	Midianites

5692.152	5082.126	6148.526	881, 3231	4623, 988	4513.126
v Qal act ptc mp	cj, v Qal impf 3mp	cj, v Hiphil impf 3mp	do, pn	prep, art, n ms	cj, v Qal impf 3mp
סֹחֲרִים	וַיִּמְשְׁכוּ	וַיַּעֲלוּ	אֶת־יוֹסֵף	מִן־הַבּוֹר	וַיִּמְכְּרוּ
sōchărîm	wayyimshekhû	wayya‘ălû	'eth-yôsēph	min-habbôr	wayyimkerû
merchants	and they pulled	and they lifted up	Joseph	from the cistern	and they sold

881, 3231	3937, 3580	904, 6465	3826B	971.526	881, 3231	4875
do, pn	prep, art, pn	prep, num	n ms	cj, v Hiphil impf 3mp	do, pn	pn
אֶת־יוֹסֵף	לַיִּשְׁמְעֵאלִים	בְּעֶשְׂרִים	כָּסֶף	וַיָּבִיאוּ	אֶת־יוֹסֵף	מִצְרָיְמָה
'eth-yôsēph	layyishme‘ē'lîm	be‘esrîm	kāseph	wayyāvî'û	'eth-yôsēph	mitsrāymāh
Joseph	to the Ishmaelites	with twenty	silver	and they brought	Joseph	to Egypt

	8178.121	7498	420, 988	2079	375, 3231	904, 988
29.	cj, v Qal impf 3ms	pn	prep, art, n ms	cj, intrj	*sub*, pn	prep, art, n ms
	וַיָּשָׁב	רְאוּבֵן	אֶל־הַבּוֹר	וְהִנֵּה	אֵין־יוֹסֵף	בַּבּוֹר
	wayyāshāv	re'ûvēn	'el-habbôr	wehinnēh	'ên-yôsēph	babbôr
	and he returned	Reuben	to the cistern	and behold	there was not of Joseph	in the cistern

7458	881, 933		8178.121	420, 250	569.121	3315
cj, v Qal impf 3ms	do, n mp, ps 3ms	**30.**	cj, v Qal impf 3ms	prep, n ms, ps 3ms	cj, v Qal impf 3ms	art, n ms
וַיִּקְרַע	אֶת־בְּגָדָיו		וַיָּשָׁב	אֶל־אֶחָיו	וַיֹּאמַר	הַיֶּלֶד
wayyiqôra‘	'eth-beghādhâv		wayyāshāv	'el-'echâv	wayyō'mar	hayyeledh
and he tore	his clothes		and he returned	to his brothers	and he said	the boy

375	603	586	603, 971.151		4089.126	881, 3930
sub, ps 3ms	cj, pers pron	intrg	pers pron, v Qal act ptc ms	**31.**	cj, v Qal impf 3mp	do, *n fs*
אֵינֶנּוּ	וַאֲנִי	אָנָה	אֲנִי־בָא		וַיִּקְחוּ	אֶת־כְּתֹנֶת
'ênennû	wa'ănî	'ānāh	'ănî-vā'		wayyiqŏchû	'eth-kethōneth
he was not	and I	where	I going		and they took	the tunic with sleeves of

3231	8250.126	7988	6008	2991.126	881, 3930
pn	cj, v Qal impf 3mp	*n ms*	n fp	cj, v Qal impf 3mp	do, art, n fs
יוֹסֵף	וַיִּשְׁחֲטוּ	שְׂעִיר	עִזִּים	וַיִּטְבְּלוּ	אֶת־הַכֻּתֹּנֶת
yôsēph	wayyishchătû	se‘îr	‘izzîm	wayyitbelû	'eth-hakkutōneth
Joseph	and they slaughtered	he-goat of	goats	and they dipped	the tunic with sleeves

904, 1879		8365.326	881, 3930	6692	971.526
prep, art, n ms	**32.**	cj, v Piel impf 3mp	do, *n fs*	art, n mp	cj, v Hiphil impf 3mp
בַּדָּם		וַיְשַׁלְּחוּ	אֶת־כְּתֹנֶת	הַפַּסִּים	וַיָּבִיאוּ
baddām		wayshallechû	'eth-kethōneth	happassîm	wayyāvî'û
in the blood		and they sent	the tunic with sleeves of	the long tunic	and they brought

420, 1	569.126	2148	4834.119	5421.531, 5167	3930
prep, n ms, ps 3mp	cj, v Qal impf 3mp	dem pron	v Qal pf 1cp	v Hiphil impv 2ms, part	art, *n fs*
אֶל־אֲבִיהֶם	וַיֹּאמְרוּ	זֹאת	מָצָאנוּ	הַכֶּר־נָא	הַכְּתֹנֶת
'el-'ăvîhem	wayyō'm^{e}rû	zō'th	mātsā'nû	hakker-nā'	hakk^{e}thōneth
to their father	and they said	this	we found	identify please	the tunic with sleeves of

1158	2000	524, 3940		5421.521	569.121	3930
n ms, ps 2ms	pers pron	cj, adv	**33.**	cj, v Hiphil impf 3ms, ps 3fs	cj, v Qal impf 3ms	*n fs*
בִּנְךָ	הִוא	אִם־לֹא		וַיַּכִּירָהּ	וַיֹּאמֶר	כְּתֹנֶת
bin^{e}khā	hiw'	'im-lō'		wayyakkîrāhh	wayyō'mer	k^{e}thōneth
your son	it	or not		and he recognized it	and he said	the tunic with sleeves of

26. And Judah said unto his brethren, What profit is it if we slay our brother, and conceal his blood?: ... secret, *Darby, Geneva* ... hide, *KJVII* ... dabble ourselves in his blood, *Fenton.*

27. Come, and let us sell him to the Ishmeelites, and let not our hand be upon him for he is our brother and our flesh. And his brethren were content: ... that guilt will no be upon us, *Fenton* ... let us not put violent hands upon him, *BB.*

28. Then there passed by Midianites merchantmen; and they drew and lifted up Joseph out of the pit, and sold Joseph to the Ishmeelites for twenty pieces of silver: and they brought Joseph into Egypt: ... twenty dollars, *Berkeley* ... twenty shekels of silver, *RSV, NKJV, NIV* ... silverlings, *Young* ... bits, *BB.*

29. And Reuben returned unto the pit; and, behold, Joseph was not in the pit; and he rent his clothes: ... giving signs of grief, *BB* ... he tore his clothes in sorrow, *Good News.*

30. And he returned unto his brethren, and said, The child is not; and I, whither shall I go?: ... where can I turn, *NRSV* ... how can I go home, *Goodspeed* ... The lad is not! and mourning, I shall grieve, and die of grief, *Fenton.*

31. And they took Joseph's coat, and killed a kid of the goats, and dipped the coat in the blood: ... young goat, *BB* ... hegoat, *NASB, Berkeley* ... buck of goats, *Darby* ... male goat, *NASB.*

32. And they sent the coat of many colours, and they brought it to their father; and said, This have we found: know now whether it be thy son's coat or no: ... we came across this, *BB* ... examine it to see whether it is your son's tunic or not, *NASB* ... do you recognize it?, *NEB, REB.*

33. And he knew it, and said, It is my son's coat; an evil beast hath devoured him; Joseph is without

37:28. The men in the caravan were Midianite merchants who had joined with the Ishmaelites for business purposes, but were also known as Ishmaelites (cf. Judg. 8:22-24).

The brothers then pulled Joseph out of the cistern and sold him to the Ishmaelites for 20 shekels (weight) of silver. (Coins were not used until the time of the Persians in the 5th century B. C.). Twenty shekels weighed about 7.3 ounces Troy weight. This was the standard price for a healthy, young slave in Bible times. A mature slave would be sold for 30 shekels, the price for which Jesus was betrayed. Joseph was brought to Egypt, the first step toward the fulfillment of the prophecy of Gen. 15:13-14.

37:29-30. Reuben was shocked and distraught when he returned to the cistern and Joseph was not there. He tore his clothes as a sign of grief and dismay. He then went to his brothers and expressed his alarm. He did not know where to go to find Joseph.

37:31-32. The brothers apparently explained that Joseph was sold. Then they slaughtered a full-grown he-goat, dipped Joseph's tunic in its blood, and sent it to Jacob. "They brought it" seems to mean they caused it to be brought, for they did not wish to face Jacob with it themselves. With it they sent a heartless, cruel message asking Jacob to identify the tunic. At the same time, they suggested their innocence by pretending they did not know for sure whose the tunic was. Even Reuben joined in with no consideration of the effect of this on his father.

37:33-34. Jacob recognized the tunic as Joseph's and jumped to the conclusion the brothers had intended. He thought Joseph was dead, surely torn in pieces by some evil wild animal. To show his grief, Jacob tore his clothes and wrapped sackcloth around him. Sackcloth was a coarse black cloth made of goat's hair that let everyone know he was mourning over Joseph. He stayed in mourning, overwhelmed with grief, for a long time.

3231	3072.411	3072.142	404.112	7750	2516	1158
pn	v Pual pf 3ms	v Qal inf abs	v Qal pf 3fs, ps 3ms	n fs	n fs	n ms, ps 1cs
יוֹסֵף	טֹרַף	טָרֹף	אֲכָלָתְהוּ	רָעָה	חַיָּה	בְּנִי
yôsēph	tōraph	tārōph	'ăkhālāth^{e}hû	rā'āh	chayyāh	b^{e}nî
Joseph	he was torn in pieces	tearing in pieces	it ate him	evil	animal	my son

34.

904, 5158	8012	7947.121	7980	3399	7458.121
prep, n md, ps 3ms	n ms	cj, v Qal impf 3ms	n fp, ps 3ms	pn	cj, v Qal impf 3ms
בְּמָתְנָיו	שַׂק	וַיָּשֶׂם	שִׂמְלֹתָיו	יַעֲקֹב	וַיִּקְרַע
b^{e}māth^{e}nâv	saq	wayyāsem	simlōthâv	ya'ăqōv	wayyiqŏra'
on his loins	sackcloth	and he put	his clothes	Jacob	and he tore

7521	3219	6142, 1158	57.721
adj	n mp	prep, n ms, ps 3ms	cj, v Hithpael impf 3ms
רַבִּים	יָמִים	עַל־בְּנוֹ	וַיִּתְאַבֵּל
rabbîm	yāmîm	'al-b^{e}nô	wayyith'abbēl
many	days	over of his son	and he mourned

35.

3725, 1158	7251.126
adj, n mp, ps 3ms	cj, v Qal impf 3mp
כָּל־בָּנָיו	וַיָּקֻמוּ
khol-bānâv	wayyāqumû
all his sons	and they rose

569.121	3937, 5341.741	4126.321	3937, 5341.341	3725, 1351
cj, v Qal impf 3ms	prep, v Hithpael inf con	cj, v Piel impf 3ms	prep, v Piel inf con, ps 3ms	cj, *adj*, n fp, ps 3ms
וַיֹּאמֶר	לְהִתְנַחֵם	וַיְמָאֵן	לְנַחֲמוֹ	וְכָל־בְּנֹתָיו
wayyō'mer	l^{e}hithnachēm	waymā'ēn	l^{e}nachmô	w^{e}khol-b^{e}nōthâv
and he said	to be comforted	but he refused	to comfort him	and all his daughters

1	881	1098.121	8061	58	420, 1158	3706, 3495.125
n ms, ps	do, ps 3ms	cj, v Qal impf 3ms	n fs	adj	prep, n ms, ps 1cs	cj, v Qal impf 1cs
אָבִיו	אֹתוֹ	וַיֵּבְךְּ	שְׁאֹלָה	אָבֵל	אֶל־בְּנִי	כִּי־אֵרֵד
'āvîw	'ōthô	wayyēv^{e}kh	sh^{e}'ōlāh	'āvēl	'el-b^{e}nî	kî-'ērēdh
his father	him	and he wept over	to Sheol	mourning	to my son	because I will go down

36.

6799	5835	3937, 6561	420, 4875	881	4513.116	4226
pn	*n ms*	prep, pn	prep, pn	do, ps 3ms	v Qal pf 3cp	cj, art, pn
פַּרְעֹה	סְרִיס	לְפוֹטִיפַר	אֶל־מִצְרָיִם	אֹתוֹ	מָכְרוּ	וְהַמְּדָנִים
par'ōh	s^{e}rîs	l^{e}phôṭîphar	'el-mitsrāyim	'ōthô	mākh^{e}rû	w^{e}hamm^{e}dhānîm
Pharaoh	the eunuch of	to Potiphar	to Egypt	him	they sold	and the Midianites

2986	8015
art, n mp	n ms
הַטַּבָּחִים	שַׂר
hattabbāchîm	sar
the executioners	the official of

38:1

3495.121	2000	904, 6496	2030.121
cj, v Qal impf 3ms	art, dem pron	prep, art, n fs	cj, v Qal impf 3ms
וַיֵּרֶד	הַהִוא	בָּעֵת	וַיְהִי
wayyēredh	hahiw'	bā'ēth	wayhî
that he went down	the that	in the time	and it was

8428	5938	5912, 382	5371.121	250	4623, 882	3171
cj, n ms, ps 3ms	pn	prep, n ms	cj, v Qal impf 3ms	n mp, ps 3ms	prep, prep	pn
וּשְׁמוֹ	עֲדֻלָּמִי	עַד־אִישׁ	וַיֵּט	אֶחָיו	מֵאֵת	יְהוּדָה
ûsh^{e}mô	'ădhullāmî	'adh-'îsh	wayyēṭ	'echâv	mē'ēth	y^{e}hûdhāh
and his name	Adullamite	to man	and he turned aside	his brothers	from	Judah

2537
pn
חִירָה
chîrāh
Hirah

2.

8428	3793	1351, 382	3171	7495.121, 8427
cj, n ms, ps 3ms	pn	*n fs, n ms*	pn	cj, v Qal impf 3ms, adv
וּשְׁמוֹ	כְּנַעֲנִי	בַּת־אִישׁ	יְהוּדָה	וַיַּרְא־שָׁם
ûsh^{e}mô	k^{e}na'ănî	bath-'îsh	y^{e}hûdhāh	wayyar'-shām
and her name	Canaanites	the daughter of man of	Judah	and he saw there

420	971.121	4089.121	8214
prep, ps 3fs	cj, v Qal impf 3ms	cj, v Qal impf 3ms, ps 3fs	pn
אֵלֶיהָ	וַיָּבֹא	וַיִּקָּחֶהָ	שׁוּעַ
'ēlêhā	wayyāvō'	wayyiqqāchehā	shûa'
to her	and he went in	and he took her	Shua

3.

3314.122	2106.122
cj, v Qal impf 3fs	cj, v Qal impf 3fs
וַתֵּלֶד	וַתַּהַר
wattēledh	wattahar
and she gave birth	and she conceived

doubt rent in pieces: ...Joseph fell prey to beasts!, *Anchor* ... torn and eaten, *Fenton* ...eaten, *KJVII* ... torn-torn is Joseph, *Young*.

34. And Jacob rent his clothes, and put sackcloth upon his loins, and mourned for his son many days: ... sackcloth girdle, *Berkeley* ... sackcloth for his death, *Fenton* ... a long season, *Geneva*.

35. And all his sons and all his daughters rose up to comfort him; but he refused to be comforted; and he said, For I will go down into the grave unto my son mourning. Thus his father wept for him: ... the underworld, *BB* ... Sheol, *NRSV, Young, Goodspeed* ... world of the dead, *Good News*.

36. And the Midianites sold him into Egypt, unto Potiphar, an officer of Pharaoh's, and captain of the guard: ... of high position, *BB* ... a eunuch, *Geneva, NEB* ... of Pharaoh, head of the executioners, *Young* ... his head steward, *Goodspeed* ... chamberlain, *Darby*.

38:1. And it came to pass at that time, that Judah went down from his brethren: ... left his brothers, *NEB* ... parted from, *REB* ... pitched his tent near, *NAB*.

and turned in to a certain Adullamite, whose name was Hirah: ... affiliated with, *Berkeley* ... went down to stay with, *NIV* ... became a friend of, *BB*.

2. And Judah saw there a daughter of a certain Canaanite, whose name was Shuah; and he took her, and went in unto her: ... married her, *Anchor* ... had relations with her, *NAB* ... had intercourse with, *Goodspeed*.

37:35. The sons and daughters who tried to comfort Jacob would include his grandchildren. They, however, did not repent of what they had done, for they did not tell Jacob the truth nor did they send down to try to get Joseph back. Jacob rejected their efforts to comfort him and said he would go down into *Sheol* to his son mourning. Some believe Sheol means the grave. However, it is identified with Abaddon, the place of destruction (Job 26:6; 31:12; Ps. 88:11; Prov. 27:20).

Since Jacob thought Joseph was torn to pieces, he was obviously not in a grave, though he was in Sheol. In many places in the Old Testament, it is clear Sheol was a place of punishment (Ps. 9:17; cf. Num. 16:33; Job 26:6; Pss. 30:17-18; 49:13-15; 55:15; 88:11-12; Prov. 5:5; 7:27; 9:18; 15:10-11; 27:20; Isa. 38:18). Often the context refers to the anger or wrath of God (Job 14:13; Pss. 6:1, 5; 88:3, 7; 89:46, 48), and sometimes to both wrath and fire (Deut. 32:22).

Jacob had dreams God fulfilled. He should have had confidence that God would fulfill Joseph's dreams, for he had not forgotten them. Jacob must have jumped to the conclusion that Joseph had displeased God somehow and had come under God's judgment. Jacob felt responsible and felt God was punishing him by Joseph's death. Thus, Jacob believed he was also destined for Sheol, the place of punishment. Surely if he thought Joseph was in a good place, Jacob would have accepted comfort. Notice there is no record of Jacob praying or seeking God until after he received news that Joseph was alive.

37:36. Joseph might have been sold to some farmer in upper Egypt and we would never have heard of him again. But in the providence of God, he was taken to the capital city and sold to Potiphar, a eunuch of Pharaoh (Pharaoh means "great house," because he was established in the great house or royal palace). "Eunuch" came to mean any high officer or royal minister, whether a physical eunuch or not. Potiphar probably was not, for he was married. He was chief of the royal executioners, who were also the royal bodyguard. God was working on Joseph's behalf in spite of the wicked intentions of his brothers.

38:1. The kind of repetition found in 37:36 and 39:1 is a Hebrew way of showing that the material in between is a parenthesis. Note the strong contrast between 38:1 "Judah went down" and 39:1 "Joseph was brought down." Judah went down of his own accord. Joseph had no choice. The events of chapter 38 took place over a number of years, so 39:1 is a continuation of chapter 37. But chapter 38 is placed here to provide a strong contrast to the events of chapter 39. It also shows Joseph was right in what he said about his brothers mixing with Canaanite ways and religion. There was a real danger that they would be absorbed by the Canaanites and lose their place as a chosen people. It gives further reason why God allowed them to go down to Egypt later.

Judah left his brothers at Hebron and went down to Adullam in the foothills about 16 miles southwest of Jerusalem. There he became a friend of an Adullamite named Hirah ("nobility").

38:2. At Adullam he saw a Canaanite girl, the daughter of Shua ("wealth"), and took her as a wife.

1158	7410.121	881, 8428	6385		2106.122	5968	3314.122
n ms	cj, v Qal impf 3ms	do, n ms, ps 3ms	pn	**4.**	cj, v Qal impf 3fs	adv	cj, v Qal impf 3fs
בֵּן	וַיִּקְרָא	אֶת־שְׁמוֹ	עֵר		וַתַּהַר	עוֹד	וַתֵּלֶד
bēn	wayyiqŏrā'	'eth-sh^{e}mô	'ēr		wattahar	'ôdh	wattēledh
son	and he called	his name	Er		and she conceived	again	and she gave birth

1158	7410.122	881, 8428	207		3362.522	5968
n ms	cj, v Qal impf 3fs	do, n ms, ps 3ms	pn	**5.**	cj, v Hiphil impf 3fs	adv
בֵּן	וַתִּקְרָא	אֶת־שְׁמוֹ	אוֹנָן		וַתֹּסֶף	עוֹד
bēn	wattiqŏrā'	'eth-sh^{e}mô	'ônān		wattōseph	'ôdh
son	and she called	his name	Onan		and she continued	again

3314.122	1158	7410.122	881, 8428	8349	2030.111	904, 3698
cj, v Qal impf 3fs	n ms	cj, v Qal impf 3fs	do, n ms, ps 3ms	pn	cj, v Qal pf 3ms	prep, pn
וַתֵּלֶד	בֵּן	וַתִּקְרָא	אֶת־שְׁמוֹ	שֵׁלָה	וְהָיָה	בִכְזִיב
wattēledh	bēn	wattiqŏrā'	'eth-sh^{e}mô	shēlāh	w^{e}hāyāh	vikhzîv
and she gave birth	son	and she called	his name	Shelah	and it was	in Chezib

904, 3314.141	881		4089.121	3171	828	3937, 6385	1111
prep, v Qal inf con, ps 3fs	do, ps 3ms	**6.**	cj, v Qal impf 3ms	pn	n fs	prep, pn	n ms, ps 3ms
בְּלִדְתָּהּ	אֹתוֹ		וַיִּקַּח	יְהוּדָה	אִשָּׁה	לְעֵר	בְּכוֹרוֹ
b^{e}lidhtāhh	'ōthô		wayyiqqach	y^{e}hûdhāh	'ishshāh	l^{e}'ēr	b^{e}khôrô
in her giving birth	him		and he took	Judah	wife	to Er	his first-born

8428	8888		2030.121	6385	1111	3171	7737	904, 6084
cj, n ms, ps 3fs	pn	**7.**	cj, v Qal impf 3ms	pn	*n ms*	pn	adj	prep, *n fp*
וּשְׁמָהּ	תָּמָר		וַיְהִי	עֵר	בְּכוֹר	יְהוּדָה	רַע	בְּעֵינֵי
ûsh^{e}māhh	tāmār		wayhî	'ēr	b^{e}khôr	y^{e}hûdhāh	ra'	b^{e}'ênê
and her name	Tamar		and he was	Er	the firstborn of	Judah	evil	in the eyes of

3176	4322.521	3176		569.121	3171	3937, 207	971.131
pn	cj, v Hiphil impf 3ms, ps 3ms	pn	**8.**	cj, v Qal impf 3ms	pn	prep, pn	v Qal impv 2ms
יְהוָה	וַיְמִתֵהוּ	יְהוָה		וַיֹּאמֶר	יְהוּדָה	לְאוֹנָן	בֹּא
y^{e}hwāh	waymithēhû	y^{e}hwāh		wayyō'mer	y^{e}hûdhāh	l^{e}'ônān	bō'
Yahweh	and he killed him	Yahweh		and he said	Judah	to Onan	go

420, 828	250	3101.331	882	7251.531	2320
prep, *n fs*	n ms, ps 2ms	cj, v Piel impv 2ms	prep, ps 3fs	v Hiphil impv 2ms	n ms
אֶל־אֵשֶׁת	אָחִיךָ	וְיַבֵּם	אֹתָהּ	וְהָקֵם	זֶרַע
'el-'ēsheth	'āchîkhā	w^{e}yabbēm	'ōthāhh	w^{e}hāqēm	zera'
to the wife of	your brother	and fulfill your brother-in-law duty	with her	and cause to rise	seed

3937, 250		3156	207	3706	3940	3937	2030.121
prep, n ms, ps 2ms	**9.**	cj, v Qal impf 3ms	pn	cj	neg part	prep, ps 3ms	v Qal impf 3ms
לְאָחִיךָ		וַיֵּדַע	אוֹנָן	כִּי	לֹּא	לּוֹ	יִהְיֶה
l^{e}'āchîkhā		wayyēdha'	'ônān	kî	lō'	lô	yihyeh
for your brother		but he knew	Onan	that	not	to him	it would be

2320	2030.111	524, 971.111	420, 828	250	8273.311	800
art, n ms	cj, v Qal pf 3ms	cj, v Qal pf 3ms	prep, *n fs*	n ms, ps 3ms	cj, v Piel pf 3ms	n fs
הַזָּרַע	וְהָיָה	אִם־בָּא	אֶל־אֵשֶׁת	אָחִיו	וְשִׁחֵת	אַרְצָה
hazzāra'	w^{e}hāyāh	'im-bā'	'el-'ēsheth	'āchîw	w^{e}shichēth	'arysāh
the seed	and it was	whenever he went	to the wife of	his brother	that he spoiled	on the ground

3937, 1153	5598.141, 2320	3937, 250		7778.121	904, 6084	3176
prep, neg part	v Qal inf con, n ms	prep, n ms, ps 3ms	**10.**	cj, v Qal impf 3ms	prep, n fp	pn
לְבִלְתִּי	נְתָן־זֶרַע	לְאָחִיו		וַיֵּרַע	בְּעֵינֵי	יְהוָה
l^{e}viltî	n^{e}thān-zera'	l^{e}'āchîw		wayyēra'	b^{e}'ênê	y^{e}hwāh
to not	to give seed	to his brother		and it was evil	in the eyes of	Yahweh

866	6449.111	4322.521	1612, 881		569.121	3171	3937, 8888
rel part	v Qal pf 3ms	cj, v Hiphil impf 3ms	cj, do, ps 3ms	11.	cj, v Qal impf 3ms	pn	prep, pn
אֲשֶׁר	עָשָׂה	וַיָּמֶת	גַּם־אֹתוֹ		וַיֹּאמֶר	יְהוּדָה	לְתָמָר
'ăsher	'āsāh	wayyāmeth	gam-'ōthô		wayyō'mer	y^{e}hûdhāh	l^{e}thāmār
which	he did	and he killed	also him		and he said	Judah	to Tamar

3738	3553.132	496	941, 1041, 1	5912, 1461.121	8349
n fs, ps 3ms	v Qal impv 2fs	n fs	prep, *n ms*, n ms, ps 2fs	prep, v Qal impf 3ms	pn
כַּלָּתוֹ	שְׁבִי	אַלְמָנָה	בֵית־אָבִיךְ	עַד־יִגְדַּל	שֵׁלָה
kallāthô	sh^{e}vî	'almānāh	vêth-'āvîkh	'adh-yighdāl	shēlāh
his daughter-in-law	remain	widow	in the house of your father	until he grows up	Shelah

3. And she conceived, and bare a son; and he called his name Er.

4. And she conceived again, and bare a son; and she called his name Onan.

5. And she yet again conceived, and bare a son; and called his name Shelah: ... addeth again, *Young.*

and he was at Chezib, when she bare him: ... the birth took place, *BB* ... then she ceased to be child-bearing, *Fenton* ... ceased to bear children, *NEB.*

6. And Judah took a wife for Er his firstborn, whose name was Tamar.

7. And Er, Judah's firstborn, was wicked in the sight of the LORD and the LORD slew him: ... put him to death, *NRSV, BB* ... the Ever-Living caused him to die, *Fenton.*

8. And Judah said unto Onan, Go in unto thy brother's wife, and marry her, and raise up seed to thy brother: ... fulfilling the duty of a brother-in-law, and thus maintain your brother's line, *Anchor.*

9. And Onan knew that the seed should not be his: ... seeing that the offspring would not be his, *BB.*

and it came to pass, when he went in unto his brother's wife, that he spilled it on the ground: ... let it go to waste on the ground every time, *Anchor* ... spilled the sperm, *Berkeley* ... destroyed it to the earth, *Young.*

lest that he should give seed to his brother: ... preserve his brothers line, *NAB* ... raise up descendants for, *NCB* ... so as not to give his brother a family, *Goodspeed.*

10. And the thing which he did displeased the LORD: wherefore he slew him also: ... took his life, too, *Anchor.*

11. Then said Judah to Tamar his daughter in law, Remain a widow at thy father's house, till Shelah my son be grown: for he said, Lest peradventure he die also, as his brethren did: ... she may also kill him like his brothers, *Fenton.*

38:3-5. Over the next few years, his wife bore three sons to Jacob, Er ("watching"), Onan ("strong"), and Shelah ("a sprout"). By the time Shelah was born, Jacob had moved to Chezib, also called Achzib ("deceitful"), a few miles back in the direction of Hebron.

38:6-7. When Er was old enough, Judah arranged a marriage with a Canaanite woman named Tamar ("palm tree"). That Er was wicked in the sight of the LORD probably means he became involved in Canaanite idolatry. God brought judgment and death upon him for this. He died childless.

38:8. Judah then asked Onan to perform the duty of a brother-in-law by marrying Tamar and raising a child who would be the heir of Er and carry on his line. This custom was common all through the Middle East in ancient times as Nuzi tablets show. It is often called Levirate marriage (from the Latin *levir*, "a husband's brother") and was later incorporated into the Law of Moses (Deut. 25:5-10). It was allowed only when a brother died without leaving any children.

38:9-10. Onan married Tamar, but whenever he went in to her, he spilled the semen on the ground in order to keep from having a child by her. He did this because he did not want to father a child who would not be considered his, but who would become the legal heir of his brother. This lack of brotherly love was evil in the eyes of the Lord, so the Lord brought judgment on him and caused him to die also. (It was not the spilling of the seed that was evil, but the refusal to father a child who would be his brother's.)

38:11. Judah sent Tamar back to her father's house in Adullam, telling her to remain a widow until Shelah was old enough to marry her. Judah, however, was afraid that Shelah would die also, and probably never intended to let him fulfill the levirate law.

1158	3706	569.111	6678, 4322.121	1612, 2000	3626, 250	2050.122
n ms, ps 1cs	cj	v Qal pf 3ms	cj, v Qal impf 3ms	cj, pers pron	prep, n mp, ps 3ms	cj, v Qal impf 3fs
בְנִי	כִּי	אָמַר	פֶּן־יָמוּת	גַּם־הוּא	כְּאֶחָיו	וַתֵּלֶךְ
v^{e}nî	kî	'āmar	pen-yāmûth	gam-hû'	k^{e}'echâv	wattēlekh
my son	because	he said	otherwise he will die	also he	like his brothers	and she went

8888	3553.122	941, 1041	1		7528.126	3219
pn	cj, v Qal impf 3fs	prep, *n ms*	n ms, ps 3fs		cj, v Qal impf 3mp	art, n mp
תָּמָר	וַתֵּשֶׁב	בֵּית	אָבִיהָ	**12.**	וַיִּרְבּוּ	הַיָּמִים
tāmār	wattēshev	bêth	'āvîhā		wayyirbû	hayyāmîm
Tamar	and she dwelled	in the house of	her father		and they increased	the days

4322.122	1351, 8214	828, 3171	5341.221	3171	6148.121
cj, v Qal impf 3fs	n fs, pn	n fs, pn	cj, v Niphal impf 3ms	pn	cj, v Qal impf 3ms
וַתָּמָת	בַּת־שׁוּעַ	אֵשֶׁת־יְהוּדָה	וַיִּנָּחֶם	יְהוּדָה	וַיַּעַל
wattāmāth	bath-shûa'	'ēsheth-y^{e}hûdhāh	wayyinnāchem	y^{e}hûdhāh	wayya'al
and she died	the daughter of Shua	wife of Judah	and he was comforted	Judah	and he went up

6142, 1525.152	6887	2000	2537	7751	5938	8883
prpe, *v Qal act ptc mp*	n fs, ps 3ms	pers pron	cj, pn	n ms, ps 3ms	art, pn	pn
עַל־גֹּזְזֵי	צֹאנוֹ	הוּא	וְחִירָה	רֵעֵהוּ	הָעֲדֻלָּמִי	תִּמְנָתָה
'al-gōz^{e}zê	tsō'nô	hû'	w^{e}chîrāh	rē'ēhû	hā'ădhullāmî	timnāthāh
beside the shearers of	his sheep	he	and Hirah	his friend	the Adullamite	to Timnah

	5222.621	3937, 8888	3937, 569.141	2079	2624	6148.151
	cj, v Hophal impf 3ms	prep, pn	prep, v Qal inf con	intrj	n ms, ps 2fs	v Qal act ptc ms
13.	וַיֻּגַּד	לְתָמָר	לֵאמֹר	הִנֵּה	חָמִיךְ	עֹלֶה
	wayyuggadh	l^{e}thāmār	lē'mōr	hinnēh	chāmîkh	'ōleh
	and it was told	to Tamar	saying	behold	your father-in-law	going up

8883	3937, 1525.141	6887		5681.122	933	497
pn	prep, v Qal inf con	n fs, ps 3ms		v Qal impf 3fs	*n mp*	n fs, ps 3fs
תִּמְנָתָה	לָגֹז	צֹאנוֹ	**14.**	וַתָּסַר	בִּגְדֵי	אַלְמְנוּתָהּ
thimnāthāh	lāgōz	tsō'nô		wattāsar	bigh^{e}dhê	'alm^{e}nûthāhh
to Timnah	to shear	his sheep		and she took off	the clothes of	her widowhood

4623, 6142	3803.322	904, 7086	6190.722	3553.122	904, 6860
prep, prep, ps 3fs	cj, v Piel impf 3fs	prep, art, n ms	cj, v Hithpael impf 3fs	cj, v Qal impf 3fs	prep, *n ms*
מֵעָלֶיהָ	וַתְּכַס	בַּצָּעִיף	וַתִּתְעַלָּף	וַתֵּשֶׁב	בְּפֶתַח
mē'ālêhā	watt^{e}khas	batstsā'îph	wattith^{e}'allāph	wattēshev	b^{e}phethach
from on her	and she covered	with a shawl	and she wrapped herself	and she sat	by the entrance of

6095	866	6142, 1932	8883	3706	7495.112	3706, 1461.111
pn	rel part	prep, *n ms*	pn	cj	v Qal pf 3fs	cj, v Qal pf 3ms
עֵינַיִם	אֲשֶׁר	עַל־דֶּרֶךְ	תִּמְנָתָה	כִּי	רָאֲתָה	כִּי־גָדַל
'ênayim	'ăsher	'al-derekh	timnāthāh	kî	rā'ăthāh	kî-ghādhal
Enaim	which	on the road	to Timnah	because	she saw	that he had grown up

8349	2026	3940, 5598.212	3937	3937, 828		7495.121
pn	cj, pers pron	neg part, v Niphal pf 3fs	prep, ps 3ms	prep, n fs		cj, v Qal impf 3ms, ps 3fs
שֵׁלָה	וְהִוא	לֹא־נִתְּנָה	לוֹ	לְאִשָּׁה	**15.**	וַיִּרְאֶהָ
shēlāh	w^{e}hiw'	lō'-nitt^{e}nāh	lô	l^{e}'ishshāh		wayyir'ehā
Shelah	but she	not she was given	to him	for a wife		and he saw her

3171	2913.121	3937, 2265.153	3706	3803.312	6686
pn	cj, v Qal impf 3ms, ps 3fs	prep, v Qal act ptc fs	cj	v Piel pf 3fs	n mp, ps 3fs
יְהוּדָה	וַיַּחְשְׁבֶהָ	לְזוֹנָה	כִּי	כִסְּתָה	פָּנֶיהָ
y^{e}hûdhāh	wayyachsh^{e}vehā	l^{e}zônāh	kî	khiss^{e}thāh	panêhā
Judah	and he thought her	for a prostitute	because	she covered	her face

16.

5371.121	420	420, 1932	569.121	1957.132, 5167	971.125	420
cj, v Qal impf 3ms	prep, ps 3fs	prep, art, n ms	cj, v Qal impf 3ms	v Qal impv 2fs, part	v Qal impf 1cs	prep, ps 2fs
וַיֵּט	אֵלֶיהָ	אֶל־הַדֶּרֶךְ	וַיֹּאמֶר	הָבָה־נָּא	אָבוֹא	אֵלַיִךְ
wayyēṯ	'ēlêhā	'el-hadderekh	wayyō'mer	hāvāh-nā'	'āvô'	'ēlayikh
and he turned in	to her	by the road	and he said	come please	I will go in	to you

3706	3940	3156.111	3706	3738	2000	569.122
cj	neg part	v Qal pf 3ms	cj	n fs, ps 3ms	pers pron	cj, v Qal impf 3fs
כִּי	לֹא	יָדַע	כִּי	כַלָּתוֹ	הִוא	וַתֹּאמֶר
kî	lō'	yādha'	kî	khallāthô	hiw'	wattō'mer
for	not	he knew	that	his daughter-in-law	she	and she said

4242, 5598.123, 3937	3706	971.123	420		569.121	609
intrg, v Qal impf 2ms, prep, ps 1cs	cj	v Qal impf 2ms	prep, ps 1cs	**17.**	cj, v Qal impf 3ms	pers pron
מַה־תִּתֶּן־לִי	כִּי	תָּבוֹא	אֵלָי		וַיֹּאמֶר	אָנֹכִי
mah-titten-lî	kî	thāvô'	'ēlāy		wayyō'mer	'ānōkhî
what will you give to me	that	you will come in	to me		and he said	I

And Tamar went and dwelt in her father's house: ... parental home, *Berkeley*.

12. And in process of time the daughter of Shuah Judah's wife died; and Judah was comforted, and went up unto his sheepshearers to Timnath, he and his friend Hirah the Adullamite: ... After Judah completed the period of mourning, *NAB* ... recovered from his grief, *NIV*.

13. And it was told Tamar, saying, Behold thy father in law goeth up to Timnath to shear his sheep: ... news of it was brought to Tamar, *Goodspeed*.

14. And she put her widow's garments off from her, and covered her with a vail, and wrapped herself, : ... widow's weeds, *Berkeley, Fenton, NEB* ... to disguise herself, *Anchor, NIV, Berkeley* ... perfumed herself, *NEB*.

and sat in an open place, which is by the way to Timnath; for she saw that Shelah was grown, and she was not given unto him to wife: ... Enaim,
Anchor, BB, NRSV ... where the road forks, *REB* ... opening by the wells, *Fenton*.

15. When Judah saw her, he thought her to be an harlot; because she had covered her face: ... prostitute, *NRSV* ... since her face was veiled, *Berkeley*.

16. And he turned unto her by the way, and said, Go to, I pray thee, let me come in unto thee: ... let me lie with you, *Anchor* ... let me have intercourse with you, *Goodspeed, NCB, NAB*.

(for he knew not that she was his daughter in law.) And she said, What wilt thou give me, that thou mayest come in unto me?: ... pay me, *Anchor*.

17. And he said, I will send thee a kid from the flock: ... of the goats or sheep, *Fenton*.

And she said, Wilt thou give me a pledge, till thou send it?: ... surety, *Goodspeed* ... guarantee, *Anchor*.

38:12. A few years later Judah's wife died. After a time of mourning, Judah was comforted and proceeded to go about his shepherding business with his friend Hirah. At the time of sheepshearing they went to Timnath (also called Timnah) about 10 miles west of Bethlehem, where the shearers were working.

38:13-14. Because Shelah was now old enough to marry her and was not given to her as a husband, Tamar decided on a drastic plan. When she heard Judah was going to Timnath, she took off her widow's clothes and covered herself with a shawl, wrapping it around her. Then she went ahead and sat by the gate of Enaim ("double springs," not "an open place"), a village on the road to Timnath. She knew Judah would pass by there.

38:15. When Judah saw her with her face covered, he thought she was a prostitute, but not an ordinary prostitute. Verse 21 uses a different word, *qedheshah,* which literally means "a holy woman." This is what Canaanites called religious prostitutes who considered their sex acts as religious acts devoted to some Canaanite god or goddess.

38:16-19. Judah knew what he was doing when he asked to have sex with the woman. That is, he knew this was part of Canaanite religion and that the Canaanites would consider that he was doing this as an act of worship to one of their gods

8365.125	1454, 6008	4623, 6887	569.122	524, 5598.123	6402	5912
v Qal impf 1cs	n ms, n fp	prep, art, n fs	cj, v Qal impf 3fs	cj, v Qal impf 2ms	n ms	adv
אֲשַׁלַּח	גְּדִי־עִזִּים	מִן־הַצֹּאן	וַתֹּאמֶר	אִם־תִּתֵּן	עֵרָבוֹן	עַד
'ăshallach	g^{e}dhî-'izzîm	min-hatstsō'n	wattō'mer	'im-tittēn	'ērāvôn	'adh
I will send	kid of the goats	from the flock	and she said	if you will give	pledge	until

8365.141		569.121	4242	6402	866	5598.125, 3937
v Qal inf con, ps 2ms	**18.**	cj, v Qal impf 3ms	intrg	art, n ms	rel part	v Qal impf 1cs, prep, ps 2fs
שָׁלְחֶךָ		וַיֹּאמֶר	מָה	הָעֵרָבוֹן	אֲשֶׁר	אֶתֶּן־לָךְ
shāl^{e}chekhā		wayyō'mer	māh	hā'ērāvôn	'ăsher	'etten-lākh
your sending		and he said	what	the pledge	which	I will give to you

569.122	2460	6870	4431	866	904, 3135
cj, v Qal impf 3fs	n ms, ps 2ms	cj, n ms, ps 2ms	cj, n ms, ps 2ms	rel part	prep, n fs, ps 2ms
וַתֹּאמֶר	חֹתָמְךָ	וּפְתִילֶךָ	וּמַטְּךָ	אֲשֶׁר	בְּיָדֶךָ
wattō'mer	chōthām^{e}khā	ûph^{e}thîlekhā	ûmatt^{e}khā	'ăsher	b^{e}yādhekhā
and she said	your signet-ring	and your cord	and your staff	which	in your hand

5598.121, 3937	971.121	420	2106.122	3937
cj, v Qal impf 3ms, prep, ps 3fs	cj, v Qal impf 3ms	prep, ps 3fs	cj, v Qal impf 3fs	prep, ps 3ms
וַיִּתֶּן־לָהּ	וַיָּבֹא	אֵלֶיהָ	וַתַּהַר	לוֹ
wayyitten-lāhh	wayyāvō'	'ēlêhā	wattahar	lô
and he gave to her	and he went in	to her	and she conceived	for him

	7251.122	2050.122	5681.122	7086	4623, 6142	3980.122
19.	cj, v Qal impf 3fs	cj, v Qal impf 3fs	v Qal impf 3fs	n ms, ps 3fs	prep, prep, ps 3fs	cj, v Qal impf 3fs
	וַתָּקָם	וַתֵּלֶךְ	וַתָּסַר	צְעִיפָהּ	מֵעָלֶיהָ	וַתִּלְבַּשׁ
	wattāqām	wattēlekh	wattāsar	ts^{e}'îphāhh	mē'ālêhā	wattilbash
	and she rose	and she went	and she took off	her shawl	from on her	and she put on

933	497		8365.121	3171	881, 1454	6008	904, 3135
n mp	n fs, ps 3fs	**20.**	cj, v Qal impf 3ms	pn	do, *n ms*	art, n fp	prep, *n fs*
בִּגְדֵי	אַלְמְנוּתָהּ		וַיִּשְׁלַח	יְהוּדָה	אֶת־גְּדִי	הָעִזִּים	בְּיַד
bigh^{e}dhê	'alm^{e}nûthāhh		wayyishlach	y^{e}hûdhāh	'eth-g^{e}dhî	hā'izzîm	b^{e}yadh
the clothes of	her widowhood		and he sent out	Judah	the kid of	the goats	in the hand of

7751	5938	4089.141	6402	4623, 3135	828	3940
n ms, ps 3ms	art, pn	prep, v Qal inf con	art, n ms	prep, *n fs*	art, n fs	cj, neg part
רֵעֵהוּ	הָעֲדֻלָּמִי	לָקַחַת	הָעֵרָבוֹן	מִיַּד	הָאִשָּׁה	וְלֹא
rē'ēhû	hā'ădhullāmî	lāqachath	hā'ērāvôn	miyyadh	hā'ishshāh	w^{e}lō'
his friend	the Adullamite	to receive	the pledge	from the hand of	the woman	but not

4834.111		8068.121	881, 596	4887	3937, 569.141	347
v Qal pf 3ms, ps 3fs	**21.**	cj, v Qal impf 3ms	do, *n mp*	n ms, ps 3fs	prep, v Qal inf con	intrg
מְצָאָהּ		וַיִּשְׁאַל	אֶת־אַנְשֵׁי	מְקֹמָהּ	לֵאמֹר	אַיֵּה
m^{e}tsā'āhh		wayyish'al	'eth-'anshê	m^{e}qōmāhh	lē'mōr	'ayyēh
he found her		and he asked	the men of	her place	saying	where

7228	2000	904, 6095	6142, 1932	569.126	3940, 2030.112
art, n fs	pers pron	prep, art, pn	prep, art, n ms	cj, v Qal impf 3mp	neg part, v Qal pf 3fs
הַקְּדֵשָׁה	הִוא	בָעֵינַיִם	עַל־הַדָּרֶךְ	וַיֹּאמְרוּ	לֹא־הָיְתָה
haqq^{e}dhēshāh	hiw'	vā'ênayim	'al-haddārekh	wayyō'm^{e}rû	lō'-hāy^{e}thāh
the temple prostitute	she	by Enaim	on the road	and they said	not she was

904, 2172	7228		8178.121	420, 3171	569.121	3940
prep, dem pron	n fs	**22.**	cj, v Qal impf 3ms	prep, pn	cj, v Qal impf 3ms	neg part
בָזֶה	קְדֵשָׁה		וַיָּשָׁב	אֶל־יְהוּדָה	וַיֹּאמֶר	לֹא
vāzeh	qŏdhēshāh		wayyāshāv	'el-y^{e}hûdhāh	wayyō'mer	lō'
on this	temple prostitute		so he returned	to Judah	and he said	not

4834.115	1612	596	4887	569.116	3940, 2030.112	904, 2172
v Qal pf 1cs, ps 3fs	cj, cj	*n mp*	art, n ms	v Qal pf 3cp	neg part, v Qal pf 3fs	prep, dem pron
מְצָאתִיהָ	וְגַם	אַנְשֵׁי	הַמָּקוֹם	אָמְרוּ	לֹא־הָיְתָה	בָזֶה
m^{e}tsā'thîhā	w^{e}gham	'anshê	hammāqôm	'ām^{e}rû	lō'-hāy^{e}thāh	vāzeh
I found her	and also	the men of	the place	they said	not she was	on this

7228		569.121	3171	4089.122, 3937	6678	2030.120
n fs	**23.**	cj, v Qal impf 3ms	pn	v Qal juss 3fs, prep, ps 3fs	cj	v Qal impf 1cp
קְדֵשָׁה		וַיֹּאמֶר	יְהוּדָה	תִּקַּח־לָהּ	פֶּן	נִהְיֶה
qŏdhēshāh		wayyō'mer	y^{e}hûdhāh	tiqqach-lāhh	pen	nihyeh
temple prostitute		and he said	Judah	let her take for herself	otherwise	we will be

3937, 973	2079	8365.115	1454	2172	887	3940	4834.113
prep, n ms	intrj	v Qal pf 1cs	art, n ms	art, dem pron	cj, pers pron	neg part	v Qal pf 2ms, ps 3fs
לָבוּז	הִנֵּה	שָׁלַחְתִּי	הַגְּדִי	הַזֶּה	וְאַתָּה	לֹא	מְצָאתָהּ
lāvûz	hinnēh	shālachtî	hagg^{e}dhî	hazzeh	w^{e}'attāh	lō'	m^{e}tsā'thāhh
for contempt	behold	I sent	the kid	the this	and you	not	you found her

18. And he said, What pledge shall I give thee? And she said, Thy signet, and thy bracelets, and thy staff that is in thine hand: ... your ring, *Fenton* ... thy cloke, *Geneva* ... your seal and its cord, *NEB, NAB, REB* ... signet and cord, *NCB, Berkeley, RSV.*

And he gave it her, and came in unto her, and she conceived by him.

19. And she arose, and went away, and laid by her vail from her, and put on the garments of her widowhood: ... widow's weeds, *NEB, Fenton, Berkeley.*

20. And Judah sent the kid by the hand of his friend the Adullamite, to receive his pledge from the woman's hand: but he found her not.

21. Then he asked the men of that place, saying, Where is the harlot: ... townspeople, *NRSV* ... votary, *Anchor* ... separated one, *Young* ... temple-prostitute, *Goodspeed, NASB, REB.*

that was openly by the way side? And they said, There was no harlot in this place: ... where the road forks, *REB, NEB* ... has never been, *Anchor, NAB.*

22. And he returned to Judah, and said, I cannot find her; and also the men of the place said, that there was no harlot in this place.

23. And Judah said, Let her take it to her, lest we be shamed: ... Let her keep my pledge, or we shall get a bad name, *NEB* ... become a laughingstock, *NAB, REB, NASB* ... be ridiculed, *Berkeley, NCB* ... dispised, *Young* ... incur a scandal, *Goodspeed.*

behold, I sent this kid, and thou hast not found her: ... I did try to pay her, but couldn't find her, *Good News.*

24. And it came to pass about three

---

or goddesses. But he did not know it was his daughter-in-law. She asked what he would give her as payment for her letting him have what he wanted, and he promised to send her a young goat from his flock. When she asked for something as a pledge that would guarantee he would send her the kid, he asked her to name what she wanted. She asked first for something very personal, his signet ring that would probably be inscribed with his name, the special twisted cord that was probably used to hang it around his neck, and his shepherd's staff. He proceeded to give it to her, had sex with her, and she became pregnant by him. Then she went home, put away the veil and put on the clothes that marked her as a widow.

38:20-21. When Judah sent the young goat by his friend Hirah in order to get back the signet ring, cord, and staff, he did not find her. When he asked some men who belonged to the place where the religious prostitute was who was at Enaim by the roadside, they denied that there was any religious prostitute there.

38:22-23. When Hirah told this to Judah, Judah said to let her take it to herself, that is, let her keep it, otherwise we will become a laughingstock (i.e. if we keep asking people where she is). Then, emphatically, Judah said he had sent the kid, that is, he had fulfilled his part of the bargain, but Hirah had not found her.

38:24. When it became obvious that Tamar was pregnant, someone told Judah she had illicit intercourse and was pregnant by prostitution. Judah immediately called for her to be brought out for execution, to be burned to death for this sin.

24.	2030.121	3626, 4623, 8421	2414	5222.621	3937, 3171	3937, 569.141
	cj, v Qal impf 3ms	prep, prep, num	n mp	cj, v Hophal impf 3ms	prep, pn	prep, v Qal inf con
	וַיְהִי	כְּמִשְׁלֹשׁ	חֳדָשִׁים	וַיֻּגַּד	לִיהוּדָה	לֵאמֹר
	wayhî	k^{e}mishlōsh	chădhāshîm	wayyuggadh	lîhûdhāh	lē'mōr
	and it was	after three	months	that it was told	to Judah	saying

2265.112	8888	3738	1612	2079	2107
v Qal pf 3fs	pn	n fs, ps 2ms	cj, cj	intrj	adj
זָנְתָה	תָּמָר	כַּלָּתֶךָ	וְגַם	הִנֵּה	הָרָה
zān^{e}thāh	tāmār	kallāthekhā	w^{e}gham	hinnēh	hārāh
she committed prostitution	Tamar	your daughter-in-law	and also	behold	pregnant

3937, 2267	569.121	3171	3428.533	8041.222	25.	2000
prep, n mp	cj, v Qal impf 3ms	pn	v Hiphil impv 2mp, ps 3fs	v Niphal impf 3fs		pers pron
לִזְנוּנִים	וַיֹּאמֶר	יְהוּדָה	הוֹצִיאוּהָ	וְתִשָּׂרֵף		הִוא
liznûnîm	wayyō'mer	y^{e}hûdhāh	hôtsî'ûhā	w^{e}thishshārēph		hiw'
by prostitution	and he said	Judah	bring her out	and she will be burned		she

3428.657	2026	8365.112	420, 2624	3937, 569.141	3937, 382
v Hophal ptc fs	cj, pers pron	v Qal pf 3fs	prep, n ms, ps 3fs	prep, v Qal inf con	prep, n ms
מוּצֵאת	וְהִיא	שָׁלְחָה	אֶל־חָמִיהָ	לֵאמֹר	לְאִישׁ
mûtsē'th	w^{e}hî'	shāl^{e}chāh	'el-chāmîhā	lē'mōr	l^e'îsh
being brought out	and she	she sent	to her father-in-law	saying	to man

886, 431	3937	609	2107	569.122	5421.531, 5167	3937, 4449
rel part, dem pron	prep, ps 3ms	pers pron	adj	cj, v Qal impf 3fs	v Hiphil impv 2ms, part	prep, intrg
אֲשֶׁר־אֵלֶּה	לוֹ	אָנֹכִי	הָרָה	וַתֹּאמֶר	הַכֶּר־נָא	לְמִי
'ăsher-'ēlleh	lô	'ānōkhî	hārāh	wattō'mer	hakker-nā'	l^{e}mî
which these	by him	I	pregnant	and she said	identify please	to whom

2460	6870	4431	431	26.	5421.521	3171
art, n fs	cj, art, n mp	cj, art, n ms	art, dem pron		cj, v Hiphil impf 3ms	pn
הַחֹתֶמֶת	וְהַפְּתִילִים	וְהַמַּטֶּה	הָאֵלֶּה		וַיַּכֵּר	יְהוּדָה
hachōthemeth	w^{e}happ^{e}thîlîm	w^{e}hammatteh	hā'ēlleh		wayyakkēr	y^{e}hûdhāh
the signet-ring	and the cord	and the staff	the these		and he recognized	Judah

569.121	6927.112	4623	3706, 6142, 3772	3940, 5598.115	3937, 8349
cj, v Qal impf 3ms	v Qal pf 3fs	prep, ps 1cs	cj, prep, adv	neg part, v Qal pf 1cs, ps 3fs	prep, pn
וַיֹּאמֶר	צָדְקָה	מִמֶּנִּי	כִּי־עַל־כֵּן	לֹא־נְתַתִּיהָ	לְשֵׁלָה
wayyō'mer	tsādh^{e}qāh	mimmennî	kî-'al-kēn	lō'-n^{e}thattîhā	l^{e}shēlāh
and he said	she is righteous	more than me	because	not I gave her	to Shelah

1158	3940, 3362.111	5968	3937, 3156.141	27.	2030.121
n ms, ps 1cs	cj, neg part, v Qal pf 3ms	adv	prep, v Qal inf con, ps 3fs		cj, v Qal impf 3ms
בְנִי	וְלֹא־יָסַף	עוֹד	לְדַעְתָּהּ		וַיְהִי
v^{e}nî	w^{e}lō'-yāsaph	'ôdh	l^{e}dha'ăttāh		wayhî
my son	and not he did again	again	to have relations with her		and it was

904, 6496	3937, 3314.141	2079	8751	904, 1027	28.	2030.121
prep, *n fs*	prep, v Qal inf con, ps 3fs	cj, intrj	n mp	prep, n fs, ps 3fs		cj, v Qal impf 3ms
בְּעֵת	לְלִדְתָּהּ	וְהִנֵּה	תְאוֹמִים	בְּבִטְנָהּ		וַיְהִי
b^e'ēth	lidhtāhh	w^{e}hinnēh	th^e'ômîm	b^{e}vitnāhh		wayhî
in the time of	for her giving birth	and behold	twins	in her womb		and it was

904, 3314.141	5598.121, 3135	4089.122	3314.353	7489	6142, 3135
prep, v Qal inf con, ps 3fs	cj, v Qal impf 3ms, n fs	cj, v Qal impf 3fs	art, v Piel ptc fs	cj, v Qal impf 3fs	prep, n fs, ps 3ms
בְלִדְתָּהּ	וַיִּתֶּן־יָד	וַתִּקַּח	הַמְיַלֶּדֶת	וַתִּקְשֹׁר	עַל־יָדוֹ
v^{e}lidhtāhh	wayyitten-yādh	wattiqqach	hamyalledheth	wattiqŏshōr	'al-yādhô
in her giving birth	that he put hand	and she took	the midwife	and she tied	on his hand

8528	3937, 569.141	2172	3428.111	7518		2030.121	3626, 8178.551
adj	prep, v Qal inf con	dem pron	v Qal pf 3ms	adj		cj, v Qal impf 3ms	prep, v Hiphil ptc ms
שָׁנִי	לֵאמֹר	זֶה	יָצָא	רִאשֹׁנָה	29.	וַיְהִי	כְּמֵשִׁיב
shānî	lē'mōr	zeh	yātsā'	ri'shōnāh		wayhî	k^{e}mēshîv
red thread	saying	this	he went out	first		and it was	when bringing back

3135	2079	3428.111	250	569.122	4242, 6805.113
n fs, ps 3ms	cj, intrj	v Qal pf 3ms	n ms, ps 3ms	cj, v Qal impf 3fs	intrg, v Qal pf 2ms
יָדוֹ	וְהִנֵּה	יָצָא	אָחִיו	וַתֹּאמֶר	מַה־פָּרַצְתָּ
yādhô	w^{e}hinnēh	yātsâ'	'āchîw	wattō'mer	mah-pāratstā
his hand	then behold	he came out	his brother	and she said	how have you made a breach

6142	6806	7410.121	8428	6807		313	3428.111
prep, ps 2ms	n ms	cj, v Qal impf 3ms	n ms, ps 3ms	pn		cj, adv	v Qal pf 3ms
עָלֶיךָ	פָּרֶץ	וַיִּקְרָא	שְׁמוֹ	פָּרֶץ	30.	וְאַחַר	יָצָא
'ālêykhā	pārets	wayyiqōrā'	sh^{e}mô	pārets		w^{e}'achar	yātsā'
concerning you	a breach	and he called	his name	Perez		and afterward	he came out

250	866	6142, 3135	8528	7410.121	8428	2313
n ms, ps 3ms	rel part	prep, n fs, ps 3ms	art, adj	cj, v Qal impf 3ms	n ms, ps 3ms	pn
אָחִיו	אֲשֶׁר	עַל־יָדוֹ	הַשָּׁנִי	וַיִּקְרָא	שְׁמוֹ	זָרַח
'āchîw	'ăsher	'al-yādhô	hashshānî	wayyiqōrā'	sh^{e}mô	zārach
his brother	which	on his hand	the red thread	and he called	his name	Zerah

months after, that it was told Judah, saying, Tamar thy daughter in law hath played the harlot: ... acting like a loose woman, *BB.*

and also, behold, she is with child by whoredom. And Judah said, Bring her forth, and let her be burnt: ... cremated, *Berkeley.*

25. When she was brought forth, she sent to her father in law, saying, By the man, whose these are, am I with child: and she said, Discern, I pray thee, whose are these, the signet, and bracelets, and staff: ... Please verify, *Anchor* ... Please note whose these are, *Goodspeed.*

26. And Judah acknowledged them, and said, She hath been more righteous than I: ... more in the right than I am, *NEB* ... more virtuous, *Fenton.*

because that I gave her not to Shelah my son. And he knew her again no more: ... I have failed in my obligation to her, *Good News* ... did not have intercourse with her again, *NEB*, *REB.*

27. And it came to pass in the time of her travail, that, behold, twins were in her womb: ... At the time of her delivery, *Berkeley* ... twin boys, *NIV.*

28. And it came to pass, when she travailed, that the one put out his hand: and the midwife took and bound upon his hand a scarlet thread, saying, This came out first: ... crimson, *Anchor* ... red, *BB* ... should be born first, *Goodspeed.*

29. And it came to pass, as he drew back his hand, that, behold, his brother came out: and she said, How hast thou broken forth? this breach be upon thee: therefore his name was called Pharez: ... how have you forged your way through?, *Goodspeed* ...What an opening you have made for yourself!, *BB* ... and he was names Perez, *NIV.*

38:25-26. When Tamar was brought out for execution, she sent to Judah and asked him to identify the signet ring, the twisted cord, and the shepherd's staff belonging to the man who had made her pregnant. Judah then admitted she was more righteous (that is, more in the right) than he, for he had failed to keep his word and give her to Shelah to be his wife. Judah did not take her as a wife and did not have relations with her again. It is implied that Judah learned a lesson from this and never did anything like that again.

38:28-29. Tamar gave birth to twins. One of the twins put out his hand and the midwife tied a crimson thread on his hand to identify him as the firstborn. The vivid crimson or scarlet dye for the thread was obtained from eggs of the shield-louse deposited on oak leaves. But that twin pulled back his hand and the other was born first, This, she said, was a breach or a bursting out, and so she named him Perez ("a breach," "a bursting out," "a rupture"). He became the ancestor of King David (Ruth 4:18-22), and of Jesus (Matt. 1:3, 6).

39:1	3231	3495.611	4875	7353.121	6561	5835
	cj, pn	v Hophal pf 3ms	pn	v Qal impf 3ms, ps 3ms	pn	*n ms*
	וְיוֹסֵף	הוּרַד	מִצְרָיְמָה	וַיִּקְנֵהוּ	פּוֹטִיפַר	סְרִיס
	weyôsēph	hûradh	mitsrāymāh	wayyiqōnēhû	pôṭîphar	serîs
	now Joseph	he was brought down	to Egypt	and he bought him	Potiphar	the eunuch of

6799	8015	2986	382	4874	4623, 3135
pn	*n ms*	art, n mp	*n ms*	pn	prep, *n fs*
פַּרְעֹה	שַׂר	הַטַּבָּחִים	אִישׁ	מִצְרִי	מִיַּד
par'ōh	sar	hattabbāchîm	'îsh	mitsrî	miyyadh
Pharaoh	the chief of	the executioners	man of	Egyptians	from the hand of

3580	866	3495.516	8427	2.	2030.121	3176
art, pn	rel part	v Hiphil pf 3cp, ps 3ms	adv		cj, v Qal impf 3ms	pn
הַיִּשְׁמְעֵאלִים	אֲשֶׁר	הוֹרִדֻהוּ	שָׁמָּה		וַיְהִי	יְהוָה
hayyishme'ē'lîm	'ăsher	hôridhuhû	shāmmāh		wayhî	yehwāh
the Ishmaelites	who	they brought him down	to there		and He was	Yahweh

882, 3231	2030.121	382	7014.551	2030.121	904, 1041	112
prep, pn	cj, v Qal impf 3ms	n ms	v Hiphil ptc ms	cj, v Qal impf 3ms	prep, *n ms*	n ms, ps 3ms
אֶת־יוֹסֵף	וַיְהִי	אִישׁ	מַצְלִיחַ	וַיְהִי	בְּבֵית	אֲדֹנָיו
'eth-yôsēph	wayhî	'îsh	matslîach	wayhî	bevêth	'ădhōnâv
with Joseph	and he became	man	successful	and he was	in the house of	his master

4874	3.	7495.121	112	3706	3176	882	3725	886, 2000
art, pn		cj, v Qal impf 3ms	n ms, ps 3ms	cj	pn	prep, ps 3ms	cj, adj	rel part, pers pron
הַמִּצְרִי		וַיַּרְא	אֲדֹנָיו	כִּי	יְהוָה	אִתּוֹ	וְכֹל	אֲשֶׁר־הוּא
hammitsrî		wayyare'	'ădhōnâv	kî	yehwāh	'ittô	wekhōl	'ăsher-hû'
the Egyptian		and he saw	his master	that	Yahweh	with him	and all	that he

6449.151	3176	7014.551	904, 3135	4.	4834.121	3231
v Qal act ptc ms	pn	v Hiphil ptc ms	prep, n fs, ps 3ms		cj, v Qal impf 3ms	pn
עֹשֶׂה	יְהוָה	מַצְלִיחַ	בְּיָדוֹ		וַיִּמְצָא	יוֹסֵף
'ōseh	yehwāh	matslîach	beyādhô		wayyimtsā'	yôsēph
doing	Yahweh	making successful	by his hand		and he found	Joseph

2682	904, 6084	8664.321	881	6734.521	6142, 1041
n ms	prep, n fd, ps 3ms	v Piel impf 3ms	do, ps 3ms	cj, v Hiphil impf 3ms, ps 3ms	prep, n ms, ps 3ms
חֵן	בְּעֵינָיו	וַיְשָׁרֶת	אֹתוֹ	וַיַּפְקִדֵהוּ	עַל־בֵּיתוֹ
chēn	be'ênâv	wayshāreth	'ōthô	wayyaphqidhēhû	'al-bêthô
favor	in his eyes	and he waited on	him	and he appointed him	over his house

3725, 3552, 3937	5598.111	904, 3135	5.	2030.121	4623, 226	6734.511
cj, adj, sub, prep, ps 3ms	v Qal pf 3ms	prep, n fs, ps 3ms		cj, v Qal impf 3ms	prep adv	v Hiphil pf 3ms
וְכָל־יֶשׁ־לוֹ	נָתַן	בְּיָדוֹ		וַיְהִי	מֵאָז	הִפְקִיד
wekhol-yesh-lô	nāthan	beyādhô		wayhî	mē'āz	hiphqîdh
and all there was to him	he put	in his hand		and it was	from then	he appointed

881	904, 1041	6142	3725, 866	3552, 3937	1313.321	3176
do, ps 3ms	prep, n ms, ps 3ms	cj, prep	adj, rel part	sub, prep, ps 3ms	cj, v Piel impf 3ms	pn
אֹתוֹ	בְּבֵיתוֹ	וְעַל	כָּל־אֲשֶׁר	יֶשׁ־לוֹ	וַיְבָרֶךְ	יְהוָה
'ōthô	bevêthô	we'al	kol-'ăsher	yesh-lô	wayevārekh	yehwāh
him	over his household	and over	all which	there was to him	and He blessed	Yahweh

881, 1041	4874	904, 1600	3231	2030.121	1318	3176
do, *n ms*	art, pn	prep, prep	pn	cj, v Qal impf 3ms	*n fs*	pn
אֶת־בֵּית	הַמִּצְרִי	בִּגְלַל	יוֹסֵף	וַיְהִי	בִּרְכַּת	יְהוָה
'eth-bêth	hammitsrî	bighlal	yôsēph	wayhî	birkath	yehwāh
the house of	the Egyptian	on account of	Joseph	and it was	the blessing of	Yahweh

904, 3725, 866	3552, 3937	904, 1041	904, 7898		6013.121
prep, *adj*, rel part	sub, prep, ps 3ms	prep, art, n ms	cj, prep, art, n ms		cj, v Qal impf 3ms
בְּכָל־אֲשֶׁר	יֶשׁ־לוֹ	בַּבַּיִת	וּבַשָּׂדֶה	**6.**	וַיַּעֲזֹב
b^{e}khāl-'ăsher	yesh-lô	babbayith	ûvassādheh		wayya'ăzōv
over all which	there was to him	in the house	and in the field		so he left

3725, 866, 3937	904, 3135, 3231	3940, 3156.111	882	4114	3706
adj, rel part, prep, ps 3ms	prep, *n ms*, pn	cj, neg part, v Qal pf 3ms	prep, ps 3ms	indef pron	cj
כָּל־אֲשֶׁר־לוֹ	בְּיַד־יוֹסֵף	וְלֹא־יָדַע	אִתּוֹ	מְאוּמָה	כִּי
kol-'ăsher-lô	b^{e}yadh-yôsēph	w^{e}lō'-yāda'	'ittô	m^{e}'ûmāh	kî
all which to him	in the hand of Joseph	and not he knew	with him	anything	except

524, 4035	886, 2000	404.151	2030.121	3231	3413, 8717
cj, art, n ms	rel part, pers pron	v Qal act ptc ms	cj, v Qal impf 3ms	pn	adj, *n ms*
אִם־הַלֶּחֶם	אֲשֶׁר־הוּא	אוֹכֵל	וַיְהִי	יוֹסֵף	יְפֵה־תֹאַר
'im-hallechem	'ăsher-hû'	'ôkhēl	wayhî	yôsēph	y^{e}phēh-thō'ar
only the bread	that he	eating	and he was	Joseph	handsome of form

30. And afterward came out his brother, that had the scarlet thread upon his hand: and his name was called Zarah.

39:1. And Joseph was brought down to Egypt; and Potiphar, an officer of Pharaoh, captain of the guard, an Egyptian, bought him of the hands of the Ishmeelites, which had brought him down thither: ... eunuch, *Geneva, NEB, Young* ... courtier, *NAB, Berkeley, Anchor* ... chamberlain, *Darby* ... chief (head) steward, *Geneva, NAB, Anchor* ... head of the executioners, *Young.*

2. And the LORD was with Joseph, and he was a prosperous man; and he was in: ... lived in, *NEB, Berkeley, NCB* ... assigned to, *NAB.*

the house of his master the Egyptian: ... steward to his master, *Fenton.*

3. And his master saw that the LORD was with him, and that the LORD made all that he did to prosper in his hand: ... giving him success in all that he undertook, *NEB* ... making everything he did go well, *BB.*

4. And Joseph found grace in his sight, and he served him: ... favor, *NRSV, NIV, NASB* ... took a fancy to, *Anchor* ... high opinion of, *BB* ... personal attendant (servant), *Goodspeed, Anchor* ... ruler of his house, *Geneva* ... he was honest towards him, *Fenton.*

and he made him overseer over his house, and all that he had he put into his hand: ... superintendent, *Goodspeed, Berkeley* ... became his orderly, *Berkeley* ... all his possessions, *Anchor.*

5. And it came to pass from the

38:30. The boy with the crimson thread on his hand was named Zerah ("shining like the red rays of the dawn," probably a reference to the brightness of the crimson thread).

39:1. Notice again the contrast with 38:1. Judah was free and his sin was his own choice. The dark picture of his sin in chapter 38 makes the purity of Joseph in the following account stand out all the more. Joseph was a slave and he was about to be tested again and again. The first test was to see how he would react when he was made a slave to Potiphar. As the captain of the king's bodyguard and chief executioner, Potiphar must have been a man who was severe and not easy to please.

39:2-3. Instead of becoming bitter, Joseph trusted the LORD. His confidence in God's promises must have made him willing to commit his way to the LORD (Ps. 37:5). He must have done everything he was asked to do as unto the LORD. Thus, the LORD was with Joseph and honored his faith and faithfulness by making him successful in his tasks in the household of his master. Potiphar could not help noticing this. Perhaps Joseph gave testimony to the LORD. So Potiphar recognized that Joseph's God was making him successful in all he was doing.

39:4-6. Because Joseph found favor in Potiphar's eyes, he made him his personal attendant. Later, he made him overseer of his household and over everything he had. That is, he became the business manager with responsibility over all Potiphar's possessions. It was not uncommon for a trusted slave to be made a personal business manager (cf. the case of Eliezer, Gen. 15:2). From that time the LORD blessed everything Potiphar owned, in his house and in his field or farm property--on

3413	4920		2030.121	313	1745	431
cj, *adj*	n ms	**7.**	cj, v Qal impf 3ms	adv	art, n mp	art, dem pron
וִיפֵה	מַרְאֶה		וַיְהִי	אַחַר	הַדְּבָרִים	הָאֵלֶּה
wîphēh	mar'eh		wayhî	'achar	haddevārîm	hā'ēlleh
and handsome of	appearance		and it was	after	the matters	the these

5558.122	828, 112	881, 6084	420, 3231	569.122	8311.131
cj, v Qal impf 3fs	*n fs*, n mp, ps 3ms	do, n fd, ps 3fs	prep, pn	cj, v Qal impf 3fs	v Qal impv 2ms
וַתִּשָּׂא	אֵשֶׁת־אֲדֹנָיו	אֶת־עֵינֶיהָ	אֶל־יוֹסֵף	וַתֹּאמֶר	שִׁכְבָה
wattissā'	'ēsheth-'ădhōnâv	'eth-'ênêhā	'el-yôsēph	wattō'mer	shikhvāh
that she lifted up	the wife of his master	her eyes	to Joseph	and she said	lie down

6196		4126.321	569.121	420, 828	112	2075	112
prep, ps 1cs	**8.**	cj, v Piel impf 3ms	cj, v Qal impf 3ms	prep, n fs	n ms, ps 3ms	intrj	n ms, ps 1cs
עִמִּי		וַיְמָאֵן	וַיֹּאמֶר	אֶל־אֵשֶׁת	אֲדֹנָיו	הֵן	אֲדֹנִי
'immî		waymā'ēn	wayyō'mer	'el-'ēsheth	'ădhōnâv	hēn	'ădhōnî
with me		but he refused	and he said	to the wife of	his master	behold	my master

3940, 3156.111	882	4242, 904, 1041	3725	866, 3552, 3937	5598.111
neg part, v Qal pf 3ms	prep, ps 1cs	intrg, prep, art, n ms	cj, adj	rel part, sub, prep, ps 3ms	v Qal pf 3ms
לֹא־יָדַע	אִתִּי	מַה־בַּבָּיִת	וְכֹל	אֲשֶׁר־יֶשׁ־לוֹ	נָתַן
lō'-yādha'	'ittî	mah-babbāyith	wekhōl	'ăsher-yesh-lô	nāthan
not he knows	with me	what in the house	and all	which there is to him	has he put

904, 3135		375	1448	904, 1041	2172	4623	3940, 2910.111
prep, n fs, ps 1cs	**9.**	sub, ps 3ms	adj	prep, art, n ms	art, dem pron	prep, ps 1cs	cj, neg part, v Qal pf 3ms
בְּיָדִי		אֵינֶנּוּ	גָּדוֹל	בַּבַּיִת	הַזֶּה	מִמֶּנִּי	וְלֹא־חָשַׂךְ
beyādhî		'ênennû	ghādhôl	babbayith	hazzeh	mimmennî	welō'-chāsakh
in my hand		he is not	greater	in the house	the this	more than me	and not he withheld

4623	4114	3706	524, 881	904, 866	879, 828	351	6449.125
prep, ps 1cs	indef pron	cj	cj, do, ps 2fs	prep, rel part	pers pron, n fs, ps 3ms	cj, intrg	v Qal impf 1cs
מִמֶּנִּי	מְאוּמָה	כִּי	אִם־אוֹתָךְ	בַּאֲשֶׁר	אַתְּ־אִשְׁתּוֹ	וְאֵיךְ	אֶעֱשֶׂה
mimmennî	me'ûmāh	kî	'im-'ôthākh	ba'ăsher	'atte-'ishtô	we'êkh	'e'ĕseh
from me	anything	that	except you	because	you his wife	and how	will I do

7750	1448	2148	2490.115	3937, 435		2030.121
art, n fs	art, adj	art, dem pron	cj, v Qal pf 1cs	prep n mp	**10.**	cj, v Qal impf 3ms
הָרָעָה	הַגְּדֹלָה	הַזֹּאת	וְחָטָאתִי	לֵאלֹהִים		וַיְהִי
hārā'āh	haggedhōlāh	hazzō'th	wechāṯā'thî	lē'lōhîm		wayhî
the evil	the great	the this	and would I sin	against God		and it was

3626, 1744.341	420, 3231	3219	3219	3940, 8471.111	420	3937, 8311.141
prep, v Qal inf con, ps 3fs	prep, pn	n ms	n ms	cj, neg part, v Qal pf 3ms	prep, ps 3fs	prep, v Qal inf con
כְּדַבְּרָהּ	אֶל־יוֹסֵף	יוֹם	יוֹם	וְלֹא־שָׁמַע	אֵלֶיהָ	לִשְׁכַּב
kedhabberāhh	'el-yôsēph	yôm	yôm	welō'-shāma'	'ēlêhā	lishkav
as her speaking	to Joseph	day	day	that not he listened	to her	to lie

703	3937, 2030.141	6196		2030.121	3626, 3219	2172	971.121
prep, ps 3fs	prep, v Qal inf con	prep, ps 3fs	**11.**	cj, v Qal impf 3ms	prep, art, n ms	art, dem pron	cj, v Qal impf 3ms
אֶצְלָהּ	לִהְיוֹת	עִמָּהּ		וַיְהִי	כְּהַיּוֹם	הַזֶּה	וַיָּבֹא
'etslāhh	lihyôth	'immāhh		wayhî	kehayyôm	hazzeh	wayyāvō'
beside her	to be	with her		and it was	like the day	the this	and he went

1041	3937, 6449.141	4536	375	382	4623, 596	1041
art, n fs	prep, v Qal inf con	n fs, ps 3fs	cj, *sub*	n ms	prep, *n mp*	art, n ms
הַבַּיְתָה	לַעֲשׂוֹת	מְלַאכְתּוֹ	וְאֵין	אִישׁ	מֵאַנְשֵׁי	הַבַּיִת
habbaythāh	la'ăsôth	mela'khtô	we'ên	'îsh	mē'anshê	habbayith
to the house	to do	his work	and there was not	man	of the men of	the house

8427	904, 1041		8945.122	904, 933	3937, 569.141	8311.131
adv	prep, art, n ms	**12.**	cj, v Qal impf 3fs, ps 3ms	prep, n ms, ps 3ms	prep, v Qal inf con	v Qal impv 2ms
שָׁם	בַּבָּיִת		וַתִּתְפְּשֵׂהוּ	בְּבִגְדוֹ	לֵאמֹר	שִׁכְבָה
shām	babbāyith		wattithp^{e}sēhû	b^{e}vigh^{e}dhô	lē'mōr	shikhvāh
there	in the house		and she seized him	by his garment	saying	lie down

6196	6013.121	933	904, 3135	5308.121	3428.121
prep, ps 1cs	cj, v Qal impf 3ms	n ms, ps 3ms	prep, n fs, ps 3fs	cj, v Qal impf 3ms	cj, v Qal impf 3ms
עִמִּי	וַיַּעֲזֹב	בִּגְדוֹ	בְּיָדָהּ	וַיָּנָס	וַיֵּצֵא
'immî	wayya'ăzōv	bigh^{e}dhô	b^{e}yādhāhh	wayyānās	wayyētsē'
with me	and he left	his garment	in her hand	and he fled	and he went out

time that he had made him overseer in his house, and over all that he had, that the LORD blessed the Egyptian's house for Joseph's sake; and the blessing of the LORD was upon all that he had in the house, and in the field: ... because of Joseph, *NIV*... inside and outside, *Anchor*.

6. And he left all that he had in Joseph's hand; and he knew not aught he had, save the bread which he did eat: ... concerned himself with nothing, *NEB* ... made no inquiry what he had, *Fenton* ... was concerned about nothing except the food he ate, *NCB*.

And Joseph was a goodly person, and well favoured: ... fair, *Geneva* ... handsome and good looking, *NEB*, *RSV*, *NRSV*, *Goodspeed* ... strikingly handsome in countenance and body, *NAB*.

7. And it came to pass after these things, that his master's wife cast her eyes upon Joseph; ... took notice of him, *NEB* ... looked with desire, *NASB* ... ogled, *Berkeley* ... infatuated, *REB*.

and she said, Lie with me: ... come to bed with me, *NIV*.

8. But he refused, and said unto his master's wife, Behold, my master wotteth not what is with me in the house, and he hath committed all that he hath to my hand: ... knows not what is in his house, *Fenton* ... committed all his property to my charge, *Goodspeed* ... has trusted me with all he has, *REB*.

9. There is none greater in this house than I: ... He is not greater in this house than I am, *NRSV*, *ASV*.

neither hath he kept back any thing from me but thee, because thou art his wife: how then can I do this great wickedness, and sin against God?: ... great crime, *Goodspeed*.

10. And it came to pass, as she spake to Joseph day by day, that he hearkened not unto her, to lie by her, or to be with her: ... tried to entice him, *NAB* ... solicited, *Fenton* ... cajoled, *Anchor* ... to keep her company, *Berkeley*.

11. And it came to pass about this time, that Joseph went into the house to do his business; and there was none of the men of the house there within. ... came to her apartment with a message for her, *Fenton* ... attend his duties, *NIV* ...

account of Joseph (for Joseph's sake). So completely did Potiphar trust Joseph, that he turned all of his household and personal business over to him without asking Joseph to give any account of it to him. Potiphar carried out his duties for the Pharaoh and paid no attention to anything at home except to enjoy the food he ate. This was important preparation for Joseph. The 17-year-old boy who was sold into Egypt needed several years to learn how to handle business affairs before he could fulfill the dreams God had given him.

39:7-9. The second great test that came to Joseph was the test of personal purity. He was away from home, a handsome young man who was a slave with no rights. It would have been easy for him to yield to temptation when Potiphar's wife enticed him. Probably no one would have known. But Joseph refused. Potiphar had put him over all the other servants and given him access to everything in the household except her, for she was Potiphar's wife. Then Joseph revealed the secret of his keen sense of responsibility and of his victory in this great test. He could not do this great evil for it would be a sin, not just against his master, but against God. Joseph's relation to God was the secret of his victory over temptation to sin.

39:10-12. Day after day Potiphar's wife kept trying to entice Joseph to have sex with her. He kept refusing to do so, or even to be with her. He avoided her as much as possible and would not even give her his friendly company. But one day when Joseph came into the house to do his usual tasks and no one else was around, Potiphar's wife grabbed hold of him by his outer garment and commanded him to lie down with her. But he left his outer garment in her hand and fled out of the house.

2445		2030.121	3626, 7495.141	3706, 6013.111	933	904, 3135
art, n ms	**13.**	cj, v Qal impf 3ms	prep, v Qal inf con, ps 3fs	cj, v Qal pf 3ms	n ms, ps 3ms	prep, n fs, ps 3fs
הַחוּצָה		וַיְהִי	כִּרְאוֹתָהּ	כִּי־עָזַב	בִּגְדוֹ	בְּיָדָהּ
hachûtsāh		wayhî	kir'ôthāhh	kî-'āzav	bigh^{e}dhô	b^{e}yādhāhh
outside		and it was	when her seeing	that he left	his garment	in her hand

5308.121	2445		7410.122	3937, 596	1041	569.122	3937
cj, v Qal impf 3ms	art, n ms	**14.**	cj, v Qal impf 3fs	prep, *n mp*	n ms, ps 3fs	cj, v Qal impf 3fs	prep, ps 3mp
וַיָּנָס	הַחוּצָה		וַתִּקְרָא	לְאַנְשֵׁי	בֵּיתָהּ	וַתֹּאמֶר	לָהֶם
wayyānās̱	hachûtsāh		wattiqŏrā'	l^{e}'anshê	vêthāhh	wattō'mer	lāhem
and he fled	outside		then she called	to the men of	her house	and she said	to them

3937, 569.141	7495.133	971.511	3937	382	5888	3937, 6978.341
prep, v Qal inf con	v Qal impv 2mp	v Hiphil pf 3ms	prep, ps 1cp	*n ms*	pn	prep, v Piel inf con
לֵאמֹר	רְאוּ	הֵבִיא	לָנוּ	אִישׁ	עִבְרִי	לְצַחֶק
lē'mōr	r^{e}'û	hēvî'	lānû	'îsh	'ivrî	l^{e}tsacheq
saying	see	he brought	for us	the man of	Hebrews	to mock

904	971.111	420	3937, 8311.141	6196	7410.125	904, 7249
prep, ps 1cp	v Qal pf 3ms	prep, ps 1cs	prep, v Qal inf con	prep, ps 1cs	cj, v Qal impf 1cs	prep, n ms
בָּנוּ	בָּא	אֵלַי	לִשְׁכַּב	עִמִּי	וָאֶקְרָא	בְּקוֹל
bānû	bā'	'ēlay	lishkav	'immî	wā'eqŏrā'	b^{e}qôl
us	he came	to me	to lie	with me	but I called	with voice

1448		2030.121	3626, 8471.141	3706, 7597.515	7249	7410.125
adj	**15.**	cj, v Qal impf 3ms	prep, v Qal inf con, ps 3ms	cj, v Hiphil pf 1cs	n ms, ps 1cs	cj, v Qal impf 1cs
גָּדוֹל		וַיְהִי	כְשָׁמְעוֹ	כִּי־הֲרִימֹתִי	קוֹלִי	וָאֶקְרָא
gādhôl		wayhî	kh^{e}shām^{e}'ô	kî-h^{e}rîmōthî	qôlî	wā'eqŏrā'
great		and it was	when his hearing	that I raised	my voice	and I called

6013.121	933	703	5308.121	3428.121	2445
cj, v Qal impf 3ms	n ms, ps 3ms	prep, ps 1cs	cj, v Qal impf 3ms	cj, v Qal impf 3ms	art, n ms
וַיַּעֲזֹב	בִּגְדוֹ	אֶצְלִי	וַיָּנָס	וַיֵּצֵא	הַחוּצָה
wāyyā'ăzōv	bigh^{e}dhô	'etslî	wayyānās̱	wayyētsē'	hachûtsāh
then he left	his garment	beside me	and he fled	and he went out	outside

	5299.522	933	703	5912, 971.141	112	420, 1041
16.	cj, v Hiphil impf 3fs	n ms, ps 3ms	prep, ps 3fs	prep, v Qal inf con	n ms, ps 3ms	prep, n fs, ps 3ms
	וַתַּנַּח	בִּגְדוֹ	אֶצְלָהּ	עַד־בּוֹא	אֲדֹנָיו	אֶל־בֵּיתוֹ
	wattannach	bigh^{e}dhô	'etslāhh	'adh-bô'	'ădhōnâv	'el-bêthô
	and she put	his garment	beside her	until coming	his master	to his house

	1744.322	420	3626, 1745	431	3937, 569.141	971.111, 420
17.	cj, v Piel impf 3fs	prep, ps 3ms	prep, art, n mp	art, dem pron	prep, v Qal inf con	v Qal pf 3ms, prep, ps 1cs
	וַתְּדַבֵּר	אֵלָיו	כַּדְּבָרִים	הָאֵלֶּה	לֵאמֹר	בָּא־אֵלַי
	watt^{e}dhabbēr	'ēlâv	kadd^{e}vārîm	hā'ēlleh	lē'mōr	bā'-'ēlay
	and she spoke	to him	like the words	the these	saying	he came in to me

5860	5888	866, 971.513	3937	3937, 6978.341	904
art, n ms	art, pn	rel part, v Hiphil pf 2ms	prep, ps 1cs	prep, v Piel inf con	prep, ps 1cs
הָעֶבֶד	הָעִבְרִי	אֲשֶׁר־הֵבֵאתָ	לָנוּ	לְצַחֶק	בִּי
hā'evedh	hā'ivrî	'ăsher-hēvē'thā	lānû	l^{e}tsacheq	bî
the slave	the Hebrew	which you bought	to us	to mock	me

	2030.121	3626, 7597.541	7249	7410.125	6013.121	933
18.	cj, v Qal impf 3ms	prep, art, v Hiphil inf con	n ms, ps 1cs	cj, v Qal impf 1cs	cj, v Qal impf 3ms	n ms, ps 3ms
	וַיְהִי	כַּהֲרִימִי	קוֹלִי	וָאֶקְרָא	וַיַּעֲזֹב	בִּגְדוֹ
	wayhî	kahrîmî	qôlî	wā'eqŏrā'	wayya'ăzōv	bigh^{e}dhô
	and it was	when my raising	my voice	and I called	then he left	his garment

703	5308.121	2445		2030.121	3626, 8471.141	112
prep, ps 1cs	cj, v Qal impf 3ms	art, n ms	**19.**	cj, v Qal impf 3ms	prep, v Qal inf con	n ms, ps 3ms
אֶצְלִי	וַיָּנָס	הַחוּצָה		וַיְהִי	כִּשְׁמֹעַ	אֲדֹנָיו
'etslî	wayyānās̱	hachûtsah		wayhî	khishmōa'	'ădhōnâv
beside me	and he fled	outside		and it was	when hearing	his master

881, 1745	828	866	1744.312	420	3937, 569.141	3626, 1745
do, *n mp*	n fs, ps 3ms	rel part	v Piel pf 3fs	prep, ps 3ms	prep, v Qal inf con	prep, art, n mp
אֶת־דִּבְרֵי	אִשְׁתּוֹ	אֲשֶׁר	דִּבְּרָה	אֵלָיו	לֵאמֹר	כַּדְּבָרִים
'eth-divrê	'ishtô	'ăsher	dibb^{e}rāh	'ēlâv	lē'mōr	kadd^{e}vārîm
the words of	his wife	which	she spoke	to him	saying	about the things

431	6449.111	3937	5860	2835.121	653
art, dem pron	v Qal pf 3ms	prep, ps 1cs	n ms, ps 2ms	cj, v Qal impf 3ms	n ms, ps 3ms
הָאֵלֶּה	עָשָׂה	לִי	עַבְדֶּךָ	וַיִּחַר	אַפּוֹ
hā'ēlleh	'āsāhh	lî	'avdekhā	wayyichar	'appô
the these	he did	to me	your slave	then it became hot	his nose

house(hold) servants, *NAB*, *Anchor.*

12. And she caught him by his garment: ... cloak, *NEB*, *NIV* ... wrapper, *Fenton* ... coat, *Berkeley*, *BB*, *Anchor* ... loincloth, *REB*.

saying, Lie with me: and he left his garment in her hand, and fled, and got him out: ... and fled away naked, *Fenton*.

13. And it came to pass, when she saw that he had left his garment in her hand, and was fled forth: ... outside, *NRSV*, *Anchor*, *NKJV* ... ran out of the house, *NIV* ... fled naked, *Fenton*.

14. That she called unto the men of her house, and spake unto them, saying, See, he hath brought in an Hebrew unto us to mock us: ... house(hold) servants, *Anchor*, *Goodspeed* ... foreign fellow, *Fenton* ... violate, *Goodspeed* ... play with, *Young* ... make sport of, *BB*, *NIV*, *NASB*, *NAB* ... insult, *NRSV.*

he came in unto me to lie with me, and I cried with a loud voice: ... broke in, *Anchor* ... rape me, *Good News*, *REB* ... violate me, *Fenton* ... screamed, *NASB* ... shrieked out, *Fenton*.

15. And it came to pass, when he heard that I lifted up my voice and cried, that he left his garment with me, and fled: ... away naked, *Fenton* ... out of the house, *NIV*.

16. And she laid up his garment by her, until his lord came home: ... kept his, *NEB*.

17. And she spake unto him according to these words, saying, The Hebrew servant: ... repeated her tale, *NEB* ... bondman, *Darby.*

which thou hast brought unto us, came in unto me to mock me: ... molest, *Berkeley* ... to make an object of insult, *REB* ... abuse, *KJVII.*

18. And it came to pass, as I lifted up my voice and cried, that he left his garment with me, and fled out: ... fled away naked, *Fenton*.

19. And it came to pass, when his master heard the words of his wife, which she spake unto him, saying, After this manner did thy servant to me: ... this is the way your servant treated me, *Goodspeed*.

39:13-15. Potiphar's wife must have been very angry because Joseph spurned her advances. The outer garment Joseph left in her hand gave her an idea of how to get even. She called the men of her house, that is, to the other servants, who were probably Egyptian. She said her husband had brought in a Hebrew to mock us, and she lied, saying Joseph came in to rape her and when she raised her voice and called loudly (the call the men heard), he fled out of the house, leaving his outer garment beside her. Actually, he fled before she called, and she was holding the garment when he fled.

39:16-18. She waited with the garment beside her until Joseph's master came home. Then she repeated the lies she had told the other men of the household, again emphasizing that Joseph was a Hebrew slave, a foreigner.

39:19. When Potiphar heard his wife's story of what Joseph did, he became hot with anger. Part of that anger may have been against Joseph. Part of it must have been because he had to punish Joseph since all the household knew what his wife had said. This would mean he would lose the best business manager he ever had.

20.	4089.121	112	3231	881	5598.121	420, 1041
	cj, v Qal impf 3ms	*n mp*	pn	do, ps 3ms	cj, v Qal impf 3ms, ps 3ms	prep, *n ms*
	וַיִּקַּח	אֲדֹנֵי	יוֹסֵף	אֹתוֹ	וַיִּתְּנֵהוּ	אֶל־בֵּית
	wayyiqqach	'ădhōnê	yôsēph	'ōthô	wayyitt^{e}nēhû	'el-bêth
	and he took	the master of	Joseph	him	and he put him	into the house of

5654	4887	866, 629	4567	646.156	2030.121, 8427
art, n ms	*n ms*	rel part, *n mp*	art, n ms	v Qal pass ptc mp	cj, v Qal impf 3ms, adv
הַסֹּהַר	מְקוֹם	אֲשֶׁר־אֲסוּרֵי	הַמֶּלֶךְ	אֲסוּרִים	וַיְהִי־שָׁם
hassōhar	m^{e}qôm	'ăsher-'ăsûrê	hammelekh	'ăsûrîm	wayhî-shām
the prison	the place	which the prisoners of	the king	imprisoned	and he was there

904, 1041	5654	21.	2030.121	3176	882, 3231	5371.121	420
prep, *n ms*	art, n ms		cj, v Qal impf 3ms	pn	prep, pn	cj, v Qal impf 3ms	prep, ps 3ms
בְּבֵית	הַסֹּהַר		וַיְהִי	יְהוָה	אֶת־יוֹסֵף	וַיֵּט	אֵלָיו
b^{e}vêth	hassōhar		wayhî	y^{e}hwāh	'eth-yôsēph	wayyēt	'ēlâv
in the house of	the prison		and he was	Yahweh	with Joseph	and he extended	to him

2721	5598.121	2682	904, 6084	8015	1041, 5654
n ms	cj, v Qal impf 3ms	n ms, ps 3ms	prep, *n fp*	*n ms*	*n ms*, art, n ms
חָסֶד	וַיִּתֵּן	חִנּוֹ	בְּעֵינֵי	שַׂר	בֵּית־הַסֹּהַר
chāsedh	wayyittēn	chinnô	b^{e}'ênê	sar	bêth-hassōhar
steadfast love	and he gave	the favor of him	in the eyes of	the official of	the house of the prison

22.	5598.121	8015	1041, 5654	904, 3135, 3231	881	3725, 629
	cj, v Qal impf 3ms	*n ms*	*n ms*, art, n ms	prep, *n ms*, pn	do	*adj*, art, n mp
	וַיִּתֵּן	שַׂר	בֵּית־הַסֹּהַר	בְּיַד־יוֹסֵף	אֵת	כָּל־הָאֲסִירִם
	wayyittēn	sar	bêth-hassōhar	b^{e}yadh-yôsēph	'ēth	kol-hā'ăsîrim
	and he placed	the chief of	the house of the prison	in the hand of Joseph		all the prisoners

866	904, 1041	5654	881	3725, 866	6449.152	8427	2000
rel part	prep, *n ms*	art, n ms	cj, do	*adj*, rel part	v Qal act ptc mp	adv	pers pron
אֲשֶׁר	בְּבֵית	הַסֹּהַר	וְאֵת	כָּל־אֲשֶׁר	עֹשִׂים	שָׁם	הוּא
'ăsher	b^{e}vêth	hassōhar	w^{e}'ēth	kol-'ăsher	'ōsîm	shām	hû'
which	in the house of	the prison	and	all which	things being done	there	he

2030.111	6449.151	23.	375	8015	1041, 5654	7495.151
v Qal pf 3ms	v Qal act ptc ms		*sub*	*n ms*	*n ms*, art, n ms	v Qal act ptc ms
הָיָה	עֹשֶׂה		אֵין	שַׂר	בֵּית־הַסֹּהַר	רֹאֶה
hāyāh	'ōseh		'ên	sar	bêth-hassōhar	rō'eh
it was	doing		there was not	the chief of	the house of the prison	seeing

881, 3725, 4114	904, 3135	904, 866	3176	882	866, 2000
do, *adj*, indef pron	prep, n fs, ps 3ms	prep, rel part	pn	prep, ps 3ms	cj, rel part, pers pron
אֶת־כָּל־מְאוּמָה	בְּיָדוֹ	בַּאֲשֶׁר	יְהוָה	אִתּוֹ	וַאֲשֶׁר־הוּא
'eth-kol-m^{e}'ûmāh	b^{e}yādhô	ba'ăsher	y^{e}hwāh	'ittô	wa'ăsher-hû'
all of anything	in his hand	in which	Yahweh	with him	and that he

6449.151	3176	7014.551	40:1	2030.121	313	1745	431
v Qal act ptc ms	pn	v Hiphil ptc ms		cj, v Qal impf 3ms	adv	art, n mp	art, dem pron
עֹשֶׂה	יְהוָה	מַצְלִיחַ		וַיְהִי	אַחַר	הַדְּבָרִים	הָאֵלֶּה
'ōseh	y^{e}hwāh	matslîach		wayhî	'achar	hadd^{e}vārîm	hā'ēlleh
doing	Yahweh	bringing success		and it was	after	the matters	the these

2490	5126	4567, 4875	659	3937, 112
v Qal pf 3cp	*n ms*	*n ms*, pn	cj, art, v Qal act ptc ms	prep, n mp, ps 3mp
חָטְאוּ	מַשְׁקֵה	מֶלֶךְ־מִצְרַיִם	וְהָאֹפֶה	לַאֲדֹנֵיהֶם
chāt^{e}'û	mashqēh	melekh-mitsrayim	w^{e}hā'ōpheh	la'ădhōnêhem
they offended	the cup-bearer of	the king of Egypt	and the baker	to their master

3937, 4567	4875		7395.121	6799	6142	8530	5835	6142
prep, *n ms*	pn		cj, v Qal impf 3ms	pn	prep	*num*	n mp, ps 3ms	prep
לְמֶלֶךְ	מִצְרָיִם	**2.**	וַיִּקְצֹף	פַּרְעֹה	עַל	שְׁנֵי	סָרִיסָיו	עַל
l^emelekh	mitsrāyim		wayyiqŏtsōph	par'ōh	'al	sh^enê	sārîsāv	'al
to the king of	Egypt		and he was angry	Pharaoh	at	the two of	his eunuchs	at

8015	5126	6142	8015	659.152		5598.121	881
n ms	art, n mp	cj, prep	*n ms*	art, v Qal act ptc mp		cj, v Qal impf 3ms	do, ps 3mp
שַׂר	הַמַּשְׁקִים	וְעַל	שַׂר	הָאוֹפִים	**3.**	וַיִּתֵּן	אֹתָם
sar	hammashqîm	w^e'al	sar	hā'ôphîm		wayyittēn	'ōthām
the chief of	the cup-bearers	and at	the chief of	the bakers		and he placed	them

that his wrath was kindled: ... blazed, *Goodspeed* ... enraged, *Anchor, NAB.*

20. And Joseph's master took him, and put him into the prison: ... roundhouse, *Young* ... tower-house ... Round Tower, *NEB, Darby, Fenton* ... guardhouse, *REB.*

a place where the king's prisoners were bound: and he was there in the prison: ... state, *Goodspeed, Berkeley* ... kept in chains, *BB.*

21. But the LORD was with Joseph, and shewed him mercy: ... kept faith in him, *NEB* ... steadfast love, *NRSV* ... kindness, *Young.*

and gave him favour in the sight of the keeper of the prison: ... made him his friend, *BB* ... good graces, *Goodspeed* ... governor, *NEB* ... chief jailer, *NAB, NASB, NRSV, Anchor* ... commander, *Fenton* ... warden, *NIV.*

22. And the keeper of the prison committed to Joseph's hand all the prisoners that were in the prison; and whatsoever they did there, he was the doer of it: ... everything that had to be done, was done under his management, *NAB* ... directed their work, *REB.*

23. The keeper of the prison looked not to any thing that was under his hand; because the LORD was with him, and that which he did, the LORD made it to prosper: ... did not supervise, *Anchor* ... did not superintend anything, *Fenton.*

40:1. And it came to pass after these things, that the butler: ... cup-bearer, *Darby, REB, NASB* ... butler (only), *Fenton* ... servant who had the care of the wine, *BB.*

of the king of Egypt and his baker had offended their lord the king of Egypt: ... bread-maker, *BB.*

2. And Pharaoh was wroth: ... angry, *Goodspeed, NKJV, RSV* ... furious, *NASB* ... enraged, *Fenton.*

39:20. Putting Joseph in the prison house where the king's prisoners were kept was not the severe penalty one would expect for the crime Potiphar's wife had accused him of. It was unusual for a slave to be sent to a place where government officials who had displeased Pharaoh would be kept. It may be that Potiphar was aware of his wife's tendencies and may have doubted the accusation. So he gave Joseph the lightest punishment possible, though without any hope of release.

39:21-22. It was another test, after having been the business manager with many privileges and comparative honor, to be put in prison. The dreams of ruling must have seemed far away now. He had been slandered and dropped into a situation worse than being a slave. Yet he accepted it without saying a word or attempting to justify or defend himself. What an example of suffering according to the will of God (1 Pet. 4:19)! Then the LORD showed He was with Joseph by extending His covenant love and giving him favor with the chief official who was over the prison (and who was a subordinate officer under Potiphar). So the prison overseer put all the other prisoners under Joseph's care. Thus, whatever was done there, Joseph planned it and Joseph carried it out. This was another step in God's preparation of Joseph. He had to learn how to deal with and direct difficult people before he could be used in the place God had for him.

39:23. The overseer of the prison then left everything to Joseph's care and direction because the LORD was with him and brought success to all he did. This seems to imply that Joseph's witness to the LORD was known by all.

40:1-3. After Joseph was given this authority and a measure of freedom within the prison, Pharaoh's chief cupbearer (whose office made him an important advisor of the king) and his chief baker sinned against him; that is, they were guilty of some offense. Because Pharaoh was angry with them, he put them in the custody of the house (or office) of his chief executioner, and they were taken to the prison house where Joseph was imprisoned.

904, 5110	1041	8015	2986	420, 1041	5654
prep, *n ms*	*n ms*	*n ms*	art, n mp	prep, *n ms*	art, n ms
בְּמִשְׁמַר	בֵּית	שַׂר	הַטַּבָּחִים	אֶל־בֵּית	הַסֹּהַר
b^{e}mishmar	bêth	sar	hatabbāchîm	'el-bêth	hassōhar
in the custody of	the house of	the official of	the executioners	to the house of	the prison

4887	866	3231	646.155	8427		6734.121	8015
n ms	rel part	pn	v Qal pass ptc ms	adv	**4.**	cj, v Qal impf 3ms	*n ms*
מְקוֹם	אֲשֶׁר	יוֹסֵף	אָסוּר	שָׁם		וַיִּפְקֹד	שַׂר
m^{e}qôm	'ăsher	yôsēph	'āsûr	shām		wayyiphqōdh	sar
place	which	Joseph	imprisoned	there		and he appointed	the chief of

2986	881, 3231	882	8664.321	881	2030.126	3219
art, n mp	do, pn	prep, ps 3mp	v Piel impf 3ms	do, ps 3mp	cj, v Qal impf 3mp	n mp
הַטַּבָּחִים	אֶת־יוֹסֵף	אִתָּם	וַיְשָׁרֶת	אֹתָם	וַיִּהְיוּ	יָמִים
hattabbāchîm	'eth-yôsēph	'ittām	wayshāreth	'ōthām	wayyihyû	yāmîm
the executioners	Joseph	with them	and he waited on	them	and they were	days

904, 5110		2593.126	2573	8530	382	2573	904, 4050
prep, n ms	**5.**	cj, v Qal impf 3mp	n ms	num, ps 3mp	n ms	n ms, ps 3ms	prep, n ms
בְּמִשְׁמָר		וַיַּחַלְמוּ	חֲלוֹם	שְׁנֵיהֶם	אִישׁ	חֲלֹמוֹ	בְּלַיְלָה
b^{e}mishmār		wayyachalmû	chălôm	sh^{e}nêhem	'îsh	chălōmô	b^{e}laylāh
in custody		and they dreamed	dream	the two of them	each	his dream	in night

259	382	3626, 6879	2573	5126	659
num	n ms	prep, *n ms*	n ms, ps 3ms	art, n ms	cj, art, v Qal act ptc ms
אֶחָד	אִישׁ	כְּפִתְרוֹן	חֲלֹמוֹ	הַמַּשְׁקֶה	וְהָאֹפֶה
'echādh	'îsh	k^{e}phithrôn	chălōmô	hammashqeh	w^{e}hā'ōpheh
one	each	according to the interpretation of	his dream	the cup-bearer	and the baker

866	3937, 4567	4875	866	646.156	904, 1041	5654
rel part	prep, *n ms*	pn	rel part	v Qal pass ptc mp	prep, *n ms*	art, n ms
אֲשֶׁר	לְמֶלֶךְ	מִצְרַיִם	אֲשֶׁר	אֲסוּרִים	בְּבֵית	הַסֹּהַר
'ăsher	l^{e}melekh	mitsrayim	'ăsher	'ăsûrîm	b^{e}vêth	hassōhar
who	to the king of	Egypt	who	imprisoned	in the house of	the prison

	971.121	420	3231	904, 1269	7495.121	881	2079
6.	cj, v Qal impf 3ms	prep, ps 3mp	pn	prep, art, n ms	cj, v Qal impf 3ms	do, ps 3mp	cj, intrj, ps 3mp
	וַיָּבֹא	אֲלֵיהֶם	יוֹסֵף	בַּבֹּקֶר	וַיַּרְא	אֹתָם	וְהִנָּם
	wayyāvō'	'ălêhem	yôsēph	babbōqer	wayyar^{e}'	'ōthām	w^{e}hinnām
	and he went	to them	Joseph	in the morning	and he saw	them	and behold they

2280.552		8068.121	881, 5835	6799	866	882	904, 5110
v Qal act ptc mp	**7.**	cj, v Qal impf 3ms	do, *n mp*	pn	rel part	prep, ps 3ms	prep, *n ms*
זֹעֲפִים		וַיִּשְׁאַל	אֶת־סְרִיסֵי	פַּרְעֹה	אֲשֶׁר	אִתּוֹ	בְמִשְׁמַר
zō'ăphîm		wayyish'al	'eth-s^{e}rîsê	phar'ōh	'ăsher	'ittô	v^{e}mish^{e}mar
ones dejected		and he asked	the eunuchs of	Pharaoh	who	with him	in the custody of

1041	112	3937, 569.141	4211	6686	7737	3219		569.126
n ms	n ms, ps 3ms	prep, v Qal inf con	intrg	n mp, ps 2mp	adj	art, n ms	**8.**	cj, v Qal impf 3mp
בֵּית	אֲדֹנָיו	לֵאמֹר	מַדּוּעַ	פְּנֵיכֶם	רָעִים	הַיּוֹם		וַיֹּאמְרוּ
bêth	'ădhōnâv	lē'mōr	maddûa'	p^{e}nêkhem	rā'îm	hayyôm		wayyō'mrû
the house of	his master	saying	why	your faces	bad	today		and they said

420	2573	2593.119	6876.151	375	881	569.121
prep, ps 3ms	n ms	v Qal pf 1cp	v Qal act ptc ms	*sub*	do, ps 3ms	cj, v Qal impf 3ms
אֵלָיו	חֲלוֹם	חָלַמְנוּ	וּפֹתֵר	אֵין	אֹתוֹ	וַיֹּאמֶר
'ēlâv	chălôm	chālamnû	ûphōthēr	'ên	'ōthô	wayyō'mer
to him	dream	we dreamed	and interpreter	there is not of	it	and he said

420 prep, ps 3mp	3231 pn	3940 intrg part, neg part	3937, 435 prep n mp	6879 n mp	5807.333, 5167 v Piel impv 2mp, part	3937 prep, ps 1cs
אֲלֵהֶם	יוֹסֵף	הֲלוֹא	לֵאלֹהִים	פִּתְרֹנִים	סַפְּרוּ־נָא	לִי
'ălēhem	yôsēph	h^{e}lô'	lē'lōhîm	pithrōnîm	sapp^{e}rû-nā'	lî
to them	Joseph	are not	to God	interpretations	tell please	to me

9.

5807.321 cj, v Piel impf 3ms	8015, 5126 *n ms*, art, n mp	881, 2573 do, n ms, ps 3ms	3937, 3231 prep, pn	569.121 cj, v Qal impf 3ms	3937 prep, ps 3ms
וַיְסַפֵּר	שַׂר־הַמַּשְׁקִים	אֶת־חֲלֹמוֹ	לְיוֹסֵף	וַיֹּאמֶר	לוֹ
waysappēr	sar-hammasqîm	'eth-chălōmô	l^{e}yôsēph	wayyō'mer	lô
and he told	the chief of the cup-bearers	his dream	to Joseph	and he said	to him

against two of his officers: ... his two courtiers, *Anchor, NAB* ... two eunuchs, *NEB, Young* ... servants, *BB.*

against the chief of the butlers, and against the chief of the bakers: ... chief wine-servant, *BB* ... chief of the cooks, *Fenton* ... bread-maker, *BB.*

3. And he put them in ward in the house of the captain of the guard: ... custody, *NRSV* ... head (chief) steward, *Goodspeed, NAB, Anchor* ... commander, *Fenton* ... chief of executioners, *Young.*

into the prison, the place where Joseph was bound: ... tower-house, *Darby* ... guardhouse, *REB* ... jail, *NASB* ... round-tower (house), *NEB, Young* ... imprisoned, *Darby.*

4. And the captain of the guard charged Joseph with them, and he served them: ... remitted, *Fenton* ... attended, *NIV* ... ministered, *ASV* ... waited on, *Goodspeed.*

and they continued a season in ward: ... after they had been in custody with them some time, *NIV* ... many days under restraint, *Fenton.*

5. And they dreamed a dream both of them, each man his dream in one night, each man according to the interpretation of his dream, the butler and the baker of the king of Egypt, which were bound in the prison: ... on the same night, *BB* ... each dream with its own meaning, *NRSV, Anchor, NAB* ... dreams with a special sense, *BB, NEB, NKJV* ... each dream had a separate appearance, *Fenton* ... personal significance, *Berkeley.*

6. And Joseph came in unto them in the morning, and looked upon them, and, behold, they were sad: ... troubled, *RSV, RSV* ... dejected, *Anchor, NEB, NASB* ... pining gloom, *Fenton* ... dispirited, *REB* ... worried, *Goodspeed.*

7. And he asked Pharaoh's officers that were with him in the ward of his lord's house, saying, Wherefore look ye so sadly to day?: ... Why do you look so sad today?, *KJVII* ... downcast, *NRSV, RSV* ... and sorrowful, *Fenton* ... woebegone, *Berkeley.*

8. And they said unto him, We have dreamed a dream, and there is no interpreter of it. And Joseph said unto them, Do not interpretations belong to God? tell me them, I pray you: ... surely, *NAB, Anchor* ... the sense of dreams, *BB.*

9. And the chief butler told his dream to Joseph, and said to him, In my dream, behold, a vine was

40:4. Potiphar, the captain of the guard, knew that the chief cupbearer and the chief baker could be restored to favor with the king. It would be wise for him to take the best care of them possible under the circumstances, lest they be restored and have a grudge against him. So Potiphar showed he had not forgotten Joseph's good work and wonderful attitude, and he appointed Joseph to be with them, that is, as a personal servant to see to their needs. So Joseph waited on them while they remained for a long time in custody. This was another test, for instead of overseeing the prisoners, he was limited to humble service to these two men.

40:5. One night both the chief cupbearer and the chief baker had a dream. Each one felt it needed an interpretation, because the dreams were odd.

40:6-7. The next morning Joseph noticed they were dejected. Though they were guilty and he was not, he did not resent them. Instead he showed a spirit of concern and compassion as he asked them why they looked so bad.

40:8. When they told him they had dreamed a dream and had no access to an interpreter, Joseph gave a witness without hesitation. This is evidence that he must have given his witness often before. So Joseph declared that interpretations belong to God and asked them to please tell him the dream.

40:9-11. The chief cupbearer was the first to tell his dream. In the dream he saw a grapevine with three branches that seemed to be budding. Then the growth speeded up, blossoms came out, grapes ripened. Then he saw himself with

904, 2573	2079, 1655	3937, 6686		904, 1655	8421	8031
prep, n ms, ps 1cs	cj, intrg, n fs	prep, n mp, ps 1cs	**10.**	cj, prep, art, n fs	num	n mp
בַּחֲלוֹמִי	וְהִנֵּה־גֶפֶן	לְפָנָי		וּבַגֶּפֶן	שְׁלֹשָׁה	שָׂרִיגִם
bachlômî	wehinnēh-ghephen	lephānāy		ûvaggephen	shelōshāh	sārîghim
in my dream	and behold a vine	before me		and on the vine	three	branches

2026	3626, 6775.153	6148.112	5511	1344.516	838	6252
cj, pers pron	prep, v Qal act ptc fs	v Qal pf 3fs	n ms, ps 3fs	v Hiphil pf 3cp	n mp, ps 3fs	n mp
וְהִיא	כְפֹרַחַת	עָלְתָה	נִצָּהּ	הִבְשִׁילוּ	אַשְׁכְּלֹתֶיהָ	עֲנָבִים
wehî'	khephorachath	'ālethāh	nitstsāhh	hivshîlû	'ashkelōthêhā	'ănāvîm
and it	as one budding	it came up	its blossoms	they ripened	clusters	grapes

	3683	6799	904, 3135	4089.125	881, 6252	7923
11.	cj, *n fs*	pn	prep, n fs, ps 1cs	cj, v Qal impf 1cs	do, art, n mp	cj, v Qal impf 1cs
	וְכוֹס	פַּרְעֹה	בְּיָדִי	וָאֶקַּח	אֶת־הָעֲנָבִים	וָאֶשְׂחַט
	wekhôs̱	par'ōh	beyādhî	wā'eqqach	'eth-hā'ănāvîm	wā'eschaṯ
	and the cup of	Pharaoh	in my hand	and I took	the grapes	and I squeezed

881	420, 3683	6799	5598.125	881, 3683	6142, 3834	6799
do, ps 3mp	prep, *n fs*	pn	cj, v Qal impf 1cs	do, art, n fs	prep, *n fs*	pn
אֹתָם	אֶל־כּוֹס	פַּרְעֹה	וָאֶתֵּן	אֶת־הַכּוֹס	עַל־כַּף	פַּרְעֹה
'ōthām	'el-kôs̱	par'ōh	wā'ettēn	'eth-hakkôs̱	'al-kaph	par'ōh
them	to the cup of	Pharaoh	and I put	the cup	on the hand of	Pharaoh

	569.121	3937	3231	2172	6879	8421	8031
12.	cj, v Qal impf 3ms	prep, ps 3ms	pn	dem pron	n ms, ps 3ms	*num*	art, n mp
	וַיֹּאמֶר	לוֹ	יוֹסֵף	זֶה	פִּתְרֹנוֹ	שְׁלֹשֶׁת	הַשָּׂרִגִים
	wayyō'mer	lô	yôsēph	zeh	pithrōnô	shelōsheth	hassārighîm
	and he said	to him	Joseph	this	its interpretation	the three of	the branches

8421	3219	2062		904, 5968	8421	3219	5558.121	6799
num	n mp	pers pron	**13.**	prep, adv	num	n mp	v Qal impf 3ms	pn
שְׁלֹשֶׁת	יָמִים	הֵם		בְּעוֹד	שְׁלֹשֶׁת	יָמִים	יִשָּׂא	פַּרְעֹה
shelōsheth	yāmîm	hēm		be'ôdh	shelōsheth	yāmîm	yissā'	phar'ōh
three	days	they		in still	three	days	he will lift up	Pharaoh

881, 7513	8178.511	6142, 3774	5598.113	3683, 6799
do, n ms, ps 2ms	cj, v Hiphil pf 3ms, ps 2ms	prep, n ms, ps 2ms	cj, v Qal pf 2ms	*n fs*, pn
אֶת־רֹאשֶׁךָ	וַהֲשִׁיבְךָ	עַל־כַּנֶּךָ	וְנָתַתָּ	כוֹס־פַּרְעֹה
'eth-rō'shekhā	wahshîvekhā	'al-kannekhā	wenāthattā	khôs̱-par'ōh
your head	and he will restore you	concerning your office	and you will place	the cup of Pharaoh

904, 3135	3626, 5122	7518	866	2030.113	5126		3706
prep, n fs, ps 3ms	prep, art, n ms	art, adj	rel part	v Qal pf 2ms	n ms, ps 3ms	**14.**	cj
בְּיָדוֹ	כַּמִּשְׁפָּט	הָרִאשׁוֹן	אֲשֶׁר	הָיִיתָ	מַשְׁקֵהוּ		כִּי
beyādhô	kammishpāṯ	hāri'shôn	'ăsher	hāyîthā	mashqēhû		kî
in his hand	like the custom	the former	which	you were	his cup-bearer		but

524, 2226.113	882	3626, 866	3296.121	3937	6449.113, 5167
cj, v Qal pf 2ms, ps 1cs	prep, ps 2ms	prep, rel part	v Qal impf 3ms	prep, ps 2fs	cj, v Qal pf 2ms, part
אִם־זְכַרְתַּנִי	אִתְּךָ	כַּאֲשֶׁר	יִיטַב	לָךְ	וְעָשִׂיתָ־נָּא
'im-zekhartanî	'ittekhā	ka'ăsher	yîṯav	lākh	we'āsîthā-nā'
if you remember me	with you	when	it is going well	for you	then may you do please

6200	2721	2226.513	420, 6799	3428.513	4623, 1041
prep, ps 1cs	n ms	cj, v Hiphil pf 2ms, ps 1cs	prep, pn	cj, v Hiphil pf 2ms, ps 1cs	prep, art, n ms
עִמָּדִי	חָסֶד	וְהִזְכַּרְתַּנִי	אֶל־פַּרְעֹה	וְהוֹצֵאתַנִי	מִן־הַבַּיִת
'immādhî	chās̱edh	wehizkartanî	'el-par'ōh	wehôtsē'thanî	min-habbayith
with me	kindness	and you will mention me	to Pharaoh	and bring me out	from the house

2172 art, dem pron		3706, 1630.442 cj, v Pual inf abs	1630.415 v Pual pf 1cs	4623, 800 prep, *n fs*	5888 art, pn	1612, 6553 cj, cj, adv
הַזֶּה	**15.**	כִּי־גֻנֹּב	גֻּנַּבְתִּי	מֵאֶרֶץ	הָעִבְרִים	וְגַם־פֹּה
hazzeh		kî-ghunnōv	gunnavtî	mē'erets	hā'ivrîm	wegham-pōh
the this		because being stolen	I was stolen	from the land of	the Hebrews	and also here

3940, 6449.115 neg part, v Qal pf 1cs	4114 indef pron	3706, 7947.116 cj, v Qal pf 3cp	881 do, ps 1cs	904, 988 prep, art, n ms		7495.121 cj, v Qal impf 3ms
לֹא־עָשִׂיתִי	מְאוּמָה	כִּי־שָׂמוּ	אֹתִי	בַּבּוֹר	**16.**	וַיַּרְא
lō'-'āsîthî	me'ûmāh	kî-sāmû	'ōthî	babbôr		wayyare'
not I did	anything	that they put	me	in the dungeon		and he saw

8015, 659 *n ms*, art, v Qal act ptc mp	3706 cj	3005 adj	6876.111 v Qal pf 3ms	569.121 cj, v Qal impf 3ms	420, 3231 prep, pn	652, 603 cj, pers pron
שַׂר־הָאֹפִים	כִּי	טוֹב	פָּתָר	וַיֹּאמֶר	אֶל־יוֹסֵף	אַף־אֲנִי
sar-hā'ōphîm	kî	tôv	pāthār	wayyō'mer	'el-yôsēph	'aph-'ănî
the chief of the bakers	that	good	he interpreted	and he said	to Joseph	also I

before me: ... grapevine, *Good News.*

10. And in the vine were three branches: and it was as though it budded, and her blossoms shot forth; and the clusters thereof brought forth ripe grapes: ... as soon as it budded, *RSV* ... and berries grew on them, *Fenton* ... rich, *ASV* ... ready for cutting, *BB.*

11. And Pharaoh's cup was in my hand: and I took the grapes, and pressed them into Pharaoh's cup, and I gave the cup into Pharaoh's hand: ... plucked, *NEB, REB* ... squeezed, *NIV, NASB.*

12. And Joseph said unto him, This is the interpretation of it: The three branches are three days:

13. Yet within three days shall Pharaoh lift up thine head: ... pardon, *Anchor* ... honor, *BB* ... raise, *NEB* ... summon, *Goodspeed.*

and restore thee unto thy place: ... post, *NEB, Anchor, NAB* ... station, *Young, Fenton* ... office, *NRSV, NASB, ASV* ... position, *NIV, Berkeley.*

and thou shalt deliver Pharaoh's cup into his hand, after the former manner when thou wast his butler: ... as you used to do, *REB.*

14. But think on me when it shall be well with thee: ... remember me, *RSV, REB* ... when prosperity comes to you, *Goodspeed.*

and shew kindness: ... deal kindly, *Darby* ... show your gratitude to me by, *Berkeley* ... keep faith with me, *NEB.*

I pray thee, unto me, and make mention of me unto Pharaoh, and bring me out of this house: ... bringing my case to Pharoahs notice, *REB* ... liberate, *Goodspeed* ... prison, *NIV, BB.*

15. For indeed I was stolen away out of the land of the Hebrews: and here also have I done nothing that they should put me into the dungeon: ... kidnapped, *NCB* ... carried off by force, *REB* ... by treachery I was dragged, *Fenton* ... prison, *BB.*

16. When the chief baker saw that the interpretation was good: ... favorable, *NIV* ... how well he had interpreted, *Anchor* ... encouraging, *Berkeley.*

Pharaoh's cup in his hand. He took the grapes, squeezed them into Pharaoh's cup, and put the cup into Pharaoh's hand.

40:12-13. Joseph must have been looking to God for the interpretation while the chief cupbearer was telling the dream, for he gave the interpretation without hesitation. Within three days, Pharaoh would lift up the chief cupbearer's head, that is, restore him to cheerfulness by setting him free. Then he would restore him to his office as cupbearer and everything would go on as before.

40:14-15. Joseph then added a plaintive plea that if the cupbearer should remember him when it was going well with him, then let him do a kindness and mention Joseph to Pharaoh, to get him to bring him out of the prison. Joseph explained he was really stolen from the land of the Hebrews and had not done anything to cause him to be put in the dungeon. Notice that he did not ask this until after he gave the interpretation. The interpretation was given freely and unconditionally.

40:16-17. The favorable interpretation given to the chief cupbearer encouraged the chief baker to tell his dream. He saw three baskets of cake on his

904, 2573	2079	8421	5729	2854	6142, 7513		904, 5729
prep, n ms, ps 1cs	cj, intrj	*num*	*n mp*	n ms	prep, n ms, ps 1cs		cj, prep, art, n ms
בַּחֲלוֹמִי	וְהִנֵּה	שְׁלֹשָׁה	סַלֵּי	חֹרִי	עַל־רֹאשִׁי	**17.**	וּבַסַּל
bachlômî	wehinnēh	shelōshāh	sallê	chōrî	'al-rō'shî		ûvassal
in my dream	and behold	three	baskets of	cake	on my head		and in the basket

6169	4623, 3725	4120	6799	4801	659.151	5991
art, adj	prep, prep	*n ms*	pn	*n ms*	v Qal act ptc ms	cj, art, n ms
הָעֶלְיוֹן	מִכֹּל	מַאֲכַל	פַּרְעֹה	מַעֲשֵׂה	אֹפֶה	וְהָעוֹף
hā'elyôn	mikkōl	ma'ăkhal	par'ōh	ma'ăsēh	'ōpheh	wehā'ôph
the upper	some of all	the food of	Pharaoh	the work of	baker	but the birds

404.151	881	4623, 5729	4263, 6142	7513		6257.121	3231
v Qal act ptc ms	do, ps 3mp	prep, art, n ms	prep, prep	n ms, ps 1cs		cj, v Qal impf 3ms	pn
אֹכֵל	אֹתָם	מִן־הַסַּל	מֵעַל	רֹאשִׁי	**18.**	וַיַּעַן	יוֹסֵף
'ōkhēl	'ōthām	min-hassal	mē'al	rō'shî		wayya'an	yôsēph
eating	them	from the basket	on	my head		and he answered	Joseph

569.121	2172	6879	8421	5729	8421	3219	2062
cj, v Qal impf 3ms	dem pron	n ms, ps 3ms	*num*	art, n mp	*num*	n mp	pers pron
וַיֹּאמֶר	זֶה	פִּתְרֹנוֹ	שְׁלֹשֶׁת	הַסַּלִּים	שְׁלֹשֶׁת	יָמִים	הֵם
wayyō'mer	zeh	pithrōnô	shelōsheth	hassallîm	shelōsheth	yāmîm	hēm
and he said	this	its interpretation	the three of	the baskets	three	days	they

	904, 5968	8421	3219	5558.121	6799	881, 7513	4623, 6142
	prep, adv	num	n mp	v Qal impf 3ms	pn	do, n ms, ps 2ms	prep, prep, ps 2ms
19.	בְּעוֹד	שְׁלֹשֶׁת	יָמִים	יִשָּׂא	פַרְעֹה	אֶת־רֹאשְׁךָ	מֵעָלֶיךָ
	be'ôdh	shelōsheth	yāmîm	yissā'	phar'ōh	'eth-rō'shekhā	mē'ālêkhā
	in still	three	days	he will lift up	Pharaoh	your head	from you

8847.111	881	6142, 6320	404.111	5991	881, 1340	4623, 6142
cj, v Qal pf 3ms	do, ps 2ms	prep, n ms	cj, v Qal pf 3ms	art, n ms	do, n ms, ps 2ms	prep, prep, ps 2ms
וְתָלָה	אוֹתְךָ	עַל־עֵץ	וְאָכַל	הָעוֹף	אֶת־בְּשָׂרְךָ	מֵעָלֶיךָ
wethālāh	'ôthekhā	'al-'ēts	we'ākhal	hā'ôph	'eth-besārekhā	mē'ālêkhā
and he will hang	you	on tree	and they will eat	the birds	your flesh	from you

	2030.121	904, 3219	8389	3219	3314.641	881, 6799	6449.121
	cj, v Qal impf 3ms	prep, art, n ms	art, num	*n ms*	v Hophal inf con	do, pn	cj, v Qal impf 3ms
20.	וַיְהִי	בַּיּוֹם	הַשְּׁלִישִׁי	יוֹם	הֻלֶּדֶת	אֶת־פַּרְעֹה	וַיַּעַשׂ
	wayhî	bayyôm	hashshelîshî	yôm	hulledheth	'eth-par'ōh	wayya'as
	and it was	on the day	the third	the day of	being born	Pharaoh	and he made

5136	3937, 3725, 5860	5558.121	881, 7513	8015	5126
n ms	prep, *adj*, n mp, ps 3ms	cj, v Qal impf 3ms	do, *n ms*	*n ms*	art, n mp
מִשְׁתֶּה	לְכָל־עֲבָדָיו	וַיִּשָּׂא	אֶת־רֹאשׁ	שַׂר	הַמַּשְׁקִים
mishteh	lekhol-'ăvādhâv	wayyissā'	'eth-rō'sh	sar	hammashqîm
feast	for all his servants	and he lifted up	the head of	the chief of	the cup-bearers

881, 7513	8015	659.152	904, 8761	5860		8178.521
cj, do, *n ms*	*n ms*	art, v Qal act ptc mp	prep, *sub*	n mp, ps 3ms		cj, v Hiphil impf 3ms
וְאֶת־רֹאשׁ	שַׂר	הָאֹפִים	בְּתוֹךְ	עֲבָדָיו	**21.**	וַיָּשֶׁב
we'eth-rō'sh	sar	hā'ōphîm	bethôkh	'ăvādhâv		wayyāshev
and the head of	the chief of	the bakers	in the midst of	his servants		and he restored

881, 8015	5126	6142, 5126	5598.121	3683	6142, 3834
do, *n ms*	art, n mp	prep, n ms, ps 3ms	cj, v Qal pf 3ms	art, n fs	prep, *n fs*
אֶת־שַׂר	הַמַּשְׁקִים	עַל־מַשְׁקֵהוּ	וַיִּתֵּן	הַכּוֹס	עַל־כַּף
'eth-sar	hammashqîm	'al-mashqēhû	wayyittēn	hakkôs	'al-kaph
the chief of	the cup-bearers	to his position as cup-bearer	and he placed	the cup	in the hand of

6799		881	8015	659.152	8847.111	3626, 866	6876.111
pn	**22.**	cj, do	*n ms*	art, v Qal act ptc mp	v Qal pf 3ms	prep, rel part	v Qal pf 3ms
פַּרְעֹה		וְאֵת	שַׂר	הָאֹפִים	תָּלָה	כַּאֲשֶׁר	פָּתַר
par'ōh		we'ēth	sar	hā'ōphîm	tālāh	ka'ăsher	pāthar
Pharaoh		but	the chief of	the bakers	he hanged	just as	he interpreted

3937	3231		3940, 2226.111	8015, 5126	881, 3231
prep, ps 3mp	pn	**23.**	cj, neg part, v Qal pf 3ms	*n ms*, art, n mp	do, pn
לָהֶם	יוֹסֵף		וְלֹא־זָכַר	שַׂר־הַמַּשְׁקִים	אֶת־יוֹסֵף
lāhem	yôsēph		welō'-zākhar	sar-hammashqîm	'eth-yôsēph
to them	Joseph		but not he remembered	the chief of the cup-bearers	Joseph

8319.121		2030.121	4623, 7377	8523	3219	6799
cj, v Qal impf 3ms, ps 3ms	**41:1**	cj, v Qal impf 3ms	prep, *n ms*	n md	n mp	cj, pn
וַיִּשְׁכָּחֵהוּ		וַיְהִי	מִקֵּץ	שְׁנָתַיִם	יָמִים	וּפַרְעֹה
wayyishkâchēhû		wayhî	miqqēts	shenāthayim	yāmîm	ûphar'ōh
rather he forgot him		and it was	after	two years of	days	and Pharaoh

he said unto Joseph, I also was in my dream, and, behold, I had three white baskets on my head: ... three baskets of white bread, *BB*, *NASB*, *Berkeley* ... cake baskets, *NRSV*, *RSV* ... wicker baskets, *NAB*, *NCB* ... open-work baskets, *Goodspeed*.

17. And in the uppermost basket there was of all manner of bakemeats: ... highest, *Fenton* ... every kind of food which the baker prepares, *NEB*.

for Pharaoh; and the birds did eat them out of the basket upon my head: ... were pecking at, *NAB* ... top, *NEB*.

18. And Joseph answered and said, This is the interpretation thereof: The three baskets are three days:

19. Yet within three days shall Pharaoh lift up thy head from off thee: ... summon you, *Goodspeed* ... take you out of prison, *BB*.

and shall hang thee on a tree: ... hang you on a gibbet, *NCB* ... gallows, *Fenton* ... and have you impaled on a stake(pole), *NAB*, *Anchor* ... hang you on a pole, *NRSV*.

and the birds shall eat thy flesh from off thee: ... will be pecking, *NAB*, *Anchor*.

20. And it came to pass the third day, which was Pharaoh's birthday, that he made a feast unto all his servants: ... bondmen, *Darby* ... officials, *Goodspeed*, *REB*, *NIV* ... courtiers, *NCB*, *Berkeley* ... staff, *NAB*.

and he lifted up the head of the chief butler and of the chief baker among his servants: ... singled out, *Anchor* ... gave honor to, *BB*.

21. And he restored the chief butler unto his butlership again; and he gave the cup into Pharaoh's hand:

22. But he hanged the chief baker: as Joseph had interpreted to them: ... impaled, *NAB*, *Anchor*.

23. Yet did not the chief butler remember Joseph, but forgat him.

41:1. And it came to pass at the end

head, with a variety of baked goods for Pharaoh in the top basket. Birds were eating out of it.

40:18-19. The interpretation of the baker's dream was not at all favorable. Within three days Pharaoh would decapitate him and hang his body on a tree (the Hebrew can also mean on a wooden pole) as an example to warn people not to dishonor or displease Pharaoh. His body would be left there and birds would eat his flesh off his bones.

40:20-22. The third day was Pharaoh's birthday. To celebrate it, he made a great feast and invited all his servants (all the officials of his court), and he set both the chief cupbearer and the chief baker free in the midst of his servants. He apparently let them both enjoy the feast. Then he restored the chief cupbearer to his former office by putting the royal cup in his hand. But the baker he hanged, just as Joseph had said in his interpretation of their dreams.

40:23. But the cupbearer did not remember Joseph, that is, to do anything about him. Instead, he proceeded to forget him. This seems to mean that every time he did think about Joseph it was not a good time to say anything or he was too busy, so he gradually forgot him and did not think about him any more.

41:1. Two years passed. This was another test for Joseph, the test of delay, a difficult test for anyone. But God's delays are not cruel. If the chief cupbearer had told Pharaoh immediately, and

2593.151	2079	6198.151	6142, 3083		2079	4623, 3083
v Qal act ptc ms	cj, intrj	v Qal act ptc ms	prep, art, pn		cj, intrj	prep, art, pn
חֹלֵם	וְהִנֵּה	עֹמֵד	עַל־הַיְאֹר	**2.**	וְהִנֵּה	מִן־הַיְאֹר
chōlēm	wehinnēh	'ōmēdh	'al-hay'ōr		wehinnēh	min-hay'ōr
dreaming	and behold	standing	beside the Nile		and behold	from the Nile

6148.154	8124	6760	3413	4920	1304	1340
v Qal act ptc fp	num	n fp	*adj*	n ms	cj, *adj*	n ms
עֹלֹת	שֶׁבַע	פָּרוֹת	יְפוֹת	מַרְאֶה	וּבְרִיאֹת	בָּשָׂר
'ōlōth	sheva'	pārôth	yephôth	mar'eh	ûverî'ōth	bāsār
going up	seven	cows	good-looking of	appearance	and fat of	flesh

7749.127	904, 260		2079	8124	6760	311	6148.154
cj, v Qal impf 3fp	prep, art, n ms		cj, intrj	num	n fp	adj	v Qal act ptc fp
וַתִּרְעֶינָה	בָּאָחוּ	**3.**	וְהִנֵּה	שֶׁבַע	פָּרוֹת	אֲחֵרוֹת	עֹלוֹת
wattir'ênāh	bā'āchû		wehinnēh	sheva'	pārôth	'ăchērôth	'ōlôth
and they grazed	on the reeds		and behold	seven	cows	other	going up

313	4623, 3083	7737	4920	1911	1340	6198.127	703
adv, ps 3fp	prep, art, pn	*adj*	n ms	cj, *adj*	n ms	cj, v Qal impf 3fp	prep
אַחֲרֵיהֶן	מִן־הַיְאֹר	רָעוֹת	מַרְאֶה	וְדַקּוֹת	בָּשָׂר	וַתַּעֲמֹדְנָה	אֵצֶל
'achrêhen	min-hay'ōr	rā'ôth	mar'eh	wedhaqqôth	bāsār	watta'ămōdhnāh	'ētsel
after them	from the Nile	bad of	appearance	and thin of	flesh	and they stood	beside

6760	6142, 8004	3083		404.127	6760	7737	4920
art, n fp	prep, *n fs*	art, pn		cj, v Qal impf 3fp	art, n fp	*adj*	art, n ms
הַפָּרוֹת	עַל־שְׂפַת	הַיְאֹר	**4.**	וַתֹּאכַלְנָה	הַפָּרוֹת	רָעוֹת	הַמַּרְאֶה
happārôth	'al-sephath	hay'ōr		wattō'khalnāh	happārôth	rā'ôth	hammar'eh
the cows	on shore of	the Nile		and they ate	the cows	bad of	the appearance

1911	1340	881	8124	6760	3413	4920	1304
cj, *adj*	art, n ms	do	num	art, n fp	*adj*	art, n ms	cj, art, adj
וְדַקֹּת	הַבָּשָׂר	אֵת	שֶׁבַע	הַפָּרוֹת	יְפֹת	הַמַּרְאֶה	וְהַבְּרִיאֹת
wedhaqqōth	habbāsār	'ēth	sheva'	happārôth	yephōth	hammar'eh	wehabberî'ōth
and thin of	the flesh		seven	the cows	good-looking of	the appearance	and the fat

3477.121	6799		3583.121	2593.121	8529	2079
cj, v Qal impf 3ms	pn		cj, v Qal impf 3ms	cj, v Qal impf 3ms	num	cj, intrj
וַיִּיקַץ	פַּרְעֹה	**5.**	וַיִּישָׁן	וַיַּחֲלֹם	שֵׁנִית	וְהִנֵּה
wayyîqats	par'ōh		wayyîshān	wayyachlōm	shēnîth	wehinnēh
and he woke up	Pharaoh		and he was sleeping	and he dreamed	second	and behold

8124	8118	6148.154	904, 7354	259	1304	3005		2079
num	n fp	v Qal act ptc fp	prep, n ms	num	adj	cj, adj		cj, intrj
שֶׁבַע	שִׁבֳּלִים	עֹלוֹת	בְּקָנֶה	אֶחָד	בְּרִיאוֹת	וְטֹבוֹת	**6.**	וְהִנֵּה
sheva'	shibbelîm	'ōlôth	beqāneh	'echādh	berî'ôth	weṭōvôth		wehinnēh
seven	heads of grain	ones going up	on stalk	one	fat	and good		and behold

8124	8118	1911	8167.158	7205	7048.154	313
num	n fp	adj	cj, *v Qal pass ptc fp*	n ms	v Qal act ptc fp	adv, ps 3fp
שֶׁבַע	שִׁבֳּלִים	דַּקּוֹת	וּשְׁדוּפֹת	קָדִים	צֹמְחוֹת	אַחֲרֵיהֶן
sheva'	shibbelîm	daqqôth	ûshedhûphōth	qādhîm	tsōmchôth	'achrêhen
seven	heads of grain	thin	and ones scorched of	east wind	ones sprouting	after them

	1142.127	8118	1911	881	8124	8118	1304
	cj, v Qal impf 3fp	art, n fp	art, adj	do	num	art, n fp	art, adj
7.	וַתִּבְלַעְנָה	הַשִּׁבֳּלִים	הַדַּקּוֹת	אֵת	שֶׁבַע	הַשִּׁבֳּלִים	הַבְּרִיאוֹת
	wattivla'ănāh	hashshibbelîm	haddaqqôth	'ēth	sheva'	hashshibbelîm	habberî'ôth
	and they swallowed	the heads of grain	the thin		seven	the heads of grain	the fat

4529	3477.121	6799	2079	2573		2030.121	904, 1269
cj, art, adj	cj, v Qal impf 3ms	pn	cj, intrj	n ms	**8.**	cj, v Qal impf 3ms	prep, art, n ms
וְהַמְּלֵאוֹת	וַיִּיקַץ	פַּרְעֹה	וְהִנֵּה	חֲלוֹם		וַיְהִי	בַבֹּקֶר
w^{e}hamm^{e}lē'ôth	wayyîqats	par'ōh	w^{e}hinnēh	chălôm		wayhî	vabbōqer
and the full	and he woke up	Pharaoh	and behold	dream		and it was	in the morning

6717.222	7593	8365.121	7410.121	881, 3725, 2851	4875
cj, v Niphal impf 3fs	n fs, ps 3ms	cj, v Qal impf 3ms	cj, v Qal impf 3ms	do, *adj*, n mp	pn
וַתִּפָּעֶם	רוּחוֹ	וַיִּשְׁלַח	וַיִּקְרָא	אֶת־כָּל־חַרְטֻמֵּי	מִצְרַיִם
wattippā'em	rûchô	wayyishlach	wayyiqōrā'	'eth-kol-chartummê	mitsrayim
and it was troubled	his spirit	and he sent out	and he called	all of the cult priests of	Egypt

of two full years, that Pharaoh dreamed: and, behold, he stood by the river: ... the Nile, *BB*, *Anchor*, *NRSV.*

2. And, behold, there came up out of the river seven well favoured: ... sleek, *NEB*, *NRSV*, *NASB* ... beautiful, *KJVII*, *Goodspeed* ... sturdy, *Anchor.*

kine: ... cows, *NKJV*, *RSV*, *Goodspeed.*

and fatfleshed; and they fed in a meadow: ... reeds, *NEB*, *Young*, *NRSV* ... the river grass, *BB* ... rushes, *Fenton* ... marsh-grass, *NASB*, *Berkeley* ... sedge, *Goodspeed.*

3. And, behold, seven other kine came up after them out of the river, ill favoured: ... gaunt, *NEB*, *Anchor*, *NIV* ... evil, *KJVII*, ... ugly, *Anchor*, *NRSV*, *NIV.*

and leanfleshed; and stood by the other kine upon the brink of the river: ... thin and bony, *Good News.*

4. And the ill favoured and leanfleshed kine did eat up the seven well favoured and fat kine. So Pharaoh awoke.

5. And he slept and dreamed the second time: and, behold, seven ears of corn: ... grain, *ASV*, *Goodspeed*, *NKJV.*

came up upon one stalk, rank: ... fat, *Darby*, *NCB*, *NAB*, *Young*, *KJVII* ... large, *Berkeley* ... fine, *ASV*, *NCB* ... full, *REB*, *Berkeley*, *BB* ... beautiful, *Fenton* ... solid, *Anchor.*

and good: ... plump, *ASV*, *NKJV*, *RSV* ... ripe, *REB*, *NEB* ... healthy, *NAB*, *NIV*, *Anchor.*

6. And, behold, seven thin ears and blasted with the east wind sprung up after them: ... parched, *Darby* ... blighted, *NKJV*, *RSV*, *Fenton*, *NRSV* ... blighted, *Fenton* ... shriveled, *REB*, *NEB* ... scorched, *NASB*, *NIV*, *Anchor* ... wasted, *BB.*

7. And the seven thin ears devoured the seven rank and full ears. And Pharaoh awoke, and, behold, it was a dream.

8. And it came to pass in the morning that his spirit: ... mind, *REB*, *NEB.*

was troubled: ... he was so perturbed, *ASV* ... disturbed in his spirit, *Berkeley* ... oppressed, *Fenton* ... agitated, *NAB*, *Anchor.*

and he sent and called for all the magicians: ... scribes, *Darby*, *Berkeley*, *Young* ... dream-interpreters, *REB* ... writers, *Fenton* ...

Pharaoh had set Joseph free, he might still have been a slave, or he might have been sent back to Canaan. God's timing is always right. After the 2 years, Pharaoh had a dream where he saw himself standing by the river. In Egypt, this means the River Nile.

41:2-4. The dream was simple. Seven good-looking, fat cows came up from drinking at the river and began feeding on the reeds (including bulrushes, sedges, and marsh grass) on the bank. Then seven bad-looking, thin cows came up after them, stood beside the fat cows, and instead of eating the reeds, they ate the fat cows.

41:5-7. After a short period of being awake, Pharaoh went back to sleep and dreamed of seven fat, plump heads of grain (in Egypt this would be wheat) on one stalk. Then he saw seven thin heads of wheat sprouting after the fat ones. These thin ears had been scorched by the hot east wind off the desert. Then the thin heads of wheat swallowed up the fat, plump heads.

41:8. In the morning Pharaoh was disturbed in his own spirit. He was sure the dream had a meaning and the dream did not leave him with a good feeling. So he called in the soothsayer priests of Egypt (these claimed mysterious knowledge of magic, divination, and astrology; they knew all the ancient magical inscriptions and were skilled in deciphering and interpreting them) and all his wise men who knew all the latest discoveries as well as the ancient wise sayings of Egypt. None could give an interpretation.

881, 3725, 2550	5807.321	6799	3937	881, 2573	375, 6876.151
cj, do, adj, n mp	cj, v Piel impf 3ms	pn	prep, ps 3mp	do, n ms, ps 3ms	cj, sub, v Qal act ptc ms
וְאֶת־כָּל־חֲכָמֶיהָ	וַיְסַפֵּר	פַּרְעֹה	לָהֶם	אֶת־חֲלֹמוֹ	וְאֵין־פּוֹתֵר
we'eth-kol-chăkhāmêhā	waysappēr	par‘ōh	lāhem	'eth-chălōmô	we'ên-pôthēr
and all of wisemen	and he told	Pharaoh	to them	his dream	but there was not an interpreter

881	3937, 6799		1744.321	8015	5126	881, 6799	3937, 569.141
do, ps 3mp	prep, pn		cj, v Piel impf 3ms	*n ms*	art, n mp	do, pn	prep, v Qal inf con
אוֹתָם	לְפַרְעֹה	**9.**	וַיְדַבֵּר	שַׂר	הַמַּשְׁקִים	אֶת־פַּרְעֹה	לֵאמֹר
'ôthām	lephar‘ōh		wayedhabbēr	sar	hammashqîm	'eth-par‘ōh	lē'mōr
them	to Pharaoh		and he spoke	official of	the cup-bearers	Pharaoh	saying

881, 2492	603	2226.551	3219		6799	7395.111
do, n mp, ps 1cs	pers pron	v Hiphil act ptc ms	art, n ms		pn	v Qal pf 3ms
אֶת־חֲטָאַי	אֲנִי	מַזְכִּיר	הַיּוֹם	**10.**	פַּרְעֹה	קָצַף
'eth-chătā'ay	'ănî	mazkîr	hayyôm		par‘ōh	qātsaph
my faults	I	remembering	today		Pharaoh	he was angry

6142, 5860	5598.121	881	904, 5110	1041	8015
prep, n mp, ps 3ms	cj, v Qal impf 3ms	do, ps 1cs	prep, *n ms*	*n ms*	*n ms*
עַל־עֲבָדָיו	וַיִּתֵּן	אֹתִי	בְּמִשְׁמַר	בֵּית	שַׂר
‘al-‘ăvādhâv	wayyittēn	'ōthî	bemishmar	bêth	sar
concerning his servants	and he put	me	in the custody of	the house of	the official of

2986	881	881	8015	659.152		2593.120	2573
art, n mp	do, ps 1cs	cj, do	*n ms*	art, v Qal act ptc mp		cj, v Qal impf 1cp	n ms
הַטַּבָּחִים	אֹתִי	וְאֵת	שַׂר	הָאֹפִים	**11.**	וַנַּחַלְמָה	חֲלוֹם
hattabbāchîm	'ōthî	we'ēth	sar	hā'ōphîm		wannachalmāh	chălôm
the executioners	me	and	the official of	the bakers		and we dreamed	dream

904, 4050	259	603	2000	382	3626, 6879	2573
prep, n ms	num	pers pron	cj, pers pron	n ms	prep, *n ms*	n ms, ps 3ms
בְּלַיְלָה	אֶחָד	אֲנִי	וָהוּא	אִישׁ	כְּפִתְרוֹן	חֲלֹמוֹ
belaylāh	'echādh	'ănî	wāhû'	'îsh	kephithrôn	chălōmô
in night	one	I	and he	each	according to the interpretation of	his dream

2593.115		8427	882	5470	5888	5860	3937, 8015
v Qal pf 1cp		cj, adv	prep, ps 1cp	n ms	pn	n ms	prep,
חָלָמְנוּ	**12.**	וְשָׁם	אִתָּנוּ	נַעַר	עִבְרִי	עֶבֶד	לְשַׂר
chālāmnû		weshām	'ittānû	na‘ar	‘ivrî	‘evedh	lesar
we dreamed		and there	with us	young man	Hebrew	slave	to the official of

2986	5807.320, 3937	6876.121, 3937	881, 2573	382
art, n mp	cj, v Piel impf 1cp, prep, ps 3ms	v Qal impf 3ms, prep, ps 1cp	do, n mp, ps 1cp	n ms
הַטַּבָּחִים	וַנְּסַפֶּר־לוֹ	וַיִּפְתָּר־לָנוּ	אֶת־חֲלֹמֹתֵינוּ	אִישׁ
hattabbāchîm	wannesappēr-lô	wayyiphtār-lānû	'eth-chălōmōthênû	'îsh
the executioners	and we told to him	and he interpreted to us	our dreams	each

3626, 2573	6876.111		2030.121	3626, 866	6876.111, 3937
prep, n ms, ps 3ms	v Qal pf 3ms		cj, v Qal impf 3ms	prep, rel part	v Qal pf 3ms, prep, ps 1cp
כַּחֲלֹמוֹ	פָּתָר	**13.**	וַיְהִי	כַּאֲשֶׁר	פָּתַר־לָנוּ
kachlōmô	pāthâr		wayhî	ka'ăsher	pāthar-lānû
according to his dream	he interpreted		and it was	according to that	he interpreted for us

3772	2030.111	881	8178.511	6142, 3774	881	8847.111
adv	v Qal pf 3ms	do, ps 1cs	v Hiphil pf 3ms	prep, n ms, ps 1cs	cj, do, ps 3ms	v Qal pf 3ms
כֵּן	הָיָה	אֹתִי	הֵשִׁיב	עַל־כַּנִּי	וְאֹתוֹ	תָּלָה
kēn	hāyāh	'ōthî	hēshîv	‘al-kannî	we'ōthô	thālâh
so	it was	me	he restored	concerning my office	but him	he hanged

14.	8365.121 cj, v Qal impf 3ms וַיִּשְׁלַח wayyishlach and he sent	6799 pn פַּרְעֹה par'ōh Pharaoh	7410.121 cj, v Qal impf 3ms וַיִּקְרָא wayyiqŏrā' and he called	881, 3231 do, pn אֶת־יוֹסֵף 'eth-yôs̱ēph Joseph	7608.526 cj, v Hiphil impf 3mp, ps 3ms וַיְרִיצֻהוּ wayrîtsuhû and they caused him to run	4623, 988 prep, art, n ms מִן־הַבּוֹר min-habbôr from the pit

1589.321 cj, v Piel impf 3ms וַיְגַלַּח wayghallach and he shaved	2599.321 cj, v Piel impf 3ms וַיְחַלֵּף waychallēph and he changed	7980 n fp, ps 3ms שִׂמְלֹתָיו simlōthâv his clothes	971.121 cj, v Qal impf 3ms וַיָּבֹא wayyāvō' and he went	420, 6799 prep, pn אֶל־פַּרְעֹה 'el-par'ōh to Pharaoh	15.	569.121 cj, v Qal impf 3ms וַיֹּאמֶר wayyō'mer and he said

6799 pn פַּרְעֹה par'ōh Pharaoh	420, 3231 prep, pn אֶל־יוֹסֵף 'el-yôs̱ēph to Joseph	2573 n ms חֲלוֹם chălôm dream	2593.115 v Qal pf 1cs חָלַמְתִּי chālamtî I dreamed	6876.151 v Qal act ptc ms וּפֹתֵר ûphōthēr but interpreter	375 *sub* אֵין 'ên there was not of	881 do, ps 3ms אֹתוֹ 'ōthô it

holy men, *BB* … soothsayers, *Geneva.*

of Egypt, and all the wise men thereof: and Pharaoh told them his dream; but there was none that could interpret them unto Pharaoh: … sages, *Darby, NAB, NEB* … scientists, *Fenton.*

9. Then spake the chief butler unto Pharaoh, saying, I do remember my faults this day: … chief wine-servant, *BB* … chief cup-bearer, *Anchor, NRSV, NIV* … It's time to recall my faults, *NEB.*

10. Pharaoh was wroth with his servants: … angry, *Geneva,* … furious, *NASB* … bondmen, *Darby.*

and put me in ward in the captain of the guard's house, both me and the chief baker: … chief (head) steward, *NAB* … chief of executioners, *Young* … captain of the army, *BB* … general of the guard, *Fenton.*

11. And we dreamed a dream in one night, I and he; we dreamed each man according to the interpretation of his dream: … each needing it's own interpretation, *NEB* … special sense, *BB* … different significance, *Berkeley.*

12. And there was there with us a young man, an Hebrew, servant to the captain of the guard; and we told him, and he interpreted to us our dreams; to each man according to his dream he did interpret: … giving each man's dream it's own interpretation, *NEB.*

13. And it came to pass, as he interpreted to us, so it was; me he restored: … fell out, *Goodspeed* … reinstated, *NCB.*

unto mine office, and him he hanged: … impaled, *NAB, Anchor.*

14. Then Pharaoh sent and called Joseph, and they brought him hastily out of the dungeon: and he shaved himself and changed his raiment, and came in unto Pharaoh: … cause him to run out of the pit, *Young* … cut his hair, *Anchor, BB* … changed his clothes, *Darby.*

41:9-13. At this point the chief cupbearer spoke up and said he remembered his faults, the sins by which he had offended Pharaoh (40:1). He also recalled how Pharaoh was angry with the chief baker and him and how Pharoah had put them under guard in the household of the chief executioner. The prison, which the chief executioner controlled, was located on his property. (The cupbearer was not thinking of his delay in fulfilling Joseph's request here. It would have been beneath his dignity to tell Pharaoh he had wronged Joseph. He only wanted to do Pharaoh a favor to compensate for his former offense against him in case Pharaoh had not forgotten them.) Then he recounted his dream and the dream of the chief baker, and how a young Hebrew slave of the chief executioner had interpreted their dreams correctly. Joseph was about 30 years of age at this time.

41:14. Pharaoh ordered his servants to bring Joseph. Even though they made him run, they also wanted him to come before Pharaoh properly dressed and in appropriate Egyptian style so they had him shave and change his clothes. Egyptians shaved, but Hebrews did not. So Joseph shaved for the first time in his life, changed clothes to something that would be acceptable for an appearance in the palace, and ran to Pharaoh.

41:15. Pharaoh greeted Joseph with flattering words. No one could interpret his dreams, but he heard about Joseph hearing a dream to interpret it, that is, all Joseph had to do to interpret a dream was to hear it.

603	8471.115	6142	3937, 569.141	8471.123	2573	3937, 6876.141	881
cj, pers pron	v Qal pf 1cs	prep, ps 2ms	prep, v Qal inf con	v Qal impf 2ms	n ms	prep, v Qal inf con	do, ps 3ms
וַאֲנִי	שָׁמַעְתִּי	עָלֶיךָ	לֵאמֹר	תִּשְׁמַע	חֲלוֹם	לִפְתֹּר	אֹתוֹ
wa'ănî	shāma'ăttî	'ālêykhā	lē'mōr	tishma'	chălôm	liphtōr	'ōthô
and I	I heard	about you	saying	you hear	dream	to interpret	it

	6257.121	3231	881, 6799	3937, 569.141	1146	435
16.	cj, v Qal impf 3ms	pn	do, pn	prep, v Qal inf con	part, ps 1cs	n mp
	וַיַּעַן	יוֹסֵף	אֶת־פַּרְעֹה	לֵאמֹר	בִּלְעָדָי	אֱלֹהִים
	wayya'an	yôsēph	'eth-par'ōh	lē'mōr	bil'ādhāy	'ĕlōhîm
	and he answered	Joseph	Pharaoh	saying	apart from me	God

6257.121	881, 8361	6799		1744.321	6799	420, 3231	904, 2573
v Qal impf 3ms	do, *n ms*	pn	17.	cj, v Piel impf 3ms	pn	prep, pn	prep, n ms, ps 1cs
יַעֲנֶה	אֶת־שְׁלוֹם	פַּרְעֹה		וַיְדַבֵּר	פַּרְעֹה	אֶל־יוֹסֵף	בַּחֲלֹמִי
ya'ăneh	'eth-shelôm	par'ōh		wayedhabbēr	par'ōh	'el-yôsēph	bachlōmî
He will answer	peace of	Pharaoh		and he spoke	Pharaoh	to Joseph	in my dream

2079	6198.151	6142, 8004	3083		2079	4623, 3083	6148.154
intrj, ps 1cs	v Qal act ptc ms	prep, *n fs*	art, pn	18.	cj, intrj	prep, art, pn	v Qal act ptc fp
הִנְנִי	עֹמֵד	עַל־שְׂפַת	הַיְאֹר		וְהִנֵּה	מִן־הַיְאֹר	עֹלֹת
hinnî	'ōmēdh	'al-sephath	hay'ōr		wehinnēh	min-hay'ōr	'ōlōth
behold I	standing	on the shore of	the Nile		and behold	from the Nile	ones going up

8124	6760	1304	1340	3413	8717	7749.127
num	n fp	*adj*	n ms	cj, *adj*	n ms	cj, v Qal impf 3fp
שֶׁבַע	פָּרוֹת	בְּרִיאוֹת	בָשָׂר	וִיפֹת	תֹּאַר	וַתִּרְעֶינָה
sheva'	pārôth	berî'ôth	bāsār	wîphōth	tō'ar	wattir'ênāh
seven	cows	fat of	flesh	and good-looking of	appearance	and they grazed

904, 260		2079	8124	6760	311	6148.154	313	1859
prep, art, n ms	19.	cj, intrj	num	n fp	adj	v Qal act ptc fp	adv, ps 3fp	*adj*
בָּאָחוּ		וְהִנֵּה	שֶׁבַע	פָּרוֹת	אֲחֵרוֹת	עֹלוֹת	אַחֲרֵיהֶן	דַּלּוֹת
bā'āchû		wehinnēh	sheva'	pārôth	'ăchērôth	'ōlôth	'achrêhen	dallôth
on the reeds		and behold	seven	cows	another	ones going up	after them	weak of

7737	8717	4108	7828	1340	3940, 7495.115	3626, 2078
cj, *adj*	n ms	adv	cj, *adj*	n ms	neg part, v Qal pf 1cs	prep, pers pron
וְרָעוֹת	תֹּאַר	מְאֹד	וְרַקּוֹת	בָּשָׂר	לֹא־רָאִיתִי	כָּהֵנָּה
werā'ôth	tō'ar	me'ōdh	weraqqôth	bāsār	lō'-rā'îthî	khāhēnnāh
and bad of	appearance	very	and thin of	flesh	not I have seen	like them

904, 3725, 800	4875	3937, 7737		404.127	6760	7828	7737
prep, *adj, n fs*	pn	prep, art, adj	20.	cj, v Qal impf 3fp	art, n fp	art, adj	cj, art, adj
בְּכָל־אֶרֶץ	מִצְרָיִם	לָרֹעַ		וַתֹּאכַלְנָה	הַפָּרוֹת	הָרַקּוֹת	וְהָרָעוֹת
bekhol-'erets	mitsrayim	lārōa'		wattō'khalnāh	happārôth	hāraqqôth	wehārā'ôth
in all of the land of	Egypt	to the bad		and they ate	the cows	the thin	and the bad

881	8124	6760	7518	1304		971.127	420, 7419
do	num	art, n fp	art, adj	art, adj	21.	cj, v Qal impf 3fp	prep, n ms, ps 3fp
אֵת	שֶׁבַע	הַפָּרוֹת	הָרִאשֹׁנוֹת	הַבְּרִיאֹת		וַתָּבֹאנָה	אֶל־קִרְבֶּנָה
'ēth	sheva'	happārôth	hāri'shōnôth	habberi'ōth		wattāvō'nāh	'el-qirbenāh
	seven	the cows	the first	the fat		and they came	to their midst

3940	3156.211	3706, 971.116	420, 7419	4920	7737	3626, 866
cj, neg part	v Niphal pf 3ms	cj, v Qal pf 3cp	prep, n ms, ps 3fp	cj, n mp, ps 3fp	adj	prep, rel part
וְלֹא	נוֹדַע	כִּי־בָאוּ	אֶל־קִרְבֶּנָה	וּמַרְאֵיהֶן	רַע	כַּאֲשֶׁר
welō'	nôdha'	kî-vā'û	'el-qirbenāh	ûmar'êhen	ra'	ka'ăsher
but not	it would be known	that they came	to their midst	for their appearance	bad	like that

904, 8795	3477.125		7495.125	904, 2573	2079	8124
prep, art, n fs	cj, v Qal impf 1cs	**22.**	cj, v Qal impf 1cs	prep, n ms, ps 1cs	cj, intrj	num
בַּתְּחִלָּה	וָאִיקָץ		וָאֵרֶא	בַּחֲלֹמִי	וְהִנֵּה	שֶׁבַע
batt^{e}chillāh	wā'îqāts		wā'ēre'	bachlōmî	w^{e}hinnēh	sheva'
in the beginning	and I woke up		and I saw	in my dream	and behold	seven

8118	6148.154	904, 7354	259	4529	3005		2079	8124
n fp	v Qal act ptc fp	prep, n ms	num	adj	cj, adj	**23.**	cj, intrj	num
שִׁבֳּלִים	עֹלֹת	בְּקָנֶה	אֶחָד	מְלֵאֹת	וְטֹבוֹת		וְהִנֵּה	שֶׁבַע
shibblîm	'ōlōth	b^{e}qāneh	'echādh	m^{e}lē'ōth	w^{e}ṭōvôth		w^{e}hinnēh	sheva'
heads of grain	ones going up	on stalk	one	full	and good		and behold	seven

8118	7074.158	1911	8167.158	7205	7048.154	313
n fp	v Qal pass ptc fp	adj	*v Qal pass ptc fp*	n ms	v Qal act ptc fp	adv, ps 3mp
שִׁבֳּלִים	צְנֻמוֹת	דַּקּוֹת	שְׁדֻפוֹת	קָדִים	צֹמְחוֹת	אַחֲרֵיהֶם
shibblîm	ts^{e}numôth	daqqôth	sh^{e}dhuphôth	qādhîm	tsōmchôth	'achrêhem
heads of grain	withered ones	thin	scorched ones of	east wind	ones sprouting	after them

	1142.127	8118	1911	881	8124	8118	3005
24.	cj, v Qal impf 3fp	art, n fp	art, adj	do	num	art, adj	art, adj
	וַתִּבְלַעְןָ	הַשִּׁבֳּלִים	הַדַּקֹּת	אֵת	שֶׁבַע	הַשִּׁבֳּלִים	הַטֹּבוֹת
	wattivlā'ănā	hāshibb^{e}lîm	haddaqqōth	'ēth	sheva'	hashibb^{e}lîm	haṭṭōvôth
	and they swallowed	the heads of grain	the thin		seven	the heads of grain	the good

15. And Pharaoh said unto Joseph, I have dreamed a dream, and there is none that can interpret it: and I have heard say of thee, that thou canst understand a dream to interpret it: ... a report, *Fenton* ... the moment you are told, *NAB* ... that you can hear a dream and interpret it, *RSV.*

16. And Joseph answered Pharaoh, saying, It is not in me: God shall give Pharaoh an answer of peace: ... reassure, *REB* ... Apart from God, can Pharoah be given a favorable response?, *Goodspeed* ... God give Pharoah a favorable response(answer), *Berkeley*, *NCB*, *NASB* ... right answer, *NAB*, *Anchor* ... without me, God doth answer Pharoah in peace, *Young.*

17. And Pharaoh said unto Joseph, In my dream, behold, I stood upon the bank of the river:

18. And, behold, there came up out of the river seven kine, fatfleshed and well favoured; and they fed in a meadow: ... well-formed, *NAB.*

19. And, behold, seven other kine came up after them, poor and very ill favoured and leanfleshed: ... emaciated, *Anchor* ... miserable, *Fenton.*

such as I never saw in all the land of Egypt for badness: ... wretched, *Fenton* ... poor, *Goodspeed*, *NCB* ... ugly(ness), *NKJV*, *NASB*, *NAB* ... I have never seen such gaunt creatures, *NEB*, *REB.*

20. And the lean and the ill favoured kine did eat up the first seven fat kine:

21. And when they had eaten them up, it could not be known that they had eaten them; but they were still ill favoured, as at the beginning. So I awoke: ... They came and approached me, and yet I noticed as they came and drew near, *Fenton* ... they looked just as bad as before, *Anchor*, *Good News.*

22. And I saw in my dream, and, behold, seven ears came up in one stalk, full and good:

23. And, behold, seven ears, withered, thin, and blasted with the east wind, sprung up after them: ... desert wind, *Good News.*

24. And the thin ears devoured the seven good ears: and I told this unto the magicians; but there was none that could declare it to me: ... interpreters, *Berkeley*, *REB.*

41:16. Joseph could have claimed great gifts because of his God-given ability. Instead, he said it was entirely apart from him, completely beyond him, beyond any of his powers. Thus, he refused to take any credit for himself. Instead, he gave all the credit to God, God would give Pharaoh an answer that would be advantageous to him. In spite of the long delay in prison, God was still real to Joseph.

41:17-24. Pharaoh recounted the two dreams to Joseph in detail, with the addition that the seven bad-looking, thin cows were just as bad looking after eating the fat cows as they were at the beginning. Then he emphasized again that no one could explain the dreams to him.

569.125	420, 2851	375	5222.551	3937
cj, v Qal impf 1cs	prep, art, n mp	cj, *sub*	v Hiphil ptc ms	prep, ps 1cs
וָאֹמַר	אֶל־הַחַרְטֻמִּים	וְאֵין	מַגִּיד	לִי
wā'ōmar	'el-hachartummîm	w^{e}'ên	maggîdh	lî
and I said	to the cult priests	but there was not of	one who explains	to me

25.	569.121	3231	420, 6799	2573	6799	259	2000	881	866
	cj, v Qal impf 3ms	pn	prep, pn	*n ms*	pn	num	pers pron	do	rel part
	וַיֹּאמֶר	יוֹסֵף	אֶל־פַּרְעֹה	חֲלוֹם	פַּרְעֹה	אֶחָד	הוּא	אֵת	אֲשֶׁר
	wayyō'mer	yôsēph	'el-par'ōh	chălôm	par'ōh	'echādh	hû'	'ēth	'ăsher
	and he said	Joseph	to Pharaoh	dream of	Pharaoh	one	it		which

435	6449.151	5222.511	3937, 6799	26.	8124	6760	3005	8124
art, n mp	v Qal act ptc ms	v Hiphil pf 3ms	prep, pn		num	n fp	art, adj	num
הָאֱלֹהִים	עֹשֶׂה	הִגִּיד	לְפַרְעֹה		שֶׁבַע	פָּרֹת	הַטֹּבֹת	שֶׁבַע
hā'ĕlōhîm	'ōseh	higgîdh	l^{e}phar'ōh		sheva'	pārōth	hattōvōth	sheva'
God	One who does	he told	to Pharaoh		seven	cows	the good	seven

8523	2078	8124	8118	3005	8124	8523	2078	2573
n fp	pers pron	cj, num	art, n fp	art, adj	num	n fp	pers pron	n ms
שָׁנִים	הֵנָּה	וְשֶׁבַע	הַשִּׁבֳּלִים	הַטֹּבֹת	שֶׁבַע	שָׁנִים	הֵנָּה	חֲלוֹם
shānîm	hēnnāh	w^{e}sheva'	hashshibbālîm	hattōvōth	sheva'	shānîm	hēnnāh	chălôm
years	they	and seven	the heads of grain	the good	seven	years	they	dream

259	2000	27.	8124	6760	7828	7737	6148.154	313
num	pers pron		cj, *num*	art, n fp	art, adj	cj, art, adj	art, v Qal act ptc fp	adv, ps 3fp
אֶחָד	הוּא		וְשֶׁבַע	הַפָּרוֹת	הָרַקּוֹת	וְהָרָעֹת	הָעֹלֹת	אַחֲרֵיהֶן
'echādh	hû'		w^{e}sheva'	happārôth	hāraqqôth	w^{e}hārā'ōth	hā'ōlōth	'achrêhen
one	it		and the seven	the cows	the thin	and evil	going up	after them

8124	8523	2078	8124	8118	7828	8167.158
num	n fp	pers pron	cj, *num*	art, adj	art, adj	*v Qal pass ptc fp*
שֶׁבַע	שָׁנִים	הֵנָּה	וְשֶׁבַע	הַשִּׁבֳּלִים	הָרֵקוֹת	שְׁדֻפוֹת
sheva'	shānîm	hēnnāh	w^{e}sheva'	hashibb^{e}lîm	hārēqôth	sh^{e}dhuphôth
seven	years	they	and the seven	the heads of grain	the thin	the scorched of

7205	2030.126	8124	8523	7743	28.	2000	1745	866
art, adj	v Qal impf 3mp	*num*	*n fp*	n ms		pers pron	art, n ms	rel part
הַקָּדִים	יִהְיוּ	שֶׁבַע	שְׁנֵי	רָעָב		הוּא	הַדָּבָר	אֲשֶׁר
haqqādhîm	yihyû	sheva'	sh^{e}nê	rā'āv		hû'	haddāvār	'ăsher
the east	they will be	seven	years of	famine		it	the thing	which

1744.315	420, 6799	866	435	6449.151	7495.511	881, 6799
v Piel pf 1cs	prep, pn	rel part	art, n mp	v Qal act ptc ms	v Hiphil pf 3ms	do, pn
דִּבַּרְתִּי	אֶל־פַּרְעֹה	אֲשֶׁר	הָאֱלֹהִים	עֹשֶׂה	הֶרְאָה	אֶת־פַּרְעֹה
dibbartî	'el-par'ōh	'ăsher	hā'ĕlōhîm	'ōseh	her'āh	'eth-par'ōh
I spoke	to Pharaoh	what	God	about to do	He showed	Pharaoh

29.	2079	8124	8523	971.154	7882	1448	904, 3725, 800
	intrj	*num*	n fp	v Qal act ptc fp	n ms	adj	prep, *adj, n fs*
	הִנֵּה	שֶׁבַע	שָׁנִים	בָּאוֹת	שָׂבָע	גָּדוֹל	בְּכָל־אֶרֶץ
	hinnēh	sheva'	shānîm	bā'ôth	sāvā'	gādhôl	b^{e}khol-'erets
	behold	seven	years	coming	abundance	great	in all the land of

4875	30.	7251.116	8124	8523	7743	313
pn		cj, v Qal pf 3cp	*num*	*n fp*	n ms	adv, ps 3fp
מִצְרָיִם		וְקָמוּ	שֶׁבַע	שְׁנֵי	רָעָב	אַחֲרֵיהֶן
mitsrāyim		w^{e}qāmû	sheva'	sh^{e}nê	rā'āv	'achrêhen
Egypt		then they will rise	seven	years of	hunger	after them

8319.211	3725, 7882	904, 800	4875	3735.311
cj, v Niphal pf 3ms	*adj*, art, n ms	prep, *n fs*	pn	cj, v Piel pf 3ms
וְנִשְׁכַּח	כָּל־הַשָּׂבָע	בְּאֶרֶץ	מִצְרָיִם	וְכִלָּה
w^{e}nishkach	kol-hassāvā'	b^{e}'erets	mitsrāyim	w^{e}khillāh
and it will be forgotten	all the abundance	in the land of	Egypt	and it will destroy

7743	881, 800		3940, 3156.221	7882	904, 800	4623, 6681
art, n ms	do, art, n fs	**31.**	cj, neg part, v Niphal impf 3ms	art, n ms	prep, art, n fs	prep, *n ms*
הָרָעָב	אֶת־הָאָרֶץ		וְלֹא־יִוָּדַע	הַשָּׂבָע	בָּאָרֶץ	מִפְּנֵי
hārā'āv	'eth-hā'ārets		w^{e}lō'-yiwwādha'	hassāvā'	bā'ārets	mipp^{e}nê
the famine of	the land		and not it will be known	the abundance	on the land	before

7743	2000	313, 3772	3706, 3633	2000	4108		6142
art, n ms	art, dem pron	adj, prep	prep, adj	pers pron	adv	**32.**	cj, prep
הָרָעָב	הַהוּא	אַחֲרֵי־כֵן	כִּי־כָבֵד	הוּא	מְאֹד		וְעַל
hārā'āv	hahû'	'achrê-khēn	kî-khāvēdh	hû'	m^{e}'ōdh		w^{e}'al
the famine	the that	afterward	because heavy	it	very		and concerning

25. And Joseph said unto Pharaoh, The dream of Pharaoh is one: God hath shewed Pharaoh what he is about to do: ... Pharoahs dreams are one dream, *NEB* ... Pharoah's dream is simple, *Goodspeed* ... determined, *Fenton.*

26. The seven good: ... fat, *Goodspeed*, *Berkeley* ... fine, *NCB* ... healthy, *NAB*, *Anchor.*

kine are seven years; and the seven good ears are seven years: the dream is one: ... plump, *Goodspeed* ... fine, *NCB* ... healthy, *NAB*, *Anchor* ... heads, *NKJV*, *BB*.

27. And the seven thin and ill favoured: ... bad, *Darby* ... ugly, *Goodspeed*, *NKJV*, *Berkeley* ... gaunt, *RSV*, *REB*, *NEB* ... poor, *Fenton*, *BB* ... evil appearing, *KJVII.*

kine that came up after them are seven years; and the seven empty ears: ... thin, *Berkeley*, *NASB* ... worthless, *NIV* ... dry and wasted, *BB* ... of corn, *Fenton*, *NEB.*

blasted with the east wind shall be seven years of famine: ... parched, *Darby* ... shriveled, *Berkeley* ... scorched, *NASB*, *NIV*, *Anchor.*

28. This is the thing which I have spoken unto Pharaoh: What God is about to do he sheweth unto Pharaoh: ... word, *Darby* ... God has shown Pharoah what He is about to do, *NKJV*, *RSV*, *REB.*

29. Behold, there come seven years of great plenty throughout all the land of Egypt: ... bumper harvest, *REB* ... wealth of grain, *BB.*

30. And there shall arise after them seven years of famine; and all the plenty shall be forgotten in the land of Egypt; and the famine shall consume the land: ... the memory of the good years, *BB* ... ruin, *NEB*, *REB* ... ravage, *NIV*, *NASB* ... desolate, *Fenton* ... exhaust, *Berkeley.*

31. And the plenty shall not be known in the land by reason of that famine following: ... The good years will not be remembered in the land because of the famine that follows, *NEB.*

for it shall be very grievous: ... severe, *NEB*, *KJVII*, *NASB* ... very bitter, *BB.*

32. And for that the dream was doubled unto Pharaoh twice; it is because the thing is established by God, and God will shortly bring it to pass: ... that the dream was sent twice to Pharaoh in two forms means that the matter is absolutely settled by God, *Goodspeed.*

41:25-27. Joseph explained that the two dreams had one meaning. The seven good cows and the seven good heads of wheat were 7 years. The seven thin, bad-looking cows and the seven thin heads of scorched grain (and shriveled) by the east wind were 7 years of famine.

41:28. Again Joseph gave glory to God. God was showing Pharaoh what He was about to do.

41:29-31. Joseph expanded his explanation. The famine would be so great that the abundance of the previous 7 years would be forgotten and the famine would destroy the land. No one would escape the results of the famine because it would be so severe.

41:32. The repetition of the dream meant that God had firmly established it and God would do it quickly, that is, very soon.

41:33-36. Joseph then proposed a plan. Pharaoh should select a man who is perceptive and wise (that is, with practical wisdom to know what to

8521.241	2573	420, 6799	6718	3706, 3679.255	1745
v Niphal inf con	art, n ms	prep, pn	n fd	cj, v Niphal ptc ms	art, n ms
הִשָּׁנוֹת	הַחֲלוֹם	אֶל־פַּרְעֹה	פַּעֲמָיִם	כִּי־נָכוֹן	הַדָּבָר
hishshānôth	hachlôm	'el-par'ōh	pa'ămāyim	kî-nākhôn	haddāvār
the repeating of	the dream	to Pharaoh	two times	because something firm	the thing

4623, 6196	435	4257.351	435	3937, 6449.141		6498
prep, prep	art, n mp	cj, v Piel ptc ms	art, n mp	prep, v Qal inf con 3ms	**33.**	cj, adv
מֵעִם	הָאֱלֹהִים	וּמְמַהֵר	הָאֱלֹהִים	לַעֲשֹׂתוֹ		וְעַתָּה
mē'im	hā'ĕlōhîm	ûmemahēr	hā'ĕlōhîm	la'ăsōthô		we'attāh
from	God	and quickly	God	doing it		and now

7495.121	6799	382	1032.255	2550	8308.121
v Qal impf 3ms	pn	n ms	v Niphal ptc ms	cj, adj	cj, v Qal impf 3ms, ps 3ms
יֵרֶא	פַּרְעֹה	אִישׁ	נָבוֹן	וְחָכָם	וִישִׁיתֵהוּ
yērē'	phar'ōh	'îsh	nāvôn	wechākhām	wîshîthēhû
he should select	Pharaoh	man	one who is discerning	and wise	and appoint him

6142, 800	4875		6449.121	6799	6734.521	6735
prep, *n fs*	pn	**34.**	v Qal impf 3ms	pn	cj, v Hiphil impf 3ms	n mp
עַל־אֶרֶץ	מִצְרָיִם		יַעֲשֶׂה	פַּרְעֹה	וְיַפְקֵד	פְּקִדִים
'al-'erets	mitsrāyim		ya'ăseh	phar'ōh	weyaphqēdh	peqidhîm
over the land of	Egypt		he should do	Pharaoh	and he should appoint	administrators

6142, 800	2674.311	881, 800	4875	904, 8124	8523	7882
prep, art, n fs	cj, v Piel pf 3ms	do, *n fs*	pn	prep, *num*	*n fp*	art, n ms
עַל־הָאָרֶץ	וְחִמֵּשׁ	אֶת־אֶרֶץ	מִצְרַיִם	בְּשֶׁבַע	שְׁנֵי	הַשָּׂבָע
'al-hā'ārets	wechimmēsh	'eth-'erets	mitsrayim	besheva'	shenê	hassāvā'
over the land	and levy one-fifth	the land of	Egypt	in the seven	the years of	the abundance

	7192.126	881, 3725, 406	8523	3005	971.154	431
35.	cj, v Qal impf 3mp	do, adj, *n ms*	art, n fp	art, adj	art, v Qal act ptc fp	art, dem pron
	וְיִקְבְּצוּ	אֶת־כָּל־אֹכֶל	הַשָּׁנִים	הַטֹּבֹת	הַבָּאֹת	הָאֵלֶּה
	weyiqŏbbetsû	'eth-kol-'ōkhel	hashshānîm	hattōvōth	habbā'ōth	hā'ēlleh
	and they will gather	all the food of	the years	the good	the ones coming	the these

6914.126, 1277	8809	3135, 6799	406	904, 6111	8490.126
cj, v Qal impf 3mp, n ms	prep	*n fs*, pn	n ms	prep, art, n fp	cj, v Qal impf 3mp
וְיִצְבְּרוּ־בָר	תַּחַת	יַד־פַּרְעֹה	אֹכֶל	בֶּעָרִים	וְשָׁמָרוּ
weyitsberû-vār	tachath	yadh-par'ōh	'ōkhel	be'ārîm	weshāmārû
and they will pile grain	under	the hand of Pharaoh	food	in the cities	and they will keep

	2030.111	406	3937, 6736	3937, 800	3937, 8124	8523
36.	cj, v Qal pf 3ms	art, n ms	prep, n ms	prep, art, n fs	prep, *num*	*n fp*
	וְהָיָה	הָאֹכֶל	לְפִקָּדוֹן	לָאָרֶץ	לְשֶׁבַע	שְׁנֵי
	wehāyāh	hā'ōkhel	lephiqqādhôn	lā'ārets	lesheva'	shenê
	and it will be	the food	for a reserve	for the land	for the seven	the years of

7743	866	2030.127	904, 800	4875	3940, 3901.222	800
art, n ms	rel part	v Qal impf 3fp	prep, *n fs*	pn	cj, neg part, v Niphal impf 3fs	art, n fs
הָרָעָב	אֲשֶׁר	תִּהְיֶיןָ	בְּאֶרֶץ	מִצְרָיִם	וְלֹא־תִכָּרֵת	הָאָרֶץ
hārā'āv	'ăsher	tihyênā	be'erets	mitsrāyim	welō'-thikkārēth	hā'ārets
the famine	which	they will happen	in the land of	Egypt	that not it will be ruined	the land

904, 7743		3296.121	1745	904, 6084	6799	904, 6084
prep, art, n ms	**37.**	cj, v Qal impf 3ms	art, n ms	prep, *n fp*	pn	cj, prep, *n fd*
בָּרָעָב		וַיִּיטַב	הַדָּבָר	בְּעֵינֵי	פַּרְעֹה	וּבְעֵינֵי
bārā'āv		wayyîtav	haddāvār	be'ênê	phar'ōh	ûveênê
during the famine		and it seemed good	the thing	in the eyes of	Pharaoh	and in the eyes of

3725, 5860		569.121	6799	420, 5860	4834.120	3626, 2172
adj, n mp, ps 3ms	**38.**	cj, v Qal impf 3ms	pn	prep, n mp, ps 3ms	intrg part, v Qal impf 1cp	prep, dem pron
כָּל־עֲבָדָיו		וַיֹּאמֶר	פַּרְעֹה	אֶל־עֲבָדָיו	הֲנִמְצָא	כָזֶה
kol-'ăvādhâv		wayyō'mer	par'ōh	'el-'ăvādhâv	h^{e}nimtsā'	khāzeh
all his servants		and he said	Pharaoh	to his servants	can we find	like this

382	866	7593	435	904		569.121	6799	420, 3231
n ms	rel part	*n fs*	n mp	prep, ps 3ms	**39.**	cj, v Qal impf 3ms	pn	prep, pn
אִישׁ	אֲשֶׁר	רוּחַ	אֱלֹהִים	בּוֹ		וַיֹּאמֶר	פַּרְעֹה	אֶל־יוֹסֵף
'îsh	'ăsher	rûach	'ĕlōhîm	bô		wayyō'mer	par'ōh	'el-yôsēph
man	which	the Spirit of	God	on him		and he said	Pharaoh	to Joseph

311	3156.541	435	881	881, 3725, 2148	375, 1032.255
sub	v Hiphil inf con	n mp	do, ps 2ms	do, *adj*, dem pron	*sub*, v Niphal ptc ms
אַחֲרֵי	הוֹדִיעַ	אֱלֹהִים	אוֹתְךָ	אֶת־כָּל־זֹאת	אֵין־נָבוֹן
'achrê	hôdhîa'	'ĕlōhîm	'ôth^{e}khā	'eth-kol-zō'th	'ên-nāvôn
after	showing	God	you	all this	there is not one who discerns

33. Now therefore let Pharaoh look out a man discreet: ... shrewd, *NEB, Goodspeed* ... intelligent, *Young* ... discerning, *NRSV* ... firm, *Fenton* ... man of vision, *REB* ... understanding, *Geneva.*

and wise, and set him over the land of Egypt: ... good sense, *BB* ... skillful, *Fenton* ... prudent, *NCB, Berkeley, Goodspeed.*

34. Let Pharaoh do this, and let him appoint officers over the land: ... take further action ... supervisors, *Berkeley* ... overseers, *Darby, ASV, RSV* ... commissioners, *REB, NIV* ... controllers, *NEB* ... to forearm the land, *Goodspeed* ... to organize, *Anchor.*

and take up the fifth part of the land of Egypt in the seven plenteous years: ... produce, *RSV*, ... prepare the land of Egypt through the seven years of plenty, *NCB.*

35. And let them gather all the food of those good years that come: ... husband, *Fenton, Anchor.*

and lay up corn: ... grain, *Fenton, NIV, ASV.*

under the hand of Pharaoh: ... authority, *Goodspeed, NKJV.*

and let them keep food in the cities: ... guard it, *NASB, NEB* ... and fortresses, *Fenton.*

36. And that food shall be for store: ... reserve, *Goodspeed, NKJV, RSV.*

to the land against the seven years of famine, which shall be in the land of Egypt; that the land perish not through the famine: ... not be cut off, *Fenton.*

37. And the thing was good in the eyes of Pharaoh: ... the proposal commended itself, *Goodspeed, REB.*

and in the eyes of all his servants: ... bondsmen, *Darby* ... cortiers, *Goodspeed, NCB, NEB* ... officials, *REB, NIV, Anchor* ... ministers, *Fenton.*

38. And Pharaoh said unto his servants, Can we find such a one as this is: ... can we find this man's equal, *Berkeley.*

a man in whom the Spirit of God is?: ... a god, *NEB* ... divine spirit, *Anchor, NASB.*

39. And Pharaoh said unto Joseph, Forasmuch as God hath shewed thee all this, there is none so discreet and wise as thou art: ... a god, *NEB* ... God is with you in all of this, *Fenton.*

40. Thou shalt be over my house, and according unto thy word shall all my people: ... palace, *Anchor, NIV* ... shall do homage, *NASB.*

do) and appoint him over the land of Egypt. Pharaoh should also appoint administrators over the land, that is, over the harvest of the land, to take one fifth of the harvest during each of the 7 good years. They were to pile up the grain under the hand of Pharaoh (that is, by his authority) and keep it as a reserve in the various cities of Egypt. Then the land would not be ruined by the famine.

41:37-38. What Joseph said pleased Pharaoh and all of his servants (that is, the officials of his court). Though Joseph did not hint that he might be the one for task, Pharaoh then suggested they could not find a better man than this man who had the Spirit of God in him. This man was different from all the wise men of Egypt, and somehow Pharaoh recognized it was not natural excellence that made Joseph what he was.

41:39-40. Pharaoh then told Joseph that because God had shown him all this, no one was as perceptive and wise as he. He appointed Joseph

2550	3765		887	2030.123	6142, 1041	6142, 6552
cj, adj	prep, ps 2ms	**40.**	pers pron	v Qal impf 2ms	prep, n ms, ps 1cs	cj, prep, n ms, ps 2ms
וְחָכָם	כָּמוֹךָ		אַתָּה	תִּהְיֶה	עַל־בֵּיתִי	וְעַל־פִּיךָ
wechākhām	kāmôkhā		'attāh	tihyeh	'al-bêthî	we'al-pîkhā
and wise	just like you		you	you will be	over my house	and on your mouth

5583.121	3725, 6194	7828	3802	1461.125	4623		569.121
v Qal impf 3ms	*adj*, n ms, ps 1cs	adv	art, n ms	v Qal impf 1cs	prep, ps 2ms	**41.**	cj, v Qal impf 3ms
יִשַּׁק	כָּל־עַמִּי	רַק	הַכִּסֵּא	אֶגְדַּל	מִמֶּךָּ		וַיֹּאמֶר
yishshaq	kol-'ammî	raq	hakkissē'	'eghdal	mimmekhā		wayyō'mer
they will kiss	all my people	only	the throne	I will be greater	than you		and he said

6799	420, 3231	7495.131	5595.115	881	6142	3725, 800	4875
pn	prep, pn	v Qal impv 2ms	v Qal pf 1cs	do, ps 2ms	prep	*adj, n fs*	pn
פַּרְעֹה	אֶל־יוֹסֵף	רְאֵה	נָתַתִּי	אֹתְךָ	עַל	כָּל־אֶרֶץ	מִצְרָיִם
par'ōh	'el-yôsēph	re'ēh	nāthattî	'ōthekhā	'al	kol-'erets	mitsrāyim
Pharaoh	to Joseph	see	I have put	you	over	all the land of	Egypt

	5681.521	6799	881, 2995	4623, 6142	3135	5598.121	881
42.	cj, v Hiphil impf 3ms	pn	do, n fs, ps 3ms	prep, prep	n fs, ps 3ms	cj, v Qal impf 3ms	do, ps 3fs
	וַיָּסַר	פַּרְעֹה	אֶת־טַבַּעְתּוֹ	מֵעַל	יָדוֹ	וַיִּתֵּן	אֹתָהּ
	wayyāsar	par'ōh	'eth-tabba'ttô	mē'al	yādhô	wayyittēn	'ōthāhh
	and he removed	Pharaoh	his signet-ring	from	his hand	and he put	it

6142, 3135	3231	3980.521	881	933, 8668	7947.121	7535
prep, *n fs*	pn	cj, v Hiphil impf 3ms	do, ps 3ms	*n mp*, n ms	cj, v Qal impf 3ms	*n ms*
עַל־יַד	יוֹסֵף	וַיַּלְבֵּשׁ	אֹתוֹ	בִּגְדֵי־שֵׁשׁ	וַיָּשֶׂם	רְבִד
'al-yadh	yôsēph	wayyalbēsh	'ōthô	bighedhê-shēsh	wayyāsem	revidh
on the hand of	Joseph	and he clothed	him	with clothes of linen	and he put	chain of

2174	6142, 6939		7680.521	881	904, 4981	5112
art, n ms	prep, n ms, ps 3ms	**43.**	cj, v Hiphil impf 3ms	do, ps 3ms	prep, *n fs*	art, n ms
הַזָּהָב	עַל־צַוָּארוֹ		וַיַּרְכֵּב	אֹתוֹ	בְּמִרְכֶּבֶת	הַמִּשְׁנֶה
hazzāhāv	'al-tsawwā'rô		wayyarkēv	'ōthô	bemirkeveth	hammishneh
the gold	on his neck		and he caused to ride	him	on the chariot	the second

866, 3937	7410.126	3937, 6686	81	5598.142	881	6142
rel part, prep, ps 3ms	cj, v Qal impf 3mp	prep, n mp, ps 3ms	intrj	cj, v Qal inf abs	do, ps 3ms	prep
אֲשֶׁר־לוֹ	וַיִּקְרְאוּ	לְפָנָיו	אַבְרֵךְ	וְנָתוֹן	אֹתוֹ	עַל
'ăsher-lô	wayyiqŏr'û	lephānâv	'avrēkh	wenāthôn	'ōthô	'al
which to him	and they called	before him	give homage	and putting	him	above

3725, 800	4875		569.121	6799	420, 3231	603	6799
adj, *n fs*	pn	**44.**	cj, v Qal impf 3ms	pn	prep, pn	pers pron	pn
כָּל־אֶרֶץ	מִצְרָיִם		וַיֹּאמֶר	פַּרְעֹה	אֶל־יוֹסֵף	אֲנִי	פַרְעֹה
kol-'erets	mitsrāyim		wayyō'mer	par'ōh	'el-yôsēph	'ănî	phar'ōh
all the land of	Egypt		and he said	Pharaoh	to Joseph	I	Pharaoh

1146	3940, 7597.521	382	881, 3135	881, 7559	904, 3725, 800
cj, prep, ps 2ms	neg part, v Hiphil impf 3ms	n ms	do, n fs, ps 3ms	cj, do, n fs, ps 3ms	prep, *adj, n fs*
וּבִלְעָדֶיךָ	לֹא־יָרִים	אִישׁ	אֶת־יָדוֹ	וְאֶת־רַגְלוֹ	בְּכָל־אֶרֶץ
ûvil'ādhêkhā	lō'-yārîm	'îsh	'eth-yādhô	we'eth-raghlô	bekhol-'erets
and apart from you	not he will lift	man	his hand	or his foot	in all the land of

4875		7410.121	6799	8428, 3231	7123	7123
pn	**45.**	cj, v Qal impf 3ms	pn	*n ms*, pn	pn	pn
מִצְרָיִם		וַיִּקְרָא	פַרְעֹה	שֵׁם־יוֹסֵף	צָפְנַת	פַּעְנֵחַ
mitsrāyim		wayyiqrā'	phar'ōh	shēm-yôsēph	tsāphenath	pa'ănēach
Egypt		and he called	Pharaoh	the name of Joseph	Zaphenath	Paneah

5598.121, 3937	881, 635	1351, 6562	6562	3669	203	3937, 828
cj, v Qal impf 3ms, prep, ps 3ms	do, pn	*n fs*, pn	pn	*n ms*	pn	prep, n fs
וַיִּתֶּן־לוֹ	אֶת־אָסְנַת	בַּת־פּוֹטִי	פֶרַע	כֹּהֵן	אֹן	לְאִשָּׁה
wayyitten-lô	'eth-'ās̱^{e}nath	bath-pôṯî	phera'	kōhēn	'ōn	l^{e}'ishshāh
and he gave to him	Asenath	the daughter of Poti	phera	the priest of	On	for wife

3428.121	3231	6142, 800	4875		3231	1158, 8421	8523
cj, v Qal impf 3ms	pn	prep, *n fs*	pn	**46.**	cj, pn	*n ms*, num	n fs
וַיֵּצֵא	יוֹסֵף	עַל־אֶרֶץ	מִצְרָיִם		וְיוֹסֵף	בֶּן־שְׁלֹשִׁים	שָׁנָה
wayyētsē'	yôsēp̱h	'al-'erets	mitsrāyim		w^{e}yôsēp̱h	ben-sh^{e}lōshîm	shānāh
and he went out	Joseph	over the land of	Egypt		and Joseph	son of thirty	years

be ruled: only in the throne will I be greater than thou: ... armed, *Geneva* ... and all my people will depend on your every word, *NEB* ... at thy mouth do all my people kiss, *Young* ... dart at your command, *NAB.*

41. And Pharaoh said unto Joseph, See, I have set thee over all the land of Egypt: ... give you authority, *NEB, REB.*

42. And Pharaoh took off his ring: ... signet-ring, *NRSV, NIV, NAB* ... seal-ring, *Young.*

from his hand, and put it upon Joseph's hand, and arrayed him in vestures: ... garments, *NRSV, Geneva, Young* ... clothing (clothed), *KJVII, BB, Fenton* ... robes, *Goodspeed, Anchor, NIV.*

of fine linen, and put a gold chain about his neck: ... a white robe, *Fenton* ... clothes of Byssus, *Darby.*

43. And he made him to ride in the second chariot: ... the chariot of his vizier, *NAB* ... carriages, *BB* ... viceroy's chariot, *NEB.*

which he had; and they cried before him, Bow the knee: ... They shouted Abrek!, *NAB, Anchor, Geneva* ... He mounted him in his viceroy's chariot and men cried 'Make way!' before him, *REB* ... hooded chariot, *Fenton.*

and he made him ruler over all the land of Egypt: ... In this way he put him in charge of the whole land of Egypt, *NCB.*

44. And Pharaoh said unto Joseph, I am Pharaoh, and without thee shall no man lift up his hand or foot in all the land of Egypt: ... without your consent, *NKJV, RSV, REB* ... without acknowledging you, *Berkeley* ... stir, *Goodspeed.*

45. And Pharaoh called Joseph's name Zaphnathpaaneah: ... The High Treasurership, *Fenton.*

and he gave him to wife: ... in marriage (married), *RSV, Berkeley, NCB.*

over all his household and gave him authority to rule over all Pharaoh's people. They must be obedient to all Joseph's commands and directives. Pharaoh, however, would still keep his throne. He would be the only one greater than Joseph, which means Pharaoh would still have the final word.

41:41-43. Pharaoh not only told Joseph he had put him over all the land of Egypt, he gave him the symbol of his authority: his signet ring by which he stamped his signature or emblem on the clay seals that sealed documents, letters, orders, and laws. He also dressed Joseph (or had him dressed) with the fine linen clothes that the wealthy in Egypt wore and put a gold chain around his neck as another symbol of his authority and high position. Then he made him ride in his second chariot and had men shout before him, *'avrek*, which probably means "bow down," or "pay homage." Thus, his authority over the land was made complete.

41:44. Apart from Joseph, that is, without his permission no one was to do anything significant in Egypt. Joseph was given the powers of a dictator.

41:45. In order to have this authority, Joseph needed Egyptian citizenship. This was done by giving him an Egyptian name, Zaphnath-paaneah, meaning "abundance of life, nourisher of life." This was an appropriate name for his position as the prime minister who would provide for the years of famine. (Some Egyptologists, however, interpret to mean "God has spoken and he [Pharaoh and Egypt] shall live.") Then, to have the respect of the people, Joseph needed social standing. This was given him by giving him as his wife Asenath, meaning "belonging to Neith" (a goddess of Egyptian mythology). She was the daughter of Poti-pherah ("he whom the sun god gives"), the priest of On (called by the Greeks Heliopolis), a city 10 miles northeast of modern Cairo. On was a center for the worship of the sun god Ra. Its priests were almost as powerful as the Pharaoh. With his position and respect assured, Joseph went out over the land of Egypt to inspect its resources and make his plans.

904, 6198.141	3937, 6686	6799	4567, 4875	3428.121	3231
prep, v Qal inf con, ps 3ms	prep, *n mp*	pn	*n ms*, pn	cj, v Qal impf 3ms	pn
בְּעָמְדוֹ	לִפְנֵי	פַּרְעֹה	מֶלֶךְ־מִצְרָיִם	וַיֵּצֵא	יוֹסֵף
b^{e}'ām^{e}dhô	liphnê	par'ōh	melekh-mitsrāyim	wayyētsē'	yôsēph
in his standing	before	Pharaoh	the king of Egypt	and he went out	Joseph

4623, 3937, 6686	6799	5882.121	904, 3725, 800	4875		6449.122
prep, prep, *n mp*	pn	cj, v Qal impf 3ms	prep, *adj, n fs*	pn	**47.**	cj, v Qal impf 3fs
מִלִּפְנֵי	פַּרְעֹה	וַיַּעֲבֹר	בְּכָל־אֶרֶץ	מִצְרָיִם		וַתַּעַשׂ
milliphnê	phar'ōh	wayya'ăvōr	b^{e}khol-'erets	mitsrāyim		watta'as
from the presence of	Pharaoh	and he passed through	in all the land of	Egypt		and it produced

800	904, 8124	8523	7882	3937, 7347		7192.121
art, n fs	prep, *num*	*n fp*	art, n ms	prep, n mp	**48.**	cj, v Qal impf 3ms
הָאָרֶץ	בְּשֶׁבַע	שְׁנֵי	הַשָּׂבָע	לִקְמָצִים		וַיִּקְבֹּץ
hā'ārets	b^{e}sheva'	sh^{e}nê	hassāvā'	liqŏmātsîm		wayyiqŏbbōts
the earth	the seven of	the years of	the abundance	to handfuls		and he gathered

881, 3725, 406	8124	8523	866	2030.116	904, 800	4875	5598.121, 406
do, *adj, n ms*	num	n fp	rel part	v Qal pf 3cp	prep, *n fs*	pn	cj, v Qal impf 3ms, n ms
אֶת־כָּל־אֹכֶל	שֶׁבַע	שָׁנִים	אֲשֶׁר	הָיוּ	בְּאֶרֶץ	מִצְרַיִם	וַיִּתֶּן־אֹכֶל
'eth-kol-'ōkhel	sheva'	shānîm	'ăsher	hāyû	b^{e}'erets	mitsrayim	wayyitten-'ōkhel
all the food of	seven	years	which	they were	in the land of	Egypt	and he put food

904, 6111	406	7898, 6111	866	5623	5598.111	904, 8761
prep, art, n fp	*n ms*	*n ms*, art, n fs	rel part	sub, ps 3fs	v Qal pf 3ms	prep, sub, ps 3fs
בֶּעָרִים	אֹכֶל	שְׂדֵה־הָעִיר	אֲשֶׁר	סְבִיבֹתֶיהָ	נָתַן	בְּתוֹכָהּ
be'ārîm	'ōkhel	s^{e}dhēh-hā'îr	'ăsher	s^{e}vîvōthêhā	nāthan	b^{e}thôkhāhh
in the cities	the food of	the field of the city	which	to its environs	he put	in its midst

	6914.121	3231	1277	3626, 2437	3328	7528.542	4108	5912
49.	cj, v Qal impf 3ms	pn	n ms	prep, *n ms*	art, n ms	v Hiphil inf abs	adv	adv
	וַיִּצְבֹּר	יוֹסֵף	בָּר	כְּחוֹל	הַיָּם	הַרְבֵּה	מְאֹד	עַד
	wayyitsbōr	yôsēph	bār	k^{e}chôl	hayyām	harbēh	m^{e}'ōdh	'adh
	and he piled	Joseph	grain	like the sand of	the sea	making great	very	until

3706, 2403.111	3937, 5807.141	3706, 375	4709		3937, 3231	3314.411
cj, v Qal pf 3ms	prep, Qal inf con	prep, *sub*	n ms	**50.**	cj, prep, pn	v Pual pf 3ms
כִּי־חָדַל	לִסְפֹּר	כִּי־אֵין	מִסְפָּר		וּלְיוֹסֵף	יֻלַּד
kî-chādhal	lispōr	kî-'ên	mispār		ûlăyôsēph	yulladh
that he stopped	to count	because there was not	a number		and to Joseph	he was born

8530	1158	904, 3071	971.122	8523	7743	866	3314.112, 3937
num	n mp	prep, adv	v Qal impf 3fs	*n fs*	art, n ms	rel part	v Qal pf 3fs, prep, ps 3ms
שְׁנֵי	בָנִים	בְּטֶרֶם	תָּבוֹא	שְׁנַת	הָרָעָב	אֲשֶׁר	יָלְדָה־לּוֹ
sh^{e}nê	vānîm	b^{e}terem	tāvô'	sh^{e}nath	hārā'āv	'ăsher	yāl^{e}dhāh-lô
two	sons	before	it came	the year of	the famine	when	she gave birth for him

635	1351, 6562	6562	3669	203		7410.121
pn	*n fs*, pn	pn	*n ms*	pn	**51.**	cj, v Qal impf 3ms
אָסְנַת	בַּת־פּוֹטִי	פֶרַע	כֹּהֵן	אוֹן		וַיִּקְרָא
'āsnath	bath-pôṭî	phera'	kōhēn	'ôn		wayyiqŏrā'
Asenath	the daughter of Poti	phera	the priest of	On		and he called

3231	881, 8428	1111	4667	3706, 5567.311	435
pn	do, *n ms*	art, n ms	pn	cj, v Piel pf 3ms, ps 1cs	n mp
יוֹסֵף	אֶת־שֵׁם	הַבְּכוֹר	מְנַשֶּׁה	כִּי־נַשַּׁנִי	אֱלֹהִים
yôsēph	'eth-shēm	habb^{e}khôr	m^{e}nashsheh	kî-nashshanî	'ĕlōhîm
Joseph	the name of	the first-born	Manasseh	because he made me forget	God

881, 3725, 6219	881	3725, 1041	1		881	8428	8529
do, *adj*, n ms, ps 1cs	cj, do	*adj, n ms*	n ms, ps 1cs	**52.**	cj, do	*n ms*	art, num
אֶת־כָּל־עֲמָלִי	וְאֵת	כָּל־בֵּית	אָבִי		וְאֵת	שֵׁם	הַשֵּׁנִי
'eth-kol-'ămālî	w^{e}ēth	kol-bêth	'āvî		w^{e}ēth	shēm	hashshēnî
all of my hardship	and	all the house of	my father		and	the name of	the second

7410.111	688	3706, 6759.511	435	904, 800	6271
v Qal pf 3ms	pn	cj, v Hiphil pf 3ms, ps 1cs	n mp	prep, *n fs*	n ms, ps 1cs
קָרָא	אֶפְרָיִם	כִּי־הִפְרַנִי	אֱלֹהִים	בְּאֶרֶץ	עָנְיִי
qārā'	'ephrāyim	kî-hiphranî	'ĕlōhîm	b^{e}'erets	'ān^{e}yî
he called	Ephraim	because he made me fruitful	God	in the land of	my hardship

Asenath the daughter of Potipherah priest of On. And Joseph went out over: ... Joseph's fame spread, *Goodspeed* ... authority, *REB, NRSV, NEB.*

all the land of Egypt ... made a tour of, *NCB* ... Joseph at once made a survey of, *Fenton.*

46. And Joseph was thirty years old when he stood before Pharaoh king of Egypt: ... entered the service of, *Goodspeed, RSV, REB.*

And Joseph went out from the presence of Pharaoh, and went throughout all the land of Egypt: ... made a tour through, *Goodspeed* ... tour of inspection, *REB, NEB.*

47. And in the seven plenteous years the earth brought forth by handfuls: ... abundant harvest, *NEB, REB* ... overabundance, *Anchor*. . . big loads, *Fenton.*

48. And he gathered up all the food of the seven years: ... husbanded, *Anchor, NAB* ... of abundance, *NIV.*

which were in the land of Egypt, and laid up the food in the cities: the food of the field, which was round about every city, laid he up in the same: ... putting in each the food from the surrounding country, *NEB, REB.*

49. And Joseph gathered corn as the sand of the sea: ... wheate, *Geneva* ... grain, *KJVII, BB, ASV* ... stored grain in huge quantities, *NEB.*

very much, until he left numbering; for it was without number: ... quit recording it, *Berkeley.*

50. And unto Joseph were born two sons before the years of famine came, which Asenath the daughter of Potipherah priest of On bare unto him: ... before the time of need, *BB.*

51. And Joseph called the name of the firstborn Manasseh: ... Forgetfulness, *Goodspeed.*

For God, said he, hath made me forget: ... entirely, *NCB, NAB, Anchor.*

all my toil, and all my father's house: ... hardships, *Goodspeed, RSV, Berkeley* ... troubles, *REB* ... hard life, *BB* ... sufferings I endured at the hands of my family, *NAB.*

41:46. Thirteen years after Joseph was sold as a slave, he was given this high position and went out from Pharaoh to go through the land (the Hebrew may mean he went through it repeatedly).

41:47. During the 7 years of abundance, the earth produced handfuls, that is, there were bumper crops, excellent harvests, just as Joseph's interpretation of Pharaoh's dream foretold.

41:48-49. During these 7 years, Joseph gathered up all the food. This does not mean the people didn't eat. But all the grain from the fields around each city was stored in the city. So great was the harvest that the grain was piled up like the sand of the sea. He finally stopped counting because there was no number in their language to allow him to count further. (Later Greeks had no number greater than ten thousand. This was probably true of the Egyptians as well.)

41:50-52. Before the years of famine came, Joseph had two sons. The names he gave them show he was maintaining his relation to God. His exalted position did not cause him to forget God. Instead, God made him forget all the 13 years of hardship as well as all the household of his father, that is, all that they had done to him. So he named his first son Manasseh, meaning "making to forget." Then he named the second son Ephraim, "double fruit," because God had made him fruitful in the land where he endured the 13 years of hardship and suffering. By these names he was also giving testimony to his faith in God and giving praise to Him for His faithfulness. They show he now understood why God allowed so many years of hardship and training. Like Paul, he could have said, "Let us not be weary in well doing; for in due season we shall reap, if we faint not" (Gal. 6:9).

53.	3735.127	8124	8523	7882	866	2030.111	904, 800
	cj, v Qal impf 3fp	*num*	*n fp*	art, n ms	rel part	v Qal pf 3ms	prep, *n fs*
	וַתִּכְלֶינָה	שֶׁבַע	שְׁנֵי	הַשָּׂבָע	אֲשֶׁר	הָיָה	בְּאֶרֶץ
	wattikhlênāh	sheva‘	shenê	hassāvā‘	'ăsher	hāyāh	be'erets
	and they ended	the seven	the years of	the abundance	which	it was	in the land of

4875	54.	2591.527	8124	8523	7743	3937, 971.141	3626, 866
pn		cj, v Hiphil impf 3fp	*num*	*n fp*	art, n ms	prep, v Qal inf con	prep, rel part
מִצְרָיִם		וַתְּחִלֶּינָה	שֶׁבַע	שְׁנֵי	הָרָעָב	לָבוֹא	כַּאֲשֶׁר
mitsrāyim		wattechillênāh	sheva‘	shenê	hārā‘āv	lāvô'	ka'ăsher
Egypt		and they began	the seven	the years of	the famine	to come	just as

569.111	3231	2030.121	7743	904, 3725, 800	904, 3725, 800	4875
v Qal pf 3ms	pn	cj, v Qal impf 3ms	n ms	prep, *adj*, art, n fp	cj, prep, *adj*, *n fs*	pn
אָמַר	יוֹסֵף	וַיְהִי	רָעָב	בְּכָל־הָאֲרָצוֹת	וּבְכָל־אֶרֶץ	מִצְרַיִם
'āmar	yôsēph	wayhî	rā‘āv	bekhol-hā'ărātsôth	ûvkhol-'erets	mitsrayim
he said	Joseph	and it was	famine	in all the lands	but in all the land of	Egypt

2030.111	4035	55.	7742.122	3725, 800	4875	7094.121
v Qal pf 3ms	n ms		cj, v Qal impf 3fs	*adj*, *n fs*	pn	cj, v Qal impf 3ms
הָיָה	לָחֶם		וַתִּרְעַב	כָּל־אֶרֶץ	מִצְרַיִם	וַיִּצְעַק
hāyāh	lāchem		wattir‘av	kol-'erets	mitsrayim	wayyits‘aq
it was	bread		and it was hungry	all the land of	Egypt	and they cried out

6194	420, 6799	3937, 4035	569.121	6799	3937, 3725, 4875	2050.133
art, n ms	prep, pn	prep, art, n ms	cj, v Qal impf 3ms	pn	prep, *adj*, pn	v Qal impv 2mp
הָעָם	אֶל־פַּרְעֹה	לַלָּחֶם	וַיֹּאמֶר	פַּרְעֹה	לְכָל־מִצְרַיִם	לְכוּ
hā‘ām	'el-par‘ōh	lallāchem	wayyō'mer	par‘ōh	lekhol-mitsrayim	lekhû
the people	to Pharaoh	for grain	and he said	Pharaoh	to all the Egyptians	go

420, 3231	886, 569.121	3937	6449.133	56.	7743	2030.111	6142
prep, pn	rel part, v Qal impf 3ms	prep, ps 2mp	v Qal impv 2mp		cj, art, n ms	v Qal pf 3ms	prep
אֶל־יוֹסֵף	אֲשֶׁר־יֹאמַר	לָכֶם	תַּעֲשׂוּ		וְהָרָעָב	הָיָה	עַל
'el-yôsēph	'ăsher-yō'mar	lākhem	ta‘ăsû		wehārā‘āv	hāyāh	‘al
to Joseph	whatsoever he says	to you	do		and the famine	it was	on

3725, 6686	800	6858.121	3231	881, 3725, 866	904	8132.521
adj, *n mp*	art, n fs	cj, v Qal impf 3ms	pn	do, adj, rel part	prep, ps 3mp	cj, v Hiphil impf 3ms
כָּל־פְּנֵי	הָאָרֶץ	וַיִּפְתַּח	יוֹסֵף	אֶת־כָּל־אֲשֶׁר	בָּהֶם	וַיִּשְׁבֹּר
kol-penê	hā'ārets	wayyiphtach	yôsēph	'eth-kol-'ăsher	bāhem	wayyishbōr
all the surface of	the land	and he opened	Joseph	everything that	in them	and he sold grain

3937, 4875	2480.121	7743	904, 800	4875	57.	3725, 800
prep, pn	cj, v Qal impf 3ms	art, n ms	prep, *n fs*	pn		cj, *adj*, art, n fs
לְמִצְרַיִם	וַיֶּחֱזַק	הָרָעָב	בְּאֶרֶץ	מִצְרָיִם		וְכָל־הָאָרֶץ
lemitsrayim	wayyechězaq	hārā‘āv	be'erets	mitsrāyim		wekhol-hā'ārets
to the Egyptians	and it was strong	the famine	in the land of	Egypt		and all the earth

971.116	4875	3937, 8132.141	420, 3231	3706, 2480.111	7743
v Qal pf 3cp	pn	prep, v Qal inf con	prep, pn	cj, v Qal pf 3ms	art, n ms
בָּאוּ	מִצְרַיְמָה	לִשְׁבֹּר	אֶל־יוֹסֵף	כִּי־חָזַק	הָרָעָב
bā'û	mitsraymāh	lishbōr	'el-yôsēph	kî-chāzaq	hārā‘āv
they come	to Egypt	to buy grain	to Joseph	because it was strong	the famine

904, 3725, 800	42:1	7495.121	3399	3706	3552, 8134	904, 4875
prep, *adj*, art, n fs		cj, v Qal impf 3ms	pn	cj	*sub*, n ms	prep, pn
בְּכָל־הָאָרֶץ		וַיַּרְא	יַעֲקֹב	כִּי	יֶשׁ־שֶׁבֶר	בְּמִצְרָיִם
bekhol-hā'ārets		wayyar'	ya‘ăqōv	kî	yesh-shever	bemitsrāyim
in all the earth		and he saw	Jacob	that	there was grain	in Egypt

569.121	3399	3937, 1158	4066	7495.728		569.121
cj, v Qal impf 3ms	pn	prep, n mp, ps 3ms	intrg	v Hithpael impf 2mp	**2.**	cj, v Qal impf 3ms
וַיֹּאמֶר	יַעֲקֹב	לְבָנָיו	לָמָּה	תִּתְרָאוּ		וַיֹּאמֶר
wayyō'mer	ya'ăqōv	l^{e}vānâv	lāmmāh	tithrā'û		wayyō'mer
and he said	Jacob	to his sons	why	are you looking at each other		and he said

2079	8471.115	3706	3552, 8134	904, 4875	3495.133, 8427
intrj	v Qal pf 1cs	cj	*sub*, n ms	prep, pn	v Qal impf 2mp, adv
הִנֵּה	שָׁמַעְתִּי	כִּי	יֶשׁ־שֶׁבֶר	בְּמִצְרָיִם	רְדוּ־שָׁמָּה
hinnēh	shāma'ăttî	kî	yesh-shever	b^{e}mitsrāyim	r^{e}dhû-shāmmāh
behold	I heard	that	there is grain	in Egypt	go down there

52. And the name of the second called he Ephraim: ... Fruitfulness, *Goodspeed.*

For God hath caused me to be fruitful in the land of my affliction: ... misery, *Goodspeed* ... hardships, *REB, NEB* ... sorrow, *Anchor, BB* ... God has enriched me in the land of my wrongs, *Fenton.*

53. And the seven years of plenteousness, that was in the land of Egypt, were ended.

54. And the seven years of dearth: ... famine, *ASV* ... scarcity, *Berkeley.*

began to come, according as Joseph had said: and the dearth was in all lands: ... adjoining countries, *Berkeley.*

but in all the land of Egypt there was bread: ... food, *Goodspeed, REB, NCB.*

55. And when all the land of Egypt was famished: ... in need of food, *BB* ... hunger(y), *Anchor, NAB, Fenton.*

the people cried to Pharaoh for bread: and Pharaoh said unto all the Egyptians, Go unto Joseph; what he saith to you, do: ... food, *NIV, NCB, Berkeley.*

56. And the famine was over all the face of the earth: ... in every region, *NEB.*

And Joseph opened all the storehouses: ... grainery, *NEB, Berkeley, REB.*

and sold unto the Egyptians: ... corn, *NEB* ... grain, *REB, Goodspeed, BB* ... rationed, *NAB.*

and the famine waxed sore in the land of Egypt: ... severe, *NIV, NEB, Young.*

57. And all countries came into Egypt to Joseph for to buy corn: ... grain, *BB, NRSV, NIV* ... obtain rations, *Anchor.*

because that the famine was so sore in all lands: ... the famine raged, *Fenton.*

42:1. Now when Jacob saw that there was corn: ... for sale, *NCB* ... grain, *NASB, NCB, NAB* ... rations, *NAB, Anchor* ... food, *Geneva.*

41:53-54. When the 7 years of abundance ended, the 7 years of famine began to come, just as Joseph had said they would. By saying the famine was in all the lands, it means all the lands in that part of the world, the lands around Egypt. But Joseph's preparations meant that in Egypt there was bread. Bread was the major part of their diet in those days.

41:55-56. Joseph did not open the storehouses of grain until the famine became severe in Egypt and the people cried out to Pharaoh for bread. Then he sent them to Joseph, but he did not give them the grain, he sold it to them. During the years of plenty, they had prospered, so they were able to buy grain and keep their dignity, though the famine was growing steadily worse.

41:57. The famine was severe in all the earth, which probably means in all the known world, though it may have extended to every part of the earth. However, when it says all the earth came to Egypt to buy grain, it probably means all the countries around Egypt. The grain stored up from the harvest of the good years was so plentiful that Joseph was not afraid of running out of grain, so he sold it to all who came.

42:1-2. Joseph was prime minister in Egypt for 8 or 9 years before he saw the fulfillment of his first dream. It seems he did not contact his brothers when he was given this high position because he remembered how they hated him for the dreams and for the long, fancy tunic, as well as for his words. He must have wondered how much more jealous they would be if they saw him in royal robes with a gold chain around his neck and Pharaoh's signet ring on his finger. He knew if they were still jealous he could not have fellowship with them, and they might not accept his help. He apparently kept these things in mind and was ready to deal with

8132.133, 3937	**4623, 8427**	**2513.120**	**3940**	**4322.120**
cj, v Qal impf 2mp, prep, ps 1cp	prep, adv	cj, v Qal impf 1cp	cj, neg part	v Qal impf 1cp
וְשִׁבְרוּ־לָנוּ	מִשָּׁם	וְנִחְיֶה	וְלֹא	נָמוּת
w^{e}shivrû-lānû	mishshām	w^{e}nichăyeh	w^{e}lō'	nāmûth
and buy grain for us	from there	and we will live	and not	we will die

	3495.126	**250, 3231**	**6463**	**3937, 8132.141**	**1277**	**4623, 4875**
3.	cj, v Qal impf 3mp	*n mp*, pn	num	prep, v Qal inf con	n ms	prep, pn
	וַיֵּרְדוּ	אֲחֵי־יוֹסֵף	עֲשָׂרָה	לִשְׁבֹּר	בָּר	מִמִּצְרָיִם
	wayyērdhû	'ăchê-yôs̱ēph	'ăsārāh	lishbōr	bār	mimmitsrāyim
	and they went down	the brothers of Joseph	ten	to buy grain	grain	from Egypt

	881, 1175	**250**	**3231**	**3940, 8365.111**	**3399**	**882, 250**	**3706**
4.	cj, do, pn	*n ms*	pn	neg part, v Qal pf 3ms	pn	prep, n mp, ps 3ms	cj
	וְאֶת־בִּנְיָמִין	אֲחִי	יוֹסֵף	לֹא־שָׁלַח	יַעֲקֹב	אֶת־אֶחָיו	כִּי
	w^{e}'eth-binyāmîn	'ăchî	yôs̱ēph	lō'-shālach	ya'ăqōv	'eth-'echâv	kî
	but Benjamin	the brother of	Joseph	not he sent	Jacob	with his brothers	because

569.111	**6678, 7410.121**	**625**		**971.126**	**1158**	**3547**	**3937, 8132.141**
v Qal pf 3ms	cj, v Qal impf 3ms, ps 3ms	n ms	5.	cj, v Qal impf 3mp	*n mp*	pn	prep, v Qal inf con
אָמַר	פֶּן־יִקְרָאֶנּוּ	אָסוֹן		וַיָּבֹאוּ	בְּנֵי	יִשְׂרָאֵל	לִשְׁבֹּר
'āmar	pen-yiqōrā'ennû	'āsôn		wayyāvō'û	b^{e}nê	yisrā'ēl	lishbōr
he said	for fear it will happen	accident		and they went	the sons of	Israel	to buy grain

904, 8761	**971.152**	**3706, 2030.111**	**7743**	**904, 800**	**3791**
prep, *sub*	art, v Qal act ptc mp	cj, v Qal pf 3ms	art, n ms	prep, *n fs*	pn
בְּתוֹךְ	הַבָּאִים	כִּי־הָיָה	הָרָעָב	בְּאֶרֶץ	כְּנָעַן
b^{e}thôkh	habbā'îm	kî-hāyhâ	hārā'āv	b^{e}'erets	k^{e}nā'an
in the midst of	the ones going	because it was	the famine	in the land of	Canaan

	3231	**2000**	**8384**	**6142, 800**	**2000**	**8132.551**	**3937, 3725, 6194**
6.	cj, pn	pers pron	art, adj	prep, art, n fs	pers pron	art, v Hiphil ptc ms	prep, *adj, n ms*
	וְיוֹסֵף	הוּא	הַשַּׁלִּיט	עַל־הָאָרֶץ	הוּא	הַמַּשְׁבִּיר	לְכָל־עַם
	w^{e}yôs̱ēph	hû'	hashshallîṯ	'al-hā'ārets	hû'	hammashbîr	l^{e}khol-'am
	and Joseph	he	the governor	over the land	he	seller of grain	to every people of

800	**971.126**	**250**	**3231**	**8246.726, 3937**	**653**
art, n fs	cj, v Qal impf 3mp	*n mp*	pn	cj, v Hithpalel impf 3mp, prep, ps 3ms	n md
הָאָרֶץ	וַיָּבֹאוּ	אֲחֵי	יוֹסֵף	וַיִּשְׁתַּחֲווּ־לוֹ	אַפַּיִם
hā'ārets	wayyāvō'û	'ăchê	yôs̱ēph	wayyishtachwû-lô	'appayim
the earth	and they went	the brothers of	Joseph	and they bowed themselves to him	nostrils

800		**7495.121**	**3231**	**881, 250**	**5421.521**
n fs	7.	cj, v Qal impf 3ms	pn	do, n ms, ps 3ms	cj, v Hiphil impf 3ms, ps 3mp
אַרְצָה		וַיַּרְא	יוֹסֵף	אֶת־אֶחָיו	וַיַּכִּרֵם
'ār^{e}tsāh		wayyar^{e}'	yôs̱ēph	'eth-'echâv	wayyakkirēm
to the ground		and he saw	Joseph	his brothers	and he recognized them

5421.721	**420**	**1744.321**	**882**	**7482**	**569.121**
cj, v Hithpael impf 3ms	prep, ps 3mp	cj, v Piel impf 3ms	prep, ps 3mp	adj	cj, v Qal impf 3ms
וַיִּתְנַכֵּר	אֲלֵיהֶם	וַיְדַבֵּר	אִתָּם	קָשׁוֹת	וַיֹּאמֶר
wayyithnakkēr	'ălêhem	way^{e}dhabbēr	'ittām	qāshôth	wayyō'mer
but he acted like a stranger	to them	and he spoke	with them	harshly	and he said

420	**4623, 376**	**971.117**	**569.126**	**4623, 800**	**3791**	**3937, 8132.141, 406**
prep, ps 3mp	prep, adv	v Qal pf 2mp	cj, v Qal impf 3mp	prep, *n fs*	pn	prep, v Qal inf con, n ms
אֲלֵהֶם	מֵאַיִן	בָּאתֶם	וַיֹּאמְרוּ	מֵאֶרֶץ	כְּנַעַן	לִשְׁבָּר־אֹכֶל
'ălēhem	mē'ayin	bā'them	wayyō'm^{e}rû	mē'erets	k^{e}na'an	lishbār-'ōkhel
to them	from where	you came	and they said	from the land of	Canaan	to buy grain for food

8.	**5421.521**	**3231**	**881, 250**	**2062**	**3940**	**5421.516**
	cj, v Hiphil impf 3ms	pn	do, n ms, ps 3ms	cj, pers pron	neg part	v Hiphil pf 3cp, ps 3ms
	וַיַּכֵּר	יוֹסֵף	אֶת־אֶחָיו	וְהֵם	לֹא	הִכִּרֻהוּ
	wayyakkēr	yôs̱ēph	'eth-'echâv	wehēm	lō'	hikkiruhû
	and he recognized	Joseph	his brothers	but they	not	they recognized him

9.	**2226.121**	**3231**	**881**	**2573**	**866**	**2593.111**	**3937**
	cj, v Qal impf 3ms	pn	do	art, n mp	rel part	v Qal pf 3ms	prep, ps 3mp
	וַיִּזְכֹּר	יוֹסֵף	אֵת	הַחֲלֹמוֹת	אֲשֶׁר	חָלַם	לָהֶם
	wayyizkōr	yôs̱ēph	'ēth	hachlōmôth	'ăsher	chālam	lāhem
	and he remembered	Joseph		the dreams	which	he dreamed	about them

in Egypt, Jacob said unto his sons, Why do ye look one upon another?: ... stare, *REB, MLB, NASB* ... gaping, *NAB* ... Why don't you do something, *Good News* ... Why are you standing around looking at one another?, *MLB.*

2. And he said, Behold, I have heard that there is corn in Egypt: ... grain for sale, *NCB.*

get you down thither, and buy for us from thence; that we may live, and not die: ... go down there and buy from that place, *NASB* ... survive, *Anchor.*

3. And Joseph's ten brethren went down to buy corn in Egypt: ... grain, *NEB.*

4. But Benjamin, Joseph's brother: ... full, *NCB, NAB* ... the own brother, *Fenton.*

Jacob sent not with his brethren; for he said, Lest peradventure mischief befall him: ... harm, *KJVII* ... disaster, *NAB, Anchor* ... evil, *BB* ... death, *Geneva.*

5. And the sons of Israel came to buy corn among those that came: for the famine was in the land of Canaan: ... with the other purchasers, *NCB.*

6. And Joseph was the governor: ... visier, *Goodspeed* ... ruler, *Young, BB, NASB* ... regent, *Anchor* ... protector, *Fenton* ... in control, *Berkeley, MLB.*

over the land, and he it was that sold to all the people of the land: and Joseph's brethren came, and bowed down themselves before him with their faces to the earth: . . . prostrated, *Goodspeed, NCB* ... foreheads, *MLB.*

7. And Joseph saw his brethren, and he knew them, but made himself strange unto them, and spake roughly unto them; and he said unto them, Whence come ye? And they said, From the land of Canaan to buy food: ... as a stranger, *Berkeley, NKJV, Goodspeed* ... pretending not to know them, *REB, NEB* ... concealed his identity, *NAB.*

8. And Joseph knew his brethren, but they knew not him.

---

them when they came. Then the time came when they needed help. The famine was so bad that the brothers were just looking at each other, wondering what to do. Jacob saw, that is, learned, there was wheat in Egypt, so he commanded his sons to go down and buy grain to keep them alive.

42:3-4. The ten older brothers obeyed and went to Egypt, but Jacob did not let Benjamin go because he was afraid some accident might happen to him and kill him. He was still remembering what he supposed had happened to Joseph (cf. v. 36). It also shows he was giving he same preference to Benjamin he formerly gave to Joseph.

42:5-6. Others heard their was grain in Egypt, and a steady stream of people were going there to buy some. Joseph's brothers joined the crowd and went along among them. Though there was grain stored in all the cities of Egypt and Joseph managed the sale of all of it, foreigners had to come to Joseph personally as governor of the land, for he was the only one with the authority to sell to them. When the brothers came before him, they knelt down on their hands and knees and humbly bowed with their faces to the ground.

42:7-9. Joseph recognized his brothers. They probably had not changed much over the years. Joseph, however, was only 17 when they last saw him. Now he was 38 or 39 and dressed like an Egyptian. All they saw was the Egyptian governor with the Egyptian name, Zaphnath-paaneah, so they did not recognize him. He therefore acted like a stranger and spoke harshly so they would not recognize his voice. He remembered the dreams and how they had acted when he told them about it. He could not be sure how they would act now that the first dream was fulfilled and they had actually bowed down to him, something they thought they would never do. Joseph had no anger or resentment against them, as the names he gave his sons show. He wanted to reunite with his family, as later

569.121	420	7558.352	894	3937, 7495.141	881, 6413	800
cj, v Qal impf 3ms	prep, ps 3mp	v Piel ptc mp	pers pron	prep, v Qal inf con	do, *n fs*	art, n fs
וַיֹּאמֶר	אֲלֵהֶם	מְרַגְּלִים	אַתֶּם	לִרְאוֹת	אֶת־עֶרְוַת	הָאָרֶץ
wayyō'mer	'ălēhem	meraggelîm	'attem	lir'ôth	'eth-'erwath	hā'ārets
and he said	to them	spies	you	to see	the nakedness of	the land

971.117		569.126	420	3940	112	5860	971.116
v Qal pf 2mp	**10.**	cj, v Qal impf 3mp	prep, ps 3ms	neg part	n ms, ps 1cs	cj, n mp, ps 2ms	v Qal pf 3cp
בָּאתֶם		וַיֹּאמְרוּ	אֵלָיו	לֹא	אֲדֹנִי	וַעֲבָדֶיךָ	בָּאוּ
bā'them		wayyō'mrû	'ēlāv	lō'	'ădhōnî	wa'ăvādhêkhā	bā'û
you came		and they said	to him	no	my lord	but your servants	they came

3937, 8132.141, 406		3725	1158	382, 259	5348	3773	601
prep, v Qal inf con, n ms	**11.**	adj, ps 1cp	*n mp*	n ms, num	pers pron	adj	pers pron
לִשְׁבָּר־אֹכֶל		כֻּלָּנוּ	בְּנֵי	אִישׁ־אֶחָד	נָחְנוּ	כֵּנִים	אֲנַחְנוּ
lishbār-'ōkhel		kullānû	benê	'îsh-'echādh	nāchănû	kēnîm	'ănachnû
to buy grain of food		all of us	the sons of	one man	we	honest	we

3940, 2030.116	5860	7558.352		569.121	420	3940
neg part, v Qal pf 3cp	n mp, ps 2ms	v Piel ptc mp	**12.**	cj, v Qal impf 3ms	prep, ps 3mp	neg part
לֹא־הָיוּ	עֲבָדֶיךָ	מְרַגְּלִים		וַיֹּאמֶר	אֲלֵהֶם	לֹא
lō'-hāyû	'ăvādhêkhā	meraggelîm		wayyō'mer	'ălēhem	lō'
not they are	your servants	spies		and he said	to them	no

3706, 6413	800	971.117	3937, 7495.141		569.126	8530
cj, *n fs*	art, n fs	v Qal pf 2mp	prep, v Qal inf con	**13.**	cj, v Qal impf 3mp	num
כִּי־עֶרְוַת	הָאָרֶץ	בָּאתֶם	לִרְאוֹת		וַיֹּאמְרוּ	שְׁנֵים
kî-'erwath	hā'ārets	bā'them	lir'ôth		wayyō'mrû	shenêm
rather the nakedness of	the land	you came	to see		and they said	two

6461	5860	250	601	1158	382, 259	904, 800	3791
num	n mp, ps 2ms	n mp	pers pron	*n mp*	n ms, num	prep, *n fs*	pn
עָשָׂר	עֲבָדֶיךָ	אַחִים	אֲנַחְנוּ	בְּנֵי	אִישׁ־אֶחָד	בְּאֶרֶץ	כְּנָעַן
'āsār	'ăvādhêkhā	'achîm	'ănachnû	benê	'îsh-'echādh	be'erets	kenā'an
ten	your servants	brothers	we	the sons of	one man	in the land of	Canaan

2079	7277	882, 1	3219	259	375		569.121
cj, intrj	art, adj	prep, n ms, ps 1cp	art, n ms	cj, art, num	sub, ps 3ms	**14.**	cj, v Qal impf 3ms
וְהִנֵּה	הַקָּטֹן	אֶת־אָבִינוּ	הַיּוֹם	וְהָאֶחָד	אֵינֶנּוּ		וַיֹּאמֶר
wehinnēh	haqqāṭōn	'eth-'āvînû	hayyôm	wehā'echādh	'ênennû		wayyō'mer
and behold	the youngest	with our father	today	and the one	he is not		and he said

420	3231	2000	866	1744.315	420	3937, 569.141	7558.352
prep, ps 3mp	pn	pers pron	rel part	v Piel pf 1cs	prep, ps 2mp	prep, v Qal inf con	v Piel ptc mp
אֲלֵהֶם	יוֹסֵף	הוּא	אֲשֶׁר	דִּבַּרְתִּי	אֲלֵכֶם	לֵאמֹר	מְרַגְּלִים
'ălēhem	yôsēph	hû'	'ăsher	dibbartî	'ălēkhem	lē'mōr	meraggelîm
to them	Joseph	it	what	I spoke	to you	saying	spies

894		904, 2148	1010.228	2508	6799	524, 3428.128	4623, 2172
pers pron	**15.**	prep, dem pron	v Niphal impf 2mp	*n mp*	pn	cj, v Qal impf 2mp	prep, dem pron
אַתֶּם		בְּזֹאת	תִּבָּחֵנוּ	חֵי	פַרְעֹה	אִם־תֵּצְאוּ	מִזֶּה
'attem		bezō'th	tibbāchēnû	chê	phar'ōh	'im-tēts'û	mizzeh
you		by this	you will be tested	the life of	Pharaoh	if you go out	from this

3706	524, 904, 971.141	250	7277	2077		8365.133	4623
cj	cj, prep, v Qal inf con	n ms, ps 2mp	art, adj	adv	**16.**	v Qal impv 2mp	prep, ps 2mp
כִּי	אִם־בְּבוֹא	אֲחִיכֶם	הַקָּטֹן	הֵנָּה		שִׁלְחוּ	מִכֶּם
kî	'im-bevô'	'ăchîkhem	haqqāṭōn	hēnnāh		shilchû	mikkem
except	if by coming	your brother	the youngest	here		send	from you

259	4089.121	881, 250	894	646.233	1010.226
num	cj, v Qal impf 3ms	do, n ms, ps 2mp	cj, pers pron	v Niphal impv 2mp	cj, v Niphal impf 3mp
אֶחָד	וְיִקַּח	אֶת־אֲחִיכֶם	וְאַתֶּם	הֵאָסְרוּ	וְיִבָּחֲנוּ
'echādh	w^{e}yiqqach	'eth-'ăchîkhem	w^{e}attem	hē'āsrû	w^{e}yibbāchănû
one	and he will take	your brother	and you	you will be imprisoned	and they will be tested

1744	583	882	524, 3940	2508	6799	3706	7558.352
n mp, ps 2mp	intrg part, n fs	prep, ps 2mp	cj, cj, neg part	*n mp*	pn	cj	v Piel ptc mp
דִּבְרֵיכֶם	הַאֱמֶת	אִתְּכֶם	וְאִם־לֹא	חֵי	פַּרְעֹה	כִּי	מְרַגְּלִים
divrêkhem	ha'ěmeth	'itt^{e}khem	w^{e}'im-lō'	chê	phar'ōh	kî	m^{e}ragg^{e}lîm
your words	whether truth	with you	and if not	the life of	Pharaoh	that	spies

9. And Joseph remembered the dreams which he dreamed of them, and said unto them, Ye are spies; to see the nakedness of the land ye are come: ... to detect where the land lies exposed, *Berkeley, MLB* ... the weak points in our defences, *REB, NEB* ... to see the weakness of the land, *RSV, Geneva* ... where our land is unprotected, *NIV* ... undefended parts, *NASB.*

10. And they said unto him, Nay, my lord, but to buy food are thy servants come.

11. We are all one man's sons; we are true men: ... honest, *NCB, NASB, Fenton* ... right, *Young.*

thy servants are no spies: ... have never spied, *Anchor* ... have not come with any secret purpose, *BB.*

12. And he said unto them, Nay, but to see the nakedness of the land ye are come.

13. And they said, Thy servants are twelve brethren, the sons of one man in the land of Canaan; and, behold, the youngest is this day with our father, and one is not: ... is at home today, *Fenton* ... dead, *Good News, BB* ... disappeared, *NEB* ... lost, *REB.*

14. And Joseph said unto them, That is it that I spake unto you, saying, Ye are spies: . . . It is just as I told you, *NIV.*

15. Hereby ye shall be proved: ... in this manner you shall be tested, *NKJV.*

By the life of Pharaoh ye shall not go forth hence, except your youngest brother come hither: ... leave (go away from) this place, *NCB, NIV, RSV.*

16. Send one of you, and let him fetch your brother, and ye shall be kept in prison: ... bound, *ASV* ... under arrest, *Anchor, NAB* ... in bonds, *NCB.*

that your words may be proved: ... test(ed), *NASB, RSV, REB.*

whether there be any truth in you: or else by the life of Pharaoh surely ye are spies: ... your purpose is certainly secret, *BB.*

17. And he put them all together into ward three days: ... herded them, *Anchor* ... consigned, *NCB* ... custody, *Berkeley, NIV* ... guardhouse, *NAB.*

events reveal. But he knew if they were still jealous or resentful, he could have no fellowship with them. He had to test them to be sure. Egyptians were known to be suspicious of foreigners, so he proceeded to talk to them the way they probably expected Egyptians to talk. He also called them spies looking for the nakedness of the land, that is for any defenseless, unfortified places.

42:10-13. The brothers protested that they had only come to buy grain for food and that they were honest men, not spies. Joseph continued to speak harshly to them and again accused them of coming to see the nakedness of the land.

Again they protested, saying they were 12 brothers, the sons of one man, the youngest was with their father and the one was not. That is, they presumed that Joseph was dead.

42:14-16. Joseph was probably disturbed when he saw that Benjamin was not with the brothers. His first thought was that the jealousy they had for him might have been transferred to Benjamin and they might have done away with him.

Now he wanted to be sure Benjamin, his full brother, was still alive. So again he accused the brothers of being spies and swore by the life of Pharaoh that they would not be allowed to leave Egypt unless their youngest brother came. He commanded them to send one from among them to take Benjamin and bring him to Egypt while the rest of them would be kept under guard in prison until Benjamin came. This would be a test to see whether they were honest men or spies, he said.

894		636.121	881	420, 5110	8421	3219		569.121
pers pron	**17.**	cj, v Qal impf 3ms	do, ps 3mp	prep, n ms	*num*	n mp	**18.**	cj, v Qal impf 3ms
אַתֶּם		וַיֶּאֱסֹף	אֹתָם	אֶל־מִשְׁמָר	שְׁלֹשֶׁת	יָמִים		וַיֹּאמֶר
'attem		wayye'ĕsōph	'ōthām	'el-mishmār	shelōsheth	yāmîm		wayyō'mer
you		and he gathered	them	in to custody	three	days		and he said

420	3231	904, 3219	8389	2148	6449.133	2513.133	881, 435
prep, ps 3mp	pn	prep, art, n ms	art, num	dem pron	v Qal impv 2mp	v Qal impv 2mp	do, art, n mp
אֲלֵהֶם	יוֹסֵף	בַּיּוֹם	הַשְּׁלִישִׁי	זֹאת	עֲשׂוּ	וִחְיוּ	אֶת־הָאֱלֹהִים
'ălēhem	yôsēph	bayyôm	hashshelîshî	zō'th	'ăsû	wichăyû	'eth-hā'ĕlōhîm
to them	Joseph	on the day	the third	this	do	and live	God

603	3486.151		524, 3773	894	250	259	646.221
pers pron	v Qal act ptc ms	**19.**	cj, adj	pers pron	n ms, ps 2mp	num	v Niphal impf 3ms
אֲנִי	יָרֵא		אִם־כֵּנִים	אַתֶּם	אֲחִיכֶם	אֶחָד	יֵאָסֵר
'ănî	yārē'		'im-kēnîm	'attem	'ăchîkhem	'echādh	yē'āsēr
I	one who fears		if honest	you	your brother	one	he will be imprisoned

904, 1041	5110	894	2050.133	971.533	8134	7743
prep, *n ms*	n ms, ps 2mp	cj, pers pron	v Qal impv 2mp	v Hiphil impv 2mp	n ms	*n ms*
בְּבֵית	מִשְׁמַרְכֶם	וְאַתֶּם	לְכוּ	הָבִיאוּ	שֶׁבֶר	רַעֲבוֹן
bevêth	mishmarkhem	we'attem	lekhû	hāvî'û	shever	ra'ăvôn
in the house of	your prison	and you	go	bring	grain	famine of

1041		881, 250	7277	971.528	420
n mp, ps 2mp	**20.**	cj, do, n ms, ps 2mp	art, adj	v Hiphil impf 2mp	prep, ps 1cs
בָּתֵּיכֶם		וְאֶת־אֲחִיכֶם	הַקָּטֹן	תָּבִיאוּ	אֵלַי
bāttêkhem		we'eth-'ăchîkhem	haqqātōn	tāvî'û	'ēlay
your households		and your brother	the youngest	you will bring	to me

548.226	1744	3940	4322.128	6449.126, 3772
cj, v Niphal impf 3mp	n mp, ps 2mp	cj, neg part	v Qal impf 2mp	cj, v Qal impf 3mp, adv
וְיֵאָמְנוּ	דִבְרֵיכֶם	וְלֹא	תָמוּתוּ	וַיַּעֲשׂוּ־כֵן
weyē'āmenû	dhivrêkhem	welō'	thāmûthû	wayya'ăsû-khēn
then they will be verified	your words	and not	you will die	and they did so

	569.126	382	420, 250	61	845	601	6142, 250
21.	cj, v Qal impf 3mp	n ms	prep, n ms, ps 3ms	adv	adj	pers pron	prep, n ms, ps 1cp
	וַיֹּאמְרוּ	אִישׁ	אֶל־אָחִיו	אֲבָל	אֲשֵׁמִים	אֲנַחְנוּ	עַל־אָחִינוּ
	wayyō'merû	'îsh	'el-'āchîw	'ăvāl	'ăshēmîm	'ănachnû	'al-'āchînû
	and they said	each	to his brother	truly	guilty	we	concerning our brother

866	7495.119	7150	5497	904, 2706.741	420	3940
rel part	v Qal pf 1cp	*n fs*	n fs, ps 3ms	prep, v Hithpael inf con, ps 3ms	prep, ps 1cp	cj, neg part
אֲשֶׁר	רָאִינוּ	צָרַת	נַפְשׁוֹ	בְּהִתְחַנְנוֹ	אֵלֵינוּ	וְלֹא
'ăsher	rā'înû	tsārath	naphshô	behithchanănô	'ēlênû	welō'
which	we have seen	the distress of	his soul	in his pleading	to us	and not

8471.119	6142, 3772	971.112	420	7150	2148		6257.121
v Qal pf 1cp	prep, adv	v Qal pf 3fs	prep, ps 1cp	art, n fs	art, dem pron	**22.**	cj, v Qal impf 3ms
שָׁמָעְנוּ	עַל־כֵּן	בָּאָה	אֵלֵינוּ	הַצָּרָה	הַזֹּאת		וַיַּעַן
shāmā'ănû	'al-kēn	bā'āh	'ēlênû	hatstsārāh	hazzō'th		wayya'an
we listened	therefore	it came	to us	the distress	the this		and he answered

7498	881	3937, 569.141	3940	569.115	420	3937, 569.141
pn	do, ps 3mp	prep, v Qal inf con	intrg part, neg part	v Qal pf 1cs	prep, ps 2mp	prep, v Qal inf con
רְאוּבֵן	אֹתָם	לֵאמֹר	הֲלוֹא	אָמַרְתִּי	אֲלֵיכֶם	לֵאמֹר
re'ûvēn	'ōthām	lē'mōr	helō'	'āmartî	'ălēkhem	lē'mōr
Reuben	them	saying	did not	I say	to you	saying

414, 2490.128 adv, v Qal impf 2mp אַל־תֶּחֶטְאוּ 'al-techeṭ'û do not sin	904, 3315 prep, art, n ms בַּיֶּלֶד vayyeledh against the boy	3940 cj, neg part וְלֹא welō' and not	8471.117 v Qal pf 2mp שְׁמַעְתֶּם shema'ättem you listened	1612, 1879 cj, cj, n ms, ps 3ms וְגַם־דָּמוֹ wegham-dāmô and also his blood	2079 intrj הִנֵּה hinnēh behold

1938.255 v Niphal ptc ms נִדְרָשׁ nidhrāsh something to be accounted for	**23.**	2062 cj, pers pron וְהֵם wehēm and they	3940 neg part לֹא lō' not	3156.116 v Qal pf 3cp יָדְעוּ yādheû they knew	3706 cj כִּי kî that	8471.151 v Qal act ptc ms שֹׁמֵעַ shōmēa' hearing	3231 pn יוֹסֵף yôsēph Joseph

3706 cj כִּי kî because	4054.551 art, v Hiphil ptc ms הַמֵּלִיץ hammēlîts the interpreter	1033 prep, ps 3mp בֵּינֹתָם bênōthām between them	**24.**	5621.121 cj, v Qal impf 3ms וַיִּסֹּב wayyissōv and he turned	4623, 6142 prep, prep, ps 3mp מֵעֲלֵיהֶם mē'ălêhem from them	1098.121 cj, v Qal impf 3ms וַיֵּבְךְּ wayyēvekh and he wept

18. And Joseph said unto them the third day, This do, and live; for I fear God: ... revere, *Berkeley* ... you may save your lives, *Goodspeed.*

19. If ye be true men, let one of your brethren be bound in the house of your prison: go ye, carry corn for the famine of your houses: ... honest, *NIV* ... starving households, *REB*, *Goodspeed*, *Anchor.*

20. But bring your youngest brother unto me; so shall your words be verified, and ye shall not die. And they did so: ... established, *Young* ... your words will be proved true, *REB*, *NEB.*

21. And they said one to another, We are verily guilty concerning our brother: ... sins against, *Fenton*, *Geneva* ... being punished, *Anchor*, *NAB*, *NIV* ... paying the penalty, *NRSV* ... deserve to be punished, *NEB* ... we are to blame, *Goodspeed.*

in that we saw the anguish of his soul, when he besought us: ... heart, *NCB* ... grief of mind, *BB* ... pleaded, *NCB* ... begged, *KJVII* ... pity, *Fenton* ... mercy, *Goodspeed.*

and we would not hear; therefore is this distress come upon us: ... give ears to his prayers, *BB* ... trouble, *BB*, *Geneva.*

22. And Reuben answered them, saying, Spake I not unto you, saying, Do not sin against the child; and ye would not hear? therefore, behold, also his blood is required: ... retorted, *Anchor* ... reckoning for his blood, *NCB*, *NASB*, *NAB* ... upon our heads, *NEB*, *REB* ... payment for his blood has come due, *MLB.*

23. And they knew not that Joseph understood them; for he spake unto them by an interpreter: ... intermediary, *Goodspeed.*

24. And he turned himself about from them: ... withdrew, *NCB*, *Fenton.*

42:17-20. Joseph then put all ten brothers in prison under guard for three days. Then he gave them a new command by which they could stay alive. Because Joseph feared (reverenced) "the God," that is, the one true God, they could show they were honest men by leaving one brother in prison, and taking grain to feed their hungry households. Then they must bring their youngest brother, and they would not die. This implies they would die if they came back to Egypt without him.

42:21-22. The brothers then began saying to each other that they were truly guilty concerning Joseph. They had not forgotten what they had done to him. Probably the continued grief of their father (37:35) helped to keep the memory fresh. In their minds they could perhaps still hear the cries of Joseph in his distress when they were throwing him into the cistern and when they were selling him. Now they were getting what they deserved in the distress they were currently suffering. Reuben then reminded them how he begged them not to sin against the boy, and now his blood was being demanded, that is, they were held accountable.

42:23-24. The brothers were talking to each other in Hebrew, and they did not know Joseph could understand them, for he had been speaking to them through an interpreter. Joseph could not hold back his feelings, so he turned away, probably into an inner room where they could not hear him weep. When he returned, he spoke to them, probably repeating his demand that they bring Benjamin. Then he took Simeon and put chains on him before their eyes. We are not told why he chose Simeon. Perhaps he needed the additional discipline.

8178.121	420	1744.321	420	4089.121	4623, 882
cj, v Qal impf 3ms	prep, ps 3mp	cj, v Piel impf 3ms	prep, ps 3mp	cj, v Qal impf 3ms	prep, prep, ps 3mp
וַיָּשָׁב	אֲלֵהֶם	וַיְדַבֵּר	אֲלֵהֶם	וַיִּקַּח	מֵאִתָּם
wayyāshāv	'ălēhem	way^{e}dhabbēr	'ălēhem	wayyiqqach	mē'ittām
and he returned	to them	and he spoke	to them	and he took	from them

881, 8482	646.121	881	3937, 6084		6943	3231
do, pn	cj, v Qal impf 3ms	do, ps 3ms	prep, n fd, ps 3mp	25.	cj, v Piel impf 3ms	pn
אֶת־שִׁמְעוֹן	וַיֶּאֱסֹר	אֹתוֹ	לְעֵינֵיהֶם		וַיְצַו	יוֹסֵף
'eth-shim'ôn	wayye'ĕsōr	'ōthô	l^{e}'ênêhem		waytsaw	yôsēph
Simeon	and he tied up	him	before their eyes		and he commanded	Joseph

4527.326	881, 3747	1277	3937, 8178.541	3826B	382	420, 8012
v Piel impf 3mp	do, n mp, ps 3mp	n ms	cj, prep, v Hiphil inf con	n mp, ps 3mp	n ms	prep, n ms, ps 3ms
וַיְמַלְאוּ	אֶת־כְּלֵיהֶם	בָּר	וּלְהָשִׁיב	כַּסְפֵּיהֶם	אִישׁ	אֶל־שַׂקּוֹ
waymal'û	'eth-k^{e}lêhem	bār	ûlăhāshîv	kaspêhem	'îsh	'el-saqqô
and they filled	their sacks of	grain	and to put back	their silver	each	to his sack

5598.141	3937	6990	3937, 1932	6449.121	3937	3772
cj, v Qal inf con	prep, ps 3mp	n fs	prep, art, n ms	cj, v Qal impf 3ms	prep, ps 3mp	adv
וְלָתֵת	לָהֶם	צֵדָה	לַדָּרֶךְ	וַיַּעַשׂ	לָהֶם	כֵּן
w^{e}lāthēth	lāhem	tsēdhāh	laddārekh	wayya'as	lāhem	kēn
and to give	to them	provisions	for the journey	and he did	for them	so

	5558.126	881, 8134	6142, 2645	2050.126	4623, 8427
26.	cj, v Qal impf 3mp	do, n ms, ps 3mp	prep, n mp, ps 3mp	cj, v Qal impf 3mp	prep, adv
	וַיִּשְׂאוּ	אֶת־שִׁבְרָם	עַל־חֲמֹרֵיהֶם	וַיֵּלְכוּ	מִשָּׁם
	wayyis'û	'eth-shivrām	'al-chămōrêhem	wayyêl^{e}khû	mishshām
	and they lifted up	their grain	on their donkeys	and they went	from there

	6858.121	259	881, 8012	3937, 5598.141	4706	3937, 2645
27.	cj, v Qal impf 3ms	art, num	do, n ms, ps 3ms	prep, v Qal inf con	n ms	prep, art, n ms, ps 3ms
	וַיִּפְתַּח	הָאֶחָד	אֶת־שַׂקּוֹ	לָתֵת	מִסְפּוֹא	לַחֲמֹרוֹ
	wayyiphtach	hā'echādh	'eth-saqqô	lāthēth	mispô'	lachmōrô
	and he opened	the first	his sack	to give	feed	to his donkey

904, 4550	7495.121	881, 3826B	2079, 2000	904, 6552	584
prep, art, n ms	cj, v Qal impf 3ms	do, n ms, ps 3ms	cj, intrj, pers pron	prep, *n ms*	n fs, ps 3ms
בַּמָּלוֹן	וַיַּרְא	אֶת־כַּסְפּוֹ	וְהִנֵּה־הוּא	בְּפִי	אַמְתַּחְתּוֹ
bammālôn	wayyar^{e}'	'eth-kaspô	w^{e}hinnēh-hû'	b^{e}phî	'amtachtô
in the lodging place	and he saw	his silver	and behold it	in the mouth of	his sack

	569.121	420, 250	8178.611	3826B	1612	2079	904, 584
28.	cj, v Qal impf 3ms	prep, n ms, ps 3ms	v Hophal pf 3ms	n ms, ps 1cs	cj, cj	intrj	prep, n fs, ps 1cs
	וַיֹּאמֶר	אֶל־אֶחָיו	הוּשַׁב	כַּסְפִּי	וְגַם	הִנֵּה	בְאַמְתַּחְתִּי
	wayyō'mer	'el-'echâv	hûshav	kaspî	w^{e}gham	hinnēh	v^{e}'amtachtî
	and he said	to his brothers	it was returned	my silver	and also	behold	in my sack

3428.121	3949	2829.126	382	420, 250	3937, 569.141
cj, v Qal impf 3ms	n ms, ps 3mp	cj, v Qal impf 3mp	n ms	prep, n ms, ps 3ms	prep, v Qal inf con
וַיֵּצֵא	לִבָּם	וַיֶּחֶרְדוּ	אִישׁ	אֶל־אָחִיו	לֵאמֹר
wayyētsē'	libbām	wayyechr^{e}dhû	'îsh	'el-'āchîw	lē'mōr
nearly and it failed	their heart	and they trembled	each	to his brother	saying

4242, 2148	6449.111	435	3937		971.126	420, 3399	1
intrg, dem pron	v Qal pf 3ms	n mp	prep, ps 1cp	29.	cj, v Qal impf 3mp	prep, pn	n ms, ps 3mp
מַה־זֹּאת	עָשָׂה	אֱלֹהִים	לָנוּ		וַיָּבֹאוּ	אֶל־יַעֲקֹב	אֲבִיהֶם
mah-zō'th	'āsāh	'ĕlōhîm	lānû		wayyāvō'û	'el-ya'ăqōv	'ăvîhem
what this	he has done	God	to us		and they went	to Jacob	their father

800	3791	5222.526	3937	881	3725, 7424.154	882
n fs	pn	cj, v Hiphil impf 3mp	prep, ps 3ms	do	*adj*, art, v Qal act ptc fp	prep, ps 3mp
אַרְצָה	כְּנָעַן	וַיַּגִּידוּ	לוֹ	אֵת	כָּל־הַקֹּרֹת	אֹתָם
'artsāh	k^{e}nā'an	wayyaggîdhû	lô	'ēth	kol-haqqōrōth	'ōthām
to the land of	Canaan	and they reported	to him		all the happenings	with them

3937, 569.141		1744.311	382	112	800	882	7482
prep, v Qal inf con	**30.**	v Piel pf 3ms	art, n ms	*n mp*	art, n fs	prep, ps 1cp	adj
לֵאמֹר		דִּבֶּר	הָאִישׁ	אֲדֹנֵי	הָאָרֶץ	אִתָּנוּ	קָשׁוֹת
lē'mōr		dibber	hā'îsh	'ădhōnê	hā'ārets	'ittānû	qāshôth
saying		he spoke	the man	the lord of	the land	with us	harshly

5598.121	881	3626, 7558.352	881, 800		569.120	420
cj, v Qal impf 3ms	do, ps 1cp	prep, v Piel ptc mp	do, art, n fs	**31.**	cj, v Qal impf 1cp	prep, ps 3ms
וַיִּתֵּן	אֹתָנוּ	כִּמְרַגְּלִים	אֶת־הָאָרֶץ		וַנֹּאמֶר	אֵלָיו
wayyittēn	'ōthānû	kimragg^{e}lîm	'eth-hā'ārets		wannō'mer	'ēlāv
and he presented	us	as the spies of	the land		but we said	to him

and wept; and returned to them again: ... overcome with weeping, *BB* ... when he was able to speak, *NAB*, *Anchor*.

and communed with them: ... resume the conversation with them, *MLB*, *Berkeley* ... played a trick on them, *NEB*.

and took from them Simeon, and bound him before their eyes: ... put chains on, *BB* ... imprisoned, *Goodspeed*.

25. Then Joseph commanded to fill their sacks with corn: ... wagons, *Fenton* ... containers, *NAB*, *Anchor* ... receptacles, *Goodspeed* ... wheat, *Geneva*.

and to restore every man's money into his sack, and to give them provision for the way: and thus did he unto them: ... Then he gave them leave to go, and showed politeness to them, *Fenton*.

26. And they laded their asses with the corn, and departed thence: ... loaded grain on their donkeys, *NIV*.

27. And as one of them opened his sack to give his ass provender: ... food, *BB* ... feed his donkey, *REB*.

in the inn, he espied his money; for, behold, it was in his sack's mouth: ... encampment, *Anchor* ... camping place, *Goodspeed* ... resting place, *BB*.

28. And he said unto his brethren, My money is restored; and, lo, it is even in my sack: ... returned, *Berkeley* ... pack, *REB*.

and their heart failed them: ... sank, *Berkeley*, *Goodspeed* ... stopped, *Fenton* ... lost heart, *NRSV* ... became full of fear, *BB*.

and they were afraid, saying one to another, What is this that God hath done unto us?: ... horrified, *MLB* ... mystified, *NCB* ... bewildered, *REB* ... astonished, *Geneva*.

29. And they came unto Jacob their father unto the land of Canaan, and told him all that befell unto them; saying: ... their experiences, *BB*, *MLB*.

30. The man, who is the lord of the land, spake roughly to us: ... sternly, *NAB* ... put us in custody, *NAB*.

and took us for spies of the country: ... secret evil purpose, *BB*.

42:25-26. Joseph then commanded his servants to fill their sacks or containers with clean, threshed grain. (No doubt, each brother had several containers for grain since there was a large household to feed.) The servants were to put their silver back in the personal sackcloth bags (a different word than the sacks for the grain), along with provisions for the journey. The brothers were then allowed to come out of the prison, load their grain on their donkeys, and depart.

42:27-28. When the brothers stopped at a camping ground for the night, one of them opened his personal sack to feed his donkey and was shocked to see his silver, which was given to pay for the grain, was in the sack's mouth. When he told his brothers, they nearly had heart failure, and they trembled with fear. What they said to each other shows they still remembered what they had done to Joseph and felt God was punishing them for it.

42:29-34. When the brothers arrived home, they reported to Jacob all that happened to them. They called Joseph the lord of the land and told how he accused them of being spies, demanded that they leave one brother and bring their youngest brother back to him. Then they would be free to do business in the land.

3773	601	3940	2030.119	7558.352		8530, 6461	601	250
adj	pers pron	neg part	v Qal pf 1cp	v Piel ptc mp	**32.**	num pl, num	pers pron	n mp
כֵּנִים	אֲנָחְנוּ	לֹא	הָיִינוּ	מְרַגְּלִים		שְׁנֵים־עָשָׂר	אֲנַחְנוּ	אַחִים
kēnîm	'ănāchănû	lō'	hāyînû	m^{e}ragg^{e}lîm		sh^{e}nêm-'āsār	'ănachnû	'achîm
honest	we	not	we are	spies		two ten	we	brothers

1158	1	259	375	7277	3219	882, 1
n mp	n ms, ps 1cp	art, num	sub, ps 3ms	cj, art, adj	art, n ms	prep, n ms, ps 1cp
בְּנֵי	אָבִינוּ	הָאֶחָד	אֵינֶנּוּ	וְהַקָּטֹן	הַיּוֹם	אֶת־אָבִינוּ
b^{e}nê	'āvînû	hā'echādh	'ênennû	w^{e}haqqātōn	hayyôm	'eth-'āvînû
the sons of	our father	the one	he is not	and the youngest	today	with our father

904, 800	3791		569.121	420	382	112	800
prep, n fs	pn	**33.**	cj, v Qal impf 3ms	prep, ps 1cp	art, n ms	*n mp*	art, n fs
בְּאֶרֶץ	כְּנָעַן		וַיֹּאמֶר	אֵלֵינוּ	הָאִישׁ	אֲדֹנֵי	הָאָרֶץ
b^{e}'erets	k^{e}nā'an		wayyō'mer	'ēlênû	hā'îsh	'ădhōnê	hā'ārets
in the land of	Canaan		and he said	to us	the man	the lord of	the land

904, 2148	3156.125	3706	3773	894	250	259	5299.533
prep, dem pron	v Qal impf 1cs	cj	adj	pers pron	n ms, ps 2mp	art, num	v Hiphil impv 2mp
בְּזֹאת	אֵדַע	כִּי	כֵנִים	אַתֶּם	אֲחִיכֶם	הָאֶחָד	הַנִּיחוּ
b^{e}zō'th	'ēdha'	kî	khēnîm	'attem	'ăchîkhem	hā'echādh	hannîchû
by this	I will know	that	honest	you	your brother	the one	you will leave

882	881, 7743	1041	4089.133	2050.133		971.533
prep, ps 1cs	cj, do, *n ms*	n mp, ps 2mp	v Qal impv 2mp	cj, v Qal impv 2mp	**34.**	cj, v Hiphil impv 2mp
אִתִּי	וְאֶת־רַעֲבוֹן	בָּתֵּיכֶם	קְחוּ	וָלֵכוּ		וְהָבִיאוּ
'ittî	w^{e}'eth-ra'ăvôn	bāttêkhem	qōchû	wālēkhû		w^{e}hāvî'û
with me	and the famine of	your houses	take	and go		and bring

881, 250	7277	420	3156.125	3706	3940	7558.352	894
do, n ms, ps 2mp	art, adj	prep, ps 1cs	cj, v Qal impf 1cs	cj	neg part	v Piel ptc mp	pers pron
אֶת־אֲחִיכֶם	הַקָּטֹן	אֵלַי	וְאֵדְעָה	כִּי	לֹא	מְרַגְּלִים	אַתֶּם
'eth-'ăchîkhem	haqqātōn	'ēlay	w^{e}'ēdh^{e}'āh	kî	lō'	m^{e}ragg^{e}lîm	'attem
your brother	the youngest	to me	and I will know	that	not	spies	you

3706	3773	894	881, 250	5598.125	3937	881, 800
cj	adj	pers pron	do, n ms, ps 2mp	v Qal impf 1cs	prep, ps 2mp	cj, do, art, n fs
כִּי	כֵנִים	אַתֶּם	אֶת־אֲחִיכֶם	אֶתֵּן	לָכֶם	וְאֶת־הָאָרֶץ
kî	khēnîm	'attem	'eth-'ăchîkhem	'ettēn	lākhem	w^{e}'eth-hā'ārets
that	honest	you	your brother	I will give	to you	and the land

5692.128		2030.121	2062	7671.552	8012	2079, 382
v Qal impf 2mp	**35.**	cj, v Qal impf 3ms	pers pron	v Hiphil ptc mp	n mp, ps 3mp	cj, intrj, n ms
תִּסְחָרוּ		וַיְהִי	הֵם	מְרִיקִים	שַׂקֵּיהֶם	וְהִנֵּה־אִישׁ
tischārû		wayhî	hēm	m^{e}rîqîm	saqqêhem	w^{e}hinnēh-'îsh
you will do business in		and it was	they	emptying	their sack	and behold each

7154, 3826B	904, 8012	7495.126	881, 7154	3826B	2065
n ms, n ms, ps 3ms	prep, n ms, ps 3ms	cj, v Qal impf 3mp	do, *n mp*	n mp, ps 3mp	pers pron
צְרוֹר־כַּסְפּוֹ	בְּשַׂקּוֹ	וַיִּרְאוּ	אֶת־צְרֹרוֹת	כַּסְפֵּיהֶם	הֵמָּה
ts^{e}rôr-kaspô	b^{e}saqqô	wayyir'û	'eth-ts^{e}rōrôth	kaspêhem	hēmmāh
bag of his silver	in his sack	and they saw	the bags of	their silver	they

1	3486.126		569.121	420	3399	1
cj, n ms, ps 3mp	cj, v Qal impf 3mp	**36.**	cj, v Qal impf 3ms	prep, ps 3mp	pn	n ms, ps 3mp
וַאֲבִיהֶם	וַיִּירָאוּ		וַיֹּאמֶר	אֲלֵהֶם	יַעֲקֹב	אֲבִיהֶם
wa'ăvîhem	wayyîrā'û		wayyō'mer	'ălēhem	ya'ăqōv	'ăvîhem
and their father	and they were afraid		and he said	to them	Jacob	their father

881	8323.317	3231	375	8482	375	881, 1175
do, ps 1cs	v Piel pf 2mp	pn	sub, ps 3ms	cj, pn	sub, ps 3ms	cj, do, pn
אֹתִי	שִׁכַּלְתֶּם	יוֹסֵף	אֵינֶנּוּ	וְשִׁמְעוֹן	אֵינֶנּוּ	וְאֶת־בִּנְיָמִן
'ōthî	shikkaltem	yôsēph	'ênennû	w^{e}shim'ôn	'ênennû	w^{e}'eth-binyāmin
me	you have bereaved	Joseph	he is not	and Simeon	he is not	and Benjamin

4089.128	6142	2030.116	3725		569.121	7498	420, 1
v Qal impf 2mp	prep, ps 1cs	v Qal pf 3cp	adj, ps 3fp	**37.**	cj, v Qal impf 3ms	pn	prep, n ms, ps 3ms
תִּקָּחוּ	עָלַי	הָיוּ	כֻלָּנָה		וַיֹּאמֶר	רְאוּבֵן	אֶל־אָבִיו
tiqqāchû	'ālay	hāyû	khullānāh		wayyō'mer	r^{e}'ûvēn	'el-'āvîw
you will take	beside me	they are	all these		and he said	Reuben	to his father

3937, 569.141	881, 8529	1158	4322.523	524, 3940	971.525	420
prep, v Qal inf con	do, *num*	n mp, ps 1cs	v Hiphil impf 2ms	cj, adv	v Hiphil impf 1cs, ps 3ms	prep, ps 2ms
לֵאמֹר	אֶת־שְׁנֵי	בָּנַי	תָּמִית	אִם־לֹא	אֲבִיאֶנּוּ	אֵלֶיךָ
lē'mōr	'eth-sh^{e}nê	vānay	tāmîth	'im-lō'	'ăvî'ennû	'ēlêkhā
saying	the two of	my sons	you will kill	if not	I bring him	to you

5598.131	881	6142, 3135	603	8178.125	420
v Qal impv 2ms	do, ps 3ms	prep, n fs, ps 1cs	cj, pers pron	v Hiphil impf 1cs, ps 3ms	prep, ps 2ms
תְּנָה	אֹתוֹ	עַל־יָדִי	וַאֲנִי	אֲשִׁיבֶנּוּ	אֵלֶיךָ
t^{e}nāh	'ōthô	'al-yādhî	wa'ănî	'ăshîvennû	'ēlêkhā
put	him	in my hand	and I	I will bring him back	to you

31. And we said unto him, We are true men; we are no spies:

32. We be twelve brethren, sons of our father; one is not, and the youngest is this day with our father in the land of Canaan.

33. And the man, the lord of the country, said unto us, Hereby shall I know that ye are true men; leave one of your brethren here with me, and take food for the famine of your households, and be gone:

34. And bring your youngest brother unto me: then shall I know that ye are no spies, but that ye are true men: so will I deliver you your brother, and ye shall traffick in the land.

35. And it came to pass as they emptied their sacks: ... loads, *Fenton.*

that, behold, every man's bundle of money was in his sack: ... purse, *NCB* ... money-packet, *Goodspeed* ... cargo, *Fenton.*

and when both they and their father saw the bundles of money, they were afraid: ... dismayed, *NCB, NASB, NAB.*

36. And Jacob their father said unto them, Me have ye bereaved of my children: ... Must you make me childless, *NAB* ... you have robbed me of my children, *NEB, Geneva, REB.*

Joseph is not, and Simeon is not, and ye will take Benjamin away: all these things are against me: ... It is I upon whom all this falls!, *NCB* ... you would take from me all their is, *Fenton* ... always happen to me, *NAB, Anchor.*

37. And Reuben spake unto his father, saying, Slay my two sons, if I bring him not to thee: ... I now place them into your hands as a pledge, *Fenton.*

deliver him into my hand, and I will bring him to thee again: ... entrust him to my care, *NIV* ... safely, *BB.*

38. And he said, My son shall not go down with you; for his brother

42:35-36. When the brothers emptied their personal sacks, each one had the pouch or small sack of sliver in it. This made Jacob and his sons afraid. Jacob blamed the nine brothers, saying they had bereaved him of Joseph and Simeon and now they wanted to take Benjamin. He felt all these things were against him.

42:37-38. Reuben then offered to let Jacob kill his two sons if he did not bring Benjamin back to him. He was sure that if Jacob put Benjamin in his care, he would bring him back. But Jacob refused. Joseph was dead and Benjamin was left alone (that is, of Rachel's sons). Jacob was sure some accident would happen to Benjamin on the road and they would bring down his gray head in torment to Sheol. Jacob still felt that this would bring further judgment of God, like what he supposed happened to Joseph, and would send him to hell.

	569.121	3940, 3495.121	1158	6196	3706, 250	4322.151
38.	cj, v Qal impf 3ms	neg part, v Qal impf 3ms	n ms, ps 1cs	prep, ps 2mp	cj, n ms, ps 3ms	v Qal act ptc ms
	וַיֹּאמֶר	לֹא־יֵרֵד	בְּנִי	עִמָּכֶם	כִּי־אָחִיו	מֵת
	wayyō'mer	lō'-yērēdh	b^{e}nî	'immākhem	kî-'āchîw	mēth
	and he said	not he will go down	my son	with you	because his brother	dead man

2000	3937, 940	8080.255	7410.111	625	904, 1932	866
cj, pers pron	prep, n ms, ps 3ms	v Niphal ptc ms	cj, v Qal pf 3ms, ps 3ms	n ms	prep, art, n ms	rel part
וְהוּא	לְבַדּוֹ	נִשְׁאָר	וּקְרָאָהוּ	אָסוֹן	בַּדֶּרֶךְ	אֲשֶׁר
w^{e}hû'	l^{e}vaddô	nish'ār	ûqōrā'āhû	'āsôn	baderekh	'ăsher
and he	alone	one left	and it will happen	harm	on the journey	which

2050.128, 904	3495.518	881, 7939	904, 3123	8061
v Qal impf 2mp, prep, ps 3fs	cj, v Hiphil pf 2mp	do, n fs, ps 1cs	prep, n ms	n fs
תֵּלְכוּ־בָהּ	וְהוֹרַדְתֶּם	אֶת־שֵׂיבָתִי	בְּיָגוֹן	שְׁאוֹלָה
tēl^{e}khû-vāhh	w^{e}hôradhtem	'eth-sêvāthî	b^{e}yāghôn	sh^{e}'ôlāh
you will go on it	and you will bring down	my gray head	in torment	to Sheol

	7743	3633	904, 800		2030.121	3626, 866	3735.316
43:1	cj, art, n ms	adj	prep, art, n fs	**2.**	cj, v Qal impf 3ms	prep, rel part	v Piel pf 3cp
	וְהָרָעָב	כָּבֵד	בָּאָרֶץ		וַיְהִי	כַּאֲשֶׁר	כִּלּוּ
	w^{e}hārā'āv	kāvēdh	bā'ārets		wayhî	ka'ăsher	killû
	and the famine	heavy	in the land		and it was	when	they finished

3937, 404	881, 8134	866	971.516	4623, 4875	569.121	420
prep, v Qal inf con	do, art, n ms	rel part	v Hiphil pf 3cp	prep, pn	cj, v Qal impf 3ms	prep, ps 3mp
לֶאֱכֹל	אֶת־הַשֶּׁבֶר	אֲשֶׁר	הֵבִיאוּ	מִמִּצְרָיִם	וַיֹּאמֶר	אֲלֵיהֶם
le'ĕkhōl	'eth-hashshever	'ăsher	hēvî'û	mimmitsrāyim	wayyō'mer	'ălêhem
eating	the grain	which	they brought	from Egypt	then he said	to them

1	8178.133	8132.133, 3937	4746, 406		569.121	420
n ms, ps 3mp	v Qal impv 2mp	v Qal impv 2mp, prep, ps 1cp	*sub*, n ms	**3.**	cj, v Qal impf 3ms	prep, ps 3ms
אֲבִיהֶם	שֻׁבוּ	שִׁבְרוּ־לָנוּ	מְעַט־אֹכֶל		וַיֹּאמֶר	אֵלָיו
'ăvîhem	shuvû	shivrû-lānû	m^{e}'aṭ-'ōkhel		wayyō'mer	'ēlâv
their father	return	buy grain for us	little food		and he said	to him

3171	3937, 569.141	5967.542	5967.511	904	382	3937, 569.141
pn	prep, v Qal inf con	v Hiphil inf abs	v Hiphil pf 3ms	prep, ps 1cs	art, n ms	prep, v Qal inf con
יְהוּדָה	לֵאמֹר	הָעֵד	הֵעִד	בָּנוּ	הָאִישׁ	לֵאמֹר
y^{e}hûdhāh	lē'mōr	hā'ēdh	hē'idh	bānû	hā'îsh	lē'mōr
Judah	saying	warning	he warned	us	the man	saying

3940, 7495.128	6686	1153	250	882		524, 3552
neg part, v Qal impf 2mp	n mp, ps 1cs	adv	n ms, ps 2mp	prep, ps 2mp	**4.**	cj, sub, ps 2ms
לֹא־תִרְאוּ	פָּנַי	בִּלְתִּי	אֲחִיכֶם	אִתְּכֶם		אִם־יֶשְׁךָ
lō'-thir'û	phānay	biltî	'ăchîkhem	'itt^{e}khem		'im-yesh^{e}khā
not you will see	my face	except	your brother	with you		if there is among you

8365.351	881, 250	882	3495.120	8132.120	3937	406
v Piel ptc ms	do, n ms, ps 1cp	prep, ps 1cp	v Qal impf 1cp	cj, v Qal impf 1cp	prep, ps 2ms	n ms
מְשַׁלֵּחַ	אֶת־אָחִינוּ	אִתָּנוּ	נֵרְדָה	וְנִשְׁבְּרָה	לְךָ	אֹכֶל
m^{e}shallēach	'eth-'āchînû	'ittānû	nēr^{e}dhāh	w^{e}nishb^{e}rāh	l^{e}khā	'ōkhel
one sending	our brother	with us	we will go down	and we will buy grain	for you	food

	524, 375	8365.351	3940	3495.120	3706, 382	569.111
5.	cj, cj, n ms, ps 2ms	v Piel ptc ms	neg part	v Qal impf 1cp	cj, art, n ms	v Qal pf 3ms
	וְאִם־אֵינְךָ	מְשַׁלֵּחַ	לֹא	נֵרֵד	כִּי־הָאִישׁ	אָמַר
	w^{e}'im-'ên^{e}khā	m^{e}shallēach	lō'	nērēdh	kî-hā'îsh	'āmar
	but if there is not among you	one sending	not	we will go down	because the man	he said

420	3940, 7495.128	6686	1153	250	882		569.121
prep, ps 1cp	neg part, v Qal impf 2mp	n mp, ps 1cs	adv	n ms, ps 2mp	prep, ps 2mp	**6.**	cj, v Qal impf 3ms
אֵלֵינוּ	לֹא־תִרְאוּ	פָּנַי	בִּלְתִּי	אֲחִיכֶם	אִתְּכֶם		וַיֹּאמֶר
'ēlênû	lō'-thir'û	phānay	biltî	'ăchîkhem	'ittekhem		wayyō'mer
to us	not you will see	my face	except	your brother	with you		and he said

3547	4066	7778.517	3937	3937, 5222.541	3937, 382	5968
pn	intrg	v Hiphil pf 2mp	prep, ps 1cs	prep, v Hiphil inf con	prep, art, n ms	intrg part, adv
יִשְׂרָאֵל	לָמָה	הֲרֵעֹתֶם	לִי	לְהַגִּיד	לָאִישׁ	הַעוֹד
yisrā'ēl	lāmāh	herē'ōthem	lî	lehaggîdh	lā'îsh	ha'ôdh
Israel	why	you have done evil	to me	to tell	the man	is still

3937	250		569.126	8068.142	8068.111, 382	3937
prep, ps 2mp	n ms	**7.**	cj, v Qal impf 3mp	v Qal inf abs	v Qal pf 3ms, art, n ms	prep, ps 1cp
לָכֶם	אָח		וַיֹּאמְרוּ	שָׁאוֹל	שָׁאַל־הָאִישׁ	לָנוּ
lākhem	'āch		wayyō'merû	shā'ôl	shā'al-hā'îsh	lānû
to you	brother		and they said	asking	the man asked	about us

is dead, and he is left alone: ... He is all I have left, *BB*.

if mischief befall him by the way in the which ye go: ... harm, *NIV* ... accident, *Fenton* ... evil, *BB* ... death come unto him, *Geneva*.

then shall ye bring down my gray hairs with sorrow to the grave: ... hoary head, *Berkeley* ... to Sheol, *Young* ... sheol in sorrow, *Goodspeed* ... my white head down to the netherworld in grief, *NAB*.

43:1. And the famine was sore in the land: ... severe, *NKJV* ... grievous, *Darby* ... in bitter need of food, *BB* ... oppressed, *Fenton*.

2. And it came to pass, when they had eaten up the corn: ... grain, *Berkeley* ... rations, *NAB* ... food, *Fenton*.

which they had brought out of Egypt, their father said unto them, Go again, buy us a little food: ... grain, *REB* ... little more corn, *NEB*.

3. And Judah spake unto him, saying, The man did solemnly protest unto us: ... sternly warned, *Berkeley* ... warned, *NKJV* ... strictly warned, *Goodspeed* ... positively testify, *Darby* ... swore to us, *Fenton*.

saying, Ye shall not see my face, except your brother be with you: ... have audience, *Goodspeed* ... into his presence, *NEB* ... not to come before me again, *BB* ... appear in my presence, *NAB*.

4. If thou wilt send our brother with us, we will go down and buy thee food: ... If you are wise enough to, *Fenton* ... if you are ready to let our brother go with us, *Anchor*.

5. But if thou wilt not send him: ... withhold permission, *Anchor*.

we will not go down: for the man said unto us, Ye shall not see my face, except your brother be with you: ... look me not in the face, *Geneva* ... come into my presence, *NEB*.

6. And Israel said, Wherefore dealt ye so ill with me, as to tell the man whether ye had yet a brother?: ... demurred, *Berkeley* ... moaned, *MLB* ... cruel, *BB* ... evil, *Young* ... wrongfully, *NKJV* ... Why did you bring this trouble on me, *NIV* ... treat me so badly, *REB* ... make it so hard for me, *Anchor* ... treat me so shabbily, *Berkeley*.

7. And they said, The man asked us straitly of our state, and of our kindred: ... persisted, *Goodspeed* ... specifically asked, *MLB* ... questioned us in detail, *NCB* ... a number of questions, *BB* ... pointedly, *NKJV* ... about our birthplace, *Fenton* ... about ourselves and our family, *BB*.

43:1-2. When they finished the grain they brought from Egypt, the famine was still severe. Jacob then asked the brothers to go back to Egypt and buy a little grain for good.

43:3-5. Judah reminded Jacob that the man warned them strongly (implying a threat of punishment) that they could not see his face unless their brother was with them. Since they could only buy grain by coming to Joseph, not seeing his face, meant he would refuse to sell them any grain. Judah then emphasized that because of this warning they would go down to Egypt only if he would send Benjamin along with them, otherwise they would not go.

43:6-7. Jacob (Israel) then asked why they had done such a bad thing to him as to tell the man they had another brother. They told Jacob that the man asked about their family, their father, and if they had another brother and they simply answered what he asked. Surely they could not have known that he would tell them to bring their brother down because Joseph had not yet revealed his identity.

3937, 4274	3937, 569.141	5968	1	2513.111	3552
cj, prep, n fs, ps 1cp	prep, v Qal inf con	intrg part, adv	n ms, ps 2mp	v Qal pf 3ms	intrg part, adv
וּלְמוֹלַדְתֵּנוּ	לֵאמֹר	הַעוֹד	אֲבִיכֶם	חַי	הֲיֵשׁ
ûlămôladhtēnû	lē'mōr	ha'ôdh	'ăvîkhem	chay	h^{e}yēsh
and about our relatives	saying	is still	your father	he lives	is there

3937	250	5222.520, 3937	6142, 6552	1745	431
prep, ps 2mp	n ms	cj, v Hiphil impf 1cp, prep, ps 3ms	prep, *n ms*	art, n mp	art, dem pron
לָכֶם	אָח	וַנַּגֶּד־לוֹ	עַל־פִּי	הַדְּבָרִים	הָאֵלֶּה
lākhem	'āch	wannaggedh-lô	'al-pî	hadd^{e}vārîm	hā'ēlleh
to you	brother	and we told to him	on the mouth of	the words	the these

3156.142	3156.120	3706	569.121	3495.533	881, 250
intrg, v Qal inf abs	v Qal impf 1cp	cj	v Qal impf 3ms	v Hiphil impv 2mp	do, n ms, ps 2mp
הֲיָדוֹעַ	נֵדַע	כִּי	יֹאמַר	הוֹרִידוּ	אֶת־אֲחִיכֶם
h^{e}yādhôa'	nēdha'	kî	yō'mar	hôrîdhû	'eth-'ăchîkhem
could knowing	we know	that	he would say	bring down	your brother

8.	569.121	3171	420, 3547	1	8365.131	5470	882
	cj, v Qal impf 3ms	pn	prep, pn	n ms, ps	v Qal impv 2ms	art, n ms	prep, ps 1cs
	וַיֹּאמֶר	יְהוּדָה	אֶל־יִשְׂרָאֵל	אָבִיו	שִׁלְחָה	הַנַּעַר	אִתִּי
	wayyō'mer	y^{e}hûdhāh	'el-yisrā'ēl	'āvîw	shilchāh	hanna'ar	'ittî
	and he said	Judah	to Israel	his father	send	the boy	with me

7251.120	2050.120	2513.120	3940	4322.120	1612, 601
cj, v Qal impf 1cp	cj, v Qal impf 1cp	cj, v Qal impf 1cp	cj, neg part	v Qal impf 1cp	cj, pers pron
וְנָקוּמָה	וְנֵלֵכָה	וְנִחְיֶה	וְלֹא	נָמוּת	גַּם־אֲנַחְנוּ
w^{e}nāqûmāh	w^{e}nēlēkhāh	w^{e}nichăyeh	w^{e}lō'	nāmûth	gam-'ănachnû
and we will arise	and we will go	and we will live	and not	we will die	all we

1612, 887	1612, 3054	9.	609	6386.125	4623, 3135
cj, pers pron	cj, n ms, ps 1cp		pers pron	v Qal impf 1cs, ps 3ms	prep, n fs, ps 1cs
גַּם־אַתָּה	גַּם־טַפֵּנוּ		אָנֹכִי	אֶעֶרְבֶנּוּ	מִיָּדִי
gham-'attāh	gam-ṭappēnû		'ānōkhî	'e'er^{e}vennû	miyyādhî
and you	and our small children		I	I will be surety of him	of my hand

1272.323	524, 3940	971.515	420	3431.515	3937, 6686
v Piel impf 2ms, ps 3ms	cj, adv	v Hiphil pf 1cs, ps 3ms	prep, ps 2ms	cj, v Hiphil pf 1cs, ps 3ms	prep, n mp, ps 2ms
תְּבַקְשֶׁנּוּ	אִם־לֹא	הֲבִיאֹתִיו	אֵלֶיךָ	וְהִצַּגְתִּיו	לְפָנֶיךָ
t^{e}vaqōshennû	'im-lō'	h^{e}vî'ōthîw	'ēlêkhā	w^{e}hitstsaghtîw	l^{e}phānêkhā
you will seek him	if not	I bring him	to you	and set him	before you

2490.115	3937	3725, 3219	10.	3706	4020	4244.719
cj, v Qal pf 1cs	prep, ps 2ms	*adj*, art, n mp		cj	cj	v Hithpalpel pf 1cp
וְחָטָאתִי	לְךָ	כָּל־הַיָּמִים		כִּי	לוּלֵא	הִתְמַהְמָהְנוּ
w^{e}chāṭā'thî	l^{e}khā	kol-hayyāmîm		kî	lûlē'	hithmahmāhnû
then I will be at fault	to you	all the days		because	if not	we delayed

3706, 6498	8178.119	2172	6718	11.	569.121	420
cj, adv	v Qal pf 1cp	dem pron	n fd		cj, v Qal impf 3ms	prep, ps 3mp
כִּי־עַתָּה	שַׁבְנוּ	זֶה	פַעֲמָיִם		וַיֹּאמֶר	אֲלֵהֶם
kî-'attāh	shavnû	zeh	pa'ămāyim		wayyō'mer	'ălēhem
until now	we would have returned	this	two times		and he said	to them

3547	1	524, 3772	660	2148	6449.133	4089.133	4623, 2258
pn	n ms, ps 3mp	cj, adv	adv	dem pron	v Qal impv 2mp	v Qal impv 2mp	prep, *n fs*
יִשְׂרָאֵל	אֲבִיהֶם	אִם־כֵּן	אֵפוֹא	זֹאת	עֲשׂוּ	קְחוּ	מִזִּמְרַת
yisrā'ēl	'ăvîhem	'im-kēn	'ēphô'	zō'th	'ăsû	qŏchû	mizzimrath
Israel	their father	if so	then	this	do	take	from the strength of

800 art, n fs הָאָרֶץ hā'ārets the land	904, 3747 prep, n mp, ps 2mp בִּכְלֵיכֶם bikhlêkhem in your sacks	3495.533 cj, v Hiphil impv 2mp וְהוֹרִידוּ wehôrîdhû and go down	3937, 382 prep, art, n ms לָאִישׁ lā'îsh to the man	4647 n fs מִנְחָה minchāh gift of	4746 *sub* מְעַט me'at little	7159 n ms צֳרִי tserî balm	4746 cj, *sub* וּמְעַט ûme'at and little

1756 n ms דְּבַשׁ devash honey	5407 n fs נְכֹאת nekhō'th spices	4045 cj, n ms וָלֹט wālōt and myrhh	1029 n mp בָּטְנִים bātenîm pistachio nuts	8614 cj, n mp וּשְׁקֵדִים ûsheqēdhîm and almonds	**12.**	3826B cj, n ms וְכֶסֶף wekheseph and silver	5112 n ms מִשְׁנֶה mishneh double

saying, Is your father yet alive? have ye another brother? and we told him according to the tenor of these words: ... straightforwardly, *Fenton* ... demanded by the questions, *Goodspeed* ... in response, *NCB* ... we answered, *NASB.*

Could we certainly know that he would say: ... possibly, *NCB* ... how could we know, *Berkeley* ... insist, *Anchor.*

Bring your brother down?: ... to Egypt, *NEB.*

8. And Judah said unto Israel his father, Send the lad with me: ... urged, in my care, *Anchor.*

and we will arise and go: ... start at once, *REB* ... and return him alive, *Fenton.*

that we may live, and not die: ... survive, starve, *Berkeley* ... come to destruction, *BB.*

both we, and thou, and also our little ones: ... infants, *Young* ... dependants, *Goodspeed.*

9. I will be surety for him; of my hand shalt thou require him: ... stand guaranty, *Berkeley* ... I pledge myself for him, *Fenton* ... put him in my care, *BB* ... I guantee his safety, *MLB* ... hold me responsible, *NCB* ... demand him back from me, *Berkeley.*

if I bring him not unto thee, and set him before thee, then let me bear the blame for ever: ... restore him to you, *REB* ... stand condemned, *Anchor* ... guilty, *Darby* ... then banish me, for I shall have sinned against you all my days, *Fenton.*

10. For except we had lingered, surely now we had returned this second time: ... dillydallied, *NAB* ... if you had let him come, *MLB* ... we could by now have made the journey twice, *REB.*

11. And their father Israel said unto them, If it must be so now, do this: ... conceded, *MLB* ... If that is how it has to be, *Good News.*

take of the best fruits in the land in your vessels: ... choice products, *MLB* ... praised thing, *Young* ... for which our country is famous, *NEB* ... bags, *NIV* ... receptacles, *Goodspeed* ... wagons, *Fenton.*

and carry down the man a present, a little balm: ... balsam, *NEB* ... resin, *Geneva* ... perfumes, *BB.*

and a little honey: ... syrup, *NCB.*

spices: ... aromatic powder, *Berkeley* ... laudanum, *Darby* ... aromatic gum, *NASB* ... (gum) tragacanth, *REB.*

and myrrh: ... gum, *Anchor.*

nuts and almonds: ... pistachios and almonds, *NAB.*

43:8-10. Judah spoke up and made it clear that inaction would mean they, their young children, and Jacob also would die. They must rise up and go to Egypt if they wanted to live. Judah also promised to be surety for the young man (Benjamin was now about 21 years old). If he did not bring Benjamin back to Jacob, he would bear the guilt the rest of his life and be at fault to Jacob.

In contrast to Reuben, who offered his sons as surety, Judah offered himself. Already there was a change in Judah. To urge his father to let them go, Judah added that if they had not delayed they could have been back twice. Thus, there was no point in further delay.

43:11-12. Jacob recognized that this was so and commanded them to take something from the strength of the land (from the best the land produced) to put in the grain sacks as a gift for the man. These gifts should be items such as: a little balm (mastic; a pale yellow resin or gum from an evergreen tree, *Pistacia lenticus*), honey (probably grape honey, a syrup boiled down from grape juice; Egypt had bee's honey but they imported grape honey from Canaan), spices (gum traganth; from a shrub in the pea family), myrrh (not ordinary myrrh but labdanum, a sweet-smelling resin from the rock-rose, *Cistus*), pistachio nuts, and almonds. They must also take double the amount of silver that was in the mouth of their sacks. Jacob hoped that the return of their silver was an oversight.

4089.133	904, 3135	881, 3826B	8178.655	904, 6552	584
v Qal impv 2mp	prep, n fs, ps 2mp	cj, do, art, n ms	art, v Hophal ptc ms	prep, *n ms*	n fp, ps 2mp
קְחוּ	בְיֶדְכֶם	וְאֶת־הַכֶּסֶף	הַמּוּשָׁב	בְּפִי	אַמְתְּחֹתֵיכֶם
qōchû	v^{e}yedh^{e}khem	w^{e}'eth-hakkes̱eph	hammûshāv	b^{e}phî	'amt^{e}chōthêkhem
take	in your hand	and the silver	the returned	in the mouth of	your sacks

8178.528	904, 3135	193	5055	2000		881, 250
v Hiphil impf 2mp	prep, n fs, ps 2mp	adv	n ms	pers pron	**13.**	cj, do, n ms, ps 2mp
תָּשִׁיבוּ	בְיֶדְכֶם	אוּלַי	מִשְׁגֶּה	הוּא		וְאֶת־אֲחִיכֶם
tāshîvû	v^{e}yedh^{e}khem	'ûlay	mishgeh	hû'		w^{e}'eth-'ăchîkhem
you will bring back	in your hand	perhaps	oversight	it		and your brother

4089.133	7251.133	8178.133	420, 382		418	8163
v Qal impv 2mp	cj, v Qal impv 2mp	v Qal impv 2mp	prep, art, n ms	**14.**	cj, n ms	pn
קְחוּ	וְקוּמוּ	שׁוּבוּ	אֶל־הָאִישׁ		וְאֵל	שַׁדַּי
qāchû	w^{e}qûmû	shûvû	'el-hā'îsh		w^{e}'ēl	shadday
take	and arise	return	to the man		and God	Almighty

5598.121	3937	7641	3937, 6686	382	8365.311	3937
v Qal juss 3ms	prep, ps 2mp	n mp	prep, *n mp*	art, n ms	cj, v Piel pf 3ms	prep, ps 2mp
יִתֵּן	לָכֶם	רַחֲמִים	לִפְנֵי	הָאִישׁ	וְשִׁלַּח	לָכֶם
yittēn	lākhem	rachmîm	liphnê	hā'îsh	w^{e}shillach	lākhem
may he give	you	mercy	before	the man	that he will release	to you

881, 250	311	881, 1175	603	3626, 866	8323.115	8323.115
do, n ms, ps 2mp	adj	cj, do, pn	cj, pers pron	prep, rel part	v Qal pf 1cs	v Qal pf 1cs
אֶת־אֲחִיכֶם	אַחֵר	וְאֶת־בִּנְיָמִין	וַאֲנִי	כַּאֲשֶׁר	שָׁכֹלְתִּי	שָׁכָלְתִּי
'eth-'ăchîkhem	'achēr	w^{e}'eth-binyāmîn	wa'ănî	ka'ăsher	shākhōl^{e}ttî	shākhāl^{e}ttî
your brother	another	and Benjamin	but I	when	I am bereaved	I am bereaved

	4089.126	596	881, 4647	2148	5112, 3826B	4089.116
15.	cj, v Qal impf 3mp	art, n mp	do, art, n fs	art, dem pron	cj, n ms, n ms	v Qal pf 3cp
	וַיִּקְחוּ	הָאֲנָשִׁים	אֶת־הַמִּנְחָה	הַזֹּאת	וּמִשְׁנֶה־כֶּסֶף	לָקְחוּ
	wayyiqōchû	hā'ănāshîm	'eth-hamminchāh	hazzō'th	ûmishneh-kes̱eph	lāqōchû
	and they took	the men	the present	the this	and double silver	they took

904, 3135	881, 1175	7251.126	3495.126	4875	6198.126
prep, n fs, ps 3mp	cj, do, pn	cj, v Qal impf 3mp	cj, v Qal impf 3mp	pn	cj, v Qal impf 3mp
בְיָדָם	וְאֶת־בִּנְיָמִן	וַיָּקֻמוּ	וַיֵּרְדוּ	מִצְרַיִם	וַיַּעַמְדוּ
v^{e}yādhām	w^{e}'eth-binyāmin	wayyāqumû	wayyēr^{e}dhû	mitsrayim	wayya'am^{e}dhû
in their hand	and Benjamin	and they arose	and they went down	Egypt	and they stood

3937, 6686	3231		7495.121	3231	882	881, 1175	569.121
prep, *n mp*	pn	**16.**	cj, v Qal impf 3ms	pn	prep, ps 3mp	do, pn	cj, v Qal impf 3ms
לִפְנֵי	יוֹסֵף		וַיַּרְא	יוֹסֵף	אִתָּם	אֶת־בִּנְיָמִין	וַיֹּאמֶר
liphnê	yôs̱ēph		wayyar'	yôs̱ēph	'ittām	'eth-binyāmîn	wayyō'mer
before	Joseph		and he saw	Joseph	with them	Benjamin	and he said

3937, 866	6142, 1041	971.531	881, 596	1041	2983.131
prep, rel part	prep, n ms, ps 3ms	v Hiphil impv 2ms	do, art, n mp	art, n ms	cj, v Qal impv 2ms
לַאֲשֶׁר	עַל־בֵּיתוֹ	הָבֵא	אֶת־הָאֲנָשִׁים	הַבַּיְתָה	וּטְבֹחַ
la'ăsher	'al-bêthô	hāvē'	'eth-hā'ănāshîm	habbāy^{e}thāh	ût^{e}vōach
to who	over his house	bring	the men	to the house	and slaughter

2984	3679.531	3706	882	404.126	596	904, 6937
n ms	v Hiphil impv 2ms	cj	prep, ps 1cs	v Qal impf 3mp	art, n mp	prep, art, n mp
טֶבַח	וְהָכֵן	כִּי	אִתִּי	יֹאכְלוּ	הָאֲנָשִׁים	בַּצָּהֳרָיִם
ṯevach	w^{e}hākhēn	kî	'ittî	yō'kh^{e}lû	hā'ănāshîm	batstsāh^{e}rāyim
slaughtering	and prepare	because	with me	they will eat	the men	at noon

17.	6449.121 cj, v Qal impf 3ms וַיַּעַשׂ wayya'as and he made	382 art, n ms הָאִישׁ hā'îsh the man	3626, 866 prep, rel part כַּאֲשֶׁר ka'ăsher as that	569.111 v Qal pf 3ms אָמַר 'āmar he said	3231 pn יוֹסֵף yôsēph Joseph	971.521 cj, v Hiphil impf 3ms וַיָּבֵא wayyāvē' and he brought	382 art, n ms הָאִישׁ hā'îsh the man

881, 596 do, art, n mp אֶת־הָאֲנָשִׁים 'eth-hā'ănāshîm the men	904, 1041 prep, *n ms* בֵּיתָה bêthāh to the house of	3231 pn יוֹסֵף yôsēph Joseph	18.	3486.126 cj, v Qal impf 3mp וַיִּירְאוּ wayyîr'û and they were afraid	596 art, n mp הָאֲנָשִׁים hā'ănāshîm the men	3706 cj כִּי kî because

971.616 v Hophal pf 3cp הוּבְאוּ hûv'û they were brought	904, 1041 prep, *n ms* בֵּית bêth to the house of	3231 pn יוֹסֵף yôsēph Joseph	569.126 cj, v Qal impf 3mp וַיֹּאמְרוּ wayyō'm^e^rû and they said	6142, 1745 prep, *n ms* עַל־דְּבַר 'al-d^e^var over the matter of	3826B art, n ms הַכֶּסֶף hakkeseph the silver	8178.151 art, v Qal act ptc ms הַשָּׁב hashshāv the returned

12. And take double money in your hand; and the money that was brought again in the mouth of your sacks, carry it again in your hand: ... give back what was returned to you, *REB.*

peradventure it was an oversight: ... perhaps, *Goodspeed* ... mistake, *Berkeley* ... error, *BB.*

13. Take also your brother, and arise, go again unto the man: ... straight back, *NEB.*

14. And God Almighty give you mercy: ... the ruler of all, *BB* ... El Shaddai, *Anchor* ... compassion, *NASB* ... favor, *NCB* ... make him kindly disposed, *REB* ... such kindness, *Goodspeed.*

before the man, that he may send away your other brother, and Benjamin. If I be bereaved of my children, I am bereaved: ... release, *NKJV* ... robbed of my child, *Geneva* ... if I am to suffer bereavment, I shall suffer it, *Anchor* ... If my children are to be taken from me, there is no help for it, *BB.*

15. And the men took that present, and they took double money in their hand, and Benjamin; and rose up, and went down to Egypt, and stood before Joseph: ... consequently, *Fenton* ... started off, *Goodspeed* ... soon, *Anchor.*

16. And when Joseph saw Benjamin with them, he said to the ruler of his house, Bring these men home: ... steward, *NKJV...* chief, *ASV* ... invite, *Fenton* ... indoors, *NEB.*

and slay, and make ready; for these men shall dine with me at noon: ... have an animal slaughtered, *Anchor* ... butchering, *Berkeley* ... prepare a dinner, *Fenton.*

17. And the man did as Joseph bade; and the man brought the men into Joseph's house: ... did as Joseph ordered, *NKJV.*

18. And the men were afraid, because they were brought into Joseph's house; and they said: ... apprehensive, *Anchor* ... suspecting, *Berkeley.*

Because of the money that was returned in our sacks at the first time are we brought in; that he may seek occasion against us: ... have an excuse, *Fenton* ... pick a quarell against us and lay some thing to our charge, *Geneva* ... a pretext against us, *Goodspeed.*

43:13-14. Jacob finally gave them permission to take Benjamin and go, hoping that God Almighty would give them mercy before the man and that he would set their other brother free and not keep Benjamin. Then Jacob added an expression that shows he believed in God, and would commit Benjamin's future to God Almighty of whom he had just spoken even though he was still grieving over Joseph. If he was to be bereaved, he would submit to that and be bereaved.

43:15-17. With the gift, double silver, and Benjamin, the brothers went down to Egypt to Joseph. When Joseph saw them with Benjamin he told the servant who was over his household to take them to his house, butcher an animal, and prepare a meal, for these men would dine with him at noon. This was done.

43:18. None of this was explained to the brothers. So when they were brought into Joseph's house, they thought it was because of the money put back in their sacks when they were there before, and they were afraid the Egyptians were going to make a surprise attack and take them as slaves, taking their donkeys also.

904, 584	904, 8795	601	971.656	3937, 1597.741	6142
prep, n fp, ps 1cp	prep, art, n fs	pers pron	v Hophal ptc mp	prep, v Hithpael inf con	prep, ps 1cp
בְּאַמְתְּחֹתֵינוּ	בַּתְּחִלָּה	אֲנַחְנוּ	מוּבָאִים	לְהִתְגֹּלֵל	עָלֵינוּ
be'amtechōthênû	battechillāh	'ănachnû	mûvā'îm	lehithgōlēl	'ālênû
in our sacks	in the beginning	we	being brought	to fall	on us

3937, 5489.741	6142	4089.141	881	3937, 5860	881, 2645
cj, prep, v Hithpael inf con	prep, ps 1cp	cj, v Qal inf con	do, ps 1cp	prep, n mp	cj, do, n mp, ps 1cp
וּלְהִתְנַפֵּל	עָלֵינוּ	וְלָקַחַת	אֹתָנוּ	לַעֲבָדִים	וְאֶת־חֲמֹרֵינוּ
ûlăhithnappēl	'ālênû	welāqachath	'ōthānû	la'ăvādhîm	we'eth-chămōrênû
and to attack	on us	and to take	us	for slaves	and our donkeys

19.	5242.126	420, 382	866	6142, 1041	3231	1744.326
	cj, v Qal impf 3mp	prep, art, n ms	rel part	prep, *n ms*	pn	cj, v Piel impf 3mp
	וַיִּגְּשׁוּ	אֶל־הָאִישׁ	אֲשֶׁר	עַל־בֵּית	יוֹסֵף	וַיְדַבְּרוּ
	wayyiggeshû	'el-hā'îsh	'ăsher	'al-bêth	yôsēph	wayedhabberû
	and they drew near	to the man	which	over the house of	Joseph	and they spoke

420	6860	1041	20.	569.126	1031	112	3495.142
prep, ps 3ms	*n ms*	art, n ms		cj, v Qal impf 3mp	part	n ms, ps 1cs	v Qal inf abs
אֵלָיו	פֶּתַח	הַבָּיִת		וַיֹּאמְרוּ	בִּי	אֲדֹנִי	יָרֹד
'ēlâv	pethach	habbāyith		wayyō'merû	bî	'ădhōnî	yārōdh
to him	at the door of	the house		and they said	please allow me	my lord	coming down

3495.119	904, 8795	3937, 8132.141, 406	21.	2030.121	3706, 971.119
v Qal pf 1cp	prep, art, n fs	prep, v Qal inf con, n ms		cj, v Qal impf 3ms	cj, v Qal pf 1cp
יָרַדְנוּ	בַּתְּחִלָּה	לִשְׁבָּר־אֹכֶל		וַיְהִי	כִּי־בָאנוּ
yāradhnû	battechillāh	lishbār-'ōkhel		wayhî	kî-vā'nû
we came down	in the beginning	to buy grain of food		and it was	when we came

420, 4550	6858.120	881, 584	2079	3826B, 382
prep, art, n ms	cj, v Qal impf 1cp	do, n fp, ps 1cp	cj, intrj	*n ms*, n ms
אֶל־הַמָּלוֹן	וַנִּפְתְּחָה	אֶת־אַמְתְּחֹתֵינוּ	וְהִנֵּה	כֶּסֶף־אִישׁ
'el-hammālôn	wanniphtechāh	'eth-'amtechōthênû	wehinnēh	kheseph-'îsh
to the lodging place	and we opened	our sacks	and behold	the silver of each

904, 6552	584	3826B	904, 5129	8178.520	881	904, 3135
prep, *n ms*	n fs, ps 3ms	n ms, ps 1cp	prep, n ms, ps 3ms	cj, v Hiphil impf 1cp	do, ps 3ms	prep, n fs, ps 1cp
בְּפִי	אַמְתַּחְתּוֹ	כַּסְפֵּנוּ	בְּמִשְׁקָלוֹ	וַנָּשֶׁב	אֹתוֹ	בְּיָדֵנוּ
bephî	'amtachtô	kaspēnû	bemishqālô	wannāshev	'ōthô	beyādhēnû
in the mouth of	his sack	our silver	in its weight	so we returned	it	in our hand

22.	3826B	311	3495.519	904, 3135	3937, 8132.141, 406	3940	3156.119
	cj, n ms	adj	v Hiphil pf 1cp	prep, n fs, ps 1cp	prep, v Qal inf con, n ms	neg part	v Qal pf 1cp
	וְכֶסֶף	אַחֵר	הוֹרַדְנוּ	בְּיָדֵנוּ	לִשְׁבָּר־אֹכֶל	לֹא	יָדַעְנוּ
	wekheseph	'achēr	hôradhnû	veyādhēnû	lishbār-'ōkhel	lō'	yādha'ănû
	and silver	other	we brought down	in our hand	to buy grain of food	not	we know

4449, 7947.111	3826B	904, 584	23.	569.121	8361	3937
intrg, v Qal pf 3ms	n ms, ps 1cp	prep, n fp, ps 1cp		cj, v Qal impf 3ms	n ms	prep, ps 2mp
מִי־שָׂם	כַּסְפֵּנוּ	בְּאַמְתְּחֹתֵינוּ		וַיֹּאמֶר	שָׁלוֹם	לָכֶם
mî-sām	kaspēnû	be'amtechōthênû		wayyō'mer	shālôm	lākhem
who put	our silver	in our sacks		and he said	peace	to you

420, 3486.128	435	435	1	5598.111	3937	4438
adv, v Qal juss 2mp	n mp, ps 2mp	cj, *n mp*	n ms, ps 2mp	v Qal pf 3ms	prep, ps 2mp	n ms
אַל־תִּירָאוּ	אֱלֹהֵיכֶם	וֵאלֹהֵי	אֲבִיכֶם	נָתַן	לָכֶם	מַטְמוֹן
'al-tîrā'û	'ĕlōhêkhem	wē'lōhê	'ăvîkhem	nāthan	lākhem	matmôn
do not fear	your God	even the God of	your father	He put	for you	treasure

904, 584	3826B	971.111	420	3428.521	420	881, 8482
prep, n fp, ps 2mp	n ms, ps 2mp	v Qal pf 3ms	prep, ps 1cs	cj, v Hiphil impf 3ms	prep, ps 3mp	do, pn
בְּאַמְתְּחֹתֵיכֶם	כַּסְפְּכֶם	בָּא	אֵלָי	וַיּוֹצֵא	אֲלֵהֶם	אֶת־שִׁמְעוֹן
be'amtechōthêkhem	kaspekhem	bā'	'ēlāy	wayyôtsē'	'ălēhem	'eth-shim'ôn
in your sacks	your silver	it came	to me	and he brought out	to them	Simeon

	971.521	382	881, 596	904, 1041	3231	5598.121, 4448
24.	cj, v Hiphil impf 3ms	art, n ms	do, art, *n mp*	*n ms*	pn	cj, v Qal impf 3ms, n mp
	וַיָּבֵא	הָאִישׁ	אֶת־הָאֲנָשִׁים	בֵּיתָה	יוֹסֵף	וַיִּתֶּן־מַיִם
	wayyāvē'	hā'îsh	'eth-hā'ănāshîm	bêthāh	yôsēph	wayyitten-mayim
	and he brought	the man	the men of	to the house of	Joseph	and he gave water

7647.126	7559	5598.121	4706	3937, 2645		3679.526
cj, v Qal impf 3mp	n fp, ps 3mp	cj, v Qal pf 3ms	n ms	prep, art, n mp, ps 3mp	**25.**	v Hiphil impf 3mp
וַיִּרְחֲצוּ	רַגְלֵיהֶם	וַיִּתֵּן	מִסְפּוֹא	לַחֲמֹרֵיהֶם		וַיָּכִינוּ
wayyirchătsû	raghlêhem	wayyittēn	mispô'	lachmōrêhem		wayyākhînû
and they washed	their feet	and he gave	feed	to their donkeys		and they prepared

and fall upon us, and take us for bondmen, and our asses: ... to roll himself on us, *Young* ... turn against us, *Darby* ... overpower, *NIV* ... to inflict punishment, *REB* ... enslave us by treachery, *NCB* ... trump up some charge against us and victimize us, *NEB*.

19. And they came near to the steward of Joseph's house, and they communed with him at the door of the house: ... spoke with him, *NASB* ... at the verandah, *Fenton*.

20. And said, O sir, we came indeed down at the first time to buy food: ... by the Ever-Living, *Fenton* ... please listen, my lord, *NEB*.

21. And it came to pass, when we came to the inn: ... encampment, *NKJV* ... camping place, *Goodspeed* ... stopping place, *NCB*.

that we opened our sacks, and, behold, every man's money was in the mouth of his sack, our money in full weight: and we have brought it again in our hand:... top of his pack, *NRSV* ... according to its weight, *Darby* ... exact amount, *Anchor* ... full weight, *NRSV* ... back with us, *Berkeley*.

22. And other money have we brought down in our hands to buy food: we cannot tell who put our money in our sacks: ... additional, *NIV* ... We knew not that the money was there in our loads, *Fenton*.

23. And he said, Peace be to you, fear not: ... rest assured, *RSV* ... All is well with you, *Anchor* ... It's all right, he said. Don't be afraid, *NIV* ... Be quiet, *Fenton* ... Welcome to you, *MLB*.

your God, and the God of your father, hath given you treasure in your sacks: I had your money. And he brought Simeon out unto them: ... gave you a secret deposit, *Berkeley* ... given you that money secretly, *Fenton* ... I received your silver, *NIV*.

24. And the man brought the men into Joseph's house, and gave them: ... steward, *REB* ... ordered, *Fenton*.

43:19-22. The brothers then approached the man who was over the household of Joseph and who was still at the door of the house. They explained to him that they came down the first time only to buy food. Not until they came to the camping ground for the night did they discover the full weight of silver in their sacks. Now they had brought it back along with other silver to buy grain for food. They also protested that they did not know who put their silver in their sack. They wanted the man to know they had no intentions of stealing the silver.

43:23-24. The man quickly reassured them with greeting of peace and told them not to be afraid. The God who is the God of their father put treasure in their sacks for them, he said. He also said their silver came to him. This was true. It was God who prompted Joseph to have the silver put back in their sacks, and the silver did come to the overseer or manager of Joseph's household. He released Simeon and treated them as honored guests by bringing them water to wash their feet and feeding their donkeys.

43:25-26. The brothers heard, that is, they were told Joseph was coming at noon and they would eat bread (have a meal) at his house. So they prepared the gifts they had brought and presented it to him when he entered. After presenting it to him, they bowed down to the ground before him for the second time.

881, 4647	5912, 971.141	3231	904, 6937	3706	8471.116	3706, 8427
do, art, n fs	prep, v Qal inf con	pn	prep, art, n mp	cj	v Qal pf 3cp	cj, adv
אֶת־הַמִּנְחָה	עַד־בּוֹא	יוֹסֵף	בַּצָּהֳרָיִם	כִּי	שָׁמְעוּ	כִּי־שָׁם
'eth-hamminchāh	'adh-bô'	yôs̱ēph	batstsāh^{e}rāyim	kî	shām'û	kî-shām
the present	until the coming of	Joseph	at noon	because	they heard	that there

404.126	4035		971.121	3231	1041	971.526
v Qal impf 3mp	n ms	**26.**	cj, v Qal impf 3ms	pn	art, n fs	cj, v Hiphil impf 3mp
יֹאכְלוּ	לָחֶם		וַיָּבֹא	יוֹסֵף	הַבַּיְתָה	וַיָּבִיאוּ
yō'kh^{e}lû	lāchem		wayyāvō'	yôs̱ēph	habbay^{e}thāh	wayyāvî'û
they would eat	bread		and he came	Joseph	to the house	and they brought

3937	881, 4647	886, 904, 3135	1041	8246.726, 3937
prep, ps 3ms	do, art, n fs	rel part, prep, n fs, ps 3mp	art, n ms	cj, v Hithpalel impf 3mp, prep, ps 3ms
לוֹ	אֶת־הַמִּנְחָה	אֲשֶׁר־בְּיָדָם	הַבָּיְתָה	וַיִּשְׁתַּחֲווּ־לוֹ
lô	'eth-hamminchāh	'ăsher-b^{e}yādhām	habbāy^{e}thāh	wayyishtachwû-lô
to him	the present	that in their hand	to the house	and they bowed down to him

800		8068.121	3937	3937, 8361	569.121	8361
n fs	**27.**	cj, v Qal impf 3ms	prep, ps 3mp	prep, n ms	cj, v Qal impf 3ms	intrg part, n ms
אָרְצָה		וַיִּשְׁאַל	לָהֶם	לְשָׁלוֹם	וַיֹּאמֶר	הֲשָׁלוֹם
'ār^{e}tsāh		wayyish'al	lāhem	l^{e}shālôm	wayyō'mer	h^{e}shālôm
to the ground		and he asked	them	about welfare	and he said	is health

1	2292	866	569.117	5968	2508		569.126
n ms, ps 2mp	art, n ms	rel part	v Qal pf 2mp	intrg part, adv, ps 3ms	adj	**28.**	cj, v Qal impf 3mp
אֲבִיכֶם	הַזָּקֵן	אֲשֶׁר	אֲמַרְתֶּם	הַעוֹדֶנּוּ	חָי		וַיֹּאמְרוּ
'ăvîkhem	hazzāqēn	'ăsher	'ămartem	ha'ôdhennû	chāy		wayyō'm^{e}rû
your father	the old man	which	you said	is still he	alive		and they said

8361	3937, 5860	3937, 1	5968	2508	7199.126
n ms	prep, n ms, ps 2ms	prep, n ms, ps 1cp	adv, ps 3ms	adj	cj, v Qal impf 3mp
שָׁלוֹם	לְעַבְדְּךָ	לְאָבִינוּ	עוֹדֶנּוּ	חָי	וַיִּקְּדוּ
shālôm	l^{e}'avd^{e}khā	l^{e}'āvînû	'ôdhennû	chāy	wayyiqq^{e}dhû
health	to your servant	to our father	still he	alive	and they kneeled

8246.726		5558.121	6084	7495.121	881, 1175
cj, v Hithpalel impf 3mp	**29.**	cj, v Qal impf 3ms	n fp, ps 3ms	cj, v Qal impf 3ms	do, pn
וַיִּשְׁתַּחֲוֻ		וַיִּשָּׂא	עֵינָיו	וַיַּרְא	אֶת־בִּנְיָמִין
wayyishtachăwu		wayyissā'	'ênâv	wayyar$^{e'}$	'eth-binyāmîn
and they bowed down		and he lifted up	his eyes	and he saw	Benjamin

250	1158, 525	569.121	2172	250	7277
n ms, ps 3ms	*n ms*, n fs, ps 3ms	cj, v Qal impf 3ms	intrg part, dem pron	n ms, ps 2mp	art, adj
אָחִיו	בֶּן־אִמּוֹ	וַיֹּאמֶר	הֲזֶה	אֲחִיכֶם	הַקָּטֹן
'āchîw	ben-'immô	wayyō'mer	h^{e}zeh	'ăchîkhem	haqqāṭōn
his brother	the son of his mother	and he said	is this	your brother	the youngest

866	569.117	420	569.121	435	2706.121	1158
rel part	v Qal pf 2mp	prep, ps 1cs	cj, v Qal impf 3ms	n mp	v Qal impf 3ms, ps 2ms	n ms, ps 1cs
אֲשֶׁר	אֲמַרְתֶּם	אֵלָי	וַיֹּאמַר	אֱלֹהִים	יָחְנְךָ	בְּנִי
'ăsher	'ămartem	'ēlāy	wayyō'mar	'ĕlōhîm	yāchăn^{e}khā	b^{e}nî
which	you said	to me	and he said	God	may He be gracious to you	my son

	4257.321	3231	3706, 3770.216	7641	420, 250
30.	cj, v Piel impf 3ms	pn	cj, v Niphal pf 3cp	n mp, ps 3ms	prep, n ms, ps 3ms
	וַיְמַהֵר	יוֹסֵף	כִּי־נִכְמְרוּ	רַחֲמָיו	אֶל־אָחִיו
	waymahēr	yôs̱ēph	kî-nikhm^{e}rû	rachmâv	'el-'āchîw
	and he hurried	Joseph	because they were stirred up	his loving feelings	for his brother

1272	3937, 1098.141	971.121	2410	1098.121	8427
cj, v Piel impf 3ms	prep, v Qal inf con	cj, v Qal impf 3ms	art, n ms	cj, v Qal impf 3ms	adv
וַיְבַקֵּשׁ	לִבְכּוֹת	וַיָּבֹא	הַחַדְרָה	וַיֵּבְךְּ	שָׁמָּה
way^{e}vaqqēsh	livkôth	wayyāvō'	hachadhrāh	wayyēv^{e}kh	shāmmāh
and he needed	to weep	and he went	to the inner room	and he wept	to there

31.	7647.121	6686	3428.121	681.721	569.121
	cj, v Qal impf 3ms	n mp, ps 3ms	cj, v Qal impf 3ms	cj, v Hithpael impf 3ms	cj, v Qal impf 3ms
	וַיִּרְחַץ	פָּנָיו	וַיֵּצֵא	וַיִּתְאַפַּק	וַיֹּאמֶר
	wayyirchats	pānâv	wayyētsē'	wayyith'appaq	wayyō'mer
	and he washed	his face	and he went out	and he controlled himself	and he said

7947.133	4035	32.	7947.126	3937	3937, 940	3937
v Qal impv 2mp	n ms		cj, v Qal impf 3mp	prep, ps 3ms	prep, n ms, ps 3ms	cj, prep, ps 3mp
שִׂימוּ	לָחֶם		וַיָּשִׂימוּ	לוֹ	לְבַדּוֹ	וְלָהֶם
sîmû	lāchem		wayyāsîmû	lô	l^{e}vaddô	w^{e}lāhem
set	bread		and they set	to him	by himself	and for them

water, and they washed their feet; and he gave their asses provender: ... foddered, *NRSV*... feed, *REB* ... food, *Darby.*

25. And they made ready the present against Joseph came at noon: for they heard that they should eat bread there: ... prepared, *Fenton* ... had their gifts ready, *NEB* ... arrival, *Berkeley* ... in anticipation of Joseph's arrival, *Goodspeed* ... they learned, *Anchor* ... they were to dine, *NCB.*

26. And when Joseph came home they brought him the present which was in their hand into the house, and bowed themselves to him to the earth.

27. And he asked them of their welfare, and said, Is your father well, the old man of whom ye spake? Is he yet alive?: ... health, *NCB Fenton Goodspeed* ... peace, *Young* ... prosperity, *Geneva.*

28. And they answered, Thy servant our father is in good health, he is yet alive: ... thriving and still in good health, *NAB.*

And they bowed down their heads, and made obeisance: ... bowed respectfully, *NAB Anchor* ... fell down before him, *KJVII* ... prostrated themselves, *NEB* ... bending their bodies, *MLB.*

29. And he lifted up his eyes, and saw his brother Benjamin, his mother's son, and said, Is this your younger brother, of whom ye spake unto me? And he said, God be gracious unto thee, my son: ... show you mercy, *Fenton* ... be good to you, *BB* ... favor thee, *Young.*

30. And Joseph made haste; for his bowels did yearn upon his brother: ... hurried out away, *NASB* ... heart, *RSV* ... affection burned, *Fenton* ... was overcome, *NRSV* ... heart went out to his brother, *BB* ... feelings for his brother mastered him, *NEB.*

and he sought where to weep; and he entered into his chamber and wept there: ... private room, *NAB, NIV, NRSV* ... inner chamber, *Young* ... inner room, *NEB REB* ... Then Joseph made a hasty exit, for he was overcome with love for his brother and had to go out and cry, *LIVB.*

43:27-28. Joseph asked concerning the peace, or the health and well-being, of their father, and if he were still alive. The brothers probably took this as the common courtesy of a host, and their reply meant that he was well and alive. Then they kneeled and bowed down the third time.

43:29-30. When Joseph saw Benjamin, his mother's son, his only full brother, he politely asked if this were their younger brother and greeted him politely. Joseph was still being careful that his brothers would see him as the Egyptian prime minister, for he wanted to test them further. However, the sight of Benjamin stirred deep emotions of love within him, and he became so agitated that he needed to weep. He went to the innermost room of his house and wept there.

43:31-32. It was time for the meal, so he washed his face and went out to the dining room. Controlling himself, he commanded the meal to be served. But they set three separate tables in the room, one for Joseph, one for his brothers, and one for the Egyptians (probably high officials) who were eating with Joseph.

Egyptians couldn't eat a meal at the same table with the Hebrews, for they had so much prejudice that it would be detestable to them. Joseph overlooked their prejudice and was careful not to offend the Egyptians.

3937, 940	3937, 4875	404.152	882	3937, 940	3706
prep, n ms, ps 3mp	cj, prep, art, pn	art, v Qal act ptc mp	prep, ps 3ms	prep, n ms, ps 3mp	cj
לְבַדָּם	וְלַמִּצְרִים	הָאֹכְלִים	אִתּוֹ	לְבַדָּם	כִּי
lᵉvaddām	wᵉlammitsrîm	hā'ōkhᵉlîm	'ittô	lᵉvaddām	kî
by themselves	and to the Egyptians	the ones eating	with him	by themselves	because

3940	3310.126	4875	3937, 404	882, 5888	4035
neg part	v Qal impf 3mp	art, pn	prep, v Qal inf con	prep, art, pn	n ms
לֹא	יוּכְלוּן	הַמִּצְרִים	לֶאֱכֹל	אֶת־הָעִבְרִים	לֶחֶם
lō'	yûkhᵉlûn	hammitsrîm	le'ěkhōl	'eth-hā'ivrîm	lechem
not	they are able	the Egyptians	to eat	with the Hebrews	bread

3706, 8774	2000	3937, 4875		3553.126	3937, 6686	1111
cj, n fs	pers pron	prep, pn	**33.**	cj, v Qal impf 3mp	prep, n mp, ps 3ms	art, n ms
כִּי־תוֹעֵבָה	הִוא	לְמִצְרָיִם		וַיֵּשְׁבוּ	לְפָנָיו	הַבְּכֹר
kî-thô'ēvāh	hiw'	lᵉmitsrāyim		wayyēshᵉvû	lᵉphānāv	habbᵉkhōr
because detestable	it	to Egyptians		and they sat	before him	the first-born

3626, 1112	7087	3626, 7089	8867.126
prep, n fs, ps 3ms	cj, art, adj	prep, n fs, ps 3ms	cj, v Qal impf 3mp
כִּבְכֹרָתוֹ	וְהַצָּעִיר	כִּצְעִרָתוֹ	וַיִּתְמְהוּ
kivkhōrāthô	wᵉhatstsā'îr	kits'irāthô	wayyithmᵉhû
according to his birthright	and the youngest	according to his youth	and they looked in astonishment

596	382	420, 7751		5558.121	5019	4623, 882	6686
art, n mp	n ms	prep, n ms, ps 3ms	**34.**	cj, v Qal impf 3ms	n fp	prep, prep	n mp, ps 3ms
הָאֲנָשִׁים	אִישׁ	אֶל־רֵעֵהוּ		וַיִּשָּׂא	מַשְׂאֹת	מֵאֵת	פָּנָיו
hā'ănāshîm	'îsh	'el-rē'ēhû		wayyissā'	mas'ōth	mē'ēth	pānāv
the men	each	to his companion		and he lifted up	portions	from	before him

420	7528.122	5020	1175	4623, 5019	3725	2675
prep, ps 3mp	cj, v Qal impf 3fs	*n fp*	pn	prep, *n fp*	adj, ps 3mp	num
אֲלֵהֶם	וַתֵּרֶב	מַשְׂאַת	בִּנְיָמִן	מִמַּשְׂאֹת	כֻּלָּם	חָמֵשׁ
'ălēhem	wattērev	mas'ath	binyāmin	mimmas'ōth	kullām	chāmēsh
to them	and it was greater	the portion of	Benjamin	from the portions of	all of them	five

3135	8685.126	8335.126	6196		6943	881, 866
n fp	cj, v Qal impf 3mp	cj, v Qal impf 3mp	prep, ps 3ms	**44:1**	cj, v Piel impf 3ms	do, rel part
יָדוֹת	וַיִּשְׁתּוּ	וַיִּשְׁכְּרוּ	עִמּוֹ		וַיְצַו	אֶת־אֲשֶׁר
yādhôth	wayyishtû	wayyishkᵉrû	'immô		waytsaw	'eth-'ăsher
hands	and they drank	and they became drunk	with him		and he commanded	those

6142, 1041	3937, 569.141	4527.331	881, 584	596	406
prep, n ms, ps 3ms	prep, v Qal inf con	v Piel impv 2ms	do, *n fp*	art, n mp	n ms
עַל־בֵּיתוֹ	לֵאמֹר	מַלֵּא	אֶת־אַמְתְּחֹת	הָאֲנָשִׁים	אֹכֶל
'al-bêthô	lē'mōr	mallē'	'eth-'amtᵉchōth	hā'ănāshîm	'ōkhel
over his house	saying	fill	the sacks of	the men	food

3626, 866	3310.126	5558.141	7947.131	3826B, 382	904, 6552
prep, rel part	v Qal impf 3mp	v Qal inf con	cj, v Qal impv 2mp	*n ms*, n ms	prep, *n ms*
כַּאֲשֶׁר	יוּכְלוּן	שְׂאֵת	וְשִׂים	כֶּסֶף־אִישׁ	בְּפִי
ka'ăsher	yûkhᵉlûn	sᵉ'ēth	wᵉsîm	keseph-'îsh	bᵉphî
according to that	they were able	to carry	and put	the silver of each	in the mouth of

584		881, 1407	1407	3826B	7947.123	904, 6552	584
n fs, ps 3ms	**2.**	cj, do, n ms, ps 1cs	*n ms*	art, n ms	v Qal impf 2ms	prep, *n ms*	*n fs*
אַמְתַּחְתּוֹ		וְאֶת־גְּבִיעִי	גְּבִיעַ	הַכֶּסֶף	תָּשִׂים	בְּפִי	אַמְתַּחַת
'amtachtô		wᵉ'eth-gᵉvî'î	gᵉvîa'	hakkeseph	tāsîm	bᵉphî	'amtachath
his sack		and my cup	the cup of	the silver	you will put	in the mouth of	the sack of

7277	881	3826B	8134	6449.121	3626, 1745	3231
art, adj	cj, do	n ms	n ms, ps 3ms	cj, v Qal impf 3ms	prep, *n ms*	pn
הַקָּטֹן	וְאֵת	כֶּסֶף	שִׁבְרוֹ	וַיַּעַשׂ	כִּדְבַר	יוֹסֵף
haqqāṯōn	weēth	kes̱eph	shivrô	wayya'as	kidhevar	yôs̱ēph
the youngest	and	silver	his grain	and he did	according to the word of	Joseph

866	1744.311		1269	214	596	8365.416	2065
rel part	v Piel pf 3ms		art, n ms	v Qal act ptc ms	cj, art, n mp	v Pual pf 3cp	pers pron
אֲשֶׁר	דִּבֵּר	**3.**	הַבֹּקֶר	אוֹר	וְהָאֲנָשִׁים	שֻׁלְּחוּ	הֵמָּה
'ăsher	dibbēr		habbōqer	'ôr	wehā'ănāshîm	shullechû	hēmmāh
which	he spoke		the morning	becoming light	and the men	they were sent	they

31. And he washed his face, and went out, and refrained himself: ... mastered his emotions, *MLB* ... controlling himself, *Darby.*

and said, Set on bread: ... serve dinner, *Berkeley* ... serve the bread, *NKJV* ... put food before us, *BB.*

32. And they set on for him by himself, and for them by themselves: ... served, *REB* ... The meal was served, *Goodspeed* ... the brothers, *NEB* ... partook of his board, *Anchor.*

and for the Egyptians, which did eat with him, by themselves: because the Egyptians might not eat bread with the Hebrews; for that is an abomination unto the Egyptians: ... foreigners, *Fenton* ... abhorant, *Goodspeed* ... unclean, *BB* ... loathsome, *Anchor, NASB* ... disgusting, *Fenton.*

33. And they sat before him, the firstborn according to his birthright, and the youngest according to his youth: and the men marvelled: ... at his direction, *REB* ... seniority, *Anchor* ... from the oldest to the youngest, *NCB* ... arranged the men each by his relative, *Fenton* ... stared at, *Goodspeed* ... wondering, *Berkeley.*

34. And he took and sent messes unto them from before him: ... portions, *REB* ... food, *BB* ... dishes, *Fenton* ... lifted up his gifts before him, *Young* ... From his own table he sent them their courses, *Berkeley.*

but Benjamin's mess, was five times so much as any of theirs. And they drank, and were merry with him: ... feasted, *NIV* ... hilarious, *MLB,* ... drink abundantly, *Young.*

44:1. And he commanded the steward of his house, saying, Fill the men's sacks with food: ... gave orders, *NCB* ... instructions, *NIV* ... to the servant, *BB.*

as much as they can carry: ... hold, *NCB* ... bear, *Young.*

and put every man's money in his sack's mouth: ... top, *NRSV...* top of the cart, *Fenton.*

2. And put my cup, the silver cup, in the sack's mouth of the youngest, and his corn and his money: ... goblet, *NAB.*

in the sack's mouth of the youngest, and his corn money. And he did according to the word that Joseph had spoken: ... top of the load, *Fenton* ... together, *NCB* ... grain, *Darby* ... rations, *NAB.*

43:33. When the brothers were seated (probably by waiters), they noticed they were seated in order of birth from the firstborn to the youngest. This surprised them, and they looked at each other with astonishment. They could not understand how anyone knew this.

43:34. When Joseph sent the waiters with portions of food for the brothers, they brought five times as much to Benjamin. This was another test. If the brothers still had the same spirit of jealousy they had shown to Joseph, they would not have been able to enjoy the meal. But the brothers paid no attention to the favoritism shown to Benjamin. They drank (feasted) and became drunk with him. The Hebrew for drunk can mean "filled with drink." That is, they left the dinner table well satisfied.

44:1-2. Joseph commanded the servant, who was over his household, to fill the men's sack's with as much food as they could carry, put each man's silver in his sack, and put his silver chalice (goblet) in Benjamin's sack. This chalice was probably designed and ornamented especially for Joseph.

44:3-5. Soon after dawn, the brothers were sent away. But they had not gone far before Joseph commanded the overseer of his household to pursue them and ask why they had returned evil for good.

Then he was to assume they knew what they had taken and without actually mentioning the cup by saying, "Isn't this what my master drinks from, and when he practices divination, he divines with?" They were accused of evil by doing this.

In view of Joseph's close walk with God, this does not seem to mean Joseph actually practiced divination or anything else from the occult. He was

2645		2062	3428.116	881, 6111	3940	7651.516	3231
cj, n mp, ps 3mp	4.	pers pron	v Qal pf 3cp	do, art, n fs	neg part	v Hiphil pf 3cp	cj, pn
וַחֲמֹרֵיהֶם		הֵם	יָצְאוּ	אֶת־הָעִיר	לֹא	הִרְחִיקוּ	וְיוֹסֵף
wachmōrêhem		hēm	yātse'û	'eth-hā'îr	lō'	hirchîqû	weyôsēph
and their donkeys		they	they went out of	the city	not	they went far	and Joseph

569.111	3937, 866	6142, 1041	7251.131	7579.131	311	596
v Qal pf 3ms	prep, rel part	prep, n ms, ps 3ms	v Qal impv 2ms	v Qal impv 2ms	sub	art, n mp
אָמַר	לַאֲשֶׁר	עַל־בֵּיתוֹ	קוּם	רְדֹף	אַחֲרֵי	הָאֲנָשִׁים
'āmar	la'ăsher	'al-bêthô	qûm	redhōph	'achrê	hā'ănāshîm
he said	to those	over his house	rise	pursue	after	the men

5560.513	569.113	420	4066	8396.317	7750
cj, v Hiphil pf 2ms, ps 3mp	cj, v Qal pf 2ms	prep, ps 3mp	intrg	v Piel pf 2mp	n fs
וְהִשַּׂגְתָּם	וְאָמַרְתָּ	אֲלֵהֶם	לָמָּה	שִׁלַּמְתֶּם	רָעָה
wehissaghtām	we'āmarettā	'ălēhem	lāmmāh	shillamtem	rā'āh
when you catch up to them	then you will say	to them	why	did you repay	evil

8809	3009B		3940	2172	866	8685.121	112	904
prep	adj	5.	intrg part, neg part	dem pron	rel part	v Qal impf 3ms	n ms, ps 1cs	prep, ps 3ms
תַּחַת	טוֹבָה		הֲלוֹא	זֶה	אֲשֶׁר	יִשְׁתֶּה	אֲדֹנִי	בּוֹ
tachath	ṭôvāh		helô'	zeh	'ăsher	yishteh	'ădhōnî	bô
for	good		is not	this	which	he drinks	my master	with it

2000	5355.342	5355.321	904	7778.517	866	6449.117
cj, pers pron	v Piel inf abs	v Piel impf 3ms	prep, ps 3ms	v Hiphil pf 2mp	rel part	v Qal pf 2mp
וְהוּא	נַחֵשׁ	יְנַחֵשׁ	בּוֹ	הֲרֵעֹתֶם	אֲשֶׁר	עֲשִׂיתֶם
wehû'	nachēsh	yenachēsh	bô	herē'ōthem	'ăsher	'ăsîthem
and he	divining	he divines	with it	you did evil	what	you did

	5560.521	1744.321	420	881, 1745	431
6.	cj, v Hiphil impf 3ms, ps 3mp	cj, v Piel impf 3ms	prep, ps 3mp	do, art, n mp	art, dem pron
	וַיַּשִּׂגֵם	וַיְדַבֵּר	אֲלֵהֶם	אֶת־הַדְּבָרִים	הָאֵלֶּה
	wayyassighēm	waydhabbēr	'ălēhem	'eth-haddevārîm	hā'ēlleh
	and he caught up with them	and he spoke	to them	the words	the these

	569.126	420	4066	1744.321	112	3626, 1745	431
7.	cj, v Qal impf 3mp	prep, ps 3ms	intrg	v Piel impf 3ms	n ms, ps 1cs	prep, art, n mp	art, dem pron
	וַיֹּאמְרוּ	אֵלָיו	לָמָּה	יְדַבֵּר	אֲדֹנִי	כַּדְּבָרִים	הָאֵלֶּה
	wayyō'merû	'ēlāyw	lāmmāh	yedhabbēr	'ădhōnî	kaddevārîm	hā'ēlleh
	and they said	to him	why	does he speak	my lord	like the things	the these

2587	3937, 5860	4623, 6449.141	3626, 1745	2172		2075	3826B
sub	prep, n mp, ps 2ms	prep, v Qal inf con	prep, art, n ms	art, dem pron	8.	intrj	n ms
חָלִילָה	לַעֲבָדֶיךָ	מֵעֲשׂוֹת	כַּדָּבָר	הַזֶּה		הֵן	כֶּסֶף
chālîlāh	la'ăvādhêkhā	mē'ăsôth	kaddāvār	hazzeh		hēn	keseph
may it be far	for your servants	from doing	like the thing	the this		behold	silver

866	4834.119	904, 6552	584	8178.519	420	4623, 800
rel part	v Qal pf 1cp	prep, *n ms*	n fp, ps 1cp	v Hiphil pf 1cp	prep, ps 2ms	prep, *n fs*
אֲשֶׁר	מָצָאנוּ	בְּפִי	אַמְתְּחֹתֵינוּ	הֱשִׁיבֹנוּ	אֵלֶיךָ	מֵאֶרֶץ
'ăsher	mātsā'nû	bephî	'amtechōthênû	hĕshîvōnû	'ēlêkhā	mē'erets
which	we found	in the mouth of	our sacks	we brought back	to you	from the land of

3791	351	1630.120	4623, 1041	112	3826B	173	2174
pn	cj, intrg	v Qal impf 1cp	prep, *n ms*	n mp, ps 2ms	n ms	cj	n ms
כְּנָעַן	וְאֵיךְ	נִגְנֹב	מִבֵּית	אֲדֹנֶיךָ	כֶּסֶף	אוֹ	זָהָב
kenā'an	we'êkh	nighnōv	mibbêth	'ădhōnêkhā	keseph	'ô	zāhāv
Canaan	and how	could we steal	from the house of	your master	silver	or	gold

9.	**866** rel part אֲשֶׁר 'ăsher whom	**4834.221** v Niphal impf 3ms יִמָּצֵא yimmātsē' it is found	**882** prep, ps 3ms אִתּוֹ 'ittô with him	**4623, 5860** prep, n mp, ps 2ms מֵעֲבָדֶיךָ mē'ăvādhêkhā of your servants	**4322.111** cj, v Qal pf 3ms וָמֵת wāmēth then he will die	**1612, 601** cj, cj, pers pron וְגַם־אֲנַחְנוּ w^{e}gham-'ănachnû and also we

2030.120 v Qal impf 1cp נִהְיֶה nihyeh we will be	**3937, 112** prep, n ms, ps 1cs לַאדֹנִי la'dhōnî my master	**3937, 5860** prep, n mp לַעֲבָדִים la'ăvādhîm for slaves	**10.**	**569.121** cj, v Qal impf 3ms וַיֹּאמֶר wayyō'mer and he said	**1612, 6498** cj, adv גַּם־עַתָּה gam-'attāh also now	**3626, 1745** prep, n ms, ps 2mp כְדִבְרֵיכֶם kh^{e}dhivrêkhem as your words

3. As soon as the morning was light, the men were sent away, they and their asses: ... at daybreak, *NEB* ... dawn, *NIV.*

4. And when they were gone out of the city, and not yet far off: ... they had not gone far out of from the city, *NCB.*

Joseph said unto his steward, Up, follow after the men: ... mount, *Fenton* ... go at once, *NAB* ... run at once, *Goodspeed.*

and when thou dost overtake them: ... secure, *Fenton* ... catch up to them, *NIV.*

say unto them, Wherefore have ye rewarded evil for good? Why have you stolen the silver cup from me?: ... repaid, *NCB.*

5. Is not this it in which my lord drinketh, and whereby indeed he divineth?: ... taste wine, *BB* ... and prophecie, *Geneva* ... which he indeed uses for divination?, *NASB* ... gets knowledge of the future, *BB* ... observes diligently, *BB* ... He will certainly guess where it is, *NCB* ... He is very sharp-sighted. He saw what you were doing!, *Fenton.*

ye have done evil in so doing: ... wrong, *NASB* ... base, *Anchor.*

6. And he overtook them, and he spake unto them these same words: ... persued, *Fenton.*

7. And they said unto him, Wherefore saith my lord these words?: ... How can you say such things, *REB, NEB.*

God forbid that thy servants should do according to this thing: ... Heaven, *REB* ... act in such a way, *Anchor* ... Far be it from us that your servants should do such a thing, *NKJV.*

8. Behold, the money, which we found in our sacks' mouths, we brought again unto thee out of the land of Canaan: how then should we steal out of thy lord's house silver or gold?: ... remember, *Berkeley* ... top of our packs sacksloads, *REB.*

9. With whomsoever of thy servants it be found: ... If it comes to light that any of your servants has done this, *BB.*

both let him die, and we also will be my lord's bondmen: ... slaves, *Anchor* ... servants, *Young.*

10. And he said, Now also let it be according unto your words: he with whom it is found shall be my servant; and ye shall be blameless: ... go free, *MLB* ... acquited, *Young* ... exonerated, *NAB* ... innocent, *NASB.*

11. Then they speedily took down every man his sack to the ground, and opened every man his sack: ... eagerly, *Anchor* ... lowered, *NCB.*

still wanting his brothers to think of him only as the Egyptian prime minister. The Egyptians did practice divination or observe signs by putting particles of gold, silver, or drops of oil in a cup filled with water and observing the designs that were formed. Some do think Joseph did practice divination, but trusted God to guide him just as God guided some people in Bible times when they cast lots.

44:6-8. The brothers could not believe this accusation. They reminded the man that they brought back the silver they found in their sacks. Surely they would not steal silver or gold out of his master's house. ("God forbid" in KJV translates the Hebrew *chalilah,* which means "be it far from." The KJV translators put it the way they would say it in their day.)

44:9-10. The brothers were so sure that none of them were guilty, they boldly proclaimed that if he found it in anyone's sack, whoever it was would die and they would all become slaves.

The man, however, told them that only the one it was found with would be a slave, the rest would be blameless. That is, they would be free to go on their way. This was another test by Joseph for his brothers. How would the brothers react when it was found in Benjamin's sack?

3772, 2000	866	4834.221	882	2030.121, 3937	5860	894
adv, dem pron	rel part	v Niphal impf 3ms	prep, ps 3ms	v Qal impf 3ms, prep, ps 1cs	n ms	cj, pers pron
כֵּן־הוּא	אֲשֶׁר	יִמָּצֵא	אִתּוֹ	יִהְיֶה־לִּי	עָבֶד	וְאַתֶּם
ken-hû'	'ăsher	yimmātsē'	'ittô	yihyeh-lî	'āvedh	we'attem
so it	whomever	it is found	with him	he will be to me	a slave	and you

2030.128	5538		4257.326	3495.526	382	881, 584
v Qal impf 2mp	adj	11.	cj, v Piel impf 3mp	cj, v Hiphil impf 3mp	n ms	do, n fs, ps 3ms
תִּהְיוּ	נְקִיִּם		וַיְמַהֲרוּ	וַיּוֹרִדוּ	אִישׁ	אֶת־אַמְתַּחְתּוֹ
tihyû	neqiyyim		waymahrû	wayyôridhû	'îsh	'eth-'amtachtô
you will be	blameless		and they hurried	and they took down	each	his sack

800	6858.126	382	584		2769.321	904, 1448
n fs	cj, v Qal impf 3mp	n ms	n fs, ps 3ms	12.	cj, v Piel impf 3ms	prep, art, adj
אָרְצָה	וַיִּפְתְּחוּ	אִישׁ	אַמְתַּחְתּוֹ		וַיְחַפֵּשׂ	בַּגָּדוֹל
'āretsāh	wayyiphtechû	'îsh	'amtachtô		waychappēs	baggādhôl
to the ground	and they opened	each	his sack		and he searched	with the oldest

2054.511	904, 7277	3735.311	4834.221	1407	904, 584
v Hiphil pf 3ms	cj, prep, art, adj	v Piel pf 3ms	cj, v Niphal impf 3ms	art, n ms	prep, *n fs*
הֵחֵל	וּבַקָּטֹן	כִּלָּה	וַיִּמָּצֵא	הַגָּבִיעַ	בְּאַמְתַּחַת
hēchēl	ûvaqqātōn	killāh	wayyimmātsē'	haggāvîa'	be'amtachath
he began	and with the youngest	he ended	and it was found	the cup	in the sack of

1175		7458.126	7980	6227.121	382	6142, 2645
pn	13.	cj, v Qal impf 3mp	n fp, ps 3mp	cj, v Qal impf 3ms	n ms	prep, n ms, ps 3ms
בִּנְיָמִן		וַיִּקְרְעוּ	שִׂמְלֹתָם	וַיַּעֲמֹס	אִישׁ	עַל־חֲמֹרוֹ
binyāmin		wayyiqŏr'û	simlōthām	wayya'ămōs	'îsh	'al-chămōrô
Benjamin		and they tore	their clothes	and he loaded	each	on his donkey

8178.126	6111		971.121	3171	250	904, 1041	3231
cj, v Qal impf 3mp	art, n fs	14.	cj, v Qal impf 3ms	pn	cj, n mp, ps 3ms	*n ms*	pn
וַיָּשֻׁבוּ	הָעִירָה		וַיָּבֹא	יְהוּדָה	וְאֶחָיו	בֵּיתָה	יוֹסֵף
wayyāshuvû	hā'îrāh		wayyāvō'	yehûdhāh	we'echāv	bêthāh	yôsēph
and they returned	to the city		and he went	Judah	and his brothers	to the house of	Joseph

2000	5968	8427	5489.126	3937, 6686	800		569.121
cj, pers pron	adv, ps 3ms	adv	cj, v Qal impf 3mp	prep, n mp, ps 3ms	n fs	15.	cj, v Qal impf 3ms
וְהוּא	עוֹדֶנּוּ	שָׁם	וַיִּפְּלוּ	לְפָנָיו	אָרְצָה		וַיֹּאמֶר
wehû'	'ôdhennû	shām	wayyippelû	lephānâv	'āretsāh		wayyō'mer
and he	still he	there	and they fell	before him	to the ground		and he said

3937	3231	4242, 4801	2172	866	6449.117	3940
prep, ps 3mp	pn	intrg, art, n ms	art, dem pron	rel part	v Qal pf 2mp	intrg part, neg part
לָהֶם	יוֹסֵף	מָה־הַמַּעֲשֶׂה	הַזֶּה	אֲשֶׁר	עֲשִׂיתֶם	הֲלוֹא
lāhem	yôsēph	māh-hamma'ăseh	hazzeh	'ăsher	'ăsîthem	helō'
to them	Joseph	what is the deed	the this	which	you did	did not

3156.117	3706, 5355.342	5355.321	382	866	3765		569.121
v Qal pf 2mp	cj, v Piel inf abs	v Piel impf 3ms	n ms	rel part	prep, ps 1cs	16.	cj, v Qal impf 3ms
יְדַעְתֶּם	כִּי־נַחֵשׁ	יְנַחֵשׁ	אִישׁ	אֲשֶׁר	כָּמֹנִי		וַיֹּאמֶר
yedha'ăttem	kî-nachēsh	yenachēsh	'îsh	'ăsher	kāmōnî		wayyō'mer
you know	that divining	he devines	man	who	like me		and he said

3171	4242, 569.120	3937, 112	4242, 1744.320	4242, 6927.720
pn	intrg, v Qal impf 1cp	prep, n ms, ps 1cs	intrg, v Piel impf 1cp	cj, intrg, v Hithpael impf 1cp
יְהוּדָה	מַה־נֹּאמַר	לַאדֹנִי	מַה־נְּדַבֵּר	וּמַה־נִּצְטַדָּק
yehûdhāh	mah-nō'mar	la'dhōnî	mah-nedhabbēr	ûmah-nitstaddāq
Judah	what will we say	to my lord	how will we speak	or how can we prove our innocence

435	4834.111	881, 5988	5860	2079	5860	3937, 112	1612, 601
art, n mp	v Qal pf 3ms	do, *n ms*	n mp, ps 2ms	intrj, ps 1cp	n mp	prep, n ms, ps 1cs	cj, pers pron
הָאֱלֹהִים	מָצָא	אֶת־עֲוֹן	עֲבָדֶיךָ	הִנֶּנּוּ	עֲבָדִים	לַאדֹנִי	גַּם־אֲנַחְנוּ
hā'ĕlōhîm	mātsā'	'eth-'ăôn	'ăvādhêkhā	hinnennû	'ăvādhîm	lā'dhōnî	gam-'ănachnû
God	He found	the guilt of	your servants	behold we	slaves	to my lord	both we

1612	866, 4834.211	1407	904, 3135		569.121	2587	3937
cj	rel part, v Niphal pf 3ms	art, n ms	prep, n fs, ps 3ms	**17.**	cj, v Qal impf 3ms	sub	prep, ps 1cs
גַּם	אֲשֶׁר־נִמְצָא	הַגָּבִיעַ	בְּיָדוֹ		וַיֹּאמֶר	חָלִילָה	לִּי
gam	'ăsher-nimtsā'	haggāvîa'	b^eyādhô		wayyō'mer	chālîlāh	lî
and	whom it was found	the cup	in his hand		and he said	may it be far	for me

12. And he searched: ... the steward, *NIV*, ... carefully, *Darby*.

and began at the eldest, and left at the youngest: and the cup was found in Benjamin's sack: ... goblet, *NEB*, *NAB*, *Anchor*, *REB*.

13. Then they rent their clothes: ... tore, *Fenton* ... bitter grief, *BB* ... ripped their clothes in despair, *LIVB*.

and laded every man his ass, and returned to the city: ... reloaded, *NASB* ... mounted, *Fenton*.

14. And Judah and his brethren came to Joseph's house; for he was yet there: ... still, *NCB*, *NASB*, *NAB*, *NIV*.

and they fell before him: ... threw themselves, *NIV*, *NEB*, *REB*.

on the ground: ... flung themselves, *NAB*, *Anchor*, *Goodspeed*.

15. And Joseph said unto them, What deed is this that ye have done?: ... How has this occured?, *Fenton* ... How could you do such a thing?, *NAB*.

wot ye not that such a man as I can certainly divine?: ... I observe what happens around me, *Fenton* ... guess correctly, *NCB* ... find out things by divination, *NIV* ... have the power to see what is secret, *BB* ... unquestionably discover, *Berkeley*.

16. And Judah said, What shall we say unto my lord? what shall we speak? or how shall we clear ourselves?: ... justify, *Darby* ... put ourselves right in your eyes, *BB* ... prove our innocence, *Goodspeed* ... vindicate myself, *Fenton*.

God hath found out the iniquity of thy servants: ... sin, *BB* ... guilt, *RSV* ... God has uncovered our crime, *REB*.

behold, we are my lord's servants, both we, and he also with whom the cup is found: ... slaves, *MLB* ... bondmen, *Darby* ... we are in your hands, *BB*.

17. And he said, God forbid that I should do so: ... heaven, *REB* ... Far be it from me, *NKJV* ... I will do no such thing, *Berkeley*.

but the man in whose hand the cup is found, he shall be my servant; and as for you, get you up in peace unto your father: ... safe and sound, *REB*, *NAB* ... the rest of you are free, *Goodspeed* ... without hindrance, *Anchor*.

44:11-13. The brothers quickly took down their sacks and put them on the ground. The man searched each one, beginning with the oldest, thus keeping them in suspense until it was found in Benjamin's sack.

But instead of letting the man take Benjamin while they went on their way, each tore their clothes in grief. Then each one loaded his donkey, and they all returned to the city. This indicated they were changed men.

44:14-15. Judah took the leadership as they went back to Joseph's house. Joseph was still there and they fell flat on the ground before him. This showed even more humility than their previous deep bows. Joseph rebuked them sharply for the supposed deed they had done. They surely should have known that a man like him could really divine, that is, could practice divination to find out what happened to his silver chalice.

44:16. Judah again spoke up and expressed his inability to say anything to prove their innocence. God had found the guilt of Joseph's brothers, so they would all stay and become his slaves, not just the one with whom the cup was found.

At this point, Judah and his brothers apparently could not be sure whether Benjamin was guilty. Yet they were all willing to stay and be slaves along with him. They probably thought this would be just judgment for the guilt they felt for selling Joseph.

44:17. Joseph rejected their offer firmly. Only the man with whom the cup was found would be his slave. The rest must go up in peace to their father. Joseph was still testing them by giving them another opportunity to leave Benjamin behind.

4623, 6449.141	2148	382	866	4834.211	1407	904, 3135	2000
prep, v Qal inf con	dem pron	art, n ms	rel part	v Niphal pf 3ms	art, n ms	prep, n fs, ps 3ms	pers pron
מֵעֲשׂוֹת	זֹאת	הָאִישׁ	אֲשֶׁר	נִמְצָא	הַגָּבִיעַ	בְּיָדוֹ	הוּא
mē'ăsôth	zō'th	hā'îsh	'ăsher	nimtsā'	haggāvîa'	b^{e}yādhô	hû'
from doing	this	the man	whom	it was found	the cup	in his hand	he

2030.121, 3937	5860	894	6148.133	3937, 8361	420, 1
v Qal impf 3ms, prep, ps 1cs	n ms	cj, pers pron	v Qal impv 2mp	prep, n ms	prep, n ms, ps 2mp
יִהְיֶה־לִּי	עָבֶד	וְאַתֶּם	עֲלוּ	לְשָׁלוֹם	אֶל־אֲבִיכֶם
yihyeh-lî	'āvedh	w^{e}'attem	'ălû	l^{e}shālôm	'el-'ăvîkhem
he will be to me	a slave	but you	go up	in safety	to your father

18.	5242.121	420	3171	569.121	1031	112
	cj, v Qal impf 3ms	prep, ps 3ms	pn	cj, v Qal impf 3ms	part	n ms, ps 1cs
	וַיִּגַּשׁ	אֵלָיו	יְהוּדָה	וַיֹּאמֶר	בִּי	אֲדֹנִי
	wayyiggash	'ēlâv	y^{e}hûdhāh	wayyō'mer	bî	'ădhōnî
	and he drew near	to him	Judah	and he said	please allow me	my lord

1744.321, 5167	5860	1745	904, 238	112	414, 2835.121
v Piel impf 3ms, part	n ms, ps 2ms	n ms	prep, *n fp*	n ms, ps 1cs	cj, adv, v Qal impf 3ms
יְדַבֶּר־נָא	עַבְדְּךָ	דָבָר	בְּאָזְנֵי	אֲדֹנִי	וְאַל־יִחַר
y^{e}dhabber-nā'	'avd^{e}khā	khāvār	b^{e}'āznê	'ădhōnî	w^{e}'al-yichar
he will speak please	your servant	a word	in the ears of	my lord	that not it will burn

653	904, 5860	3706	3765	3626, 6799	19.	112	8068.111
n ms, ps 2ms	prep, n ms, ps 2ms	cj	prep, ps 2ms	prep, pn		n ms, ps 1cs	v Qal pf 3ms
אַפְּךָ	בְּעַבְדֶּךָ	כִּי	כָּמוֹךָ	כְּפַרְעֹה		אֲדֹנִי	שָׁאַל
'app^{e}khā	b^{e}'avdekhā	kî	khāmôkhā	k^{e}phar'ōh		'ădhōnî	shā'al
your nose	against your servant	because	like you	like Pharaoh		my lord	he asked

881, 5860	3937, 569.141	3552, 3937	1	173, 250	20.	569.120
do, n mp, ps 3ms	prep, v Qal inf con	intrg part, sub, prep, ps 2mp	n ms	cj, n ms		cj, v Qal impf 1cp
אֶת־עֲבָדָיו	לֵאמֹר	הֲיֵשׁ־לָכֶם	אָב	אוֹ־אָח		וַנֹּאמֶר
'eth-'ăvādhâv	lē'mōr	h^{e}yēsh-lākhem	'av	'ô-'āch		wannō'mer
his servants	saying	is there to you	father	or brother		and we said

420, 112	3552, 3937	1	2290.111	3315	2295	7278
prep, n ms, ps 1cs	sub, prep, ps 1cp	n ms	v Qal pf 3ms	cj, *n ms*	n mp	adj
אֶל־אֲדֹנִי	יֶשׁ־לָנוּ	אָב	זָקֵן	וְיֶלֶד	זְקֻנִים	קָטָן
'el-'ădhōnî	yesh-lānû	'av	zāqēn	w^{e}yeledh	z^{e}qunîm	qāṭān
to my lord	there is to us	father	he is old	and child of	old age	youngest

250	4322.151	3613.221	2000	3937, 940	3937, 525
cj, n ms, ps 3ms	v Qal act ptc ms	cj, v Niphal impf 3ms	pers pron	prep, n ms, ps 3ms	prep, n fs, ps 3ms
וְאָחִיו	מֵת	וַיִּוָּתֵר	הוּא	לְבַדּוֹ	לְאִמּוֹ
w^{e}'āchîw	mēth	wayyiwwāthēr	hû'	l^{e}vaddô	l^{e}'immô
and his brother	dead man	and he is left	he	alone	of his mother

1	154.111	21.	569.123	420, 5860	3495.533
cj, n ms, ps 3ms	v Qal pf 3ms, ps 3ms		cj, v Qal impf 2ms	prep, n mp, ps 2ms	v Hiphil impv 2mp, ps 3ms
וְאָבִיו	אֲהֵבוֹ		וַתֹּאמֶר	אֶל־עֲבָדֶיךָ	הוֹרִדֻהוּ
w^{e}'āvîw	'ăhēvô		wattō'mer	'el-'ăvādhêkhā	hôridhuhû
and his father	he loves him		and you said	to your servants	bring him down

420	7947.125	6084	6142	22.	569.120	420, 112
prep, ps 1cs	cj, v Qal impf 1cs	n fs, ps 1cs	prep, ps 3ms		cj, v Qal impf 1cp	prep, n ms, ps 1cs
אֵלָי	וְאָשִׂימָה	עֵינִי	עָלָיו		וַנֹּאמֶר	אֶל־אֲדֹנִי
'ēlāy	w^{e}'āsîmāh	'ênî	'ālâv		wannō'mer	'el-'ădhōnî
to me	and I will set	my eye	on him		and we said	to my lord

3940, 3310	5470	3937, 6013.141	881, 1	6013.111	881, 1
neg part, v Qal impf 3ms	art, n ms	prep, art, v Qal inf con	do, n ms, ps 3ms	cj, v Qal pf 3ms	do, n ms, ps 3ms
לֹא־יוּכַל	הַנַּעַר	לַעֲזֹב	אֶת־אָבִיו	וְעָזַב	אֶת־אָבִיו
lō'-yûkhal	hanna'ar	la'ăzōv	'eth-'āvîw	w^e'āzav	'eth-'āvîw
not he is able	the boy	to leave	his father	and should he leave	his father

4322.111		569.123	420, 5860	524, 3940	3495.121	250
cj, v Qal pf 3ms	**23.**	cj, v Qal impf 2ms	prep, n mp, ps 2ms	cj, adv	v Qal impf 3ms	n ms, ps 2mp
וָמֵת		וַתֹּאמֶר	אֶל־עֲבָדֶיךָ	אִם־לֹא	יֵרֵד	אֲחִיכֶם
wāmēth		wattō'mer	'el-'ăvādhêkhā	'im-lō'	yērēdh	'ăchîkhem
then he would die		and you said	to your servants	if not	he comes down	your brother

7277	882	3940	3362.528	3937, 7495.141	6686
art, adj	prep, ps 2mp	neg part	v Hiphil impf 2mp	prep, v Qal inf con	n mp, ps 1cs
הַקָּטֹן	אִתְּכֶם	לֹא	תֹסִפוּן	לִרְאוֹת	פָּנָי
haqqāṭōn	'itt^ekhem	lō'	thōsiphûn	lir'ôth	pānāy
the youngest	with you	not	you will do again	to see	my face

	2030.121	3706	6148.119	420, 5860	1	5222.520, 3937
24.	cj, v Qal impf 3ms	cj	v Qal pf 1cp	prep, n ms, ps 2ms	n ms, ps 1cs	cj, v Hiphil impf 1cp, prep, ps 3ms
	וַיְהִי	כִּי	עָלִינוּ	אֶל־עַבְדְּךָ	אָבִי	וַנַּגֶּד־לוֹ
	wayhî	kî	'ālînû	'el-'avd^ekhā	'āvî	wannaggedh-lô
	and it was	because	we went up	to your servant	my father	and we told to him

18. Then Judah came near: ... approached, *Fenton, NASB, NCB.*

unto him, and said, Oh my lord, let thy servant, I pray thee: ... with your permission, *Berkeley, MLB.*

speak a word in my lord's ears: ... earnestly, *NAB* ... tell you something intimate, *Berkeley* ... please listen, *REB.*

and let not thine anger burn against thy servant: ... wrath, *BB* ... be aroused, *NCB* ... do not be impatient, *Anchor.*

for thou art even as Pharaoh: ... in the place of, *BB* ... Pharaohs counterpart, *MLB* ... equal to, *NIV.*

19. My lord asked his servants, saying, Have ye a father, or a brother?

20. And we said unto my lord, We have a father, an old man, and a child of his old age, a little one; and his brother is dead: ... full, *NEB,*

and he alone is left of his mother, and his father loveth him: ... he is the only son, *BB* ... dotes, *Anchor, NAB* ... dear to, *BB.*

21. And thou saidst unto thy servants, Bring him down unto me, that I may set mine eyes upon him: ... slaves, *Fenton* ... look after, *NCB* ... so I can see him for myself, *NIV.*

22. And we said unto my lord, The lad cannot leave his father: for if he should leave his father, his father would die: ... is not able to, *Young* ... his father will not let him go, *BB.*

23. And thou saidst unto thy servants, Except your youngest brother come down with you, ye shall see my face no more: ... you shall not come into enter my presence again, *NCB* ... you cannot have audience with me again, *Goodspeed.*

24. And it came to pass when we came up unto thy servant my father, we told him the words of my lord: ... demands, *Fenton.*

25. And our father said, Go again, and buy us a little food: ... In time,

44:18. Judah then stepped closer to Joseph and gave a most powerful, moving speech of intercession that is full of compassion for his father and brother. He began by humbly begging Joseph not to be angry. He also honored Joseph as one that had a high position and great power like Pharaoh, and who thus deserved the same respect.

44:19-23. Judah next reminded Joseph of how he questioned them when they came to Egypt the first time and how they responded, telling him of their father and youngest brother. When Joseph had asked them to bring Benjamin, they pointed out his father so loved him that he would die if Benjamin would leave him. Yet Joseph made it clear that they must bring Benjamin if they wanted to see his face (and buy grain is implied). In all this speech, Judah wanted Joseph to see their honesty and integrity.

881	1745	112		569.121	1	8178.133	8132.133, 3937
do	*n mp*	n ms, ps 1cs	**25.**	cj, v Qal impf 3ms	n ms, ps 1cp	v Qal impv 2mp	v Qal impv 2mp, prep, ps 1cp
אֵת	דִּבְרֵי	אֲדֹנִי		וַיֹּאמֶר	אָבִינוּ	שֻׁבוּ	שִׁבְרוּ־לָנוּ
'ēth	divrê	'ădhōnî		wayyō'mer	'āvînû	shuvû	shivrû-lānû
	the words of	my lord		and he said	our father	return	buy grain for us

4746, 406		569.120	3940	3310.120	3937, 3495.141	524, 3552
sub, n ms	**26.**	cj, v Qal impf 1cp	neg part	v Qal impf 1cp	prep, v Qal inf con	cj, n ms
מְעַט־אֹכֶל		וַנֹּאמֶר	לֹא	נוּכַל	לָרֶדֶת	אִם־יֵשׁ
m^{e}'aṭ-'ōkhel		wannō'mer	lō'	nûkhal	lāredheth	'im-yēsh
little of food		and we said	not	we are able	to go down	unless there is

250	7277	882	3495.120	3706, 3940	3310.120
n ms, ps 1cp	art, adj	prep, ps 1cp	cj, v Qal impf 1cp	cj, neg part	v Qal impf 1cp
אָחִינוּ	הַקָּטֹן	אִתָּנוּ	וְיָרַדְנוּ	כִּי־לֹא	נוּכַל
'āchînû	haqqāṭōn	'ittānû	w^{e}yāradhnû	kî-lō'	nûkhal
our brother	the youngest	with us	then we will go down	because not	we are able

3937, 7495.141	6686	382	250	7277	375	882
prep, v Qal inf con	n mp	art, n ms	cj, n ms, ps 1cp	art, adj	sub, ps 3ms	prep, ps 1cp
לִרְאוֹת	פְּנֵי	הָאִישׁ	וְאָחִינוּ	הַקָּטֹן	אֵינֶנּוּ	אִתָּנוּ
lir'ôth	p^{e}nê	hā'îsh	w^{e}'āchînû	haqqāṭōn	'ênennû	'ittānû
to see	the face of	the man	if our brother	the youngest	he is not	with us

	569.121	5860	1	420	894	3156.117	3706	8530
27.	cj, v Qal impf 3ms	n ms, ps 2ms	n ms, ps 1cs	prep, ps 1cp	pers pron	v Qal pf 2mp	cj	num
	וַיֹּאמֶר	עַבְדְּךָ	אָבִי	אֵלֵינוּ	אַתֶּם	יְדַעְתֶּם	כִּי	שְׁנַיִם
	wayyō'mer	'avd^{e}khā	'āvî	'ēlênû	'attem	y^{e}dha'ăttem	kî	sh^{e}nayim
	and he said	your servant	my father	to us	you	you know	that	two

3314.112, 3937	828		3428.121	259	4623, 882	569.125
v Qal pf 3fs, prep, ps 1cs	n fs, ps 1cs	**28.**	cj, v Qal impf 3ms	art, num	prep, prep, ps 1cs	cj, v Qal impf 1cs
יָלְדָה־לִּי	אִשְׁתִּי		וַיֵּצֵא	הָאֶחָד	מֵאִתִּי	וָאֹמַר
yāl^{e}dhāh-lî	'ishtî		wayyētsē'	hā'echādh	mē'ittî	wā'ōmar
she bore to me	my wife		and he went out	the first	from with me	and I said

395	3072.142	3072.411	3940	7495.115	5912, 2077
adv	v Qal inf abs	v Pual pf 3ms	cj, neg part	v Qal pf 1cs, ps 3ms	cj, adv
אַךְ	טָרֹף	טֹרָף	וְלֹא	רְאִיתִיו	עַד־הֵנָּה
'akh	ṭārōph	ṭōraph	w^{e}lō'	r^{e}'îthîw	'adh-hēnnāh
surely	tearing in pieces	he was torn in pieces	and not	I will see him	again here

	4089.117	1612, 881, 2172	4623, 6196	6686	7424.111	625
29.	cj, v Qal pf 2mp	cj, do, dem pron	prep, prep	n mp, ps 1cs	cj, v Qal pf 3ms, ps 3ms	n ms
	וּלְקַחְתֶּם	גַּם־אֶת־זֶה	מֵעִם	פָּנַי	וְקָרָהוּ	אָסוֹן
	ûlăqachtem	gam-'eth-zeh	mē'im	pānay	w^{e}qārāhû	'āsôn
	if you take	also this	from	my presence	and it happens to him	harm

3495.517	881, 7939	904, 7750	8061		6498
cj, v Hiphil pf 2mp	do, n fs, ps 1cs	prep, n fs	n fs	**30.**	cj, adv
וְהוֹרַדְתֶּם	אֶת־שֵׂיבָתִי	בְּרָעָה	שְׁאֹלָה		וְעַתָּה
w^{e}hôradhtem	'eth-sêvāthî	b^{e}rā'āh	sh^{e}'ōlāh		w^{e}'attāh
then you will bring down	my gray head	in sorrow	to Sheol		and now

3626, 971.141	420, 5860	1	5470	375	882
prep, v Qal inf con, ps 1cs	prep, n ms, ps 2ms	n ms, ps 1cs	cj, art, n ms	sub, ps 3ms	prep, ps 1cp
כְּבֹאִי	אֶל־עַבְדְּךָ	אָבִי	וְהַנַּעַר	אֵינֶנּוּ	אִתָּנוּ
k^{e}vō'î	'el-'avd^{e}khā	'āvî	w^{e}hanna'ar	'ênennû	'ittānû
when my going	to your servant	my father	and the boy	he is not	with us

5497 cj, n fs, ps 3ms וְנַפְשׁוֹ w^{e}naphshô then his soul	7489.157 v Qal pass ptc fs קְשׁוּרָה qōshûrāh one bound	904, 5497 prep, n fs, ps 3ms בְּנַפְשׁוֹ v^{e}naphshô with his soul	**31.**	2030.111 cj, v Qal pf 3ms וְהָיָה w^{e}hāyāh and it will be	3626, 7495.141 prep, v Qal inf con, ps 3ms כִּרְאוֹתוֹ kir'ôthô when his seeing

3706, 375 prep, *sub* כִּי־אֵין kî-'ên that there is not of	5470 art, n ms הַנַּעַר hanna'ar the boy	4322.111 cj, v Qal pf 3ms וָמֵת wāmēth then he will die	3495.516 cj, v Hiphil pf 3cp וְהוֹרִידוּ w^{e}hôrîdhû and they will bring down	5860 n mp, ps 2ms עֲבָדֶיךָ 'ăvādhêkhā your servants

881, 7939 do, *n fs* אֶת־שֵׂיבַת 'eth-sêvath the gray head of	5860 n ms, ps 2ms עַבְדְּךָ 'avd^{e}khā your servant	1 n ms, ps 1cp אָבִינוּ 'āvînû our father	904, 3123 prep, n ms בְּיָגוֹן b^{e}yāghôn in sorrow	8061 n fs שְׁאֹלָה sh^{e}'ōlāh to Sheol	**32.**	3706 cj כִּי kî because

5860 n ms, ps 2ms עַבְדְּךָ 'avd^{e}khā your servant	6386.111 v Qal pf 3ms עָרַב 'ārav he will be surety	881, 5470 do, art, n ms אֶת־הַנַּעַר 'eth-hanna'ar the boy	4623, 6196 prep, prep מֵעִם mē'im from	1 n ms, ps 1cs אָבִי 'āvî my father	3937, 569.141 prep, v Qal inf con לֵאמֹר lē'mōr saying	524, 3940 cj, adv אִם־לֹא 'im-lō' if not

Anchor … for the family, *NAB.*

26. And we said, We cannot go down: if our youngest brother be with us, then will we go down: for we may not see the man's face, except our youngest brother be with us: … meet the man, *Berkeley* … enter the man's presence, *REB* … have audience, *Goodspeed.*

27. And thy servant my father said unto us, Ye know that my wife bare me two sons: … slave, *Fenton.*

28. And the one went out from me, and I said, Surely he is torn in pieces; and I saw him not since: … disappeared, *Anchor* … violent death, *BB* … torn by beasts, *Anchor* … by wild beasts, *NAB.*

29. And if ye take this also from me, and mischief befall him: … evil, *BB* … harm, *RSV* … calamity, *NKJV* … disaster, *NAB* … accident, *Fenton.*

ye shall bring down my gray hairs: … head, *BB* … white head, *Anchor.*

with sorrow: … misery, *NIV* … trouble, *Goodspeed* … evil, *Young.*

to the grave: … underworld, *BB* … Sheol, *NRSV.*

30. Now therefore when I come to thy servant my father, and the lad be not with us; seeing that his life is bound up in the lad's life: … his life and the boy's are one, *BB* … his life dependeth on the child's, *Geneva* … his soul is bound up in his, *Young.*

31. It shall come to pass, when he seeth that the lad is not with us, that he will die: and thy servants shall bring down the gray hairs of thy servant our father with sorrow to the grave: … hoary head, *Berkeley.*

32. For thy servant became surety for the lad unto my father: … pledged, *Anchor* … guaranteed the boy's safety, *NIV* … responsible, *BB.*

saying, If I bring him not unto thee, then I shall bear the blame: … guilty of the crime, *NCB.*

to my father for ever: … let me be banished from my father, *Fenton* … hold it against me, *NAB* … condemed, *Anchor* … let mine be the sin forever, *BB.*

44:24-29. Judah then told Joseph of their father's concerns when it became necessary for them to go again to Egypt to buy grain so they could have a little food. How he told that his wife bore two sons for him and one he was sure was torn in pieces, and if an accident happens to him so he dies, this would bring down his gray head in sorrow to Sheol.

44:30-31. Judah affirmed this was true. His father's soul or life was so closely bound together with Benjamin's that if the young man was not with them, they would indeed bring the gray hairs of their father with sorrow down to Sheol. During this plea, Judah is careful to refer to Jacob as "your servant," implying that Jacob along with the brothers were respecting Joseph's position and authority.

971.525	420	2490.115	3937, 1	3725, 3219	33.	6498
v Hiphil impf 1cs, ps 3ms	prep, ps 2ms	cj, v Qal pf 1cs	prep, n ms, ps 1cs	*adj*, art, n mp		cj, adv
אֲבִיאֶנּוּ	אֵלֶיךָ	וְחָטָאתִי	לְאָבִי	כָּל־הַיָּמִים		וְעַתָּה
'ăvî'ennû	'ēlêkhā	w^{e}chāṭā'thî	l^{e}'āvî	kāl-hayyāmîm		w^{e}'attāh
I bring him back	to you	then I will be guilty	to my father	all the days		and now

3553.121, 5167	5860	8809	5470	5860	3937, 112	5470
v Qal juss 3ms, part	n ms, ps 2ms	prep	art, n ms	n ms	prep, n ms, ps 1cs	cj, art, n ms
יֵשֶׁב־נָא	עַבְדְּךָ	תַּחַת	הַנַּעַר	עֶבֶד	לַאדֹנִי	וְהַנַּעַר
yēshev-nā'	'avd^{e}khā	tachath	hanna'ar	'evedh	la'dhōnî	w^{e}hanna'ar
let him go up	your servant	instead of	the boy	a slave	to my lord	and the boy

6148.121	6196, 250	34.	3706, 351	6148.125	420, 1	5470
v Qal impf 3ms	prep, n mp, ps 3ms		cj, intrg	v Qal impf 1cs	prep, n ms, ps 1cs	cj, art, n ms
יַעַל	עִם־אֶחָיו		כִּי־אֵיךְ	אֶעֱלֶה	אֶל־אָבִי	וְהַנַּעַר
ya'al	'im-'echâv		kî-'êkh	'e'ĕleh	'el-'āvî	w^{e}hanna'ar
he will go up	with his brothers		because how	can I go up	to my father	when the boy

375	882	6678	7495.125	904, 7737	866	4834.121	881, 1
sub, ps 3ms	prep, ps 1cs	cj	v Qal impf 1cs	prep, art, n ms	rel part	v Qal impf 3ms	do, ps 1cs
אֵינֶנּוּ	אִתִּי	פֶּן	אֶרְאֶה	בָּרָע	אֲשֶׁר	יִמְצָא	אֶת־אָבִי
'ênennû	'ittî	pen	'er'eh	vārā'	'ăsher	yimtsā'	'eth-'āvî
he is not	with me	otherwise	I will look	on the evil	which	it will find	my father

45:1	3940, 3310.111	3231	3937, 681.741	3937, 3725	5507.256	6142
	cj, neg part, v Qal pf 3ms	pn	prep, v Hithpael inf con	prep, adj	art, v Niphal ptc mp	prep, ps 3ms
	וְלֹא־יָכֹל	יוֹסֵף	לְהִתְאַפֵּק	לְכֹל	הַנִּצָּבִים	עָלָיו
	w^{e}lō'-yākhōl	yôsēph	l^{e}hith'appēq	l^{e}khōl	hannitstsāvîm	'ālâv
	then not he was able	Joseph	to control himself	to all	the ones standing	beside him

7410.121	3428.533	3725, 382	4623, 6142	3940, 6198.111	382
cj, v Qal impf 3ms	v Hiphil impv 2mp	*adj*, n ms	prep, prep	cj, neg part, v Qal pf 3ms	n ms
וַיִּקְרָא	הוֹצִיאוּ	כָל־אִישׁ	מֵעָלָי	וְלֹא־עָמַד	אִישׁ
wayyiqŏrā'	hôtsî'û	khol-'îsh	mē'ālāy	w^{e}lō'-'āmadh	'îsh
and he called	cause to go out	every man	from beside me	and not he stayed	a man

882	904, 3156.741	3231	420, 250	2.	5598.121
prep, ps 3ms	prep, v Hithpael pf 3ms	pn	prep, n ms, ps 3ms		cj, v Qal impf 3ms
אִתּוֹ	בְּהִתְוַדַּע	יוֹסֵף	אֶל־אֶחָיו		וַיִּתֵּן
'ittô	b^{e}hithwadda'	yôsēph	'el-'echâv		wayyittēn
with him	when he made himself known	Joseph	to his brothers		and he gave

881, 7249	904, 1104	8471.126	4875	8471.121	1041	6799
do, n ms, ps 3ms	prep, n ms	cj, v Qal impf 3mp	pn	cj, v Qal impf 3ms	*n ms*	pn
אֶת־קֹלוֹ	בִּבְכִי	וַיִּשְׁמְעוּ	מִצְרַיִם	וַיִּשְׁמַע	בֵּית	פַּרְעֹה
'eth-qōlô	biv^{e}khî	wayyishm^{e}'û	mitsrayim	wayyishma'	bêth	par'ōh
his voice	with weeping	and they heard	Egyptians	and it heard	the house of	Pharaoh

3.	569.121	3231	420, 250	603	3231	5968	1
	cj, v Qal impf 3ms	pn	prep, n ms, ps 3ms	pers pron	pn	intrg part, adv	n ms, ps 1cs
	וַיֹּאמֶר	יוֹסֵף	אֶל־אֶחָיו	אֲנִי	יוֹסֵף	הַעוֹד	אָבִי
	wayyō'mer	yôsēph	'el-'echâv	'ănî	yôsēph	ha'ôdh	'āvî
	and he said	Joseph	to his brothers	I	Joseph	is still	my father

2508	3940, 3310.116	250	3937, 6257.141	881	3706	963.216
adj	cj, neg part, v Qal pf 3cp	n mp, ps 3ms	prep, v Qal inf con	do, ps 3ms	cj	v Niphal pf 3cp
חָי	וְלֹא־יָכְלוּ	אֶחָיו	לַעֲנוֹת	אֹתוֹ	כִּי	נִבְהֲלוּ
chāy	w^{e}lō'-yākhlû	'echâv	la'ănôth	'ōthô	kî	nivh^{e}lû
alive	and not they were able	his brothers	to answer	him	because	they were terrified

33. Now therefore, I pray thee, let thy servant abide instead of the lad a bondman to my lord: ... slave, *Berkeley.*

and let the lad go up with his brethren: ... return, *NCB, NIV.*

34. For how shall I go up to my father, and the lad be not with me? lest peradventure I see the evil that shall come on my father: ... anguish, *NAB* ... misery, *Fenton* ... suffering, *NRSV* ... agony, *Goodspeed.*

45:1. Then Joseph could not refrain himself: ... unable to keep back his feelings, *BB* ... control his emotions, *Berkeley, MLB.*

before all them that stood by him: ... his attendants, *Goodspeed, REB, NEB* ... officers, *Fenton.*

and he cried, Cause every man to go out from me: ... everyone leave my presence, *REB, NIV.*

And there stood no man with him, while Joseph made himself known unto his brethren: ... there was no one with Joseph, *NIV.*

2. And he wept aloud: ... so loud was his weeping, *BB* ... sobs, *Anchor, NAB* ... then Joseph discovered his language to his brothers, *Fenton.*

and the Egyptians and the house of Pharaoh heard: ... news reached, *Anchor* ... it was reported to, *Fenton* ... about it, *NIV.*

3. And Joseph said unto his brethren, I am Joseph; doth my father yet live?: ... in good health, *Anchor, NAB.*

And his brethren could not answer him; for they were troubled at his presence: ... dumbfounded, *REB* ... dismayed, *RSV* ... astonished, *Geneva* ... terrified, *NIV, Fenton, NCB.*

4. And Joseph said unto his brethren, Come near to me, I pray you: ... please, *KJVII, NKJV, Berkeley* ... please come closer to me, *NASB.*

And they came near. And he said, I am Joseph your brother, whom ye sold into Egypt.

44:32-34. Because Judah became surety for Benjamin, guaranteeing his safety to his father, he begged Joseph to let him remain as his slave instead of Benjamin, and let the young man return with his brothers. He concluded with a heart-rending plea. How could he go to his father without the young man and see the evil that would come on his father.

What a complete change in attitude this was from the attitude the brothers showed when they sent Joseph's bloody tunic to their father! What a change, too, from the old Judah who sought pleasure from a pagan religious prostitute without thinking of what effect it would have on others. Repentance means a change of mind and basic attitudes. Many see that when Judah offered himself with heroic self-sacrifice as a willing substitute for Benjamin, he became a type or foreshadow of another greater Substitute who took our place on a rugged cross.

Later we read that though Joseph retained the birthright, Judah attained a leadership over his brothers, and from him came a sovereign (1 see Chron. 5:2, where the Chronicler probably had King David in mind). Judah's leadership implies strength, in this case, spiritual strength. Thus Judah, as a changed man, was God's choice to carry on the line that would lead to David and Jesus.

45:1-2. Judah's plea so stirred Joseph's emotions that he could not control himself or force himself to pretend he was a stranger any longer. Now he knew there was a genuine change in the brothers and he could trust them. So he called out a command for everyone else to leave, so that no one would stay with him while he made himself known to his brothers. To the Egyptians he must still be Zaphnath-paaneah. Then the pent-up feelings of the years, the love and longing he had for his brothers and his father, caused him to break out into loud weeping. The Egyptians outside heard it, so Pharaoh's household heard of it. To the brothers, alone in the room with Joseph, the weeping must have made them apprehensive, for they did not know what to expect.

45:3. When Joseph told the brothers who he was, his first concern was to ask gently if his father was still alive. There was no bitterness in his voice, only tender love. But the brothers could not answer. They were terrified and trembled with fear and dismay. Now they realized how foolish they had been to try to hide their sin. Now, too, they could see the resemblance to the boy they had sold and they were horrified. God had overruled and they knew their sin was against God.

45:4. Up to this time, Joseph had spoken harshly to the brothers. Thus, they may have stepped back startled when they heard him say he was Joseph. But he wanted to win their confidence and allay their fears, so he asked them to come near and again said he was Joseph, the one they had sold into Egypt.

4623, 6686		569.121	3231	420, 250	5242.133, 5167	420
prep, n mp, ps 3ms	4.	cj, v Qal impf 3ms	pn	prep, n ms, ps 3ms	v Qal impv 2mp, part	prep, ps 1cs
מִפָּנָיו		וַיֹּאמֶר	יוֹסֵף	אֶל־אֶחָיו	גְּשׁוּ־נָא	אֵלַי
mippānâv		wayyō'mer	yôsēph	'el-'echâv	geshû-nā'	'ēlay
by his presence		and he said	Joseph	to his brothers	draw near please	to me

5242.126	569.121	603	3231	250	866, 4513.117	881
cj, v Qal impf 3mp	cj, v Qal impf 3ms	pers pron	pn	n ms, ps 2mp	rel part, v Qal pf 2mp	do, ps 1cs
וַיִּגָּשׁוּ	וַיֹּאמֶר	אֲנִי	יוֹסֵף	אֲחִיכֶם	אֲשֶׁר־מְכַרְתֶּם	אֹתִי
wayyiggāshû	wayyō'mer	'ănî	yôsēph	'ăchîkhem	'ăsher-mekhartem	'ōthî
and they drew near	and he said	I	Joseph	your brother	whom you sold	me

4875		6498	414, 6321.228	414, 2835.121	904, 6084
pn	5.	cj, adv	adv, v Niphal juss 2mp	cj, adv, v Qal juss 3ms	prep, n fd, ps 2mp
מִצְרָיְמָה		וְעַתָּה	אַל־תֵּעָצְבוּ	וְאַל־יִחַר	בְּעֵינֵיכֶם
mitsrâemāh		we'attāh	'al-tē'ātsevû	we'al-yichar	be'ênêkhem
to Egypt		and now	do not grieve	and let it not be anger	in your eyes

3706, 4513.117	881	2077	3706	3937, 4376	8365.111	435
cj, v Qal pf 2mp	do, ps 1cs	adv	cj	prep, n fs	v Qal pf 3ms, ps 1cs	n mp
כִּי־מְכַרְתֶּם	אֹתִי	הֵנָּה	כִּי	לְמִחְיָה	שְׁלָחַנִי	אֱלֹהִים
kî-mekhartem	'ōthî	hēnnāh	kî	lemichăyāh	shelāchanî	'ĕlōhîm
because you sold	me	here	because	for preservation of life	he sent me	God

3937, 6686		3706, 2172	8523	7743	904, 7419	800	5968
prep, n mp, ps 2mp	6.	cj, dem pron	n md	art, n ms	prep, *n ms*	art, n fs	cj, adv
לִפְנֵיכֶם		כִּי־זֶה	שְׁנָתַיִם	הָרָעָב	בְּקֶרֶב	הָאָרֶץ	וְעוֹד
liphnêkhem		kî-zeh	shenāthayim	hārā'āv	beqerev	hā'ārets	we'ôdh
before you		because these	two years	the famine	in the midst of	the land	and still

2675	8523	866	375, 2863	7392		8365.121	435
num	n fp	rel part	*sub*, n ms	cj, n ms	7.	cj, v Qal impf 3ms, ps 1cs	n mp
חָמֵשׁ	שָׁנִים	אֲשֶׁר	אֵין־חָרִישׁ	וְקָצִיר		וַיִּשְׁלָחֵנִי	אֱלֹהִים
chāmēsh	shānîm	'ăsher	'ên-chārîsh	weqātsîr		wayyishlāchēnî	'ĕlōhîm
five	years	which	without of plowing	or harvest		and He sent me	God

3937, 6686	3937, 7947.141	3937	8086	904, 800	3937, 2513.541	3937
prep, n mp, ps 2mp	prep, v Qal inf con	prep, ps 2mp	n fs	prep, art, n fs	cj, prep, v Hiphil inf con	prep, ps 2mp
לִפְנֵיכֶם	לָשׂוּם	לָכֶם	שְׁאֵרִית	בָּאָרֶץ	וּלְהַחֲיוֹת	לָכֶם
liphnêkhem	lāsûm	lākhem	she'ērîth	bā'ārets	ûlăhachyôth	lākhem
before you	to put	for you	remnant	on the earth	and to keep alive	for you

3937, 6656	1448		6498	3940, 894	8365.117	881	2078	3706
prep, n fs	adj	8.	cj, adv	neg part, pers pron	v Qal pf 2mp	do, ps 1cs	pers pron	cj
לִפְלֵיטָה	גְּדֹלָה		וְעַתָּה	לֹא־אַתֶּם	שְׁלַחְתֶּם	אֹתִי	הֵנָּה	כִּי
liphlêṭāh	gedhōlāh		we'attāh	lō'-'attem	shelachtem	'ōthî	hēnnāh	kî
for a survivor	many		and now	not you	you sent	me	they	but

435	7947.121	3937, 1	3937, 6799	3937, 112	3937, 3725, 1041
art, n mp	cj, v Qal impf 3ms, ps 1cs	prep, n ms	prep, pn	cj, prep, n ms	prep, *adj*, n ms, ps 3ms
הָאֱלֹהִים	וַיְשִׂימֵנִי	לְאָב	לְפַרְעֹה	וּלְאָדוֹן	לְכָל־בֵּיתוֹ
hā'ĕlōhîm	waysîmēnî	le'āv	lephar'ōh	ûlă'ādhôn	lekhol-bêthô
God	and He set me	for a father	to Pharaoh	and for a master	to all his house

5090.151	904, 3725, 800	4875		4257.333	6148.133	420, 1
cj, v Qal act ptc ms	prep, *adj*, *n fs*	pn	9.	v Piel impv 2mp	cj, v Qal impv 2mp	prep, n ms, ps 1cs
וּמֹשֵׁל	בְּכָל־אֶרֶץ	מִצְרָיִם		מַהֲרוּ	וַעֲלוּ	אֶל־אָבִי
ûmōshēl	bekhol-'erets	mitsrāyim		mahrû	wa'ălû	'el-'āvî
and a ruler	in all the land of	Egypt		hurry	and go up	to my father

569.117	420	3662	569.111	1158	3231	7947.111	435
cj, v Qal pf 2mp	prep, ps 3ms	adv	v Qal pf 3ms	n ms, ps 2ms	pn	v Qal pf 3ms, ps 1cs	n mp
וַאֲמַרְתֶּם	אֵלָיו	כֹּה	אָמַר	בִּנְךָ	יוֹסֵף	שָׂמַנִי	אֱלֹהִים
wa'ămartem	'ēlâv	kōh	'āmar	binekhā	yôsēph	sāmanî	'ělōhîm
and you will say	to him	so	he said	your son	Joseph	He set me	God

3937, 112	3937, 3725, 4875	3495.131	420	414, 6198.123		3553.113
prep, n ms	prep, *adj*, pn	v Qal impv 2ms	prep, ps 1cs	adv, v Qal juss 2ms	**10.**	cj, v Qal pf 2ms
לְאָדוֹן	לְכָל־מִצְרָיִם	רְדָה	אֵלַי	אַל־תַּעֲמֹד		וְיָשַׁבְתָּ
le'ādhôn	lekhol-mitsrāyim	redhāh	'ēlay	'al-ta'ămōdh		weyāshavtā
for a lord	to all Egypt	come down	to me	do not stand still		and you will dwell

5. Now therefore be not grieved: ... disheartened, *MLB* ... distressed, *Goodspeed* ... worry, *Anchor.*

nor angry with yourselves: ... vexed, *Berkeley,* ... blame, *REB* ... displeasing in your eyes, *Young.*

that ye sold me hither: for God did send me before you to preserve life: ... And I know that with fury and rage in your eyes, you sold me, *Fenton* ... be the savior of your, *BB* ... as an instrument of survival, *Anchor.*

6. For these two years hath the famine been in: ... encircled, *Fenton* ... prevailed, *Goodspeed.*

the land: and yet there are five years, in the which there shall neither be earing: ... plowing, *NCB.*

nor harvest: ... tillage will yield no harvest, *NAB* ... yield from tilling, *Anchor* ... cutting of grain, *BB.*

7. And God sent me before you to preserve you: ... ensure, *NEB.*

a posterity in the earth, and to save your lives: ... remnant, *Goodspeed,* ... descendants, *REB* ... secure refuge, *Fenton.*

by a great deliverance: ... in a striking way, *NCB* ... keep alive for you many survivors, *NRSV* ... great escape, *Young* ... become a great nation, *BB.*

8. So now it was not you that sent me hither, but God: and he hath made me a father to Pharaoh: ... appointed, *Berkeley* ... chief counsellor, *REB.*

and lord of all his house, and a ruler throughout all the land of Egypt: ... administrator ... governor, *Fenton.*

9. Haste ye, and go up to my father, and say unto him, Thus saith thy son Joseph, God hath made me lord of all Egypt: come down unto me, tarry not: ... Go quickly, *NCB* ... hurry, *NRSV* ... do not delay, *Berkeley, REB, NKJV, MLB.*

10. And thou shalt dwell in the land of Goshen, and thou shalt be near unto me, thou, and thy children, and thy children's children, and thy flocks: ... sheep, *Fenton, Geneva, Darby.*

and thy herds, and all that thou hast: ... oxen, *Fenton* ... beasts, *Geneva* ... cattle, *Darby.*

45:5-6. Joseph saw their reaction, and told them not to grieve or find fault with themselves and not to let anger be in their eyes, that is, not to be angry with themselves for selling him to Egypt. By this he meant that his forgiveness and God's was theirs. God had a purpose. He sent Joseph ahead of them to preserve life. The famine had been in the land for 2 years and there would still be 5 more years without plowing or harvesting any crops.

45:7-8. Joseph further encouraged his brothers by drawing attention to what the grace and mercy of God had accomplished. God, in his overruling providence, sent him before them to put, constitute, or secure a remnant for them, of which Joseph would be the nucleus, and keep alive a great many survivors who would escape the results of the famine. Thus it was not the brothers, but God who sent him away. Now God had placed him in a position where he was a father, that is, an advisor and provider to Pharaoh, a master over all his household, and a ruler in all Egypt.

45:9-11. Joseph commanded the brothers to hurry and go to his father and tell him God had made him lord or master over all Egypt. His father must come down to Joseph and not delay. Joseph wanted him to live in the land of Goshen in the northeastern part of the Nile delta with his children, grandchildren, flocks, herds, and everything he possessed. Goshen was probably about 20 miles from the delta capital which was probably at Zoan (also called Tanis and Avaris at different times in Egypt's history). There he would be near Joseph, and Joseph would provide for them during the remaining 5 years of famine. Otherwise, he would become impoverished and lose all he had because of debt.

904, 800, 1705	2030.113	7427	420	887	1158	1158
prep, *n fs*, pn	cj, v Qal pf 2ms	adv	prep, ps 1cs	pers pron	cj, n mp, ps 2ms	cj, *n mp*
בְּאֶרֶץ־גֹּשֶׁן	וְהָיִיתָ	קָרוֹב	אֵלַי	אַתָּה	וּבָנֶיךָ	וּבְנֵי
ve'erets-gōshen	wehāyîthā	qārôv	'ēlay	'attāh	ûvānêkhā	ûvnê
in the land of Goshen	and you will be	near	to me	you	and your sons	and the sons of

1158	6887	1267	3725, 866, 3937		3677.315
n mp, ps 2ms	cj, n fs, ps 2ms	cj, n ms, ps 2ms	cj, adj, rel part, prep, ps 2ms	**11.**	cj, v Pilpel pf 1cs
בָנֶיךָ	וְצֹאנְךָ	וּבְקָרְךָ	וְכָל־אֲשֶׁר־לָךְ		וְכִלְכַּלְתִּי
vānêkhā	wetsō'nekhā	ûvqārekh	wekhol-'ăsher-lākh		wekhilkaltî
your sons	and your flocks	and your herds	and all which to you		and I will provide for

881	8427	3706, 5968	2675	8523	7743	6678, 3542.223
do, ps 2ms	adv	cj, adv	*num*	*n fp*	n ms	cj, v Niphal impf 2ms
אֹתְךָ	שָׁם	כִּי־עוֹד	חָמֵשׁ	שָׁנִים	רָעָב	פֶּן־תִּוָּרֵשׁ
'ōthekhā	shām	kî-'ôdh	chāmēsh	shānîm	rā'āv	pen-tiwwārēsh
you	there	because still	five	years of	famine	otherwise you will become impoverished

887	1041	3725, 866, 3937		2079	6084	7495.154
pers pron	cj, n ms, ps 2ms	cj, adj, rel part, prep, ps 2ms	**12.**	cj, intrj	n fd, ps 2mp	v Qal act ptc fp
אַתָּה	וּבֵיתְךָ	וְכָל־אֲשֶׁר־לָךְ		וְהִנֵּה	עֵינֵיכֶם	רֹאוֹת
'attāh	ûvêthekhā	wekhol-'ăsher-lākh		wehinnēh	'ênêkhem	rō'ôth
you	and your house	and all which to you		and behold	your eyes	ones that see

6084	250	1175	3706, 6552	1744.351	420
cj, *n fd*	n ms, ps 1cs	pn	cj, n ms	art, v Piel ptc ms	prep, ps 2mp
וְעֵינֵי	אָחִי	בִנְיָמִין	כִּי־פִי	הַמְדַבֵּר	אֲלֵיכֶם
we'ênê	'āchî	vinyāmîn	kî-phî	hamedhabbēr	'ălêkhem
and the eyes of	my brother	Benjamin	because my mouth	the one speaking	to you

	5222.517	3937, 1	881, 3725, 3638	904, 4875	881	3725, 866
13.	cj, v Hiphil pf 2mp	prep, n ms, ps 1cs	do, *adj*, n ms, ps 1cs	prep, pn	cj, do	adj, rel part
	וְהִגַּדְתֶּם	לְאָבִי	אֶת־כָּל־כְּבוֹדִי	בְּמִצְרַיִם	וְאֵת	כָּל־אֲשֶׁר
	wehiggadhtem	le'āvî	'eth-kol-kevôdhî	bemitsrayim	we'ēth	kol-'ăsher
	and you will tell	to my father	all my glory	in Egypt	and	all which

7495.117	4257.317	3495.517	881, 1	2078		5489
v Qal pf 2mp	cj, v Piel pf 2mp	cj, v Hiphil pf 2mp	do, n ms, ps 1cs	pers pron	**14.**	cj, v Qal impf 3ms
רְאִיתֶם	וּמִהַרְתֶּם	וְהוֹרַדְתֶּם	אֶת־אָבִי	הֵנָּה		וַיִּפֹּל
re'îthem	ûmihartem	wehôradtem	'eth-'āvî	hēnnāh		wayyippōl
you saw	and you will hurry	and you will bring down	my father	they		and he fell

6142, 6939	1175, 250	1098.121	1175	1098.111
prep, *n mp*	pn, n ms, ps 3ms	cj, v Qal impf 3ms	cj, pn	v Qal pf 3ms
עַל־צַוְּארֵי	בִנְיָמִן־אָחִיו	וַיֵּבְךְּ	וּבִנְיָמִן	בָּכָה
'al-tsawwerê	vinyāmin-'āchîw	wayyēvekh	ûvinyāmin	bākhāh
on the neck of	Benjamin his brother	and he wept	and Benjamin	he wept

6142, 6939		5583.321	3937, 3725, 250	1098.121	6142
prep, n ms, ps 3ms	**15.**	cj, v Piel impf 3ms	prep, *adj*, n mp, ps 3ms	cj, v Qal impf 3ms	prep, ps 3mp
עַל־צַוָּארָיו		וַיְנַשֵּׁק	לְכָל־אֶחָיו	וַיֵּבְךְּ	עֲלֵיהֶם
'al-tsawwā'râv		wayenashshēq	lekhol-'echâv	wayyēvekh	'ălêhem
on his neck		and he kissed	all his brothers	and he wept	on them

311	3772	1744.316	250	882		7249
cj, *sub*	adv	v Piel pf 3cp	n mp, ps 3ms	prep, ps 3ms	**16.**	cj, art, n ms
וְאַחֲרֵי	כֵן	דִּבְּרוּ	אֶחָיו	אִתּוֹ		וְהַקֹּל
we'achrê	khēn	dibberû	'echâv	'ittô		wehaqqōl
and afterward	so	they spoke	his brothers	with him		and the sound

8471.211	904, 1041	6799	3937, 569.141	971.116	250	3231
v Niphal pf 3ms	prep, *n ms*	pn	prep, v Qal inf con	v Qal pf 3cp	n mp	pn
נִשְׁמַע	בֵּית	פַּרְעֹה	לֵאמֹר	בָּאוּ	אֲחֵי	יוֹסֵף
nishma'	bêth	par'ōh	lē'mōr	bā'û	'ăchê	yôsēph
it was heard	in the house of	Pharaoh	saying	they came	the brothers of	Joseph

3296.121	904, 6084	6799	904, 6084	5860		569.121
cj, v Qal impf 3ms	prep, *n fp*	pn	cj, prep, *n fd*	n mp, ps 3ms		cj, v Qal impf 3ms
וַיִּיטַב	בְּעֵינֵי	פַּרְעֹה	וּבְעֵינֵי	עֲבָדָיו	**17.**	וַיֹּאמֶר
wayyîṯav	b^e'ênê	phar'ōh	ûv^e'ênê	'ăvādhâv		wayyō'mer
and it was pleasing	in the eyes of	Pharaoh	and in the eyes of	his servants		and he said

11. And there will I nourish: ... support, *MLB* ... provide for, *REB* ... maintain, *Darby.*

thee; for yet there are five years of famine; lest thou, and thy household, and all that thou hast, come to poverty: ... reduced to want, *REB* ... suffer no want, *Anchor* ... destitute, *NIV.*

12. And, behold, your eyes see, and the eyes of my brother Benjamin, that it is my mouth that speaketh unto you: ... I am personally conversing with you, *Berkeley* ... and that my mouth may also speak with you, *Fenton* ... You are witness of my promise, and my brother Benjamin has heard me say it, *LIVB.*

13. And ye shall tell my father of all my glory: ... honor, *REB* ... high station position, *NAB* ... power, *Fenton.*

in Egypt, and of all that ye have seen; and ye shall haste and bring down my father hither: ... cause your father to mount, *Fenton.*

14. And he fell upon his brother Benjamin's neck, and wept; and Benjamin wept upon his neck: ... threw his arms around, *NEB* ... flung himself, *Anchor.*

15. Moreover he kissed all his brethren, and wept upon them: and after that his brethren talked with him:. . . had no fear, *BB* ... only then were his brothers able to talk to him, *Anchor, NAB.*

16. And the fame thereof was heard: ... report, *KJVII* ... tidings, *Geneva* ... news was received, *NCB.*

in Pharaoh's house, saying, Joseph's brethren are come: and it pleased Pharaoh well, and his servants: ... good in the eyes of, *Young* ... ministers, *Fenton* ... courtiers, *Anchor* ... officials, *REB* ... bondmen, *Darby.*

17. And Pharaoh said unto Joseph, Say unto thy brethren, This do ye; lade your beasts: ... load, *NASB* ... pack your animals, *Berkeley, MLB.*

and go, get you, unto the land of Canaan: ... from the city, *Fenton* ... without delay, *NAB.*

18. And take your father and your households: ... families, *NCB, Berkeley, Fenton.*

and come unto me: and I will give you the good: ... best, *NCB, NASB, Berkeley* ... best land, *NAB* ... best territory, *Anchor* ... best region, *REB.*

of the land of Egypt, and ye shall eat the fat of the land: ... live, *NAB* ... enjoy, *NRSV, NEB, REB.*

45:12. Joseph as Zaphnath-Paaneah had been speaking in the Egyptian language and communicating to the brothers through an interpreter. Now he was speaking Hebrew to them with his own mouth, as all the brothers could see. This was further evidence that he was really Joseph.

45:13. Again Joseph asked his brothers to tell his father about all his glory, including his status, honor, renown, authority, prestige, impressive appearance, and of everything else they saw (concerning Joseph and his house). He wanted his father to know he was truly able to take care of him and his family. They must hurry and bring his father down to Egypt.

45:14-15. Joseph first went to Benjamin and they hugged each other, both weeping. Then he kissed each of his brothers. After this, his brothers talked freely to him. They were a united family for the first time. All the barriers between them had been broken down.

45:16-18. The report that Joseph's brothers had come reached the household of Pharaoh. Pharaoh and his court officials were pleased. Pharaoh then told Joseph to tell his brothers to load up their animals and go home to Canaan. They must take their father and their households and come to Egypt. Pharaoh would give them the best of the land and they would eat the fat (the best) of the land. This was a royal confirmation of what Joseph promised.

6799	420, 3231	569.131	420, 250	2148	6449.133	3053.133
pn	prep, pn	v Qal impv 2ms	prep, n mp, ps 2ms	dem pron	v Qal impv 2mp	v Qal impv 2mp
פַּרְעֹה	אֶל־יוֹסֵף	אֱמֹר	אֶל־אַחֶיךָ	זֹאת	עֲשׂוּ	טַעֲנוּ
par'ōh	'el-yôsēph	'ĕmōr	'el-'achêkhā	zō'th	'ăsû	ta'ănû
Pharaoh	to Joseph	say	to your brothers	this	do	load

881, 1194	2050.133, 971.133	800	3791		4089.133
do, n ms, ps 2mp	cj, v Qal impv 2mp, v Qal impv 2mp	*n fs*	pn	**18.**	cj, v Qal impv 2mp
אֶת־בְּעִירְכֶם	וּלְכוּ־בֹאוּ	אַרְצָה	כְּנָעַן		וּקְחוּ
'eth-be'îrkhem	ûlăkhû-vō'û	'artsāh	kenā'an		ûqŏchû
your beast	and go go home	to the land of	Canaan		and take

881, 1	881, 1041	971.133	420	5598.125	3937
do, n mp, ps 2mp	cj, do, n mp, ps 2mp	cj, v Qal impv 2mp	prep, ps 1cs	cj, v Qal impf 1cs	prep, ps 2mp
אֶת־אֲבִיכֶם	וְאֶת־בָּתֵּיכֶם	וּבֹאוּ	אֵלָי	וְאֶתְּנָה	לָכֶם
'eth-'ăvîkhem	we'eth-bāttêkhem	ûvō'û	'ēlāy	we'ettenāh	lākhem
your father	and your households	then come	to me	and I will give	to you

881, 3005	800	4875	404.133	881, 2561	800		887
do, adj	*n fs*	pn	cj, v Qal impv 2mp	do, *n ms*	art, n fs	**19.**	cj, pers pron
אֶת־טוּב	אֶרֶץ	מִצְרַיִם	וְאִכְלוּ	אֶת־חֵלֶב	הָאָרֶץ		וְאַתָּה
'eth-tûv	'erets	mitsrayim	we'ikhlû	'eth-chēlev	hā'ārets		we'attāh
the good of	the land of	Egypt	and eat	the fat of	the land		and you

6943.413	2148	6449.133	4089.133, 3937	4623, 800	4875
v Pual pf 2ms	dem pron	v Qal impv 2mp	v Qal impv 2mp, prep, ps 2mp	prep, *n fs*	pn
צֻוֵּיתָה	זֹאת	עֲשׂוּ	קְחוּ־לָכֶם	מֵאֶרֶץ	מִצְרַיִם
tsuwwêthāh	zō'th	'ăsû	qāchû-lākhem	mē'erets	mitsrayim
you are commanded	this	do	take for yourselves	from the land of	Egypt

5906	3937, 3054	3937, 5571	5558.117	881, 1
n fp	prep, n ms, ps 2mp	cj, prep, n fp, ps 2mp	cj, v Qal pf 2mp	do, n mp, ps 2mp
עֲגָלוֹת	לְטַפְּכֶם	וְלִנְשֵׁיכֶם	וּנְשָׂאתֶם	אֶת־אֲבִיכֶם
'ăghālôth	letappekhem	welinshêkhem	ûnesā'them	'eth-'ăvîkhem
wagons	for your little children	and for your wives	and you will carry	your father

971.117		6084	414, 2441.123	6142, 3747
cj, v Qal pf 2mp	**20.**	cj, n fs, ps 2mp	adv, v Qal impf 2ms	prep, n mp, ps 2mp
וּבָאתֶם		וְעֵינְכֶם	אַל־תָּחֹס	עַל־כְּלֵיכֶם
ûvā'them		we'ênekhem	'al-tāchōs	'al-kelêkhem
and you will come		and your eye	not you will be concerned	over your belongings

3706, 3005	3725, 800	4875	3937	2000		6449.126, 3772
cj, adj	adj, *n fs*	pn	prep, ps 2mp	pers pron	**21.**	cj, v Qal impf 3mp, adv
כִּי־טוּב	כָּל־אֶרֶץ	מִצְרַיִם	לָכֶם	הוּא		וַיַּעֲשׂוּ־כֵן
kî-tûv	kol-'erets	mitsrayim	lākhem	hû'		wayya'ăsû-khēn
because of the good	all the land of	Egypt	to you	it		and they did so

1158	3547	5598.121	3937	3231	5906	6142, 6552	6799
n mp	pn	cj, v Qal pf 3ms	prep, ps 3mp	pn	n fp	prep, *n ms*	pn
בְּנֵי	יִשְׂרָאֵל	וַיִּתֵּן	לָהֶם	יוֹסֵף	עֲגָלוֹת	עַל־פִּי	פַרְעֹה
benê	yisrā'ēl	wayyittēn	lāhem	yôsēph	'ăghālôth	'al-pî	phar'ōh
the sons of	Israel	and he gave	to them	Joseph	wagons	on the mouth of	Pharaoh

5598.121	3937	6990	3937, 1932		3937, 3725	5598.111	3937, 382
cj, v Qal pf 3ms	prep, ps 3mp	n fs	prep, art, n ms	**22.**	prep, adj, ps 3mp	v Qal pf 3ms	prep, art, n ms
וַיִּתֵּן	לָהֶם	צֵדָה	לַדָּרֶךְ		לְכֻלָּם	נָתַן	לָאִישׁ
wayyittēn	lāhem	tsēdhāh	laddārekh		lekhullām	nāthan	lā'îsh
and he gave	to them	provisions	for the journey		to all of them	he gave	to each one

2589	7980	3937, 1175	5598.111	8421	4109	3826B	2675
n fp	n fp	cj, prep, pn	v Qal pf 3ms	num	*num*	n ms	cj, num
חֲלִפוֹת	שְׂמָלֹת	וּלְבִנְיָמִן	נָתַן	שְׁלֹשׁ	מֵאוֹת	כֶּסֶף	וַחֲמֵשׁ
chăliphôth	s^{e}mālōth	ûlāvinyāmin	nāthan	sh^{e}lōsh	mē'ôth	keseph	w^{e}chămēsh
changes of	clothes	but to Benjamin	he gave	three	hundreds	silver	and five

2589	7980		3937, 1	8365.111	3626, 2148	6463	2645
n fp	n fp	**23.**	cj, prep, n ms, ps 3ms	v Qal pf 3ms	prep, dem pron	num	n mp
חֲלִפֹת	שְׂמָלֹת		וּלְאָבִיו	שָׁלַח	כְּזֹאת	עֲשָׂרָה	חֲמֹרִים
chăliphōth	s^{e}mālōth		ûlā'āvîw	shālach	k^{e}zō'th	'ăsārāh	chămōrîm
changes of	clothes		and to his father	he sent	like this	ten	male donkeys

5558.152	4623, 3005	4875	6460	888	5558.154	904, 1277
v Qal act ptc mp	prep, *adj*	pn	cj, num	n fp	v Qal act ptc fp	prep, n ms
נֹשְׂאִים	מִטּוּב	מִצְרָיִם	וְעֶשֶׂר	אֲתֹנֹת	נֹשְׂאֹת	בָּר
nōs'îm	mittûv	mitsrāyim	w^{e}'eser	'ăthōnōth	nōs'ōth	bār
bearing	of the good of	Egypt	and ten	female donkeys	loaded	with grain

19. Now thou art commanded, this do ye; take you wagons: … carts, *NCB* … charets, *Geneva.*

out of the land of Egypt for your little ones, and for your wives, and bring your father, and come: … infants, *Young* … dependants, *REB.*

20. Also regard not your stuff; for the good of all the land of Egypt is yours: … Do not be concerned about, *NCB* … furniture, *Berkeley* … belongings, *NAB* … your eye hath no pity on your vessels, *Young* … Have no regrets at leaving your possessions, *REB* … let not your eye regret your stuff, *Darby.*

21. And the children of Israel did so: … sons of Israel, *RSV* … followed these instructions, *REB.*

and Joseph gave them wagons, according to the commandment of Pharaoh, and gave them provision for the way: … from Pharaoh's arsenal, *Fenton* … food, *NEB* … vitaile, *Geneva* … journey, *Anchor.*

22. To all of them he gave each man changes of raiment: … clothes clothing, *KJVII* … festival garments, *NCB* … garments, *NKJV* … new suits, *Berkeley.*

but to Benjamin he gave three hundred pieces: … shekels, *Goodspeed* … bits, *BB.*

of silver, and five changes of raiment: … silverling, *Young* … three hundred pounds, *Fenton* … 200 dollars worth of silver, *MLB* … several, *Anchor.*

23. And to his father he sent after this manner; ten asses laden with the good things of Egypt: … riding asses the best in Mitzer, *Fenton* … best finest choice products, *Goodspeed.*

and ten she asses laden with corn: … she riding asses besides, *Fenton* … grain, *NKJV* … wheat, *Geneva.*

and bread and meat for his father by the way: … provisions, *NEB* … and food, *Darby* … sustenance, *Anchor* … with bread and meat, *Fenton.*

24. So he sent his brethren away, and they departed: and he said unto them, See that ye fall not out by the way: … not to quarrel among themselves on the road, *NEB* … do not get too excited, *Goodspeed*

45:19-20. Pharaoh emphasized that this was a command. They must take wagons from Egypt for their little children and their wives and to carry their father and come. They were not to be concerned over their belongings, for the good of all the land of Egypt would be theirs. Pharaoh was being unusually generous because of his regard for Joseph, and Pharaoh still had the final word.

45:21-23. Joseph obeyed Pharaoh and gave his brothers wagons. He also gave them provisions for the journey and gifts. To each he gave changes of clothing (the finest outer garments), but to Benjamin he gave 300 shekels weight of silver and five changes of clothing. He was still testing his brothers to be sure there was no trace of jealousy left in their hearts. Then to his father he sent a gift of ten male donkeys bearing good things of Egypt and for his father's journey to Egypt he sent ten female donkeys loaded with grain, bread, and other food.

45:24. As a final word when the brothers were leaving, Joseph asked them not to be upset on the way. He was probably afraid they might begin to accuse one another or try to fix the blame for past sins and mistakes and thus would stir up anger or cause quarreling.

4035	4332	3937, 1	3937, 1932		8365.121	881, 250
cj, n ms	cj, n ms	prep, n ms, ps 3ms	prep, art, n ms		cj, v Piel impf 3ms	do, n ms, ps 3ms
וְלֶחֶם	וּמָזוֹן	לְאָבִיו	לַדָּרֶךְ	**24.**	וַיְשַׁלַּח	אֶת־אֶחָיו
wālechem	ûmāzôn	le'āvîw	laddārekh		wayshallach	'eth-'echâv
and bread	and provisions	for his father	for the journey		and he sent	his brothers

2050.126	569.121	420	414, 7553	904, 1932		6148.126
cj, v Qal impf 3mp	cj, v Qal impf 3ms	prep, ps 3mp	adv, v Qal juss 2mp	prep, art, n ms		cj, v Qal impf 3mp
וַיֵּלֵכוּ	וַיֹּאמֶר	אֲלֵהֶם	אַל־תִּרְגְּזוּ	בַּדָּרֶךְ	**25.**	וַיַּעֲלוּ
wayyēlēkhû	wayyō'mer	'ălēhem	'al-tirgezû	baddārekh		wayya'ălû
and they went	and he said	to them	do not be upset	on the way		and they went up

4623, 4875	971.126	800	3791	420, 3399	1		5222.526
prep, pn	cj, v Qal impf 3mp	*n fs*	pn	prep, pn	n ms, ps 3mp		cj, v Hiphil impf 3mp
מִמִּצְרָיִם	וַיָּבֹאוּ	אֶרֶץ	כְּנַעַן	אֶל־יַעֲקֹב	אֲבִיהֶם	**26.**	וַיַּגִּדוּ
mimmitsrāyim	wayyāvō'û	'erets	kena'an	'el-ya'ăqōv	'ăvîhem		wayyaggidhû
from Egypt	and they came	to the land of	Canaan	to Jacob	their father		and they reported

3937	3937, 569.141	5968	3231	2513.111	3706, 2000	5090.151
prep, ps 3ms	prep, v Qal inf con	adv	pn	v Qal pf 3ms	cj, cj, pers pron	v Qal act ptc ms
לוֹ	לֵאמֹר	עוֹד	יוֹסֵף	חַי	וְכִי־הוּא	מֹשֵׁל
lô	lē'mōr	'ôdh	yôsēph	chay	wekhî-hû'	mōshēl
to him	saying	still	Joseph	he lives	and that he	ruler

904, 3725, 800	4875	6555.121	3949	3706	3940, 548.511	3937
prep, *adj, n fs*	pn	cj, v Qal impf 3ms	n ms, ps 3ms	cj	adv, v Hiphil pf 3ms	prep, ps 3mp
בְּכָל־אֶרֶץ	מִצְרָיִם	וַיָּפָג	לִבּוֹ	כִּי	לֹא־הֶאֱמִין	לָהֶם
bekhol-'erets	mitsrāyim	wayyāphāgh	libbô	kî	lō'-he'ĕmîn	lāhem
over all the land of	Egypt	and it became numb	his heart	because	not he believed	them

	1744.326	420	881	3725, 1745	3231	866	1744.311
	cj, v Piel impf 3mp	prep, ps 3ms	do	*adj, n mp*	pn	rel part	v Piel pf 3ms
27.	וַיְדַבְּרוּ	אֵלָיו	אֵת	כָּל־דִּבְרֵי	יוֹסֵף	אֲשֶׁר	דִּבֶּר
	wayedhabberû	'ēlâv	'ēth	kol-divrê	yôsēph	'ăsher	dibber
	and they spoke	to him		all the words of	Joseph	which	he spoke

420	7495.121	881, 5906	866, 8365.111	3231	3937, 5558.141	881
prep, ps 3mp	cj, v Qal impf 3ms	do, art, n fp	rel part, v Qal pf 3ms	pn	prep, v Qal inf con	do, ps 3ms
אֲלֵהֶם	וַיַּרְא	אֶת־הָעֲגָלוֹת	אֲשֶׁר־שָׁלַח	יוֹסֵף	לָשֵׂאת	אֹתוֹ
'ălēhem	wayyare'	'eth-hā'ăghālôth	'ăsher-shālach	yôsēph	lāsē'th	'ōthô
to them	then he saw	the wagons	which he sent	Joseph	to carry	him

2513.122	7593	3399	1		569.121	3547	7521
cj, v Qal impf 3fs	*n fs*	pn	n ms, ps 3mp		cj, v Qal impf 3ms	pn	intrj
וַתְּחִי	רוּחַ	יַעֲקֹב	אֲבִיהֶם	**28.**	וַיֹּאמֶר	יִשְׂרָאֵל	רַב
wattechî	rûach	ya'ăqōv	'ăvîhem		wayyō'mer	yisrā'ēl	rav
and it revived	the spirit of	Jacob	their father		and he said	Israel	enough

5968, 3231	1158	2508	2050.125	7495.125	904, 3071	4322.125
adv, pn	n ms, ps 1cs	adj	v Qal impf 1cs	cj, v Qal impf 1cs, ps 3ms	prep, adv	v Qal impf 1cs
עוֹד־יוֹסֵף	בְּנִי	חָי	אֵלְכָה	וְאֶרְאֶנּוּ	בְּטֶרֶם	אָמוּת
'ôdh-yôsēph	benî	chāy	'ēlekhāh	we'er'ennû	beterem	'āmûth
still Joseph	my son	alive	I will go	and I will see him	before	I will die

	5450.121	3547	3725, 866, 3937	971.121	916	916
	cj, v Qal impf 3ms	pn	cj, adj, rel part, prep, ps 3ms	cj, v Qal impf 3ms	pn	pn
46:1	וַיִּסַּע	יִשְׂרָאֵל	וְכָל־אֲשֶׁר־לוֹ	וַיָּבֹא	בְּאֵרָה	שָׁבַע
	wayyissa'	yisrā'ēl	wekhol-'ăsher-lô	wayyāvō'	be'ērāh	shāva'
	and he pulled out	Israel	and all which to him	and he came	to Beer	Sheba

2159.121 cj, v Qal impf 3ms וַיִּזְבַּח wayyizbach and he slaughtered	2160 n mp זְבָחִים zevāchîm sacrifices	3937, 435 prep, *n mp* לֵאלֹהֵי lē'lōhê to the God of	1 n ms, ps אָבִיו 'āvîw his father	3437 pn יִצְחָק yitschāq Isaac	**2.**	569.121 cj, v Qal impf 3ms וַיֹּאמֶר wayyō'mer and He said	435 n mp אֱלֹהִים 'ĕlōhîm God

3937, 3547 prep, pn לְיִשְׂרָאֵל leyisrā'ēl to Israel	904, 4920 prep, *n fp* בְּמַרְאֹת bemar'ōth in the visions of	4050 art, n ms הַלַּיְלָה hallaylāh the night	569.121 cj, v Qal impf 3ms וַיֹּאמֶר wayyō'mer and He said	3399 pn יַעֲקֹב ya'ăqōv Jacob	3399 pn יַעֲקֹב ya'ăqōv Jacob	569.121 cj, v Qal impf 3ms וַיֹּאמֶר wayyō'mer and he said

2079 intrj, ps 1cs הִנֵּנִי hinnēnî behold I	**3.**	569.121 cj, v Qal impf 3ms וַיֹּאמֶר wayyō'mer and He said	609 pers pron אָנֹכִי 'ānōkhî I	418 art, n ms הָאֵל hā'ēl God	435 *n mp* אֱלֹהֵי 'ĕlōhê the God of	1 n ms, ps 2ms אָבִיךָ 'āvîkhā your father	414, 3486.123 adv, Qal juss 2ms אַל־תִּירָא 'al-tîrā' do not fear

be not angry, *Young* ... don't be fretful, *Anchor.*

25. And they went up out of Egypt, and came into the land of Canaan unto Jacob their father: ... ascended to, *Fenton.*

26. And told him, saying, Joseph is yet alive, and he is governor over all the land of Egypt. And Jacob's heart fainted: ... ruler, *NASB* ... unmoved, *MLB* ... stunned, *NASB* ... quite overcome, *BB* ... heart stood still, *NKJV.*

for he believed them not: ... he could not believe him, *Fenton* ... he had no faith in it, *BB.*

27. And they told him all the words of Joseph, which he had said unto them: and when he saw the wagons which Joseph had sent to carry him, the spirit of Jacob their father revived: ... transport, *Berkeley* ... convey, *Goodspeed.*

28. And Israel said, It is enough; Joseph my son is yet alive: I will go and see him before I die: ... I am convinced, *NIV.*

46:1. And Israel took his journey with all that he had, and came to Beersheba, and offered sacrifices unto the God of his father Isaac: ... set out, *Goodspeed* ... Israel consequently marched, and all that were with him, and went to the Well of the Oath, and offered offerings to the God of his father Isaac, *Fenton.*

2. And God spake unto Israel in the visions of the night, and said, Jacob, Jacob. And he said, Here am I: ... At once, He answered, *Anchor.*

3. And he said, I am God, the God of thy father: fear not to go down

45:25-26. When the brothers came to Jacob and told him Joseph was still alive and was ruler over all Egypt, his heart turned cold and numb, that is, he went into a state of shock and his mind went blank, because he did not believe them. Probably he thought this was just another cruel trick to repay him for his own deceit. Moreover, after 22 years of mourning for Joseph, it was hard to believe Joseph was now ruling in Egypt.

45:27-28. The brothers kept telling him all that Joseph told them to. But not until he saw the wagons Joseph sent, did he finally believe. That was enough to convince him and his spirit revived, that is, he took on new life with hope and faith. Then he happily said he would go and see Joseph before he died.

46:1. Jacob started to Egypt as Israel, which may reflect a renewed confidence and faith in the God who had changed his name. Thus he went, not as a refugee or displaced person, but as the prince who had power with God and with men and who had prevailed (32:28). He also went as the head of a family who would be called Israel.

When he came to Beersheba (about two days journey from Hebron), he stopped and offered sacrifices to the God of Isaac. He probably remembered Isaac's sacrifices when God renewed the covenant promises there (26:24-25). He may have remembered how God commanded Isaac not to go to Egypt. Though he had the invitation of Joseph and Pharaoh, human approval was not enough. He wanted to be sure he was going in God's will. He probably expressed his gratitude that Joseph was alive as well.

46:2-4. In night visions God spoke to Israel, calling him Jacob. When Jacob responded, God said, "I am *the* God," that is, the one true God, the God of his father. Jacob need not be afraid to go to

4623, 3495.141	4875	3706, 3937, 1504	1448	7947.125	8427		609
prep, v Qal inf con	pn	cj, prep, n ms	adj	v Qal impf 1cs, ps 2ms	adv	**4.**	pers pron
מֵרְדָה	מִצְרַיְמָה	כִּי־לְגוֹי	גָּדוֹל	אֲשִׂימְךָ	שָׁם		אָנֹכִי
mēr^{e}dhāh	mitsraymāh	kî-l^{e}ghôy	gādhôl	'ăsîm^{e}khā	shām		'ānōkhî
of going	to Egypt	because for nation	great	I will make you	there		I

3495.125	6196	4875	609	6148.525	1612, 6148.142
v Qal impf 1cs	prep, ps 2ms	pn	cj, pers pron	v Hiphil impf 1cs	cj, v Qal inf abs
אֵרֵד	עִמְּךָ	מִצְרַיְמָה	וְאָנֹכִי	אַעַלְךָ	גַם־עָלֹה
'ērēdh	'imm^{e}khā	mitsraymāh	w^e'ānōkhî	'a'al^{e}khā	gham-'ālōh
I will go down	with you	to Egypt	and I	I will cause you to go up	also going up

3231	8308.121	3135	6142, 6084		7251.121	3399	4623, 916
cj, pn	v Qal impf 3ms	n fs, ps 3ms	prep, n fd, ps 2ms	**5.**	cj, v Qal impf 3ms	pn	prep, pn
וְיוֹסֵף	יָשִׁית	יָדוֹ	עַל־עֵינֶיךָ		וַיָּקָם	יַעֲקֹב	מִבְּאֵר
w^{e}yôsēph	yāshîth	yādhô	'al-'ênêkhā		wayyāqām	ya'ăqōv	mibb^e'ēr
and Joseph	he will put	his hand	on your eyes		and he rose up	Jacob	from Beer

916	5558.126	1158, 3547	881, 3399	1	881, 3054
pn	cj, v Qal impf 3mp	*n mp*, pn	do, pn	n ms, ps 3mp	cj, do, n ms, ps 3mp
שָׁבַע	וַיִּשְׂאוּ	בְנֵי־יִשְׂרָאֵל	אֶת־יַעֲקֹב	אֲבִיהֶם	וְאֶת־טַפָּם
shāva'	wayyis'û	v^{e}nê-yisrā'ēl	'eth-ya'ăqōv	'ăvîhem	w^e'eth-ṭappām
Sheba	and they lifted up	the sons of Israel	Jacob	their father	and their little children

881, 5571	904, 5906	866, 8365.111	6799	3937, 5558.141	881
cj, do, n fp, ps 3mp	prep, art, n fp	rel part, v Qal pf 3ms	pn	prep, v Qal inf con	do, ps 3ms
וְאֶת־נְשֵׁיהֶם	בָּעֲגָלוֹת	אֲשֶׁר־שָׁלַח	פַּרְעֹה	לָשֵׂאת	אֹתוֹ
w^e'eth-n^{e}shêhem	bā'ăghālôth	'ăsher-shālach	par'ōh	lāsē'th	'ōthô
and their wives	in the wagons	which he sent	Pharaoh	to carry	him

	4089.126	881, 4898	881, 7688	866	7697.116	904, 800
6.	cj, v Qal impf 3mp	do, n ms, ps 3mp	cj, do, n ms, ps 3mp	rel part	v Qal pf 3cp	prep, *n fs*
	וַיִּקְחוּ	אֶת־מִקְנֵיהֶם	וְאֶת־רְכוּשָׁם	אֲשֶׁר	רָכְשׁוּ	בְּאֶרֶץ
	wayyiqŏchû	'eth-miqŏnêhem	w^e'eth-r^{e}khûshām	'ăsher	rākh^{e}shû	b^e'erets
	and they took	their livestock	and their belongings	which	they acquired	in the land of

3791	971.126	4875	3399	3725, 2320	882		1158
pn	cj, v Qal impf 3mp	pn	pn	cj, *adj*, n ms, ps 3ms	prep, ps 3ms	**7.**	n mp, ps 3ms
כְּנַעַן	וַיָּבֹאוּ	מִצְרָיְמָה	יַעֲקֹב	וְכָל־זַרְעוֹ	אִתּוֹ		בָּנָיו
k^{e}na'an	wayyāvō'û	mitsrâ^{e}māh	ya'ăqōv	w^{e}khol-zar'ô	'ittô		bānâv
Canaan	and they went	to Egypt	Jacob	and all his seed	with him		his sons

1158	1158	882	1351	1351	1158	3725, 2320
cj, n mp	n mp, ps 3ms	prep, ps 3ms	n fp, ps 3ms	*n fp*	n mp, ps 3ms	cj, *adj*, n ms, ps 3ms
וּבְנֵי	בָנָיו	אִתּוֹ	בְּנֹתָיו	וּבְנוֹת	בָּנָיו	וְכָל־זַרְעוֹ
ûv^{e}nê	vānâv	'ittô	b^{e}nōthâv	ûv^{e}nôth	bānâv	w^{e}khol-zar'ô
and the sons of	his sons	with him	his daughters	and the daughters of	his sons	and all his seed

971.511	882	4875		431	8428	1158, 3547
v Hiphil pf 3ms	prep, ps 3ms	pn	**8.**	cj, dem pron	*n mp*	*n mp*, pn
הֵבִיא	אִתּוֹ	מִצְרָיְמָה		וְאֵלֶּה	שְׁמוֹת	בְּנֵי־יִשְׂרָאֵל
hēvî'	'ittô	mitsrâ^{e}māh		w^e'ēlleh	sh^{e}môth	b^{e}nê-yisrā'ēl
he brought	with him	to Egypt		and these	the names of	the sons of Israel

971.152	4875	3399	1158	1111	3399	7498
art, v Qal act ptc mp	pn	pn	cj, n mp, ps 3ms	*n ms*	pn	pn
הַבָּאִים	מִצְרַיְמָה	יַעֲקֹב	וּבָנָיו	בְּכֹר	יַעֲקֹב	רְאוּבֵן
habbā'îm	mitsraymāh	ya'ăqōv	ûvānâv	b^{e}khōr	ya'ăqōv	r^e'ûvēn
going	to Egypt	Jacob	and his sons	the first-born of	Jacob	Reuben

9.	1158 cj, *n mp* וּבְנֵי ûvnê and the sons of	7498 pn רְאוּבֵן re'ûvēn Reuben	2686 pn חֲנוֹךְ chănôkh Hanock	6641 cj, pn וּפַלּוּא ûphallû' and Pallu	2797 cj, pn וְחֶצְרוֹן wechetsrôn and Hezron	3886 cj, pn וְכַרְמִי wekharmî and Carmi	10.	1158 cj, *n mp* וּבְנֵי ûvnê and the sons of

8482 pn שִׁמְעוֹן shim'ôn Simeon	3330 pn יְמוּאֵל yemû'ēl Jemuel	3333 cj, pn וְיָמִין weyāmîn and Jamin	158 cj, pn וְאֹהַד we'ōhadh and Ohad	3308 cj, pn וְיָכִין weyākhîn and Jachin	6982 cj, pn וְצֹחַר wetsōchar and Zohar	8062 cj, pn וְשָׁאוּל weshā'ûl and Shaul

1158, 3793 *n ms*, art, pn בֶּן־הַכְּנַעֲנִית ben-hakkena'ănîth the son of the Canaanite woman	11.	1158 cj, *n mp* וּבְנֵי ûvnê and the sons of	4015 pn לֵוִי lēwî Levi	1695 pn גֵּרְשׁוֹן gērshôn Gershon	7239 pn קְהָת qŏhāth Kohath	5010 cj, pn וּמְרָרִי ûmerārî Merari

into Egypt; for I will there make of thee a great nation: ... I am El, *Anchor* ... Don't be afraid to go down to Egypt, *NIV* ... I will make of you a great nation there, *NKJV.*

4. I will go down with thee into Egypt; and I will also surely bring thee up again: ... I, The Mighty, *Fenton* ... I will see that you come back again, *BB* ... I myself will bring you back again, *Anchor* ... I will support you, *Fenton*.

and Joseph shall put his hand upon thine eyes: ... and Joseph's will be the hands that close your eyes, *REB* ... Joseph will be with you when you die, *Good News* ... after Joseph has closed your eyes, *NAB*.

5. And Jacob rose up from Beersheba: ... set out, *REB* ... The Wellof Oaths, *Fenton*.

and the sons of Israel carried Jacob their father, and their little ones: ... dependants, *NEB* ... infants, *Young*.

and their wives, in the wagons which Pharaoh had sent to carry him: ... carts, *NKJV*, *BB* ... charets, *Geneva*.

6. And they took their cattle, and their goods: ... property, *NASB*, *Fenton* ... moveable belongings, *Berkeley* ... They took the herds and the stock, *NEB*.

which they had gotten in the land of Canaan, and came into Egypt, Jacob, and all his seed with him: ... Jacob and all his descendants migrated to Egypt, *NCB*, *NAB* ... Jacob and all his race, *Fenton* ... all his offspring, *Anchor*, *NRSV.*

7. His sons, and his sons' sons with him, his daughters, and his sons' daughters: ... grandsons, *NCB* ... granddaughters, *NASB*.

and all his seed brought he with him into Egypt: ... and all his descendants migrated to Egypt, *NCB* ... all his offspring, *Anchor.*

8. And these are the names of the children of Israel, which came into Egypt, Jacob and his sons: Reuben, Jacob's firstborn.

9. And the sons of Reuben; Hanoch, and Phallu, and Hezron, and Carmi.

10. And the sons of Simeon; Jemuel, and Jamin, and Ohad, and Jachin, and Zohar, and Shaul the son of a Canaanitish woman.

11. And the sons of Levi; Gershon, Kohath, and Merari.

Egypt. God promised to make him a great nation there. God would go with him and would surely bring him back. Joseph would put his hands on his eyes to close them in death. Thus, Joseph would live and Jacob would die in peace. Jacob's going down with his family would also make possible fulfillment of the prophecy God gave Abraham (15:13-16). This journey to Egypt was an important stage in God's larger plan for the nation of Israel.

46:5-7. With this encouragement from God, Jacob rose up and went on to Egypt. His sons carried Jacob, their wives, and the little children in Pharaoh's wagons. They took everything and everyone belonging to Jacob with them.

46:8-27. The names of the sons of Jacob and their wives and children are listed, naming the children of Leah and their sons first, then the sons of Zilpah and their children and grandchildren, then the sons of Rachel with the note that the sons of Joseph were born in Egypt, then the sons of Bilhah

	1158	3171	6385	207	8349	6807	2313
12.	cj, *n mp*	pn	pn	cj, pn	cj, pn	cj, pn	cj, pn
	וּבְנֵי	יְהוּדָה	עֵר	וְאוֹנָן	וְשֵׁלָה	וָפֶרֶץ	וָזָרַח
	ûvenê	yehûdhāh	‘ēr	we'ônān	weshēlāh	wāpherets	wāzarach
	and the sons of	Judah	Er	and Onan	and Shelah	and Perez	and Zerah

4322.121	6385	207	904, 800	3791	2030.126	1158, 6807
cj, v Qal impf 3ms	pn	cj, pn	prep, *n fs*	pn	cj, v Qal impf 3mp	*n mp*, pn
וַיָּמָת	עֵר	וְאוֹנָן	בְּאֶרֶץ	כְּנַעַן	וַיִּהְיוּ	בְנֵי־פֶרֶץ
wayyāmāth	‘ēr	we'ônān	be'erets	kena‘an	wayyihyû	venê-pherets
and he died	Er	and Onan	in the land of	Canaan	and they were	the sons of Perez

2797	2639		1158	3551	8769	6557	3205	8496
pn	cj, pn	**13.**	cj, *n mp*	pn	pn	cj, pn	cj, pn	cj, pn
חֶצְרוֹן	וְחָמוּל		וּבְנֵי	יִשָּׂכָר	תּוֹלָע	וּפֻוָּה	וְיוֹב	וְשִׁמְרוֹן
chetsrôn	wechāmûl		ûvenê	yisākhār	tôlā‘	ûphuwwāh	weyôv	weshimrôn
Hezron	and Hamul		and the sons of	Issachar	Tola	and Puvah	and Job	and Shimron

	1158	2157	5825	442	3283		431	1158	3943
14.	cj, *n mp*	pn	pn	cj, pn	cj, pn	**15.**	dem pron	*n mp*	pn
	וּבְנֵי	זְבוּלֻן	סֶרֶד	וְאֵלוֹן	וְיַחְלְאֵל		אֵלֶּה	בְּנֵי	לֵאָה
	ûvenê	zevûlun	seredh	we'ēlôn	weyachle'ēl		'ēlleh	benê	lē'āh
	and the sons of	Zebulun	Sered	and Elon	and Jahleel		these	the sons of	Leah

866	3314.112	3937, 3399	904, 6549	782	881	1839	1351
rel part	v Qal pf 3fs	prep, pn	prep, pn	pn	cj, do	pn	n fs, ps 3ms
אֲשֶׁר	יָלְדָה	לְיַעֲקֹב	בְּפַדַּן	אֲרָם	וְאֵת	דִּינָה	בִתּוֹ
'ăsher	yāledhāh	leya‘ăqōv	bephaddan	'ărām	we'ēth	dînāh	vittô
which	she gave birth	for Jacob	in Paddan	Aram	and	Dinah	his daughter

3725, 5497	1158	1351	8389	8421		1158	1440
adj, n fs	n mp, ps 3ms	cj, n fp, ps 3ms	num	cj, num	**16.**	cj, *n mp*	pn
כָּל־נֶפֶשׁ	בָּנָיו	וּבְנוֹתָיו	שְׁלֹשִׁים	וְשָׁלֹשׁ		וּבְנֵי	גָד
kol-nephesh	bānâv	ûvnôthâ	shelōshîm	weshālōsh		ûvenê	ghādh
all the people of	his sons	and his daughters	thirty	and three		and the sons of	Gad

7114	2386	8206	696	6418	745	715		1158
pn	cj, pn	pn	cj, pn	pn	cj, pn	cj, pn	**17.**	cj, *n mp*
צִפְיוֹן	וְחַגִּי	שׁוּנִי	וְאֶצְבֹּן	עֵרִי	וַאֲרוֹדִי	וְאַרְאֵלִי		וּבְנֵי
tsiphyôn	wechaggî	shûnî	we'etsbōn	‘ērî	wa'ărôdhî	we'ar'ēlî		ûvenê
Ziphion	and Haggi	Shuni	and Ezbon	Eri	and Arodi	and Areli		and the sons of

862	3341	3563	3565	1309	8026	269	1158
pn	pn	cj, pn	cj, pn	cj, pn	cj, pn	n fs, ps 3mp	cj, *n mp*
אָשֵׁר	יִמְנָה	וְיִשְׁוָה	וְיִשְׁוִי	וּבְרִיעָה	וְשֶׂרַח	אֲחֹתָם	וּבְנֵי
'āshēr	yimnāh	weyishwāh	weyishwî	ûverî‘āh	weserach	'ăchōthām	ûvenê
Asher	Imnah	and Ishvah	and Ishvi	and Beriah	and Serah	their sister	and the sons of

1309	2361	4578		431	1158	2238	866, 5598.111	3969
pn	pn	cj, pn	**18.**	dem pron	*n mp*	pn	rel part, v Qal pf 3ms	pn
בְרִיעָה	חֶבֶר	וּמַלְכִּיאֵל		אֵלֶּה	בְּנֵי	זִלְפָּה	אֲשֶׁר־נָתַן	לָבָן
verî‘āh	chever	ûmalkî'ēl		'ēlleh	benê	zilpāh	'ăsher-nāthan	lāvān
Beriah	Heber	and Malchiel		these	the sons of	Zilpah	which he gave	Laban

3937, 3943	1351	3314.122	881, 431	3937, 3399	8666	6462	5497
prep, pn	n fs, ps 3ms	cj, v Qal impf 3fs	do, dem pron	prep, pn	num	num	n fs
לְלֵאָה	בִתּוֹ	וַתֵּלֶד	אֶת־אֵלֶּה	לְיַעֲקֹב	שֵׁשׁ	עֶשְׂרֵה	נָפֶשׁ
lelē'āh	vittô	wattēledh	'eth-'ēlleh	leya‘ăqōv	shēsh	‘esrēh	nāphesh
to Leah	his daughter	and she gave birth	to these	to Jacob	six	ten	people

19.	1158	7637	828	3399	3231	1175	20.	3314.221
	n mp	pn	*n fs*	pn	pn	cj, pn		cj, v Niphal impf 3ms
	בְּנֵי	רָחֵל	אֵשֶׁת	יַעֲקֹב	יוֹסֵף	וּבִנְיָמִן		וַיִּוָּלֵד
	b^{e}nê	rāchēl	'ēsheth	ya'ăqōv	yôsēph	ûvinyāmin		wayyiwwālēdh
	the sons of	Rachel	the wife of	Jacob	Joseph	and Benjamin		and he was born

3937, 3231	904, 800	4875	866	3314.112, 3937	635	1351, 6562
prep, pn	prep, *n fs*	pn	rel part	v Qal pf 3fs, prep, ps 3ms	pn	*n fs*, pn
לְיוֹסֵף	בְּאֶרֶץ	מִצְרַיִם	אֲשֶׁר	יָלְדָה־לּוֹ	אָסְנַת	בַּת־פּוֹטִי
l^{e}yôsēph	b^{e}'erets	mitsrayim	'ăsher	yāl^{e}dhāh-lô	'ās^{e}nath	bath-pôṭî
to Joseph	in the land of	Egypt	which	she gave birth for him	Asenath	the daughter of Poti

6562	3669	203	881, 4667	881, 688	21.	1158	1175	1145
pn	*n ms*	pn	do, pn	cj, do, pn		cj, *n mp*	pn	pn
פֶרַע	כֹּהֵן	אֹן	אֶת־מְנַשֶּׁה	וְאֶת־אֶפְרָיִם		וּבְנֵי	בִנְיָמִן	בֶּלַע
phera'	kōhēn	'ōn	'eth-m^{e}nashsheh	w^{e}'eth-'ephrāyim		ûv^{e}nê	vinyāmin	bela'
phera	the priest of	On	Manasseh	and Ephraim		and the sons of	Benjamin	Bela

1110	817	1660	5465	279	7515	4811	2755
cj, pn	cj, pn	pn	cj, pn	pn	cj, pn	pn	cj, pn
וָבֶכֶר	וְאַשְׁבֵּל	גֵּרָא	וְנַעֲמָן	אֵחִי	וָרֹאשׁ	מֻפִּים	וְחֻפִּים
wāvekher	w^{e}'ashbēl	gērā'	wena'ămān	'ēchî	wārō'sh	muppîm	w^{e}chuppîm
and Becher	and Ashbel	Gera	and Naaman	Ehi	and Rosh	Muppim	and Huppim

737	22.	431	1158	7637	866	3314.411	3937, 3399	3725, 5497
cj, pn		dem pron	*n mp*	pn	rel part	v Pual pf 3ms	prep, pn	*adj, n fs*
וָאָרְדְּ		אֵלֶּה	בְּנֵי	רָחֵל	אֲשֶׁר	יֻלַּד	לְיַעֲקֹב	כָּל־נֶפֶשׁ
wā'ār^{e}dd^{e}		'ēlleh	b^{e}nê	rāchēl	'ăsher	yulladh	l^{e}ya'ăqōv	kol-nephesh
and Ard		these	the sons of	Rachel	which	they were born	Jacob	all people of

12. And the sons of Judah; Er, and Onan, and Shelah, and Pharez, and Zerah: but Er and Onan died in the land of Canaan. And the sons of Pharez were Hezron and Hamul.

13. And the sons of Issachar; Tola, and Phuvah, and Job, and Shimron.

14. And the sons of Zebulun; Sered, and Elon, and Jahleel.

15. These be the sons of Leah, which she bare unto Jacob in Padanaram, with his daughter Dinah: all the souls of his sons and his daughters were thirty and three.

16. And the sons of Gad; Ziphion, and Haggi, Shuni, and Ezbon, Eri, and Arodi, and Areli.

17. And the sons of Asher; Jimnah, and Ishuah, and Isui, and Beriah, and Serah their sister: and the sons of Beriah; Heber, and Malchiel.

18. These are the sons of Zilpah, whom Laban gave to Leah his daughter, and these she bare unto Jacob, even sixteen souls.

19. The sons of Rachel Jacob's wife; Joseph, and Benjamin.

20. And unto Joseph in the land of Egypt were born Manasseh and Ephraim, which Asenath the daughter of Potipherah priest of On bare unto him.

21. And the sons of Benjamin were Belah, and Becher, and Ashbel, Gera, and Naaman, Ehi, and Rosh, Muppim, and Huppim, and Ard.

22. These are the sons of Rachel, which were born to Jacob: all the souls were fourteen.

and their children. Those who came with Jacob into Egypt numbered 66. Joseph, with his wife and two sons, brought the number of Jacob's descendants in Egypt to 70. Acts 7:15 mentions 75, because the Septuagint list adds a son and grandson of Manasseh and two sons and a grandsons of Ephraim. The Septuagint also names three sons of Benjamin and lists the others as grandsons. Some suggest neither list is meant to tell us the names of the ones who actually came down with Jacob, but rather to list those in Egypt who became heads of clans that continued to be important in Israel's history. The wives of the sons and grandsons are not listed. There may have been other small children, as well as servants. So the actual number settling in Goshen may have been considerably larger.

727	6461		1158, 1896	2459		1158	5503	3289
num	num		cj, *n mp*, pn	pn		cj, *n mp*	pn	pn
אַרְבָּעָה	עָשָׂר	**23.**	וּבְנֵי־דָן	חֻשִׁים	**24.**	וּבְנֵי	נַפְתָּלִי	יַחְצְאֵל
'arbā'āh	'āsār		ûv^{e}nêy-dhān	chushîm		ûv^{e}nê	naphtālî	yachts^{e}'ēl
four	ten		and the sons of Dan	Hushim		and the sons of	Naphtali	Jahzeel

1509	3445	8403		431	1158	1131	866, 5598.111
cj, pn	cj, pn	cj, pn		dem pron	*n mp*	pn	rel part, v Qal pf 3ms
וְגוּנִי	וְיֵצֶר	וְשִׁלֵּם	**25.**	אֵלֶּה	בְּנֵי	בִּלְהָה	אֲשֶׁר־נָתַן
w^{e}ghûnî	w^{e}yētser	w^{e}shillēm		'ēlleh	b^{e}nê	vilhāh	'ăsher-nāthan
and Guni	and Jezer	and Shillem		these	the sons of	Bilhah	which he gave

3969	3937, 7637	1351	3314.122	881, 431	3937, 3399	3725, 5497
pn	prep, pn	n fs, ps 3ms	cj, v Qal impf 3fs	do, dem pron	prep, pn	*adj, n fs*
לָבָן	לְרָחֵל	בִּתּוֹ	וַתֵּלֶד	אֶת־אֵלֶּה	לְיַעֲקֹב	כָּל־נֶפֶשׁ
lāvān	l^{e}rāchēl	bittô	wattēledh	'eth-'ēlleh	l^{e}ya'ăqōv	kol-nephesh
Laban	to Rachel	his daughter	and she gave birth	to these	for Jacob	all people of

8124		3725, 5497	971.153	3937, 3399	4875	3428.152
num		*adj*, art, n fs	art, v Qal act ptc fs	prep, pn	pn	*v Qal act ptc mp*
שִׁבְעָה	**26.**	כָּל־הַנֶּפֶשׁ	הַבָּאָה	לְיַעֲקֹב	מִצְרַיְמָה	יֹצְאֵי
shiv^{e}'āh		kol-hannephesh	habbā'āh	l^{e}ya'ăqōv	mitsraymāh	yōts'ê
seven		all the people	coming	for Jacob	to Egypt	ones coming out of

3525	4623, 3937, 940	5571	1158, 3399	3725, 5497	8666	8666
n fs, ps 3ms	prep, prep, n ms	*n fp*	*n mp*, pn	*adj, n fs*	num	cj, num
יְרֵכוֹ	מִלְּבַד	נְשֵׁי	בְנֵי־יַעֲקֹב	כָּל־נֶפֶשׁ	שִׁשִּׁים	וָשֵׁשׁ
y^{e}rēkhô	mill^{e}vadh	n^{e}shê	v^{e}nê-ya'ăqōv	kol-nephesh	shishshîm	wāshēsh
his loins	by themselves	the wives of	the sons of Jacob	all people of	sixty	and six

	1158	3231	866, 3314.411, 3937	904, 4875	5497	8530
	cj, *n mp*	pn	rel part, v Pual pf 3ms, prep, ps 3ms	prep, pn	n fs	num
27.	וּבְנֵי	יוֹסֵף	אֲשֶׁר־יֻלַּד־לוֹ	בְמִצְרַיִם	נֶפֶשׁ	שְׁנָיִם
	ûv^{e}nê	yôsēph	'ăsher-yulladh-lô	v^{e}mitsrayim	nephesh	sh^{e}nāyim
	and the sons of	Joseph	which he was born for him	in Egypt	people	two

3725, 5497	3937, 1041, 3399	971.153	4875	8124		881, 3171
adj, art, n fs	prep, *n ms*, pn	art, v Qal act ptc fs	pn	num		cj, do, pn
כָּל־הַנֶּפֶשׁ	לְבֵית־יַעֲקֹב	הַבָּאָה	מִצְרַיְמָה	שִׁבְעִים	**28.**	וְאֶת־יְהוּדָה
kol-hannephesh	l^{e}vêth-ya'ăqōv	habbā'āh	mitsraymāh	shiv'îm		w^{e}'eth-y^{e}hûdhāh
all the people	to the house of Jacob	coming	to Egypt	seventy		and Judah

8365.111	3937, 6686	420, 3231	3937, 3498.541	3937, 6686	1705	971.126
v Qal pf 3ms	prep, n mp, ps 3ms	prep, pn	prep, v Hiphil inf con	prep, n mp, ps 3ms	pn	cj, v Qal impf 3mp
שָׁלַח	לְפָנָיו	אֶל־יוֹסֵף	לְהוֹרֹת	לְפָנָיו	גֹּשְׁנָה	וַיָּבֹאוּ
shālach	l^{e}phānâv	'el-yôsēph	l^{e}hôrōth	l^{e}phānâv	gōsh^{e}nāh	wayyāvō'û
he sent	before him	to Joseph	to instruct	before him	to Goshen	and they went

800	1705		646.121	3231	4981	6148.121
n fs	pn		cj, v Qal impf 3ms	pn	n fs, ps 3ms	cj, v Qal impf 3ms
אַרְצָה	גֹּשֶׁן	**29.**	וַיֶּאְסֹר	יוֹסֵף	מֶרְכַּבְתּוֹ	וַיַּעַל
'artsāh	gōshen		wayye'ăsōr	yôsēph	merkavtô	wayya'al
to the land of	Goshen		and he harnessed	Joseph	his chariot	and he went up

3937, 7410.141, 3547	1	1705	7495.221	420	5489
prep, v Qal inf con, pn	n ms, ps	pn	cj, v Niphal impf 3ms	prep, ps 3ms	cj, v Qal impf 3ms
לִקְרַאת־יִשְׂרָאֵל	אָבִיו	גֹּשְׁנָה	וַיֵּרָא	אֵלָיו	וַיִּפֹּל
liqōra'th-yisrā'ēl	'āvîw	gōsh nāh	wayyērā'	'ēlâv	wayyippōl
to meet Israel	his father	to Goshen	and he was seen	to him	and he fell

6142, 6939 prep, n ms, ps 3ms עַל־צַוָּארָיו 'al-tsawwā'râv on his neck	1098.121 cj, v Qal impf 3ms וַיֵּבְךְּ wayyēvekh and he wept	6142, 6939 prep, n ms, ps 3ms עַל־צַוָּארָיו 'al-tsawwā'râv on his neck	5968 adv עוֹד 'ôdh a while	**30.**	569.121 cj, v Qal impf 3ms וַיֹּאמֶר wayyō'mer and he said	3547 pn יִשְׂרָאֵל yisrā'ēl Israel	420, 3231 prep, pn אֶל־יוֹסֵף 'el-yôsēph to Joseph

4322.125 v Qal impf 1cs אָמוּתָה 'āmûthāh I may die	6718 art, n fs הַפָּעַם happā'am the time	311 *sub* אַחֲרֵי 'achrê after	7495.141 v Qal inf con, ps 1cs רְאוֹתִי reothî my seeing	881, 6686 do, n mp, ps 2ms אֶת־פָּנֶיךָ 'eth-pānêkhā your face	3706 cj כִּי kî because	5968 adv, ps 2ms עוֹדְךָ 'ôdhekhā still you

2508 adj חָי chāy alive	**31.**	569.121 cj, v Qal impf 3ms וַיֹּאמֶר wayyō'mer and he said	3231 pn יוֹסֵף yôsēph Joseph	420, 250 prep, n ms, ps 3ms אֶל־אֶחָיו 'el-'echâv to his brothers	420, 1041 cj, prep, *n ms* וְאֶל־בֵּית we'el-bêth and to the house of	1 n ms, ps אָבִיו 'āvîw his father	6148.125 v Qal impf 1cs אֶעֱלֶה 'e'ĕleh I will go up

5222.525 cj, v Hiphil impf 1cs וְאַגִּידָה we'aggîdhāh and I will report	3937, 6799 prep, pn לְפַרְעֹה lephar'ōh to Pharaoh	569.125 cj, v Qal impf 1cs וְאֹמְרָה we'ōmerāh and I will say	420 prep, ps 3ms אֵלָיו 'ēlâv to him	250 n mp, ps 1cs אַחַי 'achay my brothers	1041, 1 cj, *n ms*, n ms, ps 1cs וּבֵית־אָבִי ûvêth-'āvî and the house of my father

23. And the sons of Dan; Hushim.

24. And the sons of Naphtali; Jahzeel, and Guni, and Jezer, and Shillem.

25. These are the sons of Bilhah, which Laban gave unto Rachel his daughter, and she bare these unto Jacob: all the souls were seven.

26. All the souls that came with Jacob into Egypt, which came out of his loins, besides Jacob's sons' wives, all the souls were threescore and six;

27. And the sons of Joseph, which were born him in Egypt, were two souls: all the souls of the house of Jacob, which came into Egypt, were threescore and ten.

28. And he sent Judah before him unto Joseph, to direct his face unto Goshen; and they came into the land of Goshen: ... to advise him that he was on his way to Goshen, *REB* ... to point out before him the way, *NKJV* ... to give notice before he came to Goshen, *Darby* ... to invite Joseph to meet him in Goshen, *Fenton* ... they arrived in the Goshen district, *Berkeley.*

29. And Joseph made ready his chariot: ... carriage, *BB* ... and Joseph had his chariot yoked, *REB* ... On their arrival in the land of Goshen Joseph hitched the horses to his chariot, *Goodspeed.*

and went up to meet Israel his father, to Goshen, and presented himself unto him; and he fell on his neck, and wept on his neck a good while: ... threw his arms round him, *REB* ... put his arms around his neck, weeping, *BB* ... hugged him again and again, *Berkeley.*

30. And Israel said unto Joseph, Now let me die, since I have seen thy face, because thou art yet alive: ... and know that you are still alive, *RSV* ... Now that I have seen you living again, I am ready for death, *BB.*

31. And Joseph said unto his brethren, and unto his father's

46:28. Before reaching Goshen, Jacob sent Judah ahead to give information to Joseph. This probably means Jacob wanted Joseph to guide them to the best part of Goshen.

46:29-30. Joseph responded by harnessing his chariot and going to Goshen where he fell on his father's neck, that is, he hugged him and wept while hugging him for a while. Then Israel, his father, expressed his readiness to die now that he had seen Joseph and knew he was alive. This does not mean Jacob was anxious to die. Rather, he no longer had the load of grief and the fear of dying and going to hell. Now whenever he died, he could die in peace with his hope in God. He did not die until 17 years later (47:28).

46:31-32. Joseph told his brothers and the rest of Jacob's household that he was going to report their arrival to Pharaoh and explain that the men were shepherds, men of livestock, who had come with their flocks and herds.

866	904, 800, 3791	971.116	420		596	7749.152	6887
rel part	prep, *n fs*, pn	v Qal pf 3cp	prep, ps 1cs	**32.**	cj, art, n mp	*v Qal act ptc mp*	n fs
אֲשֶׁר	בְּאֶרֶץ־כְּנָעַן	בָּאוּ	אֵלָי		וְהָאֲנָשִׁים	רֹעֵי	צֹאן
'ăsher	b^{e}'erets-k^{e}na'an	bā'û	'ēlāy		w^{e}hā'ănāshîm	rō'ê	tsō'n
which	in the land of Canaan	they came	to me		and the men	shepherds of	flocks

3706, 596	4898	2030.116	6887	1267	3725, 866	3937
cj, *n mp*	n ms	v Qal pf 3cp	cj, n fs, ps 3mp	cj, n ms, ps 3mp	cj, adj, rel part	prep, ps 3mp
כִּי־אַנְשֵׁי	מִקְנֶה	הָיוּ	וְצֹאנָם	וּבְקָרָם	וְכָל־אֲשֶׁר	לָהֶם
kî-'anshê	miqōneh	hāyû	w^{e}tsō'nām	ûv^{e}qārām	w^{e}khol-'ăsher	lāhem
because men of	livestock	they are	and their flocks	and their herds	and all which	to them

971.516		2030.111	3706, 7410.121	3937	6799	569.111
v Hiphil pf 3cp	**33.**	cj, v Qal pf 3ms	cj, v Qal impf 3ms	prep, ps 2mp	pn	cj, v Qal pf 3ms
הֵבִיאוּ		וְהָיָה	כִּי־יִקְרָא	לָכֶם	פַּרְעֹה	וְאָמַר
hēvî'û		w^{e}hāyāh	kî-yiqōrā'	lākhem	par'ōh	w^{e}'āmar
they brought		and it will be	that he will summon	you	Pharaoh	and he will say

4242, 4801		569.117	596	4898	2030.116	5860
intrg, n mp, ps 2mp	**34.**	cj, v Qal pf 2mp	*n mp*	n ms	v Qal pf 3cp	n mp, ps 2ms
מַה־מַּעֲשֵׂיכֶם		וַאֲמַרְתֶּם	אַנְשֵׁי	מִקְנֶה	הָיוּ	עֲבָדֶיךָ
mah-ma'ăsêkhem		wa'ămartem	'anshê	miqōneh	hāyû	'ăvādhêkhā
what is your work		and you will say	men of	livestock	they are	your servants

4623, 5454	5912, 6498	1612, 601	1612, 1	904, 5877	3553
prep, n mp, ps 1cp	cj, prep, adv	cj, pers pron	cj, n mp, ps 1cp	prep, prep	v Qal impf 2mp
מִנְּעוּרֵינוּ	וְעַד־עַתָּה	גַּם־אֲנַחְנוּ	גַּם־אֲבֹתֵינוּ	בַּעֲבוּר	תֵּשְׁבוּ
minn^{e}'ûrênû	w^{e}'adh-'attāh	gam-'ănachnû	gam-'ăvōthênû	ba'ăvûr	tēsh^{e}vû
from our youth	and until now	both we	and our fathers	in order that	you will dwell

904, 800	1705	3706, 8774	4875	3725, 7749.151	6887
prep, *n fs*	pn	cj, *n fs*	pn	adj, *v Qal act ptc ms*	n fs
בְּאֶרֶץ	גֹּשֶׁן	כִּי־תוֹעֲבַת	מִצְרַיִם	כָּל־רֹעֵה	צֹאן
b^{e}'erets	gōshen	kî-thô'ăvath	mitsrayim	kol-rō'ēh	tsō'n
in the land of	Goshen	because a detestable thing of	Egyptians	every shepherd of	flocks

	971.121	3231	5222.521	3937, 6799	569.121	1
47:1	cj, v Qal impf 3ms	pn	cj, v Hiphil impf 3ms	prep, pn	cj, v Qal impf 3ms	n ms, ps 1cs
	וַיָּבֹא	יוֹסֵף	וַיַּגֵּד	לְפַרְעֹה	וַיֹּאמֶר	אָבִי
	wayyāvō'	yôsēph	wayyaggēdh	l^{e}phar'ōh	wayyō'mer	'āvî
	and he went	Joseph	and he told	to Pharaoh	and he said	my father

250	6887	1267	3725, 866	3937	971.116
cj, n mp	cj, n fs, ps 3mp	cj, n ms, ps 3mp	cj, *adj*, rel part	prep, ps 3mp	v Qal pf 3cp
וְאַחַי	וְצֹאנָם	וּבְקָרָם	וְכָל־אֲשֶׁר	לָהֶם	בָּאוּ
w^{e}'achay	w^{e}tsō'nām	ûv^{e}qārām	w^{e}khol-'ăsher	lāhem	bā'û
and my brothers	and their flocks	and their herds	and all which	to them	they came

4623, 800	3791	2079	904, 800	1705		4623, 7381
prep, *n fs*	pn	cj, intrj, ps 3mp	prep, *n fs*	pn	**2.**	cj, prep, *n ms*
מֵאֶרֶץ	כְּנָעַן	וְהִנָּם	בְּאֶרֶץ	גֹּשֶׁן		וּמִקְצֵה
mē'erets	k^{e}nā'an	w^{e}hinnām	b^{e}'erets	gōshen		ûmiqōtsēh
from the land of	Canaan	and behold they	in the land of	Goshen		and from all

250	4089.111	2675	596	3431.521	3937, 6686	6799
n mp, ps 3ms	v Qal pf 3ms	num	n mp	cj, v Hiphil impf 3ms, ps 3mp	prep, *n mp*	pn
אֶחָיו	לָקַח	חֲמִשָּׁה	אֲנָשִׁים	וַיַּצִּגֵם	לִפְנֵי	פַרְעֹה
'echâv	lāqach	chămishshāh	'ănāshîm	wayyatstsighēm	liphnê	phar'ōh
his brothers	he took	five	men	and he placed them	before	Pharaoh

3.	569.121 cj, v Qal impf 3ms וַיֹּאמֶר wayyō'mer and he said	6799 pn פַּרְעֹה par'ōh Pharaoh	420, 250 prep, n ms, ps 3ms אֶל־אֶחָיו 'el-'echâv to his brothers	4242, 4801 intrg, n mp, ps 2mp מַה־מַּעֲשֵׂיכֶם mah-ma'ăsêkhem what is your work	569.126 cj, v Qal impf 3mp וַיֹּאמְרוּ wayyō'm^{e}rû and they said	420, 6799 prep, pn אֶל־פַּרְעֹה 'el-par'ōh to Pharaoh

7749.151 *v Qal act ptc ms* רֹעֵה rō'ēh shepherd of	6887 n fs צֹאן tsō'n flocks	5860 n mp, ps 2ms עֲבָדֶיךָ 'ăvādhêkhā your servants	1612, 601 cj, pers pron גַּם־אֲנַחְנוּ gam-'ănachnû both we	1612, 1 cj, n mp, ps 1cp גַּם־אֲבוֹתֵינוּ gam-'ăvôthênû and our fathers	4.	569.126 cj, v Qal impf 3mp וַיֹּאמְרוּ wayyō'm^{e}rû and they said

house; I will go up, and shew Pharaoh, and say unto him, My brethren, and my father's house, which were in the land of Canaan, are come unto me: ... who used to live in the land of Canaan have come to me, *Goodspeed* ... formerly of Canaan, *Anchor.*

32. And the men are shepherds, for their trade hath been to feed cattle; and they have brought their flocks, and their herds, and all that they have: ... for they breed livestock, *NCB* ... they have been keepers of livestock, *NASB* ... for they have been occupied with cattle, *Darby.*

33. And it shall come to pass, when Pharaoh shall call you, and shall say, What is your occupation?: ... What can you do?, *Fenton* ... What are your works?, *Young* ... What is your business?, *BB.*

34. That ye shall say, Thy servants' trade hath been about cattle: ... We your servants have bred livestock, *NCB* ... keepers of livestock, *NASB* ... They have lived with people of the fold, *Fenton.*

from our youth even until now, both we, and also our fathers: ... from the beginning until now, *NAB* ... from our boyhood on, just as our fathers did, *NIV.*

that ye may dwell in the land of Goshen; for every shepherd is an abomination unto the Egyptians: ... settle, *Berkeley* ... repugnant, *NCB* ... loathsome, *NASB* ... For the Mitzerites hate every shepherd of sheep, *Fenton* ... because shepherds are regarded as unclean by Egyptians, *REB.*

47:1. Then Joseph came and told Pharaoh, and said, My father and my brethren, and their flocks, and their herds, and all that they have are come out of the land of Canaan; and, behold, they are in the land of Goshen: ... all that they possess, *NRSV* ... Have arrived from Canaan, *NEB* ... They are now in the land of Goshen, *RSV.*

2. And he took some of his brethren even five men, and presented them unto Pharaoh: ... from among his brothers he took five men, *RSV* ... Taking five of the ablest of brothers, *Goodspeed* ... whom he had selected from their full number, *NAB* ... introduced them to Pharaoh, *Berkeley.*

3. And Pharaoh said unto his brethren, What is your occupation?: ... what is your business?, *BB*, *Fenton* ... What are your works?, *Young.*

Thy servants are shepherds, both we, and also our fathers: ... feeders of a flock, *Young* ... ancestors, *NRSV*, *NAB* ... we are shepherd like our fathers before us, *REB.*

4. They said moreover unto Pharaoh, For to sojourn in the land are we come: ... we have come

46:33-34. Joseph instructed them that when Pharaoh called them to ask their occupation, they were to tell the truth and admit they were men of livestock from their youth as were their fathers (ancestors), so that they would continue to dwell in the land of Goshen.

The Egyptians were intensive farmers and despised herdsmen. Their monuments picture shepherds as distorted, dirty, emaciated figures. Wandering shepherds with their sheep and goats could ruin their gardens so they abhorred and rejected them. This was important in God's plan, because it meant the Israelites would stay in Goshen rather than scatter and lose their identity.

47:1-2. Joseph went to Pharaoh and told him that his father, brothers, and all they owned had arrived from Canaan and were now in Goshen. But he did not wait for Pharaoh to call them. He took 5 of them and brought them before Pharaoh.

47:3-4. Pharaoh asked them what their occupation was, just as Joseph suggested he would, and they replied as they were told. They added that they came to live temporarily in Egypt because of the famine which left them without pasture for their flocks. Then they politely asked permission to live in the land of Goshen.

420, 6799	3937, 1513.141	904, 800	971.119	3706, 375	4992
prep, pn	prep, v Qal inf con	prep, art, n fs	v Qal pf 1cp	prep, *sub*	n ms
אֶל־פַּרְעֹה	לָגוּר	בָּאָרֶץ	בָּאנוּ	כִּי־אֵין	מִרְעֶה
'el-par'ōh	lāghûr	bā'ārets	bā'nû	kî-'ên	mir'eh
to Pharaoh	to sojourn	in the land	we came	because there was not	pasture

3937, 6887	866	3937, 5860	3706, 3633	7743	904, 800	3791
prep, art, n fs	rel part	prep, n mp, ps 2ms	prep, adj	art, n ms	prep, *n fs*	pn
לַצֹּאן	אֲשֶׁר	לַעֲבָדֶיךָ	כִּי־כָבֵד	הָרָעָב	בְּאֶרֶץ	כְּנָעַן
latstsō'n	'ăsher	la'ăvādhêkhā	kî-khāvēdh	hārā'āv	b^{e}'erets	k^{e}nā'an
for the flocks	which	to your servants	because heavy	the famine	in the land of	Canaan

6498	3553.126, 5167	5860	904, 800	1705	5. 569.121
cj, adv	v Qal juss 3mp, part	n mp, ps 2ms	prep, *n fs*	pn	cj, v Qal impf 3ms
וְעַתָּה	יֵשְׁבוּ־נָא	עֲבָדֶיךָ	בְּאֶרֶץ	גֹּשֶׁן	וַיֹּאמֶר
w^{e}'attāh	yēsh^{e}vû-nā'	'ăvādhêkhā	b^{e}'erets	gōshen	wayyō'mer
and now	may they dwell please	your servants	in the land of	Goshen	and he said

6799	420, 3231	3937, 569.141	1	250	971.116	420
pn	prep, pn	prep, v Qal inf con	n ms, ps 2ms	cj, n mp, ps 2ms	v Qal pf 3cp	prep, ps 2ms
פַּרְעֹה	אֶל־יוֹסֵף	לֵאמֹר	אָבִיךָ	וְאַחֶיךָ	בָּאוּ	אֵלֶיךָ
par'ōh	'el-yôsēph	lē'mōr	'āvîkhā	w^{e}'achêkhā	bā'û	'ēlêkhā
Pharaoh	to Joseph	saying	your father	and your brothers	they came	to you

6. 800	4875	3937, 6686	2000	904, 4455	800	3553.531
n fs	pn	prep, n mp, ps 2ms	pers pron	prep, *n ms*	art, n fs	v Hiphil impv 2ms
אֶרֶץ	מִצְרַיִם	לְפָנֶיךָ	הִוא	בְּמֵיטַב	הָאָרֶץ	הוֹשֵׁב
'erets	mitsrayim	l^{e}phānêkhā	hiw'	b^{e}mêṯav	hā'ārets	hôshēv
the land of	Egypt	before you	it	in the best part of	the land	cause to dwell

881, 1	881, 250	3553.126	904, 800	1705	524, 3156.113
do, n ms, ps 2ms	cj, do, n mp, ps 2ms	v Qal impf 3mp	prep, *n fs*	pn	cj, cj, v Qal pf 2ms
אֶת־אָבִיךָ	וְאֶת־אַחֶיךָ	יֵשְׁבוּ	בְּאֶרֶץ	גֹּשֶׁן	וְאִם־יָדַעְתָּ
'eth-'āvîkhā	w^{e}'eth-'achêkhā	yēsh^{e}vû	b^{e}'erets	gōshen	w^{e}'im-yādha'āttā
your father	and your brothers	let them dwell	in the land of	Goshen	and if you know

3552, 904	596, 2524	7947.113	8015	4898
cj, sub, prep, ps 3mp	*n mp*, n ms	cj, v Qal pf 2ms, ps 3mp	*n mp*	n ms
וְיֶשׁ־בָּם	אַנְשֵׁי־חַיִל	וְשַׂמְתָּם	שָׂרֵי	מִקְנֶה
w^{e}yesh-bām	'anshê-chayil	w^{e}samtām	sārê	miqŏneh
whether there is among them	men of ability	then appoint them	officials of	livestock

6142, 866, 3937	7. 971.521	3231	881, 3399	1
prep, rel part, prep, ps 1cs	cj, v Hiphil impf 3ms	pn	do, pn	n ms, ps
עַל־אֲשֶׁר־לִי	וַיָּבֵא	יוֹסֵף	אֶת־יַעֲקֹב	אָבִיו
'al-'ăsher-lî	wayyāvē'	yôsēph	'eth-ya'ăqōv	'āvîw
over which to me	and he brought	Joseph	Jacob	his father

6198.521	3937, 6686	6799	1313.321	3399	881, 6799
cj, v Hiphil impf 3ms, ps 3ms	prep, *n mp*	pn	cj, v Piel impf 3ms	pn	do, pn
וַיַּעֲמִדֵהוּ	לִפְנֵי	פַּרְעֹה	וַיְבָרֶךְ	יַעֲקֹב	אֶת־פַּרְעֹה
wayya'ămidhēhû	liphnê	phar'ōh	way^{e}vārekh	ya'ăqōv	'eth-par'ōh
and he caused him to stand	before	Pharaoh	and he blessed	Jacob	Pharaoh

8. 569.121	6799	420, 3399	3626, 4242	3219	8523	2508
cj, v Qal impf 3ms	pn	prep, pn	prpe, intrg	*n mp*	*n fp*	n ms, ps 2ms
וַיֹּאמֶר	פַּרְעֹה	אֶל־יַעֲקֹב	כַּמָּה	יְמֵי	שְׁנֵי	חַיֶּיךָ
wayyō'mer	par'ōh	'el-ya'ăqōv	kammāh	y^{e}mê	sh^{e}nê	chayyêkhā
and he said	Pharaoh	to Jacob	like what	the days of	the years of	your life

9.

569.121	3399	420, 6799	3219	8523	4175	8389
cj, v Qal impf 3ms	pn	prep, pn	*n mp*	*n fp*	n mp, ps 1cs	num
וַיֹּאמֶר	יַעֲקֹב	אֶל־פַּרְעֹה	יְמֵי	שְׁנֵי	מְגוּרַי	שְׁלֹשִׁים
wayyō'mer	ya'ăqōv	'el-par'ōh	y^{e}mê	sh^{e}nê	m^{e}ghûray	sh^{e}lōshîm
and he said	Jacob	to Pharaoh	the days of	the years of	my sojournings	thirty

4109	8523	4746	7737	2030.116	3219	8523	2508
cj, *num*	n fs	sub	cj, adj	vQal pf 3cp	*n mp*	*n fp*	n ms, ps 1cs
וּמְאַת	שָׁנָה	מְעַט	וְרָעִים	הָיוּ	יְמֵי	שְׁנֵי	חַיַּי
ûm^{e}'ath	shānāh	m^{e}'at	w^{e}rā'îm	hāyû	y^{e}mê	sh^{e}nê	chayyay
and hundred of	year	few	and evil	they have been	the days of	the years of	my life

3940	5560.516	881, 3219	8523	2508	1	904, 3219
cj, neg part	v Hiphil pf 3cp	do, *n mp*	*n fp*	*n mp*	n mp, ps 1cs	prep, *n mp*
וְלֹא	הִשִּׂיגוּ	אֶת־יְמֵי	שְׁנֵי	חַיֵּי	אֲבֹתַי	בִּימֵי
w^{e}lō'	hissîghû	'eth-y^{e}mê	sh^{e}nê	chayyê	'ăvōthay	bîmê
and not	they attained	the days of	the years of	the life of	my fathers	in the days of

to stay in this country, *REB* ... We have come to make a living in this land, *BB* ... settle as immigrants, *Goodspeed* ... live here temporarily, *Berkeley*.

for thy servants have no pasture for their flocks; for the famine is sore: ... no grass, *BB* ... famine is severe, *NKJV*.

in the land of Canaan: now therefore, we pray thee, let thy servants dwell in the land of Goshen: ... beg you, *KJVII* ... ask your majesty's leave to settle now in Goshen, *REB*.

5. And Pharaoh spake unto Joseph, saying, Thy father and thy brethren are come unto thee: ... As to your father and your brothers who have come to you, *REB* ... have joined you, *Goodspeed*.

6. The land of Egypt is before thee; in the best of the land make thy father and brethren to dwell: ... is at your disposal, *Berkeley* ... Have your father and your brothers settle in the best of the land, *Berkeley*.

in the land of Goshen let them dwell: ... Let them live in Goshen, *NIV* ... let your father and your brothers have the best of the land for their resting-place, *BB*.

and if thou knowest any men of activity among them, then make them rulers over my cattle: ... superintendent, *Fenton* ... chief herdsmen, *NEB*, *REB* ... and if you know of any able men among them, place them in charge, *NCB* ... capable men, *NASB*, *NRSV* ... qualified, *NAB* ... special ability, *NIV* ... of my own stock, *NCB*.

7. And Joseph brought in Jacob his father, and set him before Pharaoh: and Jacob blessed Pharaoh: ... Then Joseph made his father Jacob come before Pharaoh, *BB* ... greeted Pharao, *NCB* ... paid his respects to Pharaoh, *NAB* ... saluted Pharoah, *Geneva*.

8. And Pharaoh said unto Jacob, How old art thou?: ... How old are you, *NCB*.

9. And Jacob said unto Pharaoh, The days of the years of my pilgrimage are an hundred and thirty years: ... as a wayfarer, *NAB* ... The years granted add up to 130, *Anchor*.

few and evil have the days of the years of my life been: ... short and wretched has been my life, *NCB* ... few and unpleasant, *NASB* ... few and difficult, *NIV* ... small in number and full of sorrow, *BB*.

and have not attained unto the days of the years of the life of my fathers in the days of their pilgrimage: ... nor does it compare to the years my fathers lived during their pilgrimage, *NCB* ... Fewer than the years my fathers lived, *REB*.

47:5-6. Because Pharaoh delegated authority to Joseph, he then told Joseph to cause his father and brothers to dwell in the best part of the land, even let them live in the land of Goshen. Also, if Joseph knew of men of ability among them, he should appoint them as officials over Pharaoh's livestock.

47:7. Next Joseph brought in Jacob and presented him before Pharaoh. Jacob took the initiative, as if he were a king, and blessed Pharaoh.

47:8-10. When Pharaoh asked Jacob's age, Jacob called his life a sojourning, that is, he lived as a resident alien for 130 years and added that the days of the years of his life were few and evil, not in the moral sense, but in the sense of being disagreeable and full of unfavorable circumstances. He had not the length of life his fathers had. Before he left he again blessed Pharaoh.

4175		1313.321	3399	881, 6799	3428.121	4623, 3937, 6686	6799
n mp, ps 3mp	**10.**	cj, v Piel impf 3ms	pn	do, pn	cj, v Qal impf 3ms	prep, prep, *n mp*	pn
מְגוּרֵיהֶם		וַיְבָרֶךְ	יַעֲקֹב	אֶת־פַּרְעֹה	וַיֵּצֵא	מִלִּפְנֵי	פַּרְעֹה
meghûrêhem		wayevārekh	ya'ăqōv	'eth-par'ōh	wayyētsē'	milliphnê	phar'ōh
their sojournings		and he blessed	Jacob	Pharaoh	and he went out	from before	Pharaoh

	3553.521	3231	881, 1	881, 250	5598.121	3937	273
11.	cj, v Hiphil impf 3ms	pn	do, n ms, ps 3ms	cj, do, n mp, ps 3ms	cj, v Qal impf 3ms	prep, ps 3mp	n fs
	וַיּוֹשֵׁב	יוֹסֵף	אֶת־אָבִיו	וְאֶת־אֶחָיו	וַיִּתֵּן	לָהֶם	אֲחֻזָּה
	wayyôshēv	yôs̱ēph	'eth-'āvîw	we'eth-'echâv	wayyittēn	lāhem	'ăchuzzāh
	and he caused to dwell	Joseph	his father	and his brothers	and he gave	to them	property

904, 800	4875	904, 4455	800	904, 800	7774	3626, 866
prep, *n fs*	pn	prep, *n ms*	art, n fs	prep, *n fs*	pn	prep, rel part
בְּאֶרֶץ	מִצְרַיִם	בְּמֵיטַב	הָאָרֶץ	בְּאֶרֶץ	רַעְמְסֵס	כַּאֲשֶׁר
be'erets	mitsrayim	bemêṯav	hā'ārets	be'erets	ra'ămsēs̱	ka'ăsher
in the land of	Egypt	in the best part of	the land	in the land of	Rameses	according to that

6943.311	6799		3677.321	3231	881, 1	881, 250
v Piel pf 3ms	pn	**12.**	cj, v Pilpel impf 3ms	pn	do, n ms, ps 3ms	cj, do, n mp, ps 3ms
צִוָּה	פַּרְעֹה		וַיְכַלְכֵּל	יוֹסֵף	אֶת־אָבִיו	וְאֶת־אֶחָיו
tsiwwāh	phar'ōh		wayekhalkēl	yôs̱ēph	'eth-'āvîw	we'eth-'echâv
he commanded	Pharaoh		and he provided for	Joseph	his father	and his brothers

881	3725, 1041	1	4035	3937, 6552	3054		4035
cj, do	*adj, n ms*	n ms, ps	n ms	prep, *n ms*	art, n ms	**13.**	cj, n ms
וְאֵת	כָּל־בֵּית	אָבִיו	לֶחֶם	לְפִי	הַטָּף		וְלֶחֶם
we'ēth	kol-bêth	'āvîw	lechem	lephî	hattāph		welechem
and	all the house of	his father	bread	for the mouth of	the little children		and bread

375	904, 3725, 800	3706, 3633	7743	4108	3992.122	800
sub	prep, *adj*, art, n fs	prep, adj	art, n ms	adv	cj, v Qal impf 3fs	*n fs*
אֵין	בְּכָל־הָאָרֶץ	כִּי־כָבֵד	הָרָעָב	מְאֹד	וַתֵּלַהּ	אֶרֶץ
'ên	bekhol-hā'ārets	kî-khāvēdh	hārā'āv	me'ōdh	wattēlahh	'erets
there was not	in all the land	because heavy	the famine	very	and it was anxious	the land of

4875	800	3791	4623, 6681	7743		4092.321	3231
pn	cj, *n fs*	pn	prep, *n ms*	art, n ms	**14.**	cj, v Piel impf 3ms	pn
מִצְרַיִם	וְאֶרֶץ	כְּנָעַן	מִפְּנֵי	הָרָעָב		וַיְלַקֵּט	יוֹסֵף
mitsrayim	we'erets	kena'an	mippenê	hārā'āv		waylaqqēṯ	yôs̱ēph
Egypt	and the land of	Canaan	before	the famine		and he gathered	Joseph

881, 3275, 3826B	4834.255	904, 800, 4875	904, 800	3791	904, 8134
do, *adj*, art, *n ms*	art, v Niphal ptc ms	prep, *n fs*, pn	cj, prep, *n fs*	pn	prep, art, n ms
אֶת־כָּל־הַכֶּסֶף	הַנִּמְצָא	בְאֶרֶץ־מִצְרַיִם	וּבְאֶרֶץ	כְּנַעַן	בַּשֶּׁבֶר
'eth-kol-hakkes̱eph	hannimtsā'	ve'erets-mitsrayim	ûve'erets	kena'an	bashshever
all the silver	found	in the land of Egypt	and in the land of	Canaan	for the grain

866, 2062	8132.152	971.521	3231	881, 3826B	904, 1041	6799
rel part, pers pron	v Qal act part mp	cj, v Hiphil impf 3ms	pn	do, art, n ms	*n ms*	pn
אֲשֶׁר־הֵם	שֹׁבְרִים	וַיָּבֵא	יוֹסֵף	אֶת־הַכֶּסֶף	בֵּיתָה	פַּרְעֹה
'ăsher-hēm	shōverîm	wayyāvē'	yôs̱ēph	'eth-hakkes̱eph	bêthāh	phar'ōh
which they	buyers	and he brought	Joseph	the silver	to the house of	Pharaoh

	8882.121	3826B	4623, 800	4875	4623, 800	3791
15.	cj, v Qal impf 3ms	art, n ms	prep, *n fs*	pn	cj, prep, *n fs*	pn
	וַיִּתֹּם	הַכֶּסֶף	מֵאֶרֶץ	מִצְרַיִם	וּמֵאֶרֶץ	כְּנָעַן
	wayyittōm	hakkes̱eph	mē'erets	mitsrayim	ûmē'erets	kena'an
	and it was gone	the silver	from the land of	Egypt	and from the land of	Canaan

971.126	3725, 4875	420, 3231	3937, 569.141	1957.131, 3937	4035	4066
cj, v Qal impf 3mp	*adj*, pn	prep, pn	prep, v Qal inf con	v Qal impv 2ms, prep, ps 1cp	n ms	cj, intrg
וַיָּבֹאוּ	כָל־מִצְרַיִם	אֶל־יוֹסֵף	לֵאמֹר	הָבָה־לָּנוּ	לֶחֶם	וְלָמָּה
wayyāvō'û	khol-mitsrayim	'el-yôsēph	lē'mōr	hāvāh-lānû	lechem	w^{e}lāmmāh
and they went	all of Egypt	to Joseph	saying	give to us	bread	and why

4322.120	5224	3706	674.111	3826B		569.121
v Qal impf 1cp	prep, ps 2ms	cj	v Qal pf 3ms	n ms		cj, v Qal impf 3ms
נָמוּת	נֶגְדֶּךָ	כִּי	אָפֵס	כָּסֶף	**16.**	וַיֹּאמֶר
nāmûth	negdekhā	kî	'āphēs	kāseph		wayyō'mer
should we die	in the sight of you	because	it is at an end	silver		and he said

3231	1957.133	4898	5598.125	3937	904, 4898
pn	v Qal impv 2mp	n mp, ps 2mp	cj, v Qal impf 1cs	prep, ps 2mp	prep, n mp, ps 2mp
יוֹסֵף	הָבוּ	מִקְנֵיכֶם	וְאֶתְּנָה	לָכֶם	בְּמִקְנֵיכֶם
yôsēph	hāvû	miqōnêkhem	w^{e}'ett^{e}nāh	lākhem	b^{e}miqōnêkhem
Joseph	give	your livestock	and I will give	to you	for your livestock

10. And Jacob blessed Pharaoh, and went out from before Pharaoh: ... Then Jacob bade Pharao goodbye, *NCB* ... then Jacob bade Pharaoh farewell, *NAB*.

11. And Joseph placed his father and his brethren, and gave them a possession: ... made a place, *BB* ... settled, *NRSV* ... heritage, *BB* ... granted them a holding, *NRSV*.

in the land of Egypt, in the best of the land, in the land of Rameses, as Pharaoh had commanded: ... the pick of the land-the region of Rameses-as Pharaoh had commanded, *Anchor*.

12. And Joseph nourished: ... took care of, *BB* ... maintained, *Darby* ... supported, *NEB*.

his father, and his brethren, and all his father's household, with bread, according to their families: ... giving them food for the needs of their families, *BB* ... according to the number of little ones, *Darby* ... even to the young children, *Geneva*.

13. And there was no bread in all the land: ... There was no food anywhere in the land, *Goodspeed*.

for the famine was very sore, so that the land of Egypt and all the land of Canaan fainted by reason of the famine: ... and the land of Canaan were exhausted through the famine, *Darby* ... Egypt and Canaan were laid low by it, *REB*.

14. And Joseph gathered up all the money that was found in the land of Egypt, and in the land of Canaan, for the corn which they bought: and Joseph brought the money into Pharaoh's house: ... Joseph collected all the silver in Egypt and Canaan in return for the corn which the people bought, and deposited it in Pharaoh's treasury, *NEB* ... grain, *Darby*.

15. And when money failed in the land of Egypt, and in the land of Canaan, all the Egyptians came unto Joseph, and said, Give us bread: for why should we die in thy presence?: ... clamoring, *NCB* ... would you have us come to destruction before your eyes?, *BB*.

for the money faileth: ... is all gone, *Darby* ... just because our money is gone?, *Goodspeed*.

47:11-12. Joseph then settled his father and brothers, giving them property in the best part of the land, the land or district of Rameses as Pharaoh commanded. The name "Rameses" was the name of 12 later kings of Egypt. They probably took the name of the district as their name at a later time. (Some believe the name Rameses is an editorial addition added at a later time.) But the name may have changed back and forth several times over the centuries.

After settling his family, Joseph continued to provide food for them. He was especially concerned that the little children had plenty to eat and did not suffer. He would not forget the least of them.

47:13-14. Because the famine was very severe, Egypt was producing no food. This caused a great deal of anxiety in both Egypt and Canaan because it was taking all their silver to buy food. Joseph was bringing all the silver to Pharaoh's palace where it was put in his treasury.

47:15-17. When the people of Egypt and Canaan ran out of silver, the Egyptians came to Joseph and demanded food, saying "Why should we die in your presence because the silver is all gone?"

So Joseph set up a barter system where they could trade livestock of all kinds for bread (grain, food). This continued for a year.

524, 674.111	3826B		971.526	881, 4898	420, 3231
cj, v Qal pf 3ms	n ms	17.	cj, v Hiphil impf 3mp	do, n mp, ps 3mp	prep, pn
אִם־אָפֵס	כָּסֶף		וַיָּבִיאוּ	אֶת־מִקְנֵיהֶם	אֶל־יוֹסֵף
'im-'āphēs̱	kās̱eph		wayyāvî'û	'eth-miqŏnêhem	'el-yôs̱ēph
since it has come to an end	silver		and they brought	their livestock	to Joseph

5598.121	3937	3231	4035	904, 5670	904, 4898	6887
cj, v Qal impf 3ms	prep, ps 3mp	pn	n ms	prep, art, n mp	cj, prep, *n ms*	art, n fs
וַיִּתֵּן	לָהֶם	יוֹסֵף	לֶחֶם	בַּסּוּסִים	וּבְמִקְנֵה	הַצֹּאן
wayyittēn	lāhem	yôs̱ēph	lechem	bas̱s̱ûs̱îm	ûv^{e}miqŏnēh	hatstsō'n
and he gave	to them	Joseph	bread	for the horses	and for the livestock of	the flocks

904, 4898	1267	904, 2645	5273.321	904, 4035
cj, prep, *n ms*	art, n ms	cj, prep, art, n mp	cj, v Piel impf 3ms, ps 3mp	prep, art, n ms
וּבְמִקְנֵה	הַבָּקָר	וּבַחֲמֹרִים	וַיְנַהֲלֵם	בַּלֶּחֶם
ûv^{e}miqŏnēh	habbāqār	ûvachmōrîm	waynahlēm	ballechem
and for the livestock of	the cattle	and for the donkeys	and he helped them through	with the bread

904, 3725, 4898	904, 8523	2000		8882.122	8523	2000
prep, *adj*, n ms, ps 3mp	prep, art, n fs	art, dem pron	18.	cj, v Qal impf 3fs	art, n fs	art, dem pron
בְּכָל־מִקְנֵהֶם	בַּשָּׁנָה	הַהִוא		וַתִּתֹּם	הַשָּׁנָה	הַהִוא
b^{e}khāl-miqŏnēhem	bashshānāh	hahiw'		wattittōm	hashshānāh	hahiw'
for all the livestock	in the year	the that		and it ended	the year	the that

971.126	420	904, 8523	8529	569.126	3937
cj, v Qal impf 3mp	prep, ps 3ms	prep, art, n fs	art, num	cj, v Qal impf 3mp	prep, ps 3ms
וַיָּבֹאוּ	אֵלָיו	בַּשָּׁנָה	הַשֵּׁנִית	וַיֹּאמְרוּ	לוֹ
wayyāvō'û	'ēlāv	bashshānāh	hashshēnîth	wayyō'm^{e}rû	lô
and they went	to him	in the year	the second	and they said	to him

3940, 3701.320	4623, 112	3706	524, 8882.111	3826B	4898
neg part, v Piel impf 1cp	prep, n ms, ps 1cs	cj	cj, v Qal pf 3ms	art, n ms	cj, *n ms*
לֹא־נְכַחֵד	מֵאֲדֹנִי	כִּי	אִם־תַּם	הַכֶּסֶף	וּמִקְנֵה
lō'-n^{e}khachēdh	mē'ădhōnî	kî	'im-tam	hakkes̱eph	ûmiqŏnēh
not we will hide	from my lord	that	whether it has ended	the silver	and the livestock of

966	420, 112	3940	8080.211	3937, 6686	112	1153	524, 1505
art, n fs	prep, n ms, ps 1cs	neg part	v Niphal pf 3ms	prep, *n mp*	n ms, ps 1cs	adv	cj, n fs, ps 1cp
הַבְּהֵמָה	אֶל־אֲדֹנִי	לֹא	נִשְׁאַר	לִפְנֵי	אֲדֹנִי	בִּלְתִּי	אִם־גְּוִיָּתֵנוּ
habb^{e}hēmāh	'el-'ădhōnî	lō'	nish'ar	liphnê	'ădhōnî	biltî	'im-g^{e}wiyyāthēnû
the animals	to my master	not	it is left	before	my master	except	only our bodies

124		4066	4322.120	3937, 6084	1612, 601	1612	124
cj, n fs, ps 1cp	19.	intrg	v Qal impf 1cp	prep, n fd, ps 2ms	cj, pers pron	cj	n fs, ps 1cp
וְאַדְמָתֵנוּ		לָמָּה	נָמוּת	לְעֵינֶיךָ	גַּם־אֲנַחְנוּ	גַּם	אַדְמָתֵנוּ
w^{e}'adhmāthēnû		lāmmāh	nāmûth	l^{e}'ênêkhā	gam-'ănachnû	gam	'adhmāthēnû
and our land		why	should we die	to your eyes	both we	and	our land

7353.131, 881	881, 124	904, 4035	2030.120	601	124
v Qal impv 2ms, do, ps 1cp	cj, do, n fs, ps 1cs	prep, art, n ms	cj, v Qal impf 1cp	pers pron	cj, n fs, ps 1cp
קְנֵה־אֹתָנוּ	וְאֶת־אַדְמָתֵנוּ	בַּלָּחֶם	וְנִהְיֶה	אֲנַחְנוּ	וְאַדְמָתֵנוּ
qŏnēh-'ōthānû	w^{e}'eth-'adhmāthēnû	ballāchem	w^{e}nihyeh	'ănachnû	w^{e}'adhmāthēnû
buy us	and our land	for the bread	and we will be	we	and our land

5860	3937, 6799	5598.131, 2320	2513.120	3940	4322.120	124
n mp	prep, pn	cj, v Qal impv 2ms, n ms	cj, v Qal impf 1cp	cj, neg part	v Qal impf 1cp	cj, art, n fs
עֲבָדִים	לְפַרְעֹה	וְתֶן־זֶרַע	וְנִחְיֶה	וְלֹא	נָמוּת	וְהָאֲדָמָה
'ăvādhîm	l^{e}phar'ōh	w^{e}then-zera'	w^{e}nichăyeh	w^{e}lō'	nāmûth	w^{e}hā'ădhāmāh
slaves	to Pharaoh	but give us seed	so we will live	and not	we will die	and the land

3940	8460.122		7353.121	3231	881, 3725, 124	4875	3937, 6799
neg part	v Qal impf 3fs	**20.**	cj, v Qal impf 3ms	pn	do, *adj, n fs*	pn	prep, pn
לֹא	תֵשָׁם		וַיִּקֶן	יוֹסֵף	אֶת־כָּל־אַדְמַת	מִצְרַיִם	לְפַרְעֹה
lō'	thēshām		wayyiqen	yôsēph	'eth-kol-'adhmath	mitsrayim	l^{e}phar'ōh
not	it will be desolate		and he bought	Joseph	all the land of	Egypt	for Pharaoh

3706, 4513.116	4875	382	7898	3706, 2480.111	6142	7743
cj, v Qal pf 3cp	pn	n ms	n ms, ps 3ms	cj, v Qal pf 3ms	prep, ps 3mp	art, n ms
כִּי־מָכְרוּ	מִצְרַיִם	אִישׁ	שָׂדֵהוּ	כִּי־חָזַק	עֲלֵהֶם	הָרָעָב
kî-mākh^{e}rû	mitsrayim	'îsh	sādēhû	kî-chāzaq	'ălēhem	hārā'āv
because they sold	Egypt	each	his field	because it was strong	on them	the famine

2030.122	800	3937, 6799		881, 6194	5882.511	881
cj, v Qal impf 3fs	art, n fs	prep, pn	**21.**	cj, do, art, n ms	v Hiphil pf 3ms	do, ps 3ms
וַתְּהִי	הָאָרֶץ	לְפַרְעֹה		וְאֶת־הָעָם	הֶעֱבִיר	אֹתוֹ
watt^{e}hî	hā'ārets	l^{e}phar'ōh		w^{e}'eth-hā'ām	he'ĕvîr	'ōthô
and it became	the land	to Pharaoh		and the people	he caused to pass	them

16. And Joseph said, Give your cattle; and I will give you for your cattle, if money fail: ... Give up your livestock, and I will give you food for your livestock, *NASB* ... I will give you food in exchange for your livestock, *NRSV* ... I will make distribution in return for your livestock, *Anchor.*

17. And they brought their cattle unto Joseph: and Joseph gave them bread in exchange for horses, and for the flocks, and for the cattle of the herds, and for the asses: and he fed them with bread for all their cattle for that year: ... food, *NCB* ... he supplied them with food in exchange for all their stock that year, *NCB* ... he got them through that year with bread in exchange for all their livestock, *NAB.*

18. When that year was ended, they came unto him the second year, and said unto him, We will not hide it from my lord, how that our money is spent; my lord also hath our herds of cattle; there is not ought left in the sight of my lord, but our bodies, and our lands: ... the following year, *NRSV* ... There is nothing left for my lord but our bodies and our land, *NCB.*

19. Wherefore shall we die before thine eyes, both we and our land?: ... Why should we and our land perish before your eyes?, *NCB.*

buy us and our land for bread, and we and our land will be servants unto Pharaoh: ... Buy us and our land for food and we and our land will be slaves to Pharaoh, *NASB* ... then we and our land shall be in serfdom to Pharaoh, *Berkeley* ... we and our land alike will be in bondage to Pharaoh, *REB* ... we and our land shall become feudatory to Pharaoh, *Goodspeed.*

and give us seed, that we may live, and not die, that the land be not desolate ... Give us seed- corn to keep us alive, or we shall die and our land will become desert, *REB, NEB.*

20. And Joseph bought all the land of Egypt for Pharaoh; for the Egyptians sold every man his field, because the famine prevailed over them: so the land became Pharaoh's: ... the famine was cruel upon them, *Fenton* ... since the famine too much for them to bear, every Egyptian sold his field; so the land passed over to Pharaoh, *NAB.*

47:18-20. The next year the people came to Joseph and told him that since their silver and their livestock were gone, they had nothing left to offer but their bodies and their lands. To keep from dying, they offered themselves and their lands to Pharaoh. So Joseph bought all their lands, for they were willing to sell because the famine was so overpowering. Thus the land, the farm properties, became Pharaoh's.

Archaeologists have found records from earlier times in Egypt which show private ownership of property. Then records from a later time show the land was all held in the name of the Pharaoh.

47:21-22. Joseph moved the people whose lands he bought to the cities, making it easier to distribute the food to them. (The Septuagint says he reduced them to slavery, rather than he brought them into cities, however, it was not unusual for people in those days to live in cities and towns and go out to work their fields.)

The only land Joseph did not buy was the land belonging to the priests. They received an allotted portion of food from Pharaoh, so they did not need to sell their land. Since the priests had a great deal of power, Pharaoh did not want to do anything to offend them.

3937, 6111	4623, 7381	1397, 4875	5912, 7381		7828	124
prep, n fp	prep, *n ms*	*n ms*, pn	cj, prep, n ms, ps 3ms		adv	*n fs*
לֶעָרִים	מִקְצֵה	גְבוּל־מִצְרַיִם	וְעַד־קָצֵהוּ	**22.**	רַק	אַדְמַת
le'ārîm	miqŏtsēh	ghevûl-mitsrayim	we'adh-qātsēhû		raq	'adhmath
to the cities	from the end of	the boundary of Egypt	and until its end		only	the land of

3669	3940	7353.111	3706	2805	3937, 3669	4623, 882	6799
art, n mp	neg part	v Qal pf 3ms	cj	n ms	prep, art, n mp	prep, prep	pn
הַכֹּהֲנִים	לֹא	קָנָה	כִּי	חֹק	לַכֹּהֲנִים	מֵאֵת	פַּרְעֹה
hakkōhnîm	lō'	qānāh	kî	chōq	lakkōhnîm	mē'ēth	par'ōh
the priests	not	he bought	because	portion	to the priests	from	Pharaoh

404.116	881, 2805	866	5598.111	3937	6799	6142, 3772	3940
cj, v Qal pf 3cp	do, n ms, ps 3mp	rel part	v Qal pf 3ms	prep, ps 3mp	pn	prep, adv	neg part
וְאָכְלוּ	אֶת־חֻקָּם	אֲשֶׁר	נָתַן	לָהֶם	פַּרְעֹה	עַל־כֵּן	לֹא
we'ākhelû	'eth-chuqqām	'ăsher	nāthan	lāhem	par'ōh	'al-kēn	lō'
so they ate	their portion	which	he gave	to them	Pharaoh	therefore	not

4513.116	881, 124		569.121	3231	420, 6194	2075	7353.115
v Qal pf 3cp	do, n fs, ps 3mp		cj, v Qal impf 3ms	pn	prep, art, n ms	intrj	v Qal pf 1cs
מָכְרוּ	אֶת־אַדְמָתָם	**23.**	וַיֹּאמֶר	יוֹסֵף	אֶל־הָעָם	הֵן	קָנִיתִי
mākherû	'eth-'adhmāthām		wayyō'mer	yôsēph	'el-hā'ām	hēn	qānîthî
they sold	their land		and he said	Joseph	to the people	behold	I bought

881	3219	881, 124	3937, 6799	1953, 3937	2320	2319.117
do, ps 2mp	art, n ms	cj, do, n fs, ps 2mp	prep, pn	intrj, prep, ps 2mp	n ms	cj, v Qal pf 2mp
אֶתְכֶם	הַיּוֹם	וְאֶת־אַדְמַתְכֶם	לְפַרְעֹה	הֵא־לָכֶם	זֶרַע	וּזְרַעְתֶּם
'ethekhem	hayyôm	we'eth-'adhmathekhem	lephar'ōh	hē'-lākhem	zera'	ûzāra'ăttem
you	today	your land	for Pharaoh	see to you	seed	and you will sow

881, 124		2030.111	904, 8721	5598.117	2653	3937, 6799
do, art, n fs		cj, v Qal pf 3ms	prep, art, n fp	cj, v Qal pf 2mp	num	prep, pn
אֶת־הָאֲדָמָה	**24.**	וְהָיָה	בַּתְּבוּאֹת	וּנְתַתֶּם	חֲמִישִׁית	לְפַרְעֹה
'eth-hā'ădhāmāh		wehāyāh	battevû'ōth	ûnethattem	chămîshîth	lephar'ōh
the ground		and it will be	during the harvests	you will give	fifth	to Pharaoh

727	3135	2030.121	3937	3937, 2320	7898	3937, 406
cj, *num*	art, n fp	v Qal impf 3ms	prep, ps 2mp	prep, *n ms*	art, n ms	cj, prep, n ms, ps 2mp
וְאַרְבַּע	הַיָּדֹת	יִהְיֶה	לָכֶם	לְזֶרַע	הַשָּׂדֶה	וּלְאָכְלְכֶם
we'arba'	hayyādhōth	yihyeh	lākhem	lezera'	hassādeh	ûlă'ākhlekhem
and four of	the hands	they will be	for you	for the seed of	the field	and for your food

3937, 866	904, 1041	3937, 404.141	3937, 3054		569.126
cj, prep, rel part	prep, n ms, ps 2mp	cj, prep, v Qal inf con	prep, n mp, ps 2mp		cj, v Qal impf 3mp
וְלַאֲשֶׁר	בְּבָתֵּיכֶם	וְלֶאֱכֹל	לְטַפְּכֶם	**25.**	וַיֹּאמְרוּ
wela'ăsher	bevāttêkhem	wela'ĕkhōl	letappekhem		wayyō'merû
and to which	in your households	and to eat	for your little children		and they said

2513.513	4834.120, 2682	904, 6084	112	2030.119	5860
v Hiphil pf 2ms, ps 1cp	v Qal juss 1cp, n ms	prep, *n fp*	n ms, ps 1cs	cj, v Qal pf 1cp	n mp
הֶחֱיִתָנוּ	נִמְצָא־חֵן	בְּעֵינֵי	אֲדֹנִי	וְהָיִינוּ	עֲבָדִים
hechĕyithānû	nimtsā'-chēn	be'ênê	'ădhōnî	wehāyînû	'ăvādhîm
you have caused us to live	let us find favor	in the eyes of	my master	and we will be	slaves

3937, 6799		7947.121	881	3231	3937, 2805	5912, 3219	2172
prep, pn		cj, v Qal impf 3ms	do, ps 3fs	pn	prep, n ms	prep, art, n ms	art, dem pron
לְפַרְעֹה	**26.**	וַיָּשֶׂם	אֹתָהּ	יוֹסֵף	לְחֹק	עַד־הַיּוֹם	הַזֶּה
lephar'ōh		wayyāsem	'ōthāhh	yôsēph	lechōq	'adh-hayyôm	hazzeh
to Pharaoh		and he set	it	Joseph	for a statute	until today	the this

6142, 124	4875	3937, 6799	3937, 2676	7828	124	3669
prep, *n fs*	pn	prep, pn	prep, art, n ms	adv	*n fs*	art, n mp
עַל־אַדְמַת	מִצְרַיִם	לְפַרְעֹה	לַחֹמֶשׁ	רַק	אַדְמַת	הַכֹּהֲנִים
'al-'adhmath	mitsrayim	l^{e}phar'ōh	lachōmesh	raq	'adhmath	hakkōhnîm
concerning the land of	Egypt	to Pharaoh	for the fifth	only	the land of	the priests

3937, 940	3940	2030.112	3937, 6799		3553.121	3547	904, 800
prep, n ms, ps 3mp	neg part	v Qal pf 3fs	prep, pn	**27.**	cj, v Qal impf 3ms	pn	prep, *n fs*
לְבַדָּם	לֹא	הָיְתָה	לְפַרְעֹה		וַיֵּשֶׁב	יִשְׂרָאֵל	בְּאֶרֶץ
l^{e}vaddām	lō'	hāy^{e}thāh	l^{e}phar'ōh		wayyēshev	yisrā'ēl	b^{e}'erets
by themselves	not	it became	to Pharaoh		and he dwelled	Israel	in the land of

21. And as for the people, he removed them to cities from one end of the borders of Egypt even to the other end thereof: ... and Joseph reduced the people to servitude, from one end of Egypt to the other, *NIV* ... the people themselves he transferred to the towns from one end of Egypt's domain to the other, *Goodspeed* ... he transferred the people upon it to fresh villages, *Fenton.*

22. Only the land of the priests bought he not; for the priests had a portion assigned them of Pharaoh: ... ordinarie, *Geneva* ... received a regular allotment, *NIV* ... subvention, *Fenton* ... royal subsidies, *Berkeley.*

and did eat their portion which Pharaoh gave them: wherefore they sold not their lands: ... had food enough, *NIV* ... they had no need to give up their land, *BB.*

23. Then Joseph said unto the people, Behold, I have bought you this day and your land for Pharaoh: lo, here is seed for you, and ye shall sow the land: ... proclaimed to the nation, *Fenton* ... I have made you and your land this day the property of Pharaoh, *BB* ... Here is seed-corn for you. Sow the land, *REB.*

24. And it shall come to pass in the increase: ... and when the grain is cut, *BB* ... at the harvest, *RSV* ... at the ingatherings, *ASV.*

that ye shall give the fifth part unto Pharaoh, and four parts shall be your own, for seed of the field, and for your food: ... contribute one fifth to Pharaoh and keep four fifths for yourselves, *Berkeley.*

and for them of your households, and for food for your little ones: ... children, *Geneva* ... dependants, *NEB* ... infants, *Young.*

25. And they said, Thou hast saved our lives: ... kept us from death, *BB* ... Thou hast revived us, *Young.*

let us find grace in the sight of my lord, and we will be Pharaoh's servant: ... may we have grace in your eyes, *BB* ... we would thank my lord, *Goodspeed* ... if it please your lordship, we will be Pharaoh's slaves, *NEB.*

26. And Joseph made it a law over the land of Egypt unto this day: ... ordinance, *NCB* ... statute, *ASV* ... regulation, *Berkeley* ... valid, *NASB* ... So Joseph made it the constitution to this day, *Fenton.*

that Pharaoh should have the fifth part; except the land of the priests only, which became not Pharaoh's: ... of its produce should go to Pharaoh, *NAB* ... a fifth of the produce belongs to Pharaoh, *NIV* ... The land of the priest alone did not become Pharaoh's, *NRSV.*

27. And Israel dwelt in the land of Egypt, in the country of Goshen; and they had possessions therein: ... so Israel was living among the Egyptians in the land of Goshen, *BB* ... Thus Israel settled in Egypt, in Goshen, where they acquired land, *REB* ... acquired holdings, *Anchor.*

47:23-24. By this time, the 7 years of famine were coming to an end. From the remaining store of grain, Joseph gave them seed to sow the land, but because the land now belonged to Pharaoh they would be like sharecroppers and give a fifth of the harvest to Pharaoh.

This 20 percent tax was not exorbitant or unreasonable in those days when landlords in some countries took as much as 50 percent of the crops. The 80 percent remaining to the people would be their own to use for seed and for food. He mentioned seed first, because that would have to be a priority. He would not give them seed again.

47:25-26. The people accepted this and expressed their gratitude to Joseph for saving their lives. They also asked Joseph for his continuing favor, and promised to be Pharaoh's slaves. Saying they would be his slaves was a hyperbole by which meant they would be his faithful subjects.

47:27. This is a summary verse letting us know that though Israel's family came to Egypt intending to stay temporarily, they continued to live in Goshen and settled down to stay. They were prosperous and kept increasing in number.

4875	904, 800	1705	270.226	904	6759.126
pn	prep, *n fs*	pn	cj, v Niphal impf 3mp	prep, ps 3fs	cj, v Qal impf 3mp
מִצְרָיִם	בְּאֶרֶץ	גֹּשֶׁן	וַיֵּאָחֲזוּ	בָהּ	וַיִּפְרוּ
mitsrayim	b^{e}'erets	gōshen	wayyē'āchăzû	vāhh	wayyiphrû
Egypt	in the land of	Goshen	and they were settled	in it	and they were fruitful

7528.126	4108		2513.121	3399	904, 800	4875	8124
cj, v Qal impf 3mp	adv	**28.**	cj, v Qal impf 3ms	pn	prep, *n fs*	pn	num
וַיִּרְבּוּ	מְאֹד		וַיְחִי	יַעֲקֹב	בְּאֶרֶץ	מִצְרַיִם	שְׁבַע
wayyirbû	m^{e}'ōdh		waychî	ya'ăqōv	b^{e}'erets	mitsrayim	sh^{e}va'
and they increased	very		and he lived	Jacob	in the land of	Egypt	seven

6462	8523	2030.121	3219, 3399	8523	2508	8124	8523
num	n fs	cj, v Qal impf 3ms	*n mp*, pn	*n fp*	n mp, ps 3ms	num	n fp
עֶשְׂרֵה	שָׁנָה	וַיְהִי	יְמֵי־יַעֲקֹב	שְׁנֵי	חַיָּיו	שֶׁבַע	שָׁנִים
'esrēh	shānāh	wayhî	y^{e}mê-ya'ăqōv	sh^{e}nê	chayyâv	sheva'	shānîm
ten	year	and they were	the days of Jacob	the years of	his life	seven	years

727	4109	8523		7414.126	3219, 3547	3937, 4322.141
cj, num	cj, *num*	n fs	**29.**	cj, v Qal impf 3mp	, pn	prep, v Qal inf con
וְאַרְבָּעִים	וּמְאַת	שָׁנָה		וַיִּקְרְבוּ	יְמֵי־יִשְׂרָאֵל	לָמוּת
w^{e}'arbā'îm	ûm^{e}'ath	shānāh		wayyiqōr^{e}vû	y^{e}mê-yisrā'ēl	lāmûth
and forty	and hundred	years		and they drew near	the days of Israel	to die

7410.121	3937, 1158	3937, 3231	569.121	3937	524, 5167	4834.115
cj, v Qal impf 3ms	prep, n ms, ps 3ms	prep, pn	cj, v Qal impf 3ms	prep, ps 3ms	cj, part	v Qal pf 1cs
וַיִּקְרָא	לִבְנוֹ	לְיוֹסֵף	וַיֹּאמֶר	לוֹ	אִם־נָא	מָצָאתִי
wayyiqōrā'	livnô	l^{e}yôsēph	wayyō'mer	lô	'im-nā'	mātsā'thî
and he summoned	his son	Joseph	and he said	to him	if please	I have found

2682	904, 6084	7947.131, 5167	3135	8809	3525	6449.113
n ms	prep, n fd, ps 2ms	v Qal impv 2ms, part	n fs, ps 2ms	prep	n fs, ps 1cs	cj, v Qal pf 2ms
חֵן	בְּעֵינֶיךָ	שִׂים־נָא	יָדְךָ	תַּחַת	יְרֵכִי	וְעָשִׂיתָ
chēn	b^{e}'ênêkhā	sîm-nā'	yadh^{e}khā	tachath	y^{e}rēkhî	w^{e}'āsîthā
favor	in your eyes	put please	your hand	under	my loins	and you will do

6200	2721	583	414, 5167	7196.123	904, 4875		8311.115
prep, ps 1cs	n ms	cj, n fs	neg part, part	v Qal impf 2ms, ps 1cs	prep, pn	**30.**	cj, v Qal pf 1cs
עִמָּדִי	חֶסֶד	וֶאֱמֶת	אַל־נָא	תִקְבְּרֵנִי	בְּמִצְרָיִם		וְשָׁכַבְתִּי
'immādhî	chesedh	we'ĕmeth	'al-nā'	thiqōbb^{e}rēnî	b^{e}mitsrāyim		w^{e}shākhavtî
with me	loyalty	and reliability	not please	you will bury me	in Egypt		but I will lie

6196, 1	5558.113	4623, 4875	7196.113	904, 7197
prep, n mp, ps 1cs	cj, v Qal pf 2ms, ps 1cs	prep, pn	cj, v Qal pf 2ms, ps 1cs	prep, n fs, ps 3mp
עִם־אֲבֹתַי	וּנְשָׂאתַנִי	מִמִּצְרַיִם	וּקְבַרְתַּנִי	בִּקְבֻרָתָם
'im-'ăvōthay	ûn^{e}sā'thanî	mimmitsrayim	ûqōvartanî	biqōvurāthām
with my fathers	and you will carry me	from Egypt	and you will bury me	in their tomb

569.121	609	6449.125	3626, 1745		569.121	8123.231
cj, v Qal impf 3ms	pers pron	v Qal impf 1cs	prep, n mp, ps 2ms	**31.**	cj, v Qal impf 3ms	v Niphal impv 2ms
וַיֹּאמַר	אָנֹכִי	אֶעֱשֶׂה	כִדְבָרֶךָ		וַיֹּאמֶר	הִשָּׁבְעָה
wayyō'mar	'ānōkhî	'e'ĕseh	khidh^{e}vārekhā		wayyō'mer	hishshāv^{e}'āh
and he said	I	I will do	like your words		and he said	swear

3937	8123.221	3937	8246.721	3547	6142, 7513	4433
prep, ps 1cs	cj, v Niphal impf 3ms	prep, ps 3ms	cj, v Hithpalel impf 3ms	pn	prep, *n ms*	art, n fs
לִי	וַיִּשָּׁבַע	לוֹ	וַיִּשְׁתַּחוּ	יִשְׂרָאֵל	עַל־רֹאשׁ	הַמִּטָּה
lî	wayyishshāva'	lô	wayyishtachû	yisrā'ēl	'al-rō'sh	hammittāh
to me	and he swore	to him	and he bowed down	Israel	on the head of	the bed

48:1

2030.121	311	1745	431	569.121	3937, 3231	2079
cj, v Qal impf 3ms	*sub*	art, n mp	art, dem pron	cj, v Qal impf 3ms	prep, pn	intrj
וַיְהִי	אַחֲרֵי	הַדְּבָרִים	הָאֵלֶּה	וַיֹּאמֶר	לְיוֹסֵף	הִנֵּה
wayhî	'achrê	hadd^{e}vārîm	hā'ēlleh	wayyō'mer	l^{e}yôsēph	hinnēh
and it was	after	the matters	the these	and he said	to Joseph	behold

1	2571.151	4089.121	881, 8529	1158	6196	881, 4667
n ms, ps 2ms	v Qal act ptc ms	cj, v Qal impf 3ms	do, *num*	n mp, ps 3ms	prep, ps 3ms	do, pn
אָבִיךָ	חֹלֶה	וַיִּקַּח	אֶת־שְׁנֵי	בָנָיו	עִמּוֹ	אֶת־מְנַשֶּׁה
'āvîkhā	chōleh	wayyiqqach	'eth-sh^{e}nê	vānâv	'immô	'eth-m^{e}nashsheh
your father	a sick man	and he took	the two of	his sons	with him	Manasseh

and grew, and multiplied exceedingly: ... They acquired property there, were fruitful, and became very numerous, *NCB* ... were prolific and multiplied rapidly, *Berkeley.*

28. And Jacob lived in the land of Egypt seventeen years: so the whole age of Jacob was an hundred forty and seven years: ... so the length of Jacob's life was one hundred and forty-seven years, *NASB.*

29. And the time drew nigh that Israel must die: and he called his son Joseph, and said unto him, If now I have found grace in thy sight: ... the time approached, *Fenton* ... favor with you, *NCB* ... do me a favor, *Berkeley.*

put, I pray thee, thy hand under my thigh, and deal kindly and truly with me; bury me not, I pray thee, in Egypt: ... deal with me in kindness and faithfulness, *NASB* ... deal loyally and truly with me, *NRSV* ... put your hand under my thigh as a pledge of your steadfast loyalty to me, *Anchor.*

30. But I will lie with my fathers: ... but let me rest with my fathers, *NCB* ... When I lie down with my ancestors, *NRSV.*

and thou shalt carry me out of Egypt, and bury me in their buryingplace. And he said, I will do as thou hast said: ... seplulchre, *NCB, Darby* ... grave, *REB, NEB* ... bury me where they are buried, *NIV.*

31. And he said, Swear unto me. And he sware unto him. And Israel bowed: ... I will carry out your suggestion, *Berkeley* ... in worship, *REB.*

himself upon the bed's head: ... and Israel was reclining on the surface of the bed, *Fenton* ... whereupon Israel settled back on the head of his bed, *Goodspeed* ... and Israel sank down over the end of the bed, *NEB* ... and Israel worshipped as he leaned on the top of his staff, *NIV.*

48:1. And it came to pass after these things, that one told Joseph, Behold: ... word came to Joseph, *BB* ... after this Joseph was told, *NRSV.*

thy father is sick: ... The time came when Joseph was told that his father was ill, *NEB* ... your father is failing, *Anchor, NAB.*

47:28. This verse introduces the account of Jacob's last days. Moses refers to him as Jacob here since he has used Israel as the name of the whole people in the previous verse. Jacob's life was indeed shorter than that of Abraham or of Isaac. In fact, we do not read of anyone living even as long as Jacob after this. Joseph lived to be 110. Moses lived to be 120.

47:29-31. Jacob is called Israel here because he faced the prospect of death with his faith in the promise. He called Joseph to ask him to put his hand under his thigh, that is, to make an oath that he would act in covenant love and faithfulness and would please not bury him in Egypt. He wanted his body to lie with his fathers in their tomb, that is, in the cave of Machpelah. Joseph promised to do so, but Jacob insisted that Joseph swear, that is make a solemn oath. When Joseph did this, Israel bowed down on the head of his bed in praise and worship, also indicating that he was satisfied. Hebrews 11:21 says Jacob "worshiped leaning on the top of his staff." The original Hebrew text without vowels has *mtth.* The Massoretes, Jewish scholars of tradition from about A.D. 500 to 950, added vowels to read *mittah,* "bed." The writer to the Hebrews was following the Septuagint translation made by Jews before the time of Christ. They took the letters to stand for *matteh,* "staff" (as a means of support). Some believe that the Massoretes deliberately added vowels that were different here, simply because of the reference used by Christians in Hebrews 11:21.

48:1-2. When Joseph heard his father was sick, he took his two sons, Manasseh and Ephraim to go

881, 688		5222.521	3937, 3399	569.121	2079	1158	3231
cj, do, pn	**2.**	cj, v Hiphil impf 3ms	prep, pn	cj, v Qal impf 3ms	intrj	n ms, ps 2ms	pn
וְאֶת־אֶפְרָיִם		וַיַּגֵּד	לְיַעֲקֹב	וַיֹּאמֶר	הִנֵּה	בִּנְךָ	יוֹסֵף
w^{e}'eth-'ephrāyim		wayyagēdh	l^{e}ya'ăqōv	wayyō'mer	hinnēh	bin^{e}khā	yôs̲ēph
and Ephraim		and he told	to Jacob	and he said	behold	your son	Joseph

971.151	420	2480.721	3547	3553.121	6142, 4433
v Qal act ptc ms	prep, ps 2ms	cj, v Hithpael impf 3ms	pn	cj, v Qal impf 3ms	prep, art, n fs
בָּא	אֵלֶיךָ	וַיִּתְחַזֵּק	יִשְׂרָאֵל	וַיֵּשֶׁב	עַל־הַמִּטָּה
bā'	'ēlêkhā	wayyithchazzēq	yisrā'ēl	wayyēshev	'al-hammit̲t̲āh
coming	to you	and he strengthened himself	Israel	and he sat	on the bed

	569.121	3399	420, 3231	418	8163	7495.211, 420	904, 4007
3.	cj, v Qal impf 3ms	pn	prep, pn	n ms	pn	v Niphal pf 3ms, prep, ps 1cs	prep, pn
	וַיֹּאמֶר	יַעֲקֹב	אֶל־יוֹסֵף	אֵל	שַׁדַּי	נִרְאָה־אֵלַי	בְּלוּז
	wayyō'mer	ya'ăqōv	'el-yôs̲ēph	'ēl	shadday	nir'āh-'ēlay	b^{e}lûz
	and he said	Jacob	to Joseph	God	Almighty	He appeared to me	in Luz

904, 800	3791	1313.321	881		569.121	420	2079
prep, *n fs*	pn	cj, v Piel impf 3ms	do, ps 1cs	**4.**	cj, v Qal impf 3ms	prep, ps 1cs	intrj, ps 1cs
בְּאֶרֶץ	כְּנָעַן	וַיְבָרֶךְ	אֹתִי		וַיֹּאמֶר	אֵלַי	הִנְנִי
b^{e}'erets	k^{e}nā'an	way^{e}vārekh	'ōthî		wayyō'mer	'ēlay	hinnî
in the land of	Canaan	and He blessed	me		and He said	to me	behold I

6759.551	7528.515	5598.115	3937, 7235	6194
v Hiphil ptc ms, ps 2ms	cj, v Hiphil pf 1cs, ps 2ms	cj, v Qal pf 1cs, ps 2ms	prep, *n ms*	n mp
מַפְרְךָ	וְהִרְבִּיתִךָ	וּנְתַתִּיךָ	לִקְהַל	עַמִּים
maphr^{e}khā	w^{e}hirbîthikhā	ûn^{e}thattîkhā	liqhal	'ammîm
one who makes you fruitful	and I will multiply you	and I will give you	for company of	peoples

5598.115	881, 800	2148	3937, 2320	313	273	5986
cj, v Qal pf 1cs	do, art, n fs	art, dem pron	prep, n ms, ps 2ms	adv, ps 2ms	*n fs*	adv
וְנָתַתִּי	אֶת־הָאָרֶץ	הַזֹּאת	לְזַרְעֲךָ	אַחֲרֶיךָ	אֲחֻזַּת	עוֹלָם
w^{e}nāthattî	'eth-hā'ārets	hazzō'th	l^{e}zar'ăkhā	'achrêkhā	'ăchuzzath	'ôlām
and I will give	the land	the this	to your seed	after you	property of	forever

	6498	8530, 1158	3314.256	3937	904, 800	4875
5.	cj, adv	*num*, n mp, ps 2ms	art, v Niphal part mp	prep, ps 2ms	prep, *n fs*	pn
	וְעַתָּה	שְׁנֵי־בָנֶיךָ	הַנּוֹלָדִים	לְךָ	בְּאֶרֶץ	מִצְרַיִם
	w^{e}'attāh	sh^{e}nê-vānêkhā	hannôlādhîm	l^{e}khā	b^{e}'erets	mitsrayim
	and now	your two sons	the ones born	to you	in the land of	Egypt

5912, 971.141	420	4875	3937, 2062	688	4667	3626, 7498
adv, v Qal inf con, ps 1cs	prep, ps 2ms	pn	prep, ps 1cs, pers pron	pn	cj, pn	prep, pn
עַד־בֹּאִי	אֵלֶיךָ	מִצְרַיְמָה	לִי־הֵם	אֶפְרַיִם	וּמְנַשֶּׁה	כִּרְאוּבֵן
'adh-bō'î	'ēlêkhā	mitsraymāh	lî-hēm	'ephrayim	ûm^{e}nashsheh	kir'ûvēn
before my coming	to you	to Egypt	to me they	Ephraim	and Manasseh	like Reuben

8482	2030.126, 3937		4274	866, 3314.513	313
cj, pn	v Qal impf 3mp, prep, ps 1cs	**6.**	cj, n fs, ps 2ms	rel part, v Hiphil pf 2ms	adv, ps 3mp
וְשִׁמְעוֹן	יִהְיוּ־לִי		וּמוֹלַדְתְּךָ	אֲשֶׁר־הוֹלַדְתָּ	אַחֲרֵיהֶם
w^{e}shim'ôn	yihyû-lî		ûmôladht^{e}khā	'ăsher-hôladhtā	'achrêhem
and Simeon	they are to me		and your offspring	which you will bring forth	after them

3937	2030.126	6142	8428	250	7410.226
prep, ps 2ms	v Qal impf 3mp	prep	*n ms*	n mp, ps 3mp	v Niphal impf 3mp
לְךָ	יִהְיוּ	עַל	שֵׁם	אֲחֵיהֶם	יִקָּרְאוּ
l^{e}khā	yihyû	'al	shēm	'ăchêhem	yiqqār'û
to you	they will be	according to	the name of	their brothers	they will be called

and he took with him his two sons, Manasseh and Ephraim ... and came to see Jacob, *Goodspeed.*

2. And one told Jacob, and said, Behold, thy son Joseph cometh unto thee: and Israel strengthened: ... your son has come just to see you, *Goodspeed* ... rallied himself, *NIV* ... gathered his strength, *REB* ... exerted himself, *Fenton.*

and sat upon the bed: ... sat up on the bed, *NKJV* ... had himself lifted up in his bed, *BB.*

3. And Jacob said unto Joseph, God appeared unto me at Luz in the land of Canaan, and blessed me: ... the ruler of all ... in a vision, *BB* ... appeared to me on my departure from the land of Canan, *Fenton.*

4. And said unto me, Behold, I will make thee fruitful, and multiply thee: ... fertile, *BB* ... prolific, *Goodspeed* ... flourish, *Fenton* ... increase your numbers, *NIV.*

and I will make of thee a multitude of people: ... a great family of nations, *BB* ... an assembly of tribes *Anchor* ... race, *Fenton* ... until they become a host of nations, *NEB.*

and will give this land to thy seed after thee for an everlasting possession: ... I will give this land to your descendants after you as a perpetual possession, *NEB* ... a possession age-during, *Young* ... an everlasting holding, *Anchor.*

5. And now thy two sons, Ephraim and Manasseh, which were born unto thee in the land of Egypt before I came unto thee into Egypt, are mine; as Reuben and Simeon: ... I adopt your two sons, *NCB* ... no less so than Reuben and Simeon, *Anchor* ... they shall be mine ... shall be counted as my sons, *NEB.*

6. And thy issue, which thou begettest after them, shall be thine: ... progeny born to you after them, *Anchor* ... offspring, *NKJV, RSV* ... the children born to you after them shall be yours, *NCB.*

and shall be called after the name of their brethren in their inheritance: ... They shall not be called by the name of their brothers in their inheritance, *Fenton* ... If you have any more sons, the inheritance they get will come through Ephraim and Manasseh, *Good News* ... in respect of their tribal territory they will be reckoned under their elder brothers' names, *NEB.*

7. And as for me, when I came from Padan, Rachel died by me in the land of Canaan in the way: ... I want this because, *Anchor* ... when I was returning from Padan, to my sorrow Rachel died during the journey in the land of Chanaan, *NCB.*

when yet there was but a little way to come unto Ephrath; and I buried her there in the way of Ephrath; the same is Bethlehem: ... a short distance from the environs of Ephratha, *NCB* ... when there was some distance to go to Ephrath, *NASB* ... while yet a kibrath of land to enter Ephrata, *Young* ... that is, in Bethelehem, *NAB.*

---

to see him. Someone told Jacob that Joseph was coming, but did not tell him Joseph's sons were with him. This news caused Jacob to summon what strength he had left in order to rise up and sit on the edge of his bed, for he had something important he wanted to tell Joseph. When Jacob strengthened himself to do this he was called Israel as he is in most of the remaining passage.

48:3-4. Jacob first reminded Joseph of the blessing and promise God Almighty gave him at Luz (later called Bethel), when he first left home. The promise was to make him fruitful and make his descendants a congregation of peoples, that is, of the 12 tribes. Congregation (Heb. *qahal*) is used later of all Israel (1 Sam. 17:47; Ps. 22:23). The promise also included the land as the property of Israel's descendants forever.

48:5-7. Jacob then proceeded to declare his adoption of Ephraim and Manasseh as full sons of his on the same level as his first two sons, Reuben and Simeon. By this, Jacob indicated he was bypassing the older sons and was making sure that Joseph would get the double portion of the birthright. This would apply only to Ephraim and Manasseh. Any other children Joseph might have would get their inheritance through Ephraim and Manasseh. Jacob named Ephraim first in anticipation of the leadership Ephraim would have.

Then Jacob let Joseph know why he was doing this. Rachel, the wife he truly loved, died in the land of Canaan and was buried on the road to Ephrath, that is Bethlehem. Jacob wanted Joseph to know that as the oldest son of Rachel, who was Jacob's beloved, the one he intended to be his only wife, he should have the birthright with its double portion of the inheritance. However, since the customs of the time would not ordinarily allow this, Jacob found a way.

By giving Ephraim and Manasseh a full portion of the inheritance, Joseph was guaranteed the birthright (cf. 1 Chron. 5:2). Thus, Ephraim and Manasseh became the ancestors of full tribes and their names are included along with the others in the lists of the tribes of Israel.

904, 5338	**7.** 603	904, 971.141	4623, 6549	4322.112	6142
prep, n fs, ps 3mp	cj, pers pron	prep, v Qal inf con, ps 1cs	prep, pn	v Qal pf 3fs	prep, ps 1cs
בְּנַחֲלָתָם	וַאֲנִי	בְּבֹאִי	מִפַּדָּן	מֵתָה	עָלַי
b[e]nachlāthām	wa'ănî	b[e]vō'î	mippaddān	mēthāh	‘ālay
by their inheritance	and I	in my coming	from Paddan	she died	beside me

7637	904, 800	3791	904, 1932	904, 5968	3650, 800	3937, 971.141
pn	prep, *n fs*	pn	prep, art, n ms	prep, adv	*n fs*, n fs	prep, v Qal inf con
רָחֵל	בְּאֶרֶץ	כְּנַעַן	בַּדֶּרֶךְ	בְּעוֹד	כִּבְרַת־אֶרֶץ	לָבֹא
rāchēl	b[e]'erets	k[e]na‘an	badderekh	b[e]‘ôdh	kivrath-'erets	lāvō'
Rachel	in the land of	Canaan	on the journey	when still	distance of land	to go

693	7196.125	8427	904, 1932	693	2000	1074	1074
pn	cj, v Qal impf 1cs, ps 3fs	adv	prep, *n ms*	pn	pers pron	pn	pn
אֶפְרָתָה	וָאֶקְבְּרֶהָ	שָׁם	בְּדֶרֶךְ	אֶפְרָת	הִוא	בֵּית	לָחֶם
'ephrāthāh	wā'eqŏbrehā	shām	b[e]dherekh	'ephrāth	hiw'	bêth	lāchem
to Ephrathah	and I buried her	there	on the journey of	Ephrathah	that	Beth	Lehem

8. 7495.121	3547	881, 1158	3231	569.121	4449, 431
cj, v Qal impf 3ms	pn	do, *n mp*	pn	cj, v Qal impf 3ms	intrg, dem pron
וַיַּרְא	יִשְׂרָאֵל	אֶת־בְּנֵי	יוֹסֵף	וַיֹּאמֶר	מִי־אֵלֶּה
wayyar'	yisrā'ēl	'eth-b[e]nê	yôs̱ēph	wayyō'mer	mî-'ēlleh
and he saw	Israel	the sons of	Joseph	and he said	who these

9. 569.121	3231	420, 1	1158	2062	866, 5598.121, 3937
cj, v Qal impf 3ms	pn	prep, n ms, ps 3ms	n mp	pers pron	rel part, v Qal pf 3ms, prep, ps 1cs
וַיֹּאמֶר	יוֹסֵף	אֶל־אָבִיו	בָּנַי	הֵם	אֲשֶׁר־נָתַן־לִי
wayyō'mer	yôs̱ēph	'el-'āvîw	bānay	hēm	'ăsher-nāthan-lî
and he said	Joseph	to his father	my children	they	which He gave to me

435	904, 2172	569.121	4089.131, 5167	420	1313.325
n mp	prep, dem pron	cj, v Qal impf 3ms	v Qal impv 2ms, ps 3mp, part	prep, ps 1cs	cj, v Piel impf 1cs
אֱלֹהִים	בָּזֶה	וַיֹּאמַר	קָחֶם־נָא	אֵלַי	וַאֲבָרְכֵם
'ĕlōhîm	bāzeh	wayyō'mar	qāchem-nā'	'ēlay	wa'ăvārkhēm
God	on this	and he said	take them please	to me	and I will bless them

10. 6084	3547	3632.116	4623, 2293	3940	3310.121	3937, 7495.141
cj, *n fd*	pn	v Qal pf 3mp	prep, n ms	neg part	v Qal impf 3ms	prep, v Qal inf con
וְעֵינֵי	יִשְׂרָאֵל	כָּבְדוּ	מִזֹּקֶן	לֹא	יוּכַל	לִרְאוֹת
w[e]‘ênê	yisrā'ēl	kāv[e]dhû	mizzōqen	lō'	yûkhal	lir'ôth
and the eyes of	Israel	they were dull	from old age	not	he was able	to see

5242.521	881	420	5583.121	3937	2354.321
cj, v Hiphil impf 3ms	do, ps 3mp	prep, ps 3ms	cj, v Qal impf 3ms	prep, ps 3mp	cj, v Piel impf 3ms
וַיַּגֵּשׁ	אֹתָם	אֵלָיו	וַיִּשַּׁק	לָהֶם	וַיְחַבֵּק
wayyaggēsh	'ōthām	'ēlâv	wayyishshaq	lāhem	waychabbēq
and he brought near	them	to him	and he kissed	them	and he embraced

3937	**11.** 569.121	3547	420, 3231	7495.141	6686	3940
prep, ps 3mp	cj, v Qal impf 3ms	pn	prep, pn	v Qal inf con	n mp, ps 2ms	neg part
לָהֶם	וַיֹּאמֶר	יִשְׂרָאֵל	אֶל־יוֹסֵף	רְאֹה	פָנֶיךָ	לֹא
lāhem	wayyō'mer	yisrā'ēl	'el-yôs̱ēph	r[e]'ōh	phānêkhā	lō'
them	and he said	Israel	to Joseph	to see	your face	not

6663.315	2079	7495.511	881	435	1612	881, 2320
v Piel pf 1cs	cj, intrj	v Hiphil pf 3ms	do, ps 1cs	n mp	cj	do, n ms, ps 2ms
פִלַּלְתִּי	וְהִנֵּה	הֶרְאָה	אֹתִי	אֱלֹהִים	גַּם	אֶת־זַרְעֶךָ
phillāl[e]tî	w[e]hinnēh	her'āh	'ōthî	'ĕlōhîm	gam	'eth-zar‘ekhā
I expected	and behold	he showed	me	God	also	your seed

12.	3428.521	3231	881	4623, 6196	1314	8246.721
	cj, v Hiphil impf 3ms	pn	do, ps 3mp	prep, prep	n fp, ps 3ms	cj, v Hithpalel impf 3ms
	וַיּוֹצֵא	יוֹסֵף	אֹתָם	מֵעִם	בִּרְכָּיו	וַיִּשְׁתַּחוּ
	wayyôtsē'	yôsēph	'ōthām	mē'im	birkâv	wayyishtachû
	and he brought out	Joseph	them	away from	his knees	and he bowed down

3937, 653	800	13.	4089.121	3231	881, 8530	881, 688
prep, n md, ps 3ms	n fs		cj, v Qal impf 3ms	pn	do, num, ps 3mp	do, pn
לְאַפָּיו	אָרְצָה		וַיִּקַּח	יוֹסֵף	אֶת־שְׁנֵיהֶם	אֶת־אֶפְרַיִם
l^{e}'appâv	'ār^{e}tsāh		wayyiqqach	yôsēph	'eth-sh^{e}nêhem	'eth-'ephrayim
his nostrils	to the ground		and he took	Joseph	the two of them	Ephraim

904, 3332	4623, 7972	3547	881, 4667	904, 7972	4623, 3332	3547
prep, n fs, ps 3ms	prep, *n ms*	pn	cj, do, pn	prep, n ms, ps 3ms	prep, *n fs*	pn
בִּימִינוֹ	מִשְּׂמֹאל	יִשְׂרָאֵל	וְאֶת־מְנַשֶּׁה	בִשְׂמֹאלוֹ	מִימִין	יִשְׂרָאֵל
bîmînô	miss^{e}mō'l	yisrā'ēl	w^{e}'eth-m^{e}nashsheh	vismō'lô	mîmîn	yisrā'ēl
with his right	from the left of	Israel	and Manasseh	with his left	from the right of	Israel

5242.521	420	14.	8365.121	3547	881, 3332	8308.121
cj, v Hiphil impf 3ms	prep, ps 3ms		cj, v Qal impf 3ms	pn	do, n fs, ps 3ms	cj, v Qal impf 3ms
וַיַּגֵּשׁ	אֵלָיו		וַיִּשְׁלַח	יִשְׂרָאֵל	אֶת־יְמִינוֹ	וַיָּשֶׁת
wayyaggēsh	'ēlâv		wayyishlach	yisrā'ēl	'eth-y^{e}mînô	wayyāsheth
and he brought near	to him		and he put out	Israel	his right	and he placed

8. And Israel beheld Joseph's sons, and said, Who are these?: ... then Israel looked at the sons of Joseph, and said, These are mine!, *Fenton.*

9. And Joseph said unto his father, They are my sons, whom God hath given me in this place. And he said, Bring them, I pray thee, unto me, and I will bless them: ... Please lead them to me, he said,and I will bless them, *Berkeley* ... so that I may take them on my knees, *NEB.*

10. Now the eyes of Israel were dim for age, so that he could not see. And he brought them near unto him; and he kissed them, and embraced them: ... heavy, *Young* ... folding them in his arms, *BB.*

11. And Israel said unto Joseph, I had not thought to see thy face: and, lo, God hath shewed me also thy seed: ... I had no hope of seeing your face again, *BB* ... God has allowed me to see your children too, *NIV* ... progeny, *Anchor* ... offspring, *NKJV.*

12. And Joseph brought them out from between his knees, and he bowed himself with his face to the earth: ... Then Joseph removed them from Israel's knees, *NIV* ... did reverence down to the ground, *Geneva* ... Then Joseph brought them for his blessing and they bowed before his face, earthward, *Fenton* ... prostrated himself with his face to the ground, *NCB.*

13. And Joseph took them both, Ephraim in his right hand toward Israel's left hand, and Manasseh in his left hand toward Israel's right hand, and brought them near unto him: ... Ephraim on the right, that is Israel's left; and Manasseh on the left, that is Israel's right, *REB.*

14. And Israel stretched out his right hand, and laid it upon Ephraim's head, who was the younger and his left hand upon Manasseh's head, guiding his hands wittingly; for Manasseh was the firstborn: ... guided his hands wisely, *Young* ... confusing his hands, *Goodspeed* ... intentionally, *Fenton* ... crossing his hands on purpose for Manasseh was the older, *BB.*

48:8-10. Jacob was losing his sight from old age and it was not until this point that he became aware of Joseph's sons being there. Joseph gave God glory for giving him these sons, and Jacob asked him to bring them to him so he could bless them. When they came close, Jacob kissed and hugged them.

48:11-12. Jacob remembered how he never expected to see Joseph again, and now God had let him see Joseph's children. Then Joseph brought them from his knees and Joseph bowed low before his father. To do this, he took his sons away from beside Jacob's knees.

48:13-14. Then Joseph put Ephraim by Jacob's left hand and Manasseh by Jacob's right hand. Jacob, however, deliberately crossed his hands and put his right hand on Ephraim's head and his left hand on Manasseh's, though he knew Manasseh was the firstborn. (This is the Bible's first mention of laying on of hands in blessing.)

6142, 7513	688	2000	7087	881, 7972	6142, 7513	4667
prep, *n ms*	pn	cj, pers pron	art, adj	cj, do, n ms, ps 3ms	prep, *n ms*	pn
עַל־רֹאשׁ	אֶפְרַיִם	וְהוּא	הַצָּעִיר	וְאֶת־שְׂמֹאלוֹ	עַל־רֹאשׁ	מְנַשֶּׁה
'al-rō'sh	'ephrayim	w^{e}hû'	hatstā'îr	w^{e}'eth-s^{e}mō'lô	'al-rō'sh	m^{e}nashsheh
on the head of	Ephraim	and he	the younger	and his left	on the head of	Manasseh

7959.311	881, 3135	3706	4667	1111	15.	1313.321	881, 3231
v Piel pf 3ms	do, n fd, ps 3ms	cj	pn	art, n ms		cj, v Piel impf 3ms	do, pn
שִׂכֵּל	אֶת־יָדָיו	כִּי	מְנַשֶּׁה	הַבְּכוֹר		וַיְבָרֶךְ	אֶת־יוֹסֵף
sikkēl	'eth-yādhâv	kî	m^{e}nashsheh	habb^{e}khôr		way^{e}vārekh	'eth-yôsēph
he understood	his hands	that	Manasseh	the first-born		and he blessed	Joseph

569.121	435	866	2050.716	1	3937, 6686	80
cj, v Qal impf 3ms	art, n mp	rel part	v Hithpael pf 3cp	n mp, ps 1cs	prep, n mp, ps 3ms	pn
וַיֹּאמַר	הָאֱלֹהִים	אֲשֶׁר	הִתְהַלְּכוּ	אֲבֹתַי	לְפָנָיו	אַבְרָהָם
wayyō'mar	hā'ĕlōhîm	'ăsher	hithhall^{e}khû	'ăvōthay	l^{e}phānâv	'avrāhām
and he said	the God	which	they walked	my fathers	before him	Abraham

3437	435	7749.151	881	4623, 5968	5912, 3219
cj, pn	art, n mp	art, v Qal act ptc ms	do, ps 1cs	prep, adv, ps 1cs	prep, art, n ms
וְיִצְחָק	הָאֱלֹהִים	הָרֹעֶה	אֹתִי	מֵעוֹדִי	עַד־הַיּוֹם
w^{e}yitschāq	hā'ĕlōhîm	hārō'eh	'ōthî	mē'ôdhî	'adh-hayyôm
and Isaac	God	the One leading	me	all my life long	until the day

2172	16.	4534	1381.151	881	4623, 3725, 7737	1313.321
art, dem pron		art, n ms	art, v Qal act ptc ms	do, ps 1cs	prep, *adj*, n ms	v Piel juss 3ms
הַזֶּה		הַמַּלְאָךְ	הַגֹּאֵל	אֹתִי	מִכָּל־רָע	יְבָרֵךְ
hazzeh		hammal'ākh	haggō'ēl	'ōthî	mikkol-rā'	y^{e}vārēkh
the this		the Angel	the One redeeming	me	from all evil	may He bless

881, 5470	7410.221	904	8428	8428	1
do, art, n mp	cj, v Niphal juss 3ms	prep, ps 3mp	n ms, ps 1cs	cj, *n ms*	n mp, ps 1cs
אֶת־הַנְּעָרִים	וְיִקָּרֵא	בָהֶם	שְׁמִי	וְשֵׁם	אֲבֹתַי
'eth-hann^{e}'ārîm	w^{e}yiqqārē'	vāhem	sh^{e}mî	w^{e}shēm	'ăvōthay
the boys	and may it be named	among them	my name	and the name of	my fathers

80	3437	1760.126	3937, 7525.141	904, 7419	800
pn	cj, pn	cj, v Qal impf 3mp	prep, v Qal inf con	prep, *n ms*	art, n fs
אַבְרָהָם	וְיִצְחָק	וְיִדְגּוּ	לָרֹב	בְּקֶרֶב	הָאָרֶץ
'avrāhām	w^{e}yitschāq	w^{e}yidhgû	lārōv	b^{e}qerev	hā'ārets
Abraham	and Isaac	and they will become numerous	multiplying	in the midst of	the land

17.	7495.121	3231	3706, 8308.121	1	3135, 3332	6142, 7513
	cj, v Qal impf 3ms	pn	cj, v Qal impf 3ms	n ms, ps	*n fs*, n fs, ps 3ms	prep, *n ms*
	וַיַּרְא	יוֹסֵף	כִּי־יָשִׁית	אָבִיו	יַד־יְמִינוֹ	עַל־רֹאשׁ
	wayyar^{e}'	yôsēph	kî-yāshîth	'āvîw	yadh-y^{e}mînô	'al-rō'sh
	and he saw	Joseph	that he placed	his father	hand of his right	on the head of

688	7778.121	904, 6084	8881.121	3135, 1	3937, 5681.141
pn	cj, v Qal impf 3ms	prep, n fd, ps 3ms	cj, v Qal impf 3ms	*n fs*, n ms, ps 3ms	prep, v Hiphil inf con
אֶפְרַיִם	וַיֵּרַע	בְּעֵינָיו	וַיִּתְמֹךְ	יַד־אָבִיו	לְהָסִיר
'ephrayim	wayyēra'	b^{e}'ênâv	wayyithmōkh	yadh-'āvîw	l^{e}hāsîr
Ephraim	and it was noxious	in his eyes	and he took hold of	the hand of his father	to remove

881	4263, 6142	7513, 688	6142, 7513	4667	18.	569.121	3231
do, ps 3fs	prep, prep	*n ms*, pn	prep, *n ms*	pn		cj, v Qal impf 3ms	pn
אֹתָהּ	מֵעַל	רֹאשׁ־אֶפְרַיִם	עַל־רֹאשׁ	מְנַשֶּׁה		וַיֹּאמֶר	יוֹסֵף
'ōthāhh	mē'al	rō'sh-'ephrayim	'al-rō'sh	m^{e}nashsheh		wayyō'mer	yôsēph
it	from	the head of Ephraim	onto the head of	Manasseh		and he said	Joseph

420, 1	3940, 3772	1	3706, 2172	1111	7947.131	3332
prep, n ms, ps 3ms	neg part, adv	n ms, ps 1cs	cj, dem pron	art, n ms	v Qal impv 2ms	n fs, ps 2ms
אֶל־אָבִיו	לֹא־כֵן	אָבִי	כִּי־זֶה	הַבְּכֹר	שִׂים	יְמִינְךָ
'el-'āvîw	lō'-khēn	'āvî	kî-zeh	habb^{e}khōr	sîm	y^{e}mîn^{e}khā
to his father	not so	my father	because this	the first-born	put	your right hand

6142, 7513		4126.321	1	569.121	3156.115	1158	3156.115
prep, n ms, ps 3ms		cj, v Piel impf 3ms	n ms, ps	cj, v Qal impf 3ms	v Qal pf 1cs	n ms, ps 1cs	v Qal pf 1cs
עַל־רֹאשׁוֹ	19.	וַיְמָאֵן	אָבִיו	וַיֹּאמֶר	יָדַעְתִּי	בְנִי	יָדַעְתִּי
'al-rō'shô		waymā'ēn	'āvîw	wayyō'mer	yādha'ăttî	v^{e}nî	yādha'ăttî
on his head		but he refused	his father	and he said	I know	my son	I know

1612, 2000	2030.121, 3937, 6194	1612, 2000	1461.121	195	250
cj, pers pron	v Qal impf 3ms, prep, n ms	cj, cj, pers pron	v Qal impf 3ms	cj, cj	n ms, ps 3ms
גַּם־הוּא	יִהְיֶה־לְּעָם	וְגַם־הוּא	יִגְדָּל	וְאוּלָם	אָחִיו
gam-hû'	yihyeh-l^{e}'ām	w^{e}gham-hû'	yighdāl	w^{e}'ûlām	'āchîw
also he	he will be for a people	and also he	he will be great	and yet	his brother

15. And he blessed Joseph, and said, God, before whom my fathers Abraham and Isaac did walk: ... Abraham and Isaac, gave worship, *BB* ... The God in whose presence my forefathers lived, *NEB* ... before whom my fathers Abraham and Isaac walked habitually, *Young*.

the God which fed me all my life long unto this day: ... led, *RSV* ... who has been my Shepherd all my life to this day, *NIV* ... the God who appeared to me from of old, *Fenton*.

16. The Angel which redeemed me from all evil: ... delivered, *NCB* ... continually redeemed, *Berkeley* ... rescued, *REB* ... the messenger who redeemed me from all misfortunes, *Fenton*.

bless the lads; and let my name be named on them, and the name of my fathers Abraham and Isaac, and let them grow into a multitude in the midst of the earth: ... give them my power ... pour out their increase to the bounds of the earth, *Fenton* ... may my name live on in them, *NASB* ... may they grow into a great people on earth, *REB*.

17. And when Joseph saw that his father laid his right hand upon the head of Ephraim, it displeased him: and he held up his father's hand, to remove it from Ephraim's head unto Manasseh's head: ... this seemed wrong to him, *NAB* ... took hold of his fathers hand, *NCB*.

18. And Joseph said unto his father, Not so, my father: for this is the firstborn; put thy right hand upon his head: ... this is not right, *NCB*.

19. And his father refused, and said, I know it, my son, I know it: he also shall become a people, and he also shall be great: but truly his younger brother shall be greater than he, and his seed shall become a multitude of nations: ... I am doing it on purpose, my son, *BB* ... completeness of nations, *Berkeley*.

48:15-16. The blessing of the two sons was also for Joseph. Jacob began by identifying the Source of the blessing, the God before whom Abraham and Isaac lived, the One who led Jacob like a shepherd all his life long, the Angel (probably a reference to Jacob's experience at Peniel) continually redeeming Jacob from all evil (including all the harm and danger he suffered). This One would bless the young men and they will call Him by Jacob's name as well as by the name of Abraham and Isaac. That is, they would refer to Him as the God of Abraham, Isaac, and Jacob. They would become numerous, multiplying in the midst of the land (the promised land (see v. 4). That is, they would share in the blessing of Abraham. This act of blessing shows how sincere Jacob's faith in God was. (See Hebrews 11:21.)

48:17-19. In Joseph's judgment, it was unfortunate that Jacob put his right hand on his younger son, Ephraim's head. So he took hold of Jacob's right hand and tried to move it to Manasseh's head, but Jacob refused to let him. Jacob knew what he was doing, and he had prophetic foreknowledge that though Manasseh's descendants would be great, Ephraim's would be greater and become a multitude of peoples.

Throughout Genesis we have seen God choosing younger sons. God continued to do this often in Israel's later history. Gideon, David, Solomon, and many others whom God used were younger sons. Faith, along with sincere love for God, have always meant more than mere natural inheritance.

7277	1461.121	4623	2320	2030.121	4530, 1504
art, adj	v Qal impf 3ms	prep, ps 3ms	cj, n ms, ps 3ms	v Qal impf 3ms	*n ms*, art, n mp
הַקָּטֹן	יִגְדַּל	מִמֶּנּוּ	וְזַרְעוֹ	יִהְיֶה	מְלֹא־הַגּוֹיִם
haqqātōn	yighdal	mimmennû	wezar'ô	yihyeh	melō'-haggôyim
the youngest	he will be greater	than him	and his seed	it will be	multitude of nations

	1313.321	904, 3219	2000	3937, 569.141	904	1313.321
20.	cj, v Piel impf 3ms, ps 3mp	prep, art, n ms	art, dem pron	prep, v Qal inf con	prep, ps 2ms	v Piel impf 3ms
	וַיְבָרְכֵם	בַּיּוֹם	הַהוּא	לֵאמוֹר	בְּךָ	יְבָרֵךְ
	wayvārekhēm	bayyôm	hahû'	lē'môr	bekhā	yevārēkh
	and he blessed them	on the day	the that	by saying	by you	he will bless

3547	3937, 569.141	7947.121	435	3626, 688	3626, 4667
pn	prep, v Qal inf con	v Qal juss 3ms, ps 2ms	n mp	prep, pn	cj, prep, pn
יִשְׂרָאֵל	לֵאמֹר	יְשִׂמְךָ	אֱלֹהִים	כְּאֶפְרַיִם	וְכִמְנַשֶּׁה
yisrā'ēl	lē'mōr	yesimekhā	'ĕlōhîm	ke'ephrayim	wekhimnashsheh
Israel	saying	may He make you	God	like Ephraim	and like Manasseh

7947.121	881, 688	3937, 6686	4667		569.121	3547	420, 3231
cj, v Qal impf 3ms	do, pn	prep, *n mp*	pn	**21.**	cj, v Qal impf 3ms	pn	prep, pn
וַיָּשֶׂם	אֶת־אֶפְרַיִם	לִפְנֵי	מְנַשֶּׁה		וַיֹּאמֶר	יִשְׂרָאֵל	אֶל־יוֹסֵף
wayyāsem	'eth-'ephrayim	liphnê	menashsheh		wayyō'mer	yisrā'ēl	'el-yôsēph
this he put	Ephraim	before	Manasseh		and he said	Israel	to Joseph

2079	609	4322.151	2030.111	435	6196	8178.511
intrj	pers pron	v Qal act ptc ms	cj, v Qal pf 3ms	n mp	prep, ps 2mp	cj, v Hiphil pf 3ms
הִנֵּה	אָנֹכִי	מֵת	וְהָיָה	אֱלֹהִים	עִמָּכֶם	וְהֵשִׁיב
hinnēh	'ānōkhî	mēth	wehāyāh	'ĕlōhîm	'immākhem	wehēshîv
behold	I	dying	and He will be	God	with you	and He will bring back

881	420, 800	1		603	5598.115	3937	8327
do, ps 2mp	prep, *n fs*	n mp, ps 2mp	**22.**	cj, pers pron	v Qal pf 1cs	prep, ps 2ms	n ms
אֶתְכֶם	אֶל־אֶרֶץ	אֲבֹתֵיכֶם		וַאֲנִי	נָתַתִּי	לְךָ	שְׁכֶם
'ethkhem	'el-'erets	'ăvōthêkhem		wa'ănî	nāthattî	lekhā	shekhem
you	to the land of	your fathers		and I	I have given	to you	ridge

259	6142, 250	866	4089.115	4623, 3135	578	904, 2820
num	prep, n mp, ps 2ms	rel part	v Qal pf 1cs	prep, *n fs*	art, pn	prep, n fs, ps 1cs
אַחַד	עַל־אַחֶיךָ	אֲשֶׁר	לָקַחְתִּי	מִיַּד	הָאֱמֹרִי	בְּחַרְבִּי
'achadh	'al-'achêkhā	'ăsher	lāqachtî	miyyadh	hā'ĕmōrî	becharbî
one	above your brothers	which	I took	from the hand of	the Amorites	with my sword

904, 7493		7410.121	3399	420, 1158	569.121	636.233
cj, prep, n fs, ps 1cs	**49:1**	cj, v Qal impf 3ms	pn	prep, n mp, ps 3ms	cj, v Qal impf 3ms	v Niphal impv 2mp
וּבְקַשְׁתִּי		וַיִּקְרָא	יַעֲקֹב	אֶל־בָּנָיו	וַיֹּאמֶר	הֵאָסְפוּ
ûveqashtî		wayyiqōrā'	ya'ăqōv	'el-bānâv	wayyō'mer	hē'āsephû
and with my bow		and he summoned	Jacob	his sons	and he said	gather yourselves

5222.525	3937	881	866, 7410.121	882	904, 311	3219
cj, v Hiphil impf 1cs	prep, ps 2mp	do	rel part, v Qal impf 3ms	prep, ps 2mp	prep, *sub*	art, n mp
וְאַגִּידָה	לָכֶם	אֵת	אֲשֶׁר־יִקְרָא	אֶתְכֶם	בְּאַחֲרִית	הַיָּמִים
we'aggîdhāh	lākhem	'ēth	'ăsher-yiqōrā'	'ethkhem	be'achrîth	hayyāmîm
and I will tell	to you		what will happen	to you	in the end of	the days

	7192.233	8471.133	1158	3399	8471.133	420, 3547
2.	v Niphal impv 2mp	cj, v Qal impv 2mp	*n mp*	pn	cj, v Qal impv 2mp	prep, pn
	הִקָּבְצוּ	וְשִׁמְעוּ	בְּנֵי	יַעֲקֹב	וְשִׁמְעוּ	אֶל־יִשְׂרָאֵל
	hiqqāvetsû	weshim'û	benê	ya'ăqōv	weshim'û	'el-yisrā'ēl
	assemble yourselves	and hear	the sons of	Jacob	and listen	to Israel

1 n ms, ps 2mp		7498 pn	1111 n ms, ps 1cs	887 pers pron	3699 n ms, ps 1cs	7519 cj, *n fs*
אֲבִיכֶם	**3.**	רְאוּבֵן	בְּכֹרִי	אַתָּה	כֹּחִי	וְרֵאשִׁית
'ăvîkhem		re'ûvēn	beckōrî	'attāh	kōchî	wᵉrē'shîth
your father		Reuben	my first-born	you	my might	and the beginning of

202 n ms, ps 1cs	3615 *adj*	7874 n fs	3615 cj, *adj*	6007 n ms		6591 adj	3626, 4448 prep, n mp
אוֹנִי	יֶתֶר	שְׂאֵת	וְיֶתֶר	עָז	**4.**	פַּחַז	כַּמַּיִם
'ônî	yether	sᵉ'ēth	wᵉyether	'āz		pachaz	kammayim
my generative power	preeminent of	dignity	and preeminent of	strength		unstable	as water

20. And he blessed them that day, saying, In thee shall Israel bless, saying, God make thee as Ephraim and as Manasseh: and he set Ephraim before Manasseh: ... and when blessing in that period they shall say, *Fenton* ... When a blessing is pronounced in Israel, *REB* ... By you Israel will invoke blessings, *NRSV*.

21. And Israel said unto Joseph, Behold, I die; but God shall be with you, and bring you again unto the land of your fathers: ... I am about to die, *NASB* ... and restore you to the land of your fathers, *NAB* ... ancestors, *NRSV*.

22. Moreover I have given to thee one portion above thy brethren, which I took out of the hand of the Amorite with my sword and with my bow: ... therefore I give to you Shekem, *Fenton* ... I have given to you rather than to your brothers one mountain slope, *RSV* ... where I assign you one ridge of land more than your brothers, *REB* ... captured from the Amorrites, *NCB* ... As an extra legacy among your kinsfold I am leaving you the ridge I took from the Amorite with my sword and my bow, *Berkeley*.

49:1. And Jacob called unto his sons, and said, Gather yourselves together, that I may tell you that which shall befall you in the last days: ... give you news of your fate in future times, *BB* ... tell you that which shall befall you in the end of days, *MAST* ... tell you what will happen to you in days to come, *NRSV*.

2. Gather yourselves together, and hear, ye sons of Jacob; and hearken unto Israel your father: ... come near, O sons of Jacob, and give ear to the words, *BB* ... form a circle and hear, *Berkley*.

3. Reuben, thou art my firstborn, my might, and the beginning of my strength: ... the first fruit of my manly vigor, *Goodspeed* ... the crown of my passion, *Fenton* ... the first-fruit of my manhood, *NCB* ... the first issue of my vitality, *Berkley*.

the excellency of dignity, and the excellency of power: ... excelling in pride, excelling in might, *REB* ... excelling in rank and excelling in power, *NRSV* ... the abundance of exaltation and the the abundance of strength, *Young* ... excelling in beauty and excelling in strength, *Fenton* ... excessively proud and excessively fierce, *Goodspeed*.

48:20. The blessing of God would be so evident on Ephraim and Manasseh that in the future the people of Israel would bless by saying, "May God make you as Ephraim and Manasseh." In this also, Jacob put Ephraim before Manasseh.

48:21-22. Jacob realized he was about to die, but he assured Joseph God would be with him and bring him again into the land promised to Abraham and Isaac. Jacob also gave Joseph one "ridge" more than to his brothers, for Jacob took it from Amorites with his sword and his bow. (Ridge translates the Hebrew *Shechem*. Some believe Jacob went back and retook the city; others take ridge to mean "portion.") This seems to refer to an event not recorded in the Bible.

The Bible does not always give every event that happens. It often jumped over several years in the lives of Abraham, Isaac, and Jacob.

49:1-2. Before Jacob died, he gathered his sons together (probably by sending messengers to them). With prophetic insight, he told something about each one and what they and their descendants would do in the end of the days, that is, in the distant future. The chapter, beginning with verse 2, is poetic in form as shown by the use of parallelism (a rhythm of repeated ideas).

49:3-4. He began with Reuben, his firstborn, his might, the beginning of his generative power. As the firstborn, he received excellence of dignity and strength. But because he was unstable as water, Jacob could not let him have the preeminence. He showed his instability and lack of accountability by raping his father's wife (35:22; Deut. 27:20). By this he defiled his father's bed (as well as himself, Bilhah, and the family as a whole) and became unworthy of family leadership in worship.

414, 3613.523	3706	6148.113	5085	1	226
adv, v Hiphil juss 2ms	cj	v Qal pf 2ms	*n mp*	n ms, ps 2ms	adv
אַל־תּוֹתַר	כִּי	עָלִיתָ	מִשְׁכְּבֵי	אָבִיךָ	אָז
'al-tôthar	kî	'ālîthā	mishk^{e}vê	'āvîkhā	'āz
you may not have preeminence	because	you climbed into	the beds of	your father	then

2591.313	3435	6148.111		8482	4015	250	3747
v Piel pf 2ms	n ms, ps 1cs	v Qal pf 3ms	**5.**	pn	cj, pn	n mp	*n mp*
חִלַּלְתָּ	יְצוּעִי	עָלָה		שִׁמְעוֹן	וְלֵוִי	אַחִים	כְּלֵי
chillal^{e}ttā	y^{e}tsû'î	'āl^{e}h		shim'ôn	w^{e}lēwî	'achîm	k^{e}lê
you defiled	my bed	he went up		Simeon	and Levi	brothers	weapons of

2660	4517		904, 5660	420, 971.122	5497	904, 7235
n ms	n fp, ps 3mp	**6.**	prep, n ms, ps 3mp	adv, v Qal juss 3fs	n fs, ps 1cs	prep, n ms, ps 3mp
חָמָס	מְכֵרֹתֵיהֶם		בְּסֹדָם	אַל־תָּבֹא	נַפְשִׁי	בִּקְהָלָם
chāmās̱	m^{e}khērōthêhem		b^{e}s̱ōdhām	'al-tāvō'	naphshî	biqŏhālām
violence	their plans		into their council	it may not come	my soul	with their assembly

420, 3265.122	3638	3706	904, 653	2103.116	382	904, 7814
adv, v Qal juss 3fs	n fs, ps 1cs	cj	prep, n ms, ps 3mp	v Qal pf 3cp	n ms	cj, prep, n ms, ps 3mp
אַל־תֵּחַד	כְּבֹדִי	כִּי	בְאַפָּם	הָרְגוּ	אִישׁ	וּבִרְצֹנָם
'al-tēchadh	k^{e}vōdhî	kî	v^{e}'appām	hār^{e}ghû	'îsh	ûvirtsōnām
it may not be joined	my honor	because	in their anger	they killed	man	and by their will

6369.316, 8228		803.155	653	3706	6007	5887
v Piel pf 3cp, n ms	**7.**	v Qal pass ptc ms	n ms, ps 3mp	cj	n ms	cj, n fs, ps 3mp
עִקְּרוּ־שׁוֹר		אָרוּר	אַפָּם	כִּי	עָז	וְעֶבְרָתָם
'iqq^{e}rû-shôr		'ārûr	'appām	kî	'āz	w^{e}'evrāthām
they hamstrung oxen		cursed	their anger	because	strong	and their rage

3706	7481.112	2606.325	904, 3399	6571.525	904, 3547
cj	v Qal pf 3fs	v Piel impf 1cs, ps 3mp	prep, pn	cj, v Hiphil impf 1cs	prep, pn
כִּי	קָשָׁתָה	אֲחַלְּקֵם	בְּיַעֲקֹב	וַאֲפִיצֵם	בְּיִשְׂרָאֵל
kî	qāshāthāh	'ăchall^{e}qēm	b^{e}ya'ăqōv	wa'ăphîtsēm	b^{e}yisrā'ēl
because	it is fierce	I will divide them	in Jacob	and I will scatter them	in Israel

	3171	887	3142.526	250	3135	904, 6439
8.	pn	pers pron	v Hiphil impf 3mp, ps 2ms	n mp, ps 2ms	n fs, ps 2ms	prep, *n ms*
	יְהוּדָה	אַתָּה	יוֹדוּךָ	אַחֶיךָ	יָדְךָ	בְּעֹרֶף
	y^{e}hûdhāh	'attāh	yôdûkh	'achêkh	yadh^{e}kh	b^{e}'ōreph
	Judah	you	they will praise you	your brothers	your hand	on the neck of

342.152	8246.726	3937	1158	1		1514	765
v Qal act ptc mp, ps 2ms	v Hithpael impf 3mp	prep, ps 2ms	*n mp*	nn ms, ps 2ms	**9.**	*n ms*	n ms
אֹיְבֶיךָ	יִשְׁתַּחֲווּ	לְךָ	בְּנֵי	אָבִיךָ		גּוּר	אַרְיֵה
'ōy^{e}vêkh	yishtachăwû	l^{e}kh	b^{e}nê	'āvîkh		gûr	'aryēh
your enemies	they will bow down	to you	the sons of	your father		cub of	lion

3171	4623, 3073	1158	6148.113	3895.111	7547.111	3626, 765
pn	prep, n ms	n ms, ps 1cs	v Qal pf 2ms	v Qal pf 3ms	v Qal pf 3ms	prep, n ms
יְהוּדָה	מִטֶּרֶף	בְּנִי	עָלִיתָ	כָּרַע	רָבַץ	כְּאַרְיֵה
y^{e}hûdhāh	miṯṯereph	b^{e}nî	'ālîthā	kāra'	rāvats	k^{e}'aryēh
Judah	from prey	my son	you went up	he bent down	he couched down	like lion

3626, 3965	4449	7251.521		3940, 5681.121	8101	4623, 3171
cj, prep, n ms	intrg	v Hiphil impf 3ms, ps 3ms	**10.**	neg part, v Qal impf 3ms	n ms	prep, pn
וּכְלָבִיא	מִי	יְקִימֶנּוּ		לֹא־יָסוּר	שֵׁבֶט	מִיהוּדָה
ûkh^{e}lāvî'	mî	y^{e}qîmennû		lō'-yās̱ûr	shēveṯ	mîhûdhāh
and like lion	who	will cause him to rise		not it will depart	scepter	from Judah

4. Unstable as water, thou shalt not excel: ... boiling like water you lost command, *Fenton* ... never first shall you be, *NCB* ... thou art not abundant, *Young.*

because thou wentest up to thy father's bed; then defiledst thou it: he went up to my couch. ... you defiled his concubine's couch, *NEB* ... so I degraded him who went up to my couch, *Goodspeed* ... and defiled my couch to my sorrow, *NAB.*

5. Simeon and Levi are brethren; instruments of cruelty are in their habitations. ... brethern in evil, *Geneva* ... their wares are the tools of lawlessness, *Anchor* ... weapons of violence their kinship, *MAST* ... their counsels, *REB* ... deceit and force are their secret designs, *BB.*

6. O my soul, come not thou into their secret; unto their assembly, mine honour, be not thou united: ... do not share in their plot, *Berkley* ... I will never enter their circle, *Goodspeed* ... let not my being be counted in their assembly, *Torah.*

for in their anger they slew a man, and in their selfwill they digged down a wall: ... and for their pleasure even oxen were wounded, *BB* ... and at their whim they hamstrung oxen, *NRSV* ... and joyfully murdered a prince, *Fenton.*

7. Cursed be their anger, for it was fierce; and their wrath, for it was cruel: ... curse their creme, as great, and their transgression, *Fenton* ... and their wrath so relentless, *Torah.*

I will divide them in Jacob, and scatter them in Israel: ... I will let their heritage in Jacob be broken up, driving them from their places in Israel, *BB* ... For it sorely troubled Jacob, and Israel shamed, *Fenton.*

8. Judah, thou art he whom thy brethren shall praise: thy hand shall be in the neck of thine enemies; thy father's children shall bow down before thee: ... your father's sons shall do you homage, *NEB.*

9. Judah is a lion's whelp: from the prey, my son, thou art gone up: ... like a lion full of meat you have become great, my son, *BB* ... you return from the prey, *NIV* ... you have grown up on prey, *NAB.*

he stooped down, he couched as a lion, and as an old lion; who shall rouse him up?: ... like a lioness-who dares to rouse him, *NIV.*

10. The sceptre shall not depart from Judah, nor a lawgiver from between his feet: ... the mace between his legs, *NAB* ... will hold the royal scepter, and his descendants will always rule, *Good News.*

until Shiloh come; and unto him shall the gathering of the people be: ... till peace arrive and the nations obey him, *Fenton* ... while tribute is brought to him and he receives the peoples' homage, *NAB*. . . as long as men come to Shiloh; And unto him shall the obedience of the peoples be, *MAST* ... till he comes who has the right to it, and the peoples will put themselves under his rule, *BB.*

49:5-7. Simeon and Levi joined together in the massacre of the men of Shechem (34:25). Jacob now sees them as brothers with weapons of violence in their plans. Jacob would not come into their confidence, nor would his honor be joined with their assembly because they killed men in anger and deliberately chose to hamstring (cut the leg tendons of) oxen. Jacob then pronounced a curse on their arrogant anger and fierce rage (which they probably thought was righteous indignation). He would divide and scatter them in Jacob, in Israel, that is, among the other tribes. When Joshua divided the land, Simeon was scattered in the midst of the inheritance of Judah (Josh. 19:1). The tribe of Levi was given cities scattered through the remaining tribes (Josh. 21:1-40).

49:8-9. Jacob gives more attention to Judah than to any of the rest of the sons of Leah. He will live up to the meaning of his name, for his brothers will praise him. His hand on the back of the neck of his enemies means he will conquer them, and his father's descendants will bow down to him. That is, a descendant of his would take the leadership over the tribes of Israel. Judah is compared to a lion's cub, a lion, and a lioness because of future victories. The lion was a symbol of courage, power and sovereignty. The New Testament calls Jesus the Lion of the tribe of Judah (Rev. 5:5).

49:10. Now Jacob is specific. Not only would a descendant of Judah reign as king, but also the royal scepter would not depart from Judah nor would the royal scepter depart from between his feet until "Shiloh" comes. Shiloh seems to be an abbreviate expression meaning "He to whom it belongs," and thus refers to the Messiah, God's anointed Prophet, Priest, and King. The obedience of the peoples will be to Him. See Ezekiel 21:26-27 where God tells Zedekiah, the profane, wicked last king of Judah, to take off his crown. It would not be restored until the One comes to whom it rightfully belongs. The Jewish Targums interpreted this to mean "until Messiah comes." It will have its fulfillment in the Millennium when "The kingdoms of this world are become the kingdoms of our Lord, and of his Christ; and he shall reign for ever and ever" (Rev. 11:15).

2809.351	4623, 1033	7559	5912	3706, 971.121	866, 3937	3937
cj, v Poel ptc ms	prep, prep	n fd, ps 3ms	adv	cj, v Qal impf 3ms	rel part, prep, ps 3ms	cj, prep, ps 3ms
וּמְחֹקֵק	מִבֵּין	רַגְלָיו	עַד	כִּי־יָבֹא	שִׁילֹה	וְלוֹ
ûm^{e}chōqēq	mibbên	raghlâv	'adh	kîyāvō'	shîlōh	w^{e}lô
and royal scepter	from between	his feet	until	that he comes	which to him	and to him

3459	6194		636.151	3937, 1655	6114	3937, 8048
n fs	n mp	**11.**	*v Qal act ptc mp*	prep, art, n fs	n ms, ps 3ms	cj, prep, art, n fs
יִקְּהַת	עַמִּים		אֹסְרִי	לַגֶּפֶן	עִירֹה	וְלַשֹּׂרֵקָה
yiqq^{e}hath	'ammîm		'ōsrî	laggephen	'îrōh	w^{e}lassōrēqāh
obedience of	peoples		ones binding	to the vine	his donkey	and to the finest vine

1158	888	3645.311	904, 3302	3961	904, 1879, 6252
n ms	n fs, ps 3ms	v Piel pf 3ms	prep, art, n ms	n ms, ps 3ms	cj, prep, *n ms*, n mp
בְּנִי	אֲתֹנוֹ	כִּבֵּס	בַּיַּיִן	לְבֻשׁוֹ	וּבְדַם־עֲנָבִים
b^{e}nî	'ăthōnô	kibbēs	bayyayin	l^{e}vushô	ûv^{e}dham-'ănāvîm
the young of	his female donkey	he washed	in the wine	his clothes	and in the blood of grapes

5685		2547	6084	4623, 3302	3968, 8514	4623, 2560
n ms, ps 3ms	**12.**	adj	n fd	prep, n ms	cj, *adj*, n fd	prep, n ms
סוּתֹה		חַכְלִילִי	עֵינַיִם	מִיָּיִן	וּלְבֶן־שִׁנַּיִם	מֵחָלָב
sûthōh		chakhlîlî	'ênayim	miyyāyin	ûlăven-shinnayim	mēchālāv
his garments		dark	eyes	from wine	and white of teeth	from milk

	2157	3937, 2442	3328	8331.121	2000	3937, 2442	605
13.	pn	prep, *n ms*	n mp	v Qal impf 3ms	cj, pers pron	prep, *n ms*	n fp
	זְבוּלֻן	לְחוֹף	יַמִּים	יִשְׁכֹּן	וְהוּא	לְחוֹף	אֳנִיֹּת
	z^{e}vûlun	l^{e}chôph	yammîm	yishkōn	w^{e}hû'	l^{e}chôph	'ŏniyyōth
	Zebulun	toward shore of	seas	he will dwell	and he	for shore of	ships

3526	6142, 6991		3551	2645	1678	7547.151	1033
cj, n fs, ps 3ms	prep, pn	**14.**	pn	n ms	adj	v Qal act ptc ms	prep
וְיַרְכָתוֹ	עַל־צִידֹן		יִשָּׂשכָר	חֲמֹר	גָּרֶם	רֹבֵץ	בֵּין
w^{e}yar^{e}khāthô	'al-tsîdhōn		yissākhār	chămōr	gārem	rōvēts	bên
and his flank	at Sidon		Issachar	donkey	bony	couching	between

5123		7495.121	4640	3706	3005	881, 800	3706
art, n md	**15.**	cj, v Qal impf 3ms	n fs	cj	adj	cj, do, art, n fs	cj
הַמִּשְׁפְּתָיִם		וַיַּרְא	מְנֻחָה	כִּי	טוֹב	וְאֶת־הָאָרֶץ	כִּי
hammishp^{e}thāyim		wayyar^{e}'	m^{e}nuchāh	kî	tôv	w^{e}'eth-hā'ārets	kî
the saddlebags		and he will see	a resting place	that	good	and the land	that

5459.112	5371.121	8327	3937, 5628.141	2030.121
v Qal pf 3fs	cj, v Qal impf 3ms	n ms, ps 3ms	prep, v Qal inf con	cj, v Qal impf 3ms
נָעֵמָה	וַיֵּט	שִׁכְמוֹ	לִסְבֹּל	וַיְהִי
nā'ēmāh	wayyēt	shikhmô	lisbōl	wayhî
it was pleasant	and he will bend down	his shoulder	to bear	and he will become

3937, 4671, 5856.151		1896	1833.121	6194	3626, 259	8101
prep, *n ms*, v Qal act ptc ms	**16.**	pn	v Qal impf 3ms	n ms, ps 3ms	prep, *num*	*n mp*
לְמַס־עֹבֵד		דָּן	יָדִין	עַמּוֹ	כְּאַחַד	שִׁבְטֵי
l^{e}mas-'ōvēdh		dān	yādhîn	'ammô	k^{e}'achadh	shivtê
for forced labor of slave		Dan	he will judge	his people	as one of	the tribes of

3547		2030.121, 1896	5357	6142, 1932	8578	6142, 758
pn	**17.**	v Qal juss 3ms, pn	n ms	prep, n ms	n ms	prep, n ms
יִשְׂרָאֵל		יְהִי־דָן	נָחָשׁ	עֲלֵי־דֶרֶךְ	שְׁפִיפֹן	עֲלֵי־אֹרַח
yisrā'ēl		y^{e}hî-dhān	nāchāsh	'ălê-dherekh	sh^{e}phîphōn	'ălê-'ōrach
Israel		may Dan be	a serpent	on road	a horned snake	on path

5574	6357, 5670	5489	7680.151	268
art, v Qal act ptc ms	*n mp*, n ms	cj, v Qal impf 3ms	v Qal act ptc ms, ps 3ms	adv
הַנֹּשֵׁךְ	עִקְּבֵי־סוּס	וַיִּפֹּל	רֹכְבוֹ	אָחוֹר
hannōshēkh	'iqq^{e}vê-sûs	wayyippōl	rōkh^{e}vô	'āchôr
one who bites	heels of horse	and he falls	his rider	backward

18.	3937, 3568	7245.315	3176	19.	1440	1447	1496.121
	prep, n fs, ps 2ms	v Piel pf 1cs	pn		pn	n ms	v Qal impf 3ms, ps 3ms
	לִישׁוּעָתְךָ	קִוִּיתִי	יְהוָה		גָּד	גְּדוּד	יְגוּדֶנּוּ
	lîshû'āth^{e}khā	qiwwîthî	y^{e}hwāh		gādh	g^{e}dhûdh	y^{e}ghûdhennû
	for your salvation	I will wait	Yahweh		Gad	raiding party	he will raid him

11. Binding his foal unto the vine, and his ass's colt unto the choice vine; he washed his garments in wine, and his clothes in the blood of grapes: ... washing his robe in wine, *BB.*

12. His eyes shall be red with wine, and his teeth white with milk: ... darker than wine, and his teeth whiter than milk. *KJVII* ... bright as grapes, and his teeth be white as milk, *Fenton.*

13. Zebulun shall dwell at the haven of the sea; and he shall be for an haven of ships; and his border shall be unto Zidon: ... his border will extend toward Sidon, *NIV* ... and extend his legs to the fishery, *Fenton.*

14. Issachar is a strong ass couching down between two burdens: ... a sturdy ass, lounging among the ravines, *Goodspeed* ... a rawboned donkey lying between two saddlebags, *NIV* ... lying down in the cattle pens, *REB.*

15. And he saw that rest was good, and the land that it was pleasant; and bowed his shoulder to bear, and became a servant unto tribute: ... when he saw how good a settled life was, *NAB* ... submitted to forced labor, *REB* ... became a toiling serf, *Torah.*

16. Dan shall judge his people, as one of the tribes of Israel: ... like any tribe of Israel, *NCB* ... as a sceptred prince of Israel, *Fenton.*

17. Dan shall be a serpent by the way, an adder in the path, that biteth the horse heels, so that his rider shall fall backward.

18. I have waited for thy salvation, O LORD: ... for your victory trust on the Lord, *Fenton* ... I long for your deliverance, O Yehweh, *Anchor* ... I wait in hope for salvation from you, Lord, *REB.*

19. Gad, a troop shall overcome him: but he shall overcome at the last: ... Gad, an army will come against him, but he will come down on them in their flight, *BB* ... Gad is raided by raiders, and he will raid them from the rear, *REB* ... but a troop shall deceive him, *Fenton.*

49:11-12. The reign of the One to come will bring a time of peace and the simple blessings of life in the Millennium, where the vine is a symbol of prosperity and peace. Eyes darker than wine and teeth whiter than milk also speak of a fullness of health and blessing. (Some, however, apply this to the judgments of the Tribulation at the end of the age with the eyes of the Messiah full of anger against the Antichrist and the whiteness of teeth symbolizing impending judgment (cf. Rev. 19:11, 14; 20:11-13).

49:13. The brief prophecy about Zebulon tells of the tribe's residence toward the Mediterranean Sea with its northern border toward Sidon. Zebulon's border was later 10 miles from the Sea, with the tribe of Asher between it and the Mediterranean. Yet it was close enough to enjoy the abundance of the seas (Deut. 33:19) and to enable Zebulon to reach out toward the rest of the world.

49:14-15. Jacob pictured Issachar as a bony donkey crouching down between two saddlebags. He will see a good resting place and bend his shoulder to bear the burden in complete enslavement. Issachar later became subject to the Canaanites.

49:16-17. Dan will live up to his name as a judge, but as one of the tribes of Israel. This is, he will not be a judge over them or ruling them. Jacob then expresses a wish that Dan may be like a horned snake on a road or path that bites the heels of a horse, making it rare up so the rider falls backward. That is, Jacob hopes that Dan will be victorious over those who attack him.

49:18. Jacob suddenly interrupts his prophetic blessings on the tribes by proclaiming that he waited with expectation for the LORD's salvation. He pictured Judah as a lion and Dan as a horned snake. But he did not depend on their strength or abilities, nor should they. He knew that real salvation (including deliverance and the fulfillment of the promise) comes only from God.

2000	1496.121	6357	**20.**	4623, 862	8469	4035	2000
cj, pers pron	v Qal impf 3ms	n ms		prep, pn	adj	n ms, ps 3ms	cj, pers pron
וְהוּא	יָגֻד	עָקֵב		מֵאָשֵׁר	שְׁמֵנָה	לַחְמוֹ	וְהוּא
w^{e}hû'	yāghudh	'āqēv		mē'āshēr	sh^{e}mēnāh	lach^{e}mmô	w^{e}hû'
but he	he will raid	heel		from Asher	fat	his food	and he

5598.121	4729, 4567	**21.**	5503	359	8365.157	5598.151
v Qal impf 3ms	*n mp*, n ms		pn	n fs	v Qal pass ptc fs	art, v Qal act ptc ms
יִתֵּן	מַעֲדַנֵּי־מֶלֶךְ		נַפְתָּלִי	אַיָּלָה	שְׁלֻחָה	הַנֹּתֵן
yittēn	ma'ădhannê-melekh		naphtālî	'ayyālāh	sh^{e}luchāh	hannōthēn
he will give	delicacies of king		Naphtali	doe	one let loose	the one that gives

572, 8603	**22.**	1158	6759.153	3231	1158	6759.153
n mp, n ms		*n ms*	v Qal act ptc fs	pn	*n ms*	v Qal act ptc fs
אִמְרֵי־שָׁפֶר		בֵּן	פֹּרָת	יוֹסֵף	בֵּן	פֹּרָת
'imrê-shāpher		bēn	pōrāth	yôsēph	bēn	pōrāth
fawns of beauty		son of	one bearing fruit	Joseph	son of	one bearing fruit

6142, 6084	1351	7081.112	6142, 8229	**23.**	5006.326
prep, n fs	n fp	v Qal pf 3fs	prep, n ms		cj, v Piel impf 3mp, ps 3ms
עֲלֵי־עָיִן	בָּנוֹת	צָעֲדָה	עֲלֵי־שׁוּר		וַיְמָרְרֻהוּ
'ălê-'āyin	bānôth	tsā'ădhāh	'ălê-shûr		waymār^{e}ruhû
beside spring	daughters	she steps	over a wall		and they were provoked him

7525.116	7929.126	1196	2777	**24.**	3553.122
cj, v Qal pf 3cp	cj, v Qal impf 3mp, ps 3ms	*n mp*	n mp		cj, v Qal impf 3fs
וָרֹבּוּ	וַיִּשְׂטְמֻהוּ	בַּעֲלֵי	חִצִּים		וַתֵּשֶׁב
wārōbbû	wayyis̱t^{e}muhû	ba'ălê	hitstsîm		wattēshev
and they became numerous	and they hated him	owners of	arrows		but it stayed

904, 393	7493	6581.126	2307	3135	4623, 3135	47
prep, adj	n fs, ps 3ms	cj, v Qal impf 3mp	*n mp*	n fd	prep, *n fp*	*adj*
בְּאֵיתָן	קַשְׁתּוֹ	וַיָּפֹזּוּ	זְרֹעֵי	יָדָיו	מִידֵי	אֲבִיר
b^{e}'ēthān	qashtô	wayyāphōzzû	z^{e}rō'ê	yādhâv	mîdhê	'ăvîr
steady	his bow	and they were agile	the arms of	his hands	from the hands of	the Mighty One of

3399	4623, 8427	7449.151	63	3547	**25.**	4623, 418	1
pn	prep, adv	v Qal act ptc ms	*n fs*	pn		prep, *n ms*	n ms, ps 2ms
יַעֲקֹב	מִשָּׁם	רֹעֶה	אֶבֶן	יִשְׂרָאֵל		מֵאֵל	אָבִיךָ
ya'ăqōv	mishshām	rō'eh	'even	yisrā'ēl		mē'ēl	'āvîkhā
Jacob	from there	the Shepherd	the Rock of	Israel		from the God of	your father

6038.121	881	8163	1313.321	904, 1318	8452
cj, v Qal impf 3ms, ps 2ms	cj, do	pn	cj, v Piel impf 3ms, ps 2ms	prep, *n fp*	n md
וְיַעְזְרֶךָּ	וְאֵת	שַׁדַּי	וִיבָרֲכֶךָּ	בִּרְכֹת	שָׁמַיִם
w^{e}ya'ăzrekhā	w^{e}'ēth	shadday	wîvārăkhekhā	birkhōth	shāmayim
and He will help you	and	the Almighty	and He will bless you	with blessings of	heavens

4623, 6142	1318	8745	7547.153	8809	1318	8159
prep, prep	*n fp*	n fs	v Qal act ptc fs	adv	*n fp*	n md
מֵעָל	בִּרְכֹת	תְּהוֹם	רֹבֶצֶת	תָּחַת	בִּרְכֹת	שָׁדַיִם
mē'āl	birkhōth	t^{e}hôm	rōvetseth	tāchath	birkhōth	shādhayim
above	the blessings of	the deep	one lying	below	blessings of	breasts

7641	**26.**	1318	1	1428.116	6142, 1318
cj, n ms		*n fp*	n ms, ps 2ms	v Qal pf 3cp	prep, *n fp*
וָרָחַם		בִּרְכֹת	אָבִיךָ	גָּבְרוּ	עַל־בִּרְכֹת
wārācham		birkhōth	'āvîkhā	gavrû	'al-birkhōth
and the womb		the blessings of	your father	they excelled	above the blessings of

20. Out of Asher his bread shall be fat, and he shall yield royal dainties: ... bread shall be rich, *NRSV* ... shall give pleasures for a king, *Geneva* ... Asher will feast everyday, and provide dishes fit for a king, *REB.*

21. Naphtali is a hind let loose: he giveth goodly words: ... Naphtali is a free-ranging deer, *Goodspeed* ... has the gift of elopuent speech, *Fenton* ... which brings forth lovely fawns, *NAB.* ...

22. Joseph is a fruitful bough, even a fruitful bough by a well; whose branches run over the wall: ... is a fruitful son; A fruitful son by a fountain, Daughters step over the wall, *Young* ... is a young bull, A young bull at a spring, a wild-ass at Shur, *Goodspeed.*

23. The archers have sorely grieved him, and shot at him, and hated him: ... the archers have provoked him, *Darby* ... archers savagely attacked him, *REB.*

24. But his bow abode in strength, and the arms of his hands were made strong by the hands of the mighty God of Jacob from thence is the shepherd, the stone of Israel:: ... but their bows were broken by a strong one, and the cords of their arms were cut by the Strength of Jacob, by the name of the Stone of Isreal, *BB* ... yet each one's bow stayed rigid, and their arms were unsteady, By the dint of the Champion of Jacob, The Shepherd, Rock of Israel, *Anchor* ... but his bow remained steady, *NIV.*

25. Even by the God of thy father, who shall help thee; and by the Almighty, who shall bless thee with blessings of heaven above: ... by the God, the Omnipotent, may he bless you, *NCB* ... God of you father guard, *Fenton* ... With blessings of rain from above, *Good News.*

blessings of the deep that lieth under, blessings of the breasts, and of the womb: ... blessings of the abyss couching beneath, *NCB* ... With blessings below of dancing water, With the bliss of the breasts, and love!, *Fenton* ... deep waters from beneath the ground, Blessings of many cattle and children, *Good News* ... blessings of the breasts and of the fertile body, *BB.*

26. The blessings of thy father have prevailed above the blessings of my progenitors unto the utmost bound of the everlasting hills: they shall be on the head of Joseph: ... The blessings of fatherhood, yea of man and child, *Goodspeed* ... Your father's blessings are greater than the blessings of the ancient mountains, than the bounty of the age-old hills, *NIV* ... May the blessings of your father strengthen, With the bliss of the fertile vales. May the wealth of the ancient hills, *Fenton* ... the blessings of fresh grain and blossoms, The blessings of the everlasting mountains, the delights of the eternal hills. May they rest on the head of Joseph, *NAB.*

and on the crown of the head of him that was separate from his brethren: ... distinguished among his brothers, *NASB* ... More nobly crowned than his brothers!, *Fenton* ... head of the prince among his brethren, *MAST* ... brow of him who was cursed by his brothers, *Goodspeed.*

49:19. Gad will be raided by a band of raiders, but he will raid them at their heels. That is, he will turn around, attack them at the rear, and recover what they have taken.

49:20. Asher will be the source of bread that is fat, that is, the very best, compared to delicacies of a king. Moses later added, "let him dip his foot in olive oil," another symbol of rich blessing (Deut. 33:24).

49:21. Naphtali is compared to a doe let loose that bears beautiful fawns. Its freedom brings prosperity.

49:22. Joseph is given most attention of all. He is a son bearing fruit (poetic for a fruitful branch) by a spring with daughters (side branches) stepping (climbing) over the wall around the spring. This pictures a healthy grapevine and indicates prosperity.

49:23-26. Archers had a grudge against him and hated him more and more. That is, the tribe's prosperity would bring the same kind of hatred the brothers had shown against the 17-year-old Joseph. But his bow stayed steady and his arms were agile. Some take this to mean that the enemies' bows were paralyzed so could not release their arrows and that their arms shook in terror. Others take this to mean that Joseph's bow kept steady in position to shoot and his hand moved quickly back and forth discharging the arrows. This deliverance was from God, whom Jacob describes as the Mighty One, the Shepherd (who would guide and protect), the Rock of Israel (picturing God as a refuge and as dependable), the God of your father and the Almighty.

Jacob then prophesied that the Almighty would help him (that is, the descendants of Joseph), blessing him with blessings of heaven above and of the deep beneath, that is, unlimited blessings; blessings also of the breast and the womb. Jacob added that his own blessings excelled those of his progenitors, even above the desirable things on the ancient hills. They will all be on the head of Joseph, even on the crown of the head of the prince of his brothers.

2106.152 v Qal act ptc mp, ps 1cs הוֹרַי hôray my progenitors	5912, 8707 prep, *n fs* עַד־תַּאֲוַת 'adh-ta'ăwath even the desirable things of	1421 *n fp* גִּבְעֹת giv'ōth the hills of	5986 adv עוֹלָם 'ôlām antiquity	2030.127 v Qal impf 3fp תִּהְיֶיןָ tihyên they will be	3937, 7513 prep, *n ms* לְרֹאשׁ lerō'sh for the head of

3231 pn יוֹסֵף yôsēph Joseph	3937, 7221 cj, prep, *n ms* וּלְקָדְקֹד ûlăqādheqōdh and for crown of	5319 *n ms* נְזִיר nezîr prince of	250 n mp, ps 3ms אֶחָיו 'echâv his brothers	**27.**	1175 pn בִּנְיָמִין binyāmîn Benjamin	2146 n ms זְאֵב ze'ēv wolf	3072.121 v Qal impf 3ms יִטְרָף yitrāph he tears

904, 1269 prep, art, n ms בַּבֹּקֶר babbōqer in the morning	404.121 v Qal impf 3ms יֹאכַל yō'khal he eats	5913 n ms עַד 'adh prey	3937, 6394 cj, prep, art, n ms וְלָעֶרֶב welā'erev and toward evening	2606.321 v Piel impf 3ms יְחַלֵּק yechallēq he divides	8395 n ms שָׁלָל shālāl spoil	**28.**	3725, 431 *adj*, dem pron כָּל־אֵלֶּה kol-'ēlleh all these

8101 *n mp* שִׁבְטֵי shivtê the tribes of	3547 pn יִשְׂרָאֵל yisrā'ēl Israel	8530 num שְׁנֵים shenêm two	6461 num עָשָׂר 'āsār ten	2148 cj, dem pron וְזֹאת wezō'th and this	866, 1744.111 rel part, v Piel pf 3ms אֲשֶׁר־דִּבֶּר 'ăsher-dibber what he spoke	3937 prep, ps 3mp לָהֶם lāhem to them	1 n ms, ps 3mp אֲבִיהֶם 'ăvîhem their father

1313.321 cj, v Piel impf 3ms וַיְבָרֶךְ wayevārekh and he blessed	881 do, ps 3mp אוֹתָם 'ôthām them	382 n ms אִישׁ 'îsh each	866 rel part אֲשֶׁר 'ăsher which	3626, 1318 prep, n fs, ps 3ms כְּבִרְכָתוֹ kevirekhāthô according to his blessing	1313.311 v Piel pf 3ms בֵּרַךְ bērakh he blessed	881 do, ps 3mp אֹתָם 'ōthām them

29.	6943 cj, v Piel impf 3ms וַיְצַו waytsaw and he commanded	881 do, ps 3mp אוֹתָם 'ôthām them	569.121 cj, v Qal impf 3ms וַיֹּאמֶר wayyō'mer and he said	420 prep, ps 3mp אֲלֵהֶם 'ălēhem to them	603 pers pron אֲנִי 'ănî I	636.255 v Niphal ptc ms נֶאֱסָף ne'ĕsāph one gathered

420, 6194 prep, n ms, ps 1cs אֶל־עַמִּי 'el-'ammî to his people	7196.133 v Qal impv 2mp קִבְרוּ qivrû bury	881 do, ps 1cs אֹתִי 'ōthî me	420, 1 prep, n mp, ps 1cs אֶל־אֲבֹתָי 'el-'ăvōthāy to my fathers	420, 4792 prpe, art, n fs אֶל־הַמְּעָרָה 'el-hamme'ārāh to the cave	866 rel part אֲשֶׁר 'ăsher which	904, 7898 prep, *n ms* בִּשְׂדֵה bisdhēh in the field of

6317 pn עֶפְרוֹן 'ephrôn Ephron	2958 art, pn הַחִתִּי hachittî the Hittite	**30.**	904, 4792 prep, art, n fs בַּמְּעָרָה bamme'ārāh in the cave	866 rel part אֲשֶׁר 'ăsher which	904, 7898 prep, *n ms* בִּשְׂדֵה bisdhēh in the field of	4512 art, pn הַמַּכְפֵּלָה hammakhpēlāh the Machpelah	866 rel part אֲשֶׁר 'ăsher which

6142, 6686, 4613 prep, *n mp*, pn עַל־פְּנֵי־מַמְרֵא 'al-penê-mamrē' facing Mamre	904, 800 prep, *n fs* בְּאֶרֶץ be'erets in the land of	3791 pn כְּנָעַן kenā'an Canaan	866 rel part אֲשֶׁר 'ăsher which	7353.111 v Qal pf 3ms קָנָה qānāh he bought	80 pn אַבְרָהָם 'avrāhām Abraham	881, 7898 do, art, n ms אֶת־הַשָּׂדֶה 'eth-hassādheh the field

4623, 882 prep, prep מֵאֵת mē'ēth from	6317 pn עֶפְרֹן 'ephrōn Ephron	2958 art, pn הַחִתִּי hachittî the Hittite	3937, 273, 7197 prep, *n fs*, n ms לַאֲחֻזַּת־קָבֶר la'ăchuzzath-qāver for property of tomb	**31.**	8427 adv שָׁמָּה shāmmāh to there	7196.116 v Qal pf 3cp קָבְרוּ qāverû they buried	881, 80 do, pn אֶת־אַבְרָהָם 'eth-'avrāhām Abraham

881	8023	828	8427	7196.116	881, 3437	881	7549	828
cj, do	pn	n fs, ps 3ms	adv	v Qal pf 3cp	do, pn	cj, do	pn	n fs, ps 3ms
וְאֵת	שָׂרָה	אִשְׁתּוֹ	שָׁמָּה	קָבְרוּ	אֶת־יִצְחָק	וְאֵת	רִבְקָה	אִשְׁתּוֹ
w^{e}'ēth	sārāh	'ishtô	shāmmāh	qāv^{e}rû	'eth-yitschāq	w^{e}'ēth	rivqāh	'ishtô
and	Sarah	his wife	to there	they buried	Isaac	and	Rebekah	his wife

8247	7196.115	881, 3943		4898	7898	4792
cj, adv	v Qal pf 1cs	do, pn	**32.**	*n ms*	art, n ms	cj, art, n fs
וְשָׁמָּה	קָבַרְתִּי	אֶת־לֵאָה		מִקְנֵה	הַשָּׂדֶה	וְהַמְּעָרָה
w^{e}shāmmāh	qāvartî	'eth-lē'āh		miqŏnēh	hassādheh	w^{e}hamm^{e}'ārāh
and to there	I buried	Leah		the property of	the field	and the cave

866, 904	4623, 882	1158, 2953		3735.321	3399	3937, 6943
rel part, prep, ps 3ms	prep, prep	*n mp*, pn	**33.**	cj, v Piel impf 3ms	pn	prep, v Piel inf con
אֲשֶׁר־בּוֹ	מֵאֵת	בְּנֵי־חֵת		וַיְכַל	יַעֲקֹב	לְצַוֹּת
'ăsher-bô	mē'ēth	b^{e}nê-chēth		way^{e}khal	ya'ăqōv	l^{e}tsawwōth
which on it	from	the sons of Heth		and he finished	Jacob	commanding

881, 1158	636.121	7559	420, 4433	1510.121	636.221
do, n mp, ps 3ms	cj, v Qal impf 3ms	n fd, ps 3ms	prep, art, n fs	cj, v Qal impf 3ms	cj, v Niphal impf 3ms
אֶת־בָּנָיו	וַיֶּאֱסֹף	רַגְלָיו	אֶל־הַמִּטָּה	וַיִּגְוַע	וַיֵּאָסֶף
'eth-bānâv	wayye'ĕsōph	raghlâv	'el-hammiṯṯāh	wayyighwa'	wayyē'āseph
his sons	and he gathered	his feet	to the bed	and he died	and he was gathered

27. Benjamin shall ravin as a wolf: in the morning he shall devour the prey, and at night he shall divide the spoil: ... a wolf, searching for meat, *BB* ... a wolf that tears in pieces, *KJVII.*

28. All these are the twelve tribes of Israel: and this is it that their father spake unto them, and blessed them; every one according to his blessing he blessed them: ... said to them as he bade them farewell, addressing to each a parting word appropriate him, *Torah* ... when he blessed them each, *REB.*

29. And he charged them, and said unto them, I am to be gathered unto my people: bury me with my fathers in the cave that is in the field of Ephron the Hittite: ... And he gave orders to them, saying, Put me to rest with my people, *BB.*

30. In the cave that is in the field of Machpelah, which is before Mamre, in the land of Canaan, which Abraham bought with the field of Ephron the Hittite for a possession of a buryingplace.

31. There they buried Abraham and Sarah his wife; there they buried Isaac and Rebekah his wife; and there I buried Leah.

32. The purchase of the field and of the cave that is therein was from the children of Heth.

33. And when Jacob had made an end of commanding his sons, he gathered up his feet into the bed, and yielded up the ghost, and was gathered unto his people: ... stretching himself on his bed, he gave up his spirit, and went the way of his people, *BB.*

49:27. Benjamin is compared to a wolf who tears apart his prey, eats it in the morning and in the evening he divides the spoils. That is, the tribe of Benjamin would be as fierce as a wolf against their enemies and would be victorious.

49:28. Jacob's blessings for his sons were really for the 12 tribes of Israel, with each one having its own individual prophetic blessing.

49:29-32. Jacob now knew he was about to be gathered to his people, so he gave his final command for them to bury him with his fathers in the cave of Machpelah. Because they had been away for a long time, he identified this further as the one Abraham bought from Ephron and as the one where Abraham, Sarah, Isaac, Rebekah, and Leah were buried. He further emphasized that the field was bought and paid for. They had every right to bury him there, and they must make no mistake. Jacob also had in mind God's promise of the land to his descendants. So the command to bury him in that land was a final expression of his faith.

49:33. Jacob had used his last bit of strength to sit on the edge of the bed. Then he pulled his feet onto the bed, breathed his last, and was gathered to his people, that is to be with Enoch, Abraham, and other godly people who were with Lord.

420, 6194		5489	3231	6142, 6686	1	1098.121
prep, n mp, ps 3ms	**50:1**	cj, v Qal impf 3ms	pn	prep, *n mp*	n ms, ps	cj, v Qal impf 3ms
אֶל־עַמָּיו		וַיִּפֹּל	יוֹסֵף	עַל־פְּנֵי	אָבִיו	וַיֵּבְךְּ
'el-'ammâv		wayyippōl	yôsēph	'al-p^{e}nê	'āvîw	wayyēvkh
to his people		and he fell	Joseph	beside the face of	his father	and he wept

6142	5583.121, 3937		6943	3231	881, 5860
prep, ps 3ms	cj, v Qal impf 3ms, prep, ps 3ms	**2.**	cj, v Piel impf 3ms	pn	do, n mp, ps 3ms
עָלָיו	וַיִּשַּׁק־לוֹ		וַיְצַו	יוֹסֵף	אֶת־עֲבָדָיו
'ālâv	wayyishshaq-lô		waytsaw	yôsēph	'eth-'ăvādhâv
over him	and he kissed him		and he commanded	Joseph	his servants

881, 7784.152	3937, 2690.141	881, 1	2690.126	7784.152
do, art, v Qal act ptc mp	prep, v Qal inf con	do, n ms, ps 3ms	cj, v Qal impf 3mp	art, v Qal act ptc mp
אֶת־הָרֹפְאִים	לַחֲנֹט	אֶת־אָבִיו	וַיַּחַנְטוּ	הָרֹפְאִים
'eth-hārōph'îm	lachnōṯ	'eth-'āvîw	wayyachanṯû	hārōph'îm
the doctors	to embalm	his father	and they embalmed	the doctors

881, 3547		4527.126, 3937	727	3219	3706	3772	4527.126
do, pn	**3.**	cj, v Qal impf 3mp, prep, ps 3ms	num	n ms	cj	adv	v Qal impf 3mp
אֶת־יִשְׂרָאֵל		וַיִּמְלְאוּ־לוֹ	אַרְבָּעִים	יוֹם	כִּי	כֵּן	יִמְלְאוּ
'eth-yisrā'ēl		wayyiml^{e}'û-lô	'arbā'îm	yôm	kî	kēn	yiml^{e}'û
Israel		and they continued it	forty	days	because	thus	they are continued

3219	2693	1098.126	882	4875	8124	3219
n mp	art, n mp	cj, v Qal impf 3mp	prep, ps 3ms	pn	num	n ms
יְמֵי	הַחֲנֻטִים	וַיִּבְכּוּ	אֹתוֹ	מִצְרַיִם	שִׁבְעִים	יוֹם
y^{e}mê	hachnuṯîm	wayyivkû	'ōthô	mitsrayim	shiv'îm	yôm
the days of	the embalming	and they wept	with him	Egypt	seventy	days

	5882.126	3219	1107	1744.321	3231	420, 1041	6799
4.	cj, v Qal impf 3mp	n mp	n fs, ps 3ms	cj, v Piel impf 3ms	pn	prep, *n ms*	pn
	וַיַּעַבְרוּ	יְמֵי	בְכִיתוֹ	וַיְדַבֵּר	יוֹסֵף	אֶל־בֵּית	פַּרְעֹה
	wayya'avrû	y^{e}mê	v^{e}khîthô	way^{e}dhabbēr	yôsēph	'el-bêth	par'ōh
	and they passed	the days of	his mourning	and he spoke	Joseph	to the household of	Pharaoh

3937, 569.141	524, 5167	4834.115	2682	904, 6084	1744.333, 5167	904, 238
prep, v Qal inf con	cj, part	v Qal pf 1cs	n ms	prep, n fd, ps 2mp	v Piel impv 2mp, part	prep, *n fp*
לֵאמֹר	אִם־נָא	מָצָאתִי	חֵן	בְּעֵינֵיכֶם	דַּבְּרוּ־נָא	בְּאָזְנֵי
lē'mōr	'im-nā'	mātsā'thî	chēn	b^{e}'ênêkhem	dabb^{e}rû-nā'	b^{e}'āznê
saying	if please	I have found	favor	in your eyes	speak please	in the ears of

6799	3937, 569.141		1	8123.511	3937, 569.141	2079	609
pn	prep, v Qal inf con	**5.**	n ms, ps 1cs	v Hiphil pf 3ms, ps 1cs	prep, v Qal inf con	intrj	pers pron
פַרְעֹה	לֵאמֹר		אָבִי	הִשְׁבִּיעַנִי	לֵאמֹר	הִנֵּה	אָנֹכִי
phar'ōh	lē'mōr		'āvî	hishbî'anî	lē'mōr	hinnēh	'ānōkhî
Pharaoh	saying		my father	he made me swear	saying	behold	I

4322.151	904, 7197	866	3901.115	3937	904, 800	3791	8427
v Qal act ptc ms	prep, n ms, ps 1cs	rel part	v Qal pf 1cs	prep, ps 1cs	prep, *n fs*	pn	adv
מֵת	בְּקִבְרִי	אֲשֶׁר	כָּרִיתִי	לִי	בְּאֶרֶץ	כְּנַעַן	שָׁמָּה
mēth	b^{e}qivrî	'āsher	kārîthî	lî	b^{e}'erets	k^{e}na'an	shāmmāh
dying	in my tomb	which	I hewed out	for me	in the land of	Canaan	to there

7196.123	6498	6148.125, 5167	7196.125	882, 1	8178.125
v Qal impf 2ms, ps 1cs	cj, adv	v Qal impf 1cs, part	cj, v Qal impf 1cs	do, n ms, ps 1cs	cj, v Qal impf 1cs
תִּקְבְּרֵנִי	וְעַתָּה	אֶעֱלֶה־נָּא	וְאֶקְבְּרָה	אֶת־אָבִי	וְאָשׁוּבָה
tiqōbb^{e}rēnî	w^{e}'attāh	'e'ĕleh-nā'	w^{e}'eqōbb^{e}rāh	'eth-'āvî	w^{e}'āshûvāh
you will bury me	and now	I will go up please	and I will bury	my father	then I will return

6.	569.121	6799	6148.131	7196.131	881, 1	3626, 866
	cj, v Qal impf 3ms	pn	v Qal impv 2ms	cj, v Qal impv 2ms	do, n ms, ps 2ms	prep, rel part
	וַיֹּאמֶר	פַּרְעֹה	עֲלֵה	וּקְבֹר	אֶת־אָבִיךָ	כַּאֲשֶׁר
	wayyō'mer	par'ōh	'ălēh	ûqŏvōr	'eth-'āvîkhā	ka'ăsher
	and he said	Pharaoh	go up	and bury	your father	according to that

8123.511	7.	6148.121	3231	3937, 7196	881, 1	6148.126
v Hiphil pf 3ms, ps 2ms		cj, v Qal impf 3ms	pn	prep, v Qal inf con	do, n ms, ps 3ms	cj, v Qal impf 3mp
הִשְׁבִּיעֶךָ		וַיַּעַל	יוֹסֵף	לִקְבֹּר	אֶת־אָבִיו	וַיַּעֲלוּ
hishbî'ekhā		wayya'al	yôsēph	liqŏbbōr	'eth-'āvîw	wayya'ălû
he made you swear		and he went up	Joseph	to bury	his father	and they went up

881	3725, 5860	6799	2292	1041	3725	2292
do, ps 3ms	adj, *n mp*	pn	*n ms*	n ms, ps 3ms	cj, adj	*n ms*
אִתּוֹ	כָּל־עַבְדֵי	פַּרְעֹה	זִקְנֵי	בֵיתוֹ	וְכֹל	זִקְנֵי
'ittô	kol-'avdhê	phar'ōh	ziqŏnê	vêthô	w^{e}khōl	ziqŏnê
him	all the servants of	Pharaoh	the elders of	his house	and all	the elders of

50:1. And Joseph fell upon his father's face, and wept upon him, and kissed him.

2. And Joseph commanded his servants the physicians to embalm his father: and the physicians embalmed Israel: ... to make his father's body ready, folding it in linen with spices, *BB*.

3. And forty days were fulfilled for him; for so are fulfilled the days of those which are embalmed: for that was the time required for embalming, *NIV*.

and the Egyptians mourned for him threescore and ten days.

4. And when the days of his mourning were past, Joseph spake unto the house of Pharaoh, saying, If now I have found grace in your eyes, speak, I pray you, in the ears of Pharaoh, saying: ... If now I have found favor, *ASV* ... May I ask a fovour--please speak for me to Pharaoh, *REB*.

5. My father made me swear, saying, Lo, I die: ... You see that I am dying, *Berkley* ... when I die, *Anchor* ... since my father, at the point of death, made me promise on oath, *NAB*.

in my grave which I have digged for me in the land of Canaan, there shalt thou bury me. Now therefore let me go up, I pray thee, and bury my father, and I will come again.

6. And Pharaoh said, Go up, and bury thy father, according as he made thee swear: ... in accordance with your oath, *REB*.

7. And Joseph went up to bury his father: and with him went up all the servants of Pharaoh, the elders of his house: ... the senior members of his court, *Torah*.

and all the elders of the land of Egypt: ... and all the other dignitaries of Egypt, *NAB*.

8. And all the house of Joseph, and his brethren, and his father's house:

only their little ones, and their flocks, and their herds they left in the land of Goshen: except the sheep and cattle, *Fenton*.

50:1-3. After his initial expression of grief, Joseph called in the physicians who served him and they began the Egyptian process of embalming which continued for 40 days. The period of mourning continued for 30 more days, with Egypt in a state of mourning during this time out of respect for Joseph's father, and as a token of their affection and esteem for Joseph.

50:4-6. After the 70 days of mourning, Joseph asked the household of Pharaoh to tell him about the oath Jacob made Joseph swear. He did not go directly to Pharaoh probably because he was still in mourning, which might have included sackcloth and ashes. Joseph wanted permission to bury his father in the place Jacob had prepared in Canaan. Joseph also promised to return. Pharaoh gave him permission without hesitation. Even though he was a foreigner, Joseph had earned Pharaoh's full trust.

50:7-9. Joseph was still the prime minister of Egypt and highly esteemed. This is shown by Pharaoh's servants, who were the elders of his household and the elders of Egypt, traveling with Joseph to bury his father. All Joseph's brothers and their families accompanied him as well. Only the little ones, who were probably left in the care of servants, stayed behind.

800, 4875		3725	1041	3231	250	1041	1
n fs, pn	**8.**	cj, adj	n ms	pn	cj, n mp, ps 3ms	cj, n ms	n ms, ps
אֶרֶץ־מִצְרָיִם		וְכֹל	בֵּית	יוֹסֵף	וְאֶחָיו	וּבֵית	אָבִיו
'erets-mitsrāyim		wekhōl	bêth	yôsēph	we'echâv	ûvêth	'āvîw
the land of Egypt		and all	the house of	Joseph	and his brothers	and the house of	his father

7828	3054	6887	1267	6013.116	904, 800	1705
adv	n ms, ps 3mp	cj, n fs, ps 3mp	cj, n ms, ps 3mp	v Qal pf 3cp	prep, n fs	pn
רַק	טַפָּם	וְצֹאנָם	וּבְקָרָם	עָזְבוּ	בְּאֶרֶץ	גֹּשֶׁן
raq	ṭappām	wetsō'nām	ûveqārām	'āzvû	be'erets	gōshen
only	their little children	and their flocks	and their herds	they left	in the land of	Goshen

	6148.521	6196	1612, 7681	1612, 6821	2030.121	4402
9.	cj, v Hiphil impf 3ms	prep, ps 3ms	cj, n ms	cj, n mp	cj, v Qal impf 3ms	art, n ms
	וַיַּעַל	עִמּוֹ	גַּם־רֶכֶב	גַּם־פָּרָשִׁים	וַיְהִי	הַמַּחֲנֶה
	wayya'al	'immô	gam-rekhev	gam-pārashîm	wayhî	hammachneh
	and he caused to go up	with him	also chariotry	and horsemen	and it was	the company

3633	4108		971.126	5912, 1681	331B	866	904, 5885
adj	adv	**10.**	cj, v Qal impf 3mp	prep, n ms	art, pn	rel part	prep, n ms
כָּבֵד	מְאֹד		וַיָּבֹאוּ	עַד־גֹּרֶן	הָאָטָד	אֲשֶׁר	בְּעֵבֶר
kāvēdh	me'ōdh		wayyāvō'û	'adh-gōren	hā'āṭādh	'ăsher	be'ēver
impressive	very		and they went	to the threshing floor of	Atad	which	on the opposite side of

3497	5792.126, 8427	4705	1448	3633	4108	6449.121
art, pn	cj, v Qal impf 3mp, adv	n ms	adj	cj, adj	adv	cj, v Qal impf 3ms
הַיַּרְדֵּן	וַיִּסְפְּדוּ־שָׁם	מִסְפֵּד	גָּדוֹל	וְכָבֵד	מְאֹד	וַיַּעַשׂ
hayyardēn	wayyispedhû-shām	mispēdh	gādhôl	wekhāvēdh	me'ōdh	wayya'as
the Jordan	and they lamented there	lamentation	great	and grievous	very	and he made

3937, 1	60	8124	3219		7495.121	3553.151	800
prep, n ms, ps 3ms	n ms	num	n mp	**11.**	cj, v Qal impf 3ms	v Qal act part ms	art, n fs
לְאָבִיו	אֵבֶל	שִׁבְעַת	יָמִים		וַיַּרְא	יוֹשֵׁב	הָאָרֶץ
le'āvîw	'ēvel	shiv'ath	yāmîm		wayyare'	yôshēv	hā'ārets
for his father	mourning rites	seven	days		and they saw	the dwellers of	the land of

3793	881, 60	904, 1681	331B	569.126
art, pn	do, art, n ms	prep, n ms	art, pn	cj, v Qal impf 3mp
הַכְּנַעֲנִי	אֶת־הָאֵבֶל	בְּגֹרֶן	הָאָטָד	וַיֹּאמְרוּ
hakkena'ănî	'eth-hā'ēvel	beghōren	hā'āṭādh	wayyō'mrû
the Canaanites	the mourning rites	on the threshing floor of	Atad	and they said

60, 3633	2172	3937, 4875	6142, 3772	7410.111	8428	59
n ms, adj	dem pron	prep, pn	prep, adv	v Qal pf 3ms	n ms, ps 3fs	pn
אֵבֶל־כָּבֵד	זֶה	לְמִצְרָיִם	עַל־כֵּן	קָרָא	שְׁמָהּ	אָבֵל
'ēvel-kāvēdh	zeh	lemitsrāyim	'al-kēn	qārā'	shemāhh	'āvēl
a heavy mourning rite	this	for Egyptians	therefore	he called	its name	Abel

4875	866	904, 5885	3497		6449.126	1158	3937
pn	rel part	prep, n ms	art, pn	**12.**	cj, v Qal impf 3mp	n mp, ps 3ms	prep, ps 3ms
מִצְרַיִם	אֲשֶׁר	בְּעֵבֶר	הַיַּרְדֵּן		וַיַּעֲשׂוּ	בָנָיו	לוֹ
mitsrayim	'ăsher	be'ēver	hayyardēn		wayya'ăsû	vānâv	lô
Mizraim	which	on the opposite side of	the Jordan		and they did	his sons	for him

3772	3626, 866	6943.311		5558.126	881	1158	800
adv	prep, rel part	v Piel pf 3ms, ps 3mp	**13.**	cj, v Qal impf 3mp	do, ps 3ms	n mp, ps 3ms	n fs
כֵּן	כַּאֲשֶׁר	צִוָּם		וַיִּשְׂאוּ	אֹתוֹ	בָנָיו	אַרְצָה
kēn	ka'ăsher	tsiwwām		wayyis'û	'ōthô	vānâv	'artsāh
so	according to that	he commanded them		and they carried	him	his sons	to the land of

3791	7196.126	881	904, 4792	7898	4512	866	7353.111
pn	cj, v Qal impf 3mp	do, ps 3ms	prep, *n fs*	*n ms*	art, pn	rel part	v Qal pf 3ms
כְּנָעַן	וַיִּקְבְּרוּ	אֹתוֹ	בִּמְעָרַת	שְׂדֵה	הַמַּכְפֵּלָה	אֲשֶׁר	קָנָה
k^{e}na'an	wayyiqōbb^{e}rû	'ōthô	bim'ārath	s^{e}dhēh	hammakhpēlāh	'ăsher	qānâh
Canaan	and they buried	him	in the cave of	the field of	the Machpelah	which	he bought

80	881, 7898	3937, 273, 7197	4623, 882	6317	2958	6142, 6686
pn	do, art, n ms	prep, *n fs*, n ms	prep, prep	pn	art, pn	prep, *n mp*
אַבְרָהָם	אֶת־הַשָּׂדֶה	לַאֲחֻזַּת־קָבֶר	מֵאֵת	עֶפְרֹן	הַחִתִּי	עַל־פְּנֵי
'avrāhām	'eth-hassādheh	la'ăchuzzath-qever	mē'ēth	'ephrōn	hachittî	'al-p^{e}nê
Abraham	the field	for property of tomb	from	Ephron	the Hittite	facing

4613		8178.121	3231	4875	2000	250
pn	**14.**	cj, v Qal impf 3ms	pn	pn	pers pron	cj, n mp, ps 3ms
מַמְרֵא		וַיָּשָׁב	יוֹסֵף	מִצְרַיְמָה	הוּא	וְאֶחָיו
mamrē'		wayyāshāv	yôsēph	mitsraymāh	hû'	w^{e}'echâv
Mamre		and he returned	Joseph	to Egypt	he	and his brothers

3725, 6148.152	882	3937, 7196	881, 1	311	7196.111
cj, *adj*, art, v Qal act ptc mp	prep, ps 3ms	prep, v Qal inf con	do, n ms, ps 3ms	sub	v Qal pf 3ms, ps 3ms
וְכָל־הָעֹלִים	אִתּוֹ	לִקְבֹּר	אֶת־אָבִיו	אַחֲרֵי	קָבְרוֹ
w^{e}khol-hā'ōlîm	'ittô	liqōbbōr	'eth-'āvîw	'achrê	qāvrô
and all those going up	with him	to bury	his father	after	he buried him

9. And there went up with him both chariots and horsemen: and it was a very great company: ... Both chariots and charioteers went up with him, *NRSV* ... composing a formidable army, *Berkley* ... a very large caravan, *NCB*.

10. And they came to the threshingfloor of Atad, which is beyond Jordan, and there they mourned with a great and very sore lamentation: ... they gave the last honours to Jacob with great and bitter sorrow, *BB* ... a very great and solemn memorial observance, *Anchor.*

and he made a mourning for his father seven days: ... observed a seven day period of mourning, *NIV* ... and made a lamentation for his father for seven days, *Fenton*.

11. And when the inhabitants of the land, the Canaanites, saw the mourning in the floor of Atad, they said, This is a grievous mourning to the Egyptians: ... a solemn funeral, *NAB*.

wherefore the name of it was called Abelmizraim, which is beyond Jordan.

12. And his sons did unto him according as he commanded them:

13. For his sons carried him into the land of Canaan, and buried him in the cave of the field of Machpelah, which Abraham bought with the field for a possession of a buryingplace of Ephron the Hittite, before Mamre.

14. And Joseph returned into Egypt, he, and his brethren, and all that went up with him to bury his father, after he had buried his father.

The flocks and herds were also left behind, as further evidence that Joseph and his company would return soon. Joseph also brought along an armed contingent of war chariots and horsemen, to ensure their safety and rapid progress along the way. All this made a great and impressive company of people.

50:10-11. The great procession probably made a detour to avoid the Edomites and Philistines, and came to the threshing floor of Atad on the east side of the Jordan River. Since the Egyptians who were with Joseph apparently did not want to enter Canaan, this was an appropriate place for them to carry out final mourning rites for Jacob. The threshing floor was a level, hard-packed piece of ground outside of town. There they spent 7 days lamenting and carrying out great and grievous rites or customs of mourning, which probably included beating the breast and much wailing expressing their sorrow. The Canaanites who lived in the region saw these grievous mourning rites and were so impressed by them that they named the place Abel Mizraim, "Mourning of Egypt."

50:12-14. Jacob's sons obeyed his command by burying him in the cave of Machpelah. Then they returned to Egypt. But the fact that Jacob was buried in Canaan was a reminder that God would be faithful to His promises.

881, 1	15.	7495.126	250, 3231	3706, 4322.111	1	569.126
do, n ms, ps 3ms		cj, v Qal impf 3mp	*n mp*, pn	cj, v Qal pf 3ms	n ms, ps 3mp	cj, v Qal impf 3mp
אֶת־אָבִיו		וַיִּרְאוּ	אֲחֵי־יוֹסֵף	כִּי־מֵת	אֲבִיהֶם	וַיֹּאמְרוּ
'eth-'āvîw		wayyir'û	'ăchê-yôsēph	kî-mēth	'ăvîhem	wayyō'merû
his father		and they saw	the brothers of Joseph	that he died	their father	and they said

4001	7929.121	3231	8178.542	8178.521	3937
cj	v Qal impf 3ms, ps 1cp	pn	cj, v Hiphil inf abs	v Hiphil impf 3ms	prep, ps 1cp
לוּ	יִשְׂטְמֵנוּ	יוֹסֵף	וְהָשֵׁב	יָשִׁיב	לָנוּ
lû	yistemēnû	yôsēph	wehāshēv	yāshîv	lānû
probably	he bears a grudge against us	Joseph	and pay back	he will pay back	to us

881	3725, 7750	866	1621.119	882	16.	6943.326	420, 3231
do	*adj*, art, n fs	rel part	v Qal pf 1cp	prep, ps 3ms		cj, v Piel impf 3mp	prep, pn
אֵת	כָּל־הָרָעָה	אֲשֶׁר	גָּמַלְנוּ	אֹתוֹ		וַיְצַוּוּ	אֶל־יוֹסֵף
'ēth	kol-hārā'āh	'ăsher	gāmalnû	'ōthô		wayetsawwû	'el-yôsēph
	all the harm	which	we did	to him		and they sent a command	Joseph

3937, 569.141	1	6943.311	3937, 6686	4323	3937, 569.141
prep, v Qal inf con	n ms, ps 2ms	v Piel pf 3ms	prep, *n mp*	n ms, ps 3ms	prep, v Qal inf con
לֵאמֹר	אָבִיךָ	צִוָּה	לִפְנֵי	מוֹתוֹ	לֵאמֹר
lē'mōr	'āvîkhā	tsiwwāh	liphnê	môthô	lē'mōr
saying	your father	he commanded	before	his death	saying

17.	3662, 569.128	3937, 3231	588	5558.131	5167	6840	250
	adv, v Qal impf 2mp	prep, pn	intrj	v Qal impv 2ms	part	*n ms*	n mp, ps 2ms
	כֹּה־תֹאמְרוּ	לְיוֹסֵף	אָנָּא	שָׂא	נָא	פֶּשַׁע	אַחֶיךָ
	kōh-thō'merû	leyôsēph	'ānnā'	sā'	nā'	pesha'	'achêkhā
	thus you will say	to Joseph	please	forgive	please	the offence of	your brothers

2492	3706, 7750	1621.116	6498	5558.131	5167	3937, 6840
cj, n fs, ps 3mp	cj, n fs	v Qal pf 3cp, ps 2ms	cj, adv	v Qal impv 2ms	part	prep, *n ms*
וְחַטָּאתָם	כִּי־רָעָה	גְמָלוּךָ	וְעַתָּה	שָׂא	נָא	לְפֶשַׁע
wechattā'thām	kî-rā'āh	gemālûkhā	we'attāh	sā'	nā'	lephesha'
and their sin	because of harm	they did to you	and now	forgive	please	for the offence of

5860	435	1	1098.121	3231	904, 1744.341	420
n mp	*n mp*	n ms, ps 2ms	cj, v Qal impf 3ms	pn	prep, v Piel inf con	prep, ps 3ms
עַבְדֵי	אֱלֹהֵי	אָבִיךָ	וַיֵּבְךְּ	יוֹסֵף	בְּדַבְּרָם	אֵלָיו
'avedhê	'ĕlōhê	'āvîkhā	wayyēvekh	yôsēph	bedhabberām	'ēlâv
the slaves of	the God of	your father	and he wept	Joseph	during their speaking	to him

18.	2050.126	1612, 250	5489.126	3937, 6686	569.126
	cj, v Qal impf 3mp	cj, n mp, ps 3ms	cj, v Qal impf 3mp	prep, n mp, ps 3ms	cj, v Qal impf 3mp
	וַיֵּלְכוּ	גַּם־אֶחָיו	וַיִּפְּלוּ	לְפָנָיו	וַיֹּאמְרוּ
	wayyēlekhû	gam-'echâv	wayyippelû	lephānâv	wayyō'mrû
	and they came	also his brothers	and they fell	before him	and they said

2079	3937	3937, 5860	19.	569.121	420	3231
intrj, ps 1cp	prep, ps 2ms	prep, n mp		cj, v Qal impf 3ms	prep, ps 3mp	pn
הִנֶּנּוּ	לְךָ	לַעֲבָדִים		וַיֹּאמֶר	אֲלֵהֶם	יוֹסֵף
hinnennû	lekhā	la'ăvādhîm		wayyō'mer	'ălēhem	yôsēph
behold we	to you	for slaves		and he said	to them	Joseph

420, 3486.128	3706	8809	435	603	20.	894	2913.117
adv, v Qal juss 2mp	cj	intrg part, prep	n mp	pers pron		cj, pers pron	v Qal pf 2mp
אַל־תִּירָאוּ	כִּי	הֲתַחַת	אֱלֹהִים	אָנִי		וְאַתֶּם	חֲשַׁבְתֶּם
'al-tîrā'û	kî	hethachath	'ĕlōhîm	'ānî		we'attem	chăshavtem
do not fear	for	am instead of	God	I		and you	you intended

6142	7750	435	2913.111	3937, 3008	3937, 4775	6449.141
prep, ps 1cs	n fs	n mp	v Qal pf 3ms, ps 3fs	prep, n fs	prep, prep	v Qal inf con
עָלַי	רָעָה	אֱלֹהִים	חֲשָׁבָהּ	לְטֹבָה	לְמַעַן	עֲשֹׂה
'ālay	rā'āh	'ĕlōhîm	chăshāvāhh	l^eṯōvāh	l^ema'an	'ăsōh
on me	evil	God	he intended it	for good thing	for that	to do

15. And when Joseph's brethren saw that their father was dead, they said, Joseph will peradventure hate us: ... still bears a grudge against us, *NRSV* ... should be hostile towards us, *Darby* ... feels resentful, *Berkley.*

and will certainly requite us all the evil which we did unto him: ... and requires full retribution for all the harm we did him, *Berkley* ... and pays us back for all the wrongs we did to him, *NIV.*

16. And they sent a messenger unto Joseph: ... they sent messengers, *NRSV* ... they approached Joseph, *NRSV.*

saying, Thy father did command before he died, saying: ... In his last words to us before he died, your father gave us this message, *REB.*

17. So shall ye say unto Joseph, Forgive, I pray thee now, the trespass of thy brethren, and their sin; for they did unto thee evil: ... the criminal wrongdoings of your brothers, *NAB* ... the offense and guilt of your brothers, *Torah.*

and now, we pray thee, forgive the trespass of the servants of the God of thy father: ... so please, forgive the crime and faults, *Anchor* ... let the sin of the servants of your father's God have forgiveness, *BB.*

And Joseph wept when they spake unto him: ... when their message came to him, Joseph wept, *NIV.*

18. And his brethren also went and fell down before his face: ... came to him in person and prostrated themselves before him, *NCB.*

and they said, Behold, we be thy servants: ... let us be your slaves, *Anchor* ... thy bondmen, *Darby.*

19. And Joseph said unto them, Fear not: for am I in the place of God: ... am I a substitute for God, *Torah* ... can I take the place of God, *NAB.*

20. But as for you, ye thought evil against me: ... intended to do harm to me, *NRSV* ... it was in your mind to do me evil, *BB* ... set upon me for injury, *Fenton.*

but God meant it unto good: ... turned it to good, *Fenton.*

to bring to pass, as it is this day, to save much people alive: ... achieve his present end, the survival of many people, *NAB* ... preserve a numerous people, as he is doing today, *NRSV.*

50:15-17. When Joseph's brothers began to consider that their father was dead, they apparently concluded that Joseph had treated them so well only for their father's sake. Perhaps he was still holding a grudge against them, and now he would surely pay them back for throwing him into the cistern and then selling him as a slave. The brothers were still full of guilt feelings. Though they had accused one another in Joseph's presence without knowing he understood them (42:1-22), they had never made an honest, open, full confession to Joseph. Since they were afraid of what might happen, they sent a message to Joseph concerning a command they said their father made. They claimed Jacob commanded them to tell Joseph to please forgive the brothers' offense and sin--the harm they did to him. Then they begged him to please forgive them for they were the slaves, the worshipers, of the God of his father. While the messengers were telling Joseph these things, Joseph wept. The brothers had mistrusted his motives after so many years of enjoying what he provided. They understood neither his love, nor his faith in God. This broke his heart.

50:18. Without waiting for a reply, the brothers themselves came and fell down before Joseph, saying they were his slaves. They had made an honest confession and were ready to suffer the consequences.

50:19. Joseph told his brothers not to be afraid. His words show his first and primary reason why he would not seek revenge. He was not in the place of God. God said later, "Vengeance is mine; I will repay (Rom. 12:19; cf. Deut. 32:35). When we try to repay or "get even," we do not leave room for God to deal with the situation. He can make enemies into friends. Joseph's experiences were hard, but they taught him about God's love and grace. It was a future glimpse of the love that Christ would later show, that is literally "thrown beyond" knowledge. (See Eph. 3:16-19).

50:20. A second reason why Joseph didn't seek revenge, was because he could look back over the course of events and see that though the brothers intended evil, God intended it for a good purpose, to accomplish what they could see that day, and to save many people's lives.

3626, 3219	2172	3937, 2513.541	6194, 7521	21.	6498	420, 3486.128	609
prep, art, n ms	art, dem pron	prep, v Hiphil inf con	n ms, adj		cj, adv	adv, v Qal juss 2mp	pers pron
כַּיּוֹם	הַזֶּה	לְהַחֲיֹת	עַם־רָב		וְעַתָּה	אַל־תִּירָאוּ	אָנֹכִי
kayyôm	hazzeh	l^{e}hachyōth	ʿam-rāv		w^{e}ʿattāh	ʾal-tîrāʾû	ʾānōkhî
as the day	the this	to keep alive	many people		so now	do not fear	I

3677.325	881	881, 3054	5341.321	881	1744.321
v Pilpel impf 1cs	do, ps 2mp	cj, do, n ms, ps 2mp	cj, v Piel impf 3ms	do, ps 3mp	cj, v Piel impf 3ms
אֲכַלְכֵּל	אֶתְכֶם	וְאֶת־טַפְּכֶם	וַיְנַחֵם	אוֹתָם	וַיְדַבֵּר
ʾăkhalkēl	ʾethkhem	w^{e}ʾeth-tapp^{e}khem	waynachēm	ʾôthām	way^{e}dhabbēr
I will provide for	you	and your little children	and he comforted	them	and he spoke

6142, 3949	22.	3553.121	3231	904, 4875	2000	1041
prep, n ms, ps 3mp		cj, v Qal impf 3ms	pn	prep, pn	pers pron	cj, *n ms*
עַל־לִבָּם		וַיֵּשֶׁב	יוֹסֵף	בְּמִצְרַיִם	הוּא	וּבֵית
ʿal-libbām		wayyēshev	yôsēph	b^{e}mitsrayim	hûʾ	ûvêth
to their heart		and he lived	Joseph	in Egypt	he	and the household of

1	2513.121	3231	4109	6460	8523	23.	7495.121
n ms, ps	cj, v Qal impf 3ms	pn	num	cj, num	n fp		cj, v Qal impf 3ms
אָבִיו	וַיְחִי	יוֹסֵף	מֵאָה	וָעֶשֶׂר	שָׁנִים		וַיַּרְא
ʾāvîw	waychî	yôsēph	mēʾāh	wāʿeser	shānîm		wayyar^{e}ʾ
his father	and he lived	Joseph	hundred	and ten	years		and he saw

3231	3937, 688	1158	8389	1612	1158	4491	1158, 4667
pn	prep, pn	*n mp*	num	cj	*n mp*	pn	*n ms*, pn
יוֹסֵף	לְאֶפְרַיִם	בְּנֵי	שִׁלֵּשִׁים	גַּם	בְּנֵי	מָכִיר	בֶּן־מְנַשֶּׁה
yôsēph	l^{e}ʾephrayim	b^{e}nê	shillēshîm	gam	b^{e}nê	mākhîr	ben-m^{e}nashsheh
Joseph	to Ephraim	sons of	third	also	the sons of	Machir	the son of Manasseh

3314.416	6142, 1314	3231	24.	569.121	3231	420, 250	609
v Pual pf 3cp	prep, *n fp*	pn		cj, v Qal impf 3ms	pn	prep, n ms, ps 3ms	pers pron
יֻלְּדוּ	עַל־בִּרְכֵּי	יוֹסֵף		וַיֹּאמֶר	יוֹסֵף	אֶל־אֶחָיו	אָנֹכִי
yull^{e}dhû	ʿal-birkê	yôsēph		wayyōʾmer	yôsēph	ʾel-ʾechāyw	ʾānōkhî
they were born	on the knees of	Joseph		and he said	Joseph	to his brothers	I

4322.151	435	6734.142	6734.121	882	6148.511
v Qal act ptc ms	cj, n mp	v Qal inf abs	v Qal impf 3ms	prep, ps 2mp	cj, v Hiphil pf 3ms
מֵת	וֵאלֹהִים	פָּקֹד	יִפְקֹד	אֶתְכֶם	וְהֶעֱלָה
mēth	wēʾlōhîm	pāqōdh	yiphqōdh	ʾethkhem	w^{e}heʿĕlāh
dying	and God	intervening	he will intervene	with you	and he will bring up

881	4623, 800	2148	420, 800	866	8123.211	3937, 80
do, ps 2mp	prep, art, n fs	art, dem pron	prep, art, n fs	rel part	v Niphal pf 3ms	prep, pn
אֶתְכֶם	מִן־הָאָרֶץ	הַזֹּאת	אֶל־הָאָרֶץ	אֲשֶׁר	נִשְׁבַּע	לְאַבְרָהָם
ʾethkhem	min-hāʾārets	hazzōʾth	ʾel-hāʾārets	ʾăsher	nishbaʿ	l^{e}ʾavrāhām
you	from the land	the this	to the land	which	he swore	to Abraham

3937, 3437	3937, 3399	25.	8123.521	3231	881, 1158	3547
prep, pn	cj, prep, pn		cj, v Hiphil impf 3ms	pn	do, *n mp*	pn
לְיִצְחָק	וּלְיַעֲקֹב		וַיַּשְׁבַּע	יוֹסֵף	אֶת־בְּנֵי	יִשְׂרָאֵל
l^{e}yitschāq	ûlāyaʿăqōv		wayyashbaʿ	yôsēph	ʾeth-b^{e}nê	yisrāʾēl
to Isaac	and to Jacob		and he caused to swear	Joseph	the sons of	Israel

3937, 569.141	6734.142	6734.121	435	881	6148.517
prep, v Qal inf con	v Qal inf abs	v Qal impf 3ms	n mp	do, ps 2mp	cj, v Hiphil pf 2mp
לֵאמֹר	פָּקֹד	יִפְקֹד	אֱלֹהִים	אֶתְכֶם	וְהַעֲלִתֶם
lēʾmōr	pāqōdh	yiphqōdh	ʾĕlōhîm	ʾethkhem	w^{e}haʿălithem
saying	intervening	He will intervene	God	you	and you will bring up

881, 6344	4623, 2172		4322.121	3231	1158, 4109	6460
do, n fp, ps 1cs	prep, dem pron	**26.**	cj, v Qal impf 3ms	pn	*n ms*, num	cj, num
אֶת־עַצְמֹתַי	מִזֶּה		וַיָּמָת	יוֹסֵף	בֶּן־מֵאָה	וָעֶשֶׂר
'eth-'atsmōthay	mizzeh		wayyāmāth	yôsēph	ben-mē'āh	wā'eser
my bones	from this place		and he died	Joseph	son of hundred	and ten

8523	2690.126	881	7947.621	904, 751	904, 4875
n fp	cj, v Qal impf 3mp	do, ps 3ms	cj, v Hophal impf 3ms	prep, art, n ms	prep, pn
שָׁנִים	וַיַּחַנְטוּ	אֹתוֹ	וַיִּישֶׂם	בָּאָרוֹן	בְּמִצְרָיִם
shānîm	wayyachantû	'ōthô	wayyîsem	bā'ārôn	b^{e}mitsrāyim
years	and they embalmed	him	and he was put	in coffin	in Egypt

21. Now therefore fear ye not: I will nourish you, and your little ones: ... protect you and your children, *Fenton* ... provide for you and your dependants, *NCB.*

And he comforted them, and spake kindly unto them: ... speaketh unto their heart, *Young* ... and set their minds to rest, *REB* ... he reassured them, *NAB.*

22. And Joseph dwelt in Egypt, he, and his father's house: and Joseph lived an hundred and ten years: ... with all his father's family, *NIV* ... This was after Joseph returned to Mitzeraim, he and his father's family, *Fenton.*

23. And Joseph saw Ephraim's children of the third generation: the children also of Machir the son of Manasseh were brought up upon Joseph's knees: ... were placed at birth on Joseph's knees, *NIV* ... were born upon Joseph's knees, *MAST* ... he also recognized as his the children of Manasseh's son Machir, *NEB.*

24. And Joseph said unto his brethren, I die: and God will surely visit you: ... will surely remember you, *MAST* ... doth certainly inspect you, *Young* ... will keep you in mind, *BB* ... will not fail to come to your aid, *NEB* ... God will surely take care of you, *NAB.*

and bring you out of this land: ... and hath caused you to go up from this land, *Young* ... lead you out, *NAB.*

unto the land which he sware to Abraham, to Isaac, and to Jacob: ... promised on oath, *NIV.*

25. And Joseph took an oath of the children of Israel: ... made the Israelites swear, *NRSV* ... put the sons of Israel under oath, *Anchor.*

saying, God will surely visit you, and ye shall carry up my bones from hence: ... when God thus takes care of you, you must bring my bones up with you from this place, *NAB* ... God doth certainly inspect you, and ye have brought up my bones from this place, *Young* ... when God comes to your aid, you must take my bones with you from here, *NEB.*

26. So Joseph died, being an hundred and ten years old: ... a hundred and twenty years old, *Fenton.*

and they embalmed him, and he was put in a coffin in Egypt.

50:21. Joseph again encouraged his brothers not to be afraid. He would provide for them and their little children. So he comforted them and kept on speaking to their hearts. That is, he kept encouraging and reassuring them of his love and God's.

50:22-23. Joseph and all his father's household continued to live in Egypt. Joseph lived to be 110, and saw his grandchildren from Ephraim and even great-grandsons who were sons of Machir, Manasseh's son. That they were "born on Jacob's knees" means he lived to see them and treated them like his own children. (The phrase can refer to adoption, but probably does not mean that here.)

50:24. When Joseph knew he was about to die he told his brothers, that is his relatives. The contrast is emphatic. Joseph was dying, but God was not dead. Joseph's faith and confidence was that God would bring them out of Egypt to the land He swore to give to Abraham, Isaac, and Jacob.

50:25. Joseph then made the sons of Israel, that is, all the descendants of Jacob, swear an oath. God would surely intervene. He would act to fulfill His promise to give them the land of Canaan. When He did, they must carry Joseph's bones from Egypt to that land. When the Book of Hebrews catalogs the people of faith, it notes this confidence that Israel would return and this provision for his bones as the outstanding expression of Joseph's faith (Heb. 11:22).

50:26. The Book of Genesis ends with Joseph dead at 110 years of age and his body embalmed and placed in a coffin in Egypt. This coffin would be a constant reminder of their promise and of God's promise as well.

GENESIS OVERVIEW

Background

Outline

Summary

Genesis Overview

BACKGROUND

The name Genesis comes from the Greek Septuagint translation made by Jews in Alexandria about 200 years before the time of Christ. The Hebrew Bible titles the Book by its first word, *B^{e}re'shith*, "In Beginning" (meaning the furthest back beginning), and treats it as the first volume of the five-fold "Book" (singular) of Moses.

Long before New Testament times this "Book" of Moses was called the *Torah*, a Hebrew term meaning instruction or guidance. It was the guide book for Israel. The Apostle Paul called it a tutor (Gk. *paidagogos*) put in charge of Israel to guide them down through the centuries until it was time for Jesus to come (Gal. 3:24).

Genesis is indeed the Book of beginnings. In it are found the beginnings of creation, sin, divine judgment, divine revelation, divine guidance, prayer and worship, faith, prophecy, God's promises and covenants, the variety of languages and nations, and the beginnings of the chosen nation, Israel.

The Book is a teaching book with a simple basic outline (Adam, Noah, Abraham, Jacob, Joseph), a simple vocabulary, a powerful style, and a central theme that revolves around God's promise. It fits the needs of the Israelites who were about to enter the promised land. Chapter 10 gives most attention to the nations they would be in contact with when they settled in the land. God Himself gives special attention to the promise and covenant concerning the land (15:18-21; 17:7-8; 28:13-15; 35:11-12). The promise of blessing for Abraham's descendants and for all the nations of the world is repeated five times (12:3; 18:18-19; 22:17-18; 26:2-4; 28:14-15). In spite of the failures of human beings, the Book shows that God is faithful. His grace and mercy brings blessing often in spite of what people do.

Though the promise of the land was delayed, Joseph brought blessing to many nations during a great famine. God permitted Jacob to go to Egypt and promised a return to the land (46:2-4). In Egypt the Israelites prospered and began to multiply. It looked as if they were settled there. But Jacob looked ahead to the return to Canaan, and the Book ends with Joseph making provision for his bones to be carried up into the land. He expected God to fulfill His promise.

Until fairly modern times few questioned the book's authorship. The New Testament repeatedly refers to various parts of the Pentateuch as from Moses. Stephen declared Moses was educated "in all the wisdom of the Egyptians" (Acts 7;22). Archaeological discoveries in Egypt show that a young prince like Moses would have been put under tutors, would be trained in athletics and military pursuits, and would be given an active part at some level in the government.

Also important was Moses' early training from his parents (Exod. 2:9). When God revealed himself at the burning bush as "the God of Abraham, the God of Isaac, and the God of Jacob ... Moses hid his face; for he was afraid to look on God" (Exod. 3:6). Undoubtedly, from what his parents told him about Abraham, Isaac, and Jacob, Moses knew what kind of God they served.

Thus, Moses had the background and understanding to write Genesis. He also met with God again and again and was led and empowered by the Spirit of God as a prophet of God (cf. 2 Tim. 3:16; 2 Pet. 1:20-21). God gave him the revelation of the Law, and there is every reason to believe God gave him the revelation of the creation and the early history of humankind that is recorded in Genesis.

Modern literary criticism of the Pentateuch started with a French physician named Astruc (1684-1766). He decided Moses compiled Genesis from sources, some of which referred to God as *Elohim*, others used the personal name of God, *YHWH*. probably pronounced Yahweh. (The new Latin wrote the consonants YHWH as JHVH and combined them with the vowels of the Hebrew word for Lord to give the unbiblical form "Jehovah.")

Then others, such as J. G. Eichorn, J. S. Vater, and W.M.L de Wette, began to try to analyze Genesis in a very subjective way and split it into fragments. Scholars like H. Ewald and E.W. Hengstenberg defended the Mosaic authorship, pointing out that the names of God were most often used where the particular name would fit the context or purpose of what was written. The name *Elohim* being used especially when God's power is displayed. The name *Yahweh* being used where God's personal relationships or contact with humankind is being emphasized. However, so-called liberals, who denied the supernatural, continued to deny Moses' authorship.

Eventually, K. H. Graf and J. Wellhausen developed a theory, published in 1877. This theory alleged there were four documents that became the sources of the Pentateuch.

The first, the Jehovistic (J) they claimed was written in the southern kingdom of Judah about 850 B.C., supposing that writing was not invented until just before that time. Now we know that writing was invented at least by 3500 B.C., and an early Canaanite script has been found in the Sinai Peninsula. The second, the Elohistic (E), they claimed was written in the northern kingdom of Israel about 750 B.C. Then J and E were supposed to have been combined by an unknown person about 650 B.C. The third, the Deuteronomic (D), they said was written shortly after the combination of the J and E documents. This was supposedly in order to promote Josiah's reforms (621 B.C.). The fourth, the Priestly (P), they claimed was written in stages from the time of Ezekiel down to the time of Ezra. They included in this such things as details of measurement and worship which the supposed would be late. However, early writings of surrounding countries from before the time of Abraham give such details.

This JEDP theory proved attractive to those who were accepting various theories of organic evolution, and it is still standard in "liberal" seminaries. Most of their professors are so committed to the JEDP theory that they will not listen to the many objections to it that have been raised by archaeological discoveries. Nor do they bother to read scholars who have shown that the theory is unscientific and was developed by the *a priori* method, not by the *a posteriori* method scientists use. Many scholars, both Christian and Jewish (such as O. Allis, G. L. Archer, Jr., K. Kitchen, and Cyrus Gordon), have demonstrated the weaknesses of the JEDP theory, the literary integrity of the Pentateuch's history, and have shown how the Pentateuch fits the time of Moses, not the later dates that unbelievers propose.

Genesis Overview

OUTLINE

I. Adam 1:1 to 4:26
- A. Creation 1:1-2:3
  - 1. Heavens and Earth 1:1-2
  - 2. Seven Creation Days 1:3-2:3
    - a. Light 1:3-5
    - b. The Expanse 1:6-8
    - c. Dry Land and Vegetation 1:9-13
    - d. Light Bearers 1:14-19
    - e. Birds and Fish 1:20-23
    - f. Animals and Humans 1:24-31
    - g. The Seventh Day Made Holy 2:1-3
- B. Details of the Sixth Day 2:4-25
  - 1. The First Man Created 2:4-7
  - 2. Placed in the Garden 2:8-17
  - 3. Animals and Birds Named 2:18-20
  - 4. The First Woman Created 2:21-25
- C. The Temptation and Fall 3:1-24
  - 1. The Serpent Tempts 3:1-5
  - 2. The Man and the Woman Sin 3:6-8
  - 3. Judgment Pronounced 3:9-19
    - a. The Man Questioned 3:9-12
    - b. The Woman Questioned 3:13
    - c. Judgment on the Serpent 3:14-15
    - d. Judgment on the Woman 3:16
    - e. Judgment on the Man 3:17-19
  - 4. Eve Named 3:20
  - 5. Garments of Skin Provided 3:21
  - 6. Banished from the Garden 3:22-24
- D. Cain and Abel 4:1-26
  - 1. Cain and Abel Born 4:1-2
  - 2. Cain and Abel's Offerings 4:3-7
  - 3. Abel Murdered 4:8-16
  - 4. Cain's Line 4:17-24
  - 5. Seth in Abel's Place 4:25-26

II. Noah 5:1-11:26
- A. Godly Line of Seth 5:1-32
- B. Increasing Wickedness 6:1-8

C. The Command to Build an Ark 6:9-21
D. The Flood Comes 7:1-24
E. Leaving the Ark 8:1-22
F. The Rainbow Covenant 9:1-19
G. Canaan Cursed; Shem Blessed 9:20-29
H. Descendants of Noah's Sons 10:1-32
I. The Tower of Babel 11:1-9
J. Genealogy: Shem to Abram 11:10-26

III. Abraham 11:27 to 25:18
- A. Abram Taken to Haran 11:27-32
- B. Abram's Journey to Canaan 12:1-9
- C. Abram's Journey to Egypt 12:10-22
- D. Abram Separates From Lot 13:1-18
- E. Abram Rescues Lot 14:1-24
- F. God's Promise and Covenant 15:1-21
- G. Ishmael Born 16:1-16
- H. The Covenant Confirmed 17:1-27
  1. Abram Becomes Abraham 17:1-8
  2. Circumcision Instituted 17:9-14
  3. Sarai Become Sarah 17:15-22
  4. Abraham's Household Circumcised 17:23-27
- I. Sodom Destroyed and Lot Rescued 18:1 to 19:38
  1. The LORD Appears to Abraham 18:1-15
  2. Abraham Pleads for Sodom 18:16-33
  3. Sodom Destroyed and Lot Saved 19:1-38
- J. Abraham Prays For Abimelech 20:1-18
- K. Isaac Born and Ishmael Disinherited 21:1-34
- L. Abraham Tested and God Provides 22:1-24
- M. Sarah Dies 23:1-20
- N. Rebekah God's Choice For Isaac 24:1-67
- O. Abraham Dies 25:1-11
- P. Ishmael and His Sons 25:12-18

IV. Jacob 25:19 to 37:1
- A. Jacob and Esau born 25:19-28
- B. Esau Sells His Birthright 25:29-34
- C. Isaac and Abimelech 26:1-33
- D. Esau's Hittite Wives 26:34-35
- E. Jacob Steals the Blessing 27:1-46

- F. Jacob Sent to Seek a Wife 28:1-29:14
- G. Jacob Serves Laban 29:15-31:55
    1. Jacob's Marriage 29:15-30
    2. Jacob's Children 29:31-30:24
    3. Service for Wages 30:25-43
    4. Jacob to Return to Canaan 31:1-21
    5. Laban pursues Jacob 31:22-42
    6. Jacob's Covenant with Laban 31:43-55
- H. Jacob Meets Esau 32:1-33:16
    1. Preparation 32:1-21
    2. Wrestling at Peniel 32:22-32
    3. Jacob and Esau Reconciled 33:1-16
- I. Jacob at Succoth and Shechem 34:17-31
- J. Jacob Returns to Bethel 35:1-15
- K. Rachel Dies 35:16-20
- L. Jacob's Sons 35:21-26
- M. Isaac Dies 35:27-29
- N. Esau's Descendants and Edom 36:1-43
- O. Jacob Settled in Canaan 37:1

V. Joseph 37:2 to 50:26

- A. Joseph Sold into Egypt 37:2-36
- B. Judah and Tamar 38:1-30
- C. Joseph Serves Potiphar 39:1-19
- D. Joseph in Prison 39:20-40:23
- E. Interpreting Pharaoh's Dreams 41:1-36
- F. Preparing for the Famine 41:37-57
- G. Joseph's Brothers in Egypt 42:1-28
- H. Benjamin taken to Egypt 42:29-43:34
- I. Joseph's Cup 44:1-34
- J. Joseph Reveals Himself 45:1-46:27
- K. Joseph's Family Settled in Goshen 46:28-47:12
- L. Egypt's Cattle and Lands Bought 47:13-26
- M. Jacob Prepares for His Death 47:27-49:27
    1. Burial to be in Canaan 47:27-31
    2. Blessing of Ephraim and Manasseh 48:1-22
    3. Blessing of Jacob's Sons 49:1-27
- N. Jacob's Death and Burial 49:28-50:21
- O. Joseph's Death 50:22-26

SUMMARY

Early History Of God's Dealings With Humankind

Creation

Other ancient peoples had creation stories, such as the Mesopotamian *Enuma elish* ("When on high"; discovered in the ruins of Nineveh in 1873), but they exalt pagan gods and are radically different from the simplicity and majesty of the Bible's account. None of them teach a real beginning or a creation out of nothing. *Enuma elish* begins with male and female water deities, Apsu and Tiamat, who become parents of the gods. The god Ea kills Apsu. Marduk, the city god of Babylon, then kills Tiamat, splits her body and uses the two halves to form the earth and sky. Then the gods kill another god, Kingu, cut open his arteries and form humankind from his blood. The gods then mold bricks for a year and build the temple tower Esagila at Babylon and make Marduk chief of all the gods.

How different this is from Genesis which declares that in the beginning God created the heavens and the earth. We have no way of going back in time to check this, but we can join with the writer to the Hebrews who said, "By faith we understand that the universe was formed at God's command, so that what is seen was not made out of what was visible" (Heb. 11:3, NIV).

God's commands and their responses continue throughout the first chapter of Genesis. The first is dramatic--only four words in the Hebrew: be, light, and was, light. Creation continues as God gives further commands carrying out His plan in 6 days of creation. Everything is good. Everything does what it should. There is no failure on God's part. Then with His creative work finished, God ceases His work and sets the seventh day apart as holy, a reminder to those He created that we should live in holiness before Him.

Faith and Failure In Adam's Family

The remainder of the first 11 chapters deal with humankind as a whole and show the failure of the human race to obey God and give reasons for humankind's depraved condition. It begins by showing how God created the first man and woman and put them in an ideal setting in the Garden of Eden. They had everything they needed, physically, mentally, socially, and spiritually. God provided them with food, created them as perfect mates, and walked and talked with them in the cool of the afternoon breezes. But God made them responsible moral beings, creatures with the power of choice. Thus, the tree of the knowledge of good and evil was placed in the middle of the garden as a test.

When Adam and Eve failed the test, God brought judgment on them as well as the serpent that tempted them. He was merciful, however, and gave them a promise of future deliverance from the serpent. He also provided them with a covering of skins taken from a slain animal, not animals they slew, but a sacrifice that God provided.

Their failure was followed by failure in their family as Cain offered an unacceptable sacrifice, and killed his brotherout of jealousy. The death of his brother brought a curse on him and separation from Adam and Eve and the rest their family (except his wife). Cain's descendants prospered materially, but the moral breakdown and violence that developed in his family spread and eventually led to world-wide corruption and violence, and world-wide failure to do the will of God. However, there was hope in Seth's line. Faith was renewed and people began to call on the Name of the LORD, worshiping Him and calling down His blessing.

Faith and Failure in Noah's Family

By the time of Noah, the whole world was not only corrupt and full of violence, those who were wicked were working to make it worse and trying draw everyone into sharing their evil practices. Obviously, the influence of Cain's descendants and the effects of the fall had spread throughout all humankind. Even the godly line of Seth was affected (probably through intermarriage) so that Noah alone was walking with the LORD.

The sin and corruption so grieved God that He determined to send a flood to destroy humankind, but Noah found favor with Him, so He gave Noah directions to build an ark to save his family. Noah was also instructed to save two of every kind of animal and bird, with the further provision to save 7 pairs of clean animals, probably for sacrifice and for food. Rains came for 40 days, the water was high for 110 days, and then gradually went down so that Noah and his family were in the ark a total of 1 year and 10 days.

Before leaving the ark, Noah sent out a raven and a dove to see if the waters had sufficiently receded. He also took the roof off of the ark. His first act after coming out of the ark was to offer a sacrifice to give thanks to God and to express his dedication to Him.

Since the flood was world-wide, it is not strange that flood stories were passed down in various cultures. One of the oldest accounts was written down by Sumerians about 2500 B.C. Their story was later incorporated with more details in the Babylonian Gilgamesh Epic about 2000 B.C. It has some similarities to biblical account in that there is an ark, a survivor, birds are sent out, and a sacrifice is offered after coming out of the ark. But the differences are striking.

In the Sumerian and Babylonian accounts, the flood results from the caprice of the gods, who cannot agree. The ark is a cube of 120 cubits on each side, built from the reeds of the house of the hero, Utnapishtim. It has 7 stories with 9 rooms each. Utnapishtim loads it with gold, silver, the animals he owned, and his relatives. When the rain comes, the gods are terrified and cower like dogs against the wall of heaven. The flood lasts only 7 days, then a dove, swallow and raven are sent out. When the sacrifice is offered, all the gods gather round like a swarm of flies. These pagans believed the gods needed the sacrifices. Since none were offered during the flood, the gods were nearly starved to death. The gods argue about what to do with the survivors after the flood. Finally, one of them makes Utnapishtim and his wife immortal.

There is no way Moses could have purified this account to give us what we find in the Bible. Rather, it seems that some details of the flood were passed down among the Sumerians and Babylonians, but as people turned away from God, the story was encrusted with details that were polytheistic and were from human imagination. God must have revealed the truth to Moses.

The events after the flood, including

Noah's drunkenness, the curse on Canaan, and the tower of Babel show that a new beginning was not enough. The tower of Babel shows that people had put themselves on the throne, and wanted to be independent rather than submitting to the true God.

Romans 1:21-23 explains that they no longer glorified God or gave Him thanks. Their hearts were darkened; and because they needed to worship, they began making images in the form of human beings, birds, animals, and even snakes. God scattered them by supernaturally changing their languages. Romans 1:24,26 says "God gave them up to uncleanness ... unto vile affections." But God did not give up on His good purpose for humankind. He ceased dealing with humankind as a whole and He began to carry forward his plan with one man, Abraham, who responded in faith.

The History of Abraham and the Beginnings of the Chosen Line

Abraham And God's Promise

The real new beginning for humankind did not come with Noah but with Abraham. God called him out from Ur of the Chaldees.

J. E. Taylor first excavated at Ur on the west side of the Euphrates, 220 miles south of Baghdad. Major excavations were conducted by Sir Charles Leonard Woolley in 1922-34. They showed a rich, sophisticated, educated culture existed in that city in the time of Abraham. There is some evidence, however of Chaldees in northwest Mesopotamia and of another Ur north-northeast of Haran.

In either case, the evidence is that Abraham came out of a highly developed culture and was considered a merchant prince. He not only obeyed God, he entered into a personal relationship with God and became the agent of God's promises, so that the Bible calls him "the friend of God" (2 Chron. 20:7; Isa. 41:8; James 2:23).

God's promise to Abraham puts the prophecy of a great nation first, for, as the Bible emphasizes, God chose Israel to prepare the way for the redemption to come. Then God promised to bless Abraham, which implies giving him a son who would carry on his faith and would ultimately lead to the Messiah (Gal. 3:16). Another aspect of the promise was to make Abraham's name great, something that was fulfilled when Abraham became known as the father of all who believe (Rom 4:15-17; Gal. 3:6-9).

Along with these promises came the command that he must be a blessing. That is, he must conform to God's will and become empowered by God to carry His blessing to others. Then, depending on their response to the promise to Abraham, culminating its fulfillment in Jesus the Messiah, others would be either blessed or come under divine judgment.

The Bible records selected incidents in the life of Abraham to show the further development of his faith through testing. He did have faith when he left Haran to go to Canaan. But he was tested by famine, by his separation from Lot, by the delay of Isaac's birth for 25 years, by his having to disinherit Ishmael, by the delay of the promise of the land, and by the command to offer Isaac. He was not free from mistakes, as his journey to Egypt and his acceptance of Hagar as a concubine reveal. But all of his experiences helped to mature an immovable faith the New Testament sets before us as the prime example of saving faith (Rom. 4:18-25).

In Genesis 14:13, Abraham is called a Hebrew. Though Hebrew may indicate his descent from Eber, or may identify him as an immigrant from the other side of the Euphrates River, some take it to correspond to *Habiru* (an Akkadian term for people called *sa-gaz* in the Sumerian). The term seems to describe a social class of merchants, mercenary soldiers, and herdsmen throughout the ancient Middle East. This was applied to Abraham in connection with his rescue of Lot, and whatever its derivation may be, it fits the picture of Abraham's time.

Genesis 15:13 prophesies Abraham's descendants as strangers in a land not theirs for 400 years. It is then said that the fourth generation would return (15:16). This would make a generation to be over 100 years. However, the word "generation" (Heb. *dor*; Gk. *genea*) is used in a general way and is not intended to indicate exact dates.

By buying the field and the cave at Machpelah to bury Sarah, Abraham finally owned a piece of the promised land. To be buried there was a testimony to their faith in God's promise that their descendants would inherit the land. Thus Abraham, Isaac, Rebekah, Leah, and Jacob were all buried there.

As further evidence of his concern for the promise of the land, Abraham took an oath from his servant forbidding him to take Isaac back to Haran to stay. Rebekah's response to the guidance God gave the servant demonstrated her faith. Like Abraham, she had to leave her family and her land to go to the place God promised to Abraham and his descendants--which would now include hers.

Isaac

Isaac is kept in the background of the history of Jacob, just as he was in the history of Abraham. He was a promised son, but not the promised Son to come. Only chapters 26 and 27 give any details of Isaac's experiences. In the former chapter, he suffers a famine, and is then prospered. The central fact, however, is that God promises to be with him and bless him for Abraham's sake, and that others recognize the value and reality of his blessing. In chapter 27, Isaac is old and the focus is on Jacob and his struggles (just as it was from the time of his birth in chapter 25 when he was born grasping Esau's heel and later bargains for the birthright). Jacob's struggles continue from the time he deceived his father to get Esau's blessing until finally he is able to bless Pharaoh in Egypt as well as Ephraim and Manasseh and then to predict the future of all his sons.

Jacob Needs to be Changed

That Jacob is God's choice to receive the blessing of Abraham and carry on the chosen line is made clear at Bethel where God appears at the head of the ladder to heaven, promises to be with him, keep him, and bring him back to the promised land. The fact that God was with Jacob is seen by His guidance and the meeting with Rachel with whom he falls in love. However, Jacob was a man who needed to be changed. By a combination of deceitfulness and cunning, he had obtained the birthright and the blessing. He had a long time ahead to suffer from the deceitfulness and cunning of Laban as well as that of his own sons.

Laban deceived Jacob by giving him Leah

instead of Rachel after 7 years of slave labor as Laban's foreman. Then, after another 7 years of service, where Leah bore sons and Rachel was barren, Laban offered him wages but treated him unfairly for another 6 years by repeatedly changing his wages. During these 20 years, there was constant struggle between his two wives. When Rachel perceived she was barren, she offered her maid to Jacob as a concubine. The name of Bilhah's second son, Naphtali, indicates her view of the struggle (30:8).

God, however, kept his promise to be with Jacob. He showed him through a dream that he should pen up the strong female animals in Laban's herd and allow only the males to mate with them that had the markings he desired. Thus, God made Jacob prosper and at the end of the 20 years with Laban, God told him it was time to return to the promised land. God had given him sons who would be heads of the tribes of Israel. The promise to multiply his descendants was well on its way.

Jacob's wives recognized the attitude of their father had changed since Jacob had prospered and were willing to go. Rachel, however, nearly brought trouble by her deception when she stole the family gods--the teraphim. She hoped to gain the family inheritance for her husband Jacob by this trickery-- something that did not happen because the idols were later buried and left behind. Laban, however, thought Jacob was tricking him and pursued him to the hills of Gilead southeast of the Sea of Galilee. At the heap of witness they set up, they swore an oath that they would not cross a line there to go against each other.

Then Jacob prepared to meet Esau. Jacob prayed and acknowledged God's promise of help, expressing his unworthiness of God's blessing. But he still thought he should meet the situation by manipulation and by buying Esau's favor with gifts. At the River Jabbok, he was left alone, just as he was at Bethel years before. Jacob recognized the One who wrestled with him as God, which was a further fulfillment of God's promise to be with him. Having experienced the presence of God, he was ready to face Esau. God was surely with him when Esau greeted him with a hug and a kiss. Jacob then insisted that Esau keep the gifts he sent him, not as a present merely, but as a blessing (33:11). He was not giving up the blessing of Abraham. But he was recognizing that all his blessings were his because of the grace and unmerited favor of God. He was now acting like Israel. He had struggled with God and with humans and had prevailed (32:28). At the same time he was recognizing that God rules.

Jacob moved on, but did not go directly to Bethel as he had promised (28:22). Instead, he stayed first at Succoth and then moved across the Jordan River to the area of Shechem where he bought property. But buying property was not God's way of fulfilling the promise to give them the land, nor was intermarriage with the Canaanites. When the young prince, Shechem, raped Jacob's daughter, Dinah, the brothers took revenge and even used the sign of God's covenant (circumcision) as a means to trick the men of the city and bring about their murder. But it became the occasion for God to command Jacob to return to Bethel.

Jacob's pilgrimage to Bethel involved getting rid of idols and earrings which were symbols of their own position in society. No longer was Jacob a trickster and a deceiver. He came to Bethel as a humble pilgrim responding to God's command and built an altar to express his thanks to God for being with him. Then God appeared and again confirmed the blessing of Abraham and the promise of the land to him and to his descendants.

This coming back to the God who had met him at Bethel really concludes the story of Jacob. The interlude that follows tells of the death of Rachel when Benjamin was born, lists the sons of Jacob, and tells the story of Esau's wives and descendants who intermarried with the Horites and became Edomites.

Joseph, The Savior of His People from Famine

The remainder of Genesis centers its attention on Joseph, who received the birthright. But there is attention on Judah as well, for he was the one who would become the ancestor of King David and Jesus. The story provides understanding of how God brought about the preserving of the chosen people and thus the hope of the world.

Jacob's love for Joseph prompted him to give Joseph a royal tunic which quickly stirred the jealousy of Joseph's brothers. Joseph did not help the situation by telling of his brothers's sins as well as relating the dreams that appeared to exalt himself over them and his parents. When his brother's hatred made them want to kill him, Reuben wanted to save him. But it was Judah who encouraged the rest of the brothers to sell him to the merchantmen going to Egypt, thus bringing about the next step in God's plan.

Chapter 38 takes place over the next 15 or 20 years of Judah's life. This chapter is a parenthesis placed here to bring contrast to Joseph's purity and faithfulness to God seen in the next chapter. When Judah's son Er was wicked, God judged him with death. Then God brought the same judgment on Onan for refusing to submit to his responsibility to his brother and God for carrying on the multiplication of the chosen line. Then Judah withheld his third son and Er's wife, Tamar, deceived Judah and enticed him to buy her services as a religious prostitute. Jacob learned from this, and he became a changed man. Then, Perez, the younger son of Judah and Tamar became the ancestor of the line that led to King David and Jesus.

When the Bible returns to Joseph's situation in Egypt, it presents a tremendous contrast to chapter 38. Joseph was faithful, hard-working, and was blessed by God with favor and promotion in the house of Potiphar, the king's chief executioner. But Joseph became a victim of Potiphar's wife when he refused her temptations because of his loyalty to Potiphar, and above all, his loyalty to God. Prison became another test of his faith, as did his service to the chief butler and the chief baker. God confirmed his faith by giving him the correct interpretations for their dreams, but then the 2-year delay before Pharaoh's dreams was another test. Finally, God-given interpretations and God-given wisdom were recognized by Pharaoh and his court, and Joseph was made the prime minister of Egypt to administer preparations for the 7 years of famine during the 7 good years.

We do not know the Pharaoh's name, nor should we expect to find the name of Joseph or his Egyptian name Zaphnath-paaneah in Egyptian records. Joseph did everything in the name of the Pharaoh and all the orders were made official by Pharaoh's signet ring (41:42). Though it is controversial, many believe that Joseph rose to power during the early part of the Hyksos ("foreign rulers") period (1750-1550) when the Pharaohs were Asiatics. They introduced the horse and chariot to Egypt, and Joseph rode in a chariot as the king's second-in-command (41:43).

When Joseph's brothers come to buy grain they bowed down before Zaphnath-paaneah, not knowing it was Joseph. Joseph spoke to them through an interpreter, and proceeded to test them, demanding that they bring Benjamin. This was a test for Jacob as well, and he did not yield until he and his family were facing starvation. Even then it was not until Judah offered himself as a pledge to bear the blame forever that he agreed to let Benjamin go. Then, as was the case before he met Esau, Jacob sent a gift, hoping to soften the Egyptian prime minister.

Joseph did not know about Judah's pledge, so he proceeded with further tests. The seating at the dinner in Joseph's house in the order of their birth and the giving to Benjamin five times what the others received was a critical test. Though they enjoyed themselves and showed no jealousy toward Benjamin, Joseph was not sure what they would do to their youngest brother on the way home. So Joseph's silver cup was placed in Benjamin's sack, and Joseph's steward quickly followed them. The brothers claimed they were innocent and made a rash vow that if the cup was found in anyone's sack, he must die. The steward and Joseph rejected this and demanded that Benjamin remain as a slave.

Judah had truly changed. He was the one who suggested selling Joseph. He was the one who was afraid to give his youngest son to Tamar in order to continue the family line. Now he had offered himself for the sake of all of Jacob's family.

Then in Egypt, when Joseph demanded that Benjamin be left as his slave because of the silver cup placed in Benjamin's sack, Judah was the one who offered himself in Benjamin's place. This was too much for Joseph. Now he knew the repentance of his brothers was genuine, and he finally revealed who he really was.

Through Joseph, God brought blessing to Jacob and all Jacob's family. They were settled in a part of Egypt where they could retain their identity. They gained possession in it and prospered (47:11-12,27), while the rest of Egypt (except for the priests) had their lands taken over by the Pharaoh to pay for food during the famine (47:20-23).

On his deathbed, Jacob reminded Joseph of God's promise of blessing and of the land confirmed at Luz (48:3-4). Then he adopted Joseph's sons, giving the younger the preeminence, something that later history would confirm when Ephraim became the leading northern tribe in the promised land. Jacob then gave prophetic blessings to all his sons, with special attention to Judah and Joseph.

In these deathbed scenes, Israel truly lived up to his new name. He was buried in the promised land, and his example inspired Joseph to believe that God would fulfill his promises. Thus Joseph made provision for his bones to be carried up to the promised land when God would bring His people back (see Josh. 24:32). This was Joseph's final witness and it prepared the way for what God would do in the Exodus under Moses and Joshua.

APPENDICES

Explanation of Verb Stems

Translations of the Various Versions

Books of the Old and New Testaments and the Apocrypha

How the Old Testament Came to Us

Manuscripts

The Septuagint

Appendices

Appendix A

Explanation of Verb Stems

There are basically seven verb stems in the Hebrew language. Verbs are either active or passive, and they deal with past, present, or future actions or conditions. The mood of the verb relates the general meaning, but context, the relationships of words within the literary unit, always determines the final meaning.

This volume uses a verb numbering system formatted to give (1) the word number; (2) the mood; (3) the tense; and (4) the person, gender, and number. The first number is to the left of the decimal point, and the last three numbers are to the right of the decimal point. Following is a brief explanation of the numbers that occur to the right of the decimal point.

Mood (first position)

1. *Qal*--simple active verb stem. The Qal mood accounts for most of the verbs in the Old Testament. Qal usually indicates an action of the subject (*he told*). It can also indicate the state of the subject (*he was old*).

2. *Niphal*--the simple passive or reflexive counterpart of the *Qal* stem. Used passively, Niphal means the action of the verb is received by the subject (*he was told,* or, *it was told*). Although rare, Niphal is sometimes used reflexively, it means the subject performs the action of the verb upon himself or herself (*he realized*). The reflexive meaning is usually expressed using the Hithpael.

3. *Piel*--the intensive active or causative stem. The most common use of the *Piel* is as intensification of the action of the verb (*he often told,* or, *he fully explained*). It sometimes, however, is used in a causative sense like the Hiphil (*he caused to learn / he taught*).

4. *Pual*--the intensive passive counterpart of the Piel stem (*he was often told,* or, *he was completely informed,*or, *it was fully explained*).

5. *Hiphil*--the causative active counterpart of the *Qal* stem (*he caused to tell*). Sometimes it is used in a declarative sense (*he declared guilty*). Some *Hiphil* verbs are closer to the meaning of the simple active use of the *Qal* stem (*he destroyed*). Finally, some *Hiphil* verbs do not fit any of these categories, and they must be understood by their context.

6. *Hophal*--the causative passive counterpart of the *Hiphil* stem (*he was caused to tell*).

7. *Hithpael*--reflexive action (*he realized*). However, some *Hithpael* verbs are translated in a simple active sense like the *Qal* stem (*he prayed*), since the one performing the action is not transferring that action to anyone or anything else.

Tense (second position)

1. *Perfect.* The Hebrew perfect may be translated as a simple completed action (he *walked* to the store). It may also be translated as a *past perfect,* which is an action completed prior to a point of reference in past time (she gave money as *she had promised*). The perfect is translated in the present tense when the verb concerns the subject's attitude, experience, perception, or state of being (*you are old,* or, *I love you*). It may also represent action that is

viewed as completed as soon as it was mentioned (*I anoint you* as king over Israel, 2 Kings. 9:3).

When this tense is used in promises, prophecies, and threats, it commonly means that the action of the verb is certain and imminent (A star *will come* out of Jacob, Numbers 24:17). Since this use is common in the prophetic writings, it is usually called the *prophetic perfect*. It is usually translated into English as either a present or future tense verb.

Finally, when the perfect occurs with the vav conjunctive prefixed, it is usually translated in the future tense (*I will lie down* with my fathers, Genesis 47:30).

2. *Imperfect.* This tense indicates an incomplete action or state. Perhaps the most common use of the imperfect is to describe a simple action in future time (*he will reign* over you). The imperfect is also used to express habitual or customary actions in the past, present, or future (And so *he did* year by year, 1 Samuel 1:7; A son *honors* his father, Malachi 1:6; The LORD *will reign* forever and ever, Exodus 15:18). The imperfect frequently expresses contingency, and English modal auxiliaries such as *may, can, shall, might, could, should, would* and *perhaps* are used with the verb (Who is the LORD that I *should obey* his voice?, Exodus 5:2).

The modal use of the imperfect is common after the particles אֵיךְ (how) and אוּלַי (perhaps), and the interrogatives מָה (what), מִי (who), and לָמָּה (why). Two other uses of the imperfect are the *jussive* and *cohortative*.

The jussive expresses a desire for action from a third person subject (I pray *let* the king *remember* the LORD your God, 2 Samuel 14:11; *May* the LORD *lift up* his countenance unto you, Numbers 6:26). The cohortative expresses the speaker's desire or intention to act, so it occurs only in the first person singular and plural (*let me pass* through the roadblock, *let us draw near* to God).

3. *Imperative.* This tense occurs only in the second person singular and plural. The main use of the imperative is in direct commands (*Separate yourself* from me, Genesis 13:9). The imperative can also grant permission (*Go up*, and *bury* your father, according as he made you swear, Genesis 50:6). It may also disclose a request (*Give* them, I pray, a talent of silver, 2 Kings 5:22).
Imperatives may convey a wish (*May you be* the mother of thousands of millions, Genesis 24:60).
Imperatives are even used sarcastically (Come to Bethel and *transgress*, Amos 4:4).

Some uses of the imperative, however, do not carry the ordinary force of meaning. Sometimes it emphatically and vividly communicates a promise or prediction (And in the third year *sow*, and *reap*, *plant* vineyards, and *eat* the fruits thereof, 2 Kings 19:29).

4. *Infinitive.* This tense occurs in either the absolute or the construct state. Infinitives express the idea of a verb, but they are not limited by person, gender, and number. The infinitive absolute is used in several ways. It most often stands before a finite verb of the same root to intensify the certainty or force of the verbal idea (You shall *surely* die, Genesis 2:17). It also functions as a verbal noun (*slaying* cattle and *killing* sheep, Isaiah 22:13; It is not good *to eat* much honey, Proverbs 25:27). The infinitive absolute sometimes occurs after an imperative (Kill me *at once*, Numbers

11:15; Listen *diligently* to me, Isaiah 55:2). It may also occur after a verb to show continuance or repetition (*Keep on* hearing but do not understand, Isaiah 6:9; and it went *here and there*, Genesis 8:7). Frequently, it is used in place of an imperative (*Remember[ing]* the Sabbath day, Exodus 20:8). Sometimes it is used in place of a finite verb (and he *made* him ruler over all the land of Egypt, Genesis 41:43).

The infinitive construct also has several uses. It may function as the object or subject of a sentence (I know not how *to go out* or *come in*, 1 Kings 3:7; *to obey* is better than sacrifice, 1 Samuel 15:22). However, it most often occurs after ל to express purpose (he turned aside *to see*, Exodus 3:4). The infinitive construct may also occur after ל to express a gerundial meaning (The people sin against the LORD *by eating* blood, 1 Samuel 14:33). Moreover, it is frequently used in temporal clauses (*When you eat* from it, you shall surely die, Genesis 2:17).

5. *Participle* This tense in the Hebrew does not indicate person, but it does indicate gender and number. It may be either masculine or feminine, and either singular or plural. Participles may also occur in either the active or passive voice. However, only the *Qal* stem has both active and passive participles. Verbal tense is not indicated by the Hebrew participle, so it must be inferred from the context, whether it is *past*, *present*, or *future* tense. Uses of the participle include the following.

Since it is a verbal noun, a participle may indicate a continuous activity or state (I saw also the LORD *sitting* upon a throne, Isaiah 6:1). Participles may also be used as attributive or predicative adjectives. As an attributive adjective, it follows the noun it modifies, and it agrees with the noun in gender, number, and definiteness (blessed is *he who comes* in the name of the LORD, Psalm 118:26; the glory of the LORD was like a *devouring* fire, Exodus 24:17).

As a predicative adjective, the participle follows the noun it modifies, and agrees with the noun in gender and number, but it never has the definite article (the man is *standing*, the women are *standing*). When the noun is indefinite, the participle may be attributive or predicative, so context must determine the correct translation. Participles are also used as substantives (one who climbs, *climber*; one who works, *worker*; one who loves, *lover*).

Person, Gender, and Number (third position)

Person--whether the verb is *first person* (I, we), *second person* (you), or *third person* (he, she, it, they).

Gender--whether the verb is *masculine* or *feminine*.

Number--whether the verb is singular or plural (Infinitives are only indicated as construct or absolute. Participles are indicated as active or passive, masculine or feminine, and singular or plural).

Verb Identification Chart

Following is the verb identification chart used in this volume, for the three digits following the decimal of every verb. This pattern follows the usual verb chart found in Hebrew grammars.

First numeral after decimal:

1. Qal
2. Niphal
3. Piel
4. Pual
5. Hiphil
6. Hophal
7. Hithpael

Second numeral after decimal:

1. Perfect
2. Imperfect
3. Imperative
4. Infinitive
5. Participle

Third numeral after decimal:

Perfect	Imperfect	Imperative	Infinitive	Participle
1. 3ms	3ms	2ms	construct	active ms
2. 3fs	3fs	2fs	absolute	active mp
3. 2ms	2ms	2mp		active fs
4. 2fs	2fs	2fp		active fp
5. 1cs	1cs			passive ms
6. 3cp	3mp			passive mp
7. 2mp	3fp			passive fs
8. 2fp	2mp			passive fp
9. 1cp	2fp			
10.	1cp			

cs=common singular
cp=common plural
fs=feminine singular
fp=feminine plural
ms=masculine singular
mp=masculine plural

Appendices

APPENDIX B

Translations of the Various Versions

In order to provide the reader with a sample representation of many versions of the Old Testament, the following versions are compared with the King James Version. These versions are used as much as needed to illustrate various shades of meaning and main differences among the translations. All of the material could not be included. Rather the best representation of the 25 versions listed below has been used for the best.

Abbreviation:	Translation:
Anchor	Anchor Bible Commentaries
ASV	American Standard Version
BB	Dutton's Basic Bible
Berkeley	Berkeley's Version in Modern English
Darby	Darby's The Holy Scripture
Fenton	Fenton's Holy Bible
Geneva	Geneva Bible
Good News	Good News, The Bible in Today's English
Goodspeed	The Bible, An American Translation by Edgar Goodspeed
KJVII	King James Version II
LIVB	Living Bible
MAST	The Holy Scriptures According to the Masoretic Text
MLB	Modern Language Bible
MRB	The Modern Readers Bible
NAB	New American Bible
NASB	New American Standard Bible
NCB	New Catholic Bible
NEB	New English Bible
NIV	New International Version
NKJV	New King James Version
NRSV	New Revised Standard Version
REB	Revised English Bible
RSV	Revised Standard Version
Torah	A New Translation of the Holy Scriptures According to the Traditional Hebrew Text
Young	Young's Literal Translation

APPENDIX C

Books of the Old and New Testaments and the Apocrypha

Old Testament

Genesis
Exodus
Leviticus
Numbers
Deuteronomy
Joshua
Judges
Ruth
1 Samuel
2 Samuel
1 Kings
2 Kings
1 Chronicles
2 Chronicles
Ezra
Nehemiah
Esther
Job
Psalms
Proverbs
Ecclesiastes
Song of Solomon
Isaiah
Jeremiah
Lamentations
Ezekiel
Daniel
Hosea
Joel
Amos
Obadiah
Jonah
Micah
Nahum
Habakkuk
Zephaniah
Haggai
Zechariah
Malachi

New Testament

Matthew
Mark
Luke
John
Acts
Romans
1 Corinthians
2 Corinthians
Galatians
Ephesians
Philippians
Colossians
1 Thessalonians
2 Thessalonians
1 Timothy
2 Timothy
Titus
Philemon
Hebrews
James
1 Peter
2 Peter
1 John
2 John
3 John
Jude
Revelation

Books of the Apocrypha

1 & 2 Esdras
Tobit
Judith
Additions to Esther
Wisdom of Solomon
Ecclesiasticus of the Wisdom of Jesus Son of Sirach
Baruch
Prayer of Azariah and the Song of the Three Holy Children
Susanna
Bel and the Dragon
The Prayer of Manasses
Maccabees 1-4

APPENDIX D

How the Old Testament Came to Us

The Hebrew canon was written over a period of about 1,000 years (1450-400 B.C.). These books were considered inspired and therefore canonical from the time they were written. The word **canon** means a "straight edge," "rod," or "ruler." It came to mean "the rule" or "the standard" of divine inspiration and authority. The only true test of canonicity is the testimony of God regarding the authority of his own Word.

Protestants and Jews have always agreed that the thirty-nine books of the English Old Testament are canonical, although the Jews have divided them differently to form twenty-two, twenty-four, or thirty-six books. The Roman Catholic Church, since the Council of Trent in A.D. 1546, also accepts seven books of the Apocrypha (Tobit, Judith, Wisdom, Ecclesiasticus, Baruch, 1 and 2 Maccabees, and some additions to the books of Esther and Daniel) as canonical.

We no longer have access to the infallible original manuscripts (called "the autographs") of the Hebrew Scriptures. The earliest manuscripts in some cases are a thousand years removed from the original writing. However, they constitute our primary authority as to the inspired Word of God, and all copies and translations are dependent upon the best and earliest Hebrew and Aramaic manuscripts. We must review all written evidence upon which our modern editions of the Hebrew Bible are based, and have some knowledge of the wide range of evidence with which Old Testament textual criticism deals. Hebrew texts take priority in value, since God's revelation came first to Israel in the Hebrew tongue. Moreover, in the instances where very early manuscripts have been found, divine guidance is evident in the extreme accuracy of the copies.

Liberal scholars consider only the human side of the equation, thereby rejecting inspiration. From a nearly spiritually dead European church came the school of theology which developed a theory on the development of the Biblical text known as Documentary Hypothesis. With regard to the Pentateuch, the most famous of these theories is known as JEDP. Julius Wellhausen was the first significant proponent of this theory in the 1800's. Due to the rise of deistic philosophy and evolutionary science, the stage was set for historical criticism of the Bible and the rejection of the supernatural.

The Documentary Hypothesis method of document analysis was used on the works of Homer, Horace, and Shakespeare, as well as works purported to have been written by them. However, it was eventually used only to attack the validity and reliability of the Bible. The "J" document is titled as such because of the use of *Yahweh* (sometimes called Jehovah), and the "E" document is titled as such because of the use of *Elohim* for God. Whether God's name or title is used, it is speculated, determines whether that section of the first Books of the Pentateuch is from the "J" or the "E" document. It is theorized that if the entire Pentateuch were written by one person, only one name would be used for God. The dozens of etymological unifying elements threaded throughout the Pentateuch are simply ignored. The "D" document is considered a *deuteronomic work*, and the "P" document is considered primarily a *priestly editorial*. Dates of these documents are set at 950 B.C. for J, 850 B.C. for E, 625 B.C. for D, and 450 B.C. for P. The first five Books of the Bible, known for millenia as the Books of Moses, are viewed by JEDP theorists as four documents writtten over hundreds of years instead of one document written by Moses, as the Bible itself claims.

The major assumptions of the Documentary Hypothesis are (1) the guideline of divine names (Yahweh and Elohim) as evidence of diverse authorship; (2) the origin of J, E, and P as separate documents, written at different periods of time; (3) the separate origin of E as distinct from J and compared prior to J; and (4) the origin of D in the reign of Josiah (621 B.C.). As referred to above, the essential purpose of the JEDP theory was to discount the miraculous and the prophetical. However, with the discovery of the Dead Sea Scrolls, this theory has been thoroughly disproven to the point that no Bible scholar who understands the Bible to be inspired can possibly subscribe to such a theory.

The Dead Sea Scrolls have clearly pointed to the unity of the Pentateuch and moreover the unity of each book, defending the miracles and prophecies of the Bible as genuine and thoroughly accurate.

APPENDIX E

Manuscripts

The Masoretic Text

The Masoretic Text (MT) was developed A.D. 500-950, and it gave the final form to the Old Testament. It preserved in writing the oral tradition (masorah) concerning correct vowels and accents, and the number of occurrences of rare words of unusual spellings.

Vowel Pointing of YHWH

Due to Jewish fears of bringing upon themselves possible retribution for breaking the third commandment, they began refusing to pronounce the divine name. This began in Nehemiah's time. It became the normal practice to substitute the title "Lord" (adonai) for the name Yahweh when reading aloud. The Masoretes, to indicate this replacement, inserted the vowels from *Adonai* under the consonants of YaWHeH, resulting in the word YeHoWaH, which came to be pronounced as *Jehovah.* Scholars of the Renaissance period misunderstood the purpose of this vowel pointing and began pronouncing the name as *Jehovah*, rather than pronouncing the name *Yahweh* or the title *Adonai.* This erroneous pronunciation became so common that Christians generally are still unwilling to accept the correct pronunciation, Yahweh.

Qere Kethib

The terms are used to refer to textual variants that are understood though not written. The word qere means *what is read*, and the word kethib means *what is written.* (Hence--*read for what is written.*) One classic example of qere kethib is mentioned in the preceding paragraph. Therefore, although the text is *written* Yahweh, it is *read* Adonai. Qere kethibs were marginal notes written to the side of the manuscript.

The Masoretes

The Masoretes deserve much credit for their painstaking care in preserving the consonantal text that was entrusted to them. They devoted greater attention to accurately preserving the Hebrew Scriptures than has ever been given to any ancient literature in human history. They left the consonantal text exactly as it was given to them, refusing to make even the most obvious corrections. The work of the Masoretes has preserved for us a text which essentially duplicates the text considered authoritative at the time of Christ. Moreover, the Qumran evidence shows us that we have a Hebrew text that gives us a true record of God's revelation.

The Major Codices

1. British Museum Oriental 4445--a copy of the Pentateuch consonantal text (A.D. 850), vowel points added one century later, most of Genesis and Deuteronomy missing.

2. Codex Cairensus (C)--former prophets and latter prophets, copied by Aaron ben Asher (A.D. 895).

3. Leningrad MS--latter prophets (A.D. 916).

4. Leningrad MS B-19A--entire Old Testament, containing Ben Asher Masoretic

Text (A.D. 1010), faithful copy of A.D. 980 MS (since lost). This manuscript was the basis for Kittel's *Biblia Hebraica* (3rd edition and all subsequent editions).

5. Samaritan Pentateuch -- earliest MSS of this version is still in Nablus, withheld by Samaritan sectarians from publication, about 6,000 variants from MT (mostly spelling differences), contains biased sectarian insertions, no MS of the Samaritan Pentateuch known to be older than 10th century A.D.

6. Bologna Edition of the Psalter--A.D. 1477.

7. Soncino Edition of the Old Testament--(vowel-pointed) A.D. 1488.

8. Second Bomberg Edition of the Old Testament--(A.D. 1525-26) printed under the patronage of Daniel Bomberg, became basis for all modern editions up to 1929,contains text of Jacob ben Chayim, with Masorah and Rabbinical notes.

The Qumran Manuscripts

The Qumran manuscripts, or Dead Sea Scrolls, were discovered in a series of caves near the canyon of Wady Qumran, along the northwest coast of the Dead Sea. Technical identification of these documents consists of (1) a number specifying which of the caves was the scene of its discovery, (2) an abbreviation of the name of the book itself, and (3) a superscript letter indicating the order in which the manuscript came to light, as opposed to other copies of the same book. Thus the famous Dead Sea Scroll of Isaiah is labeled 1 QIs^{a}, meaning that it was the first discovered, or most important, manuscript of Isaiah found in Cave 1 at Wady Qumran. Following is a list of the most important finds at Wady Qumran.

1. Dead Sea Scroll of Isaiah (1QIs^{a})--(150-100 B.C.) entire sixty-six chapters, same family of MS as MT.

2. Habakkuk Commentary (1QpHb)--(100-50 B.C.) chapters one and two only, with commentary notes between verses, commentary is usually concerned with how each verse is fulfilled in recent (Hasmonean) history and current events.

3. Hebrew University Isaiah Scroll (1QIs^{b})--(copied ca. 50 B.C.) substantial portion of chapters 41-66, closer to MT than 1QIs^{a} is.

4. 1Q Leviticus fragments--(4th or 2nd century B.C.) a few verses each of chapters 19-22, written in paleo-Hebrew script.

5. 4Q Deuteronomy-B--32:41-43--written in hemistichs as poetry, not as prose, no date suggested.

6. 4Q Samuel-A--1 Samuel 1, 2, twenty-seven fragments (1st century B.C.).

7. 4Q Samuel-B--1 Samuel 16, 19, 21, 23 (225 B.C. or earlier).

8. 4Q Jeremiah--A (no date suggested).

9. 4Q XII-A (XII signifies a MS of the minor prophets)--(3rd century B.C.) cursive script.

10. 4Q Qoh^{a}--(2nd century B.C.) cursive text

of Ecclesiastes, derived from a source that is at least 3rd century B.C. or earlier.

11. 4Q Exodus--a fragment of chapter 1.

12. 4Q Exodus--portions of chapters 7, 29, 30, 32 (and perhaps others), written in paleo-Hebrew script.

13. 4Q Numbers--written in square Hebrew with Samaritan type expansions (after 27:33 there is an insert derived from Deuteronomy 3:21).

14. 4Q Deuteronomy-A--chapter 32 (Song of Moses).

15. 11Q Psalms--a manuscript of Psalms from cave 11, copied in formal bookhand style of the Herodian period, the bottom third of each page has been lost, thirty-three Psalms are preserved with fragments containing portions of four others. Psalms represented are 93, 101-103, 105, 109, 118, 119, 121-130, 132-146, 148- 150, and 151 from the LXX.

16. Nash Papyrus--(100-50 B.C.) contains the Decalogue and the *Shema`* (Exodus 20:1-17 and Deuteronomy 6:4-9), purchased by W. L. Nash from an Egyptian antique dealer.

The Aramaic Targums

The word *Targum* means "interpretation," and these documents became necessary because the Hebrew people lost touch with their ancestral Hebrew during the Babylonian exile and Persian empire period. First there was a need for an interpreter in the synagogue services, and later the interpretations were written down. However, there is no evidence of a written *Targum* until about A.D. 200. Because their primary purpose was for interpretation, they have limited value for textual criticism. Following is a list of several *targums*:

1. The Targum of Onkelos on the Torah --(ca. 3rd century A.D.) produced by Jewish scholars in Babylon. Traditionally assigned to a certain Onkelos, supposedly a native of Pontus. It is not quoted by extant Palestinian sources earlier than A.D. 1000.

2. The Targum of Jonathan ben Uzziel on the Prophets (i.e., Joshua-Kings, Isaiah-Malachi)--(4th century A.D.) composed in Babylonian circles. Far more free in its rendering of the Hebrew text than in Onkelos.

3. The Targum of Pseudo-Jonathan on the Torah--(ca. A.D. 650) a mixture of Onkelos and Midrashic materials.

4. The Jerusalem Targum on the Torah--(ca. A.D. 700).

APPENDIX F

The Septuagint (LXX)

The Septuagint, often noted by the Roman numerals, LXX is the Greek translation of the Hebrew Old Testament. It was translated for Greek-speaking Jews who knew no Hebrew.

It is called the LXX because it was said to have been translated by seventy, or more accurately seventy-two, Jewish scholars. This was the common Bible of New Testament times, and it is quoted frequently in the New Testament.

However, Matthew and the author of Hebrews follow a text that is closer to the MT. We must remember that the Septuagint is a *translation* of inspired Scripture, not the *original* or even a *copy* of the original. As such it is subject to error as any other translation.

It should also be noted, however, that the translators of the Septuagint were highly skilled making a Greek Old Testament that could be depended upon by the New Testament writers for quotations. When all of the Greek manuscripts are compared with the Hebrew manuscripts, a high degree of textual certainty exists in spite of some difficulties.

Bibliography

Aharoni, Yohanan. The Archeology of the Land of Israel: From the Prehistoric Beginnings to the End of the First Temple Period. trans. by Anson F. Rainey. Philadelphia: TheWestminster Press, 1982.

Allis, Oswald T. God Spake by Moses. Philadelphia: The Presbyterian and Reformed Publishing Company, 1951.

Allis, Oswald T. The Five Books of Moses: A Reexamination of the Modern Theory that the Pentateuch is a Late Compilation from Diverse and Conflicting Sources by Authors and Editors whose Identity is Completely Unknown. Philadelphia: The Presbyterian and Reformed Publishing Company, 1943.

Allis, Oswald T. The Old Testament: Its Claims and its Critics. Philadelphia: Presbyterian and Reformed Publishing Company, 1972.

Amerding, Carl E. The Old Testament and Criticism. Grand Rapids, MI: William B. Eerdmans Publishing Company, 1984.

Archer, Gleason L. Encyclopedia of Bible Difficulties. Grand Rapids, MI: Zondervan Publishing House, 1982.

Archer, Gleason L. A Survey of Old Testament Introduction, rev. ed. Chicago: Moody Press, 1964.

Barker, Kenneth, Gen. ed., The NIV Study Bible: New International Version. Grand Rapids, MI: Zondervan Bible Publishers, 1985.

Blaiklock, Edward M. and R. H. Harrison, eds., The New International Dictionary of Biblical Archeology. Grand Rapids, MI: Zondervan Publishing House, 1983.

Brown, Francis, S.R. Driver, Charles A. Briggs. The New Brown-Driver-Briggs-Gesenius Hebrew and English Lexicon. Peabody, MA: Hendickson Publishers, 1979.

Cassuto, Umberto. A Commentary on the Book of Genesis. 2 Vols., trans. by Israel Abrahams. Jerusalem: Magnes Press, 1978-84.

Craigie, Peter C. Ugarit and the Old Testament. Grand Rapids, MI: William B. Eerdmans Publishing Company, 1985.

Davis, John D. Genesis and Semitic Tradition. Grand Rapids, MI: Baker Book House, 1980.

Davis, John D. The Westminster Dictionary of the Bible. rev. by Henry Snyder Gehman. Philadelphia: The Westminster Press, 1944.

Davis, John J. Paradise to Prison: Studies in Genesis. Grand Rapids, MI: Baker Book House, 1975.

Delitzsch, Franz. A New Commentary on Genesis. 2 Vols., trans. by Sophia Taylor. Grand Rapids, MI: Kregel, 1978.

Douglas, J. D., ed., New Bible Dictionary. Wheaton, IL: Tyndale House Publishers, Inc., 1962.

Even-Shoshan, Abraham, ed., A New Concordance of the Old Testament Using the Hebrew and Aramaic Text. Grand Rapids, MI: Baker Book House, 1990.

Exell, Joseph S. and Thomas H. Leale. The Preacher's Homiletic Commentary. Vol. 1, Genesis. New York: Funk & Wagnalls Company, n.d.

Finegan, Jack. Light from the Ancient Past: The Archaeological Background of Judaism and Christianity. 2nd ed. Princeton: Princeton University Press, 1959.

Gaebelein, Frank E., ed., The Expositor's Bible Commentary. Vol. 2, Genesis, Exodus, Leviticus, Numbers, John H. Sailhamer, Walter C. Kaiser, Jr., R. Laird Harris, Ronald B. Allen. Grand Rapids, MI: Zondervan Publishing House, 1990.

Gordon, Cyrus H. "Higher Critics and the Forbidden Fruit." Christianity Today, Vol. 4, No. 4, Nov. 23, 1959, 3-5.

Gottwald, Norman K. The Hebrew Bible--a Socio-Literary Introduction. Philadelphia: Fortress Press, 1985.

Hamilton, Victor P. Handbook on the Pentateuch. Grand Rapids, MI: Baker Book House, 1982.

Bibliography

Harris, R. Laird. Inspiration and Canonicity of the Bible. Grand Rapids, MI: Zondervan Publishing House, 1957.

Harris, R. Laird, Gleason L. Archer, Jr. and Bruce K. Waltke, eds., Theological Wordbook of the Old Testament, 2 Vols. Chicago: Moody Press, 1980.

Harrison, R. K., B. K. Waltke, D. Guthrie, G. D. Fee. Biblical Criticism: Historical, Literary and Textual. Grand Rapids, MI: Zondervan Publishing House, 1980.

Harrison, R. K. Old Testament Times. Grand Rapids, MI: William B. Eerdmans Publishing Company, 1970.

Herbert, Arthur S. Genesis 12-50: Abraham and his Heirs. London: SCM Press, 1962.

Herrmann, Siegfried. Israel in Egypt. trans. by Margaret Kohl. Naperville, IL: Allenson, 1973.

Hertz, J. H., ed., The Pentateuch and Haftorahs: Hebrew Text, English Translation and Commentary. 2nd ed. London: Soncino Press, 1972.

Holladay, William L. A Concise Hebrew and Aramaic Lexicon of the Old Testament. Grand Rapids, MI: William B. Eerdmans Publishing Company, 1971.

Horton, Stanley M., ed., Systematic Theology. Springfield, MO: Logion Press, 1994.

Hunt, Ignatius. The World of the Patriarchs. Englewood Cliffs, NJ: Prentice-Hall, 1967.

Jacob, Benno. The First Book of the Bible: Genesis. trans. by Ernest I. Jacob and Walter Jacob. Jerusalem: KTAV Publishing House, 1974.

Johns, Alger F. A Short Grammar of Biblical Aramaic. Berrien Springs, MI: Andrews University Press, 1963.

Kautzch, E. and A. E. Cowley, eds., Gesenius' Hebrew Grammar. Oxford: Clarendon Press, 1910.

Keil, C. F. and F. Delitzsch. Commentary on the Old Testament. trans. by James Martin, Vol. 1. The Pentateuch. Peabody, MA: Hendrickson Publishers, 1989.

Keller, Werner. The Bible as History. 2nd rev. ed., trans. by William Neil and B. H. Rasmussen. New York: Bantam Books, 1982.

Kelley, Page H. Biblical Hebrew: An Introductory Grammar. Grand Rapids, MI: William B. Eerdmans Publishing Company, 1992.

Kidner, Derek. Genesis: An Introduction and Commentary. Downers Grove, IL: Intervarsity Press, 1972.

Koehler, Ludwig and Walter Baumgartner. The Hebrew and Aramaic Lexicon of the Old Testament. Leiden, Netherlands: E. J. Brill, 1994.

Lasor, William Sanford, David Allan Hubbard, Frederic William Bush. Old Testament Survey: The Message, Form, and Background of The Old Testament. Grand Rapids, MI: William B. Eerdmans Publishing Company, 1992.

Leupold, Herbert C. Exposition of Genesis. 2 Vols. Grand Rapids, MI: Baker Book House, 1982.

Livingston, George Herbert. The Pentateuch in its Cultural Environment. 2nd ed. Grand Rapids, MI: Baker Book House, 1988.

Mann, Thomas W. The Book of the Torah: The Narrative Integrity of the Pentateuch. Atlanta: John Knox Press, 1988.

Merrill, Eugene H. An Historical Survey of the Old Testament. Nutley, NJ: The Craig Press, 1966.

Miller, J. Maxwell and John H. Hayes. A History of Ancient Israel and Judah. Philadelphia: Westminster Press, 1986.

Bibliography

Moreland, J. P., ed., The Creation Hypothesis: Scientific Evidence for an Intelligent Designer. Downers Grove, IL: Intervarsity Press, 1977.

Newman, Robert C. and Herman J. Eckelmann, Jr. Genesis One and the Origin of the Earth. Downers Grove IL: Intervaristy Press, 1977.

Owens, John Joseph. Analytical Key to the Old Testament, Vol. 1. Grand Rapids, MI: Baker Book House, 1990.

Patten, Donald. The Biblical Flood and the Ice Epoch: A Study in Scientific History. Seattle: Pacific Meridian Publishing Company, 1966.

Patten, Donald W., ed., A Symposium on Creation VI. Seattle: Pacific Meridian Publishing Company, 1977.

Pfeiffer, Charles F., ed., Baker's Bible Atlas. Grand Rapids, MI: Baker Book House, 1961.

Pfeiffer, Charles F. Old Testament History. Grand Rapids, MI: Baker Book House, 1987.

Pfeiffer, Charles F., Howard F. Vos, John Rea, eds., Wycliffe Bible Encyclopedia. 2 Vols. Chicago: Moody Press, 1975.

Pritchard, James B., ed., The Ancient Near East: An Anthology of Texts and Pictures. Vol. 1. Princeton: Princeton University Press, 1973.

Pun, Pattle P. T. Evolution: Nature and Scripture in Conflict? Grand Rapids, MI: Zondervan Publishing House, 1982.

Rahlfs, Alfred, ed., Septuaginta. Stuttgart, Germany: Deutsche Bibelgesellschaft Stuttgart, 1935.

Ramm, Bernard. The Christian View of Science and Scripture. Grand Rapids, MI: William B. Eerdmans Publishing Company, 1978.

Rogerson, John and Philip Davies. The Old Testament World. Englewood Cliffs, NJ: Prentice-Hall, 1989.

Ross, Allen P. Creation and Blessing: A Guide to the Study and Exposition of Genesis. Grand Rapids, MI: Baker Book House, 1988.

Schoville, Keith N. *Biblical Archaeology in Focus*. Grand Rapids, MI: Baker Book House, 1982.

Schultz, Samuel J. The Old Testament Speaks. New York: Harper & Brothers, Publishers, 1960.

Segal, Moses H. *The Pentateuch: Its Composition and its Authorship and Other Biblical Studies*. Jerusalem: Magnes Press, 1967.

Seow, Choon Leong. *A Grammar for Biblical Hebrew*. Nashville, TN: Abingdon Press, 1987.

Shanks, Hershel, ed., *Ancient Israel: A Short History from Abraham to the Roman Destruction of the Temple*. Englewood Cliffs, NJ: Prentice-Hall, 1988.

Soulen, Richard N. *Handbook of Biblical Criticism*. Atlanta: John Knox Press, 1978.

Stamps, Donald C., Gen. ed., *The Full Life Study Bible*. Grand Rapids, MI: Zondervan Publishing House, 1976.

Steigers, Harld G. *A Commentary on Genesis*. Grand Rapids, MI: Zondervan Publishing House, 1976.

Thomas, W. H. Griffeth. Genesis: *A Devotional Commentary*. Grand Rapids, MI: William B. Eerdmans Publishing Company, 1946.

Van Der Woude, A. S., ed., The World of the Old Testament. trans. by Sierd Woudstra. Grand Rapids, MI: William B. Eerdmans Publishing Company, 1989.

Waltke, Bruce K. and M. O'Connor. *An Introduction to Biblical Hebrew Syntax*. Winona Lake, IN: Eisenbrauns, 1990.

Watts, J. Wash. Old Testament Teaching. Nashville, TN: Broadman Press, 1967.

Wilson, Clifford A. *In the Beginning God . . . :Answers to Questions on Genesis*. Grand Rapids, MI: Baker Book House, 1975.

Bibliography

Wiseman, Percy J. New Discoveries in Babylonia About Genesis. London: Marshall, Morgan and Scott, 1936.

Wonderly, Dan. God's Time-Records in Ancient Sediments: Evidences of Long Time Spans in Earth's History. Flint, MI: Crystal Press Publishers, 1977.

Zimmerman, Paul A., ed., Darwin, Evolution, and Creation. St. Louis: Concordia Publishing House, 1959.